Encyclopedia of Political Economy

Encyclopedia of Political Economy

edited by Phillip Anthony O'Hara

Volume 1: A–K

London and New York

First published 1999
by Routledge
11 New Fetter Lane, London, EC4P 4EE

Simultaneously published in the USA and Canada
by Routledge
29 West 35th Street, New York, NY 10001

First published in paperback 2001

Reprinted 2001

Routledge is an imprint of the Taylor & Francis Group

© 1999, 2001 Routledge

Typeset in Times by Routledge
Printed and bound in Great Britain by T.J. International Ltd, Padstow, Cornwall

All rights reserved. No part of this book may be reprinted or
reproduced or utilized in any form or by any electronic,
mechanical, or other means, now known or hereafter
invented, including photocopying and recording,
or in any information storage or retrieval system, without
permission in writing from the publishers.

British Library Cataloguing in Publication Data
A catalogue record for this book is available from the British Library

Library of Congress Cataloging-in-Publication Data
A catalog record for this book is available from the Library of Congress

PBK ISBN 0-415-24188-X (set)
PBK ISBN 0-415-24186-3 (v.1)
PBK ISBN 0-415-24187-1 (v.2)

HBK ISBN 0-415-15426-X (set)
HBK ISBN 0-415-18717-6 (v.1)
HBK ISBN 0-415-18718-4 (v.2)

Contents

Volume 1

Editorial team   vi

Foreword   xi

Preface   xiv

Acknowledgments   xvii

How to use the *Encyclopedia*   xx

List of contributors   xxviii

Entries A–K   1

Volume 2

Entries L–Z   633

Index   1275

Editorial team

Editor

Phillip Anthony O'Hara is an Associate Professor of Economics at Curtin University of Technology in Perth, Australia. He received the "Clarence Ayres Visiting International Scholar" Award from the Association for Evolutionary Economics (AFEE) in 1997–8 and is a member of the Board of Directors of AFEE. He has published in numerous international refereed journals; and has been a Visiting Professor at Marquette University in Wisconsin and a Visiting Scholar at the University of California, Riverside and California State University. His research interests are in the areas of institutionalist, radical, feminist, post-Keynesian and social political economy.

Associate editors

Deborah M. Figart is an Associate Professor of Economics at Richard Stockton College, New Jersey, USA. She is a co-author of *Contesting the Market: Pay Equity and the Politics of Economic Restructuring* (1997). She is currently serving as a Guest Editor for two journals and is one of the founding members of the International Association for Feminist Economics. In 1989–90, she was a Fulbright Scholar in Western Europe.

Marc Lavoie is a Full Professor in the Department of Economics at the University of Ottawa, Canada. He has also been a Visiting Professor at the universities of Bordeaux, Nice, Rennes, Dijon and at Curtin University. He is the author of four books, has co-edited one and has published 20 papers in various books and 60 papers in refereed journals. His interests lie in monetary economics, growth economics, the economics of sport, and all non-orthodox approaches to political economy.

Ellen Mutari is an Assistant Professor of Economics at Monmouth University in West Long Branch, New Jersey, USA. She is a co-editor of *Gender and Political Economy: Incorporating Diversity Into Theory and Policy* (1997). Her research interests include the impact of economic restructuring on gender relations and the theoretical development of feminist political economy.

Steven Pressman is a Professor of Economics and Finance at Monmouth University in West Long Branch, New Jersey, USA; North American Editor of the *Review of Political Economy*; and Treasurer of the Eastern Economic Association. He has published more than 60 articles in edited books and international refereed journals and is the author or editor of 6 books. His research centers on areas such as poverty, public finance, post-Keynesian macroeconomics and the history of economic thought.

Editorial board

John B. Davis is a Professor of Economics at Marquette University, Milwaukee, USA. He is the editor of the *Review of Social Economy* and the author of many books and journal articles. His research areas include economic methodology, the philosophy of economics, Keynes, Sraffa and classical political economy.

James Devine is a Professor of Economics at Loyola Marymount University in Los Angeles, California, USA. He is a Marxian political economist, with research interests in macroeconomics, labor issues, monetary issues, and economic history. He has published articles on high theory and on economic history, as well as on the Marxian theory of exploitation, methodology, and the microeconomics of labor–capital relations.

John T. Harvey is a Professor of Economics at Texas Christian University in Fort Worth, Texas, USA. His research interests are in international finance and macroeconomics; and his recent papers include empirical studies of exchange rate expectations, theoretical investigations of the psychology of decision making, and accounts of the evolution of the international payments system.

John S.L. McCombie is a member of the University of Cambridge and a Fellow in Economics at Downing College, Cambridge, UK. He has researched extensively on the reasons for economic growth disparities between the advanced countries; economic growth and the balance-of-payments constraint; Kaldorian growth models; the economics of Keynes; criticisms of the aggregate production function; and economic methodology.

Sabine O'Hara is Director of the PhD Program in Ecological Economics and an Assistant Professor at the Rensselaer Polytechnic Institute at Troy, New York, USA. Her research has been in ecological economics, environmental policy, social economics and sustainable development; and developing curricula and interactive teaching methods that link theory and empirical application.

Mario Seccareccia is a Full Professor in the Department of Economics at the University of Ottawa, Canada. He is also a lecturer in economics at the Labour College of Canada and has been a consultant economist for Canadian trade unions. His areas of teaching and research include labor economics, macroeconomics, monetary theory, the history of economic thought, and Canadian economic history.

Eric Shutz is an Associate Professor at Rollins College, Winter Park, Florida, USA. His areas of interest and teaching include industrial organization, Marxian economics, comparative economic systems and American political economy.

Ajit Sinha currently teaches economics at the University of Newcastle in Australia. He has published several research papers in the area of Marxian political economy. and has co-edited a special issue of *Research in Political Economy* (volume 15).

Douglas Vickers is a Professor Emeritus of Economics at the University of Massachusetts, Amherst, USA. He has authored 15 books on economics, philosophy and theology and numerous journal articles. His research has concentrated on monetary economics, the significance of time for an understanding and critique of market relationships, and the importance of ethics in the workings of institutions.

Richard D. Wolff is a Professor of Economics at the University of Massachusetts, Amherst, USA, where he has taught economic theory (including Marxian economics) at graduate and undergraduate levels. He has published numerous books and refereed journal articles. He helped to form the Association for Economic and Social Analysis (AESA) which runs international conferences on Marxian economics and publishes the journal *Rethinking Marxism*.

Editorial advisors

Hassan Bougrine is an Associate Professor of Economics at Laurentian University, Sudbury, Ontario, Canada. He has published numerous articles in refereed journals and edited books. His research interests include

Editorial team

economic growth, finance, public policy and international trade.

Mathew Forstater is a Visiting Scholar at the Jerome Levy Economics Institute of Bard College, New York, and an Assistant Professor of Economics at Gettysburg College, Pennsylvania, USA. He has published articles on employment policy, methodology, and the history of economic thought.

G.C. Harcourt is Reader in the History of Economic Theory, University of Cambridge; a Fellow of Jesus College, Cambridge, UK; and Professor Emeritus, University of Adelaide, Australia. He has authored or edited (singly or jointly) 17 books and has published over 150 articles and notes in learned journals, and chapters in books. His research areas include post-Keynesian theory and policy, analytical history of economic theory and intellectual biography. He was appointed an Officer in the General Division of the Order of Australia (AO) in 1994.

Gabrielle Meagher is a Lecturer in Political Economy in the Department of Economics at the University of Sydney. Her research interests include the future of work and employment, waged domestic labor, the political economy and philosophy of commodification, and feminist political economy.

Allen Oakley is an Associate Professor of Economics at the University of Newcastle, Australia. His main publications include a number of books, amongst which are several on Karl Marx, two on Austrian economics, one on Joseph Schumpeter and one on the political economy of Adam Smith and J.S. Mill. He is presently undertaking an analysis of the role of human agency in reconstructing economic theory.

James Ronald Stanfield is a Professor of Economics at Colorado State University, Fort Collins, USA and President of the Association for Evolutionary Economics (1998). He has published five books and over 100 articles in books and journals. His present work is focused upon the "Nurturance Gap" that is arising in the wake of the neo-liberal Great Capitalist Restoration; and an effort to integrate the work of "Original" and "New" institutional economics.

Eiman Zein-Elabdin is an Assistant Professor of Economics at Franklin and Marshall College, Lancaster, Pennsylvania, USA. Her teaching and research interests are in the areas of economic development; environmental economics; women, gender, and development; and economic philosophy.

Committee of referees

H. Sonmez Atesoglu, Clarkson University, Potsdam, New York, USA
Chris Barrett, Cornell University, Ithaca, New York, USA
Enrico Bellino, Catholic University of the Sacred Heart, Milan, Italy
Riccardo Bellofiore, University of Bergamo, Italy
Christian Bidard, University of Paris X, Nanterre, France
Harry Bloch, Curtin University of Technology, Perth, Australia
Doug M. Brown, North Arizona University, Flagstaff, Arizona, USA
Paul D. Bush, California State University, Fresno, California, USA
Michael C. Carroll, Muskingum College, Ohio, USA
John C. Cross, Point Arena, California, USA
Christine D'Onofrio, New York City, USA
Robert Dixon, University of Melbourne, Melbourne, Australia
Robert Drago, University of Wisconsin, Milwaukee, Wisconsin, USA
Amitava Krishna Dutt, University of Notre Dame, South Bend, Indiana, USA
Gary A. Dymski, University of California, Riverside, California, USA

Editorial team

Robert Field, State Government of Maryland, Baltimore, Maryland, USA
Susan Fleck, American University, Washington DC, USA
Gladys Foster, Littleton, Colorado, USA
Mason Gaffney, University of California, Riverside, California, USA
B.N. Ghosh, University of Science Malaysia, Penang, Malaysia
Eric R. Hake, Mendel University, Brno, Czech Republic
Emily P. Hoffman, Western Michigan University, Kalamazoo, Michigan, USA
Ann Jennings, Lafayette College, Easton, Pennsylvania, USA
Evan Jones, University of Sydney, Sydney, Australia
Prue Kerr, University of New South Wales, Australia
Chidem Kurdas, Hoboken, New Jersey, USA
Gilberto Tadeu Lima, Universidade Estadual de Campinas, Brazil
George Liodakis, Technical University of Crete, Chania, Greece
John Lodewijks, University of New South Wales, Sydney, Australia
Mark A. Lutz, University of Maine, Orono, Maine, USA
Gary Madden, Curtin University of Technology, Perth, Australia
Ianik Marcil, University of Montreal, Canada
Patrick Mason, University of Notre Dame, Indiana, USA
Anne Mayhew, University of Tennessee, Tennessee, USA
Gary Mongiovi, St John's University, New York, USA
Robin Neill, University of Prince Edward Island, Charlottetown, Canada
P. Paraskevaides, Center of Planning and Economic Research, Athens, Greece
Paul Phillips, University of Manitoba, Winnipeg, Canada
Riccardo Realfonzo, University of Naples, Naples, Italy
Mark Setterfield, Trinity College, Hartford, Connecticut, USA
Howard J. Sherman, University of California, Riverside, California, USA
Marie-Claire Thornton, Curtin University of Technology, Perth, Australia
Daniel Underwood, Peninsula College, Port Angeles, Washington, USA
Karl-Heinz Waldow, Government of Saxony–Anhalt, Germany
Michael D. Yates, University of Pittsburgh, Pittsburgh, Pennsylvannia, USA

Subject committee members

Institutional spheres

Corporation: Hassan Bougrine, Malcolm Sawyer, Eric Schutz
Family and gender/feminist political economy: Drucilla K. Barker, Margaret Coleman, Mary Ann Dimand, Susan Feiner, Deborah M. Figart, Prue Hyman, Joyce Jacobsen, Gabrielle Meagher, Ellen Mutari, Diana Strassman
Money, credit and finance: Gary A. Dymski, Marc Lavoie, Basil Moore, Phillip Anthony O'Hara
State and policy: Wolfgang Blaas, Steven Pressman, Mark Setterfield
Work, labor and production (capital–labor relations): Robert Drago, Deborah M. Figart, Ellen Mutari, Paul Phillips, Mario Seccareccia, Michael D. Yates
World capitalist economy: Theodore Cohn, John T. Harvey, Roberto Patricio Korzeniewicz, Phillip Anthony O'Hara, Immanuel Wallerstein

Subjects

Cycles, waves and unstable growth: James Devine, David Laibman, Phillip Anthony O'Hara, Howard J. Sherman
Development: Chris Barrett, Anthony D'Costa, Mary Ann Dimand, Amitava Krishna Dutt, B.N. Ghosh, David Ruccio, John Stoneman, Eiman Zein-Elabdin
Economic anthropology: Mathew Forstater, Polly Hill, John Lodewijks
Environment: Andrew K. Dragun, Mathew Forstater, Sabine U. O'Hara, M.A. Mohamed Salih

Editorial team

History of political economy and general themes: George Argyrous, Hassan Bougrine, Robert W. Dimand, Peter Kriesler, John Lodewijks, Steven Pressman

Methodology and philosophy: John B. Davis, Allen Oakley, Charles K. Wilber, Richard D. Wolff

Race and ethnicity: Christine D'Onofrio, Susan Feiner, Deborah M. Figart, Mathew Forstater, Patrick Mason, Ellen Mutari

Political ideology and programs: Phillip Anthony O'Hara, Steven Pressman, Eric Schutz

Schools of political economy

Evolution, change and Schumpeterian themes: Geoffrey M. Hodgson, Steve Keen, Mark Setterfield, Karl-Heinz Waldow

Feminist political economy: Drucilla K. Barker, Margaret Coleman, Mary Ann Dimand, Susan Feiner, Deborah M. Figart, Prue Hyman, Joyce Jacobsen, Gabrielle Meagher, Ellen Mutari, Diana Strassman

Institutional political economy: John Adams, Paul D. Bush, William M. Dugger, Anne Mayhew, Phillip Anthony O'Hara, James Ronald Stanfield, Charles K. Wilber

Marxist political economy: James Devine, Robert Dixon, Phillip Anthony O'Hara, Stephen Resnick, Eric Schutz, Ajit Sinha

Post-Keynesian political economy: Philip Arestis, Geoffrey C. Harcourt, Richard P. F. Holt, J.E. King, Marc Lavoie, Douglas Vickers

Social political economy: John B. Davis, Mark A. Lutz, Charles K. Wilber

Sraffian political economy: Christian Bidard, Marc Lavoie, Gary Mongiovi, Ajit Sinha

Foreword

The world has entered the age of information and communication. People face an increasing diffusion of information, at an ever faster pace, on a worldwide scale. Satellites and television bring us the latest news and events, with little or no delay, from the most remote areas, and various specialized channels attempt to bring us an analysis of this information. Almost anyone, if they have the means, can now have access to telephone lines, fax machines, electronic mail and the worldwide web, either at home or at the office. All of this enables people to gather information and to exchange opinions more easily.

Still, there is a paradox surrounding the ever-increasing importance of communication within modern civilization. While the quantity of information available has increased, and while the ability to communicate quickly and over a broad area has improved, the communication itself (the message that is supposed to be relayed) is having a harder time getting through. Perhaps this is a result of information overload, and perhaps this is due to the fact that the medium itself has become the message, as Marshall McLuhan noted many years ago.

This paradox of greater technological ease of communication and less actual communication is perhaps greatest within academia, which supposedly exists to communicate knowledge to students and colleagues. Universities are becoming full of scientists and scholars who know next to nothing besides the tools of their highly specialized sub-field, and who experience increasing difficulty communicating with those outside their narrow area of specialization.

Economics provides a good example of how professionals in an academic discipline have lost the ability to communicate. Most professional economists are no longer generalists who know a great deal about the way the economy works, and who understand important economic institutions and problems. Rather, there are macroeconomists, microeconomists, labor economists, financial economists, development economists, econometricians, historians of economic thought and so on.

Even within these different fields, individual economists have come to focus increasingly on narrower and narrower areas of specialization. For example, some labor economists focus on productivity, others on labor–management relations, others on the economic impact of labor unions, others on the rise of part-time and contingent employment, and yet others study the extent of race and gender discrimination in labor markets. In addition, over the past thirty to forty years, economists have increasingly formed themselves into different schools of thought. Each school has its own set of assumptions, each employs a different perspective on how the economy works, and each has its own vocabulary. Within macroeconomics, for example, there are more than half a dozen different approaches: traditional Keynesian, post-Keynesian, new Keynesian, Marxian, monetarist, new classical, the real business cycle approach, the French Circuit School and the South American structuralist approach.

With so many divisions by area and approach, the discipline of economics has become quite fragmented. This fragmentation has a number of undesirable consequences. Economists find it difficult to talk among themselves about economics. Likewise, they find it difficult to communicate with people who are not trained in economic analysis. The general public, which takes some notice of these things, has ceased to take economists seriously. Students, too, have become lost in the labyrinth of specialization and wars among different schools of thought. Unable to find their way though this confusing maze, they

Foreword

have increasingly made the decision not to take courses in economics and to find a saner subject of study. (Some mainstream economists are aware of the problem and one response has been the creation of the *Journal of Economic Perspectives.*)

The *Encyclopedia of Political Economy* was conceived as a means of bridging these many differences within the discipline. From the beginning, a conscious attempt was made to cover as many different areas of economics as possible. Similarly, an effort was made to make entries clear, understandable and accessible, not only to a broad range of our colleagues but also to our students. The *Encyclopedia* is thus designed to be a useful first reference source for someone who is not a specialist on a particular topic. The main purpose of the *Encyclopedia* is to help students and the general public gain access to a wide variety of ideas, and to enable them to understand the discussions and exchanges taking place in economics today.

There are limits, however, to the terrain that is covered here. The *Encyclopedia* is mainly concerned with the ideas expressed by economists who desire to revive the tradition of *political economy*. Contemporary economics has increasingly become the study of how people make rational decisions and attempt to maximize their own individual utility. While this approach surely describes some human behavior, it leaves out more than it includes. Political economists all believe that the contemporary approach underplays the most interesting and important factors that affect economic activity: how human behavior is influenced by society and how individual economic pursuits may lead to sub-optimal results for the entire economy. One goal in developing this *Encyclopedia* has been to emphasize these aspects of economic life.

As with orthodox economics, political economy has long been fragmented into more or less autonomous schools and academic associations. The *Encyclopedia* seeks to reduce this fragmentation. It brings together economists with very different perspectives on economic issues. Each entry was carefully read and commented on by people holding different opinions on the topic. As a result, individual authors were forced to make their ideas accessible to a wide range of economists and were strongly encouraged to discuss different perspectives in their entry.

The contents of the *Encyclopedia* show that a substantial amount of common ground does exist among political economists. The *Encyclopedia* also shows that there are synergistic gains to be had from trying to communicate across schools of thought and across areas of specialization. Finally, the entries that follow show that economists can communicate with non-specialists when they are pressed to do so.

The *Encyclopedia* was put together in four years after its creator, Professor Phillip O'Hara, drew up its first outline. This is a rather remarkable achievement considering the size of the book, the number of authors involved, the number of referees used and the large number of people having a say in the design and content of the *Encyclopedia*. Both of us had the opportunity and made the choice to become Associate Editors when the outline of the *Encyclopedia* was taking its final form and the first entries started to come in. This involvement with the *Encyclopedia*, along with the generosity of Professor O'Hara's home institution, Curtin University, allowed us to live for some time in the magnificent city of Perth, on the coast of Western Australia, with its ever-sunny six-month summer.

There is no doubt that this huge project, arising from such a remote city, could not have been completed in such a short time without the use of modern communication methods. Virtually all communications among participants took place through electronic mail. Information about the *Encyclopedia* and the text of all entries were sent by electronic messages to everyone who was on the subject committees (about 120 people); texts containing symbols or mathematics were delivered through attachments; discussions regarding the philosophy and outline of the *Encyclopedia*, and the content of particular entries, were conducted through an electronic network.

When we began this massive undertaking many scholars warned us about the possible dangers of the electronic revolution in communication. Lack of face-to-face communication has led, in many instances, to unpleasant communication on the Internet (the infamous "flame"). Our own experience is that the Internet allowed a decentralized and democratic decision-making process that would not have been possible in an earlier era. Decisions regarding the format and content of the *Encyclopedia* were taken after extensive discussion, often as a result of participants reaching a consensus. When no consensus could be attained, it was left to Professor O'Hara to act as the benevolent editor. The collegiality and good will demonstrated by the participants in this project, as well as the final product, give us hope that economists can again become a positive force as they seek to understand the world and communicate that understanding with others.

MARC LAVOIE
STEVEN PRESSMAN

Preface

Through the writing of original articles, this fully refereed A–Z *Encyclopedia of Political Economy* seeks to document the current state of knowledge in political economy in a succinct and eloquent manner. Special emphasis is placed on work undertaken during the 1960s–90s. The 1960s and 1970s saw a renaissance of interest in political economy and further developments have occurred into the 1980s and 1990s. There are now dozens of journals, and hundreds of books being published every year in political economy.

The time is ripe to document this explosion of knowledge in a scholarly and accessible fashion as we look towards the twenty-first century. Some of the material is based on pre-1960s developments; some is a synthesis of old and new; and some is a qualitative departure from the past. Documenting this knowledge was made possible through the collective energy and expertise of 300 international writers, editors, referees and advisers.

Approximately 450 entries are included in the *Encyclopedia* as one continuous A–Z format. It seeks to be as comprehensive as possible given the limitations of space and the knowledge of writers and referees. Writers document the nature of and show links between institutions, subject areas, concepts and schools of thought. This has led to some degree of overlap; which we condone as a necessary part of the whole process. Writers were encouraged to take a global or multi-national view, so that the entries reflect concerns beyond a particular geographical area. In many entries emphasis is placed on controversies in political economy.

The main intended audience of this work is undergraduates and graduates coming to the field for the first time. It will also be of value to scholars and professors, especially for areas in which they are not specialists. In addition, it should prove useful to politicians, public servants, political activists, business people, trade unionists and the general public.

Twenty A–Z lists formed the basis of the planning of the *Encyclopedia* (see the full lists in the section on "How to Use the *Encyclopedia*"). These lists can be divided into three types: (1) *institutional spheres*, including corporations, families, the financial system, capital–labor relations, the state and the world capitalist economy; (2) *subjects*, including unstable growth, development, anthropology, the environment, race, history of thought and methodology, plus political programs and ideologies; and (3) *schools of thought*. The scope of the whole work has been delimited primarily to evolutionary, feminist, institutional, Marxist, post-Keynesian, social and Sraffian political economy.

There are three main types of article in this work:

(1) *Concepts, principles, theories or problems*, for example, path dependency, poverty, inflation, minimal dislocation, reserve army of labor and racism.
(2) *General fields of political economy* such as money, credit and finance: major contemporary themes, institutional political economy: major contemporary themes, business cycle theories, and regional economic integration in the world economy.

Some entries are hybrids between these two typologies.

(3) *Major figures of political economy.* We have included one major person for each of the schools of thought which have a founding "father" or "mother" (Marx, Veblen, Gilman, Keynes, Schumpeter and Sraffa); and we also have a number of entries on

other major figures. After considerable debate we decided not to specialize in "intellectual biographies," however, since this has already been undertaken in the literature.

The success of political economy and therefore this work will depend on its ability to explain the pressing issues of the day. Political economy has always sought to be relevant to the political concerns of successive generations of "progressives." A central concern in political economy in the 1990s, for instance, is the relationship between economic growth, institutional change and unemployment. Another is the link between growth, development and sustainable development. A third relates to the balance of payments constraint and political forces operating in the global economy. A further critical area is the distribution of income, wealth and power on the basis of nation, class, gender and race. The *Encyclopedia* seeks to link these and other issues to concepts, theories, real world processes and policies.

Political economy has traditionally been bounded by different schools of thought. Many of the schools have developed specialist concepts, theories and methodologies. For instance, evolutionary and institutional political economy concentrate on cultural and technological change. Neo-Marxism specializes in class analysis *vis-à-vis* the production and distribution of the economic surplus. Feminism is developing a clear understanding of the relationship between gender, race and class in the social construction of the economy. Sraffians seek to develop a sophisticated critique of orthodoxy and a viable theory of production, distribution and exchange. Social political economy examines the values, assumptions and ethics underlying economics and society. Post-Keynesians examine the importance of effective demand and uncertainty in the workings of the corporation, state and world economy.

One of the benefits of the schools of thought developing their own vocabularies has been their ability to develop a detailed comprehension of certain issues and problems. Each of the schools is thus able to specialize and thereby develop a high degree of expertise. We have attempted to document this expertise. Indeed, there may be room for some continuation of these specializations.

However, the high level of expertise achieved by these schools may be reaching a point of diminishing returns, at least in some areas. Therefore, the potential exists for branching out of these specialist confines towards a cross-fertilization of ideas between schools. Such a move may expand the range and nature of hypotheses and research programs. It appears that the time is ripe for an integration of many of these specialties into a unified political economy approach. Some have specifically attempted to explore this question, and already many seeds have sprouted with scholars of various persuasions working collectively on a large number of integrative projects.

As a result, recently there has been some degree of convergence among the schools. This current work seeks to flesh out these commonalities, and thereby contribute towards some degree of unification of the traditions. We seek to cross bridges, showing interconnections where possible. The reader is directed to two entries in the *Encyclopedia*, POLITICAL ECONOMY: MAJOR CONTEMPORARY THEMES and POLITICAL ECONOMY: SCHOOLS, which discuss these commonalities and interconnections in some detail.

Some discussion of orthodox economics is included for reasons of promoting dialogue and because of the imperfect boundary between political economy and orthodox economics. Many of the entries in this work compare and contrast political economy approaches with neoclassical economics. On the avant-garde fringes of orthodoxy, in particular, various theories or approaches exist which are in some measure similar to political economy. This is true where social, evolutionary, environmental and political aspects of economics are at center stage. We have included some of these trends, but a detailed analysis of orthodox economics (including its various branches) lies outside the scope of the present work.

This project took four and a half years to

Preface

complete. During the first year, 1994, the objectives and content were delineated through discussions with members of the "subject committees" through the Internet. In the second year, writers were sought for the entries and personal interaction between many committee members was initiated to sort out remaining problems and sustain interest in the project. In the third year, 1996, most of the entries were written, refereed and in the vast majority of cases rewritten. Throughout 1997 I made a final assessment of the quality of each entry and prepared the best of them for publication. Some late entries emerged and new writers came on board to write orphan entries. Many entries were rewritten, restructured and reworked to conform to an established format and standard. I worked closely with Routledge, writers, other editors and referees in getting the entries to a publishable state. During much of 1998 the manuscript was extensively proofed and corrected.

Readers are invited to communicate with me about the *Encyclopedia*, with a view to planning a second edition of the work. Constructive comments, criticisms, and suggestions are eagerly sought. Please direct correspondence as follows:

Phillip Anthony O'Hara
Editor, *Encyclopedia of Political Economy*
Department of Economics
Curtin University of Technology
GPO Box U1987
Perth 6845 Australia
Email: noharapa@alpha2.curtin.edu.au

Acknowledgments

I wish to thank the writers, associate editors, editorial board, editorial advisers, committee of referees, subject committees, Routledge editors, colleagues at Curtin University and others for their collective efforts in bringing this *Encyclopedia of Political Economy* to fruition after four long years.

In December of 1993 the wheels of the project were set in motion when I sent out invitations to fifty eminent international scholars to join the project. The response was overwhelming. The respondents (many of whom I visited soon after in the UK and US) provided a vast array of information, suggestions and encouragement. Special mention in this respect should be given to Mario Seccareccia, Geoffrey Harcourt, Philip Arestis, Richard Wolff, Charles Wilber and Steve Keen.

Then the task arose to examine in more detail the nature of the *Encyclopedia*, and to organize a large group of people to work through all the issues. This was done mainly through electronic mail. In May of 1994, thanks to Fariba Alipour of the Harvard University Science Center, we began communicating through the "*EPE* email network," with about 120 scholars involved worldwide. Virtually every day during 1994 and early 1995 we debated the nature, substance and detailed content of the proposed *Encyclopedia*. Those who were active in the *EPE* network are listed as "Subject Committee members" and deserve a great deal of praise.

Marc Lavoie then came to Curtin University as a Visiting Professor for the first semester of 1995. He helped considerably in many ways, including enlisting many suitable writers, especially from Europe. Marc has continued his close association with the project right up until its completion. Mario Seccareccia, Ian Kerr, Peter Dawkins and Geoffrey Crocket were helpful in enticing Marc to Perth.

While I was in the USA during 1995 the *EPE* blossomed. Fariba Alipour made me feel at home at Harvard University and Boston. Mark Setterfield, Stephen Resnick and Richard Wolff were great hosts at Waltham and Amherst, respectively. By March of 1995 I had completed a draft of our statement of objectives, major themes and list of entries. This included the twenty A–Z lists of 11–35 entries each, giving a total of over 500 entries (subsequently cut to 450). The skeletal foundations of the *EPE* were thus developed.

This statement of objectives, themes and content was presented at the Eastern Economic Association conference in New York City, where we had two very successful sessions devoted to the *EPE*. This was a great opportunity for forty or so members of the committees (and others) to meet collectively and discuss the project for an extended period. Steven Pressman and John Adams, along with Anne Mayhew and Ajit Sinha, were in large measure responsible for the success of these sessions. Diana Strassman (from afar), Susan Feiner, Margaret Coleman, Alan Jarvis, Edward Elgar and George Argyrous were also helpful and encouraging. I wish to thank everyone who attended these meetings.

From there I visited John Davis at Marquette University, Milwaukee, Wisconsin, in March–April 1995 as a Visiting Professor. John arranged meetings and lunches with writers and we discussed many aspects of the project. He has been of great assistance right through the whole project. Afterwards I visited Charles Wilber, University of Notre Dame, Indiana, who suggested writers and opted to write some important entries. In San Francisco a number of writers were enlisted, including Ron Stanfield and Eric Schutz, who have subsequently helped a great deal; and thanks also to Ann

Acknowledgments

Jennings for discussions about the *Encyclopedia*.

From there, Paul D. Bush invited me to the California State University, Fresno, where he provided a great deal of assistance, something he has continued to do right up until now. It was here that Mark Barragry began the process which led to Routledge drafting the publishing contract for the *Encyclopedia*. Before coming back to Perth I visited Howard Sherman (University of California at Riverside) who as usual was a source of inspiration and accepted to write important entries.

By December 1995, the vast majority of articles had suitable writers and the third major phase of the project could begin: writing, refereeing and rewriting. Also, soon afterwards a contract was signed with Routledge, thanks mainly to the efforts of Fiona Cairns and Mark Barragry.

About this time Marc Lavoie started to act as Associate Editor in charge of refereeing entries in the areas of "post-Keynesian" and "Sraffian" schools and "money, credit and finance." Then Steven Pressman offered to join Marc by refereeing entries in the areas of "state and policy," "history of political economy and general themes" and "political programs and ideologies." (It was a delight to have Steve in Perth for a month to work on the project close at hand.) Soon after, Deborah M. Figart and Ellen Mutari were in charge of refereeing entries on "feminist political economy," "race and ethnicity" and "gender and the family." Throughout the writing, refereeing, rewriting and proofing phases of the project, the four Associate Editors have continued vigorously and systematically to evaluate entries and offer help in other ways. I thank you all a great deal!

By early 1996 the Editorial Board became formalized. John Davis, James Devine, Sabine O'Hara, John Harvey, John McCombie, Eric Schutz, Mario Seccareccia, Ajit Sinha, Douglas Vickers (whom I enjoyed having at Curtin for six weeks) and Richard Wolff, have all been invaluable members of the board in refereeing entries and offering advice and encouragement. Each of them has refereed the equivalent of about 15–30 entries. This was a demanding task, and one for which I will be eternally grateful. In addition, John Davis, John Harvey and Mario Seccareccia were of great assistance in proofing the final copy. Hassan Bougrine, Mathew Forstater, Geoffrey Harcourt, Gabrielle Meagher, Allen Oakley, James Ronald Stanfield and Eiman Zein-Elabdin were enthusiastic editorial advisers during 1995–6. Thanks also go to John Lodewijks for special assistance on several matters.

As the articles arrived they were sent through the *EPE* email network, with members returning referee reports to me. On average, each entry has been subject to three referee reports, most have been considerably rewritten by the contributor, and all have been edited and formatted by me (and some by Steven Pressman) to ensure consistency and readability in the final phase of preparing them for the publisher.

Curtin University has strongly supported the activities of the *Encyclopedia*. Ian Kerr played a major role in relation to my application for funding and discussing various aspects of the project through its entirety. Marie-Claire Thornton helped me to assess the value of entries from a student perspective. Assistance was also provided by Thorsten Stromback, Siobhan Austen, Gary Madden, Harry Bloch, George Kadmos, Michael McClure and other members of the Department of Economics, the Curtin Business School (CBS) and the Division of Research at Curtin University. Financial assistance was provided by the Research and Development Committee of the CBS and the Australian Research Council. Helpful computing assistance was provided by the staff at the CBS and the Computing Center.

At Routledge, during the writing phase of the project, Colville Wemyss and Fiona Cairns supported the project a good deal. During 1997–8 Denise Rea has been and still is a source of considerable assistance and advice through the publication phase of the project. Morgan Witzel improved the work considerably through his critical scrutiny and copy editing; Sarah Hall did a great job organizing the editing and production; and Ben Swift was very helpful on administrative matters.

Acknowledgments

Closer to home, Rhoda O'Hara and Pamela Hellens provided much encouragement, support and lighthearted moments through the evolution and development of the *Encyclopedia*.

The energy that made this *Encyclopedia* possible is the deep sense of community and commitment held by those who work in the area of political economy. There is a special sense of camaraderie amongst scholars in the field, which makes the subject very worthwhile personally, socially, academically and politically. We all seek a better world of greater social welfare, material equality, warranted knowledge, community and participation.

For this reason, the *Encyclopedia of Political Economy* is dedicated to students and scholars of political economy everywhere – past, present and future – and more generally to the future of political economy!

PHILLIP ANTHONY O'HARA

How to use the *Encyclopedia*

There are two main ways of using the *Encyclopedia*.
(1) *Browse through the entries.* This can be done according to your interest and needs at the time. Cross references within each A–Z entry will guide you to other entries of relevance. There are two types of cross reference: the first is mentioned in small capital letters within the text of each entry (LIKE THIS), and the second is listed under the heading "See also" at the end of each entry. The selected references will provide you with books and articles for further reading.
(2) *Use the twenty A–Z lists below for guidance.* These can be especially useful when studying specific units in a course that correspond to the title of each list. When doing this you should realize that the lists are simply a starting point for analysis; there are usually many other entries that are relevant in other lists. An indication of what these other entries are can be gained by noting the cross-references within the text of each entry.

A–Z lists

The *Encyclopedia* is one single A–Z format, but the lists below provide guidance when you need to study entries which have some specific relationship to each other. There are twenty A–Z lists: six relate to institutional spheres (including one on "family and gender" which includes many of the entries relevant to feminist political economy), nine relate to subjects and five relate to schools of thought.

Institutional spheres

1   Corporation

advertising and the sales effort
centralized private sector planning
competition and the average rate of profit
corporate hegemony
corporate objectives
corporation
economic power
global corporate capitalism
interlocking directorships
market structures
Nelson and Winter's analysis of the corporation
overhead costs
ownership and control of the corporation
pricing
producer and consumer sovereignty
research and development
Schumpeterian competition
social structure of accumulation: corporate
transfer pricing
transnational corporations
transnational corporations and development
Williamson's analysis of the corporation

2   Family and gender

affirmative action
class structures of households
comparable worth
domestic labor debate
ecological feminism
family wage
feminist philosophy of science
feminist political economy: history and nature
feminist political economy: major contemporary themes
feminist political economy: paradigms
feminization of poverty
feminization of poverty in the Third World
gender
gender division of labor
Gilman, Charlotte Perkins
home economics, new

How to use the Encyclopedia

household labor
household production and national income
International Association for Feminist Economics
labor and labor power
marriage
participation in the labor force
patriarchy
race, ethnicity, gender and class
reproduction paradigm
reserve army of labor: latent
sexuality
social structure of accumulation: family
waged household labor
women's wages: social construction of

3 Money, credit and finance

cashless competitive payments systems
debt crises in the Third World
endogenous money and credit
finance capital
financial crises
financial innovations
financial instability hypothesis
free banking
hedge, speculative and Ponzi finance
interest rate: fair
interest rate: natural
interest rate–profit rate link
interest rates: risk structure
interest rates: term structure
liability management
liquidity preference
Minsky's Wall Street paradigm
monetary circuit
monetary policy and central banking functions
monetary theory of production
money, credit and finance: history of
money, credit and finance: major contemporary themes
money, nature and role of
regulation and deregulation: financial
social structure of accumulation: financial
speculation
speculative bubbles and fundamental values
velocity and the money multiplier

4 State and policy

affirmative action
Bretton Woods system
budget deficit
cost–benefit analysis
democracy, political stability and economic performance
economic rationalism or liberalism
environmental policy and politics
fiscal crisis of the state
fiscal policy
free banking
free trade and protection
hysteresis
industrial relations
industry policy
inflation: conflicting claims approach
inflation: wage–cost markup approach
monetary policy and central banking functions
privatization
public choice theory
regulation and deregulation: financial
rent-seeking and vested interests
Scandinavian model
social structure of accumulation: state–citizen accord
social wage
stagflation
state and government
state and internationalization
structural adjustment policies
technology policy
trade policy
unemployment: policies to reduce
welfare state

5 Work, labor and production

cost of job loss
division of labor
efficiency wages
equilibrium rate of unemployment
Fordism and the flexible system of production
gender division of labor
health and safety in the workplace
human capital
industrial relations
internal labor markets

How to use the Encyclopedia

labor force
labor and labor power
labor market discrimination
labor markets and market power
labor process
participation in the labor force
population
productivity
reproduction paradigm
reserve army of labor
reserve army of labor: latent
segmented and dual labor markets
social structure of accumulation: capital–labor accord
social wage
Taylorism
technology
unemployment and underemployment
unions
wage determination
work, labor and production: major contemporary themes
worker participation in capitalist firms

6 World capitalist economy

balance of payments
balance of payments constraint
Bretton Woods system
class analysis of world capitalism
colonialism and imperialism: classic texts
comparative advantage and unequal exchange
core–periphery analysis
cycles and trends in the world capitalist economy
exchange rates
free trade and protection
global corporate capitalism
global crisis of world capitalism
global liberalism
hegemony in the world economy
industrialization
international competitiveness
international money and finance
international political economy
international political economy: major contemporary themes
internationalization of capital
North–South trade models
precapitalist world-systems
regional economic integration in the world economy
social capabilities and convergence
technology: globalization of
trade policy
uneven development
world-system: incorporation into
world-systems analysis

Subject areas

7 Cycles, waves and uneven growth

accumulation
business cycle theories
cyclical crisis models
economic growth
financial crises
financial instability hypothesis
Goodwin cycle and predator–prey models
Great Depression
Harrod's instability principle and trade cycles
increasing returns to scale
innovation, evolution and cycles
Kaldor's theory of the growth process
Kaleckian theory of growth
long waves of economic growth and development
Maddison's analysis of growth and development
Mitchell's analysis of business cycles
North's theory of institutional change
nutcracker theory of the business cycle
Okun's Law
political business cycles
productivity slowdown
profit squeeze analysis of crises
regulation approach
Schumpeter's theory of innovation, development and cycles
secular crisis
social structures of accumulation
transformational growth and stagnation
Verdoorn's Law

8 Development

agrarian question

brain drain
capital and the wealth of nations
classes and economic development
debt crises in the Third World
development economics: orthodox
development and the environment
development political economy: history
development political economy: major contemporary themes
development and underdevelopment: definitions
foreign aid
foreign direct investment
gender and development
human development index
import substitution and export-oriented industrialization
indigenous tenure systems
informal sector
integrated conservation and development projects
land reform
Lewis's theory of economic growth and development
military expenditure in developing countries
newly industrialized Asian nations
North–South trade models
regional economic integration in the world economy
social capabilities and convergence
staple theory of growth
structural adjustment policies
structuralist theory of development
surplus approach to development
sustainable development
transnational corporations and development
world hunger and poverty

9 Economic anthropology (as linked to political economy)

culture
disembedded economy
economic anthropology: history and nature
economic anthropology: major contemporary themes
gifts
hunter–gatherer and subsistence societies
language, signs and symbols
markets and exchange in pre-modern economies
mode of production and social formation
Polanyi's views on integration
precapitalist world-systems
substantivist–formalist debate

10 Environmental political economy

bioeconomics
common property resources
cost–benefit analysis
development and the environment
ecological feminism
ecological radicalism
ecology
entropy, negentropy and the laws of thermodynamics
environmental and ecological political economy: associations and journals
environmental and ecological political economy: major contemporary themes
environmental policy and politics
environmental valuation
evolution and coevolution
Green Party
gross domestic product and net social welfare
integrated conservation and development projects
limits to growth
natural capital
nuclear energy and nuclear war
pollution
quality of life
steady-state economy
sustainable development

11 Evolution, change and Schumpeterian themes

bioeconomics
catastrophe theory
chaos theory
circular and cumulative causation
entropy, negentropy and the laws of thermodynamics
European Association for Evolutionary Political Economy
evolution and coevolution

How to use the Encyclopedia

evolutionary economics: history
evolutionary economics: major contemporary themes
hysteresis
innovation, evolution and cycles
knowledge, information, technology and change
niches
Pasinetti's analysis of structural dynamics and growth
path dependency
research and development
Schumpeter, Joseph Alois
Schumpeter's theory of innovation, development and cycles
Schumpeterian competition
Schumpeterian political economy
systems approach
technological lock in
technology
uncertainty

12 History of political economy and general themes

Austrian school of political economy
capitalism
circular and cumulative causation
classical political economy
equilibrium, disequilibrium and non-equilibrium
Galbraith's contribution to political economy
game theory
George's contribution to political economy
Heilbroner's worldly philosophy
historical school
history of economics: societies and journals
International Confederation of Associations for the Reform of Economics
Japanese political economy
journals of political economy
Keynes and the classics debate
Keynes, John Maynard
Keynesian revolution
markets
Marxist political economy: relationship with other schools

medieval Arab-Islamic economic thought
mercantilism
monetarism
Myrdal's contribution to political economy
natural rights
neoclassical economics
neoclassical economics: critique
physiocracy
political economy
political economy: history
political economy: major contemporary themes
political economy: schools
Robinson's contribution to political economy
supply and demand: aggregate
supply and demand: microeconomic
surplus approach to political economy
traverse
value foundation of price

13 Methodology and philosophy

contradictions
critical realism
determinism and overdetermination
dialectical method
entry point
feminist philosophy of science
foundationalism and anti-foundationalism
holistic method
human action and agency
laws of political economy
Lowe's instrumental method
methodological individualism and collectivism
methodology in economics
methodology of scientific research programs
modernism and postmodernism
natural rights
normative and positive economics
paradigms
pragmatism
rationality and irrationality
rhetoric
storytelling and pattern models
time
value judgments and world views

14 Race and ethnicity

cultural capital
culture of poverty
discrimination in the housing and mortgage market
labor market discrimination
land rights movements
race, ethnicity, gender and class
race in political economy: history
race in political economy: major contemporary themes
racism
segmented and dual labor markets
slavery
Williams–Rodney thesis

15 Political ideologies and programs

alienation
anarchism
capitalist breakdown debate
exploitation
fascism
future of capitalism
ideology
labor-managed enterprises
liberation theology
market socialism
Mondragón
participatory democracy and self-management
Reaganomics and Thatcherism
republicanism
social democracy
social ownership and property
socialism and communism
socialist calculation debate
utopia
Ward–Vanek model of self-management

Schools of political economy

16 Institutional political economy

Association for Evolutionary Economics and Association for Institutionalist Thought
Ayres's contribution to political economy
capitalism
centralized private sector planning
ceremonial encapsulation
circular and cumulative causation
collective social wealth
Commons' contribution to political economy
conspicuous consumption and emulation
conventions
corporate hegemony
culture
disembedded economy
economic reasoning
Galbraith's contribution to political economy
hegemony
holistic method
individual and society
instincts
institutional change and adjustment
institutional political economy: history
institutional political economy: major contemporary themes
institutionalism: old and new
institutions and habits
instrumental value theory
minimal dislocation
neoinstitutionalism
North's theory of institutional change
pragmatism
radical institutionalism
recognized interdependence
reproduction paradigm
social fabric matrix
transaction costs
Veblen, Thorstein Bunde
Williamson's analysis of the corporation

17 Marxist political economy

Asiatic mode of production
capitalism
circuit of social capital
class
class processes
classes of capitalism
commodity fetishism
competition and the average rate of profit
composition of capital
determinism and overdetermination
dialectical method
economic power
economic surplus

How to use the Encyclopedia

exploitation and surplus value
falling rate of profit tendency
falling rate of profit tendency: temporal approaches
feudalism
finance capital
labor and labor power
labor theory of value
Marx, Karl Heinrich
Marxist political economy: history
Marxist political economy: major contemporary varieties
mode of production and social formation
monopoly capitalism
primitive accumulation
productive and unproductive labor
property
reproduction paradigm
reproduction: simple and expanded
reserve army of labor
surplus value as rent, interest and profit
transformation problem
turnover time of capital
Union for Radical Political Economics
use-value and exchange-value

18 Post-Keynesian political economy

animal spirits
circular and cumulative causation
effective demand and capacity utilization
efficiency wages
expectations
French Circuit School
Kaldor–Pasinetti models of growth and distribution
Kaldor's theory of the growth process
Kalecki, Michal
Kalecki's macro theory of profits
Kalecki's principle of increasing risk
Keynes, John Maynard
Keynesian political economy
monopoly, degree of
paradoxes
post-Keynesian political economy: history
post-Keynesian political economy: major contemporary themes
post-Keynesian theory of choice
pricing
Robinson's contribution to political economy
short-run cost curves
Sraffian and post-Keynesian linkages
time
wage and profit share
X-inefficiency
uncertainty

19 Social political economy

alienation
business ethics
capital and the wealth of nations
common property resources
community
cost–benefit analysis
crime
deontology
disembedded economy
distribution of income
ethics and morality
Gandhian political economy
health care in social economics
health inequality
human dignity
humanistic economics
individual and society
inequality
instrumental value theory
Islamic political economy
justice
language, signs and symbols
Mondragón
needs
normative and positive economics
overhead costs
Polanyi's views on integration
poverty: absolute and relative
poverty: definition and measurement
public goods, social costs and externalities
quality of life
rights
social economics: history and nature
social economics: major contemporary themes
social economics: associations and organizations
social and organizational capital
social wage
sport
urban and regional political economy: history

urban and regional political economy: major contemporary themes
value judgments and world views
welfare state
world hunger and poverty

20 Sraffian political economy

basic and non-basic commodities
Cambridge revolution
capital reversing
capital theory debates
circular production and vertical integration
competition in Sraffian political economy
corn model
gravitation and convergence
heterogeneous capital and labor
international trade in Sraffian political economy
invariable measure of value
joint production
labor theory of value
Pasinetti's analysis of structural dynamics and growth
price theory, Sraffian
profit theory in Sraffian political economy
reswitching of techniques
Sraffa, Piero
Sraffa's critique of atomism
Sraffian political economy
Sraffian and post-Keynesian linkages
surplus approach to political economy
technical change and measures of technical progress
wage theories, Sraffian

List of contributors

John Q. Adams
University of Virginia, USA

Nick Adnett
Staffordshire University, UK

Morris Altman
University of Saskatchewan, Canada

Daniele Archibugi
National Research Council, Italy

George Argyrous
University of New South Wales, Australia

H. Sonmez Atesoglu
Clarkson University, USA

Hamid Azari-Rad
Alabama State University, USA

Drucilla K. Barker
Hollins College, Virginia, USA

Chris Barrett
Cornell University, New York, USA

Enrico Bellino
Catholic University of the Sacred Heart, Italy

Riccardo Bellofiore
University of Bergamo, Italy

Raymond Benton, Jr
Loyola University Chicago, USA

Daniele Besomi
Tesserete, Switzerland

Christian Bidard
University of Paris X, France

Wolfgang Blaas
Vienna University of Technology, Austria

Harry Bloch
Curtin University of Technology, Australia

Patrick Bond
University of the Witwatersrand, South Africa

Douglas E. Booth
Marquette University, USA

Hassan Bougrine
Laurentian University, Canada

Steve Breyman
Rensselaer Polytechnic Institute, USA

Vernon M. Briggs, Jr
Cornell University, USA

Daniel W. Bromley
University of Wisconsin, USA

Doug M. Brown
North Arizona University, USA

Vivienne Brown
The Open University, UK

William Brown
University of Cambridge, UK

Anne M. de Bruin
Massey University, NZ

Dick Bryan
University of Sydney, Australia

Nancy J. Burnett
University of Wisconsin, USA

Paul D. Bush
California State University, USA

Gavan Butler
University of Sydney, Australia

Michael C. Carroll
West Virginia State College, USA

Michael R. Carter
University of Wisconsin, USA

Robert Cherry
City University of New York, USA

Duangkamon Chotikapanich
Curtin University of Technology, Australia

List of contributors

M.A. Choudhury
University of Cape Breton, Canada

Charles M.A. Clark
St John's University, USA

Theodore Cohn
Simon Fraser University, Canada

Malcolm Cook
Australian Government, Canberra, Australia

Willy Cortez
El Colegio de la Frontera Norte, Mexico

Peter Cribbett
Australian Industry Commission

John C. Cross
Berkeley, California, USA

Ben Crow
University of California, USA

Anthony D'Costa
University of Washington, USA

Christine D'Onofrio
New York City, USA

Anders Danielson
University of Lund, Sweden

Peter L. Danner
Marquette University, USA

John B. Davis
Marquette University, USA

Massimo De Angelis
University of East London, UK

George DeMartino
University of Denver, USA

Ken Dennis
University of Manitoba, Canada

Johan Deprez
Whittier College, California, USA

James Devine
Loyola Marymount University, USA

Edwin Dickens
Drew University, USA

Mary Ann Dimand
Albion College, USA

Robert W. Dimand
Brock University, Canada

Romesh Diwan
Rensselaer Polytechnic Institute, USA

Robert Dixon
University of Melbourne, Australia

Wilfred Dolfsma
Erasmus University, Netherlands

Sheila Dow
University of Stirling, UK

Paul Downward
Staffordshire University, UK

Eleanor Doyle
University College, Cork, Ireland

Robert Drago
University of Wisconsin, USA

Andrew K. Dragun
Swedish University of Agricultural Sciences, Sweden

Stavros A. Drakopoulos
University of Athens, Greece

Vassilis Droucopoulos
Center for Planning and Economic Research, Greece

William M. Dugger
University of Tulsa, USA

Gérard Duménil
Université de Paris X – Nanterre, MODEM, France

Ronald F. Duska
The American College, USA

Amitava Krishna Dutt
University of Notre Dame, USA

Gary A. Dymski
University of California, USA

Zohreh Emami
Alverno College, USA

List of contributors

Ross B. Emmett
Augustana University College, USA

David Fairris
University of California, USA

Sasan Fayazmanesh
California State University, USA

Yi Feng
Claremont Graduate University, USA

Deborah M. Figart
Richard Stockton College, New Jersey, USA

Alfredo Saad Filho
South Bank University, UK

Susan Fleck
American University, Washington DC, USA

Steve Fleetwood
De Montfort University, UK

Mathew Forstater
Gettysburg College, and Jermone Levy Economics Institute, USA

Alan Freeman
University of Greenwich, UK

Terrel Gallaway
Colorado State University, USA

Jean Gardiner
University of Leeds, UK

Shirley J. Gedeon
University of Vermont, USA

Christian Gehrke
University of Graz, Austria

S.M. Ghazanfar
University of Idaho, USA

B.N. Ghosh
University of Science, Malaysia, Penang, Malaysia

Ilene Grabel
University of Denver, USA

Warren S. Gramm
Washington State University, USA

Hugh Grant
University of Winnipeg, Canada

John Groenewegen
Erasmus University, Netherlands

Shoshana Grossbard-Shechtman
San Diego State University, USA

Robert Guttmann
Hofstra University, USA

Louis Haddad
University of Sydney, Australia

Harald Hagemann
University of Hohenheim, Germany

Eric R. Hake
Franklin and Marshall College, Pennsylvania, USA

Thomas D. Hall
DePauw University, USA

Lucia C. Hanmer
Institute of Social Studies, Netherlands

John T. Harvey
Texas Christian University, USA

Aristides N. Hatzis
University of Chicago, USA

Rod Hay
University of Western Ontario, Canada

F. Gregory Hayden
University of Nebraska, Lincoln, USA

Björn Hettne
Göteborg University, Sweden

Walter W. Hill
St Mary's College of Maryland, USA

Geoffrey M. Hodgson
Judge Institute of Management Studies, Cambridge University, UK

Emily P. Hoffman
Western Michigan University, USA

Richard P.F. Holt
Southern Oregon University, USA

List of contributors

Barbara Hopkins
Wright State University, USA

Sandra Hopkins
Curtin University of Technology, Australia

Hella Hoppe
Rheinisch-Westfalische Technische Hoschule, Germany

M.C. Howard
University of Waterloo, Canada

Peter Howells
University of East London, UK

Alan Hutton
Glasgow Caledonian University, UK

Prue Hyman
Victoria University of Wellington, New Zealand

Mario Iacobacci
Economic Studies and Policy Analysis, Canada

Aiko Ikeo
Kokugakuin University, Japan

Sidney H. Ingerman
Labor College of Canada, Canada

Alan G. Isaac
American University, Washington DC, USA

Joyce Jacobsen
Wesleyan University, USA

Therese Jefferson
Curtin University of Technology, Australia

Richard Jenkins
University of Sheffield, UK

Ann Jennings
Lafayette College, USA

Jesper Jespersen
Roskilde Universitatscenter, Denmark

Evan Jones
University of Sydney, Australia

Bruno Jossa
University of Naples, Italy

James Juniper
University of South Australia, Australia

Dilek Cetindamar Karaomerlioglu
Case Western Reserve University, USA

Elizabeth Katz
Barnard College, Columbia University, USA

Steve Keen
University of Western Sydney, Australia

Ian A. Kerr
Curtin University of Technology, Australia

J. E. King
La Trobe University, Australia

Douglas Kinnear
Colorado State Unversity, USA

Philip A. Klein
Pennsylvania State University, USA

Andrew Kliman
Pace University, USA

John Knudsen
University of Idaho, USA

Roberto Patricio Korzeniewicz
University of Maryland, USA

Aric Krause
Clarion University of Pennsylvania, USA

George Krimpas,
University of Athens, Greece

Rick Kuhn
Australian National University, Australia

Chidem Kurdas
Pennsylvania State University, USA

Heinz D. Kurz
University of Graz, Austria

Christian Lager
University of Graz, Austria

David Laibman
City University of New York, USA

Marc Lavoie
University of Ottawa, Canada

Clive Lawson
University of Cambridge, UK

Tony Lawson
University of Cambridge, UK

List of contributors

Simon Lee
University of Hull, UK

Dominique Lévy
CEPREMAP, France

Gilberto Tadeu Lima
Universidade Estadual de Campinas, Brazil

George Liodakis
Technical University of Crete, Greece

Victor D. Lippit
University of California, USA

John Lodewijks
University of New South Wales, Australia

Mark A. Lutz
University of Maine, USA

Gary Madden
Curtin University of Technology, Australia

Thanasis Maniatis
Center of Planning and Economic Research, Greece

Ianik Marcil
University of Montreal, Canada

Mike Marshall
University of East London, UK

Julie Matthaei
Wellesley College, USA

Peter Hans Matthews
Middlebury College, USA

Brent McClintock
Carthage College, USA

John McCombie
University of Cambridge, UK

Terrence McDonough
National University of Ireland, Eire

Ric McIntyre
University of Rhode Island, USA

Michael McLure
Curtin University of Technology, Australia

Gabrielle Meagher
University of Sydney, Australia

Jonathan Michie
University of London, UK

John Milios
Athens National Technical University, Greece

Marco Musella
University of Naples, Italy

Ellen Mutari
Monmouth University, Long Branch, USA

Jan Nederveen Pieterse
Institute of Social Studies, Netherlands

Robin Neill
University of Prince Edward Island, Canada

Reynold F. Nesiba
Augustana College, USA

Christopher J. Niggle
University of Redlands, USA

Eric Nilsson
California State University, San Bernardino, USA

Richard B. Norgaard
University of California, Berkeley, USA

Chris Nyland
Monash University, Victoria, Australia

Edward J. O'Boyle
Mayo Research Institute, Louisiana, USA

Phillip Anthony O'Hara
Curtin University of Technology, Australia

Rhoda Adelaide O'Hara
St James, Perth, Australia

Sabine U. O'Hara
Rensselaer Polytechnic Institute, USA

Paulette Olson
Wright State University, USA

Arrigo Opocher
University of Padova, Italy

List of contributors

Pierre Paquette
Royal Military College of Canada

Man-Seop Park
Korea University, Seoul, Korea

Steve Parsons
De Montfort University, UK

Elizabeth A. Paulin
La Salle University, USA

Janice L. Peterson
State University of New York College at Fredonia, USA

Ray Petridis
Murdoch University, Australia

Paul Phillips
University of Manitoba, Canada

H.W. Plasmeijer
Groningen State University, Netherlands

Marilyn Power
Sarah Lawrence College, USA

Robert E. Prasch
Vassar College, USA

Steven Pressman
Monmouth University, USA

Michael Rafferty
University of Western Sydney, Australia

Riccardo Realfonzo
University of Naples, Italy

Angelo Reati
European Commission, Belgium

Stephen Resnick
University of Massachusetts at Amherst, USA

Peter A. Riach
De Montfort University, UK

Colin Rogers
University of Adelaide, Australia

Alessandro Roncaglia
University of Rome, Italy

Nicholas M. Rongione
The American College, USA

Stuart Rosewarne
University of Sydney, Australia

J. Barkley Rosser, Jr
James Madison University, USA

Jochen Runde
University of Cambridge, UK

Thomas K. Rymes
Carleton University, Canada

Karin Sable
University of Puget Sound, USA

Andrea Salanti
University of Bergamo, Italy

M.A. Mohamed Salih
Institute of Social Studies, Netherlands

Muhammad Syukri Salleh
University of Science Malaysia, Penang, Malaysia

Neri Salvadori
University of Pisa, Italy

Aparna Sawhney
National Institute of Public Finance and Policy, India

Malcolm Sawyer
University of Leeds, UK

A. Allan Schmid
Michigan State University, USA

Eric Schutz
Rollins College, Florida, USA

Mario Seccareccia
University of Ottawa, Canada

Stephan Seiter
University of Hohenheim, Germany

Esther-Mirjam Sent
University of Notre Dame, USA

Mark Setterfield
Trinity College, Hartford, USA

List of contributors

Zeljko Sevic
University of Greenwich, London, UK

Jean Shackelford
Bucknell University, USA

Howard J. Sherman
University of California, USA

Steven Shulman
Colorado State University, USA

Ajit Sinha
University of Newcastle, Australia

John Smithin
York University, Canada

Clive L. Spash
University of Cambridge, UK

Brenda Spotton
York University, Canada

James Ronald Stanfield
Colorado State University, USA

Frank Stilwell
University of Sydney, Australia

Antonella Stirati
University of Siena, Italy

James Stodder
Rensselaer Polytechnic Institute, USA

Colin Stoneman
University of York, UK

Gale Summerfield
Monterey Institute of International Studies, USA

Andrea Terzi
Franklin College, Switzerland

A.P. Thirlwall
University of Kent, UK

Fred Thompson
Willamette University, USA

John F. Tomer
Manhattan College, USA

Marc R. Tool
California State University, Sacramento, USA

Harry M. Trebing
Michigan State University, USA

Andrew Tylecote
University of Sheffield, UK

Alejandro Valle Baeza
Universidad Nacional Autónoma de México, Mexico

Martti Vihanto
Turku School of Economics and Business Administration, Finland

Karl-Heinz Waldow
Government of Saxony-Anhalt, Germany

William Waller
Hobart and William Smith Colleges, USA

Immanuel Wallerstein
University of Binghamton, USA

William Waters
De Paul University, USA

William J. Weida
The Colorado College, USA

E.L. Wheelwright
University of Sydney, Australia

Howard White
Institute of Social Studies, Netherlands

Charles K. Wilber
University of Notre Dame, Indiana, USA

Rhonda M. Williams
University of Maryland, USA

Steven R. Wilson
UNIDO, Vienna International Centre, Austria

Richard D. Wolff
University of Massachusetts, USA

L. Randall Wray
University of Denver, and Jerome Levy Economics Institute, USA

Michael D. Yates
University of Pittsburgh, USA

Eiman Zein-Elabdin
Franklin and Marshall College, USA

A

accumulation

In general, accumulation refers to the buildup of assets over time by an individual, an organization, a country, or the world. Most economists exclude the accumulation of natural resources, financial assets and military assets from analysis and focus on means of production or knowledge. Thus, accumulation is typically part of macroeconomics and ECONOMIC GROWTH theory, rather than part of a zero-sum game.

There are two main visions of accumulation (see Nell 1987). The first is the tradition of Adam Smith and the neoclassical economists, in which accumulation is mostly an allocational problem, the postponement of consumption. The other tradition, corresponding to classical and Marxian interpretations of CAPITALISM, sees accumulation as a result of profit-seeking behavior, independent of any plans for future consumption. Further, in this latter view, accumulation is seen as based on prior production of a surplus product.

Adam Smith

While mercantilist economic theory and the political theory of John Locke emphasized the accumulation of money, Adam Smith stressed the importance of the "accumulation of stock" (i.e. physical means of production) and its results. For him, accumulation is based on parsimonious use of profit or rent, that is, its non-expenditure on consumption or unproductive labor. He presumed that only private entrepreneurs accumulate, while the government and the landed aristocracy only consume. Assuming an early version of "Say's Law," Smith's notion of accumulation unified both saving and investment. Accumulation allows the extent of the market to rise, encouraging the division of labor and thence productivity; it was thus at the center of promoting the wealth of nations. Smith also discussed how accumulation can increase wages, allowing the benefits of expansion to trickle down to the lowest orders of the population.

Most classical economists followed the path sketched by Smith. Unlike Smith, however, David Ricardo, John Stuart Mill and others believed accumulation would eventually stop as the economy attained a "stationary state" of effectively zero profits, when profits and interest are absorbed by land rent due to natural diminishing returns. Others, such as Thomas Malthus and J.C.L. Simonde de Sismondi, saw the possibility of underconsumption blocking accumulation.

Karl Marx

For Karl MARX, on the other hand, accumulation put the "motion" into capitalism's laws of motion. Accumulation was based on surplus value resulting from the EXPLOITATION of the proletariat by the capitalists, which was based in turn on the separation of the workers from control of the means of production and subsistence and the resultant capitalist control over production. Unlike Smith, Marx emphasized the role of fixed rather than circulating capital. However, accumulation was not simply the buildup of means of production, but also the reproduction of capitalist social relations on an wider scale, including expansion across the face of the globe (see COLONIALISM AND IMPERIALISM: CLASSIC TEXTS). This expanded reproduction (growth) inherently involved both regular "revolutionizing" of the conditions of production (technical change) and the often painful transformation of society (see REPRODUCTION PARADIGM). Marx saw the pain of social change as one factor setting the basis for a new, socialist, system of production. Capitalists face the "coercive laws" imposed by the battle of competition, driving them to accumulate on the pain of extinction.

To Marx this drive was endless, but it could and did run into barriers. As accumulation went beyond these constraints it turned into overaccumulation, which resulted in economic crises. Unlike Smith and his followers, for Marx these limitations were not natural but institutional, based in capitalism's own structure. Though Marx left his theory of crisis very incomplete (see Clarke 1994), his followers have emphasized three different types. First, crises could be due to inadequate growth of wages and consumer demand. Second, crises could be due to external limits set by the supplies of labor power and natural resources (the high employment profit squeeze). Third, crises could be due to the excessive use of means of production (the FALLING RATE OF PROFIT TENDENCY). All three involve "disproportionality," the growth of accumulation out of synchronization with the rest of the economy in a way that disrupts the growth process.

John Maynard Keynes

In contrast the neoclassical school, which arose in the late nineteenth century, did not emphasize accumulation. Heterodox thinkers such as Thorstein VEBLEN, with more dynamic perspectives, were at the margin of the economics profession. However, accumulation re-entered the spotlight towards the middle of the twentieth century. Unlike previous authors, John Maynard KEYNES clearly split the accumulation process into two distinct phases: saving and investment. Keynes rejected the classical view that saving determined investment, and reversed the line of causation. Investment itself was determined by its marginal efficiency, reflecting entrepreneurs' long-term expectations. In this view, increased efforts to save could result in the "paradox of thrift." Investment, on the other hand, helped determine aggregate demand, income received and, thus, the volume of saving.

Kalecki, Robinson and Harrod

Keynes' main analysis was static, ignoring the effects of investment on stocks of means of production and the capacity to produce. A more dynamic framework was developed by Michal KALECKI, Joan Robinson and others. For instance, in the "Cambridge equation" (developed by Kalecki and others), investment also determined the realized profit rate. For Robinson (1962), the profit rate in turn determined the rate of accumulation, implying possible equilibria, where both accumulation and profit rates were determined.

Kalecki stressed the contradictory nature of investment: it not only created demand but also capacity that required further demand increases to allow full utilization. This and other work revived the importance of the accelerator effect and also the application of mathematics to understanding macrodynamics. Within this general framework, the multiplier–accelerator approach stressed the possibilities of cyclical instability, while the growth models developed by Roy Harrod and Evsey Domar emphasized the "knife-edge" instability of macroeconomic growth (see HARROD'S INSTABILITY PRINCIPLE AND TRADE CYCLES). Not only is it unlikely that the entrepreneurs' expected growth rate equals the actual growth rate, as Harrod pointed out, but it is quite possible that the economy could involve spiralling unemployment or inflation.

Neoclassical synthesis

After the Second World War, the early fears of Alvin Hansen and others of secular crisis due to inadequate investment did not seem empirically reasonable (though these views were later echoed by the monopoly capital school; see MONOPOLY CAPITALISM). Neoclassical economists created what is often termed the "neoclassical–Keynesian synthesis". Here, full employment was assured by the intelligent application of macropolicy and/or by the automatic self-adjustment of markets. This allowed a return to Smithian conceptions in which saving determines investment, as in the Solow–Swan growth model, based on the use of the now-discredited aggregate production function (see CAPITAL THEORY DEBATES). With this theory, total product rather than the surplus product was the basis for accumulation. This emphasis on full employment growth was also shared in some "Cambridge" models produced by Nicholas Kaldor and Luigi Pasinetti.

Technical change

In Solow–Swan growth models, especially as applied in "growth accounting" exercises by Edward Denison and others, much of the growth that occurs is not due to the accumulation of physical capital but due to the accumulation of technical knowledge. Originally unexplained, technical change has been linked to the concept of HUMAN CAPITAL in recent years, as with the "new growth theory" of Paul Romer and others, who apply the aggregate production function. Alternative visions of technical development focus on the way in which abundant demand encourages supply-side growth (see VERDOORN'S LAW) or the way in which investment itself encourages technological change (Kaldor's technical progress function).

See also:

business cycle theories; capital and the wealth of nations; cultural capital; cyclical crisis models; natural capital; profit squeeze analysis of crises; social and organizational capital

Selected references

Clarke, S. (1994) *Marx's Theory of Crisis*, London: Macmillan.
Domar, E. (1946) "Capital Expansion, Rate of Growth, and Employment," *Econometrica* 14.
Harrod, R. (1939) "An Essay in Dynamic Theory," *Economic Journal* 49: 14–33.
Marx, Karl (1867–94) *Das Kapital*, published as *Capital*, 3 vols, Harmondsworth: Penguin, 1976–81.
Nell, E. (1987) "Accumulation of Capital," in J. Eatwell, M. Milgate and P. Newman (eds), *The New Palgrave: A Dictionary of Economics*, London: Macmillan, vol. 1, p. 14–19.
Robinson, J. (1962) *Essays in the Theory of Economic Growth*, London: Macmillan.
Smith, A. (1776) *An Inquiry into the Nature and Causes of the Wealth of Nations*, London: Dent & Sons, 1947.
Solow, R. (1956) "A Contribution to the Theory of Economic Growth," *Quarterly Journal of Economics* 70: 65–94.

JAMES DEVINE

advertising and the sales effort

The essence of capitalism is using money to make more money. Typically, this process entails the purchase of capital goods and raw materials, the hire of labor, the production of some good or service and, finally, the sale of the good or service for a profit. Advertising and the sales effort are those activities which promote this final phase, which Marx referred to as the realization of profits (see CIRCUIT OF SOCIAL CAPITAL). Advertising and the sales effort is one of the key aspects in the competition between firms, and is also fundamental to the overall effort to absorb the production of a demand-constrained economy.

History

In the early stages of the development of market economies, there was little apparent need to undertake much advertising. The reason was simple enough: because of the low level of economic development, the overall demand for goods and services was typically far in excess of the ability of producers to meet that demand. Hence, it is quite reasonable that CLASSICAL POLITICAL ECONOMY almost completely ignored demand as an important variable in the economy. Towards the end of the nineteenth century, however, this supply-oriented view began to change dramatically, both for economic theory and for the actual economy. The industrial revolution provided the potential for supply to catch up with demand. The sale of goods and services was no longer assured. This was as true for the individual firm as it was for the economy as a whole. In the twentieth century, advertising has become an essential factor in the operation of market economies, growing in importance as generalized affluence (the demand-constrained economy) replaced generalized poverty (the supply-constrained economy).

Advertising, competition and the firm

The role of advertising in the economics of the firm has been one of the more controversial topics in twentieth-century economic theory. Advertising seems to have a schizophrenic role in the economy. On the one hand, it is seen as providing information to consumers, and is thus viewed as increasing the level of competition between firms. However, on the other hand, the information it provides might be biased, influencing consumer preferences and lowering the perceived substitutability between competitors' products, thus lowering the level of competition.

Telser (1964) has argued that advertising has played a valuable role in providing information and increasing consumer awareness of the existence and availability of a product. Search costs are reduced as consumers are informed of product characteristics and price. Informative advertising serves to increase the extent to which consumers can substitute between products, thus increasing the price elasticity of demand for advertised products in some sectors. It can facilitate entry by new firms, who use advertising to make their product known and achieve economies of scale quicker, thus becoming competitive. Nelson (1974) claims that consumers can use the level of advertising as a signal of a product's quality. If we assume that high-quality products will experience more repeat purchases than low-quality products, it is more profitable for a firm to advertise high-quality products more heavily than low-quality products. The actual content of the advertisement is not relevant, according to this theory; the very existence of advertising is enough of a quality signal for consumers in some instances.

Persuasive advertising, critics claim, attempts to influence the tastes of consumers so as to increase their preferences for the advertised product. It can be used as a method of product differentiation, as various brands vie for consumer loyalty and attempt to increase the psychic cost of moving to an alternative product, thereby lowering the associated price elasticity of demand. Such advertising may act as a destructive barrier to entry, creating monopoly power if buyers are less receptive to new or superior products due to brand loyalty, as discussed by Kaldor (1960) and empirically supported by Comonar and Wilson (1974). Rather than increasing competition, persuasive advertising may limit it, especially if a firm spends a considerable amount to retain competitive advantage.

At the heart of the advertising debate is the concept of consumer sovereignty. Consumer sovereignty is the notion that consumers are the ultimate rulers of what happens in the market. Individual producers are powerless, having little influence on demand. They have to produce what consumers want in order to survive, and what consumers want is considered autonomous, original to the individual consumers and independent of outside influences. However, if the wants that producers are satisfying are in fact initiated or created by the producers themselves, then the case for laissez-faire capitalism must be brought into question. This is the controversial argument brought forward by John Kenneth Galbraith in *The Affluent Society* (1958) and *The New Industrial State* (1967) (see GALBRAITH'S CONTRIBUTION TO POLITICAL ECONOMY). Galbraith suggested a "revised sequence" in which producers artificially create desires, and then profitably satisfy them. These ideas have their roots in the work of Thorstein VEBLEN, who specialized in the political and social economy of consumer capitalism and the creation of tastes (see PRODUCER AND CONSUMER SOVEREIGNTY).

The empirical evidence shows that there is a strong correlation between profits and advertising (see Scherer and Ross 1990 for a summary). Given that high profits, and the high price/cost margins they often stem from, often are a sign of lower elasticities of demand, it would seem that the "advertising as persuasion" advocates have the upper hand in this debate. Clark (1989), in testing Nelson's "advertising as information" theory, could find no significant correlation between product quality and product advertising intensity. The stronger argument is that advertising contributes to creating the *perception* of quality, which is quite different from *actual* quality, especially when one takes into account the importance of CONSPICUOUS CONSUMPTION AND EMULATION.

Advertising and the macroeconomy

Economists who view the issue of advertising as a welfare problem of a possible misallocation of resources tend to have as their underlying assumption Say's Law, that the economy has a natural tendency towards full employment. Yet the general problem facing modern capitalist economies is that their ability to produce goods and services most often exceeds their institutional ability to consume goods and services. Hence the persistent problem of insufficient demand. John Maynard KEYNES suggested that government FISCAL POLICY, along with the socialization of investment, would be able to solve this inherent problem, assuming that consumption was rigidly tied to, and limited by, income. Yet, as Baran and Sweezy (1966: 124) have argued, the economic importance of advertising lies not primarily in its causing a reallocation of consumer expenditures among different commodities, but in its effect on the magnitude of aggregate effective demand and thus on the level of income and employment. Advertising thus helps to absorb the surplus production by increasing consumption. Moreover, advertising is seen as a necessary cost of doing business, further assisting the absorption of surplus production.

Conclusion

Advertising and the sales effort are important aspects of modern capitalism. They are essential tools in the protection of market power and monopoly profits (see MONOPOLY CAPITALISM). Furthermore, they assist in the absorption of surplus production and boost insufficient demand. Advertising is one of the most important influences on modern culture, helping to shape society to fit the needs of those with power.

Selected references

Baran, Paul A. and Sweezy, Paul M. (1966) *Monopoly Capital*, New York: Monthly Review.

Clark, Charles M.A. (1989) "Advertising and Quality: A Comment on Nelson's Advertising as Information," *Studi Economici* 23(2): 175–90.

Comonar, William S. and Wilson, Thomas A. (1974) *Advertising and Market Power*, Cambridge, MA: Harvard University Press.

Galbraith, John Kenneth (1958) *The Affluent Society*, Boston: Houghton Mifflin.

—— (1967) *The New Industrial State*, Boston: Houghton Mifflin.

Kaldor, Nicholas (1960) *The Economic Aspects of Advertising in Essays on Value and Distribution*, 2nd edn, London: Duckworth.

Nelson, Philip (1974) "Advertising as Information," *Journal of Political Economy* 82 (July – August): 729–54.

Scherer, F.M. and Ross, David (1990) *Industrial Market Structure and Economic Performance*, 3rd edn, Boston: Houghton Mifflin.

Telser, Lester G. (1964) "Advertising and Competition," *Journal of Political Economy* 72 (December): 547–51.

CHARLES M.A. CLARK
ELEANOR DOYLE

affirmative action

Definition and nature

Affirmative action is a term for policies, either legally mandated or voluntarily negotiated, that require taking positive actions to eliminate discrimination. This includes discrimination by demographic characteristics such as race/ethnicity, gender, age and religious affiliation in areas such as employment, the awarding of government contracts, and admission to public higher educational institutions. The general objective of affirmative action is for all groups in society to be represented to the fullest extent possible in all aspects of public life in proportion to their numbers in the society.

Affirmative action is a very controversial topic, having both ardent supporters and implacable foes. While most people of good will would agree that the concept of affirmative action is ethically noble and socially desirable, there is much opposition to it because of the effects of specific policies intended to implement affirmative action.

Opposition

Most of the opposition to affirmative action arises because an effective policy requires going beyond merely "not discriminating." Not discriminating is treating job applicants and current employees equally, without regard to their race, gender, national origin or religion. Affirmative action entails taking positive steps to create equality of opportunity for all qualified persons without regard to demographic characteristics.

Abella (1984), in discussing the status of equality of employment in Canada, notes that to many people the very words "affirmative action" constitute a semantic red flag which implies interventionist government policies, and is therefore sufficient to produce opposition. She proposes using "employment equity" as a term to mean "employment practices designed to eliminate discriminatory barriers and to provide in a meaningful way equitable opportunities in employment."

The most common claim of critics is that affirmative action constitutes "reverse discrimination," most particularly against white males. Opponents also claim that affirmative action constitutes government interference in the free working of the labor market. To these critics, nothing is more sacrosanct than the unfettered operation of "the free market." Yet, they ignore the fact that almost all modern industrialized countries "interfere" in their labor markets in ways which their society generally approves of, such as banning or restricting child labor and regulating workplace safety and working conditions.

Support

While many critics doubt the effectiveness of affirmative action, a review of twenty-six studies of the results of such policies in the USA (Badgett and Hartmann 1995) found a general pattern of improvement in the employment rate of black men. Jonathan Leonard (1991) compared the gender and racial composition of the workforces of US firms which were subject to the requirements of affirmative action with the workforces of similar firms that were not. He found that the implementation of affirmative action resulted in the employment of proportionately more women and minorities, being most effective in increasing the representation of black males and least effective for white females. Note that these changes should be regarded as progress towards proportionate representation, not as reverse discrimination against white males.

Affirmative action is mainly a phenomenon of liberal democratic industrialized societies. The actual legal status and level of effectiveness is in a constant state of flux, being affected by legislative enactments and judicial interpretations which are different in each country.

Cockburn (1991) discusses the status of affirmative action in Britain, claiming that British practice was influenced by, but was weaker than, developments in the US. As Cockburn mentions, Article 4 of the United Nations Convention of 1979 introduced an important concept. This was that positive or affirmative action for women, as a means of bringing about actual equality between women and men in the political, civil, economic, social or cultural sphere, was not to be considered as unlawful sex discrimination.

History

As mentioned, affirmative action is common in advanced capitalist economies, especially since the 1970s. The following is a brief history of affirmative action as it has developed in the USA, which provides an example of how the concept arose in one advanced industrial nation.

The first legal use of the term "affirmative action" was in Executive Order 8802, issued by President Roosevelt in 1941. The order prohibited discrimination by race in the hiring of workers by government contractors, who were then engaged in the great expansion of industrial production for the Second World War. Although there were instances of "moral suasion" being applied, there were no specific procedures for the implementation of affirmative action.

That the great increases in the hiring of women and blacks during the war was mostly due to the extreme demand for labor was shown by their rapid layoff at the end of the war. However, the undeniable evidence that women and blacks "could do the job" provided support for the concept of affirmative action.

Federal support for non-discrimination in the labor market was revitalized in 1961 by Executive Order 10925, which forbids government contractors from discrimination in employment by race, creed, or color. Executive Order 11246 of 1965 not only required federal contracts to contain clauses prohibiting employment discrimination by race, color, religion or national origin, but also required each contractor to set up an enforcement mechanism to actually oversee the implementation of affirmative action. Executive Order 11375 of 1967 added sex to the list of characteristics for which discrimination was prohibited. Therefore, "affirmative action" has become the popular name for Executive Orders 11246 and 11375.

The Office of Federal Contract Compliance Programs (OFCCP) was established in 1966 to enforce the affirmative action aspects of these executive orders. Each government contractor is required to submit an annual report which includes a comparison of the composition of the employer's work force by gender and race for each occupation with the composition of the total available labor force (local or national, depending on the occupation). The contractor is also required to set goals for integrating its work force, and timetables for meeting those goals. Non-compliance could result in loss of the contract.

It should be noted that OFCCP is distinct from the Equal Employment Opportunity Commission (EEOC), which was established to enforce Title VII of the Civil Rights Act of 1964, popularly known as "Title VII". Title VII applies to all employers who engage in *interstate* commerce and have at least twenty-five employees. It outlaws labor market discrimination by race, national origin, religion and sex in such aspects of employment as hiring, pay, promotion and training. In addition, some states have laws that are similar in intent to Title VII, outlawing workplace discrimination by employers engaged in *intrastate* commerce, and have enforcement agencies similar to the EEOC.

According to Blankenship (1993), affirmative action was developed as a means of implementing Title VII, and was aimed at integrating the workforce by race. Discrimination against women was addressed by the Equal Pay Act of 1963, which Blankenship maintains was intended to protect male employment from low-wage substitute female labor.

Affirmative action currently applies equally to gender and race. Firms and organizations that have contracts with a value of $50,000 or more from the federal government are legally required to take positive action to integrate their labor force for those groups covered by Title VII.

See also:

comparable worth; feminization of poverty; gender division of labor; race, ethnicity, gender and class; race in political economy: major contemporary themes

Selected references

Abella, Judge Rosalie Silberman (1984) *Equality in Employment: A Royal Commission Report*, Ottawa: Canadian Government Publishing Centre.
Bergmann, Barbara (1996) *In Defense of Affirmative Action*, Basic Books.
Badgett, M.V. Lee and Hartmann, Heidi I. (1995) "The Effectiveness of Equal Employment Opportunity Policies," in Margaret C. Simms (ed.), *Economic Perspectives on Affirmative Action*, Washington, DC: Joint Center for Political and Economic Studies.
Blankenship, Kim M. (1993) "Bringing Gender and Race In: U.S. Employment Discrimination Policy," *Gender and Society* 7(2): 204–26.
Cockburn, Cynthia (1991) *In the Way of Women: Men's Resistance to Sex Equality in Organizations*, New York: ILR Press.
Leonard, Jonathan (1991) "The Federal Anti-Bias Effort," in Emily P. Hoffman (ed.), *Essays on the Economics of Discrimination*, Kalamazoo, MI: W.E. Upjohn Institute for Employment Research.

EMILY P. HOFFMAN

agrarian question

Introduction and history

This debate has a long history. For instance, it is implicitly related to the argument raised by Ricardo early in the nineteenth century. According to Ricardo, if technical progress in agriculture is slower than in non-agricultural sectors, an increasing demand for agricultural products would lead, through an extensive cultivation of decreasingly fertile lands, to increasing (differential) rent, increasing agricultural prices and monetary wages, and finally to a tendency of the rate of profit to fall. Rapid technological developments during the nineteenth and twentieth centuries, however, have increased labor productivity rapidly and have shown that the Ricardian hypothesis is rather erroneous.

Karl MARX elaborated critically and developed the theory of ground rent further, arguing that landed property and rent constitute a barrier to the development of capital in agriculture. Although he pointed out the dominating tendency of capitalist development, he also argued that, in many historical circumstances, simple commodity agricultural producers may be subordinated to merchant capital, without revolutionizing the means of production or transforming the old mode of production (Marx, *Das Kapital*, vol. 3: ch. 20) (see MODE OF PRODUCTION AND SOCIAL FORMATION).

In the course of capitalist development, however, simple commodity producing peasants are subjected to the economic policy of the state (agrarian reforms, fixation of agricultural prices, etc.). This, along with the credit mechanism, plays an important role in the transformation of agricultural production. In order to suppress ground rent, with a view to guaranteeing low prices for agricultural products and a low cost of reproduction of labor power, the capitalist state has often implemented programs of agrarian reform or supported simple commodity production and small capitalist enterprises in the agricultural sector.

The agrarian question was explicitly raised for the first time in the context of the populist–Marxist debate during the late nineteenth and early twentieth centuries. In its classical form, the debate was mainly concerned with the structure and transformation of the social relations of production in the countryside, and with the barriers to capitalist development in agriculture. The classic debate encounters the critique by Bolshevik Marxists, and Lenin in particular, on the preoccupations and populist ideas of the Russian Narodniks. Lenin, in *The Development of Capitalism in*

Russia (1899), goes a few steps further than the classic Marxian proposition concerning the declining tendency of peasant farming and the advance of capitalist agriculture. He shows that the system of peasant farming does not constitute a special economic form of production, but rather an ordinary petty-bourgeois one, and that the peasantry are not antagonists of capitalism, but rather its deepest and most durable foundation.

Almost at the same time Kautsky, in his classic *Die Agrarfrage* (1899) (see Banaji 1976), qualifies the position of Marx and Lenin by pointing out that, in some countries or regions, the smallholding peasantry may persist for a long time due to weak technological scale economies or to a vertical concentration of production in agriculture which does not expropriate the peasants. As he stresses, this INDUSTRIALIZATION of agriculture subordinates smallholders to industrial capital, but does not entirely eliminate them. Chayanov, a prominent representative of Russian populism, also pointed out the same process of vertical concentration, but essentially sought a theory of the peasant economy as a specific form of production. He argued that the peasantry could take advantage of scale economies and that concentration, within certain bounds and in the form of a cooperative organization subordinated to state control, would offer the best path to agrarian development.

Postwar capitalism

In the context of post-Second World War capitalism, state intervention has significantly increased, TECHNOLOGY has acquired an even greater role in the development of agriculture, and the capitalist mode of production has further expanded in the agricultural sector of most countries. The rate of this development depends, in general and apart from the natural characteristics of land and cultural or institutional factors, on the rate and form of land concentration and its conversion into large bourgeois PROPERTY. In other words, it depends on whether the Prussian way has been followed (namely, the transformation of large pre-capitalist estates directly into large capitalist landed property), or whether LAND REFORM has divided up land and distributed it amongst small farmers (the American way). Under these circumstances, the character and forms of the agrarian question have accordingly changed. Technological changes have significantly affected the development of the agricultural sector and the terms of the agrarian question, thus constituting part of the agrarian question. This has occurred because of increasing labor productivity, which has allowed the intensive cultivation of land and reduced the employment requirements of production. Most notably, technological change has resulted in a relative decline in agriculture and hence a massive exodus of labor from agriculture.

Technological changes associated with the Green Revolution and the more recent biotechnological revolution have had significant implications for the use of land, the international division of labor, the transformation of agrarian productive relations, the instability in world markets, and the degradation or destruction of the natural environment. The transformation of the seed, from a common resource controlled by the farmer into a commodity ("input"), and the extensive use of agrochemicals and pesticides have increased farmers' dependence on the market and led to a considerable de-skilling of agricultural labor. The prevalence of monoculture (a single dominant export crop) has also resulted in an extensive reduction of genetic diversity. The apparent PRODUCTIVITY increases brought about by Green Revolution technologies are largely a myth, because the famous high-yielding seeds have to be combined with large doses of complementary inputs (fertilizers, pharmaceuticals, irrigation). The measurement of productivity by narrow private criteria does not take into account the invisible externalization of a great part of the cost stemming from the utilization of technological processes which are destructive or intensive in the use of natural resources. Technology is not evidently, as is usually assumed, socially neutral and in general unequivocally progressive. On the contrary, the use of inappropriate technology may have a detrimental impact on the agricultural sector and on some particular social classes.

Revival of debate

The revival of the populist–Marxist debate in the 1970s and early 1980s is also closely associated with the contemporary agrarian question. Neo-populist authors, with a methodological background ranging from neoclassical economics to a Chayanovian or a neo-Marxist approach, have largely assumed an undifferentiated peasantry, overstressed the persistence and viability of small family farming, and sought to theorize a specific "peasant or household mode of production." Some authors have stressed a putative efficiency and viability of small farming and have attributed it to a certain type of dualism. This dualism is functional to industrial capital, because overexploitation of family labor and cheap food produced by small farms imply the reproduction of labor power at a low cost. This dualism presumably implies a stable reproduction and a subsumption of small family farming to urban capitalism.

Marxists have criticized such neo-populist views and upheld the basic hypotheses of Marx and Lenin concerning the agrarian question. They have also presented empirical evidence showing that, despite considerable barriers, class differentiation is increasing and capitalist relations tend also to develop in agriculture. Functional dualism is considered unstable and it is assumed that the peasant tends to disapear as a social category under CAPITALISM.

New forms of the agrarian problem

Under current conditions, the agrarian question acquires potentially new forms. The Common Agricultural Policy (CAP) reforms in the context of the European Union, the last GATT agreement (1994), and their deep-reaching impact on agriculture indicate an increasing internationalization of the agrarian question. An adequate conception of the agrarian question should necessarily entail not only (1) the transformation of the social relations of production in the countryside, but also (2) the interrelation of the agricultural with the industrial or other economic sectors, (3) state intervention in agriculture and its contribution to the integration of these sectors and to the creation of the preconditions for accumulation, both in agriculture and in the economy as a whole, and (4) the current trend of state deregulation related to agriculture. It should also encompass the search towards transcending capitalism and developing an alternative agriculture.

Selected references

Banaji, J. (1976) "Summary and Selected Parts of Kautsky's *The Agrarian Question*," *Economy and Society* 5: 1–49.

Chayanov, Alexander V. (1966) *A.V. Chayanov on the Theory of the Peasant Economy*, Homewood, IL: Richard D. Irwin.

De Janvry, A. (1981) *The Agrarian Question and Reformism in Latin America*, Baltimore: Johns Hopkins University Press.

Lenin, V.I. (1899) *The Development of Capitalism in Russia*, Moscow: Progress Publishers, 1964.

—— (1976) *The Agrarian Question and the "Critics of Marx"*, Moscow: Progress Publishers.

Patnaik, U. (1979) "Neo-Populism and Marxism: The Chayanovian View of the Agrarian Question and its Fundamental Fallacy," *Journal of Peasant Studies* 6(4): 375–420.

Shiva, V. (1991) *The Violence of the Green Revolution*, London: Zed Books.

GEORGE LIODAKIS

alienation

In its most basic meaning, alienation is the detachment or separation of something important or essential from oneself. In traditional legal usage, one alienates one's property from oneself by transferring to another person one's RIGHTS to it, as in a sale or gift. Certain kinds of rights are so essential or fundamental that they are supposed to be "inalienable," i.e. they may not properly be transferred to, nor taken by, someone else. Thus when such rights are in fact alienated, profound political and moral issues are raised. The question also arises that if people's NATURAL RIGHTS may be alienated, what other essential aspects of human life, perhaps even of "human nature" itself, may also be alienated? These issues have important political economy dimensions, and have been a major concern of heterodox economists ever since Karl Marx conceived alienation to be the heart of a radical critique of CAPITALISM.

Hegel and Feuerbach

Marx's philosophical predecessor, G.W.F. Hegel, had used the concept of alienation as a central element of his philosophy of the evolution of mind or consciousness in human history. Hegel believed in an Absolute Mind or Spirit (or God) that was immanent within the natural material world. The natural world was a manifestation or expression of this Absolute Mind, an actualization or materialization of Spirit: Hegel described the world as the Absolute Mind's "alienation of itself." Humanity was part of the natural world, of course, but humanity was also a Finite Mind engaged in a gradual comprehension of the natural world in history. Hence humanity represented the Absolute Mind comprehending its own alienated self, "de-alienating" itself in the process of human history.

Feuerbach, a critical follower of Hegel, had abandoned idealism in favor of a materialist philosophy, and saw religion, including Hegel's own belief in an Absolute Spirit, as itself a kind of alienation. Humanity was actually "godly," and religion represented humanity's alienation of its own spiritual essence: people conjure up and bow down before an alien "higher being" that is pictured as embodying what are actually humanity's own inherent qualities. For Feuerbach, humanity's de-alienating itself necessitated abolishing this imagined God and comprehending His qualities as humankind's own.

Marx on alienation

Marx too wanted to "turn Hegel back on his feet," adding that in human history there are many other forms of alienation besides that manifest in religion. Marx saw these as having been brought to their highest level in capitalism, the latest and most developed form of CLASS society. In his analysis of capitalist wage labor, Marx (1844) drew clear connections between alienation in the moral and philosophical senses, and alienation in the narrower sense applied to property rights. First, in wage labor the worker produces a *product* that is immediately alien to him/her in the narrow sense, as it is the property of the capitalist. Sold by the latter for profit, which is then reinvested in capitalist enterprise, the product becomes alien to the worker also in the sense that it becomes part of the structure of domination to which the worker is subject. Workers produce the machinery and materials to whose physical nature and rhythms they must then submit directly in the workplace; and they produce the capital that, when reinvested, sustains and expands the socioeconomic system of capitalist wage labor by which they are dominated.

Second, the worker alienates his or her *labor* in the act of selling it to the capitalist in the wage labor contract. Workers thereby turn over to capitalists their life activity for the length of the workday, and with it what were formerly their own self-initiative and self-command. Having thus lost their creative self-determination for the length of the workday, workers also become to some extent alienated from their general capacity for these things, even outside of the workplace.

Having foregone some of their capacity to interrelate with the physical and social world in their own self-determined ways, workers are also alienated from *nature*, their own as well as that of the material world about them. Denied full actualization of themselves in the material world, they are equally denied a full comprehension of it, as well as of themselves as a part of it; that is, as conscious, active physical creatures.

Finally, in being alienated from the *social*

world, workers are accordingly alienated from each other. They cannot actualize themselves in fully free and self-determined relationships with each other, and hence cannot fully comprehend each other in such relationships. Furthermore, this alienation among workers extends throughout the whole of society. Workers are alienated from members of the capitalist class, since they certainly cannot relate with the latter any more freely than they can with each other. Capitalists and other non-workers are also simultaneously alienated from workers, since the latter are unable to relate freely with them.

Recent studies of alienation

More recent commentaries have taken further a number of themes intimated in Marx's analysis (Mandel and Novak 1970; Ollman 1971; Weisskopf 1971; Ellerman 1973). First, wage workers themselves must be seen as only partly the agents of the alienation of their labor since they are, at least to some extent, compelled to enter the wage labor contract (see ECONOMIC POWER). Rather than saying that workers alienate their own labor, their product and so on, it is better either to refer to members of the dominant capitalist class as the agents or initiators of the alienation to which workers are subject, or else to refer to a broad social process of alienation without any clear agents at all.

Second, there are other processes of alienation in capitalism that are historically, or at least logically, prior to those of capitalist wage labor itself. Any social system of private property, since it places manifest barriers between people, constitutes an alienation of people from each other and from a full interrelationship with their world. The DIVISION OF LABOR that necessarily accompanies MARKETS also restricts people's effective comprehension of others and of their own capacities for diverse activity. The monetization of economic relationships, reducing these to a mere "cash nexus," compounds these effects. Moreover, all class societies, not just capitalism, constructed as they are upon power relationships, involve alienation: since members of the subordinate class labor to one extent or another in the interests of members of the superior class rather than their own, in effect they forego a portion of their life activity to superiors (see EXPLOITATION).

Perhaps most important from the viewpoint of their critical implications for modern capitalism are the behavioral and psychological aspects of alienation. It is widely appreciated – not merely among Marxists – that if people's capacities for certain kinds of activities, or their opportunities for certain forms of self-actualization, are denied, then they are less likely to achieve comprehension of related aspects of their world and themselves. Even Adam Smith expressed deep concern about the "deformity" of over-specialized and over-routinized workers (Skinner 1986: 81, 97). Certainly wage labor, like other power relationships, must have repressive effects on people's personal development, and feelings of impotence and meaninglessness would seem straightforwardly implied, at least at some point in the course of people's accommodation to a subordinate relationship. Social and political passivity would also seem to follow directly, as well as various "compensatory" behaviors. For instance, religion may be an "opiate of the people," or perhaps, in more affluent capitalist societies, consumerism or other distractions may fill the same role. People's alienation from each other – widely acknowledged to be an inherent feature of all "pecuniary societies" (see VEBLEN) – would seem directly to imply not only feelings of estrangement and loneliness but also relationships of mutual indifference, competitiveness and even predation, and various "strategic behaviors" such as dishonesty and social inauthenticity.

Of course, generalized ailments and pathologies like these may have their roots in other things than capitalism *per se*. Material phenomena of modern life such as suburbanization and the automobile, television and, more recently, personal computers, have been variously blamed for such maladies perceived in society today (see MODERNISM AND POSTMODERNISM). Yet such profound changes in material life are arguably themselves determinant products of the capitalist economy (see MONOPOLY CAPITALISM). Their historical appearance may represent as much an effect of pervasive alienation as it is a cause. Perhaps only an already deeply alienated society could so enthusiastically embrace something like, for example, the Internet.

What can be done?

A secular or materialist version of the religious doctrine of "Original Sin", alienation represents a type of "fallen-ness" of humankind: humanity's estrangement not from its God but from itself and its world. So understood, it could be that alienation is to some extent an essential and unavoidable aspect of the life and consciousness of the human species (but for an alternative view, see Kovel 1988). For most Marxists, however, alienation is understood to arise specifically in "civilized" human history, reaching its nadir (so far, at least) in modern capitalism. While the implications for humanity are nonetheless radically devastating, "atonement," if there be any, can only result from the worldly action of real human beings in real material history.

What might "atonement" look like? The "opposite" of alienation must be a kind of comprehension that is the fullest possible grasping or appropriation of things, not only intellectually but emotionally and sensually, and in conscious self-directed activity. At the least, the point then must be to construct social relations conducive of such a comprehensive humanity in all people, to provide people with "the real possibility of access to all essential realms of activity... right up to the highest functional level" (Bahro 1981: 273).

See also:

hegemony; justice; participatory democracy and self-management; socialism and communism

Selected references

Bahro, Rudolph (1981) *The Alternative in Eastern Europe*, London: Verso.
Ellerman, David (1973) "Forward: Capitalism and Workers' Self-Management," in G. Hunnius, G.D. Garson and J. Case (eds), *Workers' Control: A Reader on Labor & Social Change*, New York: Vintage Books.
Kovel, Joel (1988) "Human Nature, Freedom & Spirit," in *The Radical Spirit*, London: Free Association Books, 289–305.
Mandel, Ernest and Novak, George (1970) *The Marxist Theory of Alienation*, New York: Pathfinder Press.
Marx, Karl (1844) "The Economic and Philosophic Manuscripts of 1844," trans. T.B. Bottomore, in Erich Fromm, *Marx's Concept of Man*, New York: Continuum, 1992.
Meszaros, Istvan (1970) *Marx's Theory of Alienation*, London: Merlin Press.
Ollman, Bertell (1971) *Alienation: Marx's Conception of Man in Capitalist Society*, New York: Cambridge University Press.
Schacht, Richard (1970) *Alienation*, New York: Anchor Books.
Skinner, Andrew (1986) "Introduction," in Adam Smith, *The Wealth of Nations, Books I–III*, New York: Penguin.
Weisskopf, Walter A. (1971) *Alienation and Economics*, New York: Dell.

ERIC SCHUTZ

anarchism

Anarchism includes a number of social systems or ideologies that emphasize non-hierarchical forms of organization. Anarchist systems are decentralized, distrustful of centralized authority, and often optimistic about the results of a revolutionary reorganization of society. It is possible to distinguish between two varieties of anarchism. The first is "collectivist" anarchism, which tends to support worker control, community organizations, and environmental justice, being especially critical of corporate and/or government bureaucracies. The second is "individualistic" anarchism (libertarianism), which generally supports private property, individual initiative and the coordinating potential of the "free market," being especially critical of government bureaucracies. These two typologies, however, have much in common. (Proponents of anarchism argue that the term is often misleadingly used in an everyday sense to mean disorderly or chaotic social systems.)

Theorists

The roots of anarchism can be traced back to at least the early industrial revolution. Industrialization led to the disruption of the traditional way of life, along with urbanization and increased centralization of power. In Britain, William Godwin (1756–1836) saw the emerging modern state as artificial. He had faith that humans, when acting as rational educated beings, would reject the state (without violence), and that society would evolve into small autonomous communities. He thought that a community of products would be shared based on need, since the wealthy have a duty to support those who are less well endowed. On the other hand, Max Stirner (1806–56) presented an ideal world where the individual, through force and power, would eliminate the constraints of the state.

Pierre-Joseph Proudhon (1809–65), often regarded as the founder of anarchism, was a French anarchist whose views were rooted in contemporary intellectual life. He is known for his somewhat provocative phrase "property is theft." Proudhon condemned property as the basis for permitting economic exploitation, but he recognized the ownership of the fruits of labor. He wished to see individuals bound to one another by free contract, and supported the formation of associations based on reciprocity of exchange for social services. The worth of goods was to be based on the time required to produce them. Unlike Stirner, Proudhon and his followers ("mutualists") envisioned extensive cooperative links in society, through a federal system of autonomous workers' organizations and local communities.

Like many of his contemporaries, the collectivist Michael Bakunin (1814–76) was strongly influenced by the philosopher G.W.F. Hegel. However, he saw both the state and the church as his enemies. He clearly perceived the authoritarian implications of Marxist socialism and argued as such at the International Working Men's Association. Also unlike the Marxists, he advocated workers' control of industry rather than nationalization, and abolition of the state rather than a dictatorship of the proletariat. While Proudhon emphasized rights of possession for individual peasants and peaceful evolution/action (later emphasized by Leo Tolstoy and Mahatma Ghandi), Bakunin proposed the collective ownership of the means of production and revolutionary action.

Peter Kropotkin's (1842–1921) early work in zoology influenced his collectivist political thinking. He believed that society predated man and evolved naturally as man ascended out of the animal world. Society emerged without higher authority or government, but by mutual agreement in accordance with local custom. Every member of society benefits from the customs, and people are mutually dependent on the other members. The mutual aid between members creates a great chain of connections that holds civilized society together. Unlike Proudhon but like Bakunin, Kropotkin's style of anarchistic communism relied on the common ownership of the means of production and the products of labor.

Anarchist movements before 1945

Three anarchist movements of particular interest during this period include that of the United States, the USSR and Spain. American anarchism of the late nineteenth century had both a native branch and an immigrant branch. Within the native branch, Josiah Warren was perhaps most influential. He independently reached ideas similar to those of Proudhon, and in 1846 he founded a colony called Utopia, that lasted for about twenty years.

The immigrant anarchist movement became strongest in Chicago. Due to bombing incidents in Chicago and elsewhere, many anarchists, including Emma Goldman, were expelled from the USA. Goldman was committed to direct action and a form of "decentralized socialism," calling for unrestricted liberty including freedom in personal matters. She lived in the USSR for a time but, like many others, became disillusioned and left in 1921.

The October Revolution in Russia was supported by some anarchists who believed, incorrectly as it turned out, that the soviets, or workers' councils, would embody their ideas and that the Bolsheviks would improve working conditions. Anarchism had a brief flowering in the period after the Revolution. From November 1918 until June 1919 an attempt was made, with Nestor Makhno as the leader, to create an anarchist society among the Ukrainian peasants. Temporary success was achieved but by December 1919 the Red Army reached the south, and within two years Makhno had been defeated. With the Kronstadt sailors' rebellion in March 1921, which was certainly influenced by anarchist ideas, the anarchists were eliminated.

The second brief anarchist success occurred in Spain. This movement had links to anarcho-syndicalism, which thrived in France before 1915 and represented a radical form of unionism committed to industrial militancy and ultimately, through the general strike, gaining control of the production and distribution channels of industry. The movement spread from France to Spain. General Franco's revolt in July 1936 precipitated the Spanish Civil War; the Nationalist forces were opposed by the Republicans, whose alliance ranged from anarchists (including anarcho-syndicalists), socialists and communists, to liberals. Active areas of anarchism existed during stages of the war. Catalonia, relatively distant from Madrid, successfully resisted fascism in the early phases of the war and was the main site of anarchist activity.

Despite organization and tactics being formed to resist central authority, anarchists entered the government of Catalonia in September 1936 and the Madrid government in December 1936. Eventually, however, anarchist influence waned in Catalonia in favor of the communists. With the establishment of a Fascist state in Spain following the defeat of the Republican cause in March 1939, anarchist ideas became dormant, although anarchism's influence lives on through, for instance, the MONDRAGÓN experiment.

After 1945

A generation later, the ideology of anarchism was rediscovered. The student movements of May 1968 had many recognizable left-wing elements; anarchist organizational forms appeared among a myriad of other influences, and issues such as individual cultural freedom, distrust of hierarchy and decentralization appeared in sizable sectors of the movement. In this era, anarchist elements seem to have permeated many different groups and interests, rather than necessarily existing in the pure form.

One current proponent of anarchism within the environmental movement is Murray Bookchin. He views pre-industrial society as having been in harmony with nature. Another is Noam Chomsky, who generally calls himself a "left libertarian" in his political writings (with a history of opposition to both superpowers during the Cold War). Features of anarchism have influenced most European Green parties, and more radical American environmentalists. The environmentalist goal of self-contained, self-supporting grassroots democratic societies living in harmony with both people and nature renews and expands older ideas of anarchism. Many anarcho- and ecological-feminists have revived similar viewpoints.

Economics groups of the right and the left have been influenced by anarchist-type arguments. From the 1960s to the present, radical economics groups have been to some degree under the influence of anarchist themes. This is especially true for issues such as PARTICIPATORY DEMOCRACY AND SELF-MANAGEMENT in the workplace (and many other institutions) (see Albert and Hahnel 1991) and criticism of corporate power and HEGEMONY.

Right-wing economics was also affected by a brand of anarchism (or libertarianism as it is often called), especially in the late 1970s and 1980s. This is true of the emphasis being placed on individual initiative and freedom of the individual in economic affairs (see AUSTRIAN SCHOOL OF POLITICAL ECONOMY; REAGANOMICS AND THATCHERISM.) The Libertarian Party of the United States is a right-wing party, but holds numerous ideas familiar to anarchists. It entered electoral politics, receiving approximately 490,000 votes (0.5 percent) in the 1996 US presidential election.

See also:

alienation; capitalism; exploitation; fascism; labor-managed enterprises; market socialism; socialism and communism; Ward–Vanek model of self-management

Selected references

Albert, Michael and Hahnel, Robin (1991) *The Political Economy of Participatory Economics*, Princeton, NJ: Princeton University Press.
Bookchin, Murray (1972) *Post-Scarcity Anarchism*, Montreal: Black Rose.
Carter, April (1971) *The Political Theory of Anarchism*, London and New York: Routledge/Harper & Row.
Chomsky, Noam (1969) *American Power and the New Mandarins*, New York: Vintage Books.
Ellerman, David P. (1990) *The Democratic Worker-Owned Firm: A New Model for the East and the West*, Boston: Unwin Hyman.
Roker, Rudolf (1973) *Anarchism and Anarcho-Syndicalism*, London: Freedom Press.
Woodcock, George (1967) *Anarchism: A History of Libertarian Ideas and Movements*, New York: Meridian Books.

WALTER W. HILL

animal spirits

The phrase "animal spirits" was successfully introduced into economic discourse by John Maynard KEYNES. The phrase appears only in section VII of Chapter 12 of the *General Theory*, and yet it subsequently attained great popularity among economists. With this colorful expression, he painted a compelling image for his behavioral hypothesis about entrepreneurs' investment decisions. Keynes (1936: 161) referred to "animal spirits" as "a spontaneous urge to action rather than inaction" that keeps entrepreneurial (i.e. real investment) activity going. Thus, "if animal spirits are dimmed ...enterprise will fade and die," because "individual initiative will only be adequate when reasonable calculation is supplemented and supported by animal spirits, so that the thought of ultimate loss...is put aside as a healthy man puts aside the expectation of death" (p. 162).

The expression "animal spirits" originates from early physiological theories in the Galenic tradition. Being familiar with Descartes's use of the term, Keynes attached to it the meaning of "unconscious mental action" (see Carabelli 1988: 298). Keynes may also have been familiar with the use of the phrase by David Hume (see Koppl 1991) and John Locke. As an English expression, "animal spirits" indicates a natural disposition, exuberance, nerve or courage to act. Marx (1867: 326) had used the same expression to indicate the character of a human being as a social animal who increases productivity when working in a team. Veblen's phrase the "instinct of workmanship" has a similar connotation (see INSTINCTS).

Optimism and productive investment

In economics, "animal spirits" is used in two related ways. The first reflects Keynes's original sense of the term: a characteristic of human nature that boosts investment activity, notwithstanding the uncertainty under which decisions affecting the future are being made (see UNCERTAINTY). For Keynes, entrepreneurs' readiness for risk-taking is a result of a spontaneous optimism and not the "outcome of a weighted average of quantitative benefits multiplied by quantitative probabilities" (Keynes 1936: 161). The history of CAPITALISM is the history of "individuals of sanguine temperament and constructive impulses who embarked on business as a way of life" (p. 150), ready to overlook the risk of failure. These individuals have an "innate urge to activity" (p. 163), and take "satisfaction (profit apart) in constructing a factory, a railway, a mine or a farm" (p. 150). Thus, the motive for investment arises from undertaking it as well as from its prospective yield. While entrepreneurs attach utility to investment activity and challenge, they benefit the COMMUNITY as a whole by increasing productive capacity. One can draw a parallel between the concept of "animal spirits" in Keynes, capitalists' urge to accumulate in MARX, and entrepreneurs' innovative actions in SCHUMPETER.

Investment in real assets was at the core of Keynes's theory of effective demand. The idea that entrepreneurial investment decisions did not depend on a strict mathematical expectation, but rather on a "reasonable calculation ...supplemented and supported by animal spirits" (Keynes 1936: 162), added an important qualification to his analysis of the investment decision. Economic prosperity, far from being assured at all times by an invisible hand, is dependent on a "delicate balance of spontaneous optimism" and is "excessively dependent on the political and social atmosphere which is congenial to the average business man," under which business decisions are made. Animal spirits is thus a cause for action as well as a cause of instability of investment; that is, the possibility that investment may be at an excessively high or very low level. When animal spirits are lacking, the fall of investment is unlikely "to be offset by any practicable changes in the rate of interest" (p. 164). Borrowers-entrepreneurs will stop postponing new enterprise when they recover "their good spirits" (Keynes 1931: 132–33).

Unstable real and financial activity

In the economic debate after Keynes a second meaning of the phrase "animal spirits" gained popularity, that of the unpredictable state of mind of investors in both real and financial investments. This stretches Keynes's original meaning in two directions: it broadens its scope to include financial as well as real assets, and it incorporates Keynes's notion of changes in the "state of confidence" with which investors make their forecasts (that Keynes had discussed before, and separately from, animal spirits).

The textbook treatment of Keynes's theory of investment has adopted this broader meaning. The position of the investment schedule is exogenously determined by "animal spirits," that is, by the unpredictable state of business sentiment, that make it a highly unstable demand component. Erratic human behavior can then be introduced to account for cycles where misplaced optimism drives the economy into bubbles, followed by disappointment, and subsequent over-pessimism. Similarly, stock price movements follow investors' mood and whims.

This second meaning survives in the literature despite Keynes's warning, while invoking the concept of "animal spirits," that "we should not conclude from this that everything depends on waves of irrational psychology" (Keynes 1936: 162). The problem with this use of the term is that, if economic decisions depend on the unpredictable subjective mood of investors, then one key explanatory variable – investment – remains undetermined and stock prices remain unexplained.

Neoclassical mainstream economists have rejected the relevance of "animal spirits" in either sense, because it cannot be modeled under the rational behavior hypothesis, where each agent can always solve an optimization problem. Some neoclassical economists, however, believe that animal spirits should and could be modeled formally. This approach has led to the literature on speculative bubbles (see SPECULATIVE BUBBLES AND FUNDAMENTAL VALUES) and herd behavior. Heterodox economists (such as Shackle) have emphasized the radical uncertainty implied in the concept of "animal spirits," indicating the impossibility of a policy response to the inherent instability of capitalism. Most recent post-Keynesian contributions view animal spirits as a broader notion of rationality (see Dow and Dow 1985; Kregel

1987); as a hypothesis of sensible, reasonable behavior under uncertainty, related to Keynes's *Treatise on Probability* (see Carabelli 1988). Under this latter view, animal spirits reflect the ignorance and uncertainty of investors, rather than their irrationality, thus providing the basis for designing economic policy to develop confidence and sustain animal spirits.

Selected references

Carabelli, A.M. (1988) *On Keynes's Method*, London: Macmillan.
Dow, Alexander and Dow, Sheila (1985) "Animal Spirits and Rationality," in Tony Lawson and Hashem Pesaran (eds), *Keynes' Economics: Methodological Issues*, London: Croom Helm.
Keynes, J.M. (1931) "The Great Slump of 1930," in *Essays in Persuasion*, London: Macmillan.
—— (1936) *The General Theory of Employment, Interest, and Money*, London: Macmillan.
Koppl, R. (1991) "Retrospectives: Animal Spirits," *Journal of Economic Perspectives* 5(3): 203–10. (See also related "Correspondence," *Journal of Economic Perspectives* 6(3): 207–12.)
Kregel, J.A. (1987) "Rational Spirits and the Post Keynesian Macrotheory of Microeconomics," *De Economist* 135(4): 520–32.
Marx, Karl (1867) *Das Kapital*, volume I, published as *Capital*, Volume 1, New York: International Publishers, 1967.
Matthews, R.C.O. (1984) "Keynes Lecture in Economics: Animal Spirits," *Proceedings of the British Academy* 70.

ANDREA TERZI

Asiatic mode of production

Introduction and defining characteristics

MARX formulated the concept of the Asiatic mode of production in the 1850s, along with the notions of "mode of production" and "capital," as he was developing his "critique of political economy" (see MODE OF PRODUCTION AND SOCIAL FORMATION). His major aim was to grasp the main characteristics which distinguish CAPITALISM from all other modes of production. This led him to examine the modes which precede capitalism, in newspaper articles, letters to Engels, the *Grundrisse*, *Das Kapital*, and other works. He was fascinated by the seeming lack of fundamental change undergone by certain ancient "Asian" societies, despite many changes in rulers and dynasties through the centuries. In this context, be began to explore the question of whether it is valid to distinguish such Asiatic modes from primitive communistic and feudal systems.

Three structural characteristics are said to prevail in such Asiatic modes. First, there is an absence of private PROPERTY of the means of production. Land and productive forces are communally organized in villages, although control rests with the state, usually in the person of a monarch or emperor. Second, agriculture and handicrafts are the dominant products, which are either consumed locally or allocated to the state. Non-commodity production is thus dominant. Third, the state extracts ECONOMIC SURPLUS through various taxes (or rents) in kind levied on communal production.

There is thus no exploiting class apart from the state. The state, however, does not simply extract surplus product and distribute this to the various classes linked with the monarch, such as priests, guards and other retainers. State action also contributes toward the production of surplus product through the provision of social capital, such as irrigation networks for agricultural production (Hindess and Hirst 1975) (see SOCIAL AND ORGANIZATIONAL CAPITAL). The legitimacy or ultimate power of the state or monarch is said to rest with IDEOLOGY or religion, and its ability to utilize some of the surplus for productive purposes to justify its existence. Examples of the Asiatic mode of production are not limited to Asia; in addition to the Angkorian kingdoms of Cambodia, ancient Indonesian empires and the Sung dynasty in China, they include ancient Egypt, Byzantium, and the

Aztec, Inca and Mayan empires of South America.

For most pre-capitalist modes of production, such as FEUDALISM, the ruling CLASS have economic ownership of the means of production (the land). The ruled laboring class have not been "freed" from the means of production but have the direct possession of them, i.e. the power to put them to work (to cultivate the land). In societies where the Asiatic mode of production is dominant, however, surplus labor is collectively (not privately) appropriated by the ruling class, whereas the peasants directly possess the land only under the presupposition that they belong to a village community. The appropriation of surplus labor by the ruling class thus takes the form of a tribute tax, paid to the state by all agrarian or town communities.

State officials have no heritage rights to their position, but they are appointed (and discharged) by a higher state authority. On the highest level, state authority is personified in the ruler, who is regarded as the direct representative of divine order and right. State officials appear as executive organs of the highest authority's edicts. The communities share a certain degree of autonomy from the central state authorities, as long as they pay the tribute. Communities are articulated into the Asiatic social order through the rule of a local stratum of notables and religious leaders, who guarantee the status quo in contact with district or even, in some cases, central state authorities.

Controversy associated with the Asiatic mode of production

The Asiatic Mode of Production became a subject of controversy among Marxists and communists, both for theoretical and political reasons. In the 1930s, it was doomed as a "non-scientific" and "non-Marxist" concept by official Soviet Marxists (see Mandel 1971; Brook 1989; Krader 1994). Theoretically, the concept of the Asiatic mode of production is not compatible with the mechanistic–economistic version of Marxism, which practically eliminates class struggle from the theory of social evolution, and conceives human history as an exact succession of societal forms, fully predetermined by technical progress (the "development of productive forces"). According to this scheme (which can be found in the writings of Engels, and which was codified and formed to a dogma by Soviet Marxists under Stalin), there are "five stages" (primitive communism, SLAVERY, FEUDALISM, CAPITALISM and usually also socialism), which all mankind was supposed to pass necessarily through.

Therefore, as the different modes follow each other, the Asiatic mode of production either does not exist, or is conceived to be transitory (see Godelier 1978; for a critique of these approaches, see Mandel 1971: 116–39). The problematical thesis that the Asiatic mode production refers to social forms preceding well-defined class societies is to an extent related to the fact that primitive tribal societies were also characterized by communal collective property, out of which different modes of production and respective types of class societies have emerged.

Other disputes have involved questions of whether more contemporary societies display elements of the Asiatic mode of production. With the Asiatic mode of production, for instance, the absence of private property in the legal sense does not necessarily mean the abolition also of class power and exploitation. Class exploitation of the laborers may thus attain collective forms. This idea was used by Wittfogel (1957) and Bahro (1977) when they abstracted from all structural characteristics of the Asiatic mode of production except state despotism. They reduced the "complex whole" of the Asiatic mode of production to the authoritarian state and the legal abolition of private property, forgetting communities and tribute tax. On the basis of this, they claimed that twentieth-century centrally planned societies, such as the USSR, had their origins in the Asiatic mode of production.

Other disputes include questions as to whether certain characteristics are associated with modes of production or social formations. For example, some characteristics of the productive forces in specific social formations are considered to be structural elements of the

Asiatic mode of production (see Wittfogel 1957). An example is the artificial irrigation systems of ancient India and China. Some authors consider the notion of the Asiatic mode of production too abstract from the real historical diversity of characteristics associated with the myriad of such "Asiatic" societies (see Kanth 1997).

Historical analysis shows that the dissolution of Asiatic modes of production, along with the political destabilization of Asiatic empires, may follow different directions. Consider the case, for instance, of the Ottoman Empire (Milios 1988). The increasing autonomy of Christian southern Balkan communities from Ottoman state rule led to the indirect subordination of the peasants to commercial capital, the transformation of common property into private property, the formation of a local commercial, shipowning and manufacturing bourgeoisie, and the prevalence of capitalist social relations. In other Balkan regions, the increasing power of district state officials, along with destabilization and dissolution of communities, led to the formation of feudal social forms. In all cases, historical development seems to falsify the five-stages scheme of *dogmatic* Marxism.

Conclusion

The potential exists for theoretical, historical and anthropological research on the validity or otherwise of the notion of the Asiatic mode of production and alternatives to it. This needs to be linked to related arguments about modes of production, socioeconomic formations and concrete political economies. Much work lies ahead.

See also:

economic anthropology: history and nature; Marxist political economy: history

Selected references

Bahro, Rudolf (1977) *The Alternative in Eastern Europe,*, trans. David Fernbach, London: New Left Books, 1978.
Brook, Timothy (ed.) (1989) *The Asiatic Mode of Production in China*, New York.
Godelier, Maurice (1978) *Sur les sociétés précapitalistes*, Paris.
Hindess, Barry and Hirst, Paul Q. (1975) *Pre-Capitalist Modes of Production*, London: Routledge & Kegan Paul.
Kanth, Rajani Kannepalli (1997) "The Asiatic Mode of Production: Eclipse of a Notion," in R.K. Kanth, *Against Economics: Rethinking Political Economy*, Aldershot: Ashgate.
Krader, Lawrence (1994) "Asiatische Produktionsweise," in W.F. Haug (ed.), *Historisch-Kritisches Wörterbuch des Marxismus*, vol. 1, Hamburg.
Mandel, Ernest (1971) *The Formation of the Economic Thought of Karl Marx*, New York and London: New Left Books.
Milios, Jean (1988) *Kapitalistische Produktionsweise, Nationalstaat, Imperialismus*, Athens.
Taylor, John G. (1979) *From Modernization to Modes of Production*, London: Macmillan, ch. 9.
Wittfogel, Karl (1957) *Oriental Despotism*, New Haven, CT: Yale University Press.

JOHN MILIOS

Association for Evolutionary Economics and Association for Institutional Thought

Introduction

The Association for Evolutionary Economics (AFEE) is the leading organization of institutional-evolutionary political economy in the world. It was formally instituted in 1965, and has published the *Journal of Economic Issues*, a leading journal of political economy, since 1967. Academic meetings of AFEE in the USA are part of the Allied Social Science Associations (ASSA) meetings in January of every year. The Association for Institutionalist Thought (AFIT), instituted in 1979, is a sister organization of AFEE. While AFIT was started in order to focus on unadulterated institutionalism, as opposed to the presumed eclecticism of AFEE, the two organizations now complement each other well. Their conferences are at different times of the year and usually in different places in the USA, and the vast majority of AFIT members are also members of the AFEE.

Nature of AFEE

The AFEE emerged from dissatisfaction with the American Economic Association (AEA) in the late 1950s. Some dissenting economists felt that the concerns of institutionalists were not being adequately addressed in AEA-led activities, and considered starting a specifically institutionalist organization. Bush (1991: 322) points out that this group, initially called the "Wardman Group," held its first informal "rump sessions" at the 1958 AEA meetings in Washington DC, at the Wardman Park Hotel. This became an annual event wherever the annual meetings of the AEA were being held.

In 1963, John Gambs (1963) undertook a series of interviews with forty dissenting economists in various parts of the US on the question of organization. As a result, that year the Wardman Group became formalized and in the following year the *Bulletin of the Wardman Group* was launched. An Executive Committee, consisting of John Gambs, Allan Gruchy, Robert Patton, Harry Trebing and Kendall Cockran, ran the organization which was renamed the Association for Evolutionary Economics in mid/late 1965. They launched the first *Bulletin of AFEE* in November of 1965; held the first AFEE meetings in New York during December of that year; and published the first issue of the *Journal of Economic Issues* in 1967.

AFEE members tend to adhere to the evolving and pragmatic tenets of institutional political economy (see INSTITUTIONAL POLITICAL ECONOMY: MAJOR CONTEMPORARY THEMES). They view the economy as a system of power, which is embedded in culture. Institutional change is said to occur through instrumental and ceremonial influences. Economics should address the theoretical and policy questions raised by institutional change.

The annual meetings of AFEE have produced a great deal of scholarly interaction and debate. The journal is famous for publishing articles which are readable, interesting and relevant to the world around us. Every year AFEE elects a new President (and Vice-President), a post which has, depending on the incumbent, provided considerable direction to the organization. The Veblen–Commons Award is given to a scholar who has contributed a great deal to institutional economics over many decades; various other awards are given, such as the Clarence Ayres Visiting International Scholar Award. Contacts and membership emanate from every continent, and especially close contacts are kept with the EUROPEAN ASSOCIATION FOR EVOLUTIONARY POLITICAL ECONOMY (EAEPE), which was instituted (with encouragement and assistance from AFEE members) in 1989.

The *Journal of Economic Issues* and AFIT

The *Journal of Economic Issues* has undergone four periods of editorial evolution. The first phase, 1967–71, was a period of editorial instability but was nevertheless a highly successful start for the journal. In the second phase, Warren Samuels commenced a decade at the helm beginning in 1972. He instilled a considerable degree of eclecticism into AFEE, with papers being published from a variety of institutionalist approaches and perspectives and dialogues being developed with neoclassical economics and other schools of thought. By 1981, the *Journal of Economic Issues* was in a very healthy state, with widespread circulation throughout the world, and its debates reflected real world concerns as well as methodological considerations. During this decade, 1,802 articles were submitted for publication, of which 11 percent were accepted, and the number of pages increased from 477 in 1971 to 1,127 in 1981 (see Samuels 1982). Institutional-evolutionary economics had finally come of age.

At the end of his editorial tenure, Samuels warned AFEE about the possibility of becoming sectarian, and said that his only disappointment was in being unable to stimulate the development of the existing body of institutional analysis, as distinct from repeating the themes of the past, as much as he had hoped (Samuels 1982: 313). He was nevertheless optimistic about the work of the new generation of institutional scholars, and proud of the eclectic nature of the journal.

Some members of AFEE, however, were concerned that the organization was deviating too much from its roots. This was one of the motives behind the establishment of the AFIT in 1979: to reflect the 'traditional' theory and policy concerns of institutionalism, along the lines of the work of Thorstein VEBLEN, John Commons, Wesley Mitchell, Clarence Ayres and John Dewey (see Ransom 1981; Sturgeon 1981). However, there was another motive behind AFIT, which gradually became more important: to formalize the annual meetings of institutionalists that had been ongoing within the Western Social Science Association (WSSA) since 1970.

Originally, the membership of the AFIT contained mainly those linked to the "Cactus Branch" of institutionalism: the multiple generations of scholars that were influenced, directly and indirectly, by Clarence Ayres and his associates at the University of Texas (plus an input from Allan Gruchy, John Gambs and others). It also commenced a journal, the *Review of Institutional Thought*, edited by Paul D. Bush, which went through three issues before being discontinued in 1986. At present the AFIT has members from all around the USA as well as in other countries. The concerns of AFIT regarding the eclectic direction of AFEE were allayed during the third phase of the journal, when Marc Tool commenced a decade at the helm of the *Journal of Economic Issues* in 1982. He continued the broad objectives of Samuels to some degree, but sought to deepen the traditional concerns of institutionalism as a unique school of thought.

Perhaps Tool's major achievement, apart from continuing the success of the journal through the difficult years of Reaganomics (see REAGANOMICS AND THATCHERISM), was in editing a two-volume, 1,000-page manuscript on evolutionary economics, "Foundations of Institutional Thought" and "Institutional Theory and Policy" (see the September and December 1987 issues of the *Journal of Economic Issues*; Tool 1988). This, and Hodgson, Samuels and Tool (1994) are the classic statements of the history, theory and policy of institutionalism.

Contemporary nature of the *Journal of Economic Issues* and the AFEE

The fourth phase of evolution of the *Journal of Economic Issues*, which is ongoing, commenced with Anne Mayhew's editorship in 1992. She continued the editorial policy of encouraging general and specifically institutionalist themes. In this phase, the AFEE was able to benefit from the global communications revolution. It instituted an electronic mail network discussion group on institutional economics (called AFEEMAIL) and a series of websites on the Internet; established linkages with other traditions and trends in political economy; and continued the process of internationalization (for example, through greater links with the EAEPE).

Conclusion

AFEE has for over thirty years promoted the development of institutional political economy through its many activities and functions, and AFIT has effectively supplemented these activities. The *Journal of Economic Issues* has become one of the top international journals of political economy, and the primary one in institutional economics.

See also:

international political economy: history

Selected references

Bush, Paul D. (1991) "Reflections on the Twenty-Fifth Anniversary of AFEE: Philosophical and Methodological Issues in Institutional Economics," *Journal of Economic Issues* 25(2): 321–46.

Gambs, John S. (1963) "Report on Interviews with American Economists," photocopy on file with the AFFE Secretariat.

Hodgson, Geoffrey, Samuels, Warren J. and Tool, Marc R. (eds) (1994) *The Elgar Companion to Institutional and Evolutionary Economics*, Aldershot: Edward Elgar.

Ransom, Baldwin (1981) "AFEE or AFIT: Which Represents Institutional Economics," *Journal of Economic Issues* 15(2): 521–9.

Samuels, Warren J. (1982) "Editor's Report," *Journal of Economic Issues* 16(2): 313–18.

Sturgeon, James I. (1981) "The History of the Association for Institutionalist Thought," *Review of Institutional Thought* 1(December): 40–53.

Tool, Marc. R. (1988) *Evolutionary Economics*, 2 vols, New York: M.E. Sharpe.

PHILLIP ANTHONY O'HARA

Austrian school of political economy

Austrian economics is known to many social scientists merely for the views of a few of its most prominent proponents who favor a free market economy. Austrians value individual liberty and limited government, but they also share other and often more important insights into social reality. Austrian economic theory is founded on the firm belief that the most effective means toward the goal of understanding economic phenomena is to examine them in terms of the purposive actions of individual human beings. Other characteristics of Austrian thought are emphases on the subjectivity of knowledge and the spontaneity of evolution.

Methodological individualism

Economists of the Austrian school attempt to explain social phenomena as the result of choices made by individual members of society. The central position of the human being is apparent, for example, from the main title of Ludwig von Mises's monumental *Human Action: A Treatise on Economics* published in 1949. The methodological individualism of Mises and other Austrians is often criticized for a failure to catch the essence of truly societal phenomena that defy a deduction to the choices of any individual actors in particular. Carl Menger, who was active in Austria at the end of the nineteenth century, provides an early reply to such criticisms in his *Principles of Economics*, originally published in 1871. He explains how a large number of participants in the market, acting purely for their own limited ends, give rise through an invisible-hand process to the first forms of money without anyone aiming to bring about such a beneficial social outcome. The undesigned emergence of more recent monetary institutions, such as the credit card, took place in the same way (see also FREE BANKING).

Austrian economists see no reason why a smaller or larger number of the participants in monetary evolution could not be legislators or other agents of the government. The important point is that no one is capable of determining the final outcome alone or of foreseeing its specific attributes, and that everyone contributes to the process by pursuing their own individual interests, be they selfish, altruistic or something in between. No matter what they desire, human beings are self-interested because they remain forever uncertain of each other's ends. In the ears of such fallible beings, the "public interest" sounds of necessity like little more than an empty phrase.

The insistence of the members of the Austrian school on methodological individualism is nowhere as evident as it is in their resistance to the use of aggregates in economics. For example, a leading theme in F.A. Hayek's Nobel Memorial Lecture, published in his *New Studies in Philosophy, Politics, Economics and the History of Ideas* in 1978, and belatedly also in the *American Economic Review* in 1989, is that there is not and can never be a constant correlation between macroeconomic variables such as output and employment. That relationship depends upon a multitude of various considerations about how the decisions of particular producers to change their supply of goods and services affect the number of people working in exchange for a reward in the market. Ludwig M. Lachmann elucidates the complexities of the market adjustment in *Capital, Expectations, and the Market Process* (1977). He provides the example of cinema owners who, in response to an increased demand for their services, cause a conversion of suitable tenements to cinemas. This results in a growing production of complementary capital goods such as projectors, and a thousand other changes in the structure of capital. A complete explanation of the specific consequences of such capital regrouping on the structure of production is far beyond the capacity of economic analysis. A discovery of simple correlations between some of the measured aggregate outcomes seems to be still less feasible. (See METHODOLOGICAL INDIVIDUALISM AND COLLECTIVISM.)

In a plausible line of argument, reasoning in terms of made-up aggregate variables and searching for regularities between them is acceptable in so far as such macroeconomics proves to be successful in practice. While explaining the workings of the competitive processes in the market, the economist is not too interested in the particulars of the rules that the entrepreneurs daily follow with the aim of outdoing their rivals. In a similar vein, we might accept the macroeconomists who do not even pretend to understand the deep principles of the market process, but who still succeed in predicting better than non-professionals the effect of, say, a given acceleration in the growth of total production on the rate of unemployment. The laws of macroeconomics such as OKUN'S LAW are, due to their nature, dependent upon the time and place of measurement, as everyone knows all too well, and they are a far cry from the eternal wisdoms of economics proper.

Subjectivism of knowledge

An economist no doubt benefits greatly from knowledge which he or she gains by making observations of the world around him or her. A remarkable part of the relevant information is, however, only known by the human beings whose actions are the object of economic inquiries. This privacy or subjectivism of the data of economic analysis is the second major emphasis in the Austrian school. For example, only members of the parliament themselves can know their willingness to sacrifice private interests for the good of society at large. An economic analyst is in practice capable of unearthing at least something about the intentions of human beings, either indirectly by drawing intelligent conclusions from their observed behavior or, more importantly, by imagining himself or herself in the place of the acting individuals.

Economic agents themselves make extensive use of introspection while attempting to render intelligible each other's actions and the economic order they bring about. Many economists consider the method to be unreliable, and they fear any approval constitutes an open invitation to smuggle ideological contentions into scientific reasoning. The proponents of the Austrian school tend to think that, despite the obvious problems, we cannot afford to lose access to the knowledge we can obtain only through an introspective process. Regardless of the rhetoric of the schools of thought, economists draw regularly upon introspection and display accordingly, as frustrated devotees of the positivist method occasionally complain, reluctance to reject theoretical propositions on the basis of empirical refutation alone. Austrians seem to differ from most economists in their insistence that this practice of research work be integrated into a coherent whole with the methodology of economics.

The subjectivism of many of the facts that economists use in their analyses is often considered a disadvantage of economics when compared with the natural sciences. Actually, it is just the other way round. By having a structure of mind more or less similar to that of the subject of their investigation, economists are able to have a better understanding of economic reality than the natural scientists, who lack such access to things behind the directly observable. For example, Hayek explains in *Individualism and Economic Order*, published in 1948, how little we know on the basis of objective facts about human relationships.

One among the numerous consequences of subjectivism is that the cost of a choice, or the value of the best forgone alternative, as the chooser himself feels it, is also an inherently subjective entity. Outsiders attempt to measure costs in terms of monetary or some other objective units; for example, competition authorities may seek to prove that a large corporation sets its prices in excess of the marginal cost and abuses in this way its dominant position in the market. Austrian economists usually strongly oppose this kind of discretionary policy on the grounds that no single government agent can have at their disposal the requisite knowledge of the production costs or of their social optimality. The Austrian position is vulnerable to the plausible argument of its critics that competition authorities are just as capable of introspection as the Austrian economists. In so far as the policies of the innovative government, based upon such speculation, give on average better results than *laissez-faire*, we are well-advised at least to experiment with them to promote free competition.

Entrepreneurship and evolution

A prominent and unresolved controversy in the current Austrian school concerns how deep an economist should attempt to penetrate in his inquiries into the human mind. The orthodox Austrian *apriorist* and current minority position expressed, for example, by Murray N. Rothbard (in Dolan 1976), is that ends of human beings are absolute givens; as economists, we should say of them nothing beyond what is revealed in real action. The proponents of the *empiricist* Austrian position, as Hayek intimates in *Individualism and Economic Order*, (1948) take a cautious step toward a psychological view and inquire into why individuals act in particular ways or even how they ought to act in various situations.

The open difference of opinion between the two groups of Austrian economists manifests itself, perhaps most evidently, in their views on disequilibrium. According to the pure apriorists, the plans of economic agents are to the economist always fully coordinated. In contradistinction to this extreme nihilistic view, Israel M. Kirzner explains in *Competition and Entrepreneurship*, published in 1973, how the participants in the market may fail to perceive obvious opportunities for private profit, and how they could create value, as it were, out of nothing simply by being more alert to the price differentials or plan discoordinations lurking everywhere around them. In the Austrian theory of business cycles, originally developed by Mises well in advance of the Great Depression and later translated into English as *On the Manipulation of Money and Credit* in 1978, disequilibria in the structure of capital is the main explanation for the emergence of recessions in the aftermath of the decisions of monetary authorities to overexpand the quantity of money.

When entrepreneurial economic agents manage to discover unnoticed discoordinations between their plans, knowledge of the existing state increases and, *ceteris paribus*, the economic order makes a move toward the imaginary state of general equilibrium. Human beings are also able to discover something entirely new, such as product innovations, and to create total surprises which, as Kirzner explains in *The Meaning of Market Process*, published in 1992, come to no one's mind in advance or even fall beyond anyone's wildest imagination before the event. Since it is often impossible to discern the discovery of truly novel facts, or SCHUMPETERIAN COMPETITION, from the mere coordination of already existing information, and since the distinction seldom interests the actors themselves, Austrian economists prefer to look upon entrepreneurial discovery as a general category. Calling attention to the significance of this essentially open-ended process, both to the performance of the economic order and to an understanding of its operation, is the third major emphasis in the Austrian school of economics.

Given the very nature of unforeseeable discoveries, it is not possible to search for them deliberately according to a pre-imposed plan. Hayek explains at length in *The Constitution of Liberty*, published in 1960, that the only means toward a beneficial process of social evolution seems to be to follow rules of behavior that have produced good consequences in the past. The individual members of society may make use of fairly concrete routines in their daily decisions as, for example, NELSON AND WINTER'S ANALYSIS OF THE CORPORATION accounts for in detail. On the level of law, the rules must be more abstract and create conditions in which the individuals can experiment with an unknown number of different modes of action under the law and, in this way, keep the discovery process in a constant motion.

Governments have in the past enforced laws of many different kinds. The principles of private property and other rules of the free market economy occupy a special position among all the known systems of law. The rules have proven to be useful for social evolution and human well-being in the light of very long-term experience. As a result, they tend to reappear only slightly modified, time after time under most different circumstances. The viability of the market order over time is the main reason for the confident opinions of Austrian economists on behalf of the rules of the market and against government interference with these rules. The respect for capitalist institutions finds its clearest expression in the critique of central planning, which is possible only by extensive violation of the rules of the market. The Austrians were not very successful in making their case in the famous SOCIALIST CALCULATION DEBATE of the 1920s and 1930s, but their later accounts of the discovery process make the views on the perils of arbitrary state action much easier to understand.

There are also other Austrian explanations for the vital importance of individual liberty and limited government. Rothbard asserts in *The Ethics of Liberty*, published in 1982, that the rights to private property are self-evident in the sense of being requisite for enabling human beings to be human and to act as Austrians assume (see NATURAL RIGHTS). James M. Buchanan, a public choice economist very close to the Austrian school, maintains in *Freedom in Constitutional Contract* (1977) that participants in an imaginary social contract will never unanimously approve of unlimited government.

The final results of the application of social rules are largely unintended and beyond the reach of particularized planning. The Austrian style of evolutionary economics is often sharply criticized for its plain reluctance to concede that we would often greatly benefit from deliberately designing the rules themselves, instead of waiting for the haphazard products of spontaneous evolution. The attempts at reform call for an analysis in line with consistently subjectivist principles of how we ought to modify the existing rules of law in order to provide the most favorable framework for the evolutionary forces of society. This points to one of the most promising directions for future research in the Austrian school of economics.

See also:

evolutionary economics: major contemporary themes; human action and agency; neoclassical economics

Selected references

Boettke, Peter J. (ed.) (1994) *The Elgar Companion to Austrian Economics*, Aldershot: Edward Elgar.

Dolan, Edwin G. (ed.) (1976) *The Foundations of Modern Austrian Economics*, Kansas City: Sheed & Ward.

Ebeling, Richard M. (ed.) (1991) *Austrian Economics. A Reader*, Hillsdale: Hillsdale College Press.

Kirzner, Israel M. (ed.) (1994) *Classics in Austrian Economics: A Sampling in the History of a Tradition*, 3 vols, London: William Pickering.

Littlechild, Stephen C. (ed.) (1990) *Austrian Economics*, 3 vols, Aldershot: Edward Elgar.

Rothbard, Murray N. (1982) *The Ethics of*

Liberty, Atlantic Highlands, NJ: Humanities Press.

MARTTI VIHANTO

AVERAGE RATE OF PROFIT:
see competition and the average rate of profit

Ayres's contribution to economic reasoning

Clarence Edwin Ayres (1891–1972) was the unofficial Dean of the second generation of American institutionalists. After completing his formal study in 1917, Ayres was for over a decade a rather erstwhile academician, but this changed with his appointment to the economics department of the University of Texas in 1930. During his more than thirty years there, Ayres was the leading light in the formation of the Texas School of economic mavericks (see Phillips 1989, 1995).

The Ayresian legacy consists of the development of the philosophic basis of Veblenian institutionalism and its link to the progressive modern liberal agenda in economic policy (see Stanfield and Stanfield, in Phillips 1995). Of Ayres's many books and papers, undoubtedly the most influential are his statement of the concept of economic progress (Ayres 1962) and his philosophic inquiry into the mode of reasoning appropriate to the pursuit of a reasonable society (Ayres 1961). Perhaps most significant of all, a strong oral tradition flourished and was carried away from Austin by Ayres's many students and colleagues.

Veblenian dichotomy

Ayres (1964: 61) considered the Veblenian dichotomy between knowledge, skill and tools on the one hand, and the socially structured personal relations, custom and sentiments on the other, to be "Veblen's principal bequest." Veblen's dichotomy contrasts the invidious and the non-invidious interest (Veblen 1899: 143) (see VEBLEN). The non-invidious or species interest is understood to be the common good of the "generically human." The test of "impersonal usefulness" is applied to establish that a given use of resources is non-invidious in that it "serves directly to enhance human life on the whole – whether it furthers the life process taken impartially" (Veblen 1899: 78–9). This direct contribution to the "fullness of life of the individual" is drawn in contrast to the indirect or secondary utility of goods that derives from competitive emulation and the desire to make an invidious comparison (Veblen 1899: 111). The invidious interest resides in the individual's desire to make a comparison of relative rank and status to his or her neighbors. Veblenian waste is the expenditure of a scarce resource to satisfy the desire for invidious comparison.

Much of Ayres's work was dedicated to an articulation of this dichotomy, by weaving into the institutionalist paradigm the instrumental reasoning of John Dewey. For Ayres (1961), instrumental reasoning reveals that there are a handful of basic values – freedom, abundance, equality, excellence, and security – that are more or less universally held in otherwise very diverse human societies. Another such value is democracy, the process of collective governance that serves to advance these basic values, revealed to be a universal aspiration. But, following Dewey, Ayres conceived democracy differently from the mechanical conception of majority rule. Democracy is not simply or even most importantly voting to monitor preferences and resolve preference conflicts. It is most importantly a process in which preferences are *reformed*, with the enhanced enlightenment that comes from the process of inquiry and reasoned discourse. In the instrumentalist view, the democratic process implies the merger of the social scientist and social reformer (Tilman 1987). Although his efforts in this respect remain the basis for controversy (Mayhew 1987), it is agreed that Ayres clarified the issue of values articulation and brought much-needed attention to the concerns expressed by Veblen and others with regard to the pretense of positivism in conventional economics.

Ayres's derision of the "price equals value" or "making goods equals making money" formula went somewhat further than the commonplace issue of the realism of the assumptions of perfect competition. He insisted that even competitive market prices reflect not only the prevalent pattern of income and wealth distribution, but mistakes in judgment and preferences for unhealthy and destructive products (Ayres 1962: 226–8). The central issue is that wants "are social habits" which result from emotional conditioning (Ayres 1962: 84; 1961: ch. 4). The tastes or preferences held by individuals, therefore, have no more validity than the socialization process by which they are formed. Much of the formation of relative prices may be seen as accidental and arbitrary to the logic of scarcity registered in relative prices. The neoclassical credulity, with respect to relative prices, also obscures the underlying structure of power and stratification. For Ayres, the conventional price theory is a metaphysical rationalization of the extant power and distributive configuration. The positivist stance of conventional economics is a sham. (See HEGEMONY.)

Progress and change

In his most important work, Ayres (1962) examined the nature of economic progress and sketched a program for institutional adjustment to sustain it. He baldly defined progress as "finding out how to do things, finding out how to do more things, and finding out how to do all things better" (Ayres 1962: xiii). He went on to insist that progress, thus defined, is irresistible and everywhere at war with status preoccupations and habitual sensibilities of propriety. Progress occurs through new combinations of previously unrelated technical artifacts or ideas that bear fruit in their admixture. This includes not only accretion of technical materials or tools but, more fundamentally, the spread of knowledge about material process. Hence Ayres stressed widening *participation* as the key to progress. The more people who have the capacity and opportunity to engage in the material process of inquiry and development, the greater the pool from which new combinations emerge.

Ayres sketched a strategy for progress to guide the opportunity presented in the immediate postwar period. The strategy consisted of intensive and extensive development of the New Deal (the liberal social policies associated with US President F.D. Roosevelt between 1933 and 1940, and which had long-term significance). Domestically, the principles of balancing income flows and revamping the success criteria of corporate America were to be deepened to secure universal participation in socially responsible prosperity. Internationally, Ayres called for an application of these principles in a World New Deal intended to promote global economic progress and head off the abysmal deprivation that foments disorder and military conflict (Ayres 1962: 281).

Ayres advocated the concentration-and-control strategy held in common with many institutionalists, notably Rexford Tugwell, J.K. Galbraith and William Dugger. In this view, corporate concentration of resources and power is seen to be inevitable and it is therefore necessary to institute a strategy to secure national and international social control to channel corporate behavior toward the public purpose. In order to facilitate democratic control by regulators and public opinion, Ayres viewed the open corporate book as the functional equivalent of a street light in the interest of public safety (Ayres 1962: 252–7).

Ayres and other institutionalists also agreed with Keynes about the need for a policy to counteract the fundamental tendency of finance capitalism toward macroeconomic stagnation. Creation of purchasing power by income transfers and public sector projects counteracts this tendency and rescues the potential output that would otherwise go unproduced and wasted (Ayres 1962: 259–82; Ayres 1946).

It is worth emphasizing that Ayres's concern for redistribution went well beyond the macroeconomic concern for aggregate demand; indeed, it went beyond even the humanitarian concern for the underprivileged. Progress for all would be advanced by the widening participation that income redistribution would bring about. Wider participation would magnify the opportunities for creativity and new departures in knowledge and technique. For this reason, Ayres and many institutionalists advocate some manner of guaranteed income to separate the financing of household livelihoods from its direct connection to production (Ayres 1966). Ayres (1967) thought that such bold new departures would make possible the transition from the welfare society to the creative society.

Conclusion

Ayres's contributions to institutional economics are very significant and will persist for a long time. He was fond of saying that asking the right question is the key to wisdom. Although the answers and their significance may require further inquiry for some time yet, it is certain that Ayres asked the right questions about humanity's complex socioeconomic process.

See also:

institutional policy economy: history; institutional political economy: major contemporary themes; welfare state

Selected references

Ayres, C.E. (1946) *The Divine Right of Capital*, Boston: Houghton Mifflin.

—— (1961) *Toward a Reasonable Society*, Austin: University of Texas Press.

—— (1962) *The Theory of Economic Progress*, New York: Schocken.

—— (1964) "The Legacy of Thorstein Veblen," in *Institutional Economics: Veblen, Commons, and Mitchell Reconsidered*, Berkeley, CA: University of California Press, 45–62.

—— (1966) "Guaranteed Income: An Institutionalist View," in R. Theobald (ed.), *The Guaranteed Income*, Garden City, NY: Doubleday, 169–82.

—— (1967) "Ideological Responsibility," *Journal of Economic Issues* 1(2): 3–11.

Mayhew, A. (1987) "Culture: Core Concept Under Attack," *Journal of Economic Issues* 21(2): 587–603.

Phillips, R.J. (1989) "Radical Institutionalism and the Texas School of Economics," in W.M. Dugger (ed.), *Radical Institutionalism: Contemporary Voices*, Westport, CN: Greenwood Press, 21–37.

—— (ed.) (1995) *Economic Mavericks: The Texas Institutionalists*, Greenwich, CN: JAI Press.

Tilman, R. (1987) "The Neoinstrumental Theory of Democracy," *Journal of Economic Issues* 21(3): 1379–1401.

Veblen, T.B. (1899) *The Theory of the Leisure Class*, New York: New American Library, 1953.

JAMES RONALD STANFIELD

B

balance of payments

The balance of payments depicts a nation's financial position with respect to the rest of the world. In national accounting, it is an international complement of standard national accounts. Each country's balance of payments is constructed under rules set out by the International Monetary Fund (1977). The balance of payments is divided into two accounts. The *current account* shows flows of payments into and out of the nation. It is comprised of a measurement of exports and imports of goods and services, and income flows. The *capital account* records changes in the stock of foreign-owned assets over an accounting period.

History

Earliest evidence of national payments records dates to the beginning of the seventeenth century. The more systematic recording of both the flows of funds and commodity trade developed over the eighteenth century in Britain, with the term "balance of payments" being attributed to Sir James Steuart in *An Inquiry into the Principles of Political Economy,* published in 1767 (Wasserman and Ware 1965). Early balance of payments figures were based on private estimates, with an accuracy recognized to be too low to inform national policy. Official balance of payments figures were not widely produced until the twentieth century. The United States only provided official data from 1922, the first year that the League of Nations established formal international rules for data presentation (Wasserman and Ware 1965: 105, 141).

Current balance of payments accounts are substantially as they were developed in the 1940s. This shows a strong influence of Keynesian macroeconomic categories, which remains despite the demise of Keynesian analysis in policy formation in most countries. In the postwar period, economic analysis of the balance of payments focused on integrating balance of payments into the Keynesian model. The institution of the IMF, established in 1944 at Bretton Woods, was a "Keynesian" mechanism to assist countries with balance of payments problems (see BRETTON WOODS SYSTEM).

Leaving aside the endemic current account deficits of poor countries, the industrial countries maintained small imbalances in the current account from the First World War until the end of the 1970s. In the early 1980s, however, the size of imbalances (both surpluses and deficits) increased about fourfold (Turner 1991: 9). Some countries started running sustained current account deficits while others, such as Germany and especially Japan, sustained large surpluses without systematic tendencies through exchange rate movements or government policy to move toward balance. This situation has given rise to a number of contemporary debates, both about the meaning of balance of payments figures and about national policy to deal with current account imbalance.

Accuracy of balance of payments data

Global balance of payments figures should sum to zero. Yet for most of the last twenty-five years, the world has run a current account deficit of around 2 percent. In the mid-1980s, it rose temporarily to 6 percent, associated with the turmoil around the US balance of payments crisis. The inaccuracy is thought to lie in tax avoidance in cross-national transport industries; in the intra-corporate transfers of transnational corporations; in systematic delays in payments for received goods (Bank for International Settlements 1983: 86–90); and in the reduction of trade controls in most countries, which has reduced the ease of national data collection. In the capital account, the deregulation of capital flows has similarly affected national data collection. More importantly, the development of derivatives markets for international finance has led to the rapid growth of "off-balance sheet" financing of international investment, which are generally not recorded in national balance of payments data (see FINANCIAL INNOVATIONS). Indeed, the problem here is not so much one of accuracy, but rather that the capital account provides little information about international capital transactions.

Relation between current and capital accounts

The double-entry system of book-keeping means that the balance of payments always balances. A shortfall (deficit) on the current account has to be paid for by foreign funds, and that records as an equivalent surplus (capital inflow) on the capital account. This accounting construction has created the image of the current account as the autonomous account and the capital account as accommodating imbalance in the current account. This depiction was challenged perspicaciously in the 1950s by Tsiang (1951), who disputed that capital account flows are accommodating. Tsiang argued that speculative flows are autonomous, and themselves require accommodating flows.

This observation has proved critical since the 1980s. With the rapid development of global financial markets and the internationalization of investment and borrowing, it is now highly doubtful that the capital account is accommodating to the current account. Flows recorded in the capital account are increasingly to be understood as autonomous flows, driven by corporate global investment strategies and the highly developed speculative processes of international financial markets, and not as counteracting current account imbalances. The autonomy of capital movements from trade is a significant part of the explanation as to why exchange rates do not move automatically to rectify current account imbalances. Exchange rates are increasingly a reflection of movements in the value of internationally traded financial assets, with only a partial relation to a nation's trade balance.

This situation has direct implications for national state management of a country's balance of payments. For some, particularly adherents of Keynesianism, there is a need to develop specific policies to rectify current account imbalance (especially deficits). For others, with a free-market orientation, the fact that foreign exchange markets may not sell off the currency of a country with a sustained current account deficit can be taken to indicate that a balance of payments current account deficit should not be constituted as a national "problem."

Balance of payments as a national constraint

For countries with a sustained balance of payments deficit, there developed the Keynesian conception of the current account as a constraint on national growth potential. This position has been associated most directly with the work of Tony Thirlwall (1979, 1992), as well as John McCombie and Sonmez Atesoglu. In the context of the UK economy, Thirlwall contended that output could not grow as rapidly as labor productivity should have permitted, because the relative income elasticities of demand for imports and exports would have seen the increased economic activity generating a trade deficit (see BALANCE OF PAYMENTS CONSTRAINT). Hence there is a need for national policy to address trade performance directly through national industry policy. For some, this is extended to the case of reimposition of protection against imports.

Balance of payments as a national representation

Globally integrated capital markets and the growth of transnational corporations have highlighted concerns about balance of payments data as a depiction of a national situation. Which activities of which companies are recorded in which country's balance of payments, is an issue of increasing concern. Should balance of payments figures measure the activity of nationally owned companies, or of economic activity within the nation (and how should international companies be "allocated" to countries)? In policy debate, this issue became significant in the interpretation of the rapidly growing United States current account deficit in the mid-1980s.

In 1986, for example, the US current account showed a deficit of $144 billion. However, if the figures are recalculated on the basis of nationality of companies, rather than on the basis of the location of production, the (alternative) current account recorded for the same year a surplus by the global operation of US corporations of $57 billion (Julius 1990: 81). An inquiry into the system of balance of payments accounting, chaired by Robert Baldwin and involving various branches of the US state, recommended *inter alia* that, in addition to the conventional accounts, the state publish "alternative" balance of payments data, based on the nationality of ownership of capital (Kester 1992). These data have yet to appear.

The broader and more open question which arises concerns the analytical significance of aggregating individual corporate figures to depict a national situation. What does it mean, for example, to aggregate the debt of "national" companies, and call it "national debt"? The effect of the statistical socialization of private debt is to invoke national policies of austerity, as if "the nation" must collectively meet private debt repayments (Bryan 1995). This raises the question of the way in which national balance of payments data subordinate issues of domestic social and economic policy to the notion of the "collective national debt."

See also:

comparative advantage and unequal exchange; exchange rates; free trade and protection; global crisis of world capitalism; international money and finance; international political economy; internationalization of capital; state and internationalization

Selected references

Bank for International Settlements (1983) *Annual Report*, Basle: BIS.

Bryan, D. (1995) *The Chase Across the Globe: International Capital and the Contradictions for Nation States*, Boulder: Westview Press.

International Monetary Fund (1977) *Balance of Payments Manual*, 4th edn, Washington, DC: IMF.

Julius, D. (1990) *Global Companies and Public Policy: The Growing Challenge of Direct Foreign Investment*, London: Pinter.

Kester, A. (1992) *Behind the Numbers: US Trade and the World Economy*, Washington, DC: National Academy Press.

Thirlwall, A.P. (1979) "The Balance of Payments Constraint as an Explanation of International Growth Rate Differences," *Banca Nazionale del Lavoro Quarterly Review* 32(128).

—— (1992) "The Balance of Payments and Economic Performance," *National Westminster Bank Quarterly Review*, May.

Tsiang, S.C. (1951) "Balance of Payments and Domestic Flow of Income and Expenditures," *IMF Staff Papers* 1.

Turner, P. (1991) "Capital Flows in the 1980s: A Survey of Major Trends," *Bank for International Settlements Economic Papers* no. 30, Basle: BIS.

Wasserman, M.J and Ware, R.M. (1965) *The Balance of Payments: History, Methodology, Theory*, New York: Simmons-Boardman.

DICK BRYAN

balance of payments constraint

The balance of payments constrained growth model of Thirlwall (see BALANCE OF PAYMENTS) provides a demand-driven, Keynesian explanation of ECONOMIC GROWTH. In this model, economic growth is determined by the growth in aggregate demand and, in particular, by the growth in exports. In the Thirlwall model, which can be considered as a dynamic version of the Harrod foreign trade multiplier, the balance of payments position constrains the growth of aggregate demand and, thereby, the growth of the economy. The growth in exports plays a crucial role by relaxing the balance of payments constraint and allowing for expansionary aggregate demand policies.

Equations of model

The balance of payments constrained growth model of Thirlwall can be depicted with the following four equations:

$$x + p_d = m + p_f \quad (1)$$
$$m = \pi q + \phi(p_d - p_f), \quad \pi, \phi > 0 \quad (2)$$
$$x = \beta w + \alpha(p_d - p_f), \quad \beta > 0, \alpha < 0 \quad (3)$$
$$q^* = (1/\pi)x \quad (4)$$

where x is the growth rate of real exports, p_d is the growth rate of domestic prices, m is the growth rate of real imports, p_f is the growth rate of foreign prices expressed in domestic currency, q is the growth rate of real output and w is the growth rate of real world income. Equation (1) is the equilibrium condition of the model – growth rate of nominal imports equal to the growth rate of nominal exports. Equations (2) and (3) are respectively the import and export demand functions in growth rate form.

Solving equations (1)–(3) for the growth rate of output, and assuming that the growth rate of relative price is zero, $(p_d - p_f) = 0$, and substituting x for βw from equation (3), yields equation (4) – the dynamic Harrod foreign trade multiplier relation, also known as Thirlwall's Law. According to equation (4), the growth rate of real income consistent with a current account balance, q^*, depends on the income elasticity of demand for imports, π, and the growth rate of real exports.

Empirical evidence

In recent years there has been a rapid accumulation of empirical evidence drawn primarily from industrialized countries, including the United States, supportive of Thirlwall's Law and the balance of payments constrained growth model. Employing two sets of cross-section data (1953–76 and 1951–73), Thirlwall (see McCombie and Thirlwall 1994: ch. 3) was able to account for differences in economic growth among industrial countries by the dynamic foreign trade multiplier. His model and findings were challenged by McGregor and Swales (see McCombie and Thirlwall 1994: ch. 5), but the findings of McCombie (1985), Bairam (1988), and Bairam and Dempster (1991) from Asian countries lend additional favorable empirical support to Thirlwall's Law. More recently, Atesoglu (1993, 1993–4, 1994) was able to provide favorable evidence for Thirlwall's Law and the model of growth using time-series data for the United States, Canada and Germany.

The growing body of evidence in favor of the Thirlwall model indicates that this demand-oriented model of growth is not only relevant for interpreting and predicting the economic growth of small open economies such as the UK and Australia (see McCombie and Thirlwall 1994: ch. 10), but it is also relevant and becoming increasingly more so for the US, with the rise in the relative importance of international trade and finance and the persistence of current account deficits in this large open economy. Atesoglu (1995) was able to offer an explanation for the controversial issue of the slowdown in United States economic growth since the early 1970s, employing Thirlwall's model of growth. His results indicate that the fall in the rate of economic growth has been brought about mainly by an increase in the income elasticity of demand for imports.

Policy implications

The growth model of Thirlwall has straightforward but challenging policy implications for countries aspiring to have high rates of economic growth. Thirlwall's Law indicates that a rise in the economic growth rate, consistent with an equilibrium in the balance of payments, requires a reduction in the income elasticity of demand for imports or an increase in the growth rate of exports. Both of these policy objectives are difficult to achieve in the increasingly open and competitive world economy. If a country is successful in raising its balance of payments equilibrium growth rate, then it can accelerate its economic growth by expansionary aggregate demand policies, while avoiding balance of payments difficulties. Thirlwall's model and the favorable body of empirical evidence provides an effective support to the export-led growth strategy.

See also:

circular and cumulative causation; Harrod's instability principle and trade cycles; Kaldor–Pasinetti models of growth and distribution; Kaldor's theory of the growth process; Verdoorn's Law

Selected references

Atesoglu, H.S. (1993) "Balance of Payments Constrained Growth: Evidence from the United States," *Journal of Post Keynesian Economics* 15 (Summer).

—— (1993–4) "Exports, Capital Flows, Relative Prices and Economic Growth in Canada," *Journal of Post Keynesian Economics* 16 (Winter).

—— (1994) "Balance of Payments Determined Growth in Germany," *Applied Economics Letters* 1.

—— (1995) "An Explanation of the Slowdown in U.S. Economic Growth," *Applied Economics Letters* 2.

Bairam, E. (1988) "Balance of Payments, the Harrod Foreign Trade Multiplier and Economic Growth: The European and North American Experience, 1970–85," *Applied Economics* 20.

Bairam, E. and Dempster, G.J. (1991) "The Harrod Foreign Trade Multiplier and Economic Growth in Asian Countries," *Applied Economics* 23.

McCombie, J.S.L. (1985) "Economic Growth, the Harrod Foreign Trade Multiplier and Hicks' Super-Multiplier," *Applied Economics* 17.

—— (1993) "Economic Growth, Trade Interlinkages, and the Balance of Payments Constraint," *Journal of Post Keynesian Economics* 15(Summer).

McCombie, J.S.L. and Thirlwall, A.P. (1994) *Economic Growth and the Balance-of-Payments Constraint*, New York: St. Martin's Press.

Thirlwall, A.P. (1979) "The Balance of Payments Constraint as an Explanation of International Growth Rate Differences," *Banca Nazionale del Lavoro Quarterly Review* no. 128 (March).

H. SONMEZ ATESOGLU

basic and non-basic commodities

Introduction

The distinction between basics and non-basics arises from the way commodities are used as the means of production in the economy as a whole. The definitions of basics and non-basics are straightforward for the single products system, where each production process produces a single distinct type of commodity. Basics are defined as those commodities which enter, directly or indirectly, into the production of all commodities (Sraffa 1960: §6). All the other commodities are non-basics.

Non-basics can be further classified into three types (Sraffa 1960: §§35, 58). First, there are those that do not enter into the production of any commodities (pure consumption goods). Second, there are those that only enter into

basic and non-basic commodities

their own production ("self-reproducing non-basics"). Third, there are those that only enter into the production of an interconnected group of non-basics.

The terms "basic commodities" and "non-basic commodities" were first introduced by Sraffa (1960), but essentially the same distinction is found in the works of Dmitriev, von Bortkiewicz and Charasoff as well as in Ricardo's (controversial) CORN MODEL. The distinction between necessaries and luxuries in classical economics is in a similar vein, but with important differences. The classical distinction is based on the social composition of final consumption. In contrast, the Sraffian distinction refers to the technical use of commodities as the means of production. Necessities are basics only if the wage is fixed at the subsistence level and advanced from capital. If as Sraffa (§§8–9) suggests, one treats the whole wage as being paid as a share of the annual net product, then necessaries are non-basics.

Properties

Basics and non-basics have different properties, which emanate mainly from the fact that the part of the economy consisting only of basics (with the corresponding production processes), called the basic system, can be completely separated from the remaining part. For the single products system, some of the different properties are as follows (Kurz and Salvadori 1995: ch. 4). For whatever composition of the net output of the economy, basics have to be available for reproducing it, while non-basics do not. If the *numéraire* consists only of basics, the following two propositions hold. First, the prices of basics do not depend on the production conditions of non-basics, while the reverse case does not hold. Second, the relationship between the wage rate and the rate of profits is determined by the production conditions of basics only. If the price of a non-basic is changed due to a specific tax on it, the prices of basics are not affected.

Sraffa defines the maximum rate of profit as the rate of profit corresponding to a zero wage rate in the basic system. One can define the maximum rate of growth similarly, corresponding to no consumption in the basic system. The standard system is a system of production processes where the various commodities are represented among its aggregate means of production in the same proportions as they are among its products. The composite commodity which bears these proportions among its components is called the standard commodity, and the ratio of the net product to the means of production in the standard system is called the standard ratio (see INVARIABLE MEASURE OF VALUE). Then, all basics and no non-basics enter into the production of the standard commodity. The maximum rate of profit, the maximum rate of growth and the standard ratio are equal to each other. In the absence of self-reproducing non-basics, the prices of basics and non-basics are positive for all non-negative rates of profits lower than the standard ratio.

Debates

The existence of self-reproducing non-basics poses some problems. Some self-reproducing non-basics may have negative prices at a profit rate below the maximum rate (Sraffa 1960: Appendix B). As a corollary, the concepts of the maximum rates of growth and profit would not be meaningful if a lower rate could be associated with a negative price of a commodity. In an attempt to resolve the first problem, Kurz and Salvadori (1995: 82–4, ch. 12) suggest the following. When a self-reproducing non-basic is not consumed, one can assume the free disposal condition, which implies a zero price. When a self-reproducing non-basic is consumed, one can assume that there is a positive price above which it will not be consumed.

In contrast, attempting to resolve both of the two problems associated with self-reproducing non-basics, Bidard (1991: ch. 4) suggests alternative definitions of the maximum rates of profit and growth. They can be defined such that they coincide with each other, but may be smaller than the standard ratio. The common maximum rate can depend on the production conditions of non-basics. However, no commodities (including self-reproducing non-basics) have negative prices for any non-negative rates of profit lower than this maximum rate.

Joint production

The intuitive criterion for the single product system fails to apply to the system of JOINT PRODUCTION (Sraffa 1960: ch. 8). In joint production, at least one commodity is produced by multiple processes, and this makes the meaning of a direct or indirect means of production ambiguous (§57). Sraffa thus suggests a less intuitive criterion, in terms of the possibility of linearly transforming both the input and the output matrices into decomposable matrices; that is, matrices which can be linearly transformed into the ones with an upper right (or lower left) corner block whose elements consist only of zeros (§60).

The Sraffa criterion is among many possible but non-equivalent ways of distinguishing between "basics" and "non-basics" (Bidard 1991: ch. 11). The ground for the distinction is that some part of the economy is independent of its remaining part, under some type of perturbation such as tax, tribute, technical change and so on. Few of the properties of basics and non-basics listed above carry over to the joint products system, and different criteria preserve different properties.

The Sraffa criterion preserves an economic property of taxation and is useful in constructing the standard commodity. The Abraham–Frois and Berrebi criterion permits an analysis of the effects of a tribute payment on activity levels. The Flaschel criterion proves useful in the analysis of the pure fixed capital system, where fixed capital is the only type of joint product. The Bidard and Wood criterion allows for land to remain non-basic even when its quality is altered by production processes. All these criteria include the one given for the single products system as a special case, where the output matrix is an identity matrix.

See also:

price theory, Sraffian; Sraffian political economy

Selected references

Bidard, C. (1991) *Prix, reproduction, rareté*, Paris: Dunod.

Kurz, Heinz and Salvadori, Neri (1995) *Theory of Production*, Cambridge: Cambridge University Press.

Sraffa, Piero (1960) *Production of Commodities by Means of Commodities*, Cambridge: Cambridge University Press.

MAN-SEOP PARK

bioeconomics

The terms "bioeconomics," "bionomics" and "economic biology" have been used by a variety of authors, with diverse agendas. What they have in common is an insistence that human socioeconomic organization involves, and in some sense depends on, the human organism in its natural environment. In addition, there is the issue of how metaphors from biology can be used in economics, and vice versa. Transfer at the metaphorical level will be discussed here, as well as some ways in which an additional, and tighter, coupling between biology and economics has been suggested.

Early history

Biology and the social sciences have interacted for centuries. In the early 1700s, Bernard Mandeville found inspiration for economics in the complex but productive order of the social insects in his *Fable of the Bees*. The Swedish biologist Carl Linnaeus used the term *Œconomy of Nature* as the title of a Latin tract of 1751. Eight years later, Adam Smith was referring to the "œconomy of nature" in his *The Theory of Moral Sentiments*. Subsequently, Charles Darwin was influenced by the economic writings of Adam Smith, Charles

Babbage and Thomas Robert Malthus. In the crucial year of 1838, when Darwin made his theoretical breakthrough and formulated the essentials of his theory of natural selection, he read Malthus's famous *Essay on the Principle of Population* and recorded this crucial inspiration in his notebooks (Hodgson 1995). The history of the Darwinian scientific revolution shows that metaphors from economics have had a crucial effect on the development of biology. Accordingly, since the inception of these sciences in their modern form, there has been a long-established transfer of ideas in both directions.

Throughout much of the nineteenth century, organic analogies were prominent in social science in the German-speaking world (Hutter 1994). With the rise of the German historical school, a strong dependence on the organic metaphor was manifest. This was particularly evident in the works of writers such as Karl Knies, Wilhelm Roscher, Paul von Lilienfeld and Albert Schäffle.

Role of Darwin and Spencer

Partly under the impact of the developing science of biology, evolutionary and biological ideas and metaphors had an especially strong impact on economics and other social sciences throughout the Western world in the last few decades of the nineteenth century. However, it would be wrong to presume that this was all to do with the popularity of Darwin. The term "social Darwinism" is misleading, at least in that respect. In the period 1870–1900, Darwin was rivalled in standing by Herbert Spencer, and Darwinism was itself in eclipse in the scientific community.

Along with many other nineteenth-century theorists, Spencer's notion of natural causation meant that explanations of social phenomena were reduced to individual and biological terms. Spencer did not make the modern distinction between biological evolution, involving the transmission of genetic information, and social or cultural evolution, in which information is transmitted by imitation and learning. Hence in modern parlance, Spencer and his followers – such as William Graham Sumner in the United States – were biological reductionists.

Marshall, Veblen and Hobson

Alfred Marshall was influenced by a number of theorists, first and foremost of whom was Spencer (Hodgson 1993). The first edition of Marshall's *Principles* was published in 1890, at the height of Spencer's prestige. Marshall saw the relevance of biological analogies for economics, yet he was unable to develop them to the full. To use the words of Brinley Thomas (in Hodgson 1995), for Marshall economic biology "remained promise rather than substance."

In contrast, Thorstein VEBLEN (1919) inclined more to Darwin than to Spencer (Hodgson 1993). Although he was aware of problems in the development of Darwin's theory, he saw in his theory of natural selection an attempt to give a full causal and non-teleological account of the evolutionary process. It was this principle that Veblen attempted to apply to economics, first with the publication of his famous essay "Why is Economics Not an Evolutionary Science?" in 1898. Veblen thus established a strong link between economics and biology, at both the methodological and metaphorical levels. For Veblen – and unlike Spencer and Sumner – socioeconomic phenomena were not reducible analytically to biological terms.

Like Marshall and Veblen, John Atkinson Hobson was strongly influenced by organic analogies, but Hobson's organicism is stronger and more sustained than that found in Marshall's work. He drew strong methodological and anti-reductionist conclusions from his own version of organicism, writing in his book *Wealth and Life* that: "An organized unity, or whole, cannot be explained adequately by an analysis of its constituent parts: its wholeness is a new product, with attributes not ascertainable in its parts, though in a sense derived from them" (Hobson 1928: 32). Hobson thus expressed the idea of emergent properties and higher, irreducible levels of analysis. Hobson forcefully rejected mechanical metaphors, seeing them as "squeezing out humanity" and denying human novelty and creativity.

Competition and cooperation

A large number of theorists drew pro-competitive and laissez-faire conclusions from the application of chosen ideas from biology to the socioeconomic sphere. However, other writers, equally influenced by biology, drew quite different conclusions. For instance, in his book *The Psychic Factors of Civilization* published in 1893, the American Lester Ward drew a distinction between the economy of nature and economics, noting that nature exhibited massive waste rather than stewardly economy. Instead of flowing straight, rivers waste energy in their meanderings; many species lay thousands of eggs, of which only a few will reach maturity. The Russian author Peter Kropotkin drew on his own field experience to publish *Mutual Aid* in 1902, showing plentiful evidence from biology that competition and scarcity are neither universal nor natural laws. It is in this context that Herman Reinheimer coined the term "bioeconomics" and published his work *Evolution by Co-operation: A Study in Bioeconomics* in 1913. Like Kropotkin, Reinheimer rejected the universality of competition in both the social and the natural spheres.

Commonalities

However, with the notable exceptions of Hobson and Veblen, what is common to many authors on both sides of the ideological debate is the acceptance of the relevance of the science of biology for our understanding of what is actual, possible and desirable in the economic sphere. Where they differed is in their understanding of the biological facts and theories, seeing different issues in the natural world as being relevant for the economy.

Decline and revival

The situation was to change radically after 1914. Throughout the Western academic world there was a strong reaction against any use of ideas from biology in the social sciences (Degler 1991). Social science was marked by the rise of behaviorist psychology and by logical positivism. Furthermore, liberal-inclined Western academia reacted against the racist, sexist and imperialistic abuses of biology by social scientists and politicians. For several decades, biology and social science parted company.

The process was reversed after the emergence of the neo-Darwinian synthesis in biology in the 1940s. In 1950, Armen Alchian made an explicit appeal to the metaphor of natural selection. This evolutionary idea was taken up and modified by Milton Friedman and others. About the same time, in 1950, the inventive heterodox economist Kenneth Boulding published his *Reconstruction of Economics*. In this work, Boulding was one of the first to emphasize that the economy was part of, and depended upon, the ecosystem.

In the postwar years, links between biology and the social sciences were gradually re-established. The publication of Edward O. Wilson's *Sociobiology* in 1975 stimulated a protracted interest in the alleged biotic foundations of human behavior. The impact of the new sociobiology on economics was rapid. Chicago neoclassical economists Gary Becker, Jack Hirshleifer and Gordon Tullock quickly followed with calls for the joining of economics with sociobiology. Notably, these presentations were individualist and reductionist, and emphasized self-interest and individual competition in the biotic as well as the economic world. Their work was redolent of much of the so-called "social Darwinism" of the end of the nineteenth century.

The Chicago bioeconomists

The Chicago bioeconomists argue that common "economic" principles bind biology to economics: "All aspects of life are ultimately governed by scarcity of resources." Not only is competition seen as the all-pervasive law of natural-economy interactions, but "the evolutionary approach suggests that self-interest is ultimately the prime motivator of human as of all life"

bioeconomics

(Hirshleifer 1982: 52). Fundamental concepts such as scarcity, competition, equilibrium and specialization were seen to play similar roles in both spheres of inquiry. Fond of quoting the statement of Marshall in his *Principles* that economics is "a branch of biology broadly interpreted," the Chicago bioeconomists reverse its meaning and try to make biology a branch of economics narrowly interpreted.

Thus, economics and biology are presumed to address common root problems which are soluble with similar or identical concepts and toolkit theories. Hence the basis for economic imperialism, "the use of economic analytical models to study all forms of social relations rather than only the market interactions of 'rational' decision makers" (Hirshleifer 1982: 52). The case for the conquest of other social sciences and biology by the "economic imperialists" rests on the presumed universality of such ideas as scarcity, competition and self-interest. The inspiration drawn from sociobiology is that the process of natural selection should result in the emergence of something like "rational economic man," providing the pretext for the invasion of biology and other sciences by the maximizing postulates of neoclassical economics (see NEOCLASSICAL ECONOMICS; RATIONALITY AND IRRATIONALITY).

One problem with the maximization idea is that it fits uneasily into an ongoing evolutionary framework. Global maximization is a concept fitting to an unreal and transparent eternity, not the incremental and imperfect adjustments in an evolutionary process. Accordingly, rather than unrelenting competition and improvement, organisms satisfice rather than maximize: they find NICHES to protect themselves from competition. Crucially, an approach based on ever-enduring preference functions cannot provide an evolutionary explanation of their origin. By fixing preferences forever, the concepts of time and process are lost.

Ecological economics

Today, the term "bioeconomics" is also associated with the very different economics of Georgescu-Roegen (1971). He asserted the value of biological as well as thermodynamic analogies and founded a distinctive version of "bioeconomics." Instead of viewing nature in the image of "economic man," where humans are regarded as part of nature and dependent upon it, Georgescu-Roegen argued that stocks of non-renewable energy and matter are finite, as is the assimilative capacity of the environment.

Like the work of Boulding, Georgescu-Roegen's work is not an attempt to imperialize biology with economics. There is now a substantial school of writers working in this area, attempting to build bridges between economics, biology and ecology. Unlike some sociobiologists and the Chicago economists, the idea is to synthesize and develop the sciences, rather to subsume one by the other (Constanza 1991; Daly and Cobb 1990). Much of this work is published in the journal *Ecological Economics*.

See also:

entropy, negentropy and the laws of thermodynamics; environmental and ecological political economy: major contemporary themes; evolution and coevolution; evolutionary economics: major contemporary themes

Selected references

Constanza, Robert (ed.) (1991) *Ecological Economics: The Science and Management of Sustainability*, New York: Columbia University Press.

Daly, Herman E. and Cobb, John B. Jr, (1990) *For the Common Good: Redirecting the Economy Towards Community, the Environment and a Sustainable Future*, London: Green Print.

Degler, C.N. (1991) *Search of Human Nature: The Decline and Revival of Darwinism in American Social Thought,* Oxford and New York: Oxford University Press.

Georgescu-Roegen, Nicholas (1971) *The Entropy Law and the Economic Process*, Cambridge, MA: Harvard University Press.

Hirshleifer, Jack (1982) "Evolutionary Models in Economics and Law: Cooperation versus

Conflict Strategies," in R.O. Zerbe, Jr and P.H. Rubin (eds), *Research in Law and Economics* 4: 1–60.

Hobson, J.A. (1928) *Wealth and Life*, London: Macmillan.

Hodgson, Geoffrey M. (1993) *Economics and Evolution: Bringing Life Back Into Economics*, Cambridge and Ann Arbor, MI: Polity Press and University of Michigan Press.

—— (ed.) (1995) *Economics and Biology*, Aldershot: Edward Elgar.

Hutter, Michael (1994) "Organism as a Metaphor in German Economic Thought," in Philip Mirowski (ed.), *Natural Images in Economic Thought: Markets Red in Tooth and Claw*, Cambridge and New York: Cambridge University Press, 289–321.

Veblen, Thorstein B. (1919) *The Place of Science in Modern Civilisation and Other Essays*, New Brunswick, NJ: Transaction Publishers, 1990.

Wilson, Edward O. (1975) *Sociobiology: The New Synthesis*, Cambridge, MA: Harvard University Press.

GEOFFREY M. HODGSON

brain drain

The migration of high-quality manpower (HQM) from less developed countries (LDCs), often called the "brain drain," has been quite prominent since the 1960s, and has been the subject of a considerable amount of theoretical and empirical discussion (see Ghosh and Ghosh 1982). The nationalist and internationalist approaches to the problem of brain drain have often led to diametrically opposed findings (Adams 1968). While to an internationalist, brain drain is a welfare-income-development-maximizing natural process, to a nationalist it is a perverse process leading to loss of income, welfare and development and to a widening of international inequality. In between these two extremes are moderates who observe that, in some situations, brain drain may lead to a reduction in individual welfare.

Typology of brain migration

It is essential to know the typology of brain migration to avoid conceptual ambiguity. There are four main types of brain migration: (1) brain drain, (2) brain overflow, (3) brain exchange and (4) brain export (Ghosh 1981). For the purpose of mutual advantage, different countries may *exchange* brains. This involves loss compensated by gains, and is based on the principle of *quid pro quo*. Brain may be exported by one country to another for earning foreign exchange. A large number of countries sending brain power abroad receive regular remittances from the emigrants, but unless remittances cover private and public costs of the migrants, the brain migration cannot be called brain *export*. The exchange price in the case of brain export is equal to the shadow price of the brain power.

Brain *overflow* is from the surplus category of high-quality manpower, and often helps LDCs to ease the problem of educated unemployment. Brain *drain* is a one-way permanent migration of productively employed people, mostly from LDCs to developed countries. The manpower involved in brain *drain* is underutilized or overutilized in the home country. The withdrawal of this strategic manpower creates dislocations and external diseconomies, and thereby retards the process of economic development of the brain-losing country. Brain drain involves the loss of strategic manpower from key positions. It seriously affects skill formation and involves the loss of money invested in education and training. Needless to say, the loss of strategic manpower adversely affects education, research and training in infrastructure-building, creative talent, present and future technology building, and the entire intellectual climate of the brain-losing country; and it creates a growth-retarding backwash effect.

Underlying forces and costs

Empirical studies on brain drain have been attempted in many countries, but the results have been variable and often contradictory

(Ghosh and Ghosh 1982). Some of the differences may be real, but many studies measure different things. All types of HQM migration cannot justifiably be brought within a single analytic umbrella, though this has been attempted in the contemporary literature on the subject. Migration of highly qualified professional manpower from LDCs, which may be called "brain migration," may be due to several different sets of underlying social, psychological and economic forces. Like the common cold, brain migration is not a single malady but a loose generic category covering a variety of specific complaints and conditions. The phenomenon of migration from LDCs can justify the use of the term "brain," but we should be cautious in using the term "drain." In fact, all brain drain constitutes brain migration, but all brain migration does not necessarily constitute brain drain.

There are many direct and indirect costs of brain drain. Lost in the drain are leadership and creative contributions to science, technology and development. The loss of critical manpower which can formulate and influence policies is a serious loss for a developing country. There may also be the loss of physical and working capital accompanying the emigrants. It has been found empirically in many studies that brain drain reduces welfare and lowers domestic production. The losses involved in brain drain (Ghosh 1981) are found to be very high indeed. Brain drain is motivated mainly by higher relative income plus better prospects and opportunities in the immigrating country. It is caused by many factors such as low domestic income, inadequate facilities for research, human capital discrimination, underemployment, lack of promotion and bleak prospects in the domestic economy. The basic causes of brain drain are income inequalities, and differences in opportunities and real earnings between low and highly developed nations.

Brain drain can be looked upon as an immoral process hampering progress in LDCs and depriving them of the badly needed HQM. It is morally obtuse in two senses: (1) the strategic manpower of LDCs is lost, and (2) no compensation is made to the brain-losing countries by the brain-receiving countries. True, remittances are repatriated in the case of brain export; but these are not adequate, regular and compulsory. The remittances are mostly used for the purpose of consumption and speculation and not for productive purposes and economic growth according to national priorities.

Brain drain has not led to an adequate compensatory payment to the brain-sending countries and it does not generally cover the public and private costs of human capital involved in brain drain, although it partly meets the private cost. However, in the cases of brain *exchange* and *export*, the remittances are quite substantial and many less developed countries, including India, Bangladesh, Pakistan, South Korea, Egypt and Yemen, have apparently gained from such remittances. However, such hot money has been mainly responsible for escalating real estate prices and speculative derivative gains, rather than helping economic growth.

Neocolonialism

The problem of brain drain was generated and intensified by the deliberate neocolonial policy of developed capitalist countries. The exploitation by these countries continues unabated, but in a different fashion. In the pre-industrial revolution period, the developed countries took away resources from their colonies in the form of physical capital; while in the post-industrial revolution period they have been draining the human capital resources from LDCs. The developed countries do not pay the public or social cost to the LDCs for losing human capital, and as such, the brain-sending countries remain losers and brain-receiving countries are gainers. Much of the technology of developed countries is being produced by skilled workers formerly from LDCs (Kabra 1976). For instance, annual immigration to the USA is equal to the annual "output" of about 5 percent of US institutions of higher education. Similarly, about 50 percent of the British National Health Service is now staffed by non-

Britons. Instead of importing raw materials, the developed countries are now importing brains (HQM) from LDCs without paying any compensation. The developed countries try to attract HQM from LDCs in many ways, for example, by changes in immigration laws, fellowships and scholarships, and so forth. Educational and cultural domination by developed countries provides further encouragement to brain drain.

It is often claimed that the developed countries have been helping the LDCs through aid and assistance. This apparently innocuous statement has to be interpreted with much caution. For instance, US FOREIGN AID to LDCs amounted to $3.1 billion in 1970; but the income gained by the United States through brain drain from LDCs amounted to $3.7 billion in the same year (UNCTAD 1974). The UNCTAD study makes it quite clear that it is really the poor countries which are, on balance, aiding the rich developed countries and not the other way round. (See also Sukhatme 1994.)

Further, the point is made that the United States sends as many experts to developing countries as it receives from them through brain drain (US Congress 1968). But while the USA does not pay a single cent for the brain obtained from LDCs, it is paid well for the services of experts who are often themselves the HQM from LDCs. This provides ample evidence to show that, in the world economy, the core–periphery relation and surplus extraction from LDCs continues unabated, although in a different form.

Policy measures

As a general rule, policies should be directed to restricting the emigration of high-quality manpower which is of strategic importance. The restructuring of wages may produce powerful stimuli to prevent brain drain. The growth of institutions catering for R&D and providing facilities and incentives in jobs and amenities of life may also be recommended for the affected LDCs. Policies should be so designed that they can reduce brain drain in the shortrun and prevent it in the longrun. With definite plans and programs, brain overflow and brain drain can partly be converted into brain export. Instead of sending out surplus HQM individually, it would be more worthwhile to send it as government-sponsored teams on prescribed terms and conditions. The brain-sending countries should carefully formulate a compensatory brain drain policy that can ensure adequate return. The remittances are in no way connected with compensation, which is based mainly on the public cost of human capital. The brain-receiving countries can pay a part of HQM's income tax to the sending country and/or a supplementary tax may be imposed on HQM. The LDCs may jointly cooperate to formulate a policy of compensation and its implementation.

The migration of workers may be reversed, provided they can be productively absorbed into the domestic economy. The emphasis should be to improve the absorption capacity and to coordinate manpower planning, education planning and development planning accordingly. However, there must be some trade-off between individual freedom and the national interest.

See also:

colonialism and imperialism: classic texts; core-periphery analysis; development political economy: major contemporary themes

Selected references

Adams, Walter (ed.) (1968) *The Brain Drain*, New York: Macmillan.

Ghosh, B.N. (1981) "Typology of Brain Migration and Some Policy Implications," *Rivista Internazionale di Scienze Economiche e Commerciali* (April).

Ghosh, B.N. and Ghosh, Rama (1982) *Economics of Brain Migration*, New Delhi: Deep & Deep Publications.

Kabra, K.N. (1976) *Political Economy of Brain Drain*, New Delhi: Arnold-Heinemann.

Sukhatme, S.P. (1994) *The Real Brain Drain*, Hyderabad, India: Orient Longman.

UNCTAD (1974) *Reverse Transfer of Technology*, New York: UNCTAD.
US Congress (90th) (1968) *Scientific Brain Drain from the Developing Countries*, Washington, DC: US Congress.

B.N. GHOSH

Bretton Woods system

In July 1944, in Bretton Woods, New Hampshire, representatives of forty-four nations met to establish the standards by which international trade and finance would be conducted once the Second World War had ended. This included not only specification of the exchange rate and payments system that would prevail, but also of provisions for helping "Third World" nations develop in the post-colonial era. In its final form, the plan was something less than its primary architects, Harry Dexter White and John Maynard KEYNES, had hoped. Nonetheless, the stability it lent to the postwar period helped create an environment conducive to recovery. But the tranquility was not to last. In the end, it appears that the exchange rate and payments mechanism contained the seeds of its own destruction, allowing and even encouraging developments to take place that led to its demise. Meanwhile, many argue that the efforts to develop emerging economies has done more harm that good (Danaher 1994). From those events, especially the massive INTERNATIONALIZATION OF CAPITAL, evolved the modern international monetary system.

The Keynes and White Plans

Independently, White in the United States and Keynes in the UK had been developing ambitious plans for the postwar international economy since the early 1940s (Shelton 1994: 24–8). Both had conceived of a system wherein exchange rate stability was a prime goal, and they shared an intense desire to engineer an arrangement that promoted cooperation and humanitarian goals. Neither favored a return to a classical gold standard. The most significant difference between their approaches was that White's scheme tended to favor incentives designed to create price stability (see INFLATION: WAGE–COST MARKUP APPROACH) within the world's economies, while Keynes wanted a system that encouraged ECONOMIC GROWTH. In the end, although a true compromise was achieved on some points, the overwhelming economic and military power of the United States led to the adoption of a largely American plan.

The Bretton Woods system

The international monetary system that emerged was a gold-exchange standard. The US dollar was fixed to gold and convertible on demand (at $35 per ounce). All other currencies were fixed to the dollar (and therefore to gold) and were allowed to fluctuate only within a narrow band. Central banks were expected to intervene in the event that their home currency moved, or threatened to move, outside that band. If a currency's value appeared to have permanently shifted well beyond the par rate, that country had the right under the articles of agreement to declare that a fundamental disequilibrium existed. The rules of the system were then supposed to allow that country some recourse (either revaluation or devaluation of their money). In addition to these exchange-rate specific regulations, Bretton Woods also established a fund from which countries could draw when facing temporary payments difficulties. At the same time, the World Bank was established to help integrate the less developed economies into the world capitalist economy. This was to be achieved through a combination of advice, direct loans and guarantees of third-party loans.

The spectacular growth of the former combatants after the war is well known. Bretton Woods was certainly not the only reason for this "miracle," especially in light of the fact that not all of its provisions (in particular, the convertibility obligations) were in full force until 1958 and that the impact of US policy, especially the Marshall Plan, was undoubtedly greater than that of the World

Bank. Nonetheless, their stabilizing presence in this particularly unpredictable period must have encouraged international trade and investment. But by the late 1960s, flaws in the exchange rate and payments system were becoming evident.

Contradictions in the system

The par rates set after the war assumed an overwhelmingly dominant US economy. At first, this proved an accurate assumption, as the USA ran large balance of payments surpluses until 1950; but as the European economies recovered, the US payments balance slipped into deficit. This deficit remained relatively small until 1958, when it began to increase sharply. Given the worldwide shortage of dollars, this was not an unwelcome development. However, as it continued well into the 1960s, and especially when the US current account went into deficit in 1968, it was soon clear that a devaluation of the dollar was necessary.

Unfortunately, a mechanism for dealing with chronic payments imbalances and adjustments of the peg was never really finalized. As suggested above, Keynes had preferred arrangements that encouraged world growth. Consequently, his recommendations for reducing imbalances were aimed every bit as much (perhaps more so) at surplus countries as at deficit ones. He believed that the accumulation of surplus affected the world economy in the same way that savings reduced demand in a domestic one. But the USA, as a likely creditor nation, balked at Keynes's plan. While White was sensitive to the problem that placing too much of the burden on the deficit country would be deflationary, it was widely believed by the US contingent that the postwar economy was likely to be very inflationary (Bernstein 1989: 30; Walter 1991: 155–6). The inability to arrive at a satisfactory compromise left them with no systematic means of addressing the issue (Walter 1991: 154–6).

Thus, when "fundamental disequilibria" did occur, there was no automatic provision for dealing with them. Even though deficit countries were allowed considerable latitude simply to declare devaluations, in practice the political implications of this kept devaluation to a minimum (at least among the developed countries). Meanwhile, surplus countries were content to accumulate reserves. To complicate matters, the US was very reluctant to devalue, given the status of the dollar as the international currency. Though an attempt was made to save Bretton Woods in 1971 (the Smithsonian Agreement), by 1973 the inability to agree on par rates led to its collapse. The reasons for its disintegration went beyond the inability to address payments imbalances efficiently. The massive internationalization of capital that had been taking place since the late 1950s and early 1960s had placed tremendous pressure on the fixed rate system. Keynes had already warned that capital controls would be necessary if central banks were to have the power to defend the parities set under Bretton Woods (Krause 1991: 62–5). He recommended these, "not merely as a feature of the transition, but as a permanent arrangement... the right to control all capital movements" (Bryant 1987: 61–2). As part of this policy, he submitted that all currency should be converted through central banks.

Although market convertibility was substituted for official convertibility, Keynes's sentiment is reflected in the articles of agreement. Under Bretton Woods, pure capital flows could be, and were, controlled. In practice, each country put in place regulations intended to "balkanize" the various national capital markets (Krause 1991: 64); but as US payments deficits caused dollars to accumulate in Europe, a combination of investors' desire to avoid the balkanizing controls along with other considerations (like US limits on deposit interest and the growth of multinational industry and finance) led to the rise of the Eurodollar market. From 1964 (the first year for which figures are available) to 1973, the Eurodollar market grew from the equivalent of $20 billion to $305 billion (Sarver 1988: 6–7). The changing importance of the US economy relative to Europe was already making the old par rates obsolete. The growing size of capital flows was now making actual and potential movements in EXCHANGE RATES much larger, unpredictable and uncontrollable. With such capital available for SPECULATION, apparent exchange rate problems could quickly become crises. By 1973, speculators had challenged and defeated every central bank, including the Federal Reserve. The internationalization of capital had the potential both to cause and to exacerbate fundamental disequilibria and, with no practical means of resolving these problems, Bretton Woods failed.

World Bank and poverty

The failure of the World Bank to answer the challenge of world poverty, while less spectacular than the collapse of Bretton Woods, has been far more tragic. The political ideology and economic approach of that institution has been so far removed from the realities of those struggling with underdevelopment that Bank plans typically focus more on controlling inflation and introducing austerity plans than they do on addressing hunger and powerlessness (Danaher 1994). The additional burden placed on so many in the Third World by the debt created during the OPEC oil embargoes makes their future even more bleak (see WORLD HUNGER AND POVERTY).

Post-Bretton Woods arrangements

Regarding international payments and exchange rates, immediately following the collapse of Bretton Woods the stage was set for the continued growth and domination of the international capital market. Today, the overwhelming majority of currency transactions are related to capital. As a consequence, policy makers are forced to consider the reaction of international financial markets to each and every policy move, lest they by "punished" by capital outflows and currency depreciation or "rewarded" with inflows and appreciation. This has meant that not only has the volume of capital led to excessive exchange rate volatility and chronic misalignment (Harvey 1995), but it has also created a deflationary bias in the system through the necessity of pleasing international investors with high interest rates and conservative economic policies (Davidson 1992–3; Grabel 1993).

No true system has evolved to take the place of Bretton Woods. Instead, most currencies of developed nations float against one another (with one major exception, as explained below) while those of developing nations are pegged, most often to the dollar. For the developed countries, which continue to dominate trade and finance, the post-Bretton Woods era has been a managed float within which currency prices are set primarily by market forces but central-bank intervention still exists. What triggers intervention depends on the economic and political objectives of the nation in question. One would think that this might create the potential for a great deal of conflict, but, generally speaking, there have been more problems associated with market-initiated movements of the exchange rates, especially those associated with capital flows and speculation. In fact, beginning with the Plaza Agreement in 1985, the central banks of France, Germany, Japan, the United Kingdom and the United States have worked within broad guidelines to cooperate in introducing some stability into foreign exchange markets. These measures have been far short of the kind that one would expect in a fixed-rate regime, but they are nonetheless indicative of the sort of disruption of which policy makers believe international capital flows are capable.

The major exception to market-determined rates among the developed countries has been the European Monetary System. This has operated as a mini-pegged system anchored to the deutschmark since 1979, and is moving toward a single currency area. Just as in Bretton Woods, events made it clear that fundamental disequilibria existed and that changes in either macroeconomic policies or pegged rates were necessary. Again, similar to events in the early 1970s, agreement over what should be done was not easily reached, and soon the massive force of speculation forced policy makers to choose quickly which paths they would follow. By 1993, this had included extensive realignments, periods of floating and exchange rate bands so wide they were "nearly tantamount to floating" (Henning 1994: 242). Only time will tell whether this can be considered a success.

Conclusion

Ironically, the major issues that have plagued international monetary systems and agreements in the fifty years since the end of the Second World War have been precisely those feared by Keynes in the early 1940s. In fixed-rate regimes, efficient means of realigning currencies remain elusive. Either the solutions tend to be deflationary, when they force deficit countries to contract their economies, or politically unpalatable, when they require currency devaluation. Perhaps Keynes was correct when he saw the only viable means to be placing the burden of adjustment on the surplus economy – a solution today urged by Paul Davidson (1992–3). Meanwhile, capital flows have proven to be disruptive in both fixed and flexible rate systems, their "discipline" severely limiting policy choices in both circumstances. Success has been just as elusive regarding the World Bank and its work with less developed nations. Not surprisingly, the failures in both arenas have their roots in economic theory. Modern policy makers are convinced that market liberalization is the key to economic growth, so that efforts to control capital flows directly, or to plan or protect the economies of emerging states, are unlikely to be forthcoming.

See also:

balance of payments; debt crises in the Third World; international money and finance; monetary policy and central banking functions

Selected references

Bernstein, Edward M. (1989) "The Search for Exchange Stability: Before and After Bretton Woods," in Omar F. Hamouda, Robin Rowley and Bernard M. Wolf (eds), *The Future of the International Monetary System: Change, Coordination or Instability?*, Armonk, NY: M.E. Sharpe, 27–34.

Bryant, Ralph C. (1987) *International Financial Intermediation*, Washington, DC: The Brookings Institution.

Danaher, Kevin (1994) *50 Years is Enough: The Case against the World Bank and the International Monetary Fund*, Boston: South End Press.

Davidson, Paul (1992–3) "Reforming the World's Money," *Journal of Post Keynesian Economics* 15(2): 153–79.

Grabel, Ilene (1993) "Crossing Borders: A Case for Cooperation in International Financial Markets," in Gerald Epstein, Julie Graham and Jessica Nembhard (eds), *Creating a New World Economy: Forces of Change and Plans of Action*, Philadelphia, PA: Temple University Press, 64–83.

Harvey, John T. (1995) "The International Monetary System and Exchange Rate Determination: 1945 to the Present," *Journal of Economic Issues* 29(2): 493–502.

Henning, C. Randall (1994) *Currencies and Politics in the United States, Germany and Japan*, Washington, DC: Institute for International Economics.

Keynes, John Maynard (1936) *The General Theory of Employment, Interest, and Money*, San Diego: Harcourt Brace Jovanovich, 1964.

Krause, Laurence A. (1991) *Speculation and the Dollar: The Political Economy of Exchange Rates*, Boulder, CO: Westview.

Sarver, Eugene (1988) *The Eurocurrency Market Handbook: The Global Eurodeposit and Related Markets*, New York: New York Institute of Finance and Prentice Hall.

Shelton, Judy (1994) *Money Meltdown: Restoring Order to the Global Currency System*, New York: The Free Press.

Walter, Andrew (1991) *World Power and World Money: The Role of Hegemony and International Monetary Order*, New York: St. Martin's Press.

JOHN T. HARVEY

budget deficit

Government budget deficits arise when government spending exceeds government tax collections. A similar notion, national debt or government debt, is the sum total of all past budget deficits accumulated by a particular country.

Bonds

Governments run deficits primarily by issuing bonds (or IOUs) that promise to pay the holder of the bond interest plus the repayment of the principal sum in the future. Short-term borrowing repays the bondholder in 3, 6 or 18 months; intermediate-term securities usually come due in 2–10 years; and long-term bonds mature in 11–30 years. Having issued these notes, governments attempt to sell them to investors. Financial institutions, central banks and wealthy individuals are the principal groups that buy these securities. The money that governments borrow enables them to spend more than they receive in tax revenues. As an alternative means of financing its deficit, governments can print money.

Keynesian fiscal policy

Until the twentieth century, conventional economic wisdom held that governments should balance their budget every year. The Great Depression of the 1930s led to the first calls for budget deficits, but it was J.M. KEYNES who first explained conceptually why economic problems would not automatically correct themselves and why deficit spending through FISCAL POLICY must be used to reduce unemployment (see UNEMPLOYMENT: POLICIES TO REDUCE).

In times of depression or recession, government tax collections inevitably decrease as national income declines, and government spending increases for social programs such as unemployment benefits. This leads to what is now called a "cyclical deficit." An attempt to close this deficit by increasing taxes or reducing spending would only make the recession worse. What was needed instead, Keynes argued, was even more spending and even larger deficits in times of high unemployment. That is, the government should run structural deficits, or budget deficits greater than those that exist due to the recession. This would stimulate spending and help to bring the recession or depression to an end. The economics of Keynes thus called for increasing deficits in times of high unemployment.

In contrast, during times of inflation or low unemployment, fiscal policy should be used to reduce spending throughout the economy. Taxes should be increased or government spending should be cut (or both), resulting in structural budget surpluses. Following this logic, most Keynesian economists advised that governments should balance their budgets, not every year but over the entire business cycle, running deficits in times of high unemployment and surpluses at other times.

Even more radical was Lerner's (1943) theory of functional finance, which recognized that it may be necessary for governments to run budget deficits at all times. For example, as a nation gets increasingly richer, its savings rate will rise. Unless government deficits make up for this shortfall in spending, stagnation and unemployment will become serious problems. Moreover, Lerner argued that budget deficits under these circumstances would not be a problem as long as people were willing to lend their extra savings to the government.

The acceptance of Keynesian economics, with its call for large budget deficits in the face of inadequate spending by the private sector, has been accompanied by large budget deficits in virtually all countries during the latter half of the twentieth century. For example, in the early 1990s budget deficits averaged between 6 and 7 percent of gross domestic product (GDP) in the European Community. A study of ten developing countries during the period 1978–88 (Easterly and Schmidt-Hebbel 1993: 219) found public sector deficits averaging between 7 and 8 percent of GDP. Even the US, whose budget deficit in the mid-1990s was only 2 to 3 percent of GDP, was running deficits averaging 4 to 5 percent of GDP during the 1980s.

Nature and critique of crowding out

Such large deficits have worried many policy makers and citizens. Economists too have expressed concern about large budget deficits, as they have increasingly moved back to pre-Keynesian ideas in the last quarter of the twentieth century. They have argued that government deficits hurt the economy by crowding out other, more important, types of spending such as business investment, consumer expenditures and net exports.

The claim that government deficits crowd out business investment is the most popular argument against budget deficits. The case here is that the government must compete with business firms for borrowed money whenever it runs a deficit. As a result, deficits increase the demand for borrowed funds, and raise interest rates. With higher interest rates, business firms borrow less money for investment purposes, and long-term economic growth suffers.

However, there are good reasons to doubt that a large degree of crowding out results from big budget deficits. First, by expanding economic activity, budget deficits increase or crowd in business investment through an increase in business confidence (Eisner 1986; Pressman 1994) during recovery and boom. Second, as Heilbroner and Bernstein (1989: 103) point out, the first link of the crowding out argument is empirically weak. During the 1980s, those G7 countries whose budget deficit increased most relative to GDP experienced the smallest increases in real interest rates, while those G7 countries whose budget deficits increased least relative to GDP experienced the largest increases in real interest rates.

It was Barro (1974) who first made the case that government budget deficits will crowd out consumer spending. He assumed that governments must repay all borrowed money in the future, and that people will spread their consumption evenly over the course of their lifetime. He argued that, since people expect higher taxes in the future to repay budget deficits incurred now, they will save more now. Hence, when governments run budget deficits, consumption will fall and total spending will not rise.

However, there are problems with both the assumptions and the predictions of this argument. First, in contrast to Barro, governments can run budget deficits indefinitely because (unlike individuals and corporations) most lenders expect that governments will exist indefinitely. Governments only have to roll over securities as they mature, which is what they do in practice. Second, savings rates declined in conjunction with rising government deficits throughout the developed world in the 1980s and early 1990s (see Pressman 1995). There is thus no evidence of a fall in consumption.

A final case of crowding out involves net exports. As international trade increases throughout the world, and as the economic world becomes more interdependent, the impact of deficit spending on the national economy is muted. This occurs for two reasons. First, the incomes generated by budget deficits are more likely to be used to purchase imported goods as economies become more interdependent. Second, deficits will increase interest rates, which in turn will increase the value of the domestic currency. This makes imports cheaper and exports more expensive. The failure of the Mitterand government to lower French unemployment in the early 1980s by running large budget deficits is commonly explained by these factors.

As with the other two cases, the crowding out argument is weak here too. First, as noted above, there has been little correlation between rising budget deficits and rising real interest rates. Thus there is no reason to expect that higher budget deficits will result in stronger national currencies. Second, developed countries trade primarily with other developed countries. Yet all the developed countries of the world experienced sharply rising budget deficits in the 1970s and 1980s. Crowding out of net exports, while possible for one or for a small subset of the major developed nations, cannot in principle occur for all of them simultaneously.

Political will to use fiscal policy

If there is a real danger in large budget deficits, it may be that they reduce the political will to use fiscal policy to remedy the problem of unemployment. Pressman (1995) presents evidence showing that the G7 countries relied less on deficit spending to cure unemployment when their budget deficits and government debt were large (the late 1970s and 1980s) than when their deficit and debt levels were low (the 1960s and early 1970s). One consequence of this deficit paranoia is that less is done to counter recessions, and so nations experience higher levels of unemployment.

Finally, the Maastricht Treaty, the first step to establishing a European Union with a common currency and central bank, requires all participants to keep their annual budget deficits within 3 percent of GDP and their national debt to less than 60 percent of GDP. As of 1993, only two nations (Ireland and Luxembourg) satisfied the former requirement, and only five satisfied the debt requirement (Germany, France, Britain, Spain, and Luxembourg). However, concerted efforts are underway to meet the Maastricht goals by the end of the twentieth century, and the political decisions made at Maastricht have led to both lower budget deficits and higher unemployment in Western Europe during the 1990s.

See also:

economic rationalism or liberalism; fiscal crisis of the state; monetary policy and central banking functions; post-Keyesian political economy: major contemporary themes; uncertainty

Selected references

Barro, R.J. (1974) "Are Government Bonds Net Worth?," *Journal of Political Economy* 82: 1095–1117.
Easterly, W. and Schmidt-Hebbel, K. (1993) "Fiscal Deficits and Macroeconomic Performance in Developing Countries," *The World Bank Research Observer* 8(2): 211–37.
Eisner, R. (1986) *How Real Is the Deficit?*, New York: Macmillan.
Heilbroner, R. and Bernstein, P. (1989) *The Debt and the Deficit: False Alarms/Real Possibilities*, New York: W.W. Norton.
Lerner, A. (1943) "Functional Finance and the Federal Debt," *Social Research* 10(February): 38–51.
Pressman, S. (1994) "The Composition of Government Spending: Does It Make Any Difference?," *Review of Political Economy* 6(2): 221–39.
—— (1995) "Deficits, Full Employment and the Use of Fiscal Policy," *Review of Political Economy* 7(2): 212–26.

STEVEN PRESSMAN

business cycle theories

Business cycles are recurrent, relatively periodic fluctuations in the level of economic activity. The word "cycle" implies persistent patterns, but because the periodicity or timing of oscillations in the economy is often irregular, many economists prefer the term "economic fluctuations." The term "trade cycle" has also been used. For our purposes, the three terms are synonyms.

Background information

Business cycles proper can be distinguished from other types of economic fluctuations, such as Kondratieff long waves (see LONG WAVES OF ECONOMIC GROWTH AND DEVELOPMENT), Kuznets mid-length cycles and "swings," building or construction cycles, and crises. Business cycle theories explain several aspects of macroeconomic behavior: (1) "regularity," or the nature of the disturbances which cause the economy to switch from expansion to contraction, and from contraction back to expansion; (2) "periodicity," the propagation mechanisms and lags which lead to major changes spreading throughout the economy and hence determine the length of the cycles; and (3) "amplitude," the intensity of the changes which condition the depth of recession and boom.

All business cycle theories are based upon one of two sharply distinct Schumpeterian "pre-analytic visions." One approach sees the economy as being essentially stable, with its normal state being one of relatively full utilization of resources, and growth in the level of output resulting from supply-side factors. Expansions or contractions in economic activity are due to exogenous shocks to the system such as technological change, fluctuations in the prices of imported goods, changes in the quantity of money in circulation, or war. If disturbed, powerful equilibrating forces, co-ordinated through changing price levels in competitive markets, quickly return the economy to its normal, high-employment growth path. Most of the classical economists appear to have held this vision, and it reappears in contemporary orthodox economics as part of the new classical economics.

In sharp contrast is the vision shared by dissenting heterodox economists, including Marx, Kalecki, Mitchell and Keynes. They saw the economy as being potentially unstable, with growth and full utilization of resources a possible but no more likely state than recession, depression or boom. Fluctuations in economic activity are seen as being due to inherent endogenous processes that take place during expansions. Furthermore, the equilibrating, stabilizing power of markets is weak and the processes slow. Although the various theories sharing this vision differ with respect to the specific disturbance variables seen as the most important proximate cause of fluctuations, most of them emphasize aggregate demand factors. In addition, many heterodox theories treat demand-side fluctuations as dialectically connected with the process of supply-side economic growth.

First phase of cycle theories

Many observers distinguish three phases in the development of cycle theory. The first phase was the period associated with the genesis of classical political economy from David Hume (in the 1750s) through to Marx (1870s). Early in the nineteenth century, economists became aware of the importance of fluctuations, beginning to interpret them as an endogenous aspect of capitalism's normal workings and to explain them by factors such as capital accumulation, aggregate demand, profits, interest rates, technological change and the distribution of income.

Thomas R. Malthus (1820) offered one of the first attempts to explain the causes of recessions ("general gluts" of unsold goods). Ricardo had defended the proposition advanced by James Mill and Adam Smith (now known as Say's Law) that recessions caused by an excess of savings over investment were illogical, and that if they did occur they would be brief, since saving (undertaken by capitalists) was primarily intended to finance capital accumulation; income not spent on consumption would be spent on capital goods. Malthus argued against Ricardo, postulating that either the failure of the purchasing power of workers to grow with productive potential, or sudden shifts in the saving rate, could cause aggregate demand to fall below potential. Ricardo was not persuaded by this "underconsumption" theory, and argued that recessions and booms were largely due to transitional strains accompanying wars and other external shocks.

Most nineteenth-century economists accepted Ricardo's view. However, there were a few exceptions, notably Thomas Tooke (who published the first serious cycle analysis in 1823), John Stuart Mill (who discussed the role of expectations and the demand for money, profits and investment in causing fluctuations in 1848), and Karl MARX.

Marx (in Volumes I (1867) and III (1894) of *Das Kapital*) developed the first coherent, fairly complete and plausible account of fluctuations. His theory stressed the role of profits and capitalist investment through an analysis of the RESERVE ARMY OF LABOR, the distribution of income between workers and capitalists and the nature of technological change. If profits fall for any reason, investment soon falls as well (because profits finance investment) and the economy moves into recession. Marx thought that crises and recessions were inevitable because the expansionary phase of the cycle sets in motion processes which eventually reduce profit rates. Four of the main factors discussed by Marx as impacting on profits during the high point of the cycle are of special interest in precipitating recession (and acting in reverse may promote recovery).

First, if the accumulation of capital is extensive, with new capital goods being similar to the old ones, then the excess demand for labor may causes wages to squeeze profits (see PROFIT SQUEEZE ANALYSIS OF CRISES) and investment falls. Second, if capitalists react to increasing wage rates, or anticipate wage increases, by investing in labor-displacing investment, increasing the capital intensity of production, then competition may eventually force prices down to the new lower costs of production precipitating declining profitability. Third, if investment is again extensive but growth does not deplete the reserve army enough for wages to rise, then working-class purchasing power may lag behind the potential to produce wage goods, thus lessening the realization of profits (underconsumption). Fourth, Marx also discussed the roles of speculation, shifts in the demand for liquidity and financial instability in cycles as potentially contributing to recessions (especially through higher interest rates and financial crises).

Second phase of cycle theories

The second phase was between the time of Marx (1870s) and Keynes (1930s), when cycle theory as a separate line of inquiry flourished. A broad consensus was reached as to the factors which contributed to or caused economic instability, and much was written on the destabilizing effects of innovation, profit expectations, financial market conditions and changes in the capital intensity of production ("roundaboutness"). This period also saw the rising perception that the instability of capitalism was increasing. Furthermore, the first serious attempts at statistical analysis of fluctuations were undertaken. In a few cases (especially Keynes), these theories suggested or implied policy proposals to reduce instability.

Important works were developed by Mikhail Tugan-Baranowski (1894), Ralph Hawtrey (1913), Dennis Robertson, (1915), Friedrich von Hayek (1933), Gottfried Haberler (1937) and Joseph SCHUMPETER (1911, 1939). Tugan-Baranowski, for instance, combined empirical work with theory by developing a "financial theory of over-investment," in which investment booms, caused by excess liquidity supplied by banks, lead to an excess capacity with respect to purchasing power. Hayek stressed the interaction of monetary and real dimensions of the economy in his theory. In his analysis, an excessive creation of money depresses the rate of interest below the "natural rate," which can distort the structure of production through the overaccumulation of capital.

SCHUMPETER'S THEORY OF INNOVATION, DEVELOPMENT AND CYCLES built upon and extended this framework. In *The Theory of Economic Development* (1911) and *Business Cycles* (1939), he called attention to the entrepreneur's energy and willingness to take risks and to innovate as factors encouraging expansions. Schumpeter's concept of "innovations" included new production technologies, new products, corporate or market restructuring, and the opening of new markets or resource supplies. In his theory, capitalism undergoes endogenous cycles through the bunching of innovations, which regularly produce greater profits and propel other firms to adopt the new methods and markets, which in turn leads to lower profit and the need for further innovation through greater competition. Credit heightens the amplitude of cycles, propelling demand during boom as general accumulation heightens in addition to new methods, and deepening the slump as chains of bankruptcy ensure thorough breaks in the credit and investment circuits. Schumpeter utilized Kitchin (3–5 years), Juglar (7–11 years) and Kondratieff (40–60 years) cycles in his analysis, whereby during long-wave downswings, every recession in the Juglar produces a deep recession as the economy is simultaneously declining in all three cycles. During long-wave upswings, recessions tend not to be deep. Since the 1970s, there has been a resurgence of interest in Schumpeterian and long-wave themes linked to short cycles.

Hawtrey stressed the importance of the cost of short-term credit, which is necessary for carrying inventories. Reductions in interest rates encourage merchants to carry larger inventories. Greater orders encourage increased production and perhaps investment in fixed capital. The expansion continues until bank reserves are depleted and credit availability declines. This "pure monetary theory" sees the initial disturbance as a surplus of liquidity in the banking system.

Dennis Robertson's version of the Marshallian "Cambridge tradition" also emphasized the importance of monetary phenomena. Both his and Hawtrey's work influenced Keynes. Keynes's cycle theory flows from his *General Theory of Employment, Interest and Money*, published in 1936, which attacked two fundamental doctrines of orthodox macroeconomics: Say's Law and the quantity theory of money. The level of economic activity is determined by entrepreneurs' investment expenditures. Investment is determined by expectations of the rate of return on new fixed capital (the "marginal efficiency of capital") and the level of long-term interest rates. Interest rates themselves are determined by the state of "liquidity preference" (which determines the proportion of financial assets wealth holders want to hold as money) and the quantity of liquid financial assets ("money"), assumed to be determined by the central bank.

Keynes argued that two sets of psychological expectations were the key to determining investment, the marginal efficiency of capital and liquidity preference, which reflected the expected market values of financial assets. Both sets of expectations are unstable due to risk and fundamental uncertainty regarding future yields of assets. This instability causes investment to fluctuate. Investment and the multiplier effect determine the level of and changes in economic activity and employment. Aggregate demand determines aggregate output, not the other way around as Smith, Say, Ricardo and James Mill believed. Falling wages and prices in recessions exacerbate the situation, since they increase pessimism regarding profits and future asset prices.

At about the same time as Keynes, Haberler's widely read and influential treatise (1937) presented a synthetic version of the state of cycle theory in the late 1930s, and KALECKI (1936–7) developed a cycle theory similar to that of Keynes. In this latter theory, investment fluctuates in an unstable fashion. Profit and the cost and availability of credit are important factors affecting investment, with profits being influenced by changes in the distribution of income. Kalecki also recognized that the state might use its ability to influence monetary and fiscal policies to change the wage–profit relationship, thus precipitating POLITICAL BUSINESS CYCLES through counter-cyclical policies. He is of great contemporary relevance to political economy, especially in relation to KALECKI'S MACRO THEORY OF PROFITS.

Third phase of cycle theories

The third phase followed the appearance of Keynes's *General Theory* in 1936. This phase of business cycle theory involves five lines of investigation. First, an important influence (both before and after the *General Theory*) was Wesley Mitchell, Director of the influential National Bureau of Economic Research (NBER) between 1920 and 1945. Mitchell influenced the analysis of leading and lagging indicators, the cost–profit relationship, and the endogenous forces of the cycle (see Mitchell 1951).

Second, Keynesians such as Paul Samuelson (1939) formalized Keynes's model and used a combination of the "multiplier" and an investment "accelerator" analysis to explain cycles. If, for instance, aggregate demand increases, investment plans are revised upward and aggregate demand accelerates to generate upswing. Eventually, as the rate of change of output fails to increase, a recession occurs. Under certain conditions this instability may be recurring in a cyclical fashion, whether damped, accelerating or recurring with a similar amplitude.

Third, monetarist economists such as Milton Friedman (writing in the 1960s), sceptical of Keynes's theory, revised the quantity theory of money and argued that fluctuations in the money stock were the principal source of instability in the short run. Fourth, by the 1980s real business cycle theory, incorporating the rational expectations hypothesis, argued that fluctuations are caused by external shocks to the economy such as dramatic changes in oil prices or the introduction of new technologies, or unanticipated changes in monetary policy. This revival of the classical view is known as "new classical economics." Lately, the real business cycle theory has been superseded by endogenous growth theory.

And fifth, contemporary post-Keynesians such as Hyman Minsky (1982), building on the work of Keynes and Kalecki, focus on the destabilizing effects of financial instability and fundamental uncertainty regarding returns to capitalist investment. Minsky's theoretical contributions emphasize the causes and consequences of financial crises and their relation to business cycles. Also, modern Marxists have adapted Marx's views, modifying them and often incorporating aspects of Keynes's and Kalecki's work (see NUTCRACKER THEORY OF THE BUSINESS CYCLE). For heterodox economists, the ultimate causes of fluctuations appear to stem from essential attributes of capitalist economies: the institution of private property, production and investment decisions guided by profit expectations, decentralized decision-making, and the interaction of uncertainty and risk. The deep recessions of the mid-1970s, the early 1980s and the early 1990s in the West have provided a spur to heterodox approaches to business cycles.

See also:

financial instability hypothesis; Mitchell's analysis of business cycles

Selected references

Glasner, David (ed.) (1997) *Business Cycles and Depressions: An Encyclopedia*, New York and London: Garland.
Haberler, Gottfried (1937) *Prosperity and Depression*, Geneva: League of Nations.
Hawtrey, Ralph G. (1913) *Currency and Credit*, London: Longman.
Hayek, Friedrich A. von (1933) *Monetary Theory and the Trade Cycle*, New York: Augustus Kelley, 1975.
Kalecki, Michal (1936–37) "A Theory of the Business Cycle," *Review of Economic Studies* 4(2): 77–7.
Malthus, Thomas R. (1820) *The Principles of Political Economy*, New York: Augustus Kelly, 1951.
Mill, John Stuart (1848) *Principles of Political Economy: With Some of their Applications to Social Philosophy*, New York: Augustus Kelly, 1965.
Minsky, Hyman P. (1982) *Can "It" Happen Again? Essays on Instability and Finance*, Armonk, NY: M.E. Sharpe.
Mitchell, Wesley (1951) *What Happens During Business Cycles: A Progress Report*, New York: NBER.
Robertson, Dennis. (1915) *A Study of Industrial Fluctuations*, London: P.S. King & Son.
Samuelson, Paul A. (1939) "Interaction Between the Multiplier Analysis and the Principle of Acceleration," *Review of Economic Statistics* 21(May): 75–8.
Schumpeter, Joseph (1911) *The Theory of Economic Development*, Oxford: Oxford University Press, 1961.
—— (1939) *Business Cycles: A Theoretical, Historical and Statistical Analysis of the Capitalist Process*, 2 vols, New York: McGraw-Hill.
Tooke, Thomas (1823) *Thoughts and Details on the High and Low Prices of the Last Thirty Years*, London: John Murray.
Tugan-Baranowski, Mikhail (1894) *Les Crises industrielles en Angleterre*, Paris: Giard & Briere, 1913.

CHRISTOPHER J. NIGGLE

business ethics

Business ethics is the discipline which applies ethical principles to the activities of business, where business is viewed as that economic enterprise which produces and distributes goods in the context of a capitalist, free market, profit-oriented system. One can find elements of business ethics as far back as the ethical writings of Plato and Aristotle, but the specific field as we know it today is a product of twentieth-century thought.

Origins and approaches

Although choosing any one date or event as the beginning of business ethics as a discipline would be to some extent arbitrary, it is not unreasonable to consider the 1959 publication of two major critiques of business school curricula in the United States as providing the initial impetus to the field. Both the Ford and Carnegie Foundations' reports assailed business education for its excessive vocationalism, for its lack of humanistic content and for its complete neglect of concern for the ethical dimension of managerial decision-making. An increasing number of corporate improprieties also spurred great interest in the study of professional ethics in general and business ethics in particular such that, by the 1990s, after the excesses of the 1980s, the formal study of ethics had become an integral part of the curriculum of nearly all professional schools.

Initially, those interested in the field focused either on issues in business and society or on ethical issues in business. The former interest found expression primarily among management faculty such as George Steiner at the University of California at Los Angeles who, for a number of years in the 1970s, hosted a conference sponsored by the General Electric Corporation. At this conference, the social, political, legal and ethical aspects of business were discussed by representatives of "Fortune 500" companies and professors from throughout the United States. Some work was also done on the development of courses and books in business and society. This broad concern with the external environment of business currently finds expression in the social issues division of the Academy of Management.

The latter interest focused more narrowly on purely ethical issues, and found expression primarily among philosophy faculty such as Norman Bowie, Richard DeGeorge and other non-philosophers, such as Clarence Walton, who published the first books and anthologies in business ethics in the 1970s. Their work led ultimately to the formation of a Society for Business Ethics, which meets annually and publishes the journal *Business Ethics Quarterly*, at time of writing under the editorship of Patricia Werhane.

A third major approach to business ethics is represented in Catholic social teachings. The Catholic Church has a long tradition of grappling with problems of economic ethics, beginning with the Fathers of the Church, running through the medieval scholastics and continuing in the twentieth century in papal encyclicals, beginning with *Rerum Novarum* in 1891 up to and including *Laborem Exercens* in 1981. This tradition found expression most recently, in the United States at least, with the publication in 1986 of the US Catholic Bishops' pastoral letter, *Economic Justice for All*. In this document, the bishops reiterated the church's position on private property, best characterized by the notion of stewardship, according to which (1) no one owns property absolutely; (2) individuals are entitled to property because of need as well as work; and (3) property rights are not simply negative rights of non-interference, but carry obligations of stewardship with them. This position is, of course, at variance with both socialist and capitalist thought, and provoked criticism from right-wing and left-wing critics alike.

Major themes in business ethics

The exact content of the field of business ethics would be difficult to demarcate without omitting some topic thought to be essential by some scholars. Nonetheless, at least three areas or themes of consideration are essential for any course in business ethics. First, some consideration of economic systems is included to clarify the environment in which business operates. Here, systems such as capitalism and socialism are analysed and evaluated, and the question of economic justice, i.e. "How should the goods and burdens of the world be distributed?" is raised. Among authors typically read on these foundational issues are John Locke, Adam Smith and Karl Marx, as well as contemporary political philosophers such as John Rawls and Robert Nozick.

Second, some consideration of the nature and purpose of business as a social institution is usually included to specify the relationships between business and other social institutions. This encompasses the question "What is the social responsibility of business?". Theories examined here range from Milton Friedman's classic contention that "the primary and only responsibility of business is to maximize profit," to the stakeholder theory of William Evan and Edward Freeman, that businesses are responsible for all those who have a stake in the business.

Third, there is usually some presentation of various ethical theories, ranging from deontological and utilitarian ethical theories to virtue ethics and social contract theories (see DEONTOLOGY). These theories are then applied to particular cases, issues or usual business practices, such as advertising, hiring, marketing, workers' rights, workers' safety, consumer rights, and community and societal rights (including the responsibility of business to the environment).

Contemporary research

This tripartite categorization is neither all-inclusive nor fixed. Contemporary research and scholarship is dynamic and different approaches and topics are being developed and added. Postmodern and feminist critiques have been applied to business practices. Narrative approaches to developing ethical models have been utilized. Much current interdisciplinary and empirically grounded work has been added. Questions shift, from "What is the right thing for businesses to do?" to questions such as "Why do good people do bad things?" or "How can one motivate people to behave correctly?". Hence, there is more and more investigation into the economic, sociological and psychological forces that impact on ethical or unethical behavior in business. In the future, one should expect a revision of the social contract that governs our understanding of business relationships with stakeholders and a redefinition of the nature of the business firm, as well as a rekindling of interest in other ethical theoretical areas as the deficiencies of the standard approaches become well recognized.

See also:

crime; ethics and morality; human dignity; needs; rights; value judgments and world views

Selected references

Beauchamp, Thomas and Bowie, Norman (1993) *Ethical Theory and Business*, 4th edn, New York: Prentice Hall.

Bowie, Norman and Duska, Ronald (1990) *Business Ethics*, 2nd edn, New York: Prentice Hall.

DeGeorge, Richard (1986) *Business Ethics*, 2nd edn, London: Macmillan.

"Economic Justice for All: A Pastoral Letter On Catholic Social Teaching and the US Economy," November 1986.

Evan, William and Freeman, R. Edward "A Stakeholder Theory of the Modern Corporation: Kantian Capitalism," mimeo.

Friedman, Milton (1962) *Capitalism and Freedom*, Chicago: University of Chicago Press.

Walton, Clarence (1967) *Corporate Social Responsibilities*, Belmont, CA: Wadsworth.

NICHOLAS M. RONGIONE
RONALD F. DUSKA

C

Cambridge revolution

Strictly speaking, we should define a "scientific revolution" according to Kuhn's (1970) analysis of the growth of (scientific) knowledge, which is based upon the notion of scientific PARADIGMS and the parallel distinction between periods of "normal science" (when scientists try to solve puzzles and anomalies within a given paradigm) and periods of "revolutionary science" (when some scientists are engaged in subverting existing paradigms and attempting to substitute them with new ones). In this sense, it would be appropriate to speak of a "Cambridge revolution" only if it were possible to characterize with some precision the involved paradigm – which does not seem to be the case. Nevertheless, economists and historians of economic thought had been employing expressions such as "marginalist revolution" or KEYNESIAN REVOLUTION well before Kuhn's methodological thesis, simply in order to emphasize major theoretical novelties (or breakdowns) in the history of the discipline.

A revolution?

Even in this looser sense, however, it is questionable if it is really pertinent to speak of a "Cambridge revolution." First of all, it must be noted that that such terms were not commonly used by adherents to the Cambridge school. It may well have been that, at times, some of them conveyed to the reader the impression of facing so strong a critique of neoclassical theory and so new an approach to some fundamental theoretical issues such as price theory, capital theory, distribution and growth that all this could be identified as a true "revolution" in economic theory (see, for instance, Harcourt 1972, Roncaglia 1978, or Joan Robinson's *Collected Economic Papers*).

Actually, however, it was Mark Blaug (1974) who employed the expression "Cambridge revolution" in the title of his pamphlet as a rhetorical device in order to dismiss Sraffian political economy for not having ultimately succeeded in attaining so ambitious a goal. For a reply to Blaug's harsh and somewhat unjustified criticism, pointing out the positive findings obtained by scholars who identify themselves with this school, the reader may see Ian Steedman's papers in de Marchi and Blaug (1991) and Moseley (1995). The personal view of the author of this entry is that the school made substantial contributions in all the fields of research referred to above, but it ultimately failed to achieve a complete "revolution" for at least two reasons.

Correspondence rules

During the CAPITAL THEORY DEBATES of the 1960s, the critique of the neoclassical aggregate production function was presented as a purely logical criticism having the indisputable force of deductive reasoning. Actually, however, the arguments about RESWITCHING, CAPITAL REVERSING and so on are fully understandable only if we are prepared to concede a number of "correspondence rules" concerning the "interpretation" of the involved algebra. Indeed, all participants to the debate seemed to agree, for instance, that one of the obvious characteristics of capital goods is their heterogeneity (otherwise one could not understand how it was possible to criticize a theory based on a one-sector model by showing that conclusions drawn from it no longer hold in a multisectoral linear model of production). For this reason, it happened that the extension of the same kind of criticism to other parts of neoclassical theory was more difficult than initially expected, simply because much less obvious "correspondence rules" were involved (see Salanti 1989).

Specific contributions

Positive contributions, important and impressive as they may have been, were confined to some specific issues, particularly to the theory of prices of production and the theory of growth and distribution (see, for instance, Harris 1978; Marglin 1984; Pasinetti 1981). In a sense they offered an interesting and original alternative, surely worthy of serious attention, to the most unsatisfactory parts of neoclassical economics. Unfortunately, this is not sufficient to supplant a fully articulated body of economic knowledge. Indeed, as Kuhn (1970) forcefully points out, a scientific revolution is successful only when it is embraced by the majority of the younger generations of scholars within a certain discipline. This happens when they perceive the possibility, in doing so, of achieving more interesting results for the development of their field of research as well as more rewarding prospects for their own academic career. This is precisely what, for a number of reasons (some of which are not yet fully understood), has not happened in the case of the so-called "Cambridge revolution." This is so in spite of the need to supplement neoclassical theory due to its difficulties and failures in many areas (see NEOCLASSICAL ECONOMICS: CRITIQUE)

See also:

Sraffian political economy

Selected references

Blaug, Mark (1974) *The Cambridge Revolution: Success or Failure?*, London: Institute of Economic Affairs.
Harcourt, Geoffrey C. (1972) *Some Cambridge Controversies in the Theory of Capital*, Cambridge: Cambridge University Press.
Harris, Donald J. (1978) *Capital Accumulation and Income Distribution*, London: Routledge & Kegan Paul.
Kuhn, Thomas S. (1970) *The Structure of Scientific Revolutions*, 2nd edn, Chicago: University of Chicago Press.
de Marchi, Neil and Blaug, Mark (eds) (1991) *Appraising Economic Theories: Studies in the Methodology of Scientific Research Programs*, Aldershot and Brookfield, VT: Edward Elgar.
Marglin, Stephen A. (1984) *Growth, Distribution, and Prices*, Cambridge, MA: Harvard University Press.
Moseley, Fred (1995) *Heterodox Economic Theories: True or False?*, Aldershot and Brookfield, VT: Edward Elgar.
Pasinetti, Luigi L. (1981) *Structural Change and Economic Growth: A Theoretical Essay on the Dynamics of the Wealth of Nations*, Cambridge: Cambridge University Press.
Roncaglia, Alessandro (1978) *Sraffa and the Theory of Prices*, New York: Wiley.
Salanti, Andrea (1989) "'Internal' Criticisms in Economic Theory: Are They Really Conclusive?," *Economic Notes* 19(1): 1–14.

ANDREA SALANTI

CAPACITY UTILIZATION: see effective demand and capacity utilization

capital reversing

In neoclassical economics, it is usually assumed that, as the preference for the present falls, more mechanized and more productive techniques of production are introduced. Capital is said to be substituted for labor. The standard story is that, as households decide to save more out of current income, the rate of interest drops, inducing capital accumulation and an increase in capital per head – capital deepening – thus leading to an increase in permanent output and consumption per head. By being thrifty now, waiting and abstinence allows for more consumption in the future. This parable links up with the notion that the rate of profit (or the rate of interest) is a measure of the relative scarcity of capital: the lower the rate of profit, the higher the capital–labor ratio. What the Cambridge capital controversies have shown is that these relationships do not necessarily hold. In particular, a lower rate of profit may be associated with a lower capital–labor ratio: capital reversing may occur when interdependences are taken into account.

Capital per head and profit rates

For a given technique but with changing prices (i.e. at different rates of profit), a positive relationship between the value of capital per head and the rate of profit is possible. This possibility came to be known as a "negative price-Wicksell effect," since it contradicted the relationship of the standard neoclassical parable. These effects, however, were not considered to be damaging to neoclassical theory, because they were being perceived as simple revaluation effects arising from price changes. This price-Wicksell effect also did not have any impact on the other fundamental relation in neoclassical capital theory, namely, the negative association between the rate of profit and consumption per head.

In the case of a choice of techniques, the discovery of RESWITCHING brought to the fore the fact that a positive relation between capital per head and the rate of profit could be associated with real phenomena. At a switch point, real wages and profit rates are identical for both techniques and hence, in a stationary state, differences in capital–labor ratios cannot be attributed to differences in prices. Following an infinitely small decrease in the rate of profit, the technique with lower capital per head (and lower consumption per head) could be adopted because it is superior to the technique with a higher capital per head. Such a paradoxical effect cannot be attributed to changing prices, but rather to a change in the quantity of capital, the form taken by the machines, or the proportions in which the different capital goods are being held. Such real effects, contradicting the neoclassical parable, are also called negative real-Wicksell effects. Broadly speaking, capital reversing may thus be associated either with negative price or real-Wicksell effects; but strictly speaking, capital reversing ought to be associated with the real effects only, as defined above.

Reswitching and capital reversing

With reswitching there is necessarily capital reversing at one of the switch points. However, capital reversing can occur without reswitching. This implies that capital reversing can arise without profit–wage curves cutting each other more than once. Because capital reversing is the phenomenon that contradicts standard neoclassical theory, the fact that reswitching is probabilistically unlikely or has rarely, if ever, been observed is irrelevant for the critique of neoclassical production and distribution theory. Capital reversing, rather than reswitching as such, is the crucial element in the critique of neoclassical theory. Reswitching only makes the consequences of capital reversing more obvious.

General phenomena of capital reversing

Capital reversing renders meaningless the neoclassical concepts of input substitution and capital or labor scarcity. It puts in jeopardy the neoclassical theory of capital and the notion of input demand curves, both at the economy and industry levels. It also puts in jeopardy the neoclassical theories of output and employment determination, as well as Wicksellian monetary theories, since they are all being deprived of stability. The consequences for neoclassical analysis are thus quite devastating. It is usually asserted that only aggregate neoclassical theory of the textbook variety – and hence macroeconomic theory, based on aggregate production functions – is affected by capital reversing. It has been pointed out, however, that when neoclassical general equilibrium models are extended to long-run equilibria, stability proofs require the exclusion of capital reversing (Schefold 1997). In that sense, all neoclassical production models would be affected by capital reversing.

While Luigi Pasinetti, in 1966, provided the first example of capital reversing, the discovery of capital reversing – or reverse capital deepening – is usually attributed to Joan Robinson, who first called it "apparently paradoxical," a "perverse behaviour," a "curious possibility," and even a "theoretical rigmarole" in her 1953 article criticizing the neoclassical production function (see ROBINSON'S CONTRIBUTION TO POLITICAL ECONOMY). Robinson gave a graphical representation of capital reversing in *The Accumulation of Capital* (1956), making references again to a "perverse case," an "analytical puzzle," and a "curiosum." On both occasions she attributed the discovery of this paradox to a comment made by her colleague Ruth Cohen. *R*everse *C*apital deepening then came to be known as the *R*uth *C*ohen curiosum, but this turned out to be an inside joke. Robinson indicated later that her description of capital reversing followed conversations with SRAFFA – which comes as no surprise given Sraffa's own presentation of reswitching in his *Production of Commodities by Means of Commodities*, where it is portrayed as a phenomenon that cannot be construed as being a fluke.

In that sense, there is thus no justification for calling "anomalous," "unnatural," "inconvenient" or "irregular" those economies that exhibit reverse capital deepening. Following the recognition that reswitching and capital reversing are general phenomena, neoclassical authors have devoted their energies to the identification of purely mathematical conditions, unjustified on economic grounds, that would exclude the appearance of these phenomena, thus obtaining "convenient" or "regular" economies, which correspond to what Luigi Pasinetti has called the "unobtrusive postulate." Another similar line of defense has been for neoclassical economists to argue that processes of production that would lead to "irregular" technologies, and hence to unstable equilibria with neoclassical price dynamics, would not be adopted in the first place and hence are irrelevant.

Empirics and abstract models

Initially, neoclassical authors such as Frank Hahn recognized that it was up to them to provide empirical evidence showing that capital reversing and the reswitching of techniques were unlikely to occur and hence were unrealistic. All participants to the controversies gradually recognized, however, as had been underlined by Robinson, that the debates had occurred within a highly abstract model set in logical rather than in historical time; that is, comparing steady states without technical progress rather than dealing with actual paths. Actual observations of capital accumulation thus could not provide direct evidence as to the likelihood, or lack of it, of paradoxical capital behaviour. Indeed, since accumulation usually proceeds with technical progress, new techniques rather than existing ones are being introduced. When the new technique is more productive than the old ones, whatever the profit rate, there can be no reswitching by definition.

A more indirect response was thus to invoke the ability of standard production functions – such as the Cobb–Douglas or the CES functions – to correlate with the data when standard neoclassical assumptions and technical progress were added to them. Some defenders of neoclassical theory thus claimed that aggregate neoclassical production and capital theories had been vindicated by the vast amount of successful regressions with good fits. However, in a series of articles that annihilated this line of argument, it was shown by Anwar Shaikh, then by Herbert Simon and later by McCombie and Dixon (1991), that statistical estimates of increasingly sophisticated production functions do little else than replicate accounting identities. Regressing data which, by construction, have not been drawn from neoclassical production functions will still yield good statistical fits of these hypothetical aggregate production functions. The econometric estimation of neoclassical production functions thus does not provide any empirical evidence that would minimize the relevance and importance of capital reversing as an internal critique of neoclassical economics.

See also:

capital theory debates; heterogeneous capital and labor; interest rate: natural; neoclassical economics: critique; Sraffian political economy; technical change and measures of technical progress

Selected references

Burmeister, Edwin (1979) "Professor Pasinetti's Unobtrusive Postulate, Regular Economies, and the Existence of a Well-Behaved Production Function," *Revue d'économie politique* 89 (5): 644–52.
Garegnani, Pierangelo (1990) "Quantity of Capital," in John Eatwell, Murray Milgate and Peter Newman (eds), *The New Palgrave: Capital Theory*, London: Macmillan, 1–78.
Harcourt, Geoffrey C. (1972) *Some Cambridge Controversies in the Theory of Capital*, Cambridge: Cambridge University Press.
Kurz, Heinz D. and Salvadori, Neri (1995) *Theory of Production: A Long-Period Analysis*, Cambridge: Cambridge University Press.
McCombie, John and Dixon, Robert (1991) "Estimating Technical Change in Aggregate Production Functions: A Critique," *International Review of Applied Economics* 5(1): 24–46.
Pasinetti, Luigi L. (1996) "Joan Robinson and Reswitching," in Maria Cristina Marcuzzo, Luigi L. Pasinetti and Alessandro Roncaglia (eds), *The Economics of Joan Robinson*, London: Routledge.
Robinson, Joan (1953) "The Production Function and the Theory of Capital," *Review of Economic Statistics* 21.
—— (1956) *The Accumulation of Capital*, London: Macmillan.
Schefold, Bertram (1997) *Normal Prices, Technical Change and Accumulation*, London: Macmillan.
Steedman, Ian (1985) "On Input Demand Curves," *Cambridge Journal of Economics* 9(2): 165–72.

MARC LAVOIE

capital theory debates

Ever since the inception of systematic economic analysis, the problem of "capital" has given rise to often heated controversies. The main reason for the controversial nature of the concept of "capital" appears to be the fact that it holds the key to an explanation of interest and profit. This became visible in early attempts to separate capital from labor and land, and correspondingly to separate profits from wages and rent; it played an important role in attacks on the canonical prohibition of interest which were founded on some concept of the "productivity" of capital, and conceived of interest as the reward for it. In the time of the classical economists, from Adam Smith to David Ricardo, the problem of capital was in the center of the theory of value and distribution. The fact that "capital," representing heterogeneously produced means of production, cannot be measured in terms of some technical or physical unit as is the case with labor and land was pointed out by Ricardo in a controversy with Torrens. Here, Ricardo stressed that the only sense that one can speak of two capitals of equal size is to mean two capitals of equal *value*. Since in a capitalist economy, "capital" occupies a central role in both production and distribution, controversies in the theory of capital carry over to all other parts of economic analysis (see Bliss 1975).

Usury, interest and profit

In antiquity and the Middle Ages, attention focused on interest on loans. Aristotle and the schoolmen considered any interest-taking as usurious and thus unjust. The making of money through profit was regarded as "unnatural," because the acquisition of money for its own sake is without limit. Aquinas noted that interest is paid for the passing of time, but since the Creator endowed all human beings alike with time, interest is to be condemned, and actually was so by canonical law. It was only during the later Middle Ages that opposition to the prohibition of usury slowly gained momentum in the West.

In his criticism of the usury laws, Turgot remarked that after land had become tradeable, money could be used to buy a plot of land which would earn its proprietor a rent. If rent was considered acceptable, so should be interest and profit. Turgot's argument pointed toward the rule according to which a given surplus product is divided among the propertied classes of society in conditions of free competition. There is a tendency toward a sharing out of the surplus in proportion to the capital employed, irrespective of whether the capital consisted of a sum of money, a plot of land or a complex of produced means of production. The idea of a uniform rate of return on capital was to become the pivotal concept around which classical and marginal economic analysis revolved.

Theories of the origin of profit

The question about the "origin" of profit (and interest), to use Böhm-Bawerk's term, was thus posed. Following his suggestion, the answers given may be grouped as follows. Apart from the above mentioned classical theory as put forward by Ricardo, there are productivity theories, utilization theories, abstinence theories, labor theories, Böhm-Bawerk's own "agio theory" (also known as the "Austrian theory of capital and interest"), and surplus or exploitation theories.

Productivity theories are essentially of two versions: static and dynamic. The static theory starts from the hypothesis that, given the technical alternatives of production, labor equipped with produced means of production is generally more productive than unassisted labor. The extra product is to be imputed to capital and will be pocketed as profit by the capital owner. Since capital is the result of saving, profits are the reward of a socially beneficial activity. This approach was to culminate in marginal productivity theory of income distribution at the end of the nineteenth century. The dynamic version of the productivity theories starts instead from the hypothesis that any accumulation of capital involves some innovation. Variants of this view were put forward, *inter alia*, by Adam Smith, Joseph Schumpeter and Frank Knight.

Utilization theories generally assume that a (durable) capital item represents two separate and valuable goods: the capital good itself and its use or utilization. Profit (or interest) is said to be the price of the latter. This view was advocated by, among others, Jean-Baptiste Say, Lord Lauderdale and Carl Menger. It was objected by Böhm-Bawerk that these theories involve double counting and therefore have to be rejected.

Abstinence theories envisage profit as a reward of the "sacrifice" engendered by the person that saves, that is, abstains from consumption. Senior goes as far as to reckon "abstinence" as a third original factor of production alongside labor and land. Against this doctrine it was objected that while saving involves abstaining from consumption, it does not involve abstaining from any kind of enjoyment, such as the acquisition of reputation and power. Moreover, the theory cannot explain a competitive rate of profit because there is no presumption that the "sacrifice" is proportional to the value of capital.

Labor theories conceive profits as a special wage, the wage paid as a compensation of the work performed by the capitalist. These theories are also unable to explain a competitive rate of profit. Moreover, they refer at best only to the income of entrepreneurs, but cannot deal with property income.

The Austrian theory of capital and interest centers around the concept of the non-neutrality of time. The main elements of Böhm-Bawerk's analysis are the concepts of "time preference" and the "superiority of more roundabout processes of production," cast in the notion of the "average period of production." As in Jevons's version of the productivity theory of profits in terms of a temporal production function, social capital was conceived as a subsistence fund and was seen to permit the adoption of more productive but also more time-consuming methods of production. Whereas consumers, due to their "preference of present goods over future goods of the same quantity," tend to prefer short processes, producers tend to favor longer, more productive ones. The rate of interest is the variable that balances these two contradictory interests. It is to the concept of the "average period of production," which was meant to express the amount of capital employed per unit of labor, that the marginal productivity condition was applied in the determination of the level of the rate of interest. Böhm-Bawerk's construction had considerable support around the turn of the century and was refined by Wicksell. However, objections were soon leveled at each of its constituent elements. In particular, the concept of the average period of production fell into disrepute; it was attacked in the 1930s and early 1940s by Morgenstern, Knight, Steindl and Hayek, who previously had been a staunch advocate of it. Two main criticisms were that the concept could not deal with fixed capital and that "more roundabout" processes need not be superior (see AUSTRIAN SCHOOL OF POLITICAL ECONOMY).

Ricardo, Marx and the social surplus

We turn now to the analyses of Ricardo and Marx. Scrutiny shows that notwithstanding important differences, they share a common analytical structure. For both authors, profits are explained in terms of the surplus product left after making allowance for the requirements of reproduction, which were conceived inclusive of the wages of labor, or "necessary consumption" as Ricardo called them. The determination of the social surplus implied taking as data (a) the system of production in use, characterized as it is by the dominant technical conditions of production of the various commodities, (b) the size and composition of the (gross) social product, and (c) the ruling real wage rate(s). In accordance with the underlying "normal" or long-period position of the economy, the capital stock was assumed to be so adjusted to the data (a)–(c) that a uniform rate of profit obtained. Thus, these authors separated the determination of profits and prices from that of quantities. The latter were considered to be determined in the analysis of accumulation and economic and social development (see EXPLOITATION AND SURPLUS VALUE).

The rate of profit was defined as the ratio between social surplus and social capital, that is, two aggregates of heterogeneous commodities. This forced the classical authors to face the problem of value. In the *Principles*, Ricardo's ingenious device to solve this problem consisted in relating the exchange-values of the commodities to the quantities of labor directly and indirectly necessary to produce them. According to Marx's causal-genetic view, the explanation of profits in terms of the surplus approach would have been trapped in circular reasoning if the value expression of either surplus or capital were to depend on the rate of profit. The measurement of both aggregates in terms of labor values, which themselves were seen to be independent of the distribution of the product, was considered a device to circumvent this difficulty and provide a non-circular determination of the rate of profit, $r = s/(c + v)$, where r is the general rate of profit, s the "surplus value" (that is, the value of the surplus product), c the value of the means of production or "constant capital," and v the value of wages or "variable capital" (see FALLING RATE OF PROFIT TENDENCY).

Hence in both Ricardo and Marx, profits are positive, if and only if wages do not exhaust the entire (net) product. The latter fact was traced back to a tendency toward an excess supply of labor which depressed wages. Whereas Ricardo explained such a tendency in terms of a (Malthusian) population mechanism, Marx traced the existence of a reserve army of labor back to the labor saving bias of technical change in capitalism (see Kurz and Salvadori 1995: ch. 15).

As is well known, neither Ricardo nor Marx succeeded in providing a general and logically coherent formulation of the surplus approach to the theory of value and distribution. Such a formulation was eventually, subsequent to the contributions of V.K. Dmitriev and L. von Bortkiewicz, put forward by Piero Sraffa (1960). He demonstrated that the data (a)–(c) suffice to determine the independent variables: the rate of profit and relative prices. In addition, Sraffa showed that, in the case in which there are alternative techniques available from which cost-minimizing producers can choose, there is no reason to presume that these techniques can be ordered according to "degrees of mechanization" (see SRAFFIAN POLITICAL ECONOMY).

Neoclassical theory of capital

The traditional, long-period, neoclassical theory of capital, as it was advocated in one version or another by Jevons, Böhm-Bawerk, Wicksell, Clark and Marshall, adopted fundamentally the same method of analysis as the classical economists, focusing attention on equilibria characterized by a uniform rate of profit and uniform rates of remuneration for all primary factors of production. The basic novelty consisted in attempting to explain all kinds of incomes symmetrically in terms of demand and supply in regard to the respective services of the respective factors of production.

More precisely, the neoclassical approach started from the following sets of data: (1) preferences of agents; (2) technical alternatives of production; and (3) initial endowments of the economy of factors of production, including a factor "capital." On the basis of these data, the theory sought to determine the prices of goods, the prices of the factor services (income distribution) and the quantities produced of the goods and those employed of the different factors. As regards the supply side of the traditional neoclassical treatment of capital, its advocates (with the notable exception of Léon Walras) were well aware of the fact that, in order to be consistent with the concept of a long-period equilibrium, the capital equipment of the economy could not be conceived as a set of given amounts of concrete produced means of production. The "quantity of capital" in given supply instead had to be expressed in value terms, allowing it to assume the physical "form" best suited to the other data of the theory. If the capital endowment were to be given in kind, only a short-period equilibrium, characterized by differential rates of return on the supply prices of the various capital items, could be established by the forces of demand and supply. However, with capital given in value terms, the phenomena of "capital reversing" and "reswitching" may involve equilibrium being unstable. This means that the theory is unable to explain normal income distribution (Harcourt 1972; Kurz and Salvadori 1995: ch. 14; see also CAPITAL REVERSING; RESWITCHING).

Before then, however, in the late 1920s and early 1930s, in order to avoid the same difficulties, Lindahl, Hicks and Hayek had suggested a move away from the long-period method toward the inter-temporal equilibrium method. Among the three, Lindahl was perhaps best aware of the inconsistency in which marginalist long-period theory was trapped. He pointed out that the received versions of "modern" capital theory "have the disadvantage that the measure of capital is made dependent on the prices of the services invested and on the rate of interest – which belong to the unknown factors of the problem" (Lindahl 1939: 317). While in long-period analysis "the prices in succeeding periods are equal to the prices in the present period and thus do not introduce any new unknowns into the problem, in the [inter-temporal analysis] they will differ more or less from the prices in the first period" (Lindahl 1939: 319). This allowed one to consider the amounts of heterogeneous capital goods in given supply at the beginning of the first period; capital did not need to be considered as a single magnitude.

Scrutiny shows that despite their break with the traditional long-period method, Lindahl, Hicks and Hayek were still concerned with long-period positions of the economic system characterized by a uniform rate of interest. A total break with traditional analysis was finally intended in the so-called Arrow–Debreu model, developed in the 1950s. Abandoning long-period analysis, however, does not seem to have been sufficient to escape the problems of capital. To see this, we have to leave the capital market and turn to the investment–savings market. In equilibrium, investment equals savings; that is, aggregate demand for the outputs of means of production equals aggregate supply. However, there is no guarantee that the equilibrium is stable. With reswitching and capital reversing, a fall (rise) in the effective rate of interest need not result in an increase (decrease) of investment demand. In short, the presence of these phenomena in a long-period analysis would be reflected, in an inter-temporal analysis, in multiple and/or unstable equilibria. This possibility questions the validity of the entire economic analysis in terms of demand and supply (for more details see Kurz and Salvadori 1995: 455–67).

See also:

Cambridge revolution; neoclassical economics

Selected references

Bliss, C.J. (1975) *Capital Theory and the Distribution of Income*, Amsterdam: North Holland.
Harcourt, G.C. (1972) *Some Cambridge Controversies in the Theory of Capital*, Cambridge: Cambridge University Press.
Kurz, H.D. and Salvadori, N. (1995) *Theory of Production: A Long-Period Analysis*, Cambridge: Cambridge University Press.
Lindahl, E. (1939) *Studies in the Theory of Money and Capital*, London: Allen & Unwin.
Sraffa, P. (1960) *Production of Commodities by Means of Commodities. Prelude to a Critique of Economic Theory*, Cambridge: Cambridge University Press.

HEINZ D. KURZ
NERI SALVADORI

capital and the wealth of nations

Capital, generally speaking, is the dynamic stock of durable structures, whatever those structures may be. Therefore investment, as a flow, is the process whereby these durable structures are created and maintained. Consumption is the destruction or utilization of capital. Capital in its many forms provides the foundation for a flow of services over time. One should differentiate between use-values and monetary values in the flow of benefits.

Capital is not a homogenous globule. There are four main forms of capital in political economy: ecological capital, social capital, human capital and private business capital.

Ecological capital

Ecological capital is the stock of all environmental and ecological resources. It is a dynamic stock involving the biosphere, the gene pool, all plant and animal species, the weather, the cycles of nature and the physical environment. Here the concern is with the long-term regeneration of the biosphere, or the long-term survival of all plants and animals plus certain environmental conditions. This view of ecological capital, based on "deep ECOLOGY," seeks to promote ecological harmony and biospecies equality.

The history of humanity, and particularly of capitalism, has seen a rapid destruction of ecological capital as the stock of human beings and fixed business capital expands inexorably. For instance, the human population of Earth has increased fivefold from one billion (1800) to five billion people (1990) (Ekins 1992: 108–109); and the per capita stock of durable private capital has increased twentyfold in the UK and fortyfold in the US between 1820 and 1991 (Maddison 1995: 143). This has occurred in tandem with forests declining from 70 percent to 30 percent of the total land area; for tropical forests, the figure is only 7 percent (Ekins 1992: 16) These tropical forests have historically supported the vast majority of

Earth's species, and are under threat around the world. It is estimated that 50–100 animal species are extinguished every day (Ekins 1992: 16.) The switch from ecological to human types of capital means that, in large measure, the growth of human-created forms of capital is derivative (see also NATURAL CAPITAL).

Social capital

Social (or institutional) capital comprises those norms, mores, relationships and organizational arrangements which help to bond people together. Some minimal degree of trust, respect, dignity and communication between people constitutes an important aspect of social capital. Durable relationships and behaviors are created within, for instance, specific sites or spheres such as families, corporations, governments, markets and nations.

Political economy has for many decades recognized that the basic substance of the economy comprises its institutions. More recently, it has been recognized that stability and flexibility in the institutions is a necessary condition for sustained economic growth and performance. When the institutions are suitable, growth and accumulation of private business capital is encouraged; and when the institutions are in disarray, such growth and accumulation tend to falter (see SOCIAL STRUCTURES OF ACCUMULATION). However, especially in the last few decades, critical forms of social capital have been destroyed. In advanced capitalist economies, people are on average investing less in family, relationship and community capital and more in human, corporate and market forms of capital (see Dollahite and Rommel 1993).

Heller (1996) examines the relationship between social and business capital in a fascinating case study of the state of Kerala in India (population 29 million people). While GDP per capita is lower in Kerala (US $260 per capita) than for India as a whole (US $310), other indicators of the standard of living in Kerala suggest that it is much higher than that of the rest of India (and within reach of much more developed nations). For instance, average life expectancy in Kerala is 70 years compared with 59 for all of India; infant mortality in Kerala is 17 per 1,000, compared with 91 per 1,000 for all of India; and adult literacy is 91 percent in Kerala, compared with 52 percent in all of India (1991 data, from Heller 1996). Heller isolates the high dynamic stock of social capital as the main reason for Kerala's relatively high standard of living (see SOCIAL AND ORGANIZATIONAL CAPITAL).

Human capital

Human capital is usually related to those skills and knowledge that are capable of general application, although "firm specific" human capital and "learning by doing" are of considerable importance (perhaps being part of "organizational capital"). A large proportion of the knowledge and skills that are incorporated in individuals emanate from collective sources, such as schools, universities, libraries, organizational structures and the like.

Since the 1950s, economists have attributed 20–50 percent of productivity growth in advanced nations to the growth of human capital (see O'Hara 1998). People with low levels of education have a much higher rate of unemployment relative to those with a high level of education.

Radical economists have taken traditional human capital theory to task for not adequately incorporating questions of class, gender and race – and more generally socioeconomic reproduction – into the analysis. For instance, Egerton (1997) found that certain occupations are in large measure "inherited." Human capital that is appropriated by individuals is not simply dependent upon the determination and energy of the individual student but also, significantly, on the help and guidance provided by parents. Egerton's conclusion is that the upper classes are better able to provide their offspring with the "CULTURAL CAPITAL" of cognitive, personal, educational, property and social network assets which bring material success.

In the USA in 1993, for instance, 0.9 percent of individuals with less than twelve years of schooling (many being "non-white") and 8.6

percent of those with four or more years of college (mostly "white") had a net worth of $500,000 or more (USCB 1997). The net worth asset ownership of US households is heavily skewed in favor of whites. Some of this is due to inequality of human (and social) capital, and some is due to discrimination.

Private business capital

This includes durable structures within corporations, such as machinery, factories, tools, warehouses, buildings and inventories. The creation of fixed capital in the form of investment plays a critical role in the generation of business cycles (see Sherman 1991), and therefore changes in the rate of unemployment. The rate of net addition to the stock of fixed capital directly influences economic booms and slumps.

Recent debates about human and social capital have downplayed the relative importance of private business capital as a proportion of total capital. By far the most important form of capital, according to the World Bank (1995), is human resources, especially human and social capital, which represent over two-thirds of all the wealth of nations.

The vast majority of these human resources (human and social capital) belong to the West. This is due to imperialistic and, more recently, economic leadership of the world economy. Most non-Western nations have historically been left out of these structures of productive, commercial and financial dominance and leadership. The flows of income tend to emanate from the dynamic stock of capital or wealth, and vastly favour the West. Some challenge to Western dominance was achieved during the period after 1970, but this has not challenged Western power or global inequality sufficiently at this point in history.

See also:

accumulation; circuit of social capital; culture; entropy, negentropy and the laws of thermodynamics; gross domestic product and net social welfare; hegemony in the world economy; human development index; institutions and habits; quality of life; technology

Selected references

Dollahite, D.C. and Rommel, J.I. (1993) "Individual and Relationship Capital: Implications for Theory and Research on Families," *Journal of Family and Economic Issues* 14(1): 27–48.

Egerton, Muriel (1997) "Occupational Inheritance: The Role of Cultural Capital and Gender," *Work, Employment and Society* 11(2): 263–82.

Ekins, Paul, with Hillman, M. and Hutchinson, R. (1992) *Wealth Beyond Measure: An Atlas of New Economics*, London: Gaia Books.

Heller, Patrick (1996) "Social Capital as a Product of Class Mobilization and State Intervention: Industrial Workers in Kerala, India," *World Development* 24(6): 1055–71.

Maddison, Angus (1995) *Explaining the Economic Performance of Nations: Essays in Time and Space*, Aldershot: Edward Elgar.

O'Hara, Phillip Anthony (1998) "Capital, the Wealth of Nations and Inequality in the Contemporary World," in Douglas Brown (ed.), *Thorstein Veblen in the Twenty First Century*, Aldershot: Edward Elgar.

Sherman, Howard (1991) *The Business Cycle: Growth and Crisis Under Capitalism*, Princeton, NJ: Princeton University Press.

USCB (US Census Bureau) (1997) *The Official Statistics: Asset Ownership of Households*: 1993, Washington DC: USCB.

World Bank (1995) *Monitoring Environmental Progress: A Report on Work in Progress*, Washington, DC: World Bank.

PHILLIP ANTHONY O'HARA

capitalism

Capitalism is a term used by political economists to designate the type of economic system extant in most of the industrialized world today. Capitalism designates a market system in which there are two main conditions. The first condition is that the vast majority of the physical means of production are privately owned; the legal rights to their use, profit and disposal are in the hands of private individuals or corporations. The second condition is that production is done by wage labor, whereby workers contract with employers to allow the latter discretion and command over their labor for a mutually agreed portion of each day, in return for a regularly paid wage, until either party declines to continue the contract (see Schweickart 1993).

Private ownership is usually in the form of individuals or corporations owning shares of transferable stock. The wage "contract" may be explicitly detailed (as in union contracts), or merely implicit; wages may be paid hourly, as "piece rates" or as salaries; and so forth. Yet this definition also helps differentiate related cases. For example, if "owners" of the means of production have rights to their profit, but control lies in the hands of the state, then FASCISM may be a better descriptive term. Similarly, if "employers" have control not only over workers' labor but also over their lives outside the workplace, then the term SLAVERY, or perhaps FEUDALISM, may be more appropriate.

A class system

That the predominant economic system in the industrially advanced world today is merely another in humankind's long history of class systems is suggested immediately in the definition of "capitalism." In principle, people would not willingly sell their daily life activity into wage employment, any more than they would sell themselves into indentured servitude, unless compelled to do so by force of circumstances (see ECONOMIC POWER). In capitalism, if one lacks ownership of means of production, or the ability to employ others to produce goods for sale in markets, then one must "choose" wage employment in order to subsist. That system, therefore, rests upon an exploitative class relationship. Those who produce do not own the means of production, but instead are employed by those who do own them, while the latter need not produce, hence may live off the surplus labor of the rest.

Alienation

As in any class system, working people's activities within capitalism are subject to others' control and discretion instead of their own. Thus arise symptoms of ALIENATION, feelings of estrangement, meaninglessness, impotence, indifference and social incompetence. These are the consequence of the class system, and not merely the result of INDUSTRIALIZATION, modernism or the secular society.

Patriarchy and racism

Critical questions, therefore, arise about the connections and interplay between capitalism and other oppressive structures extant in modern capitalist societies, such as PATRIARCHY and RACISM. A central question for critical heterodox economists is whether capitalism tends to replace patriarchy and racism with its own form of domination, or instead strengthens them as it accommodates and incorporates them into its own dynamic (see RACE, ETHNICITY, GENDER AND CLASS).

Capitalism and socialism

Among critical heterodox economists there has been much disagreement about whether specific historical and hypothetical cases are actually "capitalist." Is Sweden's economy, for example, merely a further variation on the same basic form common to such diverse cases as the USA, France and Japan, or is it something qualitatively different? A critical tendency within capitalism is for the incessant accumulation of capital. This compulsion acts as the "engine" of economic development in capitalism, directing investment in an insatiable pursuit of profit rather than other social or private concerns. This dynamic is fundamentally conditioned by the system of wage labor and private property. On these grounds, Sweden and other similar cases are arguably capitalist, despite the large degree of social provisioning (see SOCIAL DEMOCRACY).

In fact, on the basis of the primacy of the ACCUMULATION of capital, even economies as apparently different from capitalism as those of communist Yugoslavia and the former USSR have been called "capitalist." In Yugoslavia, even though the country's physical means of production were constitutionally "publicly owned," they were subject to private control (by worker-managed firms) in the context of competitive markets within which the accumulation dynamic was quite strong.

And while the accumulation dynamic in the centrally planned USSR was not impelled by market competition, a powerful accumulation dynamic of some sort clearly existed in that country, judging from its growth record. What if top-level state planners and Party leaders were seen as being self-interested, seeking to maximize personal income, power or control? If this class of bureaucrats controlled the major resources of the economy, including wage labor, with accumulation being a central dynamic of the system, is this system then one of state capitalism? Since, moreover, major similarities existed between Soviet administrative structures and the CENTRALIZED PRIVATE SECTOR PLANNING appearing in modern capitalism, the case that the USSR was ("state" or "bureaucratic") "capitalist" is perhaps not far-fetched.

Some political economists have argued that worker cooperatives are forms of socialism rather than capitalism. This is based on the notion that there is worker control of stock and decision-making and that alienation and exploitation do not exist. The wage labor–capital distinction is non-existent, and the stock of corporations are collectively owned by the workers rather than by absentee owners (see MONDRAGÓN).

See also:

capitalist breakdown debate; circuit of social capital; classes of capitalism; exploitation; mode of production and social formation; socialism and communism

Selected references

Braudel, Fernand (1981) *Capitalism and Civilization, 15th–18th Century*, 3 vols, New York: Harper & Row.
Edwards, Richard C., Reich, Michael and Weisskopf, Thomas E. (1986) *The Capitalist System*, 3rd edn, Englewood Cliffs, NJ: Prentice Hall.
Friedman, Milton (1962) *Capitalism and Freedom*, Chicago: University of Chicago Press.
Marx, Karl and Engels, Friedrich (1988) *The Communist Manifesto*, ed. F.L. Bender, New York: W.W. Norton.
Munkirs, John R. (1985) *The Transformation of American Capitalism: From Competitive Market Structures to Centralized Private Sector Planning*, New York: M.E. Sharpe.
Peterson, Janice and Brown, Doug (1994) *The Economic Status of Women under Capitalism*, Brookfield, VT: Edward Elgar.
Polanyi, Karl (1944) *The Great Transformation*, Boston: Beacon Press.
Schweickart, David (1993) *Against Capitalism*, New York: Cambridge University Press.
Sweezy, Paul (1942) *The Theory of Capitalist Development*, New York: Monthly Review Press.
Veblen, Thorstein (1899) *The Theory of the Leisure Class*, New York: Penguin, 1979.

ERIC SCHUTZ

CAPITALISM, FUTURE OF: see future of capitalism

capitalist breakdown debate

Introduction

From the 1890s, different socialist and particularly Marxist currents debated whether capitalism's economic dynamic could be sustained indefinitely and, if it could not, the mechanisms that would cause its breakdown. The main candidates for such a mechanism were disproportionalities between industries or departments of production, overproduction/underconsumption of commodities, and the tendency of the profit rate to fall.

The debate had implications for the relationship between capital accumulation on the one hand, and colonialism and imperialism (see COLONIALISM AND IMPERIALISM: CLASSIC TEXTS) and the INTERNATIONALIZATION OF CAPITAL on the other. This controversy over capitalism's tendency toward economic breakdown also involved debate over SECULAR CRISIS and the value of different CYCLICAL CRISIS MODELS. The classic debate concluded with Grossmann's 1929 contribution, but the explanation of economic crises has remained a contentious issue in Marxist and non-Marxist theory to the present.

Disproportionality and underconsumption

Mikhail Tugan-Baranovsky (1901) built on Marx's reproduction schemes in Volume II of *Das Kapital* (see REPRODUCTION, SIMPLE AND EXTENDED) to argue that economic crises were a consequence of disproportionality between different branches of production. Other major contributors to the breakdown controversy, including his opponents, similarly used these schemes as a tool to explore and expound crisis theory. Tugan maintained that speculative investment in particular could lead to some industries growing more rapidly than others which they supply or are supplied by. This eventually sends them into financial difficulties, giving rise to partial blockages in the CIRCUIT OF SOCIAL CAPITAL and, as these ramify across the economy, to a temporary cyclical crisis.

Tugan's approach provided an additional basis for Eduard Bernstein's revisionist critique of Marxism. Bernstein sought to bring German Social Democracy's rhetorically revolutionary Marxist theory into line with its practice of increasingly concentrating on the pursuit of reforms within the framework of capitalism (see SOCIAL DEMOCRACY). Bernstein supported the "civilizing" role of imperialism, and argued that it was necessary to reject what he regarded as a key feature of Marxism: that capitalism's economic mechanism leads it to breakdown.

Tugan's position, that given capitalism's tendency to restore proportionality there was no limit to capitalist growth, provided a theoretical basis for Bernstein's position.

In response Karl Kautsky, the most influential Marxist theoretician of the period, restated the orthodoxy. This was that economic crises are a necessary consequence of the difference between the level of production and the scale of working-class consumption, a mechanism known as "overproduction" or, more commonly, "underconsumption." Competition, according to this theory, leads to increasing investment in means of production, higher productivity and the production of more and more commodities at lower prices. At the same time, capitalists seek to hold wages down. Eventually, workers' consumption and that of capitalists fail to absorb the expanding volume of commodities being produced, giving rise to crises. The growth of production also drives capitalists to seek foreign markets which can, temporarily, offset a crisis. While Kautsky had argued, against Bernstein, that a theory of *periodic* crises rather than breakdown was an element of the Marxist critique of capitalism, he was not so adamant about this in his later critique (Kautsky 1902) against Tugan.

Particularly from 1906, the intellectually dominant "center" grouping in the German Social Democratic Party moved closer to the revisionists. It became increasingly hostile to proposals for mass strikes over the restricted franchise in Prussia, the largest German state, or against the rising threat of war. This shift was reflected in a more favorable attitude toward Tugan's disproportionality explanation of crises, apparent in Rudolph Hilferding's very influential *Finance Capital*, published in 1910 (see FINANCE CAPITAL).

In her work *The Accumulation of Capital* (1913), Rosa Luxemburg criticized the position of Tugan and his predecessors. Under capitalism, she held, workers and capitalists cannot consume the whole social product, notably the part destined for accumulation. This prevented the full realization of surplus value. By affirming that capitalism was indeed characterized by a tendency to economic breakdown, and providing the most systematic account of the underconsumptionist Marxist orthodoxy, she was also implicitly challenging a key rationale for the policies of the Social Democratic Party's leadership. Luxemburg also linked capitalism's breakdown tendency to imperialism (which she identified as a way of securing markets in non-capitalist areas to absorb domestic overproduction) and militarism. These arguments provided additional justification and urgency for revolutionary action which, from the point of view of Party officials of the right and center, might place its parliamentary, trade union and press routine at risk.

The prominent theoretical and parliamentary leader of Austrian Social Democracy, Otto Bauer, was aligned with the German "center." He developed Marx's (and Tugan's) reproduction schemes in a refutation of Luxemburg's position. He maintained that the process of accumulation tends to adjust to the rate of growth of the population, understood as the labor force, through economic crises which reflect transient phases of "underaccumulation" and "overaccumulation" of capital. So, while population growth sets a limit to the longer-term *rate* of accumulation, the accumulation process can continue indefinitely. Bauer saw imperialism in part as a response to the phase of overaccumulation, when production has outpaced population growth and capitalists seek new, foreign markets.

During and after the First World War, right-wing and moderate social democrats, including Hilferding himself, drew attention to the greater coordination of production and planning of economic activity undertaken by both cartels and states. These developments, they argued, were stabilizing capitalism and moderating the effects of crises by eliminating disproportion between different sectors. Many also identified a progressive and conceivably peaceful side to imperialism.

Falling rate of profit tendency

In 1929, Henryk Grossmann took issue with both the "neo-harmonist" position of Hilferding and Bauer and the underconsumptionist tradition represented by Luxemburg (although not her identification of a breakdown tendency in capitalism or its implications for socialist political practice). He developed Marx's discussion of the FALLING RATE OF PROFIT TENDENCY from the third volume of *Das Kapital*. While the relationship between this tendency and Marx's conception of capitalist crises and breakdown had been touched on in earlier discussions, it had otherwise been neglected or dismissed.

Grossmann explained how competition drives capitalists to invest a progressively rising proportion of their capital in constant capital (as opposed to variable capital), in order to increase the productivity of labor and reduce the value and hence price of the commodities they produce. Therefore, the surplus value-creating component will decline as a proportion of total outlays. Assuming that the rate at which surplus value is generated by variable capital does not change, the ratio of surplus value to total outlays, i.e. the rate of profit, will fall. By extending Bauer's own reproduction scheme over a longer period, Grossmann demonstrated that capitalism could not indefinitely maintain any specific rate of accumulation. The model eventually breaks down because insufficient surplus value is available to continue the next round of production with the same rate of accumulation, or even on the same absolute scale. This is a contradiction at the heart of the capitalist production process, which is a consequence of the most progressive aspect of capitalism, its continuing expansion of the productivity of human labor.

A number of counter-tendencies can offset the fall in the rate of profit. Grossmann extended Marx's discussion of these, including increases in the rate of surplus value, the cheapening of constant capital, a reduction in turnover time and military expenditure. He also explained imperialism and speculation primarily as responses to falling profit rates. Despite its very considerable strengths, from the 1930s Grossmann's analysis found few supporters in an international labor movement dominated by social democracy, inclined to disproportionality theory, and Stalinist communism with its underconsumptionist perspective.

Recent debates

All three of the main approaches to economic crisis have been applied to more recent developments and continue to have adherents. Baran and Sweezy's (1970) underconsumptionism was particularly influential in the North American new left. Left-wing social democratic supporters of incomes and industry policies have found succor in disproportionality theory. Harman (1984) has explained the post-Second World War boom and its demise in terms that parallel and support Grossmann's analysis. Debates have appeared, for instance, in the journals *Science and Society*, the *Review of Radical Political Economics, International Socialism* and *Capital and Class*. Modern theories, such as the SOCIAL STRUCTURES OF ACCUMULATION and REGULATION APPROACH, have significance for this debate in terms of the degree of institutionalization of relations within modern capitalism.

See also:

business cycle theories; disembedded economy; hegemony

Selected references

Baran, Paul and Sweezy, Paul (1970) *Monopoly Capital*, Harmondsworth: Penguin.
Bauer, Otto (1986) "The Accumulation of Capital," *History of Political Economy* 18(1): 88–110.
Grossmann, Henryk (1929) *The Law of Accumulation and Breakdown of the Capitalist System: Being also Theory of Crises*, London: Pluto.
Harman, Chris (1984) *Explaining the Crisis*, London: Bookmarks.
Kautsky, Karl (1902) "Krisentheorien," *Die Neue Zeit* 20: 37–47, 76–81, 110–18, 133–43.
Kuhn, Rick (1995) "Capitalism's Collapse: Henryk Grossmann's Marxism," *Science and Society* 59(2): 174–92.
Lefebvre, Henri (1976) *The Survival of Capitalism: Reproduction of the Relations of Production*, London: Allison & Busby.
Luxemburg, Rosa (1913) *The Accumulation of Capital*, London: Routledge & Kegan Paul, 1963.
Sweezy, Paul (1942) *The Theory of Capitalist Development*, New York: Monthly Review Press.
Tugan-Baranovsky, Mikhail (1901) *Studien zur Theorie und Geschichte der Handelskrisen in England*, Jena: Fischer.

RICK KUHN

cashless competitive payments systems

Interest in cashless competitive payments systems (CCPS) was stimulated in the 1980s by two developments: first, by technological innovations which opened up the prospect of making virtually all payments by electronic transfer instead of cash; and second, by deregulation of the financial system which stimulated some monetary economists to reexamine the idea of free or laissez-faire banking (see FREE BANKING). Hence, advocates of cashless payments systems are usually also advocates of laissez-faire banking, but the link is not inevitable. Cashless payments systems may be interpreted simply as a change in the medium of exchange that entails no other fundamental change in the financial system. To make this distinction the term cashless *competitive* payments systems signals that its proponents are also exponents of some form of laissez-faire banking.

Main elements

Inspiration for CCPS comes from three influential papers by Black (1970), Fama (1980) and Hall (1982). A key element of each of these papers is the idea that the medium of exchange (MOE) and the medium of account (MOA) functions of money should be separated. The argument here is that, as the MOE impinges on all markets, any imbalance between the demand and supply of money impinges on the absolute price level and undermines the stability of the MOA. Cashless competitive payments schemes are intended to eliminate this instability. The intention is to eliminate aggregate price level fluctuations by restricting price changes to changes in relative prices only. In particular, the intention is to eliminate aggregate instability through changes in liquidity preference (Greenfield and Yeager 1989). CCPS are, therefore, intended to eliminate the problems highlighted by Keynesians.

Black and Fama locate the theoretical foundations of competitive payments systems in Walrasian general equilibrium theory, while Hall (1982) suggested a definition of the MOA in terms of a composite commodity basket, with the items composing the basket to be selected on the basis of their historical price stability. The ideas of all three authors were taken up by Greenfield and Yeager (1989) who elaborated and extended them in some important respects. In particular, Greenfield and Yeager proposed a form of indirect convertibility in terms of which private banks convert the MOE, currency, into some generally acceptable redemption medium such as gold or Treasury bills.

Criticism

The Black, Fama and Hall and the Greenfield and Yeager proposals have been critically reviewed by a number of authors from a variety of perspectives. Notable critics are McCallum (1985), White (1984) and Schandt and Whittaker (1995) while support for the scheme comes from Dowd (1995). Criticism of CCPS is of two types; that relating to the theoretical analysis, and that relating to the feasibility of the proposed schemes.

Theoretical criticism of CCPS centers on its use of the Walrasian general equilibrium system and focuses on the papers by Black and Fama. For example, both Black (1970) and Fama (1980) claimed that the MOE function of money was redundant in an economy with a sophisticated accounting system and that, consequently, the *concept* of money was no longer relevant to such a system. McCallum and White, among others, note that this conclusion is not sustainable and follows from the conflation of the existence of an electronic accounting system with the existence of a Walrasian auction. The former does not imply the latter, and it is only in the latter case that the concept of money is redundant. This is the well-known result that real Walrasian general equilibrium theory should not be applied to address questions of monetary theory (Symposium on Cashless Payments Systems 1989). More recently, Ritter (1995) has shown that in the absence of an outside agent (government) to establish the "credibility" necessary for the general acceptance of otherwise worthless paper money, the existence of a fiat money equilibrium cannot be established under laissez-faire banking.

Further debate

Despite criticism of the theoretical foundations of the Black, Fama and Hall proposals, Greenfield and Yeager insist that their proposals do not rest on Walrasian foundations and are intended to be fully operational, that is, capable of implementation to an actual economy. A key element of the debate is then whether the process of indirect convertibility proposed by Greenfield and Yeager is operational. Schandt and Whittaker (1995) argue that it is not.

The issue of indirect convertibility arises because the MOA proposed by Greenfield and Yeager follows Hall and is based on a commodity basket. However, banks cannot be expected to hold and trade this commodity basket, nor would individuals be prepared to redeem currency for a commodity basket (White 1984: 711). Hence there is a need for indirect convertibility into some acceptable "redemption" medium such as gold or Treasury bills. Greenfield and Yeager propose that banknotes be convertible into a quantity of redemption medium (gold) with a value always sufficient to purchase the composite commodity bundle, irrespective of the dollar price of the latter. This keeps the one dollar note always equal to the value of the commodity basket (for an explanation of how the Greenfield and Yeager scheme might work, see Dowd (1995)). But Schandt and Whittaker (1995) argue that as the dollar prices of goods in the basket are determined in decentralized markets, changing the redemption value between dollar notes and gold will not restore commodity prices. Consequently, they suggest that the indirect convertibility proposal is best thought of as a variable commodity standard in which banks vary their redemption rate in terms of a rule based on observed commodity prices. It is in this respect that indirect convertibility is related to Irving Fisher's "compensated dollar." (On the differences between them, see Patinkin (1996).)

Conclusion

To sum up, exponents of cashless competitive payments systems are motivated by the desire to eliminate instability, which they perceive as originating from the conflation of the MOE and MOA properties of money. Despite their disclaimer, the schemes which they propose are intended to mimic the barter properties of real Walrasian general equilibrium theory. Seen from that perspective, they overlook the store of value function which always attaches to money, no matter what its form.

See also:

financial innovations

Selected references

Black, Fischer (1970) "Banking and Interest Rates in a World without Money: The Effects of Uncontrolled Banking," *Journal of Bank Research* 1 (Autumn): 9–20; reprinted in *Business Cycles and Equilibrium*, Cambridge, MA: Blackwell, 1987.

Dowd, K. (1995) "Methods of Indirect Convertibility," *Journal of Money, Credit and Banking* 27: 67–88.

Fama, Eugene F. (1980) "Banking in the Theory of Finance," *Journal of Monetary Economics* 6: 39–57.

Greenfield, Robert L. and Yeager, Leyland B. (1989) "Can Monetary Disequilibrium Be Eliminated?," *Cato Journal* 9: 405–21.

Hall, Robert (1982) "Exploration in the Gold Standard and Related Policies for Stabilizing the Dollar," in Robert E. Hall (ed.), *Inflation: Cause and Effects*, Chicago: University of Chicago Press.

McCallum, Bennet T. (1985) "Bank Deregulation, Accounting Systems of Exchange and the Unit of Account: A Critical Review," *Carnegie Rochester Conference Series on Public Policy* 23: 13–46.

Patinkin, D. (1996) "Indirect Convertibility and Irving Fisher's Compensated Dollar," *Journal of Money, Credit and Banking* 28: 130–31.

Ritter, Joseph A. (1995) "The Transition from Barter to Fiat Money," *American Economic Review* 85: 134–49.

Schandt, Norbert and Whittaker, John (1995) "Is Indirect Convertibility Impossible? Reply," *Journal of Money, Credit and Banking* 27: 297–8.

Symposium on Cashless Payments Systems (1989) *Journal of Post Keynesian Economics* 11: 360–84.

White, Lawrence H. (1984) "Competitive Payments Systems and the Unit of Account," *American Economic Review* 74: 699–712.

COLIN ROGERS

catastrophe theory

Catastrophe theory is the qualitative study of discontinuous structural change in nonlinear dynamic systems. Although much of traditional economics has assumed linearity of most functional relationships, it has become increasingly understood that this was done for simplification and convenience. Many actual functional relationships in economics are actually nonlinear, especially those involving change. Thus most dynamic economic systems are examples of nonlinear dynamic systems and can exhibit multiple equilibria and discontinuous changes.

Variables, manifold and function

Nonlinear dynamic systems can be characterized as containing a set of control, or slow, variables as well a set of state, or fast, variables. The system can be depicted, as in Figure 1, by a surface called a "manifold" (defined below). Slow variables move the system around on the manifold gradually, while fast variables move quickly to be on the manifold if they are off it. In Figure 1, C and F are control or slow variables and J is the state or fast variable. As depicted, at a certain point in the gradual changes of C and F, J suddenly drops in value as it falls from the higher part of the manifold to the lower part.

The behavior of the system is given by a potential function, with the manifold being the set of points where the first derivatives of this function with respect to the state variables equal zero. Singularities of this surface, where the second derivatives also equal zero, indicate points where qualitative structural change can occur. Catastrophe theory provides a method for classifying these points and sets of points. The structural discontinuities are called catastrophes.

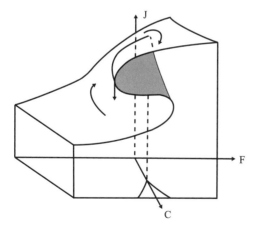

Figure 1

Simple catastrophes and behavioral patterns

Classification depends on the number of control and state variables in the system. Thom's (1972) Classification Theorem characterizes seven different elementary catastrophes, those for which the number of control variables is not greater than four and the number of state variables is not greater than two. For each one of these catastrophes there exists a generic form of its manifold. The values of the control variables for which there are singularities (catastrophes) constitute the bifurcation set. The most widely studied in political economy are the *fold*, which has one control variable and one state variable, the *cusp*, which has two control variables and one state variable, and the *butterfly*, which has four control variables and one state variable. Figure 1 above depicts the cusp catastrophe.

It is widely argued that behavioral patterns observable in the simplest of catastrophes, the two-variable fold, include bimodality, inaccessibility, sudden jumps and HYSTERESIS; and the three-variable cusp includes divergence as well. *Bimodality* means that there will be two distinct zones of values where the state variable mostly will be observed. This arises because two stable manifold zones will be discretely separated from each other by an unstable equilibrium manifold zone within which few observable states will occur. In Figure 1, the upper and lower sheets are stable zones and the middle one is unstable.

Inaccessibility refers to the unobserved unstable zone lying between the two modal stable zones, its instability rendering it inaccessible. *Sudden jumps* can occur in dynamics when control variables encounter bifurcation values, including larger structural transformation; the sudden drop in Figure 1 being such an example. *Hysteresis* arises because there is a strong tendency to remain within a stable equilibrium zone. This implies that control variables can change over wide areas continuously, and remain within their current zone. This is true even when at an earlier (or later) time, the system could have the same control variable at the same value, but the system would be in a different and distinct stable manifold zone.

In the cusp catastrophe (as in Figure 1), one control variable is normal and the other is splitting. In the figure, F is normal and C is splitting (as shown). For sufficiently low values of the splitting variable, variations of the normal variable will not intersect with the bifurcation set, and the state variable will vary continuously with continuous variation of the control variable. That is seen in the gradual increase in J that occurs after its sudden decline, which leads to a fall in C as well. At a critical value of the normal variable, increasing the splitting variable will bring the system to a cusp point, beyond which continuous variations of the normal variable will bring discontinuous jumps or decline in the state variable. This bifurcation of the equilibrium above the cusp is divergence, and can be seen in Figure 1 where the multiple sheets of the manifold appear.

Applications

Applications of catastrophe theory in political economy include Zeeman's (1974) cusp catastrophe model of stock market crashes. In this case, J is the rate of change of stock prices, F is the excess demand by fundamentalist investors (who rely on fundamental values) and C is the excess demand by chartist investors (who promote deviations of stock prices from fundamentals). Crashes happen when there is more demand by chartist speculators, who then retreat after the crash only to come on strong as prices start to accelerate again (see SPECULATIVE BUBBLES AND FUNDAMENTAL VALUES).

Other examples could be mentioned. For instance, Amson's (1975) initiation of the analysis of urban and regional structural changes uses catastrophe models. So too does Jones and Walters' (1976) model of the collapse of the Antarctic fin and blue whale stocks, as fishing boat intensity increased. Varian's (1979) model of the Kaldor trade cycle model uses the cusp catastrophe. Ho and Saunders (1980) examine a fold catastrophe model of bank failure. Casetti (1982) empirically examines a cusp catastrophe model of takeoffs into industrial growth. Rosser's (1983) application of the cusp catastrophe is related to understanding the discontinuities implied by the Cambridge capital theory paradoxes (see CAPITAL THEORY DEBATES). Fischer and Jammernegg (1986) treat a fold catastrophe associated with the emergence of STAGFLATION in the 1970s. A catastrophe examination of monopoly power is undertaken by Bonanno (1987).

Criticism and reassessment

Despite all of these efforts, the use of catastrophe theory in economics has been sharply criticized and has not been used as much in recent times as before. Among the criticisms have been the views that catastrophe theory is a fad, overused and overextended to explain too many things; that it lacks empirical content; that necessary assumptions rarely hold in reality; and that the dynamics are improperly specified. These criticisms have had their impact, and now those seeking to model discontinuities are more likely to use an alternative approach, such as self-organized criticality or spin glass models. Nevertheless, when appropriately specified models are used, catastrophe theory can sharply illuminate discontinuities in dynamic political economic systems.

In some cases, the criticisms have proven to be overblown and now look ridiculous. For instance, the Zeeman (1974) stock market crash model was ridiculed by some commentators on the ground that it allows for some less-than-perfectly rational agents who follow "chartist" strategies in financial markets. At the time, with the rational expectations revolution in full swing, this seemed a telling blow. However, subsequent research has moved in Zeeman's direction and few observers now insist that financial market participants never chase trends, expecting them to continue.

Another response to emerge from this controversy over catastrophe theory has been to argue that its best use was for deeper and more qualitative analysis. In particular, it has been argued that catastrophe theory can be viewed as a mathematical metaphor for the Hegelian dialectic (see DIALECTICAL METHOD). This has obvious implications for the potential applicability to Marxist models, although this has not been formally done. The smooth variation of a control variable, bringing about a discontinuous change in a state variable, can be viewed as representing the idea of a quantitative change bringing about a qualitative change. Thus, Thom (1972) was originally inspired substantially by the concept of morphogenesis in biology, where a developing organism exhibits emerging new organs and structures in the process of development.

Most fundamentally and generally, catastrophe-theoretic models in economics highlight the tendency to instability and sudden changes within economic systems. For political economy, this implies a foundation for deep uncertainty and an awareness of the potential fragility of economic systems (see UNCERTAINTY).

See also:

chaos theory; circular and cumulative causation; evolution and coevolution; evolutionary economics: major contemporary themes; financial crises; financial instability hypothesis; path dependency

Selected references

Amson, J.C. (1975) "Catastrophe Theory: A Contribution to the Study of Urban Systems?," *Environment and Planning B* 2: 177–221.

Bonanno, G. (1987) "Monopoly Equilibria and Catastrophe Theory," *Australian Economic Papers* 26: 197–215.

Casetti, E. (1982) "The Onset of Modern Economic Growth: Empirical Validation of a Catastrophe Model," *Papers of the Regional Science Association* 50: 9–20.

Fischer, E.O. and Jammernegg, W. (1986) "Empirical Investigation of a Catastrophe Theory Extension of the Phillips Curve," *Review of Economics and Statistics* 68: 9–17.

Ho, T. and Saunders, A. (1980) "A Catastrophe Model of Bank Failure," *Journal of Finance* 35: 1189–1207.

Jones, D.D. and Walters, C.J. (1976) "Catastrophe Theory and Fisheries Regulation," *Journal of the Fisheries Resource Board of Canada* 33: 2829–33.

Rosser, J.B., Jr (1983) "Reswitching as a Cusp Catastrophe," *Journal of Economic Theory* 31: 182–93.

Thom, R. (1972) *Stabilité Structurelle et Morphogénèse: Essai d'une Théorie Générale des Modèles*, New York: W.A. Benjamin; trans. D.H. Fowler (1975) *Structural Stability and Morphogenesis: An Outline of a General Theory of Models*, Reading: W.A. Benjamin.

Varian, H.R. (1979) "Catastrophe Theory and the Business Cycle," *Economic Inquiry* 17: 14–28.

Zeeman, E.C. (1974) "On the Unstable Behavior of the Stock Exchanges," *Journal of Mathematical Economics* 1: 39–44.

J. BARKLEY ROSSER, JR

centralized private sector planning

Centralized private sector planning (CPSP) is the organization and exchange of information on production, pricing, and financing within and between industries by the largest industrial corporations within a mixed market economy. The central planning core (CPC) consists of concentrated interests which act as corporate clearinghouses for the large industrial corporations. John Munkirs coined the term "centralized private sector planning" in the December 1983 issue of the *Journal of Economic Issues*, which was based largely on the research undertaken for his book, *The Transformation of American Capitalism*. He differentiated between mixed market economies (with structurally and functionally interdependent industries coordinated by a CPC) and competitive market structures (Munkirs 1985). Munkirs uses the term to describe this interdependence at the macro level, while using the concept of oligopolistic cooperation for analysis at the micro level. CPSP may be distinguished from central planning under "communism" by its centralized functions' being coordinated through the private sector CPC, rather than through a government-coordinated central planning agency.

Evolution of market structures

Munkirs holds that the US economy has evolved over the past two centuries from a competitive market structure to an imperfectly competitive market structure, and more recently to CPSP. The contemporary American economy has developed into "the triadic economy," consisting of a planned sector of large corporations engaged in administered pricing, a non-planned sector of smaller firms operating in competitive markets, and a government sector (Munkirs 1990). Related accounts of a triadic economy may be found in the earlier work of Gardiner Means, Robert Averitt and John Kenneth Galbraith.

At the turn of the century, John Moody (1904) provided one of the first systematic analyses of inter-corporate coordination, focusing on the trusts or holding companies of various entrepreneurs and family interests including the Rockefeller, Guggenheim and Morgan interests. Gardiner Means's work for the National Resources Committee (NRC) in the late 1930s provided a detailed analysis of corporate concentration; the emergence of a dual-sector economy divided into market and administered price sectors; and the role of corporate interest groups in inter-industry coordination in the US economy (Means 1939). The NRC study found that the managements of the larger corporations were brought together as a corporate community through a number of institutional arrangements including INTERLOCKING DIRECTORSHIPS, inter-corporate minority stockholdings, links with core financial services corporations, and relationships with major financial institutions.

Means identified a total of eight corporate interest groups: two centered around financial institutions, three organized around family interests and three clustered around certain localities. Together the eight groups owned two-thirds of the assets of the top 250 industrial corporations (Means 1939: 161). While these groups wielded significant economic power, Means stopped short of concluding there was any centralized form of private sector planning (Means 1939: 164).

Centralization in the private sector

Munkirs's theory of CPSP adopts many of the concepts and techniques used in Means's study. His distinctive contribution to the analysis of MARKET STRUCTURES is the claim that economic planning in the private sector has become much more centralized than previously recognized.

According to Munkirs, a CPC of seven large banks, four insurance companies and one diversified financial corporation provides the focus for CPSP. The activities of the CPC are not so much evidence of "banker capitalism," but of the strategic-planning role played by outside directors from the major industrial corporations in the operations of the CPC banks. These directors, with their strategic overview of the pecuniary and technological linkages in the economy, are able to engage effectively in inter-industry planning for technological as well as merger and acquisition purposes.

CPC members include, for instance, Citicorp, Chase Manhattan, J.P. Morgan, Chemical Bank, Manufacturers Hanover, Continental Illinois, First Chicago Corp., Prudential Insurance, Metropolitan, Equitable Life, New York Life and Continental Corp. Management is said to use both formal and informal planning instruments to coordinate the economic activities of major corporations, some 138 of which are analysed by Munkirs in a central planning tableau. Formal planning instruments consist of corporate stockholdings, board directorships and corporate debt, while informal mechanisms include the provision of financial services as well as bond trustee, transfer agent and registrar functions.

In order to establish greater market control, many national oligopolistic firms in a range of industries, including automobiles, air transportation, and telecommunications, have established mechanisms of international oligopolistic cooperation. These take the form of joint ventures, strategic alliances, international subcontracting, and production-sharing arrangements (Munkirs 1993). In the automobile industry, for example, international production has moved beyond horizontal and vertical integration within one firm to joint ventures and production sharing arrangements such as those formed by General Motors with Toyota, Ford with Mazda and Chrysler with Mitsubishi.

Vested interests, power and policy

A concomitant requirement of CPSP is the political influence exerted on the public sector by the CPC. Munkirs maintains that political interest groups that are representative of big business, such as the Trilateral Commission, Business Roundtable and Conference Board, work to further CPC interests (Munkirs and Ayers 1983; Munkirs and Knoedler 1987). Prominent CPC executives participate in a revolving door between elite CPC and government policy-making positions. CPC interests are also advanced through the formal structure of the US government by a plethora of industry–government advisory committees. The influence of the CPC extends to the news media and education as well (Munkirs and Knoedler 1987).

If private sector economic activity is as centralized as Munkirs' theory predicts, there are serious implications for the effectiveness of government policies. Anti-trust and regulatory policies are not simply required to contain the social costs generated by business within a particular industry, but must be devised to countervail excesses that occur between industries and which lie outside many of the traditional policy boundaries. Like Means, Munkirs contends that monetary and fiscal policies are insufficient demand-management tools for achieving macroeconomic stabilization in an economy with a high degree of CPSP (Means 1983; Munkirs and Ayers 1983). Means attributed STAGFLATION, or what he preferred to term "administrative inflation," to the administered PRICING policies of large corporations. Thus, in addition to a reconsideration of the differential impact of fiscal and monetary policies on planned and market sectors, wage and price controls need to be imposed on the largest corporations.

Aside from related work in institutional economics on corporate concentration noted above, CPSP theory suggests some parallels with Domhoff's *Who Rules America Now?* (1983). Social network analysis also seeks to document the type of interindustry coordination implied by CPSP (Mintz and Schwartz 1985). The work of Alfred Eichner and other post-Keynesians on the megacorporation and administered pricing also overlaps with Munkirs's theory of oligopolistic cooperation (Eichner 1976).

Further research

Within the institutional economics school, there is potentially some conflict between CPSP adherents and those who would see capitalism's corporate structure as the outcome of evolutionary blind drift and would allow for greater corporate competition. Little new empirical work on CPSP has been undertaken since Munkirs's initial contribution, and further elaboration and testing of the hypothesis is necessary at both the macro and micro levels. The effects of increased merger and acquisition activity and industry deregulation since 1980 raise questions as to what extent the CPC of the USA has been able to withstand greater import competition or extend its influence globally. A comparative analysis of contemporary European and Asian economies could also reveal how pervasive or otherwise CPSP is in other mixed market economies. Nonetheless, CPSP is an addition to the theoretical explanation of the tripartite economic structure of planned, market and public sectors which remains at the core of an institutionalist analysis of the contemporary mixed market economy.

See also:

corporate hegemony; economic power; ownership and control of the corporation; transnational corporations

Selected references

Domhoff, G. William (1983) *Who Rules America Now? A View for the 1980s*, New York: Simon & Schuster.
Eichner, Alfred (1976) *The Megacorp and Oligopoly*, Cambridge: Cambridge University Press.
Means, Gardiner C. (1939) *The Structure of the American Economy Part I: Basic Characteristics*, New York: A.M. Kelley, 1966.
—— (1983) "Corporate Power in the Marketplace," *Journal of Law and Economics* 26(2): 467–85.
Mintz, Beth and Schwartz, Michael (1985) *The Power Structure of American Business*, Chicago: University of Chicago Press.
Moody, John (1904) *The Truth About the Trusts*, New York: Greenwood Press, 1968.
Munkirs, John R. (1985) *The Transformation of American Capitalism*, Armonk, NY: M.E. Sharpe.
—— (1990) "The Triadic Economy (Centrally-Planned, Non-Planned and Government-Directed Sectors)," *Journal of Economic Issues* 24(2): 346–54.
—— (1993) "The Automobile Industry, Political Economy, and a New World Order," *Journal of Economic Issues* 27(2): 627–38.
Munkirs, John R. and Ayers, Michael (1983) "Political and Policy Implications of Centralized Private Sector Planning," *Journal of Economic Issues* 17(4): 969–84.
Munkirs, John R. and Knoedler, Janet T. (1987) "The Existence and Exercise of Corporate Power: An Opaque Fact," *Journal of Economic Issues* 21(4): 1679–1706.

BRENT MCCLINTOCK

ceremonial encapsulation

The principle of ceremonial encapsulation is a theoretical construct that appears in the American "neoinstitutionalist" theory of INSTITUTIONAL CHANGE AND ADJUSTMENT. It attempts to explain how technological innovations become "encapsulated" within the status and power systems of society, thereby reducing the potential instrumental efficiency such innovations can make available to the community in its problem-solving processes.

The neoinstitutionalist theory of institutional change and adjustment defines an "institution" as a set of socially prescribed patterns of correlated behavior, wherein the values of the community function as standards of judgment by which behavior is correlated (see INSTITUTIONS AND HABITS). It advances the notion that all societies manifest two separate but interrelated modes of valuation which produce these standards of judgment. These are referred to as the *instrumental* and *ceremonial* modes of valuation.

Instrumental and ceremonial modes

The instrumental mode of valuation is inherent in the tools/skills nexus of the arts and sciences that creates and sustains the life processes of the community. The values it produces as standards of judgment in the correlation of behavior are tested by the consequences of their use in enhancing the life processes of the community taken impersonally. This is referred to in the theory as the criterion of "instrumental efficiency." In contrast, the ceremonial mode of valuation produces standards of judgment (values) for the correlation of behavior in the creation and maintenance of the status and power system of the community, thereby defining and enforcing invidious distinctions among individuals and groups with respect to their presumed inherent worth as human beings (see INSTRUMENTAL VALUE THEORY).

Ceremonially warranted values are held to the test of "ceremonial adequacy," that is, whether they correlate behavior in such a way as to preserve traditional patterns of status and power that ensure the differential advantages of the few over the many. It should be noted that while the ceremonial mode of valuation rationalizes the existence of elites within the community, the processes of invidious emulation and ideological mystification ensure that the ordinary (non-elite) citizenry embrace the attendant invidious distinctions as the normal scheme of things.

A working hypothesis of American institutionalists from Thorstein B. VEBLEN (1857–1929) to Marc R. Tool (born 1921) is that the ceremonial mode of valuation tends to dominate the instrumental mode of valuation in the correlation of behavior. This creates a contradiction in human affairs, as the process of instrumental valuation contributes to a generation of innovations in the arts and sciences (called "technological innovations") that create pressure for institutional changes (called "progressive institutional changes"). Progressive institutional changes involve the substitution of instrumentally warranted values for ceremonially warranted values in the correlation of behavior. However, it is in the very nature of the dominant ceremonial value system that there should be resistance to technological innovations that are perceived (correctly or incorrectly) to threaten the existing patterns of status and power within the community.

Suppression of progressive change

Ceremonial encapsulation occurs when the community attempts to limit the impact of a technological innovation on the existing patterns of status and power. This response is most often initiated by elites whose social and economic status puts them in a position to monitor developments in the arts and sciences, but it can also arise among the ordinary citizenry who have habituated a resistance to anything that might disrupt the secure routine of their daily lives. As Veblen so clearly illustrated, both the rich and the poor (for different reasons) resist innovations (Veblen 1899: 203–5). This does not mean that technological innovations are completely prevented from entering the community's fund of knowledge. It means that some applications of the technological innovation are suppressed, thereby limiting the community's access to knowledge in its problem-solving activities.

In consequence, at any given time, a society's knowledge fund is not fully exploited in the provisioning process by which the community sustains itself. What are often perceived by the community as conditions of scarcity may very well have nothing to do with circumstances that lie beyond human discretion. Scarcity conditions arising out of ceremonial encapsulation have nothing to do with the "niggardliness of nature." They are man-made conditions that arise out of the invidious distinctions of the culture. As such, they can be eliminated, or at least substantially diminished, through the exercise of human (communal) discretion in the adoption of progressive institutional changes.

See also:

collective social wealth; culture; evolutionary economics: major contemporary themes; innovation, evolution and cycles; institutional political economy: major contemporary themes; knowledge, information, technology and change; minimal dislocation; neo-institutionalism; pragmatism; recognized interdependence; social and organizational capital; technology

Selected references

Bush, Paul D. (1986) "On the Concept of Ceremonial Encapsulation," *The Review of Institutional Thought* 3 (December): 25–45.

—— (1987) "The Theory of Institutional Change," *Journal of Economic Issues* 21 (3): 1075–1116.

Tool, Marc R. (1979) *The Discretionary Economy: A Normative Theory of Political Economy*, Santa Monica, CA: Goodyear Publishing Co.

Veblen, Thorstein B. (1899) *The Theory of the*

Leisure Class, New York: Augustus M. Kelley, 1975, especially Chapter VIII.

PAUL D. BUSH

CHANGE AND ADJUSTMENT, INSTITUTIONAL: *see* institutional change and adjustment

chaos theory

Chaos theory studies a special case of mathematical systems exhibiting non linear dynamics. Such systems endogenously generate dynamic patterns, which appear to be random but are not. They are bounded but highly erratic, reflecting a simultaneous local instability and tendency to explosiveness which conflicts with a strong bounding tendency. Although there are competing definitions of chaotic dynamics, a central feature agreed upon by all chaos theorists is that of sensitive dependence upon initial conditions (SDIC). This means that a small change in the value of a parameter or of an initial starting value can lead to a very different dynamical pattern. This condition was labeled the "butterfly effect": under the right conditions, a butterfly flapping its wings in one part of the world could induce a hurricane in another part of the world.

Conditions of chaos

A sufficient condition for the presence of SDIC is that the maximum real part of the Lyapunov exponents of a dynamical system be positive. More formally, let F be a dynamical system, $F_t(a)$ is the t-th iterate of F starting at initial condition a, D is the derivative, and $\vec{v}$ is a direction vector. Then the Lyapunov exponents are solutions to

$$L = \lim_{t \to 0} ln(\| DF_t(a)\vec{v} \|)/t \qquad (1)$$

The real parts of the Lyapunov exponents indicate rates of decay of forecastibility of the system, with that rate being very rapid if any are greater than zero (the condition of SDIC or chaotic dynamics). Thus, forecasting such systems is very difficult and only possible at best for very short intervals. This has been argued to provide a foundation for Keynesian UNCERTAINTY, and has been viewed as a severe blow to the new classical assumption of rational expectations on the part of economic agents.

Although quite a few time series have been shown possibly to exhibit such SDIC, there are no reliability measures for estimating Lyapunov exponents. Thus, no one can say for sure whether any actual time series exhibit chaotic dynamics, although a variety of candidates have been identified ranging from stock market prices to milk prices. The econometrics of these estimations is an area of intense ongoing research.

A short history

The earliest understanding of chaotic dynamics is attributed to Henri Poincaré in the late nineteenth century, in his study of celestial mechanics and above all the three-body problem. However, he rejected the implications of the idea when he encountered it, treating it as a bizarre special case to be avoided and ignored if possible. An understanding of chaotic dynamics and such related concepts as fractal dimensionality and strange attractors gradually developed through the twentieth century, with major increases in understanding coming in the 1960s and 1970s. In the mid-1970s, the term "chaos" came to be used, and it was shown that if a dynamical system generates a three-period cycle, then it is chaotic. Closely related to this is the notion that as a control parameter is varied most chaotic systems will pass through a sequence of period-doubling bifurcations, in going from a zone of convergence to a unique stable equilibrium through two-period cycles, four-period cycles and so forth, to chaotic dynamics.

Chaotic dynamics in political economy

After the mid-1970s, numerous theoretical models appeared in many areas of economics which showed the possibility of chaotic dynamics. Within microeconomics, one of the more important for political economy involved the cobweb model, which also has implications for business cycle theories (Chiarella 1988). Other important areas of political economy where chaos theory has been shown to be important include BIOECONOMICS and urban and regional political economy (Rosser 1991). Within macroeconomics directly, a variety of models in numerous areas appeared with various implications for political economy.

We can identify three broad schools of macroeconomic political economy where chaos theory has played an important role. The first is in CLASSICAL POLITICAL ECONOMY. A good example is the demonstration by Bhaduri and Harris (1987) of the possibility of chaotic dynamics within a Ricardian model. The critical tuning parameter whose variation brings about the sequence of bifurcations in the transition to chaos is determined by the relationship between the maximum marginal product of labor and the wage rate, which they call the rate of EXPLOITATION. With a high enough rate of exploitation, a stationary state can be created which is chaotic in the presence of unproduced land.

Yet another approach with many representatives is what Rosser (1991) calls the Weak New Keynesian School. Some earlier models with *ad hoc* expectations assumptions (derived from Keynes's work to some degree) are shown capable of generating chaotic dynamics if appropriately specified and tweaked. Examples include a large literature drawing on the multiplier–accelerator approach to cycles; the Kaldor trade cycle model (Lorenz 1993); the Goodwin cycle of class struggle (Pohjola 1981); and the Minsky FINANCIAL INSTABILITY HYPOTHESIS (Keen 1995).

Perhaps even more central in the disputes over macroeconomics has been the Strong New Keynesian School, which develops models assuming rational expectations and then shows that chaotic dynamics can occur within them (Grandmont 1985). This is then interpreted as demonstrating the unlikeliness of being able to form rational expectations in the first place, given the phenomenon of SDIC, and thus is seen as very destructive of the new classical approach. This result has been seen as a possible foundation for the fundamental uncertainty idea associated with post-Keynesian political economy, as well as with the newly emerging post-Walrasian school (Colander 1996) of thought.

One criticism of this idea has come from those who object to using the rational expectations assumption at all, even if merely to undermine the possibility of forming rational expectations. Thus, Mirowski (1990) has argued that such models are effectively new classical models, despite the claim that they are just the opposite. That there may be something to this argument can be seen by Grandmont's (1985) use of his model to discuss a Keynesian-style fine-tuning fiscal policy, which would presumably remove the chaotic dynamics from the economy. The idea that such a policy could be carried out seems to assume rational expectations on the part of policy makers, even though Grandmont claimed to have shown the impossibility of agents' forming rational expectations in the face of chaotic dynamics. To complicate the debate still further, some new classical economists have countered with the notion that attempted stabilization policies might actually induce chaotic dynamics in situations in which none would occur otherwise (Dwyer 1992). Needless to say, debate regarding these and other aspects of chaos theory in political economy are ongoing.

See also:

catastrophe theory; Goodwin cycle and predator-prey models; Kaldor's theory of the growth process; post-Keynesian political economy: major contemporary themes

Selected references

Bhaduri, Amit and Harris, Donald J. (1987) "The Complex Dynamics of the Simple Ricardian System," *Quarterly Journal of Economics* 102: 893–901.
Chiarella, Carl (1988) "The Cobweb Model: Its

Instability and the Onset of Chaos," *Economic Modelling* 5: 377–84.
Colander, David (ed.) (1996) *Beyond Microfoundations: Post Walrasian Macroeconomics*, New York: Cambridge University Press.
Dwyer, Gerald P., Jr (1992) "Stabilization Policy Can Lead to Chaos," *Economic Inquiry* 30: 40–46.
Grandmont, Jean-Michel (1985) "On Endogenous Competitive Business Cycles," *Econometrica* 53: 995–1045.
Keen, Steve (1995) "Finance and Economic Breakdown: Modelling Minsky's 'Financial Instability Hypothesis,' " *Journal of Post Keynesian Economics* 17: 607–35.
Lorenz, Hans-Walter (1993) *Nonlinear Dynamical Economics and Chaotic Motion*, 2nd edn, Berlin: Springer-Verlag.
Mirowski, Philip (1990) "From Mandelbrot to Chaos in Economic Theory," *Southern Economic Journal* 57: 289–307.
Pohjola, Matti T. (1981) "Stable, Cyclic and Chaotic Growth: The Dynamics of a Discrete Time Version of Goodwin's Growth Cycle," *Zeitschrift für Nationalökonomie* 41: 27–38.
Rosser, J. Barkley, Jr (1991) *From Catastrophe to Chaos: A General Theory of Economic Discontinuities*, Boston: Kluwer.

J. BARKLEY ROSSER, JR

circuit of social capital

Nature and origin

The circuit of social capital (CSC) is one of the most powerful tools in political economy, because it emphasizes the motion of capital through its various institutions and the phases of production, distribution, exchange and reproduction. In a full-blown model of CAPITALISM, it is possible to link CSC to the state, the world economy, the enterprise, the financial system and the family, as well as to the ecological environment. It can be used to examine the whole process by which commodities and classes are reproduced through time, how surplus value is created, how the institutions of capitalism link together, and what contribution each segment of the economy contributes to ECONOMIC GROWTH and unstable ACCUMULATION.

The CSC was formally developed by Karl MARX in Volume II of *Das Kapital*. This work starts with four chapters on the circuits of money capital, productive capital, commodity capital and then the circuits as a whole, respectively. This is followed, in the rest of the volume, by an analysis of circulation time, the costs of circulation, the TURNOVER TIME OF CAPITAL and, later, the famous schemas of the reproduction of capital. A major influence on Marx in the creation of the CSC was Quesnay's *Tableau économique*, which analysed the relationship between the major classes in the complex production and distribution process (see PHYSIOCRACY).

Circuit of money capital

Marx formulated three circuits of social capital, but an illustration of the circuit of money capital should suffice. The circuit of money capital includes at least four "movements": (1) M→C; (2) ...P...; (3) C'→ M' and (4) M'→M. The circuit as a whole is shown below in Figure 2 (for a more illustrative example, see Foley 1986: 67).

The circuit of money capital illustrates three "movements" of capital as they commence and end with value in the form of money. In the first movement, there is the expenditure of money (M) for the purchase of commodities (C), especially labor power and means of production: M→C.

The second movement includes the process of valorization (increase in value) within the real capitalist production process (...P...),

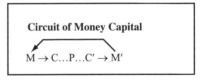

Figure 2

from which emerges commodities with a value (C′) greater than the commodities bought as inputs (C). Surplus value is equal to C′ minus C (sometimes shown as "c").

The third movement is the selling of commodities on the market (C′→M′), which includes the realization of surplus value (M′ minus M). Then, in a fourth movement, some of the resulting money (surplus value) must be regenerated back into potential money capital in order to start the circuit anew (M′→M; and possibly including an increase in credit and share capital if we expand the circuit).

Reproduction of social capital

Two of these three movements relate to the movement, flow or activation of what Marx called "formal capital" (pure exchange): the buying of production inputs (M→C) and the selling of final commodities on the market (C′→M′), the buying and selling phases. These activities, according to Marx, do not produce capital or surplus value, but rather represent "necessary costs of reproduction" of capital as a whole. They are necessary for the exchange of property rights as a form of equal exchange, and for the critical process of realizing value and surplus value on the market.

The concern with unproductive labor, then, relates to reproductive activities involved purely within the sphere of circulation. Examples include the activities of traders, book-keepers and fund managers involved in, for example, the steel industry. Marx considered these activities to be unproductive because they involve exchanges of different forms of value, equivalent exchange or commodity for money, rather than the direct process of valorization of capital. They are "necessary costs of reproduction," rather than activities which directly propel surplus value and hence real capital; they are crucial to the reproduction of capital. Hence, the exchange process is "a necessary function, because the reproduction process itself includes unproductive functions."

The movement of "real capital" (...P...), on the other hand, is an interruption to the flow of circulation *per se*, where commodities are produced by socially necessary cooperative labor. Productive labor is activated within the "hidden" abode of production to produce a surplus over and above the value of labor power and constant capital (raw materials and depreciation).

Marx implied that the productive movement in general may include at least the productive aspects of agricultural, mining, manufacturing, transportation and communication industries (however, they can include any productive sector or activity, including services). This productive activity is undertaken on the basis of the means of production, the organization of the labor process, and the product of labor being separated or alienated from the workers. Capitalist exploitation is possible when the payment of labor power is institutionally separated from the market for other commodities, and when workers are being subordinated to capital in the labor process, and are of a minimal degree of productivity (see LABOR AND LABOR POWER).

Reproduction of social capital thus expands the notions of capital and use-value to deal with the relations between the various sectors of capitalist production and circulation: the linkages; relations between production and circulation; the conditions of existence of capital; and the reproducibility of the spheres. The circuit of social capital represents social relations in effective motion over time at a system level. In order for social capital to accumulate at a fast rate, it is not sufficient for capitals of an individual branch to be operating in continuity; rather, it must have the continuity of the social process in general. (See REPRODUCTION PARADIGM.)

Extensions and modern developments

The CSC has been utilized, extended, modified and developed by an innumerable number of scholars. For instance, Ben Fine (1989) and others have utilized the CSC to understand the generation of economic crises (for example, events leading to a recession). These conditions are linked to an interruption of the CSC, be it from a lack of suitable raw materials or labor power (interrupting M→C), striking workers, conflicting managers or greater monopoly (which may interrupt the production process ...P...), declining effective demand (interrupting C'→M'), or a lack of incentive for investment or interrupted credit or cash flow (interrupting M'→M).

When the CSC is considered as a kind of method, the question arises as to how many circuits to include, how to relate the CSC to the whole of capital, whether extra circuits can be added and how that might change the analysis (if at all). Christian Palloix (1975) applies the CSC to international dimensions of capital. Kenneth Barr (1981) delineates the operations of the circuit at the level of the capitalist enterprise; he introduces a fourth movement or circuit to relate to reinvested money capital (what we have shown as M'→M), and hence whether capitalists consume the surplus individually or reinvest it. Duncan Foley (1986: ch. 5) has developed a mathematical model of the circuit of capital.

Many have used an extended form of the CSC for a macro-institutional analysis of the conditions underlying socioeconomic reproduction. David Gordon (1980) examined long waves by extending the circuit to the dominant institutions underlying SOCIAL STRUCTURES OF ACCUMULATION. James O'Connor (1984) undertook a similar task, including the three circuits of money, commodities and production capital, plus the process of consumption, and the role played by the capitalist state. Aglietta (1976) undertook a similar study, including the financial system as an additional circuit/set of institutions (see REGULATION APPROACH). These three studies have sought to understand the process of growth and accumulation (at least) over the post-1945 wave of upswing (1950s–1960s) and downswing (since the 1970s).

Conclusion

As can be seen, the CSC is a fruitful method for examining the macro-institutional relationships between the various spheres of capitalism. Many innovations in political economy have been associated with further comprehending and extending the concept. In fact, it is the fulcrum around which a detailed analysis of capitalism can be undertaken. It can be modified to help understand a myriad of social relationships and processes.

See also:

commodity fetishism; economic surplus; effective demand and capacity utilization; falling rate of profit tendency; finance capital; French Circuit School; labor theory of value; monetary circuit; productive and unproductive labor; reproduction: simple and expanded

Selected references

Aglietta, Michel (1976) *A Theory of Capitalist Regulation*, trans. David Fernbach, London: New Left Books, 1979.

Arthur, Chris (1996) "Marx's Fourth Capital Circuit," *Capital and Class* 59: 31–6.

Barr, Kenneth (1981) "On the Capitalist Enterprize," *Review of Radical Political Economics* 12 (4): 60–70.

Fine, Ben (1989) *Marx's Capital*, 3rd edn, London: Macmillan, chapters 7, 9.

Foley, Duncan (1986) *Understanding Capital: Marx's Economic Theory*, Cambridge, MA: Harvard University Press.

Gordon, David M. (1980) "Stages of Accumulation and Long Economic Cycles," in T. Hopkins and I. Wallerstein (eds), *Processes of the World-System*, London: Sage.

Levine, David (1978) "The Circuit of Capital" (ch. 4) and "The Circuit in General" (ch. 8), in David Levine, *Economic Theory: Volume One: The Elementary Relations of Economic Life*, London and Boston: Routledge & Kegan Paul, 125–53, 241–77.

O'Connor, James (1984) *Accumulation Crisis*, New York: Blackwell.

Palloix, Christian (1975) "The Internationalization of Capital and the Circuit of Social Capital," in Hugo Radice (ed.), *International Firms and Modern Imperialism*, Harmondsworth: Penguin.

Sekine, Thomas T. (1981) "The Circular Motion of Capital," *Science and Society* 45(3): 288–305.

PHILLIP ANTHONY O'HARA

circular and cumulative causation

When does a change in a variable which is part of a social system cause a significant change in the performance of that system? When is that initial change exhausted, and when does it lead to evolution of the system? To answer these questions is to have a theory of circular and cumulative causation, which is a necessary part of a theory of economic development. Cumulative causation describes a relationship between an initial change in an independent variable and the dependent variable, whereby the dependent variable in turn causes a change in the formerly independent variable in the same direction as the initial movement. This means that a small initial change can become magnified, causing a divergence in the growth of income of nations and individuals. The concept raises questions about whether the process is automatic or engenders or permits collective action.

Circularity and feedback

Circularity is at the heart of cumulativeness, for if *A* caused *B*, but *B* had no feedback to *A*, then, moving it again in the initial direction, there would be an equilibrium after the initial effect if *A* is exhausted. With feedback, however, the system evolves. The effect is cumulative if the feedback reinforces and amplifies the original change. The feedback may also transform the original variables. The evolution can be positive or negative with respect to the valued performance of the system. There can be a vicious circle (Nurkse 1953) of deterioration, or a beneficial circle of growth. Growth theorists have been interested in how to avoid low-level equilibrium where there is no circularity, or even worse, a downward spiral with negative circularity.

The literature identifies several forces and cumulative processes leading to growth or decline, which will be highlighted below. These include human capital formation, linked investments (economies of scope), export growth, effective demand and productivity, increasing returns and industrial location. The idea of cumulative causation was contained in the monetary theory of Wicksell. The money multiplier is a process by which an initial increment in money supply is spent and respent, resulting in additional money supply. A similar process occurs with income and investment multipliers. Perhaps the best-known proponent of the concept was Gunnar Myrdal, although it was developed earlier by Thorstein VEBLEN, who applied it to institutions and technology, and others.

Gunnar Myrdal and poverty

Gunnar Myrdal, a student of Wicksell, developed the concept of circular and cumulative causation beyond that of his teacher to monetary questions, economic development, and his classic study of racial inequality in the United States (see MYRDAL'S CONTRIBUTION TO POLITICAL ECONOMY). In relation to the racial question, Myrdal (1944) recognized that African-Americans were poorly educated, risk averse, had large families partly to manage risk, and saved little. These behaviors resulted in low incomes, which in turn resulted in little education and savings and contributed to prejudice and rationalized discrimination. In his 1968 study of economic development (Myrdal 1968: appendix 2), he observed the same phenomena. Low income led to low health and nutrition, which resulted in low productivity feeding back to low income. At best, the system preserved a low-level equilibrium; at worst, it got worse (see CULTURE OF POVERTY).

On the other hand, if African-Americans are able to gain (for example) more education, then this may intervene in the process and raise their standard of living. Better education may raise health, productivity, morale and income, and thereby lower discrimination; this in turn may increase education, productivity, income and lower discrimination further. A similar process of cumulative upswing can benefit underdeveloped nations, as education may enhance income, investment and prospects for the future, which in turn impact upon education and the other variables *ad infinitum*.

Myrdal pointed to the forces of stagnation and decline as well as growth. Inertia preserves low-level equilibria. Tradition, irrationality and inequality may short-circuit the self-reinforcing links noted above. Counteracting forces can be both independent of and dependent on development itself. He thought that population growth was largely independent and could defeat beneficial circularity. The terms of trade can turn against a region or a country and blunt the effects of increasing returns.

Development theorists have debated balanced versus unbalanced growth. Some have argued that the market would coordinate investments. Others have argued that leading sectors would attract complementary investment. Myrdal argued that government must coordinate lumpy investments so that firms using another firm's output as input would be on-line at the same time and avoid unused capacity. He argued that an active government could provide the necessary inter-industry links. Otherwise a firm waits to invest until its customers have made enough investments to use its output; but those input users are waiting for the first firm to ensure the supply of low-cost inputs. The lack of demand feeds back on the lack of demand.

Increasing returns to scale

Industries with increasing returns provide an opportunity for circularity and growth (see INCREASING RETURNS TO SCALE). When demand for an output increases (perhaps demand is price elastic), it allows its makers to utilize machinery which may have economies of scale, lowering unit costs. This lower price in turn increases the quantity demanded, allowing still further expansion along the decreasing cost function. This process was identified by Allyn Young (1928), following Adam Smith and arguing that specialization was associated with increasing returns. The opportunity for circularity was supplied by increasing the size of the market which in turn depended on the division of labor. As Young put it, "change becomes progressive and propagates itself in a cumulative way" (Young 1928: 533). A region with price elastic goods, produced under increasing returns, may grow faster than a region not similarly blessed. Agriculture and mining are thus at a widening disadvantage relative to manufacturing centers (see CORE–PERIPHERY ANALYSIS). This led some to advocate that developing countries should steer investment more toward manufactures than agriculture; but the resulting bottlenecks have given support to the proponents of balanced growth (for further application to developing countries, see Leibenstein (1967) and his concept of critical minimum effort).

Increasing returns creates a PATH DEPENDENCY such that a random early volume lead for one version of a product can give it a continuing cost advantage over a competitor's product, even if that latter product is technologically superior (see Arthur 1988). The feedback process is related to an aspect of CHAOS THEORY, where a small perturbation gets magnified throughout a system. Douglas North has applied the concepts of increasing returns and transaction costs to explain institutional change (see NORTH'S THEORY OF INSTITUTIONAL CHANGE). The establishment of institutions is like an investment in fixed capital, and its unit cost of use decreases with repeated use, creating a path dependency. There is learning by doing with respect to institutions as well as technology. The status quo is preserved when there are high transaction costs associated with change, even if the change can save transaction costs in other spheres. North observes that preferences are also learned, which continues the idea of circularity, first explored by MARX, VEBLEN and Myrdal, as the interaction of the mode of production and ideology, attitudes and values.

Nicholas Kaldor and Verdoorn's Law

The role of exports of manufactured goods as the engine of economic growth was observed by Nicholas Kaldor (see KALDOR'S THEORY OF THE GROWTH PROCESS). His elaboration of VERDOORN'S LAW, that a growth in output would be associated with a growth in labor productivity, has been confirmed empirically. Export-led growth has been the cornerstone of a number of successful increases in national income (see BALANCE OF PAYMENTS CONSTRAINT). Countries producing goods purchased by other countries with rising incomes (high income elasticity) can expand production to achieve economies of scale. These processes were part of Kaldor's emphasis on disequilibrium theories. A macroeconomic feedback process occurs when, in a series of linked industries, the growth in specialization of one stage leads to a growth in specialization of the preceding input stage. Thus, the efficiency of a particular industry may depend on the overall growth of manufacturing, which is not something about which the individual firm can do very much.

Effective demand

Effective demand determines the growth of output and efficiency (see EFFECTIVE DEMAND AND CAPACITY UTILIZATION). Whether it feeds back upon effective demand again depends on capital accumulation, investment and consumption. If real wages grow and lead to more demand, and investment responds, this leads in turn to higher growth of efficiency, output and wages. John Eatwell (1982: 59–60) puts it this way: a high growth of demand provides an important foundation for productivity growth which, via price and non-price factors, results in competitive success, which in turn results in high growth of demand, which results in productivity, which results in competitiveness and so on *ad infinitum*. This offers rather startling conclusions. For instance, capital is no longer scarce since it is merely output, a produced means of production depending on learning, structural and technological change, and investment. Manufacturing can generate its own capital, while the limiting factor becomes the expansion of markets, i.e. the demand for manufactures. Any pause in this circularity, such as in a business cycle, may cause the process to turn cumulatively downward (see PASINETTI'S ANALYSIS OF STRUCTURAL DYNAMICS AND GROWTH).

Spatial analysis

Theories of urban and regional political economy make use of circularity concepts to understand why a region may become a center for a new technology, without any obvious resource-based comparative advantage (see URBAN AND REGIONAL POLITICAL ECONOMY: MAJOR CONTEMPORARY THEMES). The computer industry of Silicon Valley might have developed in a number of different places. Yet, once it reaches a certain scale and the associated input producers have become established, the structure of costs is much higher in other places, because their firms are smaller and do not have the specialized input producers close by (Storper and Walker 1989). The new international trade theory points to strategic investments which a country can make to alter its comparative advantage by capturing a first mover advantage (Krugman 1991).

Counteracting forces

An example of counteracting forces set in motion by development is the argument of Mancur Olson in his *Rise and Decline of Nations*, published in 1982. Development creates a stable environment for the growth of interest groups who use their wealth to preserve their status quo advantages, even if this slows overall growth. Undesirable results of growth, such as pollution and resource destruction, may be unanticipated (see SUSTAINABLE DEVELOPMENT). Foreign exchange markets may create a limit to growth. Higher incomes may lead to an increase in imports which are not offset by an increase in exports, leading to a deficit in the current account (see BALANCE OF PAYMENTS CONSTRAINT).

Further research

Empirical research into the processes of cumulative causation presents some difficulties that are less prominent in non-circular models. It requires more insight into human cognition because some of the linkages involve expectations which can be self-fulfilling prophecies, such as the decision to invest in human capital or bail out of the stock market. Research must contend with both mechanical and cognitive transmissions of change from one variable to another. A popular theory, if believed and acted upon, can be a cause as well as the physical technology behind increasing returns. An important part of cumulative causation is the evolution of preferences as well as technologies.

Researchers continue to look for leverage points and multipliers which will feed back to and reinforce development. The role of circular and cumulative processes in the economy continues to be debated. Myrdal thought it was an argument for government planning to insure that the feedback loops were present in the right direction. He argued that individual decisions in markets were insufficient and in many cases led to vicious circles. He saw a gap between the actions of individuals and actual macro performance. Cumulative causation is non-teleological and partly random. The evolving results may be unanticipated, but are not inevitable. There is a place for different degrees of purposefulness, varieties of causality, creativity, habits and institutional routines. Some think that informed intervention could help development, but despair of governments getting it right. While modern treatments may not always use the term, the role of circular and cumulative causation in making institutions matter is supported by many contemporary theorists and practitioners.

See also:

business cycle theories; circular production and vertical integration; equilibrium, disequilibrium and non-equilibrium; evolution and coevolution; financial instability hypothesis; hysteresis; import substitution and export-oriented industrialization; innovation, evolution and cycles; institutional change and adjustment; poverty: definition and measurement; speculative bubbles and fundamental values; technology; uneven development

Selected references

Arthur, Brian (1988) "Self-Reinforcing Mechanisms in Economics," in Philip Anderson et al. (eds), *The Economy as an Evolving System*, Reading, MA: Addison-Wesley.
Eatwell, John (1982) *Whatever Happened to Britain?*, London: Duckworth and the BBC.
Kaldor, Nicholas (1978) *Further Essays on Economic Theory*, London: Duckworth.
Krugman, Paul (1991) *Geography and Trade*, Cambridge, MA: MIT Press.
Leibenstein, Harvey (1967) *Economic Backwardness and Economic Growth*, New York: Wiley.
Myrdal, Gunnar (1944) *An American Dilemma: The Negro Problem and Modern Democracy*, New York: Harper.
—— (1968) *Asian Drama: An Inquiry into the Poverty of Nations*, New York: Pantheon.
Nurkse, Ragnar (1953) *Problems of Capital Formation in Undeveloped Countries*, New York: Oxford University Press.
Storper, Michael and Walker, Richard (1989) *The Capitalist Imperative: Territory, Technology, and Industrial Growth*, New York: Blackwell.
Young, Allyn (1928) "Increasing Returns and Economic Progress," *Economic Journal* 38: 527–42.

A. ALLAN SCHMID

circular production and vertical integration

Production is a time-consuming process which might be viewed in two ways. First, production can be conceived as a *one-way avenue* leading from primary (non-producible) inputs, such as labor or land, via intermediate products to consumer goods. Since intermediate goods are used up during the process of production, the latter can be described as a causal relation between one or more inputs of original factors and final products. This view is present in the Walras–Cassel type of models as well as in the Austrian approach to the theory of production. Whereas the former views production as a point input–point output process, the latter considers also processes of the flow input–flow output type. Both models, however, neglect the existence of basic commodities, that is, commodities which enter directly or indirectly into the production of all products.

As soon as capital is taken into account it may happen that intermediate products, which emerge at a certain stage of production, are also required at preceding stages of the respective process. Thus circular processes, where a commodity enters directly or indirectly into its own production cannot in principle be avoided.

The more general approach, therefore, views production as a circular flow. This concept can be traced back to François Quesnay's *Tableau économique*, to Ricardo's corn model and to the Marxian schemes of reproduction (see REPRODUCTION: SIMPLE AND EXPANDED), as well as to the successors of these classical authors, such as Dmitriev or von Bortkiewicz. More recent contributions can be found in the works of von Neumann, Leontief, Sraffa, Pasinetti and other scholars belonging to the classical, neo-Ricardian or Sraffian schools of political economy.

While in the one-way avenue representation, intermediate products and therefore capital have disappeared, the von Neumann–Sraffa approach emphasizes production of commodities by means of commodities. Here, any flow input–flow output process is broken down into as many point input–point output processes as there are stages of production. Thus all processes constituting a system of production can be represented by matrices of inputs and outputs respectively.

When Adam Smith concluded his analysis of the component parts of prices with the proposition that the exchange-value of any commodity must resolve itself into wages, profits and rents, he had already grasped the notion of vertical integration. In order to see "at a glance" these components of the product value, Sraffa (1960: ch. 6, appendix A) used two alternative analytical tools: the reduction to dated quantities of labor and the device of sub-systems. While the former is subject to severe limitations – it can only be adopted in the case of single production or for special fixed capital systems – the sub-system approach can be applied to general (square) joint production systems as well. Sraffa proposed to subdivide the system of production in such a way that each of these sub-systems is able to produce only one kind of final product. Formalizing Sraffa's sub-systems, Pasinetti (1973) constructed vertically integrated sectors and demonstrated that prices of production can be subdivided into two components. These include (a) the costs of total labor embodied, plus (b) the profits on the value of direct and indirect capital required for the production of the respective final product. Thus, the price of a commodity j can be regarded as the sum of wages and profits that must be paid in vertically integrated "industry" j per one unit of product.

Let $\mathbf{A}$ and $\mathbf{B}$ denote square matrices for inputs and outputs respectively. Let $\mathbf{l}'$ be a row vector of homogenous labor inputs. Prices of production, $\mathbf{p}'$, must cover the cost for capital advanced, including a normal profit at rate, r, and cost for labor paid post factum at rate w. Therefore:

$$\mathbf{p'B} = (1+r)\mathbf{p'A} + w\mathbf{l'} \qquad (1)$$

Define a matrix $\mathbf{H} = \mathbf{A}(\mathbf{B}-\mathbf{A})^{-1}$ and a vector $\mathbf{v'} = \mathbf{l'}(\mathbf{B}-\mathbf{A})^{-1}$ and rewrite (1) as

$$\mathbf{p'} = r\mathbf{p'H} + w\mathbf{v'} \qquad (2)$$

This shows that the "technology" of a sub-system (or a vertically integrated sector), j, can be represented by two items. These include (a) the amount of vertically integrated labor, v_j, and (b) a composite commodity of vertically integrated productive capacity, $\mathbf{h}^j$, represented by the j-th column of matrix $\mathbf{H}$. If the system of production is all-productive – that is, if all commodities are separately producible – then $(\mathbf{B}-\mathbf{A})^{-1}$ is semi-positive and all properties of single product systems, with respect to the price system, hold.

For single product systems, i.e. if $\mathbf{B} = \mathbf{I}$, the vertically integrated labor coefficients equal the sum of the series of dated quantities of labor:

$$\mathbf{v}' = \sum \mathbf{l}'_t, \quad \text{where} \quad \mathbf{l}'_t = \mathbf{l}'\mathbf{A}' \qquad (3)$$

Thus vertical integration represents a generalization of reduction to dated quantities of labor. If not all products are basic, then $\mathbf{A}$ is decomposable. If we define away all forms of circularity – i.e. if we restrict the matrix $\mathbf{A}$ to be lower triangular (semi-positive below the principal diagonal and other elements being nought) – then the series of dated quantities of labor is finite. In this special case, the system of production may also be represented by a single Austrian process of finite duration.

Pasinetti (1988) proceeded with a dual exercise for an expanding economy. Let consumption of good i grow at its particular rate, g_i. Consequently, the intensity level of the corresponding vertically (hyper)integrated sector i at time t, represented by a vector of sectoral intensities $\mathbf{x}^i(t) = \mathbf{x}^i(0)(1+g_i)^t$ must also grow at that particular rate.

Define a vector $\mathbf{c}^i(t)$, where the i-th element denotes consumption of good i at time t, all other elements being nought. Gross outputs of vertically (hyper)integrated sector i must be equal to (1) the quantity of the consumption good, (2) the quantities of the various items required for the reproduction of capital used, and (3) the quantities of capital goods to support growth of production capacities at rate g_i, or in other words:

$$\mathbf{Bx}^i(t) = \mathbf{c}^i(t) + \mathbf{Ax}^i(t) + \mathbf{Ax}^i(t)g_i \qquad (4)$$

Therefore the vector of intensities of a vertically (hyper)integrated sector i is given by:

$$\mathbf{x}^i(t) = \left(\mathbf{B} - \mathbf{A}(1+g_i)\right)^{-1}\mathbf{c}^i(t) \qquad (5)$$

Activity levels of processes can then be calculated as the sum of all vertically hyper-integrated sectoral intensities.

In contrast to vertically integrated sectors, hyperintegrated activities must not only provide for production of the respective final good and for reproduction of capital items, but must also support the growth of vertically integrated productive capacities. For a detailed discussion of circular production see Leontief (1928), Pasinetti (1986) and Kurz and Salvadori (1995: ch. 13). A comprehensive presentation of alternative descriptions of techniques, such as vertical integration or dated quantities of labor, can be found in Pasinetti (1973, 1988) and in Kurz and Salvadori (1995: ch. 6).

See also:

basic and non-basic commodities; Pasinetti's analysis of structural dynamics and growth; price theory, Sraffian; surplus approach to political economy

Selected references

Kurz, Heinz D. and Salvadori Neri, (1995) *Theory of Production: A Long-Period Analysis*, Cambridge: Cambridge University Press.

Leontief, Wassily (1928) "Die Wirtschaft als Kreislauf," *Archiv für Sozialwissenschaft und Sozialpolitik* 60: 577–623; trans. Robert Aylett, "The Economy as a Circular Flow," *Structural Change and Economic Dynamics* 2, 1991: 181–212.

Pasinetti, Luigi L. (1973) "The Notion of Vertical Integration in Economic Analysis," *Metroeconomica* 25: 1–29.

—— (1986) "Sraffa's Circular Process and the Concept of Vertical Integration," *Political Economy: Studies in the Surplus Approach* 2: 3–16.

—— (1988) "Growing Subsystems, Vertically Hyper-integrated Sectors and the Labour Theory of Value," *Cambridge Journal of Economics* 12: 125–34.

Sraffa, Piero (1960) *Production of Commodities by Means of Commodities: Prelude to a*

Critique of Economic Theory, Cambridge: Cambridge University Press.

CHRISTIAN LAGER

class

The analysis of class and the struggles between classes has haunted political economy since its beginning. Passionate affirmations of how classes exist, interact and shape society have contested with passionate denials of the importance and even existence of classes. For example, publicists for the USA and USSR alike have insisted throughout the twentieth century, albeit for different reasons, that their own societies had "overcome class divisions" while the other had not. In the realm of theory, Marxist political economy builds its arguments on notions of class (see MARXIST POLITICAL ECONOMY: HISTORY), while the ruggedly individualist neoclassical economics refuses to grant any place for class in its theorizations.

To roil the theoretical waters still further, deep disagreements divide those – both Marxists and non-Marxists – for whom class is a social phenomenon important to understanding and changing society. Some think class has to do with PROPERTY, others with power, still others with surplus and yet others with consciousness. Moreover, devotees of these different theories of class have rarely, until recently, recognized the implications of their differences. Partly, this was because basic conceptual differences seemed less crucial (except to relatively small circles) so long as virtually all class-based theories and political movements tended to grow, gain adherents and challenge for political power. Thus, for example, from a tiny sect, Marxism – in all its varying interpretations – grew into a global, diverse movement active in virtually every country on earth.

However, the social and theoretical transformations after the Second World War, culminating in the demise of the USSR and the drastic changes in China, plunged class-based theorists and movements into a radical rethinking. They could no longer afford to jumble incompatible concepts of class together into discourses that seemed ever more confusing and ever less successful in winning adherents than class analysis deserves and all class analysts want. They had built their work on what they had assumed were agreed notions of basically different class structures (feudal, slave, communist, capitalist and so on) and revolutionary transitions among them. Now it became much more widely believed that analysis and politics would vary depending upon the different ways in which analysts understood what exactly class meant and hence what distinguished, for example, capitalist from communist class structures, and what sorts of coalitions and alliances made political sense.

Property view of class

Multiple, different and contesting concepts and politics are today the reality of what "class" means. For example, many political economists of diverse theoretical persuasions agree that class is about wealth and income. Groups of people are "classified" – become classes – according to how much wealth or income they own or receive: the rich confront the poor, the propertied oppose the propertyless. The relations and struggles among such classes shape society and drive history. Such "property theories of class" differ over what kinds of property are to count in comprising classes (for example, should this include only means of production, or liquid assets, or all property). They also differ on how fine to make their gradations. For some, the dualistic "rich versus poor" suffices; others prefer some "middle class" between polar opposites, while still others stress nuanced juxtapositions of lower-middle, upper-lower and so forth.

Such property-based conceptualizations of class have appeared in various societies across the globe for thousands of years. People not only found them useful to make sense of what was happening in their societies, but class-as-property ideas also deeply influenced their actions and so shaped the cultures, politics and economics of those societies, including the revolutions that periodically transformed them.

Power view of class

However, non-property-based definitions of class have also been with us for millennia. Among these the most widely influential "classified" people according to the power they wielded, rather than their wealth or income. For power theorists, classes were groups of people who gave orders confronting groups who followed orders: rulers versus the ruled. Class boundaries depend on the distribution of power rather than property. Power theorists disagree over which kinds of power (political, cultural, economic, or all combined) to consider in defining class boundaries. They also debate the gradations: from broad juxtapositions of the powerful to the powerless to designations of ever more nuanced classes who are powerless in some domains while powerful in others, who both give and receive orders, and who occupy middle positions.

How everyone in any society thinks about class will influence how he or she acts in and upon that society. The person who denies class altogether – perhaps believing that all social action stems ultimately from individual thoughts, feelings, and actions – will behave differently from the person who sees classes as important social actors. Likewise, the property theorist of class will behave differently from the power theorist.

For example, property theorists stress how the political economy of CAPITALISM begins with the ownership of productive property, thus defining the class structure in the property sense. Property relations determine the economic contours of capitalism: prices, profits, accumulation of capital, and crises (see Roemer 1982). In sharp contrast, power theorists focus rather on power conflicts on the job – between order-giving managers and order-takers – and at other social sites (state versus citizen, party leaders versus followers, men versus women, white versus black, and so on). In the power theorists' view, the determinant causes of economic events (prices, profits, accumulation, crises, and so on) lie in the conflicts over power which they define as class conflicts (see Bowles and Gintis 1986).

Looking back at the history of the USSR enables us to illustrate how different class concepts matter. The Bolsheviks emerged from a property-based class analytical tradition. Their 1917 revolution was primarily a radical change in property ownership, from private to collective. They thought this change would usher in socialism as a new, just social order. In contrast, a power-based class analysis might argue that socialism was thwarted because unequal distributions of power never vanished. Political power monopolized by one party yielded a ruling-versus-ruled class structure. Property and power class analysts clashed over the USSR, and hence over the lessons of its demise for the present and the future.

Surplus labor view of class

While interested in the distributions of property and power, Karl MARX defined class in yet another, different way. He argued that all societies, however they distributed property and power, also displayed particular organizations of what he termed the production, appropriation and distribution of surplus labor. This surplus labor organization had been misunderstood or, more commonly, overlooked altogether by earlier theorists. Marx's surplus labor theory of class made newly visible divisions and struggles that were central both to understanding society and to any successful breakthrough from capitalism to socialism or communism (see SOCIALISM AND COMMUNISM).

In Marx's view, all societies organize the labor without which they cannot survive into two portions. The first, which he termed necessary labor, produces output which the performers of labor demand for their own consumption. The second, which he termed surplus labor, yields a surplus product beyond what the performers consume. Every society must somehow – consciously or unconsciously, through one or another set of political, cultural, and economic mechanisms – determine who produces this surplus, who gets it into their hands ("appropriates it" in Marx's phrase), to whom these appropriators distribute it, and what such receivers do with it. Marx defined class originally as a particular set of social processes: producing, appropriating and distributing surplus labor.

Marx's definition and theory entails a class analysis yet again different from the property and power conceptions. To return to the example of the USSR, Marx's innovative theory would hold that, however dramatic and important the Bolsheviks' transformation of property distribution, they did not basically alter the class structure in the sense of who produced, who appropriated and who received the surplus labor and its products. The vast mass of Soviet citizens continued in the role of producers, not appropriators of their surplus labor (as would be the case in a surplus labor-based definition of communism); state officials replaced private citizens as appropriators. A surplus-based class analysis would argue further that, however dramatic and important a political democratization in the USSR might have been, it too – like the collectivization of property – need not have addressed or basically altered the class processes of producing, appropriating and distributing surplus labor (see Resnick and Wolff 1994).

For a surplus labor-based class theory, the transition from capitalism to communism entails the change from an exploitative class structure, where producers of the surplus are not also its appropriators and distributors, to a communism in which the producers also collectively appropriate and distribute their surplus. Such a change in the class structure is not derivative from nor guaranteed by any particular change in the distribution of property or power. Indeed, Marx's point was that to achieve and sustain collectivized property and political democracy it would be necessary to institute just such a communist structure of producing, appropriating, and distributing surplus labor.

Conclusion

The property, power and surplus labor-based conceptualizations of class are now the major contestants for the analytical loyalties of those who think class is an important component of social analysis and social change. While there are others, including theories that make self-consciousness the key determinant of whether a group of people has become a class, they are less influential than the property, power and surplus approaches. In any case, no longer do discussions proceed as if the concept of class were straightforward, something everyone could discuss as if all agreed on its meaning. Theorists cannot now combine property with power and/or surplus notions as if these were not different and as if they did not push class analyses in different directions and toward different strategies. An analytical maturity now enables a new generation of class theorists to explore how the interactions among property, power and surplus – in the context of everything else happening in a society – shape both the current evolution of capitalism and the strategies for socialist and communist transformation.

See also:

class analysis of world capitalism; class processes; classes of capitalism; classes and economic development; economic surplus; exploitation and surplus value; participatory democracy and self-management; social ownership and property; surplus approach to development; surplus approach to political economy

Selected references

Balibar, Etienne and Wallerstein, Immanuel (1991) *Race, Nation, Class: Ambiguous Identities*, London: Verso.

Bowles, Samuel and Gintis, Herbert (1986) *Democracy and Capitalism: Property, Community, and the Contradictions of Social Thought*, London: Routledge & Kegan Paul.

Callari, Antonio and Ruccio, David F. (1996) *Postmodern Materialism and the Future of Marxist Theory*, Hanover and London: Wesleyan University Press.

Gibson-Graham, J.K. (1996) *The End of Capitalism (As We Knew It)*, London and New York: Blackwell.

Marx, Karl (1867–94) *Das Kapital*, published as *Capital, Volumes 1, 2, and 3*, New York: International Publishers, 1967.

Poulantzas, Nicos (1978) *Classes in Contemporary Capitalism*, London: Verso.

Resnick, Stephen and Wolff, Richard (1987) *Knowledge and Class: A Marxian Critique of Political Economy*, Chicago: University of Chicago Press.

—— (1994) "Between State and Private Capitalism: What Was Soviet Socialism?", *Rethinking Marxism* 7 (1): 9–30.

Roberts, Bruce and Feiner, Susan (eds) (1992) *Radical Economics*, Dordrecht: Kluwer.

Roemer, John (1982) *A General Theory of Exploitation and Class*, Cambridge, MA: Harvard University Press.

RICHARD D. WOLFF

class analysis of world capitalism

In the closing decades of the twentieth century, CAPITALISM has become increasingly entrenched as the world's dominant economic system. The spread of capitalism to new areas of the world and changes in areas where capitalism was already established, linked in part to the globalization of the system, have profoundly affected the CLASS structure of world capitalism. This period has been marked by a transition to capitalism in the formerly "communist" countries and a parallel transition transforming many of the less developed countries into newly industrializing countries (often from mixed capitalist/statist systems to more "pure" forms of capitalism). Further, the evolution of capitalism in the already industrialized countries rendered obsolete the nineteenth-century image of the capitalist as captain of industry facing a mass of undifferentiated workers. The changes in the "new" and "old" capitalist countries have been tied together by the increasing globalization of production, with RESEARCH AND DEVELOPMENT, product design, headquarters coordination, component procurement and final assembly often taking place in different countries.

Controversies over class

To set the class analysis of world capitalism in this context requires further that note be taken concerning the controversies over the meaning of class. The first and more conventional view of class refers to different groups of people defined by the relations into which they enter in the processes of production, including property relations. A second, distinctive view of class has been developed by Stephen Resnick and Richard Wolff in their book *Knowledge and Class* (1987), a view based largely on their reading of volumes II and III of Marx's *Das Kapital*. Resnick and Wolff think in terms of class processes rather than in terms of classes as identifiable groups of people (see CLASS PROCESSES).

For Resnick and Wolff, the capitalist fundamental class process (CFCP) is that in which surplus labor is extracted from the direct producers. This is possible only with the support of numerous capitalist subsumed class processes which are paid for out of the initial surplus extraction. Thus capitalists must make payments of rent and interest to outsiders, hire accountants and secretaries for their own firms, and make other payments to insiders and outsiders to secure the conditions necessary to permit the CFCP to proceed. Further, a variety of non-class processes, including cultural, political, economic and natural processes, all contribute to "overdetermining" the fundamental class process (see DETERMINISM AND OVERDETERMINATION).

In considering the class analysis of world capitalism, yet another approach has also been applied. This third approach is similar to the first in that it focuses on different groups of people, distinguishing them in the first instance according to whether they appropriate significant shares of the ECONOMIC SURPLUS generated. Thus, in addition to entrepreneurial capitalists, all those, including corporate chief executives, high-priced athletes, specialist physicians who receive the surplus, corporate lawyers and others can be thought of as the principal beneficiaries of the capitalist economic order in the industrialized countries. They form distinct classes when their high incomes are transformed into property ownership and mechanisms devised to secure the inter-generational transmission of productive wealth.

There are numerous problems associated with any effort to treat classes as particular groups. From the owner of a small enterprise who works alongside his/her employees, to the corporate executive who relies primarily on his/her salary as opposed to profit income, multiple class processes carried out by single individuals make distinctive class identifications questionable. In principle, then, the Resnick–Wolff approach is theoretically preferable to its alternatives. In practice, however, assigning individuals to particular class groups can be thought of as working approximations which may ultimately be clarified through a more precise analysis of the various class and nonclass processes in which they participate. With this qualification, it is possible to analyse the class structure of world capitalism.

Taxonomy of nations

In order to do so, it is helpful to distinguish four groups of countries: (1) the already industrialized capitalist countries (AICCs); (2) the newly industrializing capitalist countries (NICCs); (3) the former communist countries in the process of transition to capitalism (the transitional countries or TCs); and (4) the non-developing Third World countries mired in poverty and governed by autocratic kleptocracies (AKs). In all countries the CFCP is taking place, but to different extents and with different subsumed class and nonclass processes providing the necessary conditions of existence. In the kleptocracies, which include much of Africa (Zaire is a notable example), the CFCP is severely limited since the arbitrary use of state power makes the security of investment questionable. The "working class" then appears throughout the world, although conflicts within this class, both intra-national and international, are often intense, especially when the competition for jobs is severe.

Appropriators of surplus value

The class differences among countries are likely to be greatest when we consider the appropriators of surplus value. In the so-called "communist" countries, the party cadres and others with privileged access to the power and resources of the state appropriated the surplus. As these countries move into transitional (to capitalism) status, economic reform involving privatization and new opportunities to establish private enterprises benefits especially those with continuing ties to state power. Although the NICCs started from a somewhat different basis, with the capitalist mode of production already existing, close connections with those holding state power remain critical. Thus in both the TCs and the NICCs, the newly emerging capitalist classes are marked by close ties to those holding state power. Ownership rights and wealth accrue to both groups, as parallel processes of privatization and the establishment of private enterprises with state financial, licensing and regulatory support proceed.

Where institutional change is especially rapid and legal frameworks to secure property rights are still in the early stages of implementation, a new "robber baron" class has emerged. Either through outright criminal activity or by taking advantage of privileged access to those holding state power, this class has created the basis for immense fortunes in both the former "communist" countries (Russia provides a clear example) and the NICCs. Latter examples range from the *chaebol* owners in South Korea, who benefited from state-provided protectionism and low-cost capital, to the family members of President Suharto in Indonesia (Engardio and Shari 1996). In addition, throughout much of Southeast Asia and in NICCs in other parts of the world, family-controlled entrepreneurial groups have amassed substantial fortunes through a combination of entrepreneurial activity and close ties to state power, with requisite payoffs to state officials or (as in the case of Mexico) their relatives. Between 1991 and 1996, the number of non-Japanese billionaire business families in Asia increased from twenty-seven to eighty-two (*Forbes* 1996: 108). This process, it should be kept in mind, is a transitional one; once wealth is amassed, it is in the interest of newly emerging elites to institutionalize their positions by securing property rights and limiting the arbitrary power of state officials.

Semi-proletariat

Part of the process of capitalist transition throughout the world involves the transformation of pre-capitalist classes into a proletariat or semi-proletariat. The semi-proletariat refers to classes that still retain ties to the land, receiving some of their subsistence from small plots in agriculture while spending a portion of their time working in capitalist enterprises. The existence of a semi-proletariat limits the level of subsistence wages that capitalists must pay, thereby increasing the surplus labor they are able to appropriate. Also in transition are the traditional landowners in much of Asia who, instead of allowing tenants to work their land (divided into small plots) for a share of the crop or fixed cash payments, are increasingly becoming capitalist farmers employing hired laborers. In the NICCs, rapid economic growth (often reaching 8 percent or more) is increasing the size of the "intermediate classes," people with specialized skills from engineering to accounting who are increasingly in demand.

Elite class status

In the AICCs, elite class status is increasingly defined by the ability to secure a disproportionate share of the economic surplus generated and to transform it into forms of productive wealth that can be transmitted inter-generationally. In contrast, in countries where capitalism is only lately on the rise (the TCs and the NICCs), modified forms of the earlier class structures of the AICCs are increasingly evident. Perhaps the most significant differences between the TCs, and NICCs on the one hand, and the AICCs, on the other, stem from (1) the greater role of the state in the TCs and NICCs, (2) the greater speed of development in many NICCs associated with higher savings rates, greater access to capital from abroad and the use of borrowed technology to accelerate industrialization, and (3) the more intense population densities in many NICCs, which force down wage rates and mandate greater semi-proletarianization as opposed to outright proletarianization.

See also:

classes of capitalism; classes and economic development; race, ethnicity, gender and class

Selected references

Engardio, Pete and Shari, Michael (1996) "The Suharto Empire," *Business Week*, August 19, 46–50.
Forbes (1996), July 15, 108–232.
Marx, Karl (1867–94) *Das Kapital*, published as *Capital*, 3 vols, New York: International Publishers, 1967.
Resnick, Stephen A. and Wolff, Richard (1987) *Knowledge and Class*, Chicago: University of Chicago Press, 109–63.
—— (1996) "Power, Property, and Class," in Victor D. Lippit (ed.), *Radical Political Economy: Explorations in Alternative Economic Analysis*, Armonk, NY: M.E. Sharpe, 140–64.
Wright, Erik Olin (1985) *Classes*, New York: Verso.

VICTOR D. LIPPITT

class processes

The notions of class and class struggle have always had a special theoretical and political place within the Marxian tradition. For Marxists, the notion of CLASS conveys the idea of EXPLOITATION in society, while class struggle denotes a struggle in society over the continued existence of that class exploitation. Informed by these ideas, the aim of Marxian theory has been twofold. It first attempts to make individuals conscious of their participation in and exploitation by a class process. Second, in so far as they gain this kind of class consciousness, it seeks to motivate individuals to eliminate that singular class exploitative process from their lives.

Class and exploitation

In Marxian theory, the concept of class classifies individuals into those who produce surplus labor and those who appropriate and then distribute that received surplus. In Volume 1 of *Das Kapital*, MARX uses this idea to introduce new questions for political economy. For instance, who in capitalism produces and appropriates this surplus? Are they the same or different individuals? In Volumes 2 and 3 of *Das Kapital*, he asks: Who in capitalism receives distributed shares of the appropriated surplus and for what reasons? In providing answers, Marx begins to specify capitalism's class structure in a new and provocative way.

No political economist prior to Marx had posed such questions about these surplus labor arrangements in society, nor had any connected an answer to the notion of exploitation in the precise way that Marx did in *Das Kapital*. Class exploitation exists in any society whenever one of the following conditions exist:

- the individual or collectivity that appropriates and then distributes the surplus is different from the individual or collectivity that produces it;
- the individual appropriator and first distributor of the surplus is the same individual that produces the surplus.

Marx thought that while feudal, slave and capitalist class arrangements have been otherwise vastly different in character, they were nonetheless remarkably similar in that they were subsumed under this first condition. Lords, masters and capitalists commonly appropriated and distributed, either as individuals or collectives, surpluses produced respectively by their serfs, slaves and wage workers. A self-exploitative class arrangement fell under this second condition: a self-employed individual appropriated and distributed the surplus produced by that same individual. Communism became the singular society that was marked by the absence of both of these conditions: the same collectivity that produced also collectively received and then distributed that surplus. Unlike FEUDALISM, SLAVERY and CAPITALISM, communist surplus appropriators were also its producers, and unlike self-exploitation, communist appropriation was always collective and never individual (see SOCIALISM AND COMMUNISM).

Marx conceived of these surplus appropriators as exploiters. In capitalism, for example, their sole function is to consume the commodity "labor power," thereby gaining access to its use-value, and hence to the value and surplus value it produced. Participating in the class process in this way, capitalists occupy a class position in which they gained for themselves a surplus value produced by workers. In other words, capitalists exploit workers. A question arose, however: How did capitalists manage to occupy and continue to occupy this class exploitative position?

Important non-class processes

The capitalists' class position and the surplus value it produces for them depend upon specific non-class processes being in place. The latter refer to a myriad of political, economic, cultural and natural processes whose combined effect created the class process and its class position for the capitalist. For example, without the chemical and biological processes provided by nature, no class process would be possible. Its existence also very much depended upon social processes being in place. While some of these are provided freely – as in the case of sunlight and air – some are not.

Capitalists, however, need to secure all of them to secure their class position. For example, without their access to means of production, workers would not be equipped with the necessary capital goods required to produce commodities. Unable to secure this process, capitalists would not be in the position to consume labor power, to put workers to work producing commodities (see LABOR AND LABOR POWER). Hence, to gain access to these means of production, they distribute a portion of their appropriated surplus in the form of dividends to their owners.

Similarly they distribute other portions of the surplus, in the form of salaries, research, advertising and capital accumulation budgets to managers, interest to bankers, fees to merchants, rents to landlords, taxes to state officials and so forth. Along with the class of owners, these different classes of managers, moneylenders, merchants, landlords and state officials receive these different forms of distributions for providing the very economic (merchanting, capital accumulating and so forth), political (supervisory), and cultural (legitimizing) processes that help to constitute the participation of capitalists in the class process and, therefore, their class position (see SURPLUS VALUE AS RENT, INTEREST AND PROFIT.)

Fundamental and subsumed class positions

Using different terms, we may summarize a society's class structure in terms of its fundamental and subsumed class positions (see Resnick and Wolff 1987). A fundamental class process refers to the production and appropriation of surplus labor and its produced products. A subsumed class process refers to the distribution of that appropriated surplus to secure a vast array of non-class processes necessary for that fundamental class process to exist. Individuals who participate in these two class processes as surplus appropriators occupy a fundamental class position, while those who receive distributed shares of the surplus for providing its condition of existence occupy subsumed class positions. One of the goals of Marxism lies in demonstrating how in any society fundamental and subsumed classes constitute and contradict one another's existence in a complex manner.

Any person may occupy one or more of these positions. For example, an individual may occupy simultaneously a fundamental class position and a number of different subsumed class positions (that is, subsumed either to him or herself or to others) as moneylender, owner of means of production, manager and so forth. Marx's own insight into this complexity is telling: "The person who applies the capital, even if he works with his own capital, breaks down into two persons, the mere owner of capital and its user; his capital itself, with respect to the categories of profit that it yields, breaks down into *owned* capital, capital *outside* the production process, which yields an interest, and capital *in* the production process, which yields profit of enterprise as capital in process" (*Das Kapital* vol. 3: 498). The key point here is not to reduce any person, including his or her thinking, motives or income, to a particular class position. Rather, Marxian theory conceives of that person's social behavior and income as always being in conflict or contradiction. This is because they are constituted by a number of different processes, in Marx's example by the fundamental class process ("the user of capital") and by the subsumed class process ("the owner of capital").

Marx used the societal adjectives of "capitalist", "feudal", "ancient" and "slave" to portray different forms of the fundamental and subsumed class processes. His notion of class struggle described struggles over existing fundamental and/or subsumed class processes that could result in the emergence of new class processes. For example, in feudalism a subsumed class of church leaders may demand, for whatever reasons, a larger share of the lords' appropriated surplus for their providing cultural processes deemed necessary for the lords' class position to exist. In reaction, lords can take a variety of different actions, each of which produces a particular consequence and dynamic for feudal society. On the one hand, lords may resist such demands, perhaps then setting in motion a struggle between lord and church over the feudal subsumed class process and continued church support for lords. On the other hand, they may finance an increased distribution to the church by reducing their distributions to one or more other feudal subsumed classes; or in one way or another expanding appropriated surpluses from feudal peasants; or some combination of the two. The first of these reactions may set in motion further new struggles in feudal society, this time between the fundamental class of feudal lords and a number of affected subsumed classes from manorial or court officials to merchants and moneylenders. The second reaction might well create a struggle between lords and peasants over the production and appropriation of feudal surplus; that is, a struggle over the relative size of that surplus or possibly even over its continued existence.

Because all of these social processes are interconnected in a seamless web of mutual effectivity, these diverse subsumed class struggles shape and are shaped by fundamental class struggles. Hence at any moment, the created interactions among them may create a rupture in feudalism, such that an entirely new class structure emerges. Marx understood such transitions from one class structure to another to be somewhat rare in human history. However, his notions of class and class struggle also led him to believe that they nonetheless had occurred periodically throughout that history, and therefore might be expected to continue to occur in the specific case of transitions from capitalisms to communisms.

See also:

class analysis of world capitalism; class structures of households; classes of capitalism; classes and economic development; mode of production and social formation

Selected references

Marx, Karl (1894) *Das Kapital*, vol. 3, published as *Capital: A Critique of Political Economy: Volume 3*, Harmondsworth: Penguin.

Resnick, S. and Wolff, R. (1987) *Knowledge and Class: A Marxian Critique of Political Economy*, Chicago: University of Chicago Press.

STEPHEN RESNICK

class structures of households

Until quite recently, political economy did not approach households as suitable sites for class analysis. At most, household activities were adjuncts to the "proper" sites of class analysis, chiefly the company, the feudal manor, the plantation or, in general, the productive enterprise. Thus, for example, households were places where the products of enterprises were demanded, consumed and/or accumulated. Households were likewise the loci of the (re)production of the gendered labor power that some of their residents sold in the waged "external" labor market, while others remained in the non-waged "internal" (household) economy.

Necessary and surplus labor in the household

However, under the intertwined stimuli of feminism and the renewal of unorthodox tendencies within Marxism after the demise of the USSR, the household itself became an object of attention for political economists. Those working within a class analytical framework focused on how production is organized (necessary and surplus labor, etc.) rather than on property and power, and began to ask and answer the following sorts of questions. Does the household itself constitute a site in society, separate from enterprises, in which class processes occur? Can households exhibit different class structures? Who occupies the different class positions in various class-structured households? Do class struggles occur within households? On the basis of constructing answers to such questions, political economists have recently also ventured to explore the complex interactions between enterprise and household class structures, and between the latter and GENDER, power and other non-class processes both within households and in the broader society (Fraad, Resnick and Wolff 1994; Gibson-Graham 1996).

This class analytical approach has found that, like enterprises, households can and do display alternative class structures that vary from time to time and place to place. That is, households are sites of production processes. As happens in enterprises, people inside households apply their brains and muscles to materials drawn from nature and convert them thereby into useful objects for consumption or for further production. Examples today would include cooking, cleaning, medical care, furniture repair, child-rearing and so on. Not surprisingly, the organization of production entails divisions between necessary and surplus household labor. Some members of households often perform both necessary and surplus labor, consume the fruits of that necessary labor, and deliver the fruits of their surplus labor to others inside such households. When that happens, an exploitative class structure exists inside the household. If and when household laborers produce and appropriate their own household surplus labor collectively, the class structure would be non-exploitative, a kind of communist household (rather like some of the "communal" households repeatedly organized and maintained by people at various times and places in human history).

Multiple class positions at different sites

Not only can households, like enterprises, exhibit alternative class structures (slave, feudal communist and so on) in their productive activities, but it is also possible for multiple class structures to coexist within a household. This too parallels the case where one enterprise employs proletarians in a capitalist class structure at one of its production sites, while also presiding over feudal plantations at another of its production sites. Husbands, wives, children, grandparents and others (not necessarily relatives) can and do occupy all manner of different single and multiple class positions inside households. In other words, they variously perform necessary and surplus labor inside households and/or appropriate such surplus labor and/or receive distributions of such surpluses.

To argue that complex class structures exist inside as well as outside households implies new ways of conducting research in political economy. The class analysis of individuals in societies becomes the examination of how they negotiate the specific patterns of different class positions that they occupy at different moments in their lives. No simplistic assumption of a one-to-one mapping of an individual with one class position survives. Instead, the norm becomes multiple rather than single class identifications for an individual. To assess how class contributes to the ideological commitments or shifts among people, entails investigations of how their participation in multiple, different class processes at the different social sites of their lives (households, enterprises and so on) together overdetermine such commitments or shifts (see DETERMINISM AND OVERDETERMINATION).

In parallel ways, the recognition of the household as itself the site of complex class structures requires a revision of the concept of class struggle. It too becomes plural. Such struggles occur in enterprises but also in households. Class struggles at one site reflect and influence those at another. Radical political organization focused on class struggle would then have to take seriously the devotion of theoretical and practical resources to analysing all these different class struggles, their interconnections and the possibilities of mobilizing their different constituencies around a shared list of social change objectives.

The presumption of households as having class structures parallel to those characterizing enterprises allows for a much more nuanced and comprehensive investigation of the relations between the two sites. No longer will it make sense to presume that what happens inside households merely reflects class structures and struggles outside it; no longer will it make sense for political economists to assess the possibilities of social transformation by examining only the economic contradictions outside the household. Instead, class analyses of societies will henceforth require assessing the class structures and dynamics both inside and outside households and the complex relations between them – or risk powerful criticism on the grounds of their being unjustifiably one-sided. In these senses, the new political economy of household class structures represents a major maturation and extension of the inherited apparatus of class analytics.

Class and non-class processes

If households are sites of class processes, differences and struggles, a new area opened for investigation, debate and organization concerns the interaction of class and non-class processes inside households. How, for example, is child-rearing affected by class struggles inside households? How do definitions of and relations between genders function as both causes and effects of household class structures? Research aimed at answering these questions is drawing the attention of growing numbers of political economists and others persuaded to take seriously the notion of the class structures of households.

Critical questions

The work of Fraad, Resnick and Wolff (1994) signals a growing maturity by including critical comments on this plural class approach by differing Marxist-feminists. For example, while Fraad, Resnick and Wolff deploy their analysis to show how and why traditional households in the United States display a specifically feudal class structure, some of their critics dispute this. The latter fear the associations with the term "feudal" that are derived from its connections to medieval Europe. They also argue that the Fraad, Resnick and Wolff focus on class may obscure the roles played within households by patriarchy and socially constructed notions of gender. These and related debates on the class structures of households and their implications suggest that a rich new analytical literature is evolving.

See also:

capitalism; domestic labor debate; feminist political economy: major contemporary themes; feudalism; patriarchy; sexuality; social structure of accumulation: family; socialism and communism

Selected references

Fraad, Harriet, Resnick, Stephen and Wolff, Richard (1994) *Bringing it all Back Home: Class, Gender, and Power in the Modern Household*, London: Pluto Press.

Gibson-Graham, J.K. (1996) *The End of Capitalism (As We Knew It): A Feminist Critique of Political Economy*, London and New York: Blackwell.

RICHARD D. WOLFF

classes of capitalism

Not until Chapter 52 of Volume III of *Das Kapital* does Marx raise the issue of the definition of social classes, asking "What makes a class?" Unfortunately no answer is forthcoming, since the manuscript stops after a few lines. However, Marx claims that this question is equivalent to the following: "What makes wage-laborers, capitalists and land-owners the formative elements of the three great social classes?" This list of "three great social classes" echoes the structure of *Das Kapital*. It refers to the position of these groups within capitalist relations of production, and the sources of their income.

As is well known, the worker sells his labor power to the capitalist for a wage corresponding to the value of labor power (see LABOR AND LABOR POWER). The capitalist appropriates the surplus labor of the worker as surplus value, which is realized as profit under various forms such as profit of enterprise and interest. Also, a fraction of the surplus value is transferred to the landowner as a rent (see SURPLUS VALUE AS RENT, INTEREST AND PROFIT). The appropriation of surplus value by the capitalist is made possible by his private ownership over the means of production and the product of labor, and his control of the LABOR PROCESS. In a similar manner, the rent flows to the landowner as a result of the private property of the soil (or any other natural resource which can be the object of private property).

This is the core of Marx's analysis of the classes of CAPITALISM, and the basic framework for the study of CLASS struggle. Capitalism is the last antagonistic mode of production, and it is the historical mission of the working class to overthrow the domination of capitalists and landowners and to create a classless society. At the beginning of the *Manifesto*, Marx stresses the explanatory power of this analytical framework: "Our epoch, the epoch of the bourgeoisie, possesses, however, this distinctive feature: it has simplified the class antagonisms. Society as a whole is splitting up more and more into two great hostile camps, into two great classes directly facing each other: Bourgeoisie and Proletariat" (Marx and Engels 1848: 100).

Class complexity

Even in the middle of the nineteenth century, class patterns were already more complex than the above statements would suggest. This complexity arises from various sources. First, the capitalist class can be divided into several categories or class factions. For example, one can distinguish between the financial capitalist, as opposed to the active industrial capitalist. The financial capitalist is the lender who transfers his capital to the active industrial capitalist in return for an interest or a dividend. Industrial capital can also be contrasted with commercial capital concerning trade and the merchant. These divisions are responsible for specific CONTRADICTIONS, internal to the ruling class. They may play important economic and political roles. In his political work, for example, Marx contends that France was governed at one point in history by a financial oligarchy.

There is, however, a second source of complexity, due to the existence of intermediary groups. The existence of these groups may reflect the continual transformations of production relations within capitalism or between capitalism and other modes of production. As Marx summarizes in Chapter 52 of *Das Kapital*, Volume III, "middle and transitional levels always conceal the boundaries."

The "petty bourgeois" has always been a crucial character in Marxist theory and the labor movement, beginning with Marx and Engels, through Lenin and Stalin and up to contemporary Marxism. The expression is usually quite pejorative: it refers to the large groups of shopkeepers, craftsmen, small farmers and so on. Their importance reflects to a large extent the still immature subsumption of the productive system within capital. These groups are hybrid, part capitalists (because of the ownership of means of production) and part workers (because of the involvement in the labor process). This intermediary position is reflected in their ambiguous attitude in class struggles. Marx repeatedly points to this conflict in his political work.

The issue of salaried intermediary groups is even more difficult to tackle. These difficulties were already present in the nineteenth century, and can be traced to Marx's analysis. They became crucial after the transformation of capitalism in the late nineteenth century and the corresponding emergence of modern capitalism.

The problem can be approached from the viewpoint of productive labor and the appropriation of surplus labor, a basic element in the determination of the working class. There is little agreement in the literature concerning Marx's concept of productive labour (see PRODUCTIVE AND UNPRODUCTIVE LABOR). Two extreme views coexist with a wide range of intermediate opinions. One conception extends the notion to all salaried workers employed by a capitalist, such as a singer, following one of Marx's examples, an engineer or a clerk. Another extreme stand reduces productive labor to the production of a commodity to be sold on the market.

A difficulty is that Marx clearly refers in his work to a number of unproductive (although useful) functions, such as "circulation expenses." These include the wages of salaried employees in charge of the metamorphoses of capital through its various forms (money capital, commodity capital and productive capital), particularly in commercial activities. Unproductive workers are thus a group (or series of groups) who are different from capitalists and productive workers. Moving upward into the hierarchy, up to higher level managers or executives, makes the problem even more thorny.

New class patterns

In this analysis, Marx foresaw the transition to a new stage of capitalism to which new class patterns correspond. He observed the early emergence of this new structure of capitalism in England. These transformations affected both the internal structure of the ruling class and new intermediary classes.

Marx's *Das Kapital*, Volume III, examines the development of large corporations ("joint stock companies"). In these firms, ownership and management are separated so that the "real traditional capitalist," who would normally undertake the joint roles of ownership and management, disappears. Marx implies that modern capitalist enterprises seem devoid of the traditional (real) capitalist. Instead, the functioning capitalist is the manager of an industrial or service enterprise, while the money capitalist becomes the manager of the bank or financial institution (Marx 1894: 512). This analysis foreshadows that of Hilferding and Lenin (see OWNERSHIP AND CONTROL OF THE CORPORATION).

The same analysis also anticipates the transformations of production relations within firms, accompanying an increase in the size of firms, known as the "managerial revolution." The transfer of capitalist functions to managers was paralleled to the development of managerial and clerical personnel in general. This revolution, which occurred at the turn of the century, is sometimes called the "corporate revolution." It combines a revolution of management, the development of corporations and financial institutions, and a specific set of relationships between the productive system in the strict sense and these financial institutions. These evolutions were progressively supplemented by a large state apparatus, in which numerous personnel are also employed.

These new class patterns of twentieth-century capitalism have always been a source of controversy within Marxist theory. Marx emphasized these new developments, but saw in the large corporation a transient organization, a stage along the road to socialism (see SOCIALISM AND COMMUNISM). Thus, he never envisioned the consequences of the rise to dominance of a new class of managers on the construction of socialism. Lenin was aware of the growing importance of these new groups, but did not elaborate on this observation. Communist parties tended to play down the differences between productive workers and other salaried employees in favor of a common front against capital (often restricted to big capital).

A number of analyses stress the emergence of a new class, in the interstices between the traditional full-fledged bourgeoisie and proletariat. This was the view presented by Rudolf Hilferding (1910). The new groups have been described as a new "petty bourgeoisie" by Poulantzas (1973). As far as they collectively assume the functions of the active capitalists, this approach conveys several relevant features of the phenomenon. Erik Olin Wright (1978) uses the concept of "objectively contradictory" class positions. Indeed, these new classes are intermediary and their class position is ambiguous, when compared with traditional class divides (see CLASS PROCESSES).

The increasing importance of intermediary groups, "middle classes," is often used as a rebuttal to interpretations of class and class struggle in the analysis of contemporary society. Society is described as a hierarchical continuum of income or power. The diminishing relative number of productive workers adds to the impact of this refutation. This view, that intermediary groups merely bridge the gap between capitalists and productive workers, is misleading.

Metamorphosis and new class contradictions

There are several aspects to this issue (Duménil 1975; Duménil and Lévy 1994). First, we confront here a metamorphosis of class patterns, not their dissolution. Second, rather than defining a new class of managerial and clerical personnel, it would be more appropriate to refer to the simultaneous emergence of this new component, and a new class contradiction within it.

From the first steps of capitalism to its modern stages, it has always been the case that the transfer of capitalist functions to salaried workers was realized in an antagonistic manner. Some functions, such as the immediate supervision of the labor process or repetitive administrative work, were delegated to subordinate personnel. With the possible assistance of the mechanization of clerical work, the working conditions of the lower section of business staff tend to reproduce the working conditions of productive workers, whereas knowledge functions are concentrated at the other end of the hierarchy within the hands of engineers and professionals.

In modern managerial capitalism the two class contradictions are combined, producing the rather complex pattern of class relations that exist at present. Indeed, much research remains to be done concerning the determination of the frontiers between the upper and lower fractions and the concrete forms implied in the combination of the two contradictions. Two questions can be raised in this latter respect. First, what is the significance of the difference between "white collar" employees lower in the corporate hierarchy, and productive workers? Second, what is the relationship between the top managerial groups and capitalist owners, the "interface" between management and ownership?

See also:

class analysis of world capitalism; class structures of households; classes and economic development

Selected references

Duménil, G. (1975) *La position de classe des cadres et employés; la fonction capitaliste parcellaire*, Grenoble: Presses Universitaires de Grenoble.

Duménil, G. and Lévy, D. (1994) "The Emergence and Functions of Managerial and Clerical Personnel in Marx's Capital," in N. Garston (ed.), *Bureaucracy: Three Paradigms*, Boston: Kluwer Academic Press, 61–81.

Hilferding, R. (1910) *Finance Capital: A Study of the Latest Phase of Capitalist Development*, London and Boston: Routledge & Kegan Paul, 1981.

Marx, K. (1894) *Das Kapital*, Volume III, published as *Capital, Volume 3*, New York: First Vintage Book Edition, 1981.

Marx, K. and Engels, F. (1848) *Manifesto of the Communist Party, Selected Works of Marx and Engels*, Moscow: Progress Publishers, 1973, 98–137.

Poulantzas, N. (1973) "Marxism and Social Classes," *New Left Review* 78: 27–54.

Wright, E. O. (1978) *Class, Crisis and the State*, London: New Left Books.

GÉRARD DUMÉNIL
DOMINIQUE LÉVY

classes and economic development

As low income economies grow, the structure of classes within them tends to change systematically: largely self-sufficient peasants may become wage workers; rural landlords may become industrial capitalists. The political and economic implications of these class transitions are many. One element within this class transition is the change in the structure of the elite or surplus-appropriating classes (see CLASS ANALYSIS OF WORLD CAPITALISM). Another is the changing position of what can be loosely termed the working class. Beginning with a property-based concept of CLASS, this entry focuses on the political economy of this latter transition.

Class transition in agriculture

Questions over the class transition in agriculture – what happens to the peasantry as agriculture capitalizes and grows? – featured prominently in debates within CLASSICAL POLITICAL ECONOMY. This is closely linked to the so-called AGRARIAN QUESTION. The nature of the class transition in the agrarian sector is important, because it shapes not only the well-being of people in rural locations, but also the nature of migration and labor supply to urban and other sectors. An agrarian economy in which the traditional peasantry is displaced and squeezed by rising land values and falling labor demand is not only one in which rural people are insecure and dependent on the vagaries of the labor market; it is also one which can push migrants out of the rural sector before the new labor market opportunities come into existence.

Within the classic European debate, which took place around the beginning of the twentieth century, the peasantry was an "awkward class" (to borrow Shanin's (1972) term). It was a numerically significant and seemingly persistent group of petty commodity producers who did not mesh easily with the binary class categories (capital and labor) of CAPITALISM. The revival of this debate in the 1970s (and its projection to the Third World), returned the awkward class to the forefront of discussions about the evolution of class structure in developing economies. The Russian populist economist Chayanov was dusted off and outfitted in more contemporary neoclassical garb. It was argued that imperfect labor markets give small peasant family labor farms a competitive advantage over labor-hiring farms, because such imperfect markets are permitted to access labor at cheap EFFICIENCY WAGES. This is due to the fact that these farms do not have to pay costs of labor supervision, or because their inability to sell their labor time freely off-farm lessened the real economic opportunity cost of family labor time.

Either way, this competitive advantage was argued to impart a stability to the awkward class, even in dynamic capitalist economies. Other analysts objected strenuously, noting that the seeming competitive advantage of peasant producers was borne of their own poverty (i.e. their inability to sell their labor off-farm), and could not hide the unfavorable access to markets and new technologies of production which foretold their coming demise as independent producers.

While this debate swirled, the world itself uncooperatively generated a puzzling array of experience. The restoration of the peasant household in China *circa* 1980 ushered in an era of rapid agrarian growth. This seemed to confirm the Asian experience, in which rapid industrialization was mounted on a base of tiny family farms. Meanwhile, rapid export-oriented growth in Latin American agriculture – spurred often by structural adjustment (see STRUCTURAL ADJUSTMENT POLICIES) – seemed in many instances to accelerate the displacement of the peasantry (Carter, Barham and Mesbah 1996). To make matters worse, some observers identified a new (doubly?) awkward class of middle-sized producers who matched with neither traditional peasant nor capitalist producers.

Endowment continuum and risk

Interestingly, when combined with insights from the economics of imperfect information, the work of John Roemer (1982) on classes has begun to yield some new and more informative insights on this puzzle of classes and economic development. The general spirit of Roemer's work is best appreciated by starting with the idea of a property or endowment continuum. Imagine all the agents who constitute an economy lined up in rank order, from poorest to richest, in terms of their ownership of productive wealth. Assuming that each agent behaves in an instrumentally rational way, Roemer then examines the competitive neoclassical general equilibrium of the economy constituted by these agents, showing that there exists correspondence between an agent's position on this continuum and his or her class as determined by any of several conventional markers (for example, exploitation status). From this rational choice perspective, class emerges from "endowment necessitated behavior," to use Jon Elster's (1985) language.

While controversial among analysts of class, endowment continuum models yield particularly rich implications when used to study class structures in low income rural economies, where labor, financial and contingency markets are thin or absent. For example, Mukesh Eswaran and Ashok Kotwal (1986) analyse the class structure of an agrarian economy. In this structure, labor supervision costs impart a labor cost advantage to small farms. Also, unequal access to the financial capital needed to finance roundabout agrarian production processes counters that advantage. The result is an equilibrium agrarian class structure characterized by the competitive coexistence of multiple classes and modes of agrarian production organization (including the awkward peasantry). Importantly, while rooted in a rational choice approach, structural considerations (including the initial distribution of property, the rules of rationed access to labor and capital markets and the nature of technology) fundamentally shape the analysis. The shape of class structure is thus ultimately endogenous and highly contingent.

Endowment continuum models offer a number of interesting directions for further analysis of classes and economic development. For example, a number of authors have noted the (awkward) persistence of contractual forms typically associated with pre-capitalist economic formations, such as share tenancy and tied labor contracts. Explicit consideration of those forms, together with more obviously modern forms of agrarian production organization such as contract farming, may yield further insight into the evolving class structure and development.

In addition, a more finely tuned appreciation of rural market structures – especially the role of risk and missing markets to deal with it – may offer further insight. Avishay Braverman and Joseph Stiglitz (1988), for example, suggest that risk may in fact break down the competitive survival capacity of the peasantry, even when characterized by labor cost advantages. In an empirical analysis of West African agriculture, Carter (1997) suggests that risk potentially appears as a motor of differentiation, even in relatively egalitarian economies. Finally, recognizing that questions of class evolution are ultimately dynamic questions, there is an emerging body of work which explicitly studies the asset accumulation logic of different classes in imperfect market environments (Carter (1998) introduces the issues).

Conclusion

Taken together, the long debate on the evolution of agrarian class structure, including this more recent work and directions, suggests that there is no simple answer to the question about the fate of the peasantry, because there is no single answer. Endowment continuum models offer an intellectually interesting bridge between rational choice and more structural approaches to political economy. Still waiting to be made is the link between this work on agrarian class transitions and work on urban labor markets and the fracturing of the urban labor class based on both skill accumulation and SEGMENTED AND DUAL LABOR MARKETS.

See also:

class processes; classes of capitalism; development political economy: history

Selected references

Braverman, Avishay and Stiglitz, Joseph (1988) "Credit Rationing, Tenancy, Productivity and Inequality," in Pranab K. Bardhan (ed.) *Economic Theory of Agrarian Institutions*, Oxford: Oxford University Press.

Carter, Michael R., (1997) "Environment, Technology and the Social Articulation of Risk," *Economic Development and Cultural Change* 45(2).

—— (1998) "On the Economics of Realizing and Sustaining an Efficient Redistribution of

Productive Assets," in Erik O. Wright (ed.), *Recasting Egalitarianism: New Rules for Accountability and Equity in Markets, Communities and States*, London: Verso.

Carter, Michael R., Barham, Bradford and Mesbah, Dina (1996) "Agro-Export Booms and the Rural Poor in Chile, Guatemala and Paraguay," *Latin American Research Review* 31(1): 33–65.

Elster, Jon (1985) *Making Sense of Marx*, Cambridge: Cambridge University Press.

Eswaran, Mukesh and Kotwal, Ashok (1986) "Access to Capital and Agrarian Production Organization," *Economic Journal* 96(2): 482–98.

Roemer, John (1982) *A General Theory of Exploitation and Class*, Cambridge, MA: Harvard University Press.

Shanin, Teodor (1972) *The Awkward Class*, Oxford: Oxford University Press.

MICHAEL R. CARTER

classical political economy

Definitions and scope

Classical political economy can be defined, first, as the political economy of the industrial revolution, a period extending from about the middle of the eighteenth century to the middle of the nineteenth century. Adam Smith and David Ricardo are the two leading figures of this era. However, the term "classical political economy" can also be used to refer to a specific approach to analysing production and distribution decisions. From this perspective, classical political economy is still alive today, and the term can be used to designate particular streams of contemporary economics.

If classical political economy is defined with reference to a specific period in the formation of economic theory, there is no difficulty in classifying economists such as Adam Smith, David Ricardo, Jean-Baptiste Say and Robert Malthus in the same category. Some analysts adopt a very broad view of the school, and see it as stretching from the Physiocrats in the 1750s (see PHYSIOCRACY) to MARX in the 1870s. One typical list includes Quesnay, Smith, Ricardo, Mill, McCulloch, Torrens, Bailey, Jones, Senior, Longfield, Babbage, Tooke and Wakefield, possibly including Marx (O'Brien 1975; Blaug 1978). This is the most frequent way that historians of economic thought define "classical political economy." However, when defined in this way it is difficult to identify a great deal of coherence in this approach.

Similarities and differences

Both Smith and Ricardo relied on a LABOR THEORY OF VALUE. However, Ricardo was critical of Smith, and Marx was critical of both Smith and Ricardo on the labor theory of value. Mill explicitly followed Ricardo's analysis of the negative wage–profit relation. Both Smith and Ricardo described a declining trend of the profit rate, although their explanations were divergent: increasing competition for Smith, and the rising cost of labor for Ricardo (in relation to the limited availability of land, on which Ricardo based his claim of a low price of corn, and therefore free trade).

Many aspects of Ricardo's work, especially concerning foreign trade and the poor laws, had an impact on contemporary debates, but it is difficult to outline a specifically classical stand on these policy issues. The same was true of Smith. His study of the DIVISION OF LABOR, and institutions in general, had important policy implications but did not lead to a set of policies accepted and promulgated by most classical economists.

A strong divide can be drawn, however, between Ricardo and Malthus over the issue of demand and Say's Law. Ricardo acknowledged situations of crisis. They were described as temporary deficiencies of capital mobility among industries, due to the slow migration of capital. However, Ricardo denied the possibility of overall gluts in the market. Malthus took the opposite stand and supported a high price for corn, and therefore high rent and lavish consumption by land owners. He wholly rejected Ricardo's view of the negative relationship between wages and profits, claiming that high wages are consistent with high profits. Whereas Ricardo was concerned with the distribution of wealth in the long term under normal conditions (a form of equilibrium), Malthus insisted on disequilibrium situations and the role of supply and demand. This focus by Malthus on market prices contrasts sharply with the focus of Smith and Ricardo on competition and natural prices.

Marx found in Smith and Ricardo the key elements for his own radical criticism of CAPITALISM: a labor theory of value (however imperfect), and a tendency towards a falling rate of profit (see FALLING RATE OF PROFIT TENDENCY). This scientific character of classical economics – deeply rooted in the labor theory of value, the basis of the theory of EXPLOITATION – was crucial in Marx's definition of the school.

Thematic coherence

Although it is difficult to find coherence when classical political economy is defined in terms of a particular time frame, things are different when the emphasis is placed on thematic content. Here, one must identify the main approach and the theoretical thrust of classical economics. This way of defining "classical political economy" is due to Marx, who applied the notion primarily to Smith and Ricardo.

According to Marx, classical economists devised a theoretical framework unveiling the true nature of capitalist relations of production (beyond the surface phenomena). This interpretation allows for a constructive approach to classical political economy (Duménil and Lévy 1993) and opens up a new agenda for research, including the following themes.

Classical political economy presents an approach to economic theory that is decidedly different from traditional economic analysis. First, this theory contains an analysis of value distinct from that of normal or equilibrium prices (see VALUE FOUNDATION OF PRICE). Second, a long-term equilibrium is defined, with equalized profit rates and associated outputs and capital stocks. In this framework, returns to scale are constant since the number of firms can be increased in the long term. This analysis is combined with that of non-reproducible resources and the category of income accruing to their owners, i.e. rent. The theory of rent assumes diminishing returns, notably on land. The issue of the stability of this equilibrium can be treated, following the classical economists, in a disequilibrium framework where economic agents react to disequilibrium (such as capitalists reacting to profitability differentials). Capital stocks are thus allocated among the various industries by capitalists, and firms modify prices and outputs in response to disequilibria between supply and demand. This broad research field can be covered, both theoretically and empirically.

CLASS analysis was a prominent feature of classical political economy. Society was viewed in terms of classes of people with particular economic functions, including workers, capitalists and landlords. Income distribution was studied by looking at the share of national income going to each class. A clearcut division of the various categories of income into wages, profits and rents, was established. The contradictory character of distribution was also acknowledged, as in the negative wage–profit relationship, and the negative relationship between profits and rents. Although Ricardo embodied in his analysis a long-term feedback effect of wages and employment on the growth of the labor force, he did not assume that labor markets would necessarily clear.

These analyses of the distribution of resources among various industries and determination of income must be supplemented by a theory of the determination of the general level of economic activity. This is where the historical legacy of classical political economy is deficient. However, both Marx and Keynes provide elements of an alternative framework, and considerable research is presently being done to add a theory of output to the classical theory of distribution (Lavoie 1992).

The three economists, Smith, Ricardo, and Marx, were concerned with the historical tendencies of capitalism, in particular the falling rate of profit tendency. They analysed technical change and its consequences, stressing in particular the role of the profit rate as a determinant of ACCUMULATION and macroeconomic stability. The historical relevance of this perspective, and its theoretical foundations, are the object of much investigation (Moseley and Wolff 1992).

Political economists (Smith and Marx, even more than Ricardo) focused on the transformation of the institutions of capitalism, or what Marx called "the transformation of relations of production." This approach was later followed by Marxist, institutionalist and evolutionary economists (see INSTITUTIONS AND HABITS). Much work remains to be done along these lines, and the future of classical political economy is positive. Much research lies ahead.

See also:

evolutionary economics: history; institutional political economy: history; Marxist political economy: history; Sraffian political economy; surplus approach to political economy

Selected references

Blaug, M. (1978) *Economic Theory in Restrospect*, Cambridge, MA: Cambridge University Press.
Duménil, G. and Lévy, D. (1993) *The Economics of the Profit Rate: Competition, Crises, and Historical Tendencies in Capitalism*, Aldershot: Edward Elgar.
Lavoie, M. (1992) "Towards a New Research Programme for Post-Keynesianism and Neo-Ricardianism," *Review of Political Economy* 4(1): 37–78.
Moseley, F. and Wolff, E. (1992) *International Perspectives on Profitability and Accumulation*, Aldershot: Edward Elgar.
O'Brien, D.P. (1975) *The Classical Economists*, London: Oxford University Press.

GÉRARD DUMÉNIL
DOMINIQUE LÉVY

collective social wealth

According to Thorstein VEBLEN, the founding father of institutional political economy, wealth generation is fundamentally a social process. This is especially true under CAPITALISM, where the material product is produced in unison in the labor process (as Marx showed) but also, and more fundamentally, due to the collective origins of knowledge, the industrial arts, TECHNOLOGY, organization and communication.

Dual theory of collective wealth

In *The Theory of the Leisure Class* (1899), Veblen developed a general theory of socioeconomic reproduction, where social wealth is maintained and regenerated through INSTITUTIONS AND HABITS based on workmanship, science and culture (and non-reproduced through business, war and emulation). A narrower theory of collective wealth is developed in *The Theory of Business Enterprise* (1904) and *Absentee Ownership* (1923), based on the division between industry (productive of wealth) and business (unproductive). In both theories, the origin of this wealth is the collective mode of organization of the community, and the degree to which this mode influences the direction of instinctual tendencies. Egalitarian conclusions about the distribution of income, wealth and power were drawn from his theories.

Positive and negative instincts

INSTINCTS were important to Veblen, but they were not seen as being purely physiological, biological or psychological; rather, they are heavily conditioned by institutions and habits. Institutions and the pattern of social behavior predicate which instincts will be manifested more than others. In Veblen's general theory, good instincts, such as "workmanship," the "parental bent" and "idle curiosity" (in order of importance), were seen as being directed toward the collective welfare or collective life process of the global society. Workmanship

111

links to the work ethic, technological knowledge and material production. The parental bent relates to the tendency of human beings to care for other people, and idle curiosity is the non-directed activity of exploration in the search for answers to life's interests ("fundamental" thinking/research is one aspect of this) (see Veblen 1914).

Unproductive processes negate collective welfare in the interests of individual gain through warfare, private profit, patriarchy and emulation. Hence the "predatory," "emulative" and "pecuniary" tendencies of human society. The predatory tendency links to the trend toward aggression, attack, war and plunder. The emulative trend is the tendency for comparison on the basis of criteria of status and prestige, and the pecuniary tendency is the tendency to make judgments on the basis of monetary standards. Unproductive activities are correlated with the manifestation of predatory, emulative and pecuniary tendencies within institutions, which discriminate in order to promote the vested interests of certain businesses, classes, tribes, nations and one or other sex.

Collective wealth exists because the elements of the social whole are organically connected in such a way that cooperation and some degree of institutional unity are needed to propel the life force of the community. Cooperation and unity will be undeveloped if the flow of workmanship, idle curiosity and parental care is at a relatively low level of development compared with pecuniary, emulative and predatory/exploitative processes. While the origin of these activities is collective, it is possible to privatize their benefits by controlling the institutions and material assets. The vested interests, Veblen theorized, gain the benefits of the community's social wealth through predation, patriarchy, war, business, emulation and inheritance.

Business activities and exploitation

Under the modern capitalism of Veblen's time, business activities (and war) were the dominant methods of gaining a share of the monetary gains from the surplus collective output. He believed that these negate collective interests by (a) slowing down production during recessions or depressions, (b) reducing output through degrees of monopolization, (c) redistributing surplus from industry to banking and the sales effort, and (d) producing output which is utilized for luxury consumption or military destruction, which are wasteful uses of COMMUNITY resources.

In Veblen's delimited theory of collective wealth, business interests are able to gain an unearned income from the EXPLOITATION of the social wealth activated within the key sectors of agriculture, manufacturing, steel and the power industry. Private ownership of capital in the key sectors is based in part on the "maintenance of law and order," which, Veblen recognized, is instituted by the military, through the schools, and indirectly by the manufacture of armaments. This wasteful activity of owning, transferring and protecting private property (business) involves turning the technological wealth to the injury of people.

In *The Vested Interests and the Common Man* (1919), Veblen's theory of exploitation is seen in relation to the practice of the vested interests controlling the collective social wealth for their own benefit, by appropriating economic surplus (for example, profit, interest, rent and surplus salaries). Collective wealth provides a rationale for creating social goods and/or equal distribution, and/or distribution according to the contribution made to workmanship. If one class receives a higher per capita share of national product than another, then to the extent that this distribution is higher than their collective contribution to workmanship or social wealth, they are exploiting the underlying population which does not receive their fair share, or are not given the resources to contribute collectively to wealth. Veblen's political solution was for some unique combination of industrial anarchism, economic planning and "community consciousness" with the dominance of positive instincts.

Conclusion

The weakest part of Veblen's theory is the analysis of instincts, which needs to be reworked in the modern institutional–evolutionary tradition. Veblen's general theory of wealth has much potential for further development (for example, to include NATURAL CAPITAL). In many respects, his analysis of industry and business is similar to the work of Karl MARX, Joseph SCHUMPETER and John Maynard KEYNES. In modern political economy, the theory of collective social wealth is related to the notions of SOCIAL AND ORGANIZATIONAL CAPITAL and SOCIAL STRUCTURES OF ACCUMULATION, and has influenced the development of INSTRUMENTAL VALUE THEORY and the theory of INSTITUTIONAL CHANGE AND ADJUSTMENT.

See also:

capital and the wealth of nations; conspicuous consumption and emulation; exploitation; inequality

Selected references

O'Hara, Philip Anthony (1993) "Veblen's Analysis of Business, Industry and the Limits of Capital: An Interpretation and Sympathetic Critique," *History of Economics Review* 20: 95–119.

Veblen, Thorstein Bunde (1899) *The Theory of the Leisure Class*, New York and London: Penguin, 1994.

—— (1904) *The Theory of Business Enterprise*, New York: Augustus M. Kelley, 1975.

—— (1914) *The Instinct of Workmanship and the State of the Industrial Arts*, New Brunswick, NJ: Transaction Books, 1990.

—— (1919) *The Vested Interests and the Common Man*, New York: Augustus M. Kelley, 1964.

—— (1923) *Absentee Ownership and Business Enterprise in Recent Times*, New York: Augustus M. Kelley, 1964.

PHILLIP ANTHONY O'HARA

colonialism and imperialism: classic texts

Introduction

Colonialism, in the recent historical sense, designates the occupation and ruling of overseas territories by European powers, for the acquisition of economic, political and military benefits. The era of colonialism began in the fifteenth century, with the "discovery" of America and of the passage to India via the Cape of Good Hope. The naval powers of the time, Portugal and Spain at first and then later Holland, France and England, also became the major colonial powers. Two types of colonies were thus created: settlement colonies for Europeans (e.g. Canada, Australia) and pre-capitalist societies ruled by European powers (e.g. India). Through military victories against its rivals, Britain became, in the eighteenth century, the world's greatest colonial power, taking under its rule India (1757), Canada and other parts of North America (1763), and later Australia (1788).

Classical political economy

Political economy, from its very beginning, was interested in colonialism. Adam Smith considered colonialism to be economically beneficial to both the colonial powers and the colonies, and he was only opposed to the exclusive (monopolistic) trade conditions which the mother countries established with their colonies. As he said: "The discovery of America...by opening a new and inexhaustible market to all the commodities of Europe... gave occasion to new divisions of labor and improvements of art, which, in the narrow circle of the ancient commerce, could never have taken place..." (Smith 1776, IV, I: 348). However, "The *exclusive* trade of the mother countries tends to diminish...both the enjoyments and industry of all those nations in general" (Smith 1776, IV, VII, part III: 467; emphasis added).

David Ricardo, criticizing Smith's approach

to international trade, pointed out, though, that a colonial power may benefit at the expense of its colony. As he said: "The trade with a colony may be so regulated that it shall at the same time be less beneficial to the colony, and more beneficial to the mother country, than a perfectly free trade" (Ricardo 1821: 231).

Marx's view

Karl MARX conceptualized colonialism as a major moment in the historical process of PRIMITIVE ACCUMULATION, and therefore as a precondition for the domination of the capitalist mode of production (CMP). As he said: "The colonial system ripened trade and navigation as in a hot-house.... The treasures captured outside Europe by undisguised looting, enslavement and murder flowed back to the mother country and were turned into capital there" (Marx 1867–94: 918). Colonialism was therefore conceived as part of the general conditions for the expanded reproduction of commercial and manufacture capitalism, until the formation of industrial capitalism.

Furthermore, Marx believed that colonialism did not automatically lead to the prevalence of the CMP in the colonies, since the latter, as well as capital ACCUMULATION, "have for their fundamental condition the annihilation of that private property which rests on the labor of the individual himself; in other words, the expropriation of the worker" (Marx 1867–94: 940). "The obstacles that the internal solidity and articulation of pre-capitalist modes of production oppose to the solvent effect of trade are strikingly apparent in the English commerce with India and China" (Marx 1867–94: 451). These social obstacles to CAPITALISM were also noticed by Smith, who claimed that a settlement colony for Europeans "advances more rapidly to wealth and greatness than any other human society" (Smith 1776, IV, VII, part II: 467), whereas in colonies "inhabited by barbarous nations... it was more difficult to displace the natives and to extend the European plantations" (Smith 1776, IV, VII, part III: 502).

New trends and the work of Hobson

The antagonism between the world's major capitalist countries led, in the last quarter of the nineteenth century, to conflicts over the re-partition of colonies and rule over unoccupied territories, a consequence of the rise of nationalism in all capitalist countries. The concentration and centralization of capital advanced rapidly, big cartels and trusts were formed, FOREIGN DIRECT INVESTMENT made its dynamic appearance in international economy, the rates of capitalist development varied in different countries, new capitalist powers (such as the USA and Japan) emerged, and all these changes were pushing towards a new equilibrium in the international relations of power. In the period 1876–1900, the colonial territories of the eight major powers increased from 46.5 million square kilometers and 314 million people to 72.9 million square kilometers and 530 million people (Sternberg 1926: 428–9).

A new term also emerged to describe the colonial empires and the antagonisms among them: "imperialism." Under this title, J.A. Hobson published in 1902 a book in which he stated that free-competition capitalism had been replaced by the era of MONOPOLY CAPITALISM, which constituted a historical period of capitalist decline and parasitism and therefore the last stage of capitalism. To defend his position about the parasitism of monopoly capitalism, Hobson, ignoring the social obstacles to capitalism in underdeveloped regions, claimed that the colonies would gradually attract production assets, mainly due to the low labor costs, thus leaving to European ruling classes the role of renters.

Hilferding, Luxemburg and Bukharin

Hobson's ideas influenced the classical Marxist theories of imperialism. However, the latter are theoretically more sophisticated and thorough than was Hobson's approach. For instance, Rudolf Hilferding, in his *Finance Capital* (1910), concentrated on the fusion of bank and industrial capital which attained then, as finance capital, its most developed ultimate form. As Hilferding said (1910: 326): "The policy of finance capital has three objectives: (1) To establish the largest possible economic territory; (2) to close this territory to foreign competition; [and] (3) to reserve it as an area of exploitation for the national monopolistic combinations."

Rosa Luxemburg, in her *Accumulation of Capital* (1913), conceived imperialism mainly as a struggle among developed capitalist countries for the domination over still unoccupied non-capitalist territories. On the basis of an underconsumptionist approach, Luxemburg thought of these territories as the major reservoir of "third party consumers," who alone could absorb that portion of surplus value, which neither capitalists nor workers could (supposedly) realize (Milios 1994).

Both Luxemburg and Nikolai Bukharin (in his *Imperialism and World Economy*, 1917) conceived capitalism as a unified world structure. In other words, they claimed that in the era of imperialism the expanded reproduction of the CMP takes place on the world scale, not on the level of each capitalist social formation. Thus, the

> World economy is one of the species of social economy in general.... The whole process of world economic life...reduces itself to...an ever widening reproduction of the relations between two classes – the class of the world proletariat on the one hand and the world bourgeoisie on the other.
> (Bukharin 1917: 27)

Lenin's view of imperialism

Lenin, in *Imperialism: The Highest Stage of Capitalism* (1917), defined imperialism as:

> capitalism in that stage of development in which the dominance of monopolies and finance capital has established itself; in which the export of capital has acquired pronounced importance; in which the division of the world among the international trusts has begun; in which the division of all territories of the globe among the biggest capitalist powers has been completed.
> (Lenin 1917: 106)

Lenin explained the intensifying contradictions among imperialist powers as being due to the UNEVEN DEVELOPMENT of capitalism, which made the formation of a stable "ultra-imperialist" alliance of capitalist powers impossible. This in turn was "giving rise to alternating forms of peaceful and non-peaceful struggle out of *one and the same* basis of imperialist connections and relations" (Lenin 1917: 144-5; original emphasis).

All of the above Marxist approaches considered colonialism to be an indispensable feature of imperialism. Lenin was sceptical of theories which place undue emphasis on the unified global nature of capitalism, and which underplay the role of nations and states. He showed that capitalism cannot be reduced to the (world) economy, by ignoring the state or the political and ideological relations of power. He emphasized that the nation state is an important influence on the way economies are organized in the normal course of capitalist development, and that there are important economic forces propelling the reproduction of nation states. Capitalist power over the working classes is at the same time economic, political and ideological, and it is "condensed" by the capitalist state in each national social formation. He thought that the articulation and intertwining of all existing capitalist powers, each of which possesses a different strength and development level, forms the world "imperialist chain," the weakest "link" of which was Russia in 1917.

Imperialism is thus a tendency to expansion of a developed capitalist power, a tendency created in the last instance by economic processes, but supported also by political and ideological processes. Major historical events such as the Second World War show that it was not the most economically developed capitalist country (the USA) which challenged the British colonial–imperialist supremacy, but Nazi Germany, i.e. an imperialist country mainly motivated by "national claims" against its neighboring states.

Lenin's analyses of imperialism, the national question and the state differ significantly from what was called the "Leninist theory of imperialism," the dogmatic version of Marxist theory formulated mainly by Soviet Marxists under Stalin and his successors. In the latter (a) the Marxist theory of the capital relation is substituted by the simplistic scheme of "the monopolies," and (b) capitalism is at a phase of mortal decline, of "rotting," stagnation and disintegration. Rather, for Lenin, the analysis of imperialism should be linked to the political economy of exchange, markets and crises (not simply "monopolies"), and imperialism may promote the growth of capitalism rather than necessarily hinder it.

More recent work

After the Second World War and the national liberation movements which followed, most former colonies won their national independence, leading to the dissolution of empires and to the end of colonialism. Most postwar Marxist approaches to imperialism consider, however, that ex-colonies and developing countries are still subordinated to imperialist countries through dependency relations. For instance, as Popov states:

> A special type of development of the countries dependent on imperialism is characteristic of the international capitalist division of labor within the framework of the world capitalist system. The dependence created by colonialism is still manifested in all the key spheres of the developing countries' economic life
>
> (Popov 1984: 119)

See also:

comparative advantage and unequal exchange; core–periphery analysis; development political economy: history; global crisis of world capitalism; hegemony in the world economy; world-systems analysis

Selected references

Bukharin, N. (1917) *Imperialism and World Economy*, London: Merlin Press, 1972.
Hilferding, R. (1910) *Finance Capital*, London: Routledge & Kegan Paul, 1981.
Lenin, V.I. (1917) *Imperialism: The Highest Stage of Capitalism: A Popular Outline*, Beijing: Foreign Languages Press, 1973.
Marx, K. (1867–94) *Das Kapital*, published as *Capital*, Volume I, Harmondsworth: Penguin, 1976; Volume III, Harmondsworth: Penguin, 1981.
Milios, J. (1994) "Marx's Theory and the Historic Marxist Controversy on Economic Crisis (1900–1937)," *Science and Society* 58(2).
Popov, Y. (1984) *Essays in Political Economy: Imperialism and the Developing Countries*, Moscow: Progress Publishers.
Ricardo, D. (1821) *The Principles of Political Economy and Taxation*, Cambridge: Cambridge University Press, 1951.
Smith, A. (1776) *An Inquiry into the Nature and Causes of the Wealth of Nations*, London: Ward, Lock & Co., no date (reprint of the 1812 edition).
Sternberg, Fritz (1926) *Der Imperialismus*, Berlin.

JOHN MILIOS

commodity fetishism

The idea of commodity fetishism emanates from the work of Karl MARX, and recognizes a critical facet of the capitalist market economy. It is explained by Marx in the *Grundrisse* (1857–8), and a special section is devoted to it in Volume I of *Das Kapital* entitled, "The Fetishism of the Commodity and Its Secret." I. I. Rubin, in his celebrated *Essays on Marx's Theory of Value*, goes so far as to say that "The theory of fetishism is, *per se*, the basis of Marx's entire economic system, and in particular of his theory of value" (Rubin 1928: 5) (see LABOR THEORY OF VALUE).

Spheres of exchange and production

The notion of commodity fetishism is probably the most difficult aspect of Marxist political economy. This is because Marx's theory differentiates between two levels of the economy. The first is the everyday world of money, exchange, commodities and price; the second is the world of value, abstract labor, production relationships and the DIVISION OF LABOR. Marx tried to show in his work that the two were inextricably linked and that a scientific analysis of political economy needs to express this linkage theoretically.

In this connection, capitalism is the first truly social system where producers and consumers are connected globally, or at least nationally or regionally. A producer of commodities, such as wheat or chairs, is likely to have competitors beyond the purely local level. The capitalist market economy tends to become more national and global in operation. This generates a social system where price is established over a wide area. Hence, much pressure is placed on producers to employ the latest techniques and processes, for otherwise they may be forced out of business. Labor is thus employed in production only when it is of a sufficient degree of efficiency and productivity. Labor and value are, therefore, no longer local but social in their form.

Commodity production therefore forces producers to employ socially necessary labor, a complex division of labor, and therefore value which is socially acknowledged. The value relation is expressed as so many units of abstract labor, that which is socially valid. Exchange thus drives producers to employ labor which is at least of average intensity and thus creates the value relation which emanates from the production relations.

Capitalism appears to be based on a relationship between things: commodities and money, markets, the rule of exchange. Indeed, one aspect of capitalism is based on relationships which reduce "the economy" to a common denominator with a "thing-like" character: what factors are worth, what the product is worth, what the market will bear, and the exchange of equivalents in the monetary form.

Marx, however, recognized that such a view of the world ignores or mystifies critical aspects of the workings of the capitalist market economy. It ignores the fact that even a predominant market economy is fundamentally affected by social relationships between people in the production process and the creation of value. Because the products of labor appear as commodities in a system of generalized exchange, production is controlled by the determination of value by socially necessary labor time. The mysterious element of the commodity is that exchange reflects the social determination of value which emanates from the social labor process.

Marx (1867: ch. 1, §4) states that at a certain historical stage of economic development, the products of human labor generally take the commodity form. Henceforth they also take the value form. At the simplest level, it is the value relation between the qualitatively equal labors of the individual producers, as expressed in the exchange value of the commodities, which is obscured by commodity fetishism.

Rubin says that "Marx did not only show that human relations were veiled by relations between things, but rather that, in the commodity economy, social production relations inevitably took the form of things and could not be expressed except through things" (Rubin 1928: 6). Marx accuses vulgar economics of fetishism, of only seeing the thing-like character of the economy, rather than the social foundations upon which the commodity form is based. Even though he praises CLASSICAL POLITICAL ECONOMY for dissolving many of the illusions created by the fetishism of vulgar economists, he criticizes them for their ahistorical analysis of the commodity and value form which they took as natural forms, eternally given.

Fetishism and surplus value

Marx discussed commodity fetishism in *Das Kapital* prior to his discussion of surplus value. Further insights into fetishism are gained by linking it to the exploitation process. It follows logically that if one were to be blinded by the surface variables of capitalism – price, exchange, wages – the process by which surplus value is produced would be ignored. However, by examining the linkages between exchange and production, one is able to comprehend more fully the operation of capitalism.

For instance, in the sphere of exchange, workers receive wages which approximate the value of their labor power. In the sphere of production, however, workers are exerting labor in the production of commodities. Because the total labor embodied in commodities is greater than the labor embodied in wage goods, there is a surplus value created by labor. On the surface, workers receive the value of labor power on the market, but when one looks at production relations it becomes clear that total labor time is greater than that necessary for reproducing wage goods. Thus, equality in exchange obscures exploitation in production, another element of the notion of commodity fetishism (see LABOR AND LABOR POWER; CIRCUIT OF SOCIAL CAPITAL).

See also:

alienation; exploitation; Marxist political economy: major contemporary varieties

Selected references

Colleti, L. (1977) "Some Comments on Marx's Theory of Value," in J. Schwartz (ed.), *The Subtle Anatomy of Capitalism*, Santa Monica, CA: Goodyear.
Hunt, E.K. (1982) "Marx's Concept of Human Nature and the Labor Theory of Value," *Review of Radical Political Economics* 14(2): 7–25.
Hussain, A. (1990) "Commodity Fetishism," in John Eatwell, Murray Milgate and Peter Newman (eds), *The New Palgrave: Marxian Economics*, London: Macmillan.
Marx, Karl (1857–8) *Grundrisse*, Harmondsworth: Penguin, 1973.
—— (1867–94) *Das Kapital*, published as *Capital*, Volume I, New York: Vintage, 1976; Volume III, New York: Vintage, 1981.
Rosdolsky, R. (1977) *The Making of Marx's Capital*, London: Pluto Press.
Rubin, I.I. (1928) *Essays on Marx's Theory of Value*, Detroit: Black and Red Books, 1973.

THANASIS MANIATIS
PHILLIP ANTHONY O'HARA

common property resources

Common property resources usually refer to ubiquitous or fugitive resources which appear to be in the public or even global domain without any clear structure of ownership or control. By their nature many so-called common property resources run the risk of being overcapitalized in their extraction, overexploited and degraded. The solution to this problem is often touted as the need to establish private property rights. However, this begs the question of the original structure of rights in the commons situation, and substantively a consideration of common property resources cannot be separated from a discussion of common property rights. Ultimately, resources traditionally classified as common property might be better identified as a function of the non-existence of institutional structure and a more appropriate use of words might be "open access resources."

Ironically, the solution to "open access resource problems" appears to be the establishment of more formal property rights structures closer to common property rights than pure private rights. In this setting, the success of managing "open access resources" depends on the decision-making processes employed by the common owners of the resource, which emphasize reciprocity and mutual trust to determine levels of resource use as well as disputes between users.

Issues of common property resources and their management have emerged over the past thirty years or so to be of particular interest to considerations of natural resource management. The interest in common property is amazingly polar. On the one hand, it is seen as the cause of many resource problems by many researchers; on the other hand, it is recognized as a fundamental solution by another large group of researchers.

Neoclassical view

The common property "problem" was originally articulated best by Hardin (1968) in terms of "the tragedy of the commons." There is an institutional difficulty associated with all forms of common property. According to the orthodox neoclassical view, the resource misallocation, overcapitalization and overexploitation of certain resources is a direct function of the non-existence of private property rights. Accordingly, common property resources have been described as resources of open access, "where anyone who wishes to do so is free to enter" (Schaefer 1957: 678), and where "no individual can be prohibited from using the resource" (Anderson 1977: 33). Further, Scott (1955: 63) observes that, "everybody's property is nobody's property," while Anderson (1977: 33–5) notes that, "no one has an exclusive claim to the resource."

The marine fishery has been the main target of the neoclassical interest in common property resources. Here the thrust of economic policy has been to create a form of private property through two means. These include, firstly, restricting entry to the fishery, and secondly, introducing an individually defined fish catch quota (which is individually transferable). Such a quota is usually defined as having all the normal characteristics of any other transferable good. As the name suggests, it should be freely transferable so that it might be employed where it produces the greatest benefit.

The belief in the neoclassical orthodoxy is that the current disastrous state of the world's marine fisheries (FAO 1994) is a product of this inability to define private property rights. In some quarters, this inability is linked to the intransigence of fishers, fishery biologists, fishery bureaucrats and politicians. The inability to define individual private property rights in such resources as the marine fishery also precludes a consideration of other neoclassical policy measures, such as the Pigovian tax. It is a strong argument against non-market approaches which might involve bureaucratic regulation of the fishery.

Alternative perspectives

However, the institutional structure of marine fisheries and some of the other so-called "common property" resources does not resemble anything approaching the widespread international experience of common property (see Jurgensmeyer and Wadley 1974). As Ciriacy-Wantrup and Bishop (1975: 715) observe, the formal legal conditions of co-equal ownership can rarely be recognized in most natural resource situations. Rather, it is usually seen that no property rights or institutional structure exist at all. Hence, the appropriate designation appears to be "unowned resources," as Ciriacy-Wantrup and Bishop observe, rather than the formal notion of "co-equal ownership" as is characterized in the "common property as a problem" approach.

Consequently, the usual depiction of "common property resources" is in fact a semantic mistake (Bromley 1992). The correct depiction of a wide range of "ubiquitous" natural resource situations should probably be "open access resources" or "common pool resources." In this setting, common property rights might be recognized in a spectrum of property rights forms varying from private property, through state property, to common property and then to open access (Bromley 1989). The distinction here is that common property is in fact "the property of individuals, not the state," and is certainly not "nobody's property." Here individuals would appear to have all the claims and privileges of private property including the right to exclude others.

While "common property" was wrongly blamed as the root of "open access" problems (the solution being private property), common property is suggested as the solution to "the problem" where private property will fail (Jurgensmeyer and Wadley 1974; Ciriacy-Wantrup and Bishop 1975). Subsequently, considerable attention has been directed to designing the appropriate structure of governance to "make the commons work" (Bromley 1992). Thus, the success of commons-type institutions is related to the processes of collective choice and the character of the actual commons organization (Ostrom 1992). Ostrom notes six propositions of commons organizational success: rule simplicity, the enforcement of rules, the existence of internally adaptive mechanisms, owners being able to sustain legal claims, the legitimacy of the organization relative to larger organizations, and that the organization is not subject to rapid exogenous change.

See also:

markets; natural capital; natural rights; property; rights; social and organizational capital

Selected references

Anderson, L.G. (1977) *The Economics of Fisheries Management*, Baltimore, MD: Johns Hopkins University Press.

Bromley, D.W. (1989) "Property Relations and Economic Development," *World Development* 17: 19–93.

—— (ed.) (1992) *Making the Commons Work; Theory, Practice and Policy*, San Francisco: ICS Press.

Ciriacy-Wantrup, S.V. and Bishop, R.C. (1975) "Common Property as a Concept in Natural Resources Policy," *Natural Resources Journal* 15(October): 713–28.

FAO (1994) *Review of the State of World Marine Fishery Resources*, Fisheries Technical Paper 335, Rome: FAO.

Hardin, G. (1968) "The Tragedy of the Commons," *Science* 162 (December).

Jurgensmeyer, J.C. and Wadley, J.B. (1974), "The Common Lands Concept: A 'Commons' Solution to a Common Environmental Problem, *Natural Resources Journal* 14: 368–81.

Ostrom, E. (1992) "The Rudiments of a Theory of the Origins, Survival and Performance of Common Property Institutions," in D.W. Bromley (ed.) (1992).

Schaefer, M.B. (1957) "Some Considerations of Population Dynamics and Economics in Relation to the Management of the Commercial Marine Fisheries," *Journal of the Fisheries Research Board of Canada* 14: 669–81.

Scott, A. (1955) "The Fishery: The Objectives of Sole Ownership," *Journal of Political Economy* 63(April): 116–24.

ANDREW K. DRAGUN

Commons' contribution to political economy

The work of John R. Commons (1862–1945) occupies a curious position in the history of economic thought. On the one hand, Commons' influence on his students, his colleagues, the nature of important American economic reforms and a distinct branch of institutional political economy was and remains enormous (see INSTITUTIONAL POLITICAL ECONOMY: HISTORY). On the other hand, his written work is regularly dismissed as obscure, unclear or merely a preoccupation with classification.

The dominant conception of Commons is probably that expressed by Seckler, who concludes that "Commons was a man one would rather have known than read" (Seckler 1975: 131). Recently, however, this conception has been challenged by a series of contributions which, although different, all draw attention to Commons' refusal to ignore the inherently "connected" nature of social reality. Much of Commons' writings can thus be understood as attempts to develop an approach (a relevant unit of analysis, conception of change, role for the economist and so on) which reflects or is consistent with this connectedness.

Scholarly career

Commons' eventful career and personal life is wonderfully detailed in his autobiography

Myself, first published in 1934. Although an "undistinguished" student, he sufficiently impressed his professors to be encouraged and helped to pursue further research at Johns Hopkins University in 1988, where he succeeded in gaining the friendship of the influential Richard T. Ely. Commons did not get a degree, however, leaving before his third year after failing a history examination. Commons then had a series of disastrous teaching appointments (Wesleyan 1890–1, Oberlin 1891–2, Indiana 1892–5 and Syracuse 1895–9, with the latter of these seeing the dissolution of his chair in sociology due to his apparent "radical tendencies"). This was followed by five years as a freelance economic researcher and statistician, before securing the appointment at Wisconsin for which he is best known.

At Wisconsin, Commons managed to gain the admiration of his students and the respect of various legislative bodies through all manner of public service. During this time he became recognized as "a...national authority and pioneer in the problems of municipalities, labor–management relations, civil legislation, the creation and management of public utilities" (Seckler 1975: 121; see also Perlman (1950) for a listing of some of Commons' more outstanding practical involvements).

Commons' interests over these years were extremely wide. Of particular importance was his preoccupation with the nature of law and property rights and their incorporation into economic theorizing. The earlier of Commons' major contributions, *The Distribution of Wealth* in 1893, *Proportional Representation* in 1896 and a series of articles under the title "A Sociological View of Sovereignty" in 1899 and 1900, were each in some way a response to the orthodox view which takes "the laws of private property for granted, assuming they are fixed and immutable" (1893: 59).

Commons' ideas developed rapidly, partly through working on his monumental historical works, which were to establish him as the foremost authority on American labor. These included *Documentary History of American Industrial Society* in 1910–11 and *History of Labor in the United States* in 1918–35, as well as the excellent "American Shoemakers, 1648–1885: A Sketch of Industrial Evolution" in 1909. His ideas also were influenced by what he liked to term his "experiments in collective action."

Commons' last three major works, *The Legal Foundations of Capitalism* in 1924, *Institutional Economics: Its Place in Political Economy* in 1934 and *The Economics of Collective Action* (posthumously published in 1950), are all attempts to systematize these more "mature" ideas. The difficulty that Commons had in systematizing his ideas in these books is well known: *The Economics of Collective Action* is itself an attempt to simplify the ideas in the previous work, *Institutional Economics*. Certainly, nowhere did Commons produce an abstract or "neat" explanation of what he was doing. Instead, he preferred to introduce a series of concepts and typologies in different contexts and with different intentions, cross-referencing and refining the concepts on the way. However, several concepts are frequently returned to and stand as good indicators of the sorts of issues that concerned Commons most.

Collective action, the transaction and working rules

For Commons, the distinction between collective action and individual action lies at the very heart of social explanation. However, his central focus of attention is not so much the collective action itself as the vast array of relationships (transactions) and rules (working rules) which structure and facilitate such action. Commons' well known typology of transactions (bargaining, managerial and rationing) arose from his attempts to articulate the main features of those relations that he viewed *ex posteriori* to be of most importance to economic activity (Lawson 1994).

For example, the *bargaining transaction* is concerned with the transfer of ownership of some property and holds between legal equals: buyers, sellers, buyers and sellers in general, actual buyer and actual seller. Any particular activity may involve standing in different relations simultaneously. For example, understanding the role of a foreman may require taking account of a bargaining relation to management (in which the foreman stands as employee), as well as a managerial (command and obedience) relation to other workers (in which the foreman stands as delegated manager). Such relations are themselves underpinned by different working rules. Working rules are the collection of laws and customs which enable activity to occur: defining different transactions, the transactions that will be undertaken, and so on.

Commons was especially interested in the processes by which working rules change. The nature of the relations involved (e.g. employer–employed, buyer–seller) generate conflicts, for instance, over the nature of competition or the employment contract involved, which are ultimately manifest in disputes over the relevant working rules. For each transaction there is some agent in a position of authority (conveyor, arbitrator, courts, state and so on), whose job it is to select the existing "good" rules in favor of "bad" ones. These changes in rules can lead to changes in the nature of the relation (transaction) itself.

Commons was particularly interested in these processes and the way they enabled the different intentions and purposes of the competing groups and those of the sanctioning group (e.g. the state) to interpenetrate, often leading to the incorporation of the interests of new groups within the state (Chasse 1986). Commons took over Darwin's term "artificial selection" to describe such processes, where intention and purpose are essential to the manner in which working rules are selected (evolve), the contrast being to a situation in which rules are the direct result of some "grand design."

Holism

Commons' refusal to ignore connections and processes of change has encouraged a view of him within economics as the archetypal holist. Although some care is necessary here (see Lawson 1996; Rutherford 1983), such an interpretation does capture a large part of Commons' methods and interests (Ramstad 1986). Commons' work is a useful example of how holistic explanation might appear.

Holistic explanation is appropriate to situations where the objects of study are internally related (that is, are constituted by the relations in which they stand). The problem in such contexts is how to "cut into" or develop methods appropriate to such connectedness (see ENTRY POINT). Commons' method of analysing relationships and processes of change linked with transactions and artificial selection is typically holistic (see HOLISTIC METHOD). However, many of his insights remain undeveloped. For example, the point of *conflict resolution* is of interest not simply as a point where intentions or purposes interpenetrate, but also because it provides such a "first cut" into an internally related social reality.

This preoccupation with interconnectedness may well explain why Commons' work continues to appeal to heterodox economists. A major challenge of economic research is that of disentangling, understanding and explaining a social world which is irreducibly internally related and dynamic. Commons' appeal lies in the fact that this challenge is one with which he was continually and fruitfully engaged.

See also:

Ayres's contribution to economic reasoning; Galbraith's contribution to political economy; institutional political economy: major contemporary themes; Mitchell's analysis of business cycles; transaction costs; Veblen

Selected references

Chasse, J.D. (1986) "John R. Commons and the Democratic State," *Journal of Economic Issues* 20: 759–84.

Commons, J.R. (1893) *The Distribution of Wealth*, New York: Macmillan.

—— (1899) "A Sociological View of Sovereignty," *American Journal of Sociology* 5 (July–November): 1–15, 155–71, 347–66.

—— (1900) "A Sociological View of Sover-

eignty," *American Journal of Sociology* 5 (January–May, July): 544–52, 683–95, 67–89.
—— (1909) "American Shoemakers, 1648–1895: A Sketch of Industrial Evolution," *Quarterly Journal of Economics* 24 (November): 39–84.
Lawson, C. (1994) "The Transformational Model of Social Activity and Economic Analysis: A Reinterpretation of the Work of J.R. Commons," *Review of Political Economy* 6 (2): 186–204.
—— (1996) "Holism and Collectivism in the Work of J.R. Commons," *Journal of Economic Issues* 30 (4): 967–84.
Perlman, S. (1950) "Introduction," in John R. Commons, *The Economics of Collective Action*, New York: Macmillan.
Ramstad, Y. (1986) "A Pragmatist's Quest for Holistic Knowledge: The Scientific Methodology of J.R. Commons," *Journal of Economic Issues* 20 (December): 1067–1105.
Rutherford, M. (1983) "J.R. Commons' Institutional Economics," *Journal of Economic Issues* 17 (September): 721–44.
Seckler, D. (1975) *Thorstein Veblen and the Institutionalists*, London: Macmillan.

CLIVE LAWSON

COMMUNISM: see socialism and communism

community

Community is often confused with neighborhood, especially families being subject to a similar socioeconomic environment and being aware of and responsive to each other's good and bad fortune. A neighborhood may actually exemplify community, but true community is more than just neighborliness.

The essence of community is a sense of belonging, which animates and bonds a group of people to espouse a common set of values and thus to act together. This spirit not only manifests itself in human interrelationships and sociality, but transcends them. By linking individual to group goals, the process of community converts personal ambitions and vocations from a lonely egocentrism to a sharing with others.

Examples of such accord include reciprocal commitments to a momentous "cause," as well as deeply felt friendships. But the natural paradigm of such bonding throughout human history is the tribe or village of indigenous peoples. In more complex societies, it is the marriage vow which mutually unites spouses, not only physically but emotionally and intentionally, so that the good of each becomes the other's good. The children of their union often become the common good of both. Ideally, all such communities provide support in times of difficulties, respite from problems, sharing in success and solace in failures.

Obviously, few marriages realize this high ideal for which many strive. This implies that community is manifested in degrees less intense and in forms less intimate and looser. It can animate a parish, a school, a club, a sports team, a workplace and even a political movement. Such diversity implies that community can inspire groups which are formed for temporary purposes, like a neighborhood cleanup, or a particular cause, like supporting AIDS research. It also suggests that community can be twisted into forms of social control which exploit rather than sustain individual members. All of the above suggests the need to examine the essential content of true community. It is a fellowship of individual persons, who share common cultural values and whose organization requires some structure and promises some continuity (see CULTURE).

People can voluntarily enter into association with others and commit themselves to them in the sense of seeking their own good in the good of the group. They must be accepted as individuals, each with his/her particular abilities, desires, talents and contributions to the group. Brainwashing or lock-step behavior is alien to true community. Indeed, each member is somebody, not just one of the crowd, and has status, a role to play, functions to perform; each is also answerable for his/her own behavior. In short, in such a group a person is at home, and can share their innermost thoughts and disagree without being ostracized. Even children who resist or reject family values retain some, if only tenuous, communal status.

Indeed, value sharing is the cement which sets community. The paramount values, specific to community, are concerns for both the personality and the individuality of all associates. In thus safeguarding personal freedom and transcendental hopes, while at the same time prizing differences in talents, interests and ambitions, community of its very nature blends diversity in such a way that all may benefit. A mark of true community is an easy working relationship among members.

On the other hand, but necessarily related to valuing its members, is esteem for the public good. This is true even though associations formed to establish, restore or maintain a public good may require their members' risking or sacrificing their individual good for the higher common good. Conversely, groups formed to defy the common good will certainly be hostile or indifferent not only to the good of other persons but also of group members. Thus criminal gangs or cabals can never achieve true community, but at best only a kind of clannishness which sacrifices individuals for gang ends. On the other hand, true community cherishes social values like respect for law and public institutions, love of country, family values and welfare, concern for the disadvantaged and social justice. As surety for furthering the common good and never putting the group's good ahead of it, true community should be transparent and open to public scrutiny.

Thus, valuing the individual person and concern for the public welfare are common to all communities. What differentiates them are the values particular communities espouse. The family, for example, generated by the spouses' mutual love and commitment, espouses the values of intimacy, sacrifice and mutual love. A parish as a worship community will stress liturgy, charity and moral development. A sports team will emphasize sportsmanship, competition and winning. So too schools, research centers, social clubs, private charities, labor unions and businesses, in developing community, will emphasize different values and evolve different structures appropriate to their respective natures and purposes.

While community, as shared value espousal, will coalesce and can dissolve in inexplicable ways, it does require some continuity and structure. Families can retain their community identity over the lifetime of the parents; children leave one by one to form communities of their own, and each family's structure evolves as circumstances and personalities direct. In other communities such as clubs, schools, parishes and associations, which endure over many lifetimes, membership must be more openly initiated and its structure more formally constituted. The authority to articulate the values and objectives of the community must be vested in some representatives, who are prepared to respond to the association's changing circumstances, all the while preserving contact with the past.

Above all, community enriches the individual's personality. Drawing support from broad human themes, religious convictions, family feeling, school spirit and neighborhood attachment, by fostering people's natural habitat of fellowship, provides a countervail against entrenched government and corporate power. The person experiences the kind of social ambience which makes it easier to posit higher values than satisfying material wants and desires, to be sensitive to what is right and due to others, and be generous with time, talent and money in helping others in need. However, the sense of community is something of the mind and heart, its natural impetus being to improve the way people live. Its values are social values.

See also:

collective social wealth; ethics and morality; gifts; health inequality; human dignity; humanistic economics; hunter–gatherer and subsistence societies; individual and society; justice; language, signs and symbols; methodological individualism and collectivism; needs; social economics: history and nature; social and organizational capital; socialism and communism

Selected references

Boswell, Jonathan (1990) *Community and the Economy: The Theory of Public Cooperation*, New York and London: Routledge.
Danner, Peter L. (1994) *Getting and Spending: A Primer in Economic Morality*, Kansas City: Sheed & Ward.
May, Rollo (1922) *Power and Innocence*, New York: Norton.
Nisbet, Robert A. (1962) *Community and Power*, New York: Galaxy.

PETER L. DANNER

comparable worth

Comparable worth, also known as "equal pay for equal value" and "pay equity," involves setting equal wages for jobs that are determined to be of equal worth to the firm. Many persons concerned with the continued pay disparity between women and men have argued in favor of such policies. Most extant equal pay policies only attempt to equalize pay within jobs, and therefore are ineffective in addressing the pay disparity linked to the different distributions of women and men across jobs (see GENDER DIVISION OF LABOR).

Generally, the type of implementation proposed is to raise wages for all holders of a job which is found to have the same number of job points under some chosen rating system as another higher-paying job. While in theory this criterion need have nothing to do with the gender composition of the job, in practice female-dominated jobs are generally found to receive lower pay than male-dominated jobs with equivalent points (England 1992).

Historical background

Equal pay for equal value had been seriously proposed since the late nineteenth century. A century later, most of the movement for equalization of pay was eclipsed by the culmination of the discussion of equal pay for equal work in the 1963 Equal Pay Act in the USA, and a series of equal pay laws in Europe in the mid-1970s. However, the expansion of public sector employment and union power, particularly in female-dominated occupations, along with increased feminist activity during the 1970s, apparently provided the conditions for a reopening of the debate.

A series of lawsuits in the late 1970s and early 1980s brought the concept of comparable worth back into serious consideration. Of special importance was the district court decision in *AFSCME* v. *Washington State* in 1983, that Washington State's pay system needed to be reworked (McCann 1994). During the same period, a number of scholarly studies documenting a relationship between gender composition of an occupation and pay were published, in particular a 1981 compilation from the National Research Council (Treiman and Hartmann 1981). Soon almost all US state governments and many local governments had commissioned pay equity studies.

Numerous books and articles on comparable worth were published by both advocates and opponents during the 1980s, with a lessened but continuing flow into the 1990s. Meanwhile, several US state and local governments and several jurisdictions in Canada have implemented comparable worth policies covering public sector employees, with extensive legislation covering both private and public sectors in the province of Ontario. The national wage-setting policy in Australia has comparable worth features. There have also been widespread efforts in Canada and the United States to implement comparable worth through collective bargaining agreements.

Economic analysis

Opponents of comparable worth (a category that includes practically all neoclassical economists) argue that advocates of comparable worth are committing the intrinsic value fallacy. In other words, there is no way to determine a priori the value of a job. In addition, they argue that wage-setting systems are both administratively and economically inefficient, creating labor shortages in some markets and an oversupply of labor in others. They tend, therefore, to promote a non-optimal factor mix throughout the economy by affecting the relative prices of capital and types of labor, and they fail to correct the fundamental labor market inefficiency caused by discrimination, that is, barriers to entry into higher-paying occupations. Therefore, it is argued, comparable worth would actually hurt some of those it is meant to help by increasing unemployment in female-dominated occupations.

Proponents, including those with feminist, institutionalist and segmentation approaches, counter these assertions. They argue that comparable worth would not supplant a market-driven system, as job valuation systems are already used widely by institutions to set wages (see WAGE DETERMINATION; WOMEN'S WAGES: SOCIAL CONSTRUCTION OF; INTERNAL LABOR MARKETS), and that there exist SEGMENTED AND DUAL LABOR MARKETS. Rather than making the system more inefficient, an existing inefficiency in the form of discrimination will have been corrected, and there will be negligible unemployment effects. Therefore, not changing the system is also unfair to particular groups of individuals, and the gains to those who are helped will more than offset the losses to those who are hurt.

Studies of existing implementations suggest a range of possible outcomes. One study of policy in the city of San Jose, California, concludes that the pay adjustments raised wages approximately 5.7 percent in female jobs and reduced employment in female jobs by about 6.6 percent relative to what it would have been (Killingsworth 1990). Another study finds significantly greater wage growth in affected jobs, and that employment growth was still higher than in surrounding cities; the targeted jobs actually experienced an increase in their proportion of female employment, implying either that the higher wages did not attract male applicants, or that hiring policies favored female applicants (Kahn 1992). In Minnesota, the gender wage ratio rose from 0.74 in 1981 to 0.82 in 1986, when implementation was completed, while employment in female jobs has grown less rapidly than the rate that would have likely occurred in the absence of wage adjustments (Sorensen 1994).

In Australia, where minimum wage rates are set nationally for many occupations and/or industries by wage tribunals, prior to the 1968 "equal pay for equal work" decision, women's minimum wages were set below men's minimum wages within occupations. In 1972, however, the equality concept was extended to include "equal pay for work of equal value." The gender earnings ratio rose from 0.76 in 1973 to 0.84 by 1978. There has been disagreement over the effects of this policy on female employment, ranging from a slight reduction (Gregory and Duncan 1981: 420–21) to negligible effects (Killingsworth 1990: 263).

It is difficult to calculate the actual gains and losses for women and men if they are making decisions in a household framework. The labor market participation of both spouses may be altered by relative wage changes, and consumption allocations may or may not map to relative contributions to family income. This interaction has been largely ignored in the existing literature (save for Beider, Bernheim, Fuchs and Shoven 1988). But the implication, addressed increasingly by feminist economists, is that rises in female wages and employment do not automatically translate into greater well-being for women.

The politicization of comparable worth has also been addressed by several authors, including the potential for raising women workers' consciousness. However, Evans and Nelson (1989) and Rhoads (1993) note the lack of awareness of many workers in Minnesota that pay adjustments were even occurring. Rhoads also cites numerous problems that have arisen in Minnesota's implementation, such as more politically powerful and better-paid occupations managing to capture most of the gains. For reasons such as these, along with the more conservative legal and political climate (Figart and Kahn 1997), comparable worth has moved to the back burner as a strategy for raising women's wages.

Selected references

Beider, Perry C., Bernheim, B. Douglas, Fuchs, Victor R. and Shoven, John B. (1988) "Comparable Worth in a General Equilibrium Model of the U.S. Economy," *Research in Labor Economics* 9: 1–52.
England, Paula (1992) *Comparable Worth: Theories and Evidence*, New York: Aldine.
Evans, Sara M. and Nelson, Barbara J. (1989) *Wage Justice: Comparable Worth and the Paradox of Technocratic Reform*, Chicago: University of Chicago Press.
Figart, Deborah M. and Kahn, Peggy (1997) *Contesting the Market: Pay Equity and the Politics of Economic Restructuring*, Detroit, MI: Wayne State University Press.
Gregory, Robert G. and Duncan, Ronald C. (1981) "The Relevance of Segmented Labor Market Theories: The Australian Experience of the Achievement of Equal Pay for Women," *Journal of Post Keynesian Economics* 3(3): 403–28.
Kahn, Shulamit (1992) "The Economic Implications of Public-Sector Comparable Worth: The Case of San Jose, California," *Industrial Relations* 31(2): 270–91.
Killingsworth, Mark R. (1990) *The Economics of Comparable Worth*, Kalamazoo, MI: W.E. Upjohn.
McCann, Michael W. (1994) *Rights at Work: Pay Equity Reform and the Politics of Legal Mobilization*, Chicago: University of Chicago Press.
Rhoads, Steven E. (1993) *Incomparable Worth: Pay Equity Meets the Market*, Cambridge: Cambridge University Press.
Sorensen, Elaine (1994) *Comparable Worth: Is It a Worthy Policy?* Princeton, NJ: Princeton University Press.
Treiman, Donald J. and Hartmann, Heidi (1981) *Women, Work, and Wages: Equal Pay for Jobs of Equal Value*, Washington, DC: National Academy Press.

JOYCE JACOBSEN

comparative advantage and unequal exchange

Comparative advantage

Ongoing debates around the relative importance of comparative advantage and unequal exchange address one of the most persistent disputes in political economy: whether markets, free from regulation, can enhance the welfare of all the agents involved in trade. Advocates of the notion of comparative advantage maintain that, by specializing in producing and trading those goods for which they have the greater cost advantage, nations and their population maximize their access to wealth and welfare. Critics of this position (including advocates of the notion of unequal exchange) argue that reliance on comparative advantage primarily serves to reproduce deep inequalities in the distribution of wealth and welfare.

Theories supporting the notion of comparative advantage can be traced to CLASSICAL POLITICAL ECONOMY. Adam Smith, in the *Wealth of Nations* (1776), situated his discussion of free trade within a broader framework, emphasizing the gains to be derived from specialization (according to natural advantage) and exchange (as an outcome of individuals pursuing their self-interest). Foreign trade (as any other form of exchange) would allow for the greater development of productive powers by expanding markets.

However, it was David Ricardo, in his *Principles of Political Economy and Taxation* in 1817, who moved to highlight labor costs as the crucial component of comparative advantage, and to emphasize that boundaries restricting the mobility of factors of production were specific to trade as a form of exchange. Due to these boundaries, according to Ricardo, nations would tend to specialize in trading those goods that could be produced with the lowest relative costs. Later, but still within the classical tradition, John Stuart Mill, in his *Principles of Political Economy* in 1848, specified the relative productivity of labor as the basis of comparative advantage (although noting that transportation costs were a significant variable shaping this advantage), and linked specialization to the relative elasticity of demand for different products.

Moving to a price theory of value, neoclassical economic models in the twentieth century sought further to specify the mechanisms through which specialization in activities, characterized by comparative advantage, maximized wealth and welfare for all involved (Ohlin 1935). In these models, trading nations specialize in producing goods that use those factors of most abundance in the country in question. Free trade leads to an equalization of factor prices across countries, and gains within countries rise most rapidly for the owners of abundant resources. Additionally, some of these models sought to establish that specialization in the production of raw materials for trade could rapidly increase productivity and investment levels, and hence provide a strong drive for economic growth as a whole. Empirical support for the notion of comparative advantage was often drawn in these studies from the earlier experience of settler nations, but there ensued considerable disputes as to the extent that these models adequately account for trade patterns in either developed or less developed countries.

Problems with comparative advantage

A deeper challenge to these models emerged in the 1950s, hand in hand with development economics. To begin with, several studies pointed to the low elasticity of demand for raw materials. Among the most influential of these studies was R. Prebisch's *The Economic Development of Latin America and its Principal Problems* in 1950. In this work, Prebisch argued that a deterioration in the terms of trade for raw materials in peripheral nations was shaped in part by differences in the relative income elasticities of manufactured and unprocessed commodities (with demand for manufactures rising faster than for raw materials). The terms of trade were also shaped by the tendency for the United States (the new hegemonic power of the postwar period) to import relatively less than England, its predecessor in this role (see CORE–PERIPHERY ANALYSIS). The argument that the gains of trade are not equally distributed between center and peripheral countries came to be known in the literature as the "Prebisch–Singer Thesis."

A complementary line of analysis emphasized that less developed countries were characterized by low-level equilibria that prevented growth. Some studies focused on the "circular relationships that afflict both the demand and the supply side of the problem of capital formation in economically backward areas" (Nurkse 1952: 571). Others focused on the dynamics of labor supplies and capitalist investments in a situation of economic dualism between a capitalist and a subsistence sector (Lewis 1954). Most of these studies sought to identify mechanisms to promote faster industrial growth, although debating whether balanced or unbalanced growth was required to break from low-level equilibria. Overall, the emphasis was placed on the differences that made these areas less likely to respond to market signals in the same manner as developed countries.

The notion that the social structure of less developed countries differed from that of more developed countries is important. It linked to a more substantive departure in the mode of characterizing the relationship between more and less developed countries. Thus Prebisch emphasized the unequal advantage derived by center and peripheral nations from their world economic linkages, as different patterns in the relative bargaining power of capital and labor in center and peripheral areas altered the outcome of exchange between the two areas (resulting in a long-run improvement of the terms of trade for center areas, but a deterioration of these terms for the periphery). From this point of view, the trajectories of center and peripheral countries were interrelated, as both sets of nations were integral to a single, worldwide system of accumulation.

While there were significant differences among many of the critics of the notion of comparative advantage, most coincided in emphasizing the role of industrialization as the key mechanism for breaking away from low-level equilibrium (although with considerable disagreement as to the type of policies that could best ensure qualitative shifts in rates of capital formation and/or entrepreneurship). Building both on these analytical perspectives and on the various alternative strategies for economic growth developed in areas such as Latin America since the 1920s, import-substitution industrialization emerged as an alternative, comprehensive strategy of development. In this strategy, state regulation had a crucial role to play in channeling resources and investments so as to provide adequate incentives for the development of a diversified national economy.

Several characteristics of the immediate postwar period have been highlighted in the literature as being conducive to a certain type of challenge to the notion of comparative advantage. For example:

- In most industrialized nations, Keynesian economics was reaching the peak of its influence, providing a receptive audience and economic discourse that portrayed the poverty of underdeveloped areas as an outcome of low-level equilibrium. Here the tension was between full employment and idle resources.
- The apparent success of the Soviet Union in using state planning and industrialization as a means of obtaining greater access to wealth and power challenged aspects of comparative advantage.
- The implementation of the Marshall Plan in postwar Europe suggested that concerted policies could indeed be effective in promoting rapid economic growth.

Radical challenges to comparative advantage

A more radical challenge to the notion of comparative advantage came from the literature that came to be known as dependency theory. While some within this literature interpreted the core–peripheral model in terms that were similar to those advanced by Prebisch, others moved to emphasize that it was in the very nature of capitalist development to produce the underdevelopment of peripheral countries. These authors generally sought to broaden the scope of Prebisch's analysis by focusing on the impact of capital flows and class relations in producing situations of underdevelopment or dependent development.

Along these lines, Emmanuel (1969) developed the argument of unequal exchange, indicating that the deterioration in the terms of trade for the products of peripheral countries was likely to take place even under conditions of perfect competition. In this model, the perfect mobility of capital ensures equal profit rates between core and peripheral countries, but restrictions upon the mobility of labor result in persistent wage-rate differences between these countries (with the institutional determination of wages being exogenous to the model, although noting that trade unions in core countries play a role in raising wages, and that higher wages provide for larger core markets). Under these conditions, the exchange of products between core and peripheral countries entails an exchange of unequal values, and hence a transfer of surplus from peripheral to core countries.

Emmanuel's model has been criticized on several fronts, including its treatment of wages as an exogenous variable, and for failing to consider potential differences in levels of productivity between core and peripheral labor. A modified interpretation of unequal exchange was provided by Amin (1970), who sought to make wage levels in core and peripheral countries endogenous to his model, and argued that the function of unequal exchange (rooted in the disarticulation of capitalist and other modes of production in peripheral areas) is to allow capital in core countries to escape a squeeze on profits. Within WORLD-SYSTEMS ANALYSIS, there has been a growing emphasis on the uneven spatial distribution of innovations and competitive pressures as a determinant of differences in the gains from trade among core, semi-peripheral and peripheral countries.

Since the 1970s, there has been a resurgence of a neoclassical emphasis on comparative advantage as a basis for organizing world production and trade (for instance, Krueger 1978). However, within this new resurgence, greater emphasis is placed on the need both for an appropriate institutional framework to allow competitive markets to function, and for states to intervene in areas where markets prove themselves inadequate (World Bank 1991).

Recent post-Keynesian approaches

Along with this trend has been the development of increasing sophistication in heterodox critique of comparative advantage and free trade. Prasch (1996), for instance, emphasizes the need to develop a realistic theory of trade based on political economy foundations. He tries to eschew the problematic assumptions of many neoclassical models of comparative advantage. These include no externalities, free and costless mobility of capital and labor, full employment of available resources, balanced trade and a fixed set of productive resources. Instead, he suggests that an alternative theory of trade should place greater emphasis on the environmental problems associated with trade, the possibility of underutilized resources, the costs of adjustment to freer trade, possible problems of deindustrialization and incorporating historical time into the analysis (including path dependency and dynamic comparative advantage).

Norman (1996) took a similar position, but went further by incorporating more realistic assumptions into his model. Attempting to develop a post-Keynesian theory of protection, he based his model on the "normal situation" of underutilized resources (including labor), historical time, two sectors of oligopoly (for finished goods with markup pricing) and competition (for primary industry with supply and demand pricing), and resource materials being more highly substitutable for domestic production than are finished goods. In this system, he found that the introduction of a differential tariff on goods produced marked increases in output but small increases in prices. Such were the outcomes of a more realistic theory incorporating an oligopoly sector, Keynesian macro-policy, and the importance of non-price competition for finished goods (see POST-KEYNESIAN POLITICAL ECONOMY: MAJOR CONTEMPORARY THEMES).

See also:

colonialism and imperialism: classic texts; free trade and protection; global crisis of world capitalism; global liberalism; import substitution and export-orientated industrialization; international political economy: major contemporary themes

Selected references

Amin, S. (1970) *L'accumulation à l'echelle mondiale*, Paris: Anthropos; trans. *Accumulation on a World Scale*, New York: Monthly Review Press, 1974.

Balassa, B. et al. (1971) *The Structure of Protection in Developing Countries*, Baltimore, MD: Johns Hopkins University Press.

Emmanuel, A. (1969) *Unequal Exchange: A Study of the Imperialism of Trade*, New York: Monthly Review Press, 1972.

Krueger, A. (1978) *Liberalization Attempts and Consequences*, Cambridge, MA: Ballinger.

Lewis, W.A. (1954) "Economic Development with Unlimited Supplies of Labor," *Manchester School of Economic and Social Studies* 22 (May): 139–91.

Norman, Neville R. (1996) "A General Post Keynesian Theory of Protection," *Journal of Post Keynesian Economics* 18(4): 509–31.

Nurkse, R. (1952) "Some International Aspects of the Problem of Economic Development," *American Economic Review* 42(2): 571–83.

Ohlin, B. (1935) *Interregional and International Trade*, Cambridge, MA: Harvard University Press.

Prasch, Robert E. (1996) "Reassessing the Theory of Comparative Advantage," *Review of Political Economy* 8(1): 37–55.

World Bank (1991) *World Development Report 1991: The Challenge of Development*, New York: Oxford University Press.

ROBERTO PATRICIO KORZENIEWICZ

competition and the average rate of profit

Competition is the struggle between different capitals to control a larger proportion of the socially produced surplus value. Viewed in this sense, it is an important element in Marxist political economy. Industrial competition includes intra-industrial and inter-industrial competition.

Transfer of surplus value

Competition is conditioned by the relationship between capital and labor, and therefore the consequences for capitalism are contradictory. The Marxist vision of competition is that it is a war between capitals, which is impossible to avoid and in which there are frequent casualties. Competition itself is not the source of surplus value, but competition enables more profit to be realized by more productive firms through surplus being transferred from less to more productive units of production.

Marx observes that increases in productivity strengthen capitalism but simultaneously impose insuperable limitations on it. The most discussed aspects of Marx's theory of competition appear in Volume III of *Das Kapital* when he analyses capital as a whole (production and circulation and the unity of the two). Here he is interested in the transformation of surplus value into profit, and other phenomena characteristic of the redistribution of surplus value between different kind of capitals (industrial, financial and commercial). Nevertheless there are important aspects in all of the volumes of *Das Kapital* which are necessary for the elaboration of a theory of competition.

General law

In Volume I of *Das Kapital* Marx states that, in order to be able to dominate the labor force, capital goods must increase at a rate greater than the rate of increase of the labor force. Marx called this an increase in the COMPOSITION OF CAPITAL. It is a basic element of the "general law of capitalist accumulation." In this law, Marx states that ACCUMULATION and competition have the consequence that social capital is concentrated in fewer hands. If capital increased more rapidly than the labor force without at the same time increasing productivity, capitalism would be a regressive form of production. Capital seeks opportunities for unlimited growth. Therefore it must unceasingly raise productivity or, which is the same, decrease the labor value incorporated into its products. "Accumulate! Accumulate!" is an imperative imposed on capital, even though the capitalists or their representatives may not be fully conscious of their motivation or its consequences.

Processes of competition

When the same products are sold at the same price, the more efficient companies are rewarded and the less efficient ones are punished. Thus, differences in efficiency are translated into differences in the rates of profit within industries. Higher rates of profit lead to growth greater than that of the industry in general, and oblige the businesses that have fallen behind to raise their productivity or disappear. Both factors contribute to a rise in the average level of productivity in the industry. This is an important aspect of competition: the tendency to reduce the amount of time necessary for production (Weeks 1981: 32).

Competition also occurs between different industries. Expansion takes place through a takeover of a completely new area of production. When a given industry wishes to have greater control over its costs, and hence increase its profits, it puts itself through a process of vertical and/or horizontal integration. Its expansion is not limited only to other businesses in the same sector; it expands into any area where an opportunity exists. Marx, like most economists, considers that these processes result in a greater homogeneity of the rates of profit between different industries. The prices at which this process could be carried out would be prices of production. Marx also maintains in Volume III of *Das Kapital* that those industries where some of the means of production are not themselves produced (such as agriculture or oil extraction) would enjoy a higher rate of profit. This is because even the least efficient producer would obtain the average rate of profit. This is another important contribution for competition theory, the Marxian theory of rent.

A series of important studies exists for the analysis of inter-industrial competition. Nikaido (1983) showed, using a qualitative analysis of differential equations, that the process of adjustment toward production prices is locally unstable. These findings cast doubt on the validity of using the concept of "prices of production" in either theoretical or empirical investigation. The problem is particularly serious for the Sraffian and Marxist theorists. However, Duménil and Lévy (1987) and other economists responded with an analysis which showed that the adjustment process could be locally stable in the case of *circulating capital*.

Concentration of capital

The third aspect of the Marxist theory of competition which is proposed by some of his followers is related to the Marxist idea of the concentration of capital. This states that, as capitalism develops, the severity of the competition diminishes and hence some of its defects disappear. However, as the economy became dominated by monopolies, the economic crises, characterized by sudden interruptions of production and a corresponding increase in unemployment, would evolve into stagnation. With less competition, the law of the FALLING RATE OF PROFIT TENDENCY would be transformed into the law of growing ECONOMIC SURPLUS. This, however, would not translate into greater growth because of the limits imposed by consumption (see Baran and Sweezy 1965).

Empirical analysis

The study of competition has given rise to a variety of empirical investigations. Duménil *et al.* (1992) have shown that the rate of profit has diminished in the United States for a very long period as a result of a rise in the organic composition of capital. Another area of empirical work is that on the tendency toward equality in rates of profit between different industries. It has been found that the greater the concentration of industry, the higher the rate of profit (Sherman 1991) although there are also findings which contradict this (Semmler 1984).

See also:

labor theory of value; monopoly capitalism; transformation problem; value foundation of price

Selected references

Baran, P. and Sweezy, Paul M. (1965) *Monopoly Capital*, New York: Monthly Review Press.

Duménil, G. and Lévy, D. (1987) "The Dynamics of Competition: A Restoration of the Classical Analysis," *Cambridge Journal of Economics* 11(2): 133–64.

Duménil, G., Glick, M. and Lévy, D. (1992) "Stages in the Development of US Capitalism: Trends in Profitability since the Civil War," in Fred Moseley and Edward N. Wolff (eds), *International Perspectives on Profitability and Accumulation*, Brookfield, VT and Aldershot: Edward Elgar.

Glick, Mark (1994) "Competition, Antitrust and Beyond," in Philip Arestis and Malcolm Sawyer (eds), *The Elgar Companion to Radical Political Economy*, Brookfield, VT and Aldershot: Edward Elgar.

Nikaido, H. (1983) "Marx on Competition," *Zeitschrift für Nationalökonomie* 43(4): 337–62.

Semmler, W. (1984) *Competition, Monopoly and Differential Profit Rates*, New York: Columbia University Press.

Sherman, Howard (1991) *The Business Cycle: Growth and Crisis Under Capitalism*, Princeton, NJ: Princeton University Press.

Weeks, John (1981) *Capital and Exploitation*, Princeton, NJ: Princeton University Press.

ALEJANDRO VALLE BAEZA

competition in Sraffian political economy

While mainstream economics deals explicitly with "competition," the same is not true for Sraffa's analysis. Nevertheless this concept plays a central role in SRAFFIAN POLITICAL ECONOMY. Thanks to some contributions of various authors subsequent to the publication of Sraffa's *Production of Commodities by Means of Commodities* in 1960, it is possible to single out some guidelines on the meaning and the working of competition in Sraffian economics. In what follows we will begin the argument in terms of a comparison between the notions of competition in neoclassical general equilibrium analysis and in Sraffian analysis in order to illustrate the peculiarities of the latter.

Neoclassical perfect competition

In standard microeconomic theory one talks of "perfect" competition in order to describe: (1) the producer's choice of the mix of inputs that minimizes the cost of production of a given output; (2) the seller's choice of the quantity of output to be sold that maximizes the profit; and (3) the process that drives each firm to select an output level that minimizes the average cost of production. For a firm whose technology can be expressed by a smooth production function, $y_t = f(\mathbf{x}_{t-1})$, where y_t is the output at time t and $\mathbf{x}_{t-1}$ the vector of inputs required at time $t-1$, perfect competition operates in such a way that the following equalities hold:

$$\frac{f_i}{f_j} = \frac{p_{i_{t-1}}}{p_{j_{t-1}}} \quad (1)$$

$$p_{y_t} = C'(\mathbf{p}_{t-1}, y_t) \quad (2)$$

$$p_{y_t} = \min_{y_t} \frac{C(\mathbf{p}_{t-1}, y_t)}{y_t} \quad (3)$$

where f_i and $p_{i_{t-1}}$ are the marginal product and the price of input i at time t; p_{y_t} is the price of output at time t; and $C(\mathbf{p}_{t-1}, y_t)$ is the total cost function (the temporal element has been introduced to settle the analysis in an inter-temporal context, which is the most appropriate to compare classical and neoclassical approaches).

Conditions (1)–(3) and Sraffian analysis

Condition (1) does have a correspondence in Sraffian economics: it concerns the problem of the choice of technique. Also, in Sraffian analysis it is assumed that for each commodity competition compels producers to adopt cost-minimizing processes. It has been shown that this behavior drives the system on the wage–profit frontier. In other words, for each given value of one of the two distributive variables, for example the wage rate, it permits the obtaining of the highest profit rate (see, for example, Pasinetti 1977: ch. 6; Kurz and Salvadori 1995: chaps 3, 5).

Condition (2) does not find a correspondence in Sraffian political economy. This condition concerns the rather controversial issue of the relationship between prices and the scale of production. In Sraffian political economy, it has been explicitly formulated only in the literature on "gravitation," to represent the adjustment process towards long-run equilibrium (see GRAVITATION AND CONVERGENCE).

Condition (3) is a long-run equilibrium condition, as it is the result of the entry/exit process of new firms in the market attracted by extra profits/losses. Here the Sraffian notion of competition departs from the neoclassical notion. Condition (3) has a correspondence in Sraffian analysis in the equation that determines the prices of production:

$$\mathbf{p} = (1+r)\mathbf{Ap} + w\mathbf{a}_0 \quad (4)$$

where $\mathbf{A}$ is the technical coefficients matrix, $\mathbf{a}_0$

is the labor input vector, r is the rate of profit and w is the wage rate.

However, two qualifications are necessary. First, in Sraffa's price equation (4) the remuneration of capital, the "profit," appears explicitly while in the cost function $C(\mathbf{p}, y)$ it is included among the other costs of production. Second, in equation (4) only one technique has been considered, represented by matrix ($\mathbf{A}$, $\mathbf{a}_0$); this technique can be assumed to be the result of a previous cost-minimizing choice.

Convergence to long-run equilibrium

At this point we can observe that equations (3) and (4) both impose an equalization between price and cost, and in both cases this is the long-run outcome of competition. In traditional microeconomics, it is the entry/exit mechanism of firms in response to the presence of extra profits that enforces this long-run equilibrium. In the Sraffian framework, the central force that drives the system towards the long-run equilibrium is the competition among capitalists in looking for the most profitable investment in the various productive sectors.

Let $\mathbf{p}^*$ be a production price system, i.e. a solution for $\mathbf{p}$ in equation (4). For any given level of w, it represents the price system that ensures the prevalence of a uniform profit rate among all sectors. If at a certain date t, a different price system, $\mathbf{p}_t$, should prevail, the resulting sectoral profit rates would be no more uniform. It would thus be profitable for capitalists to move capital from low profit rate sectors towards high profit rate sectors. This intersectoral capital mobility should decrease the supply of the former group of commodities and increase the latter. The consequent movements of market prices that change in the opposite direction, driven by supply and demand forces, should engender a long-run gravitation of the system toward or around its long-run equilibrium.

The working of this process has been recently challenged in some works, in which the classical competitive process has been formally described by means of dynamic systems. Since then, a quite large number of works has appeared in which convergence toward the classical long-run equilibrium has been proved under economically meaningful conditions. Good surveys of this literature can be found in Boggio (1992) and Duménil and Lévy (1993).

The other element that differentiates the two approaches is the fact that, in equation (3), the equalization between prices and costs is realized by the price systems of two different periods: $\mathbf{p}_t$ and $\mathbf{p}_{t-1}$. In equation (4) it is realized by the same system of prices, $\mathbf{p}^*$. This in fact is the main difference between inter-temporal general equilibrium prices and production prices. The underlying reason lies in the fact that, in Sraffian long-run equilibrium, the composition of capital has reached its long-run configuration; that is, capital goods are exactly in the proportions required to produce the final output. In neoclassical general equilibrium this is not the case, as initial endowments of capital goods are given exogenously. These discrepancies in the structure of capital affect the price system, which has to change from time to time to permit the equalization of prices to costs.

In classical long-run configuration, this equalization takes place together with (and just thanks to) the adjustments in the composition of capital in response to profitability differentials. It has also been shown (see Dana et al. 1989) that, under certain regularity conditions regarding consumers' preferences, if one considers an infinite temporal horizon, the sequence of inter-temporal general equilibrium prices converges toward a stationary configuration, the production price system. When time tends toward infinity, the influence of initial endowments tends to disappear.

Conclusion

The position of economists on all these topics is not at all uniform. Each school of thought tends to affirm the superiority of its own approach. Bliss (1975) and Hahn (1982) provide examples on the neoclassical side and Duménil and Lévy (1985) are on the classical side. An intermediate position is presented in Bidard (1991: part 3) (see also PRICE THEORY, SRAFFIAN).

Selected references

Bidard, C. (1991) *Prix, reproduction, rareté*, Paris: Dunod.
Bliss, C.J. (1975) *Capital Theory and the Distribution of Income*, Amsterdam: North Holland.
Boggio, L. (1992) "Production Prices and Dynamic Stability: Results and Open Questions," *The Manchester School* 69(3): 264–94.
Dana, R.A., Florenzano, M., Le Van, C. and Lévy, D. (1989) "Production Prices and General Equilibrium Prices: A Long-Run Property of a Leontief Economy," *Journal of Mathematical Economics* 18(3): 263–80.
Duménil, G. and Lévy, D. (1985) "The Classicals and the NeoClassicals: A Rejoinder to Frank Hahn," *Cambridge Journal of Economics* 9(4): 327–45.
—— (1993) *The Economics of the Profit Rate: Competition, Crisis, and Historical Tendencies in Capitalism*, Aldershot: Edward Elgar.
Hahn, F. (1982) "The Neo-Ricardians," *Cambridge Journal of Economics* 6(4): 353–74.
Kurz, H. and Salvadori, N. (1995) *Theory of Production*, Cambridge: Cambridge University Press.
Pasinetti, L. (1977) *Lectures on the Theory of Production*, London: Macmillan.
Sraffa, P. (1960) *Production of Commodities by Means of Commodities. Prelude to a Critique of Economic Theory*, Cambridge: Cambridge University Press.

ENRICO BELLINO

composition of capital

Introduction

That the "composition of capital" might vary both between industries or departments and over time is of crucial importance to a number of elements in MARX's economic (and social) ideas. In discussing the tendency for labor supply to outstrip labor demand, he places great emphasis on the substitution of capital for labor and also on what would today be called "labor-saving technical change." Movement over time in the composition of capital also figures prominently in his discussion of the rate of surplus value and of the rate of profit, and especially the tendency of the latter to fall even if the former is constant over time.

The composition of capital plays a pivotal role in Marx's discussion of the relationship between values and prices, particularly in his attempt to demonstrate that not only were deviations of prices from values to be expected but also that these very deviations were systematic and predictable (see TRANSFORMATION PROBLEM). Indeed Marx posited, correctly, that these deviations were related to differences in the organic composition of capital between industries (see Dixon 1988: ch. 5 for further discussion). The distinction between constant and variable capital (especially when seen in terms of embodied labor) also informs Marx's discussion of alienation and his view that "in proportion as capital accumulates, the situation of the worker, be his payment high or low, must grow worse" (Marx 1867: 799).

It was Roger Garaudy who most eloquently made the case for regarding Marx's *Das Kapital* as being, in its essence, an extension of his *Economic and Philosophic Manuscripts* of 1844. He writes:

> the relation between dead and living labor, between *being* and *having*, is the profound law of capitalist society and its development. The more *having* increases in the hands of the capitalist, the more the *being* of the worker, who is the author of it, is impoverished. It is this that Marx proves in *Capital*, under the name of the *general law of capitalist accumulation*.
> (Garaudy 1967: 60ff)

Value and technical dimensions

Marx distinguished between the "value composition of capital" and the "technical composition of capital." The clearest exposition of what he means by these terms may be found in Chapter 25 ("The General Law of Capitalist

Accumulation") of Volume I of *Das Kapital*. He writes:

> The composition of capital is to be understood in a two-fold sense. On the side of value, it is determined by the proportion in which it is divided into constant capital or value of the means of production, and variable capital or value of labor-power, the sum total of wages. On the side of material, as it functions in the process of production, all capital is divided into means of production and living labor-power. This latter composition is determined by the relation between the mass of the means of production employed, on the one hand, and the mass of labor necessary for their employment on the other. I call the former the value-composition, the latter the technical composition of capital. Between the two there is a strict correlation. To express this, I call the value-composition of capital, in so far as it is determined by its technical composition and mirrors the changes of the latter, the organic composition of capital.
> (Marx 1867: 762)

Although in this context it is clear that Marx means by the term "organic composition of capital," the ratio of constant to variable capital [c/v], at other times it would seem that he had in mind the ratio of constant to total capital [$c/(c+v)$] (Sweezy 1970: 66). Fortunately, the two are related in a systematic way. It is in Chapter 25 that Marx promulgates his "law of the progressive growth of the constant part of capital in comparison with the variable part" (Marx 1867: 773).

Concern about Marx's analysis

Many writers have expressed concern with Marx's analysis of the composition of capital. These concerns have arisen both in the context of disputes over the transformation of values into prices, and in questioning the logic behind certain predictions made by Marx. One, relatively unimportant, issue concerns the measurement of the numerator in the ratio of c to v, and in particular whether flows or stocks of capital are the relevant variable (Robinson 1942).

A second issue concerns the relationship between technological progress and the composition of capital. It is easy to show that if technological progress is capital-saving, the ratio need not move in the direction postulated by Marx in Volume I of *Das Kapital* (see Blaug 1960; Heertje 1972). Essentially this is because, as Marx himself realized (1867: 774 and elsewhere), improvements in labor productivity reduce the embodied labor content of both the means of production and workers' consumption.

However, technological progress may affect sectors differently. It may be that the ratio of produced inputs to labor in physical units tends to rise, while the labor value of produced inputs and labor power itself will tend to fall. Although this is unmistakably a rise in the technical composition of capital, in order to predict what will happen to the organic or value composition we have to know whether the second effect outweighs the first. Marx believed that it would not, and that the technical and organic compositions would both rise over time. He had no warrant for believing this.

A third area of difficulty arises once we put Marx's ideas into "Sraffian" terms. If we do, it becomes immediately evident that there will be no simple mapping from the technical to the organic composition. Indeed, some would go further and join with Steedman (1981) in questioning the necessity to work in terms of a value composition, if we wish to model macroeconomic or distributional phenomena. At the same time, there is the empirical issue of whether value and technical compositions are in fact highly correlated.

Empirical measurement

There have been very few attempts to compare movements over time in the "technical composition" with a measure of the "organic composition" based, as it should be, on embodied labor content. Those studies which have been undertaken are based on information on direct and indirect labor requirements, obtained from input–output tables. In practice, a common measure of the composition of capital is the value of intermediate inputs plus depreciation relative to the value of workers' wages or workers' consumption. Studies differ also in whose wages or consumption they include. Some include all wage and salary earners, but most include only production workers.

In his study of Puerto Rico over the period 1948–63, Wolff finds that the technical composition increased slightly more than twofold while the organic composition fell by about one-quarter. In his study of data for the US economy over the period 1947–81, Wolff finds that the technical composition increased just under twofold while the organic (value) composition remained unchanged (Wolff 1992: 104). In one sub-period (1958–67), Wolff finds that the two moved in opposite directions, with the technical composition rising by 27 percent and the value composition falling by 12 percent. Shaikh and Tonak in their important study are critical of the approach used by Wolff. Adopting a different methodology, they find that the organic composition increased by around 23 percent over the period 1948–89 in the USA, while the "orthodox counterpart, the ratio of intermediate inputs to wages" fell by 12 percent (Shaikh and Tonak 1994: 121).

See also:

falling rate of profit tendency; labor theory of value; transformation problem; turnover time of capital

Selected references

Blaug, M. (1960) "Technical Change and Marxian Economics," *Kyklos* 13: 495–512.
Dixon, R. (1988) *Production, Distribution and Value*, Brighton: Wheatsheaf Books.
Garaudy, Roger (1967) *Karl Marx: The Evolution of His Thought*, New York: International Publishers.
Heertje, A. (1972) "An Essay on Marxian Economics," *Schweizerische Zeitschrift für Volkswirtschaft und Statistik* 108: 33–45; repr. in M. Howard and J. King (eds), 1976, *The Economics of Marx*, Harmondsworth: Penguin, 219–32.
Marx, Karl (1867) *Das Kapital*, Volume I published as *Capital Volume 1*, Harmondsworth: Penguin, 1976.
Robinson, Joan (1942) *An Essay on Marxian Economics*, London; Macmillan.
Shaikh, A. and Tonak, E. (1994) *Measuring the Wealth of Nations*, New York: Cambridge University Press.
Steedman, I. (1981) "Ricardo, Marx, Sraffa," in I. Steedman *et al.*, *The Value Controversy*, London: Verso, 11–19.
Sweezy, P. (1970) *The Theory of Capitalist Development*, New York: Monthly Review Press.
Wolff, E. (1992) "Structural Change and the Movement of the Rate of Profit in the USA," in F. Mosley and E. Wolff (eds), *International Perspectives on Profitability and Accumulation*, Aldershot: Edward Elgar, 93–121.

ROBERT DIXON

conspicuous consumption and emulation

Conspicuous consumption and emulation are important concepts in institutionalist theories of social control and social criticism. Conspicuous consumption also involves technical implications in orthodox demand theory, consumer choice theory, welfare theory and the consumption function. These concepts were originally analysed by Thorstein VEBLEN in *The Theory of the Leisure Class* (1899). Much consumption is in order to obtain some kind of gratification or to avoid some kind of deprivation. Such consumption is usually thought to yield something internal to the individual consumer because of some intrinsic characteristic of the commodity consumed. This is consumption for personal satisfaction, an inner-directed process. Conspicuous consumption, on the other hand, is an outer-directed process and is done to impress others or to avoid condemnation by others. Conspicuous consumption is driven through emulation rather than by internal satisfaction derived from intrinsic characteristics of the commodity consumed. Emulation itself is the attempt to gain prestige in the eyes of others by displaying a higher than average ability to pay.

Though the technical implications are of less importance than the radical substance, those implications warrant a brief discussion before moving on to more important matters. Purely technical implications of conspicuous consumption and emulation include the bandwagon and snob effects in consumer choice theory, and the sometimes incorrectly analysed characteristics of a "Veblen good" in demand theory. With a Veblen good, utility to a consumer is assumed to be a positive function of price. This, however, does not mean that demand for such a commodity is upward sloping, since the budget constraint still yields the expected negative slope for the demand curve.

Interdependent utility functions

A far more important implication of conspicuous consumption and emulation for demand theory has to do with interdependent consumer utility functions. In orthodox neoclassical economics, utility functions are independent so the market demand for a commodity is obtained by simply adding up the quantity demanded by each consumer in the market at each possible price. Hence, market demand is the summation of individual demands. However, if the utility of one consumer is affected by the consumption of other consumers, as it is in conspicuous consumption and emulation, then market demand cannot be the summation of individual demands because each individual demand itself becomes dependent on other individual demands. A simple adding up is no longer possible when conspicuous consumption and emulation make consumer utility functions, and therefore their individual demands, interdependent.

Demonstration effect

The "demonstration effect" ("keeping up with the Joneses") is another important implication of conspicuous consumption and emulation which applies to the consumption function. A puzzle that absorbs much attention in consumption function theory is the apparent divergence between long-run and short-run consumption functions. In the short-run functions, frequently constructed from cross-sectional budget studies, the average propensity to consume declines as income rises. Such a decline implies a rising average propensity to save over time and a growing tendency toward secular stagnation unless investment or some other form of autonomous expenditure rises fast enough to absorb the rising pool of savings. But in long-run consumption functions, frequently constructed from time-series data, the average propensity to consume is generally found not to decline, so as *not* to imply a growing tendency toward secular stagnation.

The demonstration effect (linked to the relative income hypothesis of Duesenberry) easily explains the divergence by pointing out that new consumer commodities are continually being introduced into the high-budget consumer standards of the rich. Such commodities then quickly become necessary consumer goods, even for consumers who are not rich, through the demonstration effect, which is largely due to emulation. As a result, the short-run consumption function keeps shifting upwards over time as the purchase of more and more consumer goods becomes necessary to maintain good repute or to avoid bad repute in the eyes of other consumers. The continued upward shifting of the short-run function keeps the long-run average propensity to consume from falling over time. If the demonstration effect were to weaken, however, secular stagnation could set in as income rose over time. Then, massive income redistribution (egalitarianism) and/or socialization of investment (socialism) would be required to absorb the rising pool of savings.

Game theory

Conspicuous consumption and emulation have

a profoundly significant implication in welfare theory. The implication is hinted at but not developed in the demonstration effect. At the heart of orthodox economics is the belief that more is better. More commodities are better than less and can always be used to compensate the losers from economic changes that are Pareto optimal. In GAME THEORY terms, more consumption is a positive-sum game. It increases total consumer welfare. However, with conspicuous consumption and emulation, consuming more commodities may not be better. More consumption is a zero-sum game; it leaves total consumer welfare unchanged. Conspicuous consumption driven by emulation is an attempt to obtain prestige by displaying the ability to pay more than the average. But, not everybody can be above average; for those who are above average, there are also those who are below average. Those who measure up by consuming above the average, gain; but, those who fail to measure up by consuming below the average, lose. Since the sum of the gainers and the losers has to equal the average, and since the gain from being average is zero, the sum of the conspicuous consumption game itself is zero. Under some conditions – quite reasonable ones at that – the sum can even turn negative (Dugger 1985).

Social control processes

Saving the most radical and the most avoided dimension for last, conspicuous consumption and emulation serve key roles in elitist social control processes. First, they enforce a strong work ethic, particularly in the lower and working classes. Second, they replace consumer sovereignty with Galbraith's revised sequence (see GALBRAITH'S CONTRIBUTION TO POLITICAL ECONOMY). Third, they facilitate the manipulation of the values, meanings and beliefs of underlings.

The work ethic, particularly for those whose income is below the average, is reinforced by conspicuous consumption because it drives them to try to work harder and longer in order to get more income to spend on conspicuous consumption. A less than average ability to pay becomes a deprivation and, since ECONOMIC GROWTH raises the average ability to pay, growth never eases the work burden. Instead, it raises the level of expenditure required to avoid deprivation.

The revised sequence, explained by John Kenneth Galbraith in his book *The New Industrial State*, which appeared in 1967, replaces the autonomous demand that originates with consumer preferences with an induced demand that originates with producer advertising. Such advertising plays on the emulative pressures we all face and manipulates us into engaging in ever higher levels of conspicuous consumption.

The elitist manipulation of values, beliefs and meanings is facilitated by conspicuous consumption and emulation because they redirect our attention, respect and aspiration toward the elite and away from our families and friends (not only in the developed nations but also in the less developed). The intensification of our drive to rise into higher social and economic levels makes us eager to accept the values, beliefs and meanings emanating from those levels. In plain English, it makes us easily duped by elitist ideology.

Conclusion

In conclusion, the innocuous implications of conspicuous consumption and emulation have been incorporated as technical elaborations of mainstream economics without profoundly affecting the conservative nature of the mainstream. However, the less technical, more social and philosophical implications of conspicuous consumption and emulation are profoundly threatening to the mainstream.

See also:

advertising and the sales effort; corporate hegemony; institutional political economy: major contemporary themes; post-Keynesian theory of choice; producer and consumer sovereignty

Selected references

Dugger, W.M. (1985) "The Analytics of Consumption Externalities," *Review of Social Economy* 43(October).

—— (1989) "Emulation: An Institutional Theory of Value Formation," *Review of Social Economy* 47(Summer).

WILLIAM M. DUGGER

CONSUMPTION: *see* conspicuous consumption and emulation

contradictions

In modern political economy, a contradiction is an endogenously generated dysfunctional process resulting from the interaction between a positive and a negative aspect of an economic system. The positive and negative aspects (a) are inherent in the workings of the economy, (b) are necessary for each other, (c) contribute to dynamic long-term evolution and development, (d) usually heighten the cyclical amplitude of the economy and/or (e) contribute to the periodic trend toward structural crisis.

Mao Zedong on contradiction

The notion of "contradiction" is a part of the DIALECTICAL METHOD. Mao Zedong (1937) wrote an important essay entitled "On Contradiction," where he contrasted dialectical and mechanical thinking. Mechanical thinking sees things as being isolated, separate, static and one-sided, where change is external in origin and where quantitative change is privileged over qualitative change. This is a similar method to that of NEOCLASSICAL ECONOMICS. Dialectical thinking, on the other hand, examines internal relations, the interaction between processes, how internal contradictions are the essence of change and development and how quantitative changes can become so pronounced as to constitute qualitative changes. This is part of the POLITICAL ECONOMY approach.

Mao recognized that not all changes are internal in nature, that external factors (such as chance events) can influence the course of internal processes, and that processes and contradictions change over time. To study a phenomenon such as capitalism, he recognized that it is necessary to examine all sides of its tendencies and motion, and not to restrict analysis to, for example, the market by ignoring the linkage of the market to production and the reproduction of social relationships. There are many contradictions, whether primary or secondary, and they are interrelated in the dynamic process of change and motion.

Marxist political economy

In Marxist political economy, the primary contradiction of CAPITALISM is usually seen as being between the revolutionary nature of the forces of production (usually seen as the positive aspect) and the relatively static and bounded social relations of production (the negative aspect) (Glyn 1990; MARXIST POLITICAL ECONOMY: HISTORY). On the one hand, capitalism is the most revolutionary system yet seen in the promotion of new TECHNOLOGY and PRODUCTIVITY, one which enhances output and potential human welfare; but on the other hand, adequate demand for the realization of profit is limited by the institutionalized conflict between capital and labor in the spheres of production and distribution. When capital is able to substitute capital for labor, the sale of output and the realization of profit may be inhibited through inadequate effective demand; and when labor is able to increase its share of national income during business cycle upswings, profits may be similarly squeezed. The organized resistance of labor to capital is a continual threat to capital's profitability, yet the capital–labor nexus is a defining feature of capitalism.

Schumpeter

Joseph SCHUMPETER, in *Capitalism, Socialism*

and Democracy, published in 1942, saw the major contradiction of capitalism to be between the incessant development of the productive forces and the trend to greater concentration of production in the large corporation. The dynamic force of capitalism is the competitive spirit of the entrepreneur, that unconventional individual who challenges the establishment through the commercial application of new products, processes, markets, corporate structures and raw materials. Temporary monopoly profits are created, and other firms adopt these new methods as part of the dynamics of the business cycle. Schumpeter recognized that oligopoly profits become the established practices of economic life as large-scale industry and economies of scale create private bureaucracies bent on institutionalizing the innovation process. Thus, the very nature of capitalism challenges its central dynamic – entrepreneurial competition – and the predictable workings of the large corporation may lead to the possibility of a type of "socialist" system devoid of the instabilities of the old system.

Modern political economy

In modern political economy, a systemic contradiction of capitalism is related to Karl Polanyi's notion of the DISEMBEDDED ECONOMY (see Stanfield 1995). We know that capitalism is the most revolutionary system ever in the development of the productive forces and productivity; but inextricably related to this is the destruction of social safety nets, the family, pre-capitalist relations and the environment, as capitalism seeks change and dynamic growth. Capitalism necessarily engages in creative destruction, expanding on the world scale, destroying barriers in its way and confronting every obstacle in the search for markets, productivity improvements and profitability. In doing so, it tends to destroy institutions, or, more generally, social and natural capital, a significant amount of which is necessary for long-term profitability and growth of capitalism and, indeed, of all socioeconomic systems.

Recently, many political economists have sought to comprehend more specifically the institutional contradictions of economic systems. This is especially the case for the REGULATION APPROACH and the SOCIAL STRUCTURES OF ACCUMULATION analysis. The building and decaying of institutions are said to be critical to the pattern of accumulation and decline over the long wave. Institutions that are suitable for capitalism provide the foundation for relative stability in the long term, but eventually the contradictory relationships embedded in the institutions become manifest and the rate of growth declines. Contradictions are endogenously structured in the institutions and adversely affect economic performance as the potential of the institutions become exhausted.

For instance, one of the central pillars of accumulation in the 1945–70 era was US hegemony in production, commerce, finance and warfare which provided leadership and stability for the capitalist system (see HEGEMONY IN THE WORLD ECONOMY). However, as other players copied US technology and commerce and as the USA lost the Vietnam War, it was unable or unwilling to provide the same degree of leadership into the 1970s, 1980s and 1990s. This promoted uncertainty and thus adversely affected investment (see Arrighi 1982: 60). Conceptually similar contradictions were inherent in other social structures of accumulation, which led to their decline (and potential reconstruction).

Another important contradiction is that between industry and finance, about which Marx, Veblen, Keynes and Schumpeter (and their modern followers) have written much. Industry and finance are two central elements of capitalism. While to some degree they complement each other, and thereby enhance growth and ACCUMULATION, there are limits to capital relating to the institutionalized conflict between them. Industry provides the economic surplus which forms the basis of the financial system (either realized or expected), since economic surplus can be distributed from industrial profit to interest (and rent). With a rising surplus, during the middle phases of economic boom few problems arise, especially as credit expansion in turn expands industrial capital. Some degree of symbiotic unity is thus apparent. However, the credit and financial system poses sharp limits to industrial capital as interest rates rise during the boom in the cycle and thus crowd out industrial profits; as a failure to repay credit sets up chains of bankruptcy throughout industry; and as speculative bubbles in the stock and other markets lead to a sudden collapse of asset prices which adversely affects industry (see SPECULATIVE BUBBLES AND FUNDAMENTAL VALUES).

The trend in modern political economy toward a holistic study of institutions, qualitative processes and human relationships reinforces the notion that there are multiple contradictions, which overdetermine each other in the complex workings of economic systems (see Resnick and Wolff 1994). In other words, none of the sites of capitalism, such as the state, the family, production, finance or the world economy, should be given special consideration a priori in the contradictory dynamics of growth and socioeconomic reproduction. A detailed historical analysis of the dynamic motion of systems is necessary in order to ascertain the nature and trends of the contradictions. While the contradictions are endogenous, they exist both within and between sub-systems (see Pienkos 1986), while some are systemic (see Parkin 1982). Evolutionary changes occur in the nature and form of the relationships and contradictions through long historical time.

Further research

There is scope for a series of major studies into the nature of contradictions within economic systems. Such studies need to provide a taxonomy of the different types of contradictions; how they link to institutions, business cycles, long waves and phases of evolution; how the contradictions themselves have changed over time; and a thorough critical analysis and reconstruction of the notion of contradiction itself. Much work lies ahead.

See also:

business cycle theories; circular and cumulative causation; determinism and overdetermination; entropy, negentropy and the laws of thermodynamics; evolution and coevolution; falling rate of profit tendency; holistic method; long waves of economic growth and development; secular crisis; uncertainty

Selected references

Arrighi, Giovanni (1982) "A Crisis of Hegemony," in Samir Amin, Giovanni Arrighi, Andre Gunder Frank and Immanuel Wallerstein, *Dynamics of Global Crisis*, London: Macmillan.

Bell, Daniel (1976) *The Cultural Contradictions of Capitalism*, New York: Basic Books.

Bowles, Samuel and Gintis, Herbert (1986) *Democracy and Capitalism: Property, Community, and the Contradictions of Modern Social Thought*, London: Routledge & Kegan Paul, esp. ch. 4.

Center for Political Ecology (1995) *The Second Contradiction of Capitalism: Debates*, Santa Cruz: CNS/CPE.

Glyn, Andrew (1990) "Contradictions of Capitalism," in John Eatwell, Murray Milgate and Peter Newman, *The New Palgrave: Marxian Economics*, London: Macmillan.

Mao Zedong (1937) "On Contradiction," *Five Essays in Philosophy*, Beijing, 1977.

Offe, Claus (1984) *Contradictions of the Welfare State*, ed. John Keane, London: Hutchinson.

Parkin, Frank (1982) "System Contradiction and Political Transformation," in Anthony Giddens and David Held (eds), *Class, Power, and Conflict: Classical and Contemporary Debates*, London: Macmillan.

Pienkos, Andrew (1986) "Organizational Contradiction and Policy Inertia in Yugoslav Institutional Evolution," *Journal of Economic Issues* 20(2).

Resnick, Stephen A. and Wolff, Richard D. (1994) "Rethinking Complexity in Economic Theory: The Challenge of Overdetermination," in Richard W. England (ed.), *Evolutionary Concepts in Contemporary Economics*, Ann Arbor, MI: University of Michigan Press.

Stanfield, James Ronald (1995) *Economics, Power and Culture: Essays in the Development of Radical Institutionalism*, New York: St Martin's Press.

PHILLIP ANTHONY O'HARA

conventions

A convention can be broadly defined as a self-actuating impulse to follow a previously adopted course of action. Conventions are essential to handle the intricacies of everyday life, and many of our decisions are governed by conventions over which there is only occasional intervention by conscious deliberation. Conventions endow us with a manageable mechanism for retaining a pattern of behavior without having to engage continuously in global calculations involving vast amounts of information. They possess a stable and inert quality, thus tending to sustain and pass on their basic features through time. Conventional behavior can be seen as a form of boundedly rational behavior (see RATIONALITY AND IRRATIONALITY), for it is a purposeful behavior that takes into account the cognitive limitations of the decision-maker – limitations of both knowledge and computational capacity.

Shared among different traditions within political economy is a discomfort with the reductionist way decision-making is dealt with in neoclassical theory, which sees maximizing behavior as the basic postulate in any meaningful economic analysis. A crucial presupposition in neoclassical theory is that individuals are able to have an accurate understanding of the circumstances they are in, and the options they face, and have the cognitive capabilities to assess the actual best option. Political economists, in turn, by stressing the limits of human cognitive capabilities to make decisions about an unknowable future, see action as the consequence of following habits or customs (Veblen 1919), conventions (Keynes 1937), rules of thumb (Cyert and March 1963), or routines (Nelson and Winter 1982).

Propensities and attitudes

Conventional behavior figures prominently in the writings of KEYNES and the post-Keynesians. Keynes's *General Theory of Employment, Interest and Money* (1936) is a detailed exploration of the logic of economic behavior under conditions of UNCERTAINTY, a situation to be distinguished from one of probabilistic risk. As the phenomenon of uncertainty is a persistent presence, this leads to the endogenous emergence of conventions that guide decision-making, especially that associated with real and financial ACCUMULATION. As Davis (1994) put it, an important dimension of Keynes's work is its emphasis upon the dispositional nature of behavior, conventions playing an important role in structuring the varying degrees to which psychological propensities and attitudes, such as propensities to consume and hold liquid assets, are manifest in different individuals.

Unemployment and effective demand

Keynes's argument regarding unemployment (see UNEMPLOYMENT AND UNDEREMPLOYMENT) ultimately relates to his concept of conventional behavior. Unemployment is explained by the inertial evolution of conventional attitudes regarding finance and the labor market. Income and employment are then determined by the level of effective demand that this state of affairs permits. The principle of effective demand, by way of the dependence of investment upon conventional attitudes toward liquidity and prospective yields, is thus to a significant degree detached from the logic of market forces. Indeed, the important role played by conventional behavior in the dynamics of the labor market has been recently taken up by the so-called "French conventions school" (*Revue économique* 1989; Orléan 1994).

Uncertainty and ignorance

In his famous reply to early critics of the *General Theory*, Keynes (1937) criticized orthodox analysis for wrongly reducing uncertainty to probabilistic risk. By uncertainty, Keynes did not mean merely to distinguish what is known for certain from what is only probable. Rather, he meant to distinguish what is known for certain from matters about which there is no scientific basis on which to form any calculable probability whatever ("we simply do not know" – ignorance prevails). Nevertheless, Keynes added, the necessity for making decisions compels economic actors to do their best to overlook such inevitable uncertainty. One major technique devised for the purpose is to fall back on the judgment of the rest of the world that is, perhaps, better informed. By endeavoring to conform with the behavior of the majority or the average, economic actors rely on conventional judgments.

Keynes saw behavior grounded on conventions as sensible in situations where the lack of complete knowledge about the course of events does not supply better reasons for acting. Once bounded rationality is introduced into the behavior of agents, conventional behavior can be seen as a sensible way of dealing with the intricacies of decision making. Therefore, such behavior implies that the presence of fundamental uncertainty does not necessarily generate chaotic dynamics or prevent economic theorizing. Keynes admitted that being based on so flimsy a foundation, conventional judgment is subject to sudden and violent changes. It endows the economic system with some degree of stability and thus predictability, however tenuous those might be. The more robust conventions and expectations are, the less tenuous will be the systemic stability generated by economic actors falling back on conventions.

Modern political economy

Even though Keynes and the post-Keynesians focus almost exclusively on the macroeconomic implications of given conventional behaviors, knowing how these get instituted and change over time is also a relevant issue to be addressed by political economists. Admittedly, Keynes believed that conventions may change precipitately in response to unanticipated shocks, while the FINANCIAL INSTABILITY HYPOTHESIS advanced by Minsky (1975) is based on the view that financial conventions change in such a way during a boom as to worsen the fragility of the system. However, there are increasing returns, so to speak, to greater cross-fertilization among the strands in political economy on these issues. In particular, the evolutionary and institutionalist approaches to institutional change and adjustment, in which changes in institutions and habits as well as routines play a pivotal role, certainly provide a natural framework for placing Keynes's insightful notion of conventional behavior in a broader perspective.

In Bianchi's (1990) interesting approach, for instance, changes in routines result from an endogenous process of learning through search and selection. In this evolutionary context, uncertainty becomes, positively, the source of innovation and change and not only, negatively, a source of limiting behavioral rules. In the same vein, some recent evolutionary discussions on organizational routines (for example, Cohen *et al.* 1995), in which routines are seen as emergent properties of the interaction of learning and adaptation processes, are worthy of careful attention as well.

See also:

animal spirits; business cycle theories; evolutionary economics: history; expectations; monetary theory of production

Selected references

Bianchi, Marina (1990) "The Unsatisfactoriness of Satisficing: From Bounded Rationality to Innovative Rationality," *Review of Political Economy* 2(2).

Cohen, Michael *et al.* (1995) "Routines and Other Recurring Action Patterns of Organizations: Contemporary Research Issues,"

Santa Fe Institute Working Paper, November.

Cyert, Richard and March, James (1963) *A Behavioral Theory of the Firm*, Englewood Cliffs, NJ: Prentice Hall.

Davis, John (1994) *Keynes's Philosophical Development*, Cambridge: Cambridge University Press.

Keynes, John Maynard (1937) "The General Theory of Employment," *The Quarterly Journal of Economics* (February); reprinted in *The Collected Works of John Maynard Keynes*, vol. XIV, London: Macmillan, for the Royal Economic Society, 1973.

Minsky, Hyman (1975) *John Maynard Keynes*, New York: Columbia University Press.

Nelson, Richard and Winter, Sidney (1982) *An Evolutionary Theory of Economic Change*, Cambridge, MA: Harvard University Press.

Orléan, André (1994) *Analyse économique des conventions*, Paris: Presses Universitaires de France.

Revue Économique (1989) "L'Économie des conventions" (special issue), 2(2).

Veblen, Thorstein (1919) *The Place of Science in Modern Civilization and Other Essays*, New Brunswick, NJ: Transaction Publishers, 1990.

GILBERTO TADEU LIMA

CONVERGENCE: *see* gravitation and convergence

core–periphery analysis

Early work of Prebisch and associates

A highly influential contribution to the development of this line of analysis was provided by Raul Prebisch (1950), through his work at the Economic Commission for Latin America (ECLA) of the United Nations. Prebisch began using the center–periphery metaphor in the mid-1940s to emphasize the unequal advantages being derived by rich and poor nations from their world economic linkages. Prebisch argued that these linkages were characterized by a deterioration in the terms of trade for the raw materials produced in peripheral countries, attributing this deterioration to (a) the low income elasticity of demand for raw materials, and (b) differences between center (or core) and peripheral countries in the organization of labor markets, wages and prices.

According to Prebisch, the deterioration in the terms of trade for the products of peripheral nations was driven in part by differences in the relative income elasticities of manufactured and unprocessed commodities (with demand for manufactures rising faster than for raw materials). In addition, Prebisch noted recent changes in the international economy, as the United States (the new hegemonic power of the postwar period) tended to import relatively less than England (its predecessor).

Center nations were also characterized by the prevalence of oligopolistic enterprises and strong trade unions that restrict competitive pressures (see MONOPOLY CAPITALISM). Under these conditions, technological change in center nations tended to result in rising productivity and rising wages (as negotiated by strong unions), with no significant fall in prices (due to oligopolistic practices). In the periphery, on the other hand, enterprises and labor both experienced stronger competitive pressures. Technological changes enhanced competition among both enterprises and workers, resulting in falling prices for peripheral products (such as raw materials) and wages. In short, different patterns in the social organization of production in center and peripheral areas altered the outcome of exchanges between the two areas (resulting in a long-run improvement of the terms of trade for center areas, but a deterioration of these terms for the periphery). Compatible interpretations of the dynamics shaping peripheral labor markets were offered also in the 1950s by Lewis (1954) and Singer (1950).

Challenging the notion that comparative advantages alone can push peripheral nations into a path of sustained development, center and peripheral status had other implications as well. For example, while center governments gained greater leeway to implement full employment policies by expanding the money supply, the threat of monetary instability prevented peripheral governments from pursuing such policies. In this sense, center and peripheral status had direct implications for the welfare of people in these areas.

As other critical approaches to development economics advanced in the 1940s and 1950s, Prebisch's analysis was influenced by a Keynesian emphasis on the impact of idle resources as a constraint on growth. Prebisch's personal trajectory also shaped his analysis of the nature of the relationship between center and peripheral areas. As a trade negotiator and Central Bank Director in Argentina before the Second World War, he was exposed to the practical difficulties and constraints faced by peripheral states in seeking to promote economic growth through either free trade or Keynesian policies. His travels through Latin America in the 1940s are also reported to have led him to identify regional similarities in both the type of constraints limiting economic growth and the innovative state policies being implemented to promote greater industrial development.

Various dimensions of these arguments have been criticized within the literature. Several studies have challenged empirically the evidence of a secular deterioration of the terms of trade, as well as Prebisch's dichotomous focus on agriculture and industry as sources of poverty and wealth in peripheral and center nations. Critical approaches to development in the 1960s challenged the notion that industrialization and foreign investment could provide an effective path to growth in peripheral areas, and argued that Prebisch and most of his followers at ECLA failed to discuss adequately the role of the distribution of wealth and power in peripheral areas (or, for that matter, within the world economy as a whole) as crucial variables affecting patterns of growth. On the other hand, others criticized the notion that state-led industrialization and protectionism could be sustained over the long run, and argued that growth would be more likely to result from an export-led industrialization fully integrated into world markets (see IMPORT SUBSTITUTION AND EXPORT-ORIENTED INDUSTRIALIZATION).

Dependency and world-systems approaches

Many variations on the center–periphery theme were developed after Prebisch, particularly by the dependency and world-systems approaches (see WORLD-SYSTEMS ANALYSIS). Generally, these approaches traced center–periphery relations to the very origins of capitalism as a system. They argued that the exploitative character of relations between center and peripheral countries included mechanisms other than terms of trade (such as the use of financial networks or direct investments by center and transnational corporations to appropriate profits in peripheral nations).

For example, Andre Gunder Frank (1967) critiqued modernization theories of development by arguing that they failed to focus on the exploitative character of the relationship between metropoles and satellites. Organized through a chain, reaching from the largest wealthiest cities in the world to the poorest rural areas and small villages, Frank argued that this relationship served to transfer economic surplus from satellites to metropoles, thereby "underdeveloping" the satellites by draining their wealth. For Frank, underdevelopment would be most pronounced among satellites closely linked to their metropoles, and satellites would undergo the greatest development when these ties were loosened (for example, in periods of world trade disruptions).

Samir Amin (1976) distinguished peripheral from central capitalist development. He argued that capitalist development in the periphery is distorted by the predominance of export-oriented activities; the accelerated growth of non-productive service activities; the appropriation of peripheral surplus by center capital-controlling trade and financial activities; and the lack of integration among peripheral economic activities (what he called "disarticulation" between sectors).

A different variant was introduced by such

authors as Immanuel Wallerstein (1979) and Giovanni Arrighi (1994) in the world-systems approach. As with some of the previous authors, this approach emphasizes that, in a capitalist world economy characterized by a single division of labor and a multiplicity of nation-states, core and peripheral status reflects a spatial distribution of wealth, and that core and peripheral nations have been generally characterized by growing polarization. However, there are significant differences between the world-systems approach and other perspectives in their discussion of core–periphery relations. For example, the relative access of nations to wealth in the world economy is not seen (in world-systems analysis) as being directly correlated with the relative access of these nations to power in the inter-state system. World-systems analysts also emphasize the importance of semi-peripheral nations (distinct from both core and peripheral nations in their relative access to wealth) for the dynamics of change and stability within the world-system. Finally, the relationship between core and peripheral nations is analysed in terms of patterns of competition (rather than as an outcome of relative specialization in the production and trade of raw materials or manufactured goods).

Prebisch's more recent work

Prebisch (1981) and his collaborators at the Economic Commission for Latin America and the Caribbean (ECLAC) have themselves revised several aspects of the initial center–periphery formulation. While some studies continue to emphasize the importance of a long-term deterioration of the terms of trade, others move to acknowledge other factors. For example, capital flows and foreign investments, although leading to greater diversification of productive activities in the periphery, entail new forms of dependence that continue to hinder sustained peripheral development. Thus, the new technologies introduced in developing countries might not respond to peripheral needs, and the volatility of capital flows might increase the vulnerability of peripheral countries to world economic cycles. Under these conditions, the gap between core and peripheral areas is likely to continue to grow.

See also:

balance of payments constraint; class analysis of world capitalism; colonialism and imperialism: classic texts; comparative advantage and unequal exchange; development political economy: history; exchange rates; free trade and protection; global crisis of world capitalism; hegemony in the world economy; international money and finance; internationalization of capital

Selected references

Amin, Samir (1976) *Unequal Development: An Essay on the Social Formation of Peripheral Capitalism*, New York: Monthly Review Press.

Arrighi, Giovanni (1994) *The Long Twentieth Century*, New York: Verso.

Frank, Andre Gunder (1967) *Capitalism and Underdevelopment in Latin America*, New York: Monthly Review Press.

Lewis, W. Arthur (1954) "Economic Development with Unlimited Supplies of Labor," *Manchester School of Economic and Social Studies* 22(May): 139–91.

Love, Joseph L. (1980) "Raul Prebisch and the Origins of Unequal Exchange," *Latin American Research Review* 15(3): 45–72.

Prebisch, Raul (1950) *The Economic Development of Latin America and its Principal Problems*, New York: United Nations.

—— (1981) "The Latin American Periphery in the Global System of Capitalism," *CEPAL Review* 13: 143–50.

Singer, H.W. (1950) "The Distribution of Gains Between Investing and Borrowing Countries," *American Economic Review: Papers and Proceedings* 40(May): 473–85.

Wallerstein, Immanuel (1979) *The Capitalist*

World-Economy, New York: Cambridge University Press.

ROBERTO PATRICIO KORZENIEWICZ

corn model

In the 1815 *Essay on the Influence of a Low Price of Corn on the Profits of Stock* (published in Sraffa 1951–73, vol. 4), as well as in his correspondence of 1814 and early 1815, David Ricardo seems to have in mind a particular mechanism according to which "it is the profits of the farmer that regulate the profits of all other trades" (Sraffa 1951–73, vol. 6: 102). The rationale of this argument was never completely spelled out by its original author, but it has been masterfully reconstructed by SRAFFA in his introduction to *The Works and Correspondence of David Ricardo* (Sraffa 1951–73, vol. 1: xiii–lxii). It is this reconstruction that became subsequently known as the Ricardian "corn model." In Sraffa's words (vol. 1: xxxi), "...in agriculture the same commodity, namely corn, forms both the capital (conceived as composed of the subsistence necessary for workers) and the product, so that the determination of profit by the difference between total product and capital advanced, and also the determination of the ratio of this profit to the capital, is done directly between quantities of corn without any question of valuation."

Because agriculture is the sole sector which does not employ any input from other sectors, while all the other sectors must perforce use "corn" as one of their inputs (if only because they need some wage-goods for the subsistence of workers), "corn" appears as the only basic good in the system (see BASIC AND NON-BASIC COMMODITIES). Consequently, if we want to have a uniform rate of profit in all sectors of the economy, as a result of the classical mechanism of competition (see COMPETITION IN SRAFFIAN POLITICAL ECONOMY), we are led to conclude that the prices of other goods must be those prices which make the rate of profit in such sectors equated to the one determined in agriculture on the basis of physical magnitudes only. The fundamental property of the "corn model," therefore, is that the rate of profit emerges "before," and independently of, price calculations. Of course the model is based upon a particular assumption which, as was noticed at the time by Malthus, is empirically flawed. It is not true, indeed, that "corn" is produced by means of "corn" and labor alone, or moreover, that "corn" is the only wage-good consumed by workers.

According to Sraffa, however, the "corn model" may help to understand the origin and the nature of the problem of finding an invariable standard of value with which Ricardo struggled through subsequent editions of the first chapter, "On Value," of the *Principles*, and again in his last and unfinished manuscript, *Absolute Value and Exchangeable Value*. (Sraffa's interpretation prompted much debate: for a contrary position see Hollander (1973, 1979).)

Furthermore, as shown by Pasinetti (1960; see also Pasinetti 1977: ch. 1), the "corn model" may be also understood as a simplified sketch of the Ricardian vision of economic growth and its ultimate tendency toward a stationary state. Indeed, the growth of population brings about the use of less and less fertile lands which are less and less productive and, consequently, a lower and lower rate of profit. The end of the process is envisaged in a stationary state with a zero rate of profit and no further accumulation because of the particular assumptions that only profits give rise to savings and therefore investments, while rent is wholly consumed (see PROFIT THEORY IN SRAFFIAN POLITICAL ECONOMY; RENT-SEEKING AND VESTED INTERESTS).

There is no doubt that this interpretation of the "corn model" gets its analytical foundations in Sraffa's (1960) attempt to reformulate a classical theory of prices of production (see PRICE THEORY, SRAFFIAN) independently from any labor theory of value (see Sraffa 1960: Appendix D).

See also:

Sraffian political economy

Selected references

Dobb, Maurice (1973) *Theories of Value and Distribution since Adam Smith*, Cambridge: Cambridge University Press.
Eatwell, John (1975) "The Interpretation of Ricardo's 'Essay on Profits'," *Economica* 42(166): 182–7.
Garegnani, Pierangelo (1982) "On Hollander's Intepretation of Ricardo's Early Theory of Profits," *Cambridge Journal of Economics* 6 (1): 65–77.
Hollander, Samuel (1973) "Ricardo's Analysis of the Profit Rate, 1813–15," *Economica* 40(159): 260–82.
—— (1979) *The Economics of David Ricardo*, London: Heinemann.
Pasinetti, Luigi L. (1960) "A Mathematical Formulation of the Ricardian System," *Review of Economic Studies* 27(2): 78–98.
—— (1977) *Lectures on the Theory of Production*, London: Macmillan
Quadrio Curzio, Alberto (1980) "Rent, Income Distribution, and Orders of Efficiency and Rentabilty," in Luigi L. Pasinetti (ed.), *Essays on the Theory of Joint Production*, London: Macmillan, 218–40.
Sraffa, Piero (ed.) (1951–73) *The Works and Correspondence of David Ricardo*, 11 vols, Cambridge: Cambridge University Press.
—— (1960) *Production of Commodities by Means of Commodities: Prelude to a Critique of Economic Theory*, Cambridge: Cambridge University Press.

ANDREA SALANTI

corporate hegemony

The notion of corporate hegemony is one of the central elements in the radical critique of contemporary capitalist economies. It refers to the particular way in which the ownership and management of capital have become formally institutionalized at the close of the twentieth century. Corporate hegemony involves a crystallization of cultural, legal, political and ECONOMIC POWER relations that make the capitalist corporation the dominant institution and make those who control it the dominant CLASS in modern society. The economic and political power of the corporation play important roles in its HEGEMONY, but so too does the cultural power of the corporation as an institution.

Stages of corporate hegemony

Three stages can be identified in the evolution of corporate hegemony, particularly in the USA. First, at the close of the nineteenth century, corporate organization began to replace individual enterprise in most sectors involving large-scale industrial production and/or oligopolistic and monopolistic rivalry. This organization revolution spread as the ability of individual owners to finance and manage enterprises was surpassed by the growing scale of enterprises (see CORPORATION).

Second, in the early twentieth century, a separation of corporate ownership and managerial control began evolving within maturing corporate enterprises (see OWNERSHIP AND CONTROL OF THE CORPORATION). As the original owners and their heirs died out, the large blocks of stock they held passed into the hands of absentee owners (see Veblen 1923), who took no direct personal interest in managing the corporation. Their interest became purely financial, and the operational interest in the corporation passed into the hands of an increasingly professional cadre of business managers. Experience differed widely from corporation to corporation but, to varying degrees, the ownership interest lost control over the managerial interest. This loss meant a less than complete devotion to ownership's profit and the rise of the Galbraithian technostructure. It also provided financial incentives for the third and contemporary stage in the evolution of corporate hegemony.

Third, at the close of the twentieth century, the cadre of now university-trained managers is being brought back under the control of corporate ownership. Waves of corporate mergers and takeovers have strengthened the hand of the corporate ownership against corporate management by putting management under an increasingly credible threat of takeover by more aggressive outside ownership. Quite simply, this takeover threat now means that management must focus more closely on earning profits for ownership, lest it be fired by a new ownership. In the tighter focus on profit, layer after layer of managers have been fired (the euphemism is "downsizing") and those still holding onto their positions have been speeded up (the euphemism is "flexibility"). It is now possible for a few thousand managers to run several enormous, globe-spanning enterprises, all under one organizational roof (see TRANSNATIONAL CORPORATIONS). The corporation has become leaner, and meaner.

The next stage of corporate hegemony is in the future and the future is overdetermined (see DETERMINISM AND OVERDETERMINATION). Nonetheless, an irony may yield some insight into what corporate hegemony means now and where it is headed in the future. Earlier in the twentieth century, TAYLORISM speeded up the working class as the newly emerging managers took over the planning and directing of the production process. Now, at the close of the twentieth century, the worm is turning – on itself. The newly strengthened owners are driving the higher layers of management to speed up the lower layers.

Cultural processes of corporate hegemony

This organizational speeding up is being reinforced at the social level by four related cultural processes that involve value power: the power to instill values in others, even if those values run counter to their own. The four processes are emulation, contamination, subordination and mystification, and they go far beyond the mere power to sell commodities through advertising (see CONSPICUOUS CONSUMPTION AND EMULATION). More importantly, these processes focus individual behavior on the pursuit of corporate profit, by institutionalizing values that are conducive to such pursuit and by de-institutionalizing values that are not.

The leaders of a hegemonic institution are emulated by others. Emulation is the seeking of social status through competitive imitation of those with higher standing. It plays on the widespread envy felt toward those in very high corporate positions, and it allows those occupying such positions to exert status and authority claims in all walks of life, even in the spiritual, moral, political, aesthetic and intellectual realms. Emulation magnifies the value-power of corporate leaders. Since others try to be like them, such leaders find it easy to instill their values in others and to recruit others into the corporate realm.

Contamination substitutes the values from one institution for the values of a different institution. For example, it allows the values of corporate CAPITALISM to replace the values of educational institutions, and to replace the values even of the nation-state itself. If the values of corporate capitalism are destructive of educational and political values, then the widespread emulation of corporate leaders encourages such contamination.

Subordination turns the formerly independent ends of one institution into the dependent means of another. To the extent that the end or objective of schooling used to be education but is now vocational training, the ends of the school have become the means of the corporation. A hegemonic institution is able to subordinate the ends of other institutions into its means, changing them to fit its own purposes in the process.

Mystification is the usurpation of the positive symbols of one institution by another. The leaders of a hegemonic institution are able to take the positive symbols of other institutions and display them as their own, thus elevating the social standing of the hegemonic institution while lowering the standing of the others. To the extent that the symbols of democracy can be taken from the political realm and used by the corporate, then unregulated corporate investment anywhere in the world can come to mean the very essence of democratic freedom, rather than the exercise of capitalist power.

These four value-power processes (emulation, contamination, subordination and mystification) are not only enriching the cultural content of the corporation, but are also hollowing out the cultural content of non-corporate institutions and deflecting the social response to the hollowing-out into attacks on disadvantaged groups and away from movements to curb corporate power. This is particularly true for members of the so-called middle class. While the role they play in their corporation comes to mean more and more to them, the roles they play in their family, school, union, church and nation all come to mean less and less. Working longer and longer hours in less and less secure corporate jobs, time and energy devoted to family, church and community all decline. This decline in the significance of non-corporate institutions has caused real pain, but the pain has given rise to a growing right-wing reaction misdirected at the welfare state, racial and ethnic minorities, feminists and gay rights advocates, none of which are to blame for the decline. (See CAPITAL AND THE WEALTH OF NATIONS.)

Decadent capitalism

The power of the capitalist corporation has grown to such an extent that we are witnessing a new stage of capitalism, a stage in which rising corporate power is substituting for the declining dynamism of capitalism itself. "Decadent capitalism" is the new historical epoch. When capitalism is dynamic, spreading growth and positive social transformation are important social control mechanisms; but when capitalism turns decadent, the fear of unemployment and increased reliance on manipulation and coercion become far more important social control mechanisms (see UNEMPLOYMENT AND UNDEREMPLOYMENT).

This particular era of decadent capitalism may turn out to be of the mindless Veblenian variety or of the mindful Schumpeterian variety. It all depends on what purpose growing corporate power serves: the individualistic purpose critiqued by Veblen or the collectivistic purpose critiqued by Schumpeter.

Veblen's decadent capitalism involves the individualistic and uncoordinated pursuit of pecuniary value through financial SPECULATION and the individualistic pursuit of invidious distinction through emulation and conspicuous consumption. In Veblen's decadent capitalism, then, corporate power will be used for mindless waste and society will blindly drift in whatever direction the uncoordinated actions of the "captains of finance" happen to move it (Veblen 1899, 1904).

On the other hand, and opposed to Veblen, Schumpeter's decadent capitalism involves the collectivistic and coordinated pursuit of the quiet life for corporate leaders through the "groupthink" of committees and the spread of socialistic palliatives for the people. Society will move toward a suffocating normality as it stifles the creative destruction of the great innovating entrepreneurs (for a Schumpeterian variant see CENTRALIZED PRIVATE SECTOR PLANNING). Although the close of the twentieth century resembles Veblen's mindless drift into increasing individualism and waste more than it resembles Schumpeter's mindful move into collectivism and quietude, only time will disclose the true nature of the next stage of corporate hegemony (Dugger 1989).

See also:

advertising and the sales effort; Schumpterian competition

Selected references

Dugger, William M. (1989) *Corporate Hegemony*, New York: Greenwood Press.
Veblen, Thorstein Bunde (1899) *The Theory of the Leisure Class*, London: Penguin, 1994.
—— (1904) *The Theory of Business Enterprise*, Clifton, NJ: Augustus M. Kelley, 1975.
—— (1923) *Absentee Ownership and Business Enterprise in Recent Times*, Clifton, NJ: Augustus M. Kelley, 1964.

WILLIAM M. DUGGER

corporate objectives

The CORPORATION is an organization rather than an individual, and discussion of the objectives of a corporation has to consider whether it is possible to think of an organization (as opposed to an individual) having well-defined objectives. A great deal of theorizing within economics (from the different schools of thought) has treated the firm as a "black box" and as a single entrepreneur grown larger. Thus the objectives of the corporation are identified with the objectives of the single entrepreneur. In neoclassical economics, the objectives of the individual are taken to be the maximization of utility, and it is generally assumed that there is a close relationship between utility and profit, so that the objective of the entrepreneur and hence of the corporation can be taken as profit maximization (though see Scitovsky 1943).

At one level, decisions are made by people within an organization rather than by the organization itself, as the organization does not literally have a brain of its own. The weight given to the objectives of different individuals within the organization varies considerably. But, provided that more than one individual is involved in the effective decision-making, the question arises as to how the objectives of the individuals concerned are aggregated into the objectives of the organization. The "voting paradox" is relevant here (as elaborated by Arrow in the context of social choice). This is the idea that even when the rankings of the individuals over the relevant states are transitive, there is little reason to think that the rankings arrived through voting will be transitive, and in that sense it may be difficult to speak of corporate objectives.

Survival and growth

There is a sense in which an organization is both more and less than the sum of the individuals who compose it. It is less in that individuals have an interest outside of that organization. It is more in that the organization has a history, working routines, a culture and a reputation which influence the decisions made. In general, the organization will be constrained to have a positive cash flow. It can then be argued that the organization itself seeks to survive and to grow. While the individuals within an organization are likely to have an interest in its survival and growth (since, for example, their current job depends on the organization's survival), there is an imperative for the organization to survive. This was summarized by Eichner (who uses the term "megacorp" for the large corporation) when he wrote that:

> The megacorp is an organization rather than an individual.... As an organization, the megacorp's goal is to expand at the highest possible rate.... It is expansion at the highest rate possible that creates the maximum opportunities for advancement within the organization, and thus personal rewards for those who are part of the firm's decision-making structure.
>
> (Eichner 1985: 30)

Later, Eichner writes that:

> In pursuit of this goal, the megacorp can be expected to follow two behavioral rules. One of these is that it will attempt to maintain, if not actually to enlarge, its share of the market in the industries to which it already belongs while simultaneously undertaking whatever investment is necessary to lower its costs of production. The other behavioral rule is that it will attempt to expand into newer, more rapidly growing industries while simultaneously withdrawing from any older, relatively stagnant industries.
>
> (Eichner 1987: 361)

Profit maximization

The most commonly assumed corporate objective is that of profit (or value) maximization. It is justified along one of (at least) two lines. First, the corporation is supposedly run in the interests of its owners, and the benefits which they derive from the corporation are closely related to its profits. Thus profit maximization is derived from the pursuit of self-interest by the owners. Second, in a competitive market situation there is pressure on profits and, in order to secure sufficient profits for survival and growth, the corporation has to maximize profits. This maximization may occur through a calculated attempt by the controllers of the corporation to secure high profits, or through random chance, habit or some other factor. The notion of natural selection has been used to validate the maximization hypothesis according to the judgment that it equates in a broad sense to the survival conditions of the corporation (Friedman 1953). This argument by biological analogy has been variously criticized for its misuse of biology and its implicit assumptions of a stable environment (notably by Hodgson 1993).

Sales revenue maximization

The perceived separation of OWNERSHIP AND CONTROL OF THE CORPORATION raises the question as to whether the managers (or other controllers) will, willingly or otherwise, pursue the interests of the owners (which are taken to be essentially profits or dividends). The work of Baumol (1959) can be represented in terms of the objectives of the corporation being sales revenue maximization (subject to a minimum profit constraint). Sales revenue maximization is a proxy for the objectives of the managers whose salary, prestige and promotion prospects are positively related to the sales revenue of the corporation. Furthermore, the managers are viewed as the effective decision-makers (especially over issues such as PRICING and investment) and make decisions that enhance their objectives. Marris (1964) can be readily viewed as a development of this work of Baumol, in which the objective of managers, and thereby of the corporation, is growth (of sales) maximization subject to a takeover constraint. The stock market valuation is seen to be based on dividend policy (retention ratio) and growth (of profits). The takeover threat arises from an increased probability of being acquired if the valuation of the corporation is too low, which would arise from, for example, a higher retention ratio in pursuit of faster growth.

Principal–agent problem

These works are significant in two regards. First, they relate to corporations in which there is a degree of divergence between ownership and control, and hence in which the objectives of those who control set the objectives of the corporation. Second, they can be viewed as examples of what has now become formalized as a "principal–agent" problem. The owners (principals) contract the managers (agents) to undertake activities and make decisions on their behalf in a situation where the contract between the two parties is not and cannot be fully specified and monitored, and where the agent possesses information (for example, on opportunities) which the principal does not have. The principals may wish to impose their own objectives, but the pursuit of those objectives depends on the agents, who have their objectives which are imperfectly aligned with those of the principals. This again raises the issue of what is meant by corporate objectives. Do we mean the objectives of the principal which can only be carried through if the agents behave in a manner which conforms to those objectives? Further, who are the agents and who are the principals? While it has been usual to view the owners as the principals and the managers and workers as agents (reflecting the perceived legal position under capitalism), the position may be closer to one in which the managers are the principals, with the suppliers of capital and of labor as the agents. If that view were accepted, it would have profound effects for the way in which corporations are viewed: as instruments of management rather than of capital owners.

See also:

economic power; Galbraith's contribution to political economy; market structures; transnational corporations

Selected references

Baumol, W.J. (1959) *Business Behaviour, Value and Growth*, London: Macmillan.

Berle, A.A. and Means, G.C. (1932) *The Modern Corporation and Private Property*, New York: Macmillan.
Eichner, A.S. (1985) *Towards a New Economics*, New York: M.E. Sharpe.
—— (1987) *The Macrodynamics of Advanced Market Economies*, New York: M.E.Sharpe.
Friedman, M. (1953) *Essays in Positive Economics*, Chicago: University of Chicago Press.
Hodgson, G.M. (1993) *Economics and Evolution*, Cambridge: Polity Press.
Marris, R. (1964) *The Economic Theory of "Managerial" Capitalism*, London: Macmillan.
Sawyer, M. (1989) *The Challenge of Radical Political Economy*, Hemel Hempstead: Harvester-Wheatsheaf, chapters 4–6.
Scitovsky, T. (1943) "A Note on Profit Maximization," *Review of Economic Studies* 11.

MALCOLM SAWYER

corporation

The modern joint stock company or corporation has been the legal form of business enterprise through which many of the most important economic and social processes of CAPITALISM have taken place. Legally, the corporate form separates the activities and property of the firm from the private property of its owners, and limits the liability of investors over the use of their capital by the firm. Limited liability is established by creating the firm itself as a distinct legal entity that can sue and be sued. With the corporation, the firm is created as an "artificial" legal person that owns the property of the firm and is responsible for managing its activities. As Adolph Berle (1959) observed, the legal entity known as the corporation emerges as the owner of the firm's property; or, to put it another way, the creation of the corporation as legal person has meant that capital is now both the subject as well as the object of property (Kay 1991).

One hundred years ago, when the transition toward a "corporate" economy was taking place, the evolution of the modern corporation seemed to represent developments in capitalism beyond its classic form. For many of the most significant political economists writing during this transitional period, the corporation, along with a number of social upheavals occurring in the late nineteenth and early twentieth centuries, seemed to indicate that capitalism had reached a mature phase and was possibly even decaying. The corporation itself was often seen as accelerating the "socialization" of production and therefore to be a transitional form of organization. In retrospect, however, it is clear that the corporation did not represent a bridge between capitalism and some new form of society, whether it be socialist or post-capitalist, nor did it even represent the maturing or decaying of capitalism. Instead, the development of the corporation has been the evolution of the legal/institutional form of capital best suited to accumulation in changed conditions of production (Kay 1991).

Limited liability legislation: 1850s–1880s

Limited liability was developed in Britain through a series of legislative reforms in the middle of the nineteenth century, and was consolidated by the establishment of an effective system of liquidation in the 1880s (Hadden 1977). These reforms also made incorporation a relatively cheap process, even for small firms. Initially, legislative reform was concerned with the prevention of fraud, and indeed the early history of the corporation was associated with much corruption and fraud. By 1886, for instance, almost one in three public companies which had incorporated after the enactment of limited liability legislation in England in the 1850s had ended in insolvency, in many cases presumably related to corruption of various kinds. The legislative reforms had much wider implications, and they defined property rights in a manner consistent with mass production and strengthened the internal administration of capital.

Earlier forms of corporation

The corporate form, however, existed well before the middle of the nineteenth century and even longer than its use for solely commercial purposes (Bruchey 1968). In as much as modern corporations were developments of past forms of corporate or business organization, their precursors can be found in the chartered companies and unincorporated firms. Chartered corporations had existed since the 1600s, but did not exist solely for the purposes of profit. The chartered mercantile companies, such as the trading companies, helped to make possible the voyages of discovery, commerce and colonization that Marx called the period of PRIMITIVE ACCUMULATION. Chartered corporations such as the East India Company were, however, mainly a form of statutory monopoly and derived their permanence and security from individual statutory sanction. They became unstable once their monopolistic privileges were withdrawn as part of the tide of legislation inspired by a growing enthusiasm for free trade and laissez-faire in the mid-nineteenth century (Hannah 1983).

Industrial revolution

The origins of the modern corporation are usually traced to the capital and organizational requirements of industries that were developed or grew out of the industrial revolution and the factory system. As early as the second half of the eighteenth century, many of the organizational and technological requirements of the modern corporate form were already present. In 1784, for instance, Sir Robert Peel's calico printing partnership in the Midlands of England employed more than 7,000 people and used steam power and mechanical cotton looms (Hannah 1983). The representative firm, however, remained much smaller and several institutional developments in company law and stock exchange practice were still required. Most firms operated as unincorporated businesses, such as family firms and partnerships. The problems with this form of organization were that such firms lacked continuity and had a narrow capital base and uneven managerial abilities, and investors risked losing their entire wealth through losses on one activity. These features constrained the ability of unincorporated firms to grow in both scale and scope (Hadden 1977).

From the mid-nineteenth century, the development of industries such as railways, shipping and large-scale mining required a transformation in both the technical conditions of production and in the legal, financial and organizational requirements of firms. The process of incorporation occurred first in these industries, where firms were increasingly being organized through the corporate form. In the development of the leading companies of the period, it is possible to discern not just many of the institutional and organizational features of the modern corporation (Chandler and Salsbury 1968), but also the changing structure of capital accumulation and social relations. The formation of corporations for the construction and operation of railways, for instance, helped to fashion a disciplined wage labor force which, through its own consumption spending, also became a motive force of economic growth (Jenks 1944).

Industrial concentration and conglomerates

The growing number of firms that were undergoing incorporation was also accompanied by the growth in the average size of the individual business unit. By encouraging the pooling of the money of many individuals into a common unit, the corporation enabled individual firms to operate on a scale beyond the capacity or wealth of any individual or family. The average size of corporations increased under the pressure of both the growing minimum scale of production and through a series of merger waves by corporations, in Britain but especially in the United States. Industrial concentration was also often associated with the creation of conglomerate corporations with activities in several industries, coordinated by a central or head office. The movement toward industrial concentration in the late nineteenth century was historically unprecedented and created individual production enterprises on a scale that could not have been conceived a century before (Hannah 1983).

In place of open competition between many small firms, industrial concentration also encouraged forms of organized collaboration between a few large firms. Along with the end of perfect competition in product markets, a new role developed for the state in arranging these new forms of inter-firm relations. The role of the state in inter-corporate relations occurred under the rubric of what is now known as INDUSTRY POLICY or TRADE POLICY. Taken together, these developments in the decades preceding the First World War marked the end of what is usually called the competitive or laissez-faire period of capitalist history.

Ownership and control

At least as important as the development of the conditions in which corporations operated, and in relations between corporations, was a transformation in the *internal* relations of the firm. In the typical nineteenth-century private or family firm, the functions of ownership and control usually resided in one person, the entrepreneur/owner. The appearance of the corporation separated the two functions and that separation has become more pronounced over the last century. The economic and social significance of ownership and control separation that is inherent in the corporation has been one of the most controversial aspects of the corporation (Berle and Means 1932). For instance, the growing separation of ownership and control of the corporation created the need for new forms of administrative control (Chandler 1977) and consequently for a new managerial class of trained and committed staff to perform the administrative functions of the corporation. (See OWNERSHIP AND CONTROL OF THE CORPORATION.)

Transnational corporations after 1945

Since the Second World War, the development of the corporation have also been associated with the internationalization of individual corporations – with what have become known as TRANSNATIONAL CORPORATIONS. While in the early postwar period the transnational corporation was especially associated with the international spread of corporations from the United States, in recent decades corporations with activities overseas have emerged from almost all developed countries, and from a wide range of developing countries as well. Internationalization has raised questions about the relationship between the corporation and the nation-state, and created significant problems for defining the nationality of companies. Along with the much greater mobility of capital, the role of corporations in the INTERNATIONALIZATION OF CAPITAL has become an important issue for governments and researchers. (See STATE AND INTERNATIONALIZATION.)

Leverage and partnerships: 1970s–1980s

Developments during the 1970s and 1980s also changed other features of the corporation. Some of the important changes include the development of new forms of corporate organization and changing boundaries of the firm. For instance, an increasing proportion of corporate funding was being provided in the form of debt (increasing corporate gearing or leverage). Leveraged and management buyouts (LBOs and MBOs) were, perhaps, the most novel features of this financing trend. Many large firms were taken over by corporate raiders or by the firm's management, largely by using debt capital. The resulting businesses were usually corporate in form, but often had no public shareholders and were not listed or traded on organized stockmarkets. Debt financing was criticized as increasing the financial fragility of the corporate sector and widening the scope for speculative activity. (See FINANCIAL INSTABILITY HYPOTHESIS.)

Jensen (1989), however, suggested that the transformation in corporate financing resulted in a valuable organizational innovation. These new forms of corporation were helping to resolve a central weakness of the public corporation, the conflict between owners and managers. In the changed conditions of the 1970s and 1980s, the public corporation was seen as generating widespread waste and inefficiency, especially in industries where long-term growth was slow and where internally generated funds were greater than the opportunities for profitable re-investment. The public corporation was unable to resolve the conflict between shareholders and managers over the retention or payout of "free cash flow" – money in excess of that required to fund the firm's current and future profitable investment projects. Product markets and internal control systems, which should discipline the corporation, had proven inadequate. Only the capital market could extract surplus money capital from the company by converting equity into debt. Increasing the leverage of corporations through LBOs and MBOs was said to be an effective way of disciplining managers to release cash and to adopt "value-creating" policies.

In the 1970s and 1980s, developments in corporate organization also changed our understanding about the boundaries of the firm. Corporate control is now often exercised, not just through very low levels of equity, but also through non-equity forms. Many firms have also developed various forms of alliances and partnerships with each other in areas such as supply, marketing and even production. These relationships stand somewhere between control and competition. In these circumstances, the notion of the firm as a discrete entity has been qualified by the more permeable boundaries of the firm, and the changing nature of relationships between firms. These developments have directed attention not just to the nature of the institution of the corporation, but to the complex networks of interdependence between corporations; that is, to capital as a social process.

See also:

centralized private sector planning; corporate hegemony; corporate objectives; pricing

Selected references

Berle, A. (1959) *Power Without Property: A New Development in American Political Economy*, New York: Harvest Books.

Berle, A. and Means, G. (1932) *The Modern Corporation and Private Property*, New York: Harcourt Brace.

Bruchey, S. (1968) "The Quasi-Public Corporation: Corporation Historical Development," in A. Chandler, S. Bruchey and A. Galambos (eds), *The Changing Economic Order: Readings in American Business and Economic History*, New York: Harcourt Brace.

Chandler, A. (1977) *The Visible Hand: The Managerial Revolution in American Business*, Cambridge, MA: Harvard University Press.

Chandler, A. and Salsbury, S. (1968) "The Railroads: Innovators in Modern Business Administration," in A. Chandler, S. Bruchey and A. Galambos (eds), *The Changing Economic Order: Readings in American Business and Economic History*, New York: Harcourt Brace.

Hadden, T. (1977) *Company Law and Capitalism*, 2nd edn, London: Weidenfeld & Nicolson.

Hannah, L. (1983) *The Rise of the Corporate Economy*, 2nd edn, London: Methuen.

Jenks, L. (1944) "The Railroads as an Economic Force in American Development," *The Journal of Economic History* 4(May).

Jensen, M. (1989) "The Eclipse of the Public Corporation," *Harvard Business Review*, September–October.

Kay, G. (1991) "The Joint Stock Company – Notes on Machover," *Critique* 23.

MICHAEL RAFFERTY

cost–benefit analysis

Cost–benefit analysis is a means of comparing the beneficial and adverse consequences of economic decisions with a view to determining whether the expected outcomes are in the public interest. It has become a widely used method for evaluation of public projects such

cost–benefit analysis

as whether to build a new urban freeway, whether to locate a new airport at site A or site B, whether to allow more mining in an area or to preserve its environmental assets, or whether to restrict the availability of a new product with potential consumer hazards. These are the sorts of decisions to which cost–benefit analysis can be applied. Indeed, one major attraction of cost–benefit (CB) analysis is its apparent generality. As one enthusiastic proponent put it, "In principle, all kinds of public decision-making can be guided or controlled by CB analysis" (Bohm 1973: 117).

Cost–benefit analysis procedure

The basic procedure of cost–benefit analysis can be summarized in five steps:

- *Identify* all the relevant consequences of a particular public policy decision.
- *Evaluate* all the consequences in monetary terms, so as to derive values for the streams of costs and benefits expected to accrue to the society as a whole.
- *Estimate* the net present value of those costs and benefits through the application of a discount rate.
- *Compare* the net present value of the costs and the net present value of the benefits, in the form of an overall cost–benefit ratio.
- *Select* all the policy alternatives where the cost–benefit ratio is less than one; or, in the case of mutually exclusive alternatives, select the policy alternative with the lowest cost–benefit ratio.

Example

Take the construction of a new urban freeway, for example. The first step would require the analyst to list all the likely effects of its construction, on travel times for freeway users and for those on existing roads, the likely incidence and severity of traffic accidents, the impact on atmospheric pollution, the loss of flora and fauna resulting from this land use and so on. The second step would require putting a dollar value on each item, including the value of travel time saved, the value of lives lost or saved according to whether traffic accidents would be increased or reduced, and so on. The third step is to express these various streams of costs and benefits in terms of their current value equivalent, on the assumption that future costs and benefits have less weight than immediate costs and benefits. This is where the choice of a discount rate enters the calculations. The fourth step would involve comparing the discounted costs of the freeway construction with its estimated benefits, all expressed in terms of these monetary net present values. The freeway is then deemed to be socially desirable only if the benefits exceed the costs. In the case of two or more different freeway routes the preferred option would be that with the lowest cost–benefit ratio. Unless mutually incompatible, all freeways with a net benefit figure should be constructed.

Sensitivity analysis

Practitioners of cost–benefit analysis sometimes acknowledge the need for some supplementary sensitivity analysis in these calculations. Because the evaluations of costs and benefits may involve "guesstimates" with considerable margins of error, they note that the effect of differing valuations on the benefits and costs should be assessed, for example in the form of maximum and minimum estimates. Likewise, the appropriate value of the discount rate to be applied may be a matter of controversy, so the sensitivity of the overall benefits and costs to different rates of discount needs to be assessed. These supplementary calculations add to the sophistication of the analysis while reducing its apparent clarity as a tool for decision making.

Advantages

Various advantages can be claimed to arise from the application of cost–benefit analysis. First and most obviously, there are advantages in having a method which increases the consistency of decision making. The consistency is sought through a very distinctive process: "one which explicitly makes the effort to compare like with like using a single measuring rod of benefits and costs, money" (Pearce *et al.* 1989: 57). Second, there are advantages in making explicit the valuations which are often implicit in existing decision-making processes. As Abelson (1979: 197–9) argues, "In the last resort, all decisions imply that some assessment of costs and benefits is made, however intuitively. What cost–benefit analysis does, among other things, is to make these assessments explicit, and this is surely a desirable practice." Third, cost–benefit analysis has the potential to provide a basis for making the decision-making process more *transparent*. The claim here is that the openness of the decision-making process may be enhanced if the cost–benefit analyses are available for public scrutiny: debate may then take place systematically on the basis of whether appropriate valuations have been made.

Problems with cost–benefit analysis

Despite these claims to be a universal decision-making tool, cost–benefit analysis is fraught with difficulties. There follows a discussion of some of these.

Theoretical difficulties. Some problems arise from its shaky theoretical foundations. Cost–benefit analysis may be regarded as an application of welfare economics, which in turn has a close association with neoclassical microeconomic theory. It shares with those branches of economic analysis a distinctive set of assumptions about the nature of the economy and society and the influences which are relevant in assessing the determinants of community well-being. The approach embodies a utilitarian philosophy which, applied in the economic sphere, provides a restrictive basis for normative propositions about social welfare. The underlying notion of welfare derives from the neoclassical concept of "consumer surplus." A particularly thorny conceptual problem then arises because, according to neoclassical theory, individual consumers' utilities are identifiable only in ordinal rather than cardinal terms. In the language of the orthodox economists, this prohibits interpersonal comparisons of utility: hence the difficulty of weighing up the utility gained by some consumers against the disutility experienced by others.

How does one undertake the calculation of social costs/benefits unless there is a cardinal measure of each consumer's utility? Such a measure is precisely what orthodox economists deny to be possible. But if a measure of overall economic welfare is not identifiable through the aggregation of individual consumer welfares, how is an overall "social welfare function" to be identified? One is not avoiding making ethical judgments about "what is good for the community" by the use of scientific procedures: rather, implicit ethical judgments are embodied in the assumptions underlying the analysis.

Discounting. The process of discounting future costs and benefits to determine the net present value of the project being evaluated also rests on a particular assumption about the relationship between the interests of present and future generations. Discounting has a monetary logic: a dollar today is worth more than the promise of a dollar next year because of the interest that can be earned in the interim. However, environmentalists argue that by applying a discounting process to social costs, cost–benefit analysis "discriminates against future generations by saying that future costs are worth less than present costs" (Beder 1993:55–6). In the case of the freeway example, the travel time savings of current users are given a full weighting but the effects on future generations – and on future environmental conditions – are weighted less heavily because a discount rate is applied.

Selectivity. Many other practical problems recur. One of the more obvious is identifying all the relevant consequences of a particular policy or project. Any event, act or policy will tend to have an infinite number of reverberations on the economy, society and environment. The best a cost–benefit analyst can do is to identify some of the most obvious and most likely clusters of those possible consequences. But there's the rub; what then differentiates one cost–benefit analysis from another is the principles of selection, which are likely to be conditioned by, among other things, the theoretical orientation, value judgments and political commitments of each analyst.

Monetary evaluations. Placing monetary evaluations on the various consequences is also fraught with difficulties. (One is reminded of George Bernard Shaw's gibe that economists know the price of everything but the value of nothing.) Market valuations are particularly problematic. Take the cost of human life, for example, which is often a key variable in transport projects or other policies which impact, either positively or negatively, on health and safety. As Mishan (1982: 30) notes, "despite repeated expressions of dissatisfaction with the method, the most common way of calculating the economic worth of a person's life and, therefore, the loss to the economy consequent on his decease is that of discounting to the present the person's expected future earnings." The ethical bias is evident: such a calculation values life only in terms of economic contributions, and it values more cheaply the lives of the unskilled, the handicapped, the aged and so on.

Distributional issues. How to take account of distributional considerations is one of the most perplexing aspects of cost–benefit analysis. The technique compares aggregate social costs and benefits, and pays no regard to the incidence of these costs and benefits on different sections of the population. However, cost–benefit analysis does not merely avoid distributional issues: its apparent distributional neutrality may be a mask for policy recommendation with an implicit distributional bias. Thus, if consumer costs and benefits are measured by what consumers are prepared to pay for a product or to avoid potential hazards, the valuations will reflect ability to pay and hence the distribution of income. The result is an implicit distributional bias toward the *status quo*,

Various proposals have been made to correct this neglect in cost–benefit analysis of distributional considerations and/or implicit distributional bias. Bohm (1973: 111), for example, suggested either the imposition of distributional constraints (thereby imposing equity limits on an otherwise efficiency-oriented analysis) or the application of different weights to the various costs and benefits according to their distributional incidence (for example, higher weights on benefit items accruing to particular groups the government wants to support). On the former approach, Mishan (1982: 165) argues that "it is not enough that the outcome of an ideal cost–benefit analysis be positive.... It must be shown...that the resulting distributional changes are not perceptibly regressive and that no gross inequities are perpetrated." As for the more complex alternative of assigning differential weights to costs and benefits accruing to different income groups, there are major conceptual and practical difficulties in identifying the appropriate weights. The resulting benefits and costs become even more subject to disputation over the issue of whether correct weights have been applied.

Intangibles. There is a further problem with so-called intangibles. Some matters are simply too difficult to evaluate in monetary terms for the purposes of cost–benefit analysis. This illustrates a general dilemma in the application of cost–benefit analysis: the more honestly and carefully the analyst identifies the uncertain and intangible items, the more inconclusive are the results; but the more willing the analyst is to assign specific monetary values to everything, the more unreliable and potentially biased are the results. As Pearce (1983) put it:

> ...if a measure is suggested [for intangibles] the analyst is accused of attempting to measure the unmeasurable [but] if no measure is suggested, the critic argues that cost–benefit has failed to produce answers which are any better than those which would have been achieved by a simple political or planning decision.
>
> (Pearce 1983: 12)

In the freeway construction example, the possible loss of flora and fauna illustrates this dilemma: there is no agreed basis for evaluating this environmental damage in monetary terms, but not to do so imparts an anti-environmental bias into the cost–benefit analysis process.

Practical politics. What of the politics of applying cost–benefit analysis in practice? As noted earlier, one of the possible advantages of cost–benefit analysis is that it can increase the "transparency" of the decision-making process and hence provide a basis for systematic and informed public participation. However, a contrary tendency is apparent. It is that cost–benefit analysis may tend to substitute for the political process because of its image of scientific objectivity, and the typically large and technical character of cost–benefit analysis reports. In its attempt to generate a more "objective" basis for decisions, the effect of cost–benefit analysis may thereby be to reduce public participation. Self (1975: 5, 97–149) describes cost–benefit analysis as "the supreme example of econocracy," the subordination of the political process to a narrow economic reasoning.

Evidently, the more closely one examines cost–benefit analysis, the more problematic it appears. Recognizing this, it has become common to reduce the claims made on its behalf. Mishan (1982: 198), for example, stresses that cost–benefit analysis is "no more than a useful technique in the service of social decisions" and that "it is certainly not to be thought of as a part of, or substitute for, economic policy." Similarly, an OECD report (1983: 77) stresses that cost–benefit analysis "should be considered as only one input to the decision making process" and that "certainly there will be situations where a policy decision may be taken contrary to cost–benefit recommendations." This all sounds pleasantly open-minded, but it leaves the status of cost–benefit analysis quite ambiguous.

Conclusion

The theoretical underpinnings, conceptual structure and empirical aspects of cost–benefit analysis are all deeply troublesome, as already noted. The ambiguous status in the political process compounds the problems. If cost–benefit analysis is not to be decisive in the policy process, then it is necessary to determine what considerations could or should overrule it: otherwise, cost–benefit analysis has no coherent claim to making the decision-making processes more systematic and consistent. Either the use of cost–benefit analysis leads to an undemocratic "econocracy," or cost–benefit analysis tends to be redundant in relation to the essentially political character of the decision-making process. This illustrates the more general problem of trying to extend economic analysis, especially analysis based on neoclassical assumptions, to serve as a basis for practical decision-making in a political-economic context.

See also:

environmental and ecological political economy: major contemporary themes; environmental policy and politics; public goods, social costs and externalities; state and government

Selected references

Abelson, P. (1979) *Cost–Benefit Analysis and Environmental Problems*, London: Saxon House.

Beder, Sharon (1993) *The Nature of Sustainable Development*, Newham, Victoria: Scribe Publishers.

Bohm, P. (1973) *Social Efficiency*, London: Macmillan.

Mishan, E.J. (1982) *Cost–Benefit Analysis*, 3rd edn, London: George Allen & Unwin.

OECD (1983) *Product Safety: Risk Management and Cost–Benefit Analysis*, Paris: OECD.

Pearce, D.W. (1983) *Cost–Benefit Analysis*, 2nd edn, London: Macmillan.

Pearce, D.W., Markandya, Anil and Barbier, Edward B. (1989) *Blueprint for a Green Economy*, London: Earthscan.

Schmid, A.A. (1989) *Benefit–Cost Analysis: A Political Economy Approach*, San Francisco: Westview Press.

Self, P. (1975) *Econocrats and the Policy

Process: The Politics and Philosophy of Cost–Benefit Analysis, London: Macmillan.

FRANK STILWELL

cost of job loss

The cost of job loss (CJL) is the cost to workers of being permanently laid off or fired from their jobs. Job loss is costly to workers because the compensation paid to employed workers is invariably greater than the income and income equivalent available to unemployed persons.

Economic power and unemployment

CJL is *one* determinant of the ECONOMIC POWER that employers have over employees. The greater the CJL, the greater the potential punishment an employer can inflict on an employee if this employee fails to act as the employer desires. In general, the level of work effort (how hard and how well an employee works) that an employer desires is greater than that the employee would provide without coercion. A growth in CJL permits the employer to elicit still more work effort from the employees (see LABOR AND LABOR POWER; EFFICIENCY WAGES).

Schor and Bowles (1987) first elaborated the notion of CJL and indicated its importance in bargaining between employers and employees. The most important theoretical paper is Bowles (1985), which showed that the profitability of capitalist firms required that CJL be positive and that a positive CJL required the existence of involuntary unemployment. In this article, Bowles also details the interaction between CJL, employee monitoring within the firm, and the direction of technological change.

Simplified formula

The CJL is most commonly expressed as the ratio of the dollar cost of job loss to the worker's annual standard of living. One simplified formula for CJL is:

$$CJL = \frac{DU \times (Compensation - UB)}{52 \times (Compensation + SW)}$$

The numerator represents the loss of income a worker would experience due to a spell of unemployment. DU is the duration of unemployment (measured in weeks), while (Compensation − UB) is the difference between the worker's weekly compensation (wages + non-wage benefits) and what he/she would receive in weekly unemployment benefits (UB). The denominator represents the annual standard of living for an employed worker. The latter is determined by weekly employment compensation and SW, the weekly SOCIAL WAGE. The social wage is equal to the income and income equivalent available to all people in society independent of employment status.

The notion of CJL is an extension of the classical Marxian notion of the RESERVE ARMY OF LABOR. Indeed, the size of the reserve army is one determinate of CJL: as the level of unemployment grows, so too does the duration of unemployment and CJL.

Political and social influences

CJL is affected by the political and social spheres. For instance, workers' and unions' success in the political arena in expanding unemployment insurance programs will reduce CJL by increasing UB. Further, an expansion of socialized consumption (that is, SW) provided by the WELFARE STATE can lessen workers' dependence on wage labor for their survival, and thus can lead to a fall in CJL, as more of workers' standard of living is gained independently of wage labor. In either case, the outcomes of political struggles within the state can affect the relative bargaining power of employers and employees within the economy. The above simplified CJL formula is intended to focus attention on the impact of events in the political sphere on CJL. However, other economic and "non-economic" aspects can also affect CJL (see Nilsson 1997).

One criticism of the CJL literature is that it underemphasizes the role of consent (or Gramscian HEGEMONY) in capital–labor relations. The exchange between Burawoy and Wright (1990) and Bowles and Gintis (1990) clarifies this criticism.

Empirical estimation

Econometric studies using time series estimates for CJL for the post-Second World War United States have shown that changes in CJL have meaningful effects on economic behavior. For instance, Weisskopf, Bowles and Gordon (1983) demonstrated that CJL affects aggregate productivity while Bowles, Gordon and Weisskopf (1986) documented the impact of CJL on corporate profitability. Schor and Bowles (1987) showed that a fall in CJL is linked to a rise in workplace conflict. Similarly, Nilsson (1996) found that decreases in CJL provoked employer attacks on labor unions in the postwar US economy.

While CJL is a straightforward theoretical notion, complex conceptual and data issues confront those desiring to estimate CJL empirically. For instance, one needs to specify in detail what contributes to the social wage and how to value each component of the social wage. Not surprisingly, disagreements exist as to the best methodology for measuring CJL. This debate is critical because different estimation methodologies can lead to different levels and trends in CJL. For instance, Bowles, Gordon and Weisskopf (1990) report that CJL has been on a downward trend in the postwar United States, while Nilsson (1997) finds that CJL has no clear postwar trend.

Empirical work within the CJL literature has focused exclusively on the US economy. Studies of the magnitude and trends of CJL in other countries and the impact of CJL on economic behavior in these countries are needed in order to fill an important gap in the literature of political economy.

See also:

profit-squeeze analysis of crises

Selected references

Bowles, Samuel (1985) "The Production Process in a Competitive Economy: Walrasian, Neo-Hobbesian, and Marxian Models," *American Economic Review* 75(1): 16–36.

Bowles, Samuel and Gintis, Herbert (1990) "Reply to Our Critics," *Politics and Society* 18(2): 293–315.

Bowles, Samuel, Gordon, David M. and Weisskopf, Thomas E. (1986) "Power and Profits: The Social Structure of Accumulation and the Profitability of the Postwar U.S. Economy," *Review of Radical Political Economics* 18(1&2): 132–67.

—— (1990) *After the Wasteland: A Democratic Economics for the Year 2000*, Armonk, NY: M.E. Sharpe.

Burawoy, Michael and Wright, Erik Olin (1990) "Coercion and Consent in Contested Exchange," *Politics and Society* 18(2): 251–66.

Nilsson, Eric A. (1996) "The Breakdown of the U.S. Postwar System of Labor Relations," *Review of Radical Political Economics* 28(1): 20–50.

—— (1997) "The Cost of Job Loss Series: A Deconstruction/Reconstruction" California State University, San Bernadino, Working Paper No. 97-1.

Schor, Juliet B. and Bowles, Samuel (1987) "Employment Rents and the Incidence of Strikes," *Review of Economics and Statistics* 69(4): 584–92.

Weisskopf, Thomas E., Bowles, Samuel and Gordon, David M. (1983) "Hearts and Minds: A Social Model of U.S. Productivity Growth," *Brookings Papers on Economic Activity* 2: 381–441.

ERIC NILSSON

crime

Introduction

The existence of "crime" was the supposed justification for the creation of the state, according to the social contract myth theory. Of course, one wonders if "crime" exists regardless of society, or if it is just a socially constructed concept; a behavior arbitrarily characterized as such by a given society for reasons of social control. The philosophical questions induced by the problems of crime and punishment have been extensively discussed through the ages, but crime in modern societies is a major reason for a substantial decrease in the utility of citizens. This is true even in the wealthiest of countries, notably in the USA, where it is indisputably the gravest social problem. (The analysis of crime in this article does not include "crimes of passion.")

Statistical evidence on crime is abundant. For example, it was calculated that the expected cost (to the perpertrator) of a burglary in the USA is 4.8 days in prison, for murder 1.8 years, for rape 60 days, robbery 23 days and vehicle theft 1.5 days. The average expected prison sentence for a serious crime has fallen from 24 days in 1950 to 9 days in 1992. However, it is also widely accepted that statistics on crime are not completely accurate. There is a great range of criminal activities that are not (or cannot be) reported. Typical examples are white-collar crimes and sexual offences.

A reflection of social problems

The social sciences generally view crime as a reflection of social problems. Sociology, social psychology, criminology and Marxism have elaborated their theories of the criminal phenomenon. A similarity among these views is the argument that problematical social relations are an important source of criminal behavior. These problems are variously isolated as anomalous family relations, subcultures, CLASS structure and INEQUALITY.

An important argument is that blue-collar or lower-class crime is related to the existence of a competitive capitalist society, in relation to an increase in relative poverty or inequality (see POVERTY: ABSOLUTE AND RELATIVE). This is especially the case if the majority of the population is under pressure to "do better," with the poor trying to emulate the rich who engage in conspicuous consumption. Under these conditions, the greater the gap, the greater is the pressure on the lower classes to go beyond their means via credit or crimes against property. Hence, even situations when income generally increases can result in greater crime if the gap between rich and poor (in terms of relative income) increases.

David Gordon (1973) presents an interesting early radical analysis of crime. Emphasis is placed on the class structures of institutions and the class biases of the state. Gordon recognizes that an understanding of crime can be aided by situating the problem within the context of the social formation under scrutiny. In a contemporary capitalist society, particularly that of the USA, the presence of competitive pressures stimulates certain people to attempt to gain income from any source possible, within the context of their class positions, gender and opportunities.

The middle and upper classes tend to have access to sources of income and wealth which reduce their need for violence, and which make the crime less visible and offensive. For example, corporate crime and price-fixing. The lower classes, however, usually have less physical access to income and wealth and therefore tend to need more confrontation in order to obtain this wealth: examples are burglary and shoplifting. In addition, poorer classes and races are more likely to commit crimes against property because of their relative lack of income, wealth and employment.

Since the state pays more attention to lower-class crime, partly because of greater violence, members of this class find themselves representing the vast proportion of inmates in prisons (especially for long-term imprisonment). People of color are over-represented in the prison system because they are more likely to be members of the lower classes, and are also more likely to be stereotyped as criminal and charged.

Neoclassical approaches

In a seminal paper, Gary Becker (1968)

introduced rational choice as the methodology for the study of crime. He looked at criminal behavior as a labor market behavior and crime as a voluntary act, committed by people who have compared expected benefits with expected costs of the act prior to committing it. Becker proposed methods for promoting the optimal investment of social resources toward the best possible prevention and enforcement policy. This includes primarily a system of severe and fairly certain punishments. He also argued that for the costs of enforcement to be minimized, monetary fines must replace imprisonment when criminals can afford to pay the fine.

Neoclassical economic theory in general (see Becker and Landes (1974) for the seminal papers) and the school of law and economics in particular (Posner 1985) extended Becker's work by exploring criminal motives. A criminal is often a rational actor who weighs the costs and the benefits before deciding to commit a crime (see RATIONALITY AND IRRATIONALITY). The basic function in this decision is the expected cost of criminal activity. Important here is the disutility created by the penalty for the criminal act, discounted by the probability of punishment, plus the opportunity cost of using time in a more legitimate way. If the expected cost is lower than the expected benefit for the crime, the latter seems a rational (if not a reasonable) act for a risk-neutral individual; sometimes the cost is so low that even risk-aversion is compensated.

This cost–benefit calculation is also generally applied to criminal behavior as a career choice. Criminals are rational actors who have decided that crime pays off. The opportunity cost of a legitimate career is low if they are poor (since most of them are uneducated), and the expected cost is lower when they are rich (since the probability of punishment is very low). Therefore, neoclassical economists recommend that governments should manipulate incentives, opportunities, costs and benefits with the intent of making crime more costly than it presently is, by raising the expected or the opportunity cost. A better education raises the opportunity cost of crime and a moral education the expected cost, as does a more efficient police; the same is true for exemplary punishment. A less corrupt police and an independent judiciary raises the cost of the crime for the rich.

Statistical evidence seems to substantiate the theory. The increase in the probability of detention and of the severity of punishment have led to less crime. However, the greater probability of punishment is more effective, since it is accompanied by severe social sanctions, a kind of fixed cost of crime, regardless of the severity of punishment. On the other hand, prevention is more costly than a severe punishment (which is also not free, given the long prison terms). The problem is how far enforcement should go in terms of efficiency. Is it efficient to eliminate all criminal activity? Of course not, since all the resources in the world would not suffice. Consequently, the "optimal level of crime," the optimization of society's social utility function, is found where the marginal cost of the expenditures on law enforcement equals the social cost from the marginal criminal activity it constrains.

Decriminalization

Economics can also provide policy advice leading to decriminalization rather than to heavier penalties, the most typical example being drug legalization. The main result of such a policy would be a drastic reduction in drug-related crime, since criminal empires would collapse, and the addicts would not have to break the law in order to raise money for costly drugs.

See also:

business ethics; culture of poverty; distribution of income; ethics and morality; health care in social economics; health inequality; human dignity; justice; needs; neoclassical economics; public goods, social costs and externalities; race, ethnicity, gender and class; rights; social economics: major contemporary themes; social and organizational capital; welfare state

Selected references

Becker, Gary S. (1968), "Crime and Punishment: An Economic Approach," *Journal of Political Economy* 76(2): 169–217.
Becker, Gary S. and Landes, William M. (eds) (1974) *Essays in the Economics of Crime and Punishment*, New York: Columbia University Press.
Gordon, David M. (1973) "Class and the Economics of Crime," in James H. Weaver (ed.), *Modern Political Economy: Radical and Orthodox Views on Crucial Issues*, Boston: Allyn & Bacon, 256–86.
Posner, Richard A. (1985) "An Economic Theory of the Criminal Law," *Columbia Law Review* 85(6): 1193–1231.
Pyle, David J. (1995), *Cutting the Costs of Crime: The Economics of Crime and Criminal Justice*, London: Institute of Economic Affairs.

ARISTIDES N. HATZIS
PHILLIP ANTHONY O'HARA

CRISES, FINANCIAL: see financial crises

critical realism

Any position may be designated a (philosophical) *realism* that asserts the existence of some disputed kind of entity (such as black holes, quarks, class relations, the Loch Ness monster, utility, probability, economic equilibria, truth, or yetis). A *scientific realism* is a theory that the ultimate objects of scientific enquiry exist and act (mostly) quite independently of scientists and their practices (Bhaskar 1978; Lawson 1989, 1997). A *transcendental realism* is primarily a metaphysical theory constituting an account of what the world must be like before it is investigated by science, and for scientific activities to be possible. Such a realism neither turns on, nor endorses, any substantive theory. Once obtained, however, it may provide insight as to how science can be done. It may also provide an appropriate standard of comparison for those economists interested in a particular version of the question of naturalism: whether economics can be a science in the same sense as the sciences of nature (see for example Bhaskar 1978, 1989; Lawson 1994, 1997, 1998). The position systematized as *critical realism* which has recently achieved some attention in economics (see, for example, Boylan and O'Gorman 1995; Foss 1994; Lawson 1994, 1997a, 1997b; Pratten 1993) is basically a philosophy of (and for) the social sciences consistent with, and indeed in part comprising, a particular transcendental realist theory of science.

According to the transcendental realism accepted in this critical realist account, reality is structured, intransitive and open. It is *structured* in the sense of being composed in part of structures, powers, mechanisms and their tendencies which are irreducible to actualities (such as the course of events). It is *intransitive* in comprising items that exist and act independently, for the most part, of our knowledge of them. Finally, it is *open* in that regularities of the form "whenever event x then event y" are not the typical situation. Accepting this perspective, it follows that science is primarily concerned not with correlations between events or other actualities, but with uncovering the deeper structures, powers, mechanisms and their tendencies which explain the course of events and states of affairs. Thus, medical science is primarily concerned with identifying and counteracting the underlying causes of ailments rather than with the patterning of symptoms *per se*.

Critical realism has been formulated by way of questioning the extent to which the study of social phenomena can be a science in this sense. Its starting point is that interesting "event regularities" have yet to be uncovered in the social realm and seem, a priori, unlikely to be so. This is the case especially given the reality of human choice, that each person could always have acted otherwise, along with the infeasibility of experimental control in the social realm. And it has been developed through questioning whether there are specifically social structures (facilitating human agency) which a social science such as economics can uncover and/or help to understand.

Any such assessment of the possibilities for a social science of economics, so conceived, necessitates a conception not only of (1) specifically social structure, but also of (2) numerous aspects of human subjectivity more generally, together with (3) some understanding of their interconnection. It is easy to see why. In an open and structured world, all possibilities for capable human agency depend upon whatever structures and mechanisms are in place. However, any aspects of structure that can be designated "social" must (in order to be so designated) also depend in turn on human agency. Social rules, such as language systems, are like this. Both depend upon speech acts, and are a condition of the latter's possibility. Clearly, the nature of this interdependency and related features warrant further elaboration.

In opposition to individualists, on the one hand, and collectivists, on the other, critical realism emphasizes an essentially relational conception of the social. Further, in opposition to structuralists and subjectivists alike, critical realism supports a transformational conception of the agency/structure relation, whereby neither element can be identified with, explained completely in terms of, or reduced to the other.

On the *relational* conception of the social, all social forms, structures and systems, such as the economy, the state, international organizations, trade unions and households, depend upon or presuppose social relations. Of particular concern are the internally related positions into which individuals essentially slot, along with their associated practices, tasks, rights, obligations, prerogatives and so forth. On the *transformational* conception of social activity, the existence of social structure is the often unacknowledged but necessary condition for an individual act, as well as an often unintended but inevitable outcome of individual actions taken in total. Social structure, in short, is the unmotivated condition of our motivated productions, the non-created but drawn upon and reproduced/transformed condition for our daily economic/social activities.

On this critical realist conception, then, the objective of economics is to identify the structures governing some economic phenomenon of interest. Essentially this entails identifying, understanding and explaining certain practices of relevance to the phenomenon in question; that is, identifying the unacknowledged conditions of these practices, unconscious motivations and tacit skills, as well as the unintended consequences. While society and the economy are the skilled accomplishment of active agents, they remain to a degree opaque to the individuals upon whose activities they depend. The task of economics, then, is to describe the total process (whether or not adequately conceptualized by the agents involved) that must be going on for some manifest phenomenon of interest to be possible.

The essential mode of inference implicated in such a conception of science is neither induction (particular to general) nor deduction (general to particular) but retroduction or abduction (manifest phenomenon, at any one level, to "deeper" conditioning structure). For example, this essential movement of science is captured not by starting from, say, the observation of a few black ravens and inferring that all ravens must be black (induction), nor by starting with the claim that all ravens are black and deducing that the next one to be observed must be black (deduction). Rather, critical realism starts with the observation of one or more black ravens and (operating under something like a logic of analogy and metaphor) identifying a causal mechanism (most likely) intrinsic to ravens which disposes them to being black. As Peirce recognized: "[induction] never can originate any idea whatever. Nor can deduction. All the ideas of science come to it by way of abduction. Abduction consists in studying the facts and devising a theory to explain them" (Peirce 1967, vol. 5: 146).

Three further considerations bearing upon method, policy and scope also warrant emphasis. First, because critical realism acknowledges the openness of the economic world and accepts as the primary aim of science the identification and elaboration of the deeper structures that govern surface phenomena, the central criterion of theory assessment must be explanatory power, not predictive accuracy (see, for example, Bhaskar 1978; Collier 1994; Lawson 1989).

Second, critical realism recognizes both that significant event regularities are rarely in evidence in the economic sphere, and that the aim of economic science is instead to uncover relatively enduring underlying structures. Therefore, it holds that economic policy is properly concerned not with predictive control (with manipulating values of variables in the hope of controlling future events, the attempted amelioration of states of economic affairs), but with emancipation through the knowledgeable transformation of structures that govern and facilitate human action.

Third, a broadly philosophical project like critical realism does not, and cannot, licence any specific substantive theory. Specifically, the identification and understanding of any given set of structures, mechanisms and tendencies which explain human practices and other concrete phenomena are the tasks of economic science. In Lockean fashion, philosophy is essentially an under-laborer for science, including economics; it is a ground-clearing device or tendency. It does not exist apart from or detached from science, and it deals with the same reality. However, its primary task is to facilitate a set of perspectives on the nature of the economy and society, and on how to understand them. It is an essential aid to, and a meta-theoretical moment in (but not a substitute for) the empirically controlled investigations of science into the real structures that generate and govern the equally real phenomena of economic and social life.

Finally, why is the perspective and project outlined here referred to as *critical* realism? The adoption of this label is hardly novel (examples of earlier works include Durant Drake's *Essays in Critical Realism*, published in 1920, and George Dawes Hicks's *Critical Realism* in 1938), and mainly centers on the human agency-dependent nature of social structure. Specifically, because social structure is dependent upon human agency, it is open to transformation though changing human practices which in turn can be affected by criticizing the conceptions and understandings on which people act. The sciences and various philosophies are themselves social structures and practices, which are unavoidably susceptible to change through critique. In like fashion, any emergent science of economics will be part of its own field of study and thereby sensitive to and, like society at large, ultimately dependent on social criticism. Of course, it is at least conceivable that competing social philosophies will emerge which both accept the transcendental realist account of science sketched above and also recognize the dependency of social life on human conceptions (without being reducible to them), and hence on critical reason. Although the position outlined here takes the heading of critical realism, it warrants emphasis that there may in the future be numerous conceptions which would qualify equally for this ascription.

See also:

laws of political economy; method in economics; methodological individualism; normative and positive economics; pragmatism

Selected references

Bhaskar, R. (1978) *A Realist Theory of Science*, 2nd edn, Brighton: Harvester.
—— (1989) *Reclaiming Reality*, London: Verso.
Boylan, T.A. and O'Gorman, P.F. (1995) *Beyond Rhetoric and Realism in Economics: Towards a Reformulation of Economic Methodology*, London: Routledge.
Collier, A. (1994) *Critical Realism: An Introduction to Roy Bhaskar's Philosophy*, London: Verso.
Foss, N.J. (1994) "Realism and Evolutionary Economics," *Journal of Social and Evolutionary Systems* 17(1): 21–40.
Lawson, C. (1994) "The Transformation Model of Social Activity and Economic Activity: A Reinterpretation of the Work of J.R. Commons," *Review of Political Economy* 6(2).
Lawson, T. (1989) "Abstraction, Tendencies

and Stylised Facts: A Realist Approach to Economic Analysis," *Cambridge Journal of Economics* 13(1): 59–78.
——(1997)*Economics and Reality*, London: Routledge.
—— (1998) "Transcendental Realism," in J. Davis, D. Hands and U. Mäki (eds), *The Handbook of Economic Methodology*, Cheltenham: Edward Elgar.
Peirce, C.S. (1967) *Collected Papers of Charles Sanders Peirce*, ed. C. Hartshorne and P. Weiss, Cambridge, MA: Harvard University Press.
Pratten, S. (1993) "Structure, Agency and Marx's Analysis of the Labour Process," *Review of Political Economy* 5(4): 403–26.

TONY LAWSON

cultural capital

Definitions

The term "cultural capital" signifies particular kinds of knowledge, social styles, talent and abilities and is used here in the Bourdieuan sense. According to sociologist Pierre Bourdieu (1986) cultural capital comes in three states. The first, embodied cultural capital, can be understood as the ability, talent, style or even speech patterns of people in a group; for instance, a particular ethnic group. This is the embodiment of characteristics that in general are acquired over time and/or through the socialization process and tend to be the marks that distinguish one group from another. Bourdieu (1986: 244) explains embodied cultural capital as external wealth converted into an integral part of the person in such a way that it appears natural and effortless. This form of cultural capital cannot be transferred instantaneously, or bought or sold. It is acquired, yet has the appearance of being innate and frequently goes unrecognized.

The second type is objectified cultural capital, which comprises cultural goods such as pictures, books, instruments and so on. These objects can be an expression of cultural identity as well as being sold on the market for remuneration. The third form is institutionalized cultural capital, when the cultural capital is directed into structures which can enhance the group's economic position. For example, this occurs when cultural capital facilitates the creation of educational qualifications. The latter in particular is a critical determinant of the socioeconomic position of various groups.

Social inequality

Bourdieu initially developed the concept of cultural capital to explain the differences in academic achievement of children from different social strata or classes and point out how social INEQUALITY is transmitted from one generation to another (Bourdieu 1973; Bourdieu and de Saint-Martin 1974; Bourdieu and Passeron 1977). The concept provided a fresh approach to the social stratification debate in the 1970s and 1980s and the writings of Bourdieu have made an important contribution to the sociology of education.

The cultural capital of the dominant CLASS, including their language and linguistic style, values, definitions of basic knowledge and assumptions, enables this class to succeed in the educational system. Minority ethnic groups, including indigenous or first peoples and new immigrants often lack the appropriate cultural capital to achieve or secure a headstart at school. The school system itself can become the agent of the reproduction of social inequality by being responsive to the arbitrary cultural code of the dominant class and impervious to the "cultural deprivation" of the non-dominant classes (see REPRODUCTION PARADIGM). The embodied cultural capital of some individuals can be transformed and institutionalized into formal educational qualifications. This, however, often depends on social class. Empirical work on the link between social class and the progression to further or higher education has shown that students from a working class background are less likely than middle class students to move into higher education and when they do move into higher education they are less likely to select programs that lead them to the higher professions (see for example Lauder and Hughes 1990; Nash 1986).

A wider definition of human capital

Generally economists do not pay much attention to the link between culture and economic outcomes. Fortunately this is slowly changing with a few economists, such as Arjo Klamer (who is the occupant of the world's first chair in the Economics of Art and Culture, at Erasmus University, The Netherlands), acting as a catalyst for this change (see, for example, Klamer 1996).

De Bruin (1997) makes a case for examining cultural capital when seeking solutions for unemployment. In this respect it is necessary to broaden the definition of HUMAN CAPITAL to include cultural capital. Such a recognition would serve three purposes. First, it would overcome the preconception that ethnic minorities are necessarily less employable because they are lacking in human capital. Second, innovative community initiatives can recognize and utilize this dimension of human capital to provide employment for ethnic minorities. Third, it provides a theoretical underpinning for practical programs to create jobs at the community level.

For the majority of indigenous peoples of the world, the conversion of embodied cultural capital into formal educational qualifications is often slow and indirect. For dominant, especially white cultures, on the other hand, the link is often immediate and direct. Hence, there is a considerable gap in educational qualifications among ethnic groups. Employer selection of job applicants is influenced to some extent by their formal educational qualifications. Those with lower qualifications have a reduced probability of being selected from among a pool of job applicants.

A widened definition of human capital, however, recognizes the possibilities for embodied cultural capital to be harnessed and transformed to create employment for such labor market disadvantaged groups, especially through grassroots action at the micro level of the local community. This is shown to be a possibility particularly in the tourism industry (de Bruin and Dupuis 1995). Community action could not only harness cultural capital but also draw strength from a social force called "cultural energy," which could be generated by cultural expression. This force motivates and inspires people to face problems, identify solutions and participate in implementing them (Kleymeyer 1994).

See also:

accumulation; capital theory debates; capital and the wealth of nations; crime; culture of poverty; humanistic economics; language, signs and symbols; natural capital; race, ethnicity, gender and class; race in political economy: major contemporary themes; social economics: major contemporary themes; social and organizational capital

Selected references

Bourdieu, Pierre (1973) "Cultural Reproduction and Social Reproduction," in Richard Brown (ed.), *Knowledge, Education and Cultural Change*, London: Tavistock, 71–112.

—— (1986) "The Forms of Capital," in John G. Richardson (ed.), *Handbook of Theory and Research for the Sociology of Education*, New York: Greenwood Press, 241–58.

Bourdieu, Pierre and Passeron, Jean-Claude (1977) *Society, Culture and Education*, Beverley Hills, CA: Sage Publications.

Bourdieu, Pierre and de Saint-Martin, Monique (1974) "The School as a Conservative Force: Scholastic and Cultural Inequalities," in John Eggleston (ed.), *Contemporary Research in the Sociology of Education*, New York: Harper & Row, 32–46.

de Bruin, Anne (1997) "The Transformation of the Welfare State in New Zealand with Special Reference to Employment," unpublished Ph.D. thesis, Massey University, New Zealand.

de Bruin, Anne and Dupuis, Ann (1995) "A Closer Look at New Zealand's Superior Economic Performance: Ethnic Employment

Issues," *British Review of New Zealand Studies* 8: 85–97.

Klamer, Arjo (ed.) (1996) *The Value of Culture*, Amsterdam: Amsterdam University Press.

Kleymeyer, Charles (1994) "Cultural Expression and Grassroots Development," in Charles Kleymeyer (ed.), *Cultural Expression and Grassroots Development*, Boulder, CO: Lynne Rienner Publishers.

Lauder, Hugh and Hughes, David (1990) "Social Origins, Destinations and Educational Inequality,'" in John Codd, Richard Harker and Roy Nash (eds), *Political Issues in New Zealand Education*, Palmerston North: Dunmore Press.

Nash, Roy (1986) "Education and Social Inequality: The Theories of Bourdieu and Boudon with Reference to Class and Ethnic Differences in New Zealand," *New Zealand Sociology* 1(2): 121–37.

ANNE M. DE BRUIN

culture

The anthropological concept of culture is as much an object of study as "society" or "the economy." As an object of study, culture is generally conceived of as the whole way of life of a society. As an orientation, the study of "culture" sees existing institutional and social patterns as a determinant of individual behavior. This does not deny the importance of the individual, since it places the individual within a context. The object is to understand that context and how it impacts upon individual and collective behavior.

Definition and approaches

In *Primitive Culture*, Edward Burnett Tylor defined culture as "that complex whole which includes knowledge, belief, art, law, morals, customs, and any other capabilities and habits acquired by man as a member of society" (Tylor 1871: 1). The key ideas were those of continuity, creation, accumulation and transmission independently of genetic constitutions and biological characteristics.

Culture is inextricably tied to a community. It is what connects the individual with society, what the individual learns as he or she is transformed into a fully socialized member of society. Education, both formal and informal, is the process by which the individual acquires the "knowledge, customs, capabilities and habits" needed to be a fully functional "member of society." So conceived, individuals are neither wholly conditioned by the sociocultural environment, nor wholly separate from it. Although clearly interdependent, anthropology traditionally gives priority to studying how culture impacts on the individual rather than how the individual impacts on culture.

One contemporary orientation in anthropology is to see all cultures as being adapted to, and explicable through, their material environment (Harris 1979). In this sense, culture becomes not the link between the individual and society as much as it is the link between society and its material conditions of life. Culture, in this sense, is an adaptive mechanism of populations in ecosystems. Human societies are subject to the same laws of evolution as other animals species, but selection operates on the combination of culture-plus-biology. All aspects of culture contribute to the ecological adjustment of a society. From this perspective, the study of culture and the study of economy, conceived as the material conditions of existence, are inextricably linked (Jackson 1996).

Another contemporary approach breaks with the "natural science" orientation and conceives culture to be the imaginative universe by and through which people live their lives. In the same way that Papuans or Amazonians inhabit the world they imagine, so do nuclear physicists, historians of the Mediterranean in the age of Phillip II, and economists of one variety or another. The science of culture becomes an interpretive affair that borrows more from philosophy and literature than it does from natural science (Geertz 1973).

All sciences are interpretive, but the social sciences involve multiple interpretations because human beings are the objects of investigation as well as the investigators. In this tradition of inquiry, which itself has a long history (Berlin 1979), the anthropologist searches out and analyses the symbolic forms – words, images, institutions, behaviors – which different people in different places use to represent themselves to themselves, to one another and to others. Here social theorists, when studying their own society, have to interpret the behavior of others, who are themselves floundering to comprehend reality and perhaps hold versions or fragments of the theorist's perspective. This is particularly true in the case of economics.

Culture and economic organization

In his book *Industrial Evolution* (1901), Karl Buecher suggested that "savages" had no economic organization but were in a pre-economic stage of development. In response, Bronislaw Malinowski (1921) argued both that economists need to recognize that economic activities are embedded in the wider social-cultural relations of tribal life, and also that ethnologists need to acknowledge the importance of economic factors in tribal life. The fact was that people like the Trobriand Islanders, whom Malinowski had studied in great detail and whom Buecher had included in his generalizations about "savages," did have very complex forms of economic organization; they were just different from our own.

Economics and political economy

By the unqualified term "economic theory," economists normally have in mind the theory derived from the neoclassical economics of the late nineteenth century (see NEOCLASSICAL ECONOMICS). This brand of economics has little use for culture, and therefore tends to ignore it. In mainstream economics, the individual is the analytical unit from which all theorizing and explaining begins; this is not a specific individual in time and place, but rather a generic all-purpose individual seen as being similarly responsive to self-interest in all times and all places, rather than heeding specific social or cultural norms. Those who work within the neoclassical tradition assume that the patterns of behavior that they describe derive from these universal human characteristics. The cultural patterns that are time and place specific may, on occasion and regrettably, constrain behavior but are not a subject matter of concern to economists.

The prospects for a more culturally informed economics lies with non-neoclassical economists. Of the varieties of non-neoclassical theory, institutional political economy is the most culturally inclined (see INSTITUTIONAL POLITICAL ECONOMY: HISTORY). The word "culture" may not always be used, but what institutional economists mean by terms such as "mass behavior" (Wesley Mitchell), "habits of use and wont" (Thorstein VEBLEN), "collective control over individual action" (John R. Commons), "instituted process" (Karl Polanyi), or simply "institutions" (most institutional economists) is consistent with the cultural orientation. Social economists and feminists are similarly inclined. Whatever the term or phrase, the common ideas have been that (a) there is no universal, immutable human nature; (b) what economists describe are regularities of behavior; (c) regularities are specific to time and place and persist because of enculturation; and (d) that an analysis or description of the cultural context, the institutional framework within which specific economic behavior takes place, is the most important thing to study.

Some recent brands of institutionalism are at odds with cultural ideas in this sense. New institutionalism pursues the reductionist objective of explaining institutions as the product of culturally unconstrained, rational, purposive individuals, rather than as the context within which individual choice takes place.

Keynesian economics has many strands, some of which can accommodate a cultural perspective. Some argue that KEYNES turned away from scientific, Enlightenment philosophy toward a pre-Enlightenment philosophy which permits such "unscientific" practices as introspection and judgments of value (Fitzgibbons 1990). As Jackson observes, "This puts

Keynes nearer to the cultural tradition with its distrust of the crude extensions of Enlightenment philosophy to the study of human societies" (1993: 463). Another component of Keynes's economics, emphasized in much post-Keynesian political economy, is historical TIME (see POST-KEYNESIAN POLITICAL ECONOMY: HISTORY). Here again, Keynes has an affinity with the cultural tradition which is itself profoundly historical (see CONVENTIONS).

The position that culture includes "knowledge, belief, art, law, morals, customs, and any other capabilities and habits acquired by man as a member of society" opens the door for asking the question, "is economics culture-bound?" (Boulding 1970). Much in the tradition of institutional political economy has been devoted to answering this question in the affirmative, exposing the limited and restricted nature of economic theorizing because it is the product of a specific culture at a specific time (see also SUBSTANTIVIST–FORMALIST DEBATE). But to see "culture" in the more restricted sense, as a system of symbols and meanings by and through which people live their lives, casts economic theory not simply as part of a culture but as a cultural system in and of itself. The task of analysis becomes explicating the meanings that economics embodies by placing it in another interpretive framework (see Benton 1986). Much of the work exploring the RHETORIC of economics can be seen as an attempt to search out and analyse the cultural basis of inquiry.

This perspective of culture as systems of symbols and meanings also permits institutional economics, as a tradition of inquiry, to be the subject itself of cultural analysis and criticism. The real tension lies between culture and the individualistic, reductionist slant of neoclassical economics. As Mayhew expressed it, "It is obvious that culture is necessarily a creation of people and that this is so even if we accept that people are creations of the culture" (1987: 590). Theories of the mutual creation of individual and culture are usually found outside of anthropology, for example, Herbert Marcuse's *Eros and Civilization*. Similarly, the ability to reconcile the INDIVIDUAL AND SOCIETY has eluded much economic theorizing. Neoclassical economics, by eulogizing self-interest, overlooks the social character of economic activity, just as much social and anthropological thought has fallen into the trap of thinking of people as being encased in an organic entity beyond the influences of those caught up in the process. Cultural theory, and any economic theory taking a cultural perspective, should ideally be non-dualistic and non-reductionist. There can be no universal human nature determinants of human nature.

See also:

Commons's contribution to political economy; economic anthropology: major contemporary themes; evolutionary economics: major contemporary themes; holistic method; institutional political economy: major contemporary themes; institutions and habits; language, signs and symbols; methodological individualism and collectivism

Selected references

Benton, Raymond, Jr (1986) "Economics and the Loss of Meaning," *Review of Social Economy* 44: 251–67.
Berlin, Isaiah (1979) "The Counter-Enlightenment," in *Against the Current: Essays in the History of Ideas*, New York: Viking Press.
Boulding, Kenneth E. (1970) "Is Economics Culture-Bound?," *American Economic Review* 60(2): 406–11.
Buecher, Karl (1901) *Industrial Evolution*, London: George Bell & Sons.
Fitzgibbons, Athol (1990) *Keynes's Vision: A New Political Economy*, Oxford: Oxford University Press.
Geertz, Clifford (1973) *The Interpretation of Cultures*, New York: Basic Books.
Harris, Marvin (1979) *Cultural Materialism*, New York: Random House.
Jackson, William A. (1993) "Culture, Society and Economic Theory," *Review of Political Economy* 5(4): 453–69.
—— (1996) "Cultural Materialism and Institu-

tional Economics," *Review of Social Economy* 54(2): 221–44.

Malinowski, Bronislaw (1921) "The Primitive Economics of the Trobriand Islanders," *The Economic Journal* 31: 1–16.

Mayhew, Anne (1987) "Culture: Core Concept Under Attack," *Journal of Economic Issues* 21(2): 587–603.

Tylor, Edward Burnett (1871) *Primitive Culture: Researches into the Development of Mythology, Philosophy, Religion, Art and Custom*, New York: Gordon Press, 1974.

RAYMOND BENTON, JR

culture of poverty

Historical background

Since the 1950s, the culture of poverty (COP) thesis has played a contentious role in social science discourse. Loosely defined and selectively applied, it has too often provided a rationale for blaming individuals for their plight rather than focusing on structural or systemic solutions. A working definition is that there are particular attitudes, values and behaviors (such as the tendency to have a short-term planning horizon) that distinguish the poor from the non-poor, with some of these characteristics contributing toward the persistence of their poverty. This entry focuses on the particular form that culture of poverty explanations have taken historically within economics, and in particular on its role in the work of Gunnar Myrdal.

Prior to the publication of Myrdal's *An American Dilemma* in 1944, there was a broad consensus among elite social scientists that African-Americans were genetically inferior. This consensus began with the founders of the American Economics Association, Richard Ely and General Amasa Walker, and the monographs by Frederick Hoffman and Joseph Tillinghast. While many economists also used genetic explanations for the inadequacies of recent white immigrants, liberals offered a cultural explanation. While optimistic that white immigrants could be integrated into society, many, including leading labor economist John R. Commons, were pessimistic with regard to African-Americans. Commons, in *Races and Immigrants in America*, published in 1930, held open little possibility that African-Americans as a group could attain equality; only crossbreeding would allow them to rise up to the standards of European-Americans. Echoing the thoughts of Tillinghast and Hoffman, Commons believed that African-Americans were ill-prepared for freedom.

The culture of poverty explanation was first applied to the situation of African-Americans by Booker T. Washington. He contrasted the "semi-barbarous" African race with the white race that had attained "the highest civilization that the world knows." While slavery had enabled blacks to gain self-discipline and future-oriented goals, Washington believed that they were not the equal of whites at the time of emancipation (Washington 1902).

Earlier dissenters

There were of course dissenters from both the genetic and cultural inferiority viewpoints, including W.E.B. DuBois, Isaac Hourwich and Joseph Goldberger. DuBois protested racial explanations for criminality and the insensitivity of the US Census in refusing to collect lynching statistics; Goldberger fought against genetic theories of pellegra, which rationalized the malnutrition of poor blacks and whites in the South; and Hourwich defended the actions of militant workers against culture of poverty theories. Later they were joined by the group of anthropologists, including Melvin Herskovits and Otto Klineberg, who were trained by Franz Boas. Herskovits promoted the view that African civilization had great achievements, while Klineberg refuted the notion that there was statistical evidence from First World War IQ tests which demonstrated black genetic inferiority. This group, however, had little influence on social science thinking until after the Second World War.

Important building blocks

An important building block of the culture of poverty thesis was Louis Wirth's assessment of the inferior status of Jewish immigrants, in *The Ghetto*, published in 1929, and again in *Community Life and Social Policy* in 1956. He considered the urban mode of life to be difficult for rural individuals, so that crime, mental problems, suicide and alientation would be expected to be more common in the urban than compared with the rural environment. This would be the case for groups such as Eastern European Jews who, he believed, were still affected by their exclusion and suppression from mainstream society. This theory complemented the views popularized by Commons and other social reformers, who believed that unions, settlement houses and compulsory education would acculturate immigrants to American values and behavior.

With the closing of European immigration in the 1920s, African-Americans became more fully integrated into economic life and their northern migration eliminated any notion that the "negro question" was of only regional concern. Just as the culture of poverty thesis was important to those who wished to integrate European immigrants into American society, Myrdal's *An American Dilemma* articulated this thesis when the time came to integrate African-Americans.

Myrdal and Commons

Myrdal noted "the low standards of efficiency, reliability, ambition, and morals actually displayed by the average Negro" (1944: 208). Unlike the earlier liberals, however, Myrdal believed that cultural deficits were the predominant explanation. He attributed perceived African-American laziness to the paternalistic attitude of upper-class white employers, which tended "to diminish the Negroes' formal responsibilities" (1944: 550). Moreover, as a result of lower expectations, Myrdal claimed that Negro youth "is not expected to make good in the same way as white youth. And if he is not extraordinary, he will not expect it himself and will not really put his shoulder to the wheel" (1944: 643). In general, Myrdal argued that these social pathologies could be rectified through education, which would "diffuse middle class norms to the uneducated and crude Southern 'folk Negroes,' emerging out of the backwardness of slavery" (1944: 645).

Myrdal suggested that racism induced African-Americans to have less respect for laws: "Life becomes cheap and crime not so reprehensible" (1944: 959) and this hostility to whites promoted the "shielding of Negro criminals and suspects" (1944: 763). Like Wirth, who was his chief outside consultant, Myrdal pointed to the social disorganization caused by the urbanization process and accepted the views of Washington that African civilization was inferior to European culture.

For both Myrdal and Commons, culture of poverty theories were useful in arguing against radical anti-capitalist changes. Commons claimed that the more radical reforms advocated by many immigrants reflected their lack of appreciation of democratic institutions, rather than an accurate analysis of legitimate grievances. Similarly, Myrdal rejected the central need for labor market policies to overcome discriminatory hiring practices and instead focused on educational initiatives.

Commons and Myrdal stressed moderate institutional changes that were compatible with corporate interests. Their ideas provided the foundation for liberal support of the capital–labor accord between the AFL-CIO and big business reached in the 1950s, and for educational initiatives – Head Start and special minority funding – begun in the 1960s. Emphasizing full employment and migration policies, Myrdal essentially believed in the liberal notion that a rising tide lifts all boats.

While Myrdal believed that the lack of contact between whites and blacks creates stereotypes, he did not relate this to labor market policies. Only in the 1970s did this relationship find its way into labor economics through the institutional models of statistical discrimination, featured prominently in Michael Piore's presentation of the dual labor market. Due to racial stereotyping Piore claimed that many African-American men who possess the proper behavioral traits for decent jobs are forced into low-wage secondary labor markets. However, Piore suggested that once individuals enter the environment of the secondary labor market they adopt COP values. He wrote:

> Working in a world where employment is intermittent and erratic, one tends to lose habits of regularity and punctuality.... Illegitimate activity also tends to follow the intermittent work patterns prevalent in secondary employment, and the...life patterns and role models it presents...foster behavioral traits antagonistic to primary employment.
>
> (Piore 1977: 91–5)

William J. Wilson (1987) updated Myrdal's CIRCULAR AND CUMULATIVE CAUSATION analysis by which past discrimination induces African-Americans to maintain feelings of inferiority and adapt in ways that are dysfunctional; ways that are reinforced by structural black unemployment, created by the loss of inner-city manufacturing employment. Unlike Myrdal, however, he rejected claims that contemporary discrimination is primarily responsible for the problems faced by poor blacks. Indeed, Wilson suggested that the lessening of discrimination – by allowing upwardly mobile blacks to leave the inner city – has increased the social isolation of low-income African-Americans. Without middle-class role models and community institutions provided by these more affluent African-Americans, Wilson believed that the vicious cycle of poverty grows and pathological behaviors are intensified. Not surprisingly, Wilson argued against pursuing demands for further anti-discrimination legislation.

Contemporary critics

There are, of course, many contemporary economists who reject culture of poverty explanations for the situation of low-income African-Americans. Thomas Boston (1988), William Darity and Rhonda Williams demonstrate the incompatibility of culture of poverty explanations with competitive mechanisms, and believe that they function solely to rationalize proposals to scrap welfare and AFFIRMATIVE ACTION. Most importantly, left-wing critics of the culture of poverty theory believe that inequality can best be understood by looking at the culture of racism and new studies of whiteness. Roediger (1991) and Omi and Winant (1994) believe that white workers have promoted culture of poverty theories, enabling them to rationalize discrimination in the labor market: good jobs are reserved for white (male) workers. Others, including Reich, believe that the primary function of culture of poverty explanations has been to enable capitalists to divide workers along race/ethnic lines, weakening their bargaining power, as workers, for higher wages, and as citizens, for better social services.

See also:

race in political economy: history; race in political economy: major contemporary themes; segmented and dual labor markets; Williams–Rodney thesis

Selected references

Boston, Thomas (1988) *Race, Class, and Conservatism*, Boston: Unwin Hyman.
Cherry, Robert (1976) "Racial Thought and the Early Economics Profession," *Review of Social Economics* 33(October): 147–62.
—— (1995) "The Culture of Poverty Thesis and African Americans," *Journal of Economic Issues* 29(December): 1–14.
Jackson, Walter (1990) *Gunnar Myrdal and America's Conscience*, Chapel Hill, NC: University of North Carolina Press.
Jennings, Ann and Champlin, Dell (1994) "Cultural Contours of Race, Gender, and Class Distinction," in Janice Peterson and Doug Brown (eds), *The Economic Status of Women Under Capitalism*, Cheltenham: Edward Elgar.
Johnson, Guy (1944) "The Stereotype of the American Negro," in Otto Klineberg, *Char-*

acteristics of the American Negro, San Francisco: Harper & Row.

Myrdal, Gunnar (1944) *An American Dilemma: The Negro Problem and Modern Democracy*, 2 vols, New York: Pantheon.

Omi, Michael and Winant, Howard (1994) *Racial Formation in the United States*, London and New York: Routledge.

Piore, Michael (1977) "The Dual Labor Market," in David Gordon (ed.), *Problems in Political Economy*, Lexington, MA: D.C. Heath, 91–5.

Roediger, David (1991) *The Wages of Whiteness*, London: Verso.

Shulman, Steven and Darity, William (1989) *The Question of Race*, Middletown, CT: Wesleyan University Press.

Southern, David (1987) *Gunnar Myrdal and Black–White Relations*, Baton Rouge, LA: Louisiana State University Press.

Washington, Booker T. (1902) *The Future of the American Negro*, Boston.

Wilson, William J. (1987) *The Truly Disadvantaged*, Chicago: University of Chicago Press.

ROBERT CHERRY

CUMULATIVE CAUSATION: see circular and cumulative causation

cycles and trends in the world capitalist economy

Business cycles

Virtually everyone agrees that there are short-term fluctuations in the economic life of the modern world. Such fluctuations are usually called business cycles, which presumably go up and down every few years. In terms of length, they are not so different from the agricultural cycles of pre-modern times, which were generally the result of weather cycles. Such short-term cycles are what the newspapers usually mean when they talk of "recessions" and "booms," and which are manifested in short-term variations in unemployment. Central banks often respond to such variations by influencing interest rates.

Kondratieff cycles

When one speaks of longer-term cycles, the reaction of most economists is negative or at least sceptical. The view, however, that longer-run cycles do exist and play a central role in the functioning of the capitalist economy has an impressive list of advocates which spans the ideological spectrum. These longer-run cycles (45–60 years in length) are commonly called "Kondratieff cycles," after the Russian economist who wrote classic essays on the topic (1925). Among the early advocates of the importance of such cycles were J. van Gelderen, Leon Trotsky and Joseph Schumpeter. In the post-1945 period, other leading advocates include W.W. Rostow, Jay Forrester and Ernest Mandel (see LONG WAVES OF ECONOMIC GROWTH AND DEVELOPMENT).

Kondratieff's mode of analysing long cycles, which has been the dominant mode, was to examine price fluctuations in leading countries (such as the UK, France, USA and Germany) and observe parallels in the timing of rises and falls. Most authors who believe that Kondratieff cycles exist come up with similar periodizations (for a comparison of the various authors, see Goldstein (1988)). The post-1792 periodization is often equated with presumed stages in the process of INDUSTRIALIZATION: the cotton or steam era, the iron or railroad era, and so on. Sceptics have challenged the statistical bases of the tables (most notably Slutzky (1937), but see in response Reijnders (1984)). Advocates have offered a wide range of dynamics to understand the phenomenon, largely reflecting their general theoretical vantage point: terms of trade, innovations, and rate of profit explanations. There has also been debate about so-called endogenous-versus-exogenous explanations, particularly of the upturn (see Mandel 1995; Gordon 1991).

While economists have tended to see Kondratieff cycles as a phenomenon engendered by the industrial revolution (but not Schumpeter), others have pushed the phenomenon back to the sixteenth century at least (Braudel 1979; Goldstein 1988; Wallerstein 1984). This is either because they saw capitalist processes as existing earlier, or because they wished to link cycles to wars, hegemonic power shifts or value shifts.

Logistic and hegemonic cycles

Once we push the phenomenon back in time, some authors have observed a longer cycle than that of Kondratieff. Rondo Cameron (1973) has given the 100-year-plus cycles the name of "logistics," on the grounds that they have the shape of a logistic, with a rise and then a flattening. These take the form of long monetary inflations followed by long stability in nominal prices. Economic historians have long noted such phenomena, in such discussions as "the crisis of the seventeenth century" or the long inflationary rise of the twentieth century.

Finally, there have been discussions of hegemonic cycles. The argument is that the modern world has seen systematic shifts between periods in which one power created the terms of a reigning world order, and periods in which rivalry among major powers prevented any such stable situation. Some authors see three such hegemonic powers (the United Provinces, United Kingdom and United States successively); others see earlier equivalents (Arrighi 1994). How such hegemonic cycles relate to the logistics is not entirely clear. They seem to be of approximately the same length but do not seem to have the same periodization for important stretches of time (see HEGEMONY IN THE WORLD ECONOMY).

Trends in the world-economy

The concept of trends is antinomic to that of cycles. Cycles are phenomena that repeat themselves in some way. Trends are phenomena that move steadily in some direction. Neoclassical economists believe basically in the Whig interpretation of history. The trend is linear, positive and moving toward the good (perfect?) society. There is more and more commercialization, more and more urbanization, more and more creation of so-called human capital, and above all more and more acceptance/legitimation of the free market as the underpinning of the good society.

For critics of capitalism, the trends are the consequences of the contradictions of CAPITALISM. What is unilinear is the increasing intensity of the contradictions. This is the opposite of a Whig interpretation. It suggests that historical systems have lives; that is, they begin at certain moments, proceed through a historical evolution and, when the contradictions become too intense, come to an end. If one thinks of this process as having three major moments – the birth of a historical system, its ongoing life, the crisis of a historical system – then the link between cycles and trends is very easy to establish. One of the features of the ongoing life of a system is cyclical processes. As far as we know, all natural phenomena exhibit cyclical processes (the human heartbeat is an example). Also, although this is more controversial, all natural phenomena show evolving trends which, at a certain point, make it impossible for the system to continue to adjust to its environment (human aging may be taken as an example).

Complex cyclical rhythms

If we translate this into an analysis of the capitalist world-economy, we see a structure which emerged sometime in the sixteenth century (the literature on the "transition from feudalism to capitalism" is one major discussion on this emergence). We see a structure that has matured, expanded and thrived for five centuries. During this time, it is ontologically plausible and empirically verifiable that the structure has exhibited all sorts of cyclical rhythms. There is little reason a priori to doubt the possibility of multiple cycles, including the business cycle, the Kondratieffs, the hegemonic cycles, the logistics, and no doubt many others. All of these are of course subject to close empirical analysis and debate.

What we can assume is that these cycles are not mechanically uniform, because they are affected by the trends of the system. Furthermore, it can be demonstrated that the cyclical processes are themselves the origin of some, even many, of the trends. For example, if in order to get out of cyclical downturns, one required element is an expansion of effective demand, one method of obtaining such an expansion is to involve more persons on a full-time basis in the wage labor force. This is one major source of an oft-noted trend, that of "proletarianization."

The question is, what is the impact of these trends on the ability of the capitalist world economy to function? Cycles can be seen as systemic adjustments. The A-period of a cycle refers to the moments at which a system is functioning in a non-problematic way. Presumably something happens (a minor trend), which makes it unlikely that it will function unproblematically. An example often given is "overproduction." The system seems to malfunction, which may be called "crisis" or "downturn" or "disorder" or "depression." This is the B-period of a cycle. Not everyone suffers in a B-period. For some, a B-period may be a moment of great advantage; but for the majority, B-periods are viewed negatively, and many actors seek to restore what is viewed as "normality." Such a renewed "upturn" is not necessarily easy to achieve, but it has occurred repeatedly. We may envisage the steps taken as achieving middle-run normality (or a new A-phase) at the expense of taking measures which accentuate long-run contradictions (the trends). In effect, a system is buying time, which is no doubt rational; but eventually, the price has to be paid. At this point, we come to the real "systemic crisis," out of which the only result can be the replacement of the existing system by an alternative system or systems (see GLOBAL CRISIS OF WORLD CAPITALISM).

See also:

nutcracker theory of the business cycle; Schumpeter's theory of innovation, development and cycles; secular crisis; social structures of accumulation; world-systems analysis

Selected references

Arrighi, Giovanni (1994) *The Long Twentieth Century*, London: Verso.
Braudel, Fernand (1979) "A Model for the Analysis of the Decline of Italy," *Review* II(4): 647–62.
Cameron, Rondo E. (1973) "The Logistics of European Economic Growth," *Journal of European Economic History* II(1): 145–48.
Goldstein, Joshua S. (1988) *Long Cycles: Prosperity and War in the Modern Age*, New Haven: Yale University Press.
Gordon, David M. (1991). "Inside and Outside the Long Swing: The Exogeneity/Endogeneity Debate and the Social Structures of Accumulation Approach," *Review* XIV(2): 263–312.
Kondratieff, Nikolai (1925) *The Long Wave Cycle*, New York: Richardson & Snyder, 1984.
Mandel, Ernest (1980) *Long Waves of Capitalist Development: A Marxist Interpretation*, 2nd revised edn, London: Verso, 1995.
Reijnders, Jan (1984) "Perspectivistic Distortion: A Note on Some Fundamental Problems Concerning the Approximation of Trends and Trend-Cycles," *Social Science Information* 23(2).
Slutzky, E. (1937) "The Summation of Random Causes as the Source of Cyclic Processes," *Econometrica* 5: 105–46.
Wallerstein, Immanuel (1984) "Long Waves as Capitalist Process," *Review* 7(4): 559–75.

IMMANUEL WALLERSTEIN

cyclical crisis models

Models of this type occur almost entirely within Marxist political economy (see MARXIST POLITICAL ECONOMY: MAJOR CONTEMPORARY VARIETIES). The term "cyclical crisis" joins together the concepts "cycle" and "crisis," each of which often appears on its own. Thus, for example, certain works describe smooth cycles, of the multiplier/accelerator or Goodwin predator–prey types (see GOODWIN

cyclical crisis models

CYCLE AND PREDATOR–PREY MODELS). The term "crisis" denotes periodic moments of economic catastrophe or secular (long-term) undermining of capitalist reproduction (see SECULAR CRISIS), without any necessary connection to a cyclical, ebb and flow process. Cyclical crisis, on the other hand, combines a determinate cyclical movement with a moment of sharp rupture and systemic disorganization. A typical growth path for a capitalist economy experiencing cyclical crisis, as shown in Figure 3, has a smooth rising region culminating in a sharp break – the crisis – resulting in a discontinuous downward movement, or crash; this is then followed by a lingering trough and a renewed period of smooth but intensifying ACCUMULATION.

Mathematical and literary branches

Marxist economic theory has tried to grasp the reality of critical cycles in CAPITALISM: their possibility, their necessity and their directionality (contribution to and determination by long-term structural evolution). An example is the NUTCRACKER THEORY OF THE BUSINESS CYCLE. Owing to the inherent difficulty of formally modeling complex processes, however, the literature has tended to separate into mathematical and literary branches. The mathematical branch uses CATASTROPHE THEORY to describe critical cycles (cycles punctuated with crises). Little progress has been made, however, in deriving the characteristics of the model that result in catastrophes (sudden breaks, or discontinuous shifts, in the variables of interest) from underlying postulates; the models show why catastrophes must occur given the cusp, or fold, in the behavior surface, but do not explain why those cusps or folds exist in the first place. For an introduction to catastrophe theory with no Marxist interface, see Zeeman (1976).

The literary branch works within the tradition of theorizing exemplified by Marx's *Das Kapital* (e.g. Weeks 1981; Itoh 1980). In Itoh's approach, both cycles and crisis have much to do with the role of fixed capital and the credit system. In the boom, capitals are committed in fixed form and labor-saving technical change cannot occur. Accumulation is therefore capital-widening, and the demand for labor puts upward pressure on wages. At the same time, inter-capitalist competition must take on financial forms, as capitals seek to grow at each other's expense. The demand for loans pushes up the rate of interest. Capitalists are thus caught in the double pincer of rising wage rates and rising interest rates. SPECULATION lends this process a "bubble" aspect, and the bursting of the bubble explains the critical nature of the downturn. In the trough, fixed capitals are devalued and can be replaced; it is here that labor-saving, productivity-enhancing technical change enters the picture. This weakens the demand for labor and explains the protracted quality of the trough. Eventually, with fixed capital being recommitted, a new round of rapid accumulation begins.

The literary approach to cyclical crisis is able to incorporate a rich variety of elements; it is not, however, able to locate turning points precisely or provide a rigorous account of the cycle, including its critical phases. Marx had spoken of the rise in wages during the boom touching "the point at which the surplus-labor [profit] that nourishes capital is no longer supplied in normal quantity"; at this point "a reaction sets in: a smaller part of revenue is capitalized, accumulation lags, and the movement of the rise in wages receives a check" (Marx 1867: 680). The questions remain: at exactly what point does that occur? Why must the lag in accumulation take a discontinuous form?

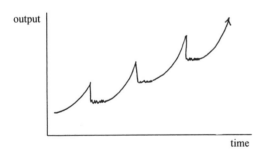

Figure 3

cyclical crisis models

Dynamic nature of investment and competition

One possible answer is explored in a model that tries to develop a middle ground between the formal-mathematical and the literary branches of the subject (see Laibman 1992: chaps 9–11). The key is the dynamic nature of the investment decision: in the intense struggle for survival that characterizes inter-capitalist competition, each capitalist must invest (accumulate) at a maximal rate when others are doing so. To fail in this regard is to fall behind in the race for markets, scale and productivity, and consequently to die. Similarly, when capital-in-general is abstaining from investment and sheltering in liquidity, the individual firm is at pains to do the same (in the words of the old business adage: "Don't panic; but if you do, be the first!"). The investment share, therefore, changes suddenly and discontinuously between a high level embodying the full frenzy of the struggle to accumulate in expectation of strong markets, and a low level (possibly zero) determined by fear of exposure and takeover in conditions of weak or declining markets.

In Figure 4, a positive relation is drawn between the growth rate of the demand for labor (vertical axis) and the unemployment rate (horizontal axis).

High unemployment weakens workers, and lagging wages produce high profit rates and consequently high rates of accumulation and labor demand; and conversely. This positive relation, however, is drawn for two cases: the upper curve of labor demand growth for the high level of the investment share, and the lower curve of labor demand growth for the low (or zero) level of the investment share. The horizontal line represents the (constant) growth rate of the labor supply. (More complex assumptions are possible, but do not add substantially to the dynamics depicted.)

At point A in Figure 4, labor demand is growing more rapidly than supply and unemployment is falling; the economy is therefore starting to move to the left along the top curve, as shown by the arrow on the curve. In this phase, the working class is becoming stronger, and profit and growth rates are falling. So long as markets are growing, however – as determined most decisively by the fact of falling unemployment – capitalists must struggle to participate in them, and investment remains at the high level.

When point B is reached, however, unemployment stops falling and markets stop growing. This, and not some undetermined "normal quantity" of profit, is what brings fear of inadequate markets and low rates of return

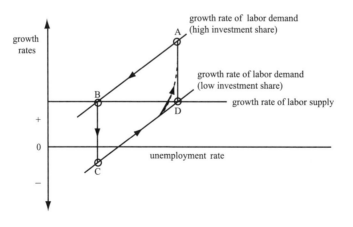

Figure 4

home to roost. Capitalists panic in the light of greater uncertainty, and the investment share drops suddenly to the lower level. The (relatively) instantaneous fall from point B to C is the moment of crisis. It is, in principle, explained by both the critical character of the movement from B to C, and the precise location of the upper turning point (B).

At C, demand for labor grows more slowly than supply (as drawn, its growth rate is actually negative). Unemployment therefore rises, and the economy moves from C toward D in the trough of the cycle. Workers are being weakened, wages are falling (relatively or absolutely) and profitability is being restored. The economy remains on the lower curve, however, owing to rising unemployment and the consequent poor EXPECTATIONS of markets. Only at D, when unemployment stabilizes, are the high profit potentials perceived by capitalists. As soon as the leap back to rapid accumulation begins, all must jump for it, on pain of extinction. The cycle returns to A, its starting point. If high profit potential begins to attract investment while unemployment is still rising, the upward leap at D may be replaced by a smooth path (shown as a dotted line in Figure 4). The upper turning point (B) may therefore be more "critical" than the lower one (D).

This model (sketched only in its essentials here) incorporates several elements described by Marx in passages often thought to be mutually contradictory. Thus, we have wage push and profit squeeze in the boom, underconsumption or demand-limiting phenomena, and biased technical change (which contributes to the shape of the relation between growth of labor demand and unemployment). When the wage share is falling, in the trough along the range from C to D, sectoral demand failure (owing to relative overextension of the consumer goods sector, relative to capital goods) may add to demand-side pressures, further postponing the recovery. Financial processes can be integrated into the story.

Conclusion

In sum, this approach points toward a synthesis of elements in the theory of cyclical crisis rather than seeking to "perfect" one theory while abandoning others (see Itoh 1980, ch. 5). It thus holds out the possibility of developing models of cyclical crisis that are both rich in structure, and rigorous in determination of the critical turning points and phases of the cycle.

See also:

business cycle theories; profit-squeeze analysis of crises

Selected references

Itoh, Makoto (1980) *Value and Crisis*, New York: Monthly Review Press.
Laibman, David (1992) *Value, Technical Change and Crisis: Explorations in Marxist Economic Theory*, Armonk, NY: M.E. Sharpe.
Marx, Karl (1867) *Das Kapital*, Volume I, published as *Capital, Volume 1*, Chicago: Charles H. Kerr & Company, 1906.
Weeks, John (1981) *Capital and Exploitation*, Princeton, NJ: Princeton University Press.
Zeeman, E.C. (1976) "Catastrophe Theory," *Scientific American* 234(4): 65–83.

DAVID LAIBMAN

D

debt crises in the Third World

It is generally accepted that developing countries regularly require external transfers to finance imports of necessary consumption and investment goods. FOREIGN AID and FOREIGN DIRECT INVESTMENT rarely cover more than a small fraction of the necessary financing. Most developing countries therefore borrow money from commercial lenders, bond holders, foreign governments or international financial institutions (IFIs) such as the World Bank, the International Monetary Fund and the regional development banks. International lending to sovereign states differs substantially from domestic lending to private borrowers. Most importantly, in the absence of a universally accepted legal system, no court can force a sovereign borrower to honor a contract. Sovereign lending thus has important strategic and political dimensions.

Definition and historical background

A debt crisis occurs when a major borrower is unable to maintain scheduled "debt servicing," that is, payment of principal and interest. The most recent international debt crisis began in August 1982, when the Mexican government informed its commercial creditors that it would not be able to continue to service its debts on schedule. Two dozen other nations made similar announcements within the year. This was not the first international debt crisis; similar episodes occurred in the 1930s and in the nineteenth century (see Suter 1992).

Shocks and policy problems

External shocks generally figured prominently in the outbreak and early phases of the 1980s debt crisis. The global oil and food price shocks of the mid-1970s stimulated extraordinary external borrowing of "petrodollars" by many developing countries. The bank deposits of OPEC nations enjoyed a sudden boom which led to increases in foreign exchange earnings. International banks seeking outlets for petrodollar deposits actively courted sovereign borrowers needing extraordinary capital inflows. In Basu's (1991) words, there was a considerable amount of "loan pushing" by lenders in the 1970s. The new bank debt of the 1970s and early 1980s was primarily dollar denominated and floating (interest) rate. Tight monetary policy in the UK and USA in the early 1980s, however, brought historically high real interest rates, a heavily overvalued dollar and the global Reagan–Thatcher recession, which hurt Third World exports to industrial economies and therefore their foreign exchange earnings. The conjuncture of these conditions pushed many debtors beyond their debt-servicing capacity.

The debt crisis was not exclusively – for some countries, hardly at all – a product of external shocks. Many borrowers were slow to adjust domestic policies to stabilize fiscal and current accounts in the wake of the external shocks of the 1970s and 1980s. Thus, through the mid-1990s, international policy-makers focused less on external shocks than on debtors' policy errors, in particular unsustainable fiscal deficits, lax monetary policy, financial repression that induced capital flight, and trade and exchange rate controls.

Phases in crisis handling

There have been three distinct phases in the

handling of the most recent Third World debt crisis. Initially, the crisis was perceived as one of illiquidity rather than insolvency. Policy makers believed the liquidity problems were of a short-term nature and relied on emergency relending, Bank for International Settlements bridge loans and rescheduling through the London and Paris Clubs for private and public creditors, respectively, to muddle through. A famous speech in late 1985 in Seoul by then US Treasury Secretary James Baker marked a turning point toward a medium-term view of debtor illiquidity. The Baker Plan emphasized concerted fresh lending by commercial creditors, general balance of payments support by the international financial institutions, and multi-year debt rescheduling by the London and Paris Clubs. The Baker Plan promised US$20 billion of new bank finance and US$9 billion of official loans, concentrated on seventeen heavily indebted middle-income countries. The strategic emphasis thus remained on liquidity and increased lender exposure, rather than solvency and debt reduction.

The primary reason for the liquidity emphasis was that substantial debt write-downs at the outset of the crisis would likely have led to widespread bank failure. Policy makers were concerned to protect the international financial system. In 1982, the nine largest US banks held Third World debt equal to about twice their capital and reserves; yet commercial banks were slow to increase loan loss provisions adequately. It was not until 1987 that major commercial banks began to provision significantly for non-performing Third World loans.

The debt crisis prompted a significant shift in the roles of the IFIs in international finance and development. It gave the IMF the mandate it had lacked since the collapse of the BRETTON WOODS SYSTEM, a decade earlier, and drew the World Bank into program (i.e. non-project) lending. The IFIs' balance of payments support was tied to borrowers' agreements to neoclassical STRUCTURAL ADJUSTMENT POLICIES that emphasized fiscal and monetary restraint, liberalized trade and exchange rate policies, privatization and export expansion.

Ironically, uncoordinated expansion of primary product exports by Third World debtors helped fuel the mid-1980s' collapse in commodity prices, that exacerbated the balance of payments and debt servicing difficulties faced by the poorest, most commodity export dependent economies.

The strategy shifted again in the late 1980s. The collapse of commodity markets caused widespread reassessment of the solvency of Third World debtors. In particular, the oil price crash of 1986 sharply reduced the repayment capacity of key debtors such as Mexico, Nigeria and Venezuela. Perhaps more importantly, by 1990 the major money center banks had reduced their Third World debt exposure to less than half of capital and reserves. Reducing the net present value of sovereign debt no longer threatened commercial bank solvency. Furthermore, it became plain that creditors were failing to meet their new money commitments under the Baker Plan. Debt forgiveness and reduction thus became an important component of new strategies to deal with debt burdens, notably the Brady Plan launched in March 1989. The Brady Plan emphasized interest reduction, debt buy-backs, conversion of bank debt to government bonds, and market-based debt swaps (for corporate equity, environmental protection and development projects). These were made possible by the rapid emergence of a secondary market in sovereign debt in the wake of bank loan-loss provisioning in 1987–9.

Some commentators claim that the evolving strategy pursued by the IFIs, commercial banks and OECD governments in dealing with the Third World debt crisis was successful. They emphasize that the external financial position of the largest middle-income debtor countries (such as Argentina, Chile, Mexico, the Philippines and Uruguay) improved markedly in the wake of the Brady Plan, as evidenced by reduced debt stock and service ratios, sharp increases in secondary market prices for their debt and, in some cases, restored access to international capital markets. Moreover, major commercial banks not only avoided collapse, they remained profitable throughout the crisis.

The supposed success of strategies to cope with the debt crisis is perhaps most manifest in the rapid growth in private capital flows to so-called "emerging markets" in the 1990s, especially in equity and securitized debt. Yet it remains unclear whether these flows are attributable to improved domestic policies and commercial creditworthiness, or to a new round of external shocks reminiscent of the mid-1970s' petrodollar recycling, in particular lower dollar interest rates that caused international capital to seek new investments. Many economists believe the Third World remains vulnerable to adverse external shocks, such as a sharp rise in dollar interest rates, and to domestic policy mismanagement, either of which might prompt a sudden exodus of portfolio investors. These risks were brought home in the Mexican financial crisis of 1994–5 and the 1997–8 crisis in Asia.

Heavily-indebted poor countries

The middle-income countries borrowed primarily from private creditors, and were the focus of international initiatives in the 1980s which saw improvement in their external debt indicators. In sharp contrast, the debt problems of a group of forty heavily indebted poor countries (HIPCs) steadily worsened over the 1980s and into the mid-1990s. The stock of HIPC debt more than tripled in US dollar terms between 1980 and 1990 and aggregate payments arrears mounted rapidly. At the end of 1994 the external debt of Sub-Saharan Africa, for instance, was one-third greater than its GNP and almost four times its export earnings. The HIPCs owed more than three-quarters of their debt stocks to other governments and the IFIs. Serious high-level discussions about an appropriate strategy for remedying the debt problems of the world's poorest countries began only in the mid-1990s. Measured by the affected human population, rather than the dollar debt stocks involved, the debt crisis remained quite serious in the mid-1990s.

Conclusion

Protracted contractionary adjustment programs made the 1980s a "lost decade" of economic growth in most heavily indebted nations, including virtually all the African and South American continents. Per capita GDP and investment rates fell across both continents, despite increased domestic savings. Moreover, although it is difficult to prove definitively, the debt crisis and associated economic adjustment measures are widely believed to have had especially severe effects on the poor. Real wages for the most part declined, the real prices of staple foods and consumer goods rose, and public provision of education, health, sanitation and other services generally receded. The debt crisis coincides with a period of severe social dislocation in much of the Third World. The costs of the debt crisis and related structural adjustment efforts seem to have been borne disproportionately by debtor nations and especially their poor.

The Third World debt crisis was the watershed development event of the 1980s and 1990s. It represented a dramatic global episode that had profound and lasting effects on international financial flow patterns, the organization and operation of the IFIs and developing country economic policy. In this respect it replaced the earlier, state-oriented development orthodoxy with a radically neo-classical vision.

See also:

financial crises; financial instability hypothesis; liability management

Selected references

Basu, Kaushik (1991) *The International Debt Problem, Credit Rationing and Loan Pushing: Theory and Experience*, Princeton: Princeton Studies in International Finance no. 70.

Cline, William R. (1995) *International Debt Reexamined*, Washington, DC: Institute for International Economics.

Eaton, Jonathan and Fernandez, Raquel (1995)

"Sovereign Debt," in Gene M. Grossman and Kenneth S. Rogoff (eds), *Handbook of International Economics*, vol. 3, Amsterdam: Elsevier Science.

Eichengreen, Barry and Lindert, Peter (eds) (1989) *The International Debt Crisis in Historical Perspective*, Cambridge, MA: MIT Press.

George, Susan (1988) *A Fate Worse Than Debt*, New York: Grove Press.

Suter, Christian (1992) *Debt Cycles in the World-Economy: Foreign Loans, Financial Crises, and Debt Settlements, 1820–1990*, San Fransisco and Oxford: Westview Press.

CHRIS BARRETT

democracy, political stability and economic performance

Two themes in the literature on the political economy of economic performance are the relationship between democracy and performance, and the relationship between political stability and performance.

Democracy and performance

Sirowy and Inkeles (1990) discuss three perspectives or schools in the study of "democracy and growth." The "conflict school" argues that democracy hinders ECONOMIC GROWTH, particularly in less developed countries. Three arguments are offered in support of this claim: (a) the dysfunctional consequences of premature democracy slow growth; (b) democracies are unable to implement policies necessary for rapid growth; and (c) democracy is incapable of pervasive state involvement for development in the present world-historical context.

In contrast, the "compatibility school" objects to these assumptions and contends that democracy enhances economic growth. These scholars maintain that democratic processes, as well as the existence and exercise of civil liberties and political rights, generate the social conditions most conducive for development.

Finally, according to the "sceptical" perspective, there is no systematic relationship between democracy and development: "regime type" means very little for economic growth. Instead, the focus should be placed on institutional structures and government development strategies, which may vary independently of the democratic character of a political system.

Empirical evidence

Despite the rich texture of the theoretical literature on the subject, cross-national empirical studies have fallen short in their attempts to reject or accept the claims made above. Some empirical studies have found no significant relationship between economic growth and democracy. Others have established a strong impact of democracy on growth. Still others have ascertained only a weak positive effect of freedom on growth, or have even discerned a weakly negative influence of freedom on growth (Feng 1997).

Similarly, the reverse effect of economic development on democracy is somewhat ambiguous. The modernization thesis that economic development is a precondition for democracy originates in Lipset's (1959) work, and is maintained by a wide range of social scientists. Empirical testing, however, has produced ambiguous results. A number of works by scholars have found that economic development emerges as a significant determinant for the degree of democracy. In contrast, others have found that increasing levels of economic development do not necessarily lead to higher levels of democracy. Additionally, it has been found that, although the effect of economic development on democracy is significant, the impact is far less pronounced than the modernization thesis would suggest.

Political stability and growth

Like the study of democracy and growth, the study of political stability and growth has also yielded contradictory findings. Alesina *et al.* (1996) find that countries with a high incidence of government collapse also have low economic growth, although they also find that low growth does not affect political instability. Londregan and Poole (1990), on the other hand, do not find evidence of reduced growth as a consequence of increased political instability. Instead, they infer from their study that low economic growth increases the probability of political instability.

In previous studies of political instability and economic performance, the concept of "major government change" is used (for example, Alesina *et al.* 1996). This covers all unconstitutional government change as well as all constitutional transfers that involve a change in the party or coalition of parties in power. Although both are categorized as major government change, unconstitutional government change and major constitutional government change can be entirely different. The former involves political regime change, in turn signaling radical political change, while the latter represents social, political and economic adjustment within the constitution.

Linkages between democracy and stability

Several studies employ simultaneous equations to investigate either the causality between growth and government change (Alesina *et al.* 1996) or between growth and democracy (Helliwell 1994), but not both. It is likely that government change and democracy are endogenous to each other in their relationships with growth. Democracies may experience typically more constitutional government transfers than dictatorships, and dictatorships may have more unconstitutional government changes than democracies. However, as stability is analytically distinct from political systems, it should be treated as such empirically (Bollen and Jackman 1989). This implies that stability and democracy should be included concurrently as separate endogenous variables in the study of economic growth. It is reasonable, then, to link growth, government change and democracy all in a simultaneous equation system to avoid the biased results of single equation estimation.

In the puzzle of the effect of democracy on growth, an important clue has been developed by Helliwell (1994), who finds that the negative but non-significant effect on growth of democracy is counterbalanced by the positive indirect effect that democracy exerts on growth through education and investment. Parallel to Helliwell's argument, an area worthy of study is the positive indirect effect of democracy on growth through the channel of political stability. Such a study can be theoretically framed and empirically carried out through a simultaneous equation model which includes growth, government change and democracy as endogenous variables (Feng 1997). While democracy may have a negative direct effect on growth, it can have a positive indirect effect on growth through its differential impacts on constitutional and unconstitutional government change.

Major constitutional government change, representing policy adjustment, may renew or spur economic growth, whereas unconstitutional government change, which generates political uncertainty, may have a negative effect on growth. Democracy has a positive impact on constitutional government change and a negative impact on unconstitutional government change. Overall, therefore, democracy can promote growth indirectly by inducing major regular government change and inhibiting irregular government change. Similarly, the critical link between economic development and democratic transitions may lie in the relationship between growth and government change. Growth may have a negative impact on irregular government change and a positive effect on regular government transfers. But while irregular government transfers may have a negative effect on democracy, major regular government change strengthens democracy (Feng 1997).

Cross-country and time-series analysis

In terms of choosing a data design, some economists (Helliwell 1994; Barro 1997) tend to adopt a cross-country analysis using annual average values of the relevant variables, while some popular scientists (Przeworski *et al.* 1997) are likely to employ a time-series cross-country strategy, where the unit of analysis is based on "per country per year." This methodological bifurcation is caused by differences in research interests between economists, who opt to study long-run aggregate relationships, and political scientists, who emphasize short-run dynamic effects.

The major drawback of the cross-country approach is that short-term dynamic change is discounted. The problem related to using the time-series approach is that the precise timing between growth and its determinants is not well specified at the high frequencies characteristic of business cycles, possibly risking misspecification. However, using a time-series approach allows for the treatment of country (i.e. fixed) effects; this is often achieved by first-differentiating all variables. The trade-offs of this practice are the loss of cross-country information and the inaccuracy of lag information. Despite these potential pitfalls, time-series analyses have an advantage in studying the dynamic change of the relationship between political and economic development. Long-run and short-run analyses, while dependent upon different research objectives, should complement each other in presenting an overall understanding of the processes of political and economic development. (See Barro 1997.)

See also:

development political economy; major contemporary themes; state and government

Selected references

Alesina, A., Özler, S., Roubini, N. and Swagel, P. (1996) "Political Instability and Economic Growth," *Journal of Economic Growth* 1.

Barro, R.J. (1997) *Determinants of Economic Growth: A Cross-Country Empirical Study*, Cambridge, MA: The MIT Press.

Bollen, K.A. and Jackman, R.W. (1989) "Democracy, Stability, and Dichotomies," *American Sociological Review* 54.

Feng, Yi (1997) "Democracy, Political Stability and Economic Growth," *British Journal of Political Science* 27.

Helliwell, J.F. (1994) "Empirical Linkages Between Democracy and Economic Growth," *British Journal of Political Science* 24.

Lipset, S.M. (1959) "Some Social Requisites of Democracy: Economic Development and Political Development," *American Political Science Review* 53.

Londregan, J.B. and Poole, K.T. (1990) "Poverty, the Coup Trap and the Seizure of Executive Power," *World Politics* 32.

Przeworski, A., Alvarez, M., Cheibub, J.A. and Limongi, F. (1997) *Democracy and Development: Political Regimes and Economic Performance, 1950–1990*, Cambridge: Cambridge University Press.

Scully, Gerald (1988) "The Institutional Framework and Economic Development," *Journal of Political Economy* 98.

Sirowy, L. and Inkeles, A. (1990) "The Effects of Democracy on Economic Growth and Inequality: A Review," *Studies in Comparative International Development* 25.

YI FENG

deontology

The ethical theorists who maintain that there are ethical concerns with actions themselves which prohibit the actions in spite of the consequences are called deontologists. The word "deontologist" comes from the Greek "*deontos*," which means "what must be done," sometimes translated into "obligation" or "duty." The foremost deontologist was the eighteenth-century philosopher Immanuel Kant.

Duty and the categorical imperative

According to Kant, human beings, like animals, have inclinations to pursue things which they "want." However, they also have two capabilities that other animals do not have: the ability to choose between alternative means or ways of achieving the goals they are inclined to, and the freedom to set aside those goals or inclinations and act from a higher motive. Although humans have inclinations for food and shelter, they can choose different means of achieving them, whereas other animals tend to follow predetermined instincts. Being able to choose alternative means to a goal makes humans somewhat different, but not significantly different from other animals. The difference that Kant thought particularly significant is that humans can act against their inclinations, for the sake of duty.

Human beings, because of their practical reason, ask the question, "what should I do?" This question can take two forms. If we are interested in fulfilling our inclinations, the question is qualified: what should I do, if I want to fulfill my inclinations? At times, however, the question is whether we should follow our inclinations or do our duty. Here the question is unqualified: it is simply, what should I do? The answers come out as rules, which Kant calls "imperatives." For Kant, all practical judgments, that is, judgments about what one ought to do, are imperatives. The qualified "oughts" he called "hypothetical" imperatives, and the unqualified "oughts" he called "categorical" imperatives.

When we make decisions based on qualified "oughts," what determines the goodness or badness is whether the decisions accomplish the goal. Human beings, unlike other animals, can be "prudent" or "imprudent" if they choose effective or ineffective means to fulfill their inclinations. Humans can be prudent, but that only gives them a hypothetical imperative, which for Kant is not an ethical imperative.

Thus, according to Kant, if one is doing something simply to fulfill a desire, then one is not acting out of a moral motive. To act morally you do something simply because it's the moral thing to do, it's your duty. These oughts of your duty are expressed in a "categorical imperative." The categorical imperative simply says, "do X," no qualifications added. If one asks, "why do X?" the answer is because it is one's duty. If one asks, "what is my duty?" Kant gives several formulae to help determine what one's duty consists of. Two of these are described below.

Formulae for determining duties

The first formula for the categorical imperative is, "act so that you can will the maxim of your action to become a universal law." The categorical imperative stresses that one must "will" the maxim to be a universal law. But for Kant, the will is practical reason and one cannot will promises not be kept, not because of unfavorable consequences but because to will thus is to involve oneself in a will contradiction.

A will contradiction essentially means having one's cake and eating it as well. In the case of promise breaking, one is willing to break a promise; but if promise breaking were universalized, no one would trust anyone so no one could make a promise to another, since a precondition of promise making is trust. Thus, to will promise breaking one must will promise making. Therein lies the contradiction.

The same sort of contradiction holds for stealing, lying, cheating, adultery and any number of other activities that we take to be immoral. It is easier for the "guilty" party to achieve his or her objective if most people do not undertake the "immoral" activity. However, that is a double standard. To will to break promises is to will other people not to break them, for if they broke promises also then promise making would be impossible. But to will others not to follow your rule is to make an exception of yourself. When we universalize, we step away from our egocentric view. We see that we are the same as others, and this is the basis for the rule of justice: "equals should be treated equally."

After this first formulation of the categorical imperative, Kant moves on to another. Unlike most other animals, whose behavior is directly influenced or limited more by instincts and genetics, human beings can transcend these limitations and be free. Humans can set projects by themselves; they are free or autonomous. Because of this, Kant calls humans "ends in themselves." They are the ones who determine their moral life; they are autonomous, self-regulating. Consequently they are special, and all alike in that they make values and ends. Since they are so special, Kant thinks there is another formula that applies: "Act so as never to treat another rational being merely as a means."

On this view, everyone is morally equal and ought to be treated with respect and HUMAN DIGNITY. Their RIGHTS ought to be respected and no one ought to be used merely as a means or instrument to bring about consequences that benefit the user. It is not justifiable to use or exploit someone to make society better. It dehumanizes by turning a fellow human being into a thing or an instrument to be used by the person exploiting. The ethical reasons that rest on concerns for justice, fairness, dignity and rights are quite often deontological in inspiration.

Conclusion

Perhaps the chief objection to Kant's deontological theory is its inability to determine what should be done when duties conflict. This deficiency was partially remedied by the twentieth-century philosopher W.D. Ross's (1939) distinction between prima facie and actual duties, and especially by the "rule utilitarian" perspective (see Smart 1967: 206–7).

See also:

business ethics; ethics and morality; humanistic economics; justice; normative and positive economics

Selected references

Kant, Immanuel (1786) *Fundamental Principles of the Metaphysics, of Morals*, 2nd edn, London, 1948.
Ross, W.D. (1939) *The Foundations of Ethics*, Oxford: Clarendon Press.
Smart, J.J.C. (1967) "Utilitarianism," in Paul Edwards (ed.), *The Encyclopedia of Philosophy*, vol. 7, London and New York: Macmillan.

RONALD F. DUSKA
NICHOLAS M. RONGIONE

determinism and overdetermination

Determinism and overdetermination are alternative ways to conceptualize, across all the domains of knowledge, how the different parts of a whole relate to one another. All economists, no matter what their theoretical orientation, deploy variants of one or the other conceptualization. However, given the limited methodological self-awareness typical among economists, there is little literature debating the strengths and weaknesses, insights and blindnesses of the competing determinist or overdeterminist presumptions underlying all their work (for three exceptions, see Roberts and Feiner 1992; Cullenberg 1994; Callari and Ruccio 1996). Yet the two offer radically different notions of how the parts of a society or economy relate to one another.

Determinisms

The many kinds of determinist social theory share a presumption (rarely made explicit) that the parts of a society or economy do not constitute (create) each other's existence; rather, they always exist independently of one another. On this basis, these parts can then be differentiated into causes and effects. The usually posited relation is unidirectional: some parts are causes which determine others as their effects. For example, in economic determinisms, economic aspects of society are thought to govern the non-economic. In political determinisms, particular powers and their distributions obtain the causal designation; and in cultural determinisms, aspects of, for example, language and consciousness are said to govern the economic and political parts of society.

Among political economists, determinist formulations usually designate some combination of political and economic parts of society as causes: for example rules governing market interactions and distributions of wealth determine the broader economy and society as their effects. The less mechanical and more subtle determinists within political economy acknowledge the possibility that effects can sometimes react back upon their causes. However, such models of simultaneous, mutual causality among parts of an economy still usually do not admit that the parts themselves are overdetermined. Only their quantitative relations (coefficients) are viewed as mutually determined. All the other dimensions of and relations among the parts are presumed to have an existence prior to and independent of these quantitative interactions.

This presumption of independently existing variables propels determinists to order which parts within any simultaneous relationship are the more determinant and which the more determined. Some within Marxian political economy thus found their way to a notion of "ultimate" or "last instance" determinism (for example, Cohen 1978). While admitting that politics and culture determine economics, as well as vice versa, they claim that the economy is "determinant in the last instance" of the non-economic aspects of social life. They weigh quanta of determination and find which is the greater.

In determinist conceptualizations, the analytical emphasis falls on finding which of the independently existing aspects are the causes – whether in the first or last instance – and showing how they produce their derived effects. For example, within some deterministic formulations of political economy, the goals are to show how property ownership ultimately causes EXPLOITATION, how the forces of production govern the relations of production, how the influence of politics and culture on the mode of production at a time and place is itself ultimately determined by that mode, and so on (see Althusser and Balibar 1970: 216–24; MODE OF PRODUCTION AND SOCIAL FORMATION).

Overdeterminisms

In contrast to all determinisms, overdetermination understands each and every part of a society or economy to be constituted by the combined effects emanating from all other parts. These diverse effects or "determinations" literally create the existence of each part. Overdetermination refers to this kind of complex causation: parts of society are understood to be the loci of combined effectivities emanating from all other parts. Because each part of a society is understood to be constituted in this way, no part or subset of parts can possibly exist by itself, independent of the effects of the others. Unlike determinisms, parts cannot be ordered into those that are only causes and those that are only their effects. All parts are always both a constituting cause and an overdetermined effect.

In overdeterminist conceptualizations, analysis would focus on how economic and non-economic aspects constitute each other's existence. For example, within some overdeterminist formulations, the point is to examine how each part – the forces or relations of culture, politics, and economics – only exists as a consequence of the combined, multiple determinations emanating from the other parts (see Resnick and Wolff 1987).

Disputes among determinists

While determinist formulations have prevailed in political economy, their proponents have disagreed over many issues. They have disputed which aspects of an economy are the ultimate causal origins and which their effects. Maurice Dobb's classic *Theories of Value and Distribution Since Adam Smith*, published in 1973, divides the entire history of economic thought into two camps. On one side, such figures as Ricardo, MARX and SRAFFA champion the system of production as cause while exchange and prices are its effects. Reversing this view, writes Dobb, NEOCLASSICAL ECONOMICS sees utility maximizing exchange as the cause, and production as among its effects. In a similar confrontation, institutionalists and macroeconomists stress the ways in which economic and social structures ultimately govern individual economic behavior. Microfoundationalists reason the other way around: individual desires and actions form the foundation upon which rest macro-level economic events. All these disputes center on which of the assumed independently existing parts are to be ordered into causes and which into their effects. There is neither discussion of nor dispute over the shared underlying presumption: determinism.

Determinist economists also debate such questions as (1) how do causes produce their effects? and (2) when multiple causes exist, which among them are, in a quantitative sense, the major causes? An entire sub-specialty arose from such debates. Econometrics divides the field deterministically into "dependent" and "independent" variables, and elaborates protocols for determining the exact relationships among them. Following these protocols is said to yield answers to how causes work their effects (directly, inversely, in complex functional relations, and so on) and also to yield measures of which cause is more and which less determinant of a particular effect.

Debates between determinists and overdeterminists

Debates between determinists and overdeterminists can and often do become rather blunt. For the overdeterminists, the determinists are like peculiar theoretical monotheists: presuming an ultimate cause, they search to find it, do so, and then show how it determines society and social change. Overdeterminists, presuming no such governing ultimate cause, believe the determinists to be experts in refining mechanisms for finding and showing what is not there. The determinists' theoretical formulations, methodological injunctions and empirical demonstrations strike overdeterminists as being founded on a very particular and partisan presumption of social wholes being nicely separable into independently existing parts which then can be ordered into causes and effects.

On the other side, determinists find overdeterminism to be impracticable or impossible, or both. If overdeterminists really mean that every part of a social whole functions as a constituent cause and overdetermined effect of every other (which overdeterminists admit they do), then how could social or economic analysis ever proceed? To understand anything about society, presuming overdetermination, one would have to analyze *every*thing about it since *every*thing plays a role in determining – or rather overdetermining – anything in that society. And analyzing everything is neither practicable nor possible. Hence, in many determinists' views, overdetermination amounts to a kind of nihilistic rejection of explanation, theory, and science *in toto* (see Gintis 1979)

The overdeterminists have published responses to this charge (Resnick and Wolff 1987). Explanation, they argue, can only ever entail connecting an object of inquiry to a very few of the many constituents that combine to overdetermine that object. In that precise sense, all explanations ever offered have been inherently partial; all have depended upon the analyst's selection of which among the infinity of overdeterminants to consider in an explanation. The distress among some theorists at their inescapable limitations and hence partiality in formulating explanations of anything often lead them to claim that their particular selections were more than matters of personal whim or cultural convention. They argued that their selections focused on those causes that were the most important in a quantitative sense: the major or essential causes rather than the secondary or inconsequential.

For the overdeterminists, this last claim – a determinism – was rejected as utterly unwarranted. To know which of the infinity of overdeterminants of any economic event were the "most important" would require comparing their effectivities quantitatively against the effectivities of all the other overdeterminants. Since the latter are infinite, this cannot be done; nor has anyone ever done it; nor would anyone undertake the task. By the time it were completed, if even possible, the relationship between effect and overdeterminants under scrutiny would long since have changed.

For overdeterminists the issue of explanation appears as follows. All theories and theorists must select from among the vast array of relevant factors a few on which to focus attention. Thus, for example, to explain rising interest rates, some theorists will focus on money supply and/or foreign trade imbalances and/or business investment plans. Other theorists will build their explanations around connecting the interest rate increase instead to political struggles among governing elites and/or individuals' changing time-preferences. Still other theorists will offer class analyses, connecting the production, appropriation and distribution of surplus labor to rising interest rates.

Each of these explanations is inherently and inescapably partial. However, that partiality may be denied by any or by all of them. This occurs in so far as each may claim that the particular set of effects on which each focuses comprises not merely some among the infinity of overdeterminants, but is rather the essential subset of effectivities that quantitatively outweighs all others and thereby deserves the name "determinant" of what is to be explained. When theories proceed in this way, they share a common commitment to determinism, albeit they may disagree on what the precise determinants are.

If one of these theories changed its commitment to overdetermination, that would entail two important differences from determinist formulations. First, the overdeterminist theory would admit its own partiality, its own focus upon a particular selection from among the infinity of overdeterminants (see ENTRY POINT) Second, the overdeterminist theory would have to explain both its own focused selection and why other theories select otherwise. In short, overdeterminist theory has to account for the extra-theoretical stakes in the coexistence and confrontations of alternative theories. In contrast, determinist theory assumes that between alternative theories the absolutely superior should and will emerge as the singular truth unless extra-theoretical forces intervene and thwart that emergence. For determinist theories, what matters is which causes account for an event in an absolutely "best" way. For overdeterminist theories, what matters is how and why different theories select different causes to construct their alternative and inescapably partial "explanations" for such an event.

Conclusion

Determinists are epistemological monists; they presume a single truth about the world, that this truth is accessible or asymptotically approachable, and that all theories aim to discover and expound that single truth. Overdeterminists are epistemological pluralists; they presume that alternative theories erect their own standards of truth, that these are incommensurable across theories and that, consequently, different theories construct, extend, correct and change their explanations of the world in different ways. In short, different theories make different senses of the world they inhabit, including making their different senses of each other as theoretical components of the world they aim to understand.

See also:

circular and cumulative causation; dialectical method; entry point; holistic method; methodology in economics; modernism and postmodernism; Myrdal's contribution to political economy; paradigms; storytelling and pattern models

Selected references

Althusser, Louis and Balibar, Etienne (1970) *Reading Capital*, London: NLB.

Callari, Antonio and Ruccio, David F. (eds) (1996) *Postmodern Materialism and the Future of Marxist Theory*, Hanover and London: Wesleyan University Press.

Cohen, G.A. (1978) *Karl Marx's Theory of History: A Defense*, Oxford: Clarendon.

Cullenberg, Stephen (1994) *The Falling Rate of*

Profit, London and Boulder, CO: Pluto Press.
Gintis, Herbert (1979) "On the Theory of Transitional Conjunctures," *Review of Radical Political Economics* 11(3): 23–31.
Resnick, Stephen and Wolff, Richard D. (1987) *Knowledge and Class: A Marxian Critique of Political Economy*, Chicago: University of Chicago Press.
Roberts, Bruce and Feiner, Susan (eds) (1992) *Radical Economics*, Boston: Kluwer Academic Publishers.

STEPHEN RESNICK
RICHARD D. WOLFF

development economics: orthodox

Orthodox approach to development

The orthodox approach to development places emphasis on getting "prices right," removing market distortions and government controls, and promoting competitive policies so that the market can automatically generate rapid growth. Contractionary macro policies and cuts in government spending are also recommended. Correspondingly, most of the blame for the poor performance of certain developing countries is placed on the shoulders of government. This approach is associated with economists such as Ian little, Anne Krueger and Bela Balassa, and institutions such as the World Bank and International Monetary Fund.

The World Bank report *Pacific Island Economies: Towards Higher Growth in the 1990s* (1991) is representative of orthodox opinion. The key argument in the report is that poor growth performance came from "an inability to adopt needed structural reforms" (World Bank 1991: 25). Growth has been inhibited by inappropriate policies, and if these policies can be reformed growth will accelerate. What exactly are these inappropriate policies? The report alleges that "the dominant role of the public sector, a general lack of competitiveness, an inward orientation, a regulatory rather than a promotional approach to private investment, and weak financial sectors all combined to stifle private sector development" (World Bank 1991: 42). There is then a "need to reduce the public sector's relative command over the economy's resources" (p. 34). Further, there is a need to "restructure the system of public enterprises" so that "liquidation should be given serious consideration" and "a program of privatization should be undertaken" and for those enterprises remaining, charges should be raised to cover costs (p. 41).

A "relatively undistorted incentives regime" should be put in place that moves the Islands away from their "inward-oriented development" and "protection from foreign competition." This involves the "dismantling of remaining...restrictions on external trade" (p. 45) and the "excessively regulatory environment" that impedes foreign direct investment: "controls on the cost and allocation of capital need to be phased out" and "capital market development" should be encouraged (pp. xi, 50–51, 64).

With respect to labor markets, there is heavy criticism of centralized wage-setting systems, which have resulted in "considerable downward rigidity in real wages" so that: "The combination of generous public sector wage awards, a high degree of unionization, and centralized wage setting, wage controls, and minimum wage restrictions have effectively severed the link between wages and productivity" (p. 44). Hence policies should be enacted to lead to "greater flexibility in the setting of private and public sector wages" and controls should be placed on "wage and salary increases or the number of government employees" in the public sector.

Once all these restrictions that "hinder private investment" are removed, and the private sector is no longer "stifled by overregulation," the dynamic forces of the private sector will be unleashed, and, combined with a surge of foreign investment, will dramatically raise rates of economic growth. "[T]he cornerstone for restoration of sustained growth will be greater participation of the private sector in investment and economic activity" (p. 64). "The private sector must take the lead" (pp. 73–4). The report considers feasible a doubling, tripling even quadrupling of annual growth rates over the decade of the 1990s if reforms are implemented.

How plausible is this scenario? Each of the suggested "reforms" can be criticized. For example, there is little agreement on whether trade liberalization packages have played an important role in the performance of outward-oriented economies. A number of countries, such as Japan, Korea, Singapore and Taiwan, have promoted exports but in an environment where imports had not been fully liberalized while government intervention played a key role (see NEWLY INDUSTRIALIZED ASIAN NATIONS).

Institutions, society and history

Lance Taylor notes the importance of differences in institutional, social and historical conditions between countries, and that the orthodox view does not take account of these differences. This failure to acknowledge differences and apply appropriate remedies leads to several consequences.

In order to promote the role of market forces, price subsidies, especially for state-owned enterprises, are often eliminated. Yet this measure usually sets up cost pressures which are difficult to contain, especially if the state-controlled prices are for key wage or investment goods.

Devaluation of the exchange rate acts to shift income distribution from workers (assumed to be low-savers) to capitalists (assumed to be high-savers). The trade balance may well then improve, particularly through reduced intermediate imports, but at a high social cost. Taylor's general point regarding austerity and devaluation is that these often do work in the sense of reducing current account imbalance, but this is achieved by reducing output and capital formation rather than through import substitution and export promotion. In other words, they are successful in so far as they retard economic growth rather than promoting it.

Taylor contends that the various parts of orthodox stabilization programs often contradict one another. In particular, trade liberalization seems at cross-purposes with devaluation and austerity, since it is likely to increase imports whereas the latter are aimed at reducing them.

Another aspect of orthodox stabilization policies is financial deregulation, which usually leads to higher interest rates. The idea behind this is that higher rates will increase domestic savings and attract foreign capital. However, even if this occurs, the reliance on imported intermediate goods means that investment will not rise so as to absorb any increase in saving. With austerity programs reducing public investment at the same time, potential savings surpluses and capital inflow "will vent in the form of reduced commodity purchases or speculation." Again policies seem to work at cross-purposes: high interest rates are intended to generate funds for capital formation yet austerity prevents them from being directed to productive uses through public sector expansion; and devaluation makes imported investment goods more expensive for the private sector.

Alternative model

Taylor believes that an alternative model would be more suited to less developed countries. The cornerstone of Taylor's approach is the significance of investment to the development process. Unless investment absorbs capital in a productive manner, other growth-oriented policies may simply fuel a speculative bubble. There is a need for the government to finance capital expenditures. If these are directed carefully, particularly into infrastructure spending, there can be significant crowding-in effects with respect to private sector investment. Public and private investment are then seen as complementary.

In addition, a strong element of price control is needed from the side of costs – wage and exchange rate freezes and caps on interest rates

– as well as attempts to keep markups in line by price checks, mobilization of public opinion and moral suasion. Taylor also supports the use of selective tariffs rather than general devaluations as a means of cutting back certain imports, such as luxuries, without affecting imports of necessary intermediate goods and without triggering inflation. Taylor favors more selective forms of state intervention such as export subsidies and import quotas.

Rigidities, lags and structure

Hollis Chenery is another development economist who questions the orthodox strategy. His "structuralist approach" attempts to identify specific rigidities, lags and other characteristics of the structure of developing economies that influence the effectiveness of traditional economic policies. A common theme is the failure of market forces and the price mechanism to produce steady growth or a desirable distribution of income. This perspective on comparative growth performances downplays the role of economic policy and highlights the general pattern underlying the growth process in all countries. This pattern is structurally determined. In brief, economies follow a logistic pattern of slow growth at low levels of income, faster growth at intermediate levels of income, falling back to slow growth at the highest levels of income. This is caused by the significant structural transformation that most economies undergo (see STRUCTURALIST THEORY OF DEVELOPMENT).

This view is presented by R.M. Sundrum (1990). He argues that in the initial stages of low income, agriculture is the most important sector both in terms of output shares and employment shares. The dominance of this sector is an important reason for the low rate of growth in this phase. In the intermediate stage of growth, the center of gravity shifts to the manufacturing sector and overall growth significantly accelerates. Manufacturing is the engine of growth. Rapid capital accumulation, technological progress and increasing returns to scale in the industrial sector lead to higher rates of growth of labor productivity in this sector than any other. In the latter stages of growth, the services sector dominates and growth slackens.

See also:

development political economy: major contemporary themes; foreign aid; gender and development; neoclassical economics: critique; North–South trade models; privatization; regulation and deregulation: financial; social capabilities and convergence; surplus approach to development; sustainable development; world hunger and poverty

Selected references

Cornia, G.A., Jolly, R. and Stewart, F. (eds) (1987) *Adjustment with a Human Face*, Oxford: Oxford University Press.

Sheahan, John (1980) "Market-Oriented Economic Policies and Political Repression in Latin America," *Economic Development and Cultural Change* 28(2): 267–91.

Sundrum, R.M. (1990) *Economic Growth in Theory and Practice*, London: Macmillan.

Taylor, Lance (1983) *Structuralist Macroeconomics: Applicable Models for the Third World*, New York: Basic Books.

—— (1988) *Varieties of Stabilization Experience: Towards Sensible Macroeconomics in the Third World*, Oxford: Clarendon Press.

Toye, John (1987) *Dilemmas of Development*, Oxford: Blackwell.

World Bank (1991) *Pacific Island Economies: Towards Higher Growth in the 1990s*, Washington, DC: World Bank Publications.

JOHN LODEWIJKS

development and the environment

Economic development offers increased private consumption, but can also degrade environmental quality due to the excessive use (or abuse) of the natural resources. The transition from a largely agrarian economy to an industrial economy often causes irreversible damage to the environment. This damage can take the form of deforestation, excessive discharges of noxious fumes into the air, discharges of sewage and of chemical, radioactive and heat wastes into water and land. The typical index of economic development measures the increase in a country's per capita output with no indication of any increase in environmental disamenities that take place in the process. Ill-defined property rights and inadequate pricing of environmental assets (atmosphere, rivers, oceans and land) typically lead to these pollution problems. (See GROSS DOMESTIC PRODUCT AND NET SOCIAL WELFARE.)

Costs of economic growth

The late 1960s witnessed a debate on the negative effects of ECONOMIC GROWTH. First, there was the depletion of energy and other natural resources due to industrialization and consumption, and second, there was the generation of waste from production and consumption. Predictions were made as to the possible LIMITS TO GROWTH in the foreseeable future, in terms of a slowdown of economic growth rate and stagnation (Meadows *et al.* 1972). In this otherwise grim forecast, optimism took the form of resource-saving technological progress and change in social attitudes (toward conservation) that would delay economic stagnation.

Recognizing the implications of environmental degradation for the survival of future generations, economists have addressed the issue of SUSTAINABLE DEVELOPMENT. This is the rate of current growth whereby the present generation can preserve the capacity for the future generation to be at least as well off as the present generation. Environmental protection can contribute to sustainability if it curtails current consumption of polluting goods and reinvests rents on non-renewable resources.

Local and global environmental problems

While the depletion of energy resources is not an immediate threat, the problem of acute environmental POLLUTION is a major concern. The nexus between growth and environmental pollution can be examined by distinguishing between local and global environmental problems.

Local problems, such as inadequate sanitation and clean water, indoor air pollution from biomass burning, and land degradation, are associated with a lack of economic development. Research has revealed an inverse relationship between these forms of pollution and income per capita (World Bank 1992), implying that economic development goes hand-in-hand with these forms of environmental quality. For outdoor pollution problems, such as atmospheric sulfur dioxide, particulate matter (concentration) and metal contamination of river basins, an inverted U-shaped relationship (environmental Kuznets curve, or EKC) was seen to exist with per capita income (Grossman and Krueger 1994). The increase in demand for environmental quality and regulatory enforcement beyond a critical level of income offset the degradation experienced in the initial stages of growth. As nations become richer, citizens are willing to pay more for improving local public goods, like air and water quality. Moreover, with technological advance, the social environmental cost of growth can be lowered, such that the EKC shifts downward over time.

Global problems, such as ozone depletion, loss of biodiversity and global warming, stem from economic expansion and increased consumption. There is indeed a trade-off between consumption and environmental quality. It is therefore pertinent to build environmental scarcity into economic decision-making, and to promote pollution-abatement technology. The rate of deforestation has also lent support to the EKC hypothesis (Panayotou 1992). EKC studies, however, ignore the underlying structural differences in the countries at different stages of growth, and the simultaneous effect of environmental degradation on economic development (Stern *et al.* 1996).

development and the environment

While the effects of economic growth on the environment are at best mixed, considering the impact of the environment on economic growth would make the "conflict" between economic development and environment less convincing. Pollution affects human health, which has a direct impact on labor PRODUCTIVITY. Although environmental protection involves both resource and transitional costs, these would be offset to some extent by a decline in health and medical costs and enhanced productivity with a cleaner environment. Moreover, environmental protection as an economic activity offers employment and income to the economy. The underlying structural factors in the development–environment nexus are briefly outlined below.

Population and urbanization

The human POPULATION has a scale effect on environmental problems. A larger population means a greater demand for food, energy and housing, which subsequently increases the discharge of wastes. However, it is a well-established fact that population growth decreases with economic growth and education; as income rises, fertility declines in the long run. Even if there exist positive income effects on fertility in the short run (due to better health conditions), in the long run the negative impact of income growth on fertility dominates. Thus for populous countries like India and China, it is essential to promote economic development in order to escape from the vicious circle of population growth, poverty and environmental degradation. These countries will also witness unprecedented demand for energy in the foreseeable future. Not surprisingly, Solow (1993) concluded that "control of population growth would probably be the best available policy on behalf of sustainability."

The economic development of a nation is marked by an increase in urbanization. A large part of the population in China and India are still rural: as of 1994, only 27 percent of the Indian population and 29 percent of the Chinese was urban (World Bank 1996: 204).

Urbanization in these countries will be a major force in increasing energy consumption, as well as vehicular pollution. Among the developed countries, energy consumption patterns with economic growth have been diverse. A study of forty-three market economies for the years 1978–80 established that several European economies have achieved per capita income comparable to the United States, but with almost one-half the US per capita energy consumption (Moroney 1989). This suggests that present-day developing economies could be set onto a growth track that is less energy intensive than that of the USA.

Government intervention

Government initiatives to promote growth, through price fixing or subsidies in sectors such as energy, agriculture and transport, often lead to harmful ecological effects. Distorting subsidies lead to an overuse of certain products and sometimes more pollution. In developing countries, agricultural subsidies for fertilizer and pesticides contribute to surface and ground water contamination from chemical runoff. Industrialized countries heavily subsidize road transport, which leads to an overuse of this mode of transportation and hence vehicular pollution. In the USA, for instance, road users pay only 79 percent of the total cost of road provisioning through taxes and tolls (Potier 1996: 6).

Structure of growth

The structure of the growth of nations has been largely biased toward polluting industries (petro-chemicals, distilleries and so on). Moreover, the pattern of international trade may have exported pollution abroad from the industrialized world. Developing countries probably subsidize the export of environmental resources or services, leading to domestic environmental degradation. Finally, with economic growth, the traditional norms of protecting local commons in these countries are typically lost. New institutional structures to protect environmental assets develop much later in the growth process, when substantial damage may already have occurred.

Conclusion

Environmental protection should be perceived as an integral part of the process of improving the quality of life. Generally, the consumption of better environmental quality is associated with the rich, but the consumption of clean air and water can be conceived as being part of the subsistence consumption bundle of the poor as well. What is needed is a growth and development process that takes the environment into account, by internalizing the social costs (both national and international) of environmental exploitation, and making provision for incentives for sustainable economic behavior.

See also:

environmental and ecological political economy: major contemporary themes; quality of life

Selected references

Dasgupta, Partha (1995) "Population, Poverty and the Local Environment," *Scientific American*, February: 40–45.
Grossman, Gene and Krueger, Alan (1994) *Economic Growth and the Environment*, NBER Working Paper no. 4634.
Meadows, D.H., Meadows, D.L., Randers, J. and Behrens, W.W. (1972) *Limits to Growth*, New York: Universe.
Moroney, John R. (1989) "Output and Energy: An International Analysis," *Energy Journal* 10(3): 1–18.
Panayotou, Theodore (1992) *Empirical Tests and Policy Analysis of Environmental Degradation at Different Stages of Economic Development*, Cambridge, MA: HIID.
Pearce, David and Warford, Jeremy (1993) *World Without End: Economics, Environment, and Sustainable Development*, Oxford: Oxford University Press.
Potier, Michel (1996) "Integrating Environment and the Economy," *The OECD Observer* 198: 6–10.
Solow, Robert (1993) "Sustainability: An Economist's Perspective" in Robert Dorfman and Nancy S. Dorfman (eds), *Economics of the Environment*, 3rd edn, New York: W.W. Norton, 179–87.
Stern, David, Common, Michael and Barbier, Edward (1996) "Economic Growth and Environmental Degradation," *World Development* 24(7): 1151–60.
World Bank *World Development Report*, annual issues, Washington, DC: World Bank.

APARNA SAWHNEY

development political economy: history

Economic development differs from ECONOMIC GROWTH in being a qualitative, as well as a quantitative, concept. Without the specification "economic," the concept of development suggests even broader connotations, such as "social," "political," or "human." This widening of the concept in different directions has made it decreasingly operational, and occasionally there appear demands for its abolition. Here the treatment is confined largely to what is usually covered by the concept "political economy," that is, the interrelationship between economic and political factors in the process of social change.

Development, as an idea of purposeful improvement of society and human well-being, has emerged in two distinct historical contexts. First, it has been concerned with the "original transition," when Europe was transformed from agrarian to industrial and rural to urban relations (see INDUSTRIALIZATION). Second, it has been interested in the post-1945 situation when "underdeveloped areas" were seen as a threat to world peace (and the liberal world order), and "development" was taken to be the remedy. Central to the latter idea is the belief that the process of societal change can be intentionally designed by a conscious agent – normally the state – rather then being an immanent historical process (which typically was the classical political economy view). Development theories can thus be distinguished by their position on a scale running from immanence to intention, or, in other words, from theories of historical transformation to utopian thinking about the good society. The theoretical core lies somewhere between the two extremes; the basic position is that the world can be changed (for the better), but only within the constraints of a given historical structure.

Classical development theory

It is thus open to discussion whether CLASSICAL POLITICAL ECONOMY (Adam Smith, David Ricardo, Thomas Malthus and Karl Marx) had a theory of development as distinct from a theory of historical transformation in the context of a *sui generis* case, namely England. On the other hand, the industrialization of England became a challenge to other countries, such as Germany, and this "modernization imperative" gave rise to the idea of "catching up," of purposeful intervention in the development process. The key author in this tradition is Friedrich List (1789–1846) who can be called the father of development theory. Also in classical development theory, as defined here, can be included all kinds of corrections and improvements of the mainstream development process which, although creative, were sometimes seen as excessively destructive. To this type of critique belong the early utopian socialists, Russian populists, social liberals and so on. As a bridge between the classical and modern traditions stands Joseph SCHUMPETER, whose main conclusion was that development was necessarily destructive in order to be creative.

Modern development theory

Modern development theory, first dominated by what was called development economics in the 1950s and 1960s, had a global scope and was from the start both normative and instrumental. It is closely associated with the idea of development strategy, a concept lacking in the classical tradition. Among the pioneers were Peter Bauer, Colin Clark, Albert Hirschman, Arthur Lewis, Gunnar Myrdal, Ragnar Nurkse, Raul Prebisch, P.N. Rosenstein Rodan, Walt Rostow, Dudley Seers, Hans Singer and Jan Tinbergen. In the Marxist tradition, major figures were Oskar Lange and Paul Baran, the father of the neo-Marxist school.

The pioneers were genuine development theorists, as they allowed themselves to have opinions about what development ought to be. As could be expected, opinions often differed. It was explicitly assumed by most theorists (Peter Bauer was an early exception) that development was a process that could and should be controlled and steered by political actors, usually the state. This explains why development has been a contested concept and development theory is an area of contending schools, the most influential of the latter being development economics, modernization theory and dependency theory.

Typically, the "development strategy" applied experiences from European economic history, both capitalist and socialist, to what became known as the Third World (in principle the former colonies). This Eurocentric bias has been countered by a number of theoretical contributions from Latin America, Africa and Asia, giving the field a truly global quality as well as changing its content. As part of the general change in the political climate from the late 1970s onwards, there has been a counterrevolution in development economics, questioning the whole interventionist project and the intention to develop.

Political economy of development

Theorizing about development has thus taken a variety of forms, and the relationship between development and political economy has been given a variety of meanings. There are theories of development within different social science disciplines (sociology, economics, geography, anthropology and political science), but there also exists "development studies" as an institutionalized interdisciplinary specialization in some countries (for example, the UK, France, the Netherlands,

Canada and the Scandinavian countries). To stress the political economy of development means, as was mentioned initially, to consider development in a broader societal context with particular (but not exclusive) emphasis on economic and political factors. As for the particular relationship between development and political economy, this has differed over time, from referring to the classical writings to neo-Marxist and dependency contributions and, later, a wider application of formal economics to non-economic fields (the "new political economy"), plus international political economy and "alternative" development theory.

Dependency theory

In the earlier theoretical phase in the 1950s, dominated by modernization theory, the external context of development was largely neglected. Development toward ultimate international interdependence was seen by the modernization theorists to be an inbuilt tendency of the market logic. Modern economic history was, according to this thesis, about the realization of the market system, both in terms of vertical deepening and horizontal expansion. Dependency theory, in contrast, did emphasize the role of external structure and was particularly concerned with its assumed perverting effects on dependent countries, which thereby became "underdeveloped." Development theory, to many of its practitioners, became "radical underdevelopment theory" and the implication of the most radical theories, for instance those of Andre Gunder Frank and the WORLD-SYSTEMS ANALYSIS (Immanuel Wallerstein), was political revolution as a precondition for genuine (socialist) development.

The global economy, in this perspective, is analyzed as a dualistic core–periphery structure (see CORE–PERIPHERY ANALYSIS) with an inherently polarizing tendency between states. This approach did not concentrate on development strategies, the ultimate rationale for development theory, concerned as they are with the task "to develop." Development theory's raison d'être was not primarily the exploration of the nature of development, but rather to intervene in the development process in order to achieve more "development" for the peripheries.

International political economy

Recently, as a consequence of what has been termed the process of globalization, the question has become how development relates to international political economy (see INTERNATIONAL POLITICAL ECONOMY: MAJOR CONTEMPORARY THEMES). Development theory has experienced a crisis emanating from its exclusive concern with the way nation-states should manage "their" economies and promote "their" national developments, as if they were independent universes. International political economy, on the other hand, typically deals with the connection between politics and economics in international relations, and the particular social order which links the two. Its underlying assumption is that any economic system presupposes a political framework of some sort. From this, it follows that the development process is structured by the world order, which raises the question of the relevance of "national developments strategies" as well as development theory as hitherto defined. Structure is typically more important than agency. The scope of action is thus limited.

By stressing national development strategy as a special case, it is implied that one can think of other actors than the state as social carriers of development strategies, and other levels of the world-system, apart from the national, at which these strategies can be carried out by a variety of actors. This perspective opens up a vast field of empirical research, case studies, comparative analysis and middle-range theorizing concerning the role of development actors in the context of a changing international political economy.

Alternative development theory

"Alternative" development theory at present deals with development, not in terms of how it actually takes place, but rather how it ought to take place. What this ultimately boils down to is the inclusion of the excluded into the development process. Alternative models are thus not born in a vacuum, but derived from negations of existing models, from a critical debate on the reality of development, from incorporating perspectives of "the excluded," and from existing utopian traditions. Of particular concern has been the neglect of ethnic minorities and aboriginal peoples in the mainstream development process, which has given rise to demands for "ethnodevelopment." Similarly, concern for the environmental consequences of "development" gave rise to the idea of "ecodevelopment" or "SUSTAINABLE DEVELOPMENT." Further, feminist critiques of development theory gradually enriched this growing tradition of critique of the mainstream and provided further ideas for alternative ends and means. Alternative development is a cry for visibility, participation and justice, which in the current world order means large-scale structural changes.

See also:

development political economy; major contemporary themes

Selected references

Caporaso, James A. and Levine, David P. (1992) *Theories of Political Economy*, New York: Cambridge University Press.
Gilpin, R. (1987) *The Political Economy of International Relations*, Princeton, NJ: Princeton University Press.
Hettne, B. (1995) *Development Theory and the Three Worlds: Towards an International Political Economy of Development*, London: Longman.
Meier, Gerald M. and Seers, Dudley (eds) (1984) *Pioneers in Development*, World Bank and Oxford University Press.
Robertson, Roland (1992) *Globalization: Social Theories and Global Culture*, London: Sage.
Staniland, Martin (1985) *What is Political Economy? A Study of Social Theory and Underdevelopment*, New Haven, CT and London: Yale University Press.
Wallerstein, Immanuel (1979) *The Capitalist World Economy*, Cambridge: Cambridge University Press.

BJÖRN HETTNE

development political economy: major contemporary themes

The political economy of development examines the problems of growth, structural change and living standards in poor countries. It emerged following the Second World War, although it has roots in CLASSICAL POLITICAL ECONOMY and its precursors. While neoclassical economics has impacted on it, especially in relation to questions of market failure and externalities, the study of development has always been influenced strongly by political economy themes. Especially important in this respect are Marxist, structuralist and institutionalist approaches (see Chenery and Srinivasan 1988–9; Behrman and Srinivasan 1995; Jameson and Wilber 1996).

Growth, distribution and poverty

Although most economists think of per capita real income as the main indicator of development, few would think of it as the sole one. The political economy tradition also stresses issues such as the DISTRIBUTION OF INCOME, poverty and the ability of an economy to satisfy basic needs. Many have focused on collective goals such as self-reliance, cultural independence, national sovereignty and SUSTAINABLE DEVELOPMENT.

Traditional themes concern the distribution of income along class lines and among income groups, focusing on the distribution of assets such as land, involvement in labor markets and the satisfaction of basic caloric requirements. A more recent emphasis has been to look within the family, at distribution by GENDER and the condition of children (for instance, child labor). Increasing attention has been given to labor standards (although some of this appears to be motivated by protectionist sentiments in rich countries). Some of the research examines the possible instrumental value of better living standards on growth. This work is linked to demand creation, HUMAN CAPITAL formation, the effect of better nutrition on PRODUCTIVITY and better income distribution alleviating market distortions.

The focus on per capita income makes ECONOMIC GROWTH one of the key issues in development. The traditional focus was on classical/Marxian themes like income distribution and savings (Lewis 1954). Subsequently, the importance of effective demand considerations – especially in semi-industrialized countries – was also stressed. This is particularly true of the modern STRUCTURALIST THEORY OF DEVELOPMENT. In drawing heavily on Kaleckian and post-Keynesian political economy (see POST-KEYNESIAN POLITICAL ECONOMY: MAJOR CONTEMPORARY THEMES), it focuses on the role of investment incentives, plus other constraints such as inelastic supplies of certain types of goods (Taylor 1991).

One particular issue that has been emphasized in this literature is the relationship between income distribution, the size of markets and growth. It is possible that a more equal distribution of income implies a higher level of consumption out of income, which increases aggregate demand. Given that investment depends on the size of the market, a higher level of investment and hence growth may result. However, if investment also depends on profitability as measured by the profit share, it is possible that a more equal distribution of income can squeeze profitability sufficiently to reduce investment, thus offsetting the demand-creating effects of higher consumption spending (see PROFIT SQUEEZE ANALYSIS OF CRISES).

Capital in its various forms

Traditionally, the political economy of development has given a great deal of emphasis to fixed capital ACCUMULATION and economic growth. However, this tendency has been criticized on four grounds. First, there is the perception that despite significant economic growth in many less-developed economies (LDCs), not much progress has been made toward fulfilling basic needs or alleviating poverty. For instance, there is evidence that in some regions (such as in the state of Kerala in India) significant strides have been made in social development at low levels of growth due to the build-up of social capital.

Second, given economic crises in many LDCs, the focus has sometimes switched from growth to stabilization to curb inflation and BALANCE OF PAYMENTS deficits. Sometimes contractionary policies have been pursued. Third, the emphasis given to capital accumulation has been criticized in the neoclassical approach, which has instead emphasized intersectoral resource allocation, efficiency and human capital issues. And finally, it has been argued that the focus on growth has diverted attention away from the issue of SUSTAINABLE DEVELOPMENT. High rates of growth have thus been achieved at the expense of destroying the natural environment; the long-run sustainability of this pattern of growth has been questioned.

Increasingly students of development, along with many other political economists, are recognizing the importance of creating many different forms of capital. They think of development in terms of the accumulation of some balanced combination of physical, social, human and natural forms of capital (see CAPITAL AND THE WEALTH OF NATIONS). Physical capital includes machines, factories, infrastructure and inventories; social capital includes institutional networks, welfare services and cooperative arrangements; HUMAN CAPITAL is the stock of skills, education and cognitive abilities; and NATURAL CAPITAL relates to the stock of forests, rivers, soils and fauna/flora.

It is often argued that economic growth and the resultant poverty alleviation have the result of reducing pressure on common property resources. Also, higher levels of development are said to make it easier for LDCs to address environmental questions and expend more resources on environmentally friendly development (see DEVELOPMENT AND THE ENVIRONMENT).

Sectoral analysis

Political economy has stressed the importance of inter-sectoral issues in the growth process. For instance, given the large size of the agricultural sector in most LDCs, the interaction between the agricultural sector and the rest of the economy has been the object of extensive scrutiny. Special reference has been given to the inter-sectoral terms of trade and resource transfers.

It has been argued that a stagnant agricultural sector reduces industrial profitability and accumulation by increasing the price of wage goods, and depressing the growth of markets. In the structuralist approach, high inflation is associated with an inelastic supply of agricultural goods. Many other inter-sectoral interactions have received attention, such as that between natural resources and the rest of the economy, between consumption and investment goods sectors, between organized and unorganized sectors, and between high-technology/productivity growth sectors and less advanced sectors.

A great deal of attention has been given to the agricultural sectors in LDCs. A special focus has been given to the relationships between conditions of land tenure (such as sharecropping) and farm size, between productivity and technological change, and between population pressure on the land and technological change and environmental degradation. Factor markets have also been emphasized, including issues relating to long-term labor contracts, rural–urban migration, high interest rates in credit markets and links between different factor markets. Given the importance of collective action in solving problems such as irrigation and overcoming market failures, ways of solving free-rider problems have been examined.

Attention has also been given to industry structure. The Kaleckian approach, using mark up PRICING, has been used as a basis for examining the determinants of the degree of monopoly power and its implications for income distribution in the industrial sector.

Open economy considerations

Open economy considerations have long played a major role in development economics. Traditionally, development economists looked on international trade and capital inflows with suspicion. Structuralists argued that LDCs were chronically plagued with balance of payments problems, due to the income-inelastic world demand for their mostly primary product exports and their price-inelastic demand for manufactured imports. The early two-gap models formalized these issues. The problem was exacerbated by the secular decline of the terms of trade of LDCs vis-à-vis the advanced economies (see NORTH–SOUTH TRADE MODELS).

Neo-Marxist and dependency theorists viewed the global system as one in which UNEVEN DEVELOPMENT made rich nations forge ahead while LDCs stagnated. The mechanisms cited included patterns of specialization in which rich countries specialized in technology-intensive sectors while LDCs, specializing in primary goods and simple manufactured goods, were denied major technological change. Moreover, flows of foreign capital from rich to poor countries (especially through TRANSNATIONAL CORPORATIONS) were seen as ultimately resulting in massive ECONOMIC SURPLUS transfers from poor to rich regions. This adversely affected domestic capital formation and enterprise in poor countries. Technology transfers were considered to be a mixed blessing, providing high royalty payments and inappropriate technology for the factor endowments of LDCs. The policy implications of these ideas were policies of import substitution and, in many countries, a restrictive attitude toward transnational corporations.

Mainstream economists have generally argued in favor of export-promotion policies in contrast to import substitution. However, the political economy view argues that the export-promotion stage can be effectively adopted usually only after the basis for INDUSTRIALIZATION has been laid by import substitution. It is pointed out that many successful export promoters have simultaneously restricted imports in relevant sectors. In recent years development economists have become much more accepting of the benefits of capital inflows (especially direct capital inflows) and technology transfers. Questions remain, however, about the stability of capital inflows (especially of footloose portfolio flows) and the effects of technology transfers on the national technological capability of host countries. Technological capacity is necessary for both autonomous technological development and effective technological learning from abroad.

Economic policy

Many preconceptions have been adopted about how states function. For instance, some early Marxists assumed that the state is a tool of the ruling class. Traditional neoclassical economists saw the state as a neutral benevolent problem-solver. More recently, public choice theorists assume that politicians try to maximize their own benefits.

The early emphasis of development economics was on active state intervention to mobilize saving and investment for capital accumulation in the modern sector. This argument was linked to import-substituting industrialization to diversify production and reduce dependence on imports, as well as to remove supply rigidities through policies such as land reform. More recently, heavy state intervention in LDCs has been seen as problematic on grounds of poor growth, macroeconomic instability and the relative decline of socialism. Mainstream economists have stressed the distortionary and rent-creating role of state intervention, and pointed to the alleged use of market-friendly policies in the East Asian NICs. (See NEWLY INDUSTRIALIZED ASIAN NATIONS.)

The political economy view argues that although excessive and low-quality state intervention has had deleterious effects in several LDCs, appropriate government intervention is necessary to overcome market distortions. Moreover, it argues convincingly that the East Asian states have been highly interventionist, especially in the use of industrial targeting and non-price interventions in the allocation of credit. High rates of inflation are viewed as being precipitated by distributional conflicts and the inelastic supply of agricultural goods, rather than by lax monetary policy (which is at worst the enabler but not the cause of inflation). The contractionary policies recommended by the IMF and many mainstream economists for dealing with macroeconomic crises have been criticized for their distributionally regressive and recessionary effects. Such effects can adversely impact on long-run growth by curtailing private and public investment spending.

The debate on government policy, which has traditionally been posed as one between the state and the markets, is now looking at the state and markets as potential complements and emphasizing the need to improve the functioning of both as facilitators of development (see Dutt *et al.* 1994). This requires a deeper understanding of the nature of markets, the state and their interaction.

The standard approach which takes markets (albeit with imperfections) for granted is beginning to be replaced by questions regarding the social basis of markets, in the form of norms and non-market institutions which regulate markets. This perspective leads to a fuller analysis of how the state can make markets more effective. An analysis of how the state operates is linked to an environment in which the state is subject to the pressures of different groups and classes, and how the quality of the bureaucracy affects economic performance. This perspective leads to questions about governance and how the state can use markets to enhance development.

See also:

classes and economic development; development political economy: history; environmental and ecological political economy: major contemporary themes; human development index; import substitution and export-oriented industrialization; international political economy: major contemporary themes; Lewis's theory of economic growth and development; state and government; structural adjustment policies

Selected references

Behrman, Jere and Srinivasan, T.N. (eds) (1995) *Handbook of Development Economics: Volume 3*, Amsterdam: North Holland.
Chenery, Hollis and Srinivasan, T.N. (eds) (1988–9) *Handbook of Development Economics: Volumes 1 and 2*, Amsterdam: North Holland.
Dutt, Amitava K., Kim, Kwan S. and Singh, Ajit (eds) (1994) *The State, Markets and Development: Beyond the Neoclassical Dichotomy*, Aldershot: Edward Elgar.
Jameson, Kenneth P. and Wilber, Charles K. (eds) (1996) *The Political Economy of Development and Underdevelopment*, 6th edn, New York: McGraw-Hill.
Lewis, W. Arthur. (1954) "Economic Development with Unlimited Supplies of Labour," *The Manchester School of Economic and Social Studies* 22(2).
Taylor, Lance (1991) *Income Distribution, Inflation and Growth: Lectures on Structuralist Macroeconomic Theory*, Cambridge, MA: MIT Press.

AMITAVA KRISHNA DUTT

development and underdevelopment: definitions

"Development" is frequently taken to be a synonym for progress. Critics of modernity (Esteva 1992) also sometimes use the term to mean modernity, or the world, and the perspective of the world, created by the industrial revolution. In these contexts, it should not be surprising that the term is the subject of much debate.

The word is also widely used in biology, psychology and other parts of the intellectual world to label processes of change. Within political economy, "development" is most frequently used to delineate the sets of social changes associated with social and economic progress in the Third (or developing) World. This use of the term became widespread after the Second World War, when the Marshall Plan for the reconstruction of Europe provided a model for directed reconstruction of production and livelihoods and much of colonial Asia and Africa gained independence.

Three principal meanings of the term may be identified. First, development is used to describe ECONOMIC GROWTH and the social transformation (of social structure, ownership and economic power) associated with economic growth (Arndt 1987: ch. 1). This meaning of development is reflected in the gross domestic product per capita rankings of economies which are produced annually by the World Bank. More specifically, this idea of development as expanding productive capacity can be denoted by a secular increase in labor PRODUCTIVITY, providing increased output of goods and services which can be used (at least in principle) to improve standards of well-being. This idea of development as economic growth (and INDUSTRIALIZATION) was shared by orthodox traditions of thought on both sides of the Cold War (Kitching 1982: ch. 1).

Second, many different observers and movements have asserted that the term should connote a broader measure of progress, including equity. For example, one view (Seers 1979) focuses on realizing human potential and identifies the following prerequisites: (1) the capacity to buy physical necessities, (2) having a job, (3) an equalization of income distribution, (4) adequate education, (5) participation in the political process and (6) belonging to an independent nation.

Third, in the 1980s and 1990s, strong alternative conceptions of progress have been articulated. Feminist movements have noted that some phases of economic development have involved increased marginalization of the productive roles of women (Sen and Grown 1988). Environmental movements have argued (Sachs 1992) that the conservation of the natural world should also have a central place in consensus notions of progress, and some conservationists have argued that the industrialized world (both the capitalist West and the formerly state-socialist East) provides an example of *over*development. Critics of modernity have questioned the utility of a universal notion of progress, and suggested that "development" is little more than a continuation of the hegemonic ideas used by colonial powers to justify their "civilization" of the non-European world. These three sets of critics of development have (with greater and lesser effect) articulated, respectively, conceptions of gender-sensitive development (Sen and Grown 1988), SUSTAINABLE DEVELOPMENT (Woodhouse 1992) and indigenous development (Hettne 1995).

"Underdevelopment" is sometimes used as a synonym for backwardness or lack of progress, but it is also associated with a school of thought about development known variously as dependency or neo-Marxism, which drew upon Latin American structuralism to criticize modernization theory. This school (see particularly Frank 1966) coined the use of the term to denote a state and a process distinctly different from backwardness. Underdevelopment, in this tradition, refers to social regression or social and economic destruction, associated archetypically with colonial rule. Recognition of the possibility, and real prevalence, of economic regression was an important innovation from this school (see also Kay 1991).

See also:

development political economy: history; development political economy: major contemporary themes; environmental and ecological political economy: major contemporary themes; feminist political economy: major contemporary themes; human development index; international political economy: major contemporary themes; modernism and postmodernism; quality of life

Selected references

Arndt, H.W. (1987) *Economic Development: The History of an Idea*, Chicago: University of Chicago Press.
Esteva, Gustavo (1992) "Development," in Wolfgang Sachs (ed.), *Development Dictionary*, London: Zed Books.
Frank, A.G. (1966) "The Development of Underdevelopment," *Monthly Review*, September.
Hettne, B. (1995) *Development Theory and the Three Worlds: Towards an International Political Economy of Development*, Essex: Longman.
Kay, C. (1991) "Reflections on the Latin American Contribution to Development Theory," *Development and Change* 22(1): 31–68.
Kitching, G. (1982) *Development and Underdevelopment in Historical Perspective*, London: Methuen.
Sachs, Wolfgang (1992) "Environment," in Wolfgang Sachs (ed.), *Development Dictionary*, London: Zed Books.
Seers, D. (1979) "The Meaning of Development," in D. Lehmann (ed.), *Development Theory: Four Critical Studies*, London: Frank Cass.
Sen, G. and Grown, C. (1988) *Development, Crises and Alternative Visions: Third World Women's Perspectives*, London: Earthscan.
Woodhouse, P. (1992) "Environmental Degradation and Sustainability,' in Tim Allen and Alan Thomas (eds) *Poverty and Development in the 1990s*, Oxford: Oxford University Press.

BEN CROW

dialectical method

Dialectics is an approach to the world that focuses on interaction and change. It has been interpreted in at least three different ways.

First view: Hegelian dialectics

The German philosopher G.W.F. Hegel asserted that the Spirit and the world are one, that everything interacts with everything else, and that the universe (consisting of the ideas of the Spirit) is ever-changing and evolving. Hegel was still a theologian operating with abstract, spiritual ideas. The effect he had on many nineteenth century intellectuals, however, was electric. To see the world as a unity of internally related processes, rather than a static place of isolated objects, made a shocking difference to the world outlook of many people, including Karl MARX and Frederick Engels. Marx used the dialectic as a flexible method with great success, but he never discussed it systematically or in detail. He did tell us quite clearly that his dialectic is the opposite of Hegel's dialectic, but that leaves considerable room for interpretation. It is obvious that Marx rejected the theological side of Hegel and all the supernatural elements in Hegel's scheme, but he did not develop the implications of a dialectic method.

Second view: Soviet dialectics

Soviet dialectics were codified as the official Soviet philosophy by Joseph Stalin, then dictator of the Soviet Union (see Stalin 1940). According to Stalin, dialectics is not only a method, but also an ontology, that is, a statement of the "laws" of the universe. Stalin's view – that dialectics is a set of "laws" – follows Hegel. A "law," as used here, means a statement of exactly how the universe will behave at all times and places.

Stalin's picture of the universe is stated in three laws. The first law is called the unity and struggle of opposites. It says that rather than random isolated things, the world consists of opposites that are part of a unified relationship. Thus, capitalism is a relationship of struggle between workers and capitalists. The second law is that quantity changes into quality and vice versa. Thus there were slow, quantitative changes in the French economy for decades or centuries that eventually led to a class struggle in the French Revolution, causing a qualitative change. The third law is called the negation of the negation. Thus, in any given process the present set of relationships (such as feudalism) is negated, leading to a new set of relationships (such as capitalism), which in turn will be negated, leading to a still higher set of relationships (such as socialism).

These three laws are very suggestive and thought-provoking, but exactly what do they mean? They appear to be generalizations about all time and space from casual and limited observations. If they are stated generally enough, they can fit any case and cannot be disproven. They achieve that untouchable status, however, by being so broad as to be meaningless when one asks any precise question about them. For example, what is an "opposite"? Are male and female or worker and capitalist "opposites," or just different? Exactly how long a time before quantitative changes lead to qualitative changes? It is nine months to give birth, but it may be ninety thousands years leading to a volcanic explosion. If, on the other hand, one tries to make the laws specific, then they no longer cover all cases. Human births and volcanic explosions have entirely different time scales, so a law covering both and specifying the time scale will be false.

Third view: contemporary Marxism

Contemporary, critical, Marxian scholars have a very different view of the dialectic than either Hegel or Stalin. The contemporary views are presented fully with lengthy sets of references in Ollman (1993) and Sherman (1995). Some contemporary Marxists would say that dialectics is really all semantic nonsense, but they are usually criticizing the Soviet form of dialectics as stated by Stalin. Many contemporary Marxists would argue that dialectics is very useful, but is limited to a method of approach and does not state the answers to all the questions of the universe. In fact, it is the usual nature of a method that it states questions to be considered, rather than any answers.

Some social scientists use an approach called

"reductionism." They reduce all explanations to one factor, such as psychology or economics, with all other factors being derivative. Dialectics opposes reductionism and encourages a holistic or relational approach as one of its most basic aspects (see HOLISTIC METHOD). The holistic approach means that one treats society as a unified organism, consisting of a set of relationships within which everything is tied to everything else. In such a conception we do not begin our investigations with separate things, but with relations. For example, one cannot understand a slave as an isolated human being with certain physical and psychological characteristics; rather, this person must be considered as part of the relation of EXPLOITATION between the slave and slave-owner. The individual life of a slave or a slave-owner must be understood within this context (see SLAVERY).

Thus, definitions such as that of "slave" are based not on the external relations of an individual to some other individuals, but on the internal relationship of the slave to the slave-owner. Conservatives may view the unemployed worker as an isolated individual with psychological problems; but the dialectical method directs our attention to the internal relations of capitalism that give rise to unemployment (see RESERVE ARMY OF LABOR). In general, the conflicts and relations considered in a dialectic approach are not external conflicts, such as the action of sunspots on the economy; rather they are internal relations, such as the tensions within capitalism that lead to contractions in economic activity.

The second major aspect of the dialectic method in contemporary Marxian political economy is the historical or evolutionary approach (see explanation and references in Ollman 1993; Sherman 1995). Society is viewed as an evolving organism, so we examine processes rather than static things and equilibrium theories. The concept of an eternal law of society, of psychology or of economics must be rejected. Each society must be examined in its historical specificity. There is no general law of how labor is exploited. Labor is exploited differently in a slave society than in a capitalist society – and woe to the naive investigator who overlooks the differences. Not only may a relationship, such as exploitation, be very different in different societies, but it may also be absent in some societies.

Thus, societies are very different in different eras and have vastly different laws of movement. A Marxian scholar will ask, how do the social laws change from an old set of socio-economic relationships to a new one? Under what conditions will there be a revolutionary change in the class relations now existing? What was the evolution (and revolution) that brought about the present society?

The three laws revisited

Given the contemporary flexible approach, each of the three so-called laws of dialectics (discussed above in the section on Stalin) must be transformed from universal, super-scientific answers to questions answerable through experience and practice. We may replace the law of unity and struggle of opposites with questions such as: In what precise ways are classes united into certain relationships and processes in a particular society? In what precise ways do they conflict with each other? What conflicts exist in society that are based on that society's social structure?

We may replace the mysterious law of the negation of the negation with questions such as: In what direction are the economic tensions, class conflicts, and ideological conflicts moving in the society? Are they moving toward a revolution, which would change the social structures causing conflict? What kind of a revolution? We may replace the abstract law of quantity and quality with questions such as: What are the incremental changes and trends within a given society – or a given process within the society – that may lead to a qualitative change in that process or in the whole society? How have past qualitative changes in our society, such as the end of slavery in the American South, led to new trends and new types of incremental changes?

Dialectics as a method

Given the contemporary flexible approach, the dialectical method leads to the use of abstraction and successive approximations. If we see society as a unified whole, composed of large numbers of complex relations, how do we sort this out and make sense of it? In research, we begin with immense amounts of details and large numbers of relations, but we abstract from these to find some specific laws of movement in each area. We may then abstract from large numbers of very specific laws to find more general ones.

An exposition of a complex social subject will generally move in the opposite direction. In order to make sense for the reader or the student, one must begin in political economy with a simple abstract model. Then one can slowly add layers of reality, getting rid of unrealistic assumptions which were necessary at the beginning. By successive approximations we arrive at a more realistic, but more complex model of society or some process of society.

Lastly, one can apply a flexible, dialectic approach as a powerful tool to end confusion within social science methodology itself. Since each methodological approach is an abstraction, it is legitimate to talk about opposites in this realm of discourse, such as theory versus fact, ethics versus science, abstract versus concrete, and so forth. These opposites do often exist as absolutes in the minds of researchers, but when applied to real problems they are false dichotomies. The dialectical approach tells us that we must learn to unify each of these pairs of apparent opposites in the real work of political economy. Thus, one must use both facts and theories at every point of the research process. Every paradigm in the social sciences constitutes a particular blend of facts, theories and ethical values. The dialectical approach tells us not to pursue the chimera of an isolated fact.

Conclusion

Contemporary Marxists reject the Soviet notion of universal laws above science as a fetter on useful research in political economy. The contemporary Marxian dialectical method, including the relational or holistic approach, the historical or evolutionary approach and the concepts of abstraction and successive approximations, can be a powerful set of tools for the use of political economy. They do not provide answers, but they are a guide to the proper questions for political economy to ask.

See also:

contradictions; determinism and overdetermination

Selected references

Ollman, Bertell (1993) *Dialectical Investigations*, New York: Routledge.
Sherman, Howard J. (1995) *Reinventing Marxism*, Baltimore, MD: Johns Hopkins University Press.
Stalin, Joseph (1940) *Dialectical and Historical Materialism*, New York: International Publishers.

HOWARD J. SHERMAN

discrimination in the housing and mortgage market

Housing and mortgage market discrimination is the adverse treatment of a home buyer, renter or mortgage applicant based solely upon his or her membership in a particular ethnic, social or racial group. In the housing market, an example would be when a realtor or leasing agent shows a white applicant more properties than a black applicant having the same housing needs, income and credit qualifications (Yinger 1995: 14). Mortgage market discrimination occurs when a minority applicant is denied a loan, charged a higher loan rate or offered a less advantageous loan contract (for example, charged a higher down-payment or higher closing costs) solely because of his or her ethnic, social or racial group membership. Redlining is a second form of mortgage market discrimination directed against a housing unit because of its location. Redlining refers to the alleged practice of bankers drawing red lines around certain low income or minority neighborhoods within which bankers refuse to make loans (see Dymski 1995). When a mortgage with a given set of applicant, property and loan characteristics is more likely to be turned down in a minority neighborhood than in a white neighborhood, redlining exists (Yinger 1995: 68).

Economic consequences

The economic consequences of these forms of discrimination are considerable. Housing and mortgage market discrimination adversely affect blacks and other people of color. They impose higher search costs for housing and perpetuate racial segregation. Racial segregation hurts people of color by limiting their access to quality education, decreasing their access to employment and impairing their potential to acquire and accumulate wealth in the form of housing. In turn, limited access to quality education, employment and home ownership lowers the prospective income levels of non-whites, increases wealth and income disparities between whites and people of color, and raises rates of poverty for non-whites (Yinger 1995). In short, housing and mortgage market discrimination has economic implications which extend far beyond the mortgage market.

Over the last two decades the academic literature on housing and mortgage market discrimination has grown rapidly. In Australia, research concerning housing finance has raised issues of GENDER inequality rarely discussed in other countries (Taylor and Jureidini 1994). In the USA, the academic literature has been written from two main points of view. Mainstream economists use a narrow definition of discrimination and a microeconomic approach to theorize about housing and mortgage market outcomes. In contrast, political economists and other empirical researchers use a broad definition of discrimination to empirically analyze housing and mortgage market data.

As a result of their different starting points and research methodologies, these two groups reach differing conclusions regarding the existence and extent of discrimination.

Traditional microeconomics

Mainstream microeconomists define discrimination narrowly as an individual's racially biased preference or action that is irrational, intentional and costly. The action is irrational in the sense that it is at odds with the presumed goal of profit maximization. The discriminating party knowingly engages in an act that increases his or her costs and/or decreases his or her income solely because of a racially biased personal preference or taste. An example of this type of mortgage market discrimination would be a banker refusing a profitable loan opportunity simply because he or she prefers not to do business with African-Americans (see Becker 1971). As a result of this narrow definition of discrimination, mainstream microeconomists rarely find evidence of housing and mortgage market discrimination. They assert that African-American and other minority borrowers are riskier borrowers since they often have lower incomes, less wealth, higher debt-to-income ratios, weaker credit ratings and less stable employment histories than white borrowers, and that these factors are difficult (if not impossible) to separate from race.

Microtheorists also assert that since data on these variables are not publicly available, only those with special access to all of the data relevant to the mortgage acceptance/denial decision can definitively determine whether or not discrimination exists. Studies using anything less than actual loan application data are viewed as incomplete. Thus, mainstream theorists often criticize empirical research on mortgage market discrimination on the grounds that there are missing variables or that the models are misspecified (see Horne 1994). From the microtheorist's perspective, even if mortgage market discrimination is detected, mainstream microeconomists would not expect it to persist, *ceteris paribus*. As all economics textbooks explain, microeconomists assume that the pursuit of profit will encourage competitors to enter the market and offer mortgages to those previously denied by bigoted lenders.

Political economy of discrimination

In contrast, political economists, empirical researchers and many involved in the legal system take a more liberal and outcome-oriented approach to mortgage market discrimination (see Nesiba 1996). For political economists, mortgage market discrimination is virtually synonymous with racially unequal outcomes. For instance, political economists concur with US law in recognizing at least three types of discrimination in lending: overt evidence of discrimination, disparate treatment and disparate impact.

Overt evidence of discrimination exists when an agent blatantly discriminates on a prohibited basis. An example would be a banker denying a loan to an African-American mortgage applicant solely because of the applicant's race. Disparate treatment exists when a lender treats a credit applicant differently based on one of the prohibited bases (race, color, religion, international origin, age, sex, marital status or receipt of income from public assistance programs). An example would be the offering of advice and counsel in the home mortgage application process to non-minority applicants, but not offering the same assistance to minority applicants.

Evidence of the third and final form of discrimination, disparate impact, occurs when a lender applies a rule or policy uniformly to all applicants, but the policy has a disproportionate adverse impact on applicants from a group protected against discrimination. An example would be a policy that states a lender will only make mortgages on homes valued over $50,000 when most of the homes in minority neighborhoods are valued at, say, $30,000. In this scenario, US law would require the lending institution to justify the "business necessity" of not making smaller mortgage loans.

As a result of this broader conception of discrimination, political economists and other empirical researchers routinely find evidence of housing and mortgage market discrimination. What these researchers find is that most whites and most blacks continue to live in neighborhoods characterized by segregation. They also find that members of minority groups fare poorly in obtaining home mortgage loans. Blacks apply proportionally for fewer mortgages than whites, yet are rejected more often. White neighborhoods receive three to four times more loans per 1,000 mortgageable structures when compared to minority neighborhoods with similar income levels (Bradbury et al. 1989). Regression analyses, using various model specifications and data sets, agree that redlining and racial variables show consistent, significant and negative coefficients (Shlay 1987). This is true even when one controls for debt obligation ratios, credit history, loan-to-value ratios and property characteristics (Munnell et al. 1992).

Mortgage lending in Boston: case study

In the USA, many regard the October 1992 Federal Reserve Bank of Boston's "Mortgage Lending in Boston: Interpreting HMDA Data" (Munnell et al. 1992) as the most persuasive study of racial discrimination in residential lending. The authors of the study attempt to address the shortcomings of earlier studies by including all relevant variables regarding a bank's loan acceptance/denial decision. Rather than using only publicly available data, the study is supplemented with actual loan application data from financial institutions in the Boston area. The authors conclude that, even given the same obligation ratios, credit histories, loan-to-value ratios and property characteristics, 17 percent of Hispanic or black residential mortgage applicants would be turned down, as opposed to 11 percent of white applicants (Munnell et al. 1992: 44).

Legislation to reduce discrimination

The legislative campaigns to eliminate discrimination in the housing and mortgage markets have been relatively recent international phenomena. In the UK, the first (1965), second (1968) and third (1976) race relations acts prohibited discrimination based on race. However, unlike the grassroots community reinvestment movement that motivated American legislation, in Britain the impetus for these acts came from large increases in the number of black immigrants moving to Britain (MacEwan 1991). In South Africa, the legislation removing apartheid as the law of the land occurred only in the 1990s. In the mid-1970s, blacks began moving into Johannesburg's inner city because of the state-housing shortage in black areas and the political crisis associated with the dissolution of apartheid (Morris 1994). In the USA, the Fair Housing Act of 1968 and Equal Credit Opportunity Act of 1974 were passed to forbid suppliers of housing, housing finance and their agents from denying housing or mortgages based on an applicant's race, color, religion, international origin, age, sex, marital status or receipt of income from public assistance. The Home Mortgage Disclosure Act (HMDA) of 1975 (significantly amended in 1989) and the Community Reinvestment Act of 1977 were passed, respectively, to increase access to bank loan records and to affirm the responsibilities banks have to local communities and individuals.

Need for a holistic method

Researchers still do not know exactly what causes the racially biased housing patterns found worldwide. A richer understanding of how housing and mortgage market disparities are created is needed if public policy is to be successful in reducing them. Developing this understanding will likely require a return to a HOLISTIC METHOD of economic research. Researchers should investigate which "rules of thumb" are being applied by lenders when making the loan approval/denial decision, and how these rules impact upon minority applicants and neighborhoods. They should evaluate the degree to which special lending and marketing programs influence the number and dollars of mortgage loans made to low and moderate income neighborhoods. Similarly, research should evaluate how borrowers, real estate agents, appraisers and mortgage insurers each influence the existence of racial disparities. In the USA, research should also be done to investigate how banking industry consolidation, average bank size, banking institution type and a lender's headquarters location influence residential lending patterns.

See also:

labor market discrimination; race in political economy: history; race in political economy: major contemporary themes; racism

Selected references

Becker, Gary (1971) *The Economics of Discrimination*, Chicago: University of Chicago Press.
Bradbury, Katherine L., Case, Carl E. and Dunham, Constance R. (1989) "Geographic Patterns of Mortgage Lending in Boston, 1982–1987," *New England Economic Review* September–October: 3–30.
Dymski, Gary A. (1995) "The Theory of Bank Redlining and Discrimination: An Exploration," *The Review of Black Political Economy* 23(3): 37–74.
Horne, David K. (1994) "Evaluating the Role of Race in Mortgage Lending," *FDIC Banking Review* Spring–Summer: 1–15.
MacEwan, Martin (1991) *Housing, Race and Law: The British Experience*, London: Routledge.
Morris, Alan (1994) "The Desegregation of Hillbrow, Johannesburg, 1978–1982," *Urban Studies* 31(6): 821–34.
Munnell, Alicia H., Browne, Lynn E., McEneaney, James and Tootell, Geoffrey M.B. (1992) "Mortgage Lending in Boston: Interpreting the HMDA Data," Federal Reserve Bank of Boston Working Paper no. 92-7.
Nesiba, Reynold F. (1996) "Racial Discrimination in Residential Lending Markets: Why Empirical Researchers Always See it and Economic Theorists Never Do," *Journal of Economic Issues* 30(1): 51–77.
Shlay, Anne B. (1987) *Credit on Color: The*

Impact of Segregation and Racial Transition on Housing Credit Flows in the Chicago SMSA from 1980–1983, Chicago: Chicago Fair Housing Alliance.

Taylor, Judy and Jureidini, Ray (1994) "The Implicit Male Norm in Australian Housing Finance," *Journal of Economic Issues* 28(2): 543–54.

Yinger, John (1995) *Closed Doors, Opportunities Lost: The Continuing Costs of Housing Discrimination*, New York: Russell Sage Foundation.

REYNOLD F. NESIBA

disembedded economy

The concept of the "disembedded economy" refers to a tendency for economic relationships to become dominant over the social relationships of kinship and polity. The concept has been variously expressed. Aristotle's distinction between natural and unnatural exchange may be regarded as an early expression. Another expression may be seen in the lamentations of MARX with regard to COMMODITY FETISHISM, ALIENATION, the subordination of human personality to production for its own sake, and the inexorable "power of money" in the world market. Werner Sombart and Max Weber, along with other members of the German HISTORICAL SCHOOL, noted that the capitalist economy turned upside down the traditional relation between economic and social life. Thorstein VEBLEN and other original institutional economists were sharply critical of the perversions wrought by pecuniary valuation upon the social economy. The most cogent expression is that associated with Karl Polanyi, and this entry will draw heavily upon Polanyi's formulation.

Reciprocity, redistribution and exchange

Economy refers to the process by which a society institutes the integration or coordination of the DIVISION OF LABOR. The assignment of individuals to particular tasks, the allotment of tools and materials to those tasks and the distribution of the real income that results are the fundamental issues of any process of divided labor. Any such integrative process requires socially structured transactions that communicate expectations and sanctions and monitor behavior. Reciprocity, redistribution and market exchange are the three known integrative patterns. Reciprocity refers to the obligatory sharing of output within a group. Redistribution requires centricity of political allegiance and involves centralized collection and allocation of income. Market exchange refers to transactions involving the transfer of ownership of equivalent values (Stanfield 1986: 3).

Reciprocity and redistribution have no particular internal logic. That is, they derive their impetus from the social and political structure that defines the individuals within social relationships and their respective rights and duties. In other words, reciprocal and redistributive transactions are embedded within social and political relationships that control the immediate transaction. Any number of customary relations can structure these transactions and vest them with the regularity necessary to sustain provisioning through time. Economies organized upon these two principles may then be said to be embedded because their relationship to society is one of subordination. Such economies may be said to be anonymous in that there is no discernible economic motivation or logic that is distinct from the cultural context of kinship and political life. The terms applied to the economy in such societies, such as "traditional economy" or "moral economy," indicate that economy was embedded in custom or moral CULTURE. These terms indicate the degree to which social position defines economic position, function and privilege.

In contrast, an economy organized primarily upon market exchange implies a far different relationship between society and economy. The market economy requires a system of price-making MARKETS in which supply and demand factors interact to establish relative prices. Note that an economy organized by market transactions, based upon relative prices that are administered by political authority or given by treaty agreements, would not constitute a pure form of market exchange, since the relative prices are not generated by price-making markets. Integration of the division of labor through transactions based on administered or treaty-based prices is accomplished by the political authorities that administer or negotiate treaty prices, not by market exchange.

Markets and pricing

Factor markets that are subject to pricing by the interaction of supply and demand are the *sine qua non* of the market economy. If factor prices are set by administration or custom ("just" prices) the integration of the division of labor is not accomplished primarily by price-making markets. Hence, in the discussion of the origin of modern CAPITALISM, it is not surprising that the primary attention focuses upon changing attitudes toward usury and entrepreneurship, alienable land and the generation of a "free" or unbonded labor force (Polanyi 1944: 6).

A system of price-making markets requires a logic and organizational force of its own. It is not surprising, then, that personal gain comes to be viewed as a specifically economic motivation and that competition comes to be regarded as an explicitly economic force for the regulation and channeling of this motivation (Polanyi 1944: 30). Particular transactions are seen as the expression of impersonal market forces and imply no underlying social or political relationship other than legal insistence upon compliance with the terms of validly executed contracts. By its harmonization of competing self-interests, the competitive process is seen as channeling the motive of gain into socially useful results. This occurs through the generation of a set of relative prices that reflect scarcity and guide decision-makers with regard to resource allocation.

This vital function of configuring prices in line with scarcity can be said to be operative because individuals can be assumed to be bargaining in their market behavior so as to achieve as favorable an outcome for themselves as possible, within the constraint of competition. That is, a bargaining mentality is essential for the operation of a market exchange economy. The operation of a market economy also requires factor mobility and a high degree of entrepreneurial freedom. Productive equipment, natural resources and labor have to be readily redeployable throughout the various economic sectors and geographic space. This is necessary so that the structured systems of transactions can operate to adjust the allocation of resources in the face of changes in the structure of relative prices. Entrepreneurs bring about this adjustment as they look to take advantage of or induce relative price changes that present profitable opportunities.

Protection from markets

Obviously the economy just described, in contrast to the traditional economy described above, is relatively unencumbered with social and political tradition and obligation. This accounts for the tremendous advance of technology and productivity in the very brief historical sojourn of thoroughgoing market exchange economies (Ward 1979). It also leads us to the familiar stresses and strains of the modern era, much of which derive from the erosion of social and COMMUNITY life by the operation of the disembedded market economy, and the concomitant social effort to guard against this erosion and reinstate social control over the economy (Polanyi 1944: 10–11).

The threat to the social existence of workers and their families by the employment insecurity of capitalism is one very evident aspect of this twofold process. Workers, and the families of workers, who are disemployed by the perennial restructuring of the market economy suffer social dislocation. Through UNIONS and political advocacy, workers seek protection against this dislocation. The threat posed to environmental and cultural continuity by the innovations and resource reallocations of the market economy leads to organizations that are dedicated to environmental protection and historical preservation. The threat of macroeconomic instability leads to political reforms to regulate financial institutions and aggregate demand. The modern CORPORATION itself is a form of protection because it serves to insulate the enterprise from the vagaries of the competitive market.

The "double movement" created by, first, the spread of the market economy and thence, second, the tendency to devise new forms of collective action to protect social existence from discontinuity, points to the political economic trajectory of capitalist development. The familiar corporate WELFARE STATE and most of the characteristic issues of the democratic industrial societies are thus revealed to be the working out of these contrary tendencies. One sees the logic of the market arrayed against the demand for social continuity in such issues as income protection policies versus labor market incentives, culture and tradition versus the entrepreneurial freedom of mass media and entertainment industry companies, and ecological sustainability versus immediate economic opportunity. Not only the movement for social democratic reform but also the appeal of socialism can be seen to be based on the desire to sustain social continuity in the face of the economic vulnerability associated with the adjustment process by which the market economy pursues an "efficient allocation of resources."

In the final analysis, the subject of the disembedded economy points to the pivotal concern for the place of economy in society. In the extreme, the logic of the market mentality may generate a nurturance gap, in which society fails to sustain the process of nurturing individuals who are capable of orderly interaction in a free society (Stanfield and Stanfield 1997; Lowe 1988). Only when its focus is squarely upon the place of economy in society can political economic thought hope to come to grips with the problems manifested in the nurturance gap.

Challenges ahead

The issues raised by the concept of the disembedded economy will continue to confront democratic industrial societies as they struggle to sustain nurturing social relationships in the context of the increasingly global thrust of the dynamic, growth-oriented market economy. Thus in the final analysis, the most important form of international competition is of the socioeconomic or political economic variety, because embedded processes are critical to the protection of the structures underlying human and ecological livelihood and meaning in a complex environment. Purely allocative or technological forms of competitiveness may lead to instability in the fragile global economy and ecology (see Heilbroner 1985), and hence need to be embedded in a stable set of relationships and processes. This is a major challenge in the years ahead for theory and policy in political economy.

See also:

business cycle theories; ceremonial encapsulation; contradictions; financial instability hypothesis; institutional political economy: major contemporary themes; institutions and habits; markets and exchange in premodern economies; Polanyi's views on integration; social economics: major contemporary themes; social structures of accumulation

Selected references

Heilbroner, R.L. (1985) *The Nature and Logic of Capitalism*, New York: W. W. Norton.

Lowe, A. (1988) *Has Freedom a Future?*, New York: Praeger.

Polanyi, K. (1944) *The Great Transformation*, New York: Rinehart; paperback edn, Boston: Beacon Press, 1957.

Stanfield, J.R. (1986) *The Economic Thought of Karl Polanyi*, London: Macmillan, and New York: St. Martin's Press.

Stanfield, J.R. and Stanfield, J.B. (1997) "Where Has Love Gone? Reciprocity, Redistribution, and the Nurturance Gap," *Journal of Socio-Economics*, April.

Ward, B. (1979) *The Conservative Economic World View*, New York: Basic Books.

JAMES RONALD STANFIELD

DISEQUILIBRIUM: see equilibrium, disequilibrium and non-equilibrium

distribution of income

The size distribution of income, or personal distribution of income, concerns the distribution of income among individuals, households or other units. It shows the entire range of income values and their observed frequencies for the population under consideration. It therefore deals with how many persons (or households) receive how much income and where their relative economic positions are.

Three methods of depiction

There are three common ways of depicting the distribution of income. The first way is by using a quantile share table, specifying population proportions and their corresponding average incomes. The second way is by using a graphical representation, the two most common of which are the histogram and the Lorenz curve. A histogram is a graph that relates the income ranges to their relative frequencies or population proportions. A Lorenz curve represents the relationship between the cumulative proportion of population and cumulative proportion of income received by that proportion of population.

The third way of representing the distribution of income is by using a formula describing a statistical distribution. The standard statistical distributions which are commonly used in describing observed income distribution data are the Pareto distribution and the Lognormal distribution. There are also other more sophisticated statistical distributions which are regularly used. They are the generalized-Beta and the generalized-Gamma families of distributions.

All three different ways of representing an income distribution can be used either with survey data on a large number of income recipients or with grouped observations. Apart from presenting the distribution of income using the three different forms, it is also useful and common to summarize the characteristics of the distribution with two measures.

Measures

The first is a measure of central location. This measure indicates where the incomes cluster or are centered. The second is a measure of variability or spread of the income. This measure is to answer the question of how unequally the income is distributed around the average.

There are three common measures of central location: the mean, the median and the mode. For a typical income distribution, the mode is less than the median which, in turn, is less than the mean. This feature has been observed and is common over time and space. It means that the most common income level (mode) is less than the income at the mid point of the population (median) which, in turn, is less than the average income (mean). A distribution with this property is called a positively skewed distribution.

Different dimensions

To observe the degree of (in)equality in the distribution of income, one can examine different dimensions. First, there are the income shares of various groups. Equally distributed income has the characteristic that each income share proportion should be equal to the proportion of population who earn that income. For example, 20 percent of the population should earn 20 percent of the total income.

The second is the Lorenz curve. This is normally represented in a unit square as shown in Figure 5. In this Figure, ACB represents a Lorenz curve.

If the total income were equally distributed among all members of the population, the

distribution of income

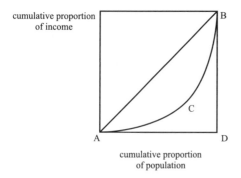

Figure 5

Lorenz curve of the distribution of income would simply be represented by the diagonal AB. In this case any 10 percent of the population would receive 10 percent of the total income. If the total income is not equally distributed, the bottom income groups will obviously enjoy a proportionately lower share of the income. Therefore, except in the case of complete equality, the Lorenz curve must be a curve which lies below the diagonal and joins the points A and B. The closer the Lorenz curve is to the diagonal, the smaller is the inequality.

For the case of comparing different income distributions, one should be aware that the Lorenz curve is an ordinal measure which provides a partial ordering of income distributions. The inequality of two or more distributions can be compared only if their Lorenz curves do not intersect. If they intersect, it is not possible to rank them. In such cases, numerical measures of inequality which can provide a comparison are needed.

Positive and normative measures

There are several measures of inequality in the literature. These measures can be classified into two groups: positive measures and normative measures. Positive measures are measures derived using statistical concepts and, as such, do not have any direct welfare implications. In contrast, normative measures are derived using social welfare functions, and these rely on value judgments. Some of the well-known positive measures are the Gini coefficient and the Theil measure. Examples of the normative measures are the Atkinson index and the Dalton index. Both the Atkinson and Dalton measures depend entirely on a properly defined welfare function. For this reason, these measures are not very popular in practice.

The Gini coefficient is closely related to the Lorenz curve. It is calculated as twice the area between the Lorenz curve and the diagonal AB. The Gini coefficient for a typical income distribution takes a value between 0 and 1. It is 0 if there is no inequality in the distribution; the Lorenz curve is the diagonal AB. It is 1 for the case of perfect inequality; the Lorenz curve is the kinked line ADB. This is the case where one person (household) receives all the income.

The Theil measure is based on the concept of entropy, which measures the information content of a particular statistical distribution. It is calculated using only the data on the population shares and the corresponding income shares of the distribution of interest. When using more than one measure to calculate inequality, it is possible that two different measures may give slightly different rankings of income distributions.

Global inequality

In recent years, more work has focused on the issue of global inequality. Some of the pioneering work has been done by Theil and his associates (Theil 1979, 1996; Theil and Seale 1994; Theil and Galvez 1995). They examined inequality across countries and tested for the convergence of real per capita income between the years 1961 and 1986. A total of 113 countries are included in the study (Theil 1996). Their finding is that international inequality increased from the early 1960s to the later 1960s, after which it remains approximately constant.

To look at the inequality in more detail, Theil (1996) divided the countries in their study into seven regions based on a distinction between temperate and tropical zones. They then decomposed the international inequality into inequality arising between regions and within regions. The finding was that the inequality between regions accounted for 86–90 percent of the international inequality, whereas the inequality within regions accounted for only 10–14 percent.

See also:

collective social wealth; health inequality; inequality; justice; needs; poverty: definition and measurement; rights

Selected references

Aitchison, J. and Brown, J.A.C. (1966) *The Lognormal Distribution*, Cambridge: Cambridge University Press.
Atkinson, A.B. (1975) *The Economics of Inequality*, Oxford: Oxford University Press.
Champernowne, D.G. (1973) *The Distribution of Income between Persons*, Cambridge: Cambridge University Press.
Cowell, F.A. (1977) *Measuring Inequality*, Oxford: Phillip Allan.
Lambert, P.J. (1993) *The Distribution and Redistribution of Income*, Manchester: Manchester University Press.
Pen, J. (1971) *Income Distribution: Facts, Theories and Policies*, New York: Praeger.
Theil, H. (1979) "World Income Inequality and Its Components," *Economics Letters* 2: 99–102.
—— (1996) *Studies in Global Econometrics: Netherlands*, Dordrecht: Kluwer Academic Publishers.
Theil, H. and Galvez, J. (1995) "On Latitude and Affluence: The Equatorial Grand Canyon," *Empirical Economics* 20: 163–6.
Theil, H. and Seale, J.L., Jr (1994) "The Geographical Distribution of World Income, 1950–1990 (Dedicated to the memory of Jan Tinbergen)," *De Economist* 142: 387–419.

DUANGKAMON CHOTIKAPANICH

division of labor

In all societies, production is a cooperative enterprise. That is, human beings take the total pool of their labor and divide it up so that no one is absolutely independent of everyone else. Put simply, a society's productive activities are divided among its members, and no one does every activity. For example, in the first mode of production, gathering and hunting, small bands of men and women divided their labor by sex, with certain activities or tasks performed primarily by men and others primarily by women (see HUNTER–GATHERER AND SUBSISTENCE SOCIETIES; GENDER DIVISION OF LABOR).

Social division of labor

The division of labor by task is common to all societies and is called the social division of labor. Prior to CAPITALISM, the social division of labor almost completely describes production. Nearly all labor is, in effect, skilled labor and there is no separation between the conception of the work and its execution. Each task or group of tasks is performed by the laborer from beginning to end. For example, hunters in the Amazon find and fell trees, shape them into boats, and then use the boats to hunt fish with bows they have also made. In their work, they exhibit the unique human ability to think and to do, to plan in advance what they are going to do, and then to execute the task. An exception to this way of working sometimes occurred in the slave mode of production, when slaves were forced to labor on large-scale public works projects such as roads. In these situations, slaves would be compelled to do repetitive unskilled labor.

Capitalist division of labor

Capitalism radically changed the division of labor. The complete detachment of the laborer from the means of production, through the conversion of the latter into private property, allowed the capitalist to impose upon the laborer a separation of the conception and the execution of work, as well as a sub-division of the labor tasks into details. The latter, which presupposes the former, is called the *detailed division of labor*. Instead of skilled workers mentally dividing their tasks into sub-tasks and performing each sub-task themselves, the capitalist now plans out the steps and assigns unskilled workers to each task.

Smith and Babbage on the detailed division of labor

Classical and neoclassical economics typically conflate the social and detailed divisions of labor, implying that the latter is no different to the former. The detailed division of labor is made to appear as a natural human development, and, in fact, one without which modern industrial society would not be possible. In his famous example of the pin factory, Adam Smith raised the detailed division of labor to the *sine qua non* of the industrial revolution (Smith 1776). By dividing the production of a straight pin into eighteen separate and unskilled details, Smith argued, the manufacturer enormously increased the productivity of the labor force. The repetition of details increased the dexterity of the workers; time was saved as a skilled worker would not have to move from sub-task to sub-task, and the simplicity of the work was an impetus to the use of machinery. Similarly, large-scale production is not possible unless there is a separation between those who direct the work and those who carry out their orders.

Smith's arguments in favor of the detailed division of labor are typical of those who cannot see the social determinants of the ways in which work is done. For is it not possible to imagine that productivity could be maintained if skilled workers did each of the steps, provided that the number of units produced was sufficiently large? Smith was unable to see that the detailed division of labor is a product of capitalism and not of mass production. The manufacturer and inventor Charles Babbage, on the other hand, saw clearly that the detailed division of labor lowers the unit cost of production because it greatly economizes on the use of skilled labor. Wherever possible, unskilled labor is employed, and this is cheaper by definition (Braverman 1974: ch. 3). In an economic system necessarily obsessed with lowering the unit costs of production, the detailed division of labor is inevitable. But it surely would be neither inevitable nor desirable in a society in which the means of production are owned in common (see SOCIALISM AND COMMUNISM).

Marxism on the detailed division of labor

In Marxist political economy, the detailed division of labor is one of the hallmarks of capitalism, with profound implications for both individual and society. First, it divides not only the labor but also the laborer. It denies the workers their innate capacity to both conceptualize and execute work. Combined with advanced mechanization, it produces the assembly-line worker who must literally disassociate himself from his or her work in order to make it through the workday (see ALIENATION). From the capitalist point of view, this is an ideal control mechanism; it makes each worker easily replaceable (see RESERVE ARMY OF LABOR), and it creates workers who subjectively feel incapable of creative labor.

Second, from a social perspective, the deformation wrought by the detailed division of labor makes the majority of people incapable of contributing solutions to capitalism's social and ecological depredations (paraphrasing Adam Smith (1776: 734–5), doing repetitive work all day makes a person as stupid as it is possible for a person to be). The meaninglessness of the detail in workers' labor also makes them susceptible to the idea that happiness can only be achieved through consumption (rather than production). Third, Smith was correct in arguing that the detailed division of labor encourages mechanization. Unfortunately, capitalist mechanization only deepens the deskilling effects of detail work by subjecting the laborer to machine pacing and by transferring knowledge from worker to machine (Braverman 1974: ch. 9).

New schemes and work teams

Naturally, the dehumanization of work breeds resistance by workers, taking forms ranging from sabotage to industrial unions. Some workers see that the homogenizing effects of detail work make it impossible for them to improve their circumstances unless they act collectively. This resistance requires employers to introduce strategies to habituate laborers to their inhuman circumstances. Today, these take the forms of job combining, work teams and monetary incentives for high quality. Some writers seem to believe that these developments spell the end of the detailed division of labor and the beginning of the growth of multi-skilled and technically sophisticated workers. However, this view is seldom based upon actually observing work. In reality, the production systems pioneered by Japanese firms have been built upon a labor process already thoroughly divided and mechanized. Sub-tasks are so devoid of skill that their combining simply means that each worker is a master of many unskilled jobs. Work teams are typically established to build company loyalty, giving the illusion of worker control without its substance (see Parker and Slaughter 1994; Graham 1995; (Fordism and the flexible system of production).

Dividing tendency

The capitalist division of labor entails many other kinds of dividing. Capitalism destroys the family economy of pre-industrial society, driving men into full-time market work and relegating married women to household labor. When women do enter the labor market, they tend to fill positions which are gender segregated. Even after years of active opposition by women, occupations and especially jobs remain remarkably segregated.

Of great importance is the "international division of labor." As the capitalist economies of Western Europe subjugated most of the rest of the world in search of wealth, markets and cheap labor, they forcibly integrated the conquered peoples into the world market. From African slaves working on Brazilian sugar plantations to Asian women putting circuits on computer chips, the world's labor power has been deformed to suit the needs of capital.

In some capitalist economies, labor is divided racially or ethnically (see RACISM; SEGMENTED AND DUAL LABOR MARKETS). The relentless drive to accumulate capital constantly divides workers spatially, as capital roams the world in search of profits. Modern technology has made workers increasingly vulnerable to this spatial redivision. It has also made possible fine time divisions, as evidenced by the increasing use of part-time and temporary labor (Yates 1994). Finally, by reducing the skill requirements of jobs, the detailed division of labor creates an enormous pool of potential workers, thereby dividing workers into those who are employed and those who are ready to take their jobs.

Conclusion

The division of labor represents a wonderful human invention, but capitalism has taken this and turned it into am implement of human oppression and degradation. The irony is that the contemporary revolution in technology has made it possible for all workers to become once again the all-round workers they once were. However, this possibility will only be realized when working men and women are sufficiently organized to force the issue (Aronowitz and DiFazio 1994).

See also:

gender division of labour; work, labour and production: major contemporary themes

Selected references

Aronowitz, Stanley and DiFazio, William (1994) *The Jobless Future: Sci-Tech and the Dogma of Work*, Minneapolis: University of Minnesota Press.

Braverman, Harry (1974) *Labor and Monopoly Capital: The Degradation of Work in the*

Twentieth Century, New York: Monthly Review Press.
Graham, Laurie (1995) *On the Line at Subaru-Isuzu: The Japanese Model and the American Worker*, Ithaca, NY: ILR Press.
Parker, Mike and Slaughter, Jane (1994) *Working Smart: A Union Guide to Participation Programs and Reengineering*, Detroit, MI: Labor Notes Books.
Smith, Adam (1776) *An Inquiry into the Nature and Causes of the Wealth of Nations*, New York: The Modern Library, 1937.
Thompson, Paul (1983) *The Nature of Work: An Introduction to Debates on the Labor Process*, London: Macmillan.
Yates, Michael D. (1994) *Longer Hours, Fewer Jobs: Employment and Unemployment in the United States*, New York: Monthly Review Press.

MICHAEL D. YATES

domestic labor debate

Nature of the debate

Domestic labor is a concept that has been used by feminists and social scientists since the 1970s to refer to unpaid work that is done by and for members of households. The domestic labor debate, which took place mainly in North America and the UK in the early to mid-1970s, explored whether and how Marxist value theory could offer a framework for analyzing the relationship between domestic labor and capital ACCUMULATION.

The domestic labor debate brought together two theoretical currents, namely feminism, which identified unpaid work in the family as a major factor in gender inequality, and the radical new left, which sought to adapt and renew Marxism. At the time, most Marxists adopted Harry Braverman's view, as expressed in *Labor and Monopoly Capital* (1974), that CAPITALISM was rapidly converting household production into commodities sold on the market for profit; and that domestic labor was a static remnant of pre-capitalist society, a latent reserve army of labor to be tapped when required by the process of capital accumulation. The domestic labor debate challenged this perspective by suggesting that household production was part of the economic infrastructure underpinning the capitalist economy (see HOUSEHOLD PRODUCTION AND NATIONAL INCOME).

Within the domestic labor debate, there were two broad approaches. One was to argue that domestic labor subsidized capitalist production through its role in the reproduction of labor power, directly enhancing capitalist profitability. The second approach was to argue that domestic labor was essential for the reproduction of labor power in capitalist society, but did not contribute to capitalist profitability (see REPRODUCTION PARADIGM).

Subsidy to capitalist production

Among those who argued that domestic labor subsidized capitalist production, there was disagreement about how to conceptualize the notion of a subsidy. In an article in *Monthly Review* in 1969, Margaret Benston argued that the support of a family was a hidden tax on the wage earner, since his wage bought the labor power of two people.

Creating surplus value. In 1972, Mariarosa Dalla Costa's article "Women and the Subversion of the Community" was published in a pamphlet by M. Dalla Costa and Selma James entitled *The Power of Women and the Subversion of the Community*. In this article, she equated domestic labor with the reproduction of labor power and argued that housework created surplus value. It was the lack of a wage that concealed the exploitation of housework by the capitalist class; hence the demand for wages for housework. Most participants in the debate rejected both the wages for housework demand and the notion that housework could be conceptualized as part of capitalist production (Malos 1980).

Performing surplus labor. John Harrison adopted an approach that was closer to Marx's concept of PRODUCTIVE AND UNPRODUCTIVE LABOR, but still involved a radical reinterpretation of the LABOR THEORY OF VALUE. Surplus value was not produced in the household, but a housewife would be performing surplus labor if the necessary labor time involved in domestic services for her husband exceeded the labor embodied in the commodities consumed by her that were purchased from his wage (Harrison 1973: 42). Although this represented an unequal exchange between husband and wife, it was assumed that housewives' surplus labor would be appropriated by the capitalist class, through paying male workers a wage that was lower than the value of their labor power. The possibility that wives consumed less and worked longer hours than husbands, and that men benefited from women's surplus labor, was raised but not explored. Subsequently, Nancy Folbre used a similar approach to explore gender inequality within the household (Folbre 1982).

Contribution to surplus value. However, the London-based Political Economy of Women group argued that domestic labor time was not comparable with Marx's concept of value or abstract labor time (Gardiner *et al.* 1975: 10). Domestic labor was not subject to capitalist production relations, nor to the market forces operating on commodity production. The value of labor power should not be redefined to include domestic labor time, but should be limited to the abstract labor time embodied in commodities entering into workers' consumption. The value of labor power and the wage paid to workers was premised on other forms of work outside capitalist production relations that provided for consumption needs, including work performed in the state sector as well as domestic labor.

Hence, domestic labor contributed to the production of surplus value by keeping the value of labor power below the total costs of its reproduction. The mechanism for this was the retention within the family of those aspects of the reproduction and maintenance of labor power which it was not cost-effective for capitalist production or the state to take over. Future trends in domestic labor would depend on the interplay of the costs of reproduction of labor, the capitalist accumulation process and the demand for female wage labor.

Rejection of subsidy notion

Some other participants in the debate rejected the notion of a subsidy. They argued that it was the role of domestic labor in the reproduction of labor power that made it an essential part of the reproduction of the capitalist mode of production, rather than any direct link between domestic labor and capitalist profitability. For Wally Seccombe (1974), the main role of domestic labor is in the production of labor power. Because labor power is a commodity, he argued that domestic labor created value. However, he rejected the view that the housewife performed surplus labor or was exploited.

Seccombe's critics argued that domestic labor was not commodity production and, therefore, could not be deemed to create value. For Susan Himmelweit and Simon Mohun, what was specific about domestic labor was that it was use-value production, not commodity production; hence the value of labor power did not include the housewife's labor. The major reason why domestic labor survived was that capitalism required workers to be free individuals selling their labor power on the market. They argued that the complete socialization of domestic labor would turn the "free" laborer into a slave, and would be inconsistent with capitalist relations of production (Himmelweit and Mohun 1977: 25).

Contribution of the debate

The domestic labor debate threw light on a number of issues. Households in industrialized capitalist societies clearly produced as well as consumed. The standard of living was not based solely on the level of wages, but also on domestically produced use-values and public services. The historical evolution of the bundle of wage goods, which constituted the value of labor power, was dependent on the degree to which domestic labor was available to process or provide substitutes for those goods.

Criticisms

The Marxist concept of value was an inadequate tool for analyzing domestic labor because its products were not exchanged on the market but consumed within the household. Domestic labor was not subject to the same pressures for increased productivity which characterized capitalist production relations (although other pressures toward greater efficiency might be present such as time constraints associated with combining domestic with wage labor).

The social relations of production in households were different from those of wage labor and needed separate investigation. Marxist theory, by equating the costs of reproduction of labor power with the consumption of wage goods, did not acknowledge the complexity of the transfers of labor and resources taking place between the household and the capitalist production sphere and within the household.

However, critics argued that the debate was limited by the narrowness of its conceptual framework and by the questions it sought to investigate. The debate neither addressed the issue of why it was women who carried out the bulk of domestic labor, nor explored the possibility that men as well as, or instead of, capitalists might be the beneficiaries (Hartmann 1979). It used an abstract, ahistorical framework to analyze an issue that needed historical and empirical investigation (Molyneux 1979). It adopted a functionalist perspective, merging notions of cause and effect and ignoring the possibility of a contradictory relationship between capitalism and the domestic sphere (Humphries 1977). It investigated social phenomena through economic categories alone, ignoring politics and sexuality.

The debate also treated domestic labor as a universal category, failing to address the different significances it might have in different societies and cultures. It gave insufficient attention to the way the combination of domestic and wage labor, rather than domestic labor alone, shaped women's experience of capitalism (Fox 1980). It focused on housework rather than childcare and on the maintenance of adult males, not on generational reproduction. It did not consider the care of elderly and disabled people. Finally, the debate did not analyze the issue of how the poverty that is linked to responsibility for domestic labor could be tackled.

Evolution beyond the debate

The debate effectively finished in the late 1970s, but many issues remained which needed further exploration. For example, the relationship between wage goods and domestic labor was clearly complex and needed historical and empirical investigation. More wage goods did not necessarily imply less domestic labor, even if they included household appliances. It was apparent that the value of labor power had become a less determinate and, arguably, less useful concept. It followed that returning to the classical political economy concept of the costs of reproduction of the laboring population might be a more fruitful approach, as Picchio argued in *Social Reproduction: the Political Economy of the Labour Market* (1992).

Limited as it was, the debate was an important attempt by feminists to develop a critique of economic theory. It identified the neglect of domestic labor within economics as being central to the discipline's marginalization of women. This theme has re-emerged within the contemporary feminist political economy literature (see Gardiner 1997). The domestic labor debate was one of the first systematic attempts on the part of feminists to rework Marxist concepts in order to explore gender divisions (see also PATRIARCHY). It provided an impetus for historical and empirical research on the social relations and economic significance of household and caring work.

See also:

class structures of households; feminist political economy: major contemporary themes; home economics: new; household labour; labor and labor power; marriage; reserve army of labor: latent; social structure of accumulation:

family; waged household labor; women's wages: social construction of

Selected references

Braverman, Harry (1974) *Labor and Monopoly Capital: The Degradation of Work in the Twentieth Century*, New York: Monthly Review Press.
Folbre, Nancy (1982) "Exploitation Comes Home: A Critique of the Marxian Theory of Family Labour," *Cambridge Journal of Economics*, December: 317–29.
Fox, B. (ed.) (1980) *Hidden in the Household*, Toronto: Women's Educational Press.
Gardiner, J. (1997) *Gender, Care and Economics*, Basingstoke: Macmillan.
Gardiner, J., Himmelweit, S. and Mackintosh, M. (1975) "Women's Domestic Labour," *Bulletin of the Conference of Socialist Economists* 4(11): 1–11.
Harrison, J. (1973) "The Political Economy of Housework," *Bulletin of the Conference of Socialist Economists*, Winter: 35–52.
Hartmann, H. (1979) "The Unhappy Marriage of Marxism and Feminism: Towards a More Progressive Union," *Capital and Class* 8(Summer): 1–33.
Himmelweit, S. and Mohun, S. (1977) "Domestic Labour and Capital," *Cambridge Journal of Economics* 1(1): 15–31.
Humphries, J. (1977) "Class Struggle and the Persistence of the Working Class Family," *Cambridge Journal of Economics* 1(3): 241–58.
Malos, E. (ed.) (1980) *The Politics of Housework*, London: Allison & Busby.
Molyneux, M. (1979) "Beyond the Domestic Labour Debate," *New Left Review* 116(July–August): 3–27.
Picchio, A. (1992) *Social Reproduction: The Political Economy of the Labour Market*, Cambridge: Cambridge University Press.
Seccombe, W. (1974) "The Housewife and Her Labour Under Capitalism," *New Left Review* 83(January–February): 3–24.

JEAN GARDINER

E

ecological feminism

Ecological feminism, or eco-feminism, is an intellectual and political movement based on a diverse group of ideas associating women and the environment, rooted in feminism, political theory, nature-based religion and environmentalism (Spretnak 1990). The term "eco-feminism" was coined by Françoise d'Eaubonne in *Le Feminisme ou La Mort* (1974), in her call on women to lead an ecological struggle that frees nature from the grip of patriarchal destruction. The most influential work in the evolution of eco-feminist ideas was Carolyn Merchant's *The Death of Nature* (1980), which traced the impact of INDUSTRIALIZATION on women and the environment in European history, and the effect of the scientific/industrial revolution on images of women and nature in European CULTURE. Merchant's work laid the basis for the central eco-feminist argument that female subordination and environmental degradation are historically and ideologically linked.

Eco-feminist activism is also concerned with violence and militarism, and the impact of modern TECHNOLOGY on reproductive health. This concern was inspired in part by the Three Mile Island nuclear plant accident in the USA, which provoked the first eco-feminist conference, "Women and Life on Earth: A Conference on Eco-Feminism in the Eighties" (Caldecott and Leland 1983). Eco-feminism also draws inspiration from women's ecological struggles worldwide, such as the Chipko movement in the Indian Himalayas and the Green Belt movement in Kenya.

Central problematic

The central problematic of eco-feminism is the relationship between women and nature, and consequently, the question of women's agency *vis-à-vis* men in environmental liberation. Some eco-feminists see an inherent biological link between women and the environment (Salleh 1984). Although not all eco-feminists agree, they generally hold women as the legitimate emancipatory agents. D'Eaubonne argued in 1974 that the only way to "save the world" is for women to destroy power structures and institute an egalitarian management system. Ynestra King – a founder of the movement – suggests that women are "the repository of a sensibility which can make a future possible" (1983: 13).

However, some eco-feminists deny that women's ecological concerns stem from their GENDER identity; some simply call for a pragmatic coalition between ecological and feminist movements (Spretnak 1990; Merchant 1980). Taking a middle ground, Heller (1990) argues that, while women are not inherently different from the rational, culture-creating man, their life experiences produce a "second nature" of "female empathy." Thus, women's leadership is justified on the basis of various positions. Common to these positions is a tendency to gloss over differences among women and to exempt them of all responsibility in ecological destruction.

Principles

According to King (1989), eco-feminism encompasses four principles: (1) that there is a dialectical link between the domination of women and that of nature; (2) that all forms of domination (such as race, gender or nature) are connected and therefore eco-feminists reject domination *in toto*; (3) ecological diversity requires a diverse, globally decentralized environmental movement; and (4) historically, women have been associated with a debased "nature," while men have been associated with "culture" because of their perceived ability to transcend nature.

Strands of eco-feminism

The diversity of views regarding these principles has produced four broad strands of eco-feminism that closely parallel the paradigmatic lines within feminism itself: liberal, cultural, social and socialist (Merchant 1992). Liberal eco-feminism is an amalgam of mainstream environmentalism and the liberal feminist critique grounded in the work of Simone de Beauvoir. This strand accepts that environmental problems reflect inadequate regulation of market society; their contention is that the environmental movement is male dominated. Cultural eco-feminism draws on Susan Griffin's *Woman and Nature*. This strand embraces rather than rejects the rational male/intuitive female dichotomy, and calls for celebrating the link between women and the natural environment. For some, this celebration extends to nature-based spirituality and religion of the Goddess (Plant 1989). Social eco-feminism is based on the anarchic, social ecology of Murray Bookchin, calling for the abolition of all economic and social hierarchies (see ANARCHISM). Social eco-feminists like King see PATRIARCHY as one of these social hierarchies. This strand rejects the claim of a unique relation between women and nature.

Socialist eco-feminism, a more recent perspective pioneered by Merchant (1992), is grounded in a Marxist critique of capitalism, arguing that the logic of accumulation that underlies capitalist patriarchy subordinates both ecology and reproduction to production, thereby exploiting both women and nature. There is considerable overlap between these different strands of eco-feminism. For instance, Vandana Shiva (1989) combines many themes. Shiva is a leading critic of development and its negative impact on women and the environment in the Third World, but she also sees an intimate relationship between women and nature. Her views partly derive from Indian cosmology where, according to her, nature is the embodiment of the "feminine principle."

Critique of environmentalism

An important contribution of eco-feminism is its critique of environmentalism, particularly the deep ecology movement. Eco-feminists argue that deep ecology is not deep enough because its call for biological egalitarianism does not extend to women (Salleh 1984). They charge that deep ecology is preoccupied with anthropocentrism (human-centeredness) as the main cause of environmental degradation, when the real problem is androcentrism, ecological destruction being male-dominated. In response, deep ecologists claim that eco-feminism itself is anthropocentric, focusing on the male–female problematic instead of the human–nature one (Fox 1989). Thus, environmentalists see eco-feminism as not sufficiently ecological. Eco-feminism represents a broadening of the feminist movement in so far as it is less self-centered and less occupied with issues of reproductive rights and equality with men, and takes on universal concerns such as environmental destruction as women's concerns.

See also:

environmental and ecological political economy: major contemporary themes; feminist political economy: major contemporary themes; race, ethnicity, gender and class; steady-state economy

Selected references

Caldecott, Léonie and Leland, Stephanie (eds) (1983) *Reclaim the Earth: Women Speak out for Life on Earth*, London: The Women's Press.

Fox, Warwick (1989) "The Deep Ecology–Ecofeminism Debate and its Parallels," *Environmental Ethics* 11 (Spring): 5–25.

Heller, Chiah (1990) "Toward a Radical

Eco-feminism," in John Clark (ed.), *Renewing the Earth: The Promise of Social Ecology*, London: Green Print.

King, Ynestra (1983) "The Eco-feminist Imperative," in Léonie Caldecott and Stephanie Leland (eds), *Reclaim the Earth: Women Speak out for Life on Earth*, London: The Women's Press.

—— (1989) "The Ecology of Feminism and the Feminism of Ecology," in Judith Plant (ed.), *Healing the Wounds: The Promise of Ecofeminism*, Philadelphia: New Society Publishers.

Merchant, Carolyn (1980) *The Death of Nature: Women, Ecology and the Scientific Revolution*, London: Harper & Row.

—— (1992) *Radical Ecology: The Search for a Livable World*, London and New York: Routledge.

Plant, Judith (ed.) (1989) *Healing the Wounds: The Promise of Ecofeminism*, Philadelphia: New Society Publishers.

Salleh, Ariel Kay (1984) "Deeper than Deep Ecology: The Eco-Feminist Connection," *Environmental Ethics* 6: 339–45.

Shiva, Vandana (1989) *Staying Alive: Women, Ecology and Development*, London: Zed Books.

Spretnak, Charlene (1990) "Ecofeminism: Our Roots and Flowering," in Irene Diamond and Gloria Orenstein (eds), *Reweaving the World: The Emergence of Ecofeminism*, San Francisco: The Sierra Club.

EIMAN ZEIN-ELABDIN

ecological radicalism

Radical ecological discourse has developed in recent times to articulate a critical elaboration of the systemic nature of environmental and ecological problems within contemporary economies. However, until recently, radical ecology has had relatively little direct impact in shaping the course of debate within political economy. This is in part because the radical ecology agenda has tended to be concentrated within the disciplines of philosophy, sociology and feminism. It is also, in part, because radical ecology has been oriented toward informing and shaping environmental struggles and mapping more ecologically-benign modes of economic and social organization, and has tended to be posed in opposition to the concerns of the dominant economic discourse. However, largely as a result of the wide grassroots appeal of radical ecology, as well as the mounting evidence of the deteriorating state of the global ecological system, conventional environmental economists and political economists have been forced to rethink the nature of economic–environment linkages.

Challenge of radical ecology

The challenge of radical ecology has prompted conventional economists to undertake a more systematic and critical appreciation of the environment. This is observable in efforts to redefine the environment as NATURAL CAPITAL, and in the growing interest in SUSTAINABLE DEVELOPMENT. The more dramatic development within the economics profession, spawned by this challenge, has been the formulation of quite different ways of posing economic–environment linkages. The developing discourse of ecological economics is founded on the interdependence of an economic and an ecological system. A similar shift in thinking has also occurred within political economy, forcing the systematic reconsideration of the nature of environmental problems as one of the anomalies of contemporary capitalist economies, as well as the more considered scrutiny of ecological systems or nature.

Environmental Marxism

Marxist political economy has long entertained an interest in documenting the environmentally destructive nature of capitalist development. Research published in the 1970s was an important catalyst in environmental struggles that saw the first wave of environmentalism. However, the import of Marxism in shaping these struggles was diminished by the tendency among Marxists to consider the environment as little more than an instrument in the progress of industrial development, captured in the notion of "man's mastery over nature." The appalling environmental record of the former communist bloc economies appeared to confirm suspicions that, beyond informing the critique of CAPITALISM and the different ways in which ACCUMULATION underscored environmental degradation, Marxism offered little guidance for indicating how to envisage an ecologically sustainable future. The growing appreciation of the environmental challenge, and the efforts to reorient the concerns of Marxist scholarship to develop a more critical engagement with environmental issues, has radically transformed this situation. The formulation of a socialist ecology has become a lively field of intellectual and political endeavor among Marxists, who have more consciously incorporated the dynamics of nature and theorizing ecology into the lexicon of historical materialism.

The main object of socialist ecology has been to theorize the dynamics of capitalist development in terms of the way in which the environment defines and shapes our material existence. In its infancy, the project was formed within and sought to build upon traditional Marxian categories. One important area of concern focused on reasserting, and inserting, nature in the LABOR PROCESS, acknowledging the natural elements drawn from the environment as essential ingredients in the production of human material existence. This has prompted the reconsideration of Marx's observations on the transformation of nature in the process of production as a metabolic process.

Production requires labor working to subject nature to its will, a process entailing the humanization of nature. Production also engenders the transformation of labor itself, because labor must first seek to understand the working of ecological processes before the EXPLOITATION of nature can commence. Also, the actual process of exploitation requires labor to adapt and to work within the biological and physical limits set by nature. The natural environment is at one and the same time the means for and the obstacle to humanity's material advancement, and this entails the naturalization of labor.

The posing of production in terms of this metabolic relation has engendered a number of avenues of inquiry. One focus has emphasized the systemic constraints on the symbiotic relation between labor and nature within capitalism. The CLASS relation that defines the organization of production is based on capital determining the terms on which nature is introduced into the production process. Nature is reduced to the status of a mere instrument, and the distinguishing feature of capitalism is that natural elements are increasingly introduced into production in the form of commodities. Nature is reified; it is both valued (in monetary terms) and devalued; and labor is alienated from nature (see ALIENATION). The imperative of capital to accumulate reinforces these processes, just as it impels capital to draw more and more natural elements under its control. Capital constantly confronts and challenges the limits of nature in its drive to accumulate, and this merely adds to the pressures on ecological systems. James O'Connor has represented this in terms of capitalism's second contradiction, the tendency for capital to undermine the natural, ecological, conditions of production, and thereby erode the natural conditions so necessary for securing accumulation (see the journal *Capitalism, Nature and Socialism*).

Another emphasis within socialist ecology has sought to build upon Marx's appreciation of the metabolism between humanity and nature. This is done by acknowledging that labor must seek to exercise some mastery over nature, but arguing that this mastery does not have to assume a destructive form. Posing labor's interaction with nature in terms of an "'eco-regulatory' mastery over nature" presents the possibility of more ecologically benign ways of organizing production. This also highlights the force of social and political struggle in defining the character of our place within and interactions with nature.

Marxist interventions have been criticized by radical ecologists for their preoccupation with production, and the tendency to define nature as an object over which humanity must exercise its mastery in the course of advancing production. Challenging the dichotomous character of this production–nature equation has been at the heart of three quite different approaches within radical ecology.

Social ecology

Social ecologists, working within an anarchist tradition, have sought to locate the systematic nature of environment problems in the hierarchical organization of the political economy. Class relations are viewed as but one dimension of the social hierarchy, based on the domination of people by people. Gender and race are two other dimensions of the oppressive and destructive structures within the political economy (see RACE, ETHNICITY, GENDER AND CLASS). The domination of nature by people is another important manifestation of the hierarchy that institutionalizes and justifies the exploitation and degradation of the natural environment. The antidote requires the abolition of this hierarchy, through the redefinition of the status of ecological systems and the reorganization of human interaction with nature. The social ecologists vision is premised on promoting ecological stewardship, working toward enhancing the integrity and complexity of nature and against control over nature, and building stronger, self-governed communities to underscore this.

Ecological feminism

This theme is reiterated within ECOLOGICAL FEMINISM. Ecological feminists shift the focus by arguing that the power relations that define women's and men's place within the political economy, their respective roles in interacting with nature, as well as the status of nature itself, are the root cause of the problem and must be contested. The more radical variant, sometimes referred to as affinity eco-feminism, contends that environmental problems arise because contemporary economies are founded on the systematic oppression of all non-male life forms. Women and nature share a mutual oppression. Women's connection with nature is grounded in this oppression, but this has deeper roots because women share some common traits with nature, most notably in birthing and nurturing reproductive or regenerative capabilities. The unsustainability of current forms of economic organization can only be redressed by constructing new ways of organization. Such new forms should build on the affinity that women have with nature, building on feminine traits in the reconstruction of the political economy.

Socialist eco-feminists

The socialist eco-feminists who have contributed to this debate take issue with the notion that there is a natural affinity between women and nature. Rather, the GENDER DIVISION OF LABOR within contemporary economies, and especially the division of labor across the public and private spheres of the economy, compounds environmental problems. The notion of maldevelopment highlights one way in which this is manifest. In less developed economies, the expansion of capitalist modes of organizing production results in women's estrangement from both nature and direct access to the material means of their existence. Capitalist development engenders environmental degradation as well as the impoverishment of women and their families. Affinity eco-feminists and socialist eco-feminists both argue that these dilemmas can only be corrected by abolishing the destructive systems of production, consumption and exchange that devalue women's worth as well as that of nature (see FEMINIST POLITICAL ECONOMY: MAJOR CONTEMPORARY THEMES).

Deep ecology

A third emphasis within radical ECOLOGY, deep ecology or transpersonal ecology, distances itself from all other conventional and radical perspectives. It argues that these are all based on an anthropocentric or human-defined and preoccupied focus on nature. Deep ecologists contend that the ecological crisis is but one aspect of a more fundamental crisis confronting humanity. The solution to this crisis lies in rebuilding connections within communities and with nature; valuing nature in its own right; and consciously organizing the political economy around the interconnectedness between all of the different elements that are essential to the livelihood, the integrity and the moral and cultural fortitude of individuals, communities and nature.

Influence of radical ecology

Radical ecology has emerged as an influence on political economy, and has considerably enlivened debate and struggles around the environment. While the contributions of eco-feminists, social eco-feminists and deep ecologists remain somewhat more marginalized than those developed within socialist ecology, the different approaches to radical ecology have much to offer in the ongoing development of political economy. This is especially evident in the preoccupations with redefining our place in nature and in considering different ways of building alternative forms of social and economic organization, such as those signaled in the interest in communitarianism, as the foundation for a sustainable ecological future.

See also:

environmental and ecological political economy: major contemporary themes; Green Party; socialism and communism

Selected references

Eckersley, Robyn (1992) *Environmentalism and Political Theory: Toward an Ecocentric Approach*, London: UCL Press.

Mellor, Mary (1992) *Breaking the Boundaries: Towards a Feminist Green Socialism*, London: Virago.

Pepper, David (1993) *Ecosocialism: From Deep Ecology to Social Justice*, London: Routledge.

STUART ROSEWARNE

ecology

Ecology is that branch of biology dealing with the interrelationships between living organisms and between organisms and their environment. Contrary to other fields within biology, ecology focuses not on individual organisms or their evolution, but on their interaction within ecosystems as both organisms and their context (animate and inanimate) of change. Human beings make use of ecosystem services as, for instance, sources of food, fuel or natural resources, or sinks for carbon absorption, nutrient cycling or water purification. Such use can only be maintained if entire systems are preserved, rather than simply the individual service deliverers.

Pure and applied ecology

In his history of ecology, Egerton (1983) distinguishes between pure ecology, as the science which seeks a generally applicable understanding of nature, and applied ecology, as the science which seeks to understand the relationship between nature and human endeavor. As organized sciences, both pure and applied ecology are relatively new fields within biology, dating back to the turn of the twentieth century and the 1940s to 1960s, respectively. In Great Britain, 1949 marks an important date for applied ecology with the government's founding of the Nature Conservancy (later the Nature Conservancy Council).

In the United States, the adoption of the National Environmental Policy Act of 1969 marks a significant date for applied ecology. It is also evidence of the growing public prominence of ecology during the 1960s, associated with the work of marine biologist Rachel Carson (1962), conservation activist David Brower, and ecologists Paul and Anne Ehrlich (1970). The contributions of these and other biologists, ecologists and conservationists not only called attention to the increasing evidence of human induced ecological destruction, but also raised questions about the underlying goals, values and direction of Western industrialized societies. Thus, the relational focus of ecology, and particularly applied ecology, cannot easily be separated from fields outside biology, such as psychology, sociology, political science, economics and ethics.

In a world of reductionist science, methodological standardization and disciplinary niches, this has meant an uneasy place for ecology within the sciences. While molecular biology and other laboratory-based disciplines gained in prestige and attention, traditional ecological subdisciplines, such as taxonomy and systematics, were not in high demand in academia. As a result, many ecologists shifted their focus from systems ecology to the more highly regarded field of population biology. In the words of Cairns and Pratt, "Additionally, a stigma was attached to applied ecology in which examination of POLLUTION problems was considered, at best, second-class science" (1995: 71).

Ecocentric perspectives and deep ecology

The more philosophical expression of the ecology movement was inspired by Aldo Leopold's "land ethic," published in *A Sand County Almanac* in 1949. Its roots go back to the ecocentric perspective and the social criticism of Henry David Thoreau, John Muir and Aldous Huxley. It argues that our ecological crisis can only be halted if we shift both our conception of reality and our actions from the currently held anthropocentric to an ecocentric world view. Ecocentrism is concerned with "the ecological integrity of the Earth and the well-being of other species, along with humans" (Sessions 1995: xi). Humans are viewed as an integral part of the biophysical world, and not as separate from or above it. The most pronounced expression of this ecocentric world view is the so-called "deep ecology" movement with its philosophical and activist strands (see GREEN PARTY; ECOLOGICAL RADICALISM).

This two-pronged focus on philosophy and activism illustrates the movement's belief that a change in the conceptual framework of the relationship between humans and the biophysical world needs to be translated into changed lifestyles, plus political and socioeconomic agendas. The term "deep ecology" was coined by the Norwegian philosopher Arne Naess in his presentation to the 1972 Third World Futures conference in Bucharest, which was published a year later under the title of *The Shallow and the Deep Long-Range Ecology Movement*. Naess distinguished between two expressions of the environmental movement: shallow environmentalism which, according to Naess, is characterized by an anthropocentrically-motivated concern for pollution, human health and resource depletion; and deep environmentalism, which is characterized by a long-range concern for "individuals, species, populations, habitats, as well as human and nonhuman cultures" (Naess 1986). In the United States, the philosophical principles of the deep ecology movement were popularized with the publication of the *Deep Ecology* platform (Devall and Sessions 1985).

Deep ecology's principles continue to be controversial. Its philosophical position of "humans as part of nature" contrasts with that of "humans in nature." While the former sees nature with all its complexity as escaping predictable human interference and control, the latter sees humans as needing to perfect nature. Critics of the deep ecology movement, such as the biologist Berry Commoner or the social ecologist Murray Bookchin, assert that deep ecology's principles are not ecocentric, but are in fact misanthropic. Commoner took issue particularly with Ehrlich's position that human overpopulation is one of the root causes of global unsustainability. Bookchin's social ecology position contends that a reorganization of human society from a hierarchical to an egalitarian social structure is essential since changed social relationships will also lead to a changed relationship between humans and their natural environment. A similar critique has come from some eco-feminists, who argue that not anthropocentrism but androcentrism is at the root of human domination and exploitation of nature (Salleh 1992), and from Third World social ecologists, who criticize deep ecologists' lack of concern for equity and social justice as expressed in overconsumption and militarism (Guha 1989).

These positions result in different responses to the ecological crisis than those proposed by the deep ecology position. Some place at the center of their concern the restructuring of human social relationships and asymmetric power structures, whether informal or institutionalized. Others call for improved human management of ecosystems and the broad-based implementation of green technology.

Influence of ecology on economics

The influence of ecology on economics is particularly evident in ecological economics, BIOECONOMICS and the debate surrounding sustainability and SUSTAINABLE DEVELOPMENT. All seek to consider economics within the context of ecological or biophysical systems and the constraints of economic theory and valuation. Here too, however, a more anthropocentric management-oriented view which seeks to integrate ecological constraints into existing conceptual frameworks can be found side by side with a more ecocentric view. The latter seeks to develop a new conception of the relationship between economic and ecological systems. Another manifestation of the ecology movement's influence on economics is bioregionalism, which seeks to assess the impact of human activity, particularly economic activity, within a specific biogeographical region or watershed. Accordingly, the sustainability or unsustainability of human economic activity cannot be evaluated in a universally applicable manner, but needs to consider specific regional characteristics such as weather patterns, geological and hydrological conditions, plant life or seasonal changes.

Pressing concerns

One of the most pressing current concerns in ecology is the rapid loss of biodiversity (Wilson 1989). Apart from more direct services like medicinal or agricultural uses, species diversity has been found to play a role in the ability of ecosystems to respond to stress, and recover from disturbances. The current trend toward the loss of biodiversity can only be halted by focusing preservation efforts on saving entire species habitats and not simply individual species. Not unrelated to biodiversity and preservation are efforts to identify indicators of ecosystem health, and to specify and prioritize ecosystem services. In addition, new approaches to conservation biology are rapidly developing, which seek to restore damaged ecosystems, instead of just chronicling species functions or their decline.

These efforts, however, may first and foremost require improved ecological literacy among policy makers and the general public. It is important for people to change their view of the ecological system from (a) the services provided by natural systems to human beings to (b) a more holistic view of ecosystem functions which promote the stability and robustness of the ecological system as a whole (which may include human beings). This requires nothing less than a fundamental change in environmental literacy and culture (see Cairns and Pratt 1995: 67).

See also:

ecological feminism; ecological radicalism; environmental and ecological political economy: major contemporary themes; evolution and coevolution; natural capital

Selected references

Cairns, John and Pratt, James (1995) "The Relationship between Ecosystem Health and Delivery of Ecosystem Services," in D.J. Rapport, C.L. Gaudet and P. Calow (eds), *Evaluating and Monitoring the Health of Large-Scale Ecosystems*: Berlin and Heidelberg: Springer-Verlag.

Carson, Rachel (1962) *Silent Spring*, Boston: Houghton Mifflin.

Devall, Bill and Sessions, George (1985) *Deep Ecology: Living as if Nature Mattered*, Salt Lake City: Gibbs Smith.

Egerton, Frank (1983) "The History of Ecology: Achievements and Opportunities," Part One, *Journal of the History of Biology* 16(3):

259–310; Part Two, *Journal of the History of Biology* 18(1): 103–43
Ehrlich, Paul and Ehrlich, Anne (1970) *Population, Resources, Environment: Issues in Human Ecology*, San Francisco: Freeman.
Guha, Ramachandra (1989) "Radical American Environmentalism and Wilderness Preservation: A Third World Critique," *Environmental Ethics* 11(1): 71–83.
Naess, Arne (1986) "The Deep Ecological Movement: Some Philosophical Aspects," *Philosophical Inquiry* 8: 10–31.
Salleh, Ariel (1992) "The Ecofeminism/Deep Ecology Debate," *Environmental Ethics* 14: 195–216.
Sessions, George (1995) *Deep Ecology for the 21st Century*, Boston and London: Shambhala.
Wilson, E.O. (1989) *Biodiversity*, Washington, DC: National Academy Press.

SABINE U. O'HARA

economic anthropology: history and nature

Background in anthropology

Anthropology as a university discipline came into its own in the late nineteenth and early twentieth centuries. There was a time when anthropology could and did define itself unambiguously as the study of primitive societies. The anthropologist studied primitive societies directly, living among them, whereas sociologists used documents and undertook statistical comparisons. The early anthropologists avoided archival or library research to concentrate on intensive field work, so they would be immersed and intellectually assimilated with the CULTURE to which they were exposed. They also studied societies as a whole: their economies, legal and political institutions, family and kinship organizations, technologies and arts.

Anthropology has a long history of involvement in development dating back to just after the First World War. Colonial governments were very interested in anthropological teaching and research, and colonial cadets were often given instruction in social anthropology at Oxford, Cambridge and London before taking up their appointments. Research institutes were established and government anthropologist posts were created in most of the British colonies. It is claimed that at least some anthropologists engaged in a kind of politically subservient anthropology at these royal institutes for the colonies or the bureaus of indigenous affairs (Huizer and Mannheim 1979). Others allege that in Africa some anthropologists were so preoccupied with African witchcraft, warfare, beer drinking, initiation rites and sex that they apparently turned a blind eye to apartheid or the Africans' involuntary migration to European-owned mines to earn money for colonial taxes. There was a similar story in the United States, where the study of American "savages" was the basic fieldwork experience for anthropologists and was actively supported by the Bureau of Indian Affairs. Ronald Meek's book *Social Science and the Ignoble Savage* (1976) is interesting in this context as it examines the heterogeneous collection of writings about the American Indians over the period 1750–1800.

Traditional anthropology was later much criticized for its ethnocentrism, racism and colonial mentality during this era. However, it must be pointed out that many of the Europeans who first encountered the natives were not racists, but saw the inferiority of natives in religious and cultural terms. The work of J.H. Boeke (1884–1956), an economist and colonial administrator in the Dutch East Indies, is often mentioned in this regard. Boeke first presented the dualistic economy notion, which has been a staple product of the economic development industry ever since. He saw sociocultural dualism as arising from values and motivations in Eastern society which were resistant to "development."

Political independence of the colonies proved an unsettling experience for anthropologists. The objects of their research began increasingly to question the usefulness of this research to them. They took offense at being called "savages," "barbarians" and "less civilized," as well as being made into mere objects of curiosity. Many of these issues led to considerable soul searching by anthropologists. There were a number of responses. Some researchers began studying traditional cultures, with a view toward preservation and defending indigenous ways of life from encroachment. Others became involved in "liberation anthropology," working among poor peasants, indigenous groups or slum dwellers. The focus now was on "development from below," "participative development" and local "self-determination," making the local people formal participants and directors of change. Many took an anti-development perspective, in the sense of objecting to rapid change and espousing a gradual evolutionary transformation rather than a consciously planned one. They were concerned about the social disruption of market immersion and the consequences for indigenous culture. Other anthropologists started to spread their wings by studying more complex societies and using modern statistical techniques and archival research.

The soul searching also forced anthropologists to be more open to other social sciences. Anthropologists realigned themselves with particular disciplines and thereby gained a better sense of intellectual direction and autonomy. This has brought some valuable contributions to the associated disciplines. Anthropologists sometimes find a closer liaison with economists, linguists, psychoanalysts or political scientists than with some in their own field.

Beginnings of economic anthropology

Turning specifically to economic anthropology, this is not a specialization, like cultural ecology, but rather a relatively common focus of several quite different theoretical approaches. These approaches involve economic behavior and are characterized more by particular pieces of work, such as Geertz's *Agricultural Involution* and Bailey's *Caste and Economic Function*.

Bronislaw Malinowski (1884–1942) is usually given credit for founding economic anthropology, and he published in the *Economic Journal* as early as 1921. He examined the ways in which "primitive" people organized their economic life and, in the 1920s and 1930s, produced intensive studies of tribal-level subsistence agricultural activities. Malinowski was the first "real" economic anthropologist in that he illustrated how much economic activity is socially motivated, how elaborate trade might become and how complex the holdings of rights and wealth were. Economic behavior was structured by a complex set of forces, duties and obligations.

In 1939–40, three books came out within a few months of each other by Firth, Goodfellow (both students of Malinowski) and Herskovits, which really got the field going in bringing the economic into anthropology. For example, Raymond Firth looked at rational allocation issues and how production and social constraints affect economic behavior. Melville Herskovits, in 1940, explored the relevance of ethnological findings for standard neoclassical economic concepts such as scarcity and efficiency. He emphasized the sociocultural context of economic behavior in tribal societies, and how this departed from the rationalistic and profit-oriented models of economic theory. Herskovits made the term "economic anthropology" popular. The most famous early exchange on the anthropology–economics connection was the Knight–Herskovits interchange in the *Journal of Political Economy* in 1941, where Frank Knight presented a critique of Herskovits' *The Economic Life of Primitive People*. Knight takes Herskovits to task for failing to recognize that there are universal principles of economy, for criticizing "economic man" concepts, and generally for the author's failure to understand economic concepts correctly.

Substantivists and formalists

The next significant milestone for economic anthropology was the work of Karl Polanyi (1886–1964). In 1961, George Dalton applied

Polanyi's ideas to anthropology proper and started a vigorous debate between the Polanyi group – the substantivists – and what were called the formalists (see SUBSTANTIVIST–FORMALIST DEBATE).

The formalist view was that economic principles of rational human action (scarcity, maximization, marginal reasoning) apply to all societies. The substantivists perceived human societies to be following various systems of organization, among which the market (based on money and prices) is only one. (The main formalist critiques of the Polanyites appear in LeClair and Schneider (1968).) At issue was whether anthropologists should adopt orthodox economics as the conceptual approach to studying peasant economies.

Anne Mayhew (1980) argues that this dispute is part of a larger issue of whether people act because of their culture, or whether culture is determined by the ways in which people act. That is, are people encased in a set of customs, or are they free to shape or mold their environment? It has been said that neoclassical economics is all about how people make choices, and anthropology is about how you do not have any choices to make.

French Marxism

Modern economic anthropology has branched out to encompass a broad range of intellectual pursuits. For example, French Marxism entered anthropology via London's University College in the early 1970s and through the establishment of the journals *Critique of Anthropology, Dialectical Anthropology* and *Economy and Society*. By far the greatest source of Marxist influence within postwar anthropology has been French structuralism. Prominent exponents include Louis Althusser, Lévi-Strauss and Maurice Godelier. Althusser stressed different modes of production (see MODE OF PRODUCTION AND SOCIAL FORMATION), while Godelier struggled with the notion of rationality and the substantivist–formalist debate. The notion of social systems was also important, and a number of contributions were made to West African ethnography. These writers played a key role in opening up Anglo economic anthropology to Marxist ideas.

Link with institutionalists

There is much synergy between economic anthropology and institutional political economy (see INSTITUTIONAL POLITICAL ECONOMY: HISTORY). We know that VEBLEN had a keen interest in anthropological findings. In the context of development studies, the work of Clarence Ayres is well known on the conflict between technology and ceremonialism (see AYRES'S CONTRIBUTION TO ECONOMIC REASONING). Other institutional economists have become deeply involved in economic anthropology and have contributed to and borrowed from this field. Neale and Mayhew (in Ortiz 1983: 14–17) mention in this regard the work of George Rosen, Anne Mayhew, Walter Neale, John Adams, James Street, Edward Van Roy, Dan Fusfeld and Ron Stanfield. There are also considerable parallels between the history of institutionalism and economic anthropology. Economic anthropologists are criticized for their excessive descriptiveness. The study of and reaction to economic anthropology gives us greater understanding about the nature of the relationship between the original and the new institutionalists (see INSTITUTIONALISM: OLD AND NEW).

Conclusion

The work of economic anthropologists has demonstrated the variety and diversity of economic behavior, while orthodox economists have been content to see universal and homogeneous actions. "Cultural analysis," says George Marcus (in Friedland and Robertson 1990: 332), "tends to make complex and obstruct any project, however sophisticated technically, that operates on reductionist assumptions and admits complex variation only within those assumptions." Gregory, in his *Gifts and Commodities*, found that the basic approach of anthropologists was reminiscent of the methods employed by the old classical political economists, Quesnay, Smith, Ricardo and Marx. Indeed, he suggested that it was the anthropologists that were the true followers of the CLASSICAL POLITICAL ECONOMY approach (Gregory 1982: 211).

It is the precise description of data in which the anthropologist immerses himself that is the distinguishing feature of the profession. Unfortunately, as Keith Hart notes, economic anthropologists have had little impact on the economics profession:

> Orthodox economics has carved out an impressive intellectual space for itself that leaves the rest of us feeling marginal and frustrated. Marginal because it is hard for us to match the formal intellectualism and public recognition that economists of the postwar period have arrogated to themselves. Frustrated because the monopoly exercised by the economics profession leaves out most of the interesting questions about the movement of economies at our time in history.
> (Friedland and Robertson 1990: 137)

See also:

disembedded economy; economic anthropology: major contemporary themes; gifts; hunter–gatherer and subsistence societies; language, signs and symbols; markets and exchange in pre-modern economies; Polanyi's views on integration

Selected references

Friedland, Roger and Robertson, A.F. (eds) (1990) *Beyond the Marketplace: Rethinking Economy and Society*, Sociology and Economics: Controversy and Integration Series, New York: Aldine de Gruyter.
Granovetter, Mark and Swedberg, Richard (eds) (1992) *The Sociology of Economic Life*, Boulder, CO: Westview Press.
Gregory, C.A. (1982) *Gifts and Commodities*, London: Academic Press.
Honigmann, John. J. (1976) *The Development of Anthropological Ideas*, Chicago: Dorsey Press.
Huizer, Gerrit and Mannheim, Bruce (eds) (1979) *The Politics of Anthropology*, World Anthropology Series, The Hague: Mouton.
Knight, Frank H. (1941) "Anthropology and Economics," *Journal of Political Economy* 49 (April): 247–68
LeClair, E.M. and Schneider, H.K. (eds) (1968) *Economic Anthropology: Readings in Theory and Analysis*, New York: Holt, Rinehart & Winston.
Mayhew, Anne (1980) "Atomistic and Cultural Analyses in Economic Anthropology," in John Adams (ed.), *Institutional Economics*, Boston: Martinus Nijhoff, 72–81.
Meek, Ronald L. (1976) *Social Science and the Ignoble Savage*, Cambridge: Cambridge University Press
Ortiz, Sutti (ed.) (1983) *Economic Anthropology: Topics and Theories*, Society for Economic Anthropology Monograph No.1, New York: University Press of America.
Swedberg, Richard (1990) *Economics and Sociology: Redefining their Boundaries, Conversations with Economists and Sociologists*, Princeton: Princeton University Press.

JOHN LODEWIJKS

economic anthropology: major contemporary themes

Economic anthropology studies non-capitalist forms of socioeconomic organization, ranging from early "primitive" and state societies to the organization of inner-city neighborhoods. The point of departure is that material production is only one aspect of the economy, especially where the economy is "embedded" in political and cultural institutions.

Although a relatively new academic discipline, economic anthropology has experienced its share of controversy, introspection, and self-doubt. Lee (1992), for instance, believes that the source of the crisis in hunter–gatherer studies relates to ambiguity or confusion as to whether it is trying to achieve a general understanding of culture, or a historically specific approach. The same can be said of contemporary anthropology, including economic anthropology. Potential conflicts between theory and empiricism, between deduction and induction, and between the search for grand systems and cultural relativism, continue to dominate discussion.

There# are three main areas of study of special relevance to political economy which have received particular attention in recent years. These are the controversy over new institutionalism, the extension of Marxist analysis to non-capitalist economic formations, and a feminist revision that evokes a more sweeping, postmodern critique of the discipline.

New institutionalism

The debate over the new institutional approach has superseded the SUBSTANTIVIST–FORMALIST DEBATE, which dominated discussion in the 1960s. Neoclassical economists assert the universal applicability of the utility-maximizing behavior of individual agents under strict assumptions about rationality. Given the pervasive market mentality to truck, barter and trade, it is necessary to explain why some individuals apparently act cooperatively and engage in non-market exchange. New institutionalists argue that there are TRANSACTION COSTS to market operations# arising out of the need to define and enforce private property rights. Instances may thus arise where non-market arrangements are an optimal means of allocating resources among self-interested individuals. Thus the practice of sharing food is described as a form of insurance in the face of highly-variable returns to individual foraging efforts. Common use of hunting territories occurs where it is too costly to enforce exclusive rights to land. Open access to agricultural land is a risk-minimizing strategy where climatic conditions lead to uncertain harvests. Customary prices are adopted where there is imperfect information over supply and demand fluctuations (see Halstead and O'Shea 1989). Apparently altruistic, cooperative behavior, therefore, may be a thinly-veiled response to risk and uncertainty.

As applied to Western cultures, new institutionalism receives its clearest articulation in the work of Douglass North (1990). High transaction costs and errors in perception may prevent markets from emerging. Moreover, since institutions evolve in relation to the culturally-determined "mental models" of individuals, inefficient non-market forms of exchange may persist. North thus emphasizes the emergence of well-defined property rights and enforcement mechanisms in the transition from FEUDALISM to CAPITALISM, and suggests that modern economic development is equally dependent upon a favorable institutional environment. The teleological approach of new institutionalism – where the culture of possessive individualism is taken as given rather than treated as a historical creation – leaves us with an uninspired caricature of human behavior, and reduces the intricacies of institutions to mere constraints upon individual action. Paralleling the demise of "new economic history," neoclassical parables in economic anthropology have failed to provide compelling depictions of human life. Custom, to use Sahlin's term, becomes merely "fetishized utility."

"Old" institutionalists have largely been dismissive of the "new." Walter Neal (1993) dubs North's seminal 1990 publication as "a strange book, even a sad one," and John Adams (1994) declares that traditional institutionalists are "winning" the battle of breaking the discipline away from individual reductionism – despite the "craw sticker" of North's sharing the Nobel Prize in Economics. Adams' optimism arises partially out of a satisfaction with empirical studies to the neglect of articulating a coherent alternative theory. (See INSTITUTIONALISM: OLD AND NEW.)

Is there a middle ground? Landa (1994) provides a richer depiction of non-market institutions by demonstrating the importance of kinship and ethnicity in trading networks, contract law and gift exchange. In an environment where the capacity to define and enforce contracts in not well developed, kinship and ethnicity are important conduits for assuring the level of trust necessary for exchange to occur. She demonstrates the potential usefulness and limitations of concepts borrowed from

New economic anthropology

The second trend follows the declaration of a "new economic anthropology" inspired by Marxism. Much of this energy arose from French Marxists, who borrowed from structural analysis in order to bring economic anthropology within the ambit of historical materialism. Since Marx's own treatment of pre-capitalist formations was expressly limited to an investigation of the historical origins of capitalism, there has been a spirited attempt by anthropologists, such as Maurice Godelier and Claude Meillassoux, to generalize Marxist analysis of non-capitalist modes of production.

The most intriguing line of inquiry concerns the interaction between capitalist and non-capitalist economies. In some instances, European expansion was limited to the sphere of circulation and the subsistence sector dictated the nature of the interaction. In other cases, the subsistence sector was transformed to serve the reproduction of the capitalist sector, while elsewhere the commodification of land and labor entailed the destruction of the subsistence sector. In the North American fur trade, for instance, aboriginal hunter–gatherers remained the principal agents of production. However, the trapping of small game for exchange redirected the economic pursuits away from cooperative hunting of larger animals. In doing so, it transformed aboriginal concepts of property rights, gender relations and political organization; and when fur resources were depleted, the aboriginal economy collapsed (Leacock 1981).

The modern application of this research is apparent in the resistance of aboriginal peoples to large-scale resource developments and other projects that encroach upon traditional subsistence pursuits. Nash (1994) argues that the continued expansion of capitalism, and its encroachment upon subsistence activities in core and peripheral economies, has been met with collective resistance ranging from the urban *barriadas* of Peru, to displaced Bolivian tin miners, to rural laborers forced off their land in Amazonia.

Feminist economic anthropology

The third prominent trend in the literature is a feminist revision that reveals a pervasive male bias and blindness in previous interpretations of various cultures. Most notable is Annette Weiner's study, *Women of Value, Men of Renown* in 1976, that revisits Malinowski's ethnography of the Trobriand Islanders, and the kula ring in particular. Malinowski's preoccupation with the activities of men, to the neglect of the primary role of women in food production, results in a misunderstanding of the dynamics of the economy. Eleanor Leacock (1981) similarly argues that the emphasis upon male activities obscures the economic and social importance of women in hunter–gatherer and farming societies, and the fluidity that marked the division of labor and social relations between genders. Nonetheless, development economics still stands accused of consistently neglecting the contribution of women to economic welfare (Hill 1986).

This feminist revision indirectly invites a postmodern critique of the entire anthropological enterprise. It evokes doubt about the "authenticity" of ethnography produced by the "participant observer," and replaces it with concern over the politics of identity, gender, and representation (Kuper 1994). This not only calls into question the opposing attempts by new institutionalism and Marxism to provide a general analytical framework, but underscores the growing disciplinary gulf between economists and anthropologists. While neoclassical economists continue to apply methodological individualism to a range of cultures, anthropologists have been more reticent in their search for a global narrative. As Mirowski observes:

> Rather than further engage the theoretical conundrums raised by exchange, gift, reciprocity, higgling, and money, it seems contemporary anthropologists have tended to regard the very project of theorizing a

subset of social experience as an illegitimate totalizing move, a disguised form of the persistent colonial imperative to dominate the Other.

(Mirowski 1994: 338–9)

This, needless to say, bodes ill for economic anthropology if cooperation between disciplines becomes more difficult to achieve.

See also:

economic anthropology: history and nature; feminist political economy: major contemporary themes; hunter–gatherer and subsistence societies; modernism and postmodernism; neoclassical economics

Selected references

Adams, John (1994) "Economy as Instituted Process: Change, Transformation, and Progress," *Journal of Economic Issues* 28: 331–55.
Clammer, John (1978) *New Economic Anthropology*, New York: St. Martin's Press.
Halstead, Paul and O'Shea, John (1989) *Bad Year Economics: Cultural Response to Risk and Uncertainty*, Cambridge: Cambridge University Press.
Hill, Polly (1986) *Development Economics on Trial: The Anthropological Case for a Prosecution*, Cambridge: Cambridge University Press.
Kuper, Adam (1994) "Culture, Identity and the Project of a Cosmopolitan Anthropology," *Man* 29: 537–54.
Landa, Janet T. (1994) *Trust, Ethnicity, and Identity: Beyond the New Institutional Economics of Ethnic Trading Networks, Contract Law, and Gift Exchange*, Ann Arbor: University of Michigan Press.
Leacock, Eleanor Burke (1981) *Myths of Male Dominance: Collected Articles on Women Cross-Culturally*, New York: Monthly Review Press.
Lee, Richard B. (1992) "Art, Science, or Politics: The Crisis in Hunter–Gatherer Studies," *American Anthropologist* 94: 31–54.
Mirowski, Philip (1994) "Tit for Tat: Concepts of Exchange, Higgling, and Barter in Two Episodes in the History of Economic Anthropology," in Neil De Marchi and Mary S. Morgan (eds), *Higgling: Transactors and their Markets*, Durham, NC: Duke University Press, 313–42.
Nash, June (1994) "Global Integration and Subsistence Insecurity," *American Anthropologist* 96: 7–30.
Neal, Walter (1993) "Review of Douglass North, *Institutions, Institutional Change, and Economic Performance*," *Economic Development and Culture Change* 41: 422–25.
North, Douglass C. (1990) *Institutions, Institutional Change and Economic Performance*, Cambridge: Cambridge University Press.

HUGH GRANT

economic growth

Definition

Economic growth has been at the center of economic reasoning since the beginnings of economics. But what does it mean? Serious arguments and counter-arguments about the arbitrariness of the various definitions abound, but there is one operational definition that is more or less generally accepted. According to this definition, economic growth refers to a sustained increase over a significant period of time in the quantity and/or quality of the goods and services produced in an economy. Ultimately, this must reflect the fact that *existing* human needs are satisfied to a greater degree than they were in the previous period. For this reason, promoting (stable?) economic growth is a main goal of public policy.

Measurement problems

From a more pragmatic perspective, official statistics define economic growth as the increase in the real (price-deflated) national product, and consequently measure it by the average annual rate of change of per capita real gross domestic product (GDP). It is widely accepted that official calculations of national income accounts suffer from serious limitations. For example, the value of GDP depends on the basis chosen for valuing individual products, and this leads to serious problems when one tries to compare different economies or different stages of the same economy over a long period of time.

There is also the problem and difficulty of how to account for depreciation (appreciation) and maintenance when calculating national income. If maintenance is caused by physical changes of the capital stock, depreciation (appreciation) can be defined as a loss (gain) of value due to a change in relative prices. While it is understood that normal wear and tear of the capital stock does impose a cost on the whole economy, it is far from obvious that changes in relative prices have the same consequence. In a class society, it can be shown that any relative price change adversely affecting one group may benefit other groups by the same amount so that, on aggregate, there may be no net change. The difficult question arises of which measure best approximates national income: GNP or net national product (NNP)? Critics of the national accounting system maintain that neither GNP nor NNP is an adequate indicator of social well-being, since they are limited to market production and do not take into account many other aspects of human life (ethics, morals, environmental quality, distribution of income and so on), nor do they take into account those activities that are carried outside of the market and government sectors (see GROSS DOMESTIC PRODUCT AND NET SOCIAL WELFARE; HUMAN DEVELOPMENT INDEX).

Theories of economic growth

Economists have been preoccupied with the behavior and tendencies of economic systems at least since the emergence of industrial capitalism. In what follows, we will refer only to those writings found in Western economic thought. Theories of growth share one common interest: how to explain the long-run course of the economy. Only a few theories have devoted their attention to studying short-run problems. Growth theorists have generally focused on two main categories of determining factors: the role of investment and the distribution of income. There are several other factors which are closely related to, and sometimes derived from, these broad categories, and they have been used in different combinations by the various conflicting theories.

Classical and Marxian approaches

The classical approach considers growth to be an outcome of capital ACCUMULATION, a process which itself depends on the functioning of the entire system. Central to this analysis is the existence of a surplus, its distribution and reinvestment. Classical economists saw a close connection between economic growth and the nature of the distribution of the surplus between industrial profit and rent. They argued that the unproductive incomes of landlords (rent) reduce the stock of funds available for investment by industrial capitalists; when the stock of capital and the rate of output cease to rise, the economy converges to a stationary state. In Smith's analysis, economic growth depended also on another strategic factor, advances in the efficiency of production. The DIVISION OF LABOR was regarded as a source of efficiency that, when combined with an increasing size of markets, generates important economies of scale and therefore stimulates further growth.

Karl MARX also emphasized the importance of reinvesting the surplus (profits), but his analysis of long-term growth was somewhat different from that of the classical economists (although some would say that his works represent the culmination of CLASSICAL POLITICAL ECONOMY). In his view, the ECONOMIC SURPLUS is divided between industrial profit interest and rent. Therefore, interest payments as well as rent can reduce profit. In Marx's economics, the rate of economic growth is affected by an array of variables, the most important being the rate of profit. The profit rate in turn is affected by technical change, wages, productive and unproductive labor, the turnover rate of capital, the length of the workday, and so on. Marx examined the factors propelling a FALLING RATE OF PROFIT TENDENCY, and also those factors counteracting this tendency. The rate of profit in capitalism undergoes marked changes through historical time and this helps to promote unstable growth, especially in relation to business cycles (see BUSINESS CYCLE THEORIES; NUTCRACKER THEORY OF THE BUSINESS CYCLE).

Standard neoclassical growth theory

Growth economics was dormant for a long time after Marx. Early neoclassical thought did not have a theory of growth; it considered society to be a collection of individuals, guided by self-interest and always trying to allocate their scarce resources among competing uses. In so doing they maximize their profits, utility and output. Harmony in the relationships between the capitalist, the landlord and the worker replaced class struggle and antagonism that characterized the classical-Marxian body of thought. The neoclassical theory of growth was later formulated and formalized by Solow (1956), among others. However, just as "the marginalist revolution" had tried to deny and disguise the social contradictions by emphasizing the notion of (static) equilibrium and optimal allocation, the Solow model has also tried to show that balanced growth along the steady-state path was the normal course of the economy. This was in opposition to early Keynesian writers such as Harrod (1939) and Domar (1946), who emphasized disequilibrium, instability and unbalanced growth.

The neoclassical model is indeed very simple, and has the advantage of lending itself to empirical analysis. It starts with a production function which assumes constant returns to scale and diminishing marginal productivity of both inputs, labor and capital. Long-run growth follows the natural rate, which is determined by growth of the labor force and technical progress, both of which are assumed to be exogenous. The steady-state growth rate is, therefore, independent of the rates of saving and investment. Given that technical progress is like manna from heaven, the neoclassical model predicts that, except for the differences which are due to different capital–labor ratios, there will be no cross-country divergence in growth rates of per capita income. Growth accounting (see Maddison 1991) attempts to measure the contributions of labor and capital to the growth of output. The residual is attributed to technical progress and referred to as the "Solow residual."

Post-Keynesian analysis of growth

The neoclassical model has received harsh criticism from post-Keynesians. Writing from different angles, post-Keynesian scholars have invariably emphasized the importance of the division of labor, technical and organizational innovations, and the role of effective demand. According to this paradigm, the driving force behind economic growth is the expansion of markets (through higher wages, higher profits, lower prices and so on). Higher demand generates dynamic INCREASING RETURNS TO SCALE through further division of labor and innovations, which improves competitiveness and stimulates further growth of output. Growth becomes a self-reinforcing and cumulative process with clear implications for cross-country (and regional) divergence (Kaldor 1970) (see CIRCULAR AND CUMULATIVE CAUSATION).

Regulation approach to growth

The post-Keynesian theory of growth can be regarded in many ways as a special case of the REGULATION APPROACH. Indeed, both post-Keynesians and regulationists share the idea that growth is demand-determined and as such owes its expansion to productivity improvements. However, for the regulation school, factors that determine productivity growth vary over time and in space, therefore leading to distinct historical phases or "productivity regimes." Moreover, aggregate demand is affected differently and its composition (internal consumption, investment and exports) will depend on whether productivity gains are distributed in the form of lower relative prices or higher wages and profits, therefore giving rise to a "demand regime." The overall growth of output and its rate of expansion depend on which component of total expenditure becomes dominant: internal consumption, investment or net exports. Long-run growth depends on the success of a combination between a "productivity regime" and a "demand regime." Such a combination is called a "regime of accumulation" (Boyer 1988).

Each regime is historically determined and lasts for as long as its stability is not undermined by the ongoing process of (technical and organizational) innovations. The exceptionally high growth that characterized most industrialized countries and lasted from the end of the Second World War until the early 1970s is called the "Fordist regime of accumulation." The PRODUCTIVITY SLOWDOWN and the decline in growth of output that started in the 1970s corresponds to the decline in the Fordist regime (and the rise in – or the possible lack of full development of – a "neo-Fordist" or "flexible regime of accumulation"). There is, therefore, a clear methodological break between post-Keynesians and regulationists, in that the latter emphasize the distinction of each phase in the growth process and reject the idea that productivity might have some unique and universal determinants.

Endogenous growth theory

One of the serious deficiencies in the standard neoclassical model is that it treats technological progress as being exogenous. Critics maintain that technical progress cannot take place in a vacuum because new technology requires new investment, both for its invention and for its application. Technical progress is not independent of investment, because firms are constantly innovating/renovating their products and processes in order to survive competition. However, technical progress does not affect only capital; it also affects the quality of labor and conditions industrial relations arrangements. For this reason, it becomes endogenous to the process of growth. The idea of endogenous technological progress can be traced back to the works of Smith, Marx, SCHUMPETER and Kaldor. Schumpeter (1911) has particularly emphasized the importance of the type of investment which enhances the quality of capital goods, that is, innovations. He argued that the implementation of "new combinations" of productive resources is the primary force that triggers economic growth.

The new "endogenous growth theory" differs from the orthodox neoclassical theory in that, by endogenizing technical change, it is able to account for the sustained growth of per capita incomes and the persistent disparities throughout most of the world (Romer 1986; Lucas 1988). The basic "endogenous growth" model incorporates HUMAN CAPITAL as a separate factor in the production function. Technological improvements or increases in the average level of human capital imply the existence of externalities and spillovers. Since not all firms invest in technological change, when leaders, for example, double their inputs by investing more in new technology, the inputs of the followers will also increase (through spillovers). Therefore, aggregate output will increase more than proportionately and, contrary to the orthodox neoclassical theory, the production function will exhibit increasing returns to scale.

This is where the "endogenous growth theory" reaches a difficult dilemma since increasing returns to scale are not consistent with perfect competition. Proponents of this theory are therefore forced either to assume a monopolistic market structure (as a necessary condition for innovation) and abandon perfect competition (a cornerstone of neoclassical theory), or to abandon increasing returns to scale, which is the novelty of the endogenous theory. Much of the recent literature in this area has been devoted to trying to make increasing returns consistent with competitive equilibrium. Another far-reaching conclusion that derives from accepting the assumption of monopolistic or oligopolistic market structures is that, due to externalities, the optimality of competitive markets is no longer guaranteed, which in turn implies that the laissez-faire policy is no longer valid. According to this theory, governments can, and should, play an active role (through taxes, subsidies, tariffs and so on) in promoting economic growth.

Is economic growth desirable?

But is economic growth always desirable? Proponents of the "no-growth society" maintain that there are critical costs of industrialization and high growth. The main costs are said to be POLLUTION, congestion, stress, CRIME and the destruction of NATURAL CAPITAL. They argue that economic growth has already done a lot of damage to the ecological system (for example, the ozone layer), and is constantly lowering the QUALITY OF LIFE, especially for future generations. For this reason, many advocate low or zero rates of economic growth (Olson and Landsberg 1973) (see ENVIRONMENTAL AND ECOLOGICAL POLITICAL ECONOMY: MAJOR CONTEMPORARY THEMES). Critics argue that if a no-growth society were to come about, it would be riddled with conflict precisely because cessation of growth would amount to conflicts over the distribution of the shrinking economic pie.

See also:

household production and national income; knowledge, information, technology and change; Maddison's analysis of growth and development; monopoly capitalism; Schumpeter's theory of innovation, development and cycles; Schumpeterian political economy; social structures of accumulation

Selected references

Boyer, R. (1988) "Formalizing Growth Regimes," in G. Dosi *et al.* (eds), *Technical Change and Economic Growth Theory*, London: Pinter.

Domar, E. (1946) "Capital Expansion, Rate of Growth and Employment," *Econometrica* 14(1).

Harrod, R.F. (1939) "Dynamic Theory," *Economic Journal* 49(1): 14–33.

Kaldor, N. (1970) "The Case for Regional Policies," *Scottish Journal of Political Economy* 17.

Lucas, R.E. (1988) "On the Mechanics of Economic Development," *Journal of Monetary Economics* 22.

Maddison, A. (1991) *Dynamic Forces in Capitalist Development*, Oxford: Oxford University Press.

Marx, K. (1867, 1885, 1894), *Das Kapital*, 3 vols, Moscow: Foreign Languages Publishing House, 1954.

Olson, M. and Landsberg, H.S. (1973) *The No-Growth Society*, New York: W.W. Norton & Company.

Ricardo, D. (1817) *Principles of Political Economy and Taxation*, London: Dent & Sons Ltd, 1973.

Romer, P.M. (1986) "Increasing Returns and Long Run Growth," *Journal of Political Economy* 94: 1002–37.

Schumpeter, J.A. (1911) *The Theory of Economic Development*, Cambridge: Cambridge University Press, 1934.

Smith, A. (1776) *An Inquiry into the Nature and Causes of the Wealth of Nations*, New York: Modern Library, 1937.

Solow, R.M. (1956) "A Contribution to the Theory of Economic Growth," *Quarterly Journal of Economics* 70(1): 65–94.

HASSAN BOUGRINE

economic power

One of the most fundamental concepts in the social sciences, power may be understood here as an individual or group's capacity to affect other individuals or groups by "altering the constraints upon their action-environments" that condition their decisions, behavior and values (Wartenberg 1990: 85). Social agents affect each other mutually, of course, but relationships in which this mutual influence is significantly asymmetric or unequal, where one agent dominates the other, are critically important. This is true not only from the normative viewpoint concerning ethics and democracy, but also from a positive viewpoint concerning how economic systems function (see NORMATIVE AND POSITIVE ECONOMICS).

All forms of power are to some extent "economic" in nature. Exercising power entails either (1) sanctioning people, that is, threatening them with a loss or offering them a promise of a gain in well-being contingent upon their making certain choices; or (2) influencing their knowledge of, or their values and preferences about, the choices available to them (Bartlett 1989; Schutz 1995). Thus the group or individual exercising power must wield "scarce resources" – at the least, time and energy. The benefits attained by exercising power are "goods or services" of one form or another that are provided, in effect, by means of the time, energy and attention of subordinates in the power relationship.

However, "economic power" is often singled out from among other forms of power as that which is involved in society's economic structures *per se*, those institutions whose primary function is allocation and distribution. Thus in modern industrial societies, economic power is most manifest in government and private bureaucracies, especially, in capitalist market economies, in corporations and the MARKET STRUCTURES that knit them together.

Mainstream economics, by and large, has been loathe to consider either corporations or markets as entities involving or manifesting power. (Bardhan (1991), which provides an excellent overview, is less disparaging.) Traditionally, neoclassical economics has treated the firm as a "black box," the social relationships inside which were of no interest. More recently, mainstream economists have begun to scrutinize these social relationships, but they continue to eschew any description of them as power relationships (see TRANSACTION COSTS; WILLIAMSON'S ANALYSIS OF THE CORPORATION).

As for the corporation's external relationships with individuals and groups in markets and other spheres of social life, neoclassical economists accept that certain circumstances may give a firm power over its customers or suppliers. Yet they consider such circumstances exceptional, and argue that the power the firm then derives is of little consequence. Neoclassical economists argue further that agents can neither subject, nor be subject to, others in any significant way in markets due to three characteristics: (a) transactions in markets are formally "voluntary"; (b) markets are more or less competitive; and (c) developed market systems allow people broad choices about their labor, leisure and consumption. Radical and other heterodox economists strongly dissent from this view.

Power relations within the firm

As a social structure, the corporation is a stratified hierarchy of command with owners or their representatives at the top, then layers of upper, middle and lower managers and, finally, production and other workers at the bottom. Some neoclassical economists view this structure as the product of a mutually agreeable relationship among individuals contracting with each other as equals in a kind of cooperative association in which they "agree" to organize themselves hierarchically in order to maximize net income (Alchian and Demsetz 1972). Yet, voluntary contractuality in a relationship does not necessarily preclude it from involving power. For example, historically, contracts of indentured servitude represented "voluntary" submissions to power. Moreover, the private corporation, in which owners and managers make decisions without democratic accountability to their employees, does not resemble the sort of organization that would be expected in a free association of equals. Instead, the structure of the corporation is most clearly an embodiment of *employer power*, that which is exercised by owners and/or managers over all employees at every level in the hierarchy.

Employer power derives partly from the threat of job termination that employers hold over employees, a threat manifest to the latter by the perennial existence of a RESERVE ARMY OF LABOR (potential employee replacements and poverty). The threat rests upon the material deprivation the employee expects to suffer with any major loss of income (see Bowles and Gintis 1990). The overwhelming majority of employees lack significant liquid or income-earning assets; the costs of finding another job may be considerable (and retraining costs can be overwhelming); and unemployment insurance and retraining and relocation subsidies are only grudgingly provided by the state in capitalist economies. As a consequence, the COST OF JOB LOSS is great and the threat is substantial.

Because these systemic features exist in all labor markets, it follows that profit income, even in "competitive equilibrium", derives at least partly from an asymmetric power relationship in such markets, that is, from the EXPLOITATION of labor. With solidarity, workers may confront their employers with countervailing power (see Galbraith 1983: 72–80), primarily by threatening to withdraw their labor services from employers (i.e. striking). This alters both their relations with employers in the firm and the larger social and political environment which conditions such relations (see UNIONS).

However, owners and managers generally may bring substantial resources to bear to prevent such a scenario. First, employers can and do structure the corporation itself such that it divides and conquers employees, including managers. The complex layering of command and privilege, and the minute definition of compensation according to experience, position, occupation, merit, race, gender, "attitude" and so forth, all militate against employee solidarity (Edwards 1979). Second, owners and managers generally have greater influence upon the cultural and political environment that underpins employer power than do those most subject to that power.

Corporate power in markets and society

It is their position on the buyers' side of a perenially glutted labor market that enables firm owners and managers to assure employee compliance with their commands (Bowles and Gintis 1990). Similar positions in other markets may privilege firms with power *vis-à-vis* other groups of transactors. For example, a firm may assume power over independent suppliers of parts or materials and effectively integrate them into its managerial command hierarchy.

One especially important instance of such power is that of lenders in financial markets. Lenders usually give regular or favored borrowers premium terms on credit (low interest-rates, easier repayment schedules and so on) as part of a strategy aimed at ensuring credit-worthy behavior. An excess demand for loans may prevail, providing a basis for lenders' invidious discrimination against certain borrowers, as occurs in residential mortgage lending. Regular business customers are thereby threatened with non-renewal of their credit lines and loss of the important advantages deriving from continuing access to business credit. Just as unemployment manifests a threat to workers, perennial credit shortage threatens borrowers with a loss of continued credit on relatively easy terms. Lenders thereby gain access to a significant non-reciprocal influence in non-financial business decision-making (see also DISCRIMINATION IN THE HOUSING AND MORTGAGE MARKET).

Another important form of threat-based power that firms may have in their market relations derives from positions of monopoly, oligopoly, or simply highly concentrated industries. In this case, customers may be threatened with complete lack of access to the product if they do not do business with the powerful corporation on its terms (monopsony conversely implies a similar threat to sellers). The "economic profits" that firms may thus extract from customers or suppliers have been extensively studied by mainstream economists.

In mainstream economics, concentrated markets are recognized as arising from contingent factors such as a maldistribution of resource ownership, government largesse or scale economies. Heterodox economists argue that monopoly/monopsony power is a primary goal of firms in dynamic market competition.

One strategy firms use in pursuit of that goal is ADVERTISING AND THE SALES EFFORT. When it is effective, advertising constitutes an exercise of *value power* (Bartlett 1989), that is, that which alters people's preferences or values, in this case concerning goods and services.

The extent of horizontal concentration, as well as vertical and conglomerate integration among ostensibly independent firms, is considerable in both the non-financial and financial sectors of modern market economies. Given the subordinacy of non-financial firms to lending institutions, a framework of coordination is therefore evident; there is a "business hierarchy" that is subject to financial hegemony (Mintz and Schwartz 1985), within which the capital allocation process occurs not by means of an "invisible hand" but instead by what amounts to CENTRALIZED PRIVATE SECTOR PLANNING.

Corporations also wield considerable power outside of the market sector for purposes of securing their goals in markets. For example, they may press for favorable treatment in labor laws affecting their power over employees; or they may press for favorable workplace safety or environmental regulations, taxes or antitrust laws. Their influence in this regard is a function of the power they can bring to bear in political and cultural affairs affecting them. Since firms are the property of their owners and top managers, this influence is effectively on behalf of these groups and constitutes an important dimension of the power of the ruling CLASS or classes in CAPITALISM.

The extra-market influence wielded by corporations, their owners and managers is crucial as an underpinning of the entire capitalist market system. Capitalism rests upon a degree of INEQUALITY in the distribution of private property that would not be sustainable were its political and social systems truly democratic. Great inequality in property distribution is equivalent to great inequality in people's rights and opportunities, and hence cannot be understood as the outcome of a truly democratic public decision on the matter. Inequality can only be sustained by power exercised on behalf of those most benefited, at the expense of the rest (Schutz 1994).

Property owners and corporate managers do indeed exercise ruling class power in capitalist society. They have more time and personal resources, along with their corporate resources, to spend in such political activities as lobbying and campaign financing than do workers or other groups. They are better able to carry out major threats of withdrawal of their "economic services" (their personal and corporate investments) in "capital strikes." They own and manage the media of public discourse and dominate other important cultural institutions such as schools, churches and opinion-making organizations.

Consequently, the values promoted in all the institutions of capitalist society are "contaminated" by and "subordinated" to those of the owning and managing classes (see CORPORATE HEGEMONY). In the mythologies they promote, for example, of the intrinsically greater worth of managers and owners relative to workers, these institutions thus tend to "mystify" rather than clarify for people the nature of their society. Their social status thus elevated, the behavior and values of owners and managers come to be widely "emulated" by those who can never hope to attain such positions. Even in many of its smallest details, then, the structure of capitalist society serves as an apparatus of "value power," functioning primarily on behalf of the property-owning and corporate managerial classes.

See also:

emulation and conspicuous consumption; hegemony; hegemony in the world economy; patriarchy; transnational corporation

Selected references

Alchian, Armen A. and Demsetz, Harold (1972) "Production, Information Cost, and Economic Organization," *American Economic Review* 62: 777–95.

Bardhan, Pranab (1991) "On the Concept of Power in Economics," *Economics and Politics* 3(3): 265–77.

Bartlett, Randall (1989) *Economics and Power: An Inquiry into Human Relations and Markets*, Cambridge: Cambridge University Press.

Bowles, Samuel and Gintis, Herbert (1990) "Contested Exchange: New Microfoundations for the Political Economy of Capitalism," *Politics and Society* 18(2): 165–222.

Edwards, Richard (1979) *Contested Terrain*, New York: Basic Books.

Galbraith, John Kenneth (1983) *The Anatomy of Power*, Boston: Houghton Mifflin.

Mintz, Beth and Schwartz, Michael (1985) *The Power Structure of American Business*, Chicago: University of Chicago Press.

Schutz, Eric (1994) "Social Power in Neo-Marxist Analyses," *Review of Radical Political Economics* 26(3): 95–102.

—— (1995) "Markets & Power," *Journal of Economic Issues* 29(4): 1147–70.

Wartenberg, Thomas E. (1990) *The Forms of Power: From Domination to Transformation*, Philadelphia: Temple University Press.

ERIC SCHUTZ

economic rationalism or liberalism

Economic rationalism

The term "economic rationalism" did not come into general use until the late 1970s. Michael Pusey (1997) defines it as "a public policy position which assumes that MARKETS and money are the only reliable means of setting values on anything, or alternatively, that economics, markets, and money can always, at least in principle, deliver better outcomes than states, bureaucracies and the law." He goes on to say that economic rationalism is generally associated with the "New Right," laissez-faire economic liberalism and mainstream Anglo-American public policy from the mid-1970s.

Through the agencies of Anglo-American dominated institutions, such as the World Bank, the International Monetary Fund and the General Agreement on Tariffs and Trade, economic rationalists have "strenuously opposed attempts by national governments to intervene in the operation of markets." Pusey concludes that they have "an inbuilt preference for small, virtual, and even token government, and a bias against the public sector and public administration generally." Their policies are inimical to "social cohesion and good government."

The central tenet of economic liberalism – as economic rationalism was called in the early decades of this century – was that the capitalist system worked best if left alone, and not interfered with by governments. Market forces would ensure this as long as there was world-wide competition. (See GLOBAL LIBERALISM.)

Keynesian revolution

In the 1920s and early 1930s, KEYNES argued that this was not the case. The evidence showed that full employment was a rare and short-lived occurrence; and investment for the long-term was being crowded out by short-term, speculative investment. Monetary policy did not work; free trade, the international mobility of capitalism, and foreign ownership of national assets were more likely to promote war than peace.

Keynes put forward these ideas in books, lectures and pamphlets, and suggested the necessary changes in policy. These included a tax on short-term speculative investment; the state taking increased responsibility for organizing investment; and a reduction if not a gradual disappearance of a rate of return on accumulated wealth. These and other policy changes were outlined in his *magnum opus*, *The General Theory of Employment, Interest, and Money* in 1936. (See SPECULATION.)

During the war years, Keynes was a negotiator for the British Government on postwar trade arrangements. He was in favor of state trading for commodities, international cartels for necessary manufactures and quantitative restrictions for non-essential manufactures. He regarded these arrangements as "future instrumentalities for orderly economic life," according to R.F. Harrod's *Life of John Maynard Keynes* (1951: 567–8). This source also shows that Keynes believed his work would, in the next decade or so, "largely revolutionize the way the world thinks about economic problems" (Harrod 1951: 462).

It did, but to the capitalist establishments of the Anglo-American world and their "high priests" of laissez-faire – the orthodox economists in the universities – his thoughts were subversive of the existing order and had to be discredited. To do this, a counter-revolution to the Keynesian one was required. This is the great strength of Richard Cockett's *Thinking the Unthinkable: Think-Tanks and the Economic Counter-Revolution* (1994); it documents in detail how and by whom this counter-revolution was made.

Mont Pelerin Society and the Atlas Foundation

Cockett shows that a key role was played by the London School of Economics (LSE) – which, ironically, was founded by Fabians – to which the doyen of the Austrian School, Professor F.A. Hayek, was appointed in 1931. Allegedly this was to offset the impact of Keynes at Cambridge and of Tawney and Laski, professors of history and politics at LSE, all of whom were regarded as "left-wing" by the "establishment." Cockett notes that:

> The debate between Hayek, the economic liberals and Keynes during the 1930s... paved the way for the formation of an international movement of economic liberals against Keynesian economics... [it] ultimately led to the development of a coherent anti-Keynesian school of economics in post-war Britain, led by the Institute of Economic Affairs, and later to Thatcherism.
> (Cockett 1994: 347)

In 1942, the Beveridge Report to the British coalition government on full employment was published, suggesting a range of measures which would be necessary in postwar Britain to achieve full employment. A year later Hayek published his *Road to Serfdom*, a reply to Beveridge, arguing that the measures necessary to achieve full employment would mean a totalitarian political system. The book became "the Bible of the Right." A condensed version was published in the *Readers Digest* in 1945, the year in which he was invited to tour the USA by the University of Chicago, which later created a special chair for him. A group of industrialists and bankers offered Hayek financial support to found a society for converting the next generation of intellectuals to the creed of economic liberalism. In 1947 the Mont Pelerin Society was formed for this purpose, taking its name from the Swiss resort in which the inaugural conference was held. This conference was attended by thirty-nine people, mostly academics with a few journalists; they included Hayek, Robbins and Popper from the LSE, Friedman and Knight from the University of Chicago, and journalists from *Fortune* and *Readers Digest*. Most of the participants were British or American. Hayek was elected President of the Society, and foreshadowed an attack on trade unions:

> If there is to be any hope of a return to a free economy the question of how the powers of trade unions can be appropriately delimited in law as well as in fact is one of the most important of all the questions to which we must give our attention.
> (Cockett 1994: 114)

The Society met about every two years, and remained semi-secret until its growing size made this difficult. By 1980, its conference at the Hoover Institute of Stanford University was attended by 600 members and guests.

Initially, the Society's ideas did not reach a very wide audience. It took a businessman to achieve that. This was Anthony Fisher, described by Milton Friedman as "the single most important person in the development of Thatcherism," who made his fortune out of broiler chicken farming and used part of it to finance the Institute of Economic Affairs (IEA). The objective of the IEA was "to propagate sound economic thought in the universities and all other educational establishments." He was knighted by Margaret Thatcher in 1988, having founded free-market think-tanks in many countries. To coordinate them, Fisher created the Atlas Economic

Research Foundation to provide a central structure; by 1991 the Foundation "claimed to have helped, created, financed or advised 78 'institutes'" in 51 countries.

Cockett remarks that "it had been a long and extraordinary road from Fisher's initial meeting with Hayek at the LSE some forty years before," and quotes Friedman's quip: "Without the IEA I doubt very much whether there would have been a Thatcherite revolution" (Cockett 1994: 307–8; 158). His conclusion is that this intellectual counter-revolution has now shot its bolt, and there is the beginning of a reaction to it. (See REAGANOMICS and THATCHERISM.)

Conclusion

Pusey (1991: 241), for example, warns that the ultimate logic of economic rationalism would lead to the internationalization of "totalitarian business democracy," which would destroy society as we know it. Chomsky (1993: 100) gives a similar warning: "In the current phase of intellectual corruption, it must be stressed that... *the economic doctrines preached by the rulers are instruments of power*, intended for others, so that they can be more efficiently robbed and exploited" (emphasis added). Hence, these "madmen in authority, who hear voices in the air, are distilling their frenzy from some academic scribbler of a few years back" (Keynes 1936: 383).

See also:

Australian school of political economy; neoclassical economics

Selected references

Chomsky, Noam (1993) *Year 501: The Conquest Continues*, London: Verso.
Cockett, Richard (1994) *Thinking the Unthinkable: Think-Tanks and the Economic Counter-Revolution*, London, HarperCollins.
Harrod, R.F. (1951) *Life of John Maynard Keynes*, London.
Keynes, John Maynard (1936) *The General Theory of Employment, Interest, and Money*, London.
Pusey, Michael (1991) *Economic Rationalism in Canberra*, Melbourne: Cambridge University Press.
—— (1997) "Economic Rationalism," in *International Encyclopedia of Public Policy and Administration*, Pittsburgh: University of Pittsburgh Press.
Rees, Stuart, Rodley, Gordon and Stilwell, Frank (eds) (1993) *Beyond the Market: Alternatives to Economic Rationalism*, Sydney: Pluto Press.
Skidelsky, Robert (1992) *John Maynard Keynes*, vol. 2, London: Macmillan.
Wheelwright, E.L. (1994) "Review of Richard Cockett, *Thinking the Unthinkable: Think-Tanks and the Economic Counter-Revolution, 1931–83*," *Journal of Australian Political Eonomy* 34 (December).

E.L. WHEELWRIGHT

economic surplus

Importance and definition

Few concepts in contemporary political economy are as important as the economic surplus. It is utilized in varying ways by all shades of political economists, be they Marxists, radicals, Sraffians, feminists, institutionalists, social economists or post-Keynesians. The surplus concept is used for explaining the dynamics of monopoly capital, technological change, economic development, GENDER relations in the household, the role of the state and financial instability, to mention just some areas.

Economic surplus can be thought of as the difference between net national income and the essential consumption requirements of the entire POPULATION. Since essential consumption requirements are socially defined (and may be, for instance, approximated by the poverty line, which differs among countries), the economic surplus can also be thought of as society's "discretionary income." It may be used for investment, luxury consumption, military activities, higher education, RESEARCH AND DEVELOPMENT, the building of monuments and churches, leisure activities, and so forth. Patterns of economic and social change depend in large part on the uses of the economic surplus, which are determined in turn by the decisions of dominant classes or groups in each society (or, historically, by colonial powers when these displaced the dominant classes).

Historical background

The concept of the economic surplus was familiar to the classical political economists, and is related to the notion of PRODUCTIVE AND UNPRODUCTIVE LABOR. David Ricardo (1963), for example, believed that workers would always tend to receive subsistence wages, leaving the dominant classes of early nineteenth-century England to struggle over the appropriation of the surplus (although he did not actually use the term "surplus," that is the thrust of his argument). Ricardo argued that if the surplus went to the capitalist class it would be invested (a necessity for competitive survival), whereas the landlord class, subject to no such pressure, tended to use the surplus for luxury housing, lavish entertaining and other unproductive pursuits. For Ricardo, then, public policies that would direct the surplus into the hands of the "progressive" capitalist class were essential to allow ECONOMIC GROWTH to take place.

Karl MARX, in Volume 1 of *Das Kapital*, published in 1867, used a variant of this concept, surplus value, which he defined as the value produced by workers when they worked beyond the time necessary to provide their essential consumption requirements (or wage goods). Surplus value was, for Marx, the source of capitalists' profits and provided the basis for his concept of exploitation.

The onset of the marginal revolution in the late 1800s, however, led to the surplus notion being discarded by orthodox economics right up until the present day. However, it remained alive in the works of Marxists, classical economists, the history of economic thought,

Thorstein VEBLEN and others. In the 1950s and 1960s, Paul Baran and Paul Sweezy revitalized scholarly work in the area by redefining the concept and placing it at the core of their critique of contemporary CAPITALISM.

Tendency of economic surplus to rise

Paul Baran presented five different variants of the concept in *The Political Economy of Growth* in 1957. However, a sixth variant, presented in *Monopoly Capital*, a work published jointly with Paul Sweezy in 1966, has received the widest exposure. It appears at the core of their effort to reassess the fundamental dynamic of contemporary capitalism. Baran and Sweezy (1966: 77) define the economic surplus as "the difference between total output and the socially necessary costs of producing total output." Whereas Marx saw the fundamental contradiction of capitalism as lying in a tendency for the rate of profit to decline, Sweezy and Baran argue that what was true of "competitive" capitalism in the nineteenth century no longer applies in the twentieth, where "monopoly" (actually oligopoly) capitalism has its own distinctive contradictions and dynamic. They argue that the core dynamic of contemporary capitalism is a tendency for the economic surplus to rise as a proportion of GDP. (See MONOPOLY CAPITALISM.)

The basis of their argument is as follows. Capitalist enterprises continue to seek profit maximization. Modern technologies, increasingly sophisticated management techniques and the vast resources of the giant modern enterprises make them capable of reducing costs more vigorously than their nineteenth-century predecessors. However, "monopoly" power enables them to compete without lowering their prices. With costs falling and prices being stable or rising, the economic surplus tends to rise over time. The result would be economic stagnation and rising unemployment, as large firms have considerable levels of underutilized capacity when demand is limited (for instance, during the 1930s). During the late 1930s through to the early 1970s, however, the modern capitalist system was organized to avoid inadequate surplus absorption by increasing unproductive expenditures on the sales effort, military expenditure and social waste. An appendix to *Monopoly Capital*, written by Joseph Phillips, attempts to quantify their argument. Phillips finds that the economic surplus in the United States rose from 46.9 percent of GNP in 1929 to 56.1 percent in 1963 (Baran and Sweezy 1966: 389) (see EFFECTIVE DEMAND AND CAPACITY UTILIZATION).

Rising or falling economic surplus?

A considerable debate has arisen concerning their thesis. Lippit (1992), for example, takes issue with a variety of the conceptual bases of Sweezy and Baran's approach, such as their treatment of only labor costs as "essential" and their neglect of environmental costs and other externalities. Lippit argues, in fact, that in the industrialized economies there is a secular tendency for the surplus to decline as "essential" consumption standards are adjusted upwards over time and negative environmental externalities rise faster than national income.

On the other hand, Michael Dawson and John Bellamy Foster (1992) broadly support the Sweezy–Baran hypothesis and extend their time span by presenting estimates showing a rise in the surplus for the period between 1963 and 1988, albeit using a slightly different methodology. It is of interest that both sides of the debate agree that the concept of the economic surplus, which has no place in conventional economic discourse, provides essential insight into the nature of contemporary capitalism.

Economic development and the environment

The concept of the economic surplus has also been used in a variety of other sub-fields of economics, most notably in economic development (see SURPLUS APPROACH TO DEVELOPMENT). Danielson (1991) and Lippit (1985) take different approaches to using the concept of the economic surplus in economic development, but they agree that it plays a critical role in the analysis of economic development; that it must be used in conjunction with an analysis of class structure to be used most fruitfully; and that the actual surplus rather than the "potential" surplus (one of Baran's forms) is the most suitable object of analysis. In environmental economics, Khan and Lippit (1993) have developed the concept of the environmentally adjusted surplus, where the economic surplus is adjusted for environmental externalities.

See also:

surplus approach to political economy

Selected references

Baran, Paul (1957) *The Political Economy of Growth*, New York: Monthly Review Press.

Baran, Paul and Sweezy, Paul (1966) *Monopoly Capital*, New York: Monthly Review Press.

Danielson, Anders (1991) "The Concept of Surplus and the Underdeveloped Countries: Critique and Suggestions," *Review of Radical Political Economics* 22: 214–30.

Davis, John B. (ed.) (1992) *The Economic Surplus in Advanced Economies*, Aldershot: Edward Elgar.

Dawson, Michael and Foster, John Bellamy (1992) "The Tendency of the Surplus to Rise," in John B. Davis (ed.), *The Economic Surplus in Advanced Economies*, Aldershot: Edward Elgar.

Foster, John Bellamy (1986) *The Theory of Monopoly Capitalism: An Elaboration of Marxian Political Economy*, New York: Monthly Review Press.

Foster, John Bellamy and Szajfer, Henryk (eds) (1984) *The Faltering Economy: The Problem of Accumulation Under Monopoly Capitalism*, New York: Monthly Review Press.

Khan, Haider and Lippit, Victor D. (1993) "The Surplus Approach and the Environment," *Review of Radical Political Economics* 25(3): 122–8.

Lippit, Victor D. (1985) "The Concept of the Surplus in Economic Development," *Review of Radical Political Economics* 17: 1–19.

—— (1992) "Reevaluating the Concept of the Surplus," in John B. Davis (ed.) *The Economic Surplus in Advanced Economies*, Aldershot: Edward Elgar.

Ricardo, David (1963) *The Principles of Political Economy and Taxation*, Homewood, IL: Irwin.

Stanfield, Ron (1973) *The Economic Surplus and Neo-Marxism*, Lexington, MA: Lexington Books.

VICTOR D. LIPPIT

effective demand and capacity utilization

The relation between effective demand and capacity utilization plays an important role in the Keynes–Kalecki macroeconomic tradition. Effective demand may be defined as the aggregate demand for goods and services which is backed by actual purchasing power (derived from owned or borrowed resources). Capacity utilization may be defined as the ratio of actual output to potential output which fully utilizes the installed capital stock of firms. Although it is difficult to do so in a precise manner (because of the problems in defining full capacity utilization), capacity utilization can be measured by the ratio of output to capital stock.

The Keynes–Kalecki tradition

Although there are a number of reasons why excess capacity can emerge in an economy (due to the shortage of other inputs which cannot be substituted by capital, or due to the inefficient use of existing capital), the Keynes–Kalecki tradition takes capacity utilization as being determined by effective demand. In this view, firms operating in an oligopolistic environment face a reduction in quantity demanded, reducing their output rather than price, the latter being determined as a stable markup on prime costs (Kalecki 1971) (see PRICING). Hence, when effective demand increases autonomously, capacity utilization increases.

Capacity utilization also affects effective demand for a number of reasons. Since output and labor employed are positively related, and the rate of profit rises with capacity utilization, a rise in capacity utilization increases consumption demand by wage earners and profit recipients, thereby increasing effective demand. An increase in capacity utilization also increases investment demand by firms, because higher capacity utilization is taken to be a signal for more buoyant markets, and indirectly because it implies an increase in the rate of profit. Not all increases in capacity utilization lead to increases in aggregate demand, however. For instance, higher capacity utilization may lead to a decline in net exports if higher output and income are associated with higher competing imports, and if higher capacity utilization (due to higher domestic demand) leads to a diminished export effort.

Indirect effects from capacity utilization to effective demand can arise due to the intervening effect of the former on income distribution. For instance, an increase in capacity utilization can affect the targeted markup charged by firms (though the direction of this effect is controversial) and the targeted real wage of workers (since higher capacity utilization reflects tighter labor markets). These changes affect the distribution of income between wages and profits. This will affect effective demand if there are different propensities to spend out of wage and profit income, for example, due to different propensities to consume out of the two types of income.

Simple model

A simple model, drawing on the work of Kalecki (1971) and Steindl (1952) and the monopoly capital school, and following Dutt (1984) and Rowthorn (1981), captures the main aspects of this two-sided relation between effective demand and capacity utilization. Consider a closed economy with unemployed labor producing a single good which can be used for both consumption and investment purposes, with two factors of production – non-depreciating capital and labor – using a fixed coefficient technology. There are two classes in the economy: workers who earn wage income and do not save, and capitalists who receive non-wage income and save a fraction of their income. Firms hold excess capacity and set price as a markup on (variable) labor costs, and invest to expand their productive capital at a higher rate when the rate of capacity utilization is higher. It follows that goods–market equilibrium implies

$$g^I = g^s \qquad (1)$$

where g^I is the ratio of investment to capital stock and g^s the ratio of saving to capital stock, and

$$g^s = sr \qquad (2)$$

$$g^I = a + bu \qquad (3)$$

where s is the rate of savings, r is the rate of profit, and u is the output–capital ratio which measures capacity utilization. A linear investment function with positive parameters, a and b, has been adopted for simplicity. The pricing assumption implies that

$$P = (1+z)Wa_0 \qquad (4)$$

where P is the price level, W the money wage, z the fixed markup rate determined by Kalecki's degree of monopoly, and a_0 the labor–output ratio. Finally, the division of total income between wages and profits implies that

$$1 = wa_0 + (r/u) \qquad (5)$$

where $w = W/P$ is the real wage. Substituting equations (4) and (5) into (2), and then (2) and (3) into (1) and solving for u, we obtain the equilibrium value of capacity utilization,

$$u^* = a/\{s[z/(1+z)] - b\}$$

Substituting this into equation (3), we obtain the equilibrium value of the rate of capital accumulation (and the rate of growth of output),

$$g^* = a + ba/\{s[z/(1+z)] - b\} \qquad (6)$$

Models of this type have several important – and somewhat surprising – implications, of which two have attracted most attention. First, the real wage is positively related to the rate of profit, given the labor–output ratio. In terms of the model, an increase in the markup, z, implies a fall in the real wage, w, which, from equation (4) is seen to be given by $1/(1+z)a_0$. Equation (6) shows that the growth rate falls when the markup rate increases, which, from equation (2) implies that since s is fixed, the equilibrium profit rate, r^*, falls. Second, the level of economic activity and the rate of growth of the economy are positively associated with the wage share, so that an improvement in income distribution may lead to an improvement in growth performance. This can be established by noting that the wage share is given by wa_0, and that a rise in the markup reduces w, u^* and g^*.

Extensions to the model

These results obviously depend on the simplifying assumptions of the model, the assumption that investment demand depends positively on the rate of capacity utilization, and the fact that excess capacity exists in the economy in equilibrium. Extensions of the model to introduce other production inputs, government activity, endogenous distributional changes, technological change, financial issues and open economy considerations alter some of the conclusions (see Taylor 1991). For instance, in the open economy, a rise in the real wage may worsen international competitiveness, reduce the trade balance and hence capacity utilization and growth.

The assumption that investment depends on the rate of capacity utilization has been generally found to be theoretically plausible and empirically supported. However, when additional variables determining investment are introduced, the results need modification. Introducing the profit *rate* as an additional determinant does not alter the conclusions, but allowing the profit *share* to affect investment demand positively may reverse them. However, the relation between effective demand and capacity utilization remain central to all these models, and under many conditions the results mentioned above continue to hold.

Criticism and defense of the models

One criticism of these models is that, in the

long run, it is unreasonable to assume that capacity utilization will be determined endogenously by effective demand and not be at some desired or "full" level. Consequently, if this latter level is exogenously fixed, the results discussed above will not hold in the long run and are therefore only of short-run significance. However, several arguments may be used in defense of the models (see, for example, Lavoie 1995). First, it can be argued that unless competition makes the markup fall whenever there is excess capacity (which is not confirmed by the available evidence), it is difficult to conceptualize a stable mechanism which will take the economy to the planned level of capacity utilization in the long run.

Second, the planned level of capacity utilization may not be exogenously given, but may depend on input prices and profit rates for Sraffian capital-theoretic, or for strategic entry-deterrence, reasons. If this is the case, under certain conditions the results of the model hold in long-run equilibrium, in which actual and planned rates of capacity utilization are equal. Finally, if the long-run equilibrium is taken not to be a position of rest but as representing an average of actual positions which shift due to parametric changes, there is no reason to expect the actual and planned levels to be equalized in that "equilibrium."

See also:

balance of payments constraint; Kalecki; Kalecki's macro theory of profits; Kaleckian theory of growth; Keynes; monopoly capitalism

Selected references

Dutt, Amitava (1984) "Stagnation, Income Distribution and Monopoly Power," *Cambridge Journal of Economics* 8(1): 25–40.

Kalecki, Michal (1971) *Selected Essays on the Dynamics of the Capitalist Economy*, Cambridge: Cambridge University Press.

Lavoie, Marc (1995) "The Kaleckian Model of Growth and Distribution and its Neo-Ricardian and Neo-Marxian Critiques," *Cambridge Journal of Economics* 19(9): 789–818.

Rowthorn, Robert (1981) "Demand, Real Wages and Growth," *Thames Papers in Political Economy*, Autumn.

Steindl, Josef (1952) *Stagnation and Maturity in American Capitalism*, Oxford: Blackwell.

Taylor, Lance (1991) *Income Distribution, Inflation and Growth*, Cambridge, MA: MIT Press.

AMITAVA KRISHNA DUTT

efficiency wages

In neoclassical terms, efficiency wages exist whenever firms find it optimal to set wages above a market-clearing level. If we conceive of a perfectly competitive labor market and a market-clearing wage, efficiency wages imply that firms choose to pay wages above that level. Involuntary unemployment, or a RESERVE ARMY OF LABOR, is an obvious implication of firms setting wages "too high."

For political economists, the term "efficiency wages" is a misnomer – "productivity-enhancing or cost-reducing wage payments" would be more correct. "Market-clearing" is also nonsensical in many political economy models. Rather, we might say that firms pay employment rents in the sense that employees strictly prefer recontracting with the firm to reentering the labor market.

The roots of efficiency wage theory are numerous, and include, for instance, what is today referred to as the "Webb effect." The first substantive modern discussion of efficiency wages appears in Leibenstein's (1957) book, where he argues that in underdeveloped countries, efficiency wage payments improve employee nutrition, and hence productivity and revenues. This model is largely ignored today. A modern theory which bears some resemblance to Leibenstein's theories is that put forth by Edward Nell (1988). He argues that if efficiency wages become more common, then cost inefficient firms (for example, due to X-INEFFICIENCY) will be forced to drop out of the market. Their market share will be taken over by cost-efficient firms that can afford to pay higher wages.

Neoclassical tradition

In the neoclassical tradition, two basic theories of efficiency wages exist: sorting and monitoring models. In the sorting model, employers cannot identify high-quality employees directly, but can attract and hold such employees through efficiency wage payments (Weiss 1991). This logic explains why firms facing declining product demand might find random layoffs more profitable than wage reductions which result in the equivalent number of voluntary redundancies. In the monitoring version (Shapiro and Stiglitz 1984), workers will shirk unless provided with both a wage rent such that dismissal is costly, and monitoring such that shirking will, with some positive probability, lead to dismissal. While both the sorting and monitoring models explain "involuntary unemployment" (although not the Keynesian variety), the monitoring model is inherently more attuned to political economy due to its inclusion of the distinction between LABOR AND LABOR POWER.

Political economy explanations

Models of efficiency wages in the political economy tradition date to Herbert Gintis (1976), who argued as follows: if firms must extract labor from labor power, then above market-clearing wages may be required; threats of dismissal and "involuntary unemployment" will both follow and be required for the successful extraction of labor by capitalists. This idea is operationally equivalent to the mainstream monitoring model of efficiency wages, though it is typically labeled a "dismissal based" model of efficiency wages.

Much later work by political economists focuses on efficiency wages (summarized in Rebitzer 1993), but three developments stand out. First is the potential role of efficiency wages within political economy theories of the LABOR PROCESS and labor segmentation.

Thinking in terms of labor control strategies (Edwards 1979), it can be argued that workers who are subject to simple control, where the immediate supervisor holds reign over rewards and punishment, also experience dismissal frequently, so they may be paid a dismissal-based efficiency wage. Workers subject to technical or bureaucratic control may also receive efficiency wages, but for reasons having to do with history and norms of fairness (discussed below). Linking these types of efficiency wages to labor market segments, it follows that low-wage, secondary sector workers receive dismissal-based efficiency wages, while high-wage, primary sector workers also receive efficiency wages. As a result, it can be argued that wages and worker efforts in the secondary sector of the economy should be more responsive to changes in macroeconomic conditions relative to other sectors.

Second, dismissal-based efficiency wages can be used to explain the productivity slowdown of the 1970s by focusing on the "cost-of-job-loss" (Bowles, Gordon and Weisskopf 1982). The COST OF JOB LOSS argument is that workers increase their efforts as the cost rises with unemployment, supervision or wages, and decrease their efforts as that cost falls. This concept offers the theoretically liberating potential for explaining how political economists understand efficiency wages. That is, the cost of job loss depends not only on the wage a worker receives from the firm, but also income and production conditions inside the family (see SOCIAL WAGE; GENDER DIVISION OF LABOR), as well as income support from the government.

Third, political economy models of efficiency wages offer a critique of capitalism as being inefficient (Bowles 1985). While there are numerous paths available for this critique, most can be reduced to the hypothesis that government policies could reduce involuntary unemployment or that LABOR-MANAGED ENTERPRISES (see PARTICIPATORY DEMOCRACY AND SELF-MANAGEMENT) could eliminate the employer–employee conflict of interest and hence improve worker welfare without reducing output.

Critiques

Critiques of efficiency wages within the political economy tradition also exist. Specifically, it can be argued that (1) the models are methodologically similar to neoclassical models with atomistic individual utility-maximizers, and so cannot account for group behavior or history, (2) an emphasis on the policy conclusion that "capitalism is inefficient" accepts the inherently conservative notion of Pareto efficiency as valid, and (3) the models do not account for unequal ECONOMIC POWER held by capitalists.

Bargaining and fairness

Alternative heterodox approaches to the relevant issues are provided by bargaining theory and theories of fairness. The bargaining approach, based on ideas from game theory, can yield efficiency wage-type results (Bowles *et al.* 1993). The disadvantage of this strategy is that it maintains methodological individualism and utility maximization. The advantages include the potential for bargaining theory to (1) explain the formation and actions of coalitions, (2) incorporate notions of economic power in a fashion permitting CLASS analysis, and (3) permit the construction of models of SOCIAL DEMOCRACY. Note, however, that efficiency wages need not consistently emerge from bargaining theory.

Turning to theories of fairness, it is possible to construct a model of efficiency wages with no threats of dismissal, but instead a promise from the firm to provide a fair share of firm revenues to workers in exchange for high levels of effort (Akerlof 1980). In this type of model, long-term employment relations may be required to seal the exchange of wages and effort. Connecting this back to labor segmentation, it can be argued that dismissal-based efficiency wages rule in the secondary segment, but that wages in primary segments (with long-term employment relations) are governed by considerations of fairness. If this argument is correct, then the recent decline of employment in the primary segments, in tandem with the expansion of secondary segment employment, implies that dismissal-based efficiency wage models will gain increasing relevance for understanding – and changing – the economy.

Acknowledgments

The author would like to thank Herbert Gintis, David Levine, Eric Nilsson, Rich Parkin and Gil Skillman.

See also:

segmented and dual labor markets; wage determination

Selected references

Akerlof, George A. (1980) "Labor Contracts as Partial Gift Exchange," *Quarterly Journal of Economics* 47(4): 543–69.

Bowles, Samuel (1985) "The Production Process in Competitive Economy: Walrasian, Neo-Hobbesian, and Marxian Models," *American Economic Review* 65(2): 16–36.

Bowles, Samuel, Gintis, Herbert and Gustafsson, Bo (eds) (1993) *Markets and Democracy: Participation, Accountability, and Efficiency*, New York: Cambridge University Press.

Bowles, Samuel, Gordon, David M. and Weisskopf, Thomas E. (1982) *Beyond the Waste Land*, New York: Doubleday.

Edwards, Richard C. (1979) *Contested Terrain*, New York: Basic Books.

Gintis, Herbert (1976) "The Nature of the Labor Exchange and the Theory of Capitalist Production," *Review of Radical Political Economy* 8(2): 36–54.

Leibenstein, Harvey (1957) *Economic Backwardness and Economic Growth*, New York: Wiley.

Nell, Edward (1988) *Prosperity and Public Spending: Transformational Growth and the Role of Government*, Boston: Unwin Hyman.

Rebitzer, James B. (1993) "Radical Political Economy and the Economics of Labor Markets," *Journal of Economic Literature* 31(3): 1394–1434.

Shapiro, Carl and Stiglitz, Joseph (1984)

"Equilibrium Unemployment as a Worker Discipline Device," *American Economic Review* 74(3): 433–44.

Weiss, Andrew (1991) *Efficiency Wages*, Oxford: Oxford University Press.

ROBERT DRAGO

EMULATION: *see* conspicuous consumption and emulation

endogenous money and credit

A central issue in post-Keynesian theory is the endogenous nature of the money supply (Lavoie 1992: 149–51). For the present purpose, it is possible to say that the stock of money is endogenous when it is determined by the demand for money, created either by the financial institutions, or by the central bank.

Exogenous versus endogenous money

The neoclassical theory of money is based on the exogenous nature of money. This hypothesis has been grounded on the assertion that central banks have full control of the money supply. However, this requires that the following conditions be satisfied: the central bank must have full control over the creation of monetary base, and the central bank, knowing the parameter of the money multiplier, must have indirect control over the creation of bank deposits.

The post-classical theories – and in particular the post-Keynesian school – consider money supply to be endogenous, mainly because it is demand determined. In the wake of some classical authors (such as Tooke), Kaldor (1939) was the first Keynesian economist to affirm the endogenous nature of money. He maintained that, if the central bank is willing to control the rate of interest, the money supply function becomes tendentially horizontal and the quantity of money changes in response to the evolution of demand (Kaldor 1939: 4). These views of Kaldor and post-Keynesians are based on the conviction that, in modern economies, there are many channels of money/credit creation not fully controlled by monetary authorities (for a clear synthesis, see Lavoie 1992: 169–92).

Channels of endogenous finance

(1) *Commercial bank discretion.* Commercial banks, playing an active role in the process of money creation, have wide margins of discretion with regard to the ratio between deposits and reserves. When the demand for loans increases, the supply of them increases as well, and this involves an increase both in bank deposits and, in many cases, also in the stock of high-powered money. This is why money supply endogeneity is sometimes defined as the situation in which the stock of money is *credit-driven*.

(2) *Financial innovation.* This channel can perhaps be considered a subset of the first channel. Wray (1990) explains endogenous money in relation to the complex game of financial institutions innovating to satisfy their clients' demand for funds, and the central bank responding by seeking to control those innovations; followed by further innovation and control, *ad infinitum* (the "innovation view"). He provides case studies of endogenous funds, including the Federal Funds Market, repurchase agreements, certificates of deposit, foreign borrowing and the discount window. Recent money substitutes may also be included here.

(3) *Central bank accommodation.* Central banks generally "accommodate" the liquidity needs of the financial system. The need for liquidity, for instance, having been created through a wage increase, is then validated by the central bank's expanding money supply. According to post-Keynesians, and differently from the neoclassical view, the main target of monetary authorities is the *stability* of the financial system. However, stability requires that the central bank accommodate the demand for reserves by commercial banks. Actually this strategy is required to avoid drastic and rapid fluctuations in the rate of interest which, as Kaldor pointed out in 1958 and in 1970, could

have very unfavorable effects on the financial markets. In particular:

- Drastic and rapid fluctuations of the rate of interest result in a higher degree of instability in bond prices, and this may substantially weaken financial institutions whose assets consist primarily of fixed-return securities.
- These fluctuations bring about an increase in the risk premia associated with the holding of fixed-return securities. This widens the difference between long-term and short-term interest rates and modifies the shape of the yield curve. As a consequence, financial markets become more speculative.
- These phenomena unfavorably affect real activity because they raise the rate of profit *required* to undertake productive investments (Kaldor 1958: 132–5).
- Moreover, if monetary authorities do not provide enough money to meet the requests of the economy, "a complete surrogate money-system and payment-system would be established, which would exist side by side with the official money" (Kaldor, 1970: 10). This would endanger the pivotal position of the central bank in the financial system.

For all these reasons, monetary authorities usually accommodate the liquidity needs coming from the economy in order to stabilize the rate of interest. Hence, according to post-Keynesians, money supply endogeneity is an unavoidable consequence of the way in which modern monetary systems work themselves out. More specifically, endogeneity is a consequence of the kind of relationships established between central banks, firms and financial institutions.

Controversy over channels

There is controversy within the post-Keynesian school over two different issues: the exact role that commercial banks and monetary authorities have with respect to the determination of money supply, and the correct analytical description of the money supply function.

With regard to the first point, some post-Keynesian economists consider the endogenous nature of money to be a consequence of the behavior of the monetary authorities ("accommodationist view"), while others claim that it is the result of the profit-maximizing behavior of the financial operators who accelerate the process of financial innovation as a reaction to restrictive monetary policy ("innovation view") (on this debate, see Wray 1990; Palley 1994).

As for the analytical description of the money supply function, some post-Keynesians describe it as a horizontal line in the money-interest graph. This is because commercial and central banks have no discretionary margins in the determination of the stock of means of payments: they can fix its price (rate of interest), but its quantity is determined by demand (Moore 1988, 1991). Other post-Keynesian authors consider instead the horizontal money supply curve as an analytical simplification of the model. They affirm that, in principle, neither the quantity of deposits nor the stock of high-powered money are variables out of the control, respectively, of commercial banks and monetary authorities.

According to the latter position, the fact that in general the monetary system accommodates the demand for liquidity coming from the non-bank operators does not imply that the system no longer controls its stock. Indeed, when the demand for money grows unexpectedly, both commercial banks and the central bank will act in such a manner as to determine a rise in the rate of interest, preventing a rise in the leverage ratio (Rousseas 1986; Musella and Panico 1995). Hence the horizontal supply function must be considered an analytical device to simplify the real way in which the financial system operates, and it is not the effect of the monetary authorities' inability to control the quantity of money in the economy (Musella and Panico 1992).

See also:

financial crises; financial innovations; financial instability hypothesis; monetary policy and

Selected references

Kaldor, N. (1939) "Speculation and Economic Activity," *Review of Economic Studies* 7(October): 1–27.

—— (1958) "Monetary Policy, Economic Stability and Growth," memorandum submitted to the Radcliffe Committee on the Working of the Monetary System, 23 June, *Principal Memoranda of Evidence*, Cmnd 827, HMSO, London, 1960, 146–53; repr. in N. Kaldor, *Essays on Economic Policy, Volume I*, London: Duckworth, 128–53.

—— (1970) "The New Monetarism," *Lloyds Bank Review* 96(July): 1–17.

Lavoie, M. (1992) *Foundations of Post-Keynesian Economic Analysis*, Aldershot: Edward Elgar.

Moore, B.J. (1988) *Horizontalist and Verticalist: The Macroeconomics of Credit Money*, Cambridge: Cambridge University Press.

—— (1991) "Has the Demand for Money been Mislaid? A Reply to 'Has Moore Become Too Horizontal?'," *Journal of Post Keynesian Economics* 14(1): 125–33.

Musella, M. and Panico, C. (1992) "Kaldor on Endogenous Money and Interest Rates," in G. Mongiovi and C. Ruhl (eds) *Macroeconomic Theory: Diversity and Convergence*, Aldershot: Edward Elgar 37–63.

—— (eds) (1995) *Introduction to Money Supply in the Economic Process*, Aldershot: Edward Elgar.

Palley, T.I. (1994) "Competing Views of the Money Supply," *Metroeconomica* 45(3): 67–88.

Rousseas, S.W. (1986) *Post-Keynesian Monetary Economics*, London: Macmillan.

Wray, L.R. (1990) *Money and Credit in Capitalist Economies*, Aldershot, UK: E. Elgar Publishing.

MARCO MUSELLA

entropy, negentropy and the laws of thermodynamics

Conservation, entropy and absolute zero

The laws of thermodynamics are important to various fields of political economy. Interest in these laws reflects the interdisciplinary nature of political economy, in particular the linkage with physics, applied mathematics and evolutionary theory. There are three main laws of thermodynamics. The first law of thermodynamics, the Law of Conservation, states that energy can be neither created nor destroyed but can undergo a change in form. This change in form can involve energy variously alternating between "motion, cohesion, electricity, light, heat and magnetism" (Peters 1993: 275). The second law of thermodynamics, the Law of Entropy, states that a closed system tends toward energy becoming increasingly unavailable for work. Hence it is said that a closed system will tend toward a maximum level of disorder or entropy over time. The third law, called the Law of Absolute Zero Temperature (or the Nernst Heat Theorem), renders the "entropies of different substances comparable, since they have the same zero entropy at absolute zero" temperature (Peters 1993: 275). (The third law is less important to our subject that the others, and hence will not be further discussed here.)

The Law of Conservation (first law), that the matter-energy of the universe is constant, leads one to the recognition that economic processes cannot alter the amount of energy and matter, but can only change their form. The Law of Entropy (second law) relates to measures of disorder. In a closed thermodynamic system, entropy is a measure of the energy unavailable for work. A closed system will move from lower toward greater states of entropy. Taken together, the first and second laws of thermodynamics describe a universe where energy and matter are constant but becoming increasingly inaccessible.

entropy, negentropy and the laws of thermodynamics

History

The study of thermodynamics is often traced back to Sadi Carnot (1796–1832). Carnot, an early nineteenth-century engineer, is famous for his inquiry into the efficiency of heat engines. "Thermodynamics thus began," Georgescu-Roegen argues, "as a physics of economic value." Referring to Carnot's work, he explains "it was the economic distinction between things having an economic value and waste which prompted the thermodynamic distinction, not conversely" (Georgescu-Roegen, in Daly and Townsend 1993: 78). In the decades that followed, the principle of the conservation of energy was commented on by Karl Griedrich Mohr and, later, by Hermann von Helmholtz. By the mid-1800s, Rudolf Clausius, building on Carnot, Joule, Kelvin and others, coined the term "entropy" and succinctly expressed what we now call the first and second laws of thermodynamics, stating: "The energy of the universe is constant," and: "The entropy of the universe tends towards a maximum" (quoted in Cardwell 1971: 273). Under the influence of Kenneth Boulding's famous article in 1966, "The Economics of the Coming Spaceship Earth" (see Daly and Townsend 1993) and Georgescu-Roegen's path-breaking book on *The Entropy Law and the Economic Process* (1971), many environmental (and other) economists became interested in the subject.

Throughput and waste

When discussing the implications of thermodynamics, economists often talk about "throughput." Throughput can be defined as "the entropic physical flow of matter-energy from nature's sources, through the human economy and back to nature's sinks" (Daly, in Daly and Townsend 1993: 326). The concept of throughput is useful in focusing attention on two important implications of the Law of Conservation. The first implication is the reminder that the economic process adds nothing to the existing quantity of matter-energy. A second implication is that waste does not simply disappear. Running a tank of gas through a car's engine reduces neither matter nor energy. As the fuel is used to perform work, availability diminishes as the fuel moves from a bound state of ordered low entropy to one of unbounded and disordered high entropy, taking the form of heat, exhaust, carbon monoxide and so on.

In this context, the significance of the first two laws of thermodynamics is more apparent when they are considered together. Each becomes increasingly constraining in the light of the other. Increased entropy would not be a concern if matter-energy could be created or there existed an unlimited stock of accessible low-entropy resources. This is not the case. Instead, the availability of low-entropy resources is an important issue. These resources are, for the most part, either solar or terrestrial. The sun provides a flow of low-entropy energy. As a source, it is limited by the rate of this flow. Earth provides a finite, low-entropy stock of both matter and energy. Such terrestrial resources are usually classified as renewable or nonrenewable. Nonrenewable resources are limited by their quantity. Renewable resources are limited by their sustainable rate of use. Thus the amount of any particular low-entropy resource is limited in some way.

The first two laws of thermodynamics are also important in understanding pollution. If it were not for entropy, the Law of Conservation would suggest that all matter and energy could be continuously recycled. The fact that waste does not disappear would therefore become a real boon to the economy. The Law of Entropy, however, ensures that this throughput now exists in a less useful form. Each transformation of throughput necessarily reduces its usability (availability or accessibility).

The Law of Conservation might lead one to wonder what is consumed by the economic process. The economy cannot consume or use up matter or energy, but it does diminish their accessibility. Each transformation of throughput necessarily leads to greater entropy of the overall system. The economy, then, consumes low entropy. There is an opportunity cost to this irreversible increase in entropy; the associated throughput could have been used for something else. For this reason, increased entropy can be viewed as an ultimate cost of economic activity (Daly 1991: 25). Much of the discussion of economics and thermodynamics revolves around the implications of these entropic costs.

Low-entropy energy asymmetries

Asymmetries exist in the supply of low-entropy energy. The flow of solar energy reaching Earth in a single year dwarfs that which could be obtained from the planet's entire endowment of fossil fuels. This enormous flow of energy, however, reaches earth in such a diffuse stream that it is difficult to harness for work (Georgescu-Roegen, in Daly and Townsend 1993: 102). Nevertheless, on Earth the sun produces wind, rain and photosynthesis. Windmills, hydroelectric generators and biofuels can be used, like the photovoltaic cell, to put solar energy to work. The asymmetry between terrestrial stock and solar flow is reflected in an asymmetry in the opportunity costs of using these low-entropy energy sources. A sunny day or a gust of wind is fleeting, and if we use them to produce work, we have not done so at the expense of future generations. It is different with fossil fuels; with these, there is an intertemporal opportunity cost. This has led some to argue that use of terrestrial energy resources should be minimized in favor of the more abundant solar source. Doing otherwise is unsustainable and, in a sense, living beyond our "budget constraint" (Daly 1991: 23).

Focusing on the higher cost of terrestrial low-entropy energy leads to critiques of a variety of modern trends. Traditional sources of energy, such as food, wood and wind, are convenient means for taking advantage of the flow of solar energy. Improved technology has made humanity more dependent on comparatively scarce terrestrial stocks, which by this measure is a backward step (Daly 1991: 22). Likewise, Georgescu-Roegen criticizes modern agricultural techniques. Many have pointed to modern agriculture as proof of the ability of human technology and genius to defeat the Malthusian specter (see, for example, De Gregori 1986: 467). However, Georgescu-Roegen argues that the increased reliance on mechanization and artificial fertilizers is "uneconomical" because it is a substitution into relatively scarce resources (Daly and Townsend 1993: 84).

Negentropy and open systems

Negentropy, or negative entropy, is also an important concept discussed by economists. Creating order out of disorder is a defining characteristic of life and civilization. Maintaining or lowering the entropy of a system requires the inflow of energy from outside that system. However, total entropy has still increased. For example, the rise of life and civilization on earth may appear, at first glance, to be contrary to the Law of Entropy: there has been an increase in the order of the terrestrial system. This was made possible by the inflow of low-entropy energy from the sun (negentropy), as Earth is an open system linked to the broader solar system and universe. The entropy of the larger, encompassing system – the solar system – has, therefore, increased. Thus, as Boulding says, evolution

> involves the creation of those extraordinary little islands of order in the cells, the plants, the animals, the human race and its artifacts, at the cost of disorder elsewhere, the elsewhere here being mainly the sun, although it may also be other parts of the earth. Another way of saying the same thing is that "evolution is pollution."
> (Boulding 1981: 151)

Policy recommendations

The implications of thermodynamics can lead to policy suggestions that are very substantial and far-reaching. Herman Daly, for example, argues that the laws of thermodynamics are among the factors that create the need for a STEADY-STATE ECONOMY. Georgescu-Roegen (in Daly and Townsend 1993: 95–6) argues that a truly steady state is impossible and that many of the arguments for such a state actually favor a declining state. Nevertheless, many of the policies advocated by Georgescu-Roegen are fully compatible with those advocated by steady-state theorists. These include ceasing weapons production, reducing world population to levels sustainable by organic agriculture, and eliminating economic polarization by aiding international development.

There are many economists, both radical and neoclassical, who do not believe that the laws of thermodynamics should cause alarm over current patterns of resource use. De Gregori (1986), for example, points out that resources are not just objects which exist at ever-increasing states of entropy. Rather, they are continuously being created. Resources must be defined in terms of the current state of technology. Technology transforms objects and phenomena into resources. As each level of technology brings a higher one within reach, this negentropic process of resource creation builds upon itself (De Gregori 1986: 467). Particular resources have always been scarce and thus limiting. However, De Gregori argues, both biological and cultural development have always been about overcoming limits and creating new resources (1986: 466–7). Toward a similar end, NEOCLASSICAL ECONOMICS points to factor substitution. As a particular resource grows relatively more scarce, rising prices will favor its replacement by a substitute.

Constraints implied by the laws

There are, one might argue, two levels of constraint imposed by the laws of thermodynamics. In the short run, specific resources – as defined by current technology – are depletable. In the long run, since all matter-energy is finite and subject to increasing entropy, all low-entropy resources and potential resources are depletable, and the substitution gambit ceases to be effective. In the former case, the issue is whether technological advance can create new resources more quickly than the old ones are depleted. In the latter case, the issue is whether it will take decades or millennia for this ultimate limit to become pressing.

Conclusion

A serious concern is that the debate will focus too much on how many commodities the economy can squeeze out of the biosphere without causing a catastrophic collapse. However, determining the upper limits to growth may be considered to be of secondary importance compared to understanding those forces which spur growth but, at the same time, reduce the QUALITY OF LIFE or the quality of the biosphere. Inquiry into such issues offers common ground for both the technophile and the Luddite. The promotion of conspicuous consumption, fashion, planned obsolescence, inequality, and the business of war and weaponry are all problems whose significance partly transcends the debate over the capacity of human genius and creativity to meet the challenges imposed by the laws of thermodynamics.

See also:

bioeconomics; development and the environment; environmental and ecological political economy: major contemporary themes; evolution and coevolution; natural capital; nuclear energy and nuclear war; sustainable development

Selected references

Boulding, Kenneth E. (1981) *Evolutionary Economics*, Beverly Hills and London: Sage Publications.

Burgenmeier, B. (ed.) (1994) *Economy, Environment, and Technology: A Socio-Economic Approach*, Armonk, NY: M.E. Sharpe.

Cardwell, D.S.L. (1971) *From Watt to Clausius: The Rise of Thermodynamics in the Early Industrial Age*, Ithaca, NY: Cornell University Press.

Daly, Herman E. (1991) *Steady-State Economics*, 2nd edn, Washington, DC: Island Press.

Daly, Herman E. and Townsend, Kenneth N. (eds) (1993) *Valuing the Earth*, Cambridge, MA: The MIT Press.

De Gregori, Thomas (1986) "Technology and

Negative Entropy," *Journal of Economic Issues* 20(2): 463–70.
—— (1987) "Finite Resources or Finite Imaginations? A Reply to John M. Gowdy," *Journal of Economic Issues* 21(1): 477–82.
Georgescu-Roegen, Nicholas (1971) *The Entropy Law and the Economic Process*, Cambridge, MA: Harvard University Press.
Gowdy, John (1987) "GAIA and Technological Utopianism: Comment on De Gregori," *Journal of Economic Issues* 21(1): 473–6.
Peters, Leo (1993) "Thermodynamics," *Collier's Encyclopedia*, New York: P.F. Collier, vol. 22.

TERREL GALLAWAY

entry point

Confronted with the infinite complexity and multi-dimensionality of such objects of analysis as society and economy, every thinker must decide where and how to begin to make sense of them. Theories differ according to which aspects of their objects they select as entry points into the complexities they seek to understand. NEOCLASSICAL ECONOMICS has, as its distinctive entry points, individual preferences, technology and initial endowments. Marxist political economy differs by selecting instead the entry point of CLASS, the processes of producing, appropriating and distributing surplus labor. Other theories (Keynesianism, institutionalism, feminism) display still other entry points such as EFFECTIVE DEMAND AND CAPACITY UTILIZATION, social organizations, GENDER and so on.

Central concerns of theories

The entry points with which a theory begins are those aspects of society that its proponents deem most worthy of attention. For example, to make sense of economics from the standpoint of individual preferences as an entry point foregrounds the roles of individuals, their psychological states of mind and their behaviors as determinants of economic events. Other aspects of those events slip, by comparison, into the background; they feature less prominently in economic explanations or even disappear altogether from them. In Marxian economic analysis, economic events are connected to class processes primarily such that individual psychologies and behaviors are accorded a secondary position. In neoclassical economics, by contrast, class processes are not rendered secondary within explanations; they are expunged altogether (see METHODOLOGICAL INDIVIDUALISM AND COLLECTIVISM).

Entry points and other phenomena

The notion of a theory's entry points includes more than the particular aspects of complex objects with which the theory begins. It extends also to the way in which the theory links those particular aspects with everything else the theory covers. For example, neoclassical theory usually links its entry points of preferences, technology and endowments to other aspects of an economic system by means of a deterministic linkage. The former are the causes that determine, for example, market prices as their effect. In this sense, the entry points of neoclassical economics include not only preferences, technology and endowments, but also determinism as the mode of linking together the parts of the economic totality to be explained.

In contrast, some Marxian economic theories likewise make determinism an entry point, but they differ from neoclassical economics by making class an entry point as well. Other Marxian economic theories differ further: they combine class processes and overdeterminism as their distinctive entry points (see DETERMINISM AND OVERDETERMINATION). That is, while they enter into their analyses of economies by focusing on class processes, they do not link class to other aspects of those economies in a deterministic manner. They do not make class the cause and other aspects the effects of class; rather, they view class and non-class aspects of economies as being overdetermined. Not only do class and non-class aspects of an economy participate in determining each other, but each is also determined by and participates in determining all the non-economic aspects of the society in which they occur.

Theories are inherently partial

One of the important implications of the concept of entry points is that all theories are inescapably partial. Each theory's entry points function like a flashlight in a dark room: some objects are illuminated, while others are thrown into the shadows. A theory's entry points limit as well as enable the analysis it can and will construct. With their different entry points, theories will differ in the understandings they reach.

Discourses and contests among theories require attention to the rationales they offer for the particular entry points they deploy. No theory can sensibly claim that its entry points include all aspects of the objects it seeks to explain. Every theory is inherently partial, an elaboration of a point of view defined as that theory's set of entry points.

Epistemology

Theoretical entry points are also matters of epistemology, the branch of philosophy concerned with how people produce knowledges. They are markers for how different human beings make their different senses of the world they inhabit. In economics, they define the different angles from which alternative theories see and construct their correspondingly different understandings. The concept of entry points not only straddles the boundary between economics and philosophy, it also shows political economists how epistemology matters to every aspect of economics.

Selected references

Resnick, Stephen and Wolff, Richard (1987) *Knowledge and Class: A Marxian Critique of Political Economy*, Chicago: University of Chicago Press.
—— (1988) "Radical Differences Among Radical Theories," *Review of Radical Political Economics* 20(2–3).

RICHARD D. WOLFF

environmental and ecological political economy: associations and journals

Economic discussions recognizing the importance of the environment and natural systems have slowly been evolving over the last century. The resource economists of the 1950s tended to regard the environment as a source of materials which required some specialized management, due to characteristics which differentiated them from manufactured goods. These economists can be viewed as being within the neoclassical school, and as having strong associations with agricultural economics. In the 1960s, environmental economics appeared in the US as a distinct discipline concerned with the growing pollution problems which were evident to the general public, even if previously ignored by academia. Journals such as *Land Economics*, refocusing on environmental economics, and the *Natural Resource Journal*, with an environmental law perspective, developed concerns about the political economy of environmental issues, although somewhat indirectly.

In the late 1970s, the US-based Association of Environmental and Resource Economists (AERE) was formed, along with an associated journal, the *Journal of Environmental Economics and Management* (JEEM). Together, resource and environmental economics explained how neoclassical models were flawed and how corrections could be made to achieve efficiency gains. The organized response in Europe was much slower, and a European Association of Environmental and Resource Economists (EAERE) was only initiated in 1991.

The AERE was initiated in 1978 by a group of US environmental and natural resource economists. Larry Ruff and Terry Ferrar had the idea of an association, and at the ASSA meetings in Dallas in December 1975 a society and a journal were initiated. The *JEEM* was established by Ralph d'Arge and Allen Kneese in cooperation with Academic Press in May 1974, and AERE later became the organization controlling the journal. Initial funding was provided in March of 1980 by The Ford Foundation, The Alfred P. Sloan Foundation, Resources for the Future, Inc. and the Resource and Environmental Economics Laboratory of the University of Wyoming. Current membership is approximately 800.

The AERE publishes a newsletter (in May and November), and runs annual workshops that were started in 1986 by President Kerry Smith. Workshop funding is provided by the US Environmental Protection Agency, The National Oceanic and Atmospheric Administration (NOAA) and the Economic Research Service of USDA. The business office of AERE has always been located at Resources for the Future (RFF) in Washington, DC. RFF provides office space free of charge and helps AERE with many other tasks. RFF itself publishes an interesting newsletter, *Resources*, which covers US environmental policy from an economic perspective.

Within the field of environmental and resource economics, discontent with the lack of policy relevance of prescriptions is often evident, but neoclassical theory maintains a dominant role. Both internal and external criticism led in the late 1980s to ecologists and economists opening more formal discussions. The result was the formation of the area called ecological economics, which attempts to take a fresh look at how economic systems interact with nature. Ecological economics is a transdisciplinary field of study that addresses the relationship between ecosystems and ecological systems in the broadest possible sense. It goes beyond conventional conceptions of scientific disciplines and attempts to integrate and synthesize many different disciplinary perspectives, in order to achieve an ecologically and economically sustainable world. An International Society for Ecological Economics (ISEE) was established in the US in 1989, and has rapidly expanded to include branches in New Zealand, Australia, South America and Europe.

ISEE is a not-for-profit organization, established in 1988, and now has more than 2,000 members in over sixty countries. The society's journal, *Ecological Economics*, is published twelve times per year, and a quarterly ecological economics bulletin is sent to members. International conferences are held biannually. Regional Chapters exist in Australia/New Zealand, Brazil, Canada, Russia and Europe. The University of Maryland's Institute for Ecological Economics (IEE) houses the Society and its journal.

The Institute has a central role in coordinating efforts of individuals and other institutes, such as the Beijer International Institute of Ecological Economics in Stockholm, Sweden, the Oikos Foundation for Ecological Economics in Siena, Italy, and the Institute for Research on Environment and Economy in Ottawa, Canada, in order to pursue research and teaching in ecological economics. Full-time IEE faculty include the Director, Dr. Costanza, Associate Director Dr. Herman Daly and Senior Fellow Dr. John Cumberland. The goals of the IEE include addressing the full range of interactions between ecological and economic systems. The Institute represents a major effort to improve the way important issues of training and research in science, economics, and public policy are approached.

The European Society for Ecological Economics (ESEE) is a new branch of the ISEE. The ESEE was officially formed in 1996, with the election of the officers of the Society held during the European Conference at the University of Versailles. The outcome was to agree on a Secretariat to be based initially at the Centre for Economics, Ethics, Environment and Development (C3ED) in France and the election of Sylvie Fauxcheux (President), Clive Spash and Jan van der Straaten (Vice-Presidents). The aims of the new Society have been established as being distinct from both the ISEE and the EAERE. As in the ISEE, the central objectives are to combine knowledge across the fields of ecology and economics, and to see that policy advice on environmental problems is formulated on this basis. In addition, the ESEE has a unique position in encouraging the social aspects of environmental policy and the wider considerations that human interaction with the environment raises. This implies a different methodology from the mainstream economic models, while allowing for a discourse on the development of a socioeconomic and ecological field of study. The journal *Environmental Values*, published by The White Horse Press and edited by Alan Holland, has become linked with the ESEE. A new series of books on ecological economics will be published by the ESEE through Edward Elgar Publishers.

The EAERE has an associated journal published by Kluwer Academic, *Environmental and Resource Economics*. The journal was started in 1991, shortly after the formal establishment of EAERE in January of that year. The EAERE is a separate organization from the US-based AERE, with independent activities, although closer links are now being formed. The secretariat for the EAERE is at the Foundazione Eni Enrico Mattei (FEEM) in Italy, which produces its own newsletter covering environmental economics and policy. The current president is Domenico Siniscalco, who is also Executive Director of FEEM.

Land Economics is a long running journal, unassociated with any society, which is worthy of special mention. Published quarterly by the University of Wisconsin Press, the journal tends to be more applied than *JEEM* (although *JEEM* has in recent years published some less mathematical and more policy oriented works). *Land Economics* was founded in 1925 as the *Journal of Land and Public Utility Economics*. The applied and policy concern has been related to land use and monetary valuation (for example, the travel cost method and contingent valuation). The current editor is Daniel Bromley. Also of special interest is the Center for Political Ecology (CPE) which has published its journal, *Capitalism, Nature and Socialism*, since the early 1990s (including much on the political economy of the environment). The CPE is headed by James O'Connor.

See also:

environmental and ecological political economy: major contemporary ithemes

CLIVE L. SPASH

environmental and ecological political economy: major contemporary themes

Environmental economics as a distinct field of inquiry emerged during the first wave of environmentalism in the 1960s. Increasing concern over the state of the natural environment during the 1980s and 1990s has revitalized interest in the development of this discourse. On the other hand, a more politically vibrant second-wave environmentalism has questioned the intellectual force of the dominant intellectual tradition shaping environmental economics, challenging the capacity of the conventional theory to identify the nature of environmental problems, let alone offer strategies for securing sustainable development. There has been a mixed response to this challenge. The boundaries of conventional environmental economics are much less clearly defined with the environment being an object of critical consideration. The emergence of ecological economics discourse signals a significant break from the conventional theory.

Intellectual foundations

The intellectual foundations of environmental economics lie within neoclassical economics and welfare economics more particularly. The conventional wisdom has generally regarded the environment as a source of physical and biological inputs into production, as a sink for absorbing the wastes and residues of production and consumption, and as an incidental element in the workings of comparatively self-contained economic systems. The introduction of the environment is posed in terms of how economic interactions with the environment impact upon the efficient allocation of resources and optimization of economic welfare. The issue of efficient utilization has generally been posed in terms of demonstrating how prices regulate rates of exploitation and the substitution of alternatives, and how market-based discounting governs the drawing down of resources through time.

The treatment of impositions on the environment has been the more intellectually interesting aspect of environment economics, as well as being much of the intellectual endeavor in the field. Many impositions are not valued within the marketplace, do not enter into individual economic calculations, and therefore detract from the efficient utilization of resources and frustrate the optimization of economic welfare. To redress this problem, conventional environmental economics advocates the "polluter pays" principle. This principle informs the design of a range of measures to address this market failure to ensure that the non-priced impositions, the economic costs of externalities, are internalized and reflected in cost structures and economic calculations. Placing a value on the costs of polluters affords some measure of identifying the compensation that would be required to maintain the economic welfare of those who suffer from the effects of the polluting activities of others, and makes for an economically efficient and optimal utilization of resources. (However, conventional environmental economics does not require that compensation be paid, merely that there is the capacity for compensation to be paid; this is especially the case in those situations where the costs associated with seeking a settlement (transaction costs) are so substantial as to eclipse the gains from compensation.)

Conventional environmental economic theory is premised on the assumption that environmental resources should be treated as distinct and discrete objects. Externalities are generally treated in a similar fashion, as discrete as well as ephemeral, treated in a sense as mere aberrations in an otherwise perfectly functioning market system. The assumption that such impositions are not the norm makes the task of promoting the optimal utilization of resources, through the internalization of costs, a comparatively simple step. However, it is one that has been the subject of much criticism, in the light of the pervasiveness of the degrading impacts on environments and the extensive drawing upon non-substitutable and unique environmental resources and amenities.

Defenders of the orthodoxy have responded to the challenges thrown up by environmental problems, and to criticisms of the adequacy of the conventional analysis, by drawing upon the development of a number of analytical techniques from other focus areas within neoclassical economics. New concerns have been taken up and a range of instruments adopted to measure the value of interactions with and impositions on the environment in an endeavor to demonstrate the relevance of environmental economics. Drawing distinctions between different aspects of the direct ways in which individuals can signal how they value the environment, such as between use values, option values and existence values, is reckoned to provide a more informed economic appreciation of the environment. Indirect valuation methods such as hedonic pricing and contingent valuation, which seek to capture some measure of the willingness of economic agents to pay for environmental goods, are other measures that have been developed to enable a computation of the monetary value of environmental resources and amenities that would not otherwise be priced in the marketplace (see ENVIRONMENTAL VALUATION).

In the course of this revitalization of environmental economics, its proponents have become more strident in asserting the merits of market-based or economic instruments over regulatory or command-and-control measures for ensuring that environmental costs and benefits are internalized in economic valuations and reflected in market prices. This has underlined the advocacy of such economic instruments as tradable emission rights, or tradable pollution permits, and the privatization of some environmental assets with a view to auctioning access to environmental goods or amenities. The institutional interventions to effect such market-based solutions are viewed as preferable to regulatory measures for securing the optimal utilization of such resources, because they do not suffer from the alleged inefficiencies that neoclassical economists associate with state intervention in the laissez-faire market.

This shift in focus has also had important ramifications in the design of environmental management. The accounting measures advocated with command-and-control techniques have had considerable purchase, most notably in environmental impact assessments. However, environmental economists appear to have become more influential in influencing the direction of much government policy. There has been increased resort to the use of economic instruments by governments largely convinced by the immediate cost savings to be had from abolishing interventionist approaches to environmental regulation.

Debates on SUSTAINABLE DEVELOPMENT have prompted more critical consideration of the notion of the environment. The conventional formulation of the environment has traditionally been conceived in terms of the environment providing a range of services necessary for economic activity which are relatively scarce in character. The different drawings from and impositions on the environment effected the scarcity of respective environmental services, but because relative scarcity is posed in terms of the environmental services being substitutable, the overall workings of the environment, let alone the integrity of ecological systems, was not a matter for consideration. In acknowledging that conventional environmental economics provides comparatively little direction for informing policy for securing sustainable development, some economists have recast the environment problematic by considering the physical limits that the environment as a whole imposes on economic activity. Several different ways of canvassing a more comprehensive appreciation of environmental constraints have been advanced, the earliest developed within the context of the first wave of environmentalism.

Challenge to the orthodoxy

Economists at the Washington-based Resources for the Future formulated the "materials-balance" model based on setting out the interconnections associated with the drawing down of resources and the various residue impositions on the environment in an input-output matrix. Their advocacy of a more cautious approach to economic interactions with the environment was reinforced with the extension of their research agenda to develop an appreciation of the uncertainty associated with environmental impacts, the irreversible consequences of many impositions of the environment, and the uniqueness and non-substitutability of some environmental amenities.

This notion of environmental constraints was further reiterated by Nicholas Georgescu-Roegen, who drew upon the laws of thermodynamics to emphasize the physically bounded nature of the economy. The first law of thermodynamics established the physical limits of the economic process, on the premise that energy and matter could neither be destroyed nor created, while the second law of thermodynamics – the so-called entropy law – pointed to the dissipation of energy and the inability of economic systems to continue to draw upon this given stock of energy and matter (see ENTROPY, NEGENTROPY AND THE LAWS OF THERMODYNAMICS).

The idea of a STEADY-STATE ECONOMY drew upon these critiques and has remained a sustained counterpoint to the preoccupations of conventional environmental economics (Daly 1990; Daly and Cobb 1989). In particular, steady-state economics has highlighted the poverty of the conventional theory's promise that the efficient utilization of resources serves as a basis for sustainable development, when the optimization of economic welfare is premised on the maintenance of economic growth and the ever-increasing drawing down of resources and ever-growing encroachments on the environment.

Conventional responses

Conventional environmental economists have responded to these critiques by seeking to expand upon and modify their conception of the environment. Some have taken up the idea of NATURAL CAPITAL, thereby acknowledging that the natural environment is more than simply a stock of resources and receptacles that facilitate economic processes, and accepting that the environment fulfils other life support functions. While these approaches embrace the idea of maintaining the stock of natural capital as a condition for sustainable development, this is generally posed in terms of the aggregate stock of natural capital, and more frequently in terms of maintaining a stock of natural capital in order to sustain the flow of environmental services to ensure sustainable economic development. Human-made capital continues to be regarded as substitutable for natural capital, thus providing the means of escaping the limits of natural capital and, in effect, reiterating the functionalist depiction of the environment (Pearce and Turner 1990; Boulding 1973).

Emergence of ecological economics

Critics of this refashioning of environmental economics to embrace the idea of natural capital have highlighted the limited purview of environmental economics by distinguishing between weak and strong sustainability. Weak sustainability captures the object of environmental economic management: maintaining the stock of natural and human-made capital in order to maintain the flow of economic services. This notion is premised on the substitutability of natural and human-made capital. By contrast, strong sustainability is premised on acknowledging the uniqueness of the natural environment, the non-substitutability of many environmental services, and the necessity to make some allowance for the uncertain implications as well as irreversible effects of our drawing down of and impositions on the environment.

This distinction is crucial in understanding the limited purview of environmental economic discourse. In contrast, a more critical engagement with the environment is evident in the developing discourse of ecological economics. Ecological economics commences with the idea of strong sustainability, and extends this to develop an appreciation of economies as being "ecologically bounded." Ecological economists contend that it is the integrity and dynamism of ecological systems, in all their complexity and diversity in life forms, biological and physical processes, that have to be sustained. Securing sustainable economic development in such a conception requires more than simply securing the stock of natural capital. It requires the more demanding objective of maintaining the diversity and complexity of ecological systems. It shifts the emphasis from one focused almost wholly on resource depletion, and resource economic management, to the biophysical limits of ecological systems as sinks capable of assimilating the economy's wastes and as the source of all material and energy inputs. This has provided a challenge to the conventional wisdom, and the force of this has gathered momentum with an array of different ways of posing the environmental problematic in an ecological economics context, especially with the publication of the journal *Ecological Economics*.

Ecological economics encompasses a disparate range of approaches to theorizing economic–ecological interactions and interdependence. Some approaches amount to little more than complements to conventional environmental economics. Much of the research and exploration in theorizing the environment under the rubric of ecological economics simply takes up the concerns of environmental economics, largely in order to make the environment a more integral and significant component of analysis (Costanza 1991). The modelling of environment–economic interactions also partly reflects this. While the environment is dealt with in a more systematic manner than is normally the case within environmental economic discourse, insofar as some models seek to integrate ecology into an essentially economic framework, there is a tendency to have as the common reference point the universal economic denominator, that is, a monetary valuation of ecological process. This is especially the case among those theorists who seek to operationalize ecological–economic models for environmental policy and management purposes, a practice that invariably reproduces many of the problems and shortcomings of conventional environmental economics (Rosewarne 1995).

There are more challenging formulations of the ecological–economic problematic that seek to link the economy and ecological systems based on symbiotic linkages that point to processes of integration or cross-fertilization. In such a schema, the economy and ecology are represented as relatively autonomous but interdependent systems. The models of the respective systems can be combined in a systems-based construct organized around the linking of accepted models that capture the dynamics of the respective systems without upsetting their integrity. Other formulations that emphasize the interdependent nature of economic and ecological processes point to the effect that interdependence has upon the form and character of the respective systems. The notion of coevolution is especially important because it requires a more fluid modeling of the economy, one that is not mechanically bound by the postulates of neoclassical economic theory (Norgaard 1994) (see EVOLUTION AND COEVOLUTION).

Other endeavors seek to formulate non-economistic ecological economic models based on reference points drawn from within an ecological framework. Mapping and monitoring energy flows through the economy and ecological systems is one such method, although as Georgescu-Roegen has observed such a reference point is not without its problems. Perhaps the more interesting and certainly more radical endeavors, although more heuristic in character, are those that seek to recast economic process in terms of more dynamic conceptions of ecological processes, such as those that are framed in terms of self-organizing ecological systems (Faber *et al.* 1995).

The more ecological economics has made ecological processes a crucial element for theorizing the interdependence of economy and ecology, the more it has challenged some of the fundamental postulates of the neoclassical economic paradigm. The most noteworthy has been the developing critique of the merits of welfare economics and, more particularly, subjective preference theory, which celebrates the artifact *homo economicus* as the pivot for defining the place, behavior and motivations of humans within environmental systems. This challenge has a long pedigree whose lineage can be found in Daly's articulation of steady-state economics. The focus on ecological systems has prompted a reorientation away from individual economic agents seeking to maximize individual economic welfare to economic agents whose *raison d'être* is COMMUNITY, part of whose purpose, indeed responsibility, is to secure the sustainability of economic interactions with ecological systems. In this refashioning of the economic problematic, it is the economy organized around the behavior of the self-interested, self-aggrandizing *homo economicus* that is held to be the cause of economically unsustainable existence.

These excursions have also engendered a critical consideration of the moral and ethical foundations of economics and economic processes. It has prompted some ecological economists to question the merits of viewing welfare simply in monetarily-defined measures. Others have built upon critiques to develop an appreciation of sustainable socioeconomic systems, which has led them to question the veracity of economics as having anything substantive to offer in informing how we can go about constructing an ecologically sustainable future. The evolution of ecological economics has entailed a radical departure from conventional environmental economics.

See also:

ecological feminism; ecological radicalism; environmental and ecological political economy: associations and journals; environmental policy and politics; quality of life

Selected references

Boulding, Kenneth (1973) "The Economics of the Coming Spaceship Earth," in Herman Daly (ed.) *Toward a Steady-State Economy*, San Francisco: W.H. Freeman.

Costanza, Robert (ed.) (1991) *Ecological Economics: The Science and Management of Sustainability*, New York: Columbia University Press.

Daly, Herman (1990) "The Economic Growth Debate: What Some Economists Have Learned But Many Have Not," *Journal of Environmental Economics and Management* 14.

Daly, Herman E. and Cobb, John B. (1989) *For the Common Good: Redirecting the Economy Toward Community, the Environment and a Sustainable Future*, 2nd edn, Boston: Beacon Press.

Faber, Malte, Manstetten, Reiner and Proops, John L.R. (1995) "On the Conceptual Foundations of Ecological Economics: A Teleological Approach," *Ecological Economics* 12(1).

Georgescu-Roegen, Nicholas (1971) *The Entropy Law and the Economic Process*, Cambridge, MA: Harvard University Press.

Norgaard, Richard (1994) *Development Betrayed: The End of Progress and a Coevolutionary Revisioning of the Future*, London and New York: Routledge

Pearce, David and Turner, R. Kerry (1990) *Economics of Natural Resources and the Environment*, Brighton: Harvester.

Rosewarne, Stuart (1993) "Selling the Environment: A Critique of Market Ecology," in Stuart Rees, Gordon Rodley and Frank Stilwell (eds), *Beyond the Market: Alternatives to Economic Rationalism*, London: Pluto Press.

—— (1995) "On Ecological Economics," *Capitalism, Nature, Socialism* 6(3).

STUART ROSEWARNE

environmental policy and politics

The history and context of environmental policies have been influenced by public concerns about the symptoms of a growing environmental crisis, such as pollution, climate change, loss of biodiversity and growing POPULATION density. Such symptoms have manifested themselves in a reduced QUALITY OF LIFE brought on by air pollution, water contamination, nuclear fallout, oil spills and nuclear, chemical and toxic waste. Questions arise concerning the consequences of the overexploitation of natural resources for environmental degradation, the ethical and moral concerns for the well-being of the human and non-human world, and the struggle for alternative ways of living in the industrialized world.

The context of environmental policies in the developing countries is influenced by their colonial past and current position in the global economic system. By and large, their environmental policies are poverty driven and related to deforestation, land degradation, overcrowded housing, ill-health, inadequate drinkable water supply, food shortages and air pollution in environmentally ill-planned industries and mega-cities. In both developing and developed economies, environmental policies have some identical objectives, for example, to govern, regulate and control human activities and their interactions with the environment in order to optimize the use of NATURAL CAPITAL, as well as to mitigate, reduce or eliminate environmental hazards and pollutants.

Prior to the 1970s, environmental policies were subsumed under a host of public policies dealing with specific sectors (agriculture, forestry, fishery, water management and so on), including measures to regulate industry and transport, to control POLLUTION, manage and dispose waste and hazardous chemicals, and so on. Today, environmental policies have become increasingly cross-sectoral, and integrated economic, social and environmental policies have been built into SUSTAINABLE DEVELOPMENT strategies (Tolba and El Kholy 1992). Anticipatory and preventive environmental policies are more common policy instruments than reactive policies.

Five main principles

Today, environmental policies are often built around some combination of five main principles (Opschoor and Turner 1994: 4):

- The "polluter pays" principle: i.e. the polluters pay the cost of meeting socially acceptable environmental quality standards.
- The prevention or precautionary principle: this explicitly recognizes the existence of uncertainty (environmental and social) and seeks to avoid irreversible damages through the imposition of a safety margin into policy; it also seeks to prevent waste generation at the source, as well as retaining some end-of-pipe measures.
- The economic efficiency/cost effectiveness principle: this applies both to the setting of standards and the design of the policy instruments for attaining them.
- The decentralization principle: to assign environmental decisions and enforcement to the lowest level of government capable of handling it, without significant residual externalities.
- The legal efficiency principle: this seeks to preclude the passage of regulations that cannot realistically be enforced.

Laws, instruments and institutions

The principles of environmental policies are operationalized through laws or legal instruments, fiscal instruments and institutions. Strategically or ideally, environmental policy laws, instruments and institutions aim at sustainable development and resource management for better environmental quality control. Environmental laws are concerned with regulating activities that have the potential to cause environmental hazards. They relate to the authorization of discharges to the environment, the containment of toxic substances, setting standards, and the licensing of emission levels and manufactured products. Regional and national environmental laws are increasingly influenced (since the late 1970s) by global environmental forums, negotiations, conventions, treaties and declarations, and the emergence of the concept of "global environmental governance" (Commission on Global Governance 1995).

Fiscal instruments include aggregate abatement costs, emission charges and tradable permits, which can be an effective means of promoting environmental quality control. Examples of socioeconomic incentives include subsidies, affordable and efficient public transport, incentive charges on emissions, demarcated bicycle tracks and walk paths. EIAs attempt to scrutinize the impact of economic projects on the environment (see Hanley and Spash 1994. All these instruments should be seen within the framework of cost-effectiveness, administrative costs and distributional impacts (Lohman 1994: 58–62).

Environmental policy institutions are often divided into national, provincial, district and local/village levels. Since the late 1970s, most countries have established environment ministries, environmental training, information and research institutions, environmental regulation and quality control institutions. Some of these institutions operate as coordinating bodies working with the public and private sectors through environmental action plans and conservation strategies. There are also self-regulating industries and business interests linked to environmentally compatible technologies.

Not all environmental quality control and environmental regulation institutions are governmental. National and transnational non-governmental organizations (NGOs), environmental pressure groups, environmental social movements, grassroots and citizen organizations provide effective environmental institutions. Non-governmental institutions plus citizen and grassroots organizations lobby, monitor, alert and pressure governments, business and industry to improve on their environmental practices or abandon environmentally damaging policies.

Sustainable development

Globally, international environmental policies have adopted sustainable development as a global objective, reinforced by the Rio Declaration and Agenda 21 in 1992, Environmental Perspective to the Year 2000 (1990) and more than 100 environmental conventions, treaties and declarations. The strategic imperative of sustainable development policies (WCED 1987: 49) includes: (1) reviving growth, (2) improving the quality of growth, (3) meeting essential needs for jobs, food, energy, water and sanitation, (4) ensuring a sustainable level of population, (5) conserving and enhancing the resource base, (6) reorienting technology and managing risk, and (7) merging the environment and economics in decision making.

Despite its noble endeavor, the notion of sustainable development has been contested by various environmental actors in the South and the North. Some Southern states and intellectuals portray sustainable development as a neo-colonial tool devised by the North to deny the South the right to development. They argue (Agarwal and Narian 1991) that since the North is responsible for most of the environmental damage caused so far, it should also be responsible for the cost of the sustainability and maintenance of the global environment. According to this school, the North has exceeded its own waste assimilative capacity, that is, the ability of the environmental life support systems, including the global commons, to accept wastes and render them harmless.

The problem is politically prompted by the question as to how to regulate the use of the global commons (seas, oceans, the atmosphere), which have historically existed as a free-access common property for the disposal of wastes unequally produced at the global level. Global environmental policies are contested on a similar basis to those on which national environmental policies are contested. That is, in terms of losers and beneficiaries from a given environmental policy orientation and the nature and consequences of the instruments used. Environmental policy instruments impact differently on different economic, social and political interests and activities. Hence, environmental policies are not politically neutral.

Free market environmentalism

Sustainable development policies are described by Eckersley (1995) as an extension to free market environmentalism which defends decentralized private choice of the market as a superior economic management system to the command and control approach. Eckersley (1995: 15) also argues that, "Free market environmentalism shares two common features with the ethos of sustainable development and structural economic policy reforms: (i) deregulation, free trade and the liberalization of the economy, and (ii) a reduction of state intervention and the liberalization of market forces."

Free market environmentalism is consistent with the current drive toward globalization and regionalization, including the emergence of competitive regional trading blocs (EEC, NAFTA, ASEAN and so on). It is criticized by more "progressive" environmentalists on the basis that its ethos may encourage excessive use of natural resources for economic growth, without due consideration to environmental destruction. This is particularly true for developing countries, which depend on primary commodity production for export because that is where their comparative advantage lies. Economic competition, according to devout environmentalists, may create political tensions between poor and rich as well as between the dominant trading blocs, if international environment policies and laws affect trade competitiveness of certain states or regions.

Tension and conflict

Environmental policies cause conflict between diverse users in the same nation, as well as interstate and regional economic bloc tensions. International environmental conflicts – interstate and regional tensions over the fulfillment or evasion of their international obligations to sustainable development as a global ideal – could result in far-reaching environmental security problems. Martinez-Alier (1991: 134–5) asserts that "the politics of environmental policies is a direct consequence of the shift of environmental costs or benefits to other social groups (national or foreign), or to future generations... as such politics determines not only environmental policy, but also the environmental agenda." The instruments used to settle these conflicts include legal instruments (international environmental law) and environmental diplomacy (environmental forums and negotiations). In short, like other public policies, environmental policies (local, national, regional or international) have a differential effect on people's welfare, employment opportunities, incomes, national interests and market competitiveness *vis-à-vis* other nations and states.

See also:

cost-benefit analysis; ecological feminism; environmental and ecological political economy: major contemporary themes; Green Party

Selected references

Agarwal, A. and Narian, S. (1991) *Global Warming in an Unequal World: A Case Study of Environmental Colonialism*, Delhi: Centre for Science and Environment.

Commission on Global Governance (1995) *Our Global Neighbourhood, Report of the Commission on Global Governance*, Oxford: Oxford University Press.

Eckersley, R. (1995) *Markets, States and the Environment: Towards Integration*, Basingstoke and London: Macmillan.

Hanley, Nick, and Spash, Clive L. (1994) *Cost-Benefit Analysis and the Environment*, Aldershot: Edward Edgar.

Lohman, Lex de Savorinin (1994) "Economic Incentives in Environmental Policy: Why are They White Ravens?" in J.P. Opschoor and R.K. Turner (eds), *Economic Incentives and Environmental Policies: Principles and Practice*, Boston and London: Kluwer Academic Publishers.

Martinez-Alier, J. (1991) "Ecological Perception and Distributional Conflict," in F.J. Dietz, F. van der Ploeg and J. van der Straaten (eds), *Environmental Policy and the Economy*, Amsterdam: North Holland.

Opschoor, J.B. and Turner, R.K. (1994) "Environmental Economics and Environmental Policy Incentives: Introduction and Overview," in J.P. Opschoor and R.K. Turner (eds), *Economic Incentives and Environmental Policies: Principles and Practice*, Boston and London: Kluwer Academic Publishers.

Tolba, M.K. and El Kholy, Osama (1992) *The World Environment 1972–1992: Two Decades for Challenge*, London and Glasgow: Chapman Hall for United Nations Environmental Programme.

WCED (1987) *Our Common Future*, Oxford: Oxford University Press.

M.A. MOHAMED SALIH

environmental valuation

At least since Alfred Marshall's *Principles of Economics* (1890), economists have been concerned that market prices present distorted signals to buyers and sellers because environmental services are not adequately included in the valuation. Factories can dump waste into the air without having to compensate others for the costs of POLLUTION. A.C. Pigou made "external costs" a central concern in his *The Economics of Welfare* (1932). K.W. Kapp argued that aggregate measures of economic performance and "progress", such as gross domestic product, were greatly distorted, in his *The Social Costs of Private Enterprise* (1950). With the rise of environmental concerns since the 1970s, amplified by the concern for the sustainability of development since the 1980s, there has been considerable interest in valuing the services of the environment. Market distortions can be reduced by including pollution costs in market prices through environmental taxes, and public decision making can be improved by including environmental values in cost–benefit analyses. Since the 1970s, both pollution taxes and environmental valuation in cost–benefit analyses have been used by national governments. During the 1990s, it became the policy of the World Bank and other international development organizations to undertake environmental valuation as systematically as possible.

Neoclassical economists have developed a variety of methods for putting monetary values on environmental services. Environmental valuation can justify important environmental measures, correct how the market works, and provide interesting insights. However, these methods have severe limitations which must be well understood.

Valuation methods

The methods used vary with the environmental issue. Frequently, values can be derived from how environmental services enter into the production of a good. Taking health as an example of a good, consider an air pollutant which causes known reductions in health, the costs of which can be calculated in terms of avoidance costs (expenditures on air cleaners, for example, by those receiving the pollutant), lost work time due to illness, and medical expenses. The value of reducing this source of air pollution would thus be at least equal to the reduction in these avoidance costs. The value of reducing air pollution is, in fact, greater than the reduction in avoidance costs, because of the annoyance of being sick and the inconvenience of having to avoid the pollutant, to say nothing of the discomfort to oneself and one's relatives of perhaps dying early. Though typically understood as minimal estimates, valuations based on the direct economic effects of pollution frequently turn out to be surprisingly high (Hanley and Spash 1993: ch. 6).

The environmental value of a scenic lake might be captured by comparing sites with different environmental characteristics. Such a "hedonic" approach might compare the values of second home properties that are adjacent to a scenic lake with those of second homes that effectively provide no access to a scenic lake, while controlling for other factors. This approach has been used to derive the cost of urban air pollution, access to parks, airport noise, earthquake risk and other environmental factors (Hanley and Spash 1993: ch. 4).

The travel cost method has been effectively used for deriving the value of recreation resources. By comparing the frequency of park visits, controlled for population level and other factors, of people at different distances (travel costs) from the recreation site, it is possible to derive a demand curve for the site. This approach assumes that, with the additional costs of a fee added on to travel costs, the frequency of visitors from each area would equal the frequency of the participants from the area with the equivalent travel costs prior to the fee. A demand curve for recreation is derived by summing the absolute participation from each area at each fee level (Hanley and Spash 1993: ch. 5).

Contingent valuation is an increasingly popular valuation method in which people are asked, within a structured interview process, how much they would be willing to pay in order to protect an environmental service. This technique has been used to value what people would have been willing to pay to protect wilderness areas, prevent oil spills such as that from the Exxon Valdez tanker off Alaska, and reduce the haze from particulates over the Grand Canyon (Hanley and Spash 1993: ch. 3).

Methodological problems in valuation

While the techniques for environmental valuation can provide critical information, frequently more than enough to justify significantly greater environmental protection measures, there are some serious methodological problems.

- *Information*. Each of the foregoing techniques presumes that people are informed about the environmental issues. But if those being exposed to an air pollutant, for example, do not know the risks of the pollutant, they will probably not spend enough on avoidance costs and, as a result, end up loosing more work time and incurring greater medical expenses. The environmental valuation, in this case, would indicate that the value of reducing the pollutant is greater than it would have been had people taken appropriate steps to avoid it in the first place. Similarly, the hedonic method would not be appropriate for valuing the effect of being located near a toxic waste site unless people knew of the dangers. In the case of contingent valuation, the researcher typically develops a statement describing the environmental issue to inform the subject before the interview. The information and choice of words used in such a statement strongly influence the subject's responses. The complexity of most environmental issues and the fact that scientists are constantly discovering new relationships between people and their environment make information assumptions especially critical.

- *Preferences*. While economists implicitly assume that preferences are somehow innate rather than socially acquired, it is absurd to argue that people have a prior preference for species not yet discovered or for things represented by abstract, socially constructed concepts such as biodiversity. Clearly, we develop preferences for such various things as environments with fewer toxic elements, hiking in the woods, and biodiversity as we learn more about them. For this reason, their values cannot be derived correctly for we are, or could be, constantly learning more. Critics of environmental protection measures similarly use this line of reasoning to argue, for example, that since future generations are likely to learn to enjoy representations of nature in cyberspace, there is little reason to protect much real nature now.
- *Separability*. The economic model assumes that goods and services are discrete units that can be bought and sold by individuals. Environmental services are not "naturally" in the market system to a large extent because they are not separable. One cannot enjoy smog-free vistas alone without others enjoying them as well. Many environmental phenomena are open access or public goods which require collective management to attain efficient amounts. Under these circumstances, an individual who is asked how much he or she would be willing to pay to protect an environmental service can only rationally respond that it depends on how much others would pay. Separability has another dimension as well. Separate nonnoxious pollutants can combine in the environment to form noxious pollutants. The smog of Los Angeles results from the interaction of different compounds. The environmental costs of any one of them depend on the existence of the others.
- *Distributional considerations*. The biggest difficulty with environmental valuation centers on who has the rights to environmental services. If environmental problems are serious, then the income from owning environmental rights makes a difference. When subjects in contingent valuation analyses are asked how much they would be willing to accept (WTA) to allow an environmental service to be degraded, they give one answer, an answer that assumes they have the right to the services and are being asked to sell it. When asked how much they are willing to pay (WTP) to protect an environmental service, which assumes they do not have the right and must purchase it, they give another answer. The two answers typically differ by a factor of three (Hanley and Spash 1993: ch. 3).

Howarth and Norgaard (1992) have shown that the efficient allocation of resources over time, including environmental services, depends on how rights are assigned between generations. If future generations are given the right to a world not threatened by human-induced climatic change, then the economic cost of greenhouse gases is greater than when future generations have no such rights.

Current environmental valuation techniques put the costs of pollution in poor neighborhoods or countries at less than the same amount of pollution in their richer counterparts. American Indians are willing to accept nuclear power plant and other wastes which richer communities shun. A World Bank official argued in 1992 that dirty industries should move to poor countries because the value of life is lower where the wages are lower (*The Economist* 1992).

The distributional concerns of environmental valuation demonstrate that economics is rarely simply a matter of efficiency. Inevitably, policy questions entail matters of economic and human RIGHTS which determine which solutions are efficient and thereby how things are valued economically. Environmental valuation will not lead to the world we will want to live in when it is too simply based on the world we do live in.

See also:

cost–benefit analysis; environmental policy and politics; Green Party; gross domestic product and net social welfare; quality of life

Selected references

The Economist (1992) "Let Them Eat Pollution," 8–14 February: 66.
Hanley, Nick and Spash, Clive L. (1993) *Cost–Benefit Analysis and the Environment*, Aldershot: Edward Elgar.
Howarth, Richard B.and Norgaard, Richard B. (1992) "Environmental Valuation under Sustainable Development," *American Economic Review* 82(2): 473–7.
Kapp, K. William (1950) *The Social Costs of Private Enterprise*, Cambridge, MA: Harvard University Press.
Marshall, Alfred (1890) *Principles of Economics*, London: Macmillan.
Pigou, A.C. (1932) *The Economics of Welfare*, 4th edn, London: Macmillan.

RICHARD B. NORGAARD

equilibrium, disequilibrium and non-equilibrium

The purpose of microeconomics is to investigate how the actions of independent agents, in a decentralized economy, can be socially compatible. This problem is that of the "invisible hand" of Adam Smith, also known as "coordination." The concept of equilibrium has been devised to account for the situation in which this coordination is accomplished.

It is possible to distinguish between two broad conceptions of equilibrium, depending on its relationship to disequilibrium. In a first definition, equilibrium is defined independently of disequilibrium; this view can be called *ex ante*. In a second view, equilibrium and disequilibrium are tightly interconnected.

Ex ante equilibrium

In the first conception, that of *ex ante* equilibrium, equilibrium describes a situation in which the plans of all economic agents are immediately compatible (supply equals demand in every market) and there is no inducement to change, since each agent maximizes its objective function.

The archetypical example is Walrasian equilibrium (Walras 1873), where equilibrium prices are given *ex ante* in all markets; agents know that it will be possible to buy or sell any quantity of any good, without rationing, at such prices. It is possible to show that, under conventional assumptions, such an equilibrium exists (there is no inconsistency in its definition). Disequilibrium has no role in this model and no disequilibrium process can be responsible for the convergence of variables toward their equilibrium values (see GRAVITATION AND CONVERGENCE).

It had been thought until recently that Walrasian tatonnement was such a process.

Usually the tatonnement process is seen as one in which historical TIME plays no role, dynamic adjustments are absent, and any exogenous shocks are equilibrated in the presence of a costless auctioneer, who ensures that economic agents have sufficient information concerning prices and quantities before trading. However, this mechanism of tatonnement toward *ex ante* equilibrium has been criticized in two respects. First, tatonnement does not necessarily converge if specific assumptions are not made concerning demand functions. Second, and more importantly, the tatonnement mechanism lacks realism. It is a centralized mechanism and must be performed prior to any actual transactions. It is a pure exchange of information between agents and a mythical auctioneer (see Vickers 1975). The project of making tatonnement more realistic has been abandoned by the mainstream.

Walrasian equilibrium is the simplest of a broad variety of equilibria, such as:

- temporary equilibrium, where some or all future markets are closed (Grandmont 1977);
- equilibrium with fixed prices, called in a rather misleading fashion "disequilibrium," where the equality between supply and demand is obtained by adjusting supply to demand (Benassy 1982);
- equilibrium with monopolistic competition, where products are differentiated depending on their producer (Chamberlin 1933);
- GAME THEORY equilibrium, where agents consider the effects of their own conduct on that of others; and
- general equilibrium with rational expectations, where agents do not necessarily know the value of all variables (due to the existence of random shocks), but they do know their law of distribution, as well as the model of the economy and the value of initial endowments. This variety is important, since it is the common orthodox reference of both new Keynesian and new classical economists.

Criticisms of *ex ante* equilibrium

Although this *ex ante* conception of equilibrium is now dominant, it is subject to several criticisms. First, let us consider criticisms deriving from the mainstream. One difficulty relates to the possible existence of multiple equilibria in the same model. Since equilibrium prices are determined *ex ante*, prior to transactions, what will happen if several equilibria exist? A second difficulty relates to complex dynamics, in particular, chaotic trajectories in intertemporal models. If such trajectories exist, the slightest uncertainty concerning initial conditions, or in the model itself, will have considerable consequences and the future will be impossible to forecast (see CHAOS THEORY). Third, the ability of economic agents to compute equilibrium trajectories is problematic. These trajectories are already very difficult to determine within theoretical models which provide a highly simplified view of the real economy.

A number of even more damaging criticisms have been formulated by heterodox economists. The notion of rational behavior is impossible to define in two situations: first, where decentralized agents interact within disequilibrium and with only limited information (they are ignorant of the true model of the economy, the law of distribution of variables and the characteristics of other agents); and second, in an environment subject to constant changes which are impossible to anticipate, i.e. confronting "radical UNCERTAINTY." Rational behavior can only be defined within highly simplistic models.

These criticisms have led to three responses: (1) the dismissal of any form of microeconomics and equilibrium by a majority of heterodox economists; (2) attempts to frame alternative microeconomics (different approaches to behaviors, and distinct definitions of equilibrium); and (3) a mixed attitude, the description of behaviors combined with the rejection of equilibrium (only trajectories are relevant).

Disequilibrium microeconomics

A number of these approaches can be described as disequilibrium microeconomics (in sharp contrast to mainstream microeconomics). A common property shared by these approaches is the notion that economic agents are not "rational" in the neoclassical sense of the term, but only manifest a "limited" or "bounded" rationality. This concept was set forth by Herbert Simon (1982). He and his followers tried to derive a theory of economic behavior from management, psychology and other sciences. Important in this respect is evolutionary economics, which borrows its concepts from biology. Here, economic agents are assumed to act according to rules and routines; a certain order prevails in the economy as a result of the selection which occurs in the market, an *ex post* process. Much work has been done along these lines concerning, for example, technical change (technical trajectories).

Adjustment defines another approach, one well adapted to the existence of disequilibrium. Agents not only act outside of equilibrium, but react to the observation of disequilibria. This includes differences between supply and demand (inventories of unsold commodities), disequilibria on capacity utilization rates, profit rate differentials among industries and so on. For example, if supply is larger than demand, a firm will diminish its price or output, or both; a rate of profit that is larger in one industry than in another will encourage capitalists to invest more in the first industry. This was the point of view of CLASSICAL POLITICAL ECONOMY, as seen in the works of Adam Smith, David Ricardo and Karl MARX. This framework of analysis has been applied to classical long-term equilibrium (with prices of production). It is also relevant in the analysis of short-term Keynesian equilibria.

A consideration of disequilibrium implies the existence of a money and credit economy where income streams and expenses do not coincide a priori. Purchasing power, under monetary form, is transferred from one economic agent to another. For example, firms distribute dividends, and the corresponding flows are not necessarily equal to profits. Households or firms hold money balances which are redistributed at each period. Money that is issued by the banking system constantly modifies this pattern. Once these disequilibrium processes have been described, one must build a model in which the interaction of many such behaviors can be studied. (See Vickers (1995) for a non-equilibrium framework.)

The natural framework of disequilibrium economics is that of *dynamic systems*. In such models, the combined effects of individual behaviors can be summarized as a recursive relationship. Here, the value of the variables at one period can be derived from their value at the previous period (or a differential equation in continuous time). This is where the diverging viewpoints mentioned above become relevant. Some analyses focus on disequilibrium trajectories, others on equilibrium – the representation of a form of order built in the system. Mathematically, the parallel issues are the existence of equilibrium and its stability, that is, the ability of a set of values of variables to converge, period after period, to an equilibrium. This convergence is synonymous with the success of coordination. If (exogenous or endogenous) shocks are introduced in a model in which a stable equilibrium exists, convergence is transformed into a process of gravitation.

Stability does not always obtain, but is subject to certain conditions. The degree of reaction to disequilibrium must be sufficient, but not excessive. For example, the problem is to what extent a firm will diminish its output (its capacity utilization rate), if its supply exceeds demand by, for example, 10 percent. A certain degree of reaction is, of course, required, but an excess reaction may prohibit convergence. When stability is not ensured, more complex trajectories can prevail. Some, such as cycles around equilibrium or chaos, may be economically significant.

See also:

business cycle theories; catastrophe theory; circular and cumulative causation; evolution and coevolution; financial instability hypothesis; hysteresis; increasing returns to scale; institutional change and adjustment; knowledge, information, technology and change; money, credit and finance: major contemporary themes; path dependency; pricing; traverse

Selected references

Benassy, J.P. (1982) *The Economics of Market Disequilibrium*, New York and London: Academic Press.
Chamberlin, E.H. (1933) *The Theory of Monopolistic Competition*, Cambridge, MA: Harvard University Press.
Grandmont, J.M. (1977) "Temporary General Equilibrium Theory," *Econometrica* 45: 535–72.
Kornai, J. (1971) *Anti-Equilibrium*, Amsterdam: North Holland.
Simon, H.A. (1982) *Models of Bounded Rationality*, Cambridge, MA: MIT Press.
Vickers, Douglas (1975) "Finance and False Trading in Non-Tatonnement Trading," *Australian Economic Papers* 14(25): 171–86.
—— (1995) *The Tyranny of the Market: A Critique of Theoretical Foundations*, Ann Arbor, MI: University of Michigan Press.
Walras, L. (1873) *Elements of Pure Economics*, London: Allen & Unwin, 1954.

GÉRARD DUMÉNIL
DOMINIQUE LÉVY

equilibrium rate of unemployment

The 1970s–1990s witnessed deep recession and high unemployment in most advanced capitalist economies. Yet any suggestion that fiscal and monetary policies be used to combat unemployment immediately raises the specter of high inflation in the minds of policy makers. This is despite the fact that inflation is at historically low rates in many nations. This perceived inflationary threat receives its support in the economics literature from the idea that there is a unique "non-accelerating inflation rate of unemployment" (NAIRU), the earlier version of which was called the "natural rate of unemployment."

NAIRU and the natural rate

In short, it is asserted that there is one particular level of equilibrium unemployment at which inflation stabilizes. According to this framework, if unemployment falls below this level, inflation will rise.

This obviously rules out any aggregate demand policies which would be thought to reduce unemployment below the NAIRU. However, NAIRU itself also induces behavior by policy makers which can lead to a self-fulfilling NAIRU prophecy. Since any decline in unemployment is interpreted by the "markets" not as a piece of good news but rather as a signal that inflation will rise, this belief therefore triggers interest rate rises which tend to push unemployment back up to what therefore becomes established as the NAIRU. Further, since inflation does not rise, this is taken as proof that this is indeed a NAIRU, regardless of what might have actually happened had unemployment been allowed to fall.

Of course, NAIRU advocates may object to being cast as opponents of active anti-unemployment policies, since they would argue that the NAIRU itself can be reduced. Most of Europe had low inflation and low unemployment in the 1950s and 1960s, and this could be interpreted in terms of these countries at that time having low NAIRUs. The fact that some countries today do have both lower unemployment and lower inflation than others could likewise be interpreted as these countries having lower NAIRUs than other countries. Thus, even within the NAIRU framework, government policies such as on skill development and training can still lower the rate of unemployment by shifting the NAIRU itself. However, despite this potential role for active government policy, much of the NAIRU framework nevertheless rests on an implicit assumption that active demand management has limited long-run benefits on the unemployment front.

Problems with an equilibrium rate

This NAIRU theory is a version of Milton Friedman's natural rate of unemployment, developed in Britain by the economists Richard Layard and Stephen Nickell. They argue that, as unemployment falls, the "bargaining wage" demanded by workers rises while the "feasible wage" which employers can afford to pay does not rise with output. This failure of the wage which employers can afford to pay to rise as output rises is based on one or both of two seriously flawed arguments.

First, it is supposed that, as firms increase their level of output, PRODUCTIVITY fails to rise and may fall. In fact, the opposite is usually the case. In times of economic expansion, output per head generally rises (it increased by 20 percent in Britain between 1984 and 1990). This increase in productivity is explained by the fact that capital is operated at a higher level of utilization as demand increases and firms invest in more modern equipment with renewed prosperity. Also, there are costs to hiring and firing (including moral costs), and this too means that productivity will rise as output expands. (See VERDOORN'S LAW.)

Indeed, the HYSTERESIS and PATH DEPENDENCY literature show that skills deteriorate during bouts of unemployment; conversely, employment will enhance worker skills and productivity. Therefore, EFFECTIVE DEMAND AND CAPACITY UTILIZATION changes which induce a recession can influence the equilibrium unemployment rate in the long run by creating more long-term unemployed. This is counter to Friedman's definition of the (equilibrium) natural rate, which is unaffected by demand. If a boom were to be influenced by demand factors, this could reduce the equilibrium unemployment rate by reducing the rate of long-term unemployment.

The more reasonable assumption is, therefore, that productivity and hence the "feasible wage" increases with output, and this destroys one of the bases for the NAIRU law. In fact, of course, the NAIRU theory could incorporate a rising feasible wage, but it would still – for the theory to hold – need to be constrained to rise less rapidly than the bargaining wage.

There may be no unique equilibrium point, or one single unemployment rate, associated with NAIRU under certain conditions. These conditions are that increased capacity utilization and, over the longer term, an increased and more technologically advanced capacity allows for growth of the feasible wage which is as great or greater than any growth in the bargaining wage. It is possible for unemployment and inflation to both decline when NAIRU conditions do not hold.

Wages and unemployment

The second string to the NAIRU bow is the argument that firms have to cut prices in order to sell more. By enabling firms to lower prices, cuts in wages and other employment costs allow them to sell more and increase employment. However, the size of the market of a firm (and hence the employment it can offer) is determined by its price *and* the price of its competitors. If the workers employed by that firm accept a lower wage, so that the firm can retain its monopoly profits at a lower price, it will be able to increase its output and its market share. However, this obtains only at the expense of other firms and the employment they offer. If all firms lower their wages, there will be no change in relative prices and no increase in demand. In fact, if this happens, the chances are that demand will decline because a general fall in wages relative to prices will have reduced the purchasing power of wage income.

The crux of the new NAIRU orthodoxy is that there is a trade-off between wages and employment. Thus Layard *et al.* ask: "Why do firms not drop their wages, so that it becomes worthwhile for them to employ the extra workers?" (1991: 11). The point, however, is that employers will tend to hire the number of workers required to produce the goods demanded, and so will not necessarily employ more just because the wage declines.

These two opposing views of the world go back to before Keynes's *General Theory*, but it was from this publication that the broadly Keynesian view – that employment was determined by output, and that output was determined by demand – came to be established in opposition to, and by the 1950s and 1960s in place of, the previous "Treasury" view. This latter view held that relative prices were the determining factor, with wage levels determining employment and this then determining output levels (Michie 1987).

Michie and Wilkinson (1992) plotted the relationship between unemployment and wages for Britain in the 1980s using changes in earnings variously measured. The results obtained could not have been more at variance with the notion of a predictable relationship between the two variables. The historical evidence for any credible relationship between the level of joblessness and the rate of inflation, or rate of change of wages, is fragile at best.

Productivity and employment

Finally, on the above points regarding productivity levels and ECONOMIC GROWTH rates, Layard *et al.* do acknowledge that their argument is being made with the assumption of "given productivity" (1991: 13). However, their analysis is then developed largely with this assumption remaining as a given. But the rate of productivity growth is, first, not given, and second, is one of the more important influences on inflation, real wages, competitiveness, output growth and employment.

Fundamentally, the reason there is no simple – or even one-way – trade-off between wages and employment is that they are not each other's sole determinant; in fact, far from it. One of the key determinants of both wage levels and employment growth is productivity growth. Successful economies will tend to have relatively high rates of productivity growth which allow, first, a relatively high proportion of input cost increases to be absorbed, with a correspondingly lower level of inflation passed on; and second, a relatively competitive economy with growing markets, output and employment. The rate of growth of real wages need play no necessary role, but in such a scenario it might be expected to be linked positively with employment.

See also:

balance of payments constraint; efficiency wages; increasing returns to scale; Kaldor's theory of the growth process; Okun's Law; reserve army of labor; unemployment and underemployment; unemployment: policies to reduce

Selected references

Layard, R., Nickell, S. and Jackman, R. (1991) *Unemployment, Macroeconomic Performance and the Labour Market*, Oxford: Oxford University Press.

Michie, J. (1987) *Wages in the Business Cycle: An Empirical and Methodological Analysis*, London and New York: Frances Pinter Publishers and Columbia University Press.

Michie, J. and Wilkinson, F. (1992) "Inflation Policy and the Restructuring of Labour Markets," in J. Michie (ed.), *The Economic Legacy: 1979–1992*, London: Academic Press.

JONATHAN MICHIE

ethics and morality

There are three ways in which ethics is important for political economy. First, economists have ethical values that help shape the way they do political economy. This builds into economic theory a particular view of how the economy does work and how it should work. Second, economic actors (consumers, workers, business owners) have moral values that help shape their behavior. Third, economic policies, INSTITUTIONS AND HABITS impact people differentially and, thus, ethical evaluations as well as economic evaluations are needed. That is, the economists' measuring rod of efficiency is insufficient by itself to evaluate policies.

Values of economic actors

Economists recently have been thinking through the implications of one of Adam Smith's key insights, namely that self-interest leads to the common good if there is sufficient competition and if most people in society have internalized a general moral law as a guide for their behavior (see Hirsch 1978; Evensky 1993). Smith believed most people, most of the time, did act within the guidelines of an internalized moral law and that those who didn't could be dealt with by the police power of the state.

One result of this rethinking is an argument by some economists that (1) people act on the basis of embodied moral values as well as from self-interest, and (2) the economy needs that ethical behavior to be efficient. The source or origin of moral values is a matter of dispute. They might be derived from a deontological position provided by religious belief or philosophic principles (see DEONTOLOGY), or from the individual having been taught to observe consequentialist norms. But this is for the philosophers to sort out.

Daniel Hausman and Michael McPherson in *Economic Analysis and Moral Philosophy*, published in 1996, recount an experiment in which wallets containing cash and identification were left in the streets of New York. Nearly half were returned to their owners intact, despite the trouble and expense for their discoverers of doing so. The effort expended and the apparently unselfish behavior demonstrated by those who returned the lost goods may, as Hausman and McPherson assert, reflect a manifest commitment to societal norms over egoistic desires. Many researchers have found the same phenomena (Dawes and Thaler 1988; Elster 1990; Frank 1988).

It is not solely for the sake of accuracy that political economists pay attention to evidence that human actions are guided by concerns not solely self-interested, but also because there are real economic consequences. Self-interest in a competitive environment is not sufficient to yield the common good. Pushed to its logical extreme, individual self-interest suggests that it would usually be in the interest of an individual to evade the rules by which other players are guided.

Under conditions of interdependence and imperfect information, rational self-interest frequently leads to socially irrational results unless that self-interest is constrained by an internalized moral code. A classic example is the situation where both the employer and worker suspect that the other cannot be trusted to honor their explicit or implicit contract. For example, the employer thinks the worker will take too many coffee breaks, spend too much time talking with other workers and generally work less than the employer thinks is owed. The worker, on the other hand, thinks the employer will try to speed up the pace of work, fire him or her unjustly if given the chance, and generally behave arbitrarily. When this is the case, the worker may tend to shirk and the employer will increase supervision to stop the expected shirking. If the workers would supervise themselves, production costs would be lower. Thus, this distrust between employer and workers reduces efficiency.

What constrains individuals from seeking solely their self-interest? One answer is that our tendency to maximize our material welfare at the expense of others is inhibited by a deeply ingrained set of moral values. There are a number of approaches used to formally represent the relation between moral values and the standard utility framework of economic theory. We must distinguish between altruistic desires and moral norms, the former being more readily incorporated into an individual's utility function. The latter might better be modeled as metapreferences or conceived of as constraints on maximization. There are difficulties with each of these approaches, which leaves the subject unsettled.

One approach to formally incorporating moral values is to treat them as preferences comparable to preferences for goods and services. An individual's compliance with a moral norm generates a sense of satisfaction adding to the agent's welfare. Concurrently, defying a norm held as important creates disutility for the individual. This formulation appears more appropriate in modeling altruistic behavior, such as purchasing a gift for one's child, than it does for an ethical norm, such as honesty, or a commitment, such as duty.

In *On Ethics and Economics* in 1987, Amartya Sen has proposed an approach in which rational individuals would have both metapreferences and ordinary preferences. Moral values regarding fairness, liberty and honesty among others make up the metapreference function, and this in turn shapes the ordering of ordinary preferences. So, for example, a person who has a strong preference to consume grapes does not buy any because of a commitment to justice for farm workers. This approach is also helpful in capturing in formal terms the internal conflict surrounding such personal choices as whether or not to smoke. An individual may simultaneously desire a cigarette (ordinary preference) and desire not to smoke in the first place (metapreference). Lutz and Lux speak of lexicographic utility functions to indicate formally that not all preferences are on the same level; for example, apples trade for oranges but not for liberty or honesty (Lutz and Lux 1979; see also Etzioni 1988).

Rather than conceiving ethical values to be preferences included among others in a standard utility function, or as metapreferences guiding the preference rankings of common goods, norms might also be seen as constraints on choices (see Etzioni 1988). As in a budget constraint, norms could be seen as externally imposing (presumably from the conscience or superego) limits on available choices. However, unlike their fiscal counterpart, norms may be violated; therefore, the limits they impose are not rigid. Also, attempts to distinguish norms-as-constraints from norms-as-preferences is often a muddy task.

Economic policies and ethical outcomes

Mainstream economics attempts to measure economic success by a policy's ability to satisfy individual consumers' preferences. This raises several important issues (see Cowen 1993). Welfare economics downplays issues of DISTRIBUTION OF INCOME to varying degrees, depending on the proposed criteria for policy making. Sometimes it is argued that only those policy changes should be made that represent Pareto improvements. However, the Pareto Rule is of limited use for policy evaluation. Since interpersonal comparisons of utility are ruled out, the only thing that can be said is that a policy which benefits someone without hurting anyone is an unambiguous gain for society. Because this type of policy is almost never possible, economists have been forced to fall back on the concept of potential Pareto improvements, for instance, in cost–benefit analysis. This is where winners gain more than losers lose and therefore, potentially, are able to make compensation so that no one loses.

Compensation schemes are very difficult to design, however, because it is so hard to identify the winners and losers. If the losers are not compensated by the winners then interpersonal comparisons of utility have been made, violating the foundational position of welfare economics. One uncomfortable result is the possibility that a few rich people gain more than many poor people lose, and the outcome is applauded. The end result is that the ethical guideline becomes a straightforward consequentialist utilitarianism. One possible definition of consequentialism is the belief that the morally relevant features of an action are its consequences, the events which result from it. Potential Pareto optimality is a special case of consequentialism, because it restricts its attention to one particular set of consequences, the effects on the utility of agents (in practice, income becomes a proxy for utility). However, it is widely recognized by moral philosophers that a wide variety of potentially important considerations are inappropriately excluded by consequentialism. Here we note only one: agent-centered restrictions.

The importance of agent-centered restrictions can be seen in the means–ends controversy. First, focusing only on the consequences ignores the fact that the means used might be morally unacceptable. A reduction of consumer goods prices by the use of child labor cannot be evaluated only by looking at consequences. Also, arguing that the consequences will be the same whether the agent acts or not does not justify the agent's actions. For example, in the mid-1980s many colleges and universities were considering divesting their portfolios of securities of companies that did business in South Africa. Many economists argued that this well-intentioned effort would be ineffectual, since other investors from around the world would provide any needed capital. This argument clearly neglected the possible relevance of agent-centered restrictions. Some have argued that the consequentialist ethic of economic theory needs to be replaced with a deontological ethic that focuses on the means not the outcomes (Etzioni 1988).

Another kind of problem overlooked by the focus on individual preference satisfaction concerns what Anderson has called the social conditions of delivery of a good (Anderson 1993: ch. 7). Mainstream economists look at the economy as instrumental for obtaining other goods, such as utility. Thus, for example, one can evaluate the desirability of free market arrangements by examining their impact on the utility of individual agents. The market itself, in this view, has no intrinsic value or dis-value; but in some cases this may be an erroneous assumption. There may be cases in which agents have a preference, not just for certain commodities, but over whether those commodities are provided by a market or by some other means.

The supply of blood provides a clear illustration of the issue (see Titmus 1970). A person is not born with a complete set of ready-made values; rather, the individual's values are socially constructed, however imperfectly, through being a part of a family, a church, a school and a particular society. If these groups expect and urge people to give their blood as an obligation of being members of the group, then that obligation becomes internalized as a moral value. Blood drives held in schools, churches, and in Red Cross facilities reinforce that sense of obligation. If commercial blood increases, the need for blood drives declines. Thus, the traditional reinforcement of that sense of obligation declines with the result that the embodied moral value atrophies. In addition, the fact that you can sell your blood creates an opportunity cost of donating it free. Finally, there is an information problem. As blood drives decline it is rational for an individual to assume that there is no need for donated blood.

The commercialization of blood giving produces a system with many shortcomings. A few of these shortcomings are the repression of expressions of altruism, increases in the danger of unethical behavior in certain areas of medicine, worsened relationships between doctor and patient, and shifts in the supply of blood from the rich to the poor. Furthermore, the commercialized blood market is more likely to distribute contaminated blood than voluntary systems. It is noteworthy that, since the AIDS crisis started in the United States, physicians regularly recommend that patients scheduled for non-emergency surgery donate their own blood in advance.

The final outcome is that a typical person must overcome imperfect information, opportunity costs and a lack of social approbation to be able to choose to donate blood. In effect, the growth of a market in blood destroys what may be a preferred system, namely, volunteerism. Another example is commercial surrogate motherhood. Anderson argues that this practice of putting motherhood on the market in effect treats children as commodities, with possibly baleful psychological effects on both the parents and the children. Such arguments counter the notion that we can determine whether the market is best simply by checking to see if it allocates goods efficiently; the market itself may be the object of preferences and norms, which must be taken into account.

Another problem of individual preference satisfaction arises when preferences are in some way based on error. Desires can spring from erroneous belief, a sense of resignation, acculturation that leads to the repression of actual needs, or a lack of information. Mainstream economists attempt to come to grips with only the last of these. They claim that it is paternalistic to argue that people make wrong choices. However, they are beginning to understand that the appeal to individual preferences has its limits. It begs the question of how these preferences are formed and it also sidesteps the reality that preferences are dependent on unreliable beliefs. People may believe that a new steel mill won't hurt the health of those downwind but if they are mistaken should their preferences still guide policy? Finally, there is a gap between what I prefer and what I actually do. I prefer not to smoke but my addiction leads me to buy cigarettes anyway. The question must be dealt with: should individually and socially undesirable preferences guide policy decisions?

See also:

business ethics; Gandhian political economy; holistic method; human dignity; humanistic economics; justice; rights; social economics: major contemporary themes; social and organizational capital; value judgments and world views

Selected references

Anderson, Elizabeth (1993) *Value in Ethics and Economics*, Cambridge, MA: Harvard University Press.

Cowen, Tyler (1993) "The Scope and Limit of Preference Sovereignty," *Economics and Philosophy* 9(2): 253–69.

Dawes, Robyn M. and Thaler, Richard H. (1988) "Cooperation," *Journal of Economic Perspectives* 2(3): 187–97.

Elster, Jon (1990) "Selfishness and Altruism," in Jane J. Mansbridge (ed.), *Beyond Self-Interest*, Chicago: University of Chicago Press.

Etzioni, Amitai (1988) *The Moral Dimension: Toward a New Economics*, New York: Free Press.

Evensky, Jerry (1993) "Ethics and the Invisible Hand," *Journal of Economic Perspectives* 7(2): 197–205.

Frank, Robert H. (1988) *Passions Within Reason: The Strategic Role of the Emotions*, New York: W.W. Norton.

Hausman, Daniel and Mc Pherson, Michael (1996) *Economic Analysis and Moral Philosophy*, Cambridge: Cambridge University Press.

Hirsch, Fred (1978) *Social Limits to Growth*, Cambridge, MA: Harvard University Press.

Lutz, Mark A. and Lux, Kenneth (1979) *The Challenge of Humanistic Economics*, Menlo Park, CA: Benjamin/Cummings Publishing Co.

Sen, Amartya (1987) *On Ethics and Economics*, Oxford: Basil Blackwell.

Titmus, Richard M. (1970) *The Gift Relationship: From Human Blood to Social Policy*, London: Allen & Unwin.

CHARLES K. WILBER

European Association for Evolutionary Political Economy (EAEPE)

EAEPE originates from a meeting at a conference in Grim's Dyke, London, on 29 June 1988. The main purpose in forming the association was to promote evolutionary, dynamic and realistic approaches to economic theory and policy. Instead of the over-formalistic and often empty theorizing of orthodox economics, the aim was to bring together the ideas of a number of theorists and theoretical traditions, and to help to develop a more realistic and adequate approach to theory and policy.

The formal round-table meeting of the association was at its first annual conference at Keswick in Cumbria, UK, on 19–22 September 1989. The EAEPE Constitution was adopted, leading to the election of a Council. The association published the first issue of its twice-yearly newsletter in January 1989.

In November 1990 the association formed a charity, the Foundation for European Economic Development. This is formally registered under the Charities Act (England and Wales) and helps with financial assistance for the EAEPE conference and other EAEPE projects. With the kind cooperation of the Kapp Foundation and the Myrdal Foundation, the association runs two annual competitions, each with a prize of £1,000.

In 1991, the EAEPE adopted a Scientific Development Plan for the Association. This designates a number of priority research areas and involves the appointment of research area coordinators. Also, in collaboration with Edward Elgar Publishing, EAEPE has produced many volumes of conference and other papers, some of which have received very positive reviews in leading academic journals. Annual conferences have been held since November 1990 in different locations across Europe.

EAEPE is a fully democratic association and has an agreed and published constitution. At each annual conference there is a membership meeting. Here, resolutions and constitutional amendments are tabled, which are then put to a postal ballot of the entire membership. At least once every two years, the membership elects a Council of fourteen persons, including a chairperson, general secretary, treasurer and newsletter editor.

At time of writing, the Honorary Presidents of the association are Janos Komai (Hungary), Luigi Pasinetti (Italy), Kurt Rothschild (Austria) and Herbert Simon (USA). Past Honorary Presidents include Nicholas Georgescu-Roegen, Edith Penrose and George Shackle.

Although membership of the association is open to anyone who accepts its constitution and rules, council members must be residents of Europe. The current council – including two co-opted members – includes academics from Austria, Belgium, the Czech Republic, Denmark, France, Italy, Germany, Greece, the Netherlands, Portugal, Sweden, Switzerland and the United Kingdom.

To become an EAEPE member a subscription is paid, the amount of which depends on income. There are substantial discounts for students and other low-income members. EAEPE membership brings a number of rights, including the right to receive the twice-yearly *EAEPE Newsletter* and to receive published EAEPE volumes at substantial discounts. At present, EAEPE does not have its own journal. However, substantial discounts have been negotiated for EAEPE members on the individual subscriptions of leading journals such as the *Cambridge Journal of Economics*, *Industrial and Corporate Change*, the *International Review of Applied Economics*, the *Review of International Political Economy* and the *Review of Political Economy*.

With the aid of a substantial grant from the European Commission, EAEPE held summer schools in 1996 (Spain), 1997 (Greece) and 1998 (Ireland). The overall theme of the three schools was "Institutions and Technology: Interdisciplinary Perspectives on European Economy and Society in an Era of Rapid Change." The summer schools were mainly for young (35 years or under) academics, postgraduates and other researchers. It is hoped to run more schools in the future.

With a membership at time of writing of around 700, EAEPE is now the foremost European association for heterodox economists and the second-largest European association of economists. EAEPE is linked with a number of other networks and has some active national chapters. In at least four European countries, EAEPE members are playing a major role in government. There are also EAEPE members in the European Parliament.

Further information is available on the EAEPE home page on the Internet: http://eaepe.tuwien.ac.at. EAEPE-published volumes are available from Edward Elgar Publishing, Gower House, Croft Road, Aldershot, Hampshire, GU1 13HR, UK.

See also:

Association for Evolutionary Economics and Association for Institutionalist Thought; evolution and coevolution; evolutionary economics: major contemporary themes; institutional political economy: major contemporary themes

Selected references

Amin, Ash and Hausner, Jerzy (1997) *Beyond Market and Hierarchy: Interactive Governance and Social Complexity*, Cheltenham: Edward Elgar.

Nielsen, Klaus and Johnson, Bjorn (1998)

Institutions and Economic Change: New Perspectives on Markets, Firms and Technology, Cheltenham: Edward Elgar.

Tylecote, Andrew and van der Straaten, Jan (1997) *Environment, Technology and Economic Growth*, Cheltenham: Edward Elgar.

GEOFFREY M. HODGSON

evolution and coevolution

Newton's mechanics of time-reversible, universal relationships provides the theoretical underpinnings of neoclassical market economics. Political economists have also incorporated the language, and implicitly the mechanisms, of physics when they speak of power, forces and root or ultimate causes. On the other hand, political economists also acknowledge the contingencies of history and the contextualities of culture and place, and for this, evolutionary theory provides an excellent formal foundation for thinking about history. Yet for a variety of historical reasons and subsequent misunderstandings, political economists have had a difficult relationship with evolutionary theory (see England 1994).

Darwin, Wallace and Spencer

In 1858, Charles Darwin and Alfred Wallace independently identified the underlying processes which could explain how change occurs in species. Gregor Mendel provided critical components that were not effectively integrated into evolutionary theory until the early 1900s. Since then, evolution has been understood in biology as a process of selection of genes in a POPULATION of a species through interaction with environmental factors. It is critically important to keep in mind that the theories of social scientists have been as important to the development of evolutionary understanding as those of biological scientists. Both Darwin and Wallace credit Thomas Malthus, parson and economist, for suggesting at the end of the eighteenth century that populations expand to their "natural" environmental limits, forcing the selection of some individuals over others. Thus a model developed as economics emerged from moral philosophy, which underlies our biological understanding of evolution.

Herbert Spencer, pre-eminent English philosopher and natural scientist as well as an important founding father of sociology, was critically important in publicly voicing opposition to creationism before Darwin and Wallace, in publicly defending their theory when it emerged, and in incorporating evolutionary theory as a basis for sociology and anthropology. Spencer's elaborations on evolution, both biological and sociological, were more often read than those of Darwin. In addition, though competition is only one of many important ways animals and plants relate to each other, the emphasis biologists have historically placed on competition rather than other types of interactions when describing selection is attributed to the dominance of economic thought in the nineteenth and twentieth centuries. Thus, whatever the appeal to either biologists or social scientists, the argument that evolutionary theory ought to be left to biologists is historically naive.

Evolutionary and coevolutionary processes

The evolutionary process is fed by random mutations or, for specific populations, by the introduction of new genetic material from another population. Selective pressure on the distribution of genetic traits is commonly understood to result in the population or species as a whole fitting its environment ever more perfectly. Evolutionary narratives explain, for example, how tortoises have been selected to be ever more fit for the aridity of desert regions. However, ever-increasing fitness, along with earlier associations of evolution with the Western idea of progress, are incorrect notions. Though relatively stable factors such as the physical environment can certainly be important, the most critical features of the environment of every species are the other species with which it interacts. Interacting species select on and coevolve with each other. In this sense, coevolution takes our understanding of ecosystems as interacting species and combines this with selection processes. The important point is that in a coevolutionary world, nothing is fixed against which progress might be gauged, nor can even a general direction be specified to facilitate prediction.

Evolutionary processes depend on trait variability so that some traits can be selected over others. For this reason, diversity is inherently a good thing within an evolutionary framework of understanding change. There are no equilibrium states for mutations and the emergence of new characteristics are presumed to be constantly taking place. Historically, significant evolutionary change was presumed to be slow and require hundreds of generations. But now it is accepted that evolution also can occur in jumps of rapid change, blurring the historic juxtaposition of evolution and revolution (Gould and Eldredge 1977).

Marx

Karl MARX expressed a close affinity to the ideas of his contemporary, Charles Darwin. Writing with Friedrich Engels, he frequently referred to evolutionary theory as an interesting basis for explaining history and grounding CLASS struggle. Yet Marx by no means converted to a Darwinian world view. His linear historical materialism, forces of production and visions of a unified socioeconomic order, to say nothing of his predictive claims as to its future, combined the dynamics and language of Newton, the unfolding processes of Hegel's DIALECTICAL METHOD and a strong progressive trajectory. Nevertheless, many find striking parallels between dialectical and evolutionary understandings of change, and had the ideas of Darwin and Wallace been more prevalent among those for whom Marx wrote, he might have projected a different narrative. Marx was sufficiently attentive to Darwinian theory to worry as early as 1862 that it could be used to rationalize the economic power of capitalists and the existence of capitalism (Hodgson 1994).

Social Darwinism

It was precisely such a rationalization that Herbert Spencer firmly planted and the American sociologist William Graham Sumner eagerly cultivated at the end of the nineteenth century. Social Darwinism misinterpreted evolutionary concepts which were still in the process of being formed in biology, combining them with the liberal value of individualism and progressive visions of the future, and propelling them along a totally different track in sociology and anthropology. A critical error was to equate evolution with progress. This justified low wages, unemployment, colonialism and imperialism, and racism, for example, as "natural" outcomes of the selection process. Since the hardship imposed selected against the economically and socially unfit, intensifying such hardship would speed human progress. It is this episode, now almost history in the social sciences yet still quite common in popular understanding, that has made the incorporation of evolutionary concepts so suspect in social theory.

Marshall, Veblen and Schumpeter

Other late nineteenth and early twentieth century economists were also taken with evolutionary ideas. Alfred Marshall argued that the mechanics of Newton were simply inadequate for describing economic organization, for which he preferred organic metaphors, or for explaining economic transformations, where evolutionary concepts were more informative. Marshall never developed these points well, arguing that formalizing biological concepts into economics would be more difficult than had been the case with mechanics, an argument reiterated by Paul Samuelson in 1947 in his *Foundations of Economic Analysis*. Nevertheless, Marshall was convinced that the future of economics was in biology, particularly in evolutionary theory.

Thorstein VEBLEN was also swayed by the ideas of Darwin and Spencer as well as by the pragmatic philosophy of one of his professors, Charles Peirce. Veblen, never having assumed so central a position within the discipline as had Marshall, was more successful in outlining a theory of socioeconomic evolution. Veblen argued that shared habits and thoughts, frequently formalized as institutions, transmitted social characteristics and slowed progressive change. However, these were also the points where social evolution did occur. Hence habits, thoughts and institutions assumed roles analogous to genes in biology, and coevolved. Some institutional economists have adopted the name "evolutionary economics" because of Veblen's use of the concept (see INSTITUTIONS AND HABITS; INSTITUTIONAL POLITICAL ECONOMY: HISTORY). Joseph SCHUMPETER also frequently espoused evolutionary arguments over those of mechanics to explain the ongoing transformation of capitalism; but he explicitly denied that the processes in economic systems paralleled those in biology (Hodgson 1994).

Boulding, Nelson and Winter

In the midst of the further mathematical formalization of the mechanics of economics, evolutionary arguments were only occasionally entertained in minor ways for several decades following the Second World War. Kenneth Boulding (1978) helped to break this trend with a expansive book which placed economic evolution within a continuum of nested evolutionary processes ranging from geophysical and biological evolution to sociocultural and scientific evolution. Boulding gave ecology and evolution such a visionary expansion that few scholars considered his grand synthesis pertinent to work in their field. Building on the subsequent discontent with the impotence of mathematical economics, Richard R. Nelson and Sidney G. Winter (1982) published a book exploring evolutionary explanations of economic growth, SCHUMPETERIAN COMPETITION and economic policy. Nelson and Winter juxtapose evolutionary and mechanical theories, but by sticking to questions already identified within orthodox economics, they stay somewhat within the mainstream (see NELSON AND WINTER'S ANALYSIS OF THE CORPORATION).

People, technology and institutions

Beginning in the 1980s, concern over the sustainability of economic development stimulated economists to explore anew how people relate to nature. John Gowdy (1994) has revitalized institutional economic analysis, arguing that people and their technologies and socioeconomic institutions have coevolved with nature. However, he argues that there are clear ecological limits within which this process can take place and that those limits now appear to have been exceeded. Richard Norgaard (1994) argues that knowledge, values, organizations, technologies and environmental systems have coevolved.

The problem is that for the past 150 years, our cultural systems have coevolved around fossil hydrocarbons instead of environmental systems, creating a significant disjuncture with the environment. This problem is compounded by the dominance of Newtonian over evolutionary understanding, limiting our ability to adapt and respond. Following evolutionary logic, Norgaard espouses cultural diversity and greater bioregional self-sufficiency over cultural homogenization and economic globalization. Like the work of Boulding, Norgaard's analysis is too expansive to pursue the questions of any particular school of thought persistently. Yet his arguments touch upon key questions in the history of political economy and challenge many of the underlying assumptions.

Problems and strengths

This brings us back to the problems that evolutionary and coevolutionary thinking bring to political economy. First, there is the central issue of power. Although Boulding (1978) ventured a chapter on the nature of power from a variety of perspectives, evolutionary social theorists have not incorporated and confronted the problem of power in the critical ways political economists have historically addressed it. Evolutionary and coevolutionary paradigms seem to be relatively ill-suited for working with power. Second, memories of social Darwinism still taint these interpretations as rationales for whatever has evolved, including power. Third, while some evolutionary interpretations of social change only include social factors, many also incorporate "natural" factors. That genes play a role in human evolution may not be controversial to biologists, but for social scientists the possible influences of genes raise deep conflicts with political beliefs and progressive visions. Environmental determinism has been especially contested by political economists. Fourth, evolutionary interpretations rationalize cultural diversity as a critical element in maintaining the evolutionary process. This clashes with progressive visions of all peoples rising together, merging to a peaceful equality rooted in scientific understanding and empowerment. Even discounting this as a rapidly fading ideal, cultural pluralists bear the burden of identifying the limits of diversity with respect to human justice and the mechanisms for maintaining cultural peace.

Closely paralleling these problems of evolution and coevolution come strengths. First, the coevolutionary pattern of explanation provides a new, coherent, systematic way of understanding how numerous things came to be related to each other, and can change. It also explains how many more things exist for short periods of time or for longer periods without achieving dominance. Second, coevolutionary interpretations provide a new way of thinking about how people affect nature and vice versa, helping us to move beyond both cultural and environmental determinism. Coevolutionary understanding can bridge our social and environmental histories and lead to new understandings of both social and environmental crises.

Western science, as the perceived dominant driver of technological, social and environmental change, is increasingly being questioned. The coevolutionary paradigm allows us to rethink the roles of Western knowledge, experiential knowledge and traditional knowledge in critically effective new ways. Third, cultural diversity appears to have regained a hold on the future in spite of global capitalism. Evolutionary and coevolutionary patterns of thinking not only help political economists question their past beliefs but help them to understand and make the best of the future we currently foresee.

See also:

bioeconomics; circular and cumulative causation; determinism and overdetermination; environmental and ecological political economy: major contemporary themes; evolutionary economics: major contemporary themes; institutional political economy: major contemporary themes; knowledge, information, technology and change

Selected references

Boulding, Kenneth E. (1978) *Ecodynamics: A New Theory of Societal Evolution*, Beverly Hills, CA and London: Sage.

England, Richard W. (ed.) (1994) *Evolutionary Concepts in Contemporary Economics*, Ann Arbor, MI: University of Michigan Press.

Gould, Stephen J. and Eldredge, Niles (1977) "Punctuated Equilibria: the Tempo and Mode of Evolution Reconsidered," *Paleobiology* 3: 115–51.

Gowdy, John M. (1994) *Coevolutionary Economics: The Economy, Society and the Environment*, Boston: Kluwer.

Greene, John C. (1981) *Science, Ideology, and World View: Essays in the History of Evolutionary Ideas*, Berkeley and Los Angeles: University of California Press.

Hodgson, Geoffrey M. (1994) "Precursors of Modern Evolutionary Economics: Marx, Marshall, Veblen, and Schumpeter," in Richard W. England (ed.), *Evolutionary Concepts in Contemporary Economics*, Ann Arbor, MI: University of Michigan Press.

Nelson, Richard R. and Winter, Sidney G. (1982) *An Evolutionary Theory of Economic Change*, Cambridge, MA: Harvard University Press.

Norgaard, Richard B. (1994) *Development Betrayed: The End of Progress and a Coevolutionary Revisioning of the Future*, London and New York: Routledge.

RICHARD B. NORGAARD

evolutionary economics: history

Before addressing its history, it must be realized that the term "evolutionary economics" has a variety of meanings. Broadly, the term is often used to refer to the study of development and change in economic systems. More narrowly, some authors use the term to refer by metaphor or analogy to biological evolution.

In economics generally speaking, there has been a widespread use of biological metaphors – such as the comparison of an economy with an organism – without necessarily addressing mechanisms of selection associated with the term "evolution" in the biological sense. Accordingly, not all use of biological metaphors in economics is "evolutionary," and neither does all use of the term "evolution" in economics invoke biology.

Individual and systemic evolution

Discussion is further complicated because, even when a biological idea of "evolution" is applied to economics, there are different understandings of the nature of evolutionary processes and emphases on different aspects of the phenomena involved. One primary division is between, on the one hand, those economists who focus on the emergence on a single convention, institution or system – such as Carl Menger's discussion of the emergence of money and Friedrich Hayek's account of the development of "spontaneous order" – and, on the other, those economists – of whom Thorstein VEBLEN is a foremost example – who address the complete and ongoing evolution of an economic system and the ongoing selection of a variety of institutions within it. In the case of the first group, who are concerned with a single entity, they are discussing something analogous to what biologists call "ontogeny": that is, the development of a single organism. The broader concept of systemic evolution embraced by Veblen and others is closer to "phylogeny": that is, the ongoing evolution of a population of organisms with a pool of genetic material that changes through time due to selection.

Physiocracy and classical economics

Political economy and theories of biological evolution have a long relationship. For example, in the eighteenth century, the French physiocratic economist François Quesnay, and in the nineteenth century, a number of members of the German historical school, all made extensive use of organic metaphors. The relationship is underlined by the crucial influence on Charles Darwin of the ideas of Adam Smith, Charles Babbage and, especially, Thomas Robert Malthus. Darwin's theory of natural selection was built on the ideas of inheritance, variation and selection. Smith's idea of the division of labor evoked variation, but Babbage – a friend of Darwin – suggested that variation must exist prior to habitual use. Darwin's theory is closer to Babbage than Smith in this respect, as Darwin saw selection as acting upon variation, rather than variation being a result of selection. Malthus hinted at the ideas of both variation and competitive selection. However, although Darwin published the *Origin of Species* in 1859, it was thirty-nine years later that a theory of economic evolution was developed that closely followed Darwin's principles.

For example, although vivid notions of economic development and change permeate Smith's *Wealth of Nations* it is not strictly a Darwinian theory. There are no corresponding principles of inheritance, variation and selection. Likewise, although Karl MARX and Charles Darwin were contemporaries, and – in a letter to Ferdinand Lasalle of 16 January 1862 – Marx proclaimed Darwin's theory as "a natural-scientific basis for the class struggle in history," neither Marx nor his collaborator, Friedrich Engels, made significant theoretical use of Darwin's ideas.

Nevertheless, the political economy of both Adam Smith and Karl Marx have strong dynamic elements and invoke important ideas of structural and institutional change. For that reason they may be legitimately described as evolutionary, as long as it is clear that that term is not used in the same sense as it is in biology.

Beginnings of Darwinian evolution in economics

Darwinian or post-Darwinian ideas of evolution in the economic sphere did not emerge for some time. This is less surprising when it is realized that, subsequent to the publication of the *Origin of Species*, Darwin's theory went into eclipse. It was only in the 1940s, when Darwin's ideas were synthesized by the geneticist Gregor Mendel, that they began to receive the degree of popular and academic acceptance that they do today. Although biological metaphors were prominent in both Anglo-American and German political economy prior to the First World War, Herbert Spencer was a more prominent influence than Darwin.

Accordingly, Alfred Marshall's economics was infused with Spencerian ideas. Although there is mention of Darwin in his classic *Principles of Economics*, first published in 1890, the acknowledged and conceptual influence of Spencer is much greater. Marshall stands out as one of the fathers of "economic biology," but not of economic evolution in a Darwinian mold.

It is in this context that Veblen's plea for a "post-Darwinian" economics, in a series of essays published in the *Quarterly Journal of Economics* from 1898 to 1900 (and republished in the collection, *The Place of Science in Modern Civilisation* (1919)), are all the more remarkable. Veblen attempted to develop a theory of socioeconomic evolution that drew upon the three Darwinian principles of inheritance, variation and selection. INSTINCTS, habits and institutions were seen as the heritable units of selection. Variation originated from the coalescence of institutions or from human invention.

Veblen's notion of evolution was phylogenetic, in that it did not confine itself to the emergence of a single institution or order, resulting from interactions within a population of given individuals. Economic evolution for VEBLEN, as for later institutional economists, involved the transformation of individuals themselves, including their preferences. Also, for Veblen, evolution was not the selection of entities in a static environment: institutions, individuals and the environment were all changed in an ongoing process of interaction. In contrast to the Marxian emphasis on the "inevitable" progression toward communism, Veblen's idea of evolution was non-teleological, involving no pre-ordained or final goal. Although the mechanisms of economic evolution were not adequately specified, Veblen's work is a towering landmark in evolutionary economics.

However, shortly after Veblen's "post-Darwinian" manifesto, the use of biological ideas in social science became increasingly under attack. In part this was a reaction against racist and sexist abuses of biology in social science by a subset of evolutionary thinkers. In addition, behaviorist ideas displaced the instinct psychology of William James and others with its explicit connections with Darwinism. Furthermore, there was a strong shift toward positivism and a rebuttal of evolutionary metaphors and allegedly intangible and unmeasurable variables. By the time of Marshall's death in 1924 and Veblen's in 1929, the dialogue between economics and biology had virtually ceased. "Economic biology" had become no more than the whisperings of a few mavericks such as the English economist John Atkinson Hobson and a number of American institutionalists.

Schumpeter

The tide of opinion against evolutionary ideas was such that even Joseph SCHUMPETER (1934: 57) accepted in 1912 that "the evolutionary idea is now discredited in our field." It is not widely recognized that Schumpeter did not embrace biological metaphors. He wrote in his *History of Economic Analysis* that "no appeal to biology would be of the slightest use" (1954: 789).

Nevertheless, Schumpeter's work remains rich in insight. He defined evolution in non-biological terms, referring essentially to structural and institutional change. The impetus behind his own version of evolutionary thinking was a lifelong project to generalize and somehow dynamize the static equilibrium thinking of neoclassical economists such as Léon Walras. Although the formulation of this project is open to criticism – especially in regard to the attempted reconciliation of evolution with the Walrasian concept of equilibrium – Schumpeter made an important contribution by keeping dynamic thinking alive during the inter-war period when the "economic biology" of both Marshall and Veblen was in a dark age. Furthermore, Schumpeter's writings on technological change and socioeconomic development have remained an inspiration for generations after his death in 1950.

Alchian, Boulding and Friedman

After the Second World War there was a partial return to biology in the social sciences. The transition was given impetus by two separate developments in biology in the 1940s and the 1970s. The first impulse was the emergence of the neo-Darwinian synthesis. The elements of this had been in place long before, but the new paradigm did not become fully established until the 1940s. A group of Darwinians working in Britain and the United States accomplished a synthesis between the theory of natural selection and Mendelian genetics. Only then did the gene became fully incorporated into the theory of evolution, giving a plausible explanation of the presumed variation of offspring and the selection of species.

The timing of Armen Alchian's famous article of 1950 is therefore apposite. Capitalizing on the triumph of a new Darwinian biology, he made an explicit appeal to the metaphor of natural selection. However, he made no reference to the earlier work of Veblen: the memory of the earlier evolutionary foray had been lost. Alchian (1950) proposed that the assumption of overt maximizing behavior by business firms is not necessary for the scientific purposes of explanation and prediction. Selective success, Alchian argued, depends on behavior and results, not motivations. If firms never actually attempted to maximize profits, "evolutionary" processes of selection and imitation would ensure the survival of the more profitable enterprises. This evolutionary idea was taken up and modified by others, including Milton Friedman (1953) who saw "natural selection" as grounds for assuming that agents act "as if" they maximize, whether or not firms and individuals actually do so.

About the same time, the heterodox economist Kenneth Boulding published his *Reconstruction of Economics* (1950). In it he borrowed "population thinking" (Metcalfe 1988) and associated models from ecology, while at the same time being careful about the limitations of biological analogies. Capital goods were represented as a population with different vintages that entered the capital fund like births and deaths of organisms in a species. In this work, Boulding was one of the first to emphasize that the economy was part of, and depended upon, the ecosystem. Boulding was thus one of the first to pioneer the notion of social and ecological coevolution (see EVOLUTION AND COEVOLUTION).

For mainstream economists, Friedman's intervention in 1953 was especially influential. It became a classic defense of the neoclassical maximization hypothesis. It used the new authority of evolutionary biology to rebut lingering doubts about that core idea. Beyond that, however, the biological analogy was little used in economics for the subsequent twenty years. Again ironically, Friedman's use of the metaphor of natural selection bolstered a key element in the mechanistic paradigm and rebutted the "evolutionary" economists of the institutional camp. In fact, Friedman had applied simplistically a half-assimilated idea from Darwinian biology to reinforce the mechanistic paradigm of neoclassical economics. Eleven years later, Sidney Winter (1964) showed that Friedman's argument had a highly limited applicability, even in evolutionary terms. One of Winter's arguments was to show that Friedman's notion of selection depended on a static environment, and neglected the interdependency of the environment and the actors within it.

Modern evolutionary bioeconomics

In economics during the 1954–74 period, by far the most important work inspired by biology was by Nicholas Georgescu-Roegen, *The Entropy Law and the Economic Process*, published in 1971. He asserted the value of biological as well as thermodynamic analogies and founded a distinctive version of BIOECONOMICS. Subsequently, the basis of a new theory of economic evolution was first outlined by Richard Nelson and Sydney Winter in an essay published in 1973 (see NELSON AND WINTER'S ANALYSIS OF THE CORPORATION).

For the social sciences as a whole, Edward O. Wilson's 1975 book *Sociobiology: The New Synthesis* was a bombshell. Its appearance stimulated a protracted interest in the alleged biotic foundations of human behavior. The book was greeted with a great deal of criticism, from both social scientists and biologists, but it nevertheless brought biology back onto the social science agenda.

The impact of the new sociobiology on economics was rapid. Neoclassical economists such as Gary Becker, Jack Hirshleifer and Gordon Tullock quickly followed with calls for the joining of economics with sociobiology. Notably these presentations were individualist and reductionist, and emphasized self-interest and individual competition in the biotic as well as the economic world.

Although the genesis of Nelson and Winter's *Evolutionary Theory of Economic Change* (1982) had much to do with the growing prestige of biology and the re-introduction of biological metaphors into social science, their work is quite different from that of the Becker–Hirshleifer–Tullock school. Nelson and Winter reject the notion that human behavior is wholly or largely determined by the genes. Their perspective is complex and interactionist, involving different levels and units of selection, and ongoing interaction between individuals, institutions and their socioeconomic environment.

At about this time, an evolutionary approach was also developed by Boulding (1981). This built on his earlier work on biological analogies, but it is significant that his fully fledged evolutionary theory did not emerge in its developed form until the late 1970s. This is later than in other social sciences, particularly anthropology, where the word "evolution" became quite common in the 1960s. The author has found no more than twenty relevant works encountered in economics from 1914 to 1980 inclusive which have the words "evolution" or "evolutionary" in their title or subtitle. About half of these appear in the years 1970–80. In contrast, the number in the decade or so after 1982 is well into three figures.

The revival of usage of "evolutionary" terminology also affected the economists of the AUSTRIAN SCHOOL OF POLITICAL ECONOMY. As in economics in general, references to biology are minimal in writings of the Austrian school prior to the 1960s. It was Hayek who began to bring evolutionary metaphors into Austrian school economics in the last thirty years of his life. Such ideas are found in essays published in the 1960s, and expressed in a more extended form in later works (Hayek 1988).

Conclusion

On the whole, modern evolutionary economics has already inspired major contributions to economic policy, particularly in the areas of technological change and strategic management. Further, it shows signs of polarization between, on the one hand, those that employ formalistic, mathematical tools and, on the other hand, those that rely on more discursive and historically rooted approaches.

See also:

entropy, negentropy and the laws of thermodynamics; evolutionary economics: major contemporary themes; institutions and habits

Selected references

Alchian, Armen A. (1950) "Uncertainty, Evolution and Economic Theory," *Journal of Political Economy* 58(2): 211–22.

Boulding, Kenneth E. (1981) *Evolutionary Economics*, Beverly Hills, CA: Sage Publications.

Friedman, Milton (1953) "The Methodology of Positive Economics," in M. Friedman, *Essays in Positive Economics*, Chicago: University of Chicago Press, 3–43.

Hayek, Friedrich A. (1988) *The Fatal Conceit: The Errors of Socialism, The Collected Works of Friedrich August Hayek*, vol. 1, ed. W.W. Bartley III, London: Routledge.

Hodgson, Geoffrey M. (1993) *Economics and Evolution: Bringing Life Back Into Economics*, Cambridge and Ann Arbor, MI: Polity Press and University of Michigan Press.

Metcalfe, J. Stanley (1988) "Evolution and Economic Change," in Aubrey Silberston (ed.), *Technology and Economic Progress*, Basingstoke: Macmillan, 54–85.

Nelson, Richard R. and Winter, Sidney G. (1982) *An Evolutionary Theory of Economic Change*, Cambridge, MA: Harvard University Press.

Schumpeter, Joseph A. (1934) *The Theory of Economic Development: An Inquiry into Profits, Capital, Credit, Interest, and the Business Cycle*, trans. Redvers Opie from the German edition of 1911, Cambridge, MA: Harvard University Press; repr. with a new introduction by John E. Elliott, New Brunswick, NJ: Transaction, 1990.

Veblen, Thorstein B. (1919) *The Place of Science in Modern Civilisation and Other Essays*, New York: Huebsch; repr. with a new introduction by W.J. Samuels, New Brunswick, NJ: Transaction, 1990.

Winter, Sidney G. (1964) "Economic 'Natural Selection' and the Theory of the Firm," *Yale Economic Essays* 4(1): 225–72.

GEOFFREY M. HODGSON

evolutionary economics: major contemporary themes

The term "evolutionary economics" is currently applied to a confusingly wide variety of approaches within the subject. At least six main groups using the phrase can be identified.

1 A century ago Thorstein VEBLEN (1898) argued for an "evolutionary" and "post-Darwinian" economics. Institutionalists in the tradition of Veblen and John Commons frequently describe their approach as being "evolutionary economics," often using the terms "institutional" and "evolutionary" as virtual synonyms, as exemplified in the title of the Association for Evolutionary Economics – the US-based association of institutional economists.

2 Joseph SCHUMPETER in *Capitalism, Socialism and Democracy* famously described capitalist development as an "evolutionary process." Work influenced by Schumpeter is also described as "evolutionary economics," as evidenced by the title of the *Journal of Evolutionary Economics*, published by the International Joseph Schumpeter Association.

3 The approach of economists of the AUSTRIAN SCHOOL OF POLITICAL ECONOMY is often described as "evolutionary," as portrayed in Carl Menger's theory of the evolution of money and other institutions, and by the extensive use of an evolutionary metaphor from biology in the later works of Friedrich Hayek (1988), especially in relation to the concept of spontaneous order.

4 In addition, the economics of assorted writers such as Adam Smith, Karl MARX, Alfred Marshall and others is also sometimes described as "evolutionary" in character.

5 Evolutionary GAME THEORY is a prominent recent development in mathematical economics, and has been inspired by related mathematical work in theoretical biology.

6 The word "evolutionary" is sometimes attached to work in what is also described as "complexity theory," typically that associated with the Santa Fe Institute in the United States, involving applications of CHAOS THEORY and various other types of computer simulation. In this and allied simulation work the use of replicator dy-

namics, genetic algorithms, genetic programming and so on, can be found.

With such a wide variety of uses, it is unlikely that there is a single, underlying and coherent message. Indeed, the use of the word "evolutionary" in economics seems very much to be a matter of fashion. It is arguable that the increasing use of the term "evolutionary economics" today can be largely traced to the impact of Richard Nelson and Sidney Winter's classic work *An Evolutionary Theory of Economic Change* (1982), although other developments in both orthodox and heterodox economics are also important. Apart from within the institutionalist and Schumpeterian schools, the use of the word "evolutionary" did not become widespread in economics until after 1982 (see EVOLUTIONARY ECONOMICS: HISTORY).

Recent works

By the late 1980s and into the 1990s, work in this area had been broadened and accelerated by the growth in both America and Europe of various institutional and Schumpeterian approaches to economics. Some notable contributions include Norman Clark and Calestous Juma's *Long-Run Economics*, Brian Loasby's *Equilibrium and Evolution*, Joel Mokyr's *The Level of Riches*, Bart Verspagen's *Uneven Growth Between Interdependent Economies*, Ulrich's edited book on *Evolutionary Economics*, Geoffrey Hodgson's books on *Economics and Evolution* and *Economics and Biology* (see Hodgson *et al*. 1994), Richard England's edited volume on *Evolutionary Concepts in Contemporary Economics* and Jack Vromen's *Economic Evolution*. There have been notable and fruitful applications of these ideas, particularly in the sphere of technological change (e.g. Giovanni Dosi *et al*., *Technical Change and Economic Theory*, and Christopher Freeman, *The Economics of Innovation*). A substantial body of work is clearly evident. Evolutionary economics has already established an impressive research program and has had a major impact on economic policy, particularly in the areas of TECHNOLOGY policy, corporate strategy and national systems of innovation.

Bounded rationality

Although there is no single and coherent system of ideas currently under the label "evolutionary economics," a number of authors in this area follow the earlier examples of the Veblenian institutionalists and Nelson and Winter in rejecting the neoclassical assumption of the rational, utility-maximizing actor. Much use is made of Herbert Simon's (1957) concepts of "satisficing" and "bounded rationality." Several authors working in this area are inspired by metaphors taken from evolutionary biology, although their use is far from universal.

Information, learning and knowledge

The core impact of the shift from a mechanistic metaphor to one taken from evolutionary biology can be illustrated as follows. As Philip Mirowski (1989) and others have argued, neoclassical economics was founded in the 1870s on the basis of ideas and formalisms taken from nineteenth-century physics. There are no information problems in such a world. A ball bearing "seeks out" the lowest point in a hemispherical cup, as if it "knew" where the optimum position (and possible stable equilibrium) could be found. Likewise, the lack of information problems in neoclassical economics means that the rational optimizers can readily choose the "best" option available from a known set of alternatives.

In an evolutionary paradigm, the problem is quite different. Agents do not know the set of different characteristics and behavioral alternatives that they may be able to acquire. There is not a given choice set. The evolutionary challenge is not to optimize immediately but to adapt gradually to circumstances. Those that are successful are more likely to survive. The transfer of an evolutionary metaphor to socio-economic systems thus provides a place for the process of learning. Choices are not known and given at the outset. To survive, the agent has to discover the options that are available and learn to adapt. Information problems are central.

Veblen (1919), Nelson and Winter (1982) and other authors argue that learning and knowledge are largely about the establishment of habit and routine. Habits apply to individuals; routines are regularized patterns of behavior involving a group. Institutions are durable and enduring sets of routines and habits. Veblen, and later Nelson and Winter, argue that something similar to "natural selection" operates on these habits, routines and institutions, although the processes and objects of selection are quite different from those pertaining to the biotic world.

Variety, novelty and indeterminacy

The biological metaphor creates problems as well as solutions. There is nothing quite like sexual recombination in the socioeconomic world of institutions and routines. What other sources of variety and novelty could be relevant? Veblen (1914) saw "idle curiosity" as the basis of much human innovation and thus an origin of novelty and variety in the socioeconomic system (see INSTINCTS). Nelson and Winter (1982) model a "mutation" process where an agent is forced to "search" for an alternative technology.

Arguably, genuine creativity, real choices and willed changes of purpose mean that human action must contain an element of indeterminacy in the sense of an uncaused cause. Accordingly, it has been argued (for example, by Loasby 1976: 9) that the neoclassical idea of behavior being programmed by fixed preference functions does not admit genuine choice. Yet the idea of an "uncaused cause" is widely rejected, even in biology. Most natural and social scientists assume that every event must have a prior cause. (See DETERMINISM AND OVERDETERMINATION.)

Non-linear dynamics and chaos theory

The development of non-linear dynamics and chaos theory raise additional questions about indeterminacy and the meaning of novelty (Hodgson 1995). Chaos theory suggests that, even if the world is deterministic, we would have to treat it as if it were indeterministic and unpredictable. Even if novelty is caused, it may appear as entirely spontaneous and free. Thus, the very distinction between determinacy and indeterminacy is undermined. We can never know for sure if any event is caused or uncaused. A number of key and well known features emerge. First, the chaos literature blurs the boundary between randomness and determinism. Second, precise predictability is confounded by the high degree of sensitivity to initial parameter values. Third, this sensitivity means that there is PATH DEPENDENCY and thus history matters. Fourth, bifurcations and "butterfly effects" also suggest and reinforce a notion of irreversibility. Fifth, the amplification of small fluctuations can provide endless novelty. Sixth, chaotic systems can exhibit emergent, higher-order properties. Seventh, chaos theory challenges the reductionist view that a system can be understood by breaking it down and studying each of its component parts.

The capacity to mimic novelty, irreversibility and emergent properties may suggest that non-linear systems and chaos theory provide the formal, mathematical apparatus for the new evolutionary economics. Yet such a development would undermine the emphasis on novelty. Even if chaotic systems can seemingly generate novelty, they are limited by their own formal assumptions. Even a stochastic process constrains the variance and defines a given parametric space. By its nature, novelty defies the boundaries of formalism. To endogenize the novelty-creating process within a formal framework is to limit greatly the set of possible novel outcomes.

Notably, in making a distinction between "formal" and "appreciative" theorizing, Nelson and Winter (1982: 45–8) argue that formal modeling should play a significant but not a central role. Instead, as in appreciative theorizing, the overriding concern is with empirical grounding and richness. Their emphasis is on the guidance and conceptual framing of empirical study, rather than the development of mathematical formalism itself.

Individuals, groups and institutions

Another important debate transfers almost directly from biology to social science, and concerns the units of selection, levels of analysis and emergent properties. On the one hand, there is in biology a debate over whether biotic behavior can be reduced analytically to the genetic composition of the organism concerned. It is thus argued that the gene is the unit of selection in the evolutionary process. This notion of "genetic reductionism" is opposed by a varied group of biologists that argue that there are emergent properties at higher levels that are not reducible to genes. Additional units of selection may apply, from individuals and groups up to species (Hodgson 1995; Sober 1984).

Likewise, in the social sciences, a large group of theorists argue for a version of reductionism widely known as "methodological individualism," which holds that socioeconomic phenomena must be explained entirely in terms of the individuals involved. Individuals are taken as the only units of analysis. An opposing view, advanced by "old" (or "neo"-) institutionalists and others, is that the use of higher units of analysis, notably institutions, is inevitable and desirable. Accordingly, later writers in this tradition stress the importance of emergent properties and the insurmountable difficulties involved in reductionism.

Conclusion

What is currently described as "evolutionary economics" encompasses both sides of the above debate, as well as embracing quite different views on the role of mathematical formalism in economic theory. It remains to be seen if "evolutionary economics" will itself evolve into a multiplicity of different species.

See also:

bioeconomics; circular and cumulative causation; European Association for Evolutionary Political Economy; evolution and coevolution; holistic method; institutional political economy: major contemporary themes; institutions and habits; knowledge, information, technology and change; methodological individualism and collectivism; Nelson and Winter's analysis of the corporation

Selected references

Hayek, Friedrich A. (1988) *The Fatal Conceit: The Errors of Socialism. The Collected Works of Friedrich August Hayek*, vol.1, ed. W.W. Bartley III, London: Routledge.

Hodgson, Geoffrey M. (1995) "The Evolution of Evolutionary Economics," *Scottish Journal of Political Economy* 42(4): 469–88.

Hodgson, Geoffrey M., Samuels, Warren J. and Tool, Marc R. (eds) (1994) *The Elgar Companion to Institutional and Evolutionary Economics*, Aldershot: Edward Elgar.

Loasby, Brian J. (1976) *Choice, Complexity and Ignorance: An Enquiry into Economic Theory and the Practice of Decision Making*, Cambridge: Cambridge University Press.

Mirowski, Philip (1989) *More Heat Than Light: Economics as Social Physics, Physics as Nature's Economics*, Cambridge: Cambridge University Press.

Nelson, Richard R. and Winter, Sidney G. (1982) *An Evolutionary Theory of Economic Change*, Cambridge, MA: Harvard University Press.

Saviotti, Pier Paolo and Metcalfe, J. Stanley (eds) (1991) *Evolutionary Theories of Economic and Technological Change: Present Status and Future Prospects*, Reading: Harwood.

Simon, Herbert A. (1957) *Models of Man: Social and Rational. Mathematical Essays on Rational Human Behavior in a Social Setting*, New York: Wiley.

Sober, Elliott (ed.) (1984) *Conceptual Issues in Evolutionary Biology: An Anthology*, Cambridge, MA: MIT Press.

Veblen, Thorstein B. (1898) "Why Is Economics Not an Evolutionary Science?," *Quarterly Journal of Economics* 12(3): 373–97; repr. in Veblen (1919).

—— (1914) *The Instinct of Workmanship, and the State of the Industrial Arts*, New York: Augustus Kelley; repr. with a new introduction by M.G. Murphey, New Brunswick, NJ: Transaction Books, 1990.

—— (1919) *The Place of Science in Modern*

Civilisation and Other Essays, New York: Huebsch; repr. with a new introduction by W.J. Samuels, New Brunswick, NJ: Transaction, 1990.

GEOFFREY M. HODGSON

exchange rates

Despite the foreign currency market's status as the world's largest market, economics is woefully short of a comprehensive explanation of its operations. Within orthodox economics, the results of empirical tests of the most popular models have been so discouraging that Mark Taylor has written: "there seems to be little professional disagreement with the view that, as a guide to the short-run behavior of the major exchange rates, exchange rate models based on macro fundamentals have largely failed" (Taylor 1995b: 28–9). Meanwhile heterodox economists, while writing extensively on INTERNATIONAL POLITICAL ECONOMY, development and monetary arrangements, have generally ignored the specifics of exchange rate determination. This is unfortunate, because it would seem that post-Keynesian and institutional political economy, in particular, would be well suited to the task.

Fundamentals and efficiency

The failure of orthodox economists to formulate a satisfactory explanation of exchange rate determination is related primarily to their predilection with the idea that "fundamental" forces must be responsible for currency price determination. The fundamentals are those variables that, if allowed to determine exchange rates, guarantee an efficient market and the optimal allocation of world resources (see SPECULATIVE BUBBLES AND FUNDAMENTAL VALUES). This core concept has created two problems for neoclassicism. First, since "efficiency" and "optimality" are a function of the independent, subjective and, unfortunately, unobservable utility functions of all market participants, it is never clear whether the empirical failure of a fundamentals-based model is because the basic theory is flawed or simply that the researcher has incorrectly specified "the" fundamental variables. This indeterminacy has tended to insulate the theory from rejection.

Second, more important than this problem has been the powerful normative undercurrent associated with the fundamentals-based approach. While, technically, the fundamentals are limited only to being whatever the market participants decide they are (based on their utility functions), in practice there is a very strong tendency to associate them with those variables that would lead to the most efficient patterns of trade and investment. Thus, the specification of the fundamentals in mainstream economic models has been restricted to those factors that economists have thought "should" determine exchange rates. Not only has this been unduly restrictive in general, but as the INTERNATIONALIZATION OF CAPITAL has increased and brought into the foreign exchange market more and more disparate players, the problem has become worse.

For many years, even as the foreign currency market began to approximate, more closely, Keynes' view of a musical-chairs style asset market – what neoclassical economist H. Visser tellingly refers to as "Keynes' *gloomy view*" (Visser 1989: 24; emphasis added) – orthodoxy clung tightly to the fundamentals-based approach. By the mid-1990s, however, there had definitely been a shift in neoclassical thought. The overwhelming evidence against the core concept had become irrefutable. To add to the list of failures of full-fledged models of exchange rate determination came new research (involving technical analysis and tests of direct observations of market participants' EXPECTATIONS) that rejected market efficiency and rational expectations. The renunciation of the fundamentals as determinants of exchange rates has been far less than complete, however.

Rather than seeking new tools of analysis to explain the phenomena, mainstream economics has kept the same tools and simply narrowed the focus. Current neoclassical thought holds that the fundamentals-based approach (whatever those fundamentals may be) properly characterizes long-term exchange rate determination, but that "irrational" forces are too important in the short run for economists to have much to say about that time horizon. Hence, the fundamentals have survived, but the short run has been abandoned (the outstanding exception being microstructure studies; see Taylor 1995b: 39–41).

Heterodox work

Meanwhile, little substantial work has been attempted in heterodox economics. Most post Keynesian research, for example, while touching on the fact that freely floating exchange rates are likely to be quite volatile as market participants adjust portfolios in response to changes in expectations, is primarily concerned with the macroeconomic effects of various international payments regimes. The details of exchange rate determination are usually ignored. For the most part, Marxist economists have hesitated to offer an explanation of exchange rates *per se*. This is due to the conviction that there exists a "contradiction between the nationality of state regulation ... and the internationality of accumulation ... [since] exchange rates cannot be understood outside of the political expression of contradictions between different parts of capital" (Bryan 1995: 79–80).

Bandwagon effects. There are a few exceptions. Stephan Schulmeister (1987), though he opts for a fundamentals-style explanation of the long run ("medium run" in his terminology), has developed an outstanding model of short-term exchange rate fluctuations. Based in part on Keynes' view of asset markets, Schulmeister explains exchange rates by outlining the structure of the market and the behavior of currency dealers (focusing on how the market does work rather than on how it "should"). He finds that the peculiar pattern of price movements (a series of upward and downward runs around a mean) are the consequence of bandwagon and cash-in effects and the fact that currency dealers simultaneously hold both short- and long-term expectations of future prices. Short-run volatility is due to the tenuous nature of the expectations held. Schulmeister argues that, in the long-run, rates fluctuate in response to more stable factors such as current account imbalances and interest rate differentials.

Speculative bubbles. Laurence Krause (1991), though the primary aim of his book is to recommend reform of the international monetary system, also develops a simple model of exchange rates. He constructs an explanation of speculative bubbles which he bases on the work of Ragnar Nurkse, John Maynard Keynes and Nicholas Kaldor. Krause contends that SPECULATION in foreign currency is very likely to be destabilizing and that, given this, the effect of shocks of an economic and political nature can lead to wide swings away from traditional macroeconomic fundamentals. The core of his approach is Keynes's asset market view, as summarized by Krause's statement that, in this environment, speculators "do not need to forecast the market's fundamentals to be successful because they can still profit by forecasting correctly the behavior of their fellow speculators" (Krause 1991: 33). He believes that this is the case because speculation is no longer a marginal activity in the market.

Expectations. Most recently, John Harvey has worked to build a heterodox explanation of exchange rate determination (1991, 1993a, 1993b). Like Schulmeister and Krause, he sets out to explain the phenomenon which orthodoxy finds most elusive: short-term currency price movements. He begins with the premise that is now well accepted even in neoclassical literature, that the vast majority of daily currency market activity is only indirectly related to international trade or investment. Hence it is the propensities of currency dealers themselves, not their customers, that are the most important to understand. Drawing from Schulmeister, Harvey models dealers as having two sets of expectations, each of which is based on technical and fundamental analysis (the former carrying more weight in the formation of short-term expectations, and vice versa). Harvey (1993a) also comes to the same conclusion as Krause regarding the nature of speculation in the market. Where he differs somewhat is in his emphasis of the institutional themes of ceremonial and instrumental valuing, and his belief that there is no significant difference between determinants of short- and long-run currency prices.

Beyond updating and extending the work of Schulmeister and Krause, Harvey (1993b) has tested a version of what he calls a post-Keynesian model of exchange rate determination. Using daily observations, he explains currency price movements using all the variables he believes exchange dealers find most important: economic and political news, technical analysis and psychological pressures to buy and sell, tempered by their longer-term expectations. While certainly not conclusive, his results indicate that the model tests extremely well.

Uncertainty. Neoclassicism should be applauded for coming to the conclusion that one of its core concepts did not adequately explain exchange rate behavior. It is nonetheless disturbing that this conclusion led to a change in focus rather than a search for new tools of analysis. What little has been done in heterodox thought, however, seems to fill the void left by orthodoxy quite well. But we are still well short of a comprehensive explanation. In particular, even though all the non-mainstream approaches have emphasized the role of market participants' expectations, none has offered more than an ad hoc theory of them. This may seem a daunting task, but the groundwork has already been done in psychology. The extensive theoretical and empirical study of Amos Tversky and Daniel Kahneman (1992) has allowed them to produce a model of decision making under uncertainty far superior to that used by economists. This model is consistent with many of the phenomena seen in the foreign exchange market. It would seem that the next logical step for heterodox economists in this area would be to adapt that model to the specifics of the exchange market, so as to provide a viable explanation for the "irrationalities" of the foreign exchange market.

See also:

Bretton Woods system; international money and finance

Selected references

Bryan, Dick (1995) *The Chase Across the Globe: International Accumulation and the Contradictions for Nation States*, Boulder, CO: Westview Press.

Harvey, John T.(1991) "A Post Keynesian View of Exchange Rate Determination," *Journal of Post Keynesian Economics* 14(1): 61–71.

—— (1993a) "Daily Exchange Rate Variance," *Journal of Post Keynesian Economics* 15(4): 515–40.

—— (1993b) "The Institution of Foreign Exchange Trading," *Journal of Economic Issues* 27(3): 679–98.

Krause, Laurence A. (1991) *Speculation and the Dollar: The Political Economy of Exchange Rates*, Boulder, CO: Westview Press.

Schulmeister, Stephan (1987) *An Essay on Exchange Rate Dynamics*, Research Unit Labour Market and Employment, Discussion Paper 87-8, Berlin: Wissenschaftzentrum Berlin für Sozialforschung.

Taylor, Mark P. (1995a) "Exchange Rate Modelling and Macro Fundamentals: Failed Partnership or Open Marriage?," *British Review of Economic Issues* 17(42): 1–41.

—— (1995b) "The Economics of Exchange Rates," *Journal of Economic Literature* 33: 13–47.

Tversky, Amos and Kahneman, Daniel (1992) "Advances in Prospect Theory: Cumulative Representation of Uncertainty," *Journal of Risk and Uncertainty* 5: 297–323.

Visser, H. (1989) "Exchange Rate Theories," *De Economist* 137(1).

JOHN T. HARVEY

expectations

All but the most trivial of economic activities require that individuals (a) predict the outcomes associated with the choices available to them, and then (b) choose a course of action based on those forecasts. Both processes are manifestations of reasoning on the part of the economic agent. Thus, expectations, choice and rationality are very closely related concepts in economic theory and in reality.

That expectations play such a central role is well recognized by all schools of thought. However, the relative emphasis placed on modelling them (directly or indirectly) varies considerably with both the context of the study and the characteristics and biases of the research program in question. It is the latter that is of most interest here.

Neoclassical view

The neoclassical view of expectations (and decision making) is strongly influenced by their belief that market systems are, unless proven otherwise, optimal and efficient. They further contend that human beings are by nature rational utility-maximizers. This characterization of human behavior is, however, rather open-ended. The confidence of neoclassical economists in the efficacy of free markets leads them to define rational utility-maximization in a unique manner consistent with the assumption that market solutions are optimal.

For example, orthodox economists contend that rational economic agents who are free to make their own decisions will, on average, make the "right" one. In other words, they will choose the option that would maximize their utility given the average outcome. This view is formalized in expected utility theory (also known as rational choice or subjective utility theory) and can be illustrated with a simple example. Imagine the following choices: (a) one alternative that promised a 10 percent chance of a gain of $500 (and a 90 percent chance of no gain) and (b) another that gave a 20 percent chance of a gain of $2,000 (and an 80 percent chance of no gain). The rational actor would choose the second. This is so because, assuming a large enough number of trials, the first choice would yield a gain of $50 on average (one gain of $500 per ten trials) while the second would give $400 (one gain of $2,000 per five trials).

The orthodox economic view of expectations is very similar, also assuming that rational economic agents will be "right" on average.

The theory of rational expectations (see Lucas and Sargent 1981; Muth 1961) intentionally makes no attempt to explain how expectations are formed. It contends that whatever the process, rationality, combined with the discipline of the market, must (after a period of learning) lead to a situation in which any persistent forecasting errors are eliminated. This is so because, if the expectations were biased by a repeated error, the error would represent profitable information that could and would be exploited. Thus, any remaining errors must be entirely random.

Rational expectations and expected utility have become vital empirical and theoretical research tools in neoclassical economics (though there are criticisms from within neoclassicism). It is no coincidence that they are consistent with the basic themes of the PARADIGMS within which they were developed (a characteristic of normal scientific research that is certainly not limited to neoclassicism). They justify a market system in that they show that rational, utility-maximizing individuals who are given the freedom to choose will, on average, select the alternatives most consistent with their welfare.

Post-Keynesian views

Post-Keynesian economists have been highly critical of the so-called "rational expectations revolution." Because they draw their inspiration from KEYNES, post-Keynesians have tended to focus on factors consistent with their belief that market systems are inherently unstable and prone to instability. With respect to expectations, the most important factors in this regard are UNCERTAINTY and non-ergodicity.

Paul Davidson argues that, in order for rational expectations to hold true, it must be possible to create probability distributions of future events based on those from the past (Davidson 1982–3). But this can only be accomplished if we can assume that the processes that create events in the economy (if that is a valid analogy in the first place) do not change over time, i.e. if the economic world is ergodic. If the world is in fact non-ergodic and the processes do change over time, then it is impossible to draw accurate inferences from the past about the future, especially with sufficient precision to build probability distributions. This is exactly what Sir John Hicks and G.L.S. Shackle have argued, the latter in terms of the "crucial decision." When a person (for example, an entrepreneur) makes a choice that forever changes the circumstances in which future choices must be made, that person has made a crucial decision: "In other words, crucial choice involves, *by definition*, situations where the very performance of choice destroys the existing distribution functions" (Davidson 1982–3: 192). This makes rational expectations impossible.

In building their explanation of expectations, post-Keynesians argue that the future is uncertain. Uncertainty causes the expectations of economic agents to be tenuous and subject to sudden and violent change. In general, it is argued that fundamental uncertainty forces agents to adopt different methods of decision-making than would be appropriate under circumstances typically assumed in neoclassicism (i.e. absolute or probabilistic certainty). Because they lack adequate information for decision-making, market participants are forced, by the necessity of action, to rely on present circumstances as being a reliable guide to those in the future (even though they know they are not). Only in so far as they have specific reasons to expect otherwise do they stray from this convention. The basis for such specific reasons can never be more than vague, however (again because of uncertainty), and thus sudden and violent changes in the conventional valuation are quite possible. Keynes's view is summarized by Geoff Hodgson: "Actions flow from judgements about the future (which often lack a firm, objective empirical foundation) as well as from observation of 'the convention' that is formed by the action of others" (Hodgson 1985: 13).

The sort of calm rationality described by expected utility theory cannot exist under uncertainty. Keynes goes so far as to say that if "mathematical expectation" were the only source of direction, then "enterprise will fade and die" (Keynes 1936: 162). Our sense of spontaneous optimism, or ANIMAL SPIRITS, prompts us to action, despite the serious lack of information regarding the likely outcomes.

Institutionalist views

Institutionalist economists have no argument with the post-Keynesian stand, except that they see it as incomplete. On this matter Hodgson writes:

> In Keynes' work there is also a failure to consider the processes through which expectations are formed and the social culture and structures which give them colour and substance. This omission is not untypical of the overwhelming majority of economic theorists, but it is all the more acute for Keynes who made uncertainty and expectations central to his analysis.
> (Hodgson 1985: 16)

In particular, institutionalists see the lack of emphasis on society and CULTURE as a weakness: "The nature and structure of economic institutions is at least as relevant as 'psychology' in the determination of expectations" (Hodgson 1985: 17). At this stage, little has been done to address this shortcoming, but it is nonetheless interesting that the institutionalists' predilection with the social organization of economic activity is apparent in their view of expectations.

Marxist views

MARX did not write a great deal about expectations, nor have his followers. Nevertheless, as Claudio Sardoni has argued, Marxist theory must at least implicitly assume Keynes-like expectations, especially with respect to the existence of uncertainty. The role that this plays in Marx's theory is, as in the post-Keynesian, in making the economy unstable. In particular, it creates the possibility of hoarding, thus breaking Say's Law (Sardoni 1991: 219–39).

Conclusion

For all four schools of thought, central paradigmatic themes play an important role in the modeling of expectations. Perhaps this should not be surprising, given the importance of expectations to economic activity. Indeed, neoclassicism would have a difficult time explaining the ability of independent agents to achieve optimality in the presence of uncertainty, as would post-Keynesians in modeling a world of volatility within the framework of rational choice and expectations. Which is most accurate? Obviously, that is not a question that can be easily answered. It is interesting to note, however, that the extensive theoretical and empirical work done in psychology on the subject of expectations and decision-making shares far more with the post-Keynesian and institutionalist traditions than with the neoclassical (see Kahneman and Tversky 1979).

See also:

conventions; institutional political economy: major contemporary themes; Marxist political economy: contemporary varieties; neoclassical economics; post-Keynesian political economy: major contemporary themes; post-Keynesian theory of choice; time

Selected references

Davidson, Paul (1982–3) "Rational Expectations: A Fallacious Foundation for Studying Crucial Decision-Making Processes," *Journal of Post Keynesian Economics* 5(2): 182–98.

Hodgson, G.M. (1985) "Persuasion, Expectations and the Limits to Keynes," in Tony Lawson and Hasham Pesaran (eds), *Keynes' Economics: Methodological Issues*, Armonk, NY: M.E. Sharpe, 10–45.

——(1988) *Economics and Institutions: A Manifesto for a Modern Institutional Economics*, Philadelphia: University of Philadelphia Press.

Kahneman, D. and Tversky, A. (1979) "Prospect Theory: An Analysis of Decision Under Risk," *Econometrica* 47(March): 263–91.

Keynes, J.M. (1936) *The General Theory of Employment, Interest and Money*, San Diego, CA: Harcourt Brace Jovanovich, 1964.

Lucas, R.E. and Sargent, T.J. (1981) *Rational Expectations and Econometric Practices*, Minneapolis: University of Minnesota Press.

Muth, J.F. (1961) "Rational Expectations and the Theory of Price Movements," *Econometrica* 29: 315–35.

Sardoni, C. (1991) "Marx and Keynes: The Critique of Say's Law," in G.A. Caravale (ed.), *Marx and Modern Analysis*, vol. 2, *The Future of Capitalism and the History of Thought*, Aldershot: Edward Elgar, 219–39.

JOHN T. HARVEY

exploitation

In a sense, "taking advantage of" or "selfishly using" other people is precisely the sort of behavior assumed to be the norm by mainstream neoclassical economics. There, market transactors are seen as forthrightly using each other in pure, unabashed self-interest, and odious as this universalized self-seeking may seem, no one is harmed by it, at least not in competitive markets where an "invisible hand" is said to turn it to the best interest of all.

Nature of exploitation

Heterodox political economists, however, understand "exploitation" quite differently. Some would argue that not only is self-oriented utility-maximization immoral, even in ideal circumstances (see ETHICS AND MORALITY), but it is also contrary to rationality, being antithetical to the survival needs of a highly social human species. Moreover, as heterodox economists use the term, "exploitation" designates a fundamentally unbalanced relationship: the "exploiter" has some form of power over the other person – perhaps based on a threat of physical or emotional abuse, or fraud or other deception –

exploitation

and uses it to get the other person to do things that are not in his/her own interest, but in the exploiter's interest instead. The "subordinate" may or may not be aware that some of his/her time or energy is being diverted for someone else's use, but in either case would not consent to it if permitted some voice in the matter.

Thus, exploitation means taking for one's own advantage some of the very "life-activity" of another person or getting the other person to labor for oneself rather than for his/her own or community purposes. Most mainstream economists would doubt that exploitation, so defined, exists in any great degree in free market systems, although they do acknowledge that firms with ECONOMIC POWER due to imperfect MARKET STRUCTURES may "exploit" their customers or employees. Heterodox economists, however, are committed to investigating several varieties of exploitation and find them pervasive, and even systemic, in the capitalist economy, just as they are elsewhere.

One variety links to social CLASS, in which subordinate class members labor for a dominant class by virtue of a lack of access to society's means of production. Another variety relates to racial exploitation, in which members of one racial or ethnic group are similarly compelled to labor for another. A third variety links to PATRIARCHY, where women and perhaps children are exploited by men. Finally, there is colonialism and imperialism, in which people of one society or nation are exploited by those of another.

Class exploitation

Of these, probably the best understood among economists is class-based exploitation. Its analysis is in many ways a model for that of the other forms, and some would even subsume the other forms as special cases of it. A dominant CLASS compels or induces a working class to produce a surplus of goods and services, i.e. above and beyond what working class people themselves need for "subsistence." The surplus is appropriated by the dominant class, hence represents the product of a portion of workers' labor that they have expended not for themselves but for the dominant class. Because some kind of power structure is necessarily involved, part of the surplus must go to sustaining that structure, for example, for the subsistence and other material needs of people in the "command hierarchy," in police and adjudication institutions, in ideological activities and so on. The rest of the surplus is then available to the dominant class for personal or collective consumption or for investment (see EXPLOITATION AND SURPLUS VALUE; PRODUCTIVE AND UNPRODUCTIVE LABOR).

In principle, it is possible to measure the extent or the rate of exploitation in a class society, for example, by the amount of labor time workers spend producing the surplus, relative to that spent on the "necessary" portion of their product (Marx 1867). So measured, the extent of exploitation may be increased *ceteris paribus* by increasing the hours of work per day (or per year) or the intensity with which workers labor, by increasing the PRODUCTIVITY of labor, or by reducing workers' material livelihood. In the last case, in principle, the rate of exploitation may be so greatly increased that the working class is superexploited, i.e the workers' portion of their total product is reduced to something less than they require for subsistence (Mandel 1970: 455). Of course, such a circumstance cannot last for long, and increasing the rate of exploitation by these or other means might require a greater expenditure on strengthening the requisite power structure than may be warranted by the additional surplus returned to the dominant class.

In general, the rate of exploitation in a society at a point in time is determined by the whole complexity of factors underlying both the PRODUCTIVITY of labor and the balance of the "class struggle" (see CLASS PROCESSES). Besides thus indicating the state of an important set of social relations, the rate of exploitation is a crucial determinant of an economy's capacity for growth (see SURPLUS APPROACH TO DEVELOPMENT) and, particularly in capitalist economies, of the rate of profit as well (see FALLING RATE OF PROFIT TENDENCY).

Obviously SLAVERY and FEUDALISM are examples of class-based exploitation, and nearly all Western political economists would agree that so too are modern Soviet-type "communist" economies (but see SOCIALISM AND COMMUNISM). Despite neoclassical economists' general disregard for the claim, CAPITALISM is arguably an economy of class-based exploitation. Property income, the hallmark of capitalism, is not a "reward for productive work," but is instead a share of the economy's total product received solely as a function of property ownership (see SURPLUS VALUE AS RENT, INTEREST AND PROFIT) and access to it is, of course, highly unequal.

Racial exploitation, patriarchy and imperialism are closely connected with the phenomenon of social class. Classes have often been partly defined along lines of gender and/or "foreign-ness," and all these forms of exploitation probably arose together and reinforced each other in the pre-history of human "civilization". Today, however, these modes of exploitation are considerably differentiated.

Gender exploitation

Men's exploitation of women rests mainly upon unequal access to means of economic and personal enrichment and positions of status and influence, even in the most advanced societies today, on account of legal, cultural and other institutional arrangements. In the paid labor force, a GENDER DIVISION OF LABOR – arising from socialization in youth, school "tracking" and so on – places women disproportionately in subordinate and low-wage occupations. Thanks to these inequalities in society at large, power relations arise within the household, where they in turn engender an "unequal exchange" of domestic labor between men and women. Violence may also play a role in subduing women in the household, and their inferior position there then reinforces their disadvantaged status in the larger society by permitting them to be more easily exploited in the paid labor force. Lower wages for women than for men follow directly, even in the same occupations, with women being thereby subject to a higher rate of exploitation in wage labor – which, of course, reinforces the adverse power relations and exploitation to which they are subject within the family.

Racial and ethnic exploitation

Similar processes are at work in racial and ethnic exploitation. Legal and extra-legal discrimination places ethnic groups in disadvantaged positions in external and INTERNAL LABOR MARKETS, housing markets, schooling and so on. This leads to major disparities in their and their offspring's accumulated wealth, culture and HUMAN CAPITAL. This in turn reinforces their segregation into subordinate and low-paying occupations, and strengthens attitudes and practices of RACISM toward them among more privileged groups. While many would contend that capitalism *per se* has nothing to do with race and gender exploitation, clearly it is arguable that it has historically propagated rather than mitigated both forms.

Colonial exploitation

Capitalism is also implicated in the modern history of colonial expansionism (see PRIMITIVE ACCUMULATION). In general, exploitation in colonialism occurs by overtly coercive means: the colonizer simply takes the colony's products and resources without any pretense of offering anything in exchange. In imperialism, at least that of the late twentieth century, the means of exploitation are much more complex. One country may subtly apply political and military power to dominate the other country's TRADE POLICY and other policies on financial and investment flows, EXCHANGE RATES, taxes, labor relations and so on; or it may merely take advantage of an industrially undeveloped country's inherently retarded position in competitive world markets (see COMPARATIVE ADVANTAGE AND UNEQUAL EXCHANGE). In either case, the outcome is a retardation or reversal in the subordinate country's development, due to the appropriation of its economic surplus by the dominant country (and perhaps the latter's allied "comprador" classes in the subordinate country) (see UNEVEN DEVELOPMENT).

Legitimization of exploitation

Exploitation is invariably rationalized by those benefiting from it (see IDEOLOGY). For example, dominant classes may argue that economic development requires a surplus product for investment, and class-based exploitation (especially the capitalist kind) is the most effective means of appropriating one. Of course, it must still be shown that those in the working class (or perhaps their offspring) will themselves benefit from the growth process – and that, most importantly, they consent to it. Alternatively, the dominant groups may argue that they "deserve" their status in one way or another; subordinates are, for example, "innately inferior." The analysis of exploitation shows quite clearly, however, that the disadvantaged are in that position not on account of any "inferiority" at all, but by having been subjugated to others' advantage. Progress toward a congenial human society can only begin by acknowledging this.

See also:

colonialism and imperialism: classic texts; inequality; labour market discrimination; race in political economy: major contemporary themes

Selected references

Barone, Charles (1985) *Marxist Thought on Imperialism*, Armonk, NY: M.E. Sharpe.
Boss, Helen (1990) *Theories of Surplus and Transfer: Parasites and Producers in Economic Thought*, Boston: Unwin Hyman.
Delphy, Christine and Leonard, Diana (1992) *Familial Exploitation: A New Analysis of Marriage in Contemporary Western Societies*, Cambridge: Polity Press.
Mandel, Ernest (1970) *Marxist Economic Theory*, New York: Monthly Review Press.
Marx, Karl (1867) *Das Kapital*, vol. 1, New York: Vintage Books, 1977.
Roemer, John E. (1988) *Free to Lose*, Cambridge, MA: Harvard University Press.
Walby, S. (1990) *Theorizing Patriarchy*, Oxford: Blackwell.

ERIC SCHUTZ

exploitation and surplus value

Introduction

Exploitation – the idea that some person or group in society is able to acquire something in return for nothing – has generated controversy in political economy for over a hundred years. Perhaps the key difference between the competing Marxist and non-Marxist theories can be traced to their opposed views on this very issue. For Marxist political economy, the rewards of capitalists (e.g. industrial profit) are gained on the basis of their exploitation of workers. The elimination of that exploitation should be added to society's social agenda. In stark contrast, NEOCLASSICAL ECONOMICS holds that the rewards of capitalists are exactly equal to what they have contributed to make those received rewards possible. Workers cannot be exploited (if they receive their marginal product) because their wages are equal to the value they add to production.

The claim that capitalists exploit workers is only part of the Marxist thesis. A related idea asserts that today's capitalist exploitation is merely a different form of a common CLASS exploitation that has bedeviled societal arrangements throughout human history. Particularly disturbing is the notion that CAPITALISM shares class exploitation in common with what are often held (by capitalists) to be backward if not despised systems, such as FEUDALISM and SLAVERY. Its presumed presence in capitalism serves to undermine what otherwise are taken to be its progressive economic and political accomplishments.

Still another related idea holds that capitalist exploitation is the source for what other dominant classes in society receive as their rewarded incomes. For the most part, merchants, industrial managers, state officials, corporate owners, landlords and moneylenders live indirectly off the value produced by but not returned to workers. The surplus value produced by workers is first received by a class of capitalists, who then distribute it to these other classes in order to gain from them the necessary conditions enabling the initial exploitation to take place (see CLASSES OF CAPITALISM). Marx used this idea to ridicule the non-Marxist claim that these other classes – like the capitalists – receive their respective incomes for adding new value to what workers alone add (Marx 1894: 956–7). Let us examine why his logic led him to believe that this claim is logically impossible.

Source of capitalist exploitation

The source of capitalist exploitation is found in Marx's theory of surplus value, presented in his three volumes of *Das Kapital*. His words are clear enough: "The rate of surplus value is therefore an exact expression for the degree of exploitation of labor power by capital, or of the worker by the capitalist" (Marx 1867: 326). While his overriding aim in *Das Kapital* is to explain exploitation in capitalism, the argument begins there in an unexpected way. Marx starts by constructing a world of fairness, equity and equality in which the exploitation of one human being by another seems unlikely. For example, in the economic arena, all goods produced by labor, deemed by society to be useful and destined for sale – called commodities – exchange for precisely what they are worth, no more and no less. Their worth is measured by what Marx defines as the socially necessary abstract labor time required for their production. For example, if five hours of abstract labor are required to produce a box of apples, and two and one-half hours to produce a shirt, then in the market two shirts exchange for one box of apples.

If this kind of equivalent exchange exists among all produced commodities, how can a surplus value arise? No individual or group can take unfair market advantage of another when exchange is always assumed to be one of equivalents. This Ricardian problem (named after David Ricardo, the political economist who first theorized it) receives a new answer from Marx (see Dobb 1973: 146–7).

First of all, Marx constructed a world of equivalent exchanges. Then, in an ironic twist to his argument, he returned to the world of use values to seek the source of surplus value. Unlike the social arena of exchange, however, the consumption of commodities involves a very private relationship between buyers and their purchased commodities. His theory of surplus value begins by peeking into this private domain of a commodity's use value to its buyer. Is there a particular kind of use value that could account for value and hence surplus value? Since Marx already has assumed that abstract labor is the source of value and exchange value, he has specified the potential value-creating substance in this abstract labor. However, Marx also has created a problem for his proposed solution: parallel to all use values, abstract labor cannot be purchased or sold. Marx's answer is to invent a new commodity called labor power which has an exchange value and a use value of abstract labor (see LABOR AND LABOR POWER).

The stage is now set for him to explain the source of surplus value and, hence, exploitation. A capitalist purchases the commodity labor power and, similar to all purchased commodities, buys it at its value. In exchange, the worker is not cheated by the capitalist: he or she receives a sum of value (in wages) exactly equal to what that sold labor-power commodity is worth.

The workday and labor time

For example, suppose the workday is ten hours, and the commodity being produced by workers is apples. Imagine it takes workers five hours to produce enough apples to equal in value terms their wage, which ensures their sustenance. It thus takes the value equivalent of one box of food (representing five hours of embodied abstract labor) to reproduce a

exploitation and surplus value

worker's labor power (their laboring capacity). The capitalist provides the worker with that equivalent value sum, for that is precisely the value of labor power. Receiving this wage, the worker purchases the required consumer goods at their value. Thus, "necessary labor time," that which is necessary for the daily and generational reproduction of labor power, represents five hours.

Parallel to sellers of any commodity, workers sell their labor power for its exchange value (five hours of abstract labor), thereby alienating its use-value (potential abstract labor) to the buyer. The capitalist as buyer acquires this use-value, consumes it productively by putting the worker to work for our assumed ten hours (to produce, in this case, two boxes of apples), and hence, as its consumer, receives whatever value results. If the resulting value of these newly produced commodities containing abstract labor is greater than the cost of gaining it, namely the cost of labor power (one box of apples), then capitalist consumption is productive of a surplus value (see PRODUCTIVE AND UNPRODUCTIVE LABOR). This surplus belongs to the capitalist buyer and consumer of labor power, for it is always the buyer and never the seller that acquires a commodity's use-value.

Thus, the workday (W) is divided into necessary labor time (N), representing five hours producing one box of apples, and surplus labor time (S) of an extra five hours producing one box of apples: W = N + S = 5 + 5. When the goods are sold on the market, the necessary labor time is transformed into wages, or what Marx called variable capital, and the surplus labor time is transformed into surplus value. Workers thus work twice as long as they need to for their sustenance. The surplus value is thus ultimately created in production, pending its sale on the market. The capitalist receives this surplus value of five abstract labor hours and its product of one box of apples for doing absolutely nothing other than consuming the commodity called labor power.

Marx concludes that capitalists receive in production the product of someone else's labor without their giving anything in return. In this example, it is an unpaid labor of five hours: capitalists exploit workers. A measure of this exploitation is the quantum of value received in the privacy of their production space relative to the value paid in the openness of the market: the ratio of unpaid to paid labor. Thus the rate of exploitation (e) is surplus value (s) divided by variable capital (v) multiplied by 100:

$$e = (s/v)(100)$$

In this case it is 100 percent: $5/5 \times 100 = 100\%$ assuming that hours of 'labour time' correspond to the same units of 'value'.

Marxist theory reveals to workers and others in society what otherwise would be a very private, concealed act of exploitation (see COMMODITY FETISHISM). Capitalists receive a reward (a surplus in the form of "profit"), not as some have claimed because they plunder or cheat workers, and not as others have argued because they take risks, own property, postpone consumption, manage a business or work hard. Rather, it is because they are in a position in society in which they can merely consume workers' labor power and hence acquire its value and surplus value-creating use-value.

Exploiting labor

To enter into that exploiting position, however, is an entirely different matter. Entry may require would-be-capitalists to engage in or benefit from a variety of diverse actions or events, including risk taking or good fortune, owning or inheriting property, investing in productive assets or plundering. Further, once firmly established in that position, capitalists need to secure and reproduce it by distributing their appropriated surplus to the classes of merchants, landlords, moneylenders, corporate managers and so on. The latter's receipt of shares of the already appropriated surplus value is the reason why Marx ridiculed the idea that these classes added new value that they then received in return (see SURPLUS VALUE AS RENT, INTEREST AND PROFIT).

Entering into and *securing* the capitalist exploiting position are very different activities from what occurs once the position is securely held. Once firmly held, the only function of the capitalist is to appropriate a surplus produced by workers, that is, to consume labor power unproductively. These different functions are often conflated or the exploiting function denied altogether in non-Marxist theory, with the consequence that the value received by capitalists is understood to be a reward for property ownership, luck, or for their doing something directly productive. The alternative Marxist lesson is to understand how these different classes function: workers, not capitalists, owners or landlords, produce value and surplus value. Hence for workers to end their exploitation, they need to be in a new class position in which they will be the ones to consume their own labor power. As in Marx's day, that new position still remains to be accomplished today.

See also:

domestic labor debate; economic surplus; exploitation; participatory democracy and self-management; socialism and communism; surplus approach to development; surplus approach to political economy; wage determination

Selected references

Boss, Helen (1990) *Theories of Surplus and Transfer: Parasites and Producers in Economic Thought*, Boston: Unwin Hyman.

Dobb, Maurice (1973) *Theories of Value and Distribution Since Adam Smith*, Cambridge: Cambridge University Press.

Marx, Karl (1867–94) *Das Kapital*, Volumes I and II, published as *Capital, Volumes 1 and 3*, Harmondsworth: Penguin, 1976, 1979.

STEPHEN RESNICK

F

falling rate of profit tendency

CLASSICAL POLITICAL ECONOMY was centrally concerned with the distribution of the social product between the major classes of capitalism, and the unstable growth of output. David Ricardo, for instance, developed a theory in which the rate of profit declined toward zero in the accumulation process as corn became more expensive with the onset of diminishing returns to agriculture. Marx's analysis of the falling rate of profit (FRP) in the *Grundrisse*, *Theories of Surplus Value* and *Das Kapital* constituted a sympathetic critique of Ricardo's theory. It was Marx who devised a law of the falling rate of profit, and then posited counter-tendencies. The debate about the falling rate of profit has lasted one hundred years, and its analysis holds a central place in modern political economy in one form or another.

Contradictions and limits of capitalism

The recent (1973) publication in English of Marx's *Grundrisse*, his first major work in political economy (written for self-clarification), has given us new insight into the problem. In this work, Marx explains that the contradictions of capitalism are numerous and that each of them exerts some influence over the rate of profit. He also devised a "six-book plan" for his ideal system of political economy, of which *Das Kapital* was to be the first book: the books were to cover (1) capital, (2) wage labor, (3) landed property, (4) the state and (5) foreign trade, and (6) the world market and crises (see MARX'S METHODOLOGY OF POLITICAL ECONOMY). The implication is that the rate of profit needs to be situated within each of these successive books to gain a total view of the matter. However, Marx himself never got very far into this project.

In the *Grundrisse*, the path of capitalist evolution and transformation is seen as being dynamic, unpredictable and unstable. Here, more than in any other work, Marx examines the rate of profit dialectically as being involved in notions of the barriers and limits to capital (see Lebowitz 1976), a decentered totality (see Cullenberg 1994), the major CONTRADICTIONS of capitalism, and the question of the historically transitory nature of the system (see CAPITALIST BREAKDOWN DEBATE). Marx repeatedly says that capitalism has a progressive side and a contradictory side, and that these two sides are inextricably linked. Hence, the immanent forces of capitalism endogenously create their own barriers and limits, which periodically threaten the reproduction of the system and thereby affect the rate of profit.

The "positive" aspect of capitalism is the incessant trend toward the accumulation of capital both in terms of new techniques and additions to the current stock of buildings, factories, machines and so on. Increases in productivity thus potentially provide material benefit to people. The "negative" aspect of capitalism emanates from the capital accumulation process itself. In the development of new methods of production, firms which are unable to compete are left to bankruptcy, workers are made redundant and the social and material environment is continually ravaged by the forces of "progress." Both aspects of capitalism are endogenously ingrained in the system, and thus represent a classic contradiction.

These problems, for Marx, are manifest in technical limits and barriers to the rate of profit. For instance, he showed that this innovation and accumulation increases surplus labor time, but at a decreasing rate over time (*Grundrisse* 1857–8: 335–6). This decline in "marginal surplus labor time" represents a limit to the maximum rate of profit. This limit propels capitalism to expand on a world scale, extend markets, promote credit and create new needs for people in order to promote the turnover of capital, and thereby attempt (temporarily) to surmount the barriers of production which inhibit profitability (*Grundrisse* 1857–8: 408). However, by trying to surmount the limits to profitability in this way, the seeds are sown for even greater crises as credit failure leads to chains of bankruptcy, trade failure leads to a general world crisis, and the new needs may fail to be internalized by the population due to lack of demand or other factors. The *Grundrisse* does not lead one to accept the view of a continual long-term fall in the rate of profit. Rather, changes in the rate of profit are tendential, cyclical, perhaps long-term in nature, but never of a linear or simplistic nature.

Rate of profit definitions

In *Das Kapital*, Marx was rather limited methodologically to discussing the rate of profit in relation to production, circulation and the unity of the two. What emerged was a simple series of models in which the rising trend of innovation and accumulation leads to a lower rate of profit due to increases in the organic COMPOSITION OF CAPITAL. As firms innovate and reap high profits, other firms begin to adopt the techniques even though the rate of profit will decline in the long run through this competitive process (a question arises as to whether this "micro" process is valid at the "macro" level). This trend is countered periodically by forces which increase the rate of profit.

The value rate of profit, (p), is defined as the flow of surplus value (s) divided by constant (c) and variable (v) capital: $p = \{s/(c+v)\}$. Through the rearranging of terms, this formula can be shown as

$$p = (s/v)/\{(c/v)+1\}.$$

Thus, the rate of profit is positively related to the rate of surplus value (s/v) and inversely related to the organic composition of capital (c/v). Growing mechanization, innovation and concentration of capital may lead to a rise in the capital/labor ratio (technical composition of capital) and the value of constant capital divided by variable capital (organic composition of capital). If only variable capital produces surplus value, then, if c/v rises faster than s/v, the general rate of profit will decline over time. Constant capital includes the value of fixed capital and raw materials. Variable capital is the value of the consumption goods utilized by workers – the value of labor power (see LABOR AND LABOR POWER). The rate of profit will decline if innovation is labor saving, and if raw material and fixed capital costs do not decline. All this assumes that values are proportional to prices of production and market prices (see TRANSFORMATION PROBLEM).

Counteracting forces

Even in *Das Kapital*, however, Marx was interested in the dialectical movement between the forces reducing the rate of profit and the forces countering these tendencies (*Das Kapital* III: chaps 13–15). Over the business cycle and in the longer run, counteracting tendencies to the fall come into play which historically have a critical role in increasing the rate of profit. The most important counteracting tendencies are (a) an increase in the rate of absolute surplus value (e.g. an increase in the number of hours in the working day), (b) a reduction of wages, (c) cheapening of capital goods and raw materials, (d) an increase in the RESERVE ARMY OF LABOR (which could increase productivity as workers fear losing their jobs), (e) an expansion of the TURNOVER TIME OF CAPITAL on the world market, and (f) a decline in the rate of interest. Real movements in the rate of profit, therefore, depend on the relative forces involved.

Debate and modern perspectives

Historically, the notion of the tendency of the rate of profit to fall has been subject to a long and heated debate. Some attempts have been made to subject the rising organic composition of capital hypothesis to empirical analysis, which has cast doubt on the importance of this variable relative to others. For instance, Joseph Gilman in *The Falling Rate of Profit* in 1957 found that the organic composition of capital (c/v) increased in the USA between 1849 and 1919, but that it was relatively stable between 1919 and 1939. Weisskopf (1979) found that the rising share of wages in national income in the 1970s adversely affected the rate of profit more than other factors. Some other studies have shown mixed results. In general, modern research has cast doubt on the notion that the organic composition of capital necessarily rises.

The Okishio Theorem represents a critique of simplistic falling rate of profit models. This theorem demonstrates technically that innovation does not have the effect of reducing the rate of profit unless real wages rise (see Bowles 1981). Other models have shown the rate of profit falling as wages rise. Paul Sweezy in the *The Theory of Capitalist Development* in 1942 critiqued the FRP theory and developed an alternative notion of the rising economic surplus with Paul Baran in *Monopoly Capital* in 1965. Modern work has been affected by the cyclical, wave-like and tendential motion of capitalism since the Second World War. The boom of the 1950s and 1960s and the deep recessions of the 1970s–1990s have recast the FRP debate into the search for answers to real world problems of accumulation, growth and profitability, plus the destructive environmental and social consequences of this system.

In the continuing debate, the rate of profit is closely linked with investment. Expected profit is a major determinant of investment and growth. The rate of profit is affected by (a) the power of the labor movement (wages and productivity); (b) the organic composition of capital; (c) the turnover time of capital (a critical factor often ignored); (d) the ratio of PRODUCTIVE AND UNPRODUCTIVE LABOR (although unproductive labor may be necessary for the absorption of the surplus); and (e) the interest rate on financial assets (in the distribution of surplus value between industrial and banking capital). The declining rate of profit since the 1970s, in most advanced capitalist economies, is due to some combination of these variables, and much of the debate is an attempt to ascertain which of these are more important. A lively body of scholarly work has emerged.

Generally, in relation to business cycle dynamics, profit rates increase just before the onset of upswings in economic activity, and decline just before the upper turning point as the recession approaches. Capitalists tend to accumulate capital at more than average rates during the upswing; however, the upswing sets in process trends which tend to reduce the rate of profit (higher raw material prices, interest rates and, often, wages). Capitalism also undergoes long waves and secular movements, and the rate of profit must be scrutinized in these contexts.

In conclusion, the traditional debate around the law of the falling rate of profit has evolved into a critical analysis of the major factors affecting profit, accumulation and growth in tandem with the destructive social and environmental consequences of capital (more research is needed on the links between these processes). A constructive series of debates has emerged.

See also:

competition and the average rate of profit; cyclical crisis models; Kalecki's macro theory of profits; nutcracker theory of the business cycle; profit-squeeze analysis of crises; regulation approach; secular crisis; social structures of accumulation; surplus value as rent, interest and profit

Selected references

Bowles, Samuel (1981) "Technical Change and the Profit Rate: A Simple Proof of the Okishio Theorem," *Cambridge Journal of Economics* 5: 183–6.

Cullenberg, Stephen (1994) *The Falling Rate of Profit: Recasting the Marxian Debate*, Boulder, CO: Pluto Press.

Fitchenbaum, Rudy (1988) "'Business Cycles,'

Turnover and the Rate of Profit: An Empirical Test of Marxian Crisis Theory," *Eastern Economic Journal* 13(3).

Glyn, A. and Sutcliffe, B. (1972) *British Capitalism, Workers and the Profit Squeeze*, London: Penguin.

Lebowitz, Michael A. (1976) "Marx's Falling Rate of Profit: A Dialectical View," *Canadian Journal of Economics* 9: 232–54.

Marglin, Stephen A. and Schor, Juliet B. (1993) *The Postwar Golden Age of Capitalism: Reinterpreting the Postwar Experience*, Oxford: Clarendon Press.

Marx, Karl (1857–8) *Grundrisse*, Harmondsworth: Penguin, 1973.

Moseley, Fred (1991) *The Falling Rate of Profit in the Postwar United States Economy*, London: Macmillan.

Sherman, Howard (1992) *The Business Cycle*, Princeton: Princeton University Press.

Weisskopf, T. (1979) "Marxian Crisis Theory and the Rate of Profit in the Postwar US Economy," *Cambridge Journal of Economics*, December 1979.

Wolff, Edward N. (1987) *Growth, Accumulation, and Unproductive Activity: An Analysis of the Postwar U.S. Economy*, Cambridge: Cambridge University Press.

PHILLIP ANTHONY O'HARA

falling rate of profit tendency: temporal approaches

Karl MARX regarded his explanation of the falling rate of profit tendency as a critical law of modern political economy. However, only since the GREAT DEPRESSION has it assumed a significant role in Marxist discussions of capital accumulation and economic crises. Both before and since, moreover, most Marxist and non-Marxist writers have argued that a falling profit rate tendency fails to result from a coherent, rigorous application of Marx's value theory. They thus deny that accumulation and crises can be legitimately theorized in terms of Marx's law.

In the wake of Okishio's (1961) work, this view has won near-universal acceptance. Yet more recent research has shown that, when Marx's value theory is interpreted in temporal terms, not by means of simultaneous equations, it does corroborate his law of the tendential fall in the profit rate.

Simultaneous and temporal approaches

Under rather general conditions, Okishio's and subsequent research seemingly shows that, given profit rate equalization, technical changes which raise the innovating firm's profit rate (calculated using current prices) cannot lower the economy-wide profit rate. If real wages also rise, a falling profit rate may accompany the technical change, but the fall is actually caused by the wage increase, not labor-saving innovation itself as Marx claimed in *Das Kapital* III, part 3.

These demonstrations depend, however, on the "unobtrusive postulate" that input prices are determined simultaneously with – i.e. constrained to equal – output prices. Ernst (1982) showed that, if the values of commodities fall continually, labor-saving innovation can lead to a falling uniform profit rate under conditions in which the "Okishio theorem" says it must rise. Other researchers have arrived independently at the same result, and have also shown how a temporal interpretation of Marx's value categories results in the falling path of commodity prices (or values) needed for the falling profit rate (see Kliman 1996; Freeman 1996).

When values (or the labor-time equivalents of money prices) decline, a falling profit rate is more likely when fixed capital is valued at historical cost, rather than current cost. Yet the temporalist results do not depend on a particular method of fixed capital valuation or from any special set of assumptions. Rather, they stem from a completely different value calculation. Even if one abstracts from fixed capital, as Okishio's original contribution did, the temporalist profit rate may fall while the simultaneous rate rises.

Example of temporal approach

We offer the following example as a substantiation of this claim (not as a model of the actual accumulation process). In period t, A_{i_t} tons of iron and L_{i_t} labor-hours produce X_{i_t} tons of iron; and A_{w_t} tons of iron and L_{w_t} labor-hours produce X_{w_t} bushels of wheat. P_{i_t}, P_{w_t} and $P_{i_{t+1}}$, $P_{w_{t+1}}$ are period t's input and output prices, respectively, measured in "labor-hours" per unit of output. Assume a uniform real wage rate of b_t bushels of wheat per labor-hour and a uniform profit rate, r_t. Each sector's aggregate output price equals its "cost-price" (expenditures) times "1 plus the profit rate":

$$P_{i_{t+1}} X_{i_t} = (P_{i_t} A_{i_t} + P_{w_t} b_t L_{i_t})(1 + r_t) \quad (1)$$

$$P_{w_{t+1}} X_{w_t} = (P_{i_t} A_{w_t} + P_{w_t} b_t L_{w_t})(1 + r_t) \quad (2)$$

According to the "temporal single-system" interpretation of Marx's theory, aggregate surplus value (or profit), as measured in labor-time, equals living labor extracted $(L_{i_t} + L_{w_t})$ minus the sum of value advanced as wages $(P_{w_t} b_t L_{i_t} + P_{w_t} b_t L_{w_t})$. Hence, although this interpretation has sometimes been thought to allow profit to arise independently of EXPLOITATION AND SURPLUS VALUE, it implies precisely that profit is positive only if workers supply more labor than the labor-time equivalent of their money wages. The aggregate profit rate, surplus value divided by capital advanced, is thus:

$$r_t = \frac{(L_{i_t} + L_{w_t}) - (P_{w_t} b_t L_{i_t} + P_{w_t} b_t L_{w_t})}{(P_{i_t} A_{i_t} + P_{w_t} b_t L_{i_t}) + (P_{i_t} A_{w_t} + P_{w_t} b_t L_{w_t})} \quad (3)$$

Assume that both sectors use 10 percent more iron input and produce 10 percent more output each period, but extract only 1.2 percent more labor. In this case, the technical COMPOSITION OF CAPITAL and labor productivity both rise continually. Holding the real wage rate constant at $b = 11/32$, each innovation would increase profit rates at current prices. Further assume that $A_{i_0} = 44$, $L_{i_0} = 11$, $X_{i_0} = 55$, $A_{w_0} = 24$, and $X_{w_0} = 30$, and that period t_0 input and output prices are equal ($P_{i_{t_0}} = P_{i_{t_1}} = 2.2$; $P_{w_{t_0}} = P_{w_{t_1}} = 0.8$).

Given these assumptions, if equations (1) and (2) were converted into simultaneous equations by replacing the input prices on the right-hand sides with output prices (which would render (3) both redundant and wrong), the profit rate would rise monotonically from 21.21 percent to 25 percent. Yet equations (1) through (3) imply that prices in both sectors fall continually, and the profit rate, initially equal to 21.21 percent, falls monotonically to 15 percent. Since this conclusion contradicts the Okishio theorem without violating any of its stated premises, it undermines the theorem.

Because this example is not a model of capital accumulation, its monotonically declining profit rate is not a prediction that the actual profit rate is incapable of rebounding. If, in response to falling profitability, technical change slackens, the temporalist interpretation suggests that the profit rate will rise. Crises also restore profitability by devaluing and destroying old capital no longer able to be employed profitably, as do collapsing prices that eliminate the overvaluation of capital which arises in "boom" times. These additional results are consonant with Marx's theory that crises are the mechanism by which the tendential fall in the profit rate is periodically overcome (see *Das Kapital* III, ch. 15).

Critique of simultaneous approach

Not only do simultaneous and temporalist profit rates diverge systematically even when fixed capital is disregarded, but the divergence does not depend on particular assumptions concerning rates of growth or technical change, number of sectors, profit and wage rate differentials, etc. Although temporalist results have been challenged on the ground that "unrealistic" examples are used to illustrate the divergence, such criticisms overlook the fact that systems such as (1)–(3) express a different theory of economic relations than do their simultaneous determination counterparts, and therefore yield different results under almost every set of assumptions. If input and output prices are determined simultaneously, the profit rate is a function of use-values (technical and real wage coefficients) alone, not the extraction of surplus labor in production. In system (1)–(3), however, the level of the profit rate depends crucially on surplus-labor extraction.

We suggest that simultaneous conclusions correspond to a theory in which use-value, not labor-time, is the substance of value, and the profit rate measures the expansion of use-value, not the expansion of capital value through the extraction of surplus labor. Because prior research has employed comparative static methods, which prevent value magnitudes from moving in opposition to use-value magnitudes, the elemental difference between the two theories has been obscured until recently. But historical-time examples reveal it clearly.

Consider a corn model, in which wages equal zero, all corn output is reinvested as seedcorn, and extraction of living labor is constant each year. Since the value of last year's output equals the constant capital invested plus the value added by living labor and, since all output is reinvested, this year's constant capital likewise equals last year's constant capital plus the value added. It thus follows trivially from Marx's theory that constant capital (equal here to total capital) increases continually and, since the value added by living labor (equal here to surplusvalue) is constant, the profit rate, surplus value divided by total capital, declines continually.

Yet if each year's corn output is 25 percent greater than corn input, the simultaneous profit rate is a constant 25 percent. This conception of profitability thus seems to resemble both the neoclassical capital-productivity theory of the interest rate and Ricardo's explanation of profit rate movements in terms of physical productivity, which, in Marx's view, "flees from economics to seek refuge in organic chemistry" (1857–8: 754).

Selected references

Ernst, John R. (1982) "Simultaneous Valuation Extirpated: A Contribution to the Critique of the Neo-Ricardian Concept of Value," *Review of Radical Political Economics* 14(2): 85–94.

Freeman, Alan (1996) "Price, Value and Profit – A Continuous, General Treatment," in Alan Freeman and Guglielmo Carchedi (eds), *Marx and Non-Equilibrium Economics*, Cheltenham: Edward Elgar.

Kliman, Andrew (1996) "A Value-Theoretic Critique of the Okishio Theorem," in Alan Freeman and Guglielmo Carchedi (eds), *Marx and Non-Equilibrium Economics*, Cheltenham: Edward Elgar.

Marx, Karl (1857–8) *Grundrisse: Foundations of the Critique of Political Economy*, New York: Vintage, 1973.

Okishio, Nobuo (1961) "Technical Changes and the Rate of Profit," *Kobe University Economic Review* 7: 85–99.

ANDREW KLIMAN
ALAN FREEMAN

family wage

The family wage is an ideological construct which expresses the idea that male breadwinners should earn a wage sufficient to support a family. The concept emerged during political and economic struggles in the nineteenth and early twentieth centuries in industrialized countries such as England and the United States. It was articulated by trade unions, middle-class reformers, social investigators and policy makers, serving as the basis for key legislative initiatives. Family wage ideology was historically linked to protective legislation such as the Factory Acts (1833, 1847 and 1874) in England. These initiatives limited the work hours of women and children, and thus women's access to employment in certain jobs and industries (Rose 1992). The consequences of family wage policies and protective legislation were (1) married women's decreased labor force participation; (2) segregated employment in lower-paid jobs for those women who were in the paid labor force, and (3) the promulgation of women's economic dependence on male breadwinners (see also Lewis 1984; Horrell and Humphries 1995).

Family wage ideology

May (1982) has suggested that the family wage ideology contained two elements, and the relationship between these two components is crucial to understanding political and economic struggles to achieve the family wage. First, the family wage represented a demand for subsistence and survival for working-class families. Second, it was based on and reinforced emerging social relations which posited separate spheres for men and women. Thus, the debate over the family wage has centered on whether it was a unified working-class strategy, or a means by which male workers gained privileges at the expense of working women. It has been a lightning rod for debates over the relationship between class and gender struggles.

Humphries (1977a, 1977b) explicitly articulated the position that the family wage was a working-class strategy for minimizing family members' labor force participation while maintaining family income. Her discussion was grounded in Marx's contention that wages do not reflect individual workers' productivity, but are the result of historical conflict between classes (see LABOR AND LABOR POWER). Although acknowledging that the family wage may have reinforced sexism in the long run, Humphries viewed the restriction of female labor supply (accompanied by the demand for a family wage) as the only strategy which could also mobilize support from bourgeois ideology. Her argument that patriarchal family structures resulted from working-class strategy was a response to the DOMESTIC LABOR DEBATE, especially those who argued that the family persisted primarily because it was functional for capitalism.

However, Humphries's account has been criticized for emphasizing class struggle over gender conflict. These critics emphasize two problems: (1) they stress the gendered impact of the policies and (2) they deny that working-class women and men were unified in support of a family wage strategy. Humphries is accused of assuming a unity of interests within the working-class family. Married women's economic dependency bestowed power upon male breadwinners within the household (Hartmann and Markusen 1980; Sen 1980). Further, family wage policies lowered the wages in women's occupations. By focusing on the benefits for married couples, her analysis ignores the situation of women who needed to stay in the labor force, especially unmarried and widowed women workers (Sen 1980). Benenson (1991) and Rose (1992) document instances of English working-class women's active resistance to the family wage doctrine, especially in the textile industry.

Benenson (1991) also argues that family wage ideology reinforced divisions among the working class. Asserting that the real purpose of the family wage was women's exclusion from well-paid jobs, the primary beneficiaries were skilled male artisans who already earned breadwinner wages. Therefore, married women's exclusion from paid employment hurt low-income families whose male workers were considered unskilled; these families depended upon pooling workers' wages. Benenson contradicts the contention that restricting women's labor supply raised wages for these male workers to the level formerly earned by multiple wage earners. He concludes that, since the family wage was achievable for only a small segment of the working class, it operated primarily at the level of ideology (see also May 1982; Rose 1992).

Class and gender

Both visions of the family wage center on the material interests and strategic alliances which shaped the development of capitalist labor markets and the GENDER DIVISION OF LABOR within families. However, more recent interpretations emphasize that class and gender are interrelated. For example, the rhetoric of the family wage was founded on definitions of masculinity as wage-earning and femininity as homemaking, which indicate that gender was fundamental to the construction of class relations. Frader (1996) argues that "the right to provide subsistence to a family was a male right," based upon workers' status as fathers and family providers. These constructions of masculinity are also racialized, since men of color are generally excluded from breadwinner jobs and married women of color's labor force participation is a social norm. Based on these analyses, feminist political economists have argued that the family wage should be de-gendered and that all workers should earn a breadwinner's wage.

See also:

marriage; patriarchy; race, ethnicity, gender and class; social wage; wage determination; women's wages: social construction of

Selected references

Benenson, Harold (1991) "The 'Family Wage' and Working Women's Consciousness in Britain, 1880–1914," *Politics and Society* 19(1): 71–108.

Frader, Laura L. (1996) "Engendering Work and Wages: The French Labor Movement and the Family Wage," in Laura L. Frader and Sonya O. Rose (eds), *Gender and Class in Modern Europe*, Ithaca, NY: Cornell University Press.

Hartmann, Heidi I. and Markusen, Ann R. (1980) "Contemporary Marxist Theory and Practice: A Feminist Critique," *Review of Radical Political Economics* 12(2): 87–94.

Horrell, Sara and Humphries, Jane (1995) "Women's Labour Force Participation and the Transition to the Male-Breadwinner Family, 1790–1865," *Economic History Review* 48(1): 89–117.

Humphries, Jane (1977a) "Class Struggle and the Persistence of the Working Class Family," *Cambridge Journal of Economics* 1: 241–58.

—— (1977b) "The Working Class Family, Women's Liberation, and Class Struggle: The Case of Nineteenth Century British History," *Review of Radical Political Economics* 9(3): 25–41.

Lewis, Jane (1984) *Women in England, 1870–1950: Sexual Divisions and Social Change*, Bloomington, IN: Indiana University Press.

May, Martha (1982) "The Historical Problem of the Family Wage: The Ford Motor Company and the Five Dollar Day," *Feminist Studies* 8(2): 399–424.

Rose, Sonya O. (1992) *Limited Livelihoods: Gender and Class in Nineteenth-Century England*, Berkeley: University of California Press.

Sen, Gita (1980) "The Sexual Division of Labor and the Working-Class Family: Towards a Conceptual Synthesis of Class Relations and the Subordination of Women," *Review of Radical Political Economics* 12(2): 76–86.

ELLEN MUTARI

fascism

The word "fascism" derives from *"fascio"*, a bundle of rods that symbolizes strength in unity. Fascism as a social system has a minimal generic base with many national variations. It is possible to differentiate between "authoritarian fascism" (hard shoe) and "democratic fascism" (soft shoe fascism). Both forms can be popular and even supported by the majority of the population. However, while the authoritarian variety eventually disposes of national elections, the democratic form has such a strong position of HEGEMONY that it thrives in the popular mood of national elections. Both forms strive to expand their military and economic power beyond their national borders, where possible, and seek to form a strong national consensus which challenges alternatives to social change.

Authoritarian fascism

Common elements of authoritarian fascism include:

- an authoritarian, police-state politics based on extreme nationalism, a strong fascist party, persecution of certain groups and, usually, the personality cult of the leader;

- a corporate capitalist economy, with private companies nominally controlling most of the industrial and financial assets, and the centralized state commanding the power to settle industrial disputes and promoting a strategic national INDUSTRY POLICY;
- a peculiar fascist form of cultural hegemony. Fascism often emerges from an environment of problematical economic conditions, such as very high UNEMPLOYMENT AND UNDEREMPLOYMENT and inflation. Under these conditions, it is easier to appeal to the popular mind of greater national identity; the scapegoating of certain ethnic, religious and other groups; the need for strong leadership; the importance of traditional family life; and anti-intellectualism.

All these are underpinned by numerous negations. Fascism is anti-liberal, anti-communist, anti-socialist, anti-union, anti-conservative and, commonly, anti-Semitic. The word "fascism," introduced by workers in Sicilian sulfur mines in the 1890s, was adopted by Mussolini in 1922. The fundamentals of fascist doctrine and practice evolving within nineteenth century European philosophy (Fichte, Nietzsche, Gobineau, Pareto and others) became formalized in the late 1920s with Hitler's National Socialism. Fascistic ideology and politics appeared in most European nations. Four major variants (in addition to Italy and Germany) were presented in Austria, Spain, Hungary and Romania (see Payne 1995: 245). Other minor movements appeared in France, Belgium, Holland, Scandinavia, Switzerland, Czechoslovakia, Finland, Portugal, Greece, Yugoslavia, the Baltic States, Bulgaria, Ireland and Great Britain.

Germany's defeat in the First World War and the punitive reparations program generated wide and deep discontent. The failure of the Weimar Republic to solve domestic problems of inflation and unemployment provided the initial example of the fascistic litany: "democracy can't work." Hitler's "populist" support, encompassing workers, capitalists and the bulk of the middle class, was grounded on the propagandistic quest for *lebensraum*, which rationalized military-based production and employment programs alongside the scapegoating of Jews. Hitler's Germany (1933–45) and Mussolini's Italy (1929–45) represent the only purely fascist political regimes. Franco's rule through the Spanish experience incorporated several interacting strains of rightist politics.

Fascism, capitalism and socialism

An early preoccupation with CAPITALISM as a cause of fascism can be replaced by a recognition of ongoing symbiotic associations between capitalism as a system and fascistic principles and practice (Gramm 1980: 414–5). Nevertheless, there is an extensive literature that finds credible connections between fascist programs and capitalist interests: "The drive toward economic self-sufficiency... high priority given to rearmament... savage repression of socialist parties and labor movements, lent support to the idea that the fascist state was, in the economic sphere, a tool of 'business interests'" (Milward 1976: 381). In *Business As a System of Power* in 1943, Robert A. Brady detailed power linkages between concentrated, peak business organizations and government in the leading industrial nations. Karl Polanyi averred in *The Great Transformation* in 1944 that fascism, along with socialism, had its origins in a market economy that became dysfunctional (see DISEMBEDDED ECONOMY).

At least two classifications have been used for fascism. First, the term "totalitarian" included both (capitalistic) fascism and (Soviet-style) communism. Both were police states with little effective personal freedom, especially for certain groups. The second classification presents a four-dimensional "isms" schema: liberal and authoritarian capitalism, and liberal and authoritarian socialism. Definitionally, these are ideal types. The two capitalisms are represented by historical examples: the United Kingdom and the United States from 1860s–present (liberal capitalism), and Nazi Germany and Fascist Italy (authoritarian capitalism; fascism). The possibility of liberal socialism is presented in examples such as the

fascism

kibbutz, Mondragón and the Scandinavian "middle way." Soviet-style systems represent authoritarian socialism.

Fascist elements in modern culture and politics

In 1968, Daniel Fusfeld described the main elements of what he called "fascist democracy in the United States." The ideological elements historically included the popular notions of pure nationalism, militant anti-communism and messianic democracy. The corporate state was dominant, with big business having most of the power, the state providing symbiotic support and the unions being included in the pact (at least until the 1980s). With a tight knit of hegemonic control mechanisms being in place, the universities could be bought out by the corporations, Keynesian policies could help to preserve stability (for a time) and the masters could exercise control with the support of the population (no matter what party was in "power"). US fascism was forward looking, with major military interventions throughout the globe and a vigorous policy of global business expansion. Since the late 1960s, elements of fascism have changed somewhat in the US.

In 1980, Bertram Gross argued that fascism "was happening" in the United States. A twenty-first century "soft-shoe fascism" can be administered with minimal physical violence; sufficient restraint can be found in systematic, token repression plus politico-social thought control and economic-based fear. Cold War surveillance of subversives, expanded to data banks on consumers and workers, can be further extended via the revolution in genetics. A national data bank available to private and public agencies can develop ultra-efficient screening of individuals for livelihood and security, based on their physical and mental abilities and disabilities. Most elements of the "fascist outlook" identified by William Ebenstein in *Today's Isms: Communism, Fascism, Capitalism and Socialism* in 1961 are present in late twentieth-century capitalism. These include a "distrust of reason, denial of basic human equality... lies and violence, government by... elite... racialism and imperialism, [and] opposition to international law and order" (1961: 105). The dominant factor, particularly for the United States, is the breakdown of law.

Conforming to international law became a matter of Cold War convenience for the USA. Internally, hate and fear generated by Cold War conformity and repression have exacerbated and generalized a century-long pattern of large corporate dominance (Gramm 1973: 577–80). Property rights for big business became absolute; legal rights for the poor atrophied. Punitive and racist punishment, requisite extended imprisonment, subversion of the judicial process, the revival of the death penalty and overcrowded prisons all reflect a growing climate of acceptable brutality which threatens the civil rights of citizens. For the political right, crime became the communism of the post-Cold War era: that is, the principal means for exploiting the fear of social decay and endemic racism. A society with a high ratio of minorities who have experienced prison conditions tends to indicate the presence of a police state.

Prospective fascist policy will not be generated by blackshirts, skinheads or death camps. Its vitality will build on actions within an existing power structure, actions that are essentially subtle and indirect. "While fascism as a distinctive political movement is dead, many of its ideological formulations... can be found in many contemporary movements... sometimes where we least expect it" (Linz 1976: 104). British laborite references to Thatcherism as "stockingfoot fascism" captured contemporary reflections that Orwell's *1984* was becoming real, and right on time. Many "national front" and "one nation" political groupings in the West, and totalitarian regimes in the underdeveloped or developing world, have certain characteristics in common with fascist ideology and practice.

Some who doubt the possibility of neo-fascism in advanced capitalism find that "the danger is great and growing that a new kind of fascism... can again develop" (in Payne 1995:

518) in the Third World industrialization process. A. James Gregor has identified Italian fascism "as a prototype of the mass-mobilizing developmental dictatorship designed to achieve...modernization" (in Payne 1995: 459). There is an alienating, authoritarian commonality in the deterioration of socially-grounded working conditions in the United States, and there is exploitative, slave-like labor within certain Third World capitalisms.

See also:

capitalism; class analysis of world capitalism; colonialism and imperialism: classic texts; economic power; feudalism; military expenditure in developing countries; social democracy; socialism and communism; state and government

Selected references

Ebenstein, William (1961) *Today's Isms: Communism, Capitalism, Fascism and Socialism*, New York: Prentice Hall.
Fusfeld, Daniel (1968) "Fascist Democracy in the United States," *Conference Papers of the Union for Radical Political Economics*, Philadelphia: URPE.
Gramm, Warren S. (1973) "Industrial Capitalism and the Breakdown of the Liberal Rule of Law," *Journal of Economic Issues* 7(4): 577–603.
—— (1980) "Oligarchic Capitalism: Arguable Reality, Thinkable Future?", *Journal of Economic Issues* 14(2): 411–32.
Gross, Bertram (1980) *Friendly Fascism*, New York: M. Evans.
Laqueur, Walter (ed.) (1976) *Fascism: A Reader's Guide*, Berkeley, CA: University of California Press.
Linz, Juan J. (1976) "Some Notes Toward a Comparative Study of Fascism in Sociological Historical Perspective," in Walter Laqueur (ed.), *Fascism: A Reader's Guide*, Berkeley, CA: University of California Press, 3–121.
Milward, Alan S. (1976) "Fascism and the Economy," in Walter Laqueur (ed.), *Fascism: A Reader's Guide*, Berkeley, CA: University of California Press, 379–412.
Payne, Stanley G. (1995) *A History of Fascism, 1914–1945*, Madison, WI: University of Wisconsin Press.

WARREN S. GRAMM

feminist philosophy of science

The notion of science as an objective enterprise – value free, politically neutral, and GENDER blind – is being contested on a variety of fronts. The feminist critique reveals that modern science, with its ideals of detachment and domination, displays a distinctly androcentric bias. There are three main categories of feminist philosophy of science that emerge from this critique: feminist empiricism, feminist standpoint epistemology and postmodern feminist epistemology. All start from the observation that science is a socially constructed activity: the social location, status and gender of scientists and scientific communities all play a significant role in determining the methods and practices of science. Throughout much of the history of Western science, women and people of color have not been part of scientific communities, and this exclusion has influenced which questions are deemed appropriate for scientific inquiry, what types of research methods are employed and what evidence counts in evaluating hypotheses.

Feminist empiricism

Feminist empiricism has its origins in the work of feminist scholars in biology and the social sciences who recognized that the answers to many questions involving sex and gender reflected a distinct androcentric and/or sexist bias (see Tuana 1989). Moreover, many questions concerning women's lives and bodies either were not answerable within mainstream theory, or had received inadequate attention from the mainstream scientific establishment. They believed that the scientific method was not the problem; the problem was that researchers were not following it. Sexism and androcentrism can be eliminated from science if researchers rigorously follow the existing norms of scientific methodology. Many feminist practitioners in the social and natural sciences today subscribe to this view (see NEOCLASSICAL ECONOMICS: CRITIQUE for an examination of feminist empiricism in economics).

Feminist standpoint epistemology

Feminist standpoint epistemology calls for a more radical change in the conception of good science. In this view, all knowledge is socially situated; there is no one position that is value neutral and objective (see VALUE JUDGMENTS AND WORLD VIEWS). It has its roots in Marx's dialectical materialism which holds that material conditions structure the way we apprehend the world (see DIALECTICAL METHOD; MARXIST POLITICAL ECONOMY: MAJOR CONTEMPORARY VARIETIES). Hartsock (1983) argues that, if material life is structured in fundamentally opposing ways for two different groups, then the vision of each will represent an inversion of the other, and in systems of domination the vision of the rulers will be partial and distorted. The institutionalized GENDER DIVISION OF LABOR structures men's and women's lives differently and forms the basis of a feminist standpoint. A feminist standpoint is neither objective nor ethically neutral. Since it is rooted in the material conditions of women's lives, it is epistemologically privileged and offers a more humane vision of the relationships between people and between people and the natural world.

Object-relations theory posits a psychoanalytic explanation for the difference in male and female apprehensions of the world, and the way that those apprehensions have influenced scientific practice. Keller (1985) argues that the equation of knowledge and power is linked to the masculine developmental process. In learning to become males, boys must learn that they are fundamentally different from their mothers, and in learning this difference boys come to perceive that the self and the object world are separate and distinct. Pervasive in the masculinist world view is the construction of the self in opposition to another. It is this psychological construction of the self that lies behind the persona of the scientist as an autonomous, disinterested observer, and the notion that the purpose of science is to gain control over the object of study.

Harding (1995) argues that feminist standpoint epistemology provides the foundation for the notion of "strong objectivity." Ideally, the concept of impartial, unbiased, value-free research should eliminate social values and prejudices from science. In practice, however, it eliminates only those values that differ among researchers. Shared values within the scientific community will not be questioned. To the extent that the community excludes women and people of color, implicit assumptions about RACE, ETHNICITY, GENDER AND CLASS will not be apparent. Strong objectivity rejects the ideal of value neutrality, and extends the notion of the scientific method to include an examination of hidden cultural assumptions that remain invisible from the standpoint of the dominant groups. Strong objectivity is necessary if science is to escape containment by the interests and values of the powerful.

A similar position is found in a philosophically grounded version of feminist empiricism (see Longino 1990; Nelson 1990). They hold that knowledge is not constructed by individuals using the scientific method, but rather by individuals in dialogic communities. It is within the context of these communities that scientists' observations, theories, hypotheses and patterns of reasoning are shaped and modified. Background assumptions and values partially define what it is to be a member of that COMMUNITY. Thus, effective criticism and, by extension, good science require alternative points of view. The crucial difference between these feminist empiricists and standpoint theorists is that the empiricists reject the claim that the standpoint of oppressed groups is epistemologically privileged.

Postmodern feminism

Postmodern feminism argues that both feminist standpoint epistemology and feminist empiricism are flawed because they require an uncritical appropriation of Enlightenment ideals (see Flax 1992; Haraway 1990). Postmodernism contests the central assumptions of the Enlightenment meta-narrative, and rejects the notion of innocent knowledge: that is, knowledge that is separate from power and works for the benefit of all. Truth, reason, universality and objectivity are seen as mere artifacts created by humans rather than transcendental truths. Truth is an effect of discourse rather than an apprehension of the real. Thus any transcendent authorization of meaning is lost, and with it the ontology which grounds Western epistemology (see MODERNISM AND POSTMODERNISM).

Order is imposed on the world through the use of binary oppositions – nature/culture, female/male, reason/emotion – which create the necessary boundaries between order and chaos. Haraway argues that the boundary maintaining images generated by the modern episteme are inadequate for today's realities. She suggests that a feminist science must begin with a new episteme and politics. It must address the fact that our world is characterized by massive insecurity and a common failure of subsistence networks for the most vulnerable, and these conditions are inseparable from the social relations of science and TECHNOLOGY. She suggests that feminist science look to the possibilities of new unities based on affinities rather than essential characteristics.

See also:

feminist political economy: major contemporary themes; holistic method

Selected references

Flax, Jane (1992) "The End of Innocence," in Judith Butler and Joan W. Scott (eds), *Feminists Theorize the Political*, New York: Routledge.
Haraway, Donna (1990) "A Manifesto for Cyborgs: Science, Technology, and Socialist Feminism in the 1980's," in Linda J. Nicholson (ed.), *Feminism/Postmodernism*, New York: Routledge.
Harding, Sandra (1991) *Whose Science? Whose Knowledge? Thinking From Women's Lives*, Ithaca, NY: Cornell University Press.
——(1995) "Can Feminist Thought Make Economics More Objective?", *Feminist Economics* 1(1): 7–32.
Hartsock, Nancy (1983) *Money, Sex and Power: Toward a Feminist Historical Materialism*, Boston: Northeastern University Press.
Keller, Evelyn Fox (1985) *Reflections on Gender and Science*, New Haven, CN: Yale University Press.
Longino, Helen (1990) *Science as Social Knowledge*, Princeton: Princeton University Press.
Nelson, Lynn Hankinson (1990) *Who Knows: From Quine to a Feminist Empiricism*, Philadelphia: Temple University Press.
Tuana, Nancy (1989) *Feminism and Science*, Bloomington, IN: Indiana University Press.

DRUCILLA K. BARKER

feminist political economy: history and nature

Feminist political economy is a counter-disciplinary approach to understanding the way in which GENDER has been culturally constructed and intertwined with the processes of CLASS formation, race and other forms of social identity to support women's disadvantaged social position. The history and nature of feminist political economy is complex because feminism is not a monolithic mode of analysis. Feminism is compatible with a variety of philosophical perspectives reflecting the many positions from which PATRIARCHY has been challenged.

During the nineteenth and early twentieth centuries, the traditions of liberalism, socialism and institutionalism informed feminist thinking. Each perspective offered a partial description and explanation of women's disadvantaged social position and strategy for change. Gender as an analytic category dominates early feminist writings. A recognition of the interlocking categories of race, class, sexuality and so on is less evident.

Liberal feminist perspectives

The liberal perspective holds a concept of human nature that locates individual uniqueness in the capacity for rationality. Accordingly, women's true capacity for reason and potential for autonomy and freedom is limited by laws and customs which exclude them from the public sphere. Women's oppression is understood as a cultural lag. Modern society with its technology, democracy and material wealth provides the preconditions for women's liberation. Justice, therefore, requires the elimination of gender discrimination, and strategies for change emphasize equal opportunity and individual action – in particular, education and political participation. The goal is to reform CAPITALISM through rational persuasion rather than activism.

The liberal perspective is often traced to John Stuart Mill's *The Subjection of Women* in 1868, which focused on the consequences of women's lack of citizenship. Mill argued for the legal, economic and political emancipation of women. He noted the injustice of confining women to domestic drudgery and to economic dependency on men, and questioned the alleged differences in male and female natures. Nevertheless, Mill did not support married women's employment, arguing that most liberated women would choose marriage and motherhood over other competing careers.

Harriet Taylor, Mill's collaborator and occasional co-author, disagreed. In *Enfranchisement of Women* in 1851, Taylor insisted that every woman work to become an equal partner with her husband. Here Taylor reveals her classism: working-class women often had no such option. Nevertheless, Taylor's analysis is more progressive than that of Mill. She challenged the ideology of separate spheres and argued for women's unconditional claims to property, earnings, inheritance and other social privileges enjoyed by men.

Mill and Taylor anticipated the arguments of (a) environmentalists, arguing against growth for growth's sake; (b) the theories of SEGMENTED AND DUAL LABOR MARKETS, formulating a theory of non-competing groups to explain the wage–skill differential; and (c) the feminist critique of science, insisting on the epistemological necessity of including women's experiences in scientific inquiry (see FEMINIST PHILOSOPHY OF SCIENCE).

Barbara Bodichon joined Mill and Taylor in the British suffrage movement. Bodichon was the first woman to write a treatise on working women. She challenged the Factory Acts and women's exclusion from trade UNIONS, and supported equal pay for equal work, property and marriage rights, better education and new employment opportunities for women. In *Women and Work* in 1857, Bodichon emphasized the importance of women's economic independence and challenged the belief that women take jobs from men, since they were occupationally segregated. She argued instead for full employment. She is credited with the earliest formulation of the crowding hypothesis. Women were "crowded" into fewer occupations than men, creating an oversupply of labor in those occupations to which women were relegated. Women's wages were therefore low because of an excess of supply over demand.

Participants in the 1890–1923 debate over equal pay for equal work were also informed by liberalism (see COMPARABLE WORTH). Millicent Garrett Fawcett provided the earliest theory of non-competing groups to explain wage–gender differentials. Ada Heather-Bigg confronted familial power imbalances, arguing for married women's right to employment. Harriet Martineau, supporter of abolitionism and suffrage, analogized SLAVERY with women's position in marriage. Noting the social pressure on women toward marriage and motherhood, Martineau argued for women's education to promote equality in marriage. William Smart questioned the dichotomy between women's customary wage and men's FAMILY WAGE. Smart, Edwin Cannan and Eleanor Rathbone recognized segmentation and the undervaluation of women's work as causes of women's lower wages.

Socialist feminist perspective

The socialist perspective in feminist thought is evident in pre-Marxist socialism, Marxism, radical socialism and reform socialism. All shared a Marxist concept of human nature that human fulfillment is found in free productive activity. However, until the DOMESTIC LABOR DEBATE in the 1970s, the non-Marxists were alone in extending the concept of productive labor to include the historically dynamic forms of sexuality and procreation. All were critical of capitalist institutions and sought a new socioeconomic order as the precondition for women's liberation. They were equally concerned with the needs and interests of working-class and middle-class women, and criticized the suffrage movement for its myopic focus on the vote. All supported women's expanded citizenship as a vehicle for changing society, but they questioned the idea that freedom and equality – for either men or women – could be achieved under CAPITALISM.

The pre-Marxist socialists such as William Thompson and Anna Wheeler rejected the theoretical foundation of CLASSICAL POLITICAL ECONOMY – most notably, competitive individualism. They advocated cooperative community models of social organization. They questioned the theoretical contradiction between a market system based on competitive individualism and family life based on paternal benevolence. Could men be self-interested in the public sphere, yet altruistic in the private sphere? Could women – confined to domestic drudgery – compete equally with men in the labor market? Challenging familial patriarchy, they argued for the rights of women and children, and demanded an expansion of women's democratic rights in the public sphere. They also challenged Malthus' assertion that contraception was immoral. Advocating contraception, communities of cooperation and collectivization of domestic labor, the pre-Marxist socialists greatly influenced the nineteenth-century birth control, trade union and cooperative movements.

A classic essay in the Marxist tradition is Friedrich Engels's *The Origin of the Family, Private Property and the State* (1884). Based to some degree on Karl Marx's *Ethnological Notebooks*, Engels offered one of the first critiques of marriage and family structure linked to the class structure of society. For Engels, the patriarchal family was founded on the wife's domestic slavery which originated with the overthrow of maternal rights and the creation of private property. For the bourgeoisie, the intergenerational assurance of the transmission of patrilineal property necessitated private control of women's sexuality. No similar basis for control existed among the propertyless. Hence, the proletarian family was exonerated from harboring gender inequality. The source of women's oppression remained outside gender relations in the relations of production. Gender inequality served the interests of capital, not men. Thus, the precondition for women's liberation was their participation in social production as wage laborers. Women's proletarianization would make them class conscious and capable of forging revolutionary alliances required for the abolition of capitalism. In revolutionary society, women would engage in social production and monogamous marriage based on love would develop.

Unlike Marxists, many radical socialists did not romanticize gender relations within proletarian marriages, recognizing instead how class and gender act as co-determining factors of women's oppression. Through their activism in working-class movements, they observed firsthand the brutalizing impact of marriage on women living in poverty. They sought to improve economic conditions for women and children in urban areas.

August Bebel's *Women and Socialism* in 1910 highlighted the interdependency of class and gender oppression by providing a detailed historical account of the emergence of patriarchal and capitalist hierarchies. For Bebel, women's economic dependency resulted from the lack of property rights, arbitrary laws, and cultural and religious norms designed to privilege men. Increasing the numbers of bourgeois women in social production would not assist working-class women suffering from economic exploitation, damaged health and marital misery. Bebel warned that civil equality would not abolish sex slavery in marriage and the economic dependency of wives. He addressed the merits of vegetarianism, the connection between unsafe abortions and women's health risks, and the link between fertility decline and women's improved economic status. Convinced that bourgeois society was incapable of liberating women, he articulated a vision of women's position under socialism.

For anarchist Emma Goldman, not only economic factors but also sexual and reproductive factors – such as marriage, sexual repression, enforced childbearing and the patriarchal family – were basic to women's oppression. As a trade union organizer and activist in the free motherhood and contraception campaigns, Goldman was committed to the struggle for freedom in some socialist future. She disagreed with the suffragist position that emancipation would have a purifying effect on society's institutions. If male qualities operated to enslave women, then these qualities were partly responsible. Women idolized those qualities in men. True liberation meant changing women's consciousness, freeing women from such ideals. Noting women's double day, where women work for wages and then undertake most of the housework as well, Goldman argued that emancipation meant more than independence at the typewriter earning subsistence pay. In the tradition of bread and roses, she insisted that women earn enough to afford books, entertainment, free love and free motherhood without the sanction of church or state.

In *Concerning Women* in 1926, Suzanne LaFollette exposed the use of legal barriers to exclude women from lucrative industrial employment, arguing against protective legislation for women on the grounds that safe standards should be extended to all workers. Like Martineau, LaFollette equated women's position in marriage to slavery and listed the legally enforced economic disadvantages suffered by married women. She emphasized how the state, in favor of the owning class, discriminated against the propertyless and argued that, until this fundamental discrimination was challenged and women's rights as human beings were established, women's emancipation remained problematic.

Reform socialism represents a unique blend of liberalism and socialism. The term "reform" refers to its political nature. It was a white, middle-class progressive politics lacking class and race consciousness. Charlotte Perkins Gilman's *Women and Economics* in 1898 is representative of this tradition. Being equally committed to women's rights and socialism, Gilman emphasized the interconnections of sexual and economic oppression, and attempted to define a cooperative and humane social order. Florence Kelley, the first English translator of Engels's *The Condition of the Working Class in England*, articulated a concern for the "human element" in production and challenged unregulated industrial capitalism. She was devoted to child labor legislation, improvement of the living conditions of women and children, and the establishment of standards for consumer goods.

Institutional feminism

The feminist content of institutionalism is especially evident in Thorstein VEBLEN's *The Theory of the Leisure Class* (1899). Veblen's critique of pecuniary CULTURE includes an indictment of women's status as objects of vicarious leisure and consumption. His critique of dualism in cultural thought is foundational to contemporary feminist political economy. Many institutionalists have recently rediscovered the feminist element in institutionalism.

Conclusion

Contributions to feminist political economy are extensive and expanding as feminist scholars are rediscovering the previously ignored or marginalized writings of Sadie Alexander, Jane Marcet, Edith Abbott, Sophonisba Preston Breckinridge, Mabel Newcomer and Grace Abbott, among others. A historical understanding of feminism helps to provide a rich foundation for its further development.

See also:

class structures of households; ecological feminism; feminist political economy: major contemporary themes; feminist political economy: paradigms; gender division of labor; global liberalism; socialism and communism

Selected references

Dimand, Mary Ann, Dimand, Robert and Forget, Evelyn (1995) *Women of Value: Feminist Essays on the History of Women in Economics*, Aldershot: Edward Elgar.

Folbre, Nancy (1993) "Socialism, Feminist and Scientific," in Marianne Ferber and Julie Nelson (eds), *Beyond Economic Man: Feminist Theory and Economics*, Chicago: Chicago University Press.

Jaggar, Alison and Rothenberg, Paula (1984) *Feminist Frameworks: Alternative Theoretical Accounts of the Relations Between Women and Men*, New York: McGraw-Hill.

Pujol, Michele (1992) *Feminism and Anti-Feminism in Early Economic Thought*, Aldershot: Edward Elgar.

Rossi, Alice (ed.) (1973) *The Feminist Papers: From Adams to de Beauvoir*, New York: Bantam Books.

Spender, Dale (ed.) (1983) *Feminist Theorists: Three Centuries of Key Women Thinkers*, New York: Pantheon Books.

PAULETTE OLSON

feminist political economy: major contemporary themes

Introduction

Feminist political economy developed out of the shortcomings of some other approaches to POLITICAL ECONOMY. Those who failed to see women's lives reflected in economic theory turned to feminist political economy to expose the GENDER bias of neoclassical models (see NEOCLASSICAL ECONOMICS: CRITIQUE). However, gender bias has not been limited to neoclassical economics. Feminists have found that Marxist political economy, for example, has tended not to adequately address gender differences within the classes, and has subordinated gender to CLASS in both analysis and struggle. Marxism has tended to emphasize production at the expense of reproduction, failing to adequately explain the materialist basis of social relations of reproduction, which, unlike production, are not sex-blind (Himmelweit 1984) (see REPRODUCTION PARADIGM). Furthermore, Marxism failed to explain gender discrimination in the labor market (Hartmann 1976).

Feminist political economists use eclectic elements from the methodologies of various political economy schools and other disciplines. They develop theories of the economy that reflect the varied experiences of women, highlight the oppression of women, and develop policy recommendations for promoting "liberation." Rather than relying on extreme assumptions of individual agency or material determination, feminist political economists grant women some agency while pointing out that social relations place different constraints on one's actions depending not just on sex, but also class, race, age, sexual orientation and so on.

For example, Nancy Folbre (1994) utilizes aspects of both Marxist and neoclassical theory, as well as interdisciplinary feminist theory, to present a framework for feminist political economy based on structures of constraint. Folbre's structural factors include assets from the Marxist tradition, preferences from the neoclassical tradition and rules and norms from both. The agents in her model include neoclassical agents and chosen groups, as well as Marxist classes and class-like groups. Nevertheless, feminist political economists disagree on the applicability of any specific tradition to feminist analysis (see the journal *Feminist Economics* for examples).

Philosophy of science

Some feminist political economists use FEMINIST PHILOSOPHY OF SCIENCE to analyze how gender bias can appear in an "objective" science. As Strassmann and Polanyi (1995) point out, recognizing that all knowledge is situated socially opens the door for the analysis of rhetoric that shows that power and self-interest are aspects of the construction of knowledge. Feminist political economists are divided between those who want to develop new measures of validity for economic theory, and those in the postmodernism tradition who reject all judgments of the value of competing theories (see MODERNISM AND POSTMODERNISM).

The feminist critique of science includes a critique of Cartesian dualism, where reality is divided into two mutually exclusive all encompassing categories. The distinction between positive and normative is an example of dual categories in economics. Another dualism often criticized by feminists is the dualism between the public marketplace and the private family.

The public/private dualism highlights the neglect of the family or household as a topic of inquiry. This dualism and the association of women with the family define women as irrelevant to the economy. Women's productive and reproductive roles are ignored. Women are devalued throughout the economy. Furthermore, the construction of separable spheres assumes away any interaction between the household and the market place. It also distorts our understanding of human behavior. Individual actors are often modeled as selfish in the public sphere and altruistic in the private sphere. Feminists argue that human behavior in the marketplace and in the family exhibit elements of selfishness and altruism. However, the identification of dualisms in feminist analyses has been criticized by Williams (1993) for the tendency to ignore the racialization of gender categories. For example, black men are often stereotyped as not being rational, and black women have historically engaged in paid reproductive labor that is simultaneously in the household and in the market.

Households

Research on households provides an example of feminist efforts to expand the scope of topics considered appropriate for economics, even though not all household economics is feminist. Rather than modeling households with individual utility functions, some feminist economists utilize bargaining models to investigate conflict in household decision making. However, Janet Seiz (1995) points out that formal models are incomplete and must be complemented by qualitative analyses. Elizabeth Katz (1991) offers an alternative to traditional game-theoretic models, based on three aspects of household negotiation: (a) differential access to resources outside the household, (b) negotiation within the household and (c) the benefits that accrue to individuals as a result of these decisions.

Many feminists build on Marxism to draw a link between the oppression of the working class under CAPITALISM and the oppression of women under PATRIARCHY. In the DOMESTIC LABOR DEBATE, Marxist-feminists have argued that male control of women in the household was supported by and necessary for capitalism. Alternatively, Ferguson and Folbre (1981) have shown that patriarchy could conflict with capitalism by denying capitalists another source of cheap labor and requiring a family wage. Understanding the complex relationship between economic institutions and women's oppression remains an important topic as feminist political economists work to evaluate economic transitions.

These debates highlight unpaid work and the importance of this work to the economy. Feminists are debating how to measure this work (see HOUSEHOLD PRODUCTION AND NATIONAL INCOME). Feminists continue to research the changes in the nature and amount of unpaid work in economies undergoing structural transformation as part of the evaluation of economic policy. Women's burden of unpaid work divides feminist economists from different perspectives. Some feminist economists believe that commoditization of domestic work is necessary for women to have equal access to the labor market, while others have raised concerns about the demise of caring that results from the expansion of market relations.

Feminist political economists, invoking postcolonial theory, emphasize the problematic relationships between white employers and dark-skinned maids.

Wages, work and labor market

Women's lower wages, occupational segregation, and their secondary status in the labor market have received extensive attention from feminist political economists. Neoclassical economists explain this mainly with HUMAN CAPITAL theory. Institutionalists and radicals explain it with SEGMENTED AND DUAL LABOR MARKETS. For many feminists, neoclassical theory is too dependent on a supply and demand framework to explain adequately the determination of wages (see WOMEN'S WAGES: SOCIAL CONSTRUCTION OF and WAGE DETERMINATION). Neoclassical theory assumes that the value of a person's work in the market is based on their marginal product. This underplays questions raised by feminist activists struggling for COMPARABLE WORTH; and the role played by gender and other social categories in the social process, whereby work becomes recognized as "skilled" or "unskilled." Unlike many neoclassical theories, feminist political economists seek to explain the origins of discriminatory tastes and preferences. In accordance with labor market segmentation theorists, who point to the importance of both "pre-" and "post-entry" discrimination, feminists have shown how attitudes about gender differences affect hiring practices. For example, beliefs that men are "more technological" affect women's access to jobs that provide training and promotion opportunity in the Scottish electronics industry (Goldstein 1992).

Feminists question the reduction of work life to quantifiable qualities. While traditional labor economics emphasizes wage determination and productivity, feminists investigate qualitative aspects of work life as well. The causal relationship between work structures and women's ability to combine work and family responsibilities is one aspect of the quality of work that mainstream economists have ignored (see Figart 1997). Policies that have mandated equality of opportunity are only the first step to increasing women's access to labor markets. Feminist political economists argue that the organization of production and social reproduction will also have to change for gender equity to be achieved and power to be redistributed within the household. Sexual harassment is another aspect of the work environment of concern to feminists.

Development and the environment

GENDER AND DEVELOPMENT is another major area of concern for feminist political economists. Development economists in the 1970s described women as unproductive dependants in need of welfare. Currently, arguments for development programs targeting women must be couched in efficiency terms to be accepted. Women are now recognized as producers. However, feminists recognize the limitations of this analysis. Government policies must also challenge the authority men have over women. Feminists also point to the need for women to control property and resources as a condition for liberation (Agarwal 1994).

Feminist political economists borrow from ECOLOGICAL FEMINISM to investigate the relationship between the environment and development. Eco-feminists argue that theories ignoring the productive capacity of nature (see NATURAL CAPITAL) are derived from the same ideology as theories ignoring the (re)productive capacity of women. Nature and women are perceived as passive, unproductive and dependent. The habit of ignoring the environment in economic theories has led to unsustainable development policies. Feminists have pointed out that women, as those primarily responsible for maintenance of the family, have been the primary losers in environmental destruction. Logging has forced women to walk farther for fuel for cooking fires. Displacing traditional agriculture with commercial agribusiness decreases a woman's ability to feed her family.

Feminist economists also question ECO-

NOMIC GROWTH as the only goal of economic development, even in its relatively benign SUSTAINABLE DEVELOPMENT form. Growth of gross domestic product is such a poor measure of human welfare that it is a poor goal for economic policy. Many feminist political economists focus on developing human capabilities as a goal. Post-colonial feminists have also begun to question the concept of sustainable development as another argument for Western men to "manage" economic processes in the countries of the South. The concept of sustainable development does not question the path of development, or whose interests are served by development, or how development affects the distribution of control over resources and power in society.

In fact, traditional wisdom about private property, combined with the idea that development must be environmentally sustainable, frequently leads to the conclusion that environmental resources are better off in the hands of multinational corporations rather than in the collective ownership of a tribe or village using it for subsistence. Feminists have suggested the concept of "sustainable livelihoods" to emphasize survival of the people rather than survival of the development process as the goal (see HUMAN DEVELOPMENT INDEX).

Conclusion

The project of developing economic theories that address feminist concerns is necessarily broad. It is a common misconception that a feminist perspective is limited to the study of women in households and labor markets. Gender analyses of macroeconomics are examples of the broad significance of incorporating gender into economic analysis. The most developed aspects of feminist macroeconomics include the valuation of unpaid reproductive work in national income accounts, patterns of employment and cycles in industrial economies, and feminist critiques of macroeconomic structural adjustment policies (Cagatay et al. 1995). Work in this area includes not only research on the impact of structural adjustment on women, but the implications for macroeconomic outcomes of neglecting gender differences and reproductive work in models of the economy.

Feminist political economists have also pointed out the biases in empirical research. Categories such as "head of household" force data to conform to patriarchal ideals and obscure reality. Feminist researchers need to collect new data to measure previously neglected economic processes and feminist categories. Lastly, it is important to note that models which incorporate gender only as a dummy variable isolate the effect of gender on economic processes to a shift of the intercept or coefficient of a regression. Feminist theory argues that gender is socially constructed. Therefore, gender should not be treated simply as an exogenous variable (see Redmount 1995).

See also:

feminist political economy: history and nature; feminist political economy: paradigms; household labor; race, ethnicity, gender and class; social structure of accumulation: family

Selected references

Agarwal, B. (1994) "Gender and Command Over Property: A Critical Gap in Economic Analysis and Policy in South Asia," *World Development* 22(10): 1455–78.

Cagatay, N., Elson, D. and Grown, C. (eds) (1995) *Gender, Adjustment and Macroeconomics*, special issue of *World Development* 23(11).

Ferguson, A. and Folbre, N. (1981) "The Unhappy Marriage of Patriarchy and Capitalism," in L. Sargent (ed.), *Women and Revolution*, Boston: South End.

Figart, Deborah M. (1997) "Gender as More Than a Dummy Variable: Feminist Approaches to Discrimination," *Review of Social Economy* 55(1): 1–32.

Folbre, N. (1994) *Who Pays for the Kids?*, London: Routledge.

Goldstein, N. (1992) "Gender and the Restructuring of High-Tech Multinational Cor-

porations: New Twists to an Old Story," *Cambridge Journal of Economics* 16: 269–84.
Hartmann, H. (1976) "Capitalism, Patriarchy, and Job Segregation by Sex," *Signs* 1(3).
Himmelweit, S. (1984) "The Real Dualism of Sex and Class," *Review of Radical Political Economics* 16(1): 167–84.
Katz, E. (1991) "Breaking the Myth of Harmony: Theoretical and Methodological Guidelines to the Study of Rural Third World Households," *Review of Radical Political Economics* 23(3–4): 37–56.
Redmount, Esther (1995) "Toward a Feminist Econometrics," in Edith Kuiper and Jolande Sap (eds), *Out of the Margin: Feminist Perspectives on Economics*, London: Routledge.
Seiz, J. (1995) "Bargaining Models, Feminism, and Institutionalism," *Journal of Economic Issues* 29(2): 609–18.
Strassmann, D. and Polanyi, L. (1995) "The Economist as Storyteller," in Edith Kuiper and Jolande Sap (eds), *Out of the Margin: Feminist Perspectives on Economics*, London: Routledge.
Williams, R. (1993) "Race, Deconstruction, and the Emergent Agenda of Feminist Economic Theory," in M. Ferber and J. Nelson (eds), *Beyond Economic Man*, Chicago: University of Chicago Press.

BARBARA HOPKINS

feminist political economy: paradigms

The recent flourishing of feminist economics has brought together a group of economists and others with the common purpose of eradicating androcentric bias from the discipline. However, this diverse group of scholars employs a variety of paradigms. While some feminist economists have been seeking to reform and refine neoclassical models, others have found refuge in broader definitions of political economy. There is no unified perspective on the relationship between feminist political economy and other schools of economic thought. In particular, it is unclear whether feminist economics constitutes its own paradigm or continues to define itself primarily as a critique of the prevailing schools.

A reigning paradigm

More than the other social sciences and humanities, economics has been a discipline dominated by a reigning paradigm. Like the discipline itself, a neoclassical approach to feminist economics can be defined by method. Neoclassical feminist economists have utilized traditional economic tools in order to broaden the subject of economic discourse. For example, traditional economic methodologies have been applied to the analysis of the household (see HOME ECONOMICS, NEW) and discrimination in the labour market.

Neoclassical feminist economics views the discipline's orthodoxy as fundamentally sound, yet seeks to reform its content. Frances Woolley (1993) defines the agenda of feminist neoclassical economics as: (1) to document differences in the well-being of men and women; (2) to advocate policies which will promote equity; and (3) to conduct research free from androcentric bias. The last focuses on eliminating stylized facts based upon masculine bias and rendering women's experiences visible within economic theory. Jane Humphries (1995) refers to this approach as affirmative action within economics.

Critical stance to neoclassicism

However, much of feminist economics takes a more critical stance toward many of the premises, categories and methods of neoclassical economics (see, for example, Ferber and Nelson 1993; Hyman 1994; Kuiper and Sap 1995). Taking a cue from the work of feminist philosophers of science, feminist economists view economic discourse as a social practice with concrete historical origins. This new feminist work challenges the gendered assumptions guiding the neoclassical paradigm, arguing for transformation rather than reform.

feminist political economy: paradigms

The intellectual framework for this perspective relies heavily upon the work of feminist scholars outside the discipline of economics, especially women's and gender studies where postmodernism in various forms has evolved into a principal mode of feminist analysis.

Broader theoretical approaches

Yet even before the recent wave of feminist economics, there has always been a sizable contingent within the discipline who have embraced broader theoretical approaches and methodologies, including Marxists, institutionalists, social economists and post-Keynesians. Those who work outside the prevailing paradigm tend to accept the following premises: that markets are flawed, that neoclassical models lack historical and cross-cultural perspective, and that traditional economic methodologies are too limiting. Like feminist thought, political economy is less rigid in its disciplinary boundaries. Further, most political economists reject treating the economy as an ahistorical, disembodied entity subject to a series of natural laws. They also question the form of economic rationality posited by neoclassical economists as the basis of behavior.

Uniqueness and synthesis

Feminist political economists recognize this shared critical perspective toward mainstream theoretical constructs, but also assert that feminist analyses provide unique contributions to economic and social theory. Feminist political economy is in many ways an act of synthesis: the creative combustion of insights drawn from diverse intellectual standpoints in the hope of generating new illumination. Because they take inspiration from so many sources, the work of feminist political economists reflects a range of interests, principles and methodologies (see Figart 1997; Mutari *et al.* 1997).

Marxism, patriarchy and reproduction

Feminists, including feminist political economists, have long grappled with their relationship with an intellectual tradition which seems to provide important insights into the process of social change: Marxism (see for example DOMESTIC LABOR DEBATE; RESERVE ARMY OF LABOR; FAMILY WAGE). Many feminists have remained dissatisfied with analyses which subsume women's issues within Marxist analysis. In a series of landmark articles, Heidi Hartmann (1979, 1981 repr. in Humphries 1995) suggested that reliance upon Marxist categories (such as class, reserve army of labor and wage laborer) could not explain why women were the ones who did domestic labor or occupied low-wage jobs. Marx's analytic categories were gender-blind. Expanding upon the work of radical feminists, Hartmann utilized the concept of PATRIARCHY as a social and economic structure which interacted with capitalism. This structural analysis became the basis for socialist feminism.

Some feminist political economists criticized socialist feminism (or dual systems theory) for positing capitalism and patriarchy as autonomous systems. Instead, Jane Humphries and Jill Rubery (1984) presented a theory of the "relative autonomy" of social reproduction, building on the methodological approach of French Marxist Louis Althusser. They viewed the interaction between production and reproduction as a dialectical and historically contingent process (see WOMEN'S WAGES: SOCIAL CONSTRUCTION OF).

Institutionalist feminists

Institutionalist feminists point out that American radical institutionalists, with Veblenian roots, reject both the neoclassical paradigm of individual choice and the economic determinism of traditional Marxism, both of which are problematic for feminism (Peterson and Brown 1994). Because institutionalist theory has traditionally rejected the pursuit of universal laws of causation as well as narrow concepts of materialism, there is an affinity between institutionalism and postmodern GENDER theory. Poststructural accounts of the interaction of RACE, ETHNICITY, GENDER AND CLASS (and, more recently, sexuality, nation and age) permit feminist political economists to address complex variations in institutional arrangements and social norms.

Structures of collective constraint

Folbre (1994: 53) conceptualizes gender, race, class, nation, sexuality and age as "structures of collective constraint" rather than as autonomous systems, in order to highlight the interaction between different dimensions of collective identity and action. She also maintains room for a structural definition of patriarchy as "a variable set of structures of collective constraint based on gender, age, and sexual preference" (Folbre 1994: 74). Folbre posits feminist political economy as neither neoclassical nor Marxist, borrowing insights from both traditions while embracing neither.

Conclusion

The concepts of patriarchy, reproduction and gender, as well as the identification of the household as an economic realm, are among the major contributions that feminist economists have made to the discipline. As feminists apply new categories and frameworks to traditional fields of economics, applied research within all schools of thought will likely benefit. In the meantime, debate continues about the extent to which feminists should draw upon any or all existing paradigms.

See also:

feminist philosophy of science; feminist political economy: history and nature; feminist political economy: major contemporary themes; neoclassical economics: critique; poverty: absolute and relative; poverty: definition and measurement; world hunger and poverty

Selected references

Ferber, Marianne A. and Nelson, Julie A. (1993) *Beyond Economic Man: Feminist Theory and Economics*, Chicago: University of Chicago Press.

Figart, Deborah M. (1997) "Gender as More than a Dummy Variable: Feminist Approaches to Discrimination," *Review of Social Economy* 55(1): 1–32.

Folbre, Nancy (1994) *Who Pays for the Kids? Gender and the Structures of Constraint*, London: Routledge.

Hartmann, Heidi I. (1979) "The Unhappy Marriage of Marxism and Feminism: Towards a More Progressive Union," *Capital and Class* 8: 1–33.

Humphries, Jane (ed.) (1995) *Gender and Economics*, International Library of Critical Writings in Economics, Aldershot and Brookfield, VT: Edward Elgar.

Humphries, Jane and Rubery, Jill (1984) "The Reconstitution of the Supply Side of the Labour Market: The Relative Autonomy of Social Reproduction," *Cambridge Journal of Economics* 8(4): 331–46.

Hyman, Prue (1994) *Women and Economics: A New Zealand Feminist Perspective*, Wellington: Brigit Williams Books.

Kuiper, Edith and Sap, Jolande (eds) (1995) *Out of the Margin: Feminist Perspectives on Economics*, London: Routledge.

Mutari, Ellen, Boushey, Heather and Fraher, William, IV (1997) *Gender and Political Economy: Incorporating Diversity into Theory and Policy*, Armonk, NY: M.E. Sharpe.

Peterson, Janice and Brown, Doug (eds) (1994) *The Economic Status of Women Under Capitalism*, Aldershot and Brookfield, VT: Edward Elgar.

Woolley, Frances (1993) "The Feminist Challenge to Neoclassical Economics," *Cambridge Journal of Economics* 17(4): 485–500.

DEBORAH M. FIGART
ELLEN MUTARI

feminization of poverty

Nature of the problem

The "feminization of poverty" thesis argues that women are disproportionately represented among the poor in many countries of the world. Often the argument is made that the level of female poverty increased disproportionately in the late 1960s and 1970s, and possibly into the 1980s and 1990s in some nations (see Allen 1992). The empirical validity of the feminization of poverty thesis as a historical trend is controversial in Australia and Britain, where women have remained a stable majority of the poor in recent decades (Cass 1988; Wright 1993). However, there is agreement that women are overrepresented among the poor in a considerable portion of the developed world and most of the developing world (see FEMINIZATION OF POVERTY IN THE THIRD WORLD).

In the US, the increase in female poverty was brought to the attention of poverty researchers and policy makers in 1978 by sociologist Diana Pearce. Until 1965, less than one-third of all poor persons lived in households headed by females; by 1980, one half of all poor persons lived in female headed households (see Rodgers 1986). Pearce argued that, in spite of the increasing LABOR FORCE PARTICIPATION and increasing economic independence of women, poverty was "rapidly becoming a female problem." She stressed that, while many women were poor because they lived in poor male-headed families, an increasing number of women were "becoming poor in their own right," raising the question of "what are the economic and social consequences of being female that result in higher rates of poverty?" (Pearce 1978: 28–9).

During the 1980s, feminist scholars from a variety of disciplines debated this question. The common theme uniting these analyses was the argument that female poverty was fundamentally different to male poverty and required a different approach to anti-poverty policy. It was argued that while male poverty was largely caused by unemployment and solved by the increased availability of jobs, the causes of female poverty were more complex and less likely to be ameliorated through economic growth alone (Stallard *et al.* 1983; Sarvasy and Van Allen 1984).

Sources of female poverty

Analysis has focused on three sources of female poverty: (a) demographic changes (reflected in changes in family structure), (b) labor market inequalities and (c) inadequate (and often inappropriate) social welfare programs. Demographic factors, such as increased rates of divorce and unmarried motherhood, increased the economic vulnerability of women and their children. Where women are the heads of households, the full force of women's relative disadvantage in the labor market collides with their responsibility for domestic labor and child care, in a context where child support and welfare payments are often insufficient (a subject which was debated in depth in the March 1989 issue of the *Journal of Economic Issues*).

Although women could no longer rely on the economic security provided by the male FAMILY WAGE, they had to seek income in a labor market shaped by this IDEOLOGY (Ehrenreich and Piven 1984). The view of women as secondary workers relegated them to contingent, secondary-sector jobs. Labor market discrimination and occupational segregation kept women's wages below men's wages and below what was necessary to support a family (Pearce 1978; Ehrenreich and Piven 1984). Thus, women were increasingly faced with an "unjust dual role": the need to "combine unpaid domestic labor with underpaid wage labor" (Sarvasy and Van Allen 1984: 92; Stallard *et al.* 1983: 51).

Role of the welfare state

In an environment of such economic insecurity, the WELFARE STATE comes to play an increasingly important role in the lives of women. In the US, Pearce (1978) described the welfare system as a "workhouse without walls," perpetuating women's poverty through its subsidization of low-wage jobs and its reinforcement of the dual labor market. Others, such as Ehrenreich and Piven (1984), saw the welfare state playing a more positive role, providing at least some economic security to women through the benefits it offered and the employment it created. The cuts in social spending made by the Reagan administration in the 1980s were seen as a serious threat to the well-being of poor women and children in the USA (Stallard et al. 1983).

In Australia, female sole parents have a much lower rate of participation in the labor force than married women or male sole parents, and so are much more likely to rely on government pensions and benefits for their income. Recent changes to policy concerning sole parents have provided incentives for labor market participation, but reliance on benefits still predominates (see Cass 1988). In Sweden, relatively generous social provision means that, although women are socially and economically disadvantaged relative to men, absolute poverty of female-headed households is rare (see Allen 1992).

Critique

In addition to providing an analysis of female poverty, the "feminization of poverty" literature sought to mobilize women around a common economic agenda. Although this work succeeded in increasing public awareness of the plight of poor women and children, Julianne Malveaux argued that it was also a "poignant reminder that some problems generate attention only when white people are involved" (Malveaux 1985: 7). Critics of the "feminization of poverty" analysis argue that in its attempt to present a common agenda for women, it focused too narrowly on the issue of gender and ignored other issues of critical importance to many poor women.

The most serious criticism of the "feminization of poverty" analysis is that it excludes (or downplays) the importance of race and class in the impoverishment of women. Numerous critics of this analysis have argued that its fundamental premise – that female poverty is a relatively new and unique phenomenon – ignores the histories of working-class women and women of color (see Burnham 1985). The exclusion of male poverty from the analysis is seen to distort the nature of poverty in many communities, while the emphasis on male–female inequality obscures the serious inequalities that exist between women (Malveaux 1985). It is argued that a policy agenda for women that ignores the importance of race and class will not serve the needs of many poor women.

Conclusion

The economic trends posited in the "feminization of poverty" thesis underscore the economic vulnerability of women and raise important economic policy challenges. The "feminization of poverty" analysis and its critics also raise important theoretical challenges for feminist scholarship and progressive political economy. A serious challenge facing political economists today is the development of inclusive modes of analysis that capture the complex interaction between gender, race and class in the economy. More recent analyses of the "feminization of poverty" have made attempts to address these issues more fully, but much work remains to be done.

See also:

informal sector; race in political economy: major contemporary themes; Reaganomics and Thatcherism; world hunger and poverty

Selected references

Allen, Tuovi (1992) "Economic Development and the Feminisation of Poverty," in Nancy Folbre, Barbara Bergman, Bina Agarwal and Mario Floro (eds), *Women's Wages in the World Economy*, New York: New York University Press.

Burnham, Linda (1985) "Has Poverty Been Feminized in Black America?," *The Black Scholar* 16(2): 214–24.

Cass, Bettina (1988) "The Feminisation of Poverty," in Barbara Caine, E.A. Grosz and Marie de Lepervanche (eds), *Crossing Boundaries: Feminisms and the Critique of Knowledges*, Sydney: Allen & Unwin.

Ehrenreich, Barbara and Piven, Frances Fox (1984) "The Feminization of Poverty: When the 'Family Wage System' Breaks Down," *Dissent* 31(2): 162–70.

Goldberg, Gertrude and Kremen, Eleanor (eds) (1990) *The Feminization of Poverty: Only in America?*, New York: Praeger.

Malveaux, Julianne (1985) "The Economic Interests of Black and White Women: Are They Similar?," *Review of Black Political Economy* 14(1): 5–27.

Pearce, Diana (1978) "The Feminization of Poverty: Women, Work, and Welfare," *Urban and Social Change Review* 2(1–2): 28–36.

Rodgers, Harrell, Jr (1986) *Poor Women, Poor Families: The Economic Plight of America's Female-Headed Households*, Armonk, NY: M.E. Sharpe.

Sarvasy, Wendy and Van Allen, Judith (1984) "Fighting the Feminization of Poverty: Socialist-Feminist Analysis and Strategy," *Review of Radical Political Economics* 16(2): 89–110.

Stallard, Karin, Ehrenreich, Barbara and Sklar, Holly (1983) *Poverty in the American Dream: Women and Children First*, Boston: South End Press.

Wright, Robert E. (1993) "A Feminization of Poverty in Great Britain? A Clarification," *Review of Income and Wealth* 39(1): 111–12.

JANICE L. PETERSON

feminization of poverty in the Third World

The "feminization of poverty" thesis argues that women are disproportionately represented among the poor. Poverty is broadly defined as an absence of minimal human material well-being or capabilities that are generally accepted as being desirable or valuable; it is, therefore, a multi-dimensional concept. Its dimensions include, for example, the ability to meet basic needs, to own and use human and physical capital, to have good health and to be assured of fundamental civil and human rights.

Income

In 1993, 1.3 billion people lived in poverty in the developing world, surviving on less than US $1 a day (World Bank 1996). Of these 1.3 billion, it is estimated that 70 percent are female (UNDP 1995). One recent study of rural poverty in forty-one countries found that the number of poor women increased by 47 percent between 1965–70 and 1988, compared to a 30 percent increase in the number of poor men (Jaizairy *et al.* 1992). Another study of twenty-one countries found women were described as poorer than men in virtually all of the countries and that, with a few exceptions, rural female-headed households were poorer and more vulnerable than other rural households (SIDA 1996). Studies of Nigeria, Kenya and Zambia show that female-headed farming households hold less land, are relatively undercapitalized and have lower levels of education, compared to male-headed households (Saito 1994). Indeed, although the characteristics of female-headed households are highly heterogeneous, in many third-world countries the emergence of increasing numbers of female-headed households is part of the dynamic of the feminization of poverty.

Health

Other support for the FEMINIZATION OF POVERTY thesis comes from health-related data, which is thought to reflect the uneven intra-household distribution of income and other household resources, including food. For example, adult women suffer more than men from malnutrition, including iodine deficiency, iron deficiency anemia and stunting caused by protein malnutrition. The evidence for a feminization of child poverty from child malnutrition data is more mixed, with malnutrition more prevalent among boys than girls in sub-Saharan Africa and more prevalent in girls than boys in Latin America and the Caribbean and some Asian countries (UNDP 1995). In the sense that the ultimate absence of well being and capability is the curtailment of life expectancy for non-biological reasons, demographic data provide further support for the "feminization of poverty" thesis.

The missing population

At birth females, for biological reasons, can be expected to live longer than males. Normally, then, the number of females in the total population outweighs the number of males. However, in China, plus South and West Asia this pattern is reversed, since there are only 94 females for every 100 males. One implication of these, and other, demographic data for developing regions, is that more than 100 million women are missing from the world's population (Sen 1990).

Causes

Academic researchers from a range of disciplines are currently engaged in analyzing the causes of the feminization of poverty in developing countries. The common theoretical theme in their work is that an understanding of gender relations is needed to analyze the differential impact of ECONOMIC GROWTH or recession on poverty and welfare. Gender relations are the socially determined relations that differentiate male and female situations.

One important research area is the effect that IMF/World Bank-sponsored structural adjustment programs (SAPs) have on the feminization of poverty. SAPs are a set of policies designed to initially stabilize and later promote growth in economies with chronic and deteriorating BALANCE OF PAYMENTS and BUDGET DEFICIT problems. Some have argued that SAP policies have been instrumental in causing a deterioration of the position of the poor in general and poor women in particular (Watkins 1995). Others argue that such welfare deterioration stems from the combined effects of the worsening international economic environment and inappropriate polices pursued by governments in the late 1970s and 1980s. In this view, without structural adjustment the situation of the poor, and, implicitly, poor women, would have been even worse (Lele 1991).

There is, however, an emerging consensus that the effectiveness of adjustment polices is limited by their failure to consider gender relations, and that women have borne a disproportionate amount of the cost of adjustment (World Bank 1995; Elson 1991). In most countries undergoing adjustment there is pressure on women to increase the time they spend in both paid and unpaid work. SAPs commonly reduce or eliminate government subsidies, privatize government enterprises and retrench civil servants. Price increases of many basic goods, higher rates of unemployment and higher schools fees and health care charges typically accompany at least the initial phases of structural adjustment.

An inflexible GENDER DIVISION OF LABOR means that women act as "shock absorbers" or "safety nets" in the system, working longer hours in order to try to maintain their families' standard of living. For example, time use studies in sub-Saharan Africa show that in Kenya women's working week averages 41 hours compared to 26 hours for men. In Cameroon, a woman's total weekly labor averages 64 hours, while for men the corresponding amount is 32 hours (Hanmer et al. 1997), and a study of poor urban communities in the Philippines, Mexico, Zambia and Hungary found that women average 13–16 hours a week on unwaged household work over and above childcare, compared to men's 5 or fewer hours a week on household tasks (Moser 1996).

Currently, academic researchers within and outside the World Bank are investigating how structural adjustment policies can be made more gender sensitive. At the country and regional level, other researchers are investigating the gender specific nature of poverty, including the implications of the growing number of households headed by women.

Data sources

Relevant regional data are published by the World Bank in its report, *Poverty Reduction and the World Bank: Progress and Challenges in the 1990s*. Also, the World Bank's *Poverty Assessments* for various countries give nationally specific poverty data, and sometimes include gender-disaggregated data. Nationally specific income poverty data are also contained in the World Bank's annual report, *Social Indicators of Development*. The UN Statistical Division

(UNSTAT) has compiled "Women's Indicators and Statistics" (WISTAT), a CD-ROM database of data and projections for 1970–2025. Also useful are UNSTAT (1994) *Women's Indicators and Statistics, version 3*, Department for Economic and Social Information and Policy Analysis, New York: UN; UNDP (various years) "Human Development Report," New York: UN; and UN (1995) *The World's Women 1995*, New York: UN.

Selected references

Elson, D. (ed.) (1991) *Male Bias in the Development Process*, Manchester: Manchester University Press.
Hanmer, L., Pyatt, G. and White, H. (1997) *Poverty in Sub-Saharan Africa: What Can We Learn from the World Bank's Poverty Assessments?*, The Hague: Institute of Social Studies Advisory Services.
Jaizairy, Idriss, Almagir, M. and Panuccio, T. (1992) *The State of Rural Poverty: An Inquiry into Its Causes and Consequences*, New York: New York University Press for the International Fund for Agricultural Development (IFAD).
Lele, U. (1991) "Women, Structural Adjustment and Transformation: Some Lessons and Questions from the Africa Experience," in Christina Gladwin (ed.), *Structural Adjustment and African Women Farmers*, Gainsville, FL: University of Florida Press.
Moser, C. (1996) *Confronting Crisis*, World Bank Monograph, Washington, DC: World Bank.
Saito, Katerine (1994) "Raising the Productivity of Women Farmers in Sub-Saharan Africa," World Bank Discussion Papers no. 230, Africa Technical Department Series, Washington, DC: World Bank.
Sen, A. (1990) "More Than 100 Million Women Are Missing," *New York Review of Books* 37(20): 61–6.
SIDA (1996) *Promoting Sustainable Livelihoods*, Stockholm: Kalmarsund Tryck.
UNDP (1995) *Human Development Report*, Oxford: Oxford University Press.
Watkins, K. (1995) *Oxfam Poverty Report*, Oxford: Oxfam.
World Bank (1995) *Towards Gender Equality*, Washington, DC: World Bank.
—— (1996) *Poverty Reduction and the World Bank*, Washington, DC: World Bank.

LUCIA C. HANMER

feudalism

Feudalism is the MODE OF PRODUCTION AND SOCIAL FORMATION combining "juridical serfdom and military protection of the peasantry by a social class of nobles, enjoying monopoly of law and private rights of justice, within a political framework of fragmented sovereignty" (Anderson 1974: 407). It characterized Western Europe from the end of the tenth century until the fifteenth century, with variants in Eastern Europe and Japan. The roots of Western feudalism are to be found in the fragmentation of the old Carolingian Empire. Its full emergence was gradual. Its main characteristics were as follows.

Main characteristics

An important class was the peasant-serf who tilled the land but were not its *de jure* owners. PROPERTY rights were held by the monarch who, through a hierarchy of lords and vassals, would assign rights of use of the land to the serf in return for aid, counsel and military services in time of war. Feudal hierarchy was thus accompanied by a fragmentation of sovereignty. Friction and conflict existed not only between landlords and peasants but also among landlords, who would seek to expand the number of their vassals at the expense of each other.

Usually, one-third of the size of the fief land was held by the lord, and the rest was left to the peasants. Through politico-legal methods of coercion, the lords would extract economic surplus in the form of labor services, rents in kind or dues by the peasants. Thus:

> If labour rent is extracted, that part is spent tilling the lord's demesne, instead of his own plot; alternatively, or in addition, some of

the effort the serf expends on his own and on the common land is directed to raising produce he will deliver to the lord's table, or sell to provide money for the lord's coffers. Nothing is more obvious than that a definite quantity of the fruits of his labour goes to his master.

(Cohen 1978: 333)

In return, the lords were expected to provide safety from incursions and protection from famine, and to dispense justice.

The serfs commanded their tools and owned animals, but their mobility was restricted and they could not dispose of their movable goods (for example, beasts). When the land passed to other hands the serf passed with it to the new lord. There were also tenants who had freedom of movement and disposal of movable goods, and a fair degree of rights on land. In addition, many pastures, forests, quarries, fisheries and wells were controlled as common rights by the village community at large.

The village community was basically self-contained. Production was mostly for use, not for sale. Few products (exceptions being salt, metal objects and millstones) were acquired from the outside. Merchants' clientele was mainly the feudal aristocracy. With no profitable market located in one place and no local representatives, the merchant had to travel in an extended area as an itinerant peddler.

As merchants tended to use towns, so artisans tended to cluster within the city walls. Artisans formed guilds, that is, trade associations which acted as units of self-defense and solidarity; imposed discipline by fixing prices, quality and labor standards; and regulated dealings. This sheltered profits from competition. It also created a class of hired servants and journeymen, on whom guild and town legislation imposed severe regulations, controlling wages and enjoining strict obedience to the master. Thus emerged "the possibility of profit being made, and capital in consequence accumulated, from direct investment in the employment of wage-labour" (Dobb 1946: 119). Yet only in some Flemish and Italian towns were there, as early as 1200, signs of actual capitalist penetration into production.

Did feudalism, as opposed to SLAVERY, create more favorable conditions for the development of productive forces? Only partly. Technological development was minimal and sporadic and did not keep pace with increasing population. The peasants pursued the rational economic strategy of subsistence production (rather than production for the market), diversification (rather than specialization), and minimizing risk (rather than achieving efficiency). This required no heavy productive investment and no important innovation in agricultural methods and techniques to improve yields. Landlords also had small inducement to carry out investments and encourage innovation.

A viable prospect was colonization by opening up new lands, which did occur in the twelfth and thirteenth centuries. However, the lords had two additional opportunities: they could fight wars against other lords, and they could forcefully extract from peasants higher rents in kind or in money and greater labor services. "The nobility was a landowning class whose profession was war: its social vocation was not an external accretion but an intrinsic function of its economic position; warfare was not the 'sport' of princes, it was their fate" (Anderson 1974: 31–2). However, this required investment in military men and weaponry, not in productive equipment.

Feudalism saw a period of increasing POPULATION (the total population of Western Europe went up from approximately 20 million in 950 to 54 million in 1348, the year of the Black Death) and decreasing wages:

[The] lords were induced to commute labour services for money rents and to cultivate their demesnes using wage labour or to lease them. But low wages and high land prices also reduced the incentive to opt for capital-using, labour-saving innovations, in favour of maintaining the old labour-intensive, labour squeezing methods–although now on the basis of hired labour rather than villein services.

(Brenner 1982: 35)

Yet such EXPLOITATION produced surpluses which found their way to the growing urban centers:

> If the population had not been more numerous than before and the cultivated area more extensive; if the fields had not become capable of yielding bigger and more frequent harvests; how could so many weavers, dyers or cloth-shearers have been brought together in towns and provided with a livelihood?
> (Bloch 1961: 70)

Conflict and transition

Social tension, conflict and peasant revolts against the power of the lords (and to a lesser extent urban confrontations) were frequent and at times developed into widespread rebellion, especially in late feudalism. In the fourteenth century, feudalism faced a prolonged period of crisis. Extensions of the cultivated area finally reached land of poor quality, while the oldest lands were exhausted. The extension of arable farming into natural pastures reduced the amount of fodder, hindered the raising of stock and deprived agriculture of manure and traction power.

The urban economy was also severely affected by the scarcity of money, due mainly to the shortage of metals. Even before the onset of the Black Death, population levels had begun a sharp decline. This, together with peasant uprisings, resulted in the diminution of the surplus in lords' hands as well as of commercial profits. This in turn brought an *intensified* surplus, exerting pressure on the peasants by freezing wages, restricting mobility, increasing fiscal exaction, as well as intensifying inter-lord competition.

There was also an opposite strategy: lords acceded to peasant demands, leased vacant lands for cash, accepted payments for canceling labor obligations and rented out their demesnes. Thus, certain landlords were transformed into rentiers, while some peasants became copyholders:

> It was the poorest among the peasantry who performed wage-labor. But even they usually derived part of their subsistence from an acre or two which they held in the openfields or from a small plot of land which surrounded their cottage. And for these cottagers and laborers, the end of the fourteenth century saw not only a rise in agricultural wages but also freedom from the most odious servile obligations. By the end of the fifteenth century, the mass of peasants were free from serfdom.
> (Lazonick 1974:15)

The artisan's workshop did not remain intact. The putting-out system emerged in the fifteenth century, which involved peasants working at home for the merchants. Merchants preferred this arrangement because the cost of production decreased, taxes were smaller and restrictions by the urban guilds circumvented. Moreover, they would extend credit to the peasant-craftsman, supply him with raw materials and dictate quantity and quality of the product.

Transition from feudalism to capitalism

The issue of the transition of feudalism to CAPITALISM has been a controversial one. Many stimuli, dubbed external to the development of the agrarian society, have been put forward by mainstream historians. The following factors figure prominently: the growth of production for exchange and trade, the development of a monetized economy, growth of the market, the rise of urban centers and the pattern of demographic change. Against this tradition, some Marxist historians have maintained the primacy of internal prime movers. They have assigned explanatory preponderance either to the relations of production and the process of class struggle or to the development of productive forces. There have recently been attempts to reconcile these two views within the Marxist tradition.

Selected references

Anderson, Perry (1974) *Lineages of the Absolutist State*, London: Verso, 1979.

Bloch, Marc (1961) *Feudal Society*, London: Routledge & Kegan Paul.
Brenner, Robert (1982) "The Agrarian Roots of European Capitalism," *Past and Present* 97: 16–113.
Cohen, G.A. (1978) *Karl Marx's Theory of History: A Defence*, Oxford: Clarendon Press.
Dobb, Maurice (1946) *Studies in the Development of Capitalism,*, London: Routledge & Kegan Paul, 1963.
Hindess, Barry and Hirst, Paul Q. (1975) *Pre-Capitalist Modes of Production*, London: Routledge & Kegan Paul.
Hilton, Rodney (1985) "Towns in English Feudal Society," in Rodney Hilton, *Class Conflict and the Crisis of Feudalism: Essays in Medieval Social History*, London: The Hambledon Press, 175–86.
Hilton, Rodney et al. (1976) *The Transition from Feudalism to Capitalism*, London: Verso, 1982.
Kula, Witold (1962) *An Economic Theory of the Feudal System: Towards a Model of the Polish Economy 1500–1800*, London: New Left Books, 1976.
Lazonick, William (1974) "Karl Marx and Enclosures in England," *Review of Radical Political Economics* 6(Summer): 1–59.

VASSILIS DROUCOPOULOS
GEORGE KRIMPAS

finance capital

In 1910 a young medic, Rudolf Hilferding, published *Finance Capital*. In this work he viewed finance capital as a specific historic phase of capitalism in which there is an intimate connection between banking, commercial and industrial interests and where the hegemony of high finance prevails. In 1915, Bukharin used the phrase "the coalescence of industrial and bank capital," and in 1917, Lenin termed finance capital "the merging of industrial with bank capital." The terms used in these definitions are not substantially different (Brewer 1980: 103–9; Howard and King 1989: ch. 5). Nor are they much different from modern-day conceptions of finance capital (Sweezy 1972: 143). These definitions each emphasize institutional power bloc characteristics of finance, at the expense of drawing attention to the vulnerability implicit in financial relations.

New forms of financial organization

This was understandable, perhaps, since during the period from 1870 to 1920 it appeared that a new institutional form, "finance capital," had achieved hegemony over the entire world economy (Sweezy 1972: 179). Evidence was found in the concentration and centralization of the major financial institutions; the organization of cartels of industrial capitalists, often by financiers; the exercise of financial control over corporate development more generally; and the powerful impetus of financiers in imperialism, manipulation of state policies and the formation of ideologies. Indeed, many political economists believed that banks and other financial institutions had actually pushed capitalism into a new and perhaps final stage, the era of monopoly, imperialist, finance capitalism. The leading Marxist theorists of the first decades of the twentieth century (Hilferding, Kautsky, Bauer, Bukharin, Lenin and others) adopted this broad argument, although there was conflict about whether this final stage was one of strength or one of decay (Tickten 1986).

However, the banks that were supposedly at the center of power in this new era of capitalism suffered tremendous bankruptcies, culminating in system-wide crashes that left the financial system in tatters during the GREAT DEPRESSION of the 1930s. Nonetheless, until then the theory of finance capital had much to recommend it. Hilferding, for example, contended that the problem of rising overaccumulation in highly concentrated branches and sectors of production could be displaced, thanks to the coordination functions of finance capital, into the more competitive, non-cartelized sectors of the economy. Thus for Hilferding (1910: 298), intensified uneven sectoral development during crisis would not generate further destabilization of the economy, but rather stabilization through deepening cartelization. The subsequent shake-out of the smaller producers would permit the finance capital cartel to increase the level of industrial concentration and survive the broader downturn.

Institutional stability

Indeed, Hilferding posited that several factors "militating against a banking crisis" would combine with finance capital's increasing range to ensure that conditions of crisis could be ameliorated. Those factors included, first, the ability of finance capital to manage and share risk effectively; second, the belief that a strong gold reserve and other state regulatory policies could shore up the creditworthiness of the system; third, a decline in the volume and importance of speculative activity (at the powerful urging of key institutions of finance capital); and fourth, the ability of joint-stock companies to continue to produce during a downturn because production need not realize an immediate return. Hilferding (1910: 291) concluded that it was "sheer dogmatism to oppose the banks' penetration of industry...as a danger to the banks."

Hilferding (1910: 180) even expressed faith that the centralization and concentration process would result in an "increasingly dense network of relations between the banks and industry...[which] would finally result in a single bank or a group of banks establishing control over the entire money capital. Such a 'central bank' would then exercise control over social production as a whole." Bukharin (1917: 73) also predicted a "gigantic combined enterprise under the tutelage of the financial kings and the capitalist state, an enterprise which monopolises the national market." Politically this was extremely important, for it justified seeking a route to socialism that entailed the socialization of capitalist relations via finance. At one point Hilferding (1910: 368) even asserted that, "taking possession of six large Berlin banks would mean taking possession of the most important spheres of large scale industry, and would greatly facilitate the initial phases of socialist policy during the transition period, when capitalist accounting might still prove useful."

Hilferding was German Finance Minister later in his career (for a few weeks in 1923, and in 1928–9), and was considered a reformist Marxist in the Bernstein/Kautsky tradition. On this point his greatest subsequent rival, Henryk Grossmann (1929:198), offered scathing comment: "Hilferding needed this construction of a 'central bank' to ensure some painless, peaceful road to socialism, to his 'regulated' economy." Even as German Finance Minister (under difficult circumstances in the late 1920s) Hilferding failed in any such mission. Yet notwithstanding emerging problems with the finance capital concept (such as the collapse, not strengthening, of financial empires), even as late as 1931 Hilferding maintained his thesis (Sweezy 1942: 298).

Critique of "finance capital"

Where did Hilferding go wrong in miscalculating the power of finance capital? According to de Brunhoff, Hilferding made a critical mistake that led him to dissociate money and the credit system ("money as an instrument of hoarding" is ignored, she complained). "This dissociation has probably been one of the reasons for the overestimation of the role of 'finance capital'" (1976: xiv).

Further objections emerge to the internal logic of Hilferding's "finance capital," as well as to its contemporary relevance. He underplayed the extent to which, for instance, finance was utilized for the financing of labor power as against means of production (especially through pension, insurance, consumer credit and government sources), and the rise in the social wage.

In addition, Hilferding's conclusion ran contrary even to much of his own prior analysis. First, the same problems in the productive sector that lead to falling profit rates also force banks to look further afield, geographically and sectorally, in order to maintain lending and a healthy deposit base, which brings added risk. Second, rather than declining in importance, financial speculation tends to increase dramatically prior to the climax of a crisis. Third,

Hilferding's argument that joint-stock companies were relatively immune from downturns was contradicted by his analysis of how vital credit was to the smooth operation of stock exchanges. As Sweezy (1942: 267) observed, "Hilferding mistakes a transitional phase of capitalist development for a lasting trend." The transitional phase was one of recovery from the 1870s–1890s financial crises; these crises would emerge again during the early 1930s and 1970s–1990s.

See also:

capitalism; capitalist breakdown debate; financial crises; financial instability hypothesis; money, credit and finance: major contemporary themes; monopoly capitalism; speculation

Selected references

Brewer, A. (1980) *Marxist Theories of Imperialism: A Critical Survey*, London: Routledge & Kegan Paul.
Bukharin, N.I. (1917) *Imperialism and the World Economy*, New York: Monthly Review, 1972.
de Brunhoff, S. (1976) *Marx on Money*, New York: Urizen Books.
Grossman, H. (1929) *The Law of Accumulation and Breakdown of the Capitalist System*, London: Pluto, 1992.
Hilferding, R. (1910) *Finance Capital*, London: Routledge & Kegan Paul, 1981.
Howard, M.C. and King, J. (1989), *A History of Marxian Economics*, vol. 1, Princeton: Princeton University Press.
Lenin, V.I. (1917) *Imperialism*, Moscow: Progress Publishers, 1986.
Sweezy, P. (1942) *The Theory of Capitalist Development*, New York: Monthly Review, 1968.
—— (1972) "The Resurgence of Finance Capital: Fact or Fancy?," *Socialist Revolution* 1(8).
Tickten, H. (1986), "The Transitional Epoch, Finance Capital and Britain: The Political Economy of Declining Capitalism," *Critique* 16.

PATRICK BOND

financial crises

Financial crises occur when relatively large groups of people panic in a financial market, disposing of assets in order to meet payment obligations, or in response to the threat of a financial institution becoming insolvent, or the threat of an asset market collapse. They tend to occur during recessions in the short cycle in the context of long-wave downswings (for example, in the 1970s–1990s), when instability and uncertainty are higher than average. They are usually precipitated by spectacular bankruptcies. Wolfson (1994) has produced the most detailed political economy view of financial crises, through an examination of the crises of 1966, 1970, 1974, 1980, 1982, 1984, 1987 and 1991 in the USA. His work links the work of institutionalists, post-Keynesians and Marxists.

Mishkin, a more traditional economist, defines a financial crisis as "a disruption to financial markets in which adverse selection and moral hazard problems become much worse, so that financial markets are unable to efficiently channel funds to those who have the most productive investment opportunities" (Mishkin 1992: 117–18). Adverse selection occurs when clients with a bad credit risk are more likely to be selected to borrow money; moral hazard occurs when there are incentives for borrowers to engage in risky projects in which the lender bears most of the cost if the project fails. In Mishkin's analysis of financial crises, typically a combination of increases in interest rates, a stock market decline and an increase in uncertainty cause adverse selection and moral hazard to increase and GDP to decline. This then leads to a "bank panic," which worsens adverse selection, moral hazard and GDP. During very difficult times, such as during the GREAT DEPRESSION, this may additionally lead to a debt-deflation process (see Fisher 1933), with a declining general price level and greater uncertainty.

Long-wave downswings

Financial crises, along with DEBT CRISES IN THE

financial crises

THIRD WORLD, tend to occur during long-wave downswings due to two forces. First, a long-wave upswing provides the foundation for optimistic expectations to expand long-term investment plans, but in abstraction from the potential for deep recessions as the memory of the last great collapse becomes more opaque (the "Minsky effect"). Firms engage in debt on the basis of high expected profits in the future. Second, once the forces of long-wave downswing emerge (for example, destabilizing SOCIAL STRUCTURES OF ACCUMULATION), debt and interest burdens become magnified as profitability declines (the "cost effect"). In the USA, for instance, financial crises were absent in the long wave upswing of the 1950s and 1960s (despite the credit crunch of 1966), but very common during the long wave downswing of the 1970s–1990s.

For Wolfson (1993), an understanding of recent financial crises must be seen historically as part of the breakdown in the financial social structure of accumulation (see SOCIAL STRUCTURE OF ACCUMULATION: FINANCIAL). During the 1930s and 1940s in the United States a new system emerged, comprising government protection (deposit insurance and lender of last resort) and restrictions on competition (controls on interest rates, segmented financial structures, and the prohibition of interstate banking). This system worked well during the 1950s and 1960s, but broke down after the 1960s and continues to experience problems into the 1990s. Government protection and competition rose simultaneously into the 1970s–1990s, so that now there are fewer opportunities for stable profits and more attempts to support failed banks. However, financial crises are also contributed to by the general economic environment, which since the 1960s has been one of greater uncertainty and the destabilization of institutions.

Early phases of recession

The vast majority of financial crises in the USA during the 1970s–1990s occurred in the early phases of recession. Typically, according to Wolfson (1994), during business cycle upswings (in long-wave downswings) corporations build up their levels of debt, overhead costs and expectations in abstraction from the possibility of recession. Higher interest rates, wages and material costs and tighter monetary policy during the last year of upswing reduce the rate of profit, but investment continues at a reasonably high level (with additional debt), until the declining profit is expected to be continuing into the future.

Then the rate of investment declines markedly, leading to recession, and the corporations have difficulty repaying the interest and principal sum from the debt, leading to defaults. Banks rely more on purchased funds which have lower reserve requirements (e.g. large negotiable certificates of deposit, Eurodollar borrowings, repurchase agreements and federal funds), but these are often volatile and become more expensive over time. By this time, in the early stages of recession, the financial system is especially fragile and a negative surprise event, which normally would have no such adverse influence, typically initiates a financial crisis in this vulnerable environment. The surprise event upsets normal finance and reduces the flow of credit, leading to potential chains of bankruptcy. The crisis subsides when lender of last resort facilities come into play (see Wolfson 1994: ch. 11).

Issues raised by financial crises

The recurrence of financial crises since the early 1970s raises three issues. First, the monetary authorities prevented the financial crises from spreading by providing institutions that defaulted, or were at risk of defaulting, with the finance they needed to meet their payment obligations. Did the monetary authorities thus resolve the financial crises, or did they exacerbate underlying structural problems of which the financial crises are manifestations or symptoms? In some of the heterodox literature, the lender of last resort interventions of the monetary authorities add inflationary pressures to fragile underlying structures.

The second issue raised by the recurrence of financial crises is whether they are monetary or real phenomena. Whereas Marxists and institutionalists have historically considered financial crises to be real phenomena, because forces at work within the manufacturing sector of the economy cause actual profits to fall, post-Keynesians argue that, because of the ease with which investments (based on overly optimistic expectations of future profits) can be financed, financial crises can occur even if actual profits are not declining. However, the heterodox work of Wolfson (1994) and others supports an eclectic view which combines the forces of optimistic expectations with increasing costs (declining profitability). Heterodox work in the area is thus converging as financial crises are seen to be the result of both "monetary" and "real" forces.

The third issue relates to the role of the monetary authorities in the crisis. Post-Keynesians like Wojnilower (1980) agree with Charles Kindleberger that financial crises are caused by the ready availability of credit to finance investments based on overly optimistic expectations of future profits. However, Wojnilower argues that the monetary authorities reward speculation when they increase the supply of money in order to halt the spread of financial crises. Wojnilower argues that bailing out defaulting institutions tempts more people to undertake speculative investments during the next period of prosperity. Consequently, each succeeding cycle of boom and bust will be characterized by greater financial fragility (that is, greater debt-to-equity ratios, shorter term debt structures and less liquid assets), until the monetary authorities finally allow a financial crisis to run its course, as they did during the Great Depression of the early 1930s, forcing the speculators into bankruptcy and letting entrepreneurs who kept their debt low and their liquidity high buy the speculators' assets at fire sale prices.

Wojnilower is post-Keynesian in the sense that he attributes the recurrence of financial crises to increasing financial fragility, but he is rare among post-Keynesians in arguing that eliminating financial fragility calls for allowing financial crises to run their course. Wolfson is more representative of the post-Keynesian literature in that he links the increasing financial fragility, and thus the recurrence of financial crises, to changes in the institutional structure of the financial sector of the economy and a periodic deterioration in the rate of profit on investment in the general economy. His proposals for reform of the financial system include greater prudential supervision, enhanced public investment in financial institutions and local community representatives on the board of directors of financial institutions (Wolfson 1993).

See also:

endogenous money and credit; financial innovations; financial instability hypothesis; liability management

Selected references

Fisher, Irving (1933) "The Debt-Deflation Theory of Great Depressions," *Econometrica* 1: 337–57.

Kindleberger, Charles P. (1978) *Manias, Panics, and Crashes*, New York: Basic Books.

Minsky, Hyman P. (1975) *John Maynard Keynes*, New York: Columbia University Press.

Mishkin, Frederic (1992) "Anatomy of a Financial Crisis," *Journal of Evolutionary Economics* 2: 115–30.

Wojnilower, Albert M. (1980) "The Central Role of Credit Crunches in Recent Financial History," *Brookings Papers on Economic Activity* 2: 277–326.

Wolfson, Martin H. (1993) "The Evolution of the Financial System and the Possibilities for Reform," in Gary Dymski, Gerald Epstein and Robert Pollin (eds), *Transforming the U.S. Financial System: Equity and Efficiency for the 21st Century*, Armonk, NY and London: M.E. Sharpe.

—— (1994) *Financial Crises: Understanding the Postwar U.S. Experience*, 2nd edn, Armonk, NY: M.E. Sharpe.

EDWIN DICKENS
PHILLIP ANTHONY O'HARA

financial innovations

Financial innovations (FIs) are understood as the introduction of new financial instruments, technologies and operating practices by financial institutions. They are developed in order to increase profitability, and often to avoid restrictions imposed by existing regulations. Many exist to correct market imperfections. The critical thing about them for the macroeconomy is not so much their introduction, but rather their spread throughout the economy (Podolski 1986). A FI eventually becomes a regular financial instrument, or *modus operandi*, when the regulator sanctions it and the financial sector accepts it.

Developments during 1960s–1990s

Modern FIs are linked to developments from the 1960s through to the 1990s. Particularly in the 1960s and 1970s, the regulated banking sector started introducing new financial instruments to avoid the application of reserve requirements and interest rates ceilings. In the 1960s there appeared certificates of deposit (CDs), Eurodollars and liability management practices (Wojnilower 1980). In the 1970s and 1980s monetary targets were missed and the M1 monetary aggregate lost its purpose. A number of FIs contributed to the missed aggregates, notably negotiable order of withdrawal accounts (NOW), automatic transfer accounts (ATS), money market mutual funds (MMMFs), repurchase agreements (RPs) and, from 1982, money market deposit accounts.

These technological advancements allowed the introduction of new transfer technologies which reduced transaction costs and increased the speed and efficiency of the monetary circuit. While credit cards were an innovation of the 1950s, this technological development allowed the further spread of "plastic card banking" (Podolski 1986) in the form of "electronic fund transfer at point of sale" (EFTPOS). This was planned to provide the automatic settlement of bills incurred in trade outlets through a system of electronic fund transfer (EFT), based on the use of a plastic card. Technological advancements have contributed to making the financial sector more contestable and subject to easy entry and exit. It has also increased the systemic risk.

In the 1980s and 1990s, FIs have mainly been the result of extensive financial engineering. The financial agents combine existing financial instruments and operating practices, creating new institutional arrangements, in order to cope mostly with increased financial volatility. Stock options and future contracts on interest rates have spread especially quickly. There was also a wave of securitization, the practice where banks transform part of their assets into stripped marketable securities.

There is no general theory of FIs. The pioneer in researching this phenomenon was Silber (1975), who saw FIs as attempts by corporations to reduce regulatory constraints. Miller (1986) defines FIs as the "unforecastable improvements" of the existing instruments and practices. FIs are often the response of the financial sector to challenging external shocks. Van Horne (1985) pointed out that "real" FIs contribute significantly to market efficiency and/or eliminate existing market deficiencies. A number of other finance scholars point out that financial agents introducing FIs earn extra profit, create niche markets and provide a significant low cost advantage over competitors. However, these microeconomic perspectives tend to ignore the wider macro influence of the FIs.

Endogenous money and instability

The introduction of FIs creates significant problems in a macroeconomy. In order to control the money supply the central bank imposes control over the monetary base or influences demand for credit through its influence on interest rates. This is completely feasible with the concept of exogenous money supply. It seems, however, insufficient to explain FIs. FIs are much more explainable if the concept of endogenous money is endorsed (Wray 1990). According to the structuralist view of endogenous money, reserve banks regulate financial institutions, and financial institutions continually innovate partly in order to circumvent these regulations, by creating new sources of finance which are not controlled by the reserve bank. Over time the reserve bank instigates suitable controls and later institutions innovate further, followed by more control, and so on. (See ENDOGENOUS MONEY AND CREDIT.)

A financial or institutional innovation, according to Minsky (1957, 1985), enables an existing quantity of monetary base to cover greater expenditures. FIs affect the existing portfolios of financial institutions, as they appear as illiquid assets replacing more liquid items in portfolios (cash, public bonds, some short-term bank debts, and so on). This contributes to the financial instability of the system, since it increases systemic risk. According to Minsky, financial institutions innovate primarily in expansionary phases of the cycle ("good times," in Wray's words), generating capital gain when asset prices are pushed higher.

Minsky strongly advocates the supervision of bank's balance sheets, in order to tackle the problem of endogenously induced instability. He relates FIs to tight monetary policy. With restrictive measures introduced during the high point in a cycle, the interest rate raises, liquid balance decreases and velocity increases. Financial institutions then tend to try and innovate in order to meet the increased demand for loans. Central banks must thus decrease aggregate reserves sufficiently to compensate for the rise in velocity which results from innovations (Minsky 1957) (see FINANCIAL INSTABILITY HYPOTHESIS).

According to Lavoie (1992), when central banks are reluctant to accommodate money demand and interest rates rise, economic agents look to other instruments and institutions. They thus avoid the higher opportunity cost, and FI occurs in order to satisfy the demand. Consequently, the introduction of FIs leads to a reduction in banks' reserves. Large firms with spare money balances can lend directly to other commercial customers, and shift money accounts from regulated financial institutions to non-regulated ones (near-banks). Electronic networks and information technology also reduce the need for cash.

See also:

cashless competitive payments systems; liability management; monetary policy and central banking functions; regulation and deregulation: financial

Selected references

Dymski G. and Pollin, R. (eds) (1994) *New Perspectives in Monetary Macroeconomics: Explorations in the Tradition of Hyman P. Minsky*, Ann Arbor, MI: University of Michigan Press.

Lavoie, M. (1992) *Foundations of Post-Keynesian Economic Analysis*, Aldershot: Edward Elgar.

Miller, M.H. (1986) "Financial Innovation: The Last Twenty Years and the Next," *Journal of Financial and Quantitative Analysis* 21(4): 459–71.

Minsky, H.P. (1957) "Central Banking and Money Market Changes," *Quarterly Journal of Economics* 71(2): 171–87.

—— (1985) "The Financial Instability Hypothesis: A Restatement," in P. Arestis and T. Skouras, *Post Keynesian Economic Theory: A Challenge to Neoclassical Economics*, Brighton: Wheatsheaf Books.

Podolski, T. (1986) *Financial Innovation and the Money Supply*, Oxford: Blackwell.

Sevic, Z. (1995) *The Concept of the Financial System: An Institutional Financial Economics Approach*, mimeo, University of Dundee.

Silber, W.L. (1975) *Financial Innovation*, Lexington, MA: Lexington Books.

Van Horne, J.C. (1985) "Of Financial Innovations and Excesses," *Journal of Finance* 40(3): 621–31.

Wojnilower, A.M. (1980) "The Central Role of Credit Crunches in Recent Financial History," *Brookings Papers on Economic Activity* 2: 277–326.

Wray, L.R. (1990) *Money and Credit in*

Capitalist Economies: The Endogenous Money Approach, Aldershot: Edward Elgar.

ZELJKO SEVIC

financial instability hypothesis

Hyman Minsky's "financial instability hypothesis" (FIH) is an explanation for the most calamitous event which can befall a capitalist economy: a depression. It also explains why a depression has not occurred since the 1930s; why periods of high boom in a cycle can be unstable and lead to recession; and it provides an unconventional interpretation of the 1975–85 phenomenon of combined high inflation and high unemployment (stagflation). In contrast to most theories of economics, the FIH explicitly considers the role of finance in a developed capitalist economy.

Dynamics of the upswing

The theory is set in historical TIME, with a cycle beginning when the economy has just returned to steady growth after a recent slump. The memory of crisis means that both firms and banks are conservative, so that the only projects initiated are those whose expected cash flows exceed debt repayment commitments at all times. However, this combination of conservative investments and a growing economy means that most investments succeed, which leads both firms and banks to believe that their previous levels of risk aversion were too high. The revision of risk premiums leads to a higher rate of investment, which increases the rate of economic growth, leading to a boom.

More external finance is needed to fund the increased level of investment, and these funds are forthcoming because the banking sector shares the increased optimism of investors (Minsky 1982: 121). The accepted debt-to-equity level rises, liquidity decreases and the growth of credit accelerates. This initial wave of increased investment meets with success as the investment accelerator propels higher growth, and the increased money supply underwrites speculative ventures.

Euphoria and panic

This ushers in what Minsky terms "the euphoric economy" (1982: 120–4), where both lenders and borrowers believe that the future is assured. Asset prices start to spiral upwards, since capitalist expectations are crystallized in the prices they are willing to pay for capital assets, and this allows the emergence of "Ponzi financiers." These are speculators who borrow heavily to purchase assets, generating debt commitments which always exceed the income generated by those assets, but who profit by selling those assets on a rising market. Their insensitivity to interest rates helps fuel an endogenous rise in rates, which pushes investments which had been conservatively financed into the speculative range where debt commitments exceed earnings for the early stage of a project.

More importantly, it converts some investments which were merely speculative into "Ponzi" investments, thus forcing the sale of these assets to enable debt to be repaid. This sudden entry of new sellers into the assets market brings to a halt the upward spiral of asset prices, forcing Ponzi investors to sell assets at a loss. Suddenly these once darlings of the finance sector go bankrupt, abruptly terminating the mood of euphoria and replacing it with panic. Asset prices collapse, investment ceases and the boom becomes a slump. What happens from this point on depends on the rate of inflation in the goods market, the size of the government sector, and the actions of central banks.

If the rate of inflation is low, then debts accumulated during the boom cannot be repaid during the slump, leading to a chain of debt-induced bankruptcies and a depression. If inflation is high, then rising prices enable most debts to be repaid, even though turnover is depressed, as in the 1975–85 experience of stagflation.

Barriers to depression

The key feature of the modern economy which prevents a depression is, according to the FIH, big government: "A cumulative debt deflation process that depends on a fall of profits for its realization is quickly halted when government is so big that the deficit explodes when income falls" (Minsky 1982: xx).

This fiscal barrier to depression is bolstered by the "lender of last resort" actions of the central bank, which expands the monetary base and loosens fiduciary strictures in times of crisis to prevent a run on the banks. However, while prompt action by central banks can help avoid a liquidity crisis, this runs the risk that the speculative boom may simply transfer from one class of assets to another (Minsky 1982: 68,152), as happened with the stock market crash of 1987, when the focus of speculation moved from shares to real estate.

Theoretical foundations of the FIH

There are four main foundations of the financial instability hypothesis. The first is Fisher's concept of a debt deflation (Fisher 1933). The second is KALECKI'S PRINCIPLE OF INCREASING RISK. The third is Keynes's awareness of UNCERTAINTY and the consequently fragile herd nature of capitalist EXPECTATIONS; the concept of a finance demand for money; and the argument that there are two price levels in capitalism (Keynes 1937). The fourth is the post-Keynesian theory of ENDOGENOUS MONEY AND CREDIT.

Fisher argued that a debt deflation could occur when overconfidence leads capitalists to borrow heavily during a boom, generating debt commitments which cannot be repaid during the ensuing slump. Kalecki asserted that capitalist investment was limited, not by decreasing returns to scale, market size and conditions, as in conventional economics, but by the reality that risk increases as the size of a debt-financed investment rises.

KEYNES spoke eloquently of the need for CONVENTIONS to guide behavior in the face of a future which is fundamentally unknowable. In consequence, investors assume that present conditions will prevail, that the existing pattern of prices is correct and that the conventional wisdom concerning the future will be vindicated. With such flimsy foundations, investor expectations are subject to sudden and violent changes, leading to rapid changes in the propensity to invest.

While Keynes's argument that investment determines savings is well-known, in 1937 he argued that the provision of bank finance itself regulates the pace of investment (1937: 247). Though Keynes did not make the link, this perspective is coupled with the view that the money supply is endogenous. The complete Keynesian causal chain thus runs from bank loans, to the investment that loans finance, to the income the investment generates, and finally to the savings which result from that income – a complete reversal of the neoclassical position that savings determine investment.

In a novel argument, Keynes saw investment as being motivated by the difference between the cost of producing an investment, and the capitalized value of the income stream that investment was expected to generate. The former is based upon the current pattern of costs; the latter is based upon capitalist expectations of future earnings. There are thus two price levels in capitalism, with the latter price level liable to vary much more than the former, rising during booms and falling during slumps.

Minsky's contribution has been to weave these many threads of analysis into a coherent and compelling whole. In his later works (Minsky 1982: 68–9), he has argued that the fully developed financial instability hypothesis can be regarded as a far more legitimate expression of Keynes's analysis than the neoclassical synthesis.

Influence on economics

Minsky's analysis has had little impact on mainstream economics, though there have been some attempts to generate Minskian results using mainstream theory, in particular by arguing that financial instability occurs because of asymmetric information because borrowers know more about the viability of their proposed investments than do lenders. This is a return to seeing macroeconomic instability as due to "imperfections in the goods, labor and capital markets" (Gatti and Gallegatii, in Fazzari and Papadimitriou 1992: 134). This has been heavily criticized by post-Keynesian theorists (Fazzari and Papadimitriou 1992: 6), who point out that the Minsky hypothesis assumes that lenders and borrowers have shared expectations of the future. It can also be seen as an attempt to avoid the issue of fundamental uncertainty, which is so much a part of post-Keynesian thinking.

Minsky's work has affected economists in many heterodox schools, not just the post-Keynesians, but also institutional, evolutionary and Marxist economists, who continue to develop the work he initiated. The *Journal of Economic Issues* and the *Journal of Post Keynesian Economics*, in particular, are venues in which Minsky's theories continue to be developed and discussed. There is little doubt that his work will live long past his death in 1996.

See also:

business cycle theories; financial crises; hedge, speculative and Ponzi finance; interest rates: risk structure; monetary policy and central banking functions; social structure of accumulation: financial

Selected references

Dymski, Gary and Pollin, Robert (eds) (1994) *New Perspectives in Monetary Macroeconomics: Explorations in the Tradition of Hyman P. Minsky*, Ann Arbor, MI: University of Michigan Press.

Fazzari, S. and Papadimitriou, D.B. (eds) (1992) *Financial Conditions and Macroeconomic Performance: Essays in Honor of Hyman P. Minsky*, Armonk, NY: M.E. Sharpe.

Fisher, I. (1933) "The Debt Deflation Theory of Great Depressions," *Econometrica* 337–55.

Keen, S. (1995) "Finance and Economic Breakdown: Modelling Minsky's 'Financial Instability Hypothesis'," *Journal of Post Keynesian Economics* 17(4): 607–35.

Keynes, John Maynard (1937) "Alternative Theories of the Rate of Interest," *Economic Journal* 241–52.

Minsky, H.P. (1975) *John Maynard Keynes*, New York: Columbia University Press.

—— (1982) *Can "It" Happen Again?*, Armonk, NY: M.E. Sharpe.

—— (1986) *Stabilizing an Unstable Economy*, New Haven, CT: Yale University Press.

—— (1992) "Hyman P. Minsky (born 1919)," in Philip Arestis and Malcolm Sawyer (eds), *A Biographical Dictionary of Dissenting Economists*, Aldershot: Edward Elgar.

Semmler, Willi (eds) (1989) *Financial Dynamics and Business Cycles: New Perspectives*, Armonk, N.Y. and London: M.E. Sharpe.

Wray, L.R. (1990) *Money and Credit in Capitalist Economies: The Endogenous Money Approach*, Aldershot: Edward Elgar.

STEVE KEEN

fiscal crisis of the state

Introduction

The "fiscal crisis of the state" is a manifestation of a pervasive feature of all capitalist political economies. This is the attempt by business to socialize the costs of investment and production while privatizing the benefits. More specifically, there is a fiscal crisis of the state in so far as there is a chronic tendency for the revenues of the state to fall short of its expenditures. The concern is with chronic (structural) deficits, as opposed to the cyclical deficits which John Maynard KEYNES in particular argued are, in and of themselves, benign events with which we can all be quite comfortable (see BUDGET DEFICIT).

Arguably, fiscal crises of nation states have been significant within almost all of the advanced capitalist political economies throughout the period of global stagnation that began in the mid-1970s. This represents the downswing of the long wave, although the fiscal crisis of the US began earlier, during the Vietnam War. Fiscal crises may in general be understood as the way in which crises of profitability within the private sector since the late 1960s have displayed themselves when they have been transferred successfully onto the shoulders of the public sector.

Social capital and social expenses

The term "fiscal crisis of the state" was popularized with the publication of a book of this title by James O'Connor (1973). Some of what he wrote concerning the expenditure side is similar to the arguments of Adolph Wagner in the 1890s (see Wagner 1958). O'Connor constructed an elaborate argument to explain why, in modern times, the expenditures of the state should persistently tend to outgrow its revenues.

There are two sorts of expenditures, according to O'Connor. The first are social capital expenditures, which support capital accumulation in general. Social capital expenditures include both social consumption and social investment such as infrastructural investments which complement private projects. Social investment will tend not to be provided by private firms because of their scale, complexity or the incapacity of the market to coordinate independent private decisions. The extent of social investment is said by O'Connor to have been increasing, because the scale and complexity of the typical project have been growing.

Social consumption covers the public provision and/or partial financing of goods such as housing and preventative health care, for the reproduction of workers' capacity to labor. Employers are understandably anxious to avoid paying for necessary consumption in pay packets. O'Connor expected social consumption expenditure to increase in relation to GDP.

The second set of expenditures consists of social expenses, which serve to legitimize the activities of modern CAPITALISM. Given that the livelihood of workers and the fortunes of small businesses are often upset in the course of capitalist development, the state must frequently undertake great compensatory and ameliorative expenditures, such as the provision of some sort of social security net. The two sets of expenditures, social expenses and social capital expenditures, are represented as tending to grow in tandem.

O'Connor might have given more attention to another sort of transfer payment by the state, namely that which is directed to the underwriting and protection of private investments (Butler 1980). There is a sound argument to the effect that the need for this sort of transfer is also growing through time (Mandel 1975).

Funding constraint

There are two sources of funds, apart from borrowings, from which the state may obtain the finance to cover its expenditures. Both of these are tightly constrained. The first is taxation revenue, which is constrained by tactics of avoidance and evasion, which seem more "legitimate" the higher the tax burden (at least in the eyes of the society's elites concerning their own shares of the burden). The second is operating surpluses of state enterprises, which are constrained by pressures for the PRIVATIZATION of state operations, especially those that are evidently profitable.

If the level of deficit financing grows in relation to the extent to which public investments raise national output, the severity of the fiscal crisis is increased. By the same token, if the deficit is financed by means of borrowing abroad there may be a tendency for the borrowing nation's currency to depreciate (unless of course the currency is a reserve currency which is accepted by the lender as a means of debt servicing). This is a problem where the net impact of depreciation on the profitability of producing significant, internationally traded commodities is negative. It is impossible to argue, though, that a fiscal deficit must necessarily worsen the current account of the balance of payments (an argument commonly attempted in the name of the "twin deficits" thesis).

Even if it seems to the business community

that the twin deficits argument does hold, there would be no consensus as to what fiscal strategy is appropriate. Budget balancing for business usually means a reduction in social expenses rather than of public investment or those transfers that are necessary to underwrite and protect private investments. However, there would be some sections of the business community (especially those producing commodities that are not internationally tradable) that would want to see deficit budgeting retained in order to sustain aggregate demand. Moreover, for the financial sector of the business community the continued creation of government debt ensures a growth of instruments on which they can look forward to turning a profit.

Political significance

In any country in which there is more than one significant level of government (perhaps particularly in federations), the fiscal crisis of the state has become a major part of politics. Each level of government has become intent on transferring the fiscal crisis to the other. Nation states have withdrawn from the operation of business enterprises in favor of brokerage deals involving private corporations as operators. It has remained necessary for nation-states to coordinate infrastructural projects; but they coordinate the financial and technical contributions of private enterprises with the inducement of guaranteed profits over some period like thirty years.

To be sure, the state thereby escapes a considerable financial burden, but only at a cost and only for the time being. The cost is a loss of political legitimacy in the eyes of citizens who must pay for the use of the infrastructure regardless of their capacity to pay. The financial rub for the state is that once ownership of the infrastructure reverts to the state, it becomes the state's responsibility to demolish obsolete and worn-out bridges and the like, as well as to coordinate upgrading for the next era.

Over the past couple of decades, from the mid-1970s, the emergence of fiscal crises has provided another weapon for those who would redistribute power within capitalist societies away from "the common person." After all, it has been the hope and the promise of social democrats and other reformers for the state to redistribute income to the collectivity and to alter the market's distribution of income and wealth. In other words, the persistence of fiscal crises has provided neo-liberals with a weapon to combat the social democratic program of redistribution.

See also:

economic rationalism or liberalism; fiscal policy; industry policy; Reaganomics and Thatcherism; social democracy; social and organizational capital; state and government; welfare state

Selected references

Butler, Gavan (1980) "The State and the Disposition of the Social Surplus," *Journal of Australian Political Economy* 9(November): 25–33.
Groenewegen, Peter (1979) *Public Finance in Australia: Theory and Practice*, Sydney: Prentice Hall.
Mandel, Ernest (1975) *Late Capitalism*, London: New Left Books, ch. 17.
Miller, John A. (1986) "The Fiscal Crisis of State Reconsidered: Two Views of the State and the Accumulation of Capital in the Postwar Economy," *Review of Radical Political Economics* 18 (1&2): 236–60.
O'Connor, James (1973) *The Fiscal Crisis of the State*, New York: St. Martin's Press.
Wagner, Adolph (1958) "Three Extracts on Public Finance," in R.A. Musgrave and A.T. Peacock (eds), *Classics in the Theory of Public Finance*, London: Macmillan for the International Economics Association.

GAVAN BUTLER

fiscal policy

Fiscal policy refers to government tax and spending changes made to improve economic performance. These changes can be used to generate more jobs and an economic expansion during a recession. Government tax and spending changes can also slow down spending to help counter inflation. These tools were first advocated by John Maynard KEYNES (1936) in the 1930s as a means to end the Great Depression facing the world economy; thus fiscal policy is frequently referred to as "Keynesian fiscal policy" or "Keynesian economic policy." In general, there are two types of fiscal policy: discretionary and non-discretionary (automatic).

Discretionary fiscal policy

Walter Heller (1967) called discretionary fiscal policy "fine tuning." This involves the national government deciding to cut taxes during a recession and then passing a tax cut bill. This would result in greater consumer spending. Alternatively, the government can pass a bill to increase its expenditures. In either case, there would be more spending in the economy, increased production by businesses to meet this additional demand and more workers hired. During times of inflation, these policies would be employed in reverse. Tax increases and cuts in government spending reduce the amount of money people have to spend. This reduces total demand and inflationary pressures in the economy.

History provides numerous instances where discretionary fiscal policy was employed to improve economic performance. The Second World War has frequently been cited as evidence that government spending is an effective policy tool to end depressions. The Kennedy–Johnson tax cut of 1964 has been heralded as evidence that the "age of Keynes" arrived in the United States shortly after the Second World War (Lekachman 1966).

However, discretionary fiscal policy also has its critics. One important criticism of discretionary fiscal policy is that it will be manipulated for political reasons and thus create rather than mitigate business cycles. Tufte (1978) has demonstrated that high unemployment levels right before an election will hurt incumbents and help challengers. He has also shown that politicians recognize this fact and tend to expand the national economy just before an election year. Then after the election, when inflation becomes a problem, tight fiscal policies are employed to slow down the economy (see POLITICAL BUSINESS CYCLES).

A second criticism of discretionary fiscal policy is that government officials react too slowly to changing economic circumstances. Political wrangling will make it impossible to implement tax cuts in a timely manner or put spending programs into effect quickly. Things will be even worse if taxes have to rise or if spending must be cut. Politicians, likely to fear the political consequences of these actions, will do nothing at all; or they will stall as long as possible and hope that the inflationary problems go away on their own.

The Kennedy–Johnson tax cut of 1964 illustrates the difficulties of timing. In 1960 the United States economy was sluggish, and unemployment had risen to 6 percent from 4 percent in the 1950s. Many Keynesian economists in the USA called for tax cuts or greater government spending. Persuaded by these Keynesians, Senator Kennedy ran for President promising a tax cut. Although Kennedy won the 1960 Presidential election, he could not get Congress to cut taxes. Not until 1964, when Lyndon Johnson was President, did Congress finally pass a tax cut; and its main impact on the US economy did not take effect until 1965. However, the US economy in 1965 was very different from the US economy in 1960. Unemployment was below 4 percent and inflation, which no one was worried about in 1960, had begun to accelerate in 1965. Thus what had been the right policy for the US economy in 1960 when candidate Kennedy was running for President had become the wrong policy by 1965, when the tax cut that Kennedy had proposed five years earlier was beginning to have an impact on the US economy.

fiscal policy

Non-discretionary fiscal policy

If elected officials cannot be trusted to pass appropriate tax and spending changes in a timely manner, or if politicians are concerned more with their own re-election than with long-term economic performance, some other type of fiscal policy becomes necessary. This second type of fiscal policy is usually referred to as "non-discretionary fiscal policy," and the policy tools themselves are usually referred to as "automatic" or "built-in" stabilizers. These are programs that lead automatically (without any legislative decisions or action) to greater government spending or to tax cuts whenever unemployment rises. These are also programs that automatically lead to reductions in government spending or tax increases whenever inflation increases. Albert Hart (1945) was the first to use the term, but Richard Musgrave (see Musgrave and Miller 1948; Musgrave and Musgrave 1989) is most responsible for popularizing the notion of built-in stabilizers and pushing for their implementation.

Important examples of automatic fiscal policy include unemployment insurance, welfare programs, and a progressive income tax. Consider unemployment insurance. When an economy is doing fine and unemployment rates are low, the government spends very little money on unemployment benefits and it collects a good deal of money in unemployment insurance premiums. However, as workers start to be laid off, spending on unemployment insurance immediately rises. No spending bill must be passed in order for this spending to take place. Rather, the spending takes place automatically because most laid off workers qualify for these unemployment benefits.

Welfare and other social insurance programs work in a similar fashion. When economic times are bad, these programs provide income to those people lacking jobs and income. This generates extra spending in the economy, which contributes to economic expansion and job creation. On the other hand, as more jobs are created and as unemployment falls, social welfare expenditures will fall. This is all for the good, since as the economy expands, inflation rather than unemployment becomes the most pressing economic problem, and the correct economic policy is to reduce total expenditures.

Finally, a progressive income tax system functions as an automatic, or built-in, economic stabilizer. With a progressive tax system, tax rates rise as income levels increase. In times of inflation, incomes generally increase, and people get used to buying higher priced goods as well as bidding up the price of goods. However, a progressive tax system puts a damper on this process. As the income of households rise, households get pushed into higher tax brackets and pay greater fractions of their income in taxes. This constrains the amount of extra money that households have to spend. With less money to spend, households contribute less to the inflation problem. The individual income tax system thus tends to restrain inflationary forces.

Similarly, in times of recession a progressive tax system dampens the decline in spending that results from layoffs. Consider a family with two earners, one of whom is laid off. The loss of income and spending power for the family will be first and foremost the lost wages from the job loss. But with a progressive tax system, reduced family income will mean that the family member who continues working will owe considerably less in taxes. This will give the family more disposable income and the family will thus be able to spend more money.

One implication of fiscal policy is that if countries tend to experience recessions and bouts of high unemployment, then they will have to run budget deficits all the time. Fiscal policy says that in times of high unemployment governments should increase spending, cut taxes, or both. Thus governments need to run budget deficits in times of economic recession. However, high deficit and debt levels in many developed countries have frightened investors, government officials and the general public. As a result, fiscal policy has been used less and less in the late twentieth century as deficit and debt levels have risen. This reduced use of fiscal policy has been cited (Pressman 1995) as one reason for the slower economic growth and higher unemployment experienced by developed countries in the last quarter of the twentieth century.

See also:

budget deficit; fiscal crisis of the state; Keynesian political economy; Keynesian revolution; monetary policy and central banking functions; social wage; state and internationalization; welfare state

Selected references

Hart, Albert G. (1945) "Model Building and Fiscal Policy," *American Economic Review* 35(September): 531–58.
Heller, Walter (1967) *New Dimensions of Political Economy*, New York: W.W. Norton.
Keynes, John Maynard (1936) *The General Theory of Employment, Interest and Money*, New York: Harcourt Brace & World.
Lekachman, Robert (1966) *The Age of Keynes*, New York: McGraw-Hill.
Musgrave, Richard A. and Miller, Merton H. (1948) "Built-in Flexibility," *American Economic Review* 38(March): 122–8.
Musgrave, Richard A. and Musgrave, Peggy B. (1989) *Public Finance in Theory and Practice*, 5th edn, New York: McGraw-Hill.
Pressman, Steven (1995) "Deficits, Full Employment and the Use of Fiscal Policy," *Review of Political Economy* 7(2): 212–26.
Tufte, Edward (1978) *The Political Control of the Economy*, Princeton, NJ: Princeton University Press.

STEVEN PRESSMAN

Fordism and the flexible system of production

Introduction

Fordism refers to the system of mass production and consumption characteristic of highly developed capitalist economies during the 1940s–1960s. Under Fordism, mass consumption combined with mass production to produce sustained economic growth and widespread material advancement. The 1970s–1990s have been a period of slower growth and increased income inequality. During this period, the system of organization of production and consumption has, perhaps, undergone another transformation, which when mature may propel another burst of economic growth. This new system is often referred to as the "flexible system of production" (FSP) or the "Japanese management system." On the production side, FSP is characterized by dramatic reductions in information costs and overheads, total quality management, just-in-time inventory control and leaderless work groups. On the consumption side, it is characterized by the globalization of consumer goods markets, faster product life cycles, and far greater product/market segmentation and differentiation.

Fordism

The term "Fordism" reflects Henry Ford's role in the rise of the American automobile industry, and the associated transformation of the United States in the early decades of the twentieth century. The US economy evolved from an agricultural, craft-based economy to an industrial, mass production economy. The latter was based on economies of scale and scope and giant organizations built upon functional specialization and minute divisions of labor. This transformation also engendered a variety of public policies, institutions and governance mechanisms intended to mitigate the failures of market capitalism, and to reform modern industrial arrangements and practices (Polanyi 1944).

Ford's main contributions to mass production were in the realm of process engineering. The hallmark of the Fordist production system was the moving, or continuous, assembly line in which each assembler performed a single, repetitive task. Ford's production system enabled labor productivity to increase tenfold and auto prices to be cut by more than half. Ford and many other industries achieved massive economies of scale and coordination through vertical integration (see Chandler 1977).

In the 1920s and 1930s, General Motors enhanced Fordism through innovations in marketing and organization. Especially influential was the multi-divisional (M-form) organizational structure, in which each major operating division serves a distinct product market; and a radically decentralized administrative control structure (Chandler 1977). Within each of its operating divisions, however, GM was organized and operated like Ford – or any other mass-production manufacturer.

In this system, assemblers were as interchangeable as parts. The system rested on the presumption that production activities should be simplified to the nth degree and controlled from above; that engineering and administrative functions be delegated to staff specialists; and the exercise of judgment be given to management. This required armies of middle managers and staff specialists, whose job it was to gather and process quantities of data for top management to use to coordinate activities, allocate resources and set strategy.

Ford's mass-production system always had critics. Surprisingly, one of the first was Frederick Taylor, who coined the term "Fordism". Taylor directed his criticism at the de-skilling of assembly line workers, likening Ford's assemblers to trained gorillas. Fordist assembly-line work is unpleasant; it is physically demanding, requires high levels of concentration, and can be excruciatingly boring. According to the somewhat stylized facts, Ford solved the problem of labor turnover by doubling pay. Other manufacturers emulated Ford's wage policies, along with his production methods. They paid premium wages for putting up with what Antonio Gramsci in *Americanismo e Fordismo* (1929–32) considered to be uninspiring, boring and repetitive work.

Regardless of the means, unskilled assembly workers eventually reaped substantial gains from increased industrial productivity – a 40 percent reduction in working hours and a massive increase in wages. In the English-speaking world, industrial unions fought for and won supracompetitive wages for their members, sometimes on their own, sometimes in cooperation with other unions and sometimes in collusion with specific firms. In the social market economies of Northern Europe, workers did even better. Coordinated wage setting between national associations of employers and national labor organizations, usually led by blue-collar unions, achieved both high wages and considerable income equality, almost without strikes (Scharpf 1991). According to Aglietta (1976) this helped to propel mass consumption, mass production's complement, thereby completing the Fordist system as a "mode of accumulation."

The ability of unskilled manufacturing employees to gain and hold supracompetitive wages probably depended primarily upon their political power. By the 1950s, the rise of mass production had made them the largest single group in every developed capitalist economy. Labor unions emerged as the best-organized and often the most powerful political force. Their preferences were reflected not only in labor laws, but in public policy generally. They were the architects and chief supporters of the postwar Keynesian WELFARE STATE, with its goals of full employment, social security and income parity. Indeed, some refer to the welfare state as the Fordist state (see Albo *et al.* 1993).

Aglietta (1976: 120–1) shows how Fordism promoted strikes and absenteeism and how its dehumanizing aspects got in the way of productivity growth and product quality. These trends were clearly evident by the late 1960s and 1970s. Fordism was also challenged, as Tylecote (1995) illustrates, by the maturation of its TECHNOLOGY, the rise of biotechnology and the information revolution. Thus the 1970s–1990s represent to many authors a transitional phase to something new, the FSP, which is heavily dependent on new technologies and institutions. (See REGULATION APPROACH.)

Flexible system of production

Flexible production, perhaps the second great transformation in the organization of work of this century, was, like mass production, brought to our attention by a revolution in the automobile industry. In this revolution, mass production and its champion, the mighty General Motors, were utterly routed by the "Toyota Production System." However, this transformation did not really start in the automobile business. IBM, for example, combined total quality management (TQM), lean manufacturing, just-in-time (JIT) delivery and price-based costing twenty years before Eiji Toyoda and Taiichi Ohno implemented the Toyota Production System.

Flexible production rests on the following presumptions: a competitive edge cannot be gained by treating workers like machines; production workers can perform most functions better than staff specialists (lean manufacturing); every process should be performed perfectly (TQM), thus reducing the need for buffer stocks (JIT) and producing a higher quality end-product (Piore and Sabel 1985). Like Fordism, this second transformation may extend well beyond process engineering, transforming not only how we make things but also how we live and what we consume. It appears to be driven primarily by reductions in communications, logistics and information processing costs (Reschenthaler and Thompson 1996).

Today, an organization that can afford a computer workstation and software can have first-class functional overhead systems. Not long ago, these systems were available only to giants. Moreover, computerized product design and manufacture permit organizations to produce customized services at mass-production prices. As a result, many large companies are mimicking their smaller competitors by shrinking head offices, removing layers of bureaucracy and concentrating on core businesses. Some of the new FSP firms, such as Nike, do nothing themselves but market products; they contract out all other activities.

Information technology has also given rise to new modes of internal organization, which emphasize multidisciplinary teams, whose members work together from the start of a job to its completion. This is in part because modern information systems and expert systems make it efficient to push the exercise of judgment down to the teams that do an organization's work. As Shoshana Zuboff explains in *The Age of the Smart Machine* published in 1988, efficient operations in the modern workplace call for a more equal distribution of knowledge, authority, and responsibility.

At present, single product organizations are often organized as virtual networks; and multi-product organizations are organized as alliances of networks. The system used by IBM at its plant in Dallas, Texas, is the quintessential example of a virtual network, or self-organizing system. Everyone in the organization plays the part of customer or provider, depending on the transaction, and the entire plant has been transformed into a network of dyads and exchanges. Johnson & Johnson is an example of a multi-product business that has organized itself into a loose alliance of networks, sharing only its top management and information system, a set of core competencies and a common culture.

Flexible production reduces the demand for unskilled labor, since it requires numerate and literate workers capable of a high degree of self-direction. As a consequence, the percentage of unskilled industrial workers in the labor force in the developed world has been falling for decades. Decreased numbers have been reflected in political decline and also in falling relative – or, in some cases, real – wages. Increasingly, workers are forced to choose between full employment (the US choice) and job security (Western Europe).

Moreover, mass production's declining significance has been accompanied by a decline in mass consumption. Instead of standardized products designed and manufactured for the lowest common denominator, final products reflect a far wider array of preferences and pocketbooks. This too has probably exacerbated the trend to further real income inequality.

Conclusion

The FSP has by no means permeated every

aspect of industry, and in an ongoing fashion many authors are still closely scrutinizing the nature and validity of "flexible production" (see the Summer 1993 issue of *Capital and Class* for several articles; and WORK, LABOR AND PRODUCTION: MAJOR CONTEMPORARY THEMES). Nevertheless, debates on the FSP are very lively and represent one of the most interesting and relevant aspects of modern political economy.

See also:

capital–labour accord; labour process; social structure of accumulation; Taylorism

Selected references

Aglietta, Michel (1976) *A Theory of Capitalist Regulation: The US Experience*, trans. from the French by David Fernbach, London: New Left Books, 1979.

Albo, Gregory, Langille, David and Panitch, Leo (eds) (1993) *A Different Kind of State?* Toronto: Oxford University Press.

Chandler, Alfred Dupont (1977) *The Visible Hand: The Managerial Revolution in American Business*, Cambridge, MA: Belknap.

Kaplinsky, Raphael (1994) *Easternization: The Spread of Japanese Management Techniques to LDCs*, London: Frank Cass.

Mansfield, Edwin (1992) "Flexible Manufacturing Systems: Economic Effects in Japan, United States, and Western Europe," *Japan and the World Economy* 2: 1–16.

Piore, M.J. and Sabel, Charles F. (1985) *Das Ende der Massenproduktion*, Berlin: Wagenbach.

Polanyi, Karl (1944) *The Great Transformation*, Boston: Beacon Press, 1985.

Reschenthaler, G.B. and Thompson, Fred (1996) "The Information Revolution and the New Public Management," *Journal of Public Administration Research and Theory* 6(1): 125–44.

Scharpf, Fritz Wilhelm (1991) *Crisis and Choice in European Social Democracy*, trans. from the German by Ruth Crowley and Fred Thompson Ithaca, NY: Cornell University Press.

Tylecote, Andrew (1995) "Technological and Economic Long Waves and their Implications for Employment," *New Technology, Work and Employment* 10(1): 3–18.

FRED THOMPSON

foreign aid

Foreign aid comprises concessional finance and subsidized goods and services to developing countries to be used for development purposes. A more precise definition is used by the donors' club, the Development Assistance Committee (DAC). According to the DAC, the funds must:

- come from official sources, which excludes funds raised by non-governmental organizations (NGOs), private voluntary organizations (PVOs), but not those channeled through NGOs by official agencies;
- be intended for developmental purposes, ruling out military aid and flows with a mainly commercial intent, such as export credits;
- have a high degree of concessionality (formally defined as a grant element of 25 percent or more); and
- be to a country on Part I of the DAC's "List of Aid Recipients," which includes all low and middle income countries.

International flows satisfying all four conditions are classified as Official Development Assistance (ODA); those satisfying all but the concessionality condition are labeled Official Development Finance (ODF).

History

The rise of aid has been a post-1945 phenomenon, though it has its precursor in the programs carried out by colonial authorities, such as the successive Colonial Welfare and Development Acts of the United Kingdom. The origins of aid are normally ascribed to three factors. First, there was the success of United States' Marshall Plan aid to Europe (explicitly emulated, for example, in the Colombo Plan for Asia). Second, there was the first wave of independence in Asia in the late 1940s; African independence in the 1960s gave a renewed impetus to aid programs. The Cold War was the third factor, as the superpowers used aid as one instrument to obtain influence and secure the position of "friendly regimes" (friendly to the relevant superpower, that is, but usually less so to the people they ruled).

The nature of aid has changed as the above trends have evolved. Point Four of President Truman's inaugural address in 1949 launched the United States aid program and during the 1950s the United States was the major donor, accounting for about two-thirds of all aid. The situation changed somewhat following Krushchev's announcement, at the Twentieth Party Congress in 1956, of an expanded Soviet aid program. The second wave of independence in the 1960s contributed to two important changes in the aid scene. First was the rise of bilateral donors, as flows to former colonies became institutionalized into the nascent aid program. Second has been the growth of the UN system and the growing demands for changes in the global economic system, including increased aid.

Control over aid finance

While there has been a proliferation of multilateral institutions (whose share of ODA grew to over 20 percent in the first half of the 1970s and has fluctuated around that level since), donor countries have successfully resisted developing country control over most aid programs and policy. Three examples may be mentioned. First, the UN's Special Fund for Economic Development (SUNFED) never materialized; instead the soft-loan window of the World Bank, the International Development Association (IDA), was created in 1961. Second, the various attempts of the UN Conference on Trade and Development (UNCTAD) to influence aid policy have been rebuffed, this role being taken by the DAC (founded as the Development Assistance Group in 1960). While the UN system works on a one-country one-vote system, the World Bank voting system is biased against developing countries and the DAC simply excludes them altogether. A more recent example is the Special Program for Africa, which discusses the modalities of aid and the design of STRUCTURAL ADJUSTMENT POLICIES to which the aid is linked. African governments are not represented at these meetings. The practice of excluding recipients from discussions of aid policy contrasts with the period of the Marshall Plan, in which the OEEC (the forerunner of the OECD) was responsible for allocation of the funds and monitoring their use, with the donor, the US, an equal member with the recipient European countries.

Perspectives from the left and the right

Commentators on aid fall into three groups. First are critics from the left who use a dependency theory framework to argue that the role of aid is to draw developing countries into the international capitalist system. Traditionally, aid helped build infrastructure to allow for the export of primary commodities and, more recently, structural adjustment programs have openly driven developing countries onto international markets so they can pay their debts to Western banks, regardless of the adverse consequences for the poor and the environment (see, for example, Hayter and Watson 1985). Equally damning of aid are critics from the right, but for the very different reason that, since most aid flows through government, it necessarily strengthens the role of the state and disrupts the market. This argument was made by Friedman in the 1950s and voiced on several occasions by Bauer (for example, Bauer 1991: ch. 4).

Macroeconomic impact

The last category is a rather broad center which comprises the aid effectiveness debate. A major part of the aid effectiveness debate has concerned aid's macroeconomic impact. Using a Harrod–Domar model, in which growth is determined by the rate of capital investment, Chenery and Strout (1966) presented a two-gap model, which showed that aid could alleviate both the savings and foreign exchange constraints and so facilitate higher growth. Critics, notably Griffin (1970), argued that the empirical data in fact show no relationship between aid and growth, which may be explained by the fact that aid both reduces domestic savings and reduces the efficiency of investment.

Other adverse macroeconomic effects of aid have been suggested, such as discouraging government tax collection and the Dutch disease (i.e. reducing exports, most likely by an appreciation of the real exchange rate). Mosley (1987) has pointed to a macro–micro paradox, since these rather pessimistic conclusions at the macroeconomic level seem to conflict with the rather more positive picture at the micro (project) level, where donor evaluations conclude that most projects are successful. Various resolutions of this paradox are possible, including that either, or both, macro or micro studies are wrong. Evidence from country case studies suggests that aid may have had a more positive macroeconomic role than suggested by cross-country estimates, since aid does positively affect imports and investment which are important determinants of growth (White 1997).

Impact on poverty

The aid effectiveness debate has also addressed the issue of aid's impact on poverty. Although poverty alleviation is frequently cited as a major motivation for aid, it is in fact difficult to say how much aid is directly used to help the poor; though it is likely that 15–20 percent is a generous estimate. We have even less evidence on how the poor have benefited from most aid transfers, but there are a number of biases in aid programs that have limited their effectiveness in this regard. Commentators on aid from across the spectrum agree that it is subject to political and commercial pressures in the donor country. These pressures affect which countries receive aid (Israel and Egypt are major beneficiaries of US aid) and what types of project they finance (donors are keener to fund high-tech urban roads than rural feeder roads built using labor-intensive techniques). Moreover, donor credibility in encouraging governments to target the poor is undermined when donors themselves use aid for other purposes.

Conclusion

Increasing the poverty impact of aid remains one of the major challenges for research and practice. Others argue that there is a need to reinvent international cooperation beyond aid, and to find new ways of ensuring international security in the post-Cold War era. Nonetheless, it is likely that aid flows will remain an important feature of the international economic system for some time to come, especially in relation to the poorer countries of the world.

See also:

debt crises in the Third World; inequality

Selected references

Bauer, Peter (1991) *The Development Frontier: Essays in Applied Economics*, Brighton: Harvester Wheatsheaf.

Chenery, Hollis B. and Strout, Alan M. (1966) "Foreign Assistance and Economic Development," *American Economic Review* 56(4): 679–733.

Griffin, Keith (1970) "Foreign Capital, Domestic Savings and Economic Development," *Bulletin of the Oxford University Institute of Economics and Statistics* 32(2): 99–112.

Hayter, Teresa and Watson, Catherine (1985) *Aid: Rhetoric and Reality*, London: Pluto Press.

Mosley, Paul (1987) *Overseas Aid: Its Defence and Reform*, Brighton: Wheatsheaf.

White, Howard (ed.) (1997) *Aid and Macroeconomic Performance: Theory, Empirical*

Evidence and Four Country Cases, London: Macmillan.

HOWARD WHITE

foreign direct investment

Foreign direct investment (FDI) denotes the export of productive, non-loan capital from one country to another. It includes, therefore, capital exports for the establishment of subsidiary or joint venture companies, for company mergers and so on, and is related to the formation of TRANSNATIONAL CORPORATIONS. FDI is usually identified by ownership of at least 10 percent of the equity in an enterprise, and it covers claims that are intended to remain outstanding for more than one year. Loans between an associated company or subsidiary and a mother company are in most cases considered by international statistics to be FDI. FDI constitutes one of the major components of the capital accounts of a nation's balance of payments.

Although FDI attained a significant role in the international economy in the first decade of the twentieth century, the real boom took place after the Second World War. From 1946 up to the 1980s, the major FDI exporting country was the USA (which took the lead from the traditional prewar FDI exporter, the UK). With the exception of these two countries and Japan (which had restrictions on inward FDI), the other important capital exporting countries (Germany, the Netherlands, France and Canada) were, at least until the mid-1970s, net capital importers as inward FDI exceeded outward FDI in value. In the 1990s Japan became the world's major FDI exporter, while the UK became a net FDI importer.

Innovative eclectic contributions

Each of the major heterodox perspectives has contributed something useful to the study of FDI, as has orthodox economics. Neoclassical economists struggled for some time to explain FDI, the primary stumbling block being the absence of a suitable answer to the question: Why would a firm choose FDI, the most expensive option, over exporting or licensing? A revolution of sorts took place when Stephen Hymer (1976) suggested that firms undertaking FDI were not, as previously assumed, perfect competitors. Thus, the higher cost of transacting abroad was not sufficient to drive them out of the market. Furthermore, they may gain specific advantages from locating internationally (something a perfect competitor, by definition, could not do).

The most productive extension of Hymer's theory has been that orchestrated by John Dunning (1977). Dunning insists that only an eclectic approach can hope to explain fully the phenomenon of FDI. Theories from economics, sociology, political science and the business disciplines may each have something substantial to contribute to a complete understanding. His broad-minded attitude is not typical of neoclassical research, wherein analyses originating outside economics are often discounted as unscientific. Nonetheless, he has been quite persuasive and influential.

Post-Keynesian and institutional views

Post-Keynesians have not felt the need to rewrite FDI theory, but one improvement which they have made is to substitute Alfred Eichner's model of oligopoly for that of the mainstream. In addition, the post-Keynesian focus on the role of UNCERTAINTY has had useful applications in FDI theory, especially with regard to exchange rate movements (see Harvey 1989–90).

Most institutionalist research has been confined to studies of FDI in developing countries (although there are exceptions). Unlike neoclassical economists, institutionalists do not view economic behavior as natural and therefore identical across social groups. Instead, because it is learned, the structure of each economy must be carefully studied before it can be understood. Hence, not only do institutionalists resist the temptation to use the same approach in every context, but they also treat economic theory as a manifestation of cultural biases and folkviews. For example, it is argued that the mainstream bias in favor of free markets has led them to the erroneous conclusions that, first, the modern industrial economies developed more quickly when they were the recipients of inward FDI, and second, that today's Third World countries therefore need FDI to spur their development process (Mayhew 1996). As a consequence, it is quite often the case that the welfare of those being "helped" by FDI is lowered rather than raised.

For instance, Jansen (1995) has studied the effects of FDI on GDP, private investment, foreign debt, inflation and the current account for Thailand in the 1980s and early 1990s. The conclusions were mixed. On the one hand, FDI contributed to a substantial increase in GDP and private investment, and a considerable dampening of inflation through increases in supply. Jansen adds, however, that without increases in FDI these variables would have rebounded from the low levels of the mid-1980s recession anyway. On the negative side, FDI increased the import dependency of the economy, especially through the import of capital goods. This led to a much higher level of external debt to balance the external accounts. Also, greater FDI increased considerably the outflow of profit and dividend payments to parent companies and the like. Thus, FDI is by no means the godsend that some analysts have argued.

Marxist views

Marxists share the concern of institutionalists, albeit for quite different reasons. Classical Marxist theories of imperialism provided the first explanations of FDI. Two such approaches stand out. First, there is the "surplus of capital" approach. This claims that, in industrial countries, while the volume of capital intended for accumulation increases rapidly, investment opportunities contract, forcing the export of capital (Hilferding 1981: 234). The second is the "colonial extra profits" approach. This claims that colonial or lowly developed (low wage) countries become a source of extra profits by reducing the cost price of industrial products. Therefore, it is these territories which can have great importance for the most powerful capitalist groups (Hilferding 1981: 328). However, the reality is that most FDI takes place among developed countries. Investment opportunities have not contracted in the industrial countries, and the comparatively low productivity of labor in many slowly-developing Third World countries has resulted in a low profit rate, despite low labor or raw materials costs (Milios 1989).

While determining why these two approaches have not worked may be interesting, the far more important issue for Marxists is explaining FDI among sectors of developed capitalist countries. FDI among industrial countries and its correlation with international trade was penetratingly investigated in Germany by several authors, who claim that the Marxist law of value functions in a modified way on the world market (see Busch *et al.* 1984). FDI is undertaken, they claim, by enterprises of a national economy which initially possess a leading position in the world market. This sector acquires extra profits by exporting commodities to foreign markets, where local producers possess a lower labor PRODUCTIVITY. These extra profits of the country with the higher labor productivity are, however, soon eroded through an overvaluation of its national currency resulting from its trade balance surpluses. Correspondingly, trade deficits lead to a devaluation of the currency of the less developed country. The advanced country's position in the foreign market is threatened by local producers, unless transposition of production in this foreign market (that is, FDI) takes place.

Therefore, currency devaluation acts protectively for the less developed industrial country as a whole and initiates inward FDI. However, sectors of this less advanced country with labor productivity exceeding the country's average can acquire, through this exchange rate mechanism, a profit advantage in international trade. The erosion of this advantage in international competition (for example, through opposite exchange rate adjustments) may lead to flows of FDI from less developed to more developed countries. FDI ceases to be mainly one-directional and becomes cross-directional, as productivity gaps between industrial countries diminish.

See also:

development political economy: major contemporary themes; international political economy

Selected references

Busch, K. (1974) *Die Multinationalen Konzerne. Zur Analyse der Weltmarktbewegung des Kapitals*, Frankfurt.
Busch, K., Grunert, G. and Tobergte, W. (1984) *Strukturen der Kapitalistischen Weltökonomie*, Saarbrücken.
Dunning, J.H. (1977) "Trade, Location of Economic Activity and the MNE: A Search for an Eclectic Approach," in B. Ohlin, P.O. Hesselborn and P.M. Wijkman (eds), *The International Allocation of Economic Activity*, London: Macmillan.
Harvey, J.T. (1989–90) "The Determinants of Direct Foreign Investment," *Journal of Post Keynesian Economics* 12(2): 260–72.
Hilferding, R. (1981) *Finance Capital*, London.
Hymer, S. (1976) *The International Operations of National Firms: A Study of Direct Foreign Investment*, Cambridge, MA: MIT Press.
Jansen, Karel (1995) "The Macroeconomic Effects of Direct Foreign Investment: The Case of Thailand," *World Development* 23(2): 193–210.
Mayhew, A. (1996) "Foreign Investment, Economic Growth, and Theories of Value," in John Adams and A. Scaperlanda (eds), *The Institutional Economics of the International Economy*, Boston: Kluwer.
Milios, J. (1989) "The Problem of Capitalist Development," in M. Gottdiener and N. Komninos (eds), *Capitalist Development and Crisis Theory*, London and New York: St Martin's Press.

JOHN MILIOS
JOHN T. HARVEY

foundationalism and anti-foundationalism

Definitions

When one questions how knowledge is systematized and in which ways scientific beliefs are justified, foundationalism and anti-foundationalism have to be discussed. The foundationalist approach holds that the structure of knowledge is a linear, hierarchical chain formation. Basic, immediately justified axioms exist from which all further beliefs derive. These derived views are then justified as well. Anti-foundationalists deny the existence of verifiable axioms and emphasize "the overall coherence of beliefs which does not depend on basic beliefs" (Rector 1991: 208).

Foundationalism

Radical foundationalism is rooted in the Greek philosophical tradition. Since the advent of Euclidean geometry, the axiomatic-deductive method has strongly influenced the ideal of a science based on self-evident axioms (Rescher 1979: 40ff). In the seventeenth century, during the emergence of modern Western philosophy, the French philosopher René Descartes adopted this ideal (Crook 1991: 168, 174ff). According to his rational philosophy, all scientific knowledge must be reduced to indisputable beliefs. Methodological scepticism brought him to his archetypal *fundamentum inconcussum*: *Cogito ergo sum* (I think, therefore I am). The axiom reflects his dualistic, hierarchical world view, where the mental world (*res cogitans*) is superior to the physical world (*res extensa*). All of Descartes's further beliefs are anchored in this basic axiom. The beliefs are deductively derived, objective, certain, universal and supposedly value-free (Rescher 1979: 202ff). Every rational individual will, it was thought, arrive at this clear and distinct basic axiom.

Rescher, a twentieth century anti-foundationalist, compared the foundationalist idea to a pyramid: "These axiomatic theses are the foundation on which rests the apex of the vast inverted pyramid that represents the total body of knowledge" (Rescher 1979: 41). Present-day foundationalists, such as Chisholm, gave up such a "rigidly *deductive* basis," but retained a weakened form of foundationalist thinking (Rescher 1979: 43). They renounce immediate, self-evident axioms and assume self-justifying, self-warranted beliefs (Rector 1991: 203).

Many neoclassical economists are methodological positivists and adhere to a foundationalist view, assuming that economics can generate objective, unbiased knowledge. They believe that this method can separate science from non-science (Rector 1991: 205; Lance and May 1995: 978). Although positivism differs from the rationalist, deductive approach of foundationalism, since it follows an empiricist, inductive method, both accept "that evidence can only give us probabilistic confirmation of theory" and that "a good deal can still be known by an agent considered in abstraction from any element of his or her context" (Lance and May 1995: 979) (see NORMATIVE AND POSITIVE ECONOMICS).

Falsification

During the mid-twentieth century, foundationalist approaches were increasingly criticized. The critical rationalism of Popper represents a principal anti-foundationalist position. According to Popper, all knowledge is provisional and cannot be verified. Popper did not follow the principle of sufficient, inductive justification. He developed the principle that all knowledge can only be falsified. Thus he excluded contradictions and errors, some sort of cognitive quality control. Falsification distinguishes science from non-science, the latter of which cannot be falsified (Backhouse 1994).

Coherence theory and pragmatism

Coherence theory, represented by works of Rescher and BonJour, is considered to be a crucial anti-foundationalist approach. In this approach, justification "comes to mean not 'derived from basic (or axiomatic) knowledge,' but rather 'appropriately interconnected with the rest of what is known'" (Rescher 1979: 75). The fitting together of knowledge is the only source of justification. Such an interrelated network model is inherently stable. Where in the linear model one change can make the pyramid crumble, this is not the case in the web model.

PRAGMATISM, the philosophical background of Veblenian institutional political economy, incorporates an anti-foundationalist view of knowledge formation (Mirowski 1987). Knowledge is not based on isolated beliefs, but is understood in a system of thought that is socially constructed. As with the HISTORICAL SCHOOL, science is further embedded in its historical environment. Pragmatism rejects absolute basic beliefs, the bifurcation of the world, and is orientated more at consensus. Hence "truth involves beliefs being coherent, with knowledge being relative to the presuppositions of a given community" (Backhouse 1994: 19). As a consequence, pragmatism rejects atomism, decontextualization of knowledge and reductionism, and follows a more HOLISTIC METHOD (Rector 1991: 208; Rorty 1979).

Feminist and interpretative approaches

Feminist and interpretative economics are two present strands of thought that seem innovative in this discussion. Interpretative economics assumes that "shared contexts of languages and traditions" constitute the social network in which our beliefs are formed and justified through the coherence of our interpretations. Gadamer's hermeneutic philosophy is a major source of inspiration, focusing on the role of language in science (Rector 1991: 215). FEMINIST PHILOSOPHY OF SCIENCE is partly linked to this discussion (Nelson 1996). Feminists underline the notion that science creates contextualized knowledge and criticize gender-biased foundations in economic epistemology, methodology and theory (Nelson 1996).

See also:

determinism and overdetermination; dialectical

method; language, signs and symbols; methodology in economics; modernism and postmodernism

Selected references

Backhouse, Roger E. (ed.) (1994) *New Directions in Economic Methodology*, London and New York: Routledge.
BonJour, Laurence (1985) *The Structure of Empirical Knowledge*, Cambridge, MA: Harvard University Press.
Crook, Stephen (1991) *Modernist Radicalism and its Aftermath: Foundationalism and Anti-Foundationalism in Radical Social Theory*, London and New York: Routledge.
Lance, Mark and May, Todd (1995) "Beyond Foundationalism and Its Opposites. Toward a Reasonal Ethics for Progressive Action," *American Behavioural Scientist* 38(7): 976–89.
Mirowski, Philip (1987) "The Philosophical Basis of Institutional Economics," *Journal of Economic Issues* 21(3): 1001–1038.
Nelson, Julie A. (1996) *Feminism, Objectivity, and Economics*, London and New York: Routledge.
Rector, Ralph A. (1991) "The Economics of Rationality and the Rationality of Economics," in Don Lavoie (ed.), *Economics and Hermeneutics*, London and New York: Routledge.
Rescher, Nicholas (1979) *Cognitive Systematization: A Systems-Theoretic Approach to a Coherent Theory of Knowledge*, Oxford: Blackwell.
Rorty, Richard (1979) *Philosophy and the Mirror of Nature*, Princeton, NJ: Princeton University Press.
Rosenthal, Sandra B. (1992) "Pragmatism and the Reconstruction of Metaphysics: Toward a New Understanding of Foundations," in Tom Rockmore and Beth J. Singer (eds), *Antifoundationalism Old and New*, Philadelphia: Temple University Press.

HELLA HOPPE

free banking

The free banking school supports a free-market monetary system based on the ideas of classical liberalism and laissez-faire thought. In a free banking regime, there would be no central bank and no exercise of monetary policy, and there would be many media of exchange bearing market-determined rates of interest. The government would not control or define the supply of base money as it currently does; rather, base (or outside) money would most likely be gold or some other tradable precious metal. A laissez-faire banking system would require a clearing house, but it need not be public. The most prominent advocates of free (unregulated competitive) banking are Kevin Dowd (1989, 1993), David Glasner (1989), Friedrich A. Hayek (1978), Steven Horwitz (1992), George Selgin (1993), and Lawrence White (1989). The fundamental argument is that there is no *economic* reason for the monopolized issue of bank notes by a central bank. A competitively supplied stock of bank notes and demand deposits convertible into gold or other base money would better serve the needs of traders to circulate commodities, and at the same time guarantee price stability and provide the self-correcting impulses to avert FINANCIAL CRISES and bank runs.

Structure of a free banking regime

In a free banking regime, banks would be permitted to issue their own brand of bank notes as well as demand deposits (checking accounts). They would both circulate and serve as means of payment. Even though there would be no legal reserve requirement, the free banking school argues that a competitively supplied stock of money would not be over-issued over time. Banks must pay a competitive return on their liabilities, and bank notes that are over-issued would be returned to the issuing bank either for redemption into base money (reserves) or conversion into interest-bearing demand deposits. All banks compete for liabilities in order to make loans. Competition among issuing banks implies that any one bank interested in issuing more of its own liabilities must raise the interest rate it pays to attract depositors and/or lower the interest rate it charges to attract loan applications. Faced with increasing marginal costs of maintaining its liabilities and decreasing marginal returns on additional loans, any profit-maximizing bank attempting to expand would issue its liabilities only up to the point where the marginal return on an additional loan equals the marginal cost of acquiring funds. Hence, the profit motive coupled with competition will limit individual banks to the issue of liabilities with stable purchasing power.

If a bank expects to maintain customer loyalty to its bank note and demand deposit liabilities, it must be prepared to redeem them on demand into base money. Any bank with insufficient reserves to redeem its liabilities stands to lose customers, and if illiquidity persists, may be forced to close. The incentive to hold sufficient reserves to meet redemption demands – especially when there is no central bank to issue emergency funds – provides additional force to the argument that banks will not over-issue money.

Money creation is treated in free banking literature as a transfer mechanism which mobilizes savings and injects them into the spending stream via investment. Savers supply loanable funds and investors demand them; the bank simply creates claims to its pool of reserves for savers and lends them to investors, thereby stabilizing spending. Saving is viewed as a simultaneous act of demanding bank liabilities and supplying loanable funds, because the willingness of savers to hold bank liabilities is a willingness to permit the bank to lend its reserves to investors. Money creation or destruction occurs endogenously when there is a change in the desire to save or invest. For example, a decrease in the desire to save would indicate that individuals desire to exchange bank liabilities for outside money. Reserves would fall, loans would be called in, the money supply would shrink and interest rates would rise.

Free banking proponents prefer the discipline of the gold standard to control domestic prices over government or central bank attempts to control money issue. The gold standard would automatically correct for trade imbalances between countries. Deficit countries would see an outflow of gold, the domestic money supply would fall and, with it, domestic prices would decline as well. The fall in the domestic price level would signal a return of bank notes to the issuing banks, so that the public's desired stock of real money would determine the desired nominal stock (White 1989: 28).

Crises of confidence

For a variety of reasons, the competitive banks may find themselves in a situation where the value of their loans and other assets have fallen below the value of their liabilities, creating insolvency. The possibility of bank insolvency raises the questions of whether a crisis of confidence in one of several banks can create a "contagion effect" that triggers system-wide bank runs, and how self-correcting mechanisms will operate. This is especially important, since the free banking system is composed only of private banks with no designated lender of last resort, and with no "ultimate" means of payment (such as a Federal Reserve Note) to respond to a system-wide rush to something other than inside (private bank) money.

Some proponents of free banking believe that banks will create their own inter-bank market for lending emergency reserves, organized possibly through the clearing house. Others propose the suspension of specie or outside money payment through the use of "option clauses" during bank panics (Rockoff 1986; Selgin 1993).

Glasner (1989: 197) proposes that in the event of illiquidity that competitive banks could gradually convert demand deposits into equity claims, or collateralized deposits. These "equity deposits" would be backed by bank capital and highly liquid assets such as Treasury bills or commercial paper; the money supply would include circulating shares to a bank-owned money market mutual funds. In the event of a fall in the value of the equity backing the deposits, the bank would draw on existing capital and/or purchase additional capital.

Ultimate failure to raise sufficient capital to cover its guarantee to depositors would lead to the liquidation of the shares and a shrinking of the money supply with depositors bearing the ultimate risk of holding the money.

Critique of free banking

Many economists question the assumptions of price flexibility that underpin the free banking theory. Keynesian and post-Keynesian theorists, for example, believe that price rigidities in labor and product markets may prevent stabilizing forces from re-establishing full employment equilibrium, and rather than moving toward stability, industrial overproduction may be accompanied by increased financial instability. In short, money is not neutral and, in order to stabilize employment and income, monetary policy is necessary.

Minsky (1982) argues that instability is an observed and normal result of capitalism and that intervention must be undertaken to guide market developments. Short-run profit expectations and competitive pressures drive firms to increase investment until they have expanded to a level beyond the growth of effective demand. Enabled by a willing credit market, many firms reach the peak of the business cycle heavily indebted. The resulting financial instability places great pressures on the financial system. Raising short-term interest rates can affect the liquidity, profitability and solvency of financial institutions, leading them to refuse to re-finance corporate debt, with the result of forcing them and their creditors into bankruptcy. To avoid subjecting the economy to such a crisis, Minsky argues that at this juncture a central bank is needed to serve as a lender of last resort to provide necessary liquidity.

The notion that private interests and calculations will yield the socially desirable results – and in this case that private banks will issue just the right amount of money needed to produce and circulate real output – also relies heavily on the assumption of perfect competition. The supply and demand of private bank money is said to be determined by the variations in the spread between the rate of interest banks charge borrowers and the rate they pay to depositors. In a competitive banking regime, private bank money will not be over-issued because the marginal cost of buying liabilities rises while the marginal revenue of each additional loan sold declines. However, this is not convincing. There is as much reason to expect that free banking would tend toward oligopoly or monopoly. Economies of scale and scope may be so prevalent in banking that marginal costs remain below average costs. In order to reduce borrowing and lending risks, free banks may be enticed to merge or enter into price fixing, market sharing or other collusive activities that reduce their lending risks, lower borrowing costs and even out cash flow, but which can conceal the overall economy's move toward greater financial fragility.

See also:

monetary policy and central banking functions; money, credit and finance: major contemporary themes; regulation and deregulation: financial

Selected references

Dowd, Kevin (1989) *The State and the Monetary System*, Oxford: Philip Allan.
—— (1993) *Laissez-Faire Banking*, London: Routledge.
Glasner, David (1989) *Monetary Evolution, Free Banking, and Economic Order*, Cambridge: Cambridge University Press.
Hayek, Friedrich A. (1978) *Denationalization of Money*, London: Institute of Economic Affairs.
Horwitz, Steven (1992) *Monetary Evolution, Free Banking, and Economic Order*, Boulder, CO: Westview.
Minsky, Hyman (1982) *Can "It" Happen Again?*, Armonk, NY: M.E. Sharpe.
Rockoff, Hugh (1986) "Institutional Requirements for Stable Free Banking," *Cato Journal* 6(2): 617–34.
Selgin, George (1993) "In Defense of Bank Suspension," *Journal of Financial Services Research* 7: 347–64.

Selgin, George and White, Lawrence H. (1994) "How Would the Invisible Hand Handle Money?," *Journal of Economic Literature* 32: 1718–49.

White, Lawrence H. (1989) *Competition and Currency*, New York: New York University Press.

SHIRLEY J. GEDEON

free trade and protection

Few would debate the proposition that most economists support free trade as the policy option most conducive to maximizing the economic welfare of any given society, that is, of maximizing real gross domestic product per capita or welfare. What is less evident, and often lost in the midst of fervent debates on free trade and protection, is that mainstream economic theory in no way rules out protection as a welfare maximizing policy option for an economy when the appropriate conditions are met. It is true, however, that protectionist instruments are typically rejected, since the conditions meriting protection (in the form of production or consumption subsidies or taxes) may fail to materialize in the real world. Whether or not one can justify protection from an economic perspective becomes an empirical question of whether or not a particular economy warrants protection as a means of maximizing the economic welfare of its populace.

Stylized historical facts

What are the stylized facts relating to protection and ECONOMIC GROWTH? The most detailed available information is for tariffs. Historically, few economies developed outside of what were often significant tariff barriers. Indeed, in Europe, only 14 percent of historical time over the century and a half between 1810 and 1960 was characterized by relatively low tariffs. The period 1860–92 stands out as the only period of freer trade in Europe until the post-Second World War era, with freer trade peaking from 1866 to 1877. The only clear and important exception to this rule was Great Britain, where economic development was already well entrenched by the mid-eighteenth century when Britain abandoned its centuries-old protectionist policies in favor of free trade.

Outside of Europe, the use of protectionist policy was even more severe. For example, the United States was the world's leading protectionist nation until the end of the Second World War, when it emerged as the world's leading economy. Canada, which was evolving into a major industrial power, also developed behind relatively high tariff walls. Moreover, historically, eras of high tariffs tend to coincide with relatively high rates of per capita GDP growth, and eras of low tariffs often coincide with low rates of economic growth. This was especially true of many of the less developed countries, which were forced by the leading colonial powers of the nineteenth and early twentieth centuries, Great Britain being the leader among them, to adopt freer trade regimes (Bairoch 1989).

However, in the post-Second World War period, with the signing of the General Agreement on Tariffs and Trade (GATT), per capita growth had reached its highest historical rates and tariffs and transportation costs fell to their lowest historical levels (Bhagwati 1988). Nonetheless, governments in many of the successfully developing economies, including Japan, have used non-tariff protectionist instruments to foster economic development. In general, therefore, the facts suggest no negative correlation between protection and growth and often quite the opposite.

Argument for free trade

Theoretical arguments supporting free trade stem from positions favoring trade and the expansion of trade. Following from the theoretical and rhetorical foundations established by David Ricardo, it is argued that trade allows different economies to take advantage of their particular comparative advantages by opening their doors to the exchange of commodities. In the absence of trade, specialization would diminish, reducing productivity and, thereby,

372

real per capita output. If perfect competition prevails in all markets and the price mechanism is efficient, such that market prices reflect social costs and benefits, policies which tend to reduce trade or distort the free market pattern of trade, production and consumption will reduce economic welfare.

Effects of a tariff

Under free trade, where the importing country cannot affect the world price for imports, a world price for imports prevails in the home market. If one nation introduces a tariff on imports (per unit or percentage) then, *ceteris paribus*, the quantity demanded of imports will decline consistent with the price elasticity of demand for imports (relative to domestic goods). This may shift demand from imports to domestic goods, thus increasing domestic employment and production. The current account position may also improve as imports are reduced and exports expanded. Self-sufficiency may be an ancilliary advantage from tariffs.

However, domestic consumers will be charged a higher price for imports, reducing their consumer surplus. It is also possible that retaliation will occur such that the importing nation places a tariff on the exports of the tariff-imposing nation. This may lead to a whole series of retaliations. It is also true that if domestic producers utilize many imported inputs that are charged a tariff – such as capital goods and materials – then domestic production may be adversely affected to some degree.

Market failure and protection

When protection counteracts a market failure, it becomes a welfare-enhancing policy choice. In fact, one can calculate a tariff rate which is optimal in the sense that it maximizes a nation's per capita income or welfare level (at the expense of those nations whose terms of trade deteriorate due to the imposition of a tariff). Unfortunately, such policies may give rise to a beggar-thy-neighbor cycle, whereby the nation initially imposing the tariff will see its policy met with a retaliatory tariff against its exports. However, Amsden (1989) and Hikino and Amsden (1994) have argued that market prices are inefficient and government must intervene to promote development. Such was the case recently in Japan and South Korea, for example, using non-tariff policy instruments.

Subsidies or taxation in place of tariffs

Imagine the introduction of a subsidy or a tax reduction to encourage import replacement industries, instead of a tariff. In this case, output would be increased without affecting the price of these commodities and, therefore, not negatively affecting consumers in the manner which tariffs necessarily do. The government realizes its objectives without generating the welfare losses produced by tariffs.

Infant industry argument

The classic case for protection is the infant industry argument, where market imperfections are considered to be of a temporary nature, requiring temporary government intervention (see the classic argument of Friedrich List 1841). The argument is that PRODUCTIVITY growth in industry exceeds that in other sectors of the economy, agriculture in particular, and that industries in newly developing countries could only effectively compete with those in the already developed economies if their industries received some initial support from government in the form of tariffs or subsidies. It takes time for entrepreneurs and workers to acquire the knowledge to drive unit costs down to competitive levels – an argument consistent with the theoretical work of Kenneth Arrow on "learning by doing" (1961–2). Only industries which were expected to become competitive in time, they argued, should receive such support.

Protection for infant industries can only be justified in mainstream theory if the expected future benefits of these industries, in terms of productivity gains, exceed the costs of the efforts needed to kick-start them. These net benefits, appropriately discounted, must exceed what is expected to accrue from the industrial structure developing under conditions of free trade. Moreover to justify protectionist measures in the first instance, capital markets should be inefficient, the social rates of return from protection should exceed the private rates of return, or entrepreneurs should be highly risk adverse.

Reducing involuntary unemployment

John Maynard KEYNES (1936) argued in favor of tariffs as a means of increasing domestic employment in a world where involuntary unemployment is typical. By reducing imports, tariffs are expected to generate balance of trade surpluses, shifting aggregate demand to the domestic market and thereby increasing the equilibrium level of domestic employment. However, as critics point out (see above) and as Keynes well recognized, such tariffs can result in retaliation and, therefore, to a beggar-my-neighbor cycle. As with an optimal tariff, demand-side tariff policy can be effective only if there is no retaliation: if one set of countries in effect agrees to finance another set of countries' trade surpluses by incurring trade deficits.

Post-Keynesian analysis of protection

Two recent papers by Prasch (1996) and Norman (1996) provide considerable insight into comparative advantage theory and protectionism. Prasch shows that the orthodox theory of comparative advantage is based on some dubious assumptions such as full employment, free mobility of resources within a nation and balanced trade between nations. Particularly problematic is the usual abstraction from the problem of effective demand and unemployment.

Norman's conclusions are remarkably similar. He then develops a model in which more practical assumptions are made and the economy is situated in historical time. A two sector model is used, with oligopoly markups characterizing finished goods producers and competitive markets in primary sector goods. He found that importable materials were more highly substitutable for domestic production than finished goods. Under conditions of underutilized resources and positive policies the introduction of a tariff on both types of goods resulted in little retaliation, a major increase in growth and little price pressure.

Increasing returns to scale

Recent developments in economic theory build upon the notion of INCREASING RETURNS TO SCALE to argue in favor of protection to foster economic growth (Arthur 1990; Krugman 1990), while the standard international trade models assume constant returns. The key argument here is that initial entrants into an industry, subject to increasing returns, gain a first-mover advantage in the sense that their unit costs will be relatively low compared with those of new entrants whose initial market is relatively small. The new entrants into increasing returns industries, in less developed countries, for example, might not be successful unless they receive some initial protection from government, until they acquire the market to realize economies of scale. This scenario can easily fit into the infant industry argument.

Conclusion

Clearly, although most economists tend to dismiss protection in any form as inefficient and ineffective instruments of economic development and growth, mainstream theory itself is not inconsistent with well-calculated protectionist measures designed to correct for potential market failures where the ensuing resource reallocation is expected to yield a higher level of per capita income and economic welfare. In effect, contemporary economic theory neither condones nor condemns protectionist economic policy, although it makes a strong case against the use of tariffs. Even here, a case can be made for tariffs given significant costs in using subsidies and taxes to engage in protection. The theory simply forewarns the policy maker to assess carefully the costs and benefits of protectionism when the policy objectives relate directly to the economic welfare of a population since protection, in and of itself, is no panacea for the economic woes of a nation. Choosing or rejecting protectionism should be an empirical, not an ideological, question; informed by economic theory and economic history.

See also:

balance of payments; balance of payments constraint; Bretton Woods system; colonialism and imperialism: classic texts; comparative advantage and unequal exchange; development political economy: major contemporary themes; international political economy

Selected references

Altman, Morris (1990) "Interfirm, Interregional, and International Differences in Labor Productivity: Variations in the Levels of 'X-Inefficiency' as a Function of Differential Labor Costs," in Mark Perlman and Klaus Weiermair (eds), *Studies in Economic Rationality: X-Efficiency Examined and Extolled*, Ann Arbor: University of Michigan Press, 323–50.
Amsden, Alice (1989) *Asia's Next Giant: South Korea and Late Industrialization*, Oxford: Oxford University Press.
Arrow, Kenneth J. (1961–2) "The Economic Implications of Learning by Doing," *Review of Economic Studies* 29: 155–73.
Arthur, W. Brian (1990) "Positive Feedbacks in the Economy," *Scientific American*, February: 92–9.
Bairoch, Paul (1989) "European Trade Policy, 1815–1914," in Peter Mathias and Sydney Pollard (eds), *The Cambridge Economic History of Europe, Vol. 8: The Industrial Economies: The Development of Economic and Social Policies*, Cambridge: Cambridge University Press, 1–160.
Barratt Brown, Michael (1974) *The Economics of Imperialism*, Harmondsworth: Penguin.
Bhagwati, Jagdish N. (1971) "The Generalized Theory of Distortions and Welfare," in Jagdish N. Bhagwati *et al.* (eds), *Trade, Balance of Payments and Growth*, Amsterdam and London: North Holland, 69–90.
—— (1988) *Protectionism*, Cambridge, MA: MIT Press.
Hikino, Takashi and Amsden, Alice H. (1994) "Staying Behind, Stumbling Back, Sneaking Up, Soaring Ahead: Late Industrialization in Historical Perspective," in William J. Baumol, Richard R. Nelson and Edward N. Wolff (eds), *Convergence of Productivity: Cross-National Studies and Historical Evidence*, New York: Oxford University Press, 285–315.
Keynes, J.M. (1936) *The General Theory of Employment, Interest and Money*, London: Macmillan.
Krugman, Paul R. (1990) *Rethinking International Trade*, Cambridge, MA: MIT Press.
List, Friedrich (1841) *The National System of Political Economy*, London: Longmans & Co. Translated by S.S. Lloyd.
Norman, Neville, R. (1996) "A General Post Keynesian Theory of Protection," *Journal of Post Keynesian Econmics* 18(4), Summer, 509–31.
Prasch, Robert E. (1996) "Reassessing the Theory of Comparative Advantage," *Review of Political Economy*, 8(1), 37–54.

MORRIS ALTMAN

French Circuit School

History and background

In the history of economic thought, descriptions of the capitalistic economic process periodically re-emerge in a monetary circuit vein. This approach – the origins of which go back to PHYSIOCRACY in France – was developed in the nineteenth century, in particular by MARX. However, the analysis of the monetary circuit is applied, particularly in the first forty years of the 1900s, through the subsequent and unconnected works of writers such as Wicksell,

French Circuit School

SCHUMPETER and Fanno. The representation of the economic process as a monetary circuit is at the center of the Keynesian project of building a MONETARY THEORY OF PRODUCTION (Realfonzo 1998).

Between the end of the 1950s and the beginning of the 1960s, the analysis of the monetary circuit was taken up once more in France in the work of J. Le Bourva, and has been subsequently developed by B. Schmitt. At present, the French Circuit School does not consist of a unified body of thought, so it may well be inappropriate to refer to it as a "school." It is possible, in fact, to divide it into two main groups. The first and largest group works in Dijon and Freiburg following the teachings of Schmitt. Cencini, Gnos and Sadigh are among those who take part in this group. The second group works in Paris under the guidance of A. Parguez, who has been for many years the editor of *Monnaie et Production*. In addition to these two groups, it is necessary to mention F. Poulon, whose work appeared mainly in the 1980s in Bordeaux.

The Circuit School has been the subject of much debate in France, stimulated by the works of M. Aglietta, R. Arena, A. Barrère, C. Benetti, J. Cartelier and M. De Vroey. On the other hand, it is worth pointing out that the "circuit of money" theory has also been taken up outside of France, particularly in Italy by A. Graziani. Following on from Graziani's work, others including R. Bellofiore and M. Messori have supported the "circuit of money" theory; it has also been taken up by Canadian French-speaking economists such as M. Lavoie and M. Seccareccia.

Recent works by monetary circuit economists show several affinities with the currents within the post-Keynesian tradition, which stresses the monetary nature of the capitalistic economy (Davidson, Kaldor, Minsky, Weintraub). In particular, these works are very close to B. Moore's horizontalism approach, according to which the money supply is potentially unlimited and the interest rate is exogenous. These works have been of growing interest to British economists (Cripps, Godley) and have led to interesting attempts at comparison (see Deleplace and Nell 1996). What follows deals specifically with the work of the French economists.

Parguez and Poulon use an approach which is close to that followed by the Italian and Canadian economists. In contrast, the Schmitt school has attempted to develop an independent general theory, paying particular attention to the problems of international payments (Lavoie 1987; Graziani 1994).

Theoretical foundations

Following the theoretical tradition of the monetary theory of production, the French economists agree on four cardinal theoretical points. First, they reject methodological individualism in favor of an analysis which presumes a hierarchy and roles between macroeconomic agents. For instance, in this system banks create money, firms make production decisions and workers provide the labor power. Second, they reject the traditional approach of simultaneous equilibria in favor of a sequential analysis. Third, they adopt an analysis of ENDOGENOUS MONEY AND CREDIT. Finally, they reject the marginalist theory of distribution.

They describe the monetary circuit, separating it into logical phases from the opening to the closing of the circuit. First, banks create money in order to satisfy firms' production finance demands (initial finance). Then firms acquire labor power in the market. After that, the productive process becomes activated. Following this, workers spend their income on consumption goods and securities (final finance). Finally, firms reimburse the initial debt to the banks (for a general analysis see MONETARY CIRCUIT; CIRCUIT OF SOCIAL CAPITAL).

The French theorists agree that the initial creation of money, in favor of firms, is finalized upon payment of money wages, which were bargained with the workers. Parguez stresses that, although banks' credit potential is theoretically unlimited, the banking system cannot create more money than is demanded. On the contrary, banks can ration credit. This thesis is not in contradiction with horizontalist principles.

On the question of the nature of money, the French theorists reject the theory of commodity money in favor of a theory of "symbol money." Schmitt defines money as a "triadic" entity, existing on three poles (bank, firm, worker) at the same time. He rejects Parguez and Poulon's notion that money "circulates" from one agent to another. According to Schmitt, money is an asset liability and it contrasts with commodities, which are net assets. Schmitt and his followers deduce from the fact that money is "triadic" that it is destroyed at the same time as it is created. Conversely, according to Parguez and Poulon, money is destroyed only when firms pay their debts to the banks.

The French theorists stress that money becomes integrated into production through the payment of wages. Schmitt maintains that the payment of wages is an instantaneous operation and production may be considered instantaneous but not void in its duration. These ideas pave the way for the "quantic theory," formulated by the Schmitt "school." According to Schmitt, money monetizes production but does not finance it. (Not all circuitists accept this theory.)

The French theorists, in line with Keynes, stress that in the labor market exclusively money wages are bargained. The level of real wages is known only at the end of production, when consumption goods are put up for sale. In this way, they point out that workers (and trade unions) have no power in establishing real wages in the labor market. Upon payment of wages, the banks debit the firms' accounts and credit the workers' accounts. Here, Schmitt differentiates between "initial deposits" and "induced deposits." Parguez shows that, in cases where workers do not spend all their wages buying commodities or securities, money presents itself as a stock. The establishment of money stocks makes firms incapable of extinguishing their debt to the banks. Money stocks are constituted only at the end of the circuit.

A widely debated issue concerns the making of money profit. Hypothesizing no state sector and no increase in money balances, firms collect the wages bill and remain the owners of the investment goods produced. In order for money profit to be made, Poulon and Parguez assume that firms take out extra loans with the banks.

Controversy within the "School"

There is significant disagreement among the French theorists as to the time scale of the circuit. According to Schmitt, the monetary circuit is instantaneous. Schmitt and Cencini talk about "quantic time" with regards to this. Conversely, Poulon measures the time of the circuit by the temporal difference which separates the financing of firms by the banks (the opening of the circuit) from the reimbursement of debt (the closing of the circuit). According to Parguez, the time of the circuit is provided by the period necessary to achieve an equal balance between savings and investments.

There is also significant disagreement as to the question of "crises" among the supporters of the circuit theory. Schmitt puts forward a new interpretation of Say's Law. By contrast, Poulon points out that crisis takes place each time firms are unable to pay their debts to the banks, despite the fact that they turn to the finance market.

See also:

money, credit and finance: major contemporary themes; political economy: history

Selected references

Deleplace, G. and Nell, E.J. (eds) (1996) *Money in Motion: The Post Keynesian and Circulation Approaches*, London: Macmillan.

Graziani A. (1994) *La teoria monetaria della produzione*, Arezzo: Banca popolare dell'Etruria e del Lazio.

Lavoie, M. (1987) "La teoria del circuito monetario," *Metamorfosi* 5: 7–36.

—— (1992) *Foundations of Post-Keynesian Economic Analysis*, Aldershot: Edward Elgar.

Parguez, A. (1984) "La dynamique de la monnaie," *Economies et Sociétés*, serie *Monnaie et Production*, 28(4): 83–118.

Poulon, F. (1982) *Macroéconomie approfondie*, Paris: Cujas.

Realfonzo, R. (1998) *Money and Banking. Theory and Debate (1900–1940)*, Edward Elgar.

Schmitt, B. (1975) *Théorie unitaire de la monnaie, nationale et internationale*, Albeuve: Edizioni Castella.

RICCARDO REALFONZO

future of capitalism

The topic examined here is the viability of capitalism. In other words, can capitalism survive as the world's dominant social order? If not, what changes must occur for it to be displaced? Capitalism has taken a variety of forms over the years (see Heilbroner 1993, 1988). However, in every variant it retains four identifying characteristics:

- the existence of markets as the dominant allocative mechanism;
- an inner logic provided by the drive toward the accumulation of capital ($M \to C \to M'$) within the CIRCUIT OF SOCIAL CAPITAL;
- the existence of wage labor and a class of business owners and financiers (capitalists) (see CLASS);
- the *relative* separation of power between the public (state) and private (economy) realms.

If the above are necessary for the existence of capitalism, then it stands to reason that if capitalism is to be replaced, then at least one of the above must be displaced.

Main characteristics of capitalism

Markets are the visible surface of capitalism. They are the conduits through which economic goods and services are allocated. Further, the price movements which arise from the market process provide some indication as to what a society values and desires. Unfortunately, these market price movements, as studied by neoclassical theorists, tell us little about the true nature of capitalism. Market prices simply reflect the underlying currents of social behavior; they are an epiphenomenon (Stanfield 1979).

For example, we often hear that markets are becoming more bearish, bullish, global, or less competitive. Markets may even suffer failures, speculative bubbles or catastrophic meltdowns. Is it really the market that changed? What actually changed is some social, political or behavioral aspect of the market participants. Market prices are simply the footprints that capitalism leaves behind. Therefore, the secret to capitalism's longevity cannot be found with conventional market analysis. A more complete understanding lies in the secrets of the drive to accumulate and the bifurcated power structure of capitalism.

If markets provide the external face of capitalism, then the drive to accumulate capital is the internal dynamic. All firms are in the business of accumulating capital. They do not accumulate merely to consume or enhance their wealth. Their sole function is continually to generate additional ECONOMIC SURPLUS for their owners. Firms are owned by individuals or groups of investors (capitalists) who willingly offer a portion of their private wealth to these business enterprises. In return, they expect the firm to generate profits consistently through the efficient production of goods and services, and provide them with an acceptable return on their investment. This return can only be realized if the firm can survive within its own competitive market. Products have very distinct life cycles, so if the producing firms are to survive (and continue to provide dividends) they must constantly look for ways of increasing their market share.

Capitalist firms must continually introduce new products and enter new markets if they wish to continue. This consistent need to expand is a hallmark of capitalism. It leads to commodification and technological innovation. Capitalism's forward looking character is the direct result of this constant need to accumulate. Further, it instills a remarkable resilience to the system. Capitalism is in constant change and often outgrows or adapts to social problems which can plague more static social formations.

Associated with this is the institution of wage labor. The payment of wages for labor power and the exploitation of labor by capital is a critical condition for the system (see LABOR AND LABOR POWER). Without a class of wage laborers employed by the owners or controllers of capital the system would not exist. Wage labor is necessary not only to produce the surplus but also as a source of demand to realize the surplus.

During the long boom phase of advanced capitalist development (1945–70), average workers were remunerated a good deal more than was necessary to reproduce labor power, which resulted in a dual expansion of both the capital and consumer goods sectors. However, the contradictions of expanding the power of labor led to a backlash, the rise of conservative governments and a sustained drop in effective demand. During the 1970s–1990s, capital and the state have been trying to find a new set of institutional relationships to enhance accumulation. This has not yet been successful, despite various changes such as deregulation, privatization, internationalization and the like.

Capitalism does not exist in a single configuration. There is much variety in the current forms of capitalism. What makes each capitalist regime unique is the degree of separation of powers between the public and private realms. Even today, as we look around the globe, what separates Japanese capitalism from European capitalism is not the differences in markets, accumulation or wage labor, but rather the degree of cooperation between the public and private sectors. American capitalism has a greater separation of power than many other capitalist systems. This stems directly from the individualist ideology inherent in the American system. Joint cooperatives such as the European Airbus would be very difficult to construct within the American capitalist system.

A future without capitalism?

Any configuration that capitalism may take in the future will depend on the interaction of the four defining characteristics associated with markets, accumulation, wage labor and the separation of power. Will capitalism be the dominant order for the next thousand years? This seems unlikely. The simple truth is that civilizations fall. Several possibilities exist for the demise of or transformation beyond capitalism (see Harvey 1982; Block 1990; Dowd 1993), as follows.

- Some believe the demise of capitalism will be related to the FALLING RATE OF PROFIT TENDENCY. Capitalists simply will not have sufficient profits to expand. This may lead those adversely affected by the problem to seek major changes or revolt (see SECULAR CRISIS).
- Conversely, others see the rising rate of profit as the demise of the system. As capitalism concentrates the economic surplus, the capitalist class will simply not be able to spend enough of the profits to support the system.
- Many see capitalism falling to environmental limitations (see LIMITS TO GROWTH), global market structures which are beyond the control of any given nation state and even another world war.
- Others see an evolutionary process whereby wage labor will gradually cease to prevail. This could be due, for instance, to robotics and the computerization of production, distribution and exchange; or due to the expansion of worker cooperatives such that labor employs capital rather than the reverse (see MONDRAGÓN).
- Perhaps the decline in capitalism will emanate from the accumulation of capital and market relations destroying the institutions, relationships and environmental conditions which underlie real meaning and hope for the future (see DISEMBEDDED ECONOMY).
- Alternatively, the decline may come through people losing interest in the motive of accumulation and profit while they seek higher values and motives (see GANDHIAN POLITICAL ECONOMY).

All of these are plausible explanations for capitalism's decline.

However, capitalism does contain several endemic survival mechanisms which may allow it to thrive for a long time. One survival mechanism is the process of transformational growth, which creates new economic frontiers by radically changing the economic environment. The introduction of the automobile and railroads transformed not only the transportation sectors of the economy, but virtually every other sector as well. It provided what capitalism truly needed: a fresh exploitable frontier. It is possible, however, for these frontiers and markets to dry up.

A second survival mechanism is the power of the public sector to soften the effects of capitalism. Welfare systems, unemployment benefits and regulation structures can blunt the harsh consequences of capitalist development and help to absorb the surplus. The social unrest that might occur were capitalism to exist unabated is delayed by the social safety net. At present, at least there are major limits to the expansion of the state in this respect. However, the future may be different.

See also:

alienation; anarchism; capitalist breakdown debate; fascism; global crisis of world capitalism; market socialism; participatory democracy and self-management; social democracy; socialism and communism; transformational growth and stagnation; utopia

Selected references

Block, Fred (1990) *Postindustrial Possibilities: A Critique of Economic Discourse*, Berkeley: University of California Press.

Dowd, Douglas (1993) "Needs and Possibilities," in Douglas Dowd, *U.S. Capitalist Development Since 1776*, Armonk, NY: M.E. Sharpe.

Harvey, David (1982) *The Limits to Capital*, Oxford: Basil Blackwell.

Heilbroner, Robert L. (1988) "Capitalism," *The New Palgrave: A Dictionary of Economics*, London: Macmillan.

——(1993) *21st Century Capitalism*, New York: W.W. Norton.

Paul, Ellen Frankel, Miller, Fred D., Paul, Jeffrey and Ahrens, John (eds) (1989) *Capitalism*, Oxford: Basil Blackwell.

Seldon, Arthur (1990) *Capitalism*, Oxford: Basil Blackwell.

Stanfield, J. Ronald (1979) "Phenomena and Epiphenomena in Economics," *Journal of Economic Issues* 13(4).

MICHAEL C. CARROLL

G

Galbraith's contribution to political economy

John Kenneth Galbraith (born in Canada in 1908) was for most of his career a Professor of Economics at Harvard University; he also became a President of the American Economic Association, and served as adviser to several Presidents or Presidential candidates of the United States. A persistent theme of Galbraith's work has been the need to view the economy as an institutionalized system of power. An institution is a cluster of mores that configures power. Institutional political economy focuses on institutional adjustment – the problem of redistributing power to improve economic performance (Stanfield 1996).

The dual economy

Galbraith has emphasized the dual nature of the modern economy. He acknowledges that a significant portion of the modern economy continues to operate in a fashion similar to the textbook theory of competition. However, alongside this market sector there is an oligopolistic or administered sector which needs to be understood in terms of the exercise of discretion by powerful corporate agents.

In his 1940s essays on price control, later assembled into *A Theory of Price Control* (1952), Galbraith emphasized this dual economic structure and its significance in controlling inflation – the power to administer requires a policy of administration or direct control over the wage-price spiral. Concern with the inflationary implications of the dual economy persisted in his books on *American Capitalism* (1952) and *The Affluent Society* (1958), but in the latter book he began to shift his attention to the qualitative effects of the dual economy and the differing impact of conventional aggregate demand policy in the two sectors.

The concern for the effective control of inflation continues throughout Galbraith's later works, where he continued to advocate institutional adjustment to transfer the power to set prices away from the administered sector to public officials. Although he now admits that wage-price controls are not politically feasible, this leaves the dilemma of inflation versus recession unresolved in his model.

Power and social imbalance

In *The Affluent Society*, Galbraith elaborates other implications of power in the modern economy. He sets out the theory of social balance. The principle of social balance states that for a given level of private consumption there is an optimal size public sector; that is, public and private consumption are complementary goods. The increased utilization of automobiles must go hand in hand with increased collective provision of roads and traffic control. Suburbanization, in the wake of the automobile age, requires a far-flung government apparatus to service and protect dispersed neighborhoods. The resort to an ever-greater volume of packaged goods and disposable items necessitates more trash removal and solid waste disposal planning. Galbraith even anticipates the trend toward dual-earner households and notes that it too has implications with regard to social balance. Increased participation of both spouses in the paid labor force generates a need for more collectively regulated and provided environments to occupy the time of children.

Galbraith maintains that the preoccupation with expanding production, and the process of the creation of consumer wants that sustains it, leads toward a penurious public sector. Added to the traditional anti-government bias of market capitalist ideology, the incessant attention to private consumption obscures the need for collective action in critically important areas. He cites many examples of the deleterious effects of insufficient public sector spending, such as lack of resources being devoted to poverty relief, environmental preservation, education, playgrounds, municipal services and medical care delivery (see SOCIAL AND ORGANIZATIONAL CAPITAL; COMMON PROPERTY RESOURCES).

In his later works, for example *Economics and the Public Purpose* (1973), Galbraith refines the analysis of social imbalance, recognizing that some public sector spending is favored because it fits the interests of the powerful corporate system. Other collective wants, and indeed some significant private wants, fare badly because there is no strong voice for them among the powers that be. The technostructure, as Galbraith calls his powerful elite, promulgates a very distorted set of social priorities as it exercises undue influence upon both the public and private sectors. In his mature model, social imbalance is not so much related to the question of public versus private as that which serves the interests of the corporate elite versus that which does not. The public purpose or general interest is not well served by this social imbalance.

Revised sequence and imagery of choice

To make this case, Galbraith introduces the concepts of revised sequence and imagery of choice. The conventional wisdom in economic thought has, at its core, the competitive market which empowers the sovereign consumer or household. In this original sequence, the flow of causative influence in the production process is from households, as ultimate consumers of commodities and ultimate suppliers of resources, to the productive organizations. The original sequence conception "supports the conclusion that the individual is the ultimate source of power in the economic system" (Galbraith 1967: 226). This conception has the further implication that state regulation is, in most respects, an unnecessary violation of the sovereign rights of the individual.

With the "revised sequence" concept, Galbraith sought to shift the analytical focus to the flow of influence from producers to consumers, though he took pains to emphasize that the reverse flow of influence from the household cannot be ignored. The interest of the administered sector is put forward via advertising and other public relations activities as well as by corporate influence on the political process. The decisive significance of the revised sequence is the doubt it raises about the legitimacy of corporate decisions on the production and distribution of output and the broader consequences of corporate power in political decision-making and the media (Stanfield 1979; Dugger 1989). He seeks to lay a basis for systematic inquiry into the process of preference formation and its implications for the quality of life, a problematic sadly lacking in neoclassical economics (see PRODUCER AND CONSUMER SOVEREIGNTY).

Less controversial than the broader issue of the revised sequence, it is clear that the power of the administered sector raises serious questions about the costs of production its prices cover and the general pattern of relative prices in the modern economy. Given the power to administer prices and commit large portions of revenues to advertising and public relations activities, the doctrine of necessary prices enforced by competitive markets is seriously undermined. Significant ambiguity of costs attends the performance of the administered sector (Sraffa 1926). This ambiguity carries over into the general pattern of relative prices and casts doubt upon all decisions made upon the assumption that these prices indicate relative scarcity.

Galbraith contends that the power exercised by the corporate elite is effectively obscured by conventional economic reasoning. To designate this obscurantism, he coins the forceful phrase "imagery of choice" (Galbraith 1973a). His charge is that conventional economics is a system of belief which tends to systematically exclude "speculation on the way the large economic organizations shape social attitudes to their ends" (1967: 77). Galbraith offers the "test of anxiety" to contrast the conventional economics model to his administered economy model. The logic of this test is that a useful economics will relate to the issues about which the public is concerned or anxious. He administers the test in a number of key areas of social concern, notably, economic instability, CORPORATE HEGEMONY, INEQUALITY and POLLUTION. His general point is that, if these problems were understood to result from the exercise of power by the corporate elite, then the public response to them would be very different. Therefore, an economics that approached its subject matter as a system of power would be a more useful economics (Galbraith 1973b). He thus called for an emancipation of belief as the first step toward sensible social reform, with the educational and scientific community taking the lead in this respect.

Recent changes in capitalism

Much has changed since Galbraith articulated his model of advanced CAPITALISM. The global economy has become more integrated, with technology's dramatic reduction of the significance of space. The trade regime, which he included in his model, has fallen into disarray, and the independence of domestic social and stabilization policy has been dramatically reduced. Global capital flows have become a much more mobile and significant force on the economy. Corporate downsizing has thinned the ranks of the lower echelons of the technostructure and reduced the number of workers who enjoy the wages and security of the administered sector. Financial control of corporations has apparently risen relative to managerial control. Product cycles have been reduced, and just-in-time inventory management has spread (see FORDISM AND THE FLEXIBLE SYSTEM OF PRODUCTION).

These and other changes no doubt indicate the need for a revision and shifting emphasis within Galbraith's model, but they do not discredit the model in any fundamental way. The methodology of viewing the economy as an institutionalized system of power and the essential thesis of an increasingly administered economy remain intact. Changes in corporate CULTURE have occurred and corporate decisions have responded to an altered global and technological environment, but administrative discretion is still apparent. The co-option of the state to the corporate agenda is still of paramount concern. Likewise, the bilaterally managed trade regime is seen by many to be unstable and there is considerable opinion that a new managed trade regime is necessary. Galbraith's model will persist into the foreseeable future since it was based on studying the pattern of change involved in recent corporate capitalism. Much of this insight has been incorporated into modern political economy.

See also:

budget deficit; corporate objectives: advertising and the sales effort; corporation; economic power; political economy: major contemporary themes

Selected references

Dugger, W.M. (1989) *Corporate Hegemony*, New York: Greenwood Press.
Galbraith, J.K. (1952a) *A Theory of Price Control*, Cambridge, MA: Harvard University Press.
—— (1952b) *American Capitalism*, Boston: Houghton Mifflin.
—— (1958) *The Affluent Society*, Boston: Houghton Mifflin.
—— (1957) "Market Structure and Stabilization Policy," *Review of Economics and Statistics* 39(May): 124–33.
—— (1967) *The New Industrial State*, Boston: Houghton Mifflin.
—— (1973a) *Economics and the Public Purpose*, Boston: Houghton Mifflin.
—— (1973b) "Power and the Useful Econo-

mist," *American Economic Review* 63(March): 1–11.

Sraffa, P. (1926) "The Laws of Returns Under Competitive Conditions," *Economic Journal* 36: 535–50.

Stanfield, J.R. (1979) *Economic Thought and Social Change*, Carbondale, IL: Southern Illinois University Press.

—— (1996) *John Kenneth Galbraith*, London: Macmillan.

JAMES RONALD STANFIELD

game theory

Game theory is the formal analysis of relative power, conflict and cooperation, under a variety of rules. As a means of mathematically formalizing constitutions and power struggles, game theory is a controversial and possibly powerful device in a political economist's toolbox.

Nature of game theory

While traditional neoclassical economics assumes atomistic price-takers in competitive markets, game theoretic paradigms stress strategic choice and interdependence. In work now recognized as game-theoretic in its modeling of strategic interaction, von Stackelberg studied duopolist behavior when each firm may act as quantity taker or quantity maker, and discussed how their roles might arise. More recently, new institutionalists and other political economists have used game theory to generalize his concerns: modeling institutions (social CONVENTIONS, or MARKETS or money) as rules of the game. It is then possible to trace the effects of institutions on agent behavior, and to study INSTITUTIONAL CHANGE AND ADJUSTMENT and formation.

Within mainstream economics, a large number of works use game theory to examine MARKET STRUCTURES. Martin Shubik (reprinted in Dimand and Dimand 1997) modeled a business cycle with organized labor as a player. With various co-authors, Shubik has modeled financial institutions as rules or as the equilibria of non-cooperative games, and examined questions such as the incidence of bankruptcy under different laws. Much of WILLIAMSON'S ANALYSIS OF THE CORPORATION employs game theory, as does Eaton and Lipsey's analysis of entry barriers as exit costs for firms. Game theoretic models have been widely used to study the feasibility of governments independently setting credible monetary policy (Blackburn and Christensen 1989). Beyond economics, game theory was put to highly controversial use in formulating and supporting strategies of nuclear deterrence in the 1950s, sponsored by the US Office of Naval Research and, through the RAND Corporation, the US Air Force. As Mirowski (1991) argues, the emphasis on adversarial situations in game theory may have been influenced by extensive military funding. Games of asymmetric information were later used to model arms control and disarmament.

Modeling institutions and their formation

John von Neumann and Oskar Morgenstern's *Theory of Games and Economic Behavior* in 1944 suggested game theory as a tool for examining institutions. However, traditional game theorists have tended to ignore the fact that, in assuming particular rules or strategy sets, they install mathematized versions of institutions. While game theoretic models have been employed by political economists, much controversy surrounds the solution concept and type of game appropriate for modeling a given institution.

Schotter (1986) has divided the institution formation literature into examinations of whether rules of a game arrive at an "optimal" solution, and analyses of social institution formation. The optimal solution literature either explicitly includes a planner who decides on the system's rules or parameters, as in mechanism design models, or the economist herself acts as a planner who considers the feasibility of "efficient" institutions. The social institution formation literature descends from the concerns of Arrow's Impossibility Theorem. This area has been a focus of mathematical or public choice economists, rather than institutionalists. The analysis of mainstream economists, such as Arrow, Gibbard and Satterthwaite, has emphasized the importance of political economy as it indicates the improbability or impossibility of a public choice institution arriving at a "social maximum" or, indeed, the meaningfulness of such a concept. James Buchanan's and Gordon Tullock's development of public choice theory follows from an understanding of the strategic role of practices such as voting rules.

The literature on social formation of institutions remains underdeveloped. While Shubik and co-authors have considered the development and relative size of a monetary sector within an economy, Schotter remains dominant in the literature of institution formation. Schotter (1981) addresses problems of coordination and of the "prisoner's dilemma" type, almost entirely through use of matrix games. In coordination problems, agents benefit from matching strategies, while under prisoner's dilemma conditions they are in a destructively competitive situation. In infinite horizon models, communication between generations of agents, or the concept of punishment for deviation traditional to the theory of infinitely repeated games, determines the formation of equilibrium institutions to which the system converges. A particularly interesting matrix modeling of the Edgeworth problem of allocation in a non-convex endowment economy suggests how equilibrium institutions may depend on the priors of agents and on chance, which determines period-by-period play and thus updated priors.

Schotter (1986) takes a different though related tack. Here, an institution is society's abandonment of some pure strategies in a matrix game, where "punishment" takes the form of reversion to a fuller game. Institutions available to the society depend on the subgames the modeler assumes as alternatives, which Schotter justifies as being dependent on the ability of players to distinguish between strategies.

Feminist political economy

A major contemporary theme of feminist political economy is game theoretic modeling of intra-family resource allocation, HOUSEHOLD LABOR and the GENDER DIVISION OF LABOR in home and market in critiques of the "black box" models of Gary Becker. Phipps and Burton (1995) give useful references and precis of a number of such models. These models typically take a one-shot bargaining approach. Agents with individualistic "outside options" arrive at an interactive solution which depends on the power given by their outside options, in a situation where unpaid house service may provide a public good. Models vary as to whether the game is cooperative or non-cooperative, and the nature of the outside option employed. In some, the outside option stems from LABOR FORCE participation. In others, the outside option comes from individuals supplying household services solely to suit their own needs. Some models have explored the effects of divorce law within marriage by making the divorce payoff part of the outside option. However, feminist economists such as Janet Seiz (1995) have criticized game theoretic inquiries into household behavior as adding little to the results of analysis and focusing on spurious objectives.

Marxist political economy

Marxist use of game theoretic modeling (part of the rational choice Marxist political economy, exemplified by John Roemer and Jon Elster) remains controversial. Carling (1986) argues in favor of such work and discusses game-theoretic methods to explain the development of the institutions of CAPITALISM, and to use and quantify constructs such as SURPLUS VALUE AND EXPLOITATION, without appeal to a LABOR THEORY OF VALUE. Critics like Wood (1989) argue that by focusing on individually rational agents such models obscure the power of a capitalist class structure, and that they discard traditional Marxism's depth of historical analysis by predetermining social structures under which agents choose.

Interestingly enough, the Marxist Bertell Ollman constructed a board game based on Marxist theory, which required the formation of coalitions between players representing different classes and incorporating environmental concerns. His experiences of marketing this in a capitalist society are related in his *Class Struggle is the Name of the Game: Confessions of a Marxist Businessman*, published in 1983.

Conclusion

Game theory has been used to model economic and social institutions, permitting mathematically checkable answers to questions posed mathematically. It has opened new ways of considering the formation of institutions. Wood (1989) argues that its historical and individualistic weaknesses make it unfit it as a Marxist methodology. Mirowski (1986) discusses game theoretic institutionalism in the context of a mainstream economics he characterizes as searching for natural laws to explain all interactions; and argues that it fails. Debates over appropriate solution concepts remain unsettled, and game theory has disappointed some hopes. For instance, Schotter and Schwödiauer conclude that the modeling of externalities through game theory is fraught with difficulties, despite the fact that it is here that one would expect game theory to be of the greatest benefit.

However, approaches such as evolutionary game theory appear promising. In this paradigm, a strategy's dominance in society depends on its survival value. This depends on the payoff from playing the strategy, which depends in turn on the other strategies played at each coup. Robert Axelrod's work on the evolution of cooperation in repeated games forms an empirical examination of this process. In some such models, the strategic choices of agents is purely mechanical, so it is in a sense society that learns from the experiences of agents.

Selected references

Blackburn, Keith and Christensen, Michael (1989) "Monetary Policy and Policy Credibility," *Journal of Economic Literature* 27(2): 1–45.

Carling, Alan (1986) "Rational Choice Marxism," *New Left Review* 160: 24–62.

Dimand, Mary Ann and Dimand, Robert (eds) (1997) *Foundations of Game Theory*, 3 vols, Cheltenham and Brookfield, VT: Edward Elgar.

Mirowski, Philip (1986) "Institutions as a Solution Concept in Game Theory Context," in L. Samuelson (ed.), *Microeconomic Theory*, Dordrecht: Kluwer Nijhoff Publishing, 243–64.

—— (1991) "When Games Grow Deadly Serious: The Military Influence on the Evolution of Game Theory," in C.D. Goodwin (ed.), *Economics and National Security*, supplement to *History of Political Economy*, vol. 23, Durham, NC: Duke University Press, 227–56.

Phipps, Shelley and Burton, Peter (1995) "Social/Institutional Variables and Behavior within Households," *Feminist Economics* 1(1): 151–74.

Schotter, Andrew (1981) *The Economic Theory of Social Institutions*, Cambridge: Cambridge University Press.

—— (1986) "The Evolution of Rules," in R. Langlois (ed.), *Economics as a Process: Essays in the New Institutional Economics*, Cambridge: Cambridge University Press, 117–33.

Schotter, Andrew and Schwödiauer, Gerhard (1980) "Economics and the Theory of Games: A Survey," *Journal of Economic Literature* 80(June): 479–527.

Seiz, Janet (1995) " Bargaining Models, Feminism, and Institutionalism," *Journal of Economic Issues* 29(2): 609–18.

Wood, Ellen Meiksins (1989) "Rational Choice Marxism: Is the Game Worth the Candle?,' *New Left Review* 177: 41–88.

MARY ANN DIMAND
ROBERT W. DIMAND

Gandhian political economy

When Mahatma Gandhi started thinking in terms of dealing with British empire in India, he was quite convinced that the then economic system was also a part of imperialist rule. He therefore articulated an alternative in his first and last book, *Hind Swaraj*, written in Gujarati in 1910. It was banned for being "seditious," but later translated into many languages. Much of what we call Gandhian political economy begins with this book and its visions and ideas, refined over the years on the basis of experience and further thinking. Much of it was articulated by Gandhi himself in his speeches and writings. These have been collected in three volumes called *Economic and Industrial Life and Relations* (1957).

Nature and assumptions

A disciple of Gandhi, Narayan (1970) wrote about the relevance of Gandhian economics. In recent years Gandhian political economics has been further refined by Sethi (1979), Das (1979), Diwan and Lutz (1985), and brought up to date so as to relate to current economic problems. Literature on Gandhian economics is also published in *Gandhi Marg*; a bi-monthly magazine of the Gandhi Peace Foundation in New Delhi. A group, Swadeshi Jagran Manch, is developing policies based on these ideas and promoting them in public for adoption by a supportive government. This group has good relations with policies being promoted by Green Parties in Germany and other European countries (see GREEN PARTY).

In terms of larger ideas, Gandhian economics belongs to spiritualism. The fundamental distinction between Gandhian and CLASSICAL POLITICAL ECONOMY, of both the right and left varieties, lies in the underlying assumptions about human beings and human conduct and therefore its moral underpinnings. Huxley (1944), Illich (1973) and Schumacher (1973) articulate its reasoning in philosophical terms. In view of its embeddedness in culture, Gandhian political economy is based on a construct of an idealized community, similar to the constructs of equilibrium and perfect competition. This idealized society is one where rulers or decision makers are asked to make decisions for the people, because the decision makers have won their hearts instead of their votes or legal authority. The ruling IDEOLOGY in this idealized society is *satya* (the truth and the ruling principles of transition to this idealized society are *ahmimsa* (non-violence) and *satyagrah* (truth in action). These conditions are based on the proposition that ends are contained in the means, so that means are important in themselves. This is contrary to the idea that "ends justify means".

Five main concepts

Diwan (1982) has formulated five basic concepts of Gandhian economics, all of which are related, are of equal importance, and have spiritual underpinnings.

- *Swadeshi*. Loosely translated, *swadeshi* means self-reliance in one's place or local environment. It may be a necessary condition for ecological sustainability.
- Bread labor. This means personal action in the *swadeshi* context, and generates the distinction between (among other things) "values-in-use" and "values-in-exchange," as well as between "stranger-defined-work" and "self-defined-work."
- *Aprigraha*. This means willing surrender or non-possession which is also "possession by all." It implies a demand function with an increase in the level of minimum consumption with a general lowering of the price level.
- Trusteeship. This is best described as *sauchi*, meaning purity of character. It is laced with spirituality and requires personal integrity, honesty and sensitivity. Gandhi's life is an example of such a personal character and trusteeship. It can be articulated as a negative relationship between privilege and trusting decision making power.
- Non-exploitation and equality. Equality and non-exploitation shift the price vector by lowering the prices of necessities and raising those of luxuries.

These concepts define two different types of affluence: one where a person is surrounded by material goods only, and the second where one is surrounded by people who care about other people. This distinction between two affluences explains the divergence between ECONOMIC GROWTH and QUALITY OF LIFE in industrialized countries, which is confirmed in the USA by estimates of GPI (the genuine progress index).

Ideas and organizations

The institutions through which policies following from Gandhian economics operate include ideas and organizations. The critical ideas are that there is a "unity of life" including all matter, living and inert, and that human beings are more than physical bodies. The organizations of importance include families, face-to-face communities in a particular place, and larger populations made up of such communities. Because of the importance of these institutions, Gandhian principles imply "small is beautiful" instead of "economies of scale." Though the emphasis here is on the local level, it relates to the global economy; made up of concentric circles each defined by a community economy. Global issues are relevant even for community problems, because of the Gandhian propositions that there is an elite–people contradiction in every society, and that local elites exploit local masses while international elites exploit people all over the world.

The role of government in Gandhian economics is to maintain and develop these institutions. Since the object is to strengthen communities, the government needs to be highly decentralized. The test of every policy is not profit, employment or growth, but instead how it strengthens family and community and, through them character and sensitivity. The world today is suffering from many problems: ecological distress, family breakdown, economic inequality, CRIME and so on. The basic cause of all these problems is the destruction of communities. The research agenda for the present and immediate future is to formulate policies based on Gandhian economics in order to regenerate communities and ensure sustainability.

See also:

ethics and morality; value judgments and world views

Selected references

Das, Amritananda (1979) *Foundations of Gandhian Economics*, New York: St. Martin's Press.
Diwan, Romesh (1982) "Economics of Love: Or An Attempt at Gandhian Economics," *Journal of Economic Issues* 16(2).
—— (1991) "Gandhian Economics and Contemporary Society," *Gandhian Perspectives* 4(1): 1–28.
Diwan, Romesh and Lutz, Mark (1985) *Essays in Gandhian Economics*, New Delhi: Gandhi Peace Foundation.
Gandhi, M.K. (1910) *Hind Swaraj*, Ahmedabad: Navjivan Publishing.
—— (1957) *Economic and Industrial Life and Relations*, 3 vols, Ahmedabad: Navjivan Publishing.
Huxley, Aldous (1944) *The Perennial Philosophy*, New York: Harper & Row.
Illich, Ivan (1973) *Tools For Conviviality*, New York: Harper & Row.
Narayan, Shriman (1970) *Relevance of Gandhian Economics*, Ahmedabad: Navjivan Publishing.
Schumacher, E.F. (1973) *Small is Beautiful*, New York: Harper & Row.
Sethi, Jai Dev (1979) *Gandhi Today*, New Delhi: Vikas Publishing.

ROMESH DIWAN

gender

Gender can take on either of two distinct meanings. The first, and most obvious, is the biological; in that sense, gender is just the description of female or male. The second is the social construction of the concept referring to associations, stereotypes and social patterns concerning the differences between women and men. It is becoming more the norm to refer to biological differences as sex, and to use the word "gender" to encompass the social and cultural constructions based on differences between the sexes. Often the term "gender" is used only for the female sex, even though it more properly refers to the social construction based on sex differences (Nelson 1995).

Studying gender can be deceptively difficult. The biological difference between men and women is easily defined: sex depends upon the number of X and Y chromosomes present in genetic makeup. Gender differences hinge on a great deal more. The social construction of gender has implications about interests, behavior, value structure and even communication styles.

Joan Scott (1988) suggests that gender is both an element of social relationships and a primary way of signifying relationships of power. An example she cites is the practice by art historians of reading social implications from depictions of women and men. These depictions then signify a primary way to decode meaning and status among forms of human interactions and the reciprocity of gender and society.

Michele Barrett (1988) discusses the IDEOLOGY of gender in relation to materialism in her book *Women's Oppression Today*. Gender ideology – the social constructs revolving around masculinity and femininity – is not and cannot be completely separated from the historical and CLASS contexts in which it appears. However, placing it solely within the context of economic relations is also stifling. Gender's meaning within society is tied to the particular household structure and DIVISION OF LABOR as it has evolved historically so that ideology and materialism must intertwine.

The recognition that gender differences have implications for the practice of science has a long, if nearly hidden, history. Even before 1900, voices could be heard saying that research centered on the male experience is inadequate when dealing with issues such as household work or women's experiences in the labor market. Much of this research is sex-blind (Ferber and Nelson 1993). For instance, the Marxist theory of de-skilling and the theories of SEGMENTED AND DUAL LABOR MARKETS assign technical competency or other work attributes (that keep women in secondary jobs) by gender to explain why women are eliminated from higher paying jobs. But they underplay the essential interrelationships between gender and the workplace that may account for these differences (Beechey 1988). Another example of this is the analysis of poverty without recognition of the disproportionate representation of women (see FEMINIZATION OF POVERTY). These analyses also usually reinforce the assumptions of "natural" gender roles and the existing societal status quo. For example, women are assumed to earn less in the market place because of "their" household responsibilities and yet, women "should" spend time in the household because of the lower opportunity cost of their time (see HOME ECONOMICS, NEW; LABOUR MARKET DISCRIMINATION).

Another example of how the workplace can interact with gender norms is suggested by Wayne Lewchuk (1993). He proposes that, as assembly lines changed the nature of work, firms maximized productivity by accommodating men to tedious work by "masculinizing" these occupations so that laborers felt a sort of fraternalism between fellow workers. Therefore, they could celebrate their work even though it was monotonous, unchallenging and generally tedious. This plays to the masculine self-image as it relates to occupation and reinforces preferences for occupational segregation.

Researchers explaining the unique experiences of women, in contrast to those of men, must first recognize that there are basic differences between the sexes (Jacobsen 1994). There are two disparate views of those differences, however. Biological determinism suggests that gender differences stem, primarily, from biological differences, that is, male dominance is the natural outcome of the greater physical strength and hormonally induced aggression of the male. Biological potentiality, on the other hand, suggests that biology shapes only the potential, not the outcome. For instance, women give birth but are not necessarily a child's primary caretaker.

In essence, this is the nearly insoluble "nature versus nurture" debate that raged in psychology. The problem is compounded here because gender traits are only loosely associated with sex. For instance, there are some women who are more aggressive than some men and there are some men who are more nurturing than some women. Still, aggression is considered a male trait and nurturing is considered a female trait. Similar problems are faced by all studies involving the litany of RACE, ETHNICITY, GENDER AND CLASS, where social traits are assigned to groups characterized by such outwardly manifested signals as color, sex and social standing.

Feminist perspectives on gender differences include two basic views (Ferber and Nelson 1993). One is the maximalist or essentialist view that basic differences between the sexes are so deep, whether they are biologically or culturally based, that there exists a distinct women's culture. According to this concept, women's culture should be valued, studied and, perhaps (in the view of some more radical believers in this paradigm), should replace the existing male culture. Another view is the minimalist or contructivist paradigm which see less of a schism between the sexes. What differences are observed are attributed mainly to the imposition of social structures. Therefore, any inequities based on gender differences can be redressed through manipulation of such social structures.

Gender related research in the social sciences takes on the form of redefining both the implications of gender for science and how the form of scientific investigation shapes the meaning of gender. For instance, in political science, gender studies involves an analysis of government policy as it affects women differentially than men, and what the state's role should be to rectify this difference. Standard NEOCLASSICAL ECONOMICS has at its base the autonomous agent, totally separated from physical and social constraints. This agent's characteristics are generally centered on the male experience. Certain themes in feminist political economy seek to reintegrate this "homo economicus" (the rational, autonomous, self-interested economic agent) back into a world with interpersonal connections and as a responder to social influences.

In general, academic feminism seeks to investigate how gender shapes the course of scientific inquiry and thought. How to change the course of science to integrate women's issues and experiences is not always clear, however. There are three levels at which this debate operates (Nelson 1995). The first approach says that an increase in female representation among practitioners will redress the situation, leaving aside as unassailable both the methods and the objects of inquiry. A second strategy suggests that women's lives offer areas of study previously ignored while continuing to assume it unnecessary to alter current methodology. A third approach recognizes that current METHODOLOGY IN ECONOMICS may be too rigid and formalistic to enable the integration of the social and cultural relationships essential to the study of gender differences. This last approach suggests that the HOLISTIC METHOD, such as argument by metaphor, STORYTELLING AND PATTERN MODELS, should either augment or replace current methods.

See also:

gender and development; household production and national income; modernism and postmodernism; patriarchy

Selected references

Barrett, Michele (1988) *Women's Oppression Today: The Marxist/Feminist Encounter*, London and New York: Verso.

Beechey, Veronica (1988) "Rethinking the Definition of Work," in Jensen, Hagen and Reddy (eds), *Feminization of the Labor Force*, New York: Oxford University Press, 45–62.

Blau, Francine and Ferber, Marianne (1992) *The Economics of Women, Men, and Work*, 2nd edn, Englewood Cliffs, NJ: Prentice Hall.

Ferber, Marianne and Nelson, Julie (eds) (1993) *Beyond Economic Man*, Chicago: University of Chicago Press.

Jacobsen, Joyce (1994) *The Economics of Gender*, Oxford: Blackwell.

Lewchuk, Wayne (1993) "Men and Monotony," *Journal of Economic History* 53(4): 824–56.

Nelson, Julie (1995) "Feminism and Economics," *Journal of Economic Perspectives* 9(2): 131–48.

Scott, Joan (1988) *Gender and the Politics of History*, New York: Columbia University Press.

NANCY J. BURNETT

gender and development

GENDER is one of many neglected "social issues" of economic development that began to be addressed during the 1970s, beginning with the publication of Ester Boserup's *Women's Role in Economic Development* in 1970. Boserup asked one of the central questions that has come to shape the gender and development literature over the past twenty-five years: what is it about the economic development process that differentially incorporates and impacts upon men and women? "Gender and development" focuses on socially constructed relationships and hierarchies between men and women, such as the GENDER DIVISION OF LABOR, stratification, reproduction, political rights, ideology, roles, norms and access to resources in developing or underdeveloped nations.

Alternative approaches

Concern with the gender-based distribution of the costs and benefits of economic development has guided the so-called "equity approach" to gender and development, which saw its heyday during the United Nations' Decade for Women (1975–85). This approach, unlike its welfarist predecessor, treats women as active participants in the development process with both productive and reproductive roles to fulfill. It has the political objective of promoting gender equality, primarily through state intervention. Women's equitable participation in and benefit from economic development is not seen as a goal in and of itself; it is seen rather as a means of ensuring the "efficiency" and "effectiveness" of that development. Women are treated as an untapped resource whose (often unremunerated) labor time, productivity and fertility can all be harnessed (or controlled) to promote economic growth.

Microeconomic concerns

Within the gender and development literature, substantial attention has been paid to the cultural specificity of the household-level gender division of labor. Attention has also been given to income management patterns which call into question some of the fundamental principles of microeconomics. Traditional development strategies implicitly rest on an understanding of how microeconomic units respond to changing market-based incentives. The assumption that "household-farm-firms" are joint maximizing units has been the key to policies which manipulate wages, prices and other parameters in the hope of inducing some particular pattern of economic development.

However, an emerging literature argues that the aggregation of preferences and budget constraints across household members is extremely problematic. Some sort of a bargaining approach to household decision-making and resource allocation is probably more appropriate in a wide range of socioeconomic contexts. If the allocation of land, labor and income is based on bargaining and not joint maximization, then the expected "response elasticities" to policy changes will depend as much on the bargaining power of individual household members as on calculations of marginal optimization and comparative advantage. Policies and programs that alter gender-specific sources of bargaining power – privatization, LAND REFORM, labor legislation and credit market policies, for example – may have unintended consequences for household production and consumption profiles.

gender and development

Agricultural development

The structural, macroeconomic concerns of gender and development have focused on the impact of agricultural development and INDUSTRIALIZATION. Some attention has also been given to the related issues of migration and the urban informal sector. With regard to agricultural development, dozens of case studies across the developing world support the notion that the gender impact (and in particular the employment effect) of technological, institutional and structural change in rural areas varies with at least three interrelated phenomena. The first is initial factor endowments, that is, the relative scarcity of land, labor and capital. The second is the gender division of labor in agriculture, by crop and/or task. The third is the factor-use intensity of the specific innovation; that is, the degree to which the agricultural development process increases or decreases demand for the various factors of production.

Migration

It has long been observed that men dominate the rural to urban population flows in most of Africa and South Asia. However, Latin American women have migrated in larger numbers than men, at least since the phenomenon began to be studied in the 1940s, and rapidly industrializing East Asian countries have also drawn significant numbers of rural women into the cities (see Chant 1992). Regionally distinct push and pull factors, such as women's agricultural labor force participation and the urban demand for female labor, can explain these gender-specific patterns. Such patterns have important implications for sex ratios, household headship, and rural and urban economic survival strategies.

Formal and informal sectors

Women's participation in the formal urban labor market of developing countries has been of particular interest since the rapid expansion of labor-intensive, export-oriented manufacturing in the 1980s. The newer studies, in comparison to the 1970s literature on women and industrialization, emphasize "not so much the marginalization of women by *exclusion* from capitalist development and industrialization, but rather women's marginalization by *inclusion* and *segregation* into labour-intensive sectors with 'low wages' and 'low skills'" (Berik and Çağatay 1992: 43). Explanations of Third World employers' preference for young female workers have focused on the perceived characteristics of manual dexterity and docility, and firms' ability to practice wage discrimination based on hegemonic notions of low female labor market commitment and secondary earner status (Joekes 1987). The increasing "flexibilization" of the industrial workforce in developing countries has drawn yet more women into the manufacturing sector, within innovative production arrangements such as home-based piecework. The implications of increased urban formal sector employment for Third World women have been explored in terms of gender interests (Moser 1993). While these new jobs have often meant access to independent income and strengthened bargaining power within the home, working conditions are poor, the potential for shopfloor organizing is limited, and most developing countries have not made adequate provisions to alleviate working women's domestic responsibilities.

A substantial number of gender-focused studies have been undertaken on the urban INFORMAL SECTOR in developing countries. Feminist work in this area has emphasized the compatibility of informal sector employment and domestic work, and has characterized the sector as a reserve of cheap, flexible, unregulated labor which acts partially to subsidize (men's) formal sector employment.

Structural adjustment programs

The experience of developing countries with STRUCTURAL ADJUSTMENT POLICIES has given rise to concerns about their potential gender bias. Of special concern is the adjustment-induced relative price shifts that lead to the movement of resources from the production of non-tradable to tradable goods and services (Haddad et al. 1995). Women's ability to reallocate their labor between sectors is generally constrained by the household and workplace gender division of labor, and by gender-biased income control which limits men's ability to mobilize their wives' labor to participate in a newly profitable activity. Cutbacks in public sector services and declining food subsidies have direct implications for the amount of domestic labor that has to be performed in order to assure the reproduction and maintenance of human resources, and women must often also bear the burden of creative financial management that accompanies price and income shocks to the household economy, potentially increasing their dependency on resource transfers from their husbands to make ends meet (Elson 1991).

Property rights and the environment

A nascent body of work has begun to develop addressing the interaction of gender, PROPERTY rights and the environment. In her seminal work on South Asia, Agarwal (1994) argues that the differential levels of employment, social status and material well-being between men and women are primarily conditioned by the "gender gap" in the ownership and control of property. Rather than looking to LABOR FORCE participation as the principal indicator of the economic status of women in developing nations, independent property claims are essential to meeting both practical and strategic gender needs. Property, especially land, is an economic resource with both direct (productive) and indirect (collateral) benefits, and can serve as an important source of intra- and extra-household bargaining power. There are many obstacles to overcoming the gender gap in property rights. Some of the most important obstacles include: (1) patrilineal inheritance laws and customs; (2) post-marital residence patterns (patrilocality), which act as a disincentive for parents or communities to cede land to young women; and (3) state-led agrarian reform and privatization schemes which consolidate control and use rights and reinforce male bias in the distribution of real property.

Where natural resources are held as private property, gender-specific tenure insecurity may reduce both the demand for and supply of capital for conservation-related investments. Where these resources are held as COMMON PROPERTY RESOURCES, women's reproductive "gathering" work often makes them the most important users of communally owned forests, pastures, and water sources. However, their role in the management of these common areas – in the establishment, adaptation and sanctioning of use and exclusion rules – is typically circumscribed. There is a general failure of common property regimes to benefit fully from women's user-based knowledge of the resource in question. And the lack of gender equality in managerial control can have disastrous consequences for women during times of economic and/or ecological crisis, such as during the Great Bengal Famine of 1943 (Agarwal 1992).

Selected references

Agarwal, Bina (1992) "Gender Relations and Food Security: Coping with Seasonality, Drought, and Famine in South Asia," in Lourdes Beneria and Shelly Feldman (eds), *Unequal Burden: Economic Crises, Persistent Poverty, and Women's Work*, Boulder, CO: Westview.

—— (1994) "Gender and Command Over Property: A Critical Gap in Economic Analysis and Policy in South Asia," *World Development* 22(10): 1455–78.

Berik, Günseli and Çağatay, Nilüfer (1992) "Industrialization Strategies and Gender Composition of Manufacturing Employment in Turkey," in Nancy Folbre, Barbara Bergmann, Bina Agarwal and Maria Floro (eds), *Women's Work in the World Economy*, London: Macmillan.

Chant, Sylvia (1992) *Gender and Migration in Developing Countries*, London: Belhaven.

Elson, Diane (1991) "Male Bias in Macroeconomics: The Case of Structural Adjustment," in Diane Elson (ed.), *Male Bias in the Development Process*, Manchester and New York: Manchester University Press.

Haddad, Lawrence, Brown, Lynn R., Richter,

Andrea and Smith, Lisa (1995) "The Gender Dimensions of Economic Adjustment Policies: Potential Interactions and Evidence to Date," *World Development* 23(6): 881–96.

Joekes, Susan P. (1987) *Women in the World Economy*, Oxford: Oxford University Press.

Moser, Caroline O.N. (1993) *Gender Planning and Development: Theory, Practice and Training*, London and New York: Routledge.

ELIZABETH KATZ

gender division of labor

A division of labor by gender, within both paid and unpaid work and between them, exists in almost all societies. However, the nature of the specialized work done by women and men differs substantially by place, time and, in some cases, over the life cycle. Hence economic and cultural interpretations require a detailed analysis in a specific social context, incorporating CLASS, race and other structural variables in addition to GENDER. Much of the GENDER AND DEVELOPMENT literature attends to this need. However, some patterns with respect to particular tasks have been observed. For example, cooking, grinding grain and carrying water are more commonly female activities and hunting, weapon-making and boat-building are more commonly male. However, planting, tending and harvesting crops are less consistently allocated to one gender (Rogers 1980). Further, flexibility in the gender division of labor is not uncommon.

Biological and social dimensions

The essential biological sexual division of labor applies only to a small subset of reproductive labor, namely pregnancy, childbirth and perhaps breastfeeding. A tendency to consider natural the gender division of labor beyond these areas is an essentialist and conservative position. Most feminist analyses regard the gender division of labor as to a large extent socially constructed. Its role in the subordination of women and the perpetuation of PATRIARCHY is a contested area. Is the gender division of labor the basis of women's subordination or only a manifestation of it?

The recognition in the capitalist world that housework, and child/dependent care was unrecognized, undervalued and done predominantly by women, gave prominence to the issue of the gender division of labor (parallels arise with respect to much of women's agricultural work in the Third World). In addition to housework and caring work, household work has been broadened to include cultural, emotional, sexual and reproductive work within family relationships, again undertaken predominantly by women. The associated problems of the public–private split and the undervaluation of unpaid work have been recognized by feminist writers since the nineteenth century. Harriet Taylor's 1851 essay, *The Enfranchisement of Women*, advocated a more equal sharing of both market and household work with equal opportunity for women in paid work. While arguing for natural temperamental as well as physical differences between women and men, Thorstein Veblen, especially in *The Theory of the Leisure Class* (1899), also recognized problems with the issues of separate spheres. These included women as men's property, enforced drudgery for working class women, and institutionalized idleness for those from the upper classes.

Historical changes

The nature of the gender division of labor has undergone changes with the decline in the centrality of agriculture, the separation of home from the site of paid work, following the industrial revolution, and the decline and re-emergence of domestic service (see WAGED HOUSEHOLD LABOR). In agriculture, the impacts of modern technology and shifts from subsistence to cash cropping largely benefited men, while increasing women's work in the family and as casual labor (Boserup 1970). The home/workplace separation in manufacturing and services was never complete, with labor intensive home work constituting another gendered phenomenon. Women's paid LABOR

FORCE participation has increased, but is subject to fluctuations matching social and economic changes, including their use as a RESERVE ARMY OF LABOR (latent and actual).

Double day

Improving labor force opportunities for women has a downside. As dual-earner households became common and the "double burden" on women emerged, it has been established from time use studies since the 1970s that women work longer hours than men in most developed and developing countries studied. Further, the boundaries between work in the public and private spheres are shifting. The drive to decrease state expenditure, and reduce labor costs in the private sector has shifted work back to women through self-service retailing, health service delivery at home and increased community responsibilities (Glazer 1993).

New home economics

The division of labor is explained by the new home economics, an extension of neoclassical analysis, using the theory of comparative advantage, initially with a common household utility function (see HOME ECONOMICS, NEW). Such an advantage for women in household work and men in paid work arises either from a belief in biological differences or from observing that men earn more on average than women. According to new home economics, the specialization of roles, with men doing all or more of the market work and women all or more of the household and caring work, results simply from rational household decision making. In turn, this expectation can justify less acquisition of HUMAN CAPITAL by women, with less time in the labor force to secure an adequate rate of return, which will perpetuate their lower average earnings. Where this is based on earnings differences rather than the more contentious biological argument, the argument involves circular reasoning. It reinforces and justifies the status quo, ignoring the role of discrimination in the labor market, with female-dominated occupations being lower paid through the social construction of skill (Phillips and Taylor 1980).

Patriarchy and capitalism

In the 1970s, Marxist-feminist work on the DOMESTIC LABOR DEBATE examined the reproductive role of women in the generation of labor power and other functions. However, this debate was later seen to be somewhat narrow in its focus. Broader concerns centered on the relationship between the gender division of labor and the reproduction of structured inequality between the sexes. These inadequacies led to a materialist feminist move from unitary to dual systems theory, analyzing patriarchy and capitalism simultaneously. Two-way causal links exist between the marriage and labor markets. Women have fewer options than men in the labor market because of the institutions associated with marriage and the family (Hartmann 1976).

Surplus value is extracted from household work, with substantial losses for women through having their options reduced. Patriarchy and capitalism are seen as distinct social systems, empirically and historically intertwined. Challenging the dominance of production over the rest of human activity is one response (Himmelweit 1984). Attempts to interweave radical and Marxist feminist perspectives see patriarchy in the home as self-perpetuating and less dependent on capitalism, with an inherent hierarchical relationship despite the incidence of greater equality within a few marriages (Delphy and Leonard 1992).

Contemporaneously, some Marxist writing has focused on the household as a site of class conflict, comparable with related struggles within enterprises and with the state. An example of this work examines the female body as a site on which unmanageable contradictions are confronted, resulting for example in eating disorders (Fraad et al. 1994).

Dual systems theory has been criticized for reductionism and functionalism and for a concentration on gender and class at the expense of other structural power dimensions, particularly ethnicity. However, whether useful

gender division of labor

tri- or multi-systems theories can be developed, or a unified framework incorporating all the power dimensions has more potential (perhaps through standpoint theory), remains contested ground.

Paid work and segmentation

The gender division of labor in paid work takes the form of horizontal and vertical occupational segregation with women being largely confined to particular types of work, including those which replicate their household work, and at lower levels. Neoclassical analysis again rationalizes horizontal segregation, with women specializing in occupations in which skills depreciate less rapidly. Other aspects mentioned are differences in tastes, sex-role stereotyping, a "taste" for discrimination by employers (and/or their male employees), and the use of gender as a screening device. Employers thus can use gender as a cost-saving proxy for supposed differences in average productivity or turnover.

Screening shades into institutional and Marxist accounts of occupational segregation. In SEGMENTED AND DUAL LABOR MARKETS, women are over-represented in the secondary sector. This occurs through occupational crowding and indirect gender discrimination, plus employer monopsony power and/or trade unions' exclusionary power denying women equal access to jobs and training. INTERNAL LABOR MARKETS also have a role. However, there are no totally satisfactory explanations of the dynamics of women's over-representation in secondary markets and particular occupations, despite many excellent case studies (see Reskin 1984). Vertical segregation sees women being confined to lower rungs within occupations and hitting "glass ceilings".

Sexuality

Another aspect of the gender division of labor is the impact of compulsory heterosexuality and heterosexism. The social construction of SEXUALITY, as well as gender, varies in detail over time and between cultures, but the restriction of women to low-paid jobs tends to promote and necessitate heterosexuality. Gender complementarity linked to heterosexual roles has even less justification or rationale with recent developments in reproductive technology (Matthaei 1995). The challenges of analyzing sexuality as well as gender, in addition to inclusiveness and avoiding false universalization, are substantial. The study of lesbian and gay families, subject to different legal, social and economic factors from those of heterosexuals, could throw light on factors influencing household task specialization and the gender division of labor.

See also:

comparable worth; division of labor; family wage; feminist political economy: major contemporary themes; feminization of poverty; household labor; household production and national income; marriage

Selected references

Boserup, E. (1970) *Women's Role in Economic Development*, New York: St Martin's Press.

Delphy, C. and Leonard, D. (1992) *Familiar Exploitation: A New Analysis of Marriage in Contemporary Western Societies*, Cambridge: Polity Press.

Fraad, H., Resnick, S. and Woolf, R. (1994) *Bringing It All Back Home: Class, Gender and Power in the Modern Household*, London: Pluto Press.

Glazer, N.Y. (1993) *Women's Paid and Unpaid Labor: The Work Transfer in Health Care and Retailing*, Philadelphia: Temple University Press.

Hartmann, H. (1976) "Capitalism, Patriarchy and Job Segregation by Sex," *Signs* 1(3, part II): 137–69.

Himmelweit, S. (1984) "The Real Dualism of Sex and Class" *Review of Radical Political Economics* 16(1): 167–83.

Matthaei, J. (1995) "The Sexual Division of Labor, Sexuality and Lesbian/Gay Liberation: Towards a Marxist-Feminist Analysis

of Sexuality in U.S. Capitalism," *Review of Radical Political Economics* 27(2): 1–37.
Phillips, A. and Taylor, B. (1980) "Sex and Skill," *Feminist Review* 6: 79–88.
Reskin, B. (ed.) (1984) *Sex Segregation in the Workplace – Trends, Explanations, Remedies*, Washington: National Academy Press.
Rogers, B. (1980) *The Domestication of Women: Discrimination in Developing Societies*, London and New York: Tavistock.

PRUE HYMAN

George's contribution to political economy

Born into an impoverished family in Philadelphia in 1839, Henry George was forced to drop out of school at the age of 14 and to work in a series of unskilled jobs for low wages for several years. Eventually he found his way to California and, as a result of self-education, secured a job as a journalist. As a consequence of these personal experiences during an era when the nation was rapidly industrializing, he was struck by the fact that, as the country became wealthier, the number of people living in poverty was increasing.

Seeking to understand this paradox, George concluded that the natural right to private property – which was assumed by most economic writers – was absurd. Property, he felt, is the heritage of all people. The parallel increases of both poverty and economic progress were due to this previously unchallenged assumption about the merits of the private ownership of land. George's attack was an original perception to American writers up until this time.

Publishing a pamphlet, *Our Land and Land Policy* in 1871, and his classic book, *Progress and Poverty* in 1879, he outlined his solution: a single tax on land. In these writings, he put forth the thesis that land rents and other income derived from the use of land and its natural resources only served to enrich a small number of wealthy landowners at the expense of the welfare of the masses. Hence, the people who own the land could keep it, but all earnings above what they paid for the land could and should be taxed away. Such a tax on unearned profits would make all other taxes unnecessary and the proceeds could, in turn, be used to cure poverty.

The rationale behind George's single tax theory was drawn from principles set forth earlier by David Ricardo and his classic theory of rent. Namely, it is not necessary for any price to exceed the cost it takes to bring an existing supply of a factor of production into the market place. If the price rises above that initial cost level, the entire increase can be taxed away without endangering the availability of the factor. In the case of land, the supply is fixed; so, any increase in the value of the land or the resources found on that land can be taxed away in its entirety, without fear that the land's use or its original price will be affected. Moreover, the owner of the land cannot shift the tax on to consumers and must pay it entirely himself or herself.

Progress and Poverty was read by millions around the world and elevated George to the status of one of the most distinguished political theorists of the late nineteenth century. John Dewey considered him to be one of the most influential political philosophers of all time. He had a significant impact on other major social reformers of his era, such as Leo Tolstoy and Lloyd George. On two occasions, George sought to be elected mayor of New York City. His first effort in 1886 was unsuccessful; during his second campaign, in 1897, he died of apoplexy only a few days before the election.

His views led to the creation of single tax reform movements at the grassroots level in several western states in the United States as well as in Britain, Australia, Canada and continental Europe. Today, several economists and institutes continue to believe in the contemporary relevance of his ideas (see Gaffney and Harrison 1994a; Horner 1993).

See also:

collective social wealth; inequality

Selected references

Cord, Steven B. (1965) *Henry George: Dreamer or Realist*, Philadelphia: University of Pennsylvania Press.

Gaffney, Mason and Harrison, Fred (1994a) *The Corruption of Economics*, London: Shepheard-Walwyn in association with the Centre for Incentive Taxation.

—— (1994b) *Land Speculation and the Business Cycle*, London: Centre for Incentive Taxation.

George, Henry (1879) *Progress and Poverty*, New York: Robert Schalkenbach Foundation, 1962.

—— (1898) *Science of Political Economy*, New York: Robert Schalkenbach Foundation, 1971.

Horner, J.H. (1993) "Seeking Institutionalist Signposts in the Work of Henry George: Relevance Often Overlooked," *American Journal of Economics and Sociology* 52(2).

VERNON M. BRIGGS, JR

gifts

Gifts raise a central question for the social sciences in general and economics in particular. Are people motivated by self-interest, or are they altruistic as well? Do people give because they expect to receive something of equal worth in return or not? Can people be conceived to be rational maximizers of their personal utility, or are they other-directed as well, at times?

Probably the best answer to give for the last question is, "both." People can at times can be seen to be rational maximizers, and at times they may be altruistic or "give" for cultural and conventional reasons. Starting with the most notable writers on the topic, Mauss and Malinowski, and followed by other anthropologists, the topic of the gift has probably been one of the main reasons for the emancipation of anthropology as a science. The research of Mauss and Malinowski, published in the early decades of the twentieth century, has been a continuing source of inspiration for such research. Mauss (1925: 1) poses the central question: "What is the principle whereby the gift received has to be repaid?"

Gifts and exchanges

Some have proposed principles, a few of which will be discussed here. All of these principles aim to explain how gift giving is different from pure market transactions or *quid pro quos*. Bourdieu (1990) proposes, following Mauss (1925: 35), that time should pass between giving and repaying a gift. Schwartz (1967) allows for more ways in which imbalances of debt, essential for gift giving according to him, may be created.

Gift exchanges establish a relation between (at least) two people. According to Sahlins, there is a continuum of different types of exchanges between the giving of gifts on the one hand and pure market exchanges on the other. This is not a controversial position. What is controversial is to hold that gifts will not likely be exchanged with people that are farther removed from each other. Physical and cultural distance, but most importantly kinship distance, is what Sahlins has in mind. While De Swaan (1995) argued convincingly that identification between people at a distance is increasingly unlikely, and "global identification" improbable, there are many examples that show the controversial nature of this assumption. The boundaries that distance creates or the "dynamics of competition and exclusion," as De Swaan calls it to relate to a key discussion in sociology, can be overcome.

Message of the gift

What Sahlin's argument points to in *Stone Age Economics* (1972), however, is a central issue in the discussion on gifts. Gifts convey a message; they are not "lifeless" objects. Gifts say what kind of person the giver is, and how he or she perceives the person who receives the gift (the majority of gifts are given and received by women). When the other party in the exchange is relatively unknown, the risk of misinterpretation and insult is significant. Refraining from giving to a "stranger," or giving something impersonal, is the safe thing to do.

Gifts thus help to establish a common frame of reference (culture) needed to interpret each others' behavior. Some argue that such a frame of reference is a prerequisite for market exchanges to occur. Mauss (1925: 35) says that market exchanges arose from gift exchanges. In this respect, the observation that ethnic, religious or family communities tend to trade with each other can be understood (see, for example, Fukuyama 1995). Lévi-Strauss (1947) even contends that exchanging gifts is an important means by which to establish peace between warring parties. Is there a better example of the creation of welfare and well being?

Example of the potlatch

One of the earliest examples of gift giving studied is the potlatch of the natives of the American Northwest (and some other peoples). A potlatch (meaning "giving") was a feast or party given to celebrate or highlight an occasion or problem, in which the host gave away or destroyed some of his surplus possessions. Prestige was gained by the individual (or clan) in proportion to the amount given away or squandered. People who gave away their surplus property repeatedly were often classed as chiefs or nobles. The potlatch is, however, not the great pacifier that gift exchanging is sometimes thought to be; it is rather a grand, conspicuous giving of gifts to establish hierarchical order within groups. Gifts are now a means of competing for status (see Mauss 1925; CONSPICUOUS CONSUMPTION AND EMULATION).

Recent studies

Over the years, different settings for gift-exchange have been studied. Gifts of refuge to Jews during the Second World War, Christmas gifts and (gendered) patterns of gift giving within the family and between friends are examples. Komter (1996) presents a handy overview of (excerpts from) classic as well as new, theoretical as well as empirical studies. Recently, attention has been given to gifts in economics. Akerlof (1982) and others, for instance, have used the idea of the gift to question the conception in mainstream economics of the efficient labor market. In recent economic literature, (an implicit) link between the notion of gift giving and trust is often made, in the labor market as well as in other MARKETS. Here again the question remains: do the parties in a contract leave room for gift giving based on mutual trust because the costs of a contract that provides for every possible future development are prohibitive, or are gift giving and trust (partly) valued for their own sakes? The study of the phenomenon of gift giving cuts across disciplines. As has been briefly shown here, it is also a topic which is approached from different methodological positions.

See also:

conventions; culture; economic anthropology: major contemporary themes; language, signs and symbols

Selected references

Akerlof, G. (1982) "Labour Contracts as Partial Gift Exchange," *Quarterly Journal of Economics* 97(4): 543–69.

Bourdieu, P. (1990) "The Work of Time," in *The Logic of Practice*, Cambridge: Polity Press.

De Swaan, A. (1995) "Widening Circles of Identification: Emotional Concerns in Sociogenetic Perspective," *Theory, Culture & Society* 12: 25–39.

Fukuyama, F. (1995) *Trust – The Social Virtues and the Creation of Prosperity*, London: Hamish Hamilton.

Komter, A.E. (ed.) (1996) *The Gift – An Interdisciplinary Perspective*, Amsterdam: Amsterdam University Press.

Lévi-Strauss, C. (1947) "The Principle of Reciprocity," translated from the French by R.L. Coser and G. Frazer in L.A. Coser and B. Rosenberg (eds), *Sociological Theory: A*

Book of Readings, New York: Macmillan, 1957.

Mauss, M. (1925) *The Gift – Forms and Functions of Exchange in Archaic Societies*, translated from the French by I. Cunnison, London: Cohen & West, 1970.

Schwartz, B. (1967) "The Social Psychology of the Gift," *American Journal of Sociology* 73(1): 1–11.

WILFRED DOLFSMA

Gilman, Charlotte Perkins

Born a Beecher on her father's side and thus related to the popular minister Henry Ward Beecher and the novelist Harriet Beecher Stowe, Charlotte Perkins (1860–1935) was almost entirely self-educated – or by her account, uneducated. Using the broad but unspecialized schooling she devised for herself, she wrote verse and plays from an early age, always pursuing her primary message, that women's abilities were shackled by social INSTITUTIONS AND HABITS, and that greater social efficiency would result from a change of institutions. She communicated her views in many speeches and publications, the most important of which were *Women and Economics* (1898), *The Home: Its Work and Influence* (1903) and her one-woman periodical, *The Forerunner* (1909–16). Works such as *Herland* and *The Man-Made World: Our Androcentric Culture* first appeared in *The Forerunner* and were later republished separately.

Personal history

Perkins's attempt to fulfill the conventional roles of wife and mother in her first marriage to the artist Walter Stetson resulted in a temporary mental deterioration which only increased under the treatment of the fashionable "nerve doctor" S. Weir Mitchell. Her story "The Yellow Wallpaper" draws on this experience. She separated relatively amicably from Stetson, who later married her close friend Grace Ellery Channing, with whom he raised Katharine, his daughter by Charlotte. After Charlotte Perkins Stetson had established herself as a writer and lecturer, she married her cousin Houghton Gilman. She committed suicide in 1935 once an inoperable cancer reached an advanced and painful stage at which she could no longer work. Details of Gilman's life are available in Gilman (1935), Hill (1980) and Lane (1990).

Social institutions proposed by Gilman

Whether writing verse, stories, essays, plays, novels or monographs, or lecturing to widely disparate audiences, Gilman stressed the economic role of women in her society and the gains which could be reaped by allowing them full access to labor markets which would limit their EXPLOITATION. This theme, revolutionary enough for her time, was shared with Harriet Taylor Mill's *Enfranchisement of Women*, published in 1851. Like Taylor Mill, Gilman argued that women who could specialize in work they were suited to would be happier and more productive, as well as able to support themselves and increase social output. Most revolutionary, however, was the change in social institutions she proposed as necessary for women to gain full human rights in society: Gilman projected a social change whereby the provision of household labor would occur through the market as customarily as shoes or housing had come to be produced in the market.

With household labor (including childcare and education) being provided through the marketplace, those best at it would perform the work, and it would be worth their while to acquire HUMAN CAPITAL to work more efficiently. Thus potential gains from specialization would be realized. Like Taylor Mill, Gilman argued that men would retain dominion over tasks in which they genuinely excelled, so that they should not fear female incursion into professions they had argued were theirs by right of efficiency. Gilman seems to have felt that women would continue to perform the bulk of household service in a GENDER DIVISION OF LABOR, but supply it more efficiently. She argued that not only would gains from specialization be realized, but that substantial increases in social output would follow the realization of economies of scale and the elimination of diseconomies of scope in house-service. Moreover, freeing and paying women to supply labor of all sorts (including WAGED HOUSEHOLD LABOR) would give their work an opportunity cost, so that the efficient quantity of house-service would be traded. Women confined to unpaid work within the home not only performed low quality work at excessive cost, but produced *too much* house-service.

Role of markets and public goods

While Gilman is often classified as a socialist thinker, she specifically disavowed cooperative production of house-service because of incentive problems. In general, Gilman favored market solutions to problems of externalities for the immediate and pre-utopian future. She did not invariably advocate additional markets, however, viewing education, disease prevention and fire prevention as public goods. She saw conservation issues affecting generations yet unborn as problems of COMMON PROPERTY RESOURCES for which a philosophy of social conscience, if not the state, was necessary for an efficient outcome.

Feminist social Darwinist

Gilman had been much influenced by the works of the American sociologist Lester Ward, whose social Darwinism and gynaecocentrism she adopted in a modified form. Ward's social Darwinism might be summarized as the belief that, like other species, humans are subject to evolution but, unlike them, humans can consciously influence the direction of evolutionary change by choosing the institutions under which they live. Gynaecocentrism, the concept of women as the "race type" of the human species, implies that institutions affecting women's development crucially determine the growth of the human race. In Gilman's view, women's economic dependence on men, due to their incarceration in the home with its unpaid work, had encouraged a sexual hypertrophy which helped them as individuals to snare a male-provided food supply, but which injured the human species. The children of weak, timid, uneducated women were not only ill-educated by their mothers, but suffered biological deprivation, losing half their "social inheritance."

Women and the home

As a feminist social Darwinist, Gilman herself sought to shape the evolution of humanity by analyzing the economic roles of house-bound woman and the home itself, by arguing in favor of market-supplied house-service and the freeing of women from merely familial roles, and by the depiction of societies with new institutions in Utopian novels. *Women and Economics* and *The Home* were dedicated primarily to the definition and economic analysis of the traditional home and woman's role, and to showing the inefficiency of prevalent institutions, regardless of the pious platitudes usually uttered about them.

Women and Economics appeared a year before Thorstein VEBLEN's *Theory of the Leisure Class*, and bears affinity to it in rhetorical technique, and to some extent in matter. In it, Gilman contended that women limited to furnishing the services of food preparation, upkeep of home and clothing, and child care and education unpaid, with no specific contract, were not their husband's partners or equals but participants in a deleteriously symbiotic relationship. By comparing females of human and other species, she contended that this parasitic role was not "natural," and that there was little reason to suppose that women could not act as more complete members of the human species.

In *The Home*, Gilman analyzed the household as a factory for widely disparate activities with conflicting physical requirements and consequences. Kitchens create mess that is undesirable near rooms for entertainment, eating or sleeping, and make cleaning a perpetual and difficult task. Using the home to entertain guests interferes with the home's function as a place for rest and familial love. The inconvenient assortment of tasks fitted into the home, in fact, precludes specialization in child raising, which Gilman viewed as the family's central purpose. (Interestingly, Gilman had little to say about the inefficiency of home laundries; that service was more frequently provided by the market then than now.) The very architecture of the home accommodating these tasks condemns women to them.

Political economy of marriage

As well as proposing the freeing of women by a move to market provision of household services, Gilman contributed to the literature on the political economy of MARRIAGE, by suggesting that this would be accompanied by a new form of marriage in which parties specified in advance what they expected from the marriage rather than falling by default into a marriage embodying social norms. Women with exit rights stemming from the ability to hire their labor out in various markets, would contract radically different marriages, without the hierarchical or parasitic qualities of the traditional one. An evolutionarily superior type of family and family organization would arise.

Gilman not only argued the nature and faults of the home and women's role within it in lectures and nonfiction works, but wrote as a polemicist working for social change. Gilman illustrated the efficiency of market-provided house service in the novel *What Diantha Did,* and the properties she attributed to a transformed culture in the Utopian novels *Herland* and *Moving the Mountain,* all first published in *The Forerunner.*

Responses to Gilman

Economists of Gilman's time paid her little attention, though Caroline Hill published a twelve-page review of *The Home* in the *Journal of Political Economy.* Veblen is said to have appreciated her work, and she was on friendly terms with Edward A. Ross and the Webbs.

Although she did not sway contemporary economists, Dolores Hayden (1981) suggests that her work was an influence in experimentation with kitchenless homes and food delivery services early in the twentieth century. To Hayden, Gilman's work was flawed by her capitalism, and by her failure to unify small and rather different constituencies created by earlier advocates of the kitchenless home. Other feminists find the commodification of household service contentious. Experiments with kitchenless homes and food delivery services failed with the rise of food prices, however, and despite the advent of fast food chains, we are little closer to achieving Gilman's ideal. Where households contain women, they are still burdened with the bulk of unpaid house service.

Conclusion

Although scholars of the women's movement rediscovered Gilman in the 1960s, feminist economists have only recently begun to interest themselves in her work, which remains not only revolutionary as political economy, but revolutionary in its social recommendations. Her approach is most immediately congenial to institutional political economy: she was Veblen's contemporary and peer. Her emphasis on property rights and exchange fits, to some extent, with the AUSTRIAN SCHOOL OF POLITICAL ECONOMY, while her consideration of exploitation may interest Marxist political economists. Gilman's work opens questions ignored by nearly all economists, and useful for most interested in household allocation.

See also:

feminist political economy: major contemporary themes; gender; home economics, new; household labour

Selected references

Gilman, Charlotte Perkins (1898) *Women and Economics: The Economic Factor Between Men and Women as a Factor in Social Evolution,* repr. 1966, ed. C.N. Degler, San Fransisco: Harper Collins Torchbooks.

—— (1903) *The Home: Its Work and Influence*, New York: McClure, Phillips.
—— (1909–16) *The Forerunner* (journal).
—— (1935) *The Living of Charlotte Perkins Gilman: An Autobiography*, 1991, Madison, WI: University of Wisconsin Press.
Hayden, Dolores (1981) *The Grand Domestic Revolution*, Cambridge, MA: MIT Press.
Hill, Mary A. (1980) *Charlotte Perkins Gilman: The Making of a Radical Feminist 1860–1896*, Philadelphia: Temple University Press.
Lane, Ann J. (1979) "Introduction," in Charlotte Perkins Gilman, *Herland: A Lost Feminist Utopian Novel*, New York: Pantheon Books.

MARY ANN DIMAND

global corporate capitalism

The United Nations reports that "as much as one third of world output is under the common governance of transnational corporations, and hence potentially part of an integrated international production system – the productive core of the globalising world economy" (UNCTAD 1994). There are some 37,000 such corporations (hereafter TNCs), but 1 percent own half the corporate assets, and over 40 percent of these are based in the Anglo-American bloc. These 370 giant corporations are concentrated in six industries: oil; automobiles; chemicals and pharmaceuticals; electronics; industrial equipment; and food, beverages and tobacco. These are the major industries which, together with the finance industry, are the key levers controlling global capitalism.

The strategies of these TNCs represent the fostering of worldwide integration in a way which suits their objectives. Entire industrial sectors have virtually disappeared from much of northwestern America and Western Europe, such as steel, shipbuilding, textiles, footwear and electronics. Service industries are also affected; Swissair and Lufthansa have moved their accounts to India where computing costs are half those in the US or Western Europe. Trade unionist Dan Gallin (1994) calls this "body shopping – the upmarket end of the new international slave trade." The "downmarket end" is the leasing of entire crews for merchant ships from Burma and China, at wages which are a fraction of international minimum standards. The global economy is a great leveler, but in present circumstances, for workers in the West, it levels downward.

New class relations

The growth of these foreign investments almost everywhere has created a new international bourgeoisie, producing "client states" of international capital. The transnationalized state becomes "the executive committee of the international bourgeoisie" (see Crough and Wheelwright 1982: 173–95). Sklair (1994: 179) speaks of "a new global capitalist class" which dictates economic transnational practices, formed by a triple alliance of the host state, transnational corporations and elements of the indigenous elite, such as senior state functionaries, prominent politicians and leaders of the learned professions.

This new CLASS changes the nature of the political struggle between capital and labor, alters the role of the state and deliberately downgrades domestic industry. It engenders the belief in many countries that most indigenous practices are inferior to foreign ones, which are now called "world's best practices." New methods and new products from abroad are virtually defined as being better than indigenous ones.

Ideology of consumerism

Sklair considers that the most important IDEOLOGY now transmitted internationally is that of consumerism, which is essential for the spread of global capitalism. However, consumerism depends on advertising, which leads to the transnationalization of the local mass media and communications systems. To this we should also add the ideology of free markets and free trade, propagated in universities and think-tanks around the world, financed by big business, and even involving a "secret society" of economists, as documented over the last fifty years by Richard Cockett (1994). The ultimate logic of this ideology is that even ideas now become commodities bought and sold in the market place.

Deindustrialization

Gare (1995) emphasizes that these developments have served to undermine national identities, and have upset the previous balance of class relations. In many nations it is causing a decline in the numbers of those producing for the domestic market, which is not compensated for by the increase in those producing for export. Hence the traditional working class is shrinking, and is fighting a rearguard action without much success. This new transnational capitalist class, Gare argues, has no direction or underlying purpose – just power, control and CONSPICUOUS CONSUMPTION AND EMULATION on a massive scale. This process has effected a massive transfer of power, wealth and income from the poor to the rich, both within and between countries, and is not contributing, on balance, to human welfare. On the contrary, it is rapidly destroying the institutional conditions essential for the continued existence of humanity.

De-industrialization has meant high levels of unemployment and impoverishment for many; but for quite a few it has meant increased wealth and the "gentrification of city men," as capital has been invested less in actual production and more in the stock market, real estate and the arts. Like Sklair, Gare also emphasizes that the rise of the new class has been associated with massive expenditure by large transnationals on public relations, promoting policies favorable to their expansion, especially the ideology of the New Right advocating the emancipation of the market from all controls.

Contradictions of capitalism

With the collapse of Soviet-style "communism," the world faces a situation which has not existed since before the First World War, when capital could go anywhere looking for markets and cheap resources, including labor. This was the world about which Rosa Luxemburg wrote in her classic *The Accumulation of Capital*, published in 1913. She believed the fundamental contradiction of capitalism to be between the growing productive power and the relative shrinking of purchasing power. Within this context, two main forces were preventing capitalism from breaking down. One force was the penetration into non-capitalist areas, and the other was militarism and expenditure on armaments. Both provided markets for the massive productive power of the capitalist system.

Today, both of these "safety valves" have lost much of their effectiveness. There is significant disarmament and, with the collapse of "communism," non-capitalist areas are rapidly disappearing. The CONTRADICTIONS – which were muted by wars, hot and cold, and the emergence of large non-capitalist areas – are now re-asserting themselves. The so-called golden years of world capitalism, the quarter-century after the Second World War, turn out to be the re-armament years, the decades when anti-communist coalitions prevented too much competition.

Global instability and change

Signs of strain began to emerge in the 1970s and 1980s when groups of dominant capitalist countries, such as the G11, G7 and so on, were formed to try to coordinate their economic policies. Trade wars began to erupt again, taking the form of regional trade blocs such as NAFTA and APEC. The economic rise of Asia was led initially by Japan, and bolstered in various ways by the West as a bulwark against Chinese communism. Asia has had the highest rate of growth over the last two decades, led in the last few years by China itself.

However, the Asian financial crisis of 1997–1998 has negatively affected economic performance, especially in Indonesia and Thailand, and to a lesser extent Malaysia and other nations. It has also stimulated domestic political reform, particularly in Indonesia. The rate of economic growth in the most affected nations is likely to be more moderate in the foreseeable future. Nevertheless, Asia is still likely to be a growth area in the longer term. (See NEWLY INDUSTRIALIZED ASIAN NATIONS.)

For instance, the World Bank predicts that the OECD's share of world output will fall from 56 percent to 40 percent; nine of the top fifteen economies will be from what we now call the Third World, and all but two of these will be in Asia. This means that the extent of cheap labor entering the world market in one form or another – goods, services or migration – will be greater than ever before in the history of capitalism. Several authors not noted for their radical views consider that the transitional costs of this transformation of the world capitalist system will fall most directly on the working classes of North America, Western Europe, Japan and Australia.

For example, Neal Soss, investment banker to the First Boston Corporation, thinks that the shift in capital and technology to the Third World will undermine the value and bargaining power of labor in the "First World"; and in the USA, Europe and Japan, the middle-class dream will end. Robert Reich, the former US Secretary for Labor, warns that only a small proportion of US workers will benefit from globalization; most are likely to fall by the wayside, and America may face political instability (see Lambert 1995).

The Prime Minister of Singapore, Goh Chok Tong, has said that the collapse of the ideological iron and bamboo curtains has brought new and serious sources of polarization. The social structures that had supported four decades of industrial growth were now in the midst of great change. Also, globalization had not led to the strengthening of the multilateral system, but to increased regionalism (*International Business Asia,* Report of Fortune Global Forum, 31 March 1995).

Already there are ugly signs of the beginnings of new forms of FASCISM in some of these regions, and its half-brother, RACISM. The future historian of the latter half of the twentieth century may well conclude that it was anti-communism which held capitalism together. One can only hope that this function is not taken over by the incipient neo-fascism of the *fin de siècle,* to which the price mechanism is already adapting itself. As Clairmont writes:

> What we have seen over the last quarter of a century is the rising inequality in the world's distribution of economic power, an era that coincides with the flowering of transnational expansion..... What is gripping as we move towards the end of our current century is capitalism's crass inability to brake...the tumultuous currents of joblessness, marginalisation and permanent impoverishment.
> (Clairmont 1996)

See also:

class analysis of world capitalism; global crisis of world capitalism; global liberalism; international political economy; internationalization of capital

Selected references

Clairmont, Frederic F. (1996) *The Rise and Fall of Economic Liberalism: The Making of the Economic Gulag,* Penang: Southbound Press and Third World Network

Cockett, Richard (1994) *Thinking the Unthinkable: Think-Tanks and the Economic Counter-Revolution, 1931–83,* London: Harper Collins.

Crough, Greg and Wheelwright, E.L. (1982) *Australia: A Client State,* Melbourne: Penguin.

Gallin, Dan (1994) "Inside the New World Order," *New Politics* 5(1): 109.

Gare, Arran (1995) "Globalisation, Postmodernity, and the Environment," *Arena Journal* 4.

Harvey, Robert (1995) *The Return of the Strong: The Drift to Global Disorder,* London: Macmillan.

Hobsbawm, Eric (1994) *Age of Extremes: The Short Twentieth Century 1914–1991,* London: Michael Joseph.

Hutton, Will (1995) *The State We're In,* London: Jonathan Cape.

Lambert, R. (1995) "International Labour Standards: Challenging Globalisation Ideology," Department of Organisational and Labour Studies, University of Western Australia. Research Report.

Sklair, Lesley (ed.) (1994) *Capitalism & Development*, London: Routledge.

Smith, David A. and Borocz, Josef (1995) *A New World Order? Global Transformations in the Late Twentieth Century*, Westport, CN: Praeger.

UNCTAD (1994) *World Investment Report: TNCs, Employment and the Workplace*, Geneva: United Nations.

Wheelwright, E.L. (1986) "Marxist Analysis of Capitalism in Australia: Past, Present and Future," in Edwin Dowdy (ed.), *Marxist Policies Today in Socialist and Capitalist Countries*, St Lucia: University of Queensland Press.

E.L. WHEELWRIGHT

global crisis of world capitalism

That capitalism would one day face a systemic crisis was implicit in the views of Adam Smith and explicit in those of Karl MARX. For both, the rate of profit would fall in the long-run (see FALLING RATE OF PROFIT TENDENCY) and, since capitalism is hard to envisage without the likelihood of profit, a crisis seemed inevitable. Today, however, views are different. On the one hand, in the Marxist camp, the so-called crisis has been proclaimed quite frequently over the past 150 years, and each time the systemic difficulties have been overcome. In effect, the cyclical and wave-like rhythms of the capitalist world-economy had been mistaken for the secular trends (see CYCLES AND TRENDS IN THE WORLD CAPITALIST ECONOMY).

As a result the crisis of capitalism has become the story of the boy who cried wolf, and today there is much skepticism about the thesis, to the glee of the opponents of Marxism and the abashment of those who believe a crisis is still in the offing. On the other hand, at the same time, followers of NEOCLASSICAL ECONOMICS have long since renounced many parts of Smithian doctrine, including his belief in the tendency of the rate of profit to fall; they are now denying even the Keynesian variant that merely suggests chronic problems of effective demand. Neoclassical economists tend to have a rosy view of the future.

It is, perhaps, less relevant to review the abstract theoretical arguments than to investigate the major factors that account for profit, and to see which if any function with more difficulty today than previously. It should be noted at the outset that we are discussing here the *global* crisis of capitalism. Capitalists may find it more or less difficult to operate within particular states at particular moments, and rates of profits calculated within each of the state boundaries may go in opposite directions at a given time, but these situations are quite different from a "global" crisis of what is, after all, the mode of production of a world economy.

Assuming that individual capitalists will seek to maximize their possibilities of overall accumulation of capital in the totality of the world economy, there are four routes through which they can work to optimize the overall profit they obtain from their transactions on the world market: they can reduce wages, externalize costs, minimize state appropriation and increase monopolistic rents. It is argued below that each of these four standard sources of profit is in extra difficulty today.

Cost and productivity of labor

What accounts for differential costs of labor for the same work and the same commodity at the same rate of PRODUCTIVITY? Such differentials can only occur if there is not a perfect labor market, which it is quite clear has never existed. For one thing, for labor to move from one zone to another is often difficult and expensive, and requires permission of state authorities, especially if it involves crossing frontiers. The power of the states to segregate the interstate labor markets has resulted in different "historical" wage rates. The word "historical," as used by most economists, tends to sweep the issue under the rug, and often hides a reluctance to analyze the factors that make such historical rates differ among countries and vary over time within countries.

Over the centuries, the lowest-paid workers worldwide have tended to be recent recruits from situations of rural underemployment, for whom a steady monetary wage, however low, represented in fact greater security and real income. But over the centuries as well, such workers have, often within a generation, been able to organize sufficient alternatives that they could insist on higher rates of pay. New cohorts of low-wage labor were then needed. A basic element in the ability to locate such new cohorts has been the ability to attract previously unrecruited sectors of the world rural force living in conditions of serious underemployment. Today the world rural labor force is in free-fall diminution, going toward an asymptote of zero. This raises the question of where the recruitment base for such low-wage labor will be in the near future (see Kasaba & Tabak 1995).

Externalization of costs

The externalization of costs has been the quiet secret of capitalist accumulation. It is probably impossible for producers to make significant profits without externalizing some of their costs. We have created a whole category of presumably legitimate externalized costs which we call "infrastructure," and expect that governments, using their fiscal powers, will appropriate the money necessary to make it possible that firms externalize parts of certain kinds of costs, notably transportation, communication, the provision of energy and waste disposal. Omitted here are trade protection costs which, when externalized, become a "protection rent," which would make the case even stronger.

The most serious costs that have been externalized, however, are some costs borne by the "society" as a whole, but not necessarily heretofore by the government. These are the costs of raw material replenishment and of repairing damage to the biosphere. The expansion of world capitalism over 500 years has led to a considerable depletion of raw material sources and considerable damage to the biomass, illustrating what writers in the journal *Capitalism, Nature and Socialism* have called the "second contradiction of capitalism." Today we have a global environmental movement that is engaged in both analysis of the situation and political protest about its continuance (see GREEN PARTY; ENVIRONMENTAL AND ECOLOGICAL POLITICAL ECONOMY: MAJOR CONTEMPORARY THEMES).

The dilemma is quite straightforward. The biomass is being used up and damaged, going toward an asymptote of an irremediable situation. If this is not to occur, something must be done both to repair damage and depletion on the one hand, and to ensure that the rate of damage and depletion in the future is radically reduced, if not eliminated, on the other. Assuming this is technically possible, it will be very expensive. It can be paid for in one of two basic ways: via taxation, with a very high individual burden to which there will be serious political objection; or by requiring the internalization of costs by firms, which will cut sharply into the rate of profit.

Minimizing state appropriation

Firms, of course, always seek to contain social appropriation of their income. They never volunteer to be taxed. On the other hand, we tend to exaggerate the depth of their opposition to taxation. Capitalist firms, especially in so far as they are able to function as a collective actor, are well aware of the degree to which they need governments to assist them in obtaining profits in multiple ways (keeping down the costs of labor, arranging for the externalization of costs and so on). They also need governments to aid them against competitors, particularly against competitors located in another state. The hostility of firms to states is therefore muted and ambiguous.

Nonetheless, one should not exaggerate in the other direction either. Particular firms have constant complaints *vis-à-vis* states. The states may, in effect, be more sympathetic to their competitors. The states may function as redistributive drains on accumulated capital – drains in the direction of politicians and bureaucrats, and drains in the form of social wages to workers resident in the state.

The states are thus the locus of constant political struggle, and the *rapport de forces* is not at all stable. The issue, therefore, is whether there is some secular trend in this *rapport de forces* as it manifests itself in the various states. There does indeed seem to be a relevant secular trend, which we may call "democratization." The call for democracy is only very partially a demand for more inclusive governance structures; it is primarily a demand that somehow the overall system provide a reasonable minimum for all persons in three domains: income (via jobs and pensions), education and health. Democratization has occurred in two ways: historically speaking, larger and larger segments of the world's populations are making such demands in more vigorous and effective ways; what is considered a reasonable minimum has been constantly rising.

If firms today find it more difficult than in previous periods to contain the social appropriation of capital, it is the result of this transformation of the political and cultural arena, and not because of some change in the arena of production. But it is a very real change, nonetheless, and it affects directly the ability to accumulate capital.

Monopoly rents

Monopolistic rents have been the repeated basis of "super-profits," and probably account for a large percentage of overall accumulation of capital. Rent is often thought to be a pre-capitalist phenomenon, an anachronistic leftover from previous modes of production. This is, of course, partially true of certain forms of rent, particularly those forms deriving from the ownership of land. However, this emphasis misses the fact that rent is a central current mode of accumulating capital, and its usage has if anything expanded under capitalism.

Rent takes many forms under capitalism, but whatever the form taken it requires state acquiescence, either by direct action (expenditures, decrees, military action) or by creating the legal frameworks within which rent is possible. Indeed, it could be argued that the provision of rents is the most significant form of aid to the accumulation of capital that states provide. But the legitimacy of state structures have been called into question very seriously within the last twenty-five years. This is the result primarily of widespread disillusionment of popular forces in the capacities of the states to deliver on the long-standing promises of gradual improvement of conditions.

When this weakening of the legitimacy of the states is combined with increased pressure for state expenditures (because of the ecological problems of the biomass and because of the pressures of democratization), the governments find themselves triply squeezed by the FISCAL CRISIS OF THE STATE, which is playing a role today analogous to that played by the "crisis of seignorial revenues" in late medieval Europe. The amount of money that can be invested in providing monopolistic rents for capitalist entrepreneurs is necessarily diminished.

Global crisis of capitalism?

What one can say is that all four of the traditional sources of increasing profit on economic transactions are less available today than previously (see Hopkins and Wallerstein 1996). In this sense, there is a structural basis for the argument that the mechanisms within the system to emerge from the regular cyclical downturns may no longer be viable. There is also a basis for the argument that the very processes that have sustained the capitalist system historically are those that are undermining it today. As one moves up a curve toward an asymptote, there is less and less room to continue in the same direction.

The heart of the argument is not that capitalism has exhausted its economic mechanisms for further growth, but that it is exhausting its political and social mechanisms for maintaining the unequal distribution upon which the accumulation of capital is dependent. If this is so, one can envisage a period of extended social turmoil throughout all zones of the world economy (indeed, one might argue that we are already in such a period). In such a period of extended turmoil, the key issue is not whether or not to maintain the capitalist system as we have know it, but what shall we construct as the replacement system or systems. It is to be expected that sophisticated defenders of privilege will concentrate on putting forward an alternative system/mode of production/ historical structure that will maintain the element of unequal distribution and power, and that popular forces will press for an opposite result. There is no inherent reason to be sure that one side or the other will necessarily prevail in their opposite pressures.

Selected references

Hopkins, Terence K. and Wallerstein, Immanuel (coordinators) (1996) *The Age of Transition: Trajectory of the World-System, 1945–2025*, London and New York: Zed Books.

Kasaba, Rasat and Tabak, Faruk (1995) "Fatal Conjuncture: The Decline and Fall of the Modern Agrarian Order During the Bretton Woods Era," in P. McMichael (ed.), *Food and Agrarian Orders in the World-Economy*, Westport, CT: Greenwood Press, 79–93.

IMMANUEL WALLERSTEIN

global liberalism

Global liberalism is to be distinguished from global neoliberalism (which should be called global conservatism). The two have the same relationship that liberal ideology had to conservative ideology in the nineteenth century; constituting the difference between a centrist position and a position on the political right. Centrist liberalism combines the acceptance of the inevitability and desirability of progress with the desire to control the limits, pace and parameters of political change. This is done by giving the primary role in the change process to rational specialists, whose role is to conceive and implement appropriate reforms via legislative and administrative action.

Centrist liberalism emerged as the dominant ideology of the modern world-system in the nineteenth century and was initially a program designed to tame the "dangerous classes" (that is, the urban proletariat) of the industrial countries of Western Europe and North America. This was done by satisfying their demands in such a way that it did not threaten the basic structure of the system. In retrospect, we can say that the program was highly successful.

Global liberalism

In the twentieth century, however, a new set of "dangerous classes" made their presence felt on the political scene: the popular classes of the non-European world. It is in response to their political demands, expressed both in the Russian Revolution and in the multiple nationalist and national liberation movements across the globe, that the doctrine of global liberalism began to take shape.

There were two principal elements to global liberalism. The first was the doctrine of the "self-determination of nations." When Woodrow Wilson first made this a major theme in world affairs, he was thinking of how to create renewed order in the wake of the collapse of the three land-based European imperial structures, the Russian, Austro-Hungarian, and Ottoman Empires. Essentially, what was proposed was granting the status of sovereign state to "peoples" of a certain size, self-awareness and territorial contiguity. Self-determination was offered as an "egalitarian" idea: one people, one vote.

When the Communist International at the Baku Congress in 1920 took the lead in creating worldwide solidarity between anti-imperialist movements, they in effect accepted the program of the "self-determination of nations," extending it to the whole non-European world. After the Second World War, the United States accepted this extension and eventually imposed these views on the European colonial powers.

There was a second part to the program of global liberalism, which turned out to be more difficult to implement at the global level than it had been at the national level for the wealthier states. This was the program of limited redistribution of income, which came to be described under various labels such as the welfare state, Keynesianism or Fordism. At the global level, this program came to be known as the "economic development of underdeveloped areas," a concept that was presumably to be promoted by extensive "aid" – material and technical – by the so-called developed countries to the so-called developing countries. In the period since 1945, multiple programs of this sort were established by the United States, the USSR, the former colonial states of Western Europe, the Nordic countries and others. Some of these programs were intergovernmental, some governmental and some non-governmental.

The United Nations assumed, as one of its basic tasks, the furtherance of this global liberalism. It did this through the work of its multiple specialized agencies, its own UN Development Program, and through the multiple conferences it patronized. The 1970s were officially proclaimed by the UN as the "Decade of Development." The 1970s, however, were precisely the moment when the end of the postwar economic expansion created considerable difficulties for this concept of modulated global redistribution.

The BALANCE OF PAYMENTS squeeze on most states outside the core zone led to extensive state borrowing, at the same time as the former donor states were all cutting back on their aid programs. This was perceived as the "debt crisis," especially once borrowing states began in the 1980s to try to renege on or reduce radically their repayments. In 1977, it was proposed that Willy Brandt (Nobel laureate and former Chancellor of the Federal Republic of Germany) convene an independent commission of international figures to assess development issues and make recommendations. The Brandt Commission report, *North–South: A Programme for Survival*, represents the quintessence of restated global liberalism. It made recommendations concerning the poorest countries, hunger and food, population, disarmament, transnational corporations, the world monetary order, development finance and international organizations. A second Brandt Commission report was issued in 1983, and a similar report was published by the Socialist International Committee on Economic Policy in 1985, again chaired by Willy Brandt. All these reports were essentially ignored.

In 1990, a group of personalities from the South, under the leadership of Julius Nyerere, issued an essentially similar report, only slightly more ambitious. This report was entitled *The Challenge to the South*. It received even less attention. It was clear that all notions of global Keynesianism or a global welfare state or even extensive foreign aid programs, so high on the agenda of the late 1960s, had become out of fashion by the 1980s.

Failure of global liberalism

The failure of global liberalism to come anywhere near its promises of bridging the gap between the North and the South had led to widespread disillusionment with all problems of global reformism. A consequence of this is that there was disillusionment, not only with the liberal center, but with all the expressions of historic revolutionary forces which had proved themselves unable to force the pace on such reformism.

The collapse of national liberation movements, and then of the so-called "communist" governments in Eastern and Central Europe, reflected this turning away from global liberalism and left the field clear for the resurgence of global conservatism (neoliberalism) in its multiple forms. The role of the IMF and its enforcement of "structural adjustment" now became central to the life of non-Western states, and its ideology became pervasive in the various neo-conservative programs adopted by Western countries.

See also:

global corporate capitalism; international political economy

Selected references

Friedrich Ebert Foundation (1981) *Towards One World? International Responses to the Brandt Report*, London: Maurice Temple Smith.
Independent Commission on International Development Issues [Brandt Commission] (1980) *North–South: A Programme for Survival*, London: Pan Books.
—— (1983) *Common Crisis: North–South Co-operation for World Recovery*, Cambridge, MA: MIT Press.
Socialist International Committee on Economic Policy (1985) *Global Challenge: From Crisis to Co-operation: Breaking the North–South Stalemate*, London: Pan Books
South Commission (1990) *The Challenge to the South*, Geneva: South Commission.
The South Centre (1993) *Facing the Challenge: Responses to the Report of the South Commission*, London: Zed Books.

IMMANUEL WALLERSTEIN

Goodwin cycle and predator–prey models

Economics has a long tradition of borrowing concepts from mechanics. Richard Goodwin (1967) turned to biology, drawing an analogy between predator–prey cycles in nature and the social phenomenon of the trade cycle. Goodwin was attempting to put into mathematical form the analysis given by MARX in Chapter 25 of *Das Kapital* Volume I. Here Marx (1867: 580–81) shows that changes in economic activity are endogenously conditioned by the conflicting relations between capital and labor. In particular, over time accumulation may be adversely affected by rising wages as profitability declines; and, as this accumulation declines, wages tend to moderate, thus leading to rising profitability and accumulation over time (see RESERVE ARMY OF LABOR).

Foundations in biology

Goodwin saw this argument as being strongly akin to predator–prey analysis in biology, which explained the cyclical fluctuations that occur in both predator and prey populations over time. Mathematical biologists model such cycles by assuming that the feed available to prey is effectively limitless, so that in the absence of predators their population will grow at the constant rate. The impact of predators depends on the number of interactions between themselves and prey, which depends on how many predators there are. Predators, on the other hand, will starve to death at the constant rate in the absence of prey. The growth of predator numbers depends on their catching prey.

While the mathematics is a little complex, the situation can easily be described in words:

- an initially high number of prey and low number of predators leads to a rapid growth in the number of prey;
- the large number of prey enables the predator population to expand;
- the growing predator population reduces the prey population;
- the reduced prey population leads to the predators dying off, thus restoring the cycle.

Application to political economy

Goodwin's genius was to see that Marx's argument above can be put into a more complex but nonetheless similar cycle of causation:

- the level of output determines the rate of employment, so that a high initial level of output requires a high rate of employment;
- the rate of employment determines the rate of change of wages, so that a high rate of employment results in a high rate of change of wages;
- the level of wages determines the rate of profit, so that a high rate of change of wages means falling levels of profit;

- the rate of profit determines the level of investment, so that falling profit means low rates of investment;
- the level of investment determines the rate of growth of the capital stock, so that low rates of investment mean slow or negative growth in the capital stock;
- the capital stock determines the level of output, so that a slowly growing or declining capital stock means static or falling levels of output, which will eventually lead to falling wages.

The rate of change of employment is a positive linear function of the current level of employment, and a negative nonlinear function of the product of employment and wages share. The rate of change of wages share is a positive nonlinear function of the product of current wages share and the wage change function, and a negative linear function of the current wages share. This system can be simulated numerically, and yields a cyclical pattern in employment and wages share of output.

When these two relationships are mapped against each other (putting wages share on one axis and employment on the other), they generate a closed cycle, the graphical form of the cyclical vision sketched by Marx. The process is distinctly a non-equilibrium one. Unless the system begins with the equilibrium values for employment and wage share, it will forever gravitate around them. Unlike cycles in a linear system, the nonlinear cycles of this model have a long term impact. While the average value of wages share equals the equilibrium value, the average value of employment is lower the further the system is from equilibrium.

Significance and further developments

Marx was the inspiration for this model, and he is normally associated with an apocalyptic secular vision of capitalism, with the relative or absolute immiserisation of the working class leading to the breakdown of capitalism (see CAPITALIST BREAKDOWN DEBATE). However, in some passages such a perspective is absent, and it is likewise absent from Goodwin's model. Instead, he argued that his model supported the empirical outcome that "real wages rose, while the rate of profit remained relatively constant." This paints workers as the ultimate long-run beneficiaries of the symbiotic relationship with capitalists and the means of production.

Goodwin's model has been the inspiration for a large range of cyclical models (Desai 1973, 1995; Skott 1989; Sportelli 1995) with flavors ranging from Marxian to neoclassical. His successful transplant of the Lotka–Volterra system of equations to economics has inspired other transplants to issues such as technological substitution and finance (Keen 1995). Many of the extensions have generated models with chaotic characteristics (Keen 1995). Some discussion of the limitations of the original model can be found in Vellupillai (1979).

See also:

business cycle theories; equilibrium, disequilibrium and non-equilibrium; evolutionary economics: major contemporary themes

Selected references

Blatt, J. (1983) *Dynamic Economic Systems*, Armonk, NY: M.E. Sharpe.
Desai, M. (1973) "Growth Cycles and Inflation in a Model of the Class Struggle," *Journal of Economic Theory* 6: 527–45.
——(1995) "An Endogenous Growth-Cycle with Vintage Capital," *Economics of Planning* 28(2–3): 87–91.
Goodwin, R.M. (1967) "A Growth Cycle," in C.H. Feinstein (ed.), *Socialism, Capitalism and Economic Growth*, Cambridge: Cambridge University Press.
Isaac, A.G. (1991) "Economic Stabilization and Money Supply Endogeneity in a Conflicting Claims Environment," *Journal of Post Keynesian Economics* 14(1): 93–110.
Keen, S. (1995) "Finance and Economic Breakdown: Modelling Minsky's "Financial Instability Hypothesis'," *Journal of Post Keynesian Economics* 17(4): 607–35.

Marx, Karl (1867) *Das Kapital*, volume I, Moscow: Progress Publishers, 1954.

Semmler, W. (1986) "On Nonlinear Theories of Economic Cycles and the Persistence of Business Cycles," *Mathematical Social Sciences* 12: 47–76.

Skott, P. (1989) "Effective Demand, Class Struggle and Cyclical Growth," *International Economic Review* 30(1): 231–47.

Sportelli, M.C. (1995) "A Kolmogoroff Generalized Predator–Prey Model of Goodwin's Growth-Cycle," *Journal of Economics – Zeitschrift für Nationalökonomie* 61(1): 35–64.

Vellupillai, K. (1979) "Some Stability Properties of Goodwin's Growth Cycle," *Journal of Economics – Zeitschrift für Nationalökonomie* 39: 245–57.

STEVE KEEN

GOVERNMENT: *see* state and government

gravitation and convergence

Prices of production and market prices

There are only minor differences between the analysis of competition and the formation of prices of production by Smith, Ricardo and MARX (Smith 1776: ch. 7; Ricardo 1817: ch. 4; Marx 1894: ch. 10). For this reason, Marx's analysis can be called "classical." The three classical economists distinguished between equilibrium prices, called "natural prices" or "prices of production," and disequilibrium prices, called "market prices". Market prices are assumed to converge toward prices of production, and to gravitate around such prices if shocks recur. Prices of production correspond to the existence of a uniform profit rate in the various industries. Although this property is less well known, the prevalence of prices of production is associated with a set of outputs ("effective demands" in Smith, "social needs" in Marx), and given stocks of capital. If growth is allowed, all quantities (outputs and capital stocks) increase at the same rate, and only the proportions among industries of these amounts are maintained.

This framework of analysis is now that of modern classical economics, common to SRAFFIAN POLITICAL ECONOMY and Marxist political economy. It was used in the famous controversy concerning the so-called "transformation of values into prices of production" (see TRANSFORMATION PROBLEM). Prices of production are not part of mainstream economics, although Walras (1873) initially attempted to incorporate such prices into his framework. The definition of the long-term position, classical long-term equilibrium, is accompanied in the work of classical economists by a description of the processes which are supposed to ensure the gravitation of the variables around their equilibrium values. The centerpiece in this analysis is "capital mobility": capitalists invest more in industries where the profit rate is larger (and less where it is comparatively lower). The issue is that of the relative value of investment among industries, and not that of its aggregate value for the total economy or each capitalist.

The "classical process"

The overall "classical process" can be summarized as follows for one industry (beginning with a comparatively large profit rate):

$$\uparrow \pi \Rightarrow \uparrow I \Rightarrow \uparrow K \Rightarrow \uparrow S \Rightarrow \downarrow P \Rightarrow \downarrow \pi$$

Here, the process begins with actions which increase the surplus or profit ($\uparrow \pi$), which provides finance for greater investment (I), which in turn results in an increase in the capital stock (K). This is equivalent to an increase in supply (S), which may result in decreasing prices (P), and hence decreasing profit margins (π). A similar chain of events occurs when the profit rate is relatively small, ending up with an increased rate of profit. Thus, classical economists thought that this process would correct any profitability differential. Several important remarks can be made:

- This process refers to the actions of decentralized agents – capitalists – acting within disequilibrium. Their behavior is described in terms of adjustment to disequilibrium: they react to the observation of disequilibrium. Capitalists invest more where profit rates are larger (a first mark of disequilibrium). They diminish prices when supply is larger than demand (a second mark of disequilibrium). However, these reactions do not fully correct for disequilibrium in one period.

- No agent is in charge of setting prices at the levels that ensure a uniform profit rate. This property follows, in the average, from the interaction of individual behaviors, in which capitalists are motivated by the improvement of their profit rate.
- Both prices (including profit rates) and quantities (outputs and capital stocks) are involved in this mechanism. Disequilibrium prices (a profitability differential) induce a modification of quantities (capital stocks and outputs); a disequilibrium on quantities (a difference between supply and demand) leads to a correction of prices.

Dynamic systems

It is interesting to notice that this analysis has been modeled only recently, whereas equilibrium had already been the object of much mathematical work. The natural framework for the analysis of convergence or gravitation is that of dynamic systems. The model combines a number of behavioral equations describing how capitalists react to profitability differentials, how firms modify their prices depending on the disequilibrium between their supply and demand, and a set of structural equations. The equations account, in particular, for the distribution of income (profits destined for consumption, etc.) and the formation of demand (consumption, investment, etc.).

Such a model can be formally reduced to a relation of recursion, in which the value of the variables in one period can be expressed as a function of their value at the previous period (or a differential equation in continuous time). The issue of stability is whether, beginning with any value of the variables, the economy will converge toward equilibrium period after period. This problem is formally equivalent to that of the gravitation of variables in a vicinity of equilibrium in the presence of shocks, as long as these shocks do not affect the equilibrium values of the variables.

Convergence, or the stability of equilibrium, will obtain depending on the assumptions of the model and the degree of reaction of economic agents to disequilibrium. Reactions are represented in the model by the values of reaction coefficients of behavioral equations. For example, one such coefficient measures the percentage by which a capitalist will modify investment patterns between two industries if the profit rates differ by 1 percent. These reactions must be sufficient, but not excessive: coefficients must fall within a given interval. In most models, for any TECHNOLOGY and any rules defining the formation of demand, one can express the conditions for which reaction coefficients yield stability.

Such limits to the degree of reaction of economic agents are a basic feature of adjustment in general. For example, the driver of a car reacts to the observation of the deviation of the trajectory of his or her vehicle, turning the wheel in the appropriate direction and to a sufficient but not excessive degree. Both a deficient or an excessive reaction could be fatal.

Obtaining convergence depends on the structure of the model. Convergence is generally ensured, provided that adequate reaction to disequilibrium has been incorporated. Convergence does not prevail in two well-known models, however. The first case involves an early model by Hobuo Nikaido (1977), which was not faithful to the classical analysis of competition. Second, equilibrium is always unstable in what is known as the "pure cross-dual model." In that model, capitalists do not react to the observation of profit rates on their sales, but to a rate which would prevail under the assumption of equilibrium in the commodity market, for example, if the entire output were sold (Boggio 1985).

A number of models of classical competition are now available (see *Political Economy:*

Studies in the Surplus Approach, 1990, vol IV, nos 1–2). All share the common feature that investments among industries are functions of profitability differentials. However, they differ in several important respects. In most instances, market prices are disequilibrium prices resulting from their progressive adjustment as a function of disequilibria between supply and demand. Nonetheless, some models adopt a market clearing assumption (assuming obviously that demands are functions of prices). It is also possible to introduce a direct reaction to disequilibria between supply and demand, assuming that firms modify the quantity produced (in addition to the adjustment of prices).

For example, if supply is larger than demand, firms diminish their output, independently of the indirect effects of diminished prices on profit rates, and of profit rates on capital stocks (i.e. on productive capacity). This mechanism is very realistic and efficient *vis-à-vis* stability; it draws an interesting link between the classical and Keynesian analyses. Models also differ in more technical respects, such as the choice between discrete or continuous time, the presence of fixed capital (and the consideration of capacity utilization rates), the explicit treatment of inventories, the number of commodities or capitalists, linear or nonlinear reactions and so on.

Shocks and endogenous processes

The difference between convergence and gravitation corresponds to the possible occurrence of shocks. These shocks can be considered exogenous, but in more general frameworks they mirror other processes which can be treated endogenously. This is the case when structural change is embodied in the analysis (concerning wages, technology and so on). Such transformations may or may not affect the equilibrium values of the variables (prices of production and outputs). If they do not, the problem is that of gravitation around a given long-term equilibrium. If they do, the issue is whether the value of the variables will follow an equilibrium constantly moving from one period to the next. Classical economists, in particular Marx, who refers to the heterogeneity of capital among firms due to technical change, were aware of this problem. It can be treated formally in a more sophisticated framework (see Duménil and Lévy 1995).

See also:

classical political economy; competition in Sraffian political economy; equilibrium, disequilibrium and non-equilibrium; price theory, Sraffian; traverse

Selected references

Boggio, L. (1985) "On the Stability of Production Prices," *Metroeconomica*, 37: 241–67.
Duménil, G. and Lévy, D. (1995) "Structural Change and Prices of Production," *Structural Change and Economic Dynamics*, 6: 397–434.
Marx, K. (1894) *Das Kapital*, vol. III, New York: First Vintage Edition, 1981.
Nikaido, H. (1977) "Refutation of the Dynamic Equalization of Profit Rates in Marx's Scheme of Reproduction," Research Paper, Department of Economics, University of Southern California.
Ricardo, D. (1817) *On the Principles of Political Economy and Taxation*, Cambridge: Cambridge University Press, 1975.
Smith, A. (1776) *An Inquiry into the Nature and Causes of the Wealth of Nations*, Oxford: Clarendon Press, 1976.
Walras, L. (1873) *Elements of Pure Economics*, London: Allen & Unwin, 1954.

GÉRARD DUMÉNIL
DOMINIQUE LÉVY

Great Depression

The collapse of both the 1920s-era prosperity of the United States and the shakier growth of Germany heralded the worldwide Great Depression of the 1930s, as primary-product producers went bankrupt, trade wars flared and the banking system disintegrated. Because this series of events shook popular faith in capitalism's ability to "deliver the goods," economic historians have dedicated much research time to understanding it. In this research, most emphasis has been on either the US economy's collapse (as with Romer 1990) or the instability of the world economy (Temin 1989).

Exogenous shocks and policy failures

The dominant neoclassical view emphasizes the importance of exogenous shocks, to what is assumed to be an essentially stable system, in causing the 1929–33 collapse. Though some, like Peter Temin (1976) and Christina Romer (1990), stress the largely unexplained fall of consumption or the exogenous stock-market crash of 1929 as a shock, policy errors receive the most attention. Milton Friedman and Anna Schwartz (1965), for example, blame a "Great Contraction" of the US money supply. Others (including Romer) emphasize the US government's efforts to balance its budget in a recession, further cutting aggregate demand. Even the "international Keynesians" who stress the structural instability of the world economy in the late 1920s have this emphasis on misguided policy. While Charles Kindleberger (1986) argues that the US should have lived up to its responsibility as leader of world capitalism to stabilize the system, Temin (1989) blames the deflationary bias inherent in the dominant policy regime of the time (including the gold standard).

Underconsumptionist explanation

Leftist economists stress the inherent instability of the US and world economies of the late 1920s. Hardly any emphasize a rising organic composition of capital or a high employment profit squeeze, since there is little evidence for those hypotheses. Instead, underconsumption tendencies are stressed. Paul Baran and Paul Sweezy (1966) see underconsumption-induced depression as the normal state of MONOPOLY CAPITALISM; it was only the First World War and the 1920s automobilization of the US economy that delayed its onset. On the other hand, the regulation school (of Michel Aglietta (1979) and others) see a structural disjunction between the rising importance of mass production and the limited development of mass consumption. The depression was highly likely in the absence of a "Fordist mode of regulation."

Overproduction, underconsumption and vulnerability

James Devine (1983, 1994) attempts to synthesize the empirically – and logically – valid parts of all of these different perspectives, while reconciling underconsumption tendencies with Marx's view that capitalism tends to expand aggressively independently of the constraints set by consumer demand. He agrees with Marx's vision of capitalist accumulation, seeing competition and class antagonism as driving the system forward to expand too far, to overaccumulate, a process allowed by the credit system. The form that this overaccumulation takes depends on the institutional context.

While "labor scarcity" in the late-1960s USA implied a profit squeeze, the late-1920s "labor abundance" encouraged terms of "overinvestment relative to consumption." Rising productivity and stagnant wages imply stagnant workers' consumption but rising profit rates, as seen in the corporate sector in the late-1920s. High profit rates are hard to sustain given low workers' demand because both investment and capitalist luxury spending (the other domestic private sources of demand) tend to be more volatile than workers' consumption. In addition, fixed investment creates new capacity that implies the need for rising investment and capitalist luxury consumption. In this view, the US economy became increasingly prone to collapse as the 1920s progressed. This meant that prosperity was more vulnerable to "shocks," such as the stock market crash, which itself can be explained in terms of the late-1920s political economy, including the Minskian euphoric economy (see FINANCIAL INSTABILITY HYPOTHESIS).

After the collapse occurred, when unused

capacity, excessive debt, and pessimistic expectations blocked further ACCUMULATION, capitalist competition induced falling wages and falling consumption, resulting in an "underconsumption trap" that encouraged lasting stagnation.

Worldwide nature of the crisis

Of course, the USA is not the whole world economy. Attention to the US economy is justified by the relative stagnation of most of the rest of the industrial world and almost all of primary production (including in the USA) after the First World War. Much of the prosperity that did occur in the 1920s in countries such as Germany was dependent on US growth, so that the USA was the capstone of the world arch. The slow growth of the world also made it difficult for the USA to preserve rising profit rates by boosting net exports.

The worldwide nature of the stagnation can be explained by the nature of capitalism at the time, especially the intense contention among nation-states. The inter-imperialist rivalry that spurred the First World War also stimulated the creeping protectionism of the 1920s which turned into trade wars in the 1930s, partly as a result of the US shift toward increased protection in 1930.

The rampant "policy failures" of the interwar period were not merely a matter of ignorance of economics, but results of the world political economy. Given the incomplete rise of the USA to super power status, and the large size of that country's primary-producing sector in the 1920s, the USA could not shoulder its "Kindlebergian responsibilities" until after the Second World War. The deflationary policy consensus that Temin describes can be explained as part of the post-First World War capitalist offensive that aimed to end rampant inflation, reverse workers' gains and restore depressed profit rates. Given the ascendancy of this movement, it is no surprise that policy makers were not interested in reversing the 1929–33 collapse until it was too late, as Epstein and Ferguson (1984) show.

See also:

business cycle theories; long waves of economic growth and development; regulation approach; social structures of accumulation

Selected references

Aglietta, Michel (1979) *A Theory of Capitalist Regulation: The US Experience*, trans. by David Fernbach, London: New Left Books.
Baran, Paul and Sweezy, Paul (1966) *Monopoly Capital*, New York: Monthly Review Press.
Devine, James (1983) "Over-Investment, Underconsumption, and the Origins of the Great Depression," *Review of Radical Political Economics* 15(2): 1–27.
—— (1994) "The Causes of the 1929–33 Great Collapse: A Marxian Interpretation," *Research in Political Economy* 14: 119–94.
Epstein, Gerald and Ferguson, Thomas (1984) "Monetary Policy, Loan Liquidation, and Industrial Conflict: The Federal Reserve and the Open Market Operations of 1932," *Journal of Economic History* 44(2): 957–83.
Friedman, Milton and Schwartz, Anna Jacobson (1965) *The Great Contraction, 1929–33*, Princeton, NJ: Princeton University Press.
Journal of Economic Perspectives (1993) special issue on the Great Depression, Spring.
Kindleberger, Charles P. (1986) *The World in Depression, 1929–1939*, Berkeley: University of California Press.
Romer, Christina (1990) "The Great Crash and the Onset of the Great Depression," *Quarterly Journal of Economics* 105(3): 597–624.
Temin, Peter (1976) *Did Monetary Forces Cause the Great Depression?*, New York: W.W. Norton.
—— (1989) *Lessons from the Great Depression*, Cambridge, MA: MIT Press.

JAMES DEVINE

Green Party

Profound and overlapping changes in personal values, societies and political economies during the 1950s and 1960s provided fertile soil for the roots of Green Parties across the industrialized world. Western Greens share a "postmaterialist" set of values characterized by concern for the environment, self-actualization, women's rights, the QUALITY OF LIFE, individual liberties, and participatory democracy (Inglehart 1990). The student movements of the 1960s, ecological LIMITS TO GROWTH and STAGFLATION gave rise to the citizens' initiatives and popular movements of the 1970s. The movements of the 1970s and 1980s were composed primarily of postmaterialists, and were opposed to nuclear energy and weapons, patriarchy, and "the establishment." Social movement veterans and activists would form the core of the Greens as a new social movement and political party (Frankland and Schoonmaker 1992).

By the late 1980s, Green Parties had sprung up in the Second World, and played a central role in the collapse of "state socialism" in the Baltic Republics and the Ukraine. By the early 1990s, Green Parties had appeared also in the Third World. Their emergence paralleled a more general "greening" of established parties (in effect, an attempt to co-opt green issues) in liberal and liberalizing democracies everywhere. As the German Greens were the first, and remain the most visible and influential Green Party in the world, the following will focus on their recommendations for economic policy, ecological restructuring, and alternative energy development.

Green critique

The Green critique of modern economies is ambiguous. Some Greens, the eco-socialists, locate the roots of environmental degradation in capitalism, with its "deficit environmental financing" and endless investment–profit–investment business cycles. Other Greens point to industrialism as the culprit in the plundering of the planet. It is not that the anti-industrial Greens are trying to save capitalism, though many support limited private property rights and are able to imagine small-scale markets among worker-owned or worker-managed enterprises. Many were disenchanted with the legacy of ecosystem destruction under state socialism. The eco-socialists respond that natural despoliation under "state socialism" is explained by the lack of democracy and the growth orientation of command economies.

Green political economy

Green political economy is founded on the "four pillars" (1) ecology, (2) non-violence, (3) grassroots democracy and (4) social responsibility of green ideology, and deep concern for what the German Greens call the "natural bases of life." Six additional principles, combined with the four pillars, were elaborated by the US Greens into the "ten key values": the first four plus (5) decentralization, (6) community-based economics, (7) post-patriarchal principles, (8) respect for diversity, (9) global responsibility and (10) a future focus. Most Green parties are generally if not explicitly anti-capitalist; employing concepts like "self-realization" and "autonomy". Their economic recommendations aim to protect social reproduction from the cold winds of the market. Profoundly suspicious of ECONOMIC GROWTH and affluence, greens are critical not just of capitalism's CONTRADICTIONS, but also of technocratic attempts to control them. Greens are instead enamored of what in the USA is called "bioregionalism": decentralized, participatory, democratic, non-hierarchical, inward-looking political economies (Andruss et al. 1990).

Cooperative enterprises, valuing craftsmanship over mass production, would employ appropriate (human-scale, environmentally benign) technologies to meet genuine human needs (not desires invented by advertising). Green political economies would simultaneously avoid the exploitation of workers and nature. Being influenced by ANARCHISM to the core, bioregional villages would be situated in some natural unit like a watershed, rather than an ecologically problematic form like a state or province. Bioregions would draw on their own natural resources, rather than enmesh themselves in the global trade and monetary systems, the better to live close to the land,

and to remain within the carrying capacity of the region. Local currencies, barter and self-sufficiency would replace wage labor and dependence on remote, profit-obsessed financial institutions.

Fundamentalists and realists

The question of how to get from "here to there," how to transform environmentally rapacious industrial economies into bioregional ecotopias divide green parties. "Fundamentalists" reject any cooperation with established political parties, corporations, and the state. "Realists" argue that some interaction with the current powers-that-be is necessary to realize Green dreams. Realists are consequently willing to enter into coalition governments, to serve as ministers, and to support legislation promoted by establishment parties. The conflict between the camps has been so intense in some national Green parties, including the German, that parties have split into two or more distinct entities.

Realists rule in most Green parties, and counsel a variety of reformist measures to move CAPITALISM closer to environmental responsibility. Greens would have ecological damage factored into the costs of production. They recommend a "contamination tax" levied on industry, agriculture and vehicles relative to the damage caused (Markovits and Gorski 1993). The funds generated would be invested in RESEARCH AND DEVELOPMENT, in order to develop cleaner production and anti-pollution technology. In place of end-of-the-pipe approaches to pollution control, Green parties would outlaw many toxic and dangerous substances, institute "ecological accounting," and enforce the "delinquency principle," whereby the polluter pays for the damage and remediation (Beckenbach et al. 1985). New industrial products would be automatically suspect, and the burden of proof for their safety would shift from consumers and society to producers. Greens favor small and medium-size firms over huge multinationals. The "ecology sector" of the economy, renewable energy generation, public transport, and products made from recycled materials would receive preference (Die Grünen 1980). A Green consumer policy would provide citizens with information about production processes and commodities to help them make wise market choices. The German Greens outlined a conversion process for the German chemical industry that would dismantle especially dangerous lines of production, convert current production toward one "bearable for nature and health," and encourage the development of "soft chemistry" (Die Grünen 1986). Green energy policy demands an "immediate exit" from nuclear power. Dependence on fossil fuels would be supplanted by a reliance upon renewable energy sources like solar, wind and biomass. Conservation is privileged over construction of new power plants. Power generation would be decentralized; ideally, individual homes and apartment buildings could generate their own electricity.

Future prospects

The future prospects of Green parties as an ideological and political economic alternative to mainstream parties appear moderately bright. Enormous obstacles remain, especially in the United States, where the Greens have yet to win many elections. The main obstacles include campaign finance laws that favor corporate-backed candidates, entrenched two-party systems, and skeptical or ignorant publics. But the moves in the early 1990s toward greater accountability on the part of Green elected officials, toward more effective organization and toward structures representative of the parties' grassroots, bode well as ecological issues assume greater prominence around the world.

See also:

ecological feminism; ecological radicalism; environmental policy and politics

Selected references

Andruss, Van et al. (eds) (1990) Home! A

Bioregional Reader, Philadelphia: New Society Publishers.
Beckenbach, Niels *et al.* (1985) *Grüne Wirtschaftspolitik: Machbare Utopien*, Cologne: Kiepenheuer and Witsch.
Die Grünen (1980) *Das Bundesprogramm*, Bonn: Die Grünen.
—— (1986) *Umbauprogramm*, Bonn: Die Grünen.
Frankland, E. Gene and Schoonmaker, Donald (1992) *Between Protest & Power: The Green Party in Germany*, Boulder, CO: Westview Press.
Inglehart, Ronald (1990) *Culture Shift in Advanced Industrial Society*, Princeton, NJ: Princeton University Press.
Markovits, Andrei S. and Gorski, Philip S. (1993) *The German Left: Red, Green and Beyond*, Oxford: Oxford University Press.

STEVE BREYMAN

gross domestic product and net social welfare

Gross domestic product (GDP) or gross national product (GNP) is likely the most widely used macroeconomic indicator. GDP measures the total output of final goods and services produced in a national economy, commonly per annum, in real currency. GDP accounts were developed in the 1930s by Simon Kuznets. Kuznets's charge was to develop a tool that would allow US policy makers to more accurately assess the extent of the crisis facing the US economy in the aftermath of the Great Depression, and to provide an information base for developing successful economic policies. Kuznets started with the obvious: flows of final output produced and value added. Unaccounted for remained those parts of the economy for which statistical data was less readily available: the household sector, the underground economy and the subsistence economy. Kuznets's accounts gained wide recognition, particularly during the late 1930s when they became the basis for analyzing possible bottlenecks in US industrial production as the USA prepared for involvement in the Second World War (see Leontief 1951).

With increased use and familiarity, however, a conceptual leap became obvious: GDP accounts were not simply taken as a measure of an economy's productive capacity but as a measure of welfare. Thus, an increase in final goods and services produced came to be associated with an increase in a nation's well-being. While Kuznets himself warned against this deceptive interpretation of national accounts, it was supported by its consistency with the implicit assumptions of neoclassical welfare theory such as non-satiation and value in exchange.

Problems with GDP

Since the 1960s, the association between increased material output and increased welfare has become increasingly doubtful. Given the conflict between output in final goods and services and the negative externalities generated in the production process, the product–welfare connection has become increasingly questionable. GDP is, perhaps, a measure of potential rather than actual welfare since it relates to production itself rather than direct consumption. Even so, the neglect of stocks in national accounts results in natural resources being exhausted without any visible impact on future potential production (Repetto *et al.* 1989). This is despite the fact that resources often constitute the basis for output generation, particularly in developing countries. A second area of criticism has focused on the fact that "defensive expenditures," that is, expenditures necessary to remedy the negative effects of deteriorating social and environmental systems, are counted as positive flows in GDP accounts. Similarly, expenditures associated with offsetting the disadvantages of urbanization or with providing the technological, financial, legal and legislative services which support complex modern civilization are counted as positive flow entries. Such expenditure would more accurately be counted as intermediate entries or costs.

Third, contributions related to but provided outside the boundaries of market production, such as the physical and emotional care provided in households and communities, or the assimilative and regenerative services provided by nature, remain unaccounted for in standard national accounts. Finally, concern has focused on the limits of monetary measures as appropriate representation of both the material and non-material components of welfare.

Measures of welfare and quality of life

Given these concerns, a variety of conceptual and technical approaches have sought to correct the shortcomings of standard national accounts. Efforts at the US National Bureau of Economic Research (NBER) in the 1960s were aimed at developing improved capital accounts which would include human capital, household services and unpaid production (Eisner 1988). The American Institute of Certified Public Accountants suggested the addition of social indicators, in their publication *Social Measurement*. Zolotas (1981) developed an index of the economic aspects of welfare (EAW). World Bank economist El Serafy (1989) introduced the concept of a "user cost" for natural resources, whereby income derived from depletable resources is transformed into a permanent income stream.

David Morris proposed a physical quality of life indicator (PQLI) which he developed for the Overseas Development Council. Roefi Hueting's (1986) work also emphasizes the physical constraints to welfare creation. He suggests a physical standard of sustainable resources be formulated, such as soil erosion below the replacement rate, to account for environmentally sustainable limits. Nordhaus and Tobin (1973) developed one of the earliest comprehensive measurement alternatives to GDP with the measure of economic welfare (MEW), even though their motivation was to try to prove that taking economic welfare into account would have a negligible effect on GDP. The MEW also became the basis for the Japanese measure of net national welfare (NNW).

Index of sustainable economic welfare

More recent efforts at correcting GDP have sought to build on Norhaus and Tobin's work of developing a comprehensive index which would correct GDP accounts. First published in 1989 in the appendix to Daly and Cobb's book, *For the Common Good*, the index of sustainable economic welfare (ISEW) takes personal consumption as found in national accounts as its starting point and adjusts for income distribution. Estimates for household services, services from household durables and services from government expenditures for infrastructure, health and education are added while twelve other items are deducted. The latter include defensive expenditures of households on health care and education, commuting costs, water, air and noise pollution, loss of wetlands and farmlands and the costs imposed on future generations from depleting non-renewable resources.

A number of countries (including the United Kingdom, Denmark, Germany, the Netherlands and Austria) have since developed ISEW-type indicators which commonly include modifications of the original ISEW indicator to take account of specific categories which reflect the welfare impacts of a particular nation. The Austrian indicator, for example, reformulated the ISEW with the explicit goal of designing a measure of consumption that can be sustained in the future. In the USA, efforts at refining the ISEW are continued in the work of Defining Progress, a San Francisco-based organization which developed the genuine progress indicator (GPI). Being similarly to the ISEW, the GPI is structured around three main categories: (1) accounting for the defensive expenditures necessary to repair social destruction, (2) considering non-renewable energy resources as borrowed from future generations, and (3) accounting for shifts in the functions provided in households and civil society to the market economy. The GPI points to a dramatic difference between GDP and GPI, particularly since the 1970s. Between 1973 and 1994, for example, per capita GDP increased by 73 percent while per capita GPI fell by 45 percent.

In 1990 the United Nations Development

Program (UNDP) published yet another aggregate indicator: the HUMAN DEVELOPMENT INDEX (HDI). Like the ISEW, the HDI is viewed as an alternative to GDP. Its approach, however, is distinctly different. Based on three main components – life expectancy, literacy and purchasing power parity – the HDI develops a ranking of most of the countries of the world. Since 1991, additional categories based on environmental damage, the human freedom index and the ratio between civilian and military budgets have been considered.

The power of an aggregate indicator is obvious: it lies in its simplicity and in its similarity to the commonly used GDP. Its disadvantage is the loss of information invariably associated with the aggregation necessary to develop a single numerical indicator. In contrast, a multi-factored measure may provide more meaningful information, particularly of social and environmental categories which cannot be easily evaluated in monetary terms. The disadvantage of multi-factored measures lies in their interpretation, as some factors may show improvements while others may worsen over time.

Sustainable development and country futures indicators

The most ambitious effort at developing a multi factored indicator has come as a result of the action plan for sustainable development, Agenda 21, put forth at the United Nations Conference on Environment and Development held in Rio de Janeiro in 1992. This plan calls for the development of so-called "sustainable development indicators" (SDIs), since currently used indicators do not provide adequate guidelines for sustainable development. SDIs seek to account for three distinct categories of standards pertinent to SUSTAINABLE DEVELOPMENT: economic, social and environmental indicators. Each set of indicators is expressed in its own dimension: economic indicators in monetary terms, social indicators in human terms and environmental indicators in physical terms (Van Dieren 1995). The overall goal of the indicators is to provide a framework for sustainable intra- and intergenerational equity. Deviations of a present situation from the goals outlined in the SDIs serve both as an indicator of further development needs and as policy guidelines.

Hazel Henderson's "county futures indicators," developed in Jacksonville, Florida, in the 1980s, are another example of a set of multi-faceted indicators. Developed on the local level, they seek to promote broadly communicable and transparent indicators which invite the participation of citizens, and allow the social, cultural and environmental diversity of local communities to become evident in a selected development path. Georgescu-Roegen's critique of arithmomorphic models may be an apt reminder of the fact that changes in welfare reflect evolutionary change and thus may require more than numerically communicable information. He writes:

> To use words, instead of numbers, for truly qualitative changes cannot be represented by an arithmomorphic model. Qualities are not pre-ordered as numbers are by their own special nature. The most relevant part of history is a story told in words, even when it is accompanied by some time series that mark the passage of time.
> (Georgescu-Roegen 1979: 325)

Conclusion

Given the persistent focus on national accounts as an indicator of successful economic policy, the answer may not be in an either/or approach but instead in multiple approaches to dealing with the complexities of development in a less reductionist and more candid fashion.

See also:

environmental and ecological political economy: major contemporary themes; environmental valuation; household production and national income; natural capital; quality of life

Selected references

Daly, H. and Cobb, J. (1989) *For the Common Good*, Boston: Beacon Press.

Eisner, R. (1988) "Extended Accounts for National Income and Product," *Journal of Economic Literature* 26(December): 1611–18.

El Serafy, S. (1989) "The Proper Calculation of Income from Depletable Natural Resources," in Y. Ahmad, S. El Serafy and E. Lutz (eds), *Environmental Accounting for Sustainable Development*, Washington, DC: World Bank, 10–18.

Georgescu-Roegen, N. (1979) "Methods in Economic Science," *Journal of Economic Issues* 13(2): 317–28.

Hueting, R. (1986) "A Economic Scenario for a Conserver Economy," in P. Ekins (ed.), *The Living Economy: a New Economics in the Making*, London: Routledge & Kegan Paul, 242–56.

Leontief, W. (1951) *The Structure of the American Economy: 1919–1929*, 2nd edn, New York: Oxford University Press.

Nordhaus, W. and Tobin, J. (1973) "Is Growth Obsolete?," in M. Moss (ed.), *The Measurement of Economic and Social Performance*, New York: NBER, Columbia University Press.

Repetto, R., Magrath, W., Wells, M., Beer, C. and Rossi, F. (1989) *Wasting Assets: Natural Resources in the National Accounts*, Washington, DC: World Resources Institute.

Stockhammer, E., Hochreiter, H., Obemayr, B. and Steiner, K. (1995) "The ISEW (Index of Sustainable Economic Welfare) as an Alternative to GDP in Measuring Economic Welfare," *Ecological Economics*.

Van Dieren, W. (ed.) (1995) *Taking Nature into Account: A Report to the Club of Rome*, New York: Springer Verlag.

Zolatas, X. (1981) *Economic Growth and Declining Social Welfare*, New York: New York University Press.

SABINE U. O'HARA

H

Harrod's instability principle and trade cycles

Roy Forbes Harrod (1900–78) was educated in Oxford, where he spent most of his teaching life at Christ Church College. He was, however, familiar with Cambridge economics, having spent a term under the guidance of J.M. Keynes in 1922, and having maintained exchanges with Cambridge economists. His contributions, often first-rate and innovative, ranged through a wide variety of topics, the most important of which are economic dynamics, international economics, imperfect competition, and monetary theory and policy. He also wrote the first official biography of Keynes. (For a partial bibliography see Eltis et al. 1970; for a biographical sketch, see Phelps Brown 1980).

Economic dynamics

On the subject of economic dynamics, Harrod maintained that the right approach to the subject consists in studying, as a first stage, a cross-section of an economy in moving equilibrium. The subsequent stages would examine the behavior of the system through time (cycles, growth and secular behavior), and finally would provide policy suggestions. Harrod's notion of dynamics never gained acceptance among orthodox students of growth and cycles. His methodological remarks passed unnoticed, and his contribution was regarded as providing an equation describing (or prescribing) a path of economic growth, characterized by extreme instability along the lines of the competing notion of dynamics propounded by Frisch (1933; for comment see Besomi 1995, 1996). In the 1950s and 1960s, when growth theory was one of the hottest topics, the debates on Harrod's "growth model" mainly concentrated on the instability principle. None of the participants in these debates, however, attempted to place this principle in the context to which – according to Harrod – it belongs, namely, trade cycle theory.

Although Harrod never claimed to have gone with sufficient precision beyond the first stage of dynamics, his first systematic contribution to the subject was a trade cycle theory (Harrod 1936). This was largely based on an epistemological premise Harrod developed in 1934 as a criticism of the traditional line of attack to the problem of economic fluctuations. Trade cycle theory was approached with the supply and demand equations determining the equilibrium quantities and prices. Under the assumption of perfect competition, this equilibrium is stable and any deviation would set in motion forces tending to bring the system back to it.

However, in such a framework, in order to be able to interpret economic fluctuations as deviations from an otherwise stable equilibrium state, it is necessary to imagine that oscillations are kept alive by the permanent alternate movement of exogenous causes such as successions of periods of optimism and pessimism. Against Pigou, Harrod argued that this kind of approach cannot provide a good theory, because it simply turns some exogenous force into a *deus ex machina* on which the burden of the explanation is shifted (Harrod 1934; a similar criticism was put forward by Adolf Lowe, although Harrod was probably not aware of it).

Instability principle

Harrod maintained, instead, that a correct

approach to the cycle should consider at the outset some destabilizing element granting the possibility of movement away from equilibrium. Harrod's instability principle thus originates from the epistemological necessity of dissociating equilibrium from rest, and is a premise rather than a result of Harrod's approach. His first attempt to apply the principle attributed instability to imperfect competition (Harrod 1934), but soon after, in *The Trade Cycle* (Harrod 1936), he succeeded in providing an integrated theory based on a twofold application of the instability principle.

Harrod accepted the traditional conclusion of the stabilizing power of some of the determinants of the entrepreneur's decisions to produce a certain level of output (e.g. the diminishing utility of goods and the increasing disutility of effort). He suggested, however, that appropriate changes in the price level could offset the combined effect of the stabilizing forces. In this case, entrepreneurs would still make rational decisions and maximize their returns, but such equilibrium would no longer be tied to a state of permanent rest (Harrod 1936: ch. 1). The first application of the instability principle to the system of static determinants (i.e. the forces determining the level of output) thus aimed at making movement theoretically conceivable.

At this stage, the causes of motion and the mechanism inducing prices to behave in such an accommodating way were left unexplained. In analogy with statics, Harrod next inquired into the forces making for movement, namely, the distribution of income and the propensity to save, which determine the magnitude of the multiplying effect; and the capital intensity, determining the value of the accelerating effect. If these dynamic determinants balanced each other, continuous and regular growth would result from the interaction of the multiplier and the accelerator. However, nothing ensures that the dynamic forces balance each other. Growth itself rather tends to bring about changes which inevitably, sooner or later, upset equilibrium. The cycle consists in cumulative divergences from such a steady state, which Harrod thought to be unstable. A failure of income to keep rising would depress expectations of consumption, thus inducing, according to the accelerator, a diminishing rate of investment, and consequently – according to the multiplier – bringing forth an even larger fall in the rate of increase of income. The analogy with statics is precise: the instability principle was applied a second time to make the cycle possible, as a deviation from the equilibrium of dynamic forces (Harrod 1936: ch. 2).

In his later writings on dynamics (in particular, "An Essay in Dynamic Theory" (1939) and *Towards a Dynamic Economics* (1948)), Harrod provided a simple formula for growth rates in terms of the interaction of the multiplier and the accelerator. However, he was more concerned with his notion of dynamics than with the trade cycle: although clearly outlined, his cycle theory occupied little space in the subsequent versions.

Conclusion

In spite of Harrod's stress that instability is a condition for the trade cycle (1948: 91–3, 115), commentators interpreted the instability principle as a result to be proved or disproved, rather than as a premise of his reasoning (for a survey of the literature, see Hahn and Matthews 1964). In the earlier years, only a few authors, such as J.R. Hicks (1950) and R.M. Goodwin (1951), took up the challenge and attempted trade cycle modeling which introduced endogenous instability. The interest of Harrod's approach thus lies in the fact that it included at the outset an epistemological reflection on the possibility of trade cycle theorizing, which is lacking in the mathematically more refined models proposed since the 1930s and still prevailing today. A careful study of his original considerations could thus have saved us from the recent complaints (see, for example, Shaw 1992: 611) that modern growth theory explained growth on the grounds of exogenous causes only, and the consequent search for "endogenous" determinants of growth.

See also:

balance of payments constraint; business cycle theories; economic growth; equilibrium, disequilibrium and non-equilibrium; Goodwin cycle and predator–prey models;

Selected references

Besomi, D. (1995) "From *The Trade Cycle* to the 'Essay in Dynamic Theory': The Harrod–Keynes Correspondence, 1937–1938," *History of Political Economy* 27(2).
—— (1996) "Harrod's Dynamics in 1938: An Additional Note on the Harrod–Keynes Correspondence," *History of Political Economy* 28(2).
Eltis, W.A., Scott, M. and Wolfe, J.N. (1970) *Induction, Growth and Trade: Essays in Honour of Sir Roy Harrod*, Oxford: Clarendon Press.
Frisch, R. (1933) "Propagation Problems and Impulse Problems in Dynamic Economics," in *Economic Essays in Honour of Gustav Cassel*, London: Allen & Unwin, 171–205.
Goodwin, R.M. (1951) "The Nonlinear Accelerator and the Persistence of the Business Cycle," *Econometrica* 19(1): 1–17.
Hahn, F.H., and Matthews, R.C.O. (1964) "The Theory of Economic Growth: A Survey," *Economic Journal* 74(December): 779–902.
Harrod, R.F. (1934) "Doctrines of Imperfect Competition," *Quarterly Journal of Economics* 48, (May):442–70.
—— (1936) *The Trade Cycle*, Oxford: Oxford University Press.
—— (1939) "An Essay in Dynamic Theory," *Economic Journal* 49 (March): 14–33.
—— (1948) *Towards a Dynamic Economics*, London: Macmillan.
Hicks, J.R. (1950) *A Contribution to the Theory of the Trade Cycle*, Oxford: Clarendon Press.
Phelps Brown, H. (1980) "Sir Roy Harrod: A Biographical Memoir," *Economic Journal* 90(March): 1–33.
Shaw, G.K. (1992) "Policy Implications of Endogenous Growth Theory," *Economic Journal* 102(May): 611–21.

DANIELE BESOMI

health care in social economics

A social economics approach to health, health care and health economics begins with recognition of the special place health holds in the configuration of human NEEDS. It develops an alternative method for valuing health care to that based on market values, and proceeds to a critical examination of market institutions surrounding the provision of health care in modern economies. Among the casualties of this form of analysis are the atomistic conception of human individuals, traditional supply and demand reasoning regarding health care, and Pareto-efficiency welfare recommendations.

Human needs and health

In their comprehensive and systematic analysis of human need, Doyal and Gough (1991: 54) treat physical health and personal autonomy as the two chief preconditions for human action and interaction in any CULTURE, and thus as the two most basic human needs. Physical health in a POPULATION can be defined as the minimization of death, disability and disease. It concerns the simple question of survival and capacity for ordinary human activity. However, autonomy, as the ability to deliberate and make informed choices, also has a health dimension, as is evident in its requirements as the minimization of mental disorder, cognitive deprivation and restricted opportunities (Doyal and Gough 1991: 172). Thus, broadly speaking, health is not only at the root of any understanding of human need, but it is also subtly intertwined with our view of the human individual. Individuals, whether in economic life or other domains, act most characteristically as we

Disability-adjusted life years

Not surprisingly, then, health has been the focus of many studies of human need, including those generated by a variety of national and international organizations interested in promoting human development. For example, the World Bank's *World Development Report: Investing in Health* (1993), produced in conjunction with the World Health Organization, examines the impact of national and international public finance and public policy on the state of world health This report describes the overall burden of disease and physical impairment on a country-by-country basis, in terms of lost disability-adjusted life years (DALYs). DALYs combine the number of healthy life years lost because of premature mortality with those indirectly lost as a result of disability. One advantage of such measures as the DALY is that they provide an understanding of the health states of individuals in quantity–quality terms. Another advantage is that such measures permit us to value the benefits of health care in need-based rather than market-based terms.

Quality-adjusted life years

DALYs are one type of quality-adjusted life year (QALY) measure used in cost-utility analysis (CUA) to capture the benefits of a quantity of life years gained, weighted by a measure of quality of life, resulting from health care. QALY measures may be constructed using any number of characterizations of quality of life, such as disability, discomfort, limited functioning and so on, that allow discrimination between socially perceived levels of well-being. For example, Kind, Rosser and Williams (1982) distinguished eight categories of disability and four categories of distress to create a thirty-two-cell grid of distinguishable health states. Here the disability factors examined include such things as whether one is unconscious, bedridden, in a wheelchair, unable to perform market work or housework, go outdoors without assistance, and so on; and distress ratings were "none", "mild", "moderate" or "severe". To value these different health states, they then conducted surveys in which individuals were asked to rank these thirty-two health states numerically on a scale from 1 (perfect health) to 0 (death). The resulting median scores were used as social benchmark measures to judge the possible benefits of different types of health care according to the health states they might produce.

QALY values need to be generated through reliable survey methods, so as to reflect the broadest opinion about health needs across all groups and income classes in society. They can then offer a basis for determining how society ought to invest in alternative health care programs. For example, a given investment in early preventive care services is preferred to an equal investment in services for late-life surgical interventions that marginally improve life for a smaller number of individuals for only a few years. This is because preventative care is more likely to produce good health for many individuals for many years. The cost per QALY gained is lower for preventive care.

QALY measures compared with cost–benefit analysis

COST–BENEFIT ANALYSIS (CBA) evaluates benefits in money terms. CBA represents the benefits of alternative health investment plans in terms of the money value of days of work gained, rather than quality of life as avoidance of disability and improvements in basic human functioning. Using CBA, wealthy individuals with high incomes would be able to argue that there ought to be more investment in medical technologies that produce late-life marginal improvements for a small number of individuals, since the money benefits of their gained work days often outweigh the money benefits of work days gained by lower income individuals.

Thus, QALY measures, when designed to elicit judgments regarding basic needs, permit social valuation rather than market valuation of the benefits of health care, and such a social economics of health care combines theorization about quality of life (see, for example, Nussbaum and Sen 1993) with empirical examination of the ways individuals actually value the QUALITY OF LIFE. Moreover, since social and market valuations of the benefits of health care generally support different distributions of health care for modern economies, a social economics of health care also examines how MARKETS distort the distribution and provision of health care.

Income distribution and need fulfillment

A DISTRIBUTION OF INCOME contrary to universal need fulfillment affects high and low income individuals differently. The former pursue luxury consumption, but are able to postpone their transactions, while the latter are constrained to transact for necessities in as short a time as possible. This implies that prices for luxuries are lower and prices of necessities are higher than would be the case were income distributed to fulfill needs. At the same time, differences in income lead the market to overproduce luxuries and underproduce necessities.

Neoclassical supply and demand market analysis rejects these conclusions, because it ignores the distinction between wants and needs, and thus ignores the way in which income distribution in modern economies undermines need fulfillment. This in turn leads it to treat individuals atomistically, as if they were free of social ties that support need fulfillment, and as if differences in income were unrelated to the ability to satisfy needs. The traditional supply and demand view of markets is consequently one of free exchange between equally advantaged, single individuals. However, actual markets for health care services hardly function according to this model.

Health care providers have significantly better understanding of health care technologies than their patients. Individuals seeking health care often feel so much anxiety about their care that they wish to defer decision making to their care providers; and paying for health care often involves social and private insurance systems that separate the purchaser and consumer of health care in time and in person.

Health care institutions

A social economics approach to health and health care seeks to understand the characteristics of health care provision in terms of real world individuals who occupy different sorts of social institutional frameworks arranged to deliver and distribute health care. Though markets often play a role, they must be seen to operate within a larger context that reflects past institutional history and social values. A social economics approach may compare alternative investment strategies according to a needs-based evaluation of prospective benefits. The value of particular health care services, as determined in exchange relationships, should be seen to reflect a process of social valuation that places exchange in a history of constructing social institutions to address health needs. This broader context includes such values as fairness, HUMAN DIGNITY and responsibility as elements in a full account of welfare. Needless to say, this approach goes beyond the narrower view of welfare inherent in the Pareto view of social welfare.

See also:

health inequality; health and safety in the workplace; social economics: major contemporary themes

Selected references

Doyal, L. and Gough, I.A. (1991) *A Theory of Human Need*, New York: Guilford.

Kind, P., Rosser, R. and Williams, A. (1982) "Valuation of Quality of Life: Some Psychometric Evidence," in M. Jones-Lee (ed.), *The Value and Safety of Life*, Amsterdam: North Holland.

Nussbaum, M. and Sen, A. (1993) *The Quality of Life*, Oxford: Clarendon Press.

World Bank (1993) *World Development Report:*

Investing in Health, New York: Oxford University Press.

JOHN B. DAVIS

health inequality

Good health may be defined in specific terms as "freedom from clinically ascertainable disease" (Townsend and Davidson 1988), or generally as "a state of complete physical, mental and social well-being" (World Health Organization definition, quoted in Evans 1984: 4). Health care refers to the "set of goods and services which consumers/patients use solely or primarily because of their anticipated (positive) impact on health status" (Evans 1984: 5). Using economists' terminology, an improvement in health is the objective or outcome of the process of health care. In practice, the relationship is more complex. Improvements in health do not necessarily result from increases in the quantity or quality of health care available. Other factors, such as better nutrition, a cleaner environment, sanitation and better housing, may contribute to an improvement in health. Spending money on health care alone is not necessarily going to result in improvements in health status, particularly in richer countries. Wilkinson (1992) shows that there is a positive relationship between GDP per capita and life expectancy at birth for poor countries only.

Health and socioeconomic status

One of the significant features of improvements in health in industrialized economies over the last twenty-five years has been the inequality in the improvements across socioeconomic groups. Such findings have been recorded in the UK (Townsend and Davidson 1988; Wilkinson 1992), Australia (National Health Strategy 1992) and the United States (Haan *et al.* 1987). The relationship between health and socioeconomic status holds when socioeconomic grouping is defined by either income, education or occupational group. Moreover, the disparity of health status between socioeconomic groups is maintained when there are improvements in overall or aggregate health status of the population.

Factors affecting health differences

Turrell (1995) concluded that the majority view among researchers is that health differences between socioeconomic groups can be attributed to two main factors. These factors emphasize the holistic needs of health care. The first factor is the cultural and behavioral differences in population groups. These differences are generally proxied by educational attainment. Cultural and behavioral differences are assumed to influence mortality and morbidity because of class differences in the consumption of harmful commodities, such as refined foods, tobacco and alcohol. This is also the case for the pursuit of leisure time activities and in the utilization of preventive care, for example, vaccination, antenatal care and contraception.

The second influence includes structural and material factors, which are generally proxied by income level. These factors influence health because of the unequal distribution of resources and wealth which characterizes most societies. The economically disadvantaged have limited access to the resources needed to maintain or improve their health. They are more likely to face inferior housing conditions, such as poor sanitation and crowded, low quality accommodation. They are more likely to be unemployed or, if employed, are less likely to have control over their working environment in terms of conditions, variety of tasks and hours of work. A number of studies have recorded the disparity in health between socioeconomic groups: a more difficult task is to explain and minimize the problem.

Reasons for health inequalities

There are two main explanations for the inequalities in health. The first is the inequality in the DISTRIBUTION OF INCOME and resources. That is, relative poverty is more influential in affecting inequalities in health than absolute poverty. Improving the distribution of income is a difficult task, but nonetheless is an important political and social objective. An example of the influence of an equitable distribution of income is the Japanese economy. It has the most equitable distribution of income and the longest life expectancy of any OECD country (Marmot 1993). A significant distributional issue in the United States, which distinguishes this country among the OECD countries, is the lack of universality of health insurance coverage. Approximately 30 percent of the POPULATION in the United States currently has no health insurance coverage. As this uninsured group is concentrated in lower socioeconomic groups, the reform of health insurance arrangements would address a crucial social issue and may improve the overall health of lower socioeconomic groups.

The second factor that affects health status is the degree to which people have control over their everyday life. People in lower socioeconomic groups tend to have lower participation rates in social networks, activities and less social support; an adverse psychosocial work environment entailing less participation in decision making and more repetitive tasks; a lower sense of personal control over health; and more financial difficulties. Townsend and Davidson (1988) found that, after controlling for all other factors, such as income, education as well as behavioral and social risk factors, people in low socioeconomic groups still have poor health status. An important reason for this is the lack of control that these people have over their lives. They tend to suffer from low self esteem.

Policy implications

What are the policy implications of the presence of health inequalities across socioeconomic groups? One policy approach is to consider the access that persons in lower socioeconomic groups have to health care services. An ideal objective in the delivery of health care is the promotion of equality of utilization for equal health needs (Mooney 1986). Although this may be desirable in an ideal world, it does imply that all the individuals in a society have the same preferences (in relation to health care). This is clearly unrealistic and elitist to the extent that the imposition of equality of utilization ignores individual preferences about whether to consume or not consume health care, and how much to consume. A policy of equal utilization may be justified in circumstances such as compulsory childhood immunization, where social benefits exceed private benefits. A more realistic objective in the delivery of health care is equal access for equal need. This objective takes account of different preferences.

A more important consideration for equalizing health status across socioeconomic groups is the role of the economic and social environment in which people live. Instead of focusing on single risk factors (such as nutrition), or even multiple risk factors for a disease such as coronary heart disease (smoking, fat intake and blood pressure), we need to consider the broader environmental factors that impact on health. These factors include job security, job creation, community development and participatory processes, housing and community design, and environmental pollution. It may be, for example, that greater improvements in the health of lower socioeconomic groups may be achieved by ensuring economic stability rather than increasing health care expenditure. Better socioeconomic conditions for the lower classes will generally improve their diet and expand their knowledge of health issues. A decrease in health inequalities between socioeconomic groups will also result from the elimination of the social divide between the "haves" and "have-nots." The solution to the inequality of health lies not in the medical or health system *per se*, but in the overall economic, social and political environment.

See also:

business cycle theories; collective social wealth; economic growth; health care in social economics; needs; poverty: absolute and relative; rights; social economics: major contemporary themes; social and organizational capital;

social structures of accumulation; unemployment: policies to reduce; unemployment and underemployment; welfare state

Selected references

Evans, Robert G. (1984) *Strained Mercy: The Economics of Canadian Health Care*, Toronto: Butterworths.
Haan, M.N., Kaplan, G.A. and Camacho, T. (1987) "Poverty and Health: Prospective Evidence from the Alameda County Study," *American Journal of Epidemiology* 124: 989–98.
Marmot, Michael G. (1993) "Social Differentials in Health Within and Between Populations," in *Prosperity, Health and Well-Being*, The Eleventh Honda Foundation Discoveries Symposium, October 16–18, 1993, Toronto.
Mooney, Gavin H. (1986) *Economics, Medicine and Health Care*, Brighton: Wheatsheaf.
National Health Strategy (1992) *Enough to Make you Sick: How Income and Environment Affect Health*, Research Paper No. 1, Canberra: Australian Government Publishing Service.
Townsend, Peter and Davidson, Nic (eds) (1988) "The Black Report," in *Inequalities in Health*, London: Penguin.
Turrell, Gavin (1995) "Social Class and Health: A Summary of the Overseas and Australian Evidence," in Gillian M. Lupton and Jake M. Najman (eds), *Sociology of Health and Illness: Australian Readings*, 2nd edn, South Melbourne: Macmillan.
Wilkinson, R.G. (1992) "Income Distribution and Life Expectancy," *British Medical Journal* 304: 165–8.

SANDRA HOPKINS

health and safety in the workplace

The study of occupational health and safety is a neglected area of political economy. The dominance of mainstream economic analysis has led to a concentration on a narrow range of health and safety issues, and a failure to integrate economic influences with the sociological, psychological and institutional determinants of health and safety in the workplace. Globalization, deregulation and increases in the intensity and insecurity of employment are likely to increase the importance of health and safety issues in the future.

One impediment to the development of political economy in this area is that data are often lacking or of poor quality. Data are generally of better quality for industrial accidents than for work-related ill health. The overall cost to a developed economy of industrial accidents has been estimated at around 3 percent of GDP, though US estimates can differ by a factor of 10. Fatal industrial accident rates tend to fall as income per head rises: the fatality rate in manufacturing in Pakistan is over twenty times that for Western European and North American countries. Deindustrialization, the replacement of electro-mechanical by electronic technology, and the advances in medical techniques have all contributed to the decline in economy-wide fatal accident rates.

However, there is no such clear trend in non-fatal accident rates in manufacturing, where post-Fordism and the associated growth of small firms, self-employment and "flexible" working patterns have produced off-setting effects (see FORDISM AND THE FLEXIBLE SYSTEM OF PRODUCTION). Accident rates tend to reflect the intensity and duration of work and studies suggest that the presence of a unionized workforce lowers accident rates. Occupational health data are usually only available for certain well-publicized diseases, such as asbestosis and those prevalent among miners, but even here data are incomplete and household survey-based measures of work-related illnesses suggest huge underreporting in official data.

Mainstream analysis

Mainstream economic analyses of occupational health and safety, following Thaler and Rosen

(1975), utilize the hedonic (i.e. quality-adjusted) pricing model within the context of competitive markets. This approach models workers as choosing between job offers on the basis of the wage premiums offered by employers to undertake jobs with known health and safety characteristics. Initially firms were viewed as largely passive in this process; once worker preferences were known they merely chose the combination of wage premiums and accident-reducing safety expenditure which minimized the costs of a given output.

As a consequence of this approach, empirical work has neglected an examination of the behavior of accident incidence over time in favor of cross-sectional studies seeking to establish the existence of credible wage premiums for accident risk. Dissimilarities in the institutional and macroeconomic environments were neglected in this desire to establish the existence of a wage premium for dangerous jobs across diverse labor markets. The surveys by Viscusi (1993) and Leigh (1989) reach very different conclusions regarding the weight of evidence on the size and stability of these premiums.

The supposed existence of such premiums has been used to justify deregulation of occupational safety. Within the mainstream model, regulation of occupational health and safety either results in additional bureaucracy and administration without affecting overall levels of health and safety, or prevents workers and firms making employment contracts which are mutually beneficial. The mainstream approach has been directly incorporated into occupational health and safety legislation in many countries. Firms are often able to escape prosecution and liability for damages by arguing that the costs of accident prevention would have exceeded the gains from reducing accident risk. Such defenses are often aided by a very narrow interpretation of the costs to workers of accidents and the neglect of costs borne by society as a whole.

In some countries, notably the UK, regulatory bodies have been requested by governments to relax the enforcement of health and safety regulations in times when industry faces recession. In addition to regulations, most developed economies have either worker compensation laws which tax employers to finance payments to victims, or require employers to take out liability insurance in combination with a no-fault system of social insurance.

Minimal labor standards

Globalization and catastrophic industrial accidents, such as that at the Union Carbide plant in Bhopal, India, have added a further dimension to the debate on regulating health and safety in the workplace. Workers and employers in developed economies often share a concern that their ability to compete in world markets may be undermined by the toleration of low health and safety standards in the newly industrialized countries. The twin fears of "unfair competition" and of TRANSNATIONAL CORPORATIONS exporting unsafe production technologies to low-wage economies, has led to demands for the adoption of minimum labor standards and the inclusion of social clauses in international trade agreements (Adamy 1994). From the perspective of firms and governments in the newly industrialized countries, such demands reflect a new form of protection, by which developed economies seek to impose their value judgments, tastes and higher safety costs upon their trading competitors.

Economic power

Mainstream analysis of health and safety at work ignores the inequality of ECONOMIC POWER between workers and employers. Freedom of contract does not necessarily equate to freedom for workers to exercise the right to quit dangerous jobs. In practice, asymmetric information and distortion of accident and health statistics prevent workers from accurately assessing risks. Liquidity constraints and the costs of job changing, especially the penalties from leaving INTERNAL LABOR MARKETS in periods of high unemployment, may prevent even well-informed workers from quitting (Bowles and Gintis 1990). Recognition of the consequences of unequal power in the labor market helps to explain why in severe recessions accident rates in manufacturing can increase by up to a third. From this perspective, the higher accident rates observed among the young is not merely the consequence of inexperience and impulsiveness, but also a reflection of their inability to enter less risky jobs.

Similarly the higher accident rates found in non-unionized and fragmented workforces, such as in the construction sector, reflect the greater ability of employers to exploit workers lacking countervailing power. Radical and heterodox approaches can illuminate two other features: the difficulties which workers face in gaining compensation for accidents in the courts, and governments cutting the resources available for the enforcement of health and safety regulations in periods of economic difficulty. Both can now be interpreted as the natural consequences of CORPORATE HEGEMONY, the subservience of government and the legal system to the interests of the owning and managing classes.

Political economy's neglect of this area is ironic given that in *Das Kapital*, MARX examines in great detail the impact of CAPITALISM on occupational health and safety; an emphasis reflecting his study of the early reports of factory inspectors in Britain. This neglect is further surprising, given the criticisms which radical and other heterodox economists level at the simplistic treatment of labor–capital relations normally found in mainstream economics. It is to be anticipated that as occupational health and safety concerns gain more importance political economists will be more willing to illustrate how their unique tools of analysis can provide additional insights and understanding.

See also:

cost of job loss; exploitation; health care in social economics; health inequality; human capital; labor markets and market power; segmented and dual labor markets

Selected references

Adamy, W. (1994) "International Trade and Social Standards," *Intereconomics*, November–December: 269–77.

Bowles, S. and Gintis, H. (1990) "Contested Exchange: New Microfoundations for the Political Economy of Capitalism," *Politics and Society* 18(2): 165–222.

Leigh, J. Paul. (1989) "Compensating Wages for Jobs-Related Deaths," *Journal of Economic Issues* 23: 823–42.

Thaler, R. and Rosen, S. (1975) "The Value of Saving a Life; Evidence from the Labor Market," in N. Terleckyj (ed.) *Household Production and Consumption*, New York: NBER/Columbia University Press.

Viscusi, W. (1993) "The Value of Risks to Life and Health," *Journal of Economic Literature* 31: 1912–46.

NICK ADNETT

hedge, speculative and Ponzi finance

"Hedge", "speculative" and "Ponzi" finance denote the three different financial positions that business entities can find themselves in. The terms were coined by Hyman Minsky (1919–96) as part of his FINANCIAL INSTABILITY HYPOTHESIS. Hedge finance is a healthy financial position; speculative finance is a situation where problems are starting to emerge; and Ponzi finance is the worst position possible. Minsky explained how the nature of financial dynamics under capitalism endogenously leads the economy to move from hedge to speculative and then to Ponzi finance over time. This may lead to speculative excesses and asset price collapses, especially over the course of business cycles and long waves.

Specific definitions

We can specifically define the three financial positions as follows. Hedge finance is a situation where the business entity is able to finance both the principal sum of debt plus the interest repayments. Cash flow is therefore positive by some margin of safety. This can be shown specifically as follows (see Minsky 1974). Net cash flow is the difference between current corporate income (Y) and current corporate contractual cash commitments (C). Hedge finance is where $Y > C$ (usually by a margin of safety). The other aspect of hedge finance is long-term in nature, reflected in the balance sheet. It occurs when the stock of accumulated or capitalized income – $K(Y)$ – is greater than the accumulated contractual payment commitments over many years – $K(C)$: hence $K(Y) > K(C)$. Thus, expected revenues are greater than debt commitments in all periods.

Speculative finance takes two forms: normal speculative finance, and the more extreme Ponzi finance. Normal speculative finance occurs when companies have to borrow or sell assets to finance their interest repayments. This occurs when the company is having short-term financial difficulties, but is sound in the long run. Specifically, net cash flow is negative since current income is less than current debt flows: $Y < C$, but capitalized income is greater than capitalized debt: $K(Y) > K(C)$.

Then the financial position becomes more problematical as profit declines and interest rates increase, leading to Ponzi finance. This is the situation when long-term expectations become negative, and a large number of business entities become technically insolvent. Specifically, net cash flow is negative: $Y < C$, and capitalized income is smaller than capitalized debt: $K(Y) < K(C)$.

Historical setting

To understand the nature of these financial positions, it is useful to situate the problem historically. Imagine that we are examining the postwar era of capitalist development in an advanced capitalist economy, from the 1940s through to the 1990s. This long wave can be dissected into long wave upswing (1940s–1970s) and downswing (1970s–1990s). During the upswing, the economy is financially robust, since profits are high and interest rates are relatively low. As a result, the economy is likely to be in the hedge finance position, although it might be pushed into the normal speculative position near the peak and recession of the short cycle. Ponzi finance is not common.

However, as we move into long-wave downswing, financial fragility emerges, profitability and interest rates are lower, and debt rates are likely to be higher. During the early to middle phases of the short cycle upswings, the economy is likely to be in hedge finance, but speculative finance emerges during the high reaches of the cycle, and much Ponzi finance during the deep recessions of the mid-1970s, the early 1980s and the early 1990s. This movement into speculative and Ponzi finance became particularly pronounced during the speculative excesses of the 1980s, the stock market and property market crashes of the late 1980s and the deep recession of the early 1990s.

Endogenous process

Many heterodox authors argue that there is an endogenous periodic process leading from hedge to speculative and on to Ponzi finance. An important part of the explanation is the problem of excessive positive expectations of the future leading firms to overinvest in productive capital in relation to the long-term trend towards deep recessions. Firms finance expansion partly by debt, but as the expected profits eventually decline asset prices deteriorate sharply. Minsky places critical importance on rising interest rates during the high points in the cycles of a long wave downswing leading to the movement to even greater debt and Ponzi finance. Others (for instance, Wolfson 1992) place more emphasis on the excessive expectations declining in the face of lower profitability as asset prices deteriorate and debt rises.

Conclusion

An increasing amount of work is being undertaken on these financial positions, and especially the nature of the processes leading from hedge to speculative and then Ponzi finance.

hegemony

There is much potential here for empirical work into the nature of the financial positions through historical time.

See also:

financial crises; liability management; long waves of economic growth and development; Minsky's Wall Street paradigm

Selected references

Dymski, Gary and Pollin, Robert (1994) *New Perspectives in Monetary Macroeconomics: Explorations in the Tradition of Hyman P. Minsky*, Ann Arbor, MI: University of Michigan Press.
Minsky, Hyman (1974) "The Modelling of Financial Instability: An Introduction," *Modelling and Simulation* 5.
—— (1982) *Can "It" Happen Again: Essays on Instability and Finance*, Armonk, NY: M.E. Sharpe, ch. 10.
Wolfson, Martin (1992) *Financial Crises: Understanding the Postwar U.S. Experience*, Armonk, NY: M.E. Sharpe.

PHILLIP ANTHONY O'HARA

hegemony

Hegemony is a concept associated with political theory and the writings of the Italian social theorist Antonio Gramsci (Gramsci 1988, 1991, 1994). During the 1920s, Gramsci critically analyzed capitalism, arguing that its success by the early twentieth century was in part due to its ability to "rule by hegemony" rather than by "coercion" or brute military power (Fiori 1971). Consequently, hegemony came to mean "rule by the power of ideas," whereby a system like CAPITALISM can sustain itself without being a police state.

Hegemony frequently means the subordination of one group by another without the direct threat of violence. It should not be confused with propaganda or "brainwashing." With hegemonic rule a system can have social stability among a consenting or submissive population who is also subordinate and exploited. Such was the case, according to Gramsci, for all modern systems including capitalism.

Exploited yet conservative

Hegemony became important at the end of the nineteenth century, because many critics of capitalism realized that the "workers of the world" were not about to "unite" and overthrow their oppressors as Karl MARX had predicted a half-century earlier. Working people had made enough wage gains and improvements in their working conditions that they had "more to lose than their chains." Workers were becoming more conservative and less revolutionary as capitalism matured. Yet, socialist critics still believed it to be fundamentally unjust and exploitative. Might workers support a system that actually exploited them? What forces determined their consciousness?

Consciousness of workers

"Class consciousness," as understood by the orthodox Marxists at the turn of the century, implied that exploited workers would eventually become conscious of the capitalist system as the cause of their EXPLOITATION. Their theoretical view held that class or socialist consciousness would be a direct effect, or epiphenomenon, caused by the degraded material conditions of the working majority.

However, there was a growing suspicion that the consciousness of workers was the result of more than just the basic economic conditions that they experienced. Theorists like Karl Korsch, Georg Lukacs and Antonio Gramsci began to examine the role that culture and ideas had on workers' attitudes about capitalism. They questioned the extent to which economic conditions alone determined consciousness. Another group of German Marxists associated with what became the "Frankfurt School" (for example, Max Horkheimer, Theodore Adorno and Herbert Marcuse (Wiggerhaus 1994)) examined this same problem. They were concerned that capitalist hegemony was so effective that both the vision and realization of a more just and democratic economy would be eclipsed.

By the Second World War it appeared that workers might not only embrace capitalism but FASCISM as well. Gramsci's writings, along with the insights of the Western or neo-Marxists mentioned above, suggested that consciousness has much to do with how people "experience" their "everyday life" in capitalism. They disputed the economic determinism of orthodox Marxism. For example, workers may experience capitalism as "opportunity," as "economic freedom" or as "individual liberty," rather than as exploitation. If so, they may consider it the "best of all possible worlds." Hegemony suggests that people have differing attitudes about their economic system, depending upon how they experience it.

Cultural web

On the other hand, hegemony means that there are many ideas originating in spheres such as religion, politics, the family and social customs that together form a cultural web. This cultural web is endogenous to experience and becomes part of how someone experiences living within a given system, be it consumer capitalism or Soviet communism. The simplest way to understand hegemony is to recognize that a political economic system works well and lasts longer when its population believes in it. In the nineteenth century Marx thought that workers would quit believing in capitalism and overthrow it. In the twentieth century Gramsci and the Western Marxists have used the concept of hegemony to explain why workers have not quit believing in capitalism.

This raises related questions of why most working people in the industrial nations continue to embrace capitalism and what is the actual character of capitalist hegemony? Thorstein VEBLEN and institutional political economy have made important contributions here. Veblen maintained that all economic systems are embedded in a cultural web, and in capitalism the cultural web is primarily "pecuniary" (Veblen 1899). Pecuniary culture, for Veblen and institutionalists, is a dimension of the socialization process that occurs as people experience life. He also stated that both workers and the business class become preoccupied and fixated on their own individual status in comparison to others. In Veblen's best known book, *The Theory of the Leisure Class* (1899), he suggests that capitalism creates the cultural environment of "consumerism." People come to believe that not only is the "good life the good*s* life," but that the "good*s* life" is the ticket to winning the game of "I am better than you."

Consumerism and pecuniary culture

The logic of consumerism implies that the cultural and ideological hegemony of capitalism is based upon workers' judgment that capitalism is good because it creates a multitude of goods for both happiness and social/self-esteem. Therefore, if workers continue to hold the "more is better" attitude, and capitalism is able to produce ever higher wages for ever higher consumption, then the cultural hegemony of capitalism – that is, consumerism – creates a stable social system without the need for "rule by coercion." To the extent that people experience capitalism as the "smorgasbord of choice," with plenty of goods and "opportunities" to obtain them, then hegemony is effective.

In 1958 this institutionalist theme was further developed by John Kenneth GALBRAITH in *The Affluent Society*. In this classic statement on consumerism, Galbraith argues that the market economy has a built-in bias toward the production of private consumer goods, and, as a consequence, people begin to view their happiness and fulfillment in terms of the quantity of private goods they can buy. The downside of this, as Galbraith suggests, is that the quality of social and public life simultaneously deteriorates. So cultural hegemony continues to evoke a malleable, middle-class labor force dedicated to the maxim of "happiness through buying," while "private affluence conceals public squalor."

Shortly after Galbraith published *The Affluent Society*, one of Western Marxism's leading theoreticians, Herbert Marcuse, published his book *One Dimensional Man*. His argument paralleled Galbraith's by examining how the logic of the market creates a narrow, "one-dimensional" individual, whose life focus is almost exclusively devoted to "happiness through buying." Both of these classic statements explain how the hegemony of capitalism creates a contented labor force, still willing and able to work hard in order to buy self-esteem and happiness at capitalism's "smorgasbord of choice."

By the end of the Second World War, workers in most Western nations were willing to surrender what interest they had in meaningful, participatory work for the easier life devoted to higher wages and more consumer goods. In effect, so long as capitalism could "deliver the goods," workers would accept its faults, injustices and alienation. This becomes the central message of capitalism's "pecuniary culture" and its hegemony.

An alternative hegemony?

Yet several questions remain. Does the notion of hegemony imply that a system like capitalism cannot be changed? What forces might emerge that effectually challenge the hegemonic rule of capitalism? Further, do leftists believe that a post-capitalist economy that is fully democratic and just might also require a type of hegemony?

Most leftists since Gramsci and Veblen argue that the existence of capitalism's cultural hegemony is not monolithic. To this day, most remain sceptical that capitalism is eternal (see FUTURE OF CAPITALISM). They are convinced that social forces and popular movements will at some point reject the ideological pillar that the "good life is the good*s* life."

Veblen and Marx agreed that political economic systems are continuously evolving, and Gramsci believed that a new form of "socialist hegemony" may evolve as well (Laclau and Mouffe 1985). Now, at the close of the twentieth century, many leftists look to the ecology and environmental movements as the seeds of change (see ENVIRONMENTAL AND ECOLOGICAL POLITICAL ECONOMY: MAJOR CONTEMPORARY THEMES). The issue of global ecological sustainability has raised the prospect that quantitative growth has limits and that the QUALITY OF LIFE is more important. It is clearly possible that these movements could result in a new consciousness for the twenty-first century in which humankind asserts the values of PARTICIPATORY DEMOCRACY AND SELF-MANAGEMENT, global justice and sustainability over those associated with consumerism. If so, market hegemony might yield to a novel form of hegemony linked to justice and global sustainability.

See also:

alienation; conspicuous consumption and emulation; corporate hegemony; hegemony in the world economy; Galbraith's contribution to political economy; ideology; institutional political economy: major contemporary themes

Selected references

Agger, Ben (1979) *Western Marxism: An Introduction*, Santa Monica, CA: Goodyear.

Fiori, Guiseppe (1971) *Antonio Gramsci: Life of a Revolutionary*, New York: Dutton.

Galbraith, John Kenneth (1958) *The Affluent Society*, New York: Houghton Mifflin.

Gramsci, Antonio (1988) *A Gramsci Reader: Selected Writings 1916–1935*, ed. David Forgacs, London: Lawrence & Wishart.

—— (1991) *Prison Notebooks*, New York: Columbia University Press.

—— (1994) *Antonio Gramsci: Pre-Prison Writings*, ed. Richard Bellamy, New York: Cambridge University Press.

Laclau, Ernesto and Mouffe, Chantal (1985) *Hegemony and Socialist Strategy: Towards A Radical Democratic Politics*, London: Verso.

Marcuse, Herbert (1964) *One-Dimensional Man*, London: Routledge.

Veblen, Thorstein (1899) *The Theory of the Leisure Class*, London and New York: Penguin, 1994.

Wiggerhaus, Rolf (1994) *The Frankfurt School:*

Its History, Theories, and Political Significance, Cambridge: Polity Press.

DOUG BROWN

HEGEMONY, CORPORATE: *see* corporate hegemony

hegemony in the world economy

Definition and main issues

Derived from the Greek word for "authority," "rule," or "to lead," hegemony is most commonly deemed to exist in the world economy when one state predominates (an alternative cultural definition is also discussed below). Thus, Immanuel Wallerstein defines hegemony as "that situation in which the ongoing rivalry between the so-called "great powers" is so unbalanced that one power is truly *primus inter pares*; that is, one power can largely impose its rules and its wishes (at the very least by effective veto power) in the economic, political, military, diplomatic, and even cultural arenas" (Wallerstein 1984: 38).

Hegemonic stability theory (HST), which seeks to examine the effects of hegemony, has spawned a vast array of literature and much lively debate in the field of INTERNATIONAL POLITICAL ECONOMY. Robert Keohane introduced the term "hegemonic stability theory" in 1980, in reference to early writings on the subject by Charles Kindleberger, Robert Gilpin, and Stephen Krasner (Keohane 1980: 136–7). In its traditional version, HST asserts that a relatively open and stable international economic system is most likely to exist when there is a hegemonic state with two characteristics: it has a sufficiently large share of resources that it is able to provide leadership, and it is willing to pursue policies necessary to create and maintain a liberal economic order. As Duncan Snidal notes, a hegemon's methods of exerting leadership range from "benevolent" at one end of the spectrum to "exploitative" or "coercive" at the other end (Snidal 1985: 585–6). When a global hegemon is lacking or a hegemon is declining in power, it is more difficult – but not impossible – to maintain economic openness and stability.

Most theorists agree that hegemonic conditions have occurred at least twice, under Britain in the nineteenth century, and under the United States after the Second World War. Some writers also maintain that the United Provinces (the present-day Netherlands) was a hegemon in the mid-seventeenth century, but most feel that its influence was not comparable with British and American influence during their hegemonic periods.

According to the traditional version of hegemonic stability theory, Britain's industrial development made it the leading state in the global political economy by the 1820s, and this was also the period when Britain moved to a low-tariff policy. The repeal of the Corn Laws in 1846 opened the British market to Continental grain exports, and other European countries followed Britain's lead by reducing their own bilateral tariffs. However, British hegemony declined from the 1880s onward, and it was unable to counteract growing moves toward protectionism.

Charles Kindleberger argues that the 1929 GREAT DEPRESSION during the interwar period was particularly severe because Britain was no longer able, and the United States was not yet willing, to take hegemonic responsibility for stabilizing the global economy (Kindleberger 1973: 291–307). After the Second World War, the United States was more willing to assume the role of hegemonic leader, and as in the British hegemonic period this contributed to a new openness in the world economy and a dramatic growth of international transactions. However, American hegemonic power began to decline in the late 1960s and the early 1970s, and this resulted in growing instability and trade protectionism.

Contentious issues

As Susan Strange notes, "today there are

variants of hegemonic theory to suit most political tastes" (Strange 1987: 557). Analysts have criticized virtually all aspects of the theory, some simply calling for revisions, and others questioning the very premises of the theory. We focus here on five questions which have been major sources of division among theorists:

- What is hegemony?
- Does a hegemon contribute to economic openness and stability?
- Can an open and stable world economy exist without hegemony?
- Is US hegemony declining?
- Is there a candidate to replace the United States as global hegemon?

What is hegemony?

Regarding the first question, most international relations theorists define "hegemony" in terms of leadership by a state (or states) in the international system (as discussed above). However, the Italian Marxist Antonio Gramsci used the term "HEGEMONY" in a cultural sense to connote the complex of ideas used by social groups to assert their legitimacy and authority. While Gramsci wrote primarily about domestic politics, neo-Gramscian writers such as Robert Cox, Stephen Gill and Giovanni Arrighi have extended Gramsci's ideas on hegemony to the international level. For example, Cox writes that hegemony exists when "the dominant state creates an order based ideologically on a broad measure of consent," which ensures "the continuing supremacy of the leading state or states and leading social classes but at the same time offer[s] some measure or prospect of satisfaction to the less powerful" (Cox 1987: 7). Cox has also argued that, in this age of increasing internationalization of production and exchange, a transnational historic bloc may be developing. The main institutions in this bloc are the largest transnational corporations, international banks, international organizations such as the International Monetary Fund and World Bank, and international elements in the most powerful capitalist states.

With the development of a transnational bloc, class relations can now be viewed on a global scale. A crucial element of the transnational bloc is the power and mobility of transnational capital, which is putting both national labor and national business groups on the defensive. The neo-Gramscian views clearly enrich our understanding by focusing on aspects of hegemony which are not adequately covered in the state-centric definitions (see CLASS ANALYSIS OF WORLD CAPITALISM).

Does a hegemon promote stability?

Empirical studies of this issue have come up with mixed results. The SOCIAL STRUCTURES OF ACCUMULATION school include US hegemony in the 1940s–1960s as one of the important institutional factors promoting stable relations underlying profit and accumulation for the advanced capitalist economies. They also show that declining US hegemony in the 1970s–1990s has adversely affected the environment for growth and accumulation. Critics argue that the effects of hegemony on the top country's economic policies must be examined on a sectoral basis. It is also argued that domestic variables and other factors, such as surplus capacity, sometimes have a greater effect than hegemony on the openness of economic relations among states.

Is stability possible without hegemony?

The third question relates to the possibility of maintaining a stable and open economy in the absence of hegemony. Many critics question the traditional pessimistic predictions about the effects of hegemonic decline. For example, Robert Keohane argues that it is easier to maintain stable and open "international regimes" than it is to create them initially. While US hegemony may have been necessary to establish the trade and monetary regimes after the Second World War, the decline of US hegemony would not necessarily lead to a collapse of these regimes. Although "regimes become more difficult to supply" after hegemony, the demand for them persists because they "facilitate mutually beneficial agreements among states" (Keohane 1980: 195). Thus, the incentives to cooperate among major states may be sufficient to maintain open regimes after hegemony.

Has US hegemony declined?

Some of the most vigorous debate has surrounded the fourth question as to whether or not US hegemony is in fact declining. The earliest literature on hegemonic stability theory appeared in the 1970s, and theorists such as Robert Gilpin simply assumed that US hegemony was declining because of US economic difficulties at the time. A number of theorists continue to be "declinists," and some view the decline of hegemony as almost inevitable. For example, some world-system theorists such as Wallerstein have written about cycles of rising and declining hegemony, and the relationship between these hegemonic cycles and economic cycles (see LONG WAVES OF ECONOMIC GROWTH AND DEVELOPMENT; WORLD-SYSTEMS ANALYSIS).

In recent years, however, a number of "renewalists" have challenged the assumption that the United States is a declining hegemon. The United States, it is argued, continues to have a considerable amount of cooptive power (also referred to as "structural" or "soft" power), since it is often successful in setting the agenda and in getting others to follow its preferences. In explaining the continued US influence, renewalists often criticize declinists for failing to consider cultural and military as well as economic factors. Renewalists also emphasize the fact that, while US economic power has declined in a relative sense since the end of the Second World War, it continues to be the most important single country with the widest range of resources. Finally, some renewalists attribute current global economic problems more to divisive domestic politics in the United States than to any significant decline of American hegemonic power.

Are there candidates to replace US hegemony?

The fifth question of interest here is whether or not there is an obvious candidate to replace the United States as global hegemon. An extensive amount of literature exists on the question of whether Japan could be the next global hegemon. While some writers have taken a rather positive view of Japan's prospects, most analysts today are skeptical about Japan's ability and willingness to lead. There has also been some speculation about the European Union's leadership prospects, but problems with developing economic and monetary union indicate that the EU would have to become a far more cohesive unit than it is at present. Many analysts point to the fact that global leadership is becoming more collective in nature, and that the United States must, therefore, accept the fact that its ability to act unilaterally is declining.

Nevertheless, the multidimensional nature of US power – encompassing military, political, economic, scientific and ideological resources – gives it a strong position to lead the collectivity. Some neo-Gramscian theorists have argued, on the other hand, that transnational processes could preclude any state – or group of states – from being hegemonic. Thus, Stephen Gill has indicated that "in response to the question, 'hegemony for whom?' the answer for the next century could well be internationally mobile capital" (Gill 1993: 105).

Conclusion

The hegemonic stability theory has contributed to a wide range of discussion and debate among scholars of international political economy. This material illustrates well the linkages between economics and politics, and is an illustration of political economy at its best. Many hypotheses have emerged that link to important questions of growth, stability, world war and peace. It is a vibrant field of inquiry.

See also:

colonialism and imperialism: classic texts; core–periphery analysis; cycles and trends in the world capitalist economy; global crisis of world capitalism; global liberalism; regulation approach

Selected references

Arrighi, Giovanni (1994) *The Long Twentieth Century: Money, Power, and the Origins of Our Times*, London: Verso.

Cox, Robert W. (1987) *Production, Power, and World Order: Social Forces in the Making of History*, New York: Columbia University Press.

Gill, Stephen (1993) "Global Finance, Monetary Policy and Cooperation among the Group of Seven, 1944–92," in Philip G. Cerny (ed.), *Finance and World Politics: Markets, Regimes and States in the Post-Hegemonic Era*, London: Edward Elgar.

Gilpin, Robert (1987) *The Political Economy of International Relations*, Princeton, NJ: Princeton University Press.

Keohane, Robert O. (1980) "The Theory of Hegemonic Stability and Changes in International Economic Regimes, 1967–1977," in Ole R. Holsti, Randolph M. Siverson and Alexander L. George (eds), *Change in the International System*, Boulder, CO: Westview, 131–62.

Kindleberger, Charles P. (1973) *The World in Depression 1929–1939*, Berkeley: University of California Press.

Krasner, Stephen D. (1976) "State Power and the Structure of International Trade," *World Politics* 28(April): 317–47.

Snidal, Duncan (1985) "The Limits of Hegemonic Stability Theory," *International Organization* 39(4): 579–614.

Strange, Susan (1987) "The Persistent Myth of Lost Hegemony," *International Organization* 41(4): 551–74.

Wallerstein, Immanuel (1984) "The Three Instances of Hegemony in the History of the Capitalist World-Economy," in Immanuel Wallerstein, *The Politics of the World-Economy: The States, the Movements and the Civilizations*, London: Cambridge University Press.

THEODORE COHN

Heilbroner's worldly philosophy

"Worldly philosophy" is a term that has its origins in Robert L. Heilbroner's famous book, *The Worldly Philosophers* first published in 1952. This work is an account of the "lives, times and ideas of the great economic thinkers," written while he was still a graduate student at the New School for Social Research. Over the years, however, the term has come to be also associated with Heilbroner's own thought, itself inseparably intertwined with both his interpretation of the history of economic thought and his vision and analysis of CAPITALISM.

This 1952 work marks the beginnings of Heilbroner's public expressions of skepticism regarding mainstream economics. He is concerned with its unacceptable and damaging ahistorical, uncritical, overly formalist, methodological individualist, and positivist character. At the same time, he expresses a hope that a revived POLITICAL ECONOMY might provide a framework for a greater understanding of the deep structures of contemporary capitalism. Such an approach could serve as the basis for constructive socioeconomic and political change.

Early work

Heilbroner's early work dealt with the dramatic scenarios of CLASSICAL POLITICAL ECONOMY, especially the work of Adam Smith, David Ricardo, Thomas Malthus, Karl MARX and John Stuart Mill, as well as Joseph SCHUMPETER, Thorstein VEBLEN and John Maynard KEYNES, who are viewed as continuing the classical tradition of treating the economy as being historically and institutionally situated. The classical scenarios depicted the almost inexorable movement of the capitalist economic system, with its "laws of motion," systematic tendencies leading to some predetermined destination. Underlying the system's movement were a variety of factors, both economic and non-economic. In other words, the trajectory of the system was inseparable from both (a) the wider sociopolitical context within which the economy is situated, and (b) the subjective drives and behavioral tendencies of historical agents, which both shape and are shaped by changing socioeconomic and political structures.

Marx's analysis of capitalism is seen as being thoroughly in this tradition, but his vision of socialism as a possible alternative system represents a crucial break with the classics, concerned as it is with historical possibility. J.S. Mill is viewed as a transitional figure, insofar as his work illustrates a growing awareness of the possibility of human interference into the trajectory of the system, and thus a significant decrease in the determinacy of the trajectory. Large-scale structural and technological transformation, socioeconomic crises and the increasing presence of the state in economic affairs set the stage for Schumpeter, Veblen and Keynes, each with their own vision of the future toward which the system may be heading. Worldly philosophy, then, is very much a historical economics, in the sense of including economic history, the history of ideas and the mutual impact of material and ideological forces upon secular historical transformations.

Values and interpretation

Heilbroner's initial fascination with the worldly philosophers' prognoses led to his analyses of the economic, political, cultural and sociopsychological drives, motivations and propensities underlying production, distribution and exchange. In these investigations, Heilbroner adopted his own versions of Schumpeter's notions of "vision" and "analysis." Whereas for Schumpeter, "analysis" had a kind of "cleansing" effect, which prevented the necessarily ideological nature of the "pre-analytical cognitive act" from tainting the scientific endeavor, for Heilbroner economic theory is inescapably value laden. Biases are always present, at times lurking just beneath the surface but often emerging in the form of assumptions which determine the content of their analytical categories and the direction of their prognostications. All inquiry is necessarily interpretive. However, socioeconomic analysis is additionally complicated by the fact that the object of inquiry is human beings, who must interpret the world which they inhabit and interact with other human beings. Thus, the social inquirer operates in a context of multiple layers of interpretation, or what has been called the "double hermeneutic" (see VALUE JUDGMENTS AND WORLD VIEWS).

More often, it is the failure to employ a self-reflective and critical approach, explicitly recognizing the sociopolitical underpinnings and implications of economic inquiry, that results in blind spots for the economist. The necessarily interpretive nature of economic inquiry means that the very object of inquiry cannot be taken to be self-evident. The "economy" is an abstraction from the social totality, and thus defining "the object" is a task which will influence the nature and direction of analysis. Heilbroner has long advocated "material provisioning" as the central problematic of the political economist: that is, providing the theoretical and empirical foundations for improving the material and cultural "lot" of human beings.

Is worldly philosophy still possible?

In recent years, Heilbroner has questioned whether, under contemporary circumstances, worldly philosophy is still possible. He believes that scenarios and visions do not lend themselves to formal analytical procedures. More importantly, he believes that the economic behaviors that set the system on its path have become less dependable, while political intervention has become more strategic. An instrumental approach, in Lowe's sense, thus becomes more appropriate, with "blueprints depicting possible routes from present realities to desired destinations" replacing "scenarios depicting a future immanent in the present" (Heilbroner 1992: 381; see also Heilbroner 1994a; Heilbroner and Milberg 1995: 118ff; LOWE'S INSTRUMENTAL METHOD).

Despite his doubts, however, Heilbroner continues to express the hope that the "irrelevant scholasticism" of contemporary neoclassical economics (Heilbroner 1994b: 8) might be replaced with a reinvigorated political economy. Political economy may "perhaps [be] resurrected by a corps of dissenting economists," employing a framework that "take[s] full cognizance of the sociopolitical realities of our time, whatever the difficulties they may pose for the construction of elegant models.... [A] rekindling of the tradition of political economy is within the realm of possibility. That would indeed be a happy ending to the teachings of the worldly philosophy" (Heilbroner 1996: 336).

Selected references

Heilbroner, Robert L. (1974) *An Inquiry into the Human Prospect,* New York: W.W. Norton.
—— (1985) *The Nature and Logic of Capitalism,* New York: W.W. Norton.
—— (1990a) "Analysis and Vision in the History of Modern Economic Thought," *Journal of Economic Literature* 28: 1097–1114.
—— (1990b) "Economics as Ideology," in W. Samuels (ed.), *Economics as Discourse,* Boston: Kluwer.
—— (1992) "Is A Worldly Philosophy Still Possible?: Adolph Lowe as Analyst and Visionary," *Review of Social Economy* 50(2): 374–82.
—— (1993) *21st Century Capitalism,* New York: W.W. Norton & Co.
—— (1994a) "Writing about the Economic Future," in M.A. Bernstein and D.E. Adler (eds), *Understanding American Economic Decline,* Cambridge: Cambridge University Press.
—— (1994b) "Vision in Economic Thought," *Journal of Economic Issues* 28(2): 325–9.
—— (1996) *Teachings From the Worldly Philosophy,* New York: W.W. Norton & Co.
Heilbroner, Robert L. and Milberg, William (1995) *The Crisis of Vision in Modern Economic Thought,* Cambridge: Cambridge University Press.

MATHEW FORSTATER

heterogeneous capital and labor

It is often suggested that theorists in the tradition of Piero SRAFFA (1960) are prone to insist on the heterogeneity of capital. If this statement is to provide a useful starting point for our discussion, it must first be noted that there is, of course, no need to insist on the real-world importance of heterogeneous capital goods, or indeed of different kinds of concrete labor. What needs to be insisted on is, rather, that this heterogeneity be adequately reflected in economic theory. The basic issue therefore is not whether economic theorists should account for heterogeneous capital goods or for different types of labor, but rather whether either of these can or must be aggregated, and if so, by which method(s) such an "aggregation" (or "reduction") can or should be accomplished.

Aggregate capital

The problem of the "aggregation" of heterogeneous capital goods has been a major concern of both classical and (early) neoclassical economists alike. The very simple reason for this is that, in a capitalist economy with free competition, a uniform rate of profit on the value of capital must be obtained. Any theory of distribution, whether it is based on the neoclassical idea of relative scarcities of different factors of production or on the classical concept of a social surplus, is therefore confronted with the problem of somehow having to "aggregate" heterogeneous capital goods. In the SURPLUS APPROACH TO POLITICAL ECONOMY the general rate of profit is conceptualized, in physical terms, as the ratio between the social surplus and the social capital. Since the two commodity aggregates generally differ in composition, they cannot be compared unless they are expressed as value magnitudes.

The classical economists sought to solve this problem by relating the exchange values of the commodities to the quantities of labor directly and indirectly required to produce them, so that the two magnitudes could be expressed as different amounts of labor. However, as is well known, the determination of the general rate of profit based on labor-value reasoning is flawed: the rate of profit must rather be determined simultaneously with relative prices (Sraffa 1960). The aggregate "quantity of capital," as a value magnitude, cannot be ascertained independently of, or prior to, the distribution of income.

Aggregate capital and factors of production

Neoclassical approaches to the theory of value and distribution generally start from given initial endowments with goods and factors of production, including the endowments with capital (goods). The crucial concept in the traditional version of marginal productivity theory is that of a factor called "capital," the demand and supply of which determines the profit rate, in a similar way as the demand and supply of labor is taken to determine the wage rate. However, in order to be consistent with the concept of a long-period competitive equilibrium, the capital equipment of the economy must be expressed as a value magnitude. If it were conceived as a set of given physical amounts of capital goods, only a short-period equilibrium, characterized by differential rates of return on the supply prices of the various capital goods, could be established. The formidable problem of the marginalist approach therefore consisted of finding a "capital" aggregate, the "quantity" of which could be expressed independently of the profit rate. As the CAPITAL THEORY DEBATES of the 1960s and 1970s showed, this is not possible except in very special cases.

To avoid a common misunderstanding, it needs emphasizing that it is not only the "aggregate production function" versions of NEOCLASSICAL ECONOMICS (including, of course, not only "macro" but also "micro" production functions in which capital goods are represented by their aggregate value) which have been shown to be inconsistent. No theory that seeks to provide an explanation of long-period normal prices and the distribution of income, in terms of the balance of the supply of and demand for the services of various "factors of production," can overcome the problem associated with "capital" as a single value magnitude (Garegnani 1970). Moreover, it has recently been argued that "the difficulties associated with the demand for 'capital' in the traditional long-period versions have to be present also in the contemporary short-period versions of neoclassical theory" (Garegnani 1990: 60), i.e. those based on the methods of intertemporal or temporary equilibria. Since these versions encompass (gross) investment and (gross) saving functions, they also cannot overcome the difficulties associated with the problem of "capital" as a single magnitude (Kurz and Salvadori 1995: 464–7).

Reduction of heterogeneous labor

It is sometimes suggested that theorists in the Sraffian tradition have no good reason for emphasizing the heterogeneity of capital goods but not that of labour, and that the existence of heterogeneous labor would pose serious problems for modern classical analyses. Their good reason for this lies in the fact that different types of labor do not need to be aggregated and can receive different wages in long-period equilibrium (while capital goods have to be aggregated, in value terms, since a uniform rate of profit on the value of capital must be obtained). Heterogeneous labor can indeed be allowed for very easily in a modern classical analysis. Consider the price vector **p** of a single product system, with **A** as the $n \times n$ matrix of material inputs; **L** as the $n \times s$ matrix of labor inputs for s different types of labor; **w** as an $s \times 1$ vector of wage rates; r as the

445

(uniform) rate of profits, and **d** as a $1 \times n$ row vector which serves as a standard of value. We therefore have:

$$\mathbf{p} = (1+r)\mathbf{Ap} + \mathbf{Lw} \qquad (1)$$
$$\mathbf{dp} = 1 \qquad (2)$$

The classical economists, who sought to determine the rate of profits by using the LABOR THEORY OF VALUE, proposed to use wage differentials as "reduction coefficients," which means that the different kinds of labor are weighted by their relative wage rates, so as to obtain the well-known price system

$$\mathbf{p} = (1+r)\mathbf{Ap} + w\mathbf{l} \qquad (3)$$

with $w = w_k$, $\mathbf{l} = \mathbf{Lw}$, where **w** is an $s \times 1$ vector which consists of elements w_i/w_k for $i = 1, 2, \ldots, s$. While such a "reduction" would in general be possible at any point of time, it would be compatible with the concept of long-period positions only if the wages structure does not change with changes in the rate of profit or in the methods of production (Kurz and Salvadori 1995: 325).

It should be emphasized, however, that in order to determine the rate of profit, or to analyze surplus labor, there is no need for a "reduction" of heterogeneous labor. The classical proposition that the rate of profit depends only on real wages and the conditions of their production can, with heterogeneous labor, not only be preserved but indeed be sharpened. The rate of profit depends only on those real wages and their conditions of production which belong to the wage-making types of labor (Steedman 1980).

On the problems posed by the "reduction" of heterogeneous labor for Marx's theory of value and EXPLOITATION, see Krause (1981) who extends the "fundamental Marxian theorem" from homogeneous to heterogeneous labor. He does this by means of the so called "standard reduction," in which a uniform rate of exploitation for the different kinds of labor is implied.

Selected references

Garegnani, Pierangelo (1970) "Heterogeneous Capital, the Production Function and the Theory of Distribution," *Review of Economic Studies* 37: 407–36.

—— (1990) "Quantity of Capital," in J. Eatwell, M. Milgate and P. Newman (eds), *Capital Theory*, London: Macmillan.

Krause, Ulrich (1981) "Heterogeneous Labour and the Fundamental Marxian Theorem," *Review of Economic Studies* 48: 173–8.

Kurz, Heinz D. and Salvadori, Neri (1995) *Theory of Production: A Long-Period Analysis*, Cambridge: Cambridge University Press.

Sraffa, Piero (1960) *Production of Commodities by Means of Commodities*, Cambridge: Cambridge University Press.

Steedman, Ian (1980) "Heterogeneous Labour and 'Classical' Theory," *Metroeconomica* 32: 39–50.

CHRISTIAN GEHRKE

HETEROGENEOUS LABOR: *see* heterogeneous capital and labor

historical school

The historical approach to political economy is essentially a phenomenon of the nineteenth century. The formal distinguishing feature is methodological – the attraction to a comparative and empirical method in contrast to an abstract deductive method. However, a complementary unifying element was in the moral and political domain – concern for the potentially adverse implications of laissez-faire industrial capitalism.

Methodological stance and world view

The methodological stance was reflected in a hostility to the conceptual structure of classical economics (Cliffe Leslie 1888). Classical economics was based on the concept of "economic man" – the autonomous, rational self-interested actor. Classical economics also embodied the presumption of universalism – economic man was, if not omnipresent, the ineluctable victor on the historical stage.

A range of individuals rebelled against the mechanistic and deterministic implications of classical economics. History was their weapon. The German states were a natural home for the rise of a historical school. Indeed, some accounts associate the "historical school" purely with developments in Germany (Schumacher 1933). Against an imported classical economics, Germany juxtaposed a relatively backward economy with a sophisticated intellectual culture.

The ensuing world view emphasized the intrinsically social and organically developmental character of economic life. Rooted in the historical method was the principle of relativity: earlier practices were not to be judged purely by current concepts and values, but were to be interpreted in terms of contemporary conditions (Cunningham 1892; Ashley 1890–94). In Germany, Wilhelm Roscher (1817–94), Bruno Hildebrand (1812–78) and Karl Knies (1821–98) were early contributors to this vision.

Later adherents to the historical approach were of an activist disposition. Intellectual life was seen as instrumental to the self-conscious process of guiding the evolving system in the broader public interest. This motif is especially reflected in the establishment of the *Verein für Sozial-Politik* in 1872, involving academics closely in the "social questions" of the age. The school's members self-consciously supported conservative reform in opposition to the influence of both liberalism and socialism. Gustav von Schmoller (1838–1917) and Adolph Wagner (1835–1917) are representative figures of this generation.

Historical school in Britain

There also developed a group of individuals in Britain who could justly be characterized as a "school," in spite of predictable differences of emphasis. Richard Jones (1790–1855) was a forerunner. After mid-century, a critical mass of opinion was produced by individuals such as T.E. Cliffe Leslie (1827–82), John Ingram (1823–1907), Arnold Toynbee (1852–83), Herbert Foxwell (1849–1936), William Cunningham (1849–1919) and William Ashley (1860–1927) (Koot 1987).

The British historical economists drew their inspiration from disparate sources – from historical jurisprudence; from Auguste Comte; from a new grouping of individuals (William Tooke, William Newmarch and Thorold Rogers) employing statistics in the service of historical generalization; from the historical and comparative ingredients in the classical tradition; and from the Germans. They were as much a natural product of the age of rationalism and of the conditions thrown up by the evolution of capitalism in Britain as were the classical economists.

Land tenure

The state of agriculture was an important concern of historical economists. Cliffe Leslie condemned the forms of land tenure in both Ireland and England: in Ireland, for lack of free transferability of land and security of tenure; in England, for the inhibition to peasant proprietors, which could provide a source of political stability and a vehicle for enhancing domestic demand and balanced economic growth (Koot 1987: ch. 2). In Germany, agriculture was naturally a dominant focus for an examination of the past and of the contemporary impact of industrialization. Agriculture was thus a vehicle for both methodological and political aims, in emphasizing the continuity of past structures into the present, and as an arena for modernization to ensure more orderly socio-economic evolution under the pressures of industrialization (Koot 1987: ch. 2).

Regeneration and *Methodenstreit*

The historical economists developed a momentum in combating classical economics, and played their part in contributing to its demise. The school experienced a period of regeneration after 1870 in combating a new intellectual enemy in the form of neoclassical economics, and confronting renewed social and economic crises for which the historical economists felt they were uniquely qualified to offer remedies. Indeed, John Ingram optimistically predicted that they would ultimately dictate the nature of the discipline (Ingram 1888). In this context, a virulent debate over an appropriate methodology arose, both in Germany (led by the Austrian marginalist Karl Menger) and in Britain. The German term *"Methodenstreit"* has been applied generically to the ensuing debate, which has been crudely characterized as a conflict between the "inductive" and "deductive" methods. The crudity has facilitated the conventional interpretation that the debate was resolved by compromise and the integration of each side's emphasis into a more robust and defensible methodology.

Marginalization of the historical school

A more plausible interpretation is that of the marginalization of the historical school. The German school was tainted by its association with an absolutist political regime, and suffered by the latter's ultimate eclipse. Members of a new generation – in particular, Max Weber, whose commitment to tighter theorization and to "value-freeness" was embodied in the new discipline of sociology – went their separate ways. Nevertheless, the predilection for a holistic conceptual framework was carried over into sociology, and also imported into Italian economics and American economics via institutional political economy.

Economic history

The British school was defeated by the gradual erection of a distinct discipline of economics rooted in neoclassical principles, especially through the strategic role of Alfred Marshall (Maloney 1985). In spite of Marshall's formal pluralism of method, ensuing generations of theorists made few concessions to historical reasoning. The historical school survived, but in a new and subordinate discipline of "economic history." Such disciplinary compartmentalization rendered futile any hopes for an integrated historically-informed theory and theoretically-informed history.

The prospect of a harmonious union between the theorists and the historicists was always fanciful, as they represented opposing world views which promised permanent intra-disciplinary warfare. Behind the fundamental methodological differences was a conflict of political philosophies, essentially classical liberal versus conservative social reform. The conflict and the debate itself survived for a period, but within the confines of the new economic history discipline. This displaced debate took place on common methodological grounds (a universal commitment to historical method), but the participants were divided on ideological grounds (Koot 1993). The character of this renewed debate within economic history highlights the independent importance which ideological differences played in the theorist–historicist debate.

By the 1970s, economic history itself was subject to methodological colonization by (neoclassical) theorists. The legacy of the historical school has essentially disappeared, even from the discipline of economic history. There is some renewed interest in Europe, in the context of dissatisfaction with the achievements of "scientific rationality" (Scaff 1995). More generally, the concerns of the historical economists survive, but in the interstices of the separate disciplines of history, politics and sociology, and in some elements of heterodox political economy.

Selected references

Ashley, W.J. (1890–94) "Historical School of Economists," *Palgrave Dictionary of Political Economy*, New York: Augustus Kelley, 1963.

Cliffe Leslie, T.E. (1888) "On the Philosophical Method of Political Economy," in *Essays in Political Economy*, London: Longmans, Green.

Cunningham, W. (1892) "The Relativity of Economic Doctrine," *Economic Journal* 2(1): 1–16.

Ingram, John Kells (1888) *A History of*

Political Economy, London: A.&C. Black, 1915.

Koot, Gerard (1987) *English Historical Economics 1870–1926*, Cambridge: Cambridge University Press.

—— (1993) "Historians and Economists: The Study of Economic History in Britain ca. 1920–1950," *History of Political Economy* 25(4): 641–75.

Maloney, John (1985) *Marshall, Orthodoxy and the Professionalisation of Economics*, Cambridge: Cambridge University Press.

Scaff, L.A. (1995) "Historism in the German Tradition of Social and Economic Thought," in P. Koslowski (ed.), *The Theory of Ethical Economy in the Historical School*, Berlin: Springer-Verlag.

Schumacher, Hermann (1933) "The Historical School," *Encyclopaedia of the Social Sciences*, New York: Macmillan.

EVAN JONES

history of economics: societies and journals

Throughout the world there are more than 2,000 members of the many history of economic thought (HET) societies. At time of writing, the Society for the History of Economic Thought in Japan has over 800 members, the North American History of Economics Society has 600 members, various European Societies contain around 700 members, and the History of Economic Thought Society of Australia has around 170 members. There are also many journals that publish articles in the history of economic thought. *History of Political Economy*, edited by Craufurd Goodwin, is the foremost journal in the field. While many journals and associations are organized on a national basis, usually scholars from anywhere in the world can (and usually are encouraged to) participate in them.

North America

The North American History of Economics Society held its first annual conference in May 1974, and began publishing the *History of Economics Society Bulletin* in 1979. This publication, edited by Donald Walker, was renamed the *Journal of the History of Economic Thought* in 1990. In recent years the annual conference has attracted around 200 economists, and around 150 papers are usually presented. The series Perspectives in the History of Economic Thought (published first by Edward Elgar and now by Routledge) consists of selected papers from the annual conference. Ross Emmett manages the Society web site, located at:
http://cs.muohio.edu/~HisEcSoc/Society/

Japan

The Japanese Society for the History of Economic Thought was founded in April 1950. Its annual meeting attracts around 300 scholars to listen to around twenty papers. There are also various regional meetings in Japan. The Japanese Society has published the *Annual Bulletin* of the Society since 1963 and also produces a *Newsletter*. There is also a Japanese Society for the History of American Economic Thought. The popularity of HET in Japan partly reflects the fact that studying the history of economics is compulsory for an economics degree in many Japanese universities.

Europe

There are also some European conferences and journals, which are transnational. The *European Journal of the History of Economic Thought* was first published in September 1993 under the leadership of Heinz Kurz, Jose Luis Cardoso and Gilbert Faccarello. The European Conferences on the History of Economics (ECHE) is not a society, but an informal group of people who decided to organize conferences on the history of economic thought in Europe. In 1994, Jose Luis

history of economics: societies and journals

Cardoso, Albert Jolink, Robert Leonard and Philippe Fontaine (Michalis Psalidopoulos joined later) formed the ECHE to establish regular contacts among European historians of economic thought and to increase communication among scholars in European countries and between European and non-European scholars. The first conference was in Rotterdam in 1995 with seventy papers presented and 100 participants. In 1995, the European Society for the History of Economic Thought (ESHET) was created by older members of the profession.

Until recently, continental Europeans have had local and national meetings, but no umbrella group for their activities as a whole. The French and the Italians form the two largest communities of historians of economics in Europe. The only journal devoted to the history of economics in France is *Economies et Sociétés* (in the series *Histoire de la pensée économique*). A French association for the study of the history of economic thought was established in the mid-1980s, the Association Charles Gide pour l'Étude de la pensée économique. In Italy, the journal *Quaderni di storia dell'economia politica* was established in 1983 and was later renamed the *History of Economic Ideas*; and recently formed was the Associazione Italiana per la Storia del Pensiero Economico.

In Britain, growing interest in the history of economics started with a conference organized by Donald Winch in 1968. The British have no formal organization. They have informal and small annual conferences, often with fewer than thirty-five participants. A small number of papers are delivered at conferences, but each paper is subject to thirty minutes of detailed discussion. Unrelated to these conferences is the *History of Economic Thought Newsletter*, edited by John Vint. It began in 1969; and by 1997 had over 400 subscribers.

Australia

The History of Economic Thought Society of Australia (HESTA) was founded in 1981 by J. Wood, J. Pullen and R. Petridis. Biannual conferences were held until 1996, when annual conferences commenced. These meetings attract about thirty-five papers. The Society published the *HETSA Newsletter* and then *Bulletin* until 1991, when the *History of Economics Review* appeared under the editorship of John Lodewijks. The Centre for the Study of the History of Economic Thought at the University of Sydney, under the directorship of Peter Groenewegen, should also be noted in the Australian context.

Other journals and associations

There are a number of other journals and associations with more narrowly focused interests. The *Marshall Studies Bulletin* was first published in 1991; its managing editor is T. Raffaelli. Donald Walker was instrumental in establishing The Walras Society in 1994. This society is devoted to the study of the work of Leon Walras; it plans an information network, meetings and a journal, the *Review of Walrasian Studies*. The International Joseph A. Schumpeter Society publishes the *Journal of Evolutionary Economics*; the Veblen Society for the History and Philosophy of Economics holds regular seminars; Rick Tilman started the International Thorstein Veblen Association in 1993, which holds a biannual conference; and there are Adam Smith, John Locke and Irving Fisher societies as well. Austrian and libertarian thought is published in the *Review of Austrian Economics*, the *Critical Review* and the *Journal of Libertarian Studies*. Other journals concentrating disproportionately on particular economists or schools of thought (often from a history of thought perspective) include the *Journal of Economic Issues* (institutionalists), *Scottish Journal of Political Economy* (Smith), *Manchester School of Economics and Social Studies* (Jevons), *Feminist Economics* and the *American Journal of Economics and Sociology* (Henry George).

Due to Ingrid Rima's editorship, articles on the history of economic thought have appeared frequently in the *Eastern Economic Journal*. *Research in the History of Economic Thought and Methodology*, edited by Warren Samuels and Jeff Biddle, is an excellent venue for papers in the history of economic thought that exceed the normal page limit requirements of a journal. Finally, the New England History of Economic Thought Club (USA) was renamed in 1979 the Kress Society and meets monthly between September and May.

Conclusion

As the foregoing indicates, economists with an interest in the history of economic thought have more journals and associations than ever before in which to participate and publish. This state of affairs exists despite the fact that the history of economic thought is becoming more marginalized over time in the average university curriculum in the United States, Britain and Australia (at least). The increasingly technical nature of economics in general is responsible for this, as the history of economic thought is more conceptual and historical in its content. Hopefully the future will see a greater backlash against the excessively technical nature of economics, and the history of economic thought will develop in response. In the meantime, scholars at least have many more avenues than ever to explore colleagially, in conferences and journals, themes in the history of economic thought.

JOHN LODEWIJKS

holistic method

"Holism" is a term originally coined by the South African scholar Jan Christiaan Smuts (1926) from the Greek word "holos," meaning "whole." He applied the term in categorizing the new type of theories in the physical sciences that were gaining widespread recognition in his time. These new evolutionary or dynamic theories (Charles Darwin's theory of evolution, Henri Becquerel's theory of radioactivity, Albert Einstein's theory of relativity) had finally displaced the old, inherited mechanistic scientific theories of Newton and the pre-Darwin world. This post-Darwinian type of scientific theory conceived of the physical world as an evolving dynamic whole, as opposed to the "atomistic" theories, which held a static or deterministic view of the world. These holistic theories are essentially couched in the belief that the whole is not only greater than the sum of the parts, but that the parts are related in such a way that their functioning is conditioned by their relationship to each other.

Dynamic interdependencies

For the holist, then, explanations of reality cannot be done by the application of universal laws, with successful predictions the only form of verification. Rather, an event or action is explained by identifying its place in a pattern that characterizes the ongoing processes of change in the whole system. The rise of environmental crises has shown that the natural sciences, such as chemistry, also can get it wrong when interdependencies are not accounted for.

The use of formal methods is even more problematic in the social sciences. Economists, like other social scientists, must contend with a situation where there are a large number of relevant variables, where there is an inherent paucity of data, and where human behavior is unlike electron behavior. Holism attempts to provide coherent accounts of situations where fact, theory and values all are necessarily mixed together in reality and in the theorizing.

Institutional environment

Their approach looks behind such abstract variables of mainstream economics as savings, investment, competition, utility/profit maximization and efficiency to the attitudes and behaviors of real economic actors and to the institutional environment in which they must operate. They focus on what in their circumstances leads people or firms to save or invest. For example, traditional growth theory talks about the effect on output of changes in capital/output ratios or saving rates. Holists want to know what causes the mobilization of savings, capital and labor. Thus they are necessarily drawn to look at social, political

holistic method

and cultural factors as well as purely economic variables.

Veblen, Kaplan and Diesing

Thorstein VEBLEN, the recognized founder of the institutionalist tradition, brought this holist philosophical orientation to the study of the US economy. He conceived of the economic order as an evolving scheme of things or cultural process. His approach has remained the point of reference from which later institutionalists and other political economists have criticized the narrow "market economics of choice" espoused by mainstream economics.

Recent attention to holism from philosophers of science has led to a coherent expression of its methodology. Most notably, the works of Abraham Kaplan and Paul Diesing each contain explicit presentations of the holist model of explanation. They seek to uncover the implicit structural framework which facilitates holist theorists' explanations of reality. There is a commonality among holist theories which includes their conception of reality, the structure of their explanations, the primacy of their subject matter and their particular form of logic.

Unity, evolution and interaction

Holistic social scientists argue that social reality must be studied as a system in its natural setting. Obviously, social wholes will tend to differ greatly with respect to size, complexity, degree of self-sufficiency and relationships to the larger wholes that include them. The magnitude of the selected system may vary from the culture on the shopfloor in industrial society to a village in the developing world, or perhaps from a formal organization or institution such as the business corporation to a whole economic system. However, the crucial element of this view is the concept of relationship or unity. That is, the holist standpoint includes the belief that social systems tend to develop a characteristic wholeness or integrity. This unity may take the form of a set of values that expresses itself throughout the system, or it may be that a particular socioeconomic structure tends to condition everything else. Holists may disagree on whether this unity derives from some basic source (for example, religion, ethics, technology, personality) or from some complex interweaving of a number of factors, but all agree that the unity is there.

The implication is that the characteristics of a part are largely determined by the whole to which it belongs and by its particular relationship with the other parts in the system. Thus, if two superficially similar parts of different systems – for example, markets – are compared closely, they will be found to vary in characteristic ways. Let us take the example of markets in less-developed countries. Some economic development experts observed that people spent a large amount of time haggling over prices in local output markets in a particular peasant society. They set up a pilot project wherein a fixed price supermarket replaced the old peasant market. It was a failure because the new market did not satisfy the social intercourse provided by the old market system. Thus, superficially similar markets provided different functions in different systems, and thus the definition of efficiency also would vary between the systems.

Since holists acknowledge the organic unity of systems, they are obligated to study the whole living system rather than one part taken out of context. The context of a particular event is important because the character of any given part is largely conditioned by the whole to which it belongs and by its particular function and location in the larger system. Thus, reality for holists is viewed as a process of evolutionary change driven by the dynamic interaction between the parts and the whole (see Myrdal 1978).

Participant observation and storytelling

The approach which has achieved the greatest success in constructing holist explanations in the social sciences is case studies using what is termed the participant–observer method. The investigators become "socialized" – that is,

holistic method

they allow the subject matter to impress upon them its norms and to instill within them its categories. In remaining close to the concrete reality of the system studied, holists are in a unique position to perceive a wide variety of recurrent themes (importance of ceremony, target profits/markup pricing, etc.) that appear in a variety of contexts. As an observer, the researcher looks for themes which illuminate the system's wholeness, that is, which contribute to its individuality or oneness. It is in this sense that holists find general laws (law of demand) and universal categories (utility) especially unsuited to the task of describing the unity of the particular system unless they have been discovered by observation to be important in this particular system.

Researchers construct tentative hypotheses about parts of the system out of the recurrent themes that become obvious to them in the course of the socialization process. These hypotheses or interpretations of themes are tested by consulting a wide variety of data (previous case studies, survey data, personal observations and so forth). Gradually, as socialization proceeds, researchers become increasingly attuned to accurate perception and interpretation of the recurrent themes and formulation of validated hypotheses. Holists use this experience and the various pieces of evidence to build up a many-sided, complex picture of the subject matter. Unfortunately, this technique can never produce the rigorous certainty espoused by logical positivists; it can only indicate varying degrees of plausibility.

Eventually the holist proceeds to the last step, which is building a model. This type of model with its emphasis on recurrent themes within or around the individual system is aptly known to philosophers of science as the pattern model of explanation or story telling (see STORYTELLING AND PATTERN MODELS). It is constructed by linking hypotheses or themes in a network or pattern, with the account of a particular part emphasizing the multiplicity of connections among that part, other parts and the whole system.

Conception of reality

Another distinguishing aspect of holist methodology can be found in the structure of holistic explanations. The structure of holistic theories is concatenated (linked together) rather than hierarchical, as in formal theories. They are composed by linking several variables or factors, rather than by logically deducing an explanandum from an explanans. A concatenated theory with its various sections and subsections provides a many-sided, complex picture of the subject matter. The concatenated structure of holist explanations is necessitated in part by holists' conception of reality. Rather than saying that we understand or explain something when we can predict it, holists say that we have an explanation for something when we understand its place in the whole.

Primacy of subject matter

Since holists do not attempt to subsume their particular system under general principles applicable to all systems, their concepts are relatively concrete, particularized and close to the real system being described. The primacy of subject matter over method, then, is a crucial element of holist methodology. In contrast, formalists argue that the method is what is important and the problem is how to use that scientific method creatively to analyze any event to show that it is merely an example of a general law. Thus an agent's behavior, in whatever context, needs to be shown as an example of optimizing behavior. Holists claim that this approach distorts the subject by saying the context does not matter other than setting constraints on optimizing behavior. Holists attempt to generalize from the facts of experience about the working of the economy while formalists attempt to construct a model based on assumptions about how economic agents would behave if they acted rationally in their own self-interest.

Concepts being dialectically related

The fourth and final characteristic of holistic

concepts is that they are frequently, although not always, related dialectically. Two concepts are related dialectically when the development of one concept focuses attention on the other as an opposed concept that has been unknowingly denied or excluded by the first; or when it is discovered that the opposite concept is necessary for the validity or applicability of the first; and when it is the case that the real theoretical problem is the interrelation between the two concepts. There are many examples of dialectical logic in political economy: the ceremonial–technological dichotomy, pecuniary versus economic values, spread versus backwash effects, and so on.

One reason for the frequent occurrence of dialectical concepts in holist theories is that they serve to counterbalance the human tendency to be biased, one-sided or abstract. They make thought and theories more concrete. Researchers begin with some historically or empirically suggested theme and develop it until its shortcomings are clear enough to suggest an opposing, formally unacknowledged theme; then the new theme is developed and related back to the first. In effect, dialectic is the logic of the concrete. The fact that dialectic is a correction of one-sidedness helps explain why many holistic works are not dialectical: there is only so much time. The hope is that later researchers can combine several one-sided works into a more complex whole (see DIALECTICAL METHOD).

Limitations and appropriate uses

Holism has its limitations. First, because of their lack of precision, the use of holist concepts must be continuously monitored by reference to observation, cases, and examples. Holism separated from its empirical base easily becomes loose, uncontrolled speculation. A second problem is that the impreciseness and generality of holist concepts make any definitive verification of hypotheses impossible. As a consequence, holists must remember that these theories are always tentative and subject to change.

Use of holist pattern models appears appropriate when an explanation involves many diverse factors, each of which is important; when the patterns or connections among those factors are important; and when these patterns can be observed in the particular case under study. Use of formal theoretical models appears more appropriate when one or two factors or laws determine what is to be explained and when these factors or laws are better known and understood than the specific instance. These formal models have their uses, even by political economists, for certain types of problems. Many of the issues political economists deal with, however, are better handled by holistic methods.

Selected references

Diesing, Paul (1971) *Patterns of Discovery in the Social Sciences*, Chicago: Aldine-Atherton.

Gruchy, Allen (1947) *Modern Economic Thought: The American Contribution*, Clifton, NJ: Augustus Kelley, 1967.

Kaplan, Abraham (1964) *The Conduct of Inquiry: Methodology for Behavioral Science*, San Francisco: Chandler Publishing Co.

Myrdal, Gunnar (1978) "Institutional Economics," *Journal of Economic Issues* 12(4): 771–83.

O'Hara, Phillip Anthony (1993) "Methodological Principles of Institutional Political Economy: Holism, Evolution and Contradiction," *Methodus* 5(1): 51–71.

Phillips, D.C. (1976) *Holistic Thought in Social Science*, Stanford, CA: Stanford University Press.

Smuts, J.C. (1926) *Holism and Evolution*, New York: Macmillan.

Wilber, Charles K and Harrison, Robert S. (1978) "The Methodological Basis of Institutional Economics: Pattern Model, Storytelling, and Holism," *Journal of Economic Issues* 12(1): 61–89.

CHARLES K. WILBER

home economics, new

The new home economics (NHE) consists of economic theories and applications of NEOCLASSICAL ECONOMICS dealing with home-based decision-making. NHE expands on other economic analyses by taking account of the family connections binding households together, and by expanding the domain of economic analysis. Whereas, prior to NHE, firms and government were the sole institutions analyzed in depth by economists, since the inception of NHE neoclassical economists have been paying increasing attention to MARRIAGE and family, the institutions governing home-based decisions.

Importance of NHE

NHE has added new depth to economic analyses of household decisions which form the core of economics, such as analyses of consumption and saving, labor supply and transportation. Jacob Mincer, from Columbia University in New York, became one of the founders of NHE in the late 1950s when he and other neoclassically trained labor economists failed to explain findings on women's labor supply in the United States with theories based on individual labor/leisure trade-offs. Mincer's contribution (1962; see Mincer 1993) was based on the realization that labor supply is decided in a family context, and that time not spent in the labor force includes not only leisure, but also household labor, child care and education.

Gary Becker had been one of Mincer's colleagues at Columbia University at the time that NHE was born. Becker published an economic theory of fertility in 1961 (see Becker 1976: ch. 9). In his widely cited *Theory of Allocation of Time*, published in 1965, Becker formalized the idea that time in the home has an economic value and exported NHE to more areas of application, including consumption studies, health economics, and transportation economics. The extensive cross-fertilization of ideas between Mincer, Becker and some of their colleagues at Columbia, Becker's prominent status (he was awarded the Nobel prize in 1992) and Becker's move to the University of Chicago in 1971, have led some to call NHE the Columbia–Chicago school of home economics. Discussions of the economics of production in the home, the essential idea promoted by NHE, is now of standard use in economics, including in (generally neoclassical) economic studies of labor supply.

NHE has shown that economic analyses can enrich the study of fields often considered outside the domain of economics. Becker led the way in applying neoclassical NHE to the study of fertility, marriage (Becker 1976: ch. 11) and related topics. Growing new fields such as aspects of the economics of the family, demographic economics, GENDER, intra-household allocation and the political economy of marriage are products of NHE.

The first wave of NHE by Becker, and others following his approach, has been mostly neoclassical. Such studies typically emphasize the influence of income and wages on individual and family decisions. The impact of institutional structures and personal preferences was underemphasized in early NHE models, which also typically assumed that families make home-related decisions. Early NHE research has been challenged on two major grounds.

Assumptions being questioned

One of the central assumptions of NHE to be questioned is that of constant preferences. There is a growing awareness among economists that individual preferences cannot be assumed to be constant. INSTITUTIONS AND HABITS as well as CULTURE are important influences on decisions in the home. Laws and norms which vary across countries and ethnic groups and over time are central to our understanding of decision-making in the home (see Folbre 1994; Grossbard-Shechtman 1993). In his later work, Becker has also challenged this assumption, although not in the context of NHE.

A second assumption that many are now questioning is the assumption, typically made in NHE, that decisions are made by families.

Except for the economic analyses of marriage and divorce, including Becker's, other applications of NHE assumed family, rather than individual, decision-making. Increasing numbers of economists realize that an analysis of all home-based decisions needs to take account of the separate interests of individual household members. There are at least four independent origins to the movement from family utility models to separate utility models.

Theories of marriage based on bargaining theory and game theory were among the first challengers to the "family utility assumption." One of the major contributors to the bargaining approach to marriage has been Marjorie McElroy (McElroy and Horney 1981; see also Manser and Brown 1980). Lately, both co-operative and non-cooperative game theory have been applied to household decisions by increasing numbers of economists. A second challenge to the family utility assumption in labor applications of NHE came from Shoshana Grossbard-Shechtman (1984), a student of Becker, and the French scholar Pierre-André Chiappori (1992), who offered models of labor supply of wives and husbands assuming individual utilities. Third, family utility models, typical of the first wave of NHE, have been challenged by feminists such as Marianne Ferber and Julie Nelson (1993). These scholars were disturbed by the implicit assumptions of male dominance found in much of the early NHE literature. Fourth, the family utility assumption is rapidly losing ground as increasing numbers of empirical studies demonstrate that consumption decisions depend on who controls resources in a family.

Future of NHE

The future of NHE is uncertain at the time of writing. Some of the challengers have associated NHE with the now unpopular assumptions that were used by Becker, Mincer and most of their followers and do not see a future for NHE (see, for instance, the work of McCrate 1987). However, rejecting NHE is like throwing the baby out with the bath water. Given NHE's historical role in promoting research on home-based labor and consumption decisions, and NHE's contribution to new fields of economics such as gender, marriage, family and intra-household allocation, opposition to NHE may impede the expansion of these fields of research.

Homes are not of lesser importance to our understanding of the economy than are firms or governments. Economists who study how economic decisions are made within families should not have lower status within the economics profession than economists who focus on the allocation of resources within firms. To bring home-based decisions into the focus they deserve, economists studying such decisions need to draw on all the resources they can gather, including the theories, methods, modes of discourse, and personal connections they can find within the new home economics.

See also:

class structures of households; domestic labor debate; feminist political economy: paradigms; household labor and national production; waged household labor

Selected references

Becker, Gary S. (1976) *The Economic Approach to Human Behavior*, Chicago: University of Chicago Press.

Chiappori, Pierre-André (1992) "Collective Labor Supply and Welfare," *Journal of Political Economy* 100(3): 437–67.

Ferber, Marianne and Nelson, Julie (1993) *Beyond Economic Man: Feminist Theory and Economics*, Chicago: University of Chicago Press.

Folbre, Nancy (1994) *Who Pays for the Kids? Gender and the Structures of Constraint*, London: Routledge.

Grossbard-Shechtman, Shoshana (1984) "A Theory of Allocation of Time in Markets for Labour and Marriage," *Economic Journal* 94: 863–82.

——(1993) *On the Economics of Marriage*, Boulder, CO: Westview.

Manser, Marilyn and Brown, Murray (1980)

"Marriage and Household Decision Making: a Bargaining Analysis," *International Economic Review* 21: 31–44.

McCrate, Elaine (1987) "Trade, Merger and Employment: Economic Theory on Marriage," *Review of Radical Political Economics* 19(1): 73–89.

McElroy, Marjorie B. and Horney, M.J. (1981) "Nash Bargained Household Decisions: Toward a Generalization of the Theory of Demand," *International Economic Review* 22: 333–49.

Mincer, Jacob (1993) *Studies in Labor Supply, Collected Essays of Jacob Mincer*, vol. 2, Aldershot: Edward Elgar.

Zeitlin, Marian F. and Megaangi, Ratna (1995) "Economic Perspectives on the Family," in M.F. Zeitlin *et al.* (eds), *Strengthening the Family*, Tokyo: United Nations University Press.

SHOSHANA GROSSBARD-SHECHTMAN

household labor

Introduction

Household labor is the activation of work in and around the home, and is mostly undertaken by women. It involves a variety of duties, including child care, cleaning, washing, production, repairs, cooking, shopping, nutrition, care of adult household members, gardening, human and institutional reproduction and psychological counseling (see REPRODUCTION PARADIGM). The institutional relations of household labor are considerably variable, depending on region, ethnicity, CLASS, GENDER and history. This entry will be concerned mainly with household labor in heterosexual relationships within Western societies (although it is often difficult to generalize), with special reference given to socioeconomic and technological dimensions (see also SOCIAL STRUCTURE OF ACCUMULATION: FAMILY).

The origins of the word "economics" emanate from "household economy," but, ironically, over time household labor was excluded from the economy in most textbooks, except as a black box called "households" or "consumption." Nevertheless, over the years neoclassical, Marxist and feminist economists have debated the productive or reproductive role of households, and now many nations have a supporting national account for household production (see HOUSEHOLD PRODUCTION AND NATIONAL INCOME).

Indeed, household economics has become a specialized area in economics, and some studies show the total estimated value of household production to be very high, if declining. For instance, Jefferson (1997: 110) calculates the value of household production in Australia to have declined from 54 percent of GDP in 1976–7 to 43 percent in 1994–5, as market production took over a greater percentage of household tasks. One hypothesis is that normal GDP growth figures are misleading because they may in part represent the extent to which production is transferring from the home to capitalist market activities, rather than necessarily increasing production very much overall.

Early twentieth century

For the average working class woman in Western society, work within the home remained a burdensome task in the interwar period. There was little in the way of labor-saving devices to assist the average housewife. Some families, especially in country areas, were highly self-supporting, maintaining a flourishing vegetable garden, fruit trees and so on, and supplying to neighbors for a margin over costs. The housewife tended to preserve some of the surplus production, and her pantry shelves were stocked with a variety of preserves of high quality. Bread was often baked at home and poultry was kept for a ready supply of fresh eggs.

In many country homes there was no electricity; oil lamps were used to supply lighting, and ironing was done by heating irons on the wood-burning stove. Some foodstuffs were kept cool and fresh in a "Coolgardie safe," where water was used as part of a drip

household labor

system for the cooling effect. In larger towns, ice was delivered on a regular basis for use in ice chests to store meat and other perishables. Wood was used extensively for cooking and heating purposes and was chopped into usable portions by husbands and children. The sewing machine (and the art of knitting) was used to make clothes for the family and articles for the home. The home was in fact a hive of industry with many household members contributing a share, but most home production was managed by the wife/mother.

The washing of clothes was often performed with a large copper basin of water heated by a fire beneath (called a "copper"); household linen especially was boiled in this manner with the use of soap. More delicate clothing was washed by hand and, in some instances, with the aid of a washing board for scrubbing. Rinsing, bluing and starching completed the tasks, before hanging it all to dry. Meanwhile, for the cleaning of carpets, vacuum cleaners started to become available at this time. Gradually, some household tasks moved increasingly into the market, such as clothing, bread-making and preserves.

During the Second World War, women filled many of the waged jobs left by men. Many women's lives were changed dramatically, as they often worked both at home and in the paid workforce.

Post-1945 era

After the war, servicemen returned home and women were generally expected to go back to keeping the "home fires burning" and the meals on time. Many families suffered from the uncertainties of readjustment. However, over time a new era of optimism emerged within the family. Conditions improved into the 1950s and 1960s, along with high levels of population growth, apparent "suburban bliss," health, education and consumerism.

Also during the 1950s and 1960s, household TECHNOLOGY expanded and often became cheaper through mass production techniques and long production runs. The washing machine became standard equipment in many homes in the 1950s, apparently saving time and energy per unit item washed. Wringers gave way to spin dryers and later hot dryers. Laundromats sprang up in the suburbs. In the 1960s, the expansion of non-iron fabrics and drip-dry clothing led to a marginal saving of fuel and time. Refrigerators became more sophisticated and enabled the consumer to store more perishable goods for longer periods and hence to save on shopping time. Ovens improved, incorporating baking areas, grillers, top burners and alarms. Vacuum cleaners were now more powerful, with many attachments, gadgets and greater dust/dirt capacity. Kitchen devices such as electric beaters, blenders and cutters enabled household workers to cater for the needs of a growing family. Added to this, of course, was the growing norm of the family car, especially for upper, middle-class and upper working-class families in advanced capitalist economies.

With a pressure cooker meals could be prepared very quickly. Later this was followed by the rapid introduction of the microwave oven, which was even quicker to use. Fast foods are now readily available (but are often not conducive to good health). With the increasing dominance of supermarkets, there is a tendency for consumers to spend more, and they do the work of de-shelving and carrying the goods to the checkout, thus reducing costs for the shop owner. Families now eat out more regularly than in earlier years; the choice of restaurants and fast food outlets is expanding rapidly, as is the choice of cuisine from a variety of countries.

As women have joined the workforce in increasing numbers they have tended to eschew even further the domestic making of clothes, gardening, the growing of food, and, to some degree, cooking (all this is historically variant, depending on region). Time-saving appliances are being utilized more universally, along with the second car and the use of child-care services. There has thus been a significant transfer of activities from the home to the market.

Nevertheless, the number of hours of housework is still high. For instance, in Australia during 1992, women working full-time in the paid workforce undertook on average 29 hours of housework, compared with 15.05 hours for men undertaking full-time paid work. Women working part time undertook 44 hours of housework, compared with 15.26 hours for men in part-time paid employment (based on Jefferson 1997: 106). Figures from many other nations also show that, on average, women work more hours than men when paid and household work are combined (see Folbre 1994: 97, 274).

Anomalies

In heterosexual relationships, women tend to work for wages as well as undertake most of the not inconsiderable amount of household labor: this is called the "double day." Women often reduce their degree of (official) PARTICIPATION IN THE LABOR FORCE, attending to children in their formative years. In the case of those who leave the labor force temporarily to care for children, it is difficult to return to their previous type of work as employers often assume that their human capital has decreased. Since few men take years off from the labor force to attend to children, they do not have this problem and hence have on average greater income and employment security. This is a major anomaly, being linked to the asymmetrical distribution of housework between the sexes.

For many neoclassical and Marxist economists, historical "progress" brings women into the public realm of wage labor. Barbara Bergmann (1986) represents the view of domesticity as a "shackle." However, the "caring labor" literature questions whether commodification and proletarianization are really "progress." Women do gain access to valued material resources (through wages) that increase their bargaining power. But is greater commodity and material advance true liberation?

Some feminist economists (such as Himmelweit 1995) argue that it is problematical to adhere to the dichotomy of "work" and "non-work" (and hence possibly "labor" and "non-labor"), especially in some "relationship type" activities undertaken in the home. By using these categories of "work" and "non-work," caring and loving activities, which enhance the quality of life of people and families, may be underrated (and thereby reduced) by not fitting into the category of "work."

See also:

class structures of households; gender; gender division of labor; household production and national income; marriage; patriarchy; reserve army of labor: latent; sexuality; waged household labor

Selected references

Bergmann, Barbara (1986) *The Economic Emergence of Women*, New York: Basic Books.
Folbre, Nancy (1994) *Who Pays for the Kids? Gender and the Structures of Constraint*, London and New York: Routledge.
Himmelweit, S. (1995) "The Discovery of Unpaid Work: The Social Consequences of the Expansion of Work," *Feminist Economics* 1(2): 1–19.
Jefferson, Therese (1997) "Some Implications of the Commodification of Activities Previously Carried Out Within Households," Master of Economics thesis, LaTrobe University, Victoria, Australia.
Wagman, B. and Folbre, Nancy (1996) "Household Services and Economic Growth in the United States, 1870–1930," *Feminist Economics* 2(1): 43–66.

RHODA ADELAIDE O'HARA
PHILLIP ANTHONY O'HARA

household production and national income

Household production is a term used to describe the non-market goods and services produced by households for their own use. To distinguish household production from other household activities, a third-party criterion may be used. Specifically, productive activities are those which result in the production of goods and services which could have been provided by a third person (see Reid 1934). They have also been defined using a market definition; that is, the production by households of goods and services that could have been purchased in the market. Activities typically included in studies of household production are: food preparation and cleanup, clothing care, general housework, house, garden and car maintenance, physical care and education of household members, provision of transport to household members, purchasing goods and services, and household paperwork and management. Time spent in civic and community activities is sometimes included.

National accounts and their limitations

The production boundary established by the United Nations System of National Accounts to estimate national income excludes most household production. With some exceptions, the defining feature of a productive economic activity is that it involves a monetary exchange. The primacy given to market transactions in defining economic activity may be traced to Marshall's *Principles of Economics*, although the most famous quote illustrating the paradox posed by this definition belongs to Pigou: "Thus if a man marries his housekeeper or cook, the national income is diminished" (Pigou 1920: 32).

It has been argued that excluding household production limits the usefulness of national income estimates in significant ways. In particular, it limits knowledge of the extent of non-market production in different economies, and thus limits the comparability of national income estimates. Further, by ignoring transfers of production between market and household sectors, the comparability of national income estimates for an economy over time is diminished.

The limited scope of GDP has led to the development of other indexes of social welfare, for example, net social welfare and the index of sustainable economic welfare (see GROSS DOMESTIC PRODUCT AND NET SOCIAL WELFARE. As a measure of business activity, GDP estimates based on exchange values may be adequate, but as an estimate of social welfare or use-values production they are not.

Significance of household production

The significance of household production was recognized prior to the establishment of a national accounting framework by the United Nations. Reid (1934) stressed that by examining only market transactions, economists were neglecting a significant determinant of living standards. Kuznets (1941) and Clark (1958), both participants in the early development of national accounting methods, recognized the importance of household production and estimated its value. Hawrylyshyn (1976) has surveyed early estimates for Sweden and the United States.

However, the GREAT DEPRESSION and the Second World War led attention to be placed on the waged labor market, the commodity market and the role of the state, and on the need to reestablish sustained accumulation and growth, conventionally conceived to exclude the household. Depression and war also led the United Nations to seek the expeditious establishment of traditional national accounting procedures. These factors, and the difficulties involved in estimating the value of non-market activity, led to the exclusion of household production from these accounts.

Despite this, concern over the exclusion of household production from mainstream economic accounts has been ongoing. Clark (1958) stated that "theoretically its exclusion from national product estimates cannot be defended" and that expediently omitting it from accounts due to the difficulty of imputing a value was a "consideration that has certainly ceased to hold." The common practice of imputing rental values for owner occupied dwellings also indicates that certain imputations can be made as part of the United Nations System of National Accounts.

Renewed interest in household production

Two important developments sparked recent interest in the area of household production. Firstly, the increased participation of women in the paid workforce focused attention upon the opportunity cost of household production and increasing market provision of goods and services, once generally carried out in the household. This theme was developed in Becker's (1965) neoclassical model of time allocation, in which utility is maximized subject to the usual constraints as well as a time constraint (see HOME ECONOMICS, NEW). This gave some theoretical basis to the issue of household production in mainstream economics. While not directly focusing upon the issue of national income estimates, it did illustrate the opportunity costs involved in both market and household production.

The second and related development is associated with the rise of the feminist movement from the late 1960s. Feminists challenged the exclusion from national accounts of a major area of production carried out by women. It was claimed that economists were treating household production as being valueless because it had no price. Feminists also suspected it was because most household production is done by women (Waring 1988). The DOMESTIC LABOR DEBATE and later feminist work provided the foundation for revised estimates of national income for the United States, which include household production (see Wagman and Folbre 1996).

Valuation methods

A variety of methods for valuing household production have been developed on a piecemeal basis. So far, the most common method of valuing household production is to estimate the labor input to household production, using some form of time-use survey and then assigning an appropriate money value to this time. Two general methods of determining a money value may be discerned. The first estimates the opportunity cost of the time allocated to household production. The second uses a market replacement approach to value the labor inputs. There is an evolving body of literature covering these measurement issues and, as yet, there is no consensus on the most appropriate methods. However, studies in Australia, Canada, Finland, France and the United States have shown household production to be a significant area of activity, valued at between 30 and 50 percent of GDP as it is currently measured (see Australian Bureau of Statistics 1990).

The development of household production estimates has a number of important policy implications. They may give a more complete picture of how productive resources are allocated within an economy, how labor policy affects these resources and further insights into income distribution. However the policy implications have remained relatively unexplored within the literature, with the greater emphasis being upon the development of a satisfactory method of estimation.

In general, the significance of household production, as part of economic output, appears to be gaining wider acceptance. Moves to develop "satellite accounts" covering household production, to supplement current national income accounts, are gaining some momentum.

See also:

gender division of labor; household labor; participation in the labor force; reserve army of labor: latent; social structure of accumulation: family

Selected references

Australian Bureau of Statistics (1990) *Measuring Unpaid Work: Issues and Experimental Estimates*, Catalogue 5326.0, Canberra: Australian Bureau of Statistics.

Becker, Gary S. (1965) "A Theory of the Allocation of Time," *Economic Journal* 75(September): 493–517.

Clark, Colin (1958) "The Economics of Housework," *Bulletin of the Oxford Institute of Statistics* 20(1): 205–11.

Goldshmidt-Clermont, L. (1990) "Economic Measurement of Non-Market Household Activities: Is it Useful and Feasible?," *International Labor Review* 129(3): 279–99.

Hawrylyshyn, O. (1976) "The Value of Household Services: A Survey of Empirical Estimates," *Review of Income and Wealth* 22: 101–31.

Kuznets, Simon (1941) *National Income and its Composition 1919–1938*, New York: National Bureau of Economic Research.

Pigou (1920) *The Economics of Welfare*, 4th edn, London: Macmillan, 1932.

Reid, Margaret (1934) *Economics of Household Production*, New York: Wiley.

United Nations (1992) *A System of National Accounts*, New York: United Nations.

Wagman, B. and Folbre, N. (1996) "Household Services and Economic Growth in the United States, 1870–1930," *Feminist Economics* 2(1): 43–66.

Waring, Marilyn (1988) *If Women Counted*, San Francisco: Harper & Row.

THERESE JEFFERSON

human action and agency

Scientific explanation is generally understood to be causal explanation, such that all causes are thought to have effects and all effects are thought to have causes. This creates a fundamental problem for any discussion of human action and agency, where these are understood in terms of a human capacity to initiate new causal chains. Specifically, on the one hand we suppose that human agency has causal properties in that human action has effects on the world; yet on the other hand, we also suppose that the capacity to initiate new causal chains cannot itself be the effect of prior causes. That is, we tend to treat human action and agency as part of the world's causal order when we consider the effects of our actions, but then turn around to deny that human action and agency are part of the causal order when we speak of our capacity as agents to act freely. Thus the problem of agency is to explain how human action is both part of the causal order and simultaneously independent of that order. Philosophers regard this as the problem of freedom and determinism (for example, Nagel 1986: ch. 7).

Neoclassical approaches

Neoclassical economics approaches the problem of agency and action from a methodological individualist perspective, or from the idea that all action arises out of the choices of individuals. Accordingly, explaining human action is a matter of explaining individual choice, where this in turn, as Elster (1989) puts it, is a matter of explaining individuals' desires (or preferences) and opportunities (or constraints). For example, consumer behavior is understood in terms of what people want, given their resources. Two approaches may be distinguished. Some neoclassical economists, following Stigler and Becker (1977), argue that all people have essentially the same preferences and desires, so that choice and human action reduces to differences in opportunities. In this instance, choice may be said to be determined by the constraints and opportunities an individual has. Individual action is then explainable as an effect of those factors that cause the individual to have a particular opportunity set. However, this means that agency, understood as the capacity to initiate new causal chains and act freely, is not explained.

Other neoclassical economists allow that individuals' desires and preferences differ, but this does not make it possible to explain how choice may freely originate. On the standard view, the formal, axiomatic representation of individual objective functions fully explains the content and structure of individual desires and the preferences they generate. Thus, for any given set of opportunities, there is always a determinate response on the part of the individual, explainable in terms of that individual's desire/preference structure. That is, an individual's desires cause the "choice" an individual makes. In comparison to the Stigler–Becker view, where opportunities dictate choice, on this view desires and preferences, given an opportunity set, dictate choice. On both views, however, choice is caused by something else – namely, desires or opportunities – and individuals only fail to behave as the theory predicts if they are "irrational." Thus while, on the neoclassical view, social science explanation conforms to the standard cause-and-effect model, it does not provide an account of human action and agency.

Of course, the classic philosophical problem of freedom and determinism will not be solved in the work of social scientists; but, given the belief that human agency is a real dimension of economic life (equally presupposed by neoclassical and heterodox economists), adequate social science requires analysis that allows for the possibility of free action in human affairs. Heterodox economists thus strive to explain the economy in terms that account for how action can be relatively independent of causal frameworks in which it occurs. Two principal approaches can be distinguished.

A post-Keynesian non-ergodic world

Post-Keynesianism, especially as it emphasizes Keynes on true uncertainty, rejects the neoclassical assumption that the world is ergodic. To say that the world is ergodic is to say that its laws or basic causal relationships are unchanging. Thus, neoclassical economists focus on risk rather than uncertainty because, unlike post-Keynesians, they suppose that the probability distributions of future events are settled and knowable. Post-Keynesians hold that an economy's causal relationships may change, that consequently the probability distributions of future events are generally not knowable, and that uncertainty, not risk, needs to be incorporated into expectation formation. Moreover, the reason that post-Keynesians hold these propositions is that they believe economic reality is transmutable, that is, that it may be transformed by human action (Davidson 1996).

This understanding clearly does provide an account of agency lacking in neoclassicism. On the neoclassical view, individuals' actions are fully explainable in terms of prior causes. Empirical research aims at uncovering the arguments (preferences) in utility functions, on the assumption that these same arguments will dictate like future behavior in a world disturbed only by "exogenous shocks." On the post-Keynesian view, knowing individuals' past choices is only a partial guide to future behavior, and individuals need to be understood as agents that have the power to initiate new causal chains of events.

There are two rationales behind the post-Keynesian view. First, in a transmutable world – one that is historical and path-dependent – change in the objects of choice is necessarily associated with change in preferences. One cannot prefer A to B in a world in which A and B no longer exist, but A' and B' do. What explains the capacity of individuals to form new preferences? Though an answer to this question falls beyond the scope of political economy, it may nonetheless be said that the element of indeterminacy this capacity introduces is fully compatible with saying that individuals act as free agents. Second, in a transmutable world, human action changes the future. This implies that past events fail to dictate future events when human agency intervenes. Thus, seeing the world as non-ergodic is a direct demonstration of a capacity for free action.

Marxian and feminist views on agency

Marxism provides another type of approach to explaining human action and agency. Classical Marxism is associated with base–superstructure explanations in which it is argued that developments in a society's economic base, understood in terms of the forces and relations of production, ramify through to changes in its superstructure, understood in terms of that society's politics, culture and property relations. Thus development in the former, broadly speaking, causes developments in the latter, though with lags and reverse repercussions. This analysis has led some commentators to argue mistakenly that Marxist views of history are deterministic in the sense that an inescapable logic dictates the course of events. A more accurate conception involves saying that broad patterns of historical development, especially as reflecting the evolution of the modes of production and social formations, account for the general pattern of events. Where does human agency, then, come into this picture?.

Marx's class analysis characterized the proletariat as the universal class in the sense of being that class with no attachment to either capitalism or class society *per se*. In his view, this unique status enabled working people to understand the nature of EXPLOITATION, social forces, and generally the factors that caused them to act as wage laborers. However, this understanding also had a revolutionizing effect in that it gave them a further capacity to step outside of the causal framework of their lives. Revolutionary action, then, was free action for Marx, and the working class was a genuine agent of historical change. Though history might move in broad patterns, how it was played out at particular points of time and in specific arenas was due to free activity tied specifically to consciousness of that history.

For Marx, of course, classes, and individuals, to the extent that they act with class consciousness, are society's agents. However, Marx's general model of agency has been adopted by other heterodox thinkers for different types of agents. Feminists, for example, also hold that gaining an understanding of the causal frameworks in which individuals generally operate creates a capacity to act freely and overcome those frameworks, when they argue that women who develop an understanding of patriarchal society may transcend patriarchal relationships, and help others to do so as well. We might thus emphasize Marx's general approach as a dialectical one in assuming that a causal process may itself bring forth breaks in a causal order, here due specifically to the emergence of human agency.

Conclusion

Heterodox economists, therefore, place important emphasis on having accounts of human action, and yet also work with different strategies for explaining agency. Ironically, neoclassical economics, which begins with the methodological individualist postulate that all actions derives from individuals, lacks a clear means of arguing that individuals are indeed agents in the sense of initiating causal sequences. This would seem to be an important deficiency, since explaining the world in cause-and-effect terms ought not exclude that set of (initiating) causes due to human action and agency.

See also:

Austrian school of political economy; dialectical method; feminist political economy: major contemporary themes; holistic method; individual and society; institutions and habits; Marxist political economy: contemporary varieties; methodological individualism and collectivism; neoclassical economics; post-Keynesian political economy: major contemporary themes

Selected references

Davidson, Paul (1996) "Reality and Economic Theory," *Journal of Post Keynesian Economics* 18(4): 479–508.
Elster, Jon (1989) *Nuts and Bolts for the Social Sciences*, Cambridge: Cambridge University Press.
Nagel, Thomas (1986) *The View from Nowhere*, Oxford: Oxford University Press.
Stigler, George and Becker, Gary (1977) "De gustibus non est disputandum," *American Economic Review* 67(2): 76–90.

JOHN B. DAVIS

human capital

Origins and history

Human capital refers to the broad range of knowledge and skills possessed by individuals, making it possible for them to produce goods and services. As with physical capital, human capital is a produced means of production. But whereas physical capital can be separated from its owner, human capital naturally cannot. Consequently, its treatment as simply another form of physical capital without qualification is subject to debate.

The treatment of either human beings or their knowledge and skills as capital can be traced back to Sir William Petty who, in the late seventeenth century, estimated the monetary value of the stock of human capital in England (Kiker 1966). Karl MARX explored human capital when he defined *labor power* as "the aggregate of those mental and physical capabilities existing in...a human being, capabilities which he sets in motion whenever he produces a use-value of any kind" (Marx 1867: 270). Thorstein VEBLEN developed the notion of "workmanship," which included the stock of knowledge and skills. Adam Smith, Jean-Baptiste Say, Nassau Senior, Leon Walras, Irving Fisher and other well-known economists also deliberated upon the concept of human capital and used it to demonstrate the benefits of education, health care and migration on productivity and hence national wealth.

Further development of what was to become the neoclassical theory of human capital investment was thwarted, however, by Alfred Marshall, who argued that it was impractical to consider human resources as capital. It was not until the late 1950s and early 1960s that Theodore Schultz, Gary Becker and Jacob Mincer shook themselves free of Marshall's criticisms and began developing a theory of human capital investment that fit squarely within the established framework of neoclassical analysis (Schultz 1961; Becker 1964; Mincer 1974).

Nature of human capital

Human capital theory asserts that individuals can increase their stock of human capital through expenditures on education, training, health care, job search and migration. Increases in human capital are assumed to increase PRODUCTIVITY and, in turn, increase individual earnings. According to Becker (1964), because these expenditures occur in the current period and yield returns in future periods, they can be treated as capital investments (as opposed to consumption expenditures), and analyzed as such.

Thus, an individual will undertake expenditures to increase his or her human capital if the internal rate of return exceeds the market rate of interest. The internal rate of return is the interest rate that equates the present value of the investment's benefits (that is, the expected increase in wages and non-pecuniary satisfaction to be received over the individual's working life) with the present value of the direct and indirect costs (that is, the out-of-pocket expenses and the earnings foregone during the investment period, respectively). Anything that increases expected benefits or reduces costs will increase the internal rate of return and make the investment more attractive. Thus, an increase in the earnings of college graduates relative to high school graduates, a reduction in expected labor force intermittency, a longer expected work life, an increase in financial aid for higher education, and a reduction in foregone earnings due to recessionary conditions in the economy at the time of the investment will all increase the likelihood that an individual will invest in human capital.

Problems

Problems are routinely dismissed by developers of the theory as being inconsequential. This includes the problems associated with the inability of individuals to forecast the future and to account for non-pecuniary benefits and costs in calculating the internal rate of return; and those related to the simple fact that some individuals pursue higher education not for purposes of investment but rather for consumption. Of all the expenditures that have been classified as investments in human capital, expenditures on education and training have received the most attention at the macroeconomic level from both theorists and policy makers.

Critique by political economists

Many US economists in the 1960s used human capital theory to argue that poverty and its attendant problems could be remedied by increasing government expenditures on education and training for the poor. These expenditures would enable the poor to increase their stock of human capital, thus increasing their productivity and their earnings. While accepting that education and training are usually necessary for obtaining well paid jobs – although not necessarily for the same reasons espoused by human capital theorists – other, non-orthodox economists rejected the claim that education and training are sufficient to bring people out of poverty. These economists argued that discrimination and the segmented nature of labor markets prevented minorities and women from capturing the returns posited by human capital theory. Thus, more radical changes are called for. The ideas put forth by these economists developed into several alternative models of the labor market.

Of the alternatives, SEGMENTED AND DUAL LABOR MARKETS, in particular, were the most important to be put forward by radicals and Marxists. According to radicals and Marxists, human capital theory, in treating workers as capitalists, eliminates CLASS and class conflict as central concepts in economic analysis (Bowles and Gintis 1975). As such, human capital theory ignores the role of education in preserving the class structure of capitalist societies, and thus fails to see how the educational system helps to keep wages low and perpetuates income inequality. In addition, Marxists argue that human capital theory excludes a consideration of the social relations of production from its theory of production. In focusing solely on the technical relations of production, human capital theorists fail to recognize that capitalists organize production so as to "extract labor from workers at the lowest possible wage and prevent the formation of worker coalitions which could oppose their power" (Bowles and Gintis 1975: 6). Consequently, human capital theorists are blind to the role that gender, race and other social factors play in the organization of production, the allocation of workers among jobs, the nature of WAGE DETERMINATION, and the structure of the occupations within which they work.

Other questions

Coincident with the development of these alternative models, many economists questioned the causal links assumed to exist between the stock of human capital and productivity and between productivity and earnings. For example, some economists assert that education does not, in and of itself, increase productivity. Rather, it is the higher level of native ability, associated with educational advancement, that is really responsible. Alternatively, other economists argue that education serves simply as a "screening device" for employers who are looking for the most trainable workers.

In the job competition model (Thurow 1975), workers compete for scarce job openings not by offering their labor at lower and lower wages, but by acquiring those credentials which make them attractive to employers. In this model, high school degrees and college diplomas are not rewarded because of any education-based productivity enhancement. Rather, rewards are due to the signal diplomas send regarding the potential of the employee. Some economists, most notably Ivar Berg (1970), predict that this type of competition among workers for job openings will result in ever greater investments in education. Indeed, it may create overinvestment as workers seek to distinguish themselves through credentialism. From a public policy point of view these interpretations are highly controversial because they call into question the social benefits of increasing government expenditures on education.

As for the second link, that between productivity and earnings, human capital theorists can only infer that a causal relationship exists due to the difficulties associated with measuring individual productivity. Their inference is based upon the marginal productivity theory of wages, which asserts that workers will be paid a wage equal to their marginal product – assuming certain restrictive assumptions hold. But as many economists point out, these assumptions are never borne out. Within the labor market there exists a multitude of market imperfections (discrimination, monopolies, labor UNIONS) that preclude the equalization of wages with marginal products. Further complicating the matter is the question of whether productivity can even be attributed to individuals, since the production of numerous goods and services requires the input of many individuals working together as a team, and since knowledge and organization is built from past and present social wealth (see COLLECTIVE SOCIAL WEALTH).

The empirical evidence does suggest that some variations in individual labor market outcomes can be accounted for by variations in human capital investment. At the same time, large residuals remain. Given human capital theorists' adherence to the neoclassical theory of discrimination and rational choice, they do not attribute any significant portion of the residual to labor market discrimination. Instead, they respond by searching for omitted human capital factors and seeking better methods of measurement. Many feminists, along with other non-orthodox economists, are highly critical of this theory-saving approach (England 1982; Bergmann 1989). Despite the criticisms leveled against human capital theory, it remains at the core of neoclassical analysis. It is an integral part of the neoclassical theory, including new home economics as well as the new theory of endogenous growth.

See also:

accumulation; capital and the wealth of nations; circuit of social capital; cultural capital; economic growth; gender; home economics, new; knowledge, information, technology and change; labor and labor power; natural capital; neoclassical economics; neoclassical economics: critique; race, ethnicity, gender and class; race in political economy: major contemporary themes; racism; social and organizational capital; work, labor and production: major contemporary themes

Selected references

Becker, Gary S. (1964) *Human Capital*, New York: National Bureau of Economic Research.
Berg, Ivar (1970) *Education and Jobs: The Great Training Robbery*, New York: Praeger Publishers.
Bergmann, Barbara R. (1989) "Does the Market for Women's Labor Need Fixing?," *Journal of Economic Perspectives* 3(1): 43–60.
Bowles, Samuel and Gintis, Herbert (1975) "The Problem with Human Capital Theory: A Marxian Interpretation," *American Economic Review* 82(3): 371–92.
England, Paula (1982) "The Failure of Human Capital Theory to Explain Occupational Sex Segregation," *Journal of Human Resources* 17(3): 358–70.
Kiker, B.F. (1966) "The Historical Roots of the Concept of Human Capital," *Journal of Political Economy* 74(October): 481–99.
Marx, Karl (1867) *Das Kapital*, Volume I, published as *Capital, Volume 1*, New York: Random House, 1977.
Mincer, Jacob (1974) *Schooling, Experience, and Earnings*, New York: National Bureau of Economic Research.
Schultz, Theodore W. (1961) "Investment in Human Capital," *American Economic Review* 51(1): 1–17.
Thurow, Lester (1975) *Generating Inequality*, New York: Basic Books.

ELIZABETH A. PAULIN

human development index

The human development index (HDI) measures the performance of different nations and regions in promoting the well-being and opportunities of their inhabitants. The HDI is a composite measure of human development, comprising three dimensions of what constitutes a valued life. These are: (a) the capability to lead a long and healthy life; (b) the ability to acquire knowledge and to participate meaningfully in the life of the community; and (c) the ability to achieve human welfare via the acquisition of vital goods and services. The HDI was devised and has been computed annually by the United Nations Development Program (UNDP) since 1990, and is published in the annual *Human Development Report*.

People-oriented development philosophy

The HDI reflects what the UNDP calls a "people-oriented" notion of economic development. The HDI project reflects the trend of the 1970s and 1980s away from unidimensional and economistic measures of development, such as ECONOMIC GROWTH. This era spawned several new measures of development, such as Morris's "physical quality of life index" (PQLI). The HDI is unique, however, in that it bears the direct influence of Amartya Sen, who has argued for a focus on people's substantive freedoms to live valued lives (their "capabilities") as the most important desideratum of development programs. This sentiment underlies the composite nature of the HDI, which is intended to capture some of the most fundamental human capabilities.

The HDI combines a country's performance in longevity, measured by the average life expectancy at birth; educational attainment, measured by the adult literacy rate and the combined primary, secondary and tertiary enrolment ratio (averaged); and access to resources, measured by adjusted GDP per capita (see below), calculated in terms of purchasing power parity (PPP$).

Calculation of the HDI

The UNDP has adopted fixed minimum and maximum values for each component in computing the index. The minima are taken from the lowest observed performance among national and subnational populations over the past thirty years; the maxima are taken to be the values achievable by the best performers by the year 2020. The range for each component is as follows:

- life expectancy at birth: 25 years to 85 years;
- adult literacy: 0 percent to 100 percent;
- combined enrolment ratio: 0 percent to 100 percent;
- real GDP per capita (PPP 1992 dollars): $100 to $40,000.

For each component, the UNDP compares a country's actual achievement (distance from the minimum) against the range of what is achievable (from the minimum to the maximum). Country j's performance in each of the three major components (i) of the index is therefore given by:

$$H_{ij} = (X_{ij} - \text{Min}, X_i)/(\text{Max}\, X_i - \text{Min}\, X_i) \tag{1}$$

A country's overall HDI is simply the unweighted average of its performance in all three of the indices: the life expectancy index (*LEI*), the educational attainment index (*EAI*), and the adjusted real GDP per capita index (*RGDPI*):

$$HDI = (LEI + EAI + RGDPI)/3 \tag{2}$$

In calculating the adjusted *RGDPI*, the UNDP discounts per capita income above the world average at steeply progressive rates, using a modified version of Atkinson's utility formula (UNDP 1995: 134). This reflects the view that higher income above some threshold level exerts a diminishing marginal contribution to human development.

The computation of the HDI can be illustrated by reference to the countries in Table 1, including Canada and Niger, the highest and lowest ranking countries (respectively) in the 1995 *Human Development Report* (based on 1992 data). The virtue of having a simple measure (with fixed maxima and minima) is that it facilitates comparing levels of human development among countries and tracking country performance over time. From 1960 to 1992 the average HDI for all developing countries (for which data exist) increased from 0.26 to 0.541, and for the least developed countries, from 0.165 to 0.307, placing the latter in the low-development range despite substantial improvements. East Asia experienced the greatest advance, increasing from 0.416 to 0.861, representing a movement from low to high development.

Ethnicity indexes

As a national average, the HDI can mask substantial intra-country disparities. Beginning with the 1993 *Human Development Report*, the UNDP has undertaken disaggregated country studies by region, race and other categories. This concern with INEQUALITY reflects (in part) the view that relative inequalities may induce absolute capability failures (Sen 1992). For example, the poor in a wealthy country may find it difficult to achieve political efficacy. The results are telling. For example, South Africa earned an aggregate HDI of 0.650 in 1994. White South Africans, however, enjoyed an HDI of 0.878, which would have placed them twenty-fourth in the world, while black South Africans experienced an HDI of 0.462, placing them 123rd. In Brazil, regional disparities are of comparable magnitudes (see RACE IN POLITICAL ECONOMY: MAJOR CONTEMPORARY THEMES).

Gender indexes

The UNDP's commitment to equality is reflected also in its computation of gender and income distribution-adjusted HDIs. The gender-related development index (GDI), adopted in 1995, combines measures of a country's overall achievement and degree of gender equality (in each component of the index). In short, "the GDI is simply the HDI discounted, or adjusted downwards, for gender inequality" (UNDP 1995: 73). The 1995 *HDR* also includes a gender empowerment measure (GEM) which focuses on the level of women's economic, political and social participation.

An examination of the GDI results yields several important conclusions. First, women fare worse than men in every country in the

Table 1

	Life expectancy at birth (years)	Adult literacy rate (%)	Enrolment ratio (%)	Real GDP per capita (PPP$)	Adjusted real GDP per capita
Canada	77.4	99.0	100	20,520	5,359
USA	76.0	99.0	95	23,760	5,374
France	76.9	99.0	86	19,510	5,347
Brazil	66.3	81.9	70	5,240	5,142
Vietnam	65.2	91.9	49	1,010	1,010
India	60.4	49.9	55	1,230	1,230
Niger	46.5	12.4	14	820	820
	LEI	EAI	RGDPI	HDI	
Canada	0.87	0.99	0.98	0.950	
USA	0.85	0.98	0.99	0.937	
France	0.87	0.95	0.98	0.930	
Brazil	0.69	0.78	0.94	0.804	
Vietnam	0.67	0.78	0.17	0.539	
India	0.59	0.52	0.21	0.439	
Niger	0.36	0.13	0.13	0.207	

Source: *Human Development Report* (1992)

world. Second, the degree of gender inequality does not depend on a country's level of income: while the Nordic countries perform extremely well, for example, Japan performs rather poorly in this regard. Among poorer countries, Barbados, Cuba, Malaysia, Sri Lanka, Thailand and Jamaica are relatively good performers in promoting gender equality. Third, the GDI has risen over time virtually everywhere, although the gender gap in human development remains substantial.

Income distribution-adjusted index

The income distribution-corrected HDI presented in the 1994 *Human Development Report* weights each country's HDI by a ratio of the income share of the poorest quintile to that of the richest quintile. Among developed countries, Belgium and Germany improve their rankings following this adjustment most dramatically; among developing countries, China, Sri Lanka and Jamaica improve most significantly. In contrast, Canada, Switzerland, Australia, Brazil and Botswana all lose significant ground relative to other countries under this measure.

Controversies and further measures

Since its inception, the HDI has generated substantial controversy. Debate centers on the dimensions of life reflected in the index, the variables chosen to capture these dimensions, and measurement of the selected variables (UNDP 1993: 104–14). Alternative definitions of development naturally entail different normative judgments concerning social progress, and hence imply alternative measures. However, disagreements exist even among those who subscribe to the capabilities approach adopted by the UNDP. For example, some critics have argued that the index is marred by the omission of indicators of human and political freedom. The 1991 and 1992 editions of the *Human Development Report* grappled with this matter and reported on the UNDP's ongoing efforts to establish a freedom index. The latter was omitted from later reports because of significant normative and practical obstacles, but work continues in this area. The UNDP has also begun investigation of a "green" HDI to incorporate environmental quality in its assessments on the grounds that the quality of a community's natural environment is a powerful determinant of its own and future generations' capabilities (see GROSS DOMESTIC PRODUCT AND NET SOCIAL WELFARE).

Disputes regarding variable selection concern (for example) the adjustments made to income as a proxy for welfare, the relationship between income and the other variables, the incomparability of measures of knowledge acquisition across national borders, and the need for context-specific rather than universal measures of human development. In some instances, the UNDP has altered its choice of variables to take account of criticisms it finds compelling (for example, the introduction of enrolment data in the 1995 HDR reflects the acknowledgment of the difficulties attending cross-border literacy comparisons). In some areas it continues to explore new approaches (for example, it is examining the need for distinct indicators for developed and developing countries), while in others, it has rejected the criticism outright (for example, it refuses to view income either as a sufficient measure of development, or as a sufficient proxy for the other measures; see UNDP (1993)).

See also:

capital and the wealth of nations; cultural capital; human capital; quality of life; social and organizational capital

Selected references

Anand, Sudhir and Sen, Amartya (1994) *Human Development Index: Methodology and Measurement*, Human Development Report Office, Occasional Paper 12, New York: United Nations Development Program.

McGillivray, Mark (1991) "The Human Development Index: Yet Another Redundant Composite Development Indicator?," *World Development* 19(10): 1461–8.

Morris, D. Morris (1979) *Measuring the Condition of the World's Poor: The Physical Quality of Life Index*, New York: Pergamon.

Sen, Amartya (1992) *Inequality Reexamined*, Cambridge: Harvard University Press.

United Nations Development Program (1990–98) *Human Development Report*, New York: Oxford University Press.

GEORGE DEMARTINO

human dignity

Human dignity refers to the intrinsic worth that all persons possess by virtue of their shared humanity. The term expresses the roots of a deeply egalitarian sentiment. Without the adjective "human," dignity alone has the almost opposite connotation of "social rank," such as a community's "dignitaries." The history of the term goes back five centuries to Pico della Mirandola's *Oration on the Dignity of Man* (1486), which can be seen as a call for human emancipation from the guardianship of the medieval Church. For many years thereafter the concept was almost totally neglected in British thought from Hobbes to Bentham, although some argue that it was strong during the Reformation. It was with the German philosopher Immanuel Kant that human dignity was restored to its central place in philosophy. In Kantian ethics it assumed the place of an objective end and served as the basis of his categorical imperative: "Act in such a way that you always treat humanity, whether in your own person or in the person of another, never simply as a means, but always as an end" (Kant 1785: 94). Human dignity, for Kant, was grounded in human agency, or the capacity of free will. More recently, sophisticated philosophical justifications of the basic notion of human dignity have been offered by Mortimer Adler (1967) and Alan Gewirth (1992).

Human dignity has been central to liberal political thought, Protestantism and Catholic social thought, while its emphasis in economic thought had been limited to American social economics, especially its HUMANISTIC ECONOMICS strand (Lutz, 1998: ch. 6). Otherwise, the imperative of human dignity is usually honored in its breach. A most telling and explicit rejection of the principle of human dignity and Kant's categorical imperative can be found in Lionel Robbins's defense of Wicksteed's "non-tuism" principle of exchange: "All [non-tuism] means is that my [human] relation to [partners in exchange] does not enter into my hierarchy of ends. For me (who may be acting for myself or my friends or some civic or charitable authority), they are regarded merely as means" (Robbins 1935: 97). Clearly, respect for human dignity eludes instrumentally rational economic man. Yet human dignity obliges us to include the other as end. Moreover, it can be argued that, without the egalitarian metaphysics of human dignity, the idea of a social contract or, more generally, the naturalistic program to ground social institutions in mere social agreement is utterly incomplete. Prior to any agreement is the presupposition that every participant must have equal worth and an equal vote. Similarly, the concept of human dignity questions the creed of cultural relativity in ethics (Lutz 1995: 180).

Neoclassical economics, while recognizing and respecting the Kantian idea of mutual consent intrinsic to Kantian ethics, goes only part of the way. Consent, while necessary, is not a sufficient condition for respecting intrinsic worth. It is necessary because, by acting under someone's compulsion, one's will is not respected but rather suppressed and subordinated to the other's will: the classic case of having to serve as a mere instrument. It is not sufficient because agents can either voluntarily, or through market coercion, engage in degrading behavior. A prime example of this is the entering into of an employment contract where workers *alienate* their will, or decision-making power, to their employer for the duration of the contract. Such was recognized by the neo-Kantian philosophers of the Marburg School, especially Hermann Cohen, in early twentieth-century Germany; this provided the foundation for their advocacy of worker cooperatives, where members *delegate* their wills to management rather than alienate them to the goals of capitalist shareholders. More recently, David Ellerman has rearticulated and elaborated this point of view in arguing for economic democracy and the labor theory of property.

Further domains where respect for human dignity demands going beyond consent may include, *inter alia*, censure of adoption markets, markets for human organs, surrogate motherhood, prostitution for pimps, pornography and manipulative commercial advertising. Above all, it also can be seen as providing the very foundation for protecting the rights of future generations under the banner of SUSTAINABLE DEVELOPMENT.

See also:

community; ethics and morality; needs; participatory democracy and self-management; rights; social economics: major contemporary themes

Selected references

Adler, Mortimer (1967) *The Difference of Man and the Difference it Makes*, New York: Holt, Rinehart & Winston.

Cohen, Hermann (1907) "Ethik des Reinen Willens," from his *Collected Works*, vol. 7, part 2, Hildesheim, George Olms Verlag, 1981.

Ellerman, David (1988) "The Kantian Person/Thing Principle in Political Economy," *Journal of Economic Issues*, 22(4): 1109–22.

Gewirth, Alan (1992) "Human Dignity as the Basis of Rights," in Michael Meyer and W.A. Parent (eds) *The Constitution of Rights: Human Dignity and American Values*, Ithaca, NY: Cornell University Press, 10–28.

Kant, Immanuel (1785) *Groundwork for the Metaphysics of Morals*, trans. H.J. Paton, New York: Harper Torch Books, 1964.

Lutz, Mark A. (1995) "Centering Social Economics on Human Dignity," *Review of Social Economy* 53(2): 171–94.

——(1998)*Economics for the Common Good: Two Centuries of Social Economic Thought in the Humanistic Tradition*, London and New York: Routledge.

Pico della Mirandola, Giovanni (1486) *Oration on the Dignity of Man*, trans. A.R. Caponigri, Chicago: Henry Regnery Company, 1967.

Robbins, Lionel (1935) *The Nature and Significance of Economic Science*, 2nd edn, London: Macmillan.

Spiegelberg, Herbert (1970) "Human Dignity: A Challenge to Contemporary Philosophy," in Rubin Gotesky and Ervin Laszlo (eds), *Human Dignity*, New York: Gordon & Breach, 39–64.

MARK A. LUTZ

humanistic economics

Being part of a tradition, rather than a school, followers of this tradition in economic thought attempt to reconstruct economics on the basis of an institutional and historical approach. It is also social in the sense of recognizing the importance of the fallacy of composition, and thereby making room for a genuine macroeconomics. Such analysis is supplemented with some ethical or normative criterion representing human welfare (see Lutz 1998). Central to the project is an explicit recognition of basic human NEEDS and intrinsic HUMAN DIGNITY. As such, it forms an integral part of social economics (see SOCIAL ECONOMICS: MAJOR CONTEMPORARY THEMES).

History of humanistic economics

Historically, this perspective dates back to J.C.L. Simonde de Sismondi's *New Principles of Political Economy*, first published in 1819, which sought to reorient classical economics away from an emphasis on wealth to human welfare. In the process, Sismondi, highly critical of both Ricardian abstract analysis and Say's Law, inaugurated a macroeconomics driven by an interest in INEQUALITY in DISTRIBUTION OF INCOME and UNCERTAINTY about the future, while emphasizing disequilibrium and the socially painful adjustment process. Rejecting laissez-faire and a natural harmony among the classes, he enlisted government to protect the poor and promote the dispersion of ownership via family farms in agriculture and worker co-ownership in industry.

The humanistic approach characterized much of the work of the economic thought of John Ruskin in England and George Gunton in the United States. However, it was John Hobson whose life's work added more than anyone else's to the tradition: his rejection of Say's Law and macroeconomic thought in many ways anticipated J.M Keynes. His *Work and Wealth*, published in 1914, established the first coherent attempt at welfare analysis centered around a human standard. His famous *Imperialism: A Study*, published in 1905, was a highly critical account of colonialism and added an international dimension to humanistic economics. Moreover, like Sismondi before him, he devoted much attention to the quality of work and the human costs of competition. He also applied the humanistic perspective to methodological issues in his *Free Thought in the Social Sciences*, published in 1926, where he rejects the fact/value distinction, instrumental reason and other aspects of positivism.

E.F. Schumacher must be seen as the third giant in humanistic economic thought. After having long been a leading economist in the British state apparatus (see Hession 1986), in 1972 he published *Small is Beautiful*, a book that focused above all on the issues of scale, resource conservation and the question of technology in less developed countries. Schumacher was very much influenced by M.K. Gandhi and R.H. Tawney, both closely linked with the humanistic tradition (see GANDHIAN POLITICAL ECONOMY).

More contemporary articulations of a humanistic approach can be found, *inter alia*, in Daly and Cobb (1989), Ellerman (1992), Ginzberg (1976), Lutz and Lux (1989) and Lutz (1998). In the space provided, we shall briefly discuss the basic elements of humanistic economics.

Human image

Humanistic economics is built on an essentially Aristotelian image of the person equipped with basic material needs and the innate drive for self-realization. The basic needs of food, shelter, clothing, economic security, affiliation, self-respect and self-actualization or "authentic" personality are seen as universal, although their means of gratification are culture bound. Moreover, there are qualitative differences between basic needs meaning that for each's particular satisfaction there is no effective substitute. Similarly, the person is seen as not only having a material dimension, but also a social and moral capacity. This translates into corresponding types of motivation, including the drive for cognitive knowledge and the common good. As a corollary, the person is understood as being able to overcome self-interest in being "other-directed," or responding to moral imperatives, from which also follows that, beyond the forces of selfishness and "socialization," there is also "individuation." Such a view permits the conception of a dual self, an idea inspired by the work of Amartya Sen (see, for instance, Sen 1977), where the agent is always confronted with a choice of following his inclinations (ego self) or acting according to his or her aspirational self, that is, the kind of preferences and behavior with which we prefer to be identified (Lutz and Lux 1989: ch. 6).

Furthermore, the growth of personality is inhibited or promoted by the surrounding socioeconomic conditions and institutional framework (see INSTITUTIONS AND HABITS; INDIVIDUAL AND SOCIETY). Preference formation is largely endogenous, and is influenced by such factors as job insecurity and the perceived extent of fairness prevailing in society. Finally, it is because of the higher capacities of reason, which demarcate humanity from the rest of nature, that every person is endowed with human dignity and certain inalienable rights independent of, and prior to, social agreement. In summary, human nature is conceived in rather traditional terms, a circumstance that will not preclude the making of a progressive, even radical reconstruction of economic thought.

The reasonable person

The humanistic reconceptualization of rationality as being complex and bounded (Hamlin 1986: 22) rejects mere instrumental definitions that postulate a given end and commensurable means. Instead, agents have plural ends and multiple preference rankings, which tend to violate the orthodox completeness axiom and deny neoclassical algorithmic choice procedures. The choice between following considerations of self-interest or morality must be seen as an incommensurable and qualitative choice, a judgment. Such judgments are reasonable or unreasonable depending on whether they promote or inhibit the person's material and social satisfaction of needs, and enable moral integrity; in other words, whether or not we act in conformity with the aspirational self. In short, the humanistic counterpart of atomistic rational economic man is the socially sensitive and morally responsible "reasonable person." Spontaneous cooperation and the activation of the whole person, not merely selfish free-riding and acquisitive instincts, is important in the generation of social behavior and the activation of economic institutions (see POST-KEYNESIAN THEORY OF CHOICE).

Critical realism

Philosophically, the humanistic tradition has been adhering to a position best described as embracing transcendental or critical realism. Its metaphysical depiction of economic agents is grounded in experience and introspection, but is always open to criticism. So, for example, its representation of human nature could be criticized by successfully demonstrating that persons cannot have or do not have self-awareness manifesting in higher order preferences of an aspirational self. Similarly, since much of humanistic thought hinges on a belief that disinterested thought is attainable in principle (although rarely attained in actuality), the critic would need to make a convincing case that going beyond self-interest is impossible. More generally, it stipulates the self as an ontological category and postulates real flesh-and-bone persons having different motives and being capable of different types of social relationships, rather than axiomatic constructs in an abstract world of mathematical objective functions. The embrace of a realist stance dictates ongoing scrutiny of the assumptions underlying theorizing, while the emphasis on rational criticism makes it largely immune to recent post-positive currents questioning the very legitimacy of economic knowledge (see Lawson 1994: 125–8; Hands 1993: ch. 11).

The emphasis on grounding economics on the whole person does not preclude the recognition that self-interested action is the predominant force in today's economy. But, at the same time, altruism and commitment to principles other than self-interest are seen as distinctive human capacities that must figure in the normative considerations of constructing a meaningful political economy. Similarly economic imperialism and the "new welfare economic," both geared to the narrow goal of allocative efficiency, appear deeply problematic (see Lutz and Lux 1989: chaps 7, 9). Instead, the perspective centers on objective material needs satisfaction, non-alienating work, and the need for self-determination and workplace democracy. The stress on vital needs also paves the way for respecting the requirements of unborn generations thereby, like the earlier stress on the fallacy of composition, further rejecting METHODOLOGICAL INDIVIDUALISM.

Endogenous ethics

Making ethics endogenous to economic thinking by postulating the imperatives of human needs satisfaction and human dignity implies a critical analysis of social institutions and policies that may be summarized by the following guiding principles: egalitarian, anti-poverty, income and job security, PARTICIPATORY DEMOCRACY AND SELF-MANAGEMENT (for example, the labor theory of property), and SUSTAINABLE DEVELOPMENT. All these goals imply a rejection of laissez-faire in domestic and international commerce, without falling prey to excessive state bureaucracy.

Ideally, the socioeconomic independence of the nation, the community and the rights of future generations are to be affirmed, insulated and protected from the competitive forces of the global marketplace.

Conclusion

Based on a sound and factual analysis of the economic process that is sensitive to history and institutions and a macroeconomics worthy of its name, humanistic economics, with its focus on human needs and dignity, proposes an ethics intended to assist in the construction of a more humane economy. It can be seen as both the oldest and perhaps least developed branch of heterodox political economy. Much of its relative attractiveness will depend on an assessment of its distinctive human image, together with its four cardinal principles: economic sufficiency for all, respect for human dignity, economic democracy and ecological sustainability.

See also:

social economics: major contemporary themes

Selected references

Daly, Herman E. and Cobb, John B. (1989) *For the Common Good*, Boston: Beacon Press.
Ellerman, David (1992) *Property and Contract: The Case for Economic Democracy*, New York: Basil Blackwell.
Ginzberg, Eli (1976) *The Human Economy*, New York: McGraw-Hill.
Hamlin, Alan (1986) *Ethics, Economics and the State*, New York: St. Martin's Press.
Hands, D. Wade (1993) *Testing, Rationality and Progress*, Lanham, MD: Rowman & Littlefield Publishers.
Hession, Charles H. (1986) "E.F. Schumacher as Heir to Keynes' Mantle," *Review of Social Economy* 44(1): 1–20.
Lawson, Tony (1994) "Why Are So Many Economists So Opposed to Methodology?," *Journal of Economic Methodology* 1(1): 105–33.

Lutz, Mark A. (1998) *Economics for the Common Good: Two Centuries of Social Economic Thought in the Humanistic Tradition*, New York: Routledge.
Lutz, Mark A. and Lux, Kenneth (1989) *Humanistic Economics: The New Challenge*, New York: Bootstrap Press.
Sen, Amartya (1977) "Rational Fools: A Critique of the Behavioral Foundation of Economic Theory," *Philosophy and Public Affairs* 6: 317–44.
Sowell, Thomas (1972) "Sismondi: A Neglected Pioneer," *History of Political Economy* 4: 62–88.

MARK A. LUTZ

hunter–gatherer and subsistence societies

The enormous variety of hunter–gatherer and subsistence societies across time and space that have been documented by historians and anthropologists makes it difficult to generalize about such societies. Each is to a large extent *sui generis*. Nevertheless, it is possible to make generalizations, provided it is borne in mind that they are subject to more than the usual qualification when applied to specific cases.

There are many approaches to the study of hunter–gatherer and subsistence societies (see Wolf 1966; Nash 1966; Terray 1972; Sahlins 1974). It is proposed here to adopt an approach based on institutions, habits and customs influencing the decision-making process in these societies (see INSTITUTIONS AND HABITS). The choice of this approach is informed by the belief that a society will function and perform in the way it does for reasons of the environment, its institutions and decisions. Institutions, including customs and CONVENTIONS, are simply the product of past decisions constrained by the physical environment. In what follows, we discuss first the influence of the physical environment on the decisions and behavior of hunter–gatherers; following this, we examine the structure and procedure of decision making, the information and criteria on which decisions are based, and the incentives and motivations of individuals living in hunter–gatherer and subsistence societies.

Subsistence and the physical environment

There is a general misconception about the concept of subsistence, namely, that subsistence societies are poor and miserable. To clarify this misconception, it is useful to draw a distinction between "subsistence production" and "subsistence living" (Wharton 1963). The former refers to a self-contained and self-sufficient society, where all production is either consumed or some of it is re-invested to sustain a growing population; in either case, there would be no increase in "income" per capita. The latter, subsistence living, refers to low levels of living. The two concepts of subsistence need not go together. Indeed, historical and anthropological accounts of hunter–gatherer societies reveal that many of them are "affluent without [experiencing] abundance" (Sahlins 1974). No doubt, some hunter–gatherers are poor, by modern standards of material wealth, but they are seldom miserable.

In the hunter–gatherer and subsistence societies, it is fairly obvious that the physical environment has an enormous influence on the decisions and behavior of the COMMUNITY. In the tropics, labor becomes arduous after a few hours of work. Basic natural wants (food, shelter and clothing) are obtained with less time and energy than in colder regions. Many studies of hunter–gatherer societies show that one person's labor is often enough to feed four or five people (Sahlins 1974). Moreover, the ease or difficulty with which NEEDS are obtained affects people's attitudes and behavior. When nature is bountiful, people are carefree and prodigal. They do not plan their production and consumption in advance. Where nature is not so bountiful, people are inclined to be more frugal, far-sighted and calculating.

Evidently, environmental factors prevent certain things from being done and enable others to be accomplished, but are seldom completely binding. The extent to which environmental factors can be overcome or exploited depends on the available TECHNOLOGY, know-how and the ability to take timely but appropriate decisions. Since the available technology is quite simple, hunter–gatherers have a low capacity to manipulate or damage the environment. Indeed, they adjust their wants and needs to the environment and, thus, tend to live in harmony with it. Further, because of the determining force of customs and tradition (the social environment) there is little pressure to change technology and preferences. Hunter–gatherer and subsistence societies therefore tend to remain in a stationary state for a long period, and will remain in that state until and unless they are disturbed by external shocks.

By definition, hunter–gatherer and subsistence societies are relatively free from investment decisions. The ECONOMIC SURPLUS is usually consumed or used for ceremonial purposes. Production is for needs, not "profits." Even in the case of an agricultural subsistence society, the investment decision is quite simple. There is no UNCERTAINTY of what to do with the surplus, or where to invest it. Most decisions are routine or habitual. The structure of decision making, who is to decide or do what, is given by customs and traditions, by the accepted DIVISION OF LABOR which is predominantly by sex and age (see GENDER DIVISION OF LABOR). Thus, men usually hunt, fish, clear the land and construct dwellings, while women gather food, fetch firewood and water and do the cooking.

Customs and conventions

There may be from time to time harvest or hunting failures which call for major decisions. It is reasonable to suppose that customs and conventions would give guidance as to what is to be done when such failures occur; but in the case of an entirely new crisis or emergency, customs and conventions will often fail and a new authority may have to be improvised to deal with the new threat. If the crisis persists for a sufficiently long period, the new authority may reorganize the hunter–gatherer society on a "command" basis.

The procedure of decision making in hunter–gatherer and subsistence societies is also largely prescribed by customs and conventions. In "normal emergencies" of harvest and hunting failures, meetings of the council of elders would take place to decide what to do, or the chief (the nominal head) might announce his decision in accordance with customs and conventions. The chief may be not an executive head but rather more like the chairperson of a committee. His function is to give voice to the decisions of elders. Documented cases of hunter–gatherer and subsistence societies (Meade 1954) reveal a variety of procedures that can be ranked on a democratic–authoritarian continuum. Often several procedures are employed depending on the nature of the problem confronting the community. In case of a serious emergency, we would expect an authoritarian procedure to dominate the decision-making process.

Corresponding to the decision-making structure, there is an information structure. Since economic activity hardly changes from year to year, no new information is required to obtain subsistence. People know in their geographical location exactly when and where to hunt, fish and gather food. They also have detailed botanical knowledge required for medicinal purposes. No doubt some individuals would possess certain skills and know-how to deal with particular problems and activities. There would also be non-conformists who are inclined to take exploratory decisions and risks, and in the process acquire new knowledge that might be beneficial to the community. However, non-conformists tend to be rare in "customary" societies.

Since economic decisions are largely habitual, and are not differentiated from other decisions, they are not conducive to "rational" economic calculations. This is not to say that a rationalist, calculating attitude is inconsistent with a great deal of traditional behavior. Indeed, it would be a waste of time and energy to calculate the costs and benefits of every decision taken by the individual or the community. Further, economic relations in "customary" societies have a collective rather than an individualistic character. Kinship relations are crucial and reciprocal. Relatives have the right to make demands on successful individuals, and the individual would find it difficult to evade his obligation. For these reasons, economic activity is not directed at making "profits" through exchange, but toward the direct provision of goods and services within the community.

There are subsistence societies where economic life is organized around a non-economic purpose. In some traditional New Guinean tribes, certain payments (such as those for brides) are made only in terms of tusked pigs. As a result, the community produces a surplus of pigs over its immediate needs and consumes it in ceremonial activities (Robinson 1970). There might be economic motives behind such behavior, but they are completely enmeshed with other motives. Labor is often seen as a social service, an obligation to the community. Superficially viewed, this may seem an altruistic or cooperative behavior. However, in reality there may be a sober calculating element underlying this behavior. In the short run, it is the impact of social obligation that is observed, the frequent rendering of a service without demanding an equivalent pay-back. In the long run, however, contributions and rewards tend to even out.

Conclusion

The common view of hunter–gatherers as living on the edge of poverty is quite false. The historical and anthropological evidence suggests that most of them were better nourished and had better health and more leisure than most people in developing countries. More importantly, hunter–gatherers and subsistence societies tend to live in harmony with the physical environment, and follow a path of sustainable subsistence. Their wants are scarce and natural resources plentiful. To that extent, they are nearer to solving the economic problem than modern societies. Thanks to the "creative" function of the market, we are

hysteresis

constantly consuming a great variety of goods. Our wants have become infinite but natural resources are getting more scarce. With our current technology we are less constrained by the physical environment than are hunter–gatherer and subsistence societies. Our control over the environment may not turn out to be a complete blessing. Indeed, we could easily end up in a catastrophe.

See also:

culture; economic anthropology: major contemporary themes; individual and society; markets and exchange in pre-modern economies; methodological individualism and collectivism; Polanyi's views on integration

Selected references

Meade, Margaret (ed.) (1954) *Cultural Patterns and Technical Change*, New York: Mentor Books.
Nash, Manning (1966) *Primitive and Peasant Economic Systems*, Scranton, PA: Chandler Publishing Company.
Robinson, Joan (1970) *Freedom and Necessity*, London: George Allen & Unwin.
Sahlins, Marshall (1974) *Stone Age Economics*, London: Tavistock.
Terray, Emanuel (1972) *Marxism and Primitive Societies*, New York and London: Monthly Review Press.
Wharton, C. (1963) "The Economic Meaning of Subsistence," *Malayan Economic Review* 8(2).
Wolf, Eric (1966) *Peasants*, Englewood Cliffs, NJ: Prentice Hall.

LOUIS HADDAD

hysteresis

Hysteresis is an organizing concept that describes economic systems as they move through historical TIME. It implies that current outcomes are contingent on the past history of the systems from which they derive.

Origins

The concept of hysteresis originated in the natural sciences, where it was first used to discuss the properties of ferric metals in response to magnetization and demagnetization (Cross 1993: 54). Hysteresis has only recently been introduced into economics, although the historical contingency of economic systems and outcomes has long been recognized (Cross 1993: 68; Setterfield 1995: 4–12). Discussions of hysteresis effects became popular during the 1980s in critiques of the natural rate hypothesis – Hargreaves Heap (1980) is the earliest example – but it appears beforehand in Georgescu-Roegen's (1966) theory of consumer behavior, where current preferences are sensitive to past consumption experience. While the "history of hysteresis" is replete with specific examples of hysteresis effects, it is well to remember that hysteresis is a potential property of *any* dynamic system. It is at this more general level of abstraction, therefore, that the concept must be explored.

Different conceptions of hysteresis

Because economists are only beginning to think about hysteresis, it is not surprising to find that there are numerous conceptions of what the process involves. Each of these draws attention to some salient property of hysteresis, and each encapsulates the key principle that economic outcomes in the present depend on the path (i.e. the sequence of prior historical events) that led up to them.

Elster (1976: 374) uses the term "hysteresis" in application to systems whose outcomes can be described by reference to the past values of some variables, but which cannot be characterized by any known or, in the extreme, any conceivable equations of state. (Equations of state involve only current valued variables, whose present values would not change even if the past history of the system were different.) What hysteresis implies, then, is that we cannot understand or explain present outcomes without reference to the past. It does not mean that past events possess a literal presence in the present (which would be absurd).

For Cross (1993: 64–5), hysteresis occurs when the outcomes of a system depend on the non-dominated extremum values of past shocks to the system. A "non-dominated extremum value" is simply a local maximum (or minimum) which is bigger (smaller) than any shock which follows it. An important implication of this definition is that if "big" shocks influence future outcomes whereas subsequent smaller shocks do not, then not all history matters in the determination of current outcomes. Instead, hysteresis involves selective rather than complete history dependence. This, in turn, sets up a distinction between hysteretic and chaotic systems (see CHAOS THEORY), a key characteristic of the latter being that they are always sensitive to even small departures from initial conditions (Cross 1993: 66). Furthermore, Cross's emphasis on shocks draws attention to the possibility of external perturbations triggering hysteresis effects. This is of particular importance when these "external perturbations" take the form of deliberate policy interventions.

Finally, Setterfield (1995: 14) suggests that hysteresis exists when the long run or final value of a variable depends on the value of the variable in the past. That is, by virtue of the influence of this past value on the current alleged exogenous variables, coefficients and structural equations which characterize the system that determines the variable. Here, the focus on long run or final outcomes draws attention to the permanence of hysteresis effects. This contrasts with the transience of historical influences in systems where the past influences current outcomes in the short run, but this influence dissipates in the long run (for example, damped cycles in the multiplier–accelerator approach to cycles). The emphasis on the current value of a variable being influenced by its own past value is also significant. Rather than being the product of exogenous shocks impacting upon an otherwise unchanging economic environment, hysteresis is thus conceived as endemic to a social reality characterized by perpetual, endogenously self-sustaining, motion and change.

Formal characterizations of hysteresis

A number of different formal characterizations of hysteresis exist. Perhaps the most familiar is the linear, unit root characterization. This is so-called because hysteresis arises owing to the existence of a unit root in a first order difference equation (see Cross 1993: 66–8; Setterfield 1995: 14–15). This formalization is attractively simple, but offers few insights into the essential nature of hysteresis. It also suffers the fundamental drawback of portraying hysteresis as a special case. This is counterintuitive given the ease with which verbal models, in which the past indelibly influences future outcomes, can be formulated.

More recent contributions (Cross 1993; Setterfield 1997: ch. 2) have therefore attempted to reconstruct the formal modeling of hysteresis. In these characterizations, hysteresis involves structural change (Amable *et al.* 1995: 169–72), arising from the existence of discontinuities in the adjustment behavior of a system. For example, in Setterfield (1997: ch. 2), the hypothetical adjustment of a system away from and then back toward some initial outcome does not completely restore initial conditions within the system. Instead, the structure of the system is permanently influenced by the experience of adjustment between states. A new long-run or final outcome results, that would not otherwise have been observed were it not for the prior adjustment history of the system. An attractive feature of the model in Cross (1993) is that hysteresis arises from discontinuities *and* the process of aggregation. Outcomes in the system as a whole depend on composition effects arising from the actions of heterogeneous agents, whose individual behavior is characterized by multiple, overlapping equilibria.

The different definitions and formal characterizations of hysteresis discussed above are all broadly confluent, in so far as they all capture the essential feature of hysteresis: the propensity of current outcomes to be influenced by the historical adjustment path taken toward them. This draws attention to an important contrast between systems which involve hysteresis and those based on the conventional (in mainstream economics) organizing concept of determinate equilibrium. In the latter, the structure of a system is treated as a set of timeless data. Outcomes are fixed points, configured a priori in terms of structural data, toward which systems inexorably tend regardless of the precise adjustment path taken. With hysteresis, however, the sequentially unfolding history of a system will influence its structure and hence its outcomes. Adjustment paths therefore determine outcomes, rather than the other way around. This contrast illustrates the claim that equilibrium systems are fundamentally ahistorical, whereas systems with hysteresis reflect the tendency of present actions and events to be born of a specific past.

A form of path dependency

It may appear that hysteresis is merely a synonym for PATH DEPENDENCY. Indeed, the terms are frequently used interchangeably and this is not altogether unreasonable, since hysteresis embodies a very general treatment of path dependency. There are, however, reasons for wishing to retain a terminological distinction. First, there are multiple concepts of path dependency – including not only hysteresis, but also CIRCULAR AND CUMULATIVE CAUSATION, lock-in and so on – each of which has different properties. For example, unlike hysteresis, both cumulative causation and lock-in involve only positive feedback; that is, change that is strictly self-reinforcing (Setterfield 1995: 17–22). Second, as has been seen above, the term "hysteresis" is often connected with specific formalizations of this process, which possess distinct properties that it may not be useful to associate with the principle of path dependency in general.

Relationship to uncertainty

A further correspondence which begs inquiry is that between hysteresis and fundamental UNCERTAINTY. Hysteresis is concerned with the relationship between the present and an immutably given past, whereas uncertainty characterizes the relationship between the present and a yet-to-be-realized future. However, some authors have argued that the two concepts are related, in that hysteresis may describe precisely the sort of evolutionary characteristics of an environment in which agents are subject to fundamental uncertainty (see, for example, Katzner 1993: 339–44).

Conclusion

Although hysteresis has already been used to analyze subjects as diverse as consumer behavior (Georgescu-Roegen 1966) and growth theory (Setterfield 1997), demonstrating its importance as a tool in practical economic modeling exercises remains an important feature of research into the process. It remains to be seen whether proponents of hysteresis will succeed in encouraging its use as an organizing concept in preference to the currently dominant ahistorical equilibrium construct.

See also:

equilibrium, disequilibrium, and nonequilibrium; equilibrium rate of unemployment; evolutionary economics: major contemporary themes; increasing returns to scale

Selected references

Amable, B.J. Henry, Lordon, F. and Topol, R. (1995) "Hysteresis Revisited: A Methodological Approach," in R. Cross (ed.), *The Natural Rate of Unemployment: Reflections on 25 Years of the Hypothesis*, Cambridge: Cambridge University Press.

Cross, R. (1993) "On the Foundations of Hysteresis in Economic Systems," *Economics and Philosophy* 9: 53–74.

Elster, J. (1976) "A Note on Hysteresis in the Social Sciences," *Synthese* 33: 371–91.

Georgescu-Roegen, N. (1966) *Analytical Economics: Issues and Problems*, Cambridge, MA: Harvard University Press.

Hargreaves Heap, S.P. (1980) "Choosing the Wrong 'Natural' Rate: Accelerating Inflation or the Role of History and the Definition of Hysteresis and Decelerating Employment and Growth" *Economic Journal* 90: 611–20.

Katzner, D. (1993) "Some Notes on Related Concepts in Economic Analysis," *Journal of Post Keynesian Economics* 15: 323–46.

Setterfield, M.A. (1995) "Historical Time and Economic Theory," *Review of Political Economy* 7: 1–27.

—— (1997) *Rapid Growth and Relative Decline: Modelling Macroeconomic Systems with Hysteresis*, London: Macmillan.

MARK SETTERFIELD

ideology

Political economists worthy of their salt have always seen questions of ideology as central to their study. Ideology is a "summary set of ideas" about the nature and role of power and authority in society in the minds of people and in motion through institutions. It includes questions of justice, right and a vision for the future, especially regarding the organization of institutions. An ideology is a vision of how the system should be organized for the betterment of certain classes, groups or processes. Essential to an ideology is a policy program on the control of capital, the role of government, and the distribution of income, wealth and power.

Since political economists are interested in the interface between production, distribution, exchange, consumption, government, reproduction and nature, they need not only to have a well-formed ideology, but also to treat the subject systematically, studiously and rigorously. The world is not comprised of two camps of scientists and ideologues. Rather, the two should be seen in symbiotic unity, with various conflicts and tensions.

Political economists tend to be scholars with a passion for critical analysis and the need to be part of a progressive political movement or party. The main tools of the trade of political economists are the skills required for institutional analysis, a critical scrutiny of the dynamic motion of socioeconomic systems, and linking into a political program for the present and the future.

Ideologies in political economy

Ideology has been important to the theories and policies of political economists down the ages, including François Quesnay, Adam Smith, David Ricardo, Karl Marx, Thorstein Veblen, John Maynard Keynes, Joseph Schumpeter, Joan Robinson, Gunnar Myrdal and John Kenneth Galbraith. Good political economy is seen as comprising a serious scholarly undertaking as well as a political act: essentially, it is a fusion of the two. Scientists who claim objectivity are often seen by political economists to be accepting the status quo, assuming constant the distribution of resources and the institutional arrangements and perhaps being afraid to make political conclusions in fear of reprisals from their research sponsors or department heads.

There are many different ideological persuasions that can be activated by economists, policy makers and economic agents. They may be conservative, liberal or radical; they may be right or left wing; they may support FASCISM, CAPITALISM, SOCIAL DEMOCRACY or socialism; they may be green, gay, supporters of the right to life, or animal liberationists. Most questions in life pose dimensions of power and authority, the distribution of resources, access to information and knowledge, exploitation and unequal ECONOMIC POWER. Every part of life can be seen through the perspective of changes in the distribution of power and resources, and the ideologies and practices of classes and economic agents. It is in this field that political economists specialize.

Karl MARX's contribution to political economy was in laying bare the exploitative and contradictory dynamics of capitalism. His ideology was critical for stimulating hypotheses, theories and policy programs. Modern Marxists (following Lenin) tend to see ideology as a "way of thinking" about power and authority relationships. Ideologies often form an important part of the legitimacy necessary for hegemonic ideas and practices (see HEGEMONY).

Thorstein VEBLEN's main contribution to political economy lay in critically examining the philosophical and political preconceptions of economic agents and economists. He recognized that every study is based on such preconceptions, usually without acknowledgment by the writer. Hence scholars cannot avoid these assumptions, methods and philosophies; they should make them explicit, and they should recognize that their work will be fundamentally influenced by them. Ideology is one set of such preconceptions, and it is inextricably linked to the others (philosophical postulates and assumptions, etc.).

John Maynard KEYNES stressed the importance of social convention and the interplay of politics and economics. He saw the real test of academic work to be not simply its theoretical or empirical relevance, but also its nature and success in the political arena. He also strongly identified his own views as being against laissez-faire, Say's Law (supply creates its own demand) and full market processes. His *General Theory* was explicitly ideological in attempting to outline his theory of modern capitalism and critique of the classical doctrine; and he was especially interested (and successful) in influencing the views of economists and politicians.

The AUSTRIAN SCHOOL OF POLITICAL ECONOMY, drawing on the work of Ludwig von Mises and Friedrich von Hayek, has an ideological equivalent at the level of government: the "laissez-faire" perspective. Belief in "spontaneous" market processes and individual motives and preferences forges a very coherent ideological position and clear policy options. The policy conclusions which follow from this theory and ideology include experiments in FREE BANKING, free trade and workplace agreements (see INDUSTRIAL RELATIONS).

Ideology plays an important part in the direction of resources. There can be no doubt that the Thatcher (UK) and Reagan (USA) governments of the 1980s had very common ideological programs (see REAGANOMICS AND THATCHERISM). There was a relatively common ideology underlying Euro-Communism through the 1950s–1980s. The "Cold War" is a classic example of destructive ideological positions taken by the West and the Soviet Bloc. The rise of Islam is associated with a distinctly non-Western outlook on power and authority in the use of resources. The ideology of "White Supremacy" officially ruled South Africa for over eighty years, Germany for twenty three years, and the USA for two hundred years.

Values, assumptions and meaning

Modern political economy tends to judge theories, not simply on the basis of internal consistency, nor simply empirical validity, but also on their ideological content, and the extent to which the theory is capable of being brought to policy attention in one form or another (see Reich 1995). Many debates have surfaced concerning the role of VALUE JUDGMENTS AND WORLD VIEWS, PARADIGMS, research programs, ideologies, and language in economics and scholarly endeavor more generally speaking. These debates have in common the notion that various preconceptions of thought exist which impact on the behavior of groups of people. Questions of objective truth or empirical validity are made problematical when these preconceptions are recognized as being an inextricable part of all such work.

Ideology, normative judgments, assumptions and paradigms have much in common. For instance, an ideology is one type of normative judgment. Quite often, people and economists holding ideologies think they are upholding objective reason. Therefore, ideologies can be expressed consciously or unconsciously, and dogmatically or open-mindedly. They are better off being held as conditional and subject to modification and reorganization on the basis of greater understanding and analysis, and changing institutional conditions.

Important questions are whether ideology is causative or merely reflective of material conditions. The HOLISTIC METHOD would indicate that the two are in symbiotic interaction, with two-way feedback operating between them. A postmodern perspective recognizes that ideologies are ways of constructing meaning in a complex world. The social construction of gender, race, class and the like is a complex outcome of the reproduction of roles and conflicts, and the generation of identity emanating from holding ideologies about such roles.

Costs and benefits

Ideologies have their costs: they tend to divide people, they oversimplify, they potentially misallocate resources, and they contribute often to wars, racial conflict, environmental destruction and anxiety. Ideologies can also function as a legitimizing force, as a smokescreen to evade issues and questions, or as a substitute for lateral and creative thinking.

Ideologies also have many benefits. Joan Robinson (1964) pointed out that ideologies can stimulate research programs and hypotheses. She adds that "a society cannot exist unless its members have common feelings about what is the proper way of conducting its affairs, and these common feelings are expressed in ideology" (Robinson 1964: 9). Ideologies function as a "summary general theory," as a metaphysic that is pre-analytical, but which needs and often stimulates analysis. They enable people to come to tentative conclusions about problems with little information. They provide a forum for interaction between people of similar political philosophies, and often of different persuasions. They help initiate fundamental social, political and economic change.

Conclusion

The great force of ideology is pervasive: it represents the political coming together of groups of people to forge a relatively common program of policy issues based on shared assumptions, theories and life backgrounds. Ideology is an important part of scholarly work, electioneering and community relationships; and it helps to justify the ends of rent seekers, profiteers, exploiters, social reformers and revolutionaries of all types.

See also:

modernism and postmodernism; normative and positive economics; race, ethnicity, gender and class

Selected references

Blackburn, Robin (ed.) (1973) *Ideology in Social Science: Readings in Critical Social Theory*, Bungay: Chaucer Press.
Dobb, Maurice (1973) *Theories of Value and Distribution Since Adam Smith: Ideology and Economic Theory*, Cambridge: Cambridge University Press.
Hausman, Daniel M. (1984) *The Philosophy of Economics: An Anthology*, Cambridge: Cambridge University Press.
Johnston, Larry (1996) *Ideologies: An Analytical and Contextual Approach*, Toronto: Broadview Press.
Katouzian, Homa (1980) *Ideology and Method in Economics*, London: Macmillan.
Lange, Oskar (1963) *Political Economy: Volume One – General Problems*, London: Pergamon Press, ch. 7.
Myrdal, Gunnar (1929) *The Political Element in the Development of Economic Theory*, New York: Simon & Schuster, 1969, especially ch. 8.
Reich, Michael (1995) "Radical Economics: Successes and Failures," in Fred Moseley (ed.) *Heterodox Economic Theories: True or False*, Aldershot: Edward Elgar.
Robinson, Joan (1964) *Economic Philosophy*, Harmondsworth: Penguin.
Schumpeter, Joseph A. (1991) "Science and Ideology" in *Essays on Entrepreneurs, Innovations, Business Cycles and the Evolution of Capitalism*, ed. Richard V. Clemence, New Brunswick, NJ: Transaction Publishers.

PHILLIP ANTHONY O'HARA

import substitution and export-oriented industrialization

Introduction

Import substitution and export-orientated industrialization (ISI and EOI) are two strategies or paths for the development by nation-states of new industries. The application of the strategy of ISI (as distinct from simply levying tariffs on imports) dates from well before the beginning of the twentieth century, and re-emerged in the 1940s–1960s. The strategy of export-oriented industrialization, on the other hand, emerged at about the end of the first "development decade" of the 1960s. It has since become a banner of the forces of globalization.

In the post-Second World War period, as colonies of European nations gained formal independence and revolutionary thought gained prominence, the attention of each emergent nation-state, and of older but very poor nation-states in South America, was focused on two policies. The first was rapid industrialization as a means of securing the development of indigenous CAPITALISM. The second was the domestic production of at least some of the consumer goods which the country had come to import regularly, as an avenue for industrialization. Imported goods are goods for which there is patently a local demand. It was hoped that import substitution would be a prelude to exporting. Arguably, the accrual of knowledge of how to attract domestic customers would make it easier to attract foreign customers, and provide production experience which would lead to cost reductions and a prospect of becoming internationally competitive as an exporter. In recent years, however, it has virtually been claimed that new industries can embark on exporting *ab initio*.

Differences between ISI and EOI

ISI and EOI differ in their reliance on domestic purchasing power. ISI involves a strategy for the protection of domestic markets for local suppliers by state regulations, as distinct from "natural" means such as transport costs. This protection is provided by way of tariffs or quantitative restrictions of imports, or by various subsidies. It may commonly be accompanied by state underwriting of investments, and involves transfers of income within the local community to both the protected capitalists and the state.

EOI, in contrast, involves chiefly the removal of local impediments to the international competitiveness of industry, including the removal of any protection afforded to the local production of raw materials, intermediate goods, equipment and wage goods. EOI enables companies to ignore the impact on purchasing power of the containment of wages as a cost of production. Where the technically optimal scale of enterprise is quite large, it is likely to lead to lower costs of production than ISI.

ISI is symbolic of state programs of protection of employment and job opportunities, and of scope for the development of new enterprises from an initially small scale. It is symbolic of social democratic programs, on the one hand, and of spreading individual aspirations to become part of the ruling class, on the other. To neo-liberals, ISI symbolizes – in their terms – the whole perverse manipulation of the power of the state for private purposes that Fabian SOCIAL DEMOCRACY has let loose on the world. In contrast, EOI as a strategy is said to require no more than market-confirming actions by the state.

Evidence on protection

The neoclassical literature during the 1950s and 1960s concerned itself with quite detailed arguments in opposition to the deployment of protective tariffs as a stimulus to industrialization. For example, it was successfully argued that tariffs are inferior to combinations of subsidies and taxes where externalities warrant some intervention. However, it was conceded that the imposition of a tariff to give protection to an infant industry, rendered uncompetitive by higher costs during a period of learning by doing, might be sensible under certain conditions.

One of these conditions was whether the industry, when it matured, could increase national income sufficiently to offset the cost of the protection. The supposition here is that the market, and especially the capital market, can be mistaken in not supporting the infant industry. It was further pointed out that there was a risk that the income transferred to a protected industry would be consumed by capital owners, workers and possibly state functionaries, instead of being put into expansion and the improvement of PRODUCTIVITY.

The official version of the track record of tariffs is that it bears out the detailed neoclassical arguments against the principle of state protection of particular industries. It is claimed that too frequently protected industries remain uncompetitive. There is said to be little evidence that the demands for equipment are sufficient stimuli for the establishment of "up-stream" industries (Little *et al.* 1970). This is perhaps not surprising, in so far as the only thing the protected industries have in common is that they produce consumer goods for which there is an evident local demand. In any case, as has been pointed out also by dependency theorists, the protected import-substituting enterprises were commonly established by the same TRANSNATIONAL CORPORATIONS as supplied the imports and added little to the local communities, beyond some employment opportunities for local workers (Furtado 1983).

All the same, there is evidence that industries targeted by nation-states can be successfully established within a developing economy. People who are described by World Bank economists as revisionists are wont to argue that nation-states, such as Japan in the decades succeeding American occupation, and Taiwan and South Korea later, stimulated industrialization in the following way. They selected certain industries for special treatment by way of subsidies, state diplomatic efforts in securing raw materials, other means of protection, and the underwriting of investments. They coordinated the investments, and set performance conditions for the companies licenced to operate in the selected industries. It is argued that the nation-states did not simply set the macroeconomic parameters correctly. In their detailed direction, the officials of the nation-states are likely to have had considerable knowledge of the input–output linkages between different industries. They also worked to solve the coordination problems that thwart the exploitation of external economies which technically related industries are capable of generating for each other (Kaldor 1972).

Cumulative causation and increasing returns

It may well be that the distinction between import substitution and export-orientated industrialization in the debate about appropriate public policy for industrialization has distracted economists from a proper examination of the conditions for increasing productivity. Certainly the debate has tended persistently to be couched in static terms, notwithstanding a parallel development of ideas related to the dynamic notions of CIRCULAR AND CUMULATIVE CAUSATION and INCREASING RETURNS TO SCALE.

Two contemporary and much-quoted writers, Michael Porter and Paul Krugman, have emphasized the strength of clusters of technically related manufacturing industries in the "competitive advantage of nations." The strength ensues from increasing returns to the scale of complexes of industries, where Kaldor wrote of the increasing returns to manufacturing as a whole. The common thread is that, where a region overcomes problems in the coordination of private investments by one means or another, it can anticipate decreases in production costs, which will lead to further decreases and greater INTERNATIONAL COMPETITIVENESS.

Conclusion

It appears that the strategy of export-orientated industrialization has become a banner in the late 1990s of the forces of globalization.

Globalization connotes the destruction of all administrative barriers to international trade and investment – that is, the development of global markets for investible funds and for commodities of all sorts. In this state of affairs, large capitals are able to deploy their resources with maximum flexibility and take advantage of low-cost labor power, whenever that is likely to contribute more surely to profits than improvements in the stock of productive equipment, the skills of the workforce and the state of TECHNOLOGY.

See also:

comparative advantage and unequal exchange; development political economy: major contemporary themes; free trade and protection; global corporate capitalism; global liberalism; international political economy; newly industrialized Asian nations; structural adjustment policies; trade policy

Selected references

Furtado, Celso (1983) *Accumulation and Development: the Logic of Industrial Civilization*, Oxford: Martin Robertson.
Hirschman, A.O. (1958) *The Strategy of Economic Development*, New Haven, CT: Yale University Press.
Kaldor, Nicholas (1972) "The Irrelevance of Equilibrium Economics," *Economic Journal* 82(December): 1237–55.
Krugman, Paul (1991) *Geography and Trade*, Leuven: Leuven University Press, and Cambridge, MA: MIT Press.
Little, Ian, Scott, Maurice and Skitovsky, Tibor (1970) *Industry and Trade in Some Developing Countries: A Comparative Study*, London: Oxford University Press for the OECD Development Centre.
Porter, Michael (1990) *The Competitive Advantage of Nations*, New York: The Free Press.
Ranis, Gustav and Fei, John (1988) "Development Economics: What Next?," ch. 5 of Gustav Ranis and T. Paul Schultz (eds), *The State of Development Economics: Progress and Perspectives*, Oxford: Blackwell.
World Bank (1993) *The East Asian Miracle: Economic Growth and Public Policy*, Oxford: Oxford University Press for the World Bank.

GAVAN BUTLER

INCOME DISTRIBUTION: see distribution of income

increasing returns to scale

Increasing returns to scale or economies of scale arise at the point of production when a proportional increase in all inputs leads to a more than proportional expansion of output. With increasing returns, total factor PRODUCTIVITY rises continually as output increases. Assuming that factor prices are given, this results in monotonically declining marginal and average costs of production.

Interest in the principle of increasing returns is as old as the subject of economics itself. However, there is still considerable debate regarding the implications of increasing returns for economic activity, and how best to incorporate increasing returns into economic models.

Sources of increasing returns

A distinction is often made between static and dynamic increasing returns to scale. Static increasing returns arise from an increase in the scale of production at a point in time. For example, a $4 \times 4 \times 4$ storage facility requires four times the building materials necessary to construct a $2 \times 2 \times 2$ facility, assuming that building inputs vary in proportion to the surface area of a structure. However, storage capacity (volume) will increase eightfold in response to the fourfold increase in inputs which brought it about.

Dynamic increasing returns result from the technological and/or organizational transformation of the production process over time as the scale of production increases. There are several sources of dynamic increasing returns. The first is associated with Adam Smith's maxim in the *Wealth of Nations*, first published in 1776, that the division of labor depends on the extent of the market. Increases in output are associated with the subdivision of tasks within firms and throughout industry as a whole as production processes become vertically disintegrated. This is efficiency enhancing because it permits specialization in a particular task by skilled workers, and eliminates time wasted by transferring between tasks.

Dynamic increasing returns also arise when capital is heterogeneous, specific and lumpy, and output is demand constrained. In this situation, a demand-driven expansion of output results in efficiency gains if, as a result, firms are able to accumulate more recent vintages of capital, the economic viability of which depends on high levels of throughput. In other words, relaxation of the demand constraint permits higher levels of output at which new capital, which is more productive because it embodies technical progress, can be fully utilized.

The process of learning by doing is also associated with dynamic increasing returns. Learning by doing involves a direct relationship between the cumulative experience of performing a particular task and the efficiency with which it is performed. Experience can be accumulated simply by repeating a task at the same level of throughput. However, an increase in the number of "doers" (i.e. factor inputs capable of learning) would also increase the stock of experience within a firm and may thus be associated with a more than proportional expansion of output.

The sources of increasing returns discussed above are all internal to the firm. There also exist external economies of scale, however (see especially Alfred Marshall's *Principles of Economics* and *Industry and Trade*). These arise when productive activity by one firm has a positive effect on the productive activities of other firms. Even if each individual firm experiences constant returns to scale, an increase in production by all firms will result in increasing returns in the aggregate owing to these externalities. External economies of scale are often associated with the concentration of production in certain geographical centers. This may result in the development of physical and organizational infrastructures which complement the factor inputs of individual firms and thus enhance efficiency. However, external economies of scale may also arise when many firms, regardless of their location, produce the same line of output or use the same method of production. For example, the knowledge that individual firms possess about a production process or product line may "spill over" to other firms, enhancing the productivity of all.

Implications for economic theory: equilibrium

According to Kaldor (1972), increasing returns render general equilibrium theory of the Arrow–Debreu–MacKenzie vintage redundant, owing to the latter's assumption of constant returns to scale. It is important to note, however, that increasing returns can be reconciled with the existence of general equilibrium, as long as imperfectly competitive behavior is assumed, and the economy is "large" (i.e. there are many agents), the latter being necessary for the application of fixed point theorems.

Nevertheless, even if economies of scale do not invalidate general equilibrium theory, it is not obvious that Walrasian economics provides the best framework in which to think about increasing returns. If increasing returns are dynamic, arising only over time, they may be better conceived as an emergent property of an evolving economy engaged in processes of ACCUMULATION and structural change. On this view, the global nature of increasing returns has a temporal dimension (Setterfield 1997: ch. 3). Increasing returns cannot be realized simply by producing a sufficiently large output at any given point in time – the static view of increasing returns that is necessarily associated with the idea of a general, intertemporal equilibrium. Instead, with dynamic increasing returns, we must think of the technical possibilities for production today as being dependent on realized output levels in the past. Concepts of PATH DEPENDENCY become more useful than equilibrium constructs for describing the behavior of the economy – a conclusion which is in keeping with Kaldor's (1972, 1985) views on the ultimate redundancy of equilibrium methodology in the presence of increasing returns.

Implications for economic theory: theory of the firm and competition

According to conventional neoclassical theory, the optimum size of the firm is determined by equating marginal revenue and marginal cost. Under conditions of perfect competition, this optimum size will coincide with the point at which average cost is minimized.

With increasing returns, however, marginal and average costs decline continuously as output increases. At any given price, there is no finite optimal size of the firm. Instead, firms face the incentive to keep increasing output indefinitely. Clearly, increasing returns are incompatible with the standard neoclassical theory of the firm under conditions of perfect competition, a point which has been evident at least since Sraffa (1926).

Marshall made a number of attempts to salvage this situation. One of his postulates was that economies of scale are external to the firm. Individual firms face conventional "U-shaped" marginal and average cost curves, and increasing returns arise only in the aggregate. However, this is not compelling unless it can be shown that firms cannot merge in order to internalize external economies. Marshall also argued that increasing returns are dynamic, emerging only over time, and will eventually be offset by entrepreneurial failures which arise as aging firms are passed into the hands of ever less competent family owners. Again this is not compelling, serving only to beg the question as to why aging firms cannot hire competent managers.

While the dynamic nature of increasing returns might well prevent individual firms from becoming indefinitely large at any point in time, dynamic considerations of this nature do not fit into conventional competitive analysis in any case (see previous section). The inescapable conclusion is that increasing returns are incompatible with price taking behavior. Imperfect competition must instead be assumed. In the face of downward sloping demand schedules, the size of the individual firm is now limited by a demand constraint rather than by conditions of supply.

Implications for economic theory: short-run macroeconomic outcomes

Increasing returns have also been used as an explanation for quantity constraints at the macroeconomic level. For Weitzman (1982) and Kaldor (1983), economies of scale explain the existence of involuntary unemployment. The argument is that unemployed workers cannot alleviate quantity constraints on their labor supply by turning to self-employment, because of increasing returns to scale. Were returns to scale constant, self-employed workers would be as efficient as large-scale producers, with whom the self-employed could, therefore, plausibly compete. However, increasing returns preclude the possibility of self-employed workers being competitive *vis-à-vis* larger scale producers. This prevents the automatic eradication of unemployment through self-employment.

This argument has not met with widespread approval from post-Keynesian economists, despite its association with Nicholas Kaldor. For post-Keynesians, involuntary unemployment arises from the essential characteristics of a monetary production economy, in which the payment of factors, the act of production and the sale of output (realization of profit) are separated in historical time. Furthermore, the intermediary in this temporal separation of exchange and production activity – money – facilitates a non-commitment to goods in any period. This leads to the possibility of deficient aggregate demand at any level of output and hence, as firms revise their production decisions, the problem of involuntary unemployment. For post-Keynesians, then, the problem of involuntary unemployment stems from effective demand failures in the sphere of circulation, and not from technical features (such as increasing returns to scale) of the point of production (see also the Symposium on Increasing Returns and Unemployment Theory, published in the *Journal of Post Keynesian Economics*, 1985).

Trade, growth and regional disparities: long-run macroeconomic outcomes

Discussion of the implications of increasing returns for trade and growth dates back to Adam Smith, whose insights resonate throughout the subsequent work of Young (1928) and Kaldor (1970: 1985). For Young, the division of labor depends on the extent of the market, but the opposite is also true. The supply and demand sides of the economy interact, therefore, in an iterative process of cumulative causation. Kaldor updated this growth schema in the light of the Keynesian revolution, by arguing that the expansion of productive potential does not automatically create sufficient demand to absorb the full capacity level of output. Rather, demand conditions are relatively autonomous, and effective demand failures can interrupt the course of growth.

For Kaldor, then, the proximate cause of output growth is the expansion of demand. However, output growth stimulates productivity growth because of increasing returns to scale in manufacturing activities, a result enshrined in VERDOORN'S LAW. This improves the international competitiveness of a region's manufactures, stimulating exports and hence aggregate demand which gives rise to further growth, and so on. In this way, initial growth becomes endogenously self-sustaining, bearing out the Kaldorian association between increasing returns and path dependency discussed earlier. The model also predicts income divergence between trading regions. This occurs as manufacturing activity becomes concentrated in regional centers, which reap first mover advantages from initial growth and development that are subsequently reinforced through cumulative causation.

The links between trade, growth, regional disparities and increasing returns have recently been rediscovered by contemporary neoclassical theory, in the form of the New Trade and New Endogenous Growth literatures. These mainstream models do not faithfully reproduce Kaldor's insights, however. For example, increasing returns are sufficient but not necessary for neoclassical endogenous growth, and arise as externalities; there is no discussion of internal economies of scale (Setterfield 1994). This only serves to illustrate the point that there is still no general agreement about the precise nature and role of increasing returns in economics, much less how and where to incorporate them into economic theory.

See also:

balance of payments constraint; circular and cumulative causation; Kaldor's theory of the growth process; social and organizational capital

Selected references

Kaldor, N. (1970) "The Case for Regional Policies," *Scottish Journal of Political Economy* 18: 337–48; repr. in N. Kaldor, *Further Essays on Economic Theory*, New York: Holmes & Meier, 1978.

—— (1972) "The Irrelevance of Equilibrium Economics," *Economic Journal* 82: 1237–55.

—— (1983) "Keynesian Economics After Fifty Years," in D. Worswick and J. Trevithick (eds), *Keynes and the Modern World*, Cambridge: Cambridge University Press.

—— (1985) *Economics Without Equilibrium*, Cardiff: University College of Cardiff Press.

Setterfield, M.A. (1994) "Recent Developments in Growth Theory: a Post Keynesian View," in P. Davidson and J. Kregel (eds), *Employment Growth and Finance: Economic Reality and Economic Growth*, Aldershot: Edward Elgar.

—— (1997) *Rapid Growth and Relative Decline: Modelling Macroeconomic Dynamics with Hysteresis*, London: Macmillan

Sraffa, P. (1926) "The Laws of Returns under Competitive Conditions," *Economic Journal* 36: 535–50.

Weitzman, M. (1982) "Increasing Returns and

the Foundations of Unemployment Theory," *Economic Journal* 92: 787–804.

Young, A. (1928) "Increasing Returns and Economic Progress," *Economic Journal* 38: 527–42.

MARK SETTERFIELD

INDEX OF SUSTAINABLE ECONOMIC WELFARE: *see* gross domestic product and net social welfare

indigenous tenure systems

In the area of development studies, indigenous or customary tenure denotes a system of land ownership (or PROPERTY rights) which, at least in part, predates European colonial and other Western influences. In such systems, the various components or incidents of property rights are typically divided between two units: first, an individual or corporate household unit which uses the land for productive purposes; and second, a local social or political authority (e.g. a clan or lineage head), which maintains rights to repossess the land if improperly used, or redistribute the land as needed to other members of the relevant community. Land rights under indigenous tenure are typically not freely marketable, and are "embedded" in a complex set of social and economic relations (see DISEMBEDDED ECONOMY).

Impact on investment and productivity

The impact of indigenous tenure systems on agricultural investment and productivity has long been debated. In the 1950s, R.J. Swynnerton, an architect of British colonial land policy in East Africa, advocated the replacement of indigenous tenure by more fully privatized Western property rights regimes. This was suggested in order to bolster agriculture investment incentives, and ease the transfer of productive resources into the hands of the most capable farmers, with the remainder of the population being "freed" to join the urban-industrial proletariat. In the 1960s, President Julius Nyerere overturned indigenous tenure and land settlement patterns in Tanzania, instituting a far reaching "villagization" program as part of his design for a specifically African socialism (see Putterman 1985). Other newly independent states have pursued less radical forms of LAND REFORM.

In the 1970s and 1980s, statistics which showed declining agricultural productivity in many African economies rekindled interest in indigenous tenure systems as possible constraints on economic growth. International aid organizations (for example, the World Bank) began to consider conditioning structural adjustment loans on the reform of indigenous tenure systems, and, in response, individual land titling and registration programs were launched in a number of locations. These land reform efforts were also consistent with the neo-liberal development agenda of getting institutions "right," to match the new price incentives for agriculture which STRUCTURAL ADJUSTMENT POLICIES were imagined to create.

Theory underlying new policies

Analytically underpinning this more recent policy orientation is an evolutionary theory of property rights, following NORTH'S THEORY OF INSTITUTIONAL CHANGE. This is based on two main postulates. The first postulate is that indigenous tenure dampens incentives for investment and productivity growth. It is thought to do this especially by making individual producers (or producer units) unwilling to forego current consumption for investment in land which may be reallocated and taken away from them. The second postulate is that demand for fully privatized property rights emerges only when land becomes sufficiently scarce, and investment sufficiently productive, such that the benefits of creating and enforcing a private property regime exceed its costs. As Platteau (1996) notes in his thorough review of this literature, the policy question confronting this perspective is whether or not land is sufficiently scarce to make it worthwhile to engage in institutional midwifery of a land reform, and thus hurrying the supply of the putatively efficient private property regime; or whether it is best to wait and let the institutional evolution come to term autonomously.

Importance of indigenous tenure

Intellectual contestation of this evolutionary theory of indigenous tenure systems has emerged at several levels. The various land privatization reforms undertaken in various African locations created the opportunity to evaluate the investment and other economic gains from such reform by comparing land investment and productivity under the privatized regime with that under still existing indigenous tenure systems. Much of this research, including that sponsored by the World Bank, found little or no economic impacts to these reforms (see Bruce and Migot-Adholla 1994). These findings bolstered the case against further land reform programs, which were already under attack for creating opportunities for local elites to grab land. These reforms were also criticized for failing to recognize and thus extinguishing so-called secondary or derivative rights. (Such rights exist in a complex indigenous tenure system, where socially subordinate people may hold a secondary right to utilize a piece of land for certain purposes.)

In addition to these considerations, the evolutionary theory and its affiliated policy implications have also been challenged on the grounds that they fundamentally misrepresent the economic functioning of indigenous tenure systems. Among other things, this criticism suggests that such systems fill important risk management and other roles which market relations are ill-equipped to replace following land reform. These considerations have begun to prompt a reconsideration of the theory of institutional evolution itself, and its implication that the creation of private property rights will usher in a distributionally neutral evolution to an efficient economy. Zimmerman and Carter (1996) for example, explore the conditions under which the innovation of private property rights regime will usher in a polarized CLASS structure, as the debate on the AGRARIAN QUESTION has suggested.

See also:

collective social wealth; community; development and the environment; inequality; public goods, social costs and externalities; quality of life; social and organizational capital

Selected references

Bruce, John and Migot-Adholla, Shem (1994) *Searching for Land Tenure Security in Africa*, Boulder, CO: Kendall/Hunt Press.
Platteau, Jean-Phillipe (1996) "The Evolutionary Theory of Land Rights as Applied to Sub-Saharan Africa: A Critical Commentary," *Development and Change* 27(1): 29–86.
Putterman, Louis (1985) *Peasants, Collectives and Choice: Economic Theory and Tanzania's Villages*, New Haven, CN: JAI Press.
Zimmerman, Frederic and Carter, Michael R. (1996) "Rethinking the Demand for Institutional Innovation: Land Rights and Land Markets in the West African Sahel," University of Wisconsin Agricultural and Applied Economics Staff Paper No. 400.

MICHAEL R. CARTER

individual and society

"What is society?" and "What is the relationship between the individual and society?" are *the* central social science queries. Along with IDEOLOGY and social context, they shape the hard core of all social theory, determining what concepts will be displaced in the process of theory creation, how phenomena will be conceptualized, what is most important, and what will be the accepted ground upon which to build theories.

Unfortunately, few theorists in the history of political economy have explicitly stated their definition of society, or their conception of the relationship between individual and society.

individual and society

For most theorists it is hidden in their preconceptions, the "convictions that shape the general trend of a man's thinking without being themselves submitted to critical scrutiny" (Mitchell 1950: 203). We can discover the implicit conception of society by examining the metaphors (i.e. displaced concepts, especially those taken from the natural sciences) they use to construct their theories and by an examination of the "final terms" of their analysis (what they accept as the most basic element of social activity).

In the history of political economy, and social theory overall, there have been three conceptions of what society is (Stark 1962), each based on one of the three conceptions of nature (Clark 1992: ch. 2). The use of "nature" and metaphors from the natural sciences in the construction of social theory is to be expected, given the role of "displaced concepts" in the process of theory construction (Schon 1967; Mirowski 1988, 1989; Clark 1992: ch. 1). The three definitions of society are: society as an organism, society as a mechanism, and society as a process.

Society as organism

The view of society as an organism is an extension of the Greek view of nature. The Greeks explained and conceptualized nature by displacing the concept of the human body onto nature; thus nature was understood as a sort of body. Under this approach, the individual units are understood in relation to their place or function in the whole. Society is seen as a unity, not as a collection of entities. Individuals are much like body parts, understood according to their function in the overall society. Two examples of organic political economy are the German HISTORICAL SCHOOL and Marxist political economy.

Society as mechanism

The mechanistic view of society has its roots in the mechanical view of nature, with Isaac Newton as its greatest proponent. In this approach, society is conceived as a collection of individuals. Only the individuals really exist; society as a separate entity is a mental fiction. Society operates much like a machine, based on the workings of the individual parts of the machine. Mechanics and physics are the primary source of metaphors for displacement into economics for this view of society. Mechanistic social theorists have looked to the individual as the "final term," in that all explanations must be in terms of individual actions and motives. This adoption of methodological individualism stems from the belief that inherent in human nature are the drives and propensities which will produce social order (equilibrium) rather than chaos. Thus, the social order in mechanistic theories is also a natural order.

The mechanistic view of society has dominated both classical and neoclassical economic theory. At one level we see this in the extensive use of mechanical and physics analogies and metaphors. The market equilibrium story is a displacement of Newtonian mechanics onto economic activity, with the resultant equilibrium being determined by the balance of individual forces. It is also seen in the necessity to explain all social phenomena as the result of individual human propensities. Whenever institutions are included in the analysis, as with the so-called new institutionalists, the institutions are most often only the effects of individual behavior; rarely are they the cause of individual behavior. The net result of adopting the mechanistic view of society is that it forces theorists to exclude historical and social context from their analysis.

The most extreme form of this type of economic analysis is modern general equilibrium theory, in which neither history nor social context exists. In fact, neoclassical economists see this as a strength of their approach, and they are right if one is looking for invariant natural laws. As Werner Stark has noted:

> If the social order is likened to an equilibrium system ... then it is almost certain to be interpreted in a non historical and unhistorical spirit. An equilibrium has no history; its laws do not change with the

centuries. The formal equations in which it can be described are of timeless validity, as all purely quantitative propositions must be. Rational mechanics is a branch of mathematics and its students glory in the fact: those social theorists who wanted to model [social theory] on rational mechanics [cannot] admit the reality of developmental change.

(Stark 1962: 56–7)

Problems with organic and mechanistic approaches

While both the organic and mechanistic views of society have yielded significant insights into certain aspect of social phenomena, these insights necessarily have always been partial and incomplete. Mechanistic theories are often criticized as being underdetermined, while organic theories are seen as overdetermined. Both criticisms have merit, for organic social thought ignores free will, while mechanistic social thought ignores CULTURE. The essential limitation of each of these approaches stems from the belief that the concepts of individual and society can be separated; that a human individual can exist independent of society, or that society is somehow independent of the individual members:

> Each and every social formation is at the same time a multiplicity and a unity. We cannot speak of a society unless there are before us several human beings, and unless the lives of these human beings are in some way interconnected and interrelated, i.e., constitute a unity of some kind.
>
> (Stark 1962: 1)

Society as process

This brings us to the third definition: society as a process. Originally inspired by the evolutionary view of nature, the "society as a process" definition of society attempts to do justice "both to the real integration of social order and to the real independence of the individuals comprised by it" (Stark 1962: 1).

Such an approach tries to understand the interaction between individuals and society, cognizant of the fact that the resulting behavior is something quite different from what is observed in the natural sciences. As Stark often noted, the natural sciences attempt to understand a reality human beings find, whereas the social sciences try to understand a reality human beings create, a reality that is constantly changing.

Although political economists have often been concerned with processes, these are most often predetermined rather than creative processes. The "society as a process" approach to economic theory views society as the interaction of individuals with free will and social and cultural institutions. The institutions generate the continuity in society with their socialization function. However, the institutions are constantly evolving and adapting to changing needs and circumstances and pressures from individual actions. The actions of individuals shape and determine institutions (along with history), and institutions shape, define and influence individual actions. The outcome of this interaction is not predetermined and there is no conception of a final state of rest or natural order.

Although no school of political economy has explicitly adopted the "society as a process" definition of society, it is implicit in many heterodox schools and can even be found in some aspects of the classical economists and in Marx. When Adam Smith emphasized historical and social context, coupled with his analysis of individual actions, he came close to adopting a "society as a process" view. Modern examples of the "society as a process" approach can be seen in post-Keynesian political economy, especially in the post-Keynesians' concept of historical TIME and their rejection of long-run equilibrium; and institutional political economy, which comes closest to explicitly building a system of thought on a conception of society as a process.

Conclusion

If political economy is to understand economic

industrial relations

activity in its full historical and social context, it must start with a conception of society that explicitly acknowledges both free will and culture; it must conceive of society as a process. This entails that it must also give up the centuries old search for invariant natural laws in the economy. It is only then that economists will do justice to both the individual and society.

See also:

circular and cumulative causation; determinism and overdetermination; holistic method; institutional change and adjustment; post-Keynesian theory of choice

Selected references

Clark, Charles M.A. (1992) *Economic Theory and Natural Philosophy*, Aldershot: Edward Elgar.
Mirowski, Philip (1988) *Against Mechanism*, Totawa, NJ: Rowman & Littlefield.
—— (1989) *More Heat Than Light*, Cambridge: Cambridge University Press.
Mitchell, Wesley C. (1950) *The Backward Art of Spending Money and Other Essays*, New York: Augustus M. Kelley.
Schon, Donald (1967) *Invention and the Evolution of Ideas*, London: Tavistock Publishing.
Stark, Werner (1962) *The Fundamental Forms of Social Thought*, New York: Fordham University Press.

CHARLES M.A. CLARK

industrial relations

Industrial relations (IR) may be defined as the set of rules and institutions which determine pay and other conditions of employment. The main kinds of rules are (1) substantive rules that regulate pay and employment; (2) procedural rules that govern the making and challenging of substantive rules; and (3) disciplinary rules that deal with a breach of both of the above sets of rules. In the settlement of these rules, partially conflicting and partially common interests of workers, employers and also the public at large are involved. Hence, key institutions in IR are companies and employers' associations, trade unions and the state. The participants in IR arrive at these rules via a wide range of means, of which collective bargaining stands out. When unable to find a consensus through negotiation, industrial disputes may arise, for example, in the form of strikes and/or lockouts, unless the parties find alternative means to settle their conflicting interests by conciliation, mediation or arbitration.

Since not only the final result (wage settlement, employment conditions and so on) but also how this result was achieved have significant implications for microeconomic and macroeconomic distribution and allocation, economists have become increasingly interested in understanding industrial relations and their role in a market economy.

History of industrial relations

Modern IR emerged at the time of the industrial revolution in the second half of the eighteenth century. While IR in Europe and in North America developed in similar directions until the end of the nineteenth century, their respective paths started to diverge thereafter. It has been argued that this divergence may be traced back to labor's choice of ideology and the strategy associated with it (Adams 1995). Whereas the European trajectory is characterized by a cooperative model of mutual recognition by central organizations of employers and trade unions, developments in the United States led to a more adversarial model. The Wagner Act in the USA, while having the originally intended effect of encouraging collective bargaining, led also to the spread of the notion that unionization is only necessary where management "failed to do right" willingly. Unions came to be considered not as social partners but, rather, as a kind of punishment for managerial mistakes. Whereas the Canadian and the British IR systems may be seen as intermediate cases between the European and the US models, Japanese IR developed only after the Second World War, when the occupying forces encouraged collective bargaining as a means of democratization. In the meantime, the Wagner Act model of IR has given way to a more cooperative behavior of the social partners.

In general, it seems that IR plays a much more important role in smaller economies than in large ones. This corresponds to the proposition that the key factors leading to the institutionalization of IR were the economic vulnerability of the country (measured in terms of its dependence on world trade) and the size of the population (Armingeon 1994).

Main participants and structures

IR may be described by the intra-organizational and inter-organizational structure of their participants. Employers may either play their role as a single decision unit and/or in association with other employers. For example, it is quite usual for agreements between an employers' association and a trade union at the industry (or regional) level to be renegotiated at the firm or plant level to adjust to the requirements of a single company. Firms can do this because they have many individual sources of power at their disposal, providing them with alternatives to collective action for defending their interests. In contrast to employers, workers participate in IR mainly (but not exclusively) as part of a representative body. The most important examples are works councils (on the firm or plant level) and trade unions (on more or less all levels from the firm to the nationwide level).

The state often plays an important role in shaping the framework within which bargaining and exchange take place and in setting material regulations concerning, for instance, minimum levels of wages or working time. A further role of the state is to harmonize price and wages policies with other areas of social and economic policies. At this point the notion of *tripartite cooperation* or *tripartism* should be introduced. Though these concepts overlap with IR to some degree, tripartism has a different focus: it refers to the participation of employers' and workers' representatives in government economic and social policy-making (Trebilcock *et al.* 1994). The state (in modern welfare systems) is also a large employer. The state interacts with the other two sides in a great variety of different ways and levels. Three general variants are of particular importance. The first is liberal pluralism, related to a passive state under the principle of non-intervention. Here, state regulation is confined to creating a (modest) legal framework for bargaining between capital and labor. An example is the UK system. The second is corporatism, with active state interference, usually in consultation with the social partners; an example is the German system. The third is statism, active and direct state interference in matters of wage settlements and working conditions; an example is the French system.

The inter-organizational structure of IR may be described according to the level, mode and degree of formalization of interaction between the agents. The level of interaction, that is, the level of centralization of bargaining and setting up of agreements, varies from the micro level (firm, plant) to the meso level (industry) and the macro level. The mode of interaction may vary from a predominantly adversarial approach (UK, Australia, USA or Canada) to a social partnership approach (Nordic countries, Germany). Finally, there are quite different *levels of formalization*: there are highly formalized structures backed by legislation (Germany); "pillarized" arrangements (as in the Netherlands, Belgium and Switzerland), which attempt to sublimate religious or linguistic divisions; formal arrangements established in historic agreements (Nordic countries); and more informal structures, established by repeated procedures (for example, Austria).

Corporatism and decentralized industrial relations

Industrial relations, understood as a set of institutions, do not lend themselves easily to economic modeling. Nevertheless, IR has been successfully used as an explanatory factor in comparative studies of economic performance.

industrial relations

In particular, economists have taken up the notion of corporatism, and developed a growing literature (for example, Pekkarinen *et al.* 1992) on the following broad thesis: in the long run, countries with highly corporatist IR show a better performance in most macroeconomic targets than the average, where highly corporatist IR are defined by (a) a high degree of centralization in collective bargaining and (b) a significant involvement of the state in IR.

Four main findings emerge on the relationship between corporatist and decentralized systems. The first is that full employment may be best achieved by countries having either completely centralized or extremely decentralized bargaining structures, while the intermediate economies are likely to do worse. The second finding is that corporatist bargaining structures allow for the implementation of a (permanent) incomes policy, and therefore provide for an option to control inflation without recourse to deflationary fiscal and monetary policies. A negative (inverse) correlation between the degree of corporatism and a "misery index" (inflation/unemployment) has been established.

Third, in countries with adversarial traditions of IR, unions are less likely to cooperate with technological change than their counterparts in countries with "social partnership" traditions. Furthermore, the capability to adjust production structures to changing circumstances and to foster technical progress varies between corporatist countries, according to whether they belong rather to the inclusive (for example, Sweden) than the exclusive (for example, Austria) type of corporatism. Whereas the former type is conducive to a strategic, forward-looking way of industrial adjustment, the latter may tend to defensive industrial policies. Lastly, in general, IR seem to be important and causal in times of turbulence. In these periods, differential economic performance among corporatist countries, and between them and non-corporatist ones, may be particularly visible and can be understood by their differential institutional endowments.

Future of industrial relations

From the perspective of the late 1990s, reflections on the future of IR in the context of globalization and deregulation have raised a number of controversial issues. First, it has been asked whether intensified competition and deregulation on a worldwide scale will eventually transform industrial relations, and in what direction. For example, competition-implied techniques such as just-in-time or lean production make work stoppages disastrous, and hence return bargaining power to the workforce (Bélanger *et al.* 1994). A second question is whether common economic trends (globalization, flexible specialization and so on) will lead to the convergence of IR across market economies (convergence thesis). The "European version" of this argument proposes that European integration will lead to a convergence of IR in European Union countries. However, the empirical evidence supports a divergence rather than a convergence thesis. Neither in Europe nor on a global scale have converging economic (and/or institutional) conditions led to a convergence in IR.

A third question refers to the possibility of transferring a (successful) model of IR from one country to another. From what has been said above, it ought to be clear that IR has historically been a socially and culturally specific institution. Hence, it cannot be expected to be easily transferable from one country to another. There is no way to simply "construct" IR according to some successful blueprint. For example, recent studies on Central and Eastern European economies indicate the enormous difficulties of merely establishing the "actors" of IR, let alone getting the system to work (Haller 1996). Finally, the globalization of production and the increasing importance of multinational firms, as well as the integration of countries into economic regions (the European Union, NAFTA and so on) raises the question of supranational IR. The conclusion from the European experience seems to indicate that there is little hope of establishing a supranational IR system "from above" (i.e. by creating an institutional framework in the European Union). A "bottom-up approach" to IR, initiated by international works councils within multinational companies, seems to be the more promising strategy.

See also:

international political economy: major contemporary themes; social structure of accumulation: capital–labor accord; social structures of accumulation; unions; wage determination; work, labor and production: major contemporary themes

Selected references

Adams, R.J. (1995) *Industrial Relations Under Liberal Democracy: North America in Comparative Perspective*, Columbia, SC: University of South Carolina Press.
Armingeon, K. (1994) *Staat und Arbeitsbeziehungen: ein Internationaler Vergleich*, Opladen: Westdeutscher Verlag.
Bamber, G.J. and Lansbury, R.D. (eds) (1993) *International and Comparative Industrial Relations: A Study of Industrialized Market Economies*, 2nd edn, London: Routledge.
Bélanger, J. et al. (eds) (1994) *Workplace Industrial Relations and the Global Challenge*, Ithaca, NY: ILR Press.
Ferner, A. and Hyman, R. (eds) (1992) *Industrial Relations in the New Europe*, Cambridge: Basil Blackwell.
Haller, B. (1996) "Introduction" to "Austrian Social Partnership – A Model for Central and Eastern Europe?," *Contemporary Austrian Studies* 4: 147–50.
Landesmann, M. (1992) "Industrial Policies and Social Corporatism," in: J. Pekkarinen, et al. (eds), *Social Corporatism: A Superior Economic System?* Oxford: Clarendon Press, 242–79.
Pekkarinen, J. et al. (eds) (1992) *Social Corporatism: A Superior Economic System?* Oxford: Clarendon Press.
Sorge, A. (1995) "New Production Technologies and Changing Work Systems," in J. Van Ruysseveldt et al. (eds), *Comparative Industrial & Employment Relations*, London: Sage, 267–92.
Trebilcock, A. et al. (1994) *Towards Social Dialogue: Tripartite Cooperation in National Economic and Social Policy-making*, Geneva: International Labour Organisation.
Ulman, L. (1987) "Industrial Relations," in J. Eatwell et al. (eds), *The New Palgrave. A Dictionary of Economics*, London: Macmillan, vol. 2, 808–11.
Van Ruysseveldt, J. et al. (eds) (1995) *Comparative Industrial & Employment Relations*, London: Sage Publications.

WOLFGANG BLAAS

industrialization

Industrialization is a process which increases the share of non-agricultural, non-service output relative to national income. Statistically, the industrial sector covers manufacturing, mining, public utilities, and construction but not small-scale, unregistered (often household) manufacturing in the INFORMAL SECTOR. This structural change from agriculture to industry has its roots in Britain, the pioneer of large-scale industry. The process entails sustained investment and continuous improvements in production technologies. It is a historically determined institutional process in which social structures, statecraft and global links play a role. Because industrialization has been associated with economic prosperity, it has been a strategy of economic development in most countries. However, with the ecological effects of cumulative industrialization, the process is being reassessed as a strategy. The global industrialization record is very uneven because of the different institutional contexts found in different societies.

Industrialization has included pioneers and followers, successful catch-up and deindustrialization. In an era of global CAPITALISM, (re)industrialization is taking place in the developed and selected developing economies, using new flexible institutional and production systems (see FORDISM AND THE FLEXIBLE

industrialization

SYSTEM OF PRODUCTION). Industrialization is a complex non-linear process, neither inevitable nor impossible. It is integral to capitalist development. Industrialization is a product of institutional change and has been fostered by proactive states. Most developing countries fail to industrialize because of institutional shortcomings, themselves a product of the past, either because of too much government that stifles innovative behavior or too little of it, allowing dominant groups to capture the state for their own ends.

Paths to industrialization

There are different paths to industrialization. Early British industrialization resulted from the gradual dissolution of FEUDALISM, while late industrialization, with the exception of the erstwhile socialist bloc, has been based on rapid and deliberate introduction of capitalist production relations by the state. Irrespective of the paths traversed, industrialization has produced unprecedented levels of urbanization with a concomitant decline in agricultural employment and rural population.

Industrialization first appeared in Britain as a result of several interrelated institutional changes. Mercantile trade, warfare, peasant rebellions and the rise of towns contributed to the collapse of feudalism, while the commodification of land and uprooting of peasants created a class of owners (capitalists) and wage workers (proletariat). With the institutionalization of private PROPERTY, production for profit through market exchange gained wider currency. The incessant drive to enlarge profits (see ACCUMULATION) by lengthening the work day and introducing labor saving machinery led to CLASS conflicts. Rivalry between capitalists also increased the application of science and technology to production, while the marketization and monetization of everyday transactions forced women and children to enter the industrial LABOR FORCE. Marx astutely observed the inherent contradiction of capitalist industrialization: though the development of superior methods of factory production promised human emancipation, the exploitation of workers by owners revealed the asymmetric power between the two classes (see ECONOMIC POWER; HEGEMONY).

Geographic distribution of industrialization

Industrialization from Britain spread gradually to Europe, North America and, to a limited extent, to other English settlements. Migration, capital flows and the spread of industrial ideas were crucial to the diffusion of industry. Britain as a pioneer could penetrate far-flung markets, but the USA, Japan and European countries relied on trade barriers to nurture their industries. With imperialism, Europe and Japan restructured colonial production. As machine-based production generated ever-increasing output, colonies were transformed into raw material and food suppliers and importers of manufactures. British exports of manufactured goods (textiles, machinery) and India's exports of primary goods (cotton, jute) benefited British industrialization and contributed to the deindustrialization of India's handloom sector. In the USA, the annihilation of non-capitalist social systems, European migration, capital inflows, abundant natural resources and, later, protection of a growing domestic market provided a fertile environment for industrial takeoff. Across the Pacific, Western encroachment forced Japanese elites into creating a highly centralized nationalist state. Like Europe, Japan industrialized by reorganizing production in its East Asian colonies and protecting its domestic market. Except for some nominal change, industrialization in colonies was mostly regressive.

Imperialism and industrialization

Whether imperialism facilitated or hindered capitalist industrialization has not been definitively settled, but neither simplistic explanations of external exploitation nor the "impossibility of industrialization" thesis is tenable. Latin American nations, nominally sovereign since the mid-nineteenth century, failed to remove the Iberian social structural barriers (*hacienda* and *latifundio* systems) and to reduce the hegemony of British and US capital. In India, the maximization of British land revenues strengthened the grip of the landed gentry, moneylenders and traders, and effectively retarded industrial development. In Korea, the Japanese increased agricultural output by eliminating the Korean landed aristocracy and introduced capitalist relations through LAND REFORM. The removal of a structural barrier facilitated future Korean state-led industrialization.

The state and industrialization

Unlike Britain, governments in the USA, Germany and Japan were far more active in promoting capitalist industrialization because of increasing investment requirements and technological complexity. Large-scale industrial production for mass markets enhanced efficiency and concentrated economic power. By the early twentieth century, the emergence of American big business, the German bank-based industrial combines and the family-owned diversified Japanese conglomerates (*zaibatsu*) reflected new forms of industrial organization that no longer conformed to perfectly competitive markets (see MONOPOLY CAPITALISM). Unlike the vast American market, which allowed big business to expand rapidly, both Germany and Japan relied on state initiatives for industrialization. New-found nationalism and the widening technology gap between the early and late entrants to industrialization justified intervention. Modes of intervention included simple infant industry protection (such as tariffs and subsidies) and wage repression, as well as more complex control over credit, macroeconomic planning and strategic trade and INDUSTRY POLICY.

In all cases, industrial investment (capital formation) was increased by raising the national savings rate. By squeezing the peasants (as in the Soviet Union and Japan), favoring the industrial bourgeoisie through tight wage policy and other incentives (as in Korea) and creating public sector enterprises (as in India), states advanced late industrialization. Forced industrialization has gone the farthest where capitalist relations were the most advanced (such as Germany and Japan). Industrialization was possible where social structural fetters were removed either through revolutions (in the former Soviet Bloc and China) or by their systematic weakening through land reforms, targeting and sequencing of industry (in Japan, Korea and Taiwan), and protection of the nascent indigenous industrial class (in Brazil, Mexico and India). Other states in various ways have also introduced limited capitalist industrialization (as in Nigeria, Turkey, Malaysia and Indonesia).

Varieties of state industrial policies

The GREAT DEPRESSION of the 1930s exposed the vulnerability of the colonial structure of trade. The rise of Keynesian demand management, rapid Soviet industrialization and new-found independence prompted many former colonies to adopt a state-led, inward-looking, import-substitution industrialization (ISI) strategy. Proponents of ISI questioned international specialization based on comparative advantage, since the exporters of primary products faced declining terms of trade (prices of non-industrial exports/prices of manufacturing imports) and hence reduced income. The low income elasticity of non-industrial goods, such as coffee, and fierce competition among such suppliers severely limited expansion of production and productivity growth reduced prices rather than raised wages. Only industrialization, it was argued, could overcome such structural bottlenecks. The state therefore protected national capitalists, provided crucial industrial and infrastructural inputs, and regulated TRANSNATIONAL CORPORATIONS (TNCs). Industrial know-how was acquired either by arms-length technology transfer or via FOREIGN DIRECT INVESTMENT in TNC subsidiaries. A number of countries experienced significant structural change in favor of industry (for example, Brazil, Mexico, India and Korea).

The outcomes of state intervention are mixed but debates surrounding the appropriate role of government in industrialization continue. Neoclassical economists have incorrectly attributed rapid export-oriented industrialization of East Asia as evidence of specialization based on comparative advantage. They concluded, not incorrectly, that ISI policies in Latin America and India, among others, sheltered producers from competition and hence supported inefficient, high-cost industry. However, the alternative explanation of East Asian industrialization has been the selective promotion by the state of national business, a market-determined allocation of resources and FREE TRADE AND PROTECTION. Non-neutral state policies favored exports via subsidies and cheap credit and penalized firms which did not meet export targets. Imports were restricted to raw materials and critical technologies, and sound macroeconomic management provided stability. How did the states do this and not succumb to popular political pressures? It was the autonomy of a proactive state, and not its absence, that contributed to industrial expansion. Export orientation, though important to international competitiveness, rested heavily on institutional arrangements geared toward adapting foreign technologies and fostering local technological capability.

New developments in contemporary industrialization

The anti-state bias sweeping the world emerged at a time when the Keynesian consensus on the role of the government in the West was already weak. With general economic malaise in the West, combined with bloated budget deficits and hyper mobility of transnational capital, the regulatory role of the state was ideologically challenged. It is therefore not surprising that the ISI strategy, which failed to eradicate poverty, encouraged rent-seeking behavior, and undermined industrial competitiveness, came under attack as well. The mounting BALANCE OF PAYMENTS problems arising from anti-export policies and the foreign DEBT CRISES IN THE THIRD WORLD, resulting partly from indiscriminate borrowing, easily lent credence to the neoclassical interpretation.

Today, STRUCTURAL ADJUSTMENT POLICIES aimed at minimizing government role and maximizing private sector involvement in economic activity are perceived as the cure for development and industrialization.

The diffusion of successful and yet limited industrialization worldwide indicates that capitalist industrialization is indeed viable but not inevitable. It is the institutional differences that explain the form, pace, and direction of industrial transformation. Also, public policies do matter. Late industrialization has one advantage, namely, the ability to learn from foreign technologies. However, many developing countries have been industrializing through subcontracting low-wage, labor-intensive production, often being a part of elaborate worldwide production networks. Both technological learning and global subcontracting pose formidable challenges to employment in the older industrialized nations, pushing firms to automate even more. On the other hand, flexible systems of work organization and corporatist arrangements between business, labor, and government on neo/post-Fordist lines have created new forms of industrial governance (as in Japan, Italy and Germany) that are creating new industrial agglomerations (reindustrialization) in older industrial countries. Whether this will mitigate the competitive challenges remains to be seen. However, the speed of industrialization in Asia, with a burgeoning middle class in China and India, is likely to stretch global resources and strengthen the populist demand for SUSTAINABLE DEVELOPMENT. With the dismantling of economic barriers, the uneven diffusion of industrialization will most likely accelerate.

Selected references

Amsden, Alice H. (1989) *Asia's Next Giant: South Korea and Late Industrialization*, New York: Oxford University Press.

Bagchi, Amiya Kumar (1982) *The Political Economy of Underdevelopment*, Cambridge: Cambridge University Press.

Best, Michael H. (1990) *The New Competition:*

Institutions of Industrial Restructuring, Cambridge, MA: Harvard University Press.

Brenner, Robert (1977) "The Origins of Capitalist Development: A Critique of Neo-Smithian Marxism," *New Left Review* 104.

Chandler, Alfred D., Jr (1977) *The Visible Hand*, Cambridge, MA: Harvard University Press.

Morishima, Michio (1982) *Why Has Japan Succeeded? Western Technology and the Japanese Ethos*, Cambridge: Cambridge University Press.

Weiss, John (1988) *Industry in Developing Countries: Theory, Policy and Evidence*, London: Routledge.

ANTHONY P. D'COSTA

industry policy

In current usage, "industry policy" is the label given to those activities of government which are explicitly oriented to maintaining and enhancing the viability of industry within its territory. The practices to which it refers are as old and as pervasive as capitalism itself. Governments start industries (such as the English woolen textile industry, the Japanese auto industry); they assist industries on their way up (semiconductors), on their way to a more favorable location (autos), and on their way down (steel). Governments engineer the reconstruction of industries (textiles).

Rationale

From a superficial perspective, governments bother because they desire to boost exports or replace imports, to enhance or retain employment in a particular location (especially pursued by state and local governments), or to provide a resource or industrial base for other industries (coal, steel and semiconductors). Behind these specifics is the phenomenon of the state (more accurately, a system of states) as mediator of capitalist competition. Some capitals are "flagged" with a national specificity (subsidiaries of multinational companies may enjoy "honorary" nationhood). The state acts as a champion for nation-based capitals.

The political–economic interface also houses the "reverse" chain of causation: capital is a vehicle for political imperatives. Prussia (Mooers 1991: ch. 3), Japan (Halliday: 1975) and Taiwan (Amsden 1985) provide striking demonstrations of the conscious facilitation of capitalist development by pre-capitalist elites to perpetuate their social dominance.

Varieties of policies

What kind of policies are used? In fact, there is a wide variety, including subsidies in the form of direct grants, tax breaks and discounted credit rates, discriminatory privileges in the form of access to credit, zoning regulations and so on. These measures are often firm-specific or industry-specific. This is industry policy at its most pragmatic and narrow, and least strategic.

At a broader level, public ownership (especially of infrastructure and basic industries) and the protective tariff have been historically important vehicles for general nation-based industrial development and stability. Tariffs or quotas have been used to protect nascent industrial sectors against competition from cheaper imports, from more efficient industries in advanced countries, and from low-wage labor in "developing" countries. Protection has been much emphasized and much criticized as a defensive and ultimately counterproductive weapon (Castles 1988). However, the character of protection may be either defensive or assertive, depending on whether it is applied in conjunction with instruments supporting industrial dynamism (see FREE TRADE AND PROTECTION).

Industry policy also encompasses considerably more complex and sophisticated structures. Complexity is reflected in the scale and degree of coordination of latent linkages within and between key institutional sectors. Important potential linkages exist within the segments of industry itself. Such linkages may be horizontal, vertical or conglomerate. Sophistication is evident in the long-term commitment by the Japanese to the development of globally viable industries in, for example, automobiles, electronics and computers. The Japanese approach to "resources security" has been exemplary in its farsightedness and assertiveness. The supply and pricing of coal, for example, have been assured by the pursuit of multiple sourcing, the strategic investment in sources and cartel buying practices from the major users (such as steel companies and electricity authorities), all overseen by the relevant bureaucracies.

Strategic vision may also be evident in tailor-made industry-specific policies, exemplified by plans constructed in Australia in the 1980s. Several industries (including steel, automobiles, heavy engineering and textiles/clothing/footwear) were in a state of decay, in spite of previous tariff protection. Packages were developed in which financial or tariff assistance, under sunset clause provisions, was directed toward industrial restructuring, incorporating leverage for workforce cooperation and specific goals such as export targeting.

Government procurement can also be assertively employed, not least because governments are major customers in particular industries. Military procurement provides the most striking, if morally repugnant, arena. The Australian government has long used leverage of procurement successfully in the telecommunications industry. This government has recently transcended a pragmatic tradition in industry support with successful procurement-based development strategies in information technology and in pharmaceuticals.

Complexity is reflected in the awareness by the Japanese that the successful development of an auto industry depended upon the simultaneous development of a machine-tool industry. Complexity and sophistication are jointly reflected in the use of wages policy and housing policy by Sweden as explicit arms of industry policy. WAGE DETERMINATION has been driven by the standards of the high-productivity export sector, accompanied by adjustment assistance for "backward" sectors. Moreover, sustainable cheap housing has been used as a key foundation for lower labor costs, in turn a foundation for globally competitive industries.

Libertarian view and critics

Many of a libertarian persuasion are persuaded that such phenomena as the "Asian miracle" are attributable to such features as high savings rates, low wages and hard work. Acknowledgment of the use of industry policies is typically accompanied by claims of its counter-productive character. However, particular interests are served by the libertarian position, which act to buttress this position. These include the interests of certain global capitals and much of the finance sector. The libertarian view argues for intervention (at best) at the macroeconomic level, getting the "big picture" right for the effective operation of market forces. At the microeconomic level, the role of government is to reinforce competition. At its most pragmatic, this respectable tradition tolerates industry policies at the margin to supplant instances of "market failure."

However, the libertarian perspective distorts the political center of gravity. The question is not whether to have an industry policy but rather what kind of industry policy? Governments will have an industry policy regardless of libertarian beliefs or arguments. This imperative is neatly reflected in post-1945 Germany. The German Christian Democratic Government was both formally committed to liberalist ideals and mindful of the need to kowtow to its American supporters. Behind the rhetoric, however, the Ministry of Economics engaged in assertive industry policies: "Rarely can a Ministry so vociferously devoted to the virtues of economic liberalism and market forces have taken so vigorous a part in setting the direction and selecting the targets of economic development" (Shonfield 1965: 275).

Embodied qualities

The essential differences of industry policy are to be found in the embodied qualities – the respective quotas of pragmatism, defensiveness, strategic vision, complexity and coherence. As a generalization, the liberal inheritance of English-speaking countries has imparted a pragmatic and fragmented character to the industry policies of such countries. Where federal governments are constitutionally or institutionally inhibited, state and local governments step in to fill the void.

A striking reflection of pragmatism in the service of necessity is to be found in the USA. Federal industry policy is centered, by default, on military procurement and its offshoots (Kolko 1975; Markusen *et al.* 1991). The "military–industrial complex" is a complex meshing of the political imperative of "security" with the economic imperative of state-supported industrial development.

Industry policy, whether pragmatic and fragmented or strategic and coherent, is the workhorse of industrial development. It is necessarily complementary to the success of macroeconomic policy in the establishment of an appropriate "macro" environment for stability and accumulation under capitalist regimes.

See also:

global corporate capitalism; internationalization of capital; state and internationalization

Selected references

Amsden, Alice H. (1985) "The State and Taiwan's Economic Development," in Peter B. Evans *et al.* (eds), *Bringing the State Back In*, Cambridge: Cambridge University Press.

Barfield, Claude E. and Schambra, William A. (eds) (1986) *The Politics of Industrial Policy*, Washington: The American Enterprise Institute.

Castles, Francis (1988) *Australian Public Policy and Economic Vulnerability*, Sydney: Allen & Unwin.

Hall, Peter A. (1984) "Patterns of Economic Policy: An Organizational Approach," in Stephen Bornstein *et al.* (eds), *The State in Capitalist Europe*, London: Allen & Unwin.

Halliday, Jon (1975) *A Political History of Japanese Capitalism*, New York: Monthly Review Press.

Kolko, Gabriel (1975) *Main Currents in Modern American History*, New York: Harper & Row.

Markusen, Ann *et al.* (1991) *The Rise of the Gunbelt: The Military Remapping of Industrial America*, New York: Oxford University Press.

Mooers, Colin (1991) *The Making of Bourgeois Europe*, London: Verso.

Shonfield, Andrew (1965) *Modern Capitalism: The Changing Balance of Public and Private Power*, London: Oxford University Press.

EVAN JONES

inequality

Introduction

Inequality is a social pathology. Limiting the food consumption, clothing, housing standards, health care and education opportunities of one social group so that another group receives an ECONOMIC SURPLUS is exceptionally costly. It requires an elaborate and expensive social control apparatus and personnel. For instance, civil wars, prisons and propaganda are often required to maintain HEGEMONY. The direct cost of maintaining structured inequality is usually very high. The upper classes do not gain anywhere near as much as the other classes lose.

Such an arrangement cannot be expected to generate a great deal in the way of new productive TECHNOLOGY and new capital ACCUMULATION. The rich do not save a great percentage of national income after they have paid for their CONSPICUOUS CONSUMPTION AND EMULATION, and the negative effects on CULTURE for art and science to become mere invidious distinctions are very high. Furthermore, the opportunity costs of limiting the development and application of the oppressed group's HUMAN CAPITAL must be included in the costings.

Inequality is not instrumental. Creating inequality today is not an investment in more production tomorrow; it is not a means to a socially desired end. Inequality is a diseased

inequality

state that cripples a significant part of society with malnutrition, poor health and ignorance, nor does this crippling in the present result in robust health in the future (see HEALTH INEQUALITY).

Circular and cumulative processes

Inequality is also cumulative, not self-correcting; it tends to either get better or get worse. Although a kind of stalemate of forces may occur from time to time, inequality seldom stays the same and it never reaches a stable equilibrium. Mostly, a vicious circle of cumulatively increasing inequality, or a virtuous circle of cumulatively decreasing inequality, are actually found in the real world. Gunnar Myrdal was the first to research carefully what he called the vicious circle of poverty in his analysis of RACISM, inequality and the CULTURE OF POVERTY in *An American Dilemma*, published in 1944.

Being deprived of adequate food, clothing, shelter, health care and education, the lower classes become relatively unproductive, unhealthy, poorly clothed, and ignorant. This makes it easy for the upper classes to look down on the lower classes as inferior beings, and to undermine the latter's self-confidence and self-worth with invidious distinctions. The upper classes find it easy to take further advantage of the lower classes without feeling guilty. The lower classes often react by accepting their fate and by blaming themselves for their own shortcomings. Their even lower condition makes it easier still for the upper classes to ignore or despise them. All these processes increase the cumulative relative inequality between classes (see CIRCULAR AND CUMULATIVE CAUSATION).

Self-confidence and opportunities for the lower classes can be improved through skill development, new employment, improvements in health and cultural enhancement. The cumulative vicious circle of relative inequality stops when the contempt and arrogance of the upper classes are weakened and the wall of exclusion that encased the lower classes is cracked. Malnutrition, illness, ignorance and fatalistic self-contempt all decline among the lower classes. They become more productive and their conditions improve. This enhances their feelings of self-worth, and eventually reduces the upper classes' feelings of superiority. However, starting this cumulative upward process is problematic (see INSTITUTIONAL CHANGE AND ADJUSTMENT).

Four modes of inequality

Individuals and their choices are important, both positively and normatively. But the degree of inequality in a society is more a product of social processes than of individual choices. Four basic processes or modes of inequality are involved: (1) GENDER, (2) race, (3) nation and (4) CLASS (see Dugger 1996). Each of these social processes works to set the context and determine the limits within which individuals choose and act. Individuals do not choose to be born into a particular gender, race, nationality or class. Instead, they are taught their roles in families, schools, churches, sporting groups and other institutions.

For example, people with male genitalia are assigned and taught the male role; they do not individually create it or choose it. Likewise, people with female genitalia are assigned and taught the female role; they do not individually create or choose these gender roles. People are born to particular kinds of parents. In the United States, if any of their parents, grandparents, great-grandparents and so on were black, they are assigned to the black race and taught the role of American black. They do not individually choose it or create it. People are also born into a particular nationality and a particular class, although with some difficulty they can often change these; but, then, with some difficulty, they can change their sex too, and probably also the color of their skin.

Two roles of the state

Inequality is created by some kind of collective action, frequently that of the state (often linked with CORPORATE HEGEMONY). However, the lower classes frequently call on the state to take action against inequality. The state, then, is a great dichotomy, a Janus-faced god of both light and darkness, whose monopolization of legitimate violence makes its own collective action the strongest of all collective actions. Furthermore, this two-faced state helps to decide whose collective action is legal and whose is criminal. The Janus-state is best understood as two states at one and the same time: the welfare state and the oppressive state (see Dugger and Waller 1992.) All modern states partake of this split personality to some degree.

One state – the WELFARE STATE – takes collective action to lift up the former slaves, the women and children, the aliens, and the downtrodden working class. This state, through its collective action on behalf of the lower classes, extends the right to vote, health care systems, schools and union representation. It enlarges the numbers and the RIGHTS of citizens, turning powerless and homeless aliens into union workers, homeowners, taxpayers and voters. This state looks toward the lower classes to some degree and responds positively to their demands.

The other state – the oppressive state – takes collective action to (re)create the lower classes by reducing upward mobility and safety nets. In its milder actions it creates and defends property rights, opens tax loopholes for the rich, and grants subsidies to investors, traders and speculators. This state also takes collective action to appropriate the property of indigenous peoples or to enforce slave codes or Jim Crow laws. This state imposes poll taxes and other restrictions on voting, enforces segregation, breaks labor unions, deports aliens and even bombs and invades their homelands. This state looks toward the upper classes and responds positively to their demands. To explain inequality, both states must be brought into the analysis and state policies made central to inquiry (see Clark 1996).

Enabling myths

Enabling myths help to maintain inequality by justifying it in the minds of all classes. Supplying the upper classes with a justification for their privileges is easy enough. Enabling myths help to confirm and articulate previously held vague beliefs, particularly for members of the upper classes. For the lower classes, enabling myths are somewhat less effective in convincing them that their lowly position and relative lack of effective rights are well deserved. Nevertheless, enabling myths usually work effectively. They enable the upper classes to keep on enjoying their position and the lower classes to refrain from revolting against theirs.

Enabling myths are of two basic types. One type is a set of stereotypes about the inferiority of the lower classes and the superiority of the upper classes. Such stereotypes relate to issues such as racism, sexism, and nationalism. These stereotypes are easily debunked, but they re-emerge in new forms relatively quickly. The other type of enabling myth is cultural in nature, and includes a set of beliefs and meanings regarding the nature of the social system. The free enterprise system is one such cultural myth. The free enterprise system includes a set of beliefs and meanings powerful enough to lift a culture of greed, envy, lust and power up into the stratosphere of individual initiative, freedom, efficiency and open competition. The theoretical justification for this is provided by NEOCLASSICAL ECONOMICS, especially the version developed at institutions such as the University of Chicago and the American Enterprise Institute.

If the lower classes can be convinced that the social system is based on individual initiative, freedom, efficiency and open competition, then serious doubts arise in their minds about their own adequacy. If they have not been able to do well in such a wonderful system, then "they must not be trying hard enough or they must lack the personal abilities to do so." It must be their fault, for surely it could not be the fault of such a perfect system. If they believe this, they will not take collective action to change the system. Inequality will go unchallenged. However, if they can be convinced that their relative poverty is not of their own making, there is a chance to change the system; but powerful, hegemonic forces must be challenged before this can be successful.

See also:

ceremonial encapsulation; class; classes of capitalism; collective social wealth; community; crime; distribution of income; human dignity; individual and society; institutional political economy: history; instrumental value theory; justice; minimal dislocation; needs; radical institutionalism; socialism and communism

Selected references

Clark, Charles M.A. (1996) "Inequality in the 1980s: An Institutionalist View," in William M. Dugger, *Inequality: Radical Institutionalist Views on Race, Gender, Class and Nation*, Westport, CT: Greenwood Press.
Dugger, William M. (1996) *Inequality: Radical Institutionalist Views on Race, Gender, Class and Nation*, Westport, CT: Greenwood Press.
Dugger, William M. and Waller, William T. (eds) (1992) *The Stratified State: Radical Institutionalist Theories of Participation and Duality*, Armonk, NY: M.E. Sharpe.

WILLIAM M. DUGGER

inflation: conflicting claims approach

The conflicting claims approach is a post-Keynesian theory of inflation, with roots in the work of Michal KALECKI, Bob Rowthorn and others. For recent work in the area, see Amitava Dutt (1990: ch. 4) and Marc Lavoie (1992: 391–421). According to the conflicting claims view, inflation results when the aggregated nominal income claims of workers and firms (ignoring other costs) exceed the total income available. Workers stake their claims in the wage negotiation process, where they must pursue their real goals through the negotiation of nominal wages. The claims of firms are represented by their target pricing markup, which they pursue subject to the costs of rapid price adjustment. The claims of workers and the claims of firms conflict when the aggregated claims exceed national income. Inflation is the manifestation of this conflict.

Illustrative model

For a simple illustration, imagine workers produce 100 units of output (ignoring other costs of production), and that they think they have the power to claim 60 percent of it. Imagine also that firms think that they could claim 60 percent of this output through an appropriate markup pricing strategy. If both parties are successful in claiming in nominal terms the equivalent of 60 percent each of the initial value of net output, then prices must rise to reflect the difference between total claims and total output.

Thus, a very simple series of equations can be shown to reflect this process. Let total nominal income claimed by all parties be Y_c, the income claimed by workers W_c, and the income claimed by capitalists Π_c (as a markup):

$$Y_c = W_c + \Pi_c \quad (1)$$

Recall the basic premise of the conflicting claims model: nominal income claims (Yc) in excess of current actual nominal income (Ya) generate inflation (p). Equation (2) represents this algebraically:

$$p = f(Y_c/Y_a) \quad f' > 0 \quad (2)$$

where f represents the sensitivity of inflation to the ratio of nominal income claims to current nominal income; or the degree to which the combined claims condition inflation.

Prices do not move instantaneously to reconcile nominal income claims with nominal income, reflecting price stickiness. In addition, price inflation is not tied directly to nominal wage inflation: the conflicting claims model can reconcile short-run variations with long-run constancy of the markup.

Equation (3) presents an alternative formulation, influenced by Desai (1973) in an extension of the Goodwin (1967) growth cycle model:

$$p = f(P^T/P) \quad f' > 0 \qquad (3)$$

Here inflation is influenced by the relationship between target (P^T) and current prices (P), in relation to a reaction function, f'. The target price level is influenced by unit labor costs. Firms adjust prices in response to the ratio of target price to current price. Price adjustment is not instantaneous: firms operate in customer markets, where rapid price adjustment is associated with a loss of market share. Further, the price-setting behavior of firms is decentralized, so that price adjustments that may prove pointless in the aggregate are nevertheless individually rational.

Another popular formulation of the conflicting claims approach represents inflation as the result of a gap between capitalists' desired and actual profit shares. The underpinnings are unchanged, but the story is usually given a slightly different twist. Suppose capitalists pursue a target profit share but also experience increasing costs, perhaps in the form of lost market share. Then capitalists initiate price increases whenever the actual profit share falls short of the target.

Alternative to orthodoxy

Conflicting claims models are an alternative to the mainstream monetarist, new classical and Phillips curve models of inflation. Orthodoxy emphasizes the long-run neutrality of money, and it links long-run inflation to (policy determined) money supply changes. The conflicting claims approach does not deny that large sustained changes in the aggregate price level require large sustained changes in the aggregate money stock. Monetarists assume causation runs from money to prices, while many conflicting claims models reverse this causality. Finally, while orthodoxy tends to focus on long-run equilibrium outcomes, the conflicting claims approach deals explicitly with short-run, disequilibrium adjustments.

Conflicting claims theorists reject the mainstream characterization of price dynamics. In the conflicting claims approach, the rate of inflation is determined by the intensity of the struggle over income shares. At the level of the firm, this translates into a focus on the gap between current economic performance and the firm's targets. Quantity-constrained, price-setting firms facing a shortfall of the current profit rate from their target profit rate will raise prices.

Phillips curve wage adjustments

Conflicting claims theorists remain divided on the Phillips curve characterization of wage adjustment. When Rowthorn (1977) established the conflicting claims model as the basic formalization of post-Keynesian theories of inflation, he linked the wage level to the unemployment rate. Many later conflicting claims models include Phillips curve (or Phillips curve-related) characterizations of wage dynamics, which link wage changes to the unemployment rate (sometimes via its influence on a target wage level). Use of the Phillips curve does not produce the mainstream characterization of price adjustment, however. Rather than linking inflation directly to the unemployment rate, these conflicting claims models allow unemployment-induced wage adjustments (implied by a Phillips curve) to determine only changes in (rather than the level of) the inflation rate. While there are theoretical considerations in favor of the levels approach (particularly the Phillips curve implication that temporary changes in the unemployment rate can have permanent effects on the real wage), there is also empirical support for stable Phillips curve wage dynamics (especially in the United States).

Money and monetary policy

Conflicting claims theorists have also differed in their treatment of money. In many conflicting claims models, the monetary sector is suppressed altogether. This suppression may reflect a skepticism of even long-run links between inflation and money growth, a link found in conflicting claims models that include a formal treatment of money. When characterizing monetary policy, conflicting claims theorists most often adopt the post-Keynesian view that money growth is endogenously determined, although Rowthorn (1977) depicts long-run inflation as the end result of relatively exogenous monetary policy decisions. In either case the conflicting claims model is distinctly anti-monetarist, for it usually implies that monetary policy has important implications for the real economy, even in the long run.

The conflicting claims approach implies that monetary policy can affect income distribution. When inflation concerns loom large, monetary policy will favor profit income over wage income. This income distribution effect persists even in the long run. This result stands in distinct contrast to neoclassical models of inflation, which usually assume monetary policy has no long-run implications for the real economy. Thus the conflicting claims approach meshes with the post-Keynesian view that the distribution of income is an important policy concern and an influence on macroeconomic performance.

See also:

corporate objectives; endogenous money and credit; inflation: wage–cost markup approach; monetarism

Selected references

Burdekin, Richard, C.K. and Burkett, Paul (1996) *Distributional Conflict and Inflation: Theoretical and Historical Perspectives*, London: Routledge.

Desai, Meghnad (1973) "Growth Cycles and Inflation in a Model of the Class Struggle," *Journal of Economic Theory* 6: 527–45.

Dutt, Amitava Krishna (1990) *Growth, Distribution, and Uneven Development*, Cambridge: Cambridge University Press.

Goodwin, R.M. (1967) "A Growth Cycle," in C.H. Feinstein (ed.), *Socialism, Capitalism, and Economic Growth*, New York: Cambridge University Press.

Isaac, Alan G. (1991) "Economic Stabilization and Money Supply Endogeneity in a Conflicting Claims Environment," *Journal of Post Keynesian Economics* 14(1): 93–110.

Lavoie, Marc (1992) *Foundations of Post-Keynesian Economic Analysis*, Aldershot: Edward Elgar.

Rowthorn, R.E. (1977) "Conflict, Inflation and Money," *Cambridge Journal of Economics* 1: 215–39.

ALAN G. ISAAC

inflation: wage–cost markup approach

Inflation is a continuous rise in the general price level. The adoption of Keynesian full employment policies after the Second World War created an accommodative environment for the acceleration of wage inflation and therefore the general inflation of all prices in industrialized countries. Full employment policies were replaced with restrictive aggregate demand policies with the breakdown of the BRETTON WOODS SYSTEM of fixed EXCHANGE RATES in the early 1970s. Inflation is a problem because the acceleration of inflation triggers restrictive aggregate demand policies with the resultant rise in unemployment. Moreover, even when inflation is low by historical standards, the fear of the acceleration of inflation becomes a pretense for maintaining restrictive aggregate demand policies. There is also evidence by Bruno (1995) indicating that high rates of inflation retard economic growth. But there is also time-series evidence from the United States by Atesoglu (1998) revealing a positive long-run relation between inflation and real income. His findings suggest that the inflationary effects of expansionary policies should not hamper growth as long as inflation remains at moderate rates.

A reliable model of inflation is a prerequisite for effectively controlling inflation and designing policies which avoid the side effects of restrictive aggregate demand policies, such as an increase in unemployment. The post-Keynesian, wage–cost markup model of Weintraub (1978) emphasizes the growth of wages relative to the growth in labor PRODUCTIVITY as the main determinant of inflation. Aggregate demand, usually measured by the unemployment rate, is recognized as a determinant of the growth rate of wages in the wage–cost markup approach to inflation. However, the distribution of income and the struggle for a larger share of aggregate income by wage earners against other groups in society, is identified as the fundamental determinant of the growth rate of wages; there is a large exogenous content in the determination of wages.

The wage–cost markup inflation model of Weintraub is derived from the following identity:

$$P = KW/A \qquad (1)$$

where P is the price level, K is the average markup, W is the average money wage rate and A is average labor productivity. Equation (1) is the wage–cost markup equation; the price level is a function of markup times the unit labor costs, W/A.

The wage–cost markup model of inflation is derived from the above identity by assuming the markup to be constant and writing equation (2) in growth rate form:

$$p = w - a \qquad (2)$$

where p is the rate of inflation, w is the growth rate of wages, and a is the labor productivity growth rate. Equation (2) predicts a one-to-one relationship between the rate of inflation and the rate of growth of unit labor costs, $w - a$. For example, if the growth rate of wages is equal to 5 percent per year and the growth rate of labor productivity is equal to 2 percent per year, the rate of inflation will be equal to 3 percent per year.

There are numerous econometric estimates of the wage–cost markup model of inflation using data from various countries, and it has been the basis of the price equations in large scale econometric models. An econometric evaluation of the wage–cost markup model of inflation, using data for the United States by Atesoglu (1980), has revealed that it is superior to the quantity theory, Phillips curve and Phelps–Friedman explanations of inflation. However, the wage–cost markup theory has been criticized as a theory of inflation. The typical criticism is that the close relation reported between the inflation rate and the growth rate of wages, another price variable, is to be expected but not enlightening and that the growth rate of wages cannot be assumed to be an exogenous variable (see for example Stein 1979).

Although post-Keynesians such as Weintraub (1978: ch. 5) and Davidson (1991: ch. 8, 1994: ch. 9) identify a strong exogenous content in the determination of wages, they do not simply assume wages to be an exogenous variable and acknowledge that macroeconomic polices and the unemployment rate can affect wages. Recent post-Keynesian empirical inflation models, of Arestis and Milberg (1993–4) using data for the United States and the United Kingdom, Downward (1995) for the United Kingdom, and Atesoglu (1997) for the United States, include variables which represent the effects of the state of the economy and aggregate demand and the effects of macroeconomic policy on wages.

The policy implications of the wage–cost markup model, equation (2), for controlling inflation is clear. To avoid the acceleration of inflation, the growth rate of wages should not be larger than that of the growth in labor productivity. Given the growth rate of productivity, policy makers can control the growth rate of wages either with incomes policies (for instance, as was in place in Australia during 1983–96), or by increasing the size of the RESERVE ARMY OF LABOR through restrictive aggregate demand policies. The deep recession of 1981–2 in the United States, which became global, is a well-known example of the use of restrictive aggregate demand policy for controlling wage and price inflation. The Kennedy–Johnson voluntary income policy years of 1961–8 are an example of a successful control of inflation, when the United States economy was allowed to approach its full employment output levels (see Davidson 1994: 152).

The experience of the United States and other industrialized countries with inflation since the Second World War reveals that wage inflation, and thereby price inflation, can be controlled with the use of restrictive aggregate demand policies. Nevertheless, the price paid in terms of high unemployment and lost real output in industrialized countries is high, and slower economic growth in industrialized countries hinders the growth prospects of the less developed countries. In the 1990s it appears that many industrialized nations have lost their political will for employing incomes policies which may allow their economies to produce full employment output with price stability.

See also:

fiscal policy; inflation: conflicting claims approach; monetary policy and central banking functions; pricing; stagflation

Selected references

Arestis, P. and Milberg, W. (1993–4) "Degree of Monopoly, Pricing, and Flexible Exchange Rates," *Journal of Post Keynesian Economics* 16(2): 167–95.
Atesoglu, H.S. (1980) "Inflation and Its Acceleration: Evidence from the Postwar United States," *Journal of Post Keynesian Economics* 3(1): 105–15.
—— (1997) "A Post Keynesian Explanation of United States Inflation," *Journal of Post Keynesian Economics* 19(4):639–49
—— (1998) "Inflation and Real Income," *Journal of Post-Keynesian Economics* 20(3): 487–9.
Bruno, M. (1995) "Does Inflation Really Lower Growth?," *Finance & Development* 32(3): 35–8.
Davidson, P. (1991) *Controversies in Post Keynesian Economics*, Aldershot: Edward Elgar.
—— (1994) *Post Keynesian Macroeconomic Theory*, Aldershot: Edward Elgar.
Downward, P. (1995) "A Post Keynesian Perspective of UK Manufacturing Prices," *Journal of Post Keynesian Economics* 17(3): 403–26.
Stein, J.L. (1979) "The Acceleration of Inflation," *Journal of Post Keynesian Economics* 2(1): 33–42.
Weintraub, S. (1978) *Capitalism's Inflation and Unemployment Crisis: Beyond Monetarism and Keynesianism*, Reading, MA: Addison-Wesley.
—— (1979) "Comment on 'The Acceleration of Inflation'," *Journal of Post Keynesian Economics* 2(1): 43–8.

H. SONMEZ ATESOGLU

informal sector

Definition

The informal sector (IS) describes economic activity that takes place outside the formal norms of economic transactions established by the state and business. It is not clearly illegal in itself. Generally, the term applies to small or micro-businesses that are the result of individual or family self-employment. It includes the production and exchange of legal goods and services that involve the lack of appropriate business permits, violation of zoning codes, failure to report tax liability, non-compliance with labor regulations governing contracts and work conditions, and/or the lack of legal guarantees in relations with suppliers and clients. As such, it is conceptually, methodologically and theoretically difficult to define in terms of its precise nature, size and significance, leading some authors to criticize the term for lack of clarity (Peattie 1987; Bromley 1990).

Size and functions

Nevertheless, widespread agreement that the sector represents a growing proportion of economic activity, particularly in less developed countries (LDCs), has placed it at the center of debate about its role with respect to economic development. The informal sector appears to provide at least some economic opportunities for the urban poor and particularly for women, often providing services and commercial activities at a very low level of economic utility. This is related to the fact that the tertiary sector has often grown faster in many LDCs than the secondary (industrial) sector. It also creates a question of whether regulatory norms should be enforced at the risk of reducing these opportunities.

The term was originally coined by Hart (1970) to describe the multitude of often temporary economic strategies adopted by migrant workers in Ghana, faced with a marginal job market which, in the aggregate, responded to real social needs. Challenging the marginality literature, which had seen these survival strategies as irrelevant or even counter-productive for national development, he argues: "Planners who look primarily for entrepreneurial persons overlook those who are currently performing the entrepreneurial *function*" (Hart 1970: 115).

The International Labour Organization (ILO) and others turned to the informal sector as a potential solution to unemployment in LDCs. While still seeing it as a collection of survival strategies held back by under-capitalization, lack of skills and the small size of enterprises, they argue that the informal sector is capable of absorbing employment if these negative conditions can be reversed (Sethuraman 1981).

Entrepreneurship and super-exploitation

Going further, De Soto argues that the informal sector comprises entrepreneurial activity that is constrained from full development by the high "costs of formality" present in many LDCs. These costs include complex, time-consuming and expensive regulations that are almost impossible for small firms to observe and which tend to favor large firms. At the same time, he argues that the characteristics that the ILO and others view as symptomatic of the problems of the informal sector firms are the result of the regulatory system itself. Informal sector entrepreneurs, he argues, need to stay small and hidden to avoid detection, while they also lack legal protection for their investment, both factors creating disincentives for growth and capital investment.

Confronting these positive assessments of the informal sector, dependency and world systems theorists argue that the informal sector represents an area of disguised unemployment and super-exploitation, that is either directly tied to the formal sector through outsourcing or distribution channels or indirectly as a RESERVE ARMY OF LABOR. Formal sector firms, they argue, cut labor costs by using home workers, sweatshops, street vendors, neighborhood shopkeepers and others in the informal sector who, while nominally self-employed, are actually "disguised workers" with none of the benefits or safeguards of formal employment (Portes and Walton 1981).

To some extent, the differences between these perspectives have been muted, as scholars recognize the heterogeneity of the sector, including entrepreneurial as well as exploitative forms of economic activity (Castells *et al.* 1989; Rakowski 1994)

Development agencies in LDCs generally focus on the positive assessments of the informal sector. By providing credit and training, their goal is to promote the growth of individual firms within the sector, while ignoring the question of whether they may be inadvertently creating more exploitation and social problems as these unregulated or semi-regulated firms violate labor relations laws or safety, health and environmental regulations. They also ignore De Soto's (1986) analysis of the limits of informal sector firm growth due to the need to avoid regulatory control.

Model of a dual market

Modifying De Soto's argument, a model of the dual market behavior of the formal and informal sectors can be developed that allows us to understand the behavior and interests of IS actors. The small size of IS firms allows them to escape regulatory enforcement and thus reduce their operating costs, giving them a competitive advantage relative to larger firms that are compelled to pay regulatory costs. This can be seen as a system of "informal subsidies" that counterbalance the economies of scale of large firms and the formal subsidies and political preference that such firms may enjoy.

This creates different optimization strategies for firms in the informal sector. Most regulatory controls impose costs on labor and are most efficiently handled through capital investment or administration. Thus, formal firms are optimized when they substitute capital for labor and strive to grow large enough to capture INCREASING RETURNS TO SCALE. IS firms, on the other hand, evade the regulatory costs on labor while their capital is subject to much greater risks (because of lack of legal protection), and thus are optimized when they substitute labor for capital and remain small enough to capture economies of flexibility. Thus, the appearance of a "dual market" arises from this polarization of incentive structures. This duality also explains why informal sector activity is proportionately more common among women and the poor, since these groups are less likely to have access to the amount of capital necessary to make formality a viable economic option.

Between these two poles exists a "semi-formal" economy, comprising activities that are partly regulated, often because state officials have recognized and sanctioned a certain degree of informality in exchange for a degree of control over them. Thus, collective taxis, land invaders, street vendors and garbage collectors have, in many cases, been given either tacit or explicit permission to carry out their activity, at times in exchange for support for the current regime, but without fully bringing them within the formal system. Often, this may lead to a continual process of conflict and re-negotiation between the administration and informal actors that politicizes the sector. Another form of "semi-formality" exists in the case of partly formal firms that may use the ability to bribe officials in order to escape particular aspects of the regulatory system.

Problems of measurement

The heterogeneity of the informal sector, as well as the close linkages in some cases with formal businesses on the one hand and illegal services on the other, makes it difficult to define and measure. For example, macroeconomic estimates of the size of the informal economy cannot distinguish between "legal" ends and "illegal" ends such as prostitution, drugs, the sale of stolen goods, contraband and the production and sale of pirated goods. All of these examples involve the production and/or sale of goods or services that are illegal in themselves, but which are difficult, if not impossible, to separate out in most studies. Even at the micro-level, the sale of contraband or unlicenced products is carried out in much the same way as the sale of legal products, and thus is difficult to distinguish.

Further research

Further research is needed to determine, in particular, the conditions under which informal sector activity may be entrepreneurial or exploitative; and in which it may be positively related to economic growth or simply a reflection of the externalization of economic costs onto society and the environment. Furthermore, the political interests of IS actors and how those interests are manifested also needs to be examined in greater depth.

See also:

development political economy: major contemporary themes; household production and national income

Selected references

Bromley, Ray (1990) "A New Path to Development? The Significance and Impact of Hernando de Soto's Ideas on Underdevelopment, Production, and Reproduction," *Economic Geography* 6(October).

Castells, Manuel, Portes, Alejandro and Benton, Lauren A. (eds) (1989) *The Informal*

Economy: Studies in Advanced and Less Developed Countries, Baltimore and London: Johns Hopkins University Press.

De Soto, Hernando (1986) *The Other Path: The Invisible Revolution in the Third World*, New York: Harper & Row, 1989.

Hart, J. Keith. (1970) "Small-scale Entrepreneurs in Ghana and Development Planning," *Journal of Development Studies* 6: 104–20.

Peattie, Lisa A. (1987) "An Idea in Good Currency and How it Grew: The Informal Sector," *World Development* 15(7): 851–60.

Portes, Alejandro and Walton, John (1981) *Labor, Class and the International System*, New York: Academic Press.

Rakowski, Cathy A. (1994) "Convergence and Divergence in the Informal Sector Debate: A Focus on Latin America," *World Development* 22: 501–16.

Sethuraman, S.V. (1981) *The Urban Informal Sector in Developing Countries: Employment, Poverty and Environment*, Geneva: International Labour Organization.

JOHN C. CROSS

innovation, evolution and cycles

From the long-term viewpoint, technological change is the main determinant of economic development. New technologies increase PRODUCTIVITY, allowing greater production with lower inputs. New products and processes enhance market variety and provide new opportunities. Innovations nurture new industries which radically change the structure of the economy. But how and why are these changes generated? Are they endogenous or exogenous to economic life? How are they distributed in time, space and fields?

Although there was widespread agreement that economic mechanisms played a role in the introduction of innovations, many economists preferred to consider TECHNOLOGY as an exogenous factor. Technological change, they argued, is influenced by too many factors – social, cultural, political and even religious – to be comprehensively discussed within economic theory. Other economists, at the fringe of mainstream orthodoxy, were unhappy to leave the relationship between technology and the economy "inside a black box" (Rosenberg 1982). They stressed that economics should have a say in explaining the main determinant of economic performance. Karl MARX, Joseph SCHUMPETER and Thorstein VEBLEN were important thinkers who tried to endogenize the analysis of technology. The recent wave of evolutionary economists have continued to try and comprehend the forces creating innovation and institutional change.

Theoretical problems with innovation

Although innovations are strictly interwoven with economic life, this does not make it any easier to incorporate them into economic theory. In fact, innovations present some tricky peculiarities due to a number of factors, such as the following.

Heterogeneity. Each innovation has a different significance which makes it difficult to assess its value. The intensity of scientific knowledge cannot be used as a predictor of the economic significance of innovations. For instance, the ball-point pen, in spite of being a simple technological device, is certainly economically more relevant than the discovery of a new galaxy (at least in the short-term).

Source variety. A large number of sources nurture innovation. While some innovations are heavily based on scientific discoveries, others are not. For instance, both antibiotics and freight containers have dramatically affected the economy, although they have received very different inputs from scientific research. Some innovations are entirely embodied in new capital goods and equipment, others are simply new ideas and are, therefore, disembodied from physical production.

Uncertainty. Firms willing to innovate have to deal with the intrinsically uncertain nature of scientific and technological research. The first UNCERTAINTY they have to face is technological: will research lead to the expected results or, at least, to any commercially exploitable result? The second uncertainty is economic: what share of the market will a new product be able to conquer? How quickly will imitators be able to copy the innovation and take a share of the new market? Uncertainty generally increases with the degree of innovativeness of a project.

Changing conditions. It is difficult to predict how the benefits of an innovation will be distributed among the innovator, the users and the imitators. In some cases, the innovator manages to appropriate the full returns of his/her innovation. In other cases, she/he fails and the advantages are distributed across economic space, without providing any specific compensation. Conditions of technological appropriation vary across countries, industries and firms and they significantly affect the willingness of agents to devote their time and resources to innovative activity (see SCHUMPETERIAN COMPETITION).

Innovation, macroeconomics and cycles

The majority of efforts devoted to innovation do not lead to any significant economic impact. Most inventive and innovative activities result in failures, or in small improvements which do not influence the macroeconomic dynamics very much, although they generally generate irreplaceable and irreversible learning. This factor – learning – is often overlooked because attention is absorbed by the most successful and visible innovative projects, while the failed and less relevant ones are not often emphasized or recorded. However, a few successful innovative projects can create major modifications in the economic structure. These innovations generate the Schumpeterian "gales of creative destruction." The strength of these innovations is associated with their ability to spin off clusters of related innovations in imitators, in down-stream users, in up-stream suppliers and in related industries.

Schumpeter hypothesized about the relationship between innovation and cycles (see SCHUMPETER'S THEORY OF INNOVATION, DEVELOPMENT AND CYCLES). In more recent decades, thanks also to the availability of new and improved statistical sources on technological change, production and investment, the connections between trends in innovation and the business cycle have been empirically tested (see Freeman 1984; Tylecote 1992). Some have argued that major innovations are introduced during economic depressions, and provide scope for recovery. Others have more convincingly shown that the diffusion of innovations is strictly associated with economic recovery and prosperity (Freeman *et al.* 1982). More recently, greater insight has been gained into these relationships (see Shionoya and Perlman 1994: 157–85; also, various articles in the *Journal of Evolutionary Economics*).

In order to account for both continuity and discontinuity in technological change, Freeman *et al.* (1982) have proposed a taxonomy of innovations according to their significance. *Incremental innovations* occur at the firm level and have a limited economic impact. *Radical innovations* might substantially change the structure of an industry but not of the whole economy. *New technology systems* create new product lines and industries and dramatically affect ECONOMIC GROWTH. *Techno-economic revolutions* characterize the production methods used in each phase of capitalist development.

Long waves tend to relate to phases of transformation, each of the phases being based upon a combination of technological knowledge, production methods and institutional framework (techno-institutional regimes; see REGULATION APPROACH). An important long-wave hypothesis is that macroeconomic performance induces the introduction and diffusion of innovations, but also that radically new innovations can influence the rate and direction of economic growth (dual causation). (See LONG WAVES OF ECONOMIC GROWTH AND DEVELOPMENT.)

Structural changes and microeconomics

It is also important to examine the microeconomic behavior of firms. Economic expansion, at this level, is seen to be due to the rise of new firms which grow and prosper by generating and exploiting new technological opportunities, thus leading to structural changes in the industrial structure (see Audretsch 1995; Simonetti 1996). However, these firms are not the sole components of the industrial fabric. Also important are firms which continuously introduce minor innovations. The evolutionary theory of the innovating firm allows for a consideration, at the microeconomic level, of the cumulative path within technological change. Firms innovating incrementally and continuously might be wiped out by major changes; or they might reinvigorate their business by exploiting new technological opportunities.

Pavitt (1984) has proposed a successful taxonomy of innovating firms, consisting of five categories. The first is supplier-dominated firms, which are active in traditional industries such as clothing and furniture. These firms innovate mainly by the acquisition of machinery and equipment. The second is specialized suppliers of capital goods and equipment, who live in symbiosis with their customers. The third is science-based firms, born to exploit new discoveries in the electrical and chemical fields, where the main source of knowledge is their internal R&D laboratories. The fourth is scale-intensive firms, active in mass production industries. The fifth is the emerging information-intensive firms, which have their main source of technological accumulation in the advanced processing of data such as in banking, retailing and tourism.

Phases of industrial evolution

Firms in each of these categories emerged in different periods of industrial development, and any major wave in economic activity has led to the rise of a new form of enterprise and industrial organization. The industrial revolution led to a separation between producers of consumption goods and producers of capital goods. The new scientific discoveries which opened the second wave created new R&D-based firms and industries. TAYLORISM and Fordism, which underpinned postwar expansion, are associated with large and heavily organized firms. Currently, new information technologies are creating some new firms and organizations, based on the intensive analysis and use of data processing. Some believe that the flexible system of production is a new revolution in the technological and institutional structure and dynamics of the economy (see FORDISM AND THE FLEXIBLE SYSTEM OF PRODUCTION).

See also:

business cycle theories; capitalism; cycles and trends in the world capitalist economy; Schumpeterian political economy

Selected references

Audretsch, D.B. (1995) *Innovation and Industry Evolution*, Cambridge, MA: MIT Press.

Dosi, G. and Nelson, R. (1994) "An Introduction to Evolutionary Theories in Economics," *Journal of Evolutionary Economics* 4(3): 153–72.

Freeman, C. (ed.) (1984) *Long Waves in the World Economy*, London: Frances Pinter.

Freeman, C., Clark, J. and Soete, L. (1982) *Unemployment and Technical Innovation: A Study of Long Waves and Economic Development*, London: Frances Pinter.

Mensch, C. (1979) *Stalemate in Technology*, Cambridge, MA: Ballinger Publishing.

Pavitt, Keith (1984) "Sectoral Patterns of Technical Change: Towards a Taxonomy and a Theory," *Research Policy* 13: 343–73.

Rosenberg, N. (1976) *Perspectives on Technology*, Cambridge: Cambridge University Press.

—— (1982) *Inside the Black Box: Technology and Economy*, Cambridge: Cambridge University Press.

Shionoya, Yuichi and Perlman, Mark (eds) (1994) *Innovation in Technology, Industries, and Institutions: Studies in Schumpeterian Perspectives*, Ann Arbor, MI: Michigan University Press.

Simonetti, R. (1996) "Technical Change and Firm Growth: 'Creative Destruction' in the Fortune List, 1963–87," in E. Helmstädter and M. Perlman (eds), *Behavioral Norms, Technological Progress, and Economic Dynamics*, Ann Arbor, MI: University of Michigan Press.

Tylecote, A. (1992) *The Long Wave in the World Economy*, London: Routledge.

DANIELE ARCHIBUGI

INNOVATIONS, FINANCIAL: see financial innovations

instincts

"Instinct psychology" was one of two leading perspectives in American psychology around the turn of the century. Instincts were understood as hereditary elements in species behavior, but were never well-defined as mechanisms. Both their weakness as experimental terms, and increasing concerns with possible racist associations of biological explanations, led to their demise in psychology by 1930. Instincts remain important in institutional political economy because of their use by Thorstein VEBLEN, especially in attacks on the foundations of orthodox economics, and later by Clarence Ayres. Although the early criticisms of instincts are less persuasive today, some reconsideration of the concept could well be useful.

Instincts versus associationism

Veblen's use of instinct theory reflected his antipathy to the philosophical implications of its main rival, associationism. Associationism rested on the Humean view that sense impressions were the only source of human knowledge. It postulated that sequences of events yielded sequences of impressions that gradually became associated, as knowledge, through regular repetition. Because the influence of one factor on another was unobservable, however, "causation" was reduced to simple repeated sequence; values were also reduced to sense impressions (hedonism). Herbert Spencer's version of associationism, which J.S. Mill declared definitive, included mental associations among the acquired traits subject to Lamarckian inheritance (and "survival of the fittest") to explain progress in human knowledge over time.

Veblen strongly objected to associationism's naive empiricism, hedonism, teleology, and biological determinism. In his view, it could not admit evolutionary CIRCULAR AND CUMULATIVE CAUSATION, and its denial of intellectual faculties prior to experience eliminated any basis for making associations of "causal" regularities in experience. Nor was there any role for human purpose; purpose was animistically imputed to nature, while human beings became passive "homogeneous globules of desire." The result, also attributed by Veblen to the orthodox economics of Mill and Marshall, was incoherent and pre-Darwinian in spirit (see EVOLUTIONARY ECONOMICS: MAJOR CONTEMPORARY THEMES).

Veblen's alternative use of instinct theory, drawn partly from William James, provided the prior mental dispositions to organize human perception, ground human purposes, admit causal inferences and reject animistic teleology in nature. A more open-ended, Darwinian view of natural (and human) processes followed, while mind–body dualisms were also displaced. Instincts gave mental powers a biological basis, but Veblen specifically denied that they were reducible to "anatomical or physiological aptitudes" or genetics. Instincts permitted "consciousness and adaptation to an end aimed at" (Veblen 1914: 4). The ends themselves, and all specific human behaviors, were conditioned by the complexes of cultural habit and belief, built up on instinctual foundations over the course of social evolution. Instincts also overlapped, compounded one another, and never appeared in pure form.

Four main instincts

As innate but socially actualized elements of human purpose, instincts were the keystone of Veblen's novel orientation in social theory and his critique of both Spencer and orthodox economics. He identified four main instincts, though only two, the "parental bent" and the "predatory bent," were purposeful in their own right. The parental instinct was a communitarian tendency to care for others; the predatory instinct was a more rapacious, acquisitive, self-seeking and individualist inclination. "The instinct of workmanship," meanwhile, was "auxiliary" to other instincts and its purposes were "ulterior," "appointed... by the various other instinctive dispositions." It was the "proclivity for taking pains" and "contriving ways and means to the end sought" (Veblen 1914: 31–5). Finally there was "idle curiosity," which lacked any "utilitarian aim," but was a source of knowledge and information about the world, and could be influenced by the instinct of workmanship and set along numerous paths.

The instinct of workmanship, as a proclivity to make use of available means for various ends, was particularly important. It formed the basis for causal inferences (or Peircean abduction) that made sense of "the congeries of events," and resulted in the knowledge that made purposeful action possible. Such knowledge was always somewhat contaminated, however; first by the need to assume that the world (animistically) conformed to the powers of human understanding, and further, by the cultural inclinations and ulterior human purposes that guided inquiry. Veblen was a sharp critic of positivistic views of knowledge.

Cultural view of instincts

Veblen was aware of the contemporary criticism that instincts were scientifically imprecise and tarnished by the racial associations of biological explanations of behavior. He was not a biological reductionist, however, and did not need specific biological mechanisms for his arguments. He employed instincts because they were philosophically more satisfactory than the available alternatives in psychology. This may explain Veblen's gleeful remark to Clarence Ayres, around 1920, as attacks on instincts neared their peak, that he had never defined instincts. However, Ayres thought that Veblen had moved away from biology. Ayres reinterpreted instincts as cultural, not biological, though he also maintained that "by far [Veblen's] most important contribution was his theory of instincts" (Ayres 1958: 25).

Ayres wedded his view of cultural instincts to Dewey's instrumentalist version of PRAGMATISM to produce what is known as the "Veblenian dichotomy." He systematized Veblen's various distinctions between serviceability and waste; making goods and making money; and knowledge based on workable cause-and-effect versus cherished belief (or science versus myth), into a composite opposition between instrumental and ceremonial modes of knowledge and behavior. Ayres used the dichotomy to support a theory of INSTITUTIONAL CHANGE AND ADJUSTMENT and INSTRUMENTAL VALUE THEORY.

Ayres also mapped cultural instincts onto the dichotomy. The parental and predatory bents became one more instance of the dichotomy, while both idle curiosity and the instinct of workmanship were aligned with instrumentally warranted service to the community and authentic knowledge (science). He argued that more wasteful status interests were advanced by ceremonially adequate myths (like orthodox economics) that only mimicked authentic causal explanations. The task of science was to unmask "imposter-knowledge" and liberate social potential from past-bound myths, habits and undeserved privilege. Such accounts have received increasing criticism in recent years and some scholars view Ayres's Veblenian dichotomy as a misrepresentation of Veblen's insights. It at least overlooks Veblen's important statements about the self-contamination of the instinct of workmanship.

Current status of instincts theory

The status of instincts within institutionalism is currently uncertain. The term itself is archaic and could bear updating or replacing, but the logic it encompasses is by no means minor or obsolete. Oddly, the grounds for Veblen's view of instincts now seem more secure than the grounds for Ayres's purely cultural instincts. That human behavior, though irreducible to biology, has fundamental moorings in some (more or less universal) physiological predispositions is today an accepted principle of cognitive psychology; such irreducibility is also one expression of current philosophical views of "emergence."

In contrast, Ayres's cultural instincts, especially as represented by him in the Veblenian dichotomy, now raise serious objections. Some argue that the implied pan-cultural distinctions between "authentic" and "inauthentic" warrants (for knowledge) may be dualistic, reflecting Eurocentric or scientistic values, and/or posing threats to the concept of CULTURE that is central to institutionalism. Probably Ayres's Veblenian dichotomy is more vulnerable to charges of Eurocentric scientism than was Veblen's conception of biological instincts.

See also:

Ayres's contribution to economic reasoning; ceremonial encapsulation; collective social wealth; conspicuous consumption and emulation; corporate hegemony; disembedded economy; hegemony; institutional political economy: major contemporary themes; institutions and habits; minimal dislocation; neoinstitutionalism; radical institutionalism

Selected references

Ayres, C.E. (1958) "Veblen's Theory of Instincts Reconsidered," in D. Dowd (ed.), *Thorstein Veblen: A Critical Reappraisal*, Ithaca, NY: Cornell University Press.
Jennings, Ann and Waller, William (1998) "The Place of Biological Science in Veblen's Economics," *History of Political Economy* 30.
Mayhew, Anne (1987) "Culture: Core Concept under Attack," *Journal of Economic Issues* 21: 587–603.
Veblen, Thorstein (1900) "The Preconceptions of Economic Science III," repr. in *The Place of Science in Modern Civilization*, New York: B.W. Huebsch, 1919.

—— (1914) *The Instinct of Workmanship and the State of the Industrial Arts*, New Brunswick, NJ: Transaction Press, 1990.
Waller, William (1994), "The Veblenian Dichotomy and its Critics," in G. Hodgson, W. Samuels and M. Tool (eds), *The Elgar Companion to Institutional and Evolutionary Economics*, Aldershot: Edward Elgar.

ANN JENNINGS

institutional change and adjustment

Introduction

A diagnostic characteristic of American institutional economics, beginning with the work of Thorstein B. VEBLEN, is its attempt to incorporate an evolutionary theory of institutional change in its explanation of the structure and functioning of real world economic systems. Perhaps the most coherent theory of institutional change found in the American institutionalist literature is that line of thought, dubbed NEOINSTITUTIONALISM by Marc R. Tool, which takes its inspiration from Veblen (1899) and emerges in the works of Clarence Ayres (1944), J. Fagg Foster (1981) and Marc R. Tool (1979), among others.

The neoinstitutionalist view is grounded in the concept of CULTURE, which holds that the individual is both a product and a producer of culture in a complex, evolving social process. Individuals become "socialized" as they are indoctrinated into the mores and folkways of the culture (Tool 1979: 55). Their tastes and preferences, aspirations, conceptions of the world, ethics and beliefs in general are culturally determined, internalized and habituated. In this sense the individual is a product of culture. Nevertheless, individuals also have the capacity to exercise creative intelligence in the problem solving processes of the community. To the extent that they do so, particularly as they contribute innovations to the problem solving processes, they are producers of culture.

The culture concept lies at the heart of the neoinstitutionalist's HOLISTIC METHOD and plays a crucial role at every stage of the neoinstitutional theory of institutional change.

Instrumental value theory

A unique feature of the neoinstitutionalist theory of institutional change is that it is "an effort to extend...the theory of value into the theory of institutional adjustment" (Foster 1981: 927). Following Ayres, neoinstitutionalists combine Veblen's evolutionary economics with John Dewey's pragmatic instrumentalist theory of knowledge and value (Dewey 1938, 1939) (see PRAGMATISM). This is accomplished in part by the formulation of the (Veblenian) institutional dichotomy, which posits that all cultures exhibit two modes of valuation within their institutional structures, the instrumental and the ceremonial. Institutions are defined as socially prescribed patterns of correlated behavior. Patterns of behavior are composed of behaviors (activities) that are correlated by the values of the culture. Given the two modes of valuation within the culture, patterns of behavior are either instrumentally warranted or ceremonially warranted (Bush 1987) (see INSTRUMENTAL VALUE THEORY).

Veblen laid the foundation for the formulation of these two modes of valuation in his definition of an "invidious distinction" (Veblen 1899: 34). An invidious distinction is a distinction among individuals or groups with respect to their presumed inherent worth as human beings. Invidious distinctions form the basis of all status systems and provide the justification for the use of "force and fraud" in the conduct of human affairs (p. 273). In contrast, the non-invidious interests of the community focus on the enhancement of the life process of the community taken impersonally (p. 99).

The instrumental (non-invidious) mode of valuation is manifest in the technological processes which encompass the arts and sciences of the culture; that is, the tools–skills nexus that ranges across the fine arts and formal scientific inquiry to the most mundane applications of human intelligence to the problem solving activities of daily life. In all of these activities, human beings assess the appropriateness of a standard of judgment (value) in the correlation of behavior on the basis of whether it enhances the life process of the community taken impersonally. In other words, instrumentally warranted standards of judgment are assessed in terms of their non-invidious consequences for members of the community. By their very character, instrumental valuations are subject to critical assessment and revision as the processes of inquiry and problem solving are carried out.

The ceremonial (invidious) mode of valuation, in contrast, is manifest in the invidious distinctions that warrant patterns of status and differential advantage of some members of the community over others. Ceremonial valuations are warranted by appeals to authority, reliance on immemorial traditions, citations of holy writs and so forth. They are justified by the standard of "ceremonial adequacy," which requires conformity with existing patterns of status and power. It is the function of IDEOLOGY to mystify the rationale for the standards of ceremonial adequacy and to protect such standards from critical inquiry and revision. Neoinstitutionalists share with Veblen the belief that ceremonial valuation (and thus ceremonially warranted patterns of behavior) tends to be the dominant mode of valuation (and behavior) in all societies.

Technological dynamic

While both modes of valuation, along with the behaviors they correlate, become habituated in the behavioral patterns of the community, the inherent dynamics of technological processes in the arts and sciences, operating through the mode of instrumental valuation, create pressures for change in habitual patterns of behavior. Contemporary neoinstitutionalists refer to this as the principle of the technological dynamic. Foster (1981) used the less felicitous term the "principle of technological determination," which inadvertently conveys the mistaken impression that neoinstitutionalists are "technological determinists." However named, the principle is that technological innovation (broadly conceived as any instrumentally warranted innovation in the arts and sciences) is the dynamic process that gives rise to institutional adjustment.

Ceremonial encapsulation

The dominance of ceremonially warranted patterns of behavior affects the capacity of the community to absorb technological innovations into the problem solving processes. The invidious interests of the community resist technological innovations that cannot be "encapsulated" within the existing status and power structure. Thus, those innovations that are utilized are those that can be incorporated into patterns of behavior correlated through ceremonially warranted standards of judgment. This is known as the Principle of Ceremonial Encapsulation. CEREMONIAL ENCAPSULATION maintains the dominance of ceremonial values in the correlation of behavior that existed before the technological innovation. The process of ceremonial encapsulation is the first phase of institutional adjustment arising out of a given technological innovation.

Progressive and regressive change

"Institutional change" is the second phase of the process of institutional adjustment. It involves a change in the value structure of the institution with respect to the relative dominance of ceremonial over instrumental patterns of behavior. Institutional change can be either "progressive" or "regressive." If it is progressive, instrumentally warranted values displace ceremonially warranted values in the correlation of behavior. As the non-invidious benefits of the technological innovation are recognized within the community, the instrumentally warranted standards of judgment generated by the innovation are applied elsewhere in the community's problem-solving processes. Tool has identified progressive institutional change as the provision "of the continuity of human life and the noninvidious re-creation of community through the instrumental use of knowledge" (Tool 1979: 293).

Regressive institutional change, on the other hand, occurs when the community's response to a technological innovation is so overwhelmingly invidious that the process of ceremonial encapsulation results in an increase in the dominance of ceremonial over instrumental patterns of behavior. Such a circumstance results in the loss of instrumental efficiency in the problem solving processes as knowledge is suppressed and individuals possessing such knowledge are ostracized, driven from their professions or, in cases of extreme authoritarianism, incarcerated or executed.

Recognized interdependence

There are two broad non-invidious restraints on progressive institutional change that affect its rate and direction. Foster referred to these restraints as the principle of recognized interdependence and the principle of minimal dislocation (Foster 1981: 933–4). The principle of RECOGNIZED INTERDEPENDENCE is based on the proposition that society is composed of a seamless web of behavioral patterns that defines the "continuity" of its institutional structure. A change in any socially prescribed pattern of behavior has the potential for bringing about changes in other patterns of behavior. Thus, progressive institutional change will be constrained by the ability of individuals to perceive the nature and necessity of the contemplated changes in interdependent habitual modes of behavior. One of the most profound implications of this principle is the critical role played by public education in providing the community with the intellectual and emotional skills of adaptation necessary to sustain a progressive, democratic society.

Minimal dislocation

The principle of MINIMAL DISLOCATION is based on the proposition that technological innovation may displace instrumentally warranted behavior that is ceremonially encapsulated in the community's patterns of behavior. Clearly such losses of instrumental efficiency must be minimized if the community is to enjoy a net increase in instrumental efficiency from the new innovation. The principle of minimal dislocation has profound implications for an understanding of institutional adjustments in any culture. For instance, the application of "market shock" policies in Eastern European countries and Russia to achieve the transition from "socialism" to "capitalism" appears to have resulted in maximal dislocation of the already tattered institutional fabric of many of these countries. This could result in "regressive" rather than "progressive" institutional changes.

See also:

Ayres's contribution to economic reasoning; circular and cumulative causation; collective social wealth; conspicuous consumption and emulation; conventions; hegemony; institutional political economy: major contemporary themes; institutions and habits

Selected references

Ayres, C.E. (1944) *The Theory of Economic Progress*, 3rd edn, Kalamazoo, MI: New Issues Press, Western Michigan University, 1978.
Bush, Paul D. (1987) "The Theory of Institutional Change," *Journal of Economic Issues* 21(3): 1075–116.
Dewey, John (1938) "Logic: The Theory of Inquiry," in Jo Ann Boydston (ed.), *John Dewey: The Later Works, 1925–1953*, vol. 12, Carbondale, IL: Southern Illinois University Press, 1986.
—— (1939) "The Theory of Valuation," in Jo Ann Boydston (ed.), *John Dewey: The Later Works, 1925–1953*, vol. 13, Carbondale, IL: Southern Illinois University Press, 1988.
Foster, J. Fagg (1981) "The Papers of J. Fagg Foster," *Journal of Economic Issues* 15(4): 857–1012.
Tool, Marc R. (1979) *The Discretionary Economy: A Normative Theory of Political Economy*, Santa Monica, CA: Goodyear Publishing Co.
Veblen, Thorstein B. (1899) *The Theory of the Leisure Class*, New York: Augustus M. Kelley, 1975.

PAUL D. BUSH

institutional political economy: history

Introduction

Institutionalism emerged as an academic and political movement counter to the excessive formalism, ahistorical analysis, comparative static methods, and conservative apologia characteristic of NEOCLASSICAL ECONOMICS. In place of this, institutionalists have sought to develop an evolutionary analysis of institutions underlying production, distribution and exchange. Long-term change, historical analysis and social and political factors are seen by institutionalists to be critical to economics.

Many economists and social theorists who articulated similar criticisms and addressed similar concerns are often associated with the institutionalists (for example, Karl MARX, John Hobson and Joseph SCHUMPETER). However, it is the work of Thorstein VEBLEN along with the extremely successful and important empirical research programs of John R. Commons (1862–1945) and Wesley C. Mitchell (1874–1948), that defines institutional political economy, historically speaking.

Veblen's evolutionary economics

Thorstein Veblen's scholarship encompassed a thorough critique of neoclassical economics for its failure to be evolutionary, by which he meant its static and taxonomic character. He recommended a focus on the process of change with special emphasis on CIRCULAR AND CUMULATIVE CAUSATION, or what he called a "genetic account of cause and effect." His theoretical contribution was the result of his methodological emphasis on a cultural analysis of evolving institutions, largely drawn from his reading of anthropology, pragmatic philosophy and socialist literature. He combined this with a theory of human nature that attributed certain proclivities or INSTINCTS to human beings. The positive proclivities or instincts were idle curiosity, workmanship and the parental bent, which are largely but not exclusively directed at serviceable ends. In contrast, the predatory instinct and emulation are largely directed at disserviceable ends. His major works include *The Theory of the Leisure Class*, published in 1899, *The Theory of Business Enterprise* in 1904 and *The Instinct of Workmanship* in 1914.

Commons and collective action

A contemporary of Veblen, John R. Commons was both an academic economist and activist. He made significant contributions to the field of labor history, and drafted important labor and social welfare legislation in the state of Wisconsin that served as models for subsequent federal legislation. His contributions to institutional political economy (both old and new) centered on the concepts of transactions, working rules and going concerns, described in his *Institutional Economics*, published in 1934. These led him to explore the legal environment of transactions, the nature of collective (rather than individual) action, and the role of government in resolving social conflict among varied interests, in the *Legal Foundations of Capitalism* in 1924 and *The Economics of Collective Action* in 1950. Commons, along with Richard Ely, was central to the development of the "Wisconsin" branch of institutional political economy (See COMMONS'S CONTRIBUTION TO POLITICAL ECONOMY).

Mitchell and business cycles

Wesley Clair Mitchell, a student of Veblen at the University of Chicago, made primary contributions in the area of business cycle analysis, notably in his *Business Cycles*, published in 1913. Mitchell developed a theory in which cycles are an inherent part of the culture of a monetary economy. Mitchell's careful empirical studies of business cycles at the National Bureau of Economic Research (NBER), and the development of statistical indicators for forecasting purposes, are a legacy to the economics discipline as a whole. Mitchell's unconventional methodology, especially his use of extensive empirical and statistical analysis to provide the foundation for a HOLISTIC METHOD, led to considerable criticism of his work by mainstream economists for being "facts without theory." (See MITCHELL'S ANALYSIS OF BUSINESS CYCLES.)

Clark, Hoxie and Hamilton

The next major group of institutional political economists rose to prominence after the First World War, and it was their work which caused institutionalism to reach the peak of its influence over US economic policy in the 1930s. Their research interests were similar to the founders. John Maurice Clark (1884–1963), the son of Veblen's teacher John Bates Clark, developed the concept of OVERHEAD COSTS as a theoretical foundation for his analysis of the working of industrial economies. Clark argued that costs were not as objective as orthodox theory or business supposed. This misperception of costs led to inappropriate behavior by business enterprises. These included price discrimination, cut-throat competition and monopolistic agreements. These practices in turn required the creation of institutions to exercise social control over business enterprises to establish workable competition.

Robert Hoxie (1868–1916) made important contributions to labor economics, employing an empirical approach strongly influenced by Veblen. Later, Walton Hamilton (1881–1958) coined the term "institutional economics" in an influential *American Economic Review* article in 1919, and wrote a critical article on "Institution" in the *Encyclopaedia of Social Sciences* in 1932. He wrote extensively on the problem of social control, which he viewed as the central theoretical and practical problem

Tugwell and Means

The voluminous writings of Rexford Tugwell (1891–1979) made a significant theoretical contribution to institutional thought, particularly in the area of defining the public interest. His career also marks the high point of the influence of institutional political economy on public policy in the United States. As part of Franklin D. Roosevelt's "brain trust" and architect of "New Deal" policy in the 1930s, Tugwell influenced the direction of the evolution of the government's role in the US economy, and helped to set the terms of public policy debates for the rest of the century. He also served as Governor of Puerto Rico (1941–6).

Gardiner Means was co-author with Adoph A. Berle, Jr of the classic work *The Modern Corporation and Private Property*, published in 1932. This book both defined and documented the evolution of the separation of ownership from the control of modern corporate enterprises, thereby signaling a fundamental shift in the nature of the US economy. Means continued this work and developed more fully the role of administered prices in the modern economy, particularly emphasizing the macroeconomic consequences for employment, inflation and the character of business cycles. This work has influenced generations of institutionalists, especially in relation to the question of ownership and control and PRICING within the corporation.

Ayres and the dichotomy

In 1930, Clarence Ayres (1891–1972) began his long career at the University of Texas. The "Texas" (or "cactus") branch of institutional political economy is dominated by his influence. Ayres came to economics from an academic career in philosophy. He expanded Veblen's frequent distinctions between efficacious and predatory social habits of thought and behavior into the more formal distinction between *ceremonial* behavior and *instrumental* (or technological) behavior. Ayres applied this distinction, which came to be known as the "Veblenian dichotomy," to the problem of economic development. He argued that economic development tends to occur on the social frontier where ceremonial conventions hold less sway over behavior, and where the exigencies of life require matter of fact problem solving, in *The Theory of Economic Progress*, published in 1944.

Ayres combined John Dewey's instrumental philosophy (a variant of American PRAGMATISM) with Veblen's historical and anthropological approach. Robert Zimmerman (1888–1961), also of the "Texas" branch, added the insight that resources are not "natural" but, instead, are created through human technological behavior. Ayres combines Veblenian analysis of social valuation and the technological optimism of Dewey's instrumentalism. Marc Tool has referred to Ayres's contribution as the beginning of NEOINSTITUTIONALISM (See AYRES'S CONTRIBUTION TO ECONOMIC REASONING).

Galbraith's contribution

John Kenneth Galbraith is certainly the most prolific and influential institutional economist since Veblen. Galbraith was born in Canada, but has spent most of his professional life and career in the US. His main contributions to institutional political economy are contained in his trilogy, *The Affluent Society*, published in 1952, *The New Industrial State* in 1967 and *Economics and the Public Purpose* in 1973. He developed a model of the economy that incorporates several new hypotheses and concepts to explain the development of modern industrial market economies.

Three concepts were especially important to Galbraith. First is the concept of the "revised sequence," where firms reach forward to control markets, managing behavior and social attitudes. The second is the notion of the "technostructure," specialists who make the substantive decisions of corporations, and whose motivation is autonomy (with a secure minimum of earnings) rather than profit maximization. The third concept is "the imagery of choice," where the illusion of consumer sovereignty is maintained, despite the revised sequence. (See GALBRAITH'S CONTRIBUTION TO POLITICAL ECONOMY.)

The European connection

After the first generation of institutionalists' scholarly contributions became better known, explicit connections between the "American" school and other economists began to appear. In Europe, the German HISTORICAL SCHOOL shared many of the criticisms of orthodoxy that had motivated Veblen's critique. The influence of the economic writings of Max Weber and Emile Durkheim similarly have contributed to the development of institutional political economy in Europe. Influential Japanese economists, who studied at the University of Wisconsin and became important in the development of the Japanese economic system, were influenced directly by American institutional political economy.

Three European economists stand out as central to the overall development of institutional political economy. First, Gunnar Myrdal (1898–1987), the only institutionalist apart from Douglass North to receive a Nobel prize in economics, made significant contributions in the areas of economic development, monetary theory and social value theory. He is probably best known for his two multi-volume exemplars of institutional analysis, *The American Dilemma*, published in 1944, which focused on race relations in the US, and *Asian Drama*, published in 1968, which focused on poverty in developing nations. He has made important contributions to holistic method, including the notion of circular and cumulative change and the linkages between political, social and economic processes.

Second, the evolutionary–institutional analysis of K. William Kapp (1910–76) was ahead of its time in situating human culture within the context of a biological, ecological and material environment. This holistic scholar provided the early foundations for an open-systems approach to the dynamic interplay between economic development, QUALITY OF LIFE, entropic processes and environmental decay.

Third, the work of Karl Polanyi (1886–1964) emphasizes the historical and anthropological approach to social inquiry that was characteristic of Veblen's work. However, he builds on less speculative historical and ethnographic work than Veblen. Central to Polanyi's analysis of the evolution of market capitalism is the distinction between embedded and disembedded economies in *The Great Transformation*, published in 1944 (see DISEMBEDDED ECONOMY).

The development of a separate sphere of human behavior, distinct from other activities of social reproduction, motivated by greed, self-interest or hunger, was seen by Polanyi as the crucial element in the development of market economies in the nineteenth century. Moreover, this development enhanced the instability and increased the likelihood of failure in social reproduction and provisioning in these economies (see REPRODUCTION PARADIGM). In this sense the economics is disembedded from its social and political foundations. Polanyi also identified the "double-movement," a protective response, where other social institutions evolved to counteract these destructive elements of market economies. Protective responses associated with public policy include automatic stabilizers (unemployment benefits), discretionary policy (large budget deficits during recessions), health and safety legislation, the "lender of last resort" facility and environmental controls.

Contemporary institutionalism

There are several major figures in contemporary institutionalism. For instance, David Hamilton's work emphasizes a cultural analysis of economic theory, consumption, and poverty. Wendell Gordon's work extends institutional political economy into the area of international economics, with particular emphasis on the evolution of the United Nations as a transnational economic institution. Marc Tool extends the work of Veblen, Ayres and others in the development of INSTRUMENTAL VALUE THEORY. Warren Samuels has made major contributions to the conceptualization of power, an explication of methodological considerations within institutionalism, and has traced the connections among many disparate forms of economics and institutional political economy.

There are two major associations of institutional economists in the United States. The Association for Evolutionary Economics (AFEE), founded in 1965, publishes the *Journal of Economic Issues* and meets annually with the Allied Social Science Association in the USA. The Association for Institutional Thought (AFIT), founded in 1979, has an annual meeting in the USA each Spring. The European Association for Evolutionary Political Economy (EAEPE), founded in 1988 with encouragement and support from some AFEE members, has informal links with the *Review of Political Economy*. The European Association is more explicit in making connections across heterodox schools of thought. Among contemporary European institutionalists, Geoffrey Hodgson's work is most consistent with the themes of the institutional political economists described herein.

Two strands of institutional political economy have emerged within the last twenty years. The first is a group of radical institutionalists who follow Veblen's holistic methodology, combined with Marc Tool's emphasis on democratic *processes* of transformation. This is clearly an offshoot of the main branch of institutional political economy. William Dugger, J. Ron Stanfield and Ann Jennings are leading lights of this group. Among other things, they are especially interested in the origins, nature and egalitarian solutions to the problems created by inequality of income, wealth and power based on gender, race/ethnicity, class and national differences.

The second is the emergence of "new" institutionalism within mainstream orthodox economics. The "new" institutionalism is an amalgamation of Coasian property rights, public choice, new theories of the firm, Austrian and other variants of mainstream thought that have chosen to address the role of social institutions in economic behavior. The work of Oliver E. Williamson and the Nobel prize winner Douglass North are the closest in terms of subject matter and similar conceptual schemes to institutional political economy. Interestingly, European institutional political economists have made the most significant attempts to combine the strengths of institutional political economy with the "new" institutionalism.

Finally, recent post-Keynesian writers, particularly Philip Arestis, Marc Lavoie and Frederic Lee, have argued that institutional economics provides the microfoundations for post-Keynesian thought. This suggests that an interesting synthesis, or at least shared research agenda, may develop between these two heterodox schools. Others have discussed the linkages between institutional, feminist and neo-Marxist political economy.

See also:

corporate hegemony; culture; evolutionary economics: major contemporary themes; hegemony; institutional change and adjustment; institutional political economy: major contemporary themes; institutionalism: old and new; institutions and habits; Myrdal's contribution to political economy; Polanyi's views on integration; political economy: schools; Williamson's analysis of the corporation

Selected references

Gruchy, Allan G. (1947) *Modern Economic Thought: The American Contribution*, New York: Prentice Hall.

—— (1974) *Contemporary Economic Thought: The Contribution of Neo-Institutional Economics*, Clifton, NJ: Augustus M. Kelley.

Hodgson, Geoffrey M., Samuels, Warren J. and Tool, Marc R. (eds) (1994) *The Elgar Companion to Institutional and Evolutionary Economics*, Brookfield, VT: Edward Elgar.

Mayhew, Anne. "The Beginnings of Institutionalism," *Journal of Economic Issues* 21(3): 971–98.

Phillips, Ronnie J. (ed.) (1995) *Economic Mavericks: The Texas Institutionalists*, Greenwich, CT: JAI Press.

WILLIAM WALLER

institutional political economy: major contemporary themes

Contemporary institutional political economy (IPE) is concerned primarily with two things. First, it seeks to develop a realistic analysis of the structure and evolution of institutions in the contemporary world, including a central concern for policy analysis. These institutions include the systems of production and distribution, the corporation, the family, the financial system, and state, and the world economy, as well as specific ideologies, beliefs, values, norms and mores which influence human behavior.

Second, it seeks to develop concepts and principles which aid such institutional analysis. Examples include the notions of culture, path dependency, circular and cumulative causation and ceremonial encapsulation. These concepts and principles are historically contingent and reexamined in the light of changing conditions. Some of the concerns of IPE are common to other schools of political economy, but there are many which are distinctive to institutionalism (see Tool 1988).

Holism, pragmatism, culture and evolution

Institutionalists tend to employ a HOLISTIC METHOD in the sense that they situate the economy within an open sociopolitical system and take a broad view of problems such as inflation, unemployment, growth, development and market power. The interconnected and interdependent character of social institutions is considered a primary object of analysis.

Within the context of the holistic method, institutionalists follow the pragmatists in epistemology, emphasize CULTURE, and develop an evolutionary analysis incorporating circular and cumulative change.

IPE has been influenced by American pragmatism, especially the work of Charles Peirce and John Dewey. This has led to an understanding of the tentative character of knowledge and theories. Knowledge is viewed as being always emerging and incomplete, continuously being reconstructed through the social process of inquiry and valuation. This fits well with the inherent complexity and contingency of socioeconomic processes.

Knowledge is always evolving because the culture and institutions which impact upon it are forever changing. In fact, a core difference that separates IPE from neoclassical and some other schools of thought is the use of the concept of culture. Economic activity is seen as an integrated aspect of a social system which is organized and given coherence within a cultural system. All social institutions need to be understood and explained within their cultural contexts (see Mayhew 1994).

IPE seeks to explain the social economy as an evolving system. The emphasis is on change and the dynamics of socioeconomic behavior and activity, as developed recently by Geoffrey Hodgson and others. Collectively we may change the social and economic order, both intentionally (discretionary policy making) and inadvertently (blind drift). Concepts such as HYSTERESIS and PATH DEPENDENCY explain processes that institutionalists have always held to be central to their inquiry. These concepts relate to the importance of historical processes affecting the future course of phenomena, such as unemployment and growth. According to these notions, complex institutional relationships are irreversible. For instance, aggregate supply and demand are interdependent. A shift in demand is thus unlikely to result in a movement back to the pre-existing equilibrium position of unemployment or output. This is because aggregate demand affects long-term unemployment, the introduction of new technology and expectations about the future, which often reinforce each other because change tends to be circular and cumulative.

The nature of CIRCULAR AND CUMULATIVE CAUSATION was analyzed by Thorstein Veblen, Gunnar Myrdal and Nicholas Kaldor, and more recently by Kurt Dopfer and others. Central to this principle is the notion of a "decentered totality" (linked to postmodernism), in which there is no one basic factor precipitating change. Rather, everything is interrelated such that multifarious and complex causation operates. This is the "circular" aspect. The cumulative aspect means that changes in the system result in multiple feedback, so that the first effect induces secondary and tertiary changes, often so as to amplify the process. The result is always one of multiple causation, and often one of increasing instability, accelerated growth or a downward spiral. The dynamic outcome depends on the original push, the precise nature of interaction among the institutions, and the extent of counteracting forces.

The notion of CIRCULAR AND CUMULATIVE CAUSATION has been applied to questions such as poverty, economic growth and development. With poverty, for instance, certain ethnic minorities tend to be in a depressed state due to the cumulative interaction of many factors: lack of financial inheritance, low education, low incomes, high rates of unemployment, discrimination, problematical lifestyle, a lack of suitable role models and inadequate parental encouragement. These factors interact and often reinforce each other, which requires constant positive initiatives and programs to break the cycle of poverty.

Another example is the cumulative waves of high and low growth which have been characteristic of the long-term motion of capitalism. During the 1950s–1960s, for instance, a number of institutional and technological innovations cumulatively led to a long boom of advanced capitalism. However, contradictions emerged in many institutions and with the maturation of technology which, in a circular and cumulative fashion, led to a high level of uncertainty and instability and lowered the floor of the business cycle. As a result, the recessions of the mid-1970s, early 1980s and early 1990s were thus deeper than average in most advanced capitalist economies.

Instrumentalism and institutional change

An important aspect of contemporary institutionalism is INSTRUMENTAL VALUE THEORY. Being a normative theory, instrumentalism examines the extent to which the economic provisioning process produces and distributes goods and services so as to enhance the quality of social life through community, warranted knowledge and participation. Every institution reproduces both instrumental functions, which are productive and promote the quality of social life, and ceremonial functions which are unproductive and inhibit such life. When the ratio of instrumental divided by ceremonial functions is increasing, then socioeconomic progress is in motion.

The productive functions of institutions promote the production of goods and services necessary for the basic needs of the population, a production process which is participatory and enhancing of creative human talent, and with a minimum negative impact on the environment. The unproductive functions promote invidious distinctions between people on the basis of class, race or gender, producing goods and services which conspicuously enhance the privilege, power and distinction of a minority class. Instrumentalism seeks to enhance the recreation of positive community, the interactive participation of people in decisions which affect their livelihood, and the widespread dissemination of information and knowledge to reduce concentrations of power and environmental destruction.

Associated with instrumentalism is a theory of INSTITUTIONAL CHANGE AND ADJUSTMENT. Progressive change occurs when social and technological wealth is used to challenge the vested interests through the promotion of new methods, institutions and values which enhance community and participation. However, changes should as far as possible minimize dislocation of the existing institutions, because instrumental functions may be adversely affected. Also, changes need, where possible, to ensure that the affected population has sufficient knowledge of the nature and possible ramifications of the changes. They should also be included in the process of instituting changes; such changes should as far as possible emanate from "below."

Gender, class, race and nation

The analysis of social stratification has always been central to IPE. SEGMENTED AND DUAL LABOR MARKETS are areas where the nexus between class, gender and race is especially strong. Institutionalists who look to Marx and Veblen for inspiration have an obvious affinity for CLASS analysis. Similarly, Veblen's interest in GENDER issues and the rise of feminism has recently spurred research on many topics by Ann Jennings, Anne Mari May, Janice Peterson and others. Feminists have examined the GENDER DIVISION OF LABOR, the FEMINIZATION OF POVERTY, and the household sector, as well as developing a feminist macroeconomics. Analysis of race and ethnicity is of interest to institutionalists, although much work is still to be undertaken in this area. More generally, institutionalists have a challenge ahead of them to scrutinize the peculiarities, similarities and general relationships between class, gender and race/ethnicity (see Dugger 1996).

Corporation and labor–capital relations

Institutionalists have always been concerned with the internal operations of the corporation and the relationship between firms. The organization of the firm is important because it forms the basis of pricing, investment and employment decisions. Linkages between firms situate these practices within "oligopolistic" and "competitive" sectors of the economy. Many institutionalists employ this two-sector model, where oligopolies tend to dominate and utilize the more competitive sector as a source of demand and cheap outsourcing.

Indeed, many oligopoly firms have collectively been termed a CENTRALIZED PRIVATE SECTOR PLANNING sector by John Munkirs and others. Oligopolistic firms in industries such as telecommunications, automobiles and transportation have established some degree of international oligopolistic cooperation. This is done through joint ventures, strategic alliances, INTERLOCKING DIRECTORSHIPS, subcontracting and production-sharing arrangements.

Institutionalists have recognized the need to examine CORPORATE HEGEMONY, where firms are seen as the dominant institutions of modern capitalism. Hegemony is developed and sustained through power, employing mechanisms such as takeovers, interlocking directorates, restrictive trade practices, the separation of ownership from control and close links to politicians. Institutionalists realize that people are born into this system of power which they may take for granted and even support. Much of the support emanates from socialization and "enabling myths," which legitimize structures of domination, discrimination, exploitation and predation (see Dugger 1996).

Financial system

Veblen's focus on the relationship between business (making money) and industry (making goods and providing services) has remained central to institutional political economy. Recently, contributions to this approach have come at the interstices of institutional and post-Keynesian political economy through the work of Randy Wray, Marc Lavoie, Basil Moore and others.

The notion of ENDOGENOUS MONEY AND CREDIT, for instance, examines the way in which government control of the monetary aggregates is limited by the ability of private banks and institutions to create their own credit. One theory examines how this is linked to the process of financial innovation. When governments try to control money and credit, financial institutions tend to find ways around the controls through innovations (and established practices) which are not included in the regulations. This expands credit for a time, until the government effectively controls this new or expanded source of funds; which is followed by further innovation, and possible further control, and so on *ad infinitum*. Endogenous money thus enables businesses to reach greater heights of euphoria, which tends to intensify the instability tendencies of the system.

The FINANCIAL INSTABILITY HYPOTHESIS is a related area of interest to institutionalists. This hypothesis, developed by Hyman Minsky and extended by Martin Wolfson, Robert Pollin and others, posits the notion that financial instability is endogenous to the normal cyclical workings of capitalism. During booms in a cycle, investors tend to become quite euphoric, investing large sums on long-term projects on the basis of what usually turns out to be a short-lived expansion. Some combination of high interest rates, wages, raw material prices, monetary policy and so on tends to reduce profitability in a sustained fashion. This leads to subdued expectations of the future, reduced investment and cash flow, along with a possible recession. During the early months of recession financial crises are most likely, when asset bubbles burst and set off a potential chain of bankruptcy. "Lender of last resort" facilities have historically been the means for preventing recessions turning into depressions, according to Minsky.

World economy and development

Historically, IPE has been US-centered. However, there have been significant contributions to the study of Latin America by Wendell Gordon, James Street, Dilmus James and James Dietz. Also Wendell Gordon and John Adams have recently pushed for greater consideration of the international economy in institutional analysis, advocating reform of the United Nations as an international decision-making unit. Institutionalists interested in Latin America have combined institutional analysis with CORE–PERIPHERY ANALYSIS, examining the structural constraints on development. John Harvey has examined the short and long-term changes in exchange rates.

Policy and the state

Institutionalists generally have seen a positive role for the state in economic policy-making, since they reject a conception of the economy as having self-adjusting tendencies. The "market economy" is not inherently stable or necessarily welfare enhancing. Consequently, government is seen as an instrument for collective problem solving, although institutions and governance may be developed by other groups and interests. Innumerable studies have been undertaken on the social control of business, the nature of deregulation and regulation and the workings of public utilities.

Market systems, following the work of Karl Polanyi, tend to experience a DISEMBEDDED ECONOMY to varying degrees. This means that the economy becomes separated and distinct from civil society. The fully integrated relationships that are necessary for provisioning are upset, resulting in varying degrees of social disruption. The economy and the values and behaviors required for market transactions take precedence over other social values. This disembedded process creates difficulties in provisioning, historically leading to a protective response: the use of other social institutions to reintegrate society.

Consequently a great deal of research focuses on what have come to be called social safety nets, such as discretionary fiscal and monetary policy, unemployment benefits, health and safety issues, "lender of last resort" facilities and agreements between capital and labor. Capitalist market systems need to be counterbalanced with sufficient social capital to moderate the tendency toward high levels of uncertainty, social fragility and business cycle instability. The state and other institutions can play an important role in facilitating such social capital, in the interim before more extensive systemic changes evolve or are instituted.

See also:

Association for Evolutionary Economics and Association for Institutional Thought; evolutionary economics: major contemporary themes; individual and society; institutional political economics: history; institutionalism: old and new; hegemony; institutions and habits; journals of political economy; neoinstitutionalism; radical institutionalism; social fabric matrix.

Selected references

Adams, John and Scaperlanda, Anthony (eds) (1996) *The Institutional Economics of the International Economy*, Boston: Kluwer Academic Publishing.
Dopfer, Kurt (1991) "The Complexity of Economic Phenomena: Reply to Tinbergen and Beyond," *Journal of Economic Issues* 25(1): 39–76.
Dugger, William (ed.) (1996) *Inequality: Radical Institutionalist Views on Race, Gender, Class, and Nation*, Westport, CT: Greenwood Press.
Jennings, Ann (1994) "Toward a Feminist Expansion of Macroeconomics: Money Matters," *Journal of Economic Issues* 28(2): 555–65.
Mayhew, Anne (1994) "Culture," in Geoffrey Hodgson, Warren J. Samuels and Marc R. Tool (eds), *The Elgar Companion to Institutional and Evolutionary Economics*, vol. 1, Aldershot: Edward Elgar, 115–19.
O'Hara, Phillip Anthony (1999) *Marx, Veblen and Modern Institutional Economics: Principles and Dynamics of Capitalism*, Cheltenham: Edward Elgar.
Tool, Marc R. (ed.) (1988) *Evolutionary Economics*, 2 vols, Armonk, NY: M.E. Sharpe.
Waller, William T. (1988) "The Concept of Habit in Economic Analysis," *Journal of Economic Issues* 22(1): 113–26.

PHILLIP ANTHONY O'HARA
WILLIAM WALLER

institutionalism: old and new

Roots of institutionalism

The label "institutionalism" has long been attached to a particular heterodox tradition in economics. Founded on the work of Veblen and Commons in the early years of the twentieth century, that tradition had, at least until the early 1930s, considerable influence in American academic economics and on economic policy. By 1944, however, Clarence Ayres, then institutionalism's leading figure, had conceded that the victory of the neoclassical mainstream over the institutionalist approach was complete. Nevertheless, since the 1960s work in this tradition has undergone a revival. This has occurred within communities of scholars focused, in the USA, on the Association for Evolutionary Economics (AFEE) and the *Journal of Economic Issues* and, in Europe, on the more recently established European Association for Evolutionary Political Economy (EAEPE). These "original" or "old" institutionalists have also been labeled "neoinstitutionalists" (see NEOINSTITUTIONALISM), a category often used to include such scholars as J.K. Galbraith, Gunnar Myrdal, Clarence Ayres, Marc Tool and others. Such work remains outside the mainstream of the discipline.

New institutional economics

In parallel with this revival of the older tradition, the last twenty years have seen the emergence, in this case from roots within mainstream economics, of a "new institutional economics" (NIE), the impact of which is indicated by the award of a Nobel Prize to Douglass North, one of its leading practitioners. This development has raised much debate about possible relationships between NIE and the "original" or "old" (and continuing) institutionalist tradition (OIE). Actual dialogue between the practitioners of OIE and NIE has been much more limited. A review of some background history might suggest why.

Background and history

Institutions may be broadly defined as norms, rules, and structures that constrain, direct or guide the behavior of human actors. North distinguishes usefully between the framework of political, social and legal ground rules within which an economic order operates (its "institutional environment"), and the governance structures, such as the firm, that condition the way economic actors cooperate and compete ("institutional arrangements").

The broad concerns of the discipline of political economy in its eighteenth and early nineteenth-century origins are indicated in the title of Adam Smith's *Inquiry into the Nature and Causes of the Wealth of Nations*, first published in 1776. The interaction of economic behavior and evolving institutional environments and arrangements was central. Indeed, it can be argued that all "political economy" must involve historically-based explanations of economic phenomena, in which institutions are both part of what is to be explained and part of the explanation. While CLASSICAL POLITICAL ECONOMY did emphasize institutions and historically grounded analysis, Veblen criticized it for nor being sufficiently evolutionary in its method. From the late nineteenth century, with the evolving division of labor in the social sciences, the narrower discipline of "economics" developed into a neoclassical orthodoxy. The messy analysis of institutions has been avoided in a mainstream positivist economic "science," which came to rely increasingly on formal mathematical techniques.

Founded on classical liberalism, the neoclassical paradigm is characterized by a form of reductionism. It uses as its basic building block the concept of an abstract, self-contained, hedonistic, rational-maximizing individual, the formation of whose tastes and preferences is exogenous to economic theory. It also uses formal static equilibrium models of economic phenomena, which translate individual analysis into a social optimality. Although the "Austrian school" economists reject such a static equilibrium approach, and are more conscious of information problems, they too remain attached to the abstract individual of classical liberalism.

OIE developed in the USA as a direct reaction against the focus and method of neoclassical economics and with roots in earlier traditions of political economy. While it is difficult to specify one set of "hard core" assumptions which define OIE, a set of common characteristics can be identified. It is holistic and organic in its approach (see HOLISTIC METHOD) and the beliefs, values and actions of individuals are seen as culturally embedded (see CULTURE). The task is to describe the complexities of the organization and control of social provisioning in its historical evolution, and the central concern to understand the process of INSTITUTIONAL CHANGE AND ADJUSTMENT. Emphasis is given to power relations, legal systems and TECHNOLOGY as key explanatory elements in the formation of institutions. A skeptical and critical perspective on contemporary institutions is taken. Economics is seen as a pragmatic, evolutionary and policy science which aims to improve the functioning of the economy through institutional change.

The parallel developments labeled NIE have, over the last twenty years, covered a variety of subject matter. This includes an analysis of the firm, collective action, property rights, law, economic history as institutional history, and an approach which includes transaction cost economics, game theory, principal–agent theory and evolutionary methodology. In general, NIE attempts to render mainstream economic analysis more realistic by endogenizing institutions. The structure and evolution of economic, legal and political institutional arrangements are explained as the product (intended or unintended) of the behavior of rational-maximizing individuals.

In Williamson's transaction cost economics, for example, institutional arrangements may have a life of their own and the institutional environment may influence individual preferences. However, the form of the governance institutions through which transactions take place – markets, firms or some hybrid – is mainly explained in terms of the decisions of rational calculating individuals. While most of this work employs the kinds of formal techniques characteristic of mainstream economics, some of it adopts a more literary style (see WILLIAMSON'S ANALYSIS OF THE CORPORATION).

Relationship between OIE and NIE

Since most of the NIE lies within the neoclassical tradition (some has "Austrian" roots), the long-held mutual antagonisms between OIE and the neoclassical mainstream lead both to a tendency by OIE to reject NIE because of its neoclassical roots, and an avoidance of associations with OIE by NIE to retain its legitimacy within the mainstream.

The tag "old" is not relished by many "old" institutionalists, who neither see themselves as *passé* nor accept that NIE is "institutionalism because it does not share the fundamental characteristics of institutionalism" (Dugger 1990: 429). Most "old" institutionalists prefer the title of "original," "Veblenian," "radical" or "neo-" institutionalist. Dugger accepts that Williamson's view of the firm as a governance structure introduces new and more realistic elements into the mainstream paradigm. However, he shares a widely held view among both OIE and NIE that, because of their fundamentally different starting premises, work in these two camps cannot be integrated into a singular "institutionalism" (see also Ramstad 1996).

But is there, perhaps, a middle way? The case for a fruitful conversation between OIE and NIE has gained ground in recent years and is most persuasively argued in Rutherford (1994) (see also the special edition of the *Review of Political Economy* (1989)).

Rutherford demonstrates both that OIE and NIE as schools or paradigms are internally more eclectic and less unified than their advocates suggest, and that in analyzing institutions and institutional change they share common problems and have different, and possibly complementary, strengths and weaknesses. Clearly both individual agency and social structures and context are necessary to a satisfactory institutional economics.

The recent work of North on institutions and national economic performance recognizes that institutions are no longer necessarily efficient. This work also recognizes that non-economic factors, such as power and IDEOLOGY, may be significant in their development (see NORTH'S THEORY OF INSTITUTIONAL CHANGE). Hence the need for the closed axiomatic theoretical system of neoclassical economics to be extensively modified (see Groenewegen *et al.* 1995).

Conclusion

Institutional political economy requires a historical approach, an openness to social and political elements, and an ideological self-consciousness. NIE must significantly escape its mainstream roots to contribute to such a project. At the very least, however, OIE must allow that NIE has stimulated renewed interest in institutionalist work in all traditions.

See also:

Association for Evolutionary Economics and Association for Institutionalist Thought; Austrian school of political economy; Ayres's contribution to economic reasoning; Commons's contribution to political economy; European Association for Evolutionary Political Economy; evolutionary economics: major contemporary themes; Galbraith's contribution to political economy; institutional political economy: major contemporary themes; institutions and habits; Mitchell's analysis of business cycles; neoclassical economics; North's theory of institutional change; public choice theory; Veblen

Selected references

Dugger, W. (1990) "The New Institutionalism: New But Not Institutionalist," *Journal of Economic Issues* 24(2): 423–31.

Groenewegen, J., Kerstholt, F. and Nagelkerke, A. (1995) "On Integrating New and Old Institutionalism: Douglass North Building Bridges," *Journal of Economic Issues* 29(2): 467–75.

Hodgson, G.M. (1988) *Economics and Institutions*, Oxford: Polity Press.

Mulberg, J. (1995) *Social Limits to Economic Theory*, London: Routledge.

Ramstad, Y. (1996) "Is a Transaction a

Transaction?," *Journal of Economic Issues* 30(2): 417–25.
Review of Political Economy (1989) 1(3), special issue devoted to old and new institutionalism and including articles by G.M. Hodgson, R.N. Langlois, M. Rutherford, A. Mayhew, V. Vanberg, and C.G. Leathers.
Rutherford, M. (1994) *Institutions in Economics: The Old and the New Institutionalism*, Cambridge: Cambridge University Press.

ALAN HUTTON

institutions and habits

Thorstein VEBLEN (1919: 239) defined institutions as "settled habits of thought common to the generality of men." The institutional economist Walton Hamilton (1932: 84) elaborated this definition of an institution, in terms of "a way of thought or action of some prevalence and permanence, which is embedded in the habits of a group or the customs of a people." Notably, in the "old" institutionalism, the concept of habit plays a central role both in its definition of an institution and in its picture of human agency (Hodgson 1988).

This contrasts with the definition of an institution in post-Weberian sociology and in the "new" institutional economics, reflecting the systematic excision of the idea of habit from both mainstream economics and sociology in the 1920s (Camic 1986). Likewise, the "new" institutionalists have attempted to decouple the concepts of institution and habit. Thus, Andrew Schotter (1981: 11) writes: "A social institution is a regularity in social behavior that is agreed to by all members of society, specifies behavior in specific recurrent situations, and is either self-policed or policed by some external authority." Douglass North (1990: 3), with a slightly different definition, again overlooks habit when he says: "Institutions are the rules of the game in society or, more formally, are the humanly devised constraints that shape human interaction. In consequence they structure incentives in human exchange, whether political, social, or economic." The absence of the word "habit" or its synonyms from these definitions is not accidental.

Broad conception of institution

Despite their differences, it should be noted that all the above definitions involve a relatively broad concept of an "institution." The idea encompasses not simply organizations – such as corporations, banks and universities – but also integrated and systematic social entities such as money, language and law. The case for such a broad definition of institutions is that all such entities involve common characteristics:

- All institutions involve the interaction of agents with crucial information *feedbacks*.
- Institutions sustain, and are sustained by, *shared* expectations.
- Institutions have a number of characteristic and common *routines*.
- Although they may change and eventually die, institutions have *durable* and persistent qualities.
- Institutions typically involve processes that promote their own moral *legitimation*: that which endures is often – rightly or wrongly – seen as morally just.

In addition, the broad definition of an institution is consistent with long-standing practice in the social sciences. Organizations may be defined as a special subset of institutions, involving deliberate coordination and recognized principles of sovereignty and command.

Habits, routines and choice

The concept of habit is central to the concept of human agency adopted by the "old" institutional economics. Habit has been usefully defined as "a more or less self-actuating disposition or tendency to engage in a previously adopted or acquired form of action" (Camic 1986: 1044). A habit is a form of non-reflective behavior that arises in repetitive situations; habits are influenced by prior activity and have self-sustaining qualities.

institutions and habits

Many modern economists have addressed habit and there is a large contemporary literature on the topic in mainstream journals. However, following much earlier neoclassical precedents, such as Alfred Marshall and Philip Wicksteed, habit is often regarded as an evocation or appendage of rational choice, and is thereby explicable in its terms.

The treatment of habit by the pragmatist philosophers and instinct psychologists who influenced the early institutionalists was quite different. Here the explanatory arrow ran in the opposite direction: instead of habits being explained in terms of rational choice, rational choice was explained in terms of habits. Further, habit was linked with knowledge and belief. For Charles Sanders Peirce, the essence of belief was the establishment of habit. All ideas, including beliefs, preferences and rational modes of calculation, were regarded as adaptations to circumstances, established through the acquisition of habitual propensities (See PRAGMATISM.)

At first sight, both approaches seem feasible: habit can be regarded as the basis of rational choice, or rational choice can be seen as the procreator of habits. Leading advocates of the rational choice paradigm, such as Kenneth Arrow (1986), have accepted the possibility of an alternative approach based on habit. Strikingly, Gary Becker (1962) long ago demonstrated that an "irrational" mode of behavior, in which agents are ruled by habit and inertia, is just as capable of predicting the standard downward-sloping demand curve and the profit-seeking activity of firms.

Veblen followed his teacher Peirce, and instinct psychologists such as William James and William McDougall, in seeing all action as being permeated by habit. Veblen's emphasis on habit did not exclude an explicit notion of purposeful behavior. Contrary to a widespread misconception, an acceptance that much human activity is purposeful is prominent throughout his works.

The "old" institutionalism may be characterized principally and fundamentally by its efforts to replace the assumption of rational, maximizing behavior in an equilibrium framework, by a more open-ended, "cumulative" and "evolutionary" approach, based on the assumption that much individual action is impelled by habits and guided by rules. These ideas are prominent in the writings of other leading "old" institutionalists, including Thorstein Veblen (1919), John Commons (1934), John Maurice Clark and Wesley Mitchell.

When habits become a common part of a group or a social culture they grow into customs (Commons 1934: 45) or routines (Nelson and Winter 1982). Typically, habits are implanted in other individuals by repeated imitation. Institutions are thus formed as integrated complexes of customs and routines. Hence a self-reinforcing circle is completed: particular habits spread through society, leading to the emergence or reinforcement of institutions; and institutions foster and underline particular habits, and transmit them to new members of the group.

Habits, routines and institutions have a stable and inert quality and tend to sustain and thus "pass on" their characteristics through TIME, and from one institution to another. Learned skills become partially embedded in habits. In this respect, habits and institutions have a quality analogous to the informational fidelity of the biotic gene. Habits and routines thus preserve knowledge, particularly tacit knowledge in relation to skills, and act through time as their transmission belt. Appropriately, Veblen deployed the Darwinian metaphor of "natural selection" to consider the evolution of habits and institutions, but never regarded this process as necessarily progressive or optimal.

However, institutions themselves may change, and they have nothing like the degree of permanence of the gene. What is important is to stress the *relative* invariance and self-reinforcing character of institutions. Institutions are regarded as imposing form and social coherence upon human activity, partly through the continuing production and reproduction of habits of thought and action. This involves the creation and promulgation of conceptual schemata and learned signs and meanings. Institutions are seen as a crucial part of the cognitive processes through which sense-data are perceived and made meaningful by agents. Indeed, rationality itself is regarded as being reliant upon institutional props (Hodgson 1988).

In the "old" institutionalist view, the availability of common cognitive tools in a given culture, as well as congenital or learned dispositions for individuals to conform with other members of the same group, work together to mold and sometimes harmonize individual goals and preferences. Accordingly, preferences are not taken as given. Importantly, widespread lip-service to notions of individuality and choice may have helped to obscure the degree to which conformity or emulation occur even in modern capitalist economies. For an "old" institutionalist, such outcomes are an important part of the institutional self-reinforcing process.

Institutions: agency and structure

At first sight, the "rational choice" and "habit-based" views of institutions each stress different aspects of the same set of phenomena. More accurately, the duality is between actor and structure. Commons (1934: 69) noted that: "Sometimes an institution seems to be analogous to a building, a sort of framework of laws and regulations, within which individuals act like inmates. Sometimes it seems to mean the 'behavior' of the inmates themselves." This dilemma of viewpoint persists today. For example, North's (1990: 3) definition of institutions as "rules of the game... or... humanly devised constraints" stresses the restraints of the metaphorical prison in which the "inmates" act. In contrast, Veblen's (1919: 239) definition of an institution as "settled habits of thought common to the generality of men" seems to start not from the objective constraints but from "the inmates themselves" (their shared experiences and actions). However, as Commons himself concluded, the thrust of the "old" institutionalist approach is to see behavioral habit and institutional structure as being mutually entwined and mutually reinforcing: both aspects are relevant to the full picture. A dual stress on both agency and structure is required.

This duality of agency and structure, in which each is necessary but neither is reducible to the other, is redolent of similar arguments in sociology by Anthony Giddens, Pierre Bourdieu, Margaret Archer, Harrison White and others. What is distinctive in the "old" institutionalist variant of this approach is the way in which the connected concepts of habit and institution link and permeate both sides of the duality: both agency and structure are constituted by habits and institutions. Institutions are simultaneously both objective structures "out there," and subjective springs of human agency "in the human head." The twin concepts of habit and institution may thus help to overcome the philosophical dilemma between realism and subjectivism in social science. Actor and structure, although distinct, are thus connected in a circle of mutual interaction and interdependence.

See also:

conventions; corporation; evolutionary economics: major contemporary themes; human action and agency; individual and society; institutional change and adjustment; institutional political economy: major contemporary themes; institutionalism: old and new; methodological individualism and collectivism; Nelson and Winter's analysis of the corporation

Selected references

Arrow, Kenneth J. (1986) "Rationality of Self and Others in an Economic System," *Journal of Business* 59(October): S385–S399; repr. in Robin M. Hogarth and Melvin Reder (eds) (1987) *Rational Choice: The Contrast Between Economics and Psychology*, Chicago: University of Chicago Press.

Becker, Gary S. (1962) "Irrational Behavior and Economic Theory," *Journal of Political Economy* 70(1): 1–13.

Camic, Charles (1986) "The Matter of Habit,"

American Journal of Sociology 91(5): 1039–87.
Commons, John R. (1934) *Institutional Economics – Its Place in Political Economy*, New York: Macmillan; repr. with a new introduction by M. Rutherford, New Brunswick, NJ: Transaction, 1990.
Hamilton, Walton H. (1932) "Institution," in Edwin R.A. Seligman and A. Johnson (eds), *Encyclopaedia of the Social Sciences*, vol. 8, 84–9; repr. in Geoffrey M. Hodgson, *The Economics of Institutions*, Aldershot: Edward Elgar, 1993.
Hodgson, Geoffrey M. (1988) *Economics and Institutions: A Manifesto for a Modern Institutional Economics*, Cambridge: Polity Press, and Philadelphia: University of Pennsylvania Press.
Nelson, Richard R. and Winter, Sidney G. (1982) *An Evolutionary Theory of Economic Change*, Cambridge, MA: Harvard University Press.
North, Douglass C. (1990) *Institutions, Institutional Change and Economic Performance*, Cambridge: Cambridge University Press.
Schotter, Andrew R. (1981) *The Economic Theory of Social Institutions*, Cambridge: Cambridge University Press.
Veblen, Thorstein B. (1919) *The Place of Science in Modern Civilisation and Other Essays*, New York: Huebsch; repr. with a new introduction by W.J. Samuels, New Brunswick, NJ: Transaction, 1990.

GEOFFREY M. HODGSON

instrumental value theory

Social value theory consists of analyses of criteria of judgment in making choices about the social and economic order. Instrumental value theory is a particular formulation of social value theory developed by American institutional political economy, mainly in the last half of the twentieth century. As will become evident, it has no common content with value theory of the neoclassical paradigm.

The purpose of economic inquiry generally is to assist the community in understanding how its economic provisioning processes function to produce and distribute real income – goods and services. Social value theory provides analyses of criteria of judgment to guide the identification and resolution of problems arising in that provisioning process. Here our tasks are (a) to understand why economic inquiry and its policy applications must be normative (what ought to be) as well as positive (what actually is); (b) to explain instrumental value theory and its role in inquiry and in problem solving; (c) to critique the ambivalent social value positions of neoclassical orthodoxy; and (d) to consider the relevance and significance of instrumental value theory for politico-economic problem solving.

Relevant inquiry must be normative

All economic systems consist of a myriad of interconnected and interdependent INSTITUTIONS AND HABITS that prescribe and proscribe patterns of belief and behavior, and that correlate activity in the creation and utilization of real income. The structure of the provisioning process is constituted by institutional forms that have become habitual and routine. Such networks and coordination devices organize the diverse forms of production and exchange of goods and services. These institutions serve divergent purposes: if they are fashioned and guided by warranted knowledge – for example, in industrial production, the efficient employment of technologies and in the promotion of workmanship – they serve productive (instrumental) purposes. If they are fashioned for and guided by ceremonial deference – for example, to achieve power, acquisition of ownership or pecuniary emulation – they serve unproductive purposes (Veblen 1899: 229 and *passim*). Typically, specific institutions will exhibit, in differing proportions, both productive and unproductive purposes.

For neoinstitutionalists, problems in these provisioning processes consist of impairments, impediments, distortions or breakdowns in the structure and performance of the institutional fabric generating the flow of real income. The existence of involuntary unemployment, a maldistribution of income, extensive poverty, industrial pollution, accelerating inflation and internecine power struggles are illustrative of such impediments. In identifying problems, social value concepts are required; a normative "ought" is implied. "What is," in some demonstrable sense, is not "what ought to be." This distinction between "is" and "ought" cannot logically be conceived except as when a criterion of judgment is employed. Moreover, such criteria themselves must be generated and appraised by warranted inquiry if INSTITUTIONAL CHANGE AND ADJUSTMENT, as shifts in policy, are to resolve problems. The claim here is that instrumental value theory is a product of warranted inquiry. It is not a contrived ideological affirmation or a philosophical certitude sustaining the status quo.

Neoinstitutionlist instrumental value theory

The function of inquiry is to enhance warranted knowledge, that is, knowledge that is grounded in evidence and is logically coherent. Its role is to turn indeterminate situations (do not know, cannot act) into determinant ones (do know, can act). Which choices demonstrably facilitate the furtherance of inquiry? Which choices enhance a comprehension of circumstance and condition? Warranted inquiry consists of a succession of choices that determine its object or purpose, its mode or method, and its analytical constructs. The quest is to explain observable means–consequences connections in causal terms. Because economic inquiry is purposive, it is value-laden and normative.

Making choices in inquiry compels recourse to criteria of choice. Standards reflecting these defining choices are instrumental to the conduct of, and accord significance to, causal inquiry. Many areas of inquiry require the making of choices that are instrumental to the determination of warrant or credibility of knowledge claims. These areas include, for instance, the identification of a problem for inquiry, the quest for evidences of causality (often CIRCULAR AND CUMULATIVE CAUSATION), the creative fashioning of explanatory hypotheses, the selection and employment of tools of inquiry, the distillation of tentative and synthetic causal accounts, and the provisional assessments of the explanatory capacities of hypotheses advanced.

The general criteria employed in warranted inquiry are demonstrated pertinence, causal accounting and evidential grounding. The quest for warranted, yet tentative, truth and instrumental value are facets of the same causal inquiry process. The criterion of the furtherance of that *warranted* inquiry process is the "ought to be" for scholars.

In appraising the outcomes of institutional coordination and performance in the economy, the same sort of instrumental value judgments are required if problems of institutional malperformance are to be identified and resolved through institutional adjustments. Neoinstitutionalists have formulated an instrumental value principle to guide such appraisals. It is to do or to choose that which provides for the continuity of human life and the noninvidious re-creation of community through the instrumental use of knowledge (Tool 1986: 33–84). This social value tenet is based on pragmatic logic, reflects the continuing search for warranted knowledge, affirms the humanity of non invidiousness and implies the efficiency of democratic rule.

The criterion of continuity of human life and culture is the *sine qua non* of further inquiry and existence. Our lives are sustained only through restoration and renewal. Significant threats to that continuity – economic, political, environmental – must be (ought to be) interdicted and removed. The criterion of recreating community acknowledges the continuing and necessary interdependence of individual and culture through which lingual, behavioral, attitudinal, motivational and intellectual capabilities are acquired and enculturated. The criterion of noninvidiousness disallows the use of individual differences of race, gender, ethnicity, color etc. as determinants of participation, worth, merit, and/or contribution. The criterion of the instrumental use of knowledge affirms the need for the development and application of evidentially grounded and logically coherent processes of inquiry that establish conjugate correspondence between theory and fact and generate new, yet provisional, warranted knowledge.

Instrumental value theory, itself a product of continuing warranted inquiry and assessment, is an analytical guide both (a) to a pertinent social inquiry process based on pragmatism, and (b) to the identification, analysis and resolution of economic, political and social problems. Accordingly, neoinstitutionalists affirm ethical instrumentalism; they reject ethical abstinence (value-free inquiry), ethical relativism (given tastes and preferences) and ethical absolutism (eternal verities).

Neoclassical utility value theory

A profound and disabling ambivalence characterizes orthodox neoclassical views of social value theory. On the one hand, neoclassicists wish to be positivists and to claim a value-free perspective, an ethical abstinence posture in which inquiry questions of "what ought to be" are regarded as corruptive of scientific methodology. On the other hand, they are *de facto* normativists, and do in fact accept a utilitarian characterization of purpose for satisfying given wants and preferences. Their historical value convolutions can only be hinted at. For Marshall and his followers, utility was the meaning of value and price was its measure. The pleasure principle of maximized satisfaction of wants was accepted. Challenges to its relativism led Hicks and others, in indifference demand theory, to abandon cardinal in favor of ordinal utility and ordered preference optimization in place of utility maximization. Paretian optimality, an admitted criterion, obtains when in equilibrium some are made "better off" without making others "worse off." Axiomatic theory reduces rationality to the observance of logical axioms of choice making involving preference and indifference relations. Judgments do not involve explicit value criteria, only the observance of logical imperatives. Ordered preferences are assumed, but not explained; the implicit utilitarian content is suppressed.

Neoclassicists' claims to a positivist position, to ethical abstinence, can thus be ignored. Orthodoxy, however, is in some respects ethically relativist and in other respects ethically absolutist. As ethical relativists, they take wants, tastes and preferences as given. Values for them are noncognitive and subjective; they are relative to individuals or societies. Satisfactions, utility or welfare are to be maximized or, in later views, preferences are to be ordered and optimized, but orthodox inquiry does not address their origin, character or significance. This posture is tautological, relativistic and inapplicable. It is tautological because whatever actually occurs as market behavior is presumed to be reflective of conduct that maximizes utility or enhances ordered preferences. It is relativistic because existing wants, tastes and preferences are enshrined as desired without reference to character or consequence. It is inapplicable because it is conceptually sterile; wants, tastes and preferences have no conceptual progeny or communicable content as a concept or value referent. Accordingly, when the orthodox are compelled to employ criteria of judgment, they tend to fall back upon an ethically absolutist position of ideologically supported laissez-faire (as with "rational expectations"), competitive market forces, alleged equilibriums, or the normative use of the competitive model. The last named is endemic in orthodoxy; its commonplace reflection in Western advice to transitional economies is indicative and instructive.

Significance of instrumentalism

Instrumental value theory is implicit in the pragmatic methodological constructs that generate warranted knowledge. Instrumentalism is explicit in the conception of problems that impair the provisioning process. What do involuntary unemployment, economic instability, race and gender discrimination, environmental degradation and nonaccountable use of power have in common? They each identify what malperformance means in differing segments of the institutional fabric. In each case there is a failure to apply instrumental logic and judgments in the analysis and evaluation of institutional performance and to make restorative institutional adjustments based thereon.

Public purposes, instrumentally defined, might well include the development of reliable economic knowledge and its regular application; the continued development of the skills and capabilities of the labor force; the assurance of paid employment for all who must or wish to work; noninvidious access to education and training; a reduction of environmental degradation; the assurance of environmental sustainability and coevolutionary development; and genuinely democratic control over economic and social policy making. The pursuit of these public purposes is aborted by continuing deference to non-instrumental value judgments that elevate utility maximization, retention of achieved power, preference ordering, Paretian optima, competitive models, equilibria and the like into the role of criteria for economic policy making. Public economic purposes can be instrumentally identified and pursued.

See also:

conspicuous consumption and emulation; normative and positive economics; value judgments and world views

Selected references

Ayres, Clarence E. (1944) *The Theory of Economic Progress*, 3rd edn, Kalamazoo, MI: New Issues Press, Western Michigan University, 1978.
Dewey, John (1939) *Theory of Valuation*, Chicago: University of Chicago Press.
Tool, Marc R. (1986) *Essays in Social Value Theory*, Armonk, NY: M.E. Sharpe.
Veblen, Thorstein (1899) *The Theory of the Leisure Class*, New York: Modern Library, 1934.

MARC R. TOOL

integrated conservation and development projects

Environmental protection in the tropics, especially efforts to preserve biodiversity and to stem deforestation and desertification, are increasingly pursued in the context of integrated conservation and development projects (ICDPs). ICDPs explicitly address the nexus between poverty and environmental degradation through participatory approaches that link conservation of COMMON PROPERTY RESOURCES to the social and economic development of communities near or within protected areas.

History and nature

ICDPs emerged from the demonstrable failure of traditional protected area management techniques in most low-income countries. The "fences and fines" approach commonly inherited from the colonial powers too often fostered opposition between protected area managers and human communities in and around protected areas, leading to a surge in illegal hunting, deforestation and sometimes brutal retaliation against locals by conservation officials. The United Nations' Man and the Biosphere program, coinciding with increased emphasis by scholars and practitioners on community participation, led to a substantial rethinking of conservation strategies. Simultaneously, the development community increasingly recognized the need for environmentally SUSTAINABLE DEVELOPMENT. The conjuncture of these intellectual trends fostered widespread belief that, in order for conservation efforts to succeed, local communities must benefit materially from environmental amenities. ICDPs assume that human and non-human systems are interdependent and that the challenges of conservation and development are inextricable.

Distinctive feature of ICDPs

While there is considerable variation in the

particulars of ICDP designs, their common distinctive feature is that rural residents are induced to surrender access to, or to curtail illegal offtake of, native species and their habitats in exchange for either alternative sources of income and sustenance, or the provision of infrastructure or social services associated with an improved standard of living. Such exchanges are sometimes contractual, but whether formalized or not, the basic notion of an exchange of access for material consideration is central to all ICDPs.

There has been tremendous support for ICDPs, and participatory approaches to sustainable development in general, since the mid-1980s. Hundreds of small ICDPs have been undertaken in biosphere reserves, protected-area buffer zones and multiple-use areas, as well as dozens of larger-scale efforts involving regional land use plans and regional development projects linked to protected areas. ICDPs have been pursued by national and regional governments, international conservation and development groups and official aid agencies.

Problems with ICDPs

Despite widespread enthusiasm for ICDPs, the hundreds launched since the mid-1980s have been less successful than hoped. Some species, especially elephants, are faring better under some schemes, but there is limited evidence of significant aggregate conservation or development gains from ICDPs. Moreover, some schemes have been disrupted or even terminated by adverse environmental shocks, civil strife or reciprocal distrust between park managers and local communities.

Critiques of ICDPs emerge from several different perspectives. First, there are those who think that "ICDPs are not yet analytically or empirically sound approaches. They proceed from untested biological and economic assumptions, many of which are likely false" (Barrett and Arcese 1995: 1080). One commonly cited problem in ICDP design is a failure to recognize and understand the nature of INDIGENOUS TENURE SYSTEMS. Second, some view ICDPs as only the most recent form of neocolonial influence, wherein international agencies with financial leverage over low-income nations experiencing BALANCE OF PAYMENTS crises impose environmental conditionality, without a full appreciation of the likely consequences for the host nation. In this spirit, a prominent Malagasy scientist was quoted as saying to a major conference in Madagascar that "the people in this room know that Malagasy nature is a world heritage. We are not sure that others realize that it is our heritage" (Jolly 1980: 7). Moreover, since most ICDPs are critically dependent on foreign financing, ICDPs share important elements of FOREIGN AID dependency.

Third, the focus on the poor as agents of environmental destruction runs the risk of diverting attention from structural issues of political power and INEQUALITY of income, wealth and power. There is a crucial logical distinction to be drawn between poor rural populations carrying out environmental predation versus them causing it. Indeed, the poor suffer disproportionately from environmental degradation, as the emerging literature on environmental justice demonstrates. Fourth, while ICDPs are sometimes passionately defended as cases of local empowerment, Hill (1996) argues that ICDPs can paradoxically prove a boon for the extension of central state authority.

Conclusion

Integrated Conservation and Development Projects are complex, recent experiments in linking rural development to environmental protection. Where earlier conservation and development strategies were often accused of being excessively biocentric and anthropocentric, respectively, ICDPs are explicitly ecocentric approaches. Yet the scant evidence thus far available is inconclusive as to their efficacy in either improving the well-being of affected human populations or in protecting threatened species, habitats and resources.

Selected references

Barrett, Christopher B. and Arcese, Peter (1995) "Are Integrated Conservation-Development Projects (ICDPs) Sustainable? On the Conservation of Large Mammals in Sub-Saharan Africa," *World Development* 23(7): 1073–84.

Brandon, Katrina E. and Wells, Michael (1992) "Planning for People and Parks: Design Dilemmas," *World Development* 20(4): 557–70.

Gibson, Clark C. and Marks, Stuart A. (1995) "Transforming Rural Hunters into Conservationists: An Assessment of Community-Based Wildlife Management Programs in Africa," *World Development* 23(6): 941–57.

Hill, Kevin A. (1996) "Zimbabwe's Wildlife Utilization Programs: Grassroots Democracy or an Extension of State Power?," *African Studies Review* 39(1): 103–121.

Jolly, Alison (1980) *A World Like Our Own – Man and Nature in Madagascar*, New Haven, CT: Yale University Press.

Kiss, Agnes (ed.) (1990) *Living With Wildlife: Wildlife Resource Management with Local Participation in Africa*, World Bank Technical Paper Number 130, Washington, DC: World Bank.

Munasinghe, Mohan and McNeely, Jeffrey (eds) (1994) *Protected Area Economics and Policy*, Washington, DC: World Bank and World Conservation Union.

Wells, Michael and Brandon, Katrina, with Lee Hannah (1992) *People and Parks: Linking Protected Area Management With Local Communities*, Washington, DC: World Bank, World Wildlife Fund and USAID.

CHRIS BARRETT

interest rate: fair

Throughout much of human history, political economists and other learned thinkers have sought to identify the rate of interest that could be socially justified on equity considerations, and that would be fair to both the lender and the borrower. In recent times, the concept of a fair rate of interest has resurfaced under the (unfortunate) appellation of the "natural" rate of interest. The fair rate of interest, as we prefer to call it, ought to be contrasted both to the neoclassical conception of an equilibrium rate, as exemplified by the Wicksellian natural rate of interest, and to the rate of interest which financial investors may feel justified in invoking, given the riskiness of their debt instruments. The fair rate of interest pertains to the rate of interest that will leave unchanged the DISTRIBUTION OF INCOME between interest and non-interest income groups, regardless of lending and borrowing activities.

History of the concept

Historically, both the philosophers of antiquity and the scholastic thinkers of the Middle Ages showed great concern about what should be the interest rate norm that ought to guide decisions regarding justice and social order. In ancient Greece and Rome, as well as in Europe during the early Middles Ages, observers perceived an economy following a stationary path. Since the dominant agricultural activity was carried out without the intervention of money, except for limited exchanges at the periodic village fairs, money was nothing but a barren token that could not justify a return for its use. To extract more than the original principal of a loan, provided purely for consumption, meant a form of exploitation of human need that the medieval schoolmen classified as usury. A positive rate of interest was perceived to be a socially destructive force, whose effect would be to tip the distribution of income and wealth in favor of the community's moneylenders.

As these ancient economies began to grow commercially and credit emerged for the purpose of financing a production that would generate a financial return to the borrower, the Aristotelian view of interest came under severe attack. By the late Middle Ages, debates over a fair rate of interest became common among scholastic writers, some of whom ultimately espoused a productivity theory of interest. Since productive activities require capital goods that generate a net surplus in production, those who provide the financial instruments to secure them ought to be rewarded for having allowed others to reap a return from their abstinence. In the hands of the classical and neoclassical economists, such views formed the essence of the loanable funds theory, whose objective was to provide an explanation of the "equilibrium" rate of interest. There were writers, however, who continued to research on the concept of the fair rate.

Pasinetti's contribution

Owing largely to the work of Luigi Pasinetti (1981: ch. 8), the notion of the fair rate of interest has been revived recently and given a very precise meaning. According to him, the fair rate of interest, in real terms, should be equal to the rate of increase in the productivity of the total amount of labor that is required, directly or indirectly, to produce consumption goods and to increase productive capacity. In other words, this rate is the growth rate of multi-factor PRODUCTIVITY, which we shall call overall productivity. In an economy where the rate of profit remains constant, this growth rate would equal the growth rate of real wages. With price inflation, the fair rate of interest would be equal to the average rate of wage inflation, that is, the growth rate of overall productivity plus the rate of price inflation. The fair rate of interest thus maintains the purchasing power, in terms of command over labor hours, of funds that are borrowed or lent and preserves the intertemporal distribution of income between borrowers and lenders.

Numerical example

A numerical example may help to grasp the notion of the fair rate of interest. Take an economy with a 5 percent inflation rate. Suppose that the average wage is initially $10 an hour. Suppose furthermore that a borrower contracts a $10,000 loan. This person has thus borrowed the equivalent of 1,000 hours of labor-time. Suppose now that the average real purchasing power, i.e. overall productivity, has risen by 2 percent. Nominal wages thus have risen by 7 percent, reaching $10.70 per hour a year later. If the rate of interest charged to the borrower is also 7 percent, i.e. if it is equal to the growth rate of overall productivity plus the rate of price inflation, the borrower will have to reimburse an amount of $10,700 the next year. However, since the average nominal wage rate has now risen to $10.70 an hour, the amount given back by the borrower is still equivalent to 1,000 hours of labor-time. As long as the actual rate of interest is equal to the fair rate of interest, as defined above, the purchasing power that is being temporarily exchanged between the borrower and the lender remains constant in labor time.

Current interest rates a problem?

Pasinetti's work provides a new perspective on why scholastic writers may initially have been so opposed to any positive rate of interest. In their days, both price inflation and the rate of technical progress were presumed to be close to zero. If this was so, it would ensue that the fair rate of interest ought also to be zero. By contrast, in many industrialized countries, actual real rates of interest have been around 5 percent for the last fifteen years, with little or no increase in overall productivity. This suggests that current interest rates have greatly distorted income distribution in favor of the rentier class.

See also:

circular production and vertical integration; interest rate: natural; interest rates: risk structure; interest rates: term structure; Islamic political economy; medieval Arab-Islamic economic thought; technical change and measures of technical progress

Selected references

Noonan, John T. (1957) *The Scholastic Analysis of Usury*, Cambridge, MA: Harvard University Press.

Pasinetti, Luigi L. (1980–1) "The Rate of

Interest and the Distribution of Income in a Pure Labor Economy," *Journal of Post Keynesian Economics* 3(2): 170–82.
—— (1981) *Structural Change and Economic Growth*, Cambridge: Cambridge University Press.
Seccareccia, Mario and Lavoie, Marc (1989) "Les idées révolutionnaires de Keynes en politique économique et le déclin du capitalisme rentier," *Economie Appliquée* 42(1): 47–70.

MARC LAVOIE
MARIO SECCARECCIA

interest rate: natural

The concept of the natural rate of interest received its most sophisticated analysis at the hands of Wicksell (1898, 1906), although the underlying ideas had been formulated earlier by Henry Thornton (Leijonhufvud 1987). Wicksell treated the natural rate of interest as a real rate of interest in the sense that it equated the forces of PRODUCTIVITY and thrift, as if saving and investment were undertaken in real goods (*in natura*). (Friedman's natural rate of unemployment is the labor market analog of Wicksell's natural rate of interest generated in the "capital" market.) The natural rate of interest, so conceived, formed the foundation of Wicksell's monetary theory, which was intended to extend the quantity theory of money to an economy with banking and credit (see MONETARISM).

Equilibrium and cumulative causation

Monetary equilibrium was said to exist when the market rate of interest, determined in the market for credit, equaled the natural rate, determined by the real forces of productivity and thrift. Any discrepancy between the market and natural rates produced cumulative inflation or deflation, which could be halted only in a monetary system which held outside money. In Wicksell's pure credit economy a discrepancy between market and natural rates of interest meant that the cumulative process was unstoppable and the price level indeterminate (see CIRCULAR AND CUMULATIVE CAUSATION). An analysis of Wicksell's distinction between the market and natural rates of interest thus led to the view that, in an economy with a banking system, price stability required equality between market and natural rates of interest.

Real forces

The concept of the natural rate of interest is central to monetary theory and was adopted by both KEYNES (in the *Treatise on Money*) and Robertson (in Banking Policy and the Price Level) in the 1920s and 1930s. Robertson in particular provided the most comprehensive statement of the analysis:

> "classical"...stands for an analysis conducted on the assumption that the monetary system operates in suchwise as to interpret and not to distort the influence of "real" forces. Put loosely, I take the theory to be that on these assumptions the rate of interest depends on the demand and supply of investible funds, behind the former standing the forces of productivity, behind the latter those of thrift.
>
> (Robertson 1966: 203)

It was this theory which was attacked unconvincingly by Keynes in *The General Theory of Employment, Interest and Money*, and which now lives on as the loanable funds theory of the rate of interest.

Critique of natural rate

The durability of the loanable funds theory is surprising in view of the fact that the limitations of its foundations were well known to the Swedish followers of Wicksell. Myrdal, Lindhal and others soon realized that the concept of a natural rate, as a rate generated when saving and investment are undertaken *in natura*, cannot be generalized beyond the simple corn economy (Hansson 1982). This conclusion has been further reinforced as a result of work by

interest rate: natural

SRAFFA and the CAPITAL THEORY DEBATES of the 1960s and 1970s (Rogers 1989). Despite a recognition that the concept of the natural rate of interest is at best restricted to a corn economy, the loanable funds theory retains a major influence on how monetary economists perceive the interest rate mechanism. One reason for the failure to appreciate the consequences of the collapse of the concept of the natural rate is the tendency to treat market and natural rates as different values of the same variable as is done, for example, by Leijonhufvud (1987: 608).

However, in Wicksell's scheme they are intended to be two distinct variables. The market rate of interest is determined in the credit market and can be a real rate only in the sense that it is inflation adjusted. The natural rate of interest is a real rate in the sense that it is supposedly determined in a market in which saving and investment are undertaken *in natura*. However, the fact is that in any but the most primitive economy no such "capital" market exists; and the natural rate of interest, as envisaged by Wicksell and Robertson, does not exist either. The concept of the natural rate of interest is not merely non-operational: it is an abstract special case of no general theoretical significance. It cannot, therefore, provide the theoretical foundations for an operational loanable funds theory of the rate of interest. For further analysis of the limitations of the one commodity model, see Steedman (1994).

Significance of the critique

The significance of all this for modern interest theory is that the market interest rate is left hanging by its own bootstraps, in the sense that the forces of productivity and thrift are not sufficient to determine a unique natural rate of interest. These forces still have a role in the marginal efficiency of capital and the market for credit, but the loanable funds theory cannot be applied to determine *the* natural rate of interest. On this point, although Keynes's critique of classical interest theory was unpersuasive, his instinct was sound. It can be argued that the rejection of the classical theory of the rate of interest and its associated natural rate of interest is necessary for Keynes's analysis of unemployment equilibrium (Rogers 1996). The argument here is that Say's Law holds in long-period equilibrium in a world in which the natural rate of interest and loanable funds theory apply. This is because, in that case, the long-period inter-temporal price structure is always such that the limit to the profitable expansion of output coincides with full employment.

In Marshallian terminology, the loanable funds theory ensures that the natural rate of interest produces a demand price for capital goods which generates sufficient investment to ensure full employment in long-period equilibrium. But once the natural rate of interest is given up, a limit to the profitable expansion of output may be encountered before full employment is attained. The market rate of interest can be "wrong" because there is no "capital" market to force it into equality with the mythical natural rate. Say's Law then falls, along with the natural rate of interest. Without the natural rate of interest, the demand price of capital goods may be such that the investment generated produces insufficient effective demand to produce long-period full employment, given the other parameters of the system. This is the essence of the principle of EFFECTIVE DEMAND AND CAPACITY UTILIZATION and it highlights the significance of Keynes's rejection of the natural rate of interest in *The General Theory of Employment, Interest and Money*.

The relationship between this largely historical account of the natural rate of interest and modern developments in monetary theory is highlighted by renewed interest in the analysis of "bootstrap" equilibria and self-fulfilling prophecies by Farmer (1994) and others. Although this modern analysis is undertaken in the context of the Arrow–Debreu system, it nevertheless reveals that the concept of a "bootstraps" equilibrium can be given a rigorous analytical treatment which has important implications for the Keynesian treatment of LIQUIDITY PREFERENCE (Runde 1994).

See also:

French Circuit School; interest rate: fair; interest rate–profit rate link; interest rates: risk structure; interest rates: term structure; monetary circuit; velocity and the money multiplier

Selected references

Farmer, Roger (1994) *The Macroeconomics of Self-fulfilling Prophecies*, Cambridge MA: The MIT Press.
Hansson, Björn A. (1982) *The Stockholm School and the Development of Dynamic Method*, London: Croom Helm.
Leijonhufvud, Axel (1987) "Natural Rate and Market Rate" in John Eatwell, Murray Milgate and Peter Newman (eds), *The New Palgrave: A Dictionary of Economics*, London: Macmillan.
Robertson, Dennis (1966) *Essays in Money and Interest*, London: Fontana.
Rogers, Colin (1989) *Money, Interest and Capital*, Cambridge: Cambridge University Press.
—— (1996) "The General Theory: Existence of a Monetary Long-period Unemployment Equilibrium," in G.C. Harcourt and P. Riach (eds), *A Second Edition of The General Theory*, London: Routledge.
Runde, Jochen (1994) "Keynesian Uncertainty and Liquidity Preference," *Cambridge Journal of Economics* 18: 129–44.
Steedman, Ian (1994) "Peverse Behaviour in a One Commodity Model," *Cambridge Journal of Economics* 18: 299–311.
Wicksell, Knut (1898) *Interest and Prices*, New York: Augustus M. Kelley, 1962.
—— (1906) *Lectures on Political Economy*, vol. II, London: Routledge & Kegan Paul, 1934.

COLIN ROGERS

interest rate–profit rate link

The effectiveness of monetary policy is the point of contention in analyses of the interest rate–profit rate link. Whereas monetary policy cannot affect the value of real variables like the rate of profit in the mainstream literature, for some heterodox economists – most prominently Dobb (1973) and Panico (1988) – monetary policy affects the distribution of income, which entails changes in both the profit rate and the real wage.

Mainstream view

In the mainstream literature, profits result from the employment of capital in the production process, in much the same way that crops result from the employment of land. A diminishing marginal productivity of capital schedule is obtained by assuming that each investment in an additional unit of capital yields less profit than all preceding investments. A full-employment level of the interest rate can then be defined as the discount rate which sets the present value of the expected returns from the investment which fully employs all available factors of production equal to its supply price.

If asset holders have high LIQUIDITY PREFERENCES, due to UNCERTAINTY concerning the future, and thus prevent the actual interest rate from falling to the full-employment level, the only long-run solution is for the monetary authorities to make a credible commitment to price stability, no matter what the short-run costs in terms of unemployed factors of production. Once the administration of a tight monetary policy, despite widespread unemployment, restores the confidence of asset holders in a stable future, they will increase their propensity to save; and as the propensity to save increases, the interest rate will fall, causing more and more investments to be undertaken (see for example Milgate 1982).

Keynes's break with the mainstream

KEYNES attempted to break with this mainstream analysis of the interest rate–profit rate link by denying an autonomous role to the propensity of asset holders to save. He argued instead that, through the income multiplier, savings would passively tend toward equality with autonomous changes in investments.

interest rate–profit rate link

Therefore, there was no mechanism to prevent the economy from being in equilibrium with the present value of the expected returns from the marginal investment equal to its supply price, no matter what the level of the discount rate set by the monetary authorities. Nor was there a mechanism at work in the economy to justify placating asset holders with a tight monetary policy. For this reason, Keynes concluded that, if and when the rising liquidity preferences of asset holders prevented an easy monetary policy from pushing the interest rate toward the full-employment level, the only solution was euthanasia of the asset holders and the socialization of investment decisions.

Keynes's conclusion was not sustained by his analysis. Since he retained a conception of capital as a factor of production representable in a diminishing marginal productivity of capital schedule, the implication remained that there was a full-employment level of the interest rate that could be obtained by a sufficiently high propensity to save. The KEYNESIAN REVOLUTION was thus reduced to the claim that the market's failure to adjust to full employment, due to the uncertainty felt by asset holders concerning the future, could justify short-run stabilization policies (see Garegnani 1979: 81 and *passim*).

An alternative heterodox analysis

The only way to break with the mainstream analysis of the interest rate–profit rate link, and sustain an argument that monetary policy is not a technical means to stabilize the economy but a political means to redistribute income, is to conceive of capital as a social relationship. This relationship is between, on the one hand, people who earn wages because they sell their labor power and, on the other hand, people who earn profit because they own the means of production (see, for example, Sraffa 1960: 33 and *passim*).

When capital is conceived of as a social relationship, rather than as a factor of production yielding diminishing marginal returns, it is not the entrepreneurial skills or the risks incurred by the owners of the means of production that create profits. The owners simply have a legal right to appropriate, in the form of profits, a portion of the goods and services produced by workers. Moreover, there is a strictly inverse relationship between the rate of profit and the real wage. The owners of the means of production cannot increase the share of the total goods and services they have a right to appropriate, in the form of profits, without reducing the right of workers to their share of the social product by an equiproportional amount. Therefore, the question of the interest rate–profit rate link becomes a question of how the monetary authorities, by changing the interest rate, can change the conventions governing the relative rights of workers and owners to shares in the proceeds of production (see Dobb 1973: 271 and *passim*).

Monetary policy influences distribution

The monetary authorities certainly try to use changes in the interest rate to effect the conventions governing the DISTRIBUTION OF INCOME. For example, Dickens (1995: 92–102) shows that the US monetary authorities in the late 1950s increased the interest rate in order to undermine the convention according to which workers in the automobile and steel industries had a right to real wage increases equal to the increases in their productivity. Nonetheless, it remains an open question as to whether such efforts by the monetary authorities to redistribute income from the workers to the owners of the means of production are effective.

Panico (1988: chaps 5–6) argues that the monetary authorities successfully redistribute income by raising the interest rate. In the wake of interest rate increases, the owners stop investing in real assets – and thus cause unemployment – until workers accept the real-wage concessions necessary to bring the rate of profit to equality with the higher rate of return on financial assets, after discounting for risk and liquidity (See MONETARY POLICY AND CENTRAL BANKING FUNCTIONS.)

Rather than focusing on the effect of changes in the interest rate on investments in real assets to analyze the interest rate–profit rate link, Pivetti (1988) concentrates on the fact that the costs of financing inventories, payrolls and other working capital requirements are necessary costs of production. By raising the interest rate, the monetary authorities thus increase the normal supply prices of goods and services. The increases in normal supply prices must be passed on in higher prices for goods and services in order to sustain the normal rate of profit. If workers are slow to respond with effective demands for money wage increases to compensate for the higher prices, then the real wage falls, causing the normal rate of profit to increase with the interest rate. On the other hand, if workers have sufficient strength to prevent a fall in the real wage, then the tightening of monetary policy sets off an inflationary wage–price spiral.

For some heterodox economists, the implication that a tight monetary policy creates inflationary pressures calls into question Panico's and Pivetti's analyses of the interest rate–profit rate link (see, for example, Nell 1988: 264). Panico and Pivetti not only contradict the almost universal conviction that tight monetary policy reduces inflation; they also argue that easy monetary policy reduces inflation by creating competitive pressures on firms to pass on the lower costs of financing working capital requirements in lower prices for the goods and services they produce. The empirical evidence, called "Gibson's paradox" in the literature, supports Panico and Pivetti (see, for, example Nell 1988: 265). Nonetheless, the controversy over the interest rate–profit rate link is far from settled.

Selected references

Dickens, E. (1995) "U.S. Monetary Policy in the 1950s: A Radical Political Economic Approach," *Review of Radical Political Economics* 27(4): 83–111.
Dobb, M. (1973) *Theories of Value and Distribution since Adam Smith*, Cambridge: Cambridge University Press.
Garegnani, P. (1979) "Notes on Consumption, Investment and Effective Demand, II," *Cambridge Journal of Economics* 3: 63–82.
Milgate, M. (1982) *Capital and Employment*, London: Academic Press.
Nell, E. (1988) "Does the Rate of Interest Determine the Rate of Profit?," *Political Economy – Studies in the Surplus Approach* 4(2): 263–7.
Panico, C. (1988) *Interest and Profit in the Theories of Value and Distribution*, New York: St. Martin's Press.
Pivetti, M. (1988) "On the Monetary Explanation of Distribution: A Rejoinder to Nell and Wray," *Political Economy – Studies in the Surplus Approach* 4(2): 275–83.
Sraffa, P. (1960) *Production of Commodities by Means of Commodities*, Cambridge: Cambridge University Press.

EDWIN DICKENS

interest rates: risk structure

The Keynesian macroeconomic model is usually portrayed in textbooks with a single interest rate that both clears the money market and determines borrowing for investment. In the real world, however, different borrowers pay different interest rates in credit markets. Interest is the payment for the use of money and rates may be higher for a particular borrower, depending on the term of the loan and the perceived risk. Borrowers with long-term, risky investment projects ask lenders to take a chance that the promised interest will be paid and principal returned.

Borrower's and lender's risk

Keynes (1936: 144–5) distinguished between borrower's and lender's risk in investment (see also Fazzari 1992). Borrower's risk arises from not knowing whether the returns expected on a project will actually materialize. Lender's risk includes this "physical" risk plus the chance that the borrower will voluntarily renege, that is, default due to moral hazard. Although careful planning and diversification can ameliorate borrower's risk, it is largely unavoidable and constitutes a "real social cost"

interest rates: risk structure

of investment. However, Keynes termed lender's risk a "pure addition" to cost in a capitalist economy. Lenders' risk is incorporated into market rates. Just as there is a regular pattern of interest rates arranged by maturity – the term structure of interest rates – there is a regular pattern of interest rates arranged by risk – the risk structure of interest rates.

Risk premiums

Traditionally, the lowest risk in credit markets is associated with the debt of sovereign governments. Given the power to tax and print money, governments, at least the larger ones, are not expected to default on their obligations. In the risk structure of interest rates, the "risk-free" rate on US government bonds provides the standard against which others are measured. Corporations, however, can fail and, therefore, pay a risk premium in bond markets. Figure 6 shows the supply and demand market determination of interest on a default-free government bond (T for Treasury bond) and a risky corporate bond (of the same maturity; C for corporate bond).

The equilibrium interest rate in the Treasury bond market is i_T and in the corporate bond market i_C. The difference between i_T and i_C is the risk premium. If market participants estimate the riskiness of buying corporate bonds increasing relative to Treasury bonds, then this may result in an increase in demand for Treasury bonds (D'_T) and decrease in demand for corporate bonds (D'_C), leading to an even higher risk premium.

Sufficient funds will not be forthcoming for corporate investment unless the corporate bond rate exceeds the risk-free rate by a risk premium. Thus the market determined spread between the risky and risk-free rates incorporates the margin that Keynes attributed to lender's risk. To Keynes, this margin was a consequence of firms having to finance at least some of their investment with external funds. In addition, there is a margin for borrower's risk between the expected yield on investment projects and the risky market rate market reflecting the perceived risk to these yields.

Corporations issuing marketable debt pay different risk premiums. Lenders rely on bond rating agencies such as Moody's or Standard and Poor's in measuring ability and willingness to repay. Criteria for judging default risk include firm leverage (ratio of debt to equity), cashflow volatility and industry cyclicality. Generally, the greater the risk of a firm, the higher the rate of return (and the higher the variance of the rate of return), but also the greater the risk of default or bankruptcy. Quality ratings for securities or bonds are inversely related to the risk premium. For

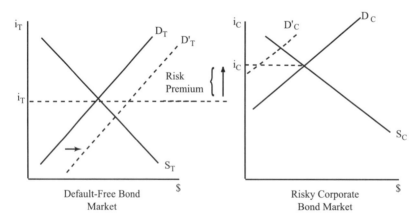

Figure 6

instance, the Standard and Poor's risk ratings, from the lowest to the highest, are shown in Table 2 with illustrative risk premiums.

The highest ratings for Bonds (Standard and Poor's AAA to BBB) are for so called "investment grade issues." Companies in default receive a C rating (not shown). The risk structure inherent in bond ratings is reflected in market rates. Spreads between "risky" interest rates paid by corporations and the US Treasury's risk-free rate widen as bond ratings decline.

Sovereign risk

With the globalization of finance, more governments and companies are borrowing across national borders. As in the US, the major bond rating agencies play an important role in assessing risk and influencing interest rates. The rating given to government issues – sovereign risk – tends also to condition the rating of firms in the same countries. Rating agencies rely on published economic data as well as other criteria which may not be quantifiable. Among the factors cited by Cantor and Packer (1996) is per capita income, which signifies an ability to repay. In addition, low external debt and a good inflation record reflect good economic policies and political stability. An expected association between both fiscal and trade deficits and poor ratings did not show up; yet countries with low ratings are forced to cut their deficits. Many authors explain how political and legal factors play a role in country risk (for instance, see Ghosh 1989). Cantor and Packer find that market rates on sovereign debt rise as ratings decline (risk increases). Some examples of sovereignty credit ratings are shown in Table 3.

At the other end of the scale from major corporations and sovereign states are smaller businesses and newer ones without a track record. Traditionally, such companies were dependent on banks for credit. But at banks, even the best customers pay an interest rate (prime rate) higher than rates on marketable securities. Banks also tend to ration credit in order to deal with moral hazard in lending. However, since the 1980s, the market for "junk" bonds has enabled firms with credit rating below BBB to bypass the banks. The rates paid on junk bonds, of course, include sizable risk premiums.

Table 2

Risk Rating S&P	Suggested Risk Premium (%)
AAA	0.2
AA	0.3
A	0.5
BBB	1.0
BB	3.0
B	6.2

Table 3

Sovereign Credit Ratings	S & P Rating: Nations
AAA (highest quality)	Austria, France, Germany, Japan
AA (high quality)	Singapore, UK, USA
A (strong payment capacity)	Belgium, Canada, Sweden, Australia, Taiwan, Ireland
BBB (adequate payment capacity)	Malaysia, Hong Kong, Malta, Thailand, Iceland, Chile
BB (speculative grade: some uncertainty)	Czech Republic, China, Indonesia, Columbia, Hungary, India, Uruguay
B (speculative: high risk)	Argentina, Mexico, Brazil, Pakistan, Turkey, Venezuela

Cantor and Packer 1996: 38, as of 29 September 1995; Dobson 1997

Risk over the business cycle

Nominal interest rates vary procyclically. However, market risk premiums tend to be countercyclical; being higher in recessions and lower during good times (especially for durables and luxury goods industries; see Saunders 1997: 193). When optimism reigns, even quite risky firms often survive; but during recessions, many risky firms and some moderately sound businesses go bankrupt. Overall, then, there is more risk of default during recession and less during the upswing in the business cycle (although some sectors such as debt collection agencies may experience procyclical movements in risk). This can be shown using Figure 6 above. With rising default risk during recession, fund supplies shift from the corporate to the government market. The increased spread of risky asset rates over the risk-free rate reflects the increased pessimism.

How important are such shifts in sentiment over the business cycle? Textbooks usually describe the economy as self-correcting, with recessions being caused by large external shocks. In Minsky's (1986) FINANCIAL INSTABILITY HYPOTHESIS, however, there are endogenous financial processes through which the economy becomes vulnerable to small shocks. The surface tranquillity of a long expansion can hide looming credit problems as leverage increases to dangerous levels. Some firms come to rely on "Ponzi" finance, in which debt accumulates relative to cash flows to cover payment commitments (Minsky 1995). Given prevailing optimism on the part of both borrowers and lenders, the deterioration in firm balance sheets and rising vulnerability to default may not initially show up in market risk premiums. At that point a shortfall of cash flows or an increase in pessimism can tip the system into recession.

The "financial accelerator" of modern financial economics (Bernanke *et al.* 1996) complements Minsky's hypothesis. Small initial shocks can be amplified near the cyclical peak when firms tend to be over-leveraged. Rising market interest rates can then have a large effect on balance sheet positions and alter the riskiness of borrowers. Due to greater information problems, smaller firms and households tend to be harder hit. Deteriorating balance sheets lead to even higher risk premiums, with greater effects on spending and production.

Event risk and leverage during boom

One cause of rising risk premiums for many companies in the 1980s was the rash of leveraged takeovers and buyouts and the like. Zimmer (1990) found that firms with low levels of leverage paid a premium for "event risk," to protect bondholders from the prospect that these firms too would be caught up in the movement to higher debt ratios (as had happened to many such firms). Zimmer shows how a curve relating interest rates to leverage flattened as the rates paid by relatively unleveraged firms started to include higher risk premiums during the boom of the late 1980s.

Real rates

Nominal interest rates in general have been both higher and more volatile in recent decades. In particular, real interest rates (nominal rates adjusted for inflation) jumped from the 1970s to the 1980s. Real rates link financial markets to spending and economic activity. Howe and Pigott (1991) show that this was a relatively permanent change in the equilibrium real rates, a change that they attribute mainly to the risk associated with rising private sector debt and financial turmoil. More generally, it appears that the whole risk structure of interest rates has shifted up recently due to a general rise in risk premiums. It is uncertain, of course, how long this will last, as risk conditions change over time.

See also:

financial crises; interest rate: natural; interest rates: term structure; Kalecki's principle of increasing risk; liquidity preference; money, credit and finance: major contemporary themes

Selected references

Bernanke, B., Gertler, M. and Gilchrist, S. (1996) "The Financial Accelerator and the Flight to Quality," *Review of Economics and Statistics* 77(1): 1–15.

Cantor, R. and Packer, F. (1996) "Determinants and Impacts of Sovereign Debt Ratings," *Economic Policy Review* 2(2): 37–53.

Dobbes, Rebecca (1997) "World Economic Analysis: Country Risk Ratings," special report published with the September 1997 edition of *Euromoney*.

Fazzari, Steven (1992) "Keynesian Theories of Investment and Finance: Neo, Post and New," in Steven Fazzari and Dimitri B. Papadimitriou (eds), *Financial Conditions and Macroeconomic Performance: Essays in Honor of Hyman P. Minsky*, Armonk, NY and London: M.E. Sharpe.

Ghosh, T.K. (1989) "Can a Country's Risk be Realistically Assessed?," *Australian Banker*, August.

Howe, H. and Pigott, C. (1991) "Determinants of Long-Term Interest Rates: An Empirical Study of Several Industrial Countries," *Quarterly Review*, Federal Reserve Bank of New York, 16(4): 12–28.

Keynes, J.M. (1936) *The General Theory of Employment, Interest and Money*, London: Macmillan.

Minsky, H.P. (1986) *Stabilizing an Unstable Economy*, New Haven, CT: Yale University Press.

—— (1995) "Longer Waves in Financial Relations: Financial Factors in the More Severe Depressions II," *Journal of Economic Issues* 29(1): 83–96.

Saunders, Anthony (1997) *Financial Institutions Management: A Modern Perspective*, Chicago and London: Irwin.

Zimmer, S.A. (1990) "Event Risk Premia and Bond Market Incentives for Corporate Leverage," *Quarterly Review*, Federal Reserve Bank of New York, 15(1): 15–30.

JOHN KNUDSEN

interest rates: term structure

The "term structure of interest rates" refers to the pattern of nominal interest rates or yields available on assets with differing periods to maturity but with uniform default risk. Prospects of default are ruled out as a possible explanation for differences in yield, isolating the effects of term. The need for uniformity of default risk leads to studies of the term structure focusing upon government bonds, treasury bills or, less frequently, interbank deposits. A plot of yields against term is known as a "time yield curve." Where numerous definitions of yield are available, yield is normally taken to mean "yield to redemption" unless otherwise specified.

The idea that term might play some part in determining the structure of interest rates has its origins in the fact that a yield curve can often be fitted quite closely to the data points. They do not, in other words, appear as a diverse scatter. Furthermore, when short-term interest rates are in what we might call a "normal" range (a point to which we return in a moment) there is a tendency for the curve to slope upward more frequently than not. There are two theories of the term structure which endeavor to account for a systematic relation between yield and term. These are the *pure expectations* theory and the *liquidity* or *term premium* theory. Two other theories, *market segmentation* and *preferred habitat*, presuppose no systematic relationship.

Pure expectations theory

The essence of the pure expectations theory is that "investors" are indifferent to holding either short-term or long-term securities. In other words, there is no inherent risk involved in buying long-term bonds rather than short-term bonds, and vice versa. This hypothesis implies that the yield curve looks exactly like a curve of expected future interest rates, or in other words, that forward rates equal expected future spot rates.

To illustrate, imagine an investor wants to buy bonds over a ten-year period, and that he or she has numerous options. For example, option 1 would be to buy a ten-year bond (long-term security); option 2 would be to buy ten one-year bonds in successive years (short-term securities); and option 3 would be to buy five two-year bonds in successive years. Imagine the investor is seriously considering options 1 and 2, which are shown below (see Kolb and Rodriguez (1992: ch. 9).

$$(1+r_{0,1})(1+r_{1,2})(1+r_{2,3})\ldots(1+r_{9,10})$$
$$=(1+r_{0,10})^{10}$$

This example shows that the investor is indifferent between holding ten one-year bonds and holding one ten-year bond, as predicted by the expectations theory. The option of holding successive short-term bonds involves buying a security in the current period (0) which matures in period one (1), shown as $(1+r_{0,1})$; then buying another security in period 1 which matures in period 2, $(1+r_{1,2})$, and so on, until the investor then buys a security in period 9 which matures in period 10 $(1+r_{9,10})$. The other option is to buy a security now (0) which matures in period 10, shown as $(1+r_{0,10})^{10}$.

If the expectations hypothesis holds, then the shape of the yield curve tells us what markets expect future short term interest rates to be. The expectations hypothesis derives a certain amount of popular support from the stylized fact that the yield curve slopes downward when short rates are historically high, and vice versa, suggesting that some notion of a "normal" level plays a part in determining expectations. Furthermore, if we add the Fisher hypothesis (that nominal rates are the sum of a stable real rate and a variable inflation premium) then we can derive implied future inflation rates from the shape of the yield curve. If the yield curve slopes upward, markets think inflation will be higher in the future and so monetary policy needs tightening.

A recent comprehensive survey of tests of the expectations theory (Shiller 1990) reports generally poor results. But some care needs to be exercised in interpreting these poor regression results. Estimations effectively include a joint hypothesis, namely that expectations determine the shape of the yield curve, and that these expectations are generally correct. The poor results may only mean that agents are very bad at estimating future interest rate changes, though adopting this interpretation in order to keep the expectations hypothesis alive raises the obvious question of why agents should make such persistent errors. An interesting and partial exception to these findings is contained in a paper by Mankiw and Miron (1986). They concluded that it was the establishment of the Federal Reserve and the subsequent manipulation of short rates by the authorities that has made it impossible for agents to derive useful information about future rates from the current long–short spread.

Liquidity or term premium hypothesis

The expectations hypothesis treats the relevant assets as being strictly homogeneous in all respects but time. The term premium hypothesis (also called the liquidity premium hypothesis) is a slight modification of the expectations theory. The earliest credit for this theory goes to Hicks (1946), who assumed that the bond market was dominated by capital risk averters. Simply put, this hypothesis indicates that, *ceteris paribus*, bond holders prefer to hold short-term (e.g. two-year) bonds rather than long-term (e.g. ten-year) bonds. This is probably because lenders are less prepared to part with their funds for longer periods, and want to avoid the sort of fluctuations in bond prices that are characteristic of long-term assets.

They are, therefore, willing to pay a premium (higher prices) for the short-term bonds as against the long-term bonds. Since bond prices and yields (interest rates) are inversely related, higher prices for short-term bonds means lower yields, and lower prices for long-term bonds means higher yields. Using the same example as above, this would mean that the return from holding ten one-year bonds would be less than holding one ten-year bond:

$$(1+r_{0,1})(1+r_{1,2})(1+r_{2,3})\ldots(1+r_{9,10})$$
$$< (1+r_{0,10})^{10}$$

Assuming future interest rates to be stable over the ten year time horizon at, say, 5 percent, the long-term bonds provide a higher rate of return than the short-term bonds in order for them to be attractive to buy. Hence the yield curve should be upward sloping to reflect the higher yielding longer-term bonds. If, on the other hand, interest rates are expected to rise in the future, then the yield curve should be steeper than what the expected interest rate would imply; and if interest rates are expected to decline substantially in the future, then the yield curve would slope downwards less than interest rates would indicate. Most evidence indicates that there does usually exist a significant liquidity or term premium (see Juttner 1990: 486–90), which contradicts the pure expectations hypothesis.

Market segmentation and preferred habitat hypotheses

In the market segmentation (Culbertson 1957) and the preferred habitat (Modigliani and Sutch 1966) hypotheses, investors are assumed to have distinct preferences between assets of differing maturities. There are several reasons for lenders (and borrowers) preferring to operate in a particular part of the maturity range. These result from a desire to match the maturity of assets and liabilities, but also from transactions costs, custom, habit and herd instincts. Banks and building societies, for example, hold government bonds as a secondary source of interest earning liquidity, and thus have a strong preference for very short-dated assets of comparative capital certainty. Insurance companies and pension funds, by contrast, have known long-term commitments and want stable income. Equally, from a firm's point of view, a series of short-term loans is not a close substitute for a long-term loan to finance a major project, because of the UNCERTAINTY introduced by the unknown rates at which short-term loans will be renewed.

The immediate consequence of segmentation is that changes in the structure of INSTITUTIONS AND HABITS will cause changes in the yield curve. If, for example, long-term insurance business grows more rapidly than deposit taking, then the demand for long-term debt will rise and yields will fall relative to those on short-term debt. But a more general and more important conclusion is that, with segmentation, the shape of the yield curve will be affected by "local" supply and demand conditions. If, for example, the government decides to issue longer-dated debt, then there must come a point at which prices will fall (and yields rise) to persuade the limited number of buyers to hold additional long-term debt. The yield curve will have a "hump" at the long end and the shape of the hump will depend upon the degree of segmentation.

Looked at from the supply (of funds) side, segmentation links changes in the yield curve to changes in LIQUIDITY PREFERENCE. An increase in liquidity preference causes lenders to shift their funds toward the shorter end of the spectrum where prices rise and yields fall. A systematic tendency to shift toward the short end during recession may be part of the explanation for short-term rates tending to follow the cycle.

The possibility that the market is significantly segmented, and that the shape of the yield curve varies with changes in the supply of and demand for assets of varying maturities, can be tested. But serious investigation of these ideas is a major undertaking, since it involves estimating structural supply and demand models for different parts of the maturity spectrum. This has not been fashionable in recent years, though attempts have been made in the past, usually in the context of trying to trace the effect of changes in debt management policies. The effects were found to be slight (Roley 1981). This is not a direct test of segmentation theories, of course. A positive finding that changes in debt sales policy changed the yield curve would have established segmentation, but the negative result does not rule it out. Much less is this a test of any role for liquidity preference.

Conclusion

The term structure literature continues to be dominated by discussion of the expectations hypothesis, in spite of the poor empirical results, for three reasons. Firstly, the prize is so large. It would be very useful to be able to forecast interest rate and above all inflation rate changes. Secondly, there is an almost inexhaustible supply of data on which (essentially the same) tests can be run. Finally, and perhaps most importantly, rejecting the expectations hypothesis involves sacrificing one or more important cornerstones of orthodox reasoning. Either agents are not rational (in switching to get the best returns) or they are working persistently with the wrong model of interest rate behavior and do not learn from their mistakes, or the market for debt instruments of various maturities is not in equilibrium or the market may be operationally inefficient. None of these is a very comforting thought for orthodox economics.

See also:

interest rate: fair; interest rate: natural; interest rate–profit rate link; interest rates: risk structure

Selected references

Culbertson, J. (1957) "The Term Structure of Interest Rates," *Quarterly Journal of Economics* 71(4).
Hicks, J.R. (1946) *Value and Capital*, 2nd edn, London: Oxford University Press.
Juttner, D.J. (1990) *Financial Markets, Interest Rates and Monetary Economics*, 2nd edn, Melbourne: Longman Cheshire.
Kolb, Robert W. and Rodriguez, Ricardo J. (1992) *Principles of Finance*, 2nd edn, Lexington, MA: D.C. Heath and Company.
Malkiel, B.G. (1966) *The Term Structure of Interest Rates*, Princeton, NJ: Princeton University Press.
Mankiw, N.G. and Miron, J.A. (1986) "The Changing Behaviour of the Term Structure of Interest Rates," *Quarterly Journal of Economics* 101.
Modigliani, F. and Sutch, R. (1966) "Innovations in Interest Rate Policy," *American Economic Review* 56: 178–97.
Roley, V. (1981) "The Determinants of the Treasury Security Yield Curve," *Journal of Finance* 36.
Shiller, R.J. (1990) "The Term Structure of Interest Rates," in B.M. Friedman and F. H. Hahn (eds), *A Handbook of Monetary Economics*, vol. 1, Amsterdam: North Holland.

PETER HOWELLS
PHILLIP ANTHONY O' HARA

interlocking directorships

Corporate boards of directors select managers and determine basic company strategy. Directors have a direct fiduciary responsibility to the shareholders who formally elect them. With diffuse stock ownership, however, corporate CEOs are often fully in charge of corporations and are able to choose members of the board, including the outside members who are supposed to supervise management (see OWNERSHIP AND CONTROL OF THE CORPORATION). Interlocking directorships, created when one director sits on two or more boards, are common and raise concerns about the ECONOMIC POWER of the interlocked corporations and the role of the multiple directors in enhancing the cohesion of a capitalist class.

General nature of interlocks

At the very least, an interlocking directorship is a non-market channel of communication between corporations. Without knowing the actual content of the communication, it is difficult to determine the significance of such interlocks for intercorporate relations and society. However, if the interlock is between two companies selling in the same market, there is good reason to suspect that the communication concerns price fixing (or some other form of collusion). If, instead, the interlocked firms buy or sell from each other, the communication could involve a preferential arrangement that increases costs to consumers. Further, when the "seller" is a bank and the "buyer" a nonfinancial corporation needing capital, communication across the interlock may facilitate bank control.

NEOCLASSICAL ECONOMICS presupposes independent, competitive firms, which means no collusive agreements to fix prices and no monopolizing mergers among rivals. Oligopolistic competitive firms, however, are interdependent and may use interlocking directorships as a sort of partial merger to manage UNCERTAINTY. Collusive agreements have long been illegal, at least in countries following British common law. Interlocking directorships could be a convenient way to accomplish the same end. Since there was no way to monitor the communication across interlocks and prevent them from being used for illegal collusion, the US Congress prohibited all horizontal interlocks; the 1914 Clayton Act expressly prohibits an individual to be a director of two corporations that are competitors.

In response to complaints from business groups about the difficulty of finding good directors, US law was amended in 1990 to exempt small companies and even large companies with little competitive overlap. The prohibitions were also eased in that an interlock is only ruled out when the firms would, if actually merged, substantially lessen competition. On the other hand, the prohibitions now cover other personnel involved in deciding competitive strategy, as well as directors. The old law had not prevented top managers, who happened not to be directors of their own company, from serving on the board of a competitor.

Horizontal and vertical interlocks

Enforcement of the legal prohibition in the USA has not been vigorous; government agencies say that the law is self-enforcing. Nevertheless, the law has probably served to reduce horizontal interlocks. Interlocking, which was present from the very beginning of incorporation in the early 1880s, reached a peak around the turn of the century and has since declined (Bunting 1977: 41).

The basic tool for intercorporate research, the "director-to-corporation matrix," can be compiled from names and affiliations of corporate directors using publicly available sources such as the Standard and Poor's Register. It shows the firms directly interlocked via their boards and the directors who, through their multiple positions, are doing the interlocking. Usually only the largest corporations are included. For example, Dooley (1969: 314) used the *Fortune* list for 1965 to find the 200 largest non-financial and 50 largest financial firms in terms of assets: 233 of these companies shared a director with another company on the list, and 1,404 of 4,007 directorships were held by multiple directors. To determine whether firms in the same industry are illegally interlocking, researchers check the SIC classification(s) of each company's business.

This exercise has little meaning unless the industry classification is at least as fine as four digits. But at that level, there are very few interlocks. Also Zajac (1988) argues that not all of the suspect cases stand up to close examination: some of the four-digit firms sharing directors are not actually competitors. Zajac also compared the 53 firms in the chemical industry, which has the most interlocks at four digits, with 53 randomly chosen firms to see whether interlocks were more likely between strategically interdependent firms in the same industry. The answer was negative. It appears that interlocking directorships are not being widely used among competing firms.

Besides the collusive potential of horizontal interlocks, vertical interlocks can also harm free markets. Independent buyers and sellers should compete freely for business. However, even large corporations face uncertainty and find their profits uncomfortably constrained by a forced interdependence with oligopolistic interlocking directorships

suppliers and customers. One way to manage the resulting profit uncertainty is through vertical acquisitions. Vertical interlocking directorships can have the same effect, according to research in the "resource dependence" tradition (Pfeffer 1987). Sending a director to a customer's board could serve to coopt that firm, as the host may be reluctant to switch away from a supplier with which it shares a director. On the other hand, a buyer may find it advantageous to use a director to infiltrate and influence a supplier. In addition, an interlocking directorship could supplement or be motivated by other existing linkages between firms, such as long-term contracts, joint ventures and interfirm stockholding, facilitating formal coordination. Interlocking directorships for all these purposes seem to be widespread. In a major study of interindustry ties, Burt (1983) found that the pattern of director interlocks matched the pattern of market constraints on the profit potential of large US firms.

Unlike those between competitors, vertical interlocks are not prohibited. However, there could be a legal problem depending on what is actually communicated through the interlock. It would be a violation of US antitrust laws to make a price agreement, over the boardroom table, in which the buyer agrees not to deal with the seller's competitors. In addition, a director in a vertical interlock could be sued by shareholders for conflict of interest.

The vertical interlocks that cause the most concern have been those between banks (and other financial companies) and non-financial corporations. The latter are, at some times more that others, dependent on banks for their capital resources in the form of debt and equity. This gives the banks great potential leverage which may be made concrete by placing directors on their clients' boards. Early in the century, J.P. Morgan and others organized "communities of interest" around large banks to monopolize major industries. Such interest groups have been difficult to detect in recent interlocks matrixes. One factor that has changed due to the 1933 Glass–Steagall Act is that American banks are no longer able to take equity positions in non-financial corporations, but banks may still be able to exercise considerable ownership power through stock held in trust accounts (see Munkirs 1985). Banks in other countries do not face the same restrictions on equity holdings. Japan has its *keiretsu*, which are fairly tightly organized around banks but which do not involve horizontal concentration. The prevalent pattern in the USA is a regional clustering with interlocks to local banks.

Nevertheless, there are numerous studies pointing out the power of the financial companies in the corporate network as highlighted in the director-to-corporation matrix. Bank boards can provide a place for directors of competing companies to meet, and be influenced. Alternatively, the bank, in sending directors to company boards, could hold down competition and boost profits. Mintz and Schwartz (1985) use the matrix to back up their contention that banks exercise a loose coordinating power within the business community which they term "financial hegemony" (see CORPORATE HEGEMONY). Munkirs (1985) goes further in describing the interlocking of the large banks and nonfinancial corporations as a system of CENTRALIZED PRIVATE SECTOR PLANNING, through which capital is allocated and major production decisions are made.

Interlocks for communication?

How important are interlocking directorates as devices for intercorporate communication? To get at the question of how interlocks might be useful to corporations, researchers have looked for corporate characteristics that lead to the establishment of interlocks. For example, Dooley's (1969: 317–18) conjecture that companies in financial difficulty try to coopt banks with a board seat has been confirmed in longitudinal studies. The extent to which firms reconstitute director ties that have been broken could also indicate their usefulness in intercorporate relations. Both financial and regional relationships have been found to be important factors in reestablishing broken ties.

However, the overall rate of reconstitution is

low. It could be that directors are appointed more for the prestige of the company than for coordination or supervision; or, for the director, the reasons for accepting a position may be personal (the pay is good). When multiple directorships are mentioned in the business press, it is to complain that directors are spread too thin and too often just go along with management's bad decisions. Japanese boards are said to be merely "honorific." Studies in the USA have shown that interlocking directorships involving CEOs sitting on each other's boards serve to raise CEO pay. In addition, a study that purports to be the first to investigate what is actually communicated through director interlocks (Haunschild 1993) shows that they facilitate imitation of strategy across corporations. In particular, a firm is more likely to make acquisitions if firms with which it interlocks have also been buying companies.

Class cohesion

There is a alternative view, especially among sociologists who study corporate structure, that what is important about the network of interlocking directorates is not so much that it is a device for intercorporate communication but is a method for maintaining class cohesion and control of business. In this class perspective, it is not important whether or not broken ties are replaced. What is important is that directors are chosen to strengthen the linkages among elite individuals and families. Managers are the instruments of directors, not the other way around as in the prevailing managerialist view. Sitting together on major corporate boards, members of the elite can ensure that firms adhere to unwritten rules of corporate conduct and do not engage in cut-throat competition.

Selected references

Bunting, David (1977) "Corporate Interlocking," *Directors & Boards* 1(4): 39–46.
Burt, Ronald S. (1983) *Corporate Profits and Cooptation: Networks of Market Constraint and Directorate Ties in the American Economy*, New York: Academic Press.
Dooley, Peter C. (1969) "The Interlocking Directorate," *American Economic Review* 59(3): 314–23.
Haunschild, Pamela R. (1993) "Interorganizational Imitation: The Impact of Interlocks on Corporate Acquisition Activity," *Administrative Science Quarterly* 38(4): 564–92.
Mintz, Beth and Schwartz, Michael (1985) *The Power Structure of American Business*, Chicago: University of Chicago Press.
Munkirs, John R. (1985) *The Transformation of American Capitalism: From Competitive Market Structures to Centralized Private Sector Planning*, Armonk, NY: M.E. Sharpe.
Pfeffer, Jeffery (1987) "A Resource Dependence Perspective on Intercorporate Relations," in Mark S. Mizruchi and Michael Schwartz (eds), *Intercorporate Relations*, Cambridge: Cambridge University Press.
Zajac, Edward J. (1988) "Interlocking Directorates as an Interorganizational Strategy: A Test of Critical Assumptions," *Academy of Management Journal* 31(2): 428–38.

JOHN KNUDSEN

internal labor markets

The theory of internal labor markets is an attempt to explain firms' hiring practices, compensation and advancement rules, and relationships to the external labor market. An internal labor market is "an administrative unit, such as a manufacturing plant, within which the pricing and allocation of labor is governed by a set of administrative rules and procedures" (Doeringer and Piore 1971: 1–2).

Definitions and background

The internal market of the individual firm is to be distinguished from the external labor market, which may be defined as the standard labor market of mainstream theory that presumes an interaction of labor demand and labor supply that establishes an equilibrium wage rate. By contrast, the internal labor market is comprised of a set of administrative rules and procedures governing entry, advancement and promotion, and tenure within the firm. The internal market contains ports of entry through which new employees may enter the firm. These ports represent the direct connection between the firm's internal labor market and the external labor market. Once a worker has entered through a port of entry, advancement, wage rates, and other conditions of employment are subject to administrative rules rather than market influences. Beyond the ports of entry, the remaining positions are filled by the promotion of workers from within the internal labor market. Thus, these jobs are partially buffered from external market forces (Doeringer and Piore 1971: 2).

The concept of an internal labor market was developed by institutionally oriented labor economists, notably Clark Kerr and John T. Dunlop. Kerr (1954), in his article "The Balkanization of Labor Markets," developed a theory not of the labor market but rather of many labor markets comprising non-competing groups, in which "Barriers to movement are set up by the skill gaps between occupations and the distance gaps between locations....lack of knowledge, the job tastes of workers, their inertia and their desire for security, and the personal predilections of employers" (Kerr 1954: 94). Kerr then explained the role of "institutional rules" in creating an "enclosure movement" in the labor market, that is, a labor market delineated by barriers dividing employment relationships into particular categories. This is a labor market characterized not by freedom of mobility, but rather by obstructions. This paper formed much of the groundwork for internal labor market analysis as well as for SEGMENTED AND DUAL LABOR MARKETS.

Job clusters and wage contours

Dunlop in 1957 extended internal labor market theory to include the concepts of "job clusters" and "wage contours." The job cluster is a group of job classifications within a firm that are linked by the production process itself or through social custom. A job cluster contains one or more "key rates" which serve as benchmarks for the rest of the firm's wage rates, which are called "associated rates." The wage contour is a group of firms that are linked through their product markets or by the labor markets in which they operate; within the wage contour are leader firms and follower firms (Dunlop 1957: 16–20). Thus, the wage contour establishes some interrelationship between firms' wage structures, while the job cluster delivers the impact of these relationships on the firm's internal wage and advancement policies. The cause–effect chain thus runs from a dominant firm or firms to the follower firms, with the influence in each firm transmitted through the key rates.

Yet, there is no single rate for any of the occupations; rather, there are just channels that influence the rates, in direct proportion to the tightness of a firm's relationship to the leader(s) in a wage contour. It is through the key rates that the external labor market, reflecting conditions of supply and demand in the wage contours, impacts the internal labor market. The external labor market is only one of many forces on a firm's internal wage structure, however, leaving the possibility that a particular firm's wage structure will not closely resemble those of other firms in the same industry and locality (see WAGE DETERMINATION).

These concepts were developed in response to the significant variations in wage rates, even for the same skills and jobs in the same geographic area, that were brought to light by wage comparison studies carried out during the Second World War (see Lester 1946). These differentials clearly contradicted the mainstream model's predictions of uniform wage rates for a given occupation in a given geographic area. The resulting theoretical explanations were mainly formulated by economists who possessed much first-hand experience in labor markets through their interactions with managers and union officials, and through direct survey research. The concept of internal labor markets, shielded from the influence of market supply and demand conditions, provided an explanation that was, for many economists, congruent with observed reality.

Growth and uses of internal labor markets

Internal labor markets have been developed in response to several factors. First and importantly, there is the need to train workers for enterprise-specific skills, which encourages the firm to develop internal rules that reward longevity and hence reduce turnover (see Thurow 1975). Second, internal labor markets developed out of union pressure for security rules, which were then emulated in non-unionized firms. Third, custom, meaning the mutual desire of workers and management for stability in the workforce and in the rules that govern the workplace, is an important factor (Doeringer and Piore 1971: II.1–II.25; Jacoby 1984: 55–7).

Internal labor market theory is particularly useful for explaining the processes of education and training within and outside of the firm, and has been expanded to include multiple internal markets within one firm as well as the role of internal markets in various types of industries and markets (see for example Doeringer and Piore 1971: ch. 1).

While this theory may be perceived as merely an extension of the theory of less-than perfectly competitive markets, it actually rejects the concept of competition as applied to labor markets (Doeringer and Piore 1971: 1); it is also distinguished by its emphasis on the demand (i.e. employers') side of the labor market as a source of wage differentials (as opposed to HUMAN CAPITAL theory's emphasis on supply-side factors, i.e. on the characteristics and choices of individual workers). While internal labor market theory is vastly different from much of contemporary labor analysis, it has nonetheless become part of the "tool kit" of most modern labor analysts (see for example Ehrenberg and Smith 1994: 158–9, ch. 11).

See also:

segmented and dual labour markets

Selected references

Doeringer, Peter B. and Piore, Michael J. (1971) *Internal Labor Markets and Manpower Analysis*, Lexington: Heath Lexington Books.

Dunlop, John T. (1957) "The Task of Contemporary Wage Theory," in John T. Dunlop (ed.), *The Theory of Wage Determination*, London: Macmillan.

Ehrenberg, Ronald G. and Smith, Robert S. (1994) *Modern Labor Economics*, New York: HarperCollins College Publishers.

Jacoby, Sanford M. (1984) "The Development of Internal Labor Markets in American Manufacturing Firms," in Paul Osterman (ed.), *Internal Labor Markets*, Cambridge, MA: The MIT Press.

Kerr, Clark (1945) "Diversity in North–South Wage Differentials and in Wage Rates Within the South," *Southern Economic Journal* 12(July).

—— (1954) "The Balkanization of Labor Markets," in *Labor Markets and Economic Opportunity*, New York: John Wiley.

Lester, Richard (1946) "Wage Diversity and its Theoretical Implications," *Review of Economics and Statistics* 28(3).

Thurow, Lester (1975) *Generating Inequality: Mechanisms of Distribution in the U.S. Economy*, New York: Basic Books.

DOUGLAS KINNEAR

International Association for Feminist Economics

The IAFFE (International Association for Feminist Economics) is a non-profit, non-governmental organization working to promote research and action on economic issues of concern to women around the world. It was founded in 1992 and (at time of writing) has 600 members from forty countries. IAFFE members include both women and men, academics and activists, and economists as well as those in other social science disciplines. The idea for IAFFE began when a small group of feminist economists confronted the fact that unlike the other social sciences, no feminist forum had developed in the economics profession. Initial interest in organizing a feminist group in economics was stimulated by panels organized for the American Economics Association meetings in 1988, 1989 and 1990. Discussions to organize a "feminist network" began in the fall of 1990.

Objectives

The IAFFE was formed to provide a forum for feminist scholars, policy makers and activists to share research and experiences. It also sought to provide a network and linkages to those who might otherwise find themselves isolated from others doing similar work. To this end, the IAFFE's objectives are to:

- foster dialogue and resource sharing among economists and others from all over the world who take feminist viewpoints;
- advance feminist inquiry into economic issues;
- educate economists, policy makers and the general public on feminist points of view on economic issues;
- foster evaluations of the underlying constructs of the economics discipline from feminist perspectives;
- aid in expanding opportunities for women, and especially women from underrepresented groups, within economics;
- promote interaction among researchers, activists and policy makers in order to improve scholarship and policy; and
- encourage the inclusion of feminist perspectives in the economic classroom.

Publications and activities

To meet these goals, the IAFFE publishes newsletters, bulletins and the journal *Feminist Economics* (published by Routledge). It organizes a mid-year conference and sponsors sessions at regional, national and international economics association meetings. It compiles bibliographies, course syllabuses and working papers on feminist economics. It also maintains an electronic mail network and web page.

See also:

feminist political economy: major contemporary themes

JEAN SHACKELFORD

international competitiveness

Definition and nature

Scott (1985) defines international competitiveness as:

> a nation state's ability to produce, distribute, and service goods in the international economy in competition with goods and services produced in other countries, and do so in a way that earns a rising standard of living. *The ultimate measure of success is not a "favorable" balance of trade, a positive current account, or an increase in the foreign reserves: it is an increase in standard of living.* To be competitive as a country means to be able to employ national resources, notably the nation's labor force, in such a way as to earn a rising level of real income through specialization and trade in the world economy.
>
> (Scott 1985: 14–15; italics added)

International competitiveness is thus a concept that must be measured in several units because it manifests itself in different spheres of the nation's economic environment. The trade balance is just one indicator of the nation's relative strength in the international economy. Additional measures of international competitiveness are the country's share in the world market in most major categories of manufactured goods, firms' profitability and real after-tax earning of workers. Singh (1990) adds another dimension to the discussion by arguing that international competitiveness of a nation is necessarily linked to improvements in the workers' rights and their working conditions.

Whether this confusion of terms is conscious or not is of no relevance at this point. What is relevant are the implications of adopting either concept of the type of economic policies that must be followed in order to become "internationally competitive." If competitiveness is reduced to positive trade balances, possible measures to improve trade performance are devaluation, reduction of real wages, worsening of labor's working conditions or any combination of them (a policy recipe followed by many less-developed economies, or LDCs). Obviously these measures are in contradiction with our definition of international competitiveness.

It is important, therefore, to determine the causes of economic strength in the international economy. Is it the result of "good" management of monetary and fiscal policies as some authors have suggested? Or is it due to the explicit and direct participation of the state in mobilizing resources toward sectors with higher possibilities of declining costs through learning, economies of scale and scope, increasing returns to scale and positive externalities?

Mainstream economists

There is agreement among economists that at the core of international competitiveness is the issue of productivity growth and technical progress. There is less agreement, however, on how productivity and technical progress can best be achieved. Mainstream economists tend to argue that productivity growth is mainly the result of a high investment rate on both physical and intangible capital. The investment rate is seen as being affected by both monetary and fiscal conditions. Hatsopoulos *et al.* (1988), for instance, in discussing the causes of the decline in US international competitiveness during the 1980s, argue that this could be traced to the decline in productivity growth caused by the low rates of investment. Investment rates were low because of the high cost of capital which, in turn, was caused by low saving rates. Both public and private savings had been affected by the way in which the US government financed its expenditures and redistributed income among the different segment of the population.

These authors argue that US fiscal policies in particular induced low private saving rates and motivated higher current at the expense of future consumption. In their view, then, fiscal and monetary policies can be used to reduce the cost of capital which will result in a higher investment rate, which in turn will lead to a higher rate of productivity growth. In an open economy with high capital mobility, the exchange rate is subject to the management of monetary and fiscal policies. To the extent that a budget deficit raises the domestic interest rate above international levels, it induces an inflow of foreign capital that will overvalue the domestic currency, causing a negative impact on the trade balance. For these reasons, these authors suggest that the best policy for improving the international competitiveness of the country is the "good" management of monetary and fiscal policies.

Economies of scale and endogenous growth

However, this view is in sharp contrast to the policy implications of the new trade theory and endogenous growth theory. Krugman (1987), for instance, noted that trade flow across countries was mainly explained by increasing returns rather than by comparative advantage. Under the presence of increasing returns, then, governments can raise national welfare by allocating resources to sectors which generate externalities or show high increasing returns. Brander and Spencer (1981) in turn argue that in some cases the nation's welfare can be raised at the expense of other countries by supporting its domestic firms in international competition.

The arguments in favor of government intervention derived from endogenous growth theory are rather similar. Romer (1986) argues that long-run economic growth is primarily driven by the accumulation of knowledge by "forward looking" profit maximizing agents. New knowledge is assumed to be the product of a research technology that exhibits diminishing returns. Investment in knowledge generates a positive externality because it cannot be perfectly patented or kept secret. Production of consumption goods, on the other hand, exhibits increasing returns with respect to the stock of knowledge. That is, knowledge may show increasing marginal product and thus grow without bound. Romer argues that even if the other inputs are held constant, "it will not be optimal to stop at some steady state where knowledge is constant and no new research is undertaken" (Romer 1986: 1003).

Institutions and technological innovations

While macroeconomic policies may have some impact on productivity growth, one should not overlook the evidence from a number of empirical studies on productivity growth and technical progress which have stressed the role played by the institutional settings and demand growth. Weiskopf et al. (1983), for example, note that worker cooperation and worker effort as well as businesses' willingness to engage in long-term investment policies are key factors in explaining productivity growth (at least in the USA). Odagiri (1994), taking the Japanese economy as a case in point, illustrates that the main factors behind the "Japanese miracle" are threefold: (a) the nature of management–worker relationships, (b) the type of cooperation and competition that exists between Japanese firms and (c) the nature of the capital market which has helped firms to obtain long-term financing without the pressures for short-term gains.

SCHUMPETER (1947) was among the first to point out that the higher the incentives for appropriating rents, the more willing firms are to devote resources toward innovative activities. He further argued that large firms were likely to undertake these activities because of their availability of resources. An excellent survey on the economics of productivity growth and technical change along the lines suggested by Schumpeter is Freeman (1994) who shows the extension of our knowledge of technical change. In particular, he reviews empirical studies done at the firm and industry levels on the determinants and diffusion of innovations and technical change (see TECHNOLOGY).

Relative power between classes

Productivity growth and technical change can only take place if firms have the possibility of selling their products. In the post-Keynesian tradition, following some of Kaldor's ideas, growth is demand driven; moreover, demand is determined by income distribution (see EFFECTIVE DEMAND AND CAPACITY UTILIZATION). Recent contributions (e.g. Skott 1989) have incorporated the Marxian notion that income distribution is the result of a CLASS struggle between workers and capitalists. The strength of workers depends on their power to set wage increases, whereas the strength of capitalists is based on their ability to pass on money wage increases in the form of higher prices. In short, the relative ECONOMIC POWER of capitalists and workers will depend on existing conditions in the goods and labor markets, and on some institutional devices that may regulate this conflict.

See also:

core–periphery analysis; hegemony in the world economy; industry policy; state and internationalization; trade policy

Selected references

Brander, James and Spencer, Barbara (1981) "Tariffs and the Extraction of Foreign Monopoly Rents Under Potential Entry," *Canadian Journal of Economics* 14: 371–89.

Freeman, Chris (1994), "The Economics of Technical Change," *Cambridge Journal of Economics* 18(5): 463–514.

Hatsopoulos, George, Krugman, Paul and Summers, Lawrence (1988) "US Competitiveness: Beyond the Trade Deficit," *Science* 241(15 July): 299–307.

Krugman, Paul R. (1987) "Is Free Trade Passé?," *Economic Perspectives* 1(2): 131–44.

Odagiri, Hirayuki (1994) *Growth through Competition, Competition through Growth*, Oxford: Clarendon Press.

Romer, Paul (1986) "Increasing Returns and Long-Run Growth," *Journal of Political Economy* 94(5): 1002–37.

Schumpeter, Joseph (1947) *Capitalism, Socialism and Democracy*, New York: Harper & Brothers.

Scott, Bruce (1985), "National Strategies: Key to International Competition," in Bruce Scott and George Lodge (eds), *US Competitiveness in the World Economy*, Cambridge, MA: Harvard Business School Press.

Singh, Ajit (1990) "Southern Competition, Labor Standards and Industrial Development in the North and the South," in Stephen Herzenberg and Jorge F. Perez-Lopez (eds), *Labor Standards and Development in the Global Economy*, Washington, DC: US Department of Labor, Bureau of International Labor Affairs.

Skott, Peter (1989) "Effective Demand, Class Struggle and Cyclical Growth," *International Economic Review* 30(1): 231–47.

Weiskopf, Thomas E., Bowles, Samuel and Gordon, David (1983) "A Social Model of US Productivity Growth," *Brookings Papers on Economic Actitivity* 2.

WILLY CORTEZ

International Confederation of Associations for the Reform of Economics

ICARE is a network of heterodox groups. Its chief function is to facilitate interaction and cooperation among the officers and memberships of scholarly associations, and related organizations, in the profession of economics. A newsletter is circulated semi-annually and contains calls for papers, information on new journals, book notices, reports on professional meetings, and other items of mutual interest. In addition, ICARE publishes an annual resource directory of journals, publishers, special projects, research centers and academic departments. An electronic bulletin board and a World Wide Web site expedite the timely exchange of information. ICARE is not an individual membership organization and its administrative functions are supported by contributions from sustaining groups.

Forces propelling ICARE

The impulse for ICARE derived from pervasive dissatisfaction with postwar trends in the discipline of economics. The exact timing of its début in the mid-1990s was a consequence of two interacting forces. The first was the rise to a near-monopoly position of what is usually called orthodox economics, a circumstance manifested as obviously as anywhere in the exclusion of non-conventional participants from the offices of the American Economic Association, the editorial boards of the profession's journals (the *American Economic Review*, the *Journal of Economic Literature* and the *Journal of Economic Perspectives*), and from access to panels at the annual conferences of the organization.

The second was the spontaneous emergence in the United States, Europe, Japan and elsewhere of new heterodox groups that actively distanced themselves from the orthodox core. Led by developments in the United States, economics had become increasingly dominated by the traditional neoclassical mainstream, to the point where it was difficult to identify more than a handful of graduate programs that did not follow the orthodox canon. Virtually all departments became controlled by a single view of what economics is about and how it should be practiced. The involuted extension of the theory of markets, frequently by applying abstruse mathematical techniques, became the *sine qua non* of the profession. Proof received louder applause than purpose. Young economists were rewarded more for adroit conformity with technical fads than the courage or creativity of their ideas. Many practitioners, including more than a few senior orthodox figures, lamented the pervasive loss of relevance, a symptom confirmed by the declining influence of economists in government and by their diminishing employment in private banks and businesses. As the end of the century approached, economics had moved into an institutionalized equilibrium trap, its own peculiar *Huis Clos*.

One conspicuous consequence of the homogenization of economics has been a loss of methodological pluralism. A second is a deflection of interest from social issues and their political context. A third is that economics as a science has lost its connections to the other social sciences; to evolutionary biology, the life sciences, and psychology; and, to its own intellectual history. In contrast to the orthodox core, as a broad generalization, ICARE participants represent a spectrum of approaches to economics, are concerned with using varied forms of analysis to confront policy issues, and are sympathetic to cross-disciplinary scholarship. They style themselves variously as institutionalists, evolutionary economists, post-Keynesians, economic rhetoricians, neo-Marxists, systems theorists, feminists, economic historians, ecological economists, historians of thought and political economists. Some are quite mathematical and empirical, others rely mostly on the logic of the written word.

History, objectives and activities

The formative meeting of ICARE was held on 13–14 September 1993, at Utrecht University in the Netherlands, under the banner "The Future of Economics." The conference was convened at the International Center for Social Economics. The structure and functions of ICARE were devised by two dozen invited participants who were involved in the leadership of American, British, and Continental heterodox associations. A preliminary organizational structure for ICARE was drafted. The accompanying statement of aims and purposes included the following items:

- to publicize and help develop a multiplicity of approaches to the scientific analysis of economic activity, within a single or multidisciplinary framework, to rival or supplement those of neoclassical orthodoxy;
- to promote a new spirit of pluralism in economics, involving critical conversation and tolerant communication among different approaches, within and across the barriers between the disciplines;
- to campaign for greater pluralism of theoretical approach in scientific debate, in the range of contributions to economics journals, and in the training and hiring of economists; and,
- to coordinate the activities of economists and economic associations who share one or more of the above aims.

In total, there are six clusters of ICARE resource groups: associations, journals, publishers, special projects, research centers and departments. Associations are scholarly organizations, most of which hold meetings annually or biannually; some are strongly national, others are markedly international. Journals may be associated with an association, or independent. In either case their editorial stance features openness to pluralism in economics. Publishers have book lists that prominently feature heterodox authors, and are actively seeking new manuscripts. They may offer special discounts to association members. Special projects include unique conferences, ongoing symposia or extraordinary publishing exercises (such as this encyclopedia). The research centers tend to be oriented toward policy analysis that relies on solid economics that may depart from and challenge the conventional orthodox wisdom. Finally, the departments offer graduate and undergraduate programs that embrace a heterogeneity of approaches to economics.

In early 1997, the ICARE resource list included thirty professional associations, thirty-two academic and policy journals, sixteen centers, nine currently active special projects, eleven publishers and sixteen departments. Not all of these groups were formally affiliated with ICARE. Heterodox economists are by no means a small fringe group, but may constitute somewhere between 20 and 40 percent of all economists who join associations and societies, depending on definitions.

To increase pluralism, diversity and methodological variety in economics, ICARE has undertaken several activities. Chief among these has been the continuing development of a system to rank journals by quality which is fair to heterodoxy. A critical activity is the dissemination of information about conferences worldwide and working papers on the ICARE newsletter and e-mail bulletin board, plus other e-mail networks. The ICARE board identified the Eastern Economic Association meetings in the USA as a trial venue for greater (joint) participation of heterodox groups, especially since heterodox economists come from many other countries to this venue. A working group within ICARE is developing solutions to the need for more heterodox exposure and joint sessions at the annual ASSA meetings in the USA, a major venue for economists worldwide; with the possibility of an additional venue being developed. ICARE is especially concerned to help junior heterodox economists increase their employment prospects and to expand collaboration among various heterodox economists.

In many countries, undergraduate enrollment in economics declined in the 1990s, due in part to the perception that the discipline has become too narrow and less concerned with the important issues of the day. The enrollment of women has been especially affected. Some feminists attribute that partly to the rational, combative and acquisitive behavior typical of orthodox theory, as distinct from heterodox concerns with social provisioning, cooperation and gender/race/class. ICARE seeks to contribute to a reversal of this trend of declining enrollments.

Conclusion

ICARE is not predicated on a style or kind of economics, nor is there a commitment to any genre of economic and social policy. There is a shared belief that orthodox economics as taught and practiced in the late twentieth century has become vapid, exclusionist and detached from its social and political milieu. The remedy for the current schism is not continuing division, but dialogue.

JOHN Q. ADAMS

international money and finance

The essence of the international capitalist economy is that it is a monetary economy (see MONETARY THEORY OF PRODUCTION). This is so even as the concept of money evolves as technology and social institutions change. Production decisions are made by those hiring inputs in return for monetary payments. Sales receipts are also sums of money. Output and employment depend upon expectations of money receipts relative to costs. Hence, the cost/availability of financial resources is of fundamental importance.

Central banking

At the national level, monetary payments mechanisms and financial intermediation are often closely interrelated, highly centralized, and dominated by a government central bank (see MONETARY POLICY AND CENTRAL BANKING FUNCTIONS). It is fiercely debated as to whether this is due to regulation as such, or "natural monopoly" characteristics in the provision of financial services. It can be argued that the need to establish confidence under conditions of uncertainty leads to the evolution of a basic monetary asset which fixes the standard of value and unambiguously represents final payment. Other exchange media also arise, but are less trustworthy and attract more confidence if convertible. Due to state power, official obligations are normally acceptable as final payment. Historically, precious metals also performed this role. However, monetary regimes in which the reserve asset is elastically supplied operate differently from commodity-based systems, with interest rate changes becoming the main rationing device.

Competing financial networks

Problems of international finance arise in a world of more than one basic monetary asset and in which international trade takes place. In the international economy, numerous competing financial networks exist, each with a different standard of value. Their interaction raises issues of exchange rate determination, interest rate policy in each bloc, and how the BALANCE OF PAYMENTS and world growth are to be financed. The competing networks were once identified with national boundaries, but the more recent phenomenon of "offshore markets" implies that use of a particular standard need not be restricted to domestic residents. The relevant economic space is, then, better defined by financial arrangements rather than geographically. Nonetheless, the same basic "international" issues arise.

In practice, there has often been a system of HEGEMONY IN THE WORLD ECONOMY, with one player dominating. The hegemon's central bank becomes effectively the world central bank and its currency the international reserve currency. Decisions taken by the main player determine the availability of financial resources to the system as whole. Examples of dominant central banks have been the nineteenth century Bank of England and the US Federal Reserve in the mid to late twentieth century. Experience shows that the rise to financial power is based on the crudest indicators of national economic success. A country claims a leading position by building up a large excess of net credits through successful trade. Once a large international credit position is achieved, its obligations are seen as rendering it uniquely trustworthy, leading to reserve currency status and concomitant influence over global interest rates.

Fixed or floating rates?

There is debate about whether EXCHANGE RATES between alternative standards should be "floating" or "fixed." Floating rates are subject to the vagaries of international financial markets. Under fixed rates, the relationship between currencies is kept within narrow limits, with domestic and foreign central banks using direct intervention and interest rate changes to keep currency values in bounds. The "managed" or "dirty" float is a hybrid regime. Exchange rates float, but the authorities take a view about the "correct" rate at any time. A final possibility would push the concept of fixed rates to its logical extreme in a currency union (such as in the evolving European Union).

The choice of exchange rate regime determines the degree of independence that individual financial networks can achieve. As different currencies are not perfect substitutes, there is usually some room to maneuver on interest rates as long as discrepancies can be accommodated by exchange rate changes. A currency union eliminates any such independence, making the global or regional economy a single unit with power over interest rates being devolved to the union central bank. The less extreme choice of a fixed rate regime also implies a relinquishing of economic power by "small open economies." Unlike a currency union, however, a fixed rate regime does leave a way out if the situation becomes intolerable, by quitting the system and floating. This occurred, for example, in the collapse of the restored gold standard in 1931, the break-up of the BRETTON WOODS SYSTEM in 1971–3 and the 1992–3 ERM crisis.

The international gold standard before 1914 was a classic example of a fixed rate regime. Each of the major currencies was convertible into a fixed quantity of gold, implying *de facto* fixed exchange rates. The period is viewed with nostalgia by advocates of "hard money," although the results in terms of price stability and growth are debated. Also, far from being an automatic mechanism regulating trade, in practice the operation of the gold standard depended heavily on the role of the Bank of England. In principle, each player should have been capable of paying out gold on demand, but this was never achieved. The system depended on the presence of a gold substitute, "as good as gold" but more readily available. Hence the part paid by the pound, confidence in which depended on Britain being a major economic power and a creditor nation.

Britain's change to debtor status after the First World War therefore meant that it was impossible to reconstruct the old system. The interwar period was one of world monetary disorder. Attempts to return to the gold standard collapsed in the world financial crisis of 1931, and the 1930s were notoriously a period of "beggar-thy-neighbor" policies.

The Bretton Woods agreement of 1944 attempted to reintroduce a semblance of stability to the system. However, the Bretton Woods era was no new gold standard. Only the US dollar was exchangeable for gold, and only by central banks. Most countries actually held a "key currency" as their international reserve, the dollar being the most important. If the gold standard was dependent on the Bank of England, the "world central bank" in the immediate postwar world was the US Fed, behind the facade of Bretton Woods institutions such as the International Monetary Fund. Bretton Woods was never as rigid as the gold standard. Exchange rates were "fixed but adjustable," a possibility which was productive of several speculative crises. The system survived until August 1971, when the USA finally cut the gold–dollar link. By early 1973 the main currencies were floating, and the contemporary "non-system" was in place.

Initially, the dollar retained a key role, but by the mid-1980s the USA was itself a debtor nation. It has been often argued that in the 1990s there is no one dominant player, but a "three-cornered" world in which the Japanese yen, German deutschmark and US dollar are each important. Recent experience tends to be regarded as unsatisfactory, both because exchange rates themselves have been volatile and because world economic performance has deteriorated. There have been calls for a return to a fixed rate system, and attempts to put this into practice on a regional basis in Europe. This debate, however, confuses cause and effect. Arguably, it has been erratic, generally deflationary, policies which have led to worsening economic conditions and volatile exchange rates, rather than the regime itself.

The exchange rate debate cuts across "party lines." For example, some economists of a broadly monetarist persuasion are now in favor of fixed rates, on the implicit assumption that the key currency nation will pursue a hard line against inflation. However, Keynesian or post-Keynesian economists may also favor fixed rates for their stability properties, and by analogy to the expansionary regime of Bretton Woods. Equally, economists at both ends of the spectrum may favor floating rates, in one case to allow for tight domestic money policies, in the other for nationally expansionary policies without a BALANCE OF PAYMENTS CONSTRAINT.

Globalization of finance

There is contemporary concern about the "globalization of financial markets" (see INTERNATIONALIZATION OF CAPITAL), a combination of rapid technical change and deregulation which has vastly increased the volume and velocity of international capital movements. It is sometimes argued that this now makes all national policy making quixotic, with ultimate power being devolved to "international bondholders" ready to move billions with a keystroke. This view is disingenuous, however, in ignoring the distinction between "perfect capital mobility" and "perfect asset substitutability." Developments in capital markets have moved the world closer to greater capital mobility but not necessarily perfect asset substitutability. The claims by domestic authorities to have "no choice" in raising interest rates because of international considerations continue to be suspicious. Frequently, they have made a clear choice to favor domestic financial interests at the expense of output and employment.

Selected references

Davidson, Paul (1991) "What International Payments Scheme Would Keynes Have Suggested for the Twenty-First Century?," in P. Davidson & J. Kregel (eds), *Economic*

Problems of the 1990s, Aldershot: Edward Elgar.
Dow, Sheila C. (forthcoming) "International Liquidity Preference and Endogenous Credit Creation," in J.T. Harvey and J. Deprez (eds), *Foundations of International Economics*, London: Routledge.
Frankel, Jeffrey A. (1992) "International Capital Mobility: A Review," *American Economic Review* 82(2): 197–202.
Smithin, John (1994) *Controversies in Monetary Economics*, Aldershot: Edward Elgar.
Smithin, John and Wolf, Bernard M. (1993) "What Would be a 'Keynesian' Approach to Currency and Exchange Rate Issues?" *Review of Political Economy* 5(3): 365–83.

JOHN SMITHIN

international political economy

Evolution and modern approaches

The historical roots of international political economy (IPE) are mercantilism, classical liberalism and Marxism. The essence of MERCANTILISM (1400–1750) included the building of a national economy through protection and state power. The basis of classical liberalism, in the work of Adam Smith (1723–90) and David Ricardo (1772–1823), was free trade, democracy institutions and economic welfare. The Marxist writings of Vladimir Lenin (1870–1924), Nikolai Bukharin (1888–1938) and Rosa Luxemburg (1871–1919) sought to examine the imperialistic workings of CAPITALISM in an era of global expansion.

After the Second World War, a basis for modern international political economy was laid by, among others, Charles Kindleberger, who offered a realistic and historical approach to IPE; Gunnar Myrdal, in his analysis of the circular and cumulative influences of trade and development; and Raul Prebisch, who claimed that the international terms of trade had turned against the less developed, raw material exporting economies, blocking their development. Forms of core–periphery analysis sought to explain the unequal power relations of world capitalism and determine their impact on the gap between rich and poor states.

Modern international political economy arose in the 1970s and 1980s out of these roots plus the political economy of development, realistic and institutional approaches to economics, international relations theory, approaches to international politics and radical political economy. Modern IPE has emerged as an active field, culminating in the commencement in the early 1990s of the *Review of International Political Economy*. Articles also continue to emanate from political science journals, such as *International Organization* and the *Review of International Studies*, as well as political economy journals such as *Capital and Class*, the *Cambridge Journal of Economics*, the *Review of Radical Political Economics*, the *Journal of Post Keynesian Economics* and the *Review* (from the Fernand Braudel Center).

The various strands of international political economy are engaging in considerable cross-fertilization of ideas, and share a surprising degree of commonality and eclecticism. For instance, the realistic liberal analysis of Robert O. Keohane (1984) and others places emphasis on institutions in a similar fashion to institutional and radical political economy; and their analysis of hegemony in the world economy enables a close dialogue with neo-Marxists, radicals (Gill 1993) and world-system analysts such as Immanuel Wallerstein. The realists' analysis of interdependencies among states enables dialogue with neo-Marxists concerning the global tendencies of capitalism. Post-Keynesian work on the balance of payments constraint, emphasizing circular and cumulative demand and technology, enables dialogue with Schumpeterians and institutionalists.

International political economy has wide and indistinct boundaries that overlap economics and political science. These approaches tend to agree on a number of methodological or substantive points. The first is the importance of a cross-disciplinary analysis of the global dynamics of modern capitalism, and the critical importance of examining complex and differential power relationships among nations and corporations. The second is the conviction that international economic relations and policies are predicated on political factors, such as the comparative power of states and the influence of domestic interest groups. The third is the special emphasis that is placed on the persistent and widening differences in per capita incomes between the world's rich and poor nations; and the role of nation size and power in explaining the division of gains to trade or investment. Lastly, they tend to agree on the necessity for understanding trade policy outcomes as the result of the conflict between classes and interest groups.

Importance of political forces

Political forces continue to shape the evolution of international economic relations. They help to determine the outcome of ongoing World Trade Organization negotiations, frame discussions of global environmental and sustainability issues, and affect the willingness of politicians and officials to reduce obstacles to trade, investment and TECHNOLOGY transfers. The halting progress of the European Union toward fiscal and monetary integration is a highly politicized process with reverberations that affect each round of European national elections. The proliferation of regional trading blocs in some respects threatens postwar progress toward global liberalization and conciliation (see REGIONAL ECONOMIC INTEGRATION IN THE WORLD ECONOMY).

Global telecommunications links and exposures constrain a range of domestic political actions available to nations, including deviations from increasingly accepted civil liberties standards. The absence of an international mechanism for chartering and regulating TRANSNATIONAL CORPORATIONS is worrisome in most IPE camps. The patchwork of national efforts to cope with mounting global environmental problems such as global warming, oceanic pollution and devastation of the rainforests is clearly incapable of establishing effective planetary policies.

Hegemony in the world economy

A convincing idea is that economic epochs feature the ascendancy of a hegemonic power, such as the Netherlands (a weak and questionable form of "dominance" during 1600–1750), Great Britain (1815–75) and the United States (1945–70) (see Arrighi 1994; Crane and Amawi 1991: ch. 8). This hegemon enjoys mutually reinforcing positions of technological, military, industrial and financial supremacy and adopts the posture of international bully or self-styled policeman. Although the hegemon benefits from its pre-eminence, this also carries certain burdens, such as preserving freedom of the seas, initiating a degree of "balance of power," "peacekeeping," sustaining technological leadership and acting as "lender of last resort" in financial panics; all behaviors that have wide international public good benefits.

Evaluating the balance between the roles of the hegemon as bully or benefactor in different eras is an important area of international political economy. The alternative to the hegemon's purveyance of global public goods is the creation of truly participatory international institutions, or of a more or less complete supranational world government, appropriately empowered and financed. Thus, the study of existing instrumentalities of global collective action, such as the International Monetary Fund, the World Bank and the various arms of the United Nations is a vital part of international political economy's field of inquiry. The challenge to create the intellectual consensus that would undergird the transition to a representative planetary state preoccupies some strands of international political economy. (See HEGEMONY IN THE WORLD ECONOMY.)

Core–periphery structure of capitalism

The principal thrust of this area is to reaffirm the continuing polarization of rich and poor economies, despite the end of the "colonial bifurcation." The primary thesis is that the core–periphery structure and its attendant mechanisms ensure that dependency relations remain in place in changed forms. A unifying feature of this component of IPE thought is the stress on perceiving the global economy as a unified whole. Its most comprehensive and credible historical explication is contained in Immanuel Wallerstein's creation of the WORLD-SYSTEMS ANALYSIS, which owes as much to the total history view of the French Annales school as to the tradition of Marxist thought. (See CORE–PERIPHERY ANALYSIS.)

Globalization of capital

Much has been written, especially since the 1980s, about the increasing globalization or INTERNATIONALIZATION OF CAPITAL. There are various dimensions to this debate, including the mobility of finance capital, the de-industrialization of advanced economies, the policy ineffectiveness of nation-states and the spread of free trade. It is true that the establishment of more or less flexible exchange rates in many areas, the spread of industrialization to Asia, developments in trade liberalization and the decline of the regulatory state has led to greater global forces. Nonetheless, capitalism was very global between 1850–1910; it then became more inward during the period 1910–50, and more recently has become more global again. Thus, more appropriate questions are: why was capitalism less global during the period 1910–50? How did the first era of globalization differ from the latest era?

Globalization in the early era was to some extent related to the imperial adventures of Britain and other European powers. Also, a global market had started to emerge, with Western Europe and the United States being major players. Much of the activity was heavily imbued with colonial and state activities, in an era of considerable international convertibility of currencies. The onset of war, revolution and subsequently depression since 1910 led most economies of the world to become more inward looking, through more protectionist and isolationist policies. In the 1940s–1950s, capitalist economies began the process of loosening the international barriers to private investment, and this process was deepened in the 1970s–1990s. During this latter period there was a backlash against active state intervention; the financial system was liberalized; and concerted attempts to open up trade (and institute regional groupings) have been instigated (see Sachs and Warner 1995).

Thus, notions that globalism is relatively new are problematical. Indeed, capitalism by its very nature has always been global to varying degrees. The system will continue to expand via investment and trade links, but as globalism reaches the limits of geographical expansion, national and local forces, centering on ethnic, regional, and religious identities, will offer countervailing responses. In addition, global environmental and labor concerns will be injected into debates over codes and standards. In a shorter time horizon, while globalism may pose problems for the state in the area of fiscal policy, and in relation to the rule of the market, the notion that the state is heavily bounded by the global forces of capitalism is to some extent exaggerated. Indeed, the state itself is a multifarious series of relationships and institutions, with diverse activities and increasingly global concerns. At a broad level, however, capitalism puts limits on the ability of the state to change the distribution relations of the system without fundamentally reconstituting the relationships underlying production and distribution. (See STATE AND INTERNATIONALIZATION.)

Comparative advantage and free trade

One of the forces driving the more recent push for globalization is the ideology of free trade and the theory of comparative advantage. Comparative advantage is based on the notion that there are advantages to be gained from specialization, and that free trade will generally enhance economies and efficiencies. Some of the assumptions used in this regard are a lack of externalities, free and costless mobility of factors, full employment, balanced trade and fixed productive resources. Many international political economists, such as Prasch (1996) and Norman (1996), have questioned these assumptions.

Particularly problematical is the assumption of fully employed resources and low or zero adjustment costs. Norman examines an economy based on oligopolistic markup pricing, two sectors incorporating finished goods and primary materials, and the degree of substitution between home and foreign goods being greater for materials than for finished goods. Under these conditions, the effects of tariffs on growth are positive and considerable but minimal on prices. The foundations of free trade are questioned; or at least it is argued that any theory of international trade should be based on realistic assumptions and analysis. Work on the BALANCE OF PAYMENTS CONSTRAINT, for instance, supplements this by recognizing the importance of effective demand in the analysis. (See FREE TRADE AND PROTECTION.)

Conclusion

More and more people and their governments perceive that the problems of the twenty-first century are to be global in nature. As this occurs, it is likely that international political economy will accelerate its growth as a critical field of study, uniting many strands of political and economic enterprises in a common purpose. Such a purpose is to make the world a safer and more prosperous place in which to live, now and in the future; although assessments of how this might happen differ somewhat between authors and approaches.

See also:

capital and the wealth of nations; class analysis of world capitalism; colonialism and imperialism: classic texts; comparative advantage and unequal exchange; cycles and trends in the world capitalist economy; exchange rates; Fordism and the flexible system of production; foreign direct investment; global corporate capitalism; global crisis of world capitalism; import substitution and export-oriented industrialization; international political economy: major contemporary themes; newly industrialized Asian nations; North–South trade models; surplus approach to development; trade policy; work, labor and production: major contemporary themes; world hunger and poverty; world-systems analysis

Selected references

Adams, John and Scaperlanda, Anthony (1996) *The Institutional Economics of the International Economy*, Boston: Kluwer.

Arrighi, Giovanni (1994) *The Long Twentieth Century: Money, Power and the Origins of Our Times*, London and New York: Verso.

Crane, George T. and Amawi, Abla (eds) (1991) *The Theoretical Evolution of International Political Economy*, New York and Oxford: Oxford University Press.

Gill, Stephen (1993) *Gramsci, Historical Materialism and International Relations*, Cambridge: Cambridge University Press.

Hirst, P. and Thompson, G. (1995) *Globalization in Question*, Cambridge: Cambridge University Press.

Keohane, Robert O. (1984) *After Hegemony: Cooperation and Discord in the World Political Economy*, Princeton, NJ: Princeton University Press.

Lake, David A. (1993) *The International Political Economy of Trade*, 3 vols, Aldershot: Edward Elgar.

McCombie, J.S.L. and Thirlwall, A.P. (1994) *Economic Growth and the Balance-of-Payments Constraint*, New York: St Martin's Press.

Norman, Neville R. (1996) "A General Post Keynesian Theory of Protection," *Journal of Post Keynesian Economics* 18(4): 509–31.

Prasch, Robert E. (1996) "Reassessing the Theory of Comparative Advantage," *Review of Political Economy* 8(1): 37–54.

Sachs, Jeffrey D. and Warner, Andrew (1995) "Economic Reform and the Process of Global Integration," *Brookings Papers on Economic Activity*, 25th Anniversary Issue, no. 1: 1–118.

Stubbs, Richard and Underhill, Geoffrey R.D. (eds) (1994) *Political Economy and the Changing Global Order*, Basingstoke: Macmillan.

Wallerstein, Immanuel. (1974–89) *The Modern World System*, 3 vols, New York: Academic Press.

JOHN Q. ADAMS
PHILLIP ANTHONY O' HARA

international political economy: major contemporary themes

Governance

If there is a single concept that unifies major themes in international political economy (IPE), it is the concept of "governance." Governance has recently supplanted "government" in debates about how best to regulate GLOBAL CORPORATE CAPITALISM. This reflects a belief that economic management is no longer the sole province of the state, but is "a function that can be performed by a wide variety of public and private, state and non-state, national and international institutions and practices" (Hirst and Thompson 1996: 184). IPE centers on the appropriate division of labor between these various institutions and practices.

Globalization

A related theme surrounds the myths and realities of globalization. Kenichi Ohmae has emphasized the importance in the international economy of flows of what he calls the four "Is": investment, industry, information technology and individual consumers. These flows, it is argued, have created a borderless world where "meaningful operational autonomy [lies with] the wealth-generating region states that lie within or across their borders." Such regions tend "to put global logic first and to function as ports of entry to the global economy" (Ohmae 1996: 142).

Others are more sanguine about the extent of globalization, its implications for governance, and the relationship between globalization and regionalization. Paul Hirst and Grahame Thompson (1996) have challenged the thesis that economic activity has become so dominated by uncontrollable global market forces that the nation state has been rendered impotent and denuded of policy choices. On the contrary, they remind us that the contemporary highly internationalized economy has been global for a long time and is in some respects less open and integrated than was the case from 1870 to 1914.

Furthermore, the world economy is far from being fully "global." Genuinely transnational corporations appear to be relatively rare. Capital mobility is not delivering a massive transfer of investment and employment from the advanced to the developing world. In any event, Europe, Japan and North America have the capacity, especially if policy is coordinated, to exert powerful governance over financial and other markets (Hirst and Thompson 1996: 2–3).

Regionalization

Another and related theme in international political economy concerns whether globalization is complementary to or in conflict with trends toward regionalization in trade and investment (Geiger and Kennedy 1996). Participation in a regional trade agreement is permitted under the articles of the World Trade Organization (WTO) but regionalization, that is, "those processes which deepen the integration of particular regional economic spaces" (Payne and Gamble 1996: 258) has raised the specter of a zero-sum conflict between regional blocs in Europe, North America and Asia characterized by exclusivity and protectionism. However, Tony Payne and Andrew Gamble have concluded that one of the most striking characteristics of such institutions is their commitment to open regionalism. Hence, the rationale of policy has been the removal rather than the erection of internal barriers to trade within the region; while simultaneously nothing has been done to aggravate protectionist sentiment externally (Payne and Gamble 1996: 251).

Liberalization

What are the implications for the governance of world trade of the establishment of the WTO, with its mandate to liberalize trade within a well-defined regulatory structure? Some tend to assume that liberalization will, in the short term, reduce inequalities among and within states; and, in the longer term, promote GLOBAL LIBERALISM around the values and institutions of liberal democracy. However, Michaela Eglin has shown how problems have arisen when China, a society and potential economic superpower which does not yet conform to these liberal values, has attempted to enter the WTO (Eglin 1997). Andrew Hurrell and Ngaire Woods have further pointed to tensions between two related trends, that is, between the reduction in the role of the state, which is implicit in the notions of liberalization and STRUCTURAL ADJUSTMENT POLICIES; and the need to maintain effective state intervention at both the national and international levels to provide the necessary economic and welfare infrastructure to manage the social consequences of liberalization (Hurrell and Woods 1995: 453) (see DISEMBEDDED ECONOMY).

Geoffrey Underhill has pointed to the divergence of opinion between those who regard INTERNATIONALIZATION OF CAPITAL as a welcome movement toward greater market competition, efficiency and flexibility; and those who view more volatile financial markets, not least those in derivatives, as potential sources of greater uncertainty and instability which are beyond the control of political authorities (Underhill 1997: 1). The collapse of established financial institutions, such as Barings and BCCI, and the damage inflicted by rogue traders upon major market makers such as Daiwa and Sumitomo, has further sharpened the debate about whether INTERNATIONAL MONEY AND FINANCE has outpaced the regulatory capacity of those charged with its supervision.

For the economies of the South, the 1995 Mexican peso crisis and the ongoing debt crisis have raised the question of whether liberalization acts to reinforce rather than reduce inequality. For the economies of the North, the creation of a single European currency, partly as a means to surmount the destabilizing impact upon economic growth of currency speculators, has led to priority being given in domestic economic policies to the narrow financial convergence criteria which are the precondition of economic and monetary union. At a time of jobless growth and mass unemployment among EU member states, this has raised the question of whose interests are being served by financial liberalization and the means chosen to manage it.

Competitiveness

A further major contemporary theme in international political economy concerns the relationship between political and social institutions and national economic performance. Recent debates have been heavily influenced by the concept of INTERNATIONAL COMPETITIVENESS. Despite its contemporary ubiquity, competitiveness has remained a problematic concept. Michael Porter, in his *Competitive Advantage of Nations*, has attributed this difficulty to the fact that "there is no generally accepted theory to explain it," with the consequence that "Innumerable characteristics of nations and firms have been proposed as important, but there has been no way of isolating and integrating the most salient ones" (Porter 1990: 12).

A recent backlash against the usefulness of the concept has been led by Paul Krugman, who has suggested that "the obsession with competitiveness is not only wrong but dangerous, skewing domestic policies and threatening the international economic system" (Krugman 1994: 44). This dangerous obsession has led to a neglect of what really matters for improving company performance and living standards. That is, namely, the rate of domestic productivity growth, which is "determined by a complex array of factors, most of them unreachable by any likely government policy" (Krugman 1994: 40). The debate over competitiveness may, therefore, be dismissed as "simply a matter of time-honored fallacies about international trade being dressed up in new and pretentious rhetoric" (Krugman 1996: 24). Despite Krugman's reservations, competitiveness has provided a valuable instrument for comparison when contemplating the changes required to improve national or corporate performance. Governments have paid increasing attention to the annual competitiveness rankings produced by the World Economic Forum and the International Institute for Management Development.

The East Asian miracle

Competitiveness rankings have consistently shown the rapidly industrializing economies of East Asia to be the top performers. Although the developmental state perspective, which identifies strong government as the prime mover of industrial modernization, remains the mainstream explanation for East Asian economic performance, it has recently been challenged both by a reaffirmation of neoclassical economics and by a focus upon the importance of the structures of civil society for economic performance.

In its report *The East Asian Miracle* (World Bank 1993), the World Bank reached an orthodox neoclassical conclusion that "In large measure the high performing Asian economies achieved high growth by getting the basics right" (World Bank 1983: 5). Indeed, it was private domestic investment and rapidly growing human capital which were the principal engines of growth, not the promotion of specific individual industries which the Bank judged had generally not been very successful. Therefore, for the World Bank, industrial policy held little promise for other developing economies.

Francis Fukuyama has also departed from the standard developmental state perspective by suggesting that it is a society's endowment of social capital, i.e. "the ability of people to work together for common purposes in groups and organizations" (Fukuyama 1995: 10), which offers the key to understanding not only economic performance and industrial organization but virtually every other aspect of social existence. It is the endowment of East Asian societies with large amounts of social capital, community and mutual trust which can account for the missing 20 percent of human behavior which Fukuyama believes neoclassical economics cannot explain.

Good government

In its *World Development Report 1997: The State in a Changing World*, the World Bank suddenly appears to wish to accord greater significance to the importance of public institutions for economic development. In a major departure from neoclassical economics, which had previously informed its notion of structural adjustment, the Bank now asserts that an "effective state" is the cornerstone of successful economies. It has defined an effective state as one which not only harnesses the energy of the private sector and individuals, but also acts as their partner and catalyst rather than restricting their partnership.

Good government is to be regarded as a vital necessity for development, rather than an expensive luxury. Indeed, without an effective state, sustainable development (both economic and social) is impossible. Although globalization poses a threat to weak or capriciously governed states, the Bank believes that it also affords the opportunity for effective, disciplined states to foster development and economic well-being.

Sustainable development

The importance attached by international political economy to SUSTAINABLE DEVELOPMENT is attested to by the publication of a vast literature. However, as the recent New York Summit demonstrated, little progress has been made toward implementation of Agenda 21, the global strategy for sustainable development which was drawn up following the United Nations Conference on Environment and Development in Rio in 1992.

Non-governmental organizations such as Oxfam have attributed this inactivity to the non-binding nature of Agenda 21, and the fact that it depends for its implementation on an unprecedented transfer of technology and finance from the North to the South. Given that the North envisaged having to finance only one quarter of the estimated $600 billion annual cost of implementation, and has provided only $742 million during the Global Environment Facility's first three years of operation, the current prospects for implementing Agenda 21 in the debt-ridden South appear very poor.

See also:

balance of payments constraint; Bretton Woods system; class analysis of world capitalism; comparative advantage and unequal exchange; gender and development; newly industrialized Asian nations; North–South trade models; structuralist theory of development; surplus approach to development; world-systems analysis

Selected references

Eglin, Michaela (1997) "China's Entry into WTO with a Little Help from the EU," *International Affairs* 73(3): 489–508.
Fukuyama, Francis (1995) *Trust: The Social Virtues and the Creation of Prosperity*, London: Hamish Hamilton.
Geiger, Till and Kennedy, Dennis (1996) *Regional Trade Blocs, Multilateralism and the GATT*, London: Pinter.
Hirst, Paul and Thompson, Grahame (1996) *Globalization in Question: The International Economy and the Possibilities of Governance*, Cambridge: Polity Press.
Hurrell, Andrew and Woods, Ngaire (1995) "Globalisation and Inequality," *Millenium* 24(3): 447–70.
Krugman, Paul (1994) "Competitiveness: A Dangerous Obsession," *Foreign Affairs* 73(2): 28–44.
—— (1996) "Making Sense of the Competitiveness Debate," *Oxford Review of Economic Policy* 12(3): 17–25.
Ohmae, Kenichi (1996) *The End of the Nation State: The Rise of Regional Economies*, London: HarperCollins.
Payne, Anthony and Gamble, Andrew (1996) "Conclusion: The New Regionalism," in A. Gamble and A. Payne (eds), *Regionalism & World Order*, London: Macmillan.
Porter, Michael (1990) *The Competitive Advantage of Nations*, London: Macmillan.
Underhill, Geoffrey (1997) "Private Markets and Public Responsibility in a Global System: Conflict and Cooperation in Transnational Banking and Securities Regulation," in G. Underhill (ed.), *The New World Order in International Finance*, London: Macmillan.

SIMON LEE

international trade in Sraffian political economy

David Ricardo, the originator of analytical trade theory, placed a central emphasis on the effect of trade on the distribution of income between wages and profits. Sraffian contributions in large measure reposition the analysis back on the Ricardian classical framework, on the ground of a "coherent" price theory.

Simple model

To present a simple account of this literature, let us consider an economy which can produce just two Sraffian basic commodities (see BASIC AND NON-BASIC COMMODITIES), by means of themselves and homogeneous labor. There are constant returns to scale and, for the sake of simplicity, only one technique is known. Denote by p and w, respectively, the price of commodity 1 and the wage (paid ex post), both in terms of commodity 2. Consider r to be the uniform rate of profit (interest), with a_{ij} being the input of commodity i per unit of j, and with l_j being the direct input of labor per unit of j. Long-period equilibrium has to satisfy the following conditions:

$$p \leqslant (1+r)(a_{11}p + a_{21}) + l_1 w$$
$$1 \leqslant (1+r)(a_{12}p + a_{22}) + l_2 w \quad (1)$$

If a strict inequality holds, the corresponding industry is not active. In autarky, both commodities have to be produced and thus both strict equalities must hold. If the system of production is "viable" (that is, capable of producing a net output), one positive relative price and one positive real wage correspond to any rate of profit lower than a maximum. Assume now that the same economy has the opportunity to trade at an internationally given relative price, p^T, with $p^T \neq p$, and that it is sufficiently small to be a price taker in the international market.

Without loss of generality, let $p < p^T$. At the new price, the second industry would not be able to pay for the autarky pair (r, w) (turning the corresponding equation into a strict inequality). The first industry would make positive pure profits (thus violating the inequality). Competition would lead the country to specialize in this latter production and to export commodity 1 in exchange for commodity 2. Moreover, r and/or w will rise until the equality between price and cost in the active industry is restored. From a strictly formal point of view, openness makes two additional "techniques" available (the method of production of commodity 1 together with an "exchange activity" giving commodity 2, at terms of trade p^T, and conversely). Therefore, the problem of determining the specialization can be thought of as a "choice of technique" problem. Accordingly, at any given p^T, one can define a "with-trade" w-r frontier, where the economy must stay in a long-period equilibrium.

Nature and significance of the results

We have here a classical view of competition and trade which contrasts sharply with the standard neoclassical view of the Heckscher–Ohlin–Samuelson (H–O–S) theory. In the classical view, the relative prices of commodities regulate profitability in the different industries and thus specialization; while in the neoclassical view, they regulate the allocation of given scarce resources and thus relative supplies. However, the Sraffian price theory generates results which are different also from Ricardo's. One of these concerns the gains or losses from trade. Let v_i be the total, direct and indirect, labor requirement per unit of net output of commodity i in autarky. If the autarky rate of profit is positive, we may have, by appropriate numbering of commodities and special cases aside, $p < v_1/v_2$. Clearly $v1/v_2$ can be interpreted as the autarkic technical rate of transformation of the two net outputs per worker. Assume now that $p < p^T$, so that commodity 1 is produced and exported in exchange for commodity 2. The trade-off between the two net outputs per worker is clearly improved with respect to autarky, if it happens that $v_1/v_2 < p^T$, but it is worsened if the inequality is reversed. Thus there can be either a gain or a loss from trade, in a comparative static sense.

This result, however, must be interpreted with care. In fact it concerns a comparison between two economies similar in all respects, but for the fact that one has always been and will be autarkic, and the other has always been and will be open to trade. The result does not concern, therefore, the effects of the opening to trade, which would call for an analysis of the *transition path*. Indeed, this latter perspective has been pursued with the result that the present value of consumption does increase with the opening to trade, if the rate of interest is equal to the rate of time preference.

International equilibrium

Turning now to an international equilibrium between two countries, we may "duplicate" system (1), distinguishing all variables and parameters with a country superscript, $k = a, b$. If technical conditions are different between countries, as assumed in the classical theories of trade, we obtain two *functions* $p^k(r^k)$. It will be clear that, in general, technical conditions alone do not determine a unique ranking of the autarky relative prices. Even if $r^a = r^b$, it may be that $p^a < p^b$ at some rates of profit, and $p^a > p^b$ at others. Therefore, both directions of trade are possible at different rates of profit. The "Ricardian comparative advantage" cannot predict the pattern of trade.

However, a "basis for trade" in a Sraffian framework by no means requires that technical conditions differ between countries. In fact, two countries with the same technology but different rates of profit will have different autarky prices, in general. This case is much stressed by the Sraffian trade theoretic literature, because it "isolates" the role of distribution. In an international equilibrium, prices and specializations are such that each country is on its with-trade w-r frontier and all commodities required for use are produced in at least one country. In a 2 × 2 framework, it is quite obvious that the international price must lie between the two autarky prices. More complex, but similar in kind, is the determination of potential equilibrium prices when there are more than two goods/countries, more goods than countries, non-tradable goods and so on.

When an international difference in income distribution is the proximate basis for trade, it becomes particularly important to ask why there can be such a difference. This involves the more general issue of an appropriate "closure" of the Sraffian system. It is, therefore, not surprising that two "closures," possibly in combination with each other, have been explored and worked out. In one or both countries either the rate of profit may be determined according to a post-Keynesian theory of growth, and/or the real wage may be determined according to a classical demographic mechanism.

In the Sraffian model of international trade, it must be remarked, there is no abundance of general and clear cut results of the kind presented by the textbook-Ricardian theory or by the traditional H–O–S theory. Indeed, the main purpose of the Sraffian model is to alert the trade theorist to the fact that a coherent view of long-period prices, which takes into account the fundamental facts of positive profit (interest) and of the use of (and trade in) heterogeneous produced inputs, implies a variety of possible comparative static properties of trade.

For this reason, a complementary part of the Sraffian approach is an analysis of the robustness of the main theorems of the standard pure theory of trade, in the formulations which allow for capital and interest. The fundamental premise is that, if "capital" and "interest" are not to be misnomers for "land" and "rent," an "endowment of capital" cannot be a physical homogeneous quantity. The only viable notion is that of an amount of value. In the long run, the physical capital goods have prices and quantities which must be determined endogenously. However, the well-known CAPITAL THEORY DEBATES have shown that both input use and commodity prices are related to input prices in completely different ways, according to whether labor is employed together with land or with heterogeneous capital. This has deep implications for the H–O–S theorems which depend crucially on monotone functions of a certain slope. In fact, the factor price equalization theorem, the Heckscher–Ohlin theorem in its price version, and the Stolper–Samuelson theorem, have been proved to be deprived of general validity and therefore of predictive power whenever heterogeneous capital is allowed for.

Reaction to Sraffian conclusions

The neoclassical theorists reacted to the Sraffian criticism mainly by questioning the relevance of a long-period (steady state) analysis of trade. The hypothesis of constantly balanced trade and the lack of emphasis on transition processes, such as the very opening to trade, are seen as severe drawbacks of the Sraffian approach. The "cost" of a coherent view of capital heterogeneity is valued more than the corresponding "benefits" by neoclassicists. Therefore, on the trade-off between "a multi-sector model in a steady state [and] a two-sector model not confined in this way" (Dixit 1981: 281), neoclassical economists prefer the latter alternative.

By contrast, on this ground, the main point stressed by the Sraffians is that some important aspects of trade, such as trade in intermediate and in capital goods, are claimed to be best analyzed in a long-period framework.

See also:

labor theory of value; price theory, Sraffa; Sraffian political economy

Selected references

Dixit, Avinash (1981) "The Export of Capital Theory," *Journal of International Economics* 11: 279–94.
Kurz, H.D. and Salvadori, Neri (1995) *Theory of Production: A Long-Period Analysis*, Cambridge: Cambridge University Press.
Mainwaring, Lynn (1984) *Value and Distribution in Capitalist Economies: An Introduction to Sraffian Economics*, Cambridge: Cambridge University Press, ch. 9.
Steedman, Ian (1979) *Trade Amongst Growing Economies*, Cambridge: Cambridge University Press.
—— (ed.) (1979) *Fundamental Issues in Trade Theory*, London: Macmillan.

ARRIGO OPOCHER

internationalization of capital

"Internationalization" in its current usage is generally applied to recent changes in the nature of capital flows which have generated a greater degree of integration of the global economy. The changes, which started in the 1970s, have involved a quantum increase in the cross-national mobility of first commodities and, particularly from the 1980s, the growth of international investment and INTERNATIONAL MONEY AND FINANCE. These changes are also referred to as "globalization."

Internationalization and globalization

Some would wish to draw a distinction between "internationalization" and "globalization" (for example, Dicken 1992: 1). In this distinction, "internationalization" involves increasing flows between national units and can be understood in terms of national BALANCE OF PAYMENTS entries (Williamson 1989). It is an analysis of increasing interaction between national economies. "Globalization," on the other hand, involves the increasing integration of economic activities located in different countries into a unified process. The terms will here be used interchangeably on the basis that, with relatively free capital mobility, there cannot be internationalization without globalization.

Capital

As a broadly-conceived description of global change, the internationalization of capital is subject to wide interpretation. The term "capital" itself has a number of meanings in political economy, from fixed capital (industry) to the Marxist concept of capital as an integration of commodities, money and production (for example, Palloix 1975). Each brings a different focus to a process of internationalization. Even within Marxism, the different ways in which the term "capital" is used (e.g. as a CLASS, or as a CIRCUIT OF SOCIAL CAPITAL) suggest different dimensions of internationalization. For instance, one can talk of the internationalization of class relations, international ACCUMULATION and international determination of value (Bryan 1995).

A focus on capital as "the corporation" privileges the role of TRANSNATIONAL CORPORATIONS and their control of international trade and investment (Jenkins 1987). A focus on the internationalization of capital accumulation, being broader in perspective, sees transnational corporations as just one aspect of internationalization. The concept of internationalization, in a Marxist framework, identifies how the growth of international trade, finance and investment, in combination, have integrated accumulation on a global scale, imposing a global criterion of profitability on all economic activity, not just (or even primarily) the activities of transnational corporations.

The emphasis here is particularly on the growth of globally-integrated financial markets, especially the development of Eurofinance markets in the 1980s. Funds raised in international capital markets increased from just over $100 billion in 1979 to over $1500 billion in 1996. The mobility of money capital associated with the growth of these markets has broken down the notion of discrete national capital markets, and seen borrowers subjected to a global process of investment allocation (Bryan 1995; Wachtel 1986). With financial markets being closely integrated, other facets of accumulation are drawn into a process of global economic calculation.

A longer-term perspective

Capital had moved "internationally" before there were "nations" (Polanyi 1944), so the distinctiveness of the process of capital movement since the 1970s needs to be clarified. It is argued, for example, that the world is now no more globally integrated than it was in the nineteenth century. As a percentage of GDP, current account imbalances and their associated capital flows were larger in the years before 1914 than in the 1980s (Turner 1991). Hence, it is argued, what needs explanation is not internationalization from the 1970s, but the decline in international integration from the 1920s to the 1970s.

The longer term perspective implicit in recognizing a history of international capital mobility is important in signaling that the contemporary process of "internationalization" should not be exaggerated. Nonetheless, the difference of the current process is substantial. Nineteenth-century internationalization was structured by the system of colonial rule. Capital flows were predominantly imperial in origin, and so were both hierarchically structured and internal to imperial systems. Moreover, the gold standard added stability to the global financial system, keeping interest rates generally lower and more stable than in the current era. As a result of both these factors, nineteenth-century international capital flows tended to be long term, associated with the opening up of new parts of the globe (see COLONIALISM AND IMPERIALISM: CLASSIC TEXTS).

The recent internationalization process, by contrast, is not on a hierarchical structure of colonial rule. Nor is there a stable international money system. The mobility of capital and of corporate operations involves capital flows into and out of all OECD countries, with flows to developing countries diminishing rapidly in importance. Most of the recent growth of capital flows has been of a short-term nature, trading on the speculative possibilities associated with exchange rate and interest rate variability (see SPECULATION). There is, therefore, now a more complex pattern of international integration of accumulation than can be found in nineteenth-century capital flows, or even from the 1960s and 1970s models of center nations using capital flows to dominate peripheral nations.

What changed from the 1970s?

Why a process of internationalization occurred from the 1970s is a subject of unresolved debate. Several key changes in the world economy did arise in the 1970s, initiating the new process of internationalization. INCREASING RETURNS TO SCALE in manufacturing, combined with Europe and Japan catching up with the US in terms of productivity, is a central element explaining the long-term growth of cross-national trade. A decline of the profit rate in the advanced industrial countries in the late 1960s and early 1970s has been seen as central to the relocation of investment (see FALLING RATE OF PROFIT TENDENCY). There is evidence of capital leaving Britain and the United States, in particular, in search of more profitable investment opportunities (Armstrong *et al.* 1991). For some analyses which focus on this process, the shift became the basis of the proposition that investment was leaving the advanced industrial countries in search of low-wage production. This was seen to be the basis of the de-industrialization of the industrial countries and the formation of a new international division of labor. Since the 1980s, however, around 85 percent of international direct investment has been between the OECD countries, and so not clearly motivated by labor costs.

Internationalization of financial markets

A further aspect of recent internationalization, and quantitatively the most significant aspect, has been the growing international integration of financial markets since the 1970s. A combination of (a) the demise of the BRETTON WOODS SYSTEM of fixed EXCHANGE RATES (generating the desire for diversified currency holdings), (b) the rapid growth of international credit markets associated initially with OPEC oil-derived surpluses, and (c) a growing demand for credit as a means to fund investment (and consumption) are essential elements of the growth of global credit markets and the internationalization of financial markets.

These factors, from the 1970s, were reinforced in the following two decades by the processes of "deregulation" of national capital controls and the development of computer and satellite technology to facilitate the transfer of financial assets. Combined, they facilitated the growth of a wide range of secondary financial markets (securitization). The developments in international financial markets and global financial mobility are a key element in the internationalization of capital from the 1970s to the present.

See also:

global corporate capitalism; state and internationalization

Selected references

Armstrong, P., Glyn, A. and Harrison, J. (1991) *Capitalism Since World War II*, Oxford: Basil Blackwell.
Bryan, D. (1995) "The Internationalization of Capital and Marxian Value Theory," *Cambridge Journal of Economics* 19: 421–40
—— (1995.) *The Chase Across the Globe: International Capital and the Contradictions for Nation States*, Boulder, CO: Westview Press.
Dicken, P. (1992) *Global Shift: The Internationalization of Economic Activity*, New York: The Guildford Press.
Jenkins, R. (1987) *Transnational Corporations and Uneven Development: The Internationalization of Capital and the Third World*, London: Methuen.
Palloix, C. (1975) "The Internationalization of Capital and the Circuit of Social Capital," in H. Radice (ed.) *International Firms and Modern Imperialism*, Harmondsworth: Penguin
Polanyi, K. (1944) *The Great Transformation: The Political and Economic Origins of Our Time*, Boston: Beacon Press
Turner, P. (1991) "Capital Flows in the 1980s: A Survey of Major Trends," *BIS Economic Papers* no. 31, Basle: Bank for International Settlements.
Wachtel, H. (1986) *The Money Mandarins: The Making of a Supra-National Economic Order*, New York: Pantheon.
Williamson, J. (1989) "International Capital Flows," in J. Eatwell, M. Millgate and P. Newman (eds), *The New Palgrave: A Dictionary of Economics*, London: Macmillan.

DICK BRYAN

invariable measure of value

The problem of an "invariable measure of value" is indissolubly connected with David Ricardo's contribution to political economy. However, it would be wrong to assume that this was only a problem of Ricardo's. Classical authors from William Petty to Ricardo sought to unravel the laws governing the growth of the wealth of nations and its distribution among the different classes in post-feudal society. They tried to come to grips with a highly complex process in which capital accumulation, population growth and technical change interacted in an environment in which the scarcity of natural resources began to make itself felt.

The rise of the nation state entailed a vivid

interest in comparisons between different countries at the same time and the same country at different times. The view gradually gained ground that the wealth of a nation depends on whether "the nation will be better or worse supplied with all the necessaries and conveniences for which it has occasion" (Smith 1776: I, 2) on a *per capita* basis. The problem of interspatial and intertemporal wealth comparisons was seen to presuppose the distinction between "value" and "riches." It was, indeed, an elaboration of this distinction which was at the center of many disputes among economists, throughout the eighteenth and at the beginning of the nineteenth century (see for example Ricardo 1951: I, 20). The problem of the measuring rod by means of which each state of society could be given an objective expression was actually present since the very inception of systematic economic analysis.

Ricardo's search for the invariable measure

In the first two editions of *the Principles of Political Economy and Taxation*, published in 1817 and 1819, Ricardo suggested taking as an invariable measure of value a commodity that would require "at all times, and under all circumstances, precisely the same quantity of labor to obtain it" (Ricardo 1951: I, 27n). If such a commodity could be found and were used as a standard of value, any variation in the value of other commodities expressed in terms of this standard would unequivocally point toward changes in the conditions of production of these commodities. Such a commodity, he added, would be "eminently useful," but he admitted that we do not have knowledge of such a commodity. Gold, he surmised, might be a commodity that comes close to fulfilling the requirement mentioned. Yet, he insisted, it would be "of considerable use towards attaining a correct theory, to ascertain what the essential qualities of [such] a standard are" (Ricardo 1951: I, 17 n.3).

In the first two editions of the *Principles*, Ricardo was clearly aware that modifications to the labor-embodied rule of relative value were necessary, due to the impact of distribution on exchange relations. However, he apparently did not think that these modifications rendered obsolete his original definition of the invariable measure. In the third edition, however, he conceded that the same difficulties encountered in determining relative prices also carried over to his attempt at defining the essential properties of an ideal standard. He argued that even if "the same quantity of labor [would] be always required to obtain the same quantity of gold, still gold would not be a perfect measure of value... because it would not be produced with precisely the same combinations of fixed and circulating capital as all other things; nor with fixed capital of the same durability; nor would it require precisely the same length of time, before it could be brought to market.... Neither gold then, nor any other commodity can ever be a perfect measure of value for all things" (Ricardo 1951: I, 44–5).

These factors were responsible for the fact that, with a change in the rate of profit (and the corresponding contrary change in the real wage rate) relative prices would change, given the technical conditions of production. In his original approach to the problem of the standard of value, Ricardo was exclusively concerned with intertemporal and interspatial comparisons, that is, measurement with respect to different technical environments. Later he became, in addition, concerned with the altogether different problem of measurement with respect to the same technical environment, but changing distributions of income. As McCulloch succinctly objected to Ricardo, attempting to kill two birds with one stone "is quite insoluble" (Ricardo 1951: IX, 69). Ricardo nevertheless insisted "that if we were in possession of the knowledge of the law which regulates the exchangeable value of commodities, we should be only one step from the discovery of a measure of absolute value" (Ricardo 1951: IX, 377). According to Sraffa, "this came close to identifying the problem of a measure with that of the law of value" (Sraffa 1951: xli).

Ricardo struggled with this problem until the end of his life, as is well documented by a complete draft and an unfinished later version of his paper "Absolute Value and Exchangeable Value." On the premise that the criterion of technological invariability is met, what does invariability with respect to variations in income distribution mean? Since "the value of all commodities resolves itself into wages and profits" (Ricardo 1951: IV, 392), the proximate answer to be given is: that commodity is invariable in value, in which the fall in the profit component is equal to the rise in the wage component (consequent upon a rise in the real wage rate and a corresponding fall in the general rate of profits). This is indeed the answer implicit in Ricardo's argument.

Contrary to Malthus, Ricardo opted for a commodity in whose production labor and capital are employed in a "medium between the two extremes," one in which only (direct) labor is applied, the other in which only capital is applied. In one place, this choice is motivated as follows: "The medium... is perhaps best adapted to the general mass of commodities; those commodities on one side of this medium, would rise in comparative value with it, with a rise in the price of labour, and a fall in the rate of profits; and those on the other side might fall from the same cause" (Ricardo 1951: VIII, 193). Consequently, some of Ricardo's efforts were directed at describing more carefully the "medium" of "the variety of circumstances under which commodities are actually produced" (Ricardo 1951: IV, 368; see also Kurz and Salvadori 1993: 103–4).

Sraffa's "solution"?

It has been frequently claimed in the literature that SRAFFA, with his concept of the "standard commodity," finally managed to solve the Ricardian problem. This view cannot be sustained. First, as the above discussion should have made clear, in Ricardo there is not just one problem, but two. As regards the problem of intertemporal and interspatial comparisons, no general solution can be found. This is implicitly made clear by Sraffa. Therefore, Ricardo was chasing after a "will o' the wisp." Second, Sraffa's ingenious device of the "Standard commodity" – which in *Production of Commodities by Means of Commodity* plays the role of a tool of analysis (Kurz and Salvadori 1993: 107–11) – could be connected only to that part of Ricardo's search for an "invariable measure of value." This of course relates to the impact of changes in distribution on relative prices, taking the technical conditions of production as given and constant (see Sraffa 1960: §23, Appendix D), where "given technical conditions" actually mean "a given technique."

See also:

classical political economy; labor theory of value; value foundation of price

Selected references

Kurz, H.D. and Salvadori, N. (1993) "The 'Standard Commodity' and Ricardo's Search for an 'Invariable Measure of Value'," in M. Baranzini and Geoffrey Harcourt (eds), *The Dynamics of the Wealth of Nations: Growth, Distribution and Structural Change. Essays in Honour of Luigi Pasinetti*, New York: St. Martin's Press, 95–123.

Ricardo, D. (1951–73) *The Works and Correspondence of David Ricardo*, 11 vols, ed. P. Sraffa in collaboration with M.H. Dobb, Cambridge: Cambridge University Press.

Smith, A. (1776) *An Inquiry into the Nature and Causes of the Wealth of Nations*, vol. 2 of *The Glasgow Edition of the Works and Correspondence of Adam Smith*, ed. R.H. Campbell, A.S. Skinner and W.B. Todd, Oxford: Oxford University Press, 1976.

Sraffa, P. (1951) "Introduction," in David Ricardo, *On the Principles of Political Economy and Taxation*, Cambridge: Cambridge University Press.

—— (1960) *Production of Commodities by Means of Commodities: Prelude to a Critique of Economic Theory*, Cambridge: Cambridge University Press.

HEINZ D. KURZ
NERI SALVADORI

Islamic political economy

Islamic political economy is the study of institutional and socioeconomic forces in the light of pervasively interactive, integrative and evolutionary processes. Such a study is based on the premise of Tawhidi epistemology, which stands for the Oneness of Allah (God) as Being and as absolute and complete stock of universal knowledge. Flows of human knowledge are thus created by the stock of knowledge and these augment cognitive forms in institutional and socioeconomic systems. By the unifying nature of knowledge flows carrying the essence of Oneness in the Stock, the principle of universal complementarity is established in institutional and socioeconomic systems.

Such unifying processes, reflecting extensive complementarities, are realized and explained by means of the tenets and instruments of Islamic law (*shari'a*). These are discovered by exercising the Islamic discursive method, called the Shuratic process, toward complementing the institutional and socioeconomic systems. The Shuratic process exists in a continuum, generating interactions, integration and creative evolution.

Islamic political economy is the study of the above-mentioned Shuratic processes in institutional, socioeconomic, microeconomic, macroeconomic, ecological and global systems. Universal complementarities with diversity are attained in Shuratic processes by means of the tenets and instruments of *shari'a*, which are in turn also evolved through such discursive media (*ahkam*).

The methodology of Islamic political economy is applied to specific issues and problems of economics, society, institutions, ecology, COMMUNITY, family, agents and the "global" order by using the principle of universal complementarity and the Shuratic process. Highly analytical formalization and policy-theoretic studies are developed by using such premises. The axiomatic base remains immutable in Tawhidi epistemology.

The methodology of Tawhidi world view explains equally processes based on Truth (knowledge induction) and Falsehood (de-knowledge). The undetermined cases between these two are treated as cognitions with limited knowledge. They are determined either as Truth or Falsehood using knowledge premised on Tawhid as the Shuratic process advances.

A contemporary advocate of such a definition of Islamic political economy is Masudul Alam Choudhury of the University of Cape Breton, Canada. Organizationally, the field of Islamic political economy was initiated in 1994 in the International Project on Islamic Political Economy (IPIPE). In 1997 this was renamed the Islamic Development Management Project (IDMP), at the School of Social Sciences, Universiti Sains Malaysia in Penang, Malaysia. The IPIPE has successfully organized two International Conferences on Islamic Political Economy. In 1997, another academic organization called the International Center of Islamic Political Economy (ICIPE), with similar objectives, was established at the Islamic University of Chittagong in Bangladesh.

See also:

collective social wealth; holistic method; institutions and habits; knowledge, information, technology and change; medieval Arab-Islamic economic thought

Selected references

Choudhury, Masudul Alam (1992) *The Principles of Islamic Political Economy – A Methodological Enquiry*, New York: St Martin's Press and London: Macmillan.

—— (1996) "Toward Islamic Political Economy at the Turn of the Century," *The American Journal of Islamic Social Sciences* 13(3): 366–81.

Choudhury, M.A. and Malik, U.A. (1992) *The Foundations of Islamic Political Economy*, New York: St Martin's Press and London: Macmillan.

Choudhury, Masudul Alam, Abdad, M.Z. and Salleh, Muhammad Syukri (eds) (1997) *Islamic Political Economy in Capitalist Globalization – An Agenda for Change*, Kuala Lumpur: Utusan Publications and Distributors and Penang: International Project on

Islamic political economy

Islamic Poltical Economy (IPIPE), School of Social Sciences, Universiti Sains Malaysia.

Khan, Mohammed A. Muqtedar (1996) "The Philosophical Foundations of Islamic Political Economy," *The American Journal of Islamic Social Sciences* 13(3): 389–400.

M.A. CHOUDHURY
MUHAMMAD SYUKRI SALLEH

J

Japanese political economy

Introduction

Occidental things and ideas, including POLITICAL ECONOMY, were quickly introduced after Japan ended its isolationist policy (1639–1854). The new government took strong leadership in the modernization of Japan after the Meiji Restoration of 1868. Japanese scholars were absorbed in translating and learning Western economic thought, although there were some who resisted Westernization and sought instead "Japaneseness" (Sugiyama 1994).

Thanks to the drastic reform in higher education in 1919–20, increasing numbers of economists tackled a wide range of economic problems and thought. The latter included MERCANTILISM, classical economics, German historical economics, Marxism and NEOCLASSICAL ECONOMICS. Moreover, the successful 1917 Socialist Revolution in Russia had some influence on the historical study of Japanese CAPITALISM in the following two decades. In 1926, Kyoto (Imperial) University started *Kyoto University Economic Review* (*KUER*), the first economics journal written in Western languages in Japan. This journal aimed at establishing the Japanese School of Economics, attempting to create a new school of economics which was to be differentiated from the Western version.

From 1945 until the mid-1960s, Marxian economists were in the majority in Japanese academia. They had a strong historical orientation, and made numerous studies on Japanese capitalism, MARX, Engels and Lenin, from the historical as well as the theoretical perspective. The history of the late developer convinced many Japanese that something was wrong with capitalism and that commercial competition for outlets, along with militarism, caused the "imperialistic" wars. That is why many Japanese had sympathy with Marxist claims and believed that the capitalist system should be modified by the state.

The German historical school

Japan shifted from free trade to protectionism in 1889, when it managed to revise unequal treaties and acquired the tariff right. The Japanese edition of List's *The National System of Political Economy* was published in the same year. Many Japanese economists visited Germany for advanced study during the period 1900–30. Tokuzo Fukuda (1874–1930) studied under Lujo Brentano around 1900, brought back a wide-angled approach to economics, and taught several leading economists of the next generation.

Marxian political economy

Hajime Kawakami (1879–1946) was sent to Europe by the Japanese government during 1913–14, and observed European culture and economic life. Returning to Japan, he began to study the problem of poverty and published his *Tale of Poverty* in 1917. This book was based on his own experience in Europe, not in Japan, and rang a warning bell for capitalist development with the widening gulf between rich and poor. The book was regarded as a good introduction to social sciences until the 1950s. Kawakami believed that a reorganization of the social system was necessary to eliminate poverty. His writings and socialist ideas captured the heart of young intellectuals. He joined the Japanese Communist Party (JCP) in 1932.

There was a major controversy over the nature of Japanese capitalism and "the coming revolution" during 1927–37 (Hoston 1986). Social democrats or non-JCP members, *Rono-ha*, believed that it would take a long time for Japan to shift to a socialist system from an early stage of capitalist system. On the other hand, JCP and ex-JCP members, *Koza-ha*, advocated a two-stage revolution: a democratic revolution first to eliminate feudal remnants, and then a socialist revolution. For example, Moritaro Yamada (1897–1980) in his *Analysis of Japanese Capitalism*, published in 1934, clarified the rapid formation of manufacture and home manufacture after 1868. For *Koza-ha* people, the imperial system was a major feudal remnant and the biggest obstacle on the road to the socialist system. Many of this group were arrested for violating the Peace Preservation Law before 1945.

After 1945, the professors who had been forced to resign from universities were reappointed. Everyone was allowed to openly study Marx, Lenin and Stalin. Marxists were confident of their analysis of Japanese capitalism, and believed that the future course of Japan would proceed according to the dictates of historical materialism. Marxist studies were part of the mainstream of economics in Japan for the next two decades. Japanese Marxian economists were historically-oriented, wrote mostly in Japanese, covered various fields of applied economics, and adapted a critical attitude toward neoclassical economics. In 1959, they established the Society of Political Economy for the study of basic theories of political economy, although they usually formed tight groups or schools.

The Uno School

The Uno School has been a minority in the Japanese Marxian community, whereas it is well known by Western counterparts. Its enthusiastic followers have been publishing in English since 1975 (Plasmeijer 1984). Kozo Uno (1897–1977) was relatively unknown when he was suddenly arrested as a political suspect and forced to leave Tohoku (Imperial) University in 1938. Uno was subsequently released and appointed professor at Tokyo in 1947. He rode on the tidal wave of Marxian economics in Japan and his heretical ideas stimulated controversy among Japanese Marxists. Avoiding political involvement, Uno basically differentiated theoretical study, historical study, and the study of actual capitalism from each other, although the last two were often mixed in the research of the Uno School. Tomohiko (Thomas) Sekine introduced Uno's reconstruction of Marxian economics to non-Japanese in 1975, and published the English version of Uno's *Principles of Political Economy* in 1980. Makoto Itoh is also a prolific writer of the Uno School, and well known to non-Japanese political economists. Chapter 1 of Itoh's *Value and Crisis* (1980) describes "The Development of Marxian Economics in Japan."

Mathematical political economy

In the 1930s, those who had been trained in neoclassical economics began to use numerical examples and mathematical tools in the study of political economy. Kei Shibata (1902–86), a student of Kawakami, was shocked by Cassel's simplified system of general equilibrium which he first learnt at economics lectures given by Yasuma Takata. Shibata started to consider the synthesis of general equilibrium theory and Marxist economics. Shibata also made critical assessments of Marx's proposition of the FALLING RATE OF PROFIT TENDENCY, due to a rising organic COMPOSITION OF CAPITAL, by using numerical examples for the technical coefficients. His papers appeared in *KUER* in 1934 and 1939. In 1961, Nobuo Okishio, trained in general equilibrium analysis, demonstrated that a cost-reducing process will not reduce the general rate of profit under the assumption of constant cost. This result is commonly known as the Shibata–Okishio Theorem (in the West it is simply known as the Okishio Theorem). In the 1980s, this line of study was pursued by Takao Fujimoto, Takashi Negishi and Eiji Hosoda (Kurz and Salvadori 1995; Ikeo 1998).

Shinzaburo Koshimura (1907–88) studied both classical and Marxist political economy at Tokyo University of Commerce (Hitotsubashi University after 1949). Koshimura, who was interested in studies of economic systems, such as Marx's reproduction schema and Quesnay's *tableau économique*, always tried to create something original and was eager to publish the results in book form. The English version of Koshimura (1956) was published under the title of *Theory of Capital Reproduction and Accumulation* in 1975. In his *Marxian Econometrics* (published in 1961 in Japanese), Koshimura applied the theory of matrices and determinants to the system of the labor theory of value.

There were other Japanese scholars who did more high-powered mathematical political economy than Koshimura. Takuma Yasui (1907–95) was a self-trained mathematical economist who was interested in dynamics and stability analysis. In 1953, Yasui formulated a Kalecki–Kaldor-type trade cycle theory by using a generalized van der Pol-type equation. Michio Morishima, who was trained in general equilibrium theory, discussed Marx with the use of the von Neumann growth model in his *Marx's Economics*, published in 1973.

Modern capitalism

Studies of the historical development of Japanese capitalism were important for political economists in the interwar and postwar period. Shigeto Tsuru played a major role in the internationalization of political economy. He studied at Harvard during the 1930s and cultivated an intellectual connection with Westerners such as Paul Baran, Paul Sweezy and Maurice Dobb. He brought both a cosmopolitan attitude and the American economic language back to Japan in 1942. Japanese political economists thus shared an interest in the analysis of economic systems with several Western counterparts.

For example, Kohachiro Takahashi (1912–82), Sweezy, Dobb, Hilton and Hill discussed the transition from feudalism to capitalism in *Science and Society* in 1950–53. They believed that they lived in the period of transition from capitalism to socialism, and were interested in earlier transitions from one social system to another. In the 1960s, Yoshihiro Takasuka (1932–91), a student of Tsuru, was an active participant in the debate over the evaluation of the rapid development of Japanese capitalism. He was critical of an incomes policy tolerating mild inflation, and conceptualized inflation as being caused by the differential rate of increase in productivity among industrial sectors. He hypothesized that, due to inflation, sectors with lower productivity could enjoy a wage rise similar to the sectors with higher rates of productivity.

Schumpeterians

Kaname Akamatsu (1896–1974) studied in Germany during 1924–6, and became especially interested in technical inventions in industry and the importance of INCREASING RETURNS TO SCALE for economic development. He observed the sequential shifting from the import of goods, including cotton textile, through to domestic production, and then to export in the development of the Japanese economy. In 1937, he advocated the theory of the "flying geese" pattern of economic growth. This states that advanced nations led underdeveloped nations through different stages of development by the diffusion of new TECHNOLOGY. Seiichi Tobata (1899–1983) studied under SCHUMPETER at Bonn in the late 1920s and became a Schumpeterian agricultural economist. He emphasized the importance of innovation and autonomy in economic activities.

Power theorist

Yasuma Takata (1883–1971) was an economist and sociologist, being called the Japanese Alfred Marshall. In the 1930s, he not only contributed to the spread of Marshallian and Walrasian ideas, but also developed the power theory of economics to modify neoclassical economics. His "power" was a social phenomenon and assumed the existence of relationships between human beings. It related to the potential to be obeyed by others, like the prestige of the nobles. Criticizing KEYNES, Takata maintained that if the unemployed do not compete for lower wages, it could be because of their resistance based on power or prestige.

Feminists

The women's liberation movement was initiated as women gradually increased their participation in the work force in Japan, like many other countries. During 1939–45, women were forced to work outside the home and fill the positions which had been occupied by men. They worked in farming but also munitions factories and heavy industry. However, these women were removed from their jobs after the war. Nevertheless, Japanese women finally acquired the same legal rights as men, including suffrage, under the occupation of the Allies during 1945–52. A number of activist women, including Kikue Yamakawa, Koko Sanpei and Setsu Tanino, cooperated to improve the social status of women. In the male-dominated community of Japanese economists, Sumiko Takahara criticized standard microeconomics, based on the assumption of individualism, in her provocative book *Challenging Male Economics*, written in 1979. She maintained that the concepts of household and family were important in political economy (see FEMINIST POLITICAL ECONOMY: MAJOR CONTEMPORARY THEMES).

Japanese political economy has thus had a long and influential history. This will continue in the future, although changes have and will continue to occur in the themes and tendencies as Japanese capitalism evolves over time.

Selected references

Hoston, Germaine A. (1986) *Marxism and the Crisis of Development in Prewar Japan*, Princeton, NJ: Princeton University Press.

Ikeo, Aiko (1996) "Marxist Economics in Japan," *Kokugakuin Keizaigaku* 44: 425–51.

—— (1998) "Classical Economics in Japan," in H. Kurz and N. Salvadori (eds), *Companion to Classical Economics*, Aldershot: Edward Elgar.

Itoh, Makoto (1980) *Value and Crisis*, London: Pluto Press.

Koshimura, Shinzaburo (1956) *Theory of Capital Reproduction and Accumulation*, ed. Jesse Schwartz, Ontario: DPG Publishing Co., 1975.

Kurz, Heinz and Salvadori, Neri (1995) *The Theory of Production*, New York: Cambridge University Press.

Morris-Suzuki, Tessa (1989) *History of Japanese Economic Thought*, London: Routledge.

Plasmeijer, Henk W. (1984) "Marxistische Ekonomie in Japan: De school van Kozo Uno," *Tijdschrift voor Politieke Ekonomie* 7: 87–105.

Sugiyama, Chuhei (1994) *Origins of Economic Thought in Modern Japan*, London: Routledge.

Takata, Yasuma (1995) *Power Theory of Economics*, trans. D.W. Anthony, London: Macmillan.

AIKO IKEO

joint production

Introduction

Joint production is the simultaneous manufacture of two or more goods in the same production process. Joint production may be intrinsic, as in the case of sheep farming where meat and wool are produced; or aggregate as in the case of multi-product firms such as banks.

For a long time, joint production was relegated to the backwaters of economic analysis as being too recherché. This situation changed with the publication of Sraffa's *Production of Commodities by Means of Commodities* in 1960. Taking up an idea of von Neumann, SRAFFA analyzed the consumption of fixed capital as a case of joint production.

As a result of this innovation, all industries could be redefined as joint producers. The joint production approach permits the reconsideration of very general problems of the classical and Marxist theories of value. It allows the incorporation (into these theories) of the analysis of fixed capital and non-producible means of production, such as land and oilfields.

Cost, fixed capital and production prices

The price of any product must be high enough both to cover the cost of its manufacture and to yield a profit. Raw materials, energy and salaries are part of the production costs of any industry. These and other similar elements are incorporated continuously and totally into the price of the product. The machinery, the buildings and the tools which are the means of production constitute the fixed capital of these firms. They have a working life of several years and must also be included in the cost of the product. Fixed capital must be replaced when it wears out. For this reason, its complete cost must be included in the price of the product being manufactured during its useful life. This situation has been resolved in different ways in the past without the intervention of economic theory.

The most common solution is to write off a given percentage of the value of the fixed capital each year. This is called linear depreciation. Using the joint production approach, every industry is considered to generate (apart from its usual products) machinery or other elements of fixed capital, aged by one year. This will have a price or labor value which reflects the years of its useful economic life which have elapsed.

With this ingenious solution, theoretical problems, such as the determination of the labor value or prices of production, may be resolved. Sraffa shows that it is possible to determine production prices, in the case of joint production. In this way, he consolidated his criticism of NEOCLASSICAL ECONOMICS (which used production functions) to show that the concept of capital is problematic.

Basing his work on the idea of joint production, Sraffa demonstrates the difficulty neoclassical theory has in arranging techniques according to their profitability. Neoclassical theory shows that technique B becomes more profitable than technique A, beyond a certain wage rate, w_0. However, Sraffa demonstrates that it is possible for technique A to become more profitable than B for higher wage rates than w_0. This is called RESWITCHING, and is a serious anomaly for orthodox theory.

To understand the joint production approach to fixed capital, let us suppose, in order to simplify the explanation, that in the production of an item of consumer goods only labor and one machine with a useful life of ten years are used. The industry involved may be divided into ten processes, all of which produce the same item by means of fixed capital of a given age and use of labor. However, in addition, each of these industries produces fixed capital, aged by one more year because of the use which it has made of it. On the basis of this economic model, it is possible to build a mathematical model which has as its unknowns embodied labor value and machines with varying ages.

When the equations are resolved, the existence of negative labor values would indicate that the process is economically unnecessary, given that the machinery has aged to a point where its continued use would consume more labor value than that which might be saved by not replacing it. Hence the physical and economic life of the machinery do not have to coincide. Thus, analyzing fixed capital in terms of joint production complicates the definition of labor value, because the labor value of the products will depend not only on the inputs but also on the economic life of the fixed capital. For this reason, Morishima and Catephores (1978: 22–58) argue that the definition of labor value may be expressed mathematically not by equations but by inequations.

Negative values and profitability

Joint production may be used without referring

to fixed capital, in order to analyze theoretical problems. For example, Steedman (1977: 150–62) has used joint production to demonstrate paradoxes such as negative values and negative surplus values, which correspond to positive prices of production. Morishima and Catephores argue that the model employed by Steedman yields negative values and surplus values because it does not eliminate the possibility of inefficient processes.

There are many other interesting conclusions to be drawn from joint production. For example, Schefold (1980) shows that the criterion of profitability can lead to the rejection of techniques which would increase consumption per capita or even result in the adoption of techniques which would reduce it. For this reason, Schefold argues that the idea of technical progress is ambivalent. At a broader level, joint production obviously links to the question of economies of scope.

See also:

labor theory of value; reswitching; technical change and measures of technical progress

Selected references

Bidard, Christian (1988) "The Falling Rate of Profit and Joint Production," *Cambridge Journal of Economics* 12(3): 355–60.
Kurz, Heinz D. and Salvadori, Neri (1995) *Theory of Production: A Long-Period Analysis*, Cambridge: Cambridge University Press.
Morishima, M. and Catephores, G. (1978) *Value Exploitation and Growth*, Maidenhead: McGraw-Hill.
Schefold, B. (1980) "Fixed Capital as a Joint Product and the Analysis of Accumulation with Different Forms of Technical Progress," in L. Pasinetti (ed.), *Essays on the Theory of Joint Production*, London: Macmillan 138–217.
Steedman, I. (1977) *Marx after Sraffa*, London: New Left Books.

ALEJANDRO VALLE BAEZA

journals of political economy

In the mid-1960s, there was no general journal which specifically attempted to develop political economy as a scholarly study of economic systems, institutions and class relations. However, the 1960s and 1970s saw a resurgence of interest in political economy, and soon many political economy journals emerged. At present, there are political economy journals on every conceivable topic and trend. The positive growth in journal outlets looks set to continue as an outlet for research.

General economics serials

General economics serials have historically been an important source of debate in political economy. All general economics journals have published papers in political economy over the years, including the *Economic Journal*, the *Journal of Political Economy* and the *American Economic Review*. Special mention should be given to the *Australian Economic Papers*, for its high political economy content when under the (joint) editorship of Geoffrey Harcourt (1963–82). Some serials originating from France, Italy, Japan and India have historically been considerably influenced by political economy. Examples include *Economie Appliquée, Economies et Sociétés, Revue d' Economie Politique, Metroeconomica, Revista Internazionale dell' Scienze e Commercial, Indian Economic Review* and the *Kobe Economic Review*. Many Spanish or Portuguese journals are also strong in political economy, including, for instance, *Pensamiento Iberoamericano: Revista de Economia Politica* (Spanish and Latin American); *Revista de Economia Politica* (Brazilian), *El Trimestre Economia* (Mexican), *Revista CEPAL Review* (Chilean), and *Revista Venezolana de Economia y Ciencias Sociales* (Venezuelan).

Socialist journals

Prior to the late 1960s, a sizable proportion of heterodox papers originated in the socialist and social economy journals. For instance, *Science and Society* commenced in 1937 as "An Independent Journal of Marxism," and has for many decades advanced the cause of scholarly debate among socialists on many diverse areas, political economy being an important one of these. For years *Monthly Review* (first published in 1949) has been edited by Paul Sweezy (one of the fathers of modern political economy) and his associates Harry Magdoff and Leo Huberman. This journal has sought to publish readable articles on theories, policies and practices of socialism and capitalism around the world.

Social economy journals

The *Review of Social Economy* (founded in 1948) was for twenty years a vehicle of the Association for Catholic Economists, specializing in the social economy of ethics, norms and human values. The *American Journal of Economics and Sociology* (founded in 1942) has always been interested in alternative themes linked to Henry George, Thorstein Veblen, the standard of living, the quality of life, the environment, worker cooperatives, normative issues, crime, health and public goods.

Resurgence in political economy in the 1960s

The 1960s saw an upsurge of interest into political economy throughout the world, especially in Britain, the USA, continental Europe and Australia. From the late 1960s onwards a procession of political economy journals have emerged; some general economics journals have come under the greater influence of political economy; and some existing heterodox journals have changed somewhat.

Journal of Economic Issues. The first fully-fledged political economy journal to emerge from this renaissance in the 1960s was the *Journal of Economic Issues* (*JEI*), published by the ASSOCIATION FOR EVOLUTIONARY ECONOMICS (AFEE) since 1967. The *JEI* is committed to the development of institutional political economy, in the tradition of Thorstein Veblen, John Commons, Wesley Mitchell, Clarence Ayres, John Kenneth Galbraith and Gunnar Myrdal. However, it has been fairly eclectic and open-minded about the inclusion of Marxist, post-Keynesian, feminist and environmentalist perspectives that run along institutional lines. The *JEI* has made an enormous contribution to the advancement of political economy for more than thirty years, especially in areas such as policy, evolutionary theory, institutions and methodology. (A closely related journal, the *Review of Institutionalist Thought*, went through three issues in the 1980s before ceasing publication.)

Review of Radical Political Economics. A couple of years after the *JEI* was founded, the *Review of Radical Political Economics* (*RRPE*) emerged under the auspices of the UNION FOR RADICAL POLITICAL ECONOMICS (URPE). Being influenced by US radical politics, feminism, Students for a Democratic Society, the Vietnam War, racial conflict, Marxism and like-minded progressives, the *RRPE* became committed to a radical analysis of modern capitalism and socialism. Writers in the *RRPE* have made major contributions to thinking on social structures of accumulation, business cycles, long waves, overdetermination, feminist economics, the economic surplus approach, discrimination, imperialism, unequal exchange, neo-Marxian political economy, economic policy and political action. In the early 1980s, the *RRPE* saw radical political economy as including Marxist, institutionalist, feminist, post-Keynesian and Cambridge economics, and it has published in all these areas, although neo-Marxian themes have historically been the main influence on the journal.

History of Political Economy. In 1969, *History of Political Economy* began its many debates of central concern to political economy. This was followed by the *Journal of the History of Economic Thought* in 1979, *History of Economics Review* in 1981, *History of Economic Ideas* in 1986 and the *European Journal of the History of Economic Thought* in 1993. The history of economics has always been an important part of the political economy tradition (see HISTORY OF ECONOMICS: SOCIETIES AND JOURNALS).

Capital and Class. In England, two main forces in the political economy movement have been the Cambridge economists and the Conference of Socialist Economists (CSE). In 1973, the CSE began to publish the *Bulletin of the Conference of Socialist Economists*, which by 1978 had changed to a more accessible name, *Capital and Class*. As with the URPE, members of the CSE became active in radical politics and in trying to comprehend the dynamic forces impacting on capitalism and socialism. The *Bulletin* and *Capital and Class* have made important contributions to social democratic or democratic socialist interpretations of world processes and economic theory. Especially notable has been work on domestic labor, the capitalist labor process, the role of the state, the international economy and questions of race and ethnicity.

Cambridge Journal of Economics. By 1977 the Cambridge Political Economy Society in the UK began publishing the *Cambridge Journal of Economics* (*CJE*). Coming from a long history of political economy at Cambridge, this journal seeks to promote work in the tradition of Karl Marx, John Maynard Keynes, Michal Kalecki, Joan Robinson and Nicholas Kaldor. It aims to focus on "theoretical, applied, interdisciplinary and methodological work, with a strong emphasis on realism of analysis, the development of critical perspectives, the provision and use of empirical evidence, and the construction of policy." The editors have been keen to publish articles on unemployment, inflation, the organization of production, distribution of income and wealth, class conflict, underdevelopment, globalization, international integration, uneven development and instability in the world economy.

Journal of Post Keynesian Economics. In 1978, with an international board, Paul Davidson and Sidney Weintraub began the *Journal of Post Keynesian Economics (JPKE)*. The original Academic Board of the *JPKE* included greats like J.K. Galbraith, Kenneth Boulding, G.C. Harcourt, Nicholas Kaldor, Gunnar Myrdal and G.L.S. Shackle. The editors seek to promote free debate into heterodox alternatives to neoclassical orthodoxy and also institutional innovations which may improve the standard of living. Also stressed is the ideological and normative basis of economics. Over the years many hundreds of themes have been explored in the *JPKE*. Special mention should be given to the work on UNCERTAINTY, money and financial instability, economic policy, investment and capital accumulation, international trade and exchange rates, and productivity and labor markets.

Review of Social Economy. Since the 1970s, the *Review of Social Economy (RSE)* has became more general and eclectic in its heterodoxy. The *RSE*'s main concerns have always been the relationship between ethics, values, human relationships and economic processes. Now these themes have a broader focus to include feminist, institutionalist, radical, Schumpeterian, environmental, neo-Marxist and behavioralist perspectives. This journal, being published now by the Association for Social Economics, is a leading force in political economy, and has a sister publication called *Forum for Social Economics*. Social economics has become a growth area, with the commencement of the *International Journal of Social Economics* in 1974, and the *Journal of Socioeconomics* (see SOCIAL ECONOMICS: ORGANIZATIONS).

Review. In the 1970s a former student of C. Wright Mills, Immanuel Wallerstein, took up a Chair at the State University of New York in Binghamton. There he set up the Fernand Braudel Center for the Study of Economies, Historical Systems and Civilizations, which in 1978 established a journal, simply called the *Review*, and which has also coordinated books of readings on the political economy of world systems. This Center and journal has established a worldwide network of scholars committed to a historical analysis of social economies within the world division of labor. A vast array of studies have been undertaken on class struggle, long waves, families, production networks, financial crises and states within the world system.

Race and development. Questions of race, ethnicity and the Third World have been of central importance to modern political economy. *Race and Class* (1959), an interdisciplinary journal of black and Third World liberation, is published by the Institute of Race Relations, London. The *Review of Black Political Economy* (1970) examines the economic status of black and Third World peoples, policies and strategies to reduce racial economic inequality. The *Review of African Political Economy* (1974) has examined imperialism and colonialism, aid, international organizations, class, race and sex, national case studies, socialism, and other topics in an African context. In addition, many journals specialize in "development," such as the *Journal of Contemporary Asia*, *World Development*, *Development and Change* and *Economic Development and Cultural Change*.

Array of journals in the 1970s, 1980s and 1990s

In the 1970s, an annual, *Research in Political Economy*, was initiated by Paul Zarembka. Some more nationally-oriented volumes emerged, such as the *Journal of Australian Political Economy* and *Studies of Political Economy* from Canada. *Politics and Society* has published some excellent studies into political economy, as has *Critical Sociology* (formerly the *Insurgent Sociologist*), and *Antipode* (a journal for radical geographers).

The 1980s and 1990s saw a continuation of the rapid expansion of political economy journals. *Economics and Philosophy* and *Methodus* (which became the *Journal of Economic Methodology* in 1994) satisfied a considerable niche for economists interested in the philosophy of science, assumptions and values. The *International Review of Applied Economics* commenced in 1987 with a mandate to concentrate on "the application of economic ideas to the real world" (including empirical work and economic policy). It is said to "adopt a broadly left-of-centre perspective on economic policy," and has proved to be a rich source of ideas and evidence in many fields. The rapid growth of environmental concerns led to the inception of *Capitalism, Socialism and Nature* in 1989 and to a number of other journals (see ENVIRONMENTAL AND ECOLOGICAL POLITICAL ECONOMY: ASSOCIATIONS AND JOURNALS).

Rethinking Marxism: A Journal of Economics, Culture, and Society. First published in 1988, this journal is published by the Association for Economic and Social Analysis. This journal has a mandate to "stimulate interest in and debate over the explanatory power and social consequences of Marxian economic, cultural and social analysis" and "encourage contributions from people in many disciplines and from a wide range of perspectives." Attempting to broaden the focus of debate, this journal has recast Marxism away from the deterministic mold toward postmodernism, class analysis and linkages between Marxism and feminism. (See MARXIST POLITICAL ECONOMY: MAJOR CONTEMPORARY VARIETIES.)

Review of Political Economy (*ROPE*). First published in 1989, *ROPE* has a broad mandate to "welcome...critical and constructive contributions within the broad traditions of political economy (including institutionalism, post-Keynesianism and other typically non-orthodox approaches) that place significant emphasis on realism of analysis." The mandate specified by the new editors in 1996 mentions in addition the importance of social, feminist, Austrian, Sraffian, econometric and mathematical perspectives on political economy. Above all else, this journal seeks to promote interaction and communication among the different schools and perspectives.

Evolutionary economics. The recent upsurge in dynamic, evolutionary and Schumpeterian political economy led to the emergence of *Structural Change and Economic Dynamics* (*SCED*) in 1990 and the *Journal of Evolutionary Economics* (*JEE*) in 1991, both of which have a strong European influence. *JEE* tends to follow the Schumpeterian trend. What is most interesting about the *SCED* are the linkages being forged between Sraffian, post-Keynesian and Schumpeterian themes relating to technological change, input–output relations and institutions.

Gender and labor. Many political economy

journals have published material on gender issues, the gender division of labor, discrimination, and segmented markets. *RRPE*, for instance, has published five special issues on the political economy of women. A major development in political economy is the recent emergence of *Feminist Economics* in 1995, which attempts a holistic analysis of gender, culture, sexuality, households, methodology and many other issues. The continuing importance of workplace democracy, the labor process, and power and inequality relations has led to the introduction of *Economic and Industrial Democracy*, *Labour and Industry*, *Work, Employment and Society*, *Prometheus* and *Gender, Work and Organization*.

International political economy. A critical area of political economy has always been the world stage. Apart from the *Review*, mentioned above, in 1994 the *Review of International Political Economy* emerged. It has already examined some critical questions, such as global hegemony, core–periphery relations, world-systems analysis and related themes. For decades global political economy issues have been discussed in journals that are stacked in the political science section of the library, such as *International Organization*, the *International Studies Quarterly* and the *Review of International Studies*. The *Journal of World-System Research*, which emerged in 1995, is the first electronic journal in political economy.

Other journals in political economy

International Papers in Political Economy, edited by Philip Arestis and Malcolm Sawyer, first appeared in 1993; its first issue was a brilliant analysis of the linkages within modern political economy. Of popular interest are *Challenge* and *Dollars and Sense*. Well worth a good look are *Kyklos*, the *New Left Review*, *Review of Austrian Economics*, *Eastern Economic Journal*, *Review of Income and Wealth*, *Review of World Economics*, *Economy and Society*, *Growth and Change*, *New Political Economy*, *Cultural Economics*, *Competition and Change* plus the numerous economic history and urban and regional journals. Also, many sociology, politics, ecology, philosophy, culture critique and business journals regularly have articles which impact on political economy. (A neoclassical or 'Austrian' influence is predominant in *Economics and Politics*, the *European Journal of Political Economy* and the *Journal of Institutional and Theoretical Economics*.)

Conclusion

Geoffrey Hodgson has examined indices of citations to heterodox journals and found some of them to be among the most cited journals in the world (notably the *Journal of Economic Issues*, and the *Cambridge Journal of Economics*). Also, the large range and breadth of modern political economy journals illustrates that political economy is in a healthy state. An increasing trend in these journals is for dialogue among different schools of thought, such as post-Keynesian, neo-Marxian, institutionalist, feminist, Sraffian, social and Schumpeterian political economy. Students choosing political economy as a career will find many outlets for serious research in an increasing number of journals. So extensive has this outlet become that the periodical *Review of Heterodox Economics* was established in 1995 by Eric Nilsson to document recent contents pages of many of these journals, working papers and the like.

See also:

political economy: major contemporary themes; political economy: schools

PHILLIP ANTHONY O'HARA

justice

Justice is generally agreed to be about treating equals equally and unequals according to their relevant inequalities, and is thus closely associated with fairness. Justice has a variety of senses, two of which need to be distinguished to understand thinking about justice in economics. *Commutative* justice concerns whether exchange is fair, such as in connection with the payment of wages and the setting of prices. *Distributive* justice concerns whether there is a fair distribution of resources, of society's benefits and burdens, and of such things as income, jobs, goods, property, taxation and social services. Both senses of justice are important in economics, but distributive justice has historically received more attention, since for many whether contracts are fair and just is often believed to depend upon whether resources are justly distributed. For example, it may be thought fair to pay one person a higher wage than another (based on skill differences) if the latter person, having greater needs, is still left with a higher after-tax income.

Distributive justice and heterodoxy

Debates regarding distributive justice revolve around different schools advocating different criteria for a just distribution of resources. With a few exceptions, however, these debates in the last half-century have only involved heterodox economists, since mainstream economists have generally ignored issues of distributive justice and restricted their normative interests to Pareto efficiency judgments. Why this is the case helps explain why heterodox economists are interested in distributive justice. Standard neoclassical models treat individuals' endowments as exogenous, and also assume that markets are generally competitive.

In contrast, heterodox economists endogenize endowments, that is, understand them to be determined by market forces and the economic process, and see market power as the rule rather than the exception. Distributive justice is thus central to heterodox economists' concerns, because understanding how societies settle on "fair" distributions of resources is inseparable from understanding how their economies operate. It is also central to heterodox concerns, because understanding the connection between the distribution of resources and the operation of the economy imparts an understanding of opportunities for social reform, a concern shared by many heterodox economists.

Perhaps not surprisingly, given their different theoretical approaches, heterodox economists emphasize different traditions with competing criteria to explain the just distribution of resources. Chief among these traditions are the Marxian view of distribution according to need, the utilitarian view of distribution according to what maximizes utility, the libertarian view that emphasizes freedom, and the Rawlsian social contract view. All have supporters among heterodox economists, and elements of each often find their way into the views of many.

Marxian view

The Marxian view is premised on a critique of capitalist society as being based on class EXPLOITATION of workers by capitalists. The capitalist system of justice is part of bourgeois society's legal and ideological requirements for capitalist production, one of the most important of which is the defense of private property in the means of production. For Marx, class oppression does not constitute a legitimate or ultimately historically viable basis for a just society, which he believed would only come about with the revolutionary appearance of communist society (Marx 1867). In such a society, resources would be distributed according to need, where generally need was a matter of human development (see SOCIALISM AND COMMUNISM). This general criterion, however, has also been defended by a variety of non-Marxists (e.g. Braybrooke 1987), with the debate over what needs individuals possess further differentiating competing views of what distributive justice requires. Indeed, for most heterodox economists, a just distribution of resources depends at least in part on addressing individual and social NEEDS.

Utilitarian theory

The utilitarian theory of just distribution is best formulated in terms of *rule* rather than *act* utilitarianism, the former being the idea that we do not judge every single action by the standard of whether it contributes to the greatest utility, but rather according to society's rules and practices on this basis (Brandt 1959). On this view, social rules are preferred that raise overall utility, irrespective, in principle, of its distribution. In practice, however, the classical utilitarians, including Jeremy Bentham, J.S. Mill and Henry Sidgwick, believed that utility is increased by having more equal distributions of resources. Earlier neoclassical economists thus used the principle of diminishing marginal utility and the concept of interpersonal comparisons of utility to argue that overall utility would be enhanced if goods and/or income were transferred from well-off individuals, for whom this would involve a modest loss of utility, to less well-off individuals, for whom this would involve a significant increase in utility. In the limit this implied that an equal DISTRIBUTION OF INCOME produces maximum utility (Pigou 1920), an egalitarian conclusion reinforced by the assumption that every person's utility counts equally.

After Lionel Robbins, however, the fact that nothing in utilitarianism in principle required any assumptions regarding distribution enabled neoclassical economists to abandon interpersonal utility comparisons and distributive justice concerns. This has not prevented many heterodox economists from arguing that a more equal distribution of resources is just, because it increases the greater good.

Libertarian thinking

Libertarian thinking about justice has been most recently associated with the views of Robert Nozick (1974). Following such thinkers as Friedrich von Hayek, Nozick's entitlement theory of justice regards economic outcomes as just if they arise from acquisitions of what was unowned or what was voluntarily transferred. Just acquisitions are those that neither violate others' rights nor their individual freedoms. This implies that the redistribution of wealth and income is only justified when it remedies previous violations of rights or freedom. Such a view naturally places heavy weight on the theory of rights and freedom, which for Nozick and most neo-Austrian economists are taken prima facie as status quo rights and freedoms associated with existing property arrangements. However, it can be argued that many current property rights are the product of forcible property expropriations in the past, and consequently that redistribution of property is often just on libertarian grounds. Moreover, while libertarians generally understand freedom in a negative sense, that is, as non-interference, a positive conception of freedom involving capacities to act would permit an even more flexible view of just redistribution.

Rawls's social contract

John Rawls's social contract view in *A Theory of Justice* (1971) develops two principles of justice that he argues rational individuals would agree to behind a hypothetical "veil of ignorance" regarding what positions they might occupy in society. The first of these, based on the idea that individuals would seek to safeguard their basic political liberties, is that "each person is to have an equal right to the most extensive basic liberty compatible with a similar liberty for others" (Rawls 1971: 60). The second is that society's social and economic institutions may allow economic inequalities only to the extent that they tend to promote the "greatest benefit of the least advantaged," and are "attached to offices and positions open to all under conditions of fair equality of opportunity" (Rawls 1971: 83). Well-being and benefit are measured not in terms of preference satisfaction but rather "primary social goods," such things as education or income that function as all-purpose resources for the variety of activities in which people engage. Thus Rawls's view is both egalitarian in its view of what a just distribution of resources involves, and yet also compatible with a market society in which individuals' transactions produce differing degrees of preference satisfaction.

There are other views of distributive justice (for example, the institutionalist view; see Tool 1979: 329–36), but these four have attracted the most attention from heterodox economists. In most cases, it is probably fair to say that heterodox economists tend to draw on each of these frameworks in some degree to explain justice. Need, utility or the greatest good, rights, freedom and equality are all notions that have a place in a full normative framework. Their integration, however, requires that distributive justice become a more central concern in economics, and that the mainstream's single-minded focus on Pareto reasoning be displaced.

See also:

crime; ethics and morality; inequality; poverty: absolute and relative

Selected references

Brandt, Richard B. (1959) *Ethical Theory*, Englewood Cliffs, NJ: Prentice Hall.

Braybrooke, David (1987) *Meeting Needs*, Princeton, NJ: Princeton University Press.

Marx, Karl (1867) *Das Kapital*, vol. 1 published as *Capital*, New York: Progress.

Nozick, Robert (1974) *Anarchy, State and Utopia*, New York: Basic Books.

Pigou, A.C. (1920) *The Economics of Welfare*, London: Macmillan.

Rawls, John (1971) *A Theory of Justice*, Cambridge, MA: Harvard University Press.

Tool, Marc R. (1979) *The Discretionary Economy: A Normative Theory of Political Economy*, Santa Monica, CA: Goodyear Publishing Company.

JOHN B. DAVIS

Kaldor–Pasinetti models of growth and distribution

These models originated in two influential papers, by Kaldor (1955-6) and Pasinetti (1962). Their distinctive characteristic is that different kinds of income – wages and profits – have different savings propensities, and they usually examine the long-run implications of the ownership of assets purchased from profit income as well as from wage income by workers.

Kaldor's model

Kaldor's model can be seen as providing an answer to Harrod's long-run problem of making the warranted rate of growth, given by s/v (where s is the average propensity to save and v the capital–output ratio), equal to the natural rate of growth (which depends on the rate of growth of labor supply and the rate of technological change), given by n. Kaldor assumes that

$$s = s_p(P/Y) + s_w(W/Y) \quad (1)$$

where s_p and s_w are the average propensities to save out of profit and wage income, respectively, assumed constant with $s_p > s_w$. P is total profits, W is total wages and Y is total income and product, all in real terms, where $Y = W + P$. He also assumes that Y is given at the full-employment level, and that I/Y, the investment share of total income (I being investment) is given autonomously, with a technologically fixed capital–output ratio, v, and an investment rate I/K which is equal to n (K being the capital stock). (Kaldor has, in several contributions, tried rather unsuccessfully to explain why, in the long run, the economy will be at full employment in terms of the buoyancy of investment demand; here we simply assume a state of full employment). The equality of savings and investment required by the clearing of the goods market then implies that the profit share of income is equal to:

$$P/Y = [1/(s_p - s_w)]nv - [s_w/(s_p - s_w)]$$

which implies that the rate of profit is given by

$$r = [1/(s_p - s_w)]n - [s_w/(s_p - s_w)]/v \quad (2)$$

In Kaldor's approach, therefore, growth is at Harrod's natural rate, and income distribution, measured by the profit share, is determined by the requirement that saving is equal to autonomous investment. If investment exceeds (is less than) savings, the price level increases (falls), which for a given money wage reduces (increases) the real wage, which increases (reduces) the profit share. Harrod's problem is solved by the fact that s varies due to variations in the distribution of income. Kaldor notes that these variations can occur if the profit share remains between certain limits determined by the lowest – perhaps subsistence – wage workers will accept, the lowest rate of profit which induces capitalists to invest, and the lowest profit share consistent with the degree of monopoly.

Although this model introduces Keynesian effective demand issues by assuming that investment is autonomous from saving, it assumes away unemployment and Keynesian multiplier effects on output and employment. An autonomous rise in investment affects only the distribution of income between wages and profits: there is forced saving in the economy to finance this higher level of investment. The model determines the distribution of income endogenously (making it depend on conditions in the goods market), but growth is determined by the exogenously given rate of labor supply growth, as in Solovian neoclassical growth models.

Pasinetti's model

Pasinetti (1962) argues that Kaldor had neglected to take into account the fact that wage earners who saved did not receive a return on their wealth. Accordingly, he modifies Kaldor's approach to take into account two sources of workers' income – from wages and from returns to wealth. In this case, equation (1) is replaced by

$$s = s_c(P_c/Y) + s_w[(W+P_w)/Y] \quad (3)$$

where s_c and s_w are the constant average propensities to save of capitalists and workers (with $s_c > s_w$), and P_c and P_w are profit income accruing to capitalists and workers, respectively. Pasinetti's criticism of Kaldor is unwarranted, since Kaldor does not distinguish between capitalists and workers but between profit and wage income (so that differential saving rates in his model can arise due to savings by firms, and not due to class differences in savings behavior). However, Pasinetti's model has attracted a great deal of attention because it addresses the important question of how the distribution of assets (between capitalists and workers) evolves in a capitalist economy, and implies that the rate of profit, when the economy grows at the natural rate, is given by

$$r \equiv P/K = n/s_c \quad (4)$$

This result has been dubbed the Pasinetti paradox or the Cambridge Theorem, which states that in steady state full employment conditions income distribution depends only on the saving rate of capitalists (and the natural rate of growth), and not on the saving rate of workers, and has been taken to demonstrate the inability of workers to influence the distribution of income in the long run (except by affecting the rate of population growth). The result can be demonstrated as follows. Assuming that capitalists and workers receive the same rate of return on their capital, given

by K_c and K_w, and noting that $I/K = n$, investment-saving equality (for goods market equilibrium) implies, using equation (3), that $n = (s_c - s_w)rk_c + s_w/v$, where $k_c = K_c/K$. Given k_c at a point in time, this equation determines the rate of profit,

$$r = (nv - s_w)/(s_c - s_w)k_c v \quad (5)$$

The dynamics of k_c over time is given by

$$\hat{k}_c = s_c r - n \quad (6)$$

where the overhat denotes time-rates of growth. Substituting equation (5) into (6) we obtain a dynamic equation for k_c, which shows that if k_c is unconstrained, it will reach a stable equilibrium at which equation (4) will be satisfied, and at which

$$k_c = s_c[v - (s_w/n)]/(s_c - s_w)v$$

However, since k_c is the capitalists' share of total capital, $0 \leqslant k_c \leqslant 1$ must hold, which requires the parameters of the model to satisfy the condition $s_w \leqslant nv \leqslant s_c$. If $s_w > nv$ the steady state value of $k_c = 0$ so that $r = n/s_w$, a result that was pointed out by Samuelson and Modigliani (1966): the euthanasia of capitalists occurs in the limit. On the other hand, if $nv > s_c$, at steady state $k_c = 1$, so that in the limit capitalists own all the capital. It should be noted that in Kaldor's model a result like equation (4), that is, $r = 1/s_p$, is obtained from equation (2) *only* when $s_w = 0$, while in Pasinetti's model it follows even when workers have positive savings.

Extensions of the literature

A large and steadily growing literature has developed which extends and modifies this model in a number of ways while continuing to assume full employment growth. The early literature considered the case of smooth neoclassical productions functions, rather than the fixed coefficients case considered here for expository simplicity. The subsequent literature – which includes contributions from Kaldor (1966) and Pasinetti (1989) – has introduced several new factors, including different rates of return for capitalists and workers, more general saving functions, internal financing of investment by firms, explicit consideration of financial assets including equity, government fiscal policy and open economy considerations (see Dalziel 1991-2, for instance). This literature has shown that the Pasinetti paradox obtains under a much wider range of conditions – though not under all – than those considered initially by Pasinetti.

Models have also been developed to depart from the neoclassical assumption of full employment, by allowing for variations in the level of unemployment and capacity utilization (see Darity 1981) making the model more consistent with Keynesian and post-Keynesian ideas. In these models both growth and income distribution are determined endogenously, unlike the Kaldor model in which growth was determined exogenously by the rate of growth of labor supply. Moreover, in these models income distribution is affected by a wider range of parameters than saving rates: for instance, in a model with excess capacity and markup pricing, Kalecki's degree of monopoly can have an effect on the long-run distribution of income (Dutt 1990). These models confirm that the rate of profit being independent of the saving rate of workers holds in a wider range of models than thought originally. Even so, it is not true in general that workers are powerless in affecting the distribution of income. For instance, in the model with markup pricing, the profit rate depends on the markup, which depends, à la Kalecki, on the relative bargaining power of workers and capitalists (see Dutt 1990).

Kaldor and Pasinetti have developed and motivated models other than the ones discussed here. For instance, Kaldor has developed models of technical change involving his technical progress function, as well as models of the interaction between primary production sectors and manufacturing sectors; and Pasinetti has developed models of structural change involving differential rates of technical change and demand growth across sectors.

See also:

circular and cumulative causation; economic growth; Kaldor's theory of the growth process; Pasinetti's analysis of structural dynamics and growth; post-Keynesian political economy: major contemporary themes; Sraffian and post-Keynesian linkages; Sraffian political economy; wage and profit share

Selected references

Dalziel, Paul (1991-2) "Does Government Activity Invalidate the Cambridge Theorem of the Rate of Profit? A Reconciliation," *Journal of Post Keynesian Economics* 14(2): 225-31.

Darity, William A. (1981) "The Simple Analytics of Neo-Ricardian Growth and Distribution," *American Economic Review* 71(6): 978-93.

Dutt, Amitava K. (1990) "Growth, Distribution and Capital Ownership: Kalecki and Pasinetti Revisited," in B. Dutta *et al.* (eds), *Economic Theory and Policy*, Delhi: Oxford University Press.

Kaldor, Nicholas (1955-6) "Alternative Theories of Distribution," *Review of Economic Studies* 23(2), repr. in N. Kaldor, *Essays on Value and Distribution*, London: Duckworth, 1960.

—— (1966) "Marginal Productivity and the Macro-economic Theories of Growth and Distribution," *Review of Economic Studies* (October): 309-19.

Pasinetti, Luigi (1962) "The Rate of Profit and Income Distribution in Relation to the Rate of Economic Growth," *Review of Economic Studies* 29(4): 267-79, reprinted in L. Pasinetti, *Growth and Income Distribution. Essays in Economic Theory*, Cambridge: Cambridge University Press, 1974.

—— (1989) "Ricardian Debt/Taxation Equivalence in the Kaldor Theory of Profits and Income Distribution," *Cambridge Journal of Economics* 13: 25-36.

Samuelson, Paul and Modigliani, F. (1966) "The Pasinetti Paradox in Neoclassical and More General Models," *Review of Economic Studies* (October): 269-301.

AMITAVA KRISHNA DUTT

Kaldor's theory of the growth process

Nicholas Kaldor (1908–86) was born in Hungary and went to the London School of Economics in 1927, where he remained on the faculty for the next twenty years. During this time, he wrote several influential papers and was one of the first economists outside Cambridge to appreciate the significance of Keynes's *General Theory*. His paper in the 1937 *Economic Journal* finally convinced Pigou of the futility of money wage cuts as a cure for unemployment. He resigned his readership at the LSE in 1947 and, after two years in Geneva, took up a fellowship at King's College, Cambridge and a lectureship in economics. He became a reader in 1952 and was appointed to a Personal Chair in 1966. At Cambridge, Kaldor, with Joan Robinson (not always harmoniously), Richard Kahn and, for a time, Luigi Pasinetti, laid many of the foundations of post-Keynesian political economy. (Thirlwall (1987) is an excellent intellectual biography of Kaldor. Kaldor's key theoretical and applied papers may be found in Targetti and Thirlwall (1989).)

Early work: 1954–66

His early theoretical work on ECONOMIC GROWTH lasted from 1954 to 1966 and was concerned with the development of a number of related closed-economy models of growth. By 1939, Harrod had developed his seminal long-run Keynesian model with the famous result that $G_w = s/C$, where G_w is the warranted growth rate (where entrepreneurs' expectations are exactly fulfilled), s is the proportion of income saved and C is the incremental capital-output ratio. There was nothing in Harrod's model to bring the warranted growth rate into line with the natural growth rate, G_n, where the latter was determined by technical change and population growth. The neoclassical solution was to allow C to vary through factor substitution in the production function. Kaldor was a trenchant critic of neoclassical growth theory which used a "smooth" production function and marginal productivity factor pricing. By contrast, he published in the *Review of Economic Studies* in 1955–6 a Keynesian macroeconomic theory of distribution (later extended by Pasinetti) which solved Harrod's problem by making s endogenous. He showed that, under plausible circumstances, the distribution of income between workers and capitalists would adjust to bring the actual and warranted growth rates into line.

The resulting debate, notably with Samuelson and Modigliani, over the KALDOR–PASINETTI MODELS OF GROWTH AND DISTRIBUTION left Kaldor's model relatively unscathed. In 1957, Kaldor published his first full-blown model of economic growth. This was to go through a number of later modifications, but the essential ingredients remained the same: namely, his theory of distribution and his novel technical progress function. The latter was initially specified as a non-linear relationship between the growth of labor productivity and growth of the capital–labor ratio (later the model was cast in a vintage framework). The function reflected Kaldor's view that it is artificial and misleading in important respects to differentiate sharply between a movement along a production function (with a given state of knowledge) and a shift in this function (with a change in the state of knowledge). The technical progress function, with its stress on "learning by doing" and induced technical change, anticipated many of the insights of the more recent models of endogenous technical change. Nevertheless, the technical progress function never really had a major impact on the growth literature, mainly because a linear version of it can be integrated to give a function resembling the conventional Cobb–Douglas production function, which it was designed to replace.

The variable s in Kaldor's approach ensured G_w was a stable growth rate, in that it would bring the economy back to that path if it were not already on it. Moreover, the distributive mechanism would also ensure that $G_w = G_n$. Full employment equilibrium growth occurred where the capital–output ratio, the share of investment, the rate of profit and the profit share were all constant. The models were thus in accord with Kaldor's "stylized facts" of economic growth. The technical progress function could also explain the secular increase in the capital–labor ratio, another stylized fact. (However, Kaldor's insistence that the equilibrium growth had to be at full employment has been described, with some justification, as "quixotic" by Harcourt (1988).)

Work after 1966

After 1966, Kaldor's ideas were painted with more of a broad brush, and he placed greater emphasis on the role of INCREASING RETURNS TO SCALE in economic growth. In his article "The Irrelevance of Equilibrium Economics," published in the *Economic Journal* in 1972, Kaldor demonstrated the radical implications of Allyn Young's (1928) paper, then almost totally ignored by the profession. (Young had been Kaldor's teacher at the London School of Economics.) First, the whole notion of equilibrium falls to the ground if increasing returns are large relative to the size of the economy. The concept of Pareto optimality becomes irrelevant because each increase in output opens up new alternatives that were not perceived before. Here, Kaldor anticipated much of the recent work on PATH DEPENDENCY and TECHNOLOGICAL LOCK-IN. Second, the capital intensity of production is not a function primarily of relative factor prices, but of the scale of production. Third, the notion of output being resource constrained is untenable, at least in the long run, since economic growth creates *pari passu* its own resources. The ACCUMULATION of capital is as much a by-product as it is the cause of development. Fast growth brings with it a rapid rate of capital accumulation and technical progress and substantial benefits from both static and dynamic increasing returns to scale. Growth becomes a process of CIRCULAR AND CUMULATIVE CAUSATION, to use Myrdal's term.

Kaldor laid particular stress on VERDOORN'S LAW (the relationship between the growth of industrial productivity and output, which has obvious similarities to the technical progress function) as providing evidence of substantial increasing returns to scale. Kaldor rejected the idea that the growth of labor supply was an exogenous determinant of growth, even for the postwar advanced countries. In the early postwar period, for many of these countries there was disguised unemployment, especially in the agricultural sector, and the demand for labor was also met by immigration and the so-called "guest workers." Since 1973, the slowdown in output growth has led to a marked increase in both disguised and officially recorded unemployment, so it is difficult to ascribe a causal role in economic growth to the labor supply.

The upward sloping output supply curve, Kaldor noted, represents the maximum output that entrepreneurs are willing to supply at any given price, whereas with increasing returns, the downward sloping supply curve represents the minimum level of output. Entrepreneurs are, in the long run, willing to meet any demand. Consequently, Say's Law is turned on its head. For industrial production, the key factor is the growth of demand. This insight led Kaldor to develop a two-sector model of growth for a closed economy. The exogenous component of demand is determined by the agricultural sector, which is subject to diminishing returns and where productivity growth is determined by the rate of land-saving innovations. In a neoclassical world, any lack of agricultural demand for industrial products would be met by an improvement in agriculture's terms of trade and hence an increase in the purchasing power of the agricultural sector in terms of industrial goods. However, Kaldor argued that industrial prices are administered prices, determined by a mark-up (see PRICING), and there is a limit beyond which industrial wages cannot or will not fall. Hence, adjustments of quantity, and not price, occur in the industrial sector and its rate of growth is determined by the growth of demand for its products from the agricultural sector, via the Hicks "super-multiplier." (The service sector was not seen as a major component of autonomous demand, as it was largely dependent on the growth of industry.)

Kaldor sketched out this demand-oriented growth model in his article "Equilibrium Theory and Growth Theory," published in the *Quarterly Journal of Economics* in 1975, but he left it to others to provide more formal statements (see Thirlwall 1987: ch. 8). As development occurs, the relative importance of agriculture diminishes and consequently the exogenous component of demand changes to that emanating from outside the region (nation), i.e. exports. However, the balance of payments may impose a constraint on demand in an open economy.

The experience of floating exchange rates in the early 1970s led Kaldor to consider nominal exchange rate adjustments to be ineffective in rectifying balance of payments deficits. Since a country cannot run a balance of payments deficit for very long, the growth of output has to adjust to bring the balance of payments into equilibrium, which may well be below the growth of productive potential. In his later writings, Kaldor stressed that growth could be restricted by a balance of payments constraint and hence was ultimately determined by the growth of exports through the workings of the (dynamic) Harrod foreign trade multiplier (McCombie and Thirlwall 1994).

Kaldor was by no means just a brilliant theoretician. He was a scathing critic of growth models with little or no empirical relevance, and in his inaugural lecture, "The Causes of the Slow Rate of Economic Growth in the United Kingdom," he put forward a number of empirical "growth laws." The most famous of these is Verdoorn's Law. The UK's poor postwar growth record was, he argued, due in large part to a labor shortage that restricted the growth of manufacturing output and hence the growth of its productivity, through the Verdoorn effect. Unlike many of the other advanced countries, the UK did not have substantial disguised unemployment in agriculture. However, Kaldor later changed his mind, arguing, on the basis of subsequent evidence, that the UK had in fact surplus labor in the tertiary sector. The UK's manufacturing output was limited by its poor export performance, and this gave rise to his later emphasis on the role of BALANCE OF PAYMENTS CONSTRAINT, noted above. He also showed that, on the basis of cross-country data, there was a strong relationship between the growth of manufacturing output and GDP, which he cited as evidence of manufacturing as "the engine of growth." Kaldor's "growth laws" have subsequently generated an enormous secondary literature (see King 1994).

Conclusion

In conclusion, it is difficult to do better than to quote from Harcourt's closing words of his eloquent obituary of Kaldor:

> Many would agree that it is a scandal that Nicholas Kaldor was never awarded the Nobel Prize for economic science.... But he was far too free a spirit to fret about it, and the insights contained in the extraordinary range of his contributions, published in eight volumes of collected economic essays, will surely allow him the last and lasting word.
> (Harcourt 1988)

Indeed, much of his work has been integrated into contemporary post-Keynesian political economy.

See also:

economic growth; Verdoorn's Law

Selected references

Harcourt, G.C. (1988) "Nicholas Kaldor, 12 May 1908–30 September 1986," *Economica* 55: 159–70; repr. in G.C. Harcourt, *Post-Keynesian Essays in Biography*, Basingstoke: Macmillan, 1993.

Kaldor, Nicholas (1961) "Capital Accumulation and Economic Growth," in F. Lutz (ed.), *The Theory of Capital*, London: Macmillan.

King, J.E. (ed.) (1994) *Economic Growth in Theory and Practice: A Kaldorian Perspective*, Aldershot: Edward Elgar.

McCombie, J.S.L. and Thirlwall, A.P. (1994) *Economic Growth and the Balance-of-Payments Constraint*, Basingstoke: Macmillan.

Targetti, F. and Thirlwall, A.P. (1989) *The Essential Kaldor*, London: Duckworth.

Thirlwall, A.P. (1987) *Nicholas Kaldor*, Brighton: Wheatsheaf Press.

Young, A.A. (1928) "Increasing Returns and Economic Growth," *Economic Journal* 38: 527–42.

JOHN McCOMBIE

Kalecki, Michal

Michal Kalecki (1899–1970) was born in Lodz, Poland. He studied engineering at Warsaw Polytechnic without graduating, and was forced by his father's financial difficulties to earn his living as a commercial journalist. Much of Kalecki's early theoretical work was published in trade papers and in the socialist press, and has only recently been translated into English. He spent seven years (1929–36) at the Institute for Business Cycle and Price Research in Warsaw, before studying in Sweden and then in England on a Rockefeller fellowship. In the late 1930s Kalecki worked in London and Cambridge, spending the war years on research at the Institute of Statistics in Oxford. In 1945 he moved briefly to Montreal to work for the International Labour Organization, and then to New York, where he was employed by the United Nations Department of Economic Affairs for almost a decade. After being subject to political pressure during the McCarthy era, Kalecki returned to Poland in 1955 as an adviser to the government and a professor in Warsaw. A non-party socialist of great integrity and intellectual independence, he enjoyed a turbulent relationship with the Polish authorities. Shortly before his death in 1970 he resigned his official positions in protest against government-sponsored anti-Semitism and the persecution of his younger colleagues.

Principle of effective demand

Kalecki's early writings are remarkable for his independent discovery of the principle of effective demand, in a two-sector, two-class model in which investment depends on expected profitability and aggregate profits are determined by the expenditure decisions of capitalists. Presented (in French) at the international conference of the Econometric Society in Leyden in 1933, and published in English in 1935, Kalecki's formal model of the trade cycle suffers from a number of technical deficiencies, but his analysis already contains (in everything but name) the central theoretical propositions of what has come to be known as Keynesian macroeconomics. Entrepreneurs, not workers or consumers, make the running and output is constrained by demand, not by supply conditions. Changes in capitalists' investment expenditures have multiplier effects on the level of output, their size being governed by the propensity to save out of profits. Instability is not an aberration, but rather the normal state for a capitalist economy. Kalecki was already, in the early 1930s, extending his analysis to the case of an open economy, for which he formulated a more sophisticated and dynamic version of the now-famous Harrod export multiplier. The influence of Marx's reproduction models is evident in all of this, along with that of contemporary cycle theorists like Aftalion. There are also some elements of mainstream neoclassical economics. Kalecki's astonishing review of the *General Theory*, not available in English until 1982, includes discussion of a representative profit-maximizing firm with a conventional U-shaped marginal cost curve.

Distribution of income

After his move to England the neoclassical element in Kalecki's thinking grew stronger, if only for a while. The 1933 profit equation determined the level of profits, in terms of capitalists' expenditures and the propensity to save. Kalecki's first attempt to develop a model of the profit share, as a function of the intensity of competition (or, inversely, the degree of monopoly), was expressed in marginalist terms. Subsequently he turned his back on orthodox price theory and reformulated the model in terms more suited to the reality of modern, oligopolistic capitalism (see PRICING). Firms set their prices by applying a mark-up to their average variable costs of production, which Kalecki assumes to be constant over a wide range of output levels. INCREASING RETURNS TO SCALE, advertising expenditures and other barriers to entry determine the degree of monopoly, which is reflected in the size of each firm's mark-up. For the whole economy, the profit share is positively related to the degree of monopoly and the price of raw materials, relatively to the wage rate; the share of wages is inversely related to these variables. The apparent constancy of relative shares over the trade cycle can now be explained, via offsetting movements in raw material prices (which always move pro-cyclically) and the degree of monopoly (which Kalecki believed to rise in depression, due to the elimination by bankruptcy of weaker firms). He used a similar argument to account for the supposed long-run constancy of relative shares over many decades.

Kalecki's model of distribution has come in for considerable criticism, and his interpretation of the historical record is not especially convincing. The underlying theory, however, has been used creatively by his disciple Josef Steindl to analyze the connection between the decline of competition and the tendency toward stagnation in twentieth-century capitalism. If the profit share (P/Y) increases, with no change in P (since investment and capitalist consumption remain constant), the level of output must fall, since $Y=(Y/P).P$. However, a decline in the intensity of competition will reduce the incentive to invest, so that a long-run tendency for the degree of monopoly to rise must lead to stagnation. This is also the fundamental proposition in Paul Baran and Paul Sweezy's analysis of the "law of the rising surplus" in *Monopoly Capital* (1965), a law which was first formulated (by Sweezy) independently of Kalecki, but is obviously compatible with the latter's ideas. (See MONOPOLY CAPITALISM.)

Policy implications

The policy implications of Kalecki's model of capitalism were examined by him in a series of articles during and immediately after the Second World War. Broadly speaking, he took the "left Keynesian" or radical social democratic position that peacetime capitalist economies were most unlikely to avoid excess capacity and heavy unemployment without a substantial redistribution of income from profits to wages and a huge expansion of (productive or unproductive) spending by the state. Kalecki subsequently attributed the long postwar boom – which he had failed to anticipate – less to the advent of the welfare state than to the Cold War. Profits, he believed, had been sustained by massive armament expenditures, financed by government borrowing. In 1943 he had been no less pessimistic about the prospects for welfare capitalism, but on different grounds. Full employment would weaken discipline in the factories, Kalecki argued, posing threats alike to profitability and to capitalist control of the workplace. Governments might initiate counter-cyclical policies in pre-election periods, but they would soon be forced by business to reverse them after the votes had been counted. Political business cycles would come to replace the more obviously economic cycles of prewar capitalism. (See POLITICAL BUSINESS CYCLES.)

Money and risk

There is not space here for a detailed discussion of the many other aspects of Kalecki's work, much of which has a surprisingly modern ring. There is, for example, an undeveloped theory of ENDOGENOUS MONEY AND CREDIT in Kalecki, which points in the direction of the MONETARY CIRCUIT theory of Augusto Graziani and others, and also casts light on the vexed questions of credit rationing and the LIQUIDITY PREFERENCE of the banks. KALECKI'S PRINCIPLE OF INCREASING RISK identified a significant constraint on the growth of the firm, and his wartime work on international monetary arrangements anticipated much of the current controversy over the respective responsibilities of deficit and surplus nations. His views on economic methodology, inflation and economic growth would also repay critical attention. Although Kalecki never ceased to work on the macroeconomics of advanced capitalism, after 1945 he was increasingly concerned with two other issues: the barriers to the development of backward areas, and the economic problems of the socialist world.

Development and socialism

Kalecki was a strong critic of the orthodox approach to economic development, attacking its reliance on the static theory of comparative advantage and the resulting neglect of what Gunnar Myrdal termed CIRCULAR AND CUMULATIVE CAUSATION. He used an essentially Marxian framework to analyze the financing of development, and argued for LAND REFORM and redistributive taxation to overcome the bottlenecks imposed by inelastic food supplies and the shortage of foreign exchange. Kalecki's influence on the STRUCTURALIST THEORY OF DEVELOPMENT, particularly in Latin America, has been considerable. His work in Poland crystallized his ideas on the economics of socialism. Although a fierce opponent of the excesses of Stalinist planning, Kalecki was always convinced that socialism had the potential ability to outperform capitalism. He constructed a formal model of socialist economic growth from which were derived detailed proposals for long, medium and short-term plans. Had Kalecki been taken more seriously by the Polish authorities, the country's economic disasters of the 1970s might well have been avoided, with incalculable political consequences.

Kalecki's influence

In the West, Kalecki's ideas have influenced a large number of heterodox political economists without ever quite forming the basis for a distinct Kaleckian school. His analysis was tirelessly propagated by Joan Robinson, who regarded Kalecki's version of the principle of effective demand as superior to that of the *General Theory*, and as the basis for a potentially powerful synthesis of Marx and Keynes. By the mid-1970s, Kalecki had become increasingly influential also among American post-Keynesians such as Sidney Weintraub, Hyman Minsky and Alfred Eichner. There were some dissenters: Paul Davidson, in particular, has always seen Kalecki as a marginal and uninteresting figure. The younger generation of fundamentalist Keynesians are equally unimpressed by his lifelong belief in closed, determinate macroeconomic systems that are – at least in principle – subject to econometric estimation. There is too little UNCERTAINTY in Kalecki for their taste, too small a role for money, too much mathematics and not enough philosophy.

The problems that Marxian political economists have with Kalecki are quite different. The affinities are obvious: Kalecki's underlying conception of capitalism as a CLASS society, subject to recurrent crises of overproduction and essentially untameable, is unmistakably Marxian in inspiration. There is a sense in which he represents the culmination of half a century of Marxian crisis theory, giving rigorous form to the intuitive arguments advanced by the underconsumptionist majority of economists in both the Second and Third Internationals; Sweezy and Steindl have honored Kalecki for precisely this reason. More orthodox Marxists, however, demur. For Kalecki, capitalism's main difficulties lie in the realization of surplus value, not in its production. He ignores the LABOR THEORY OF VALUE; his models are invariably expressed in terms of current market prices. Kalecki says nothing about EXPLOITATION or the origins of surplus value, and passes over Marx's analysis of the FALLING RATE OF PROFIT TENDENCY in total silence. Marx himself would probably have dismissed him as an intelligent, honest, vulgar economist.

Sraffian economists also object to the absence of a theory of production in Kalecki, but this time on technical grounds. Since his analysis ignores the input–output relations between different branches of the economy, its principal theoretical propositions are not securely founded. Ian Steedman has demonstrated that an increase in the degree of monopoly in one sector, for example, may lead to a lower share of profits in the output of the entire economy, and vice-versa. Thus paradoxes may arise in Kaleckian models that are analogous to the phenomena of capital reversing and reswitching which destroy the coherence of neoclassical economics. Some Sraffians would go further, arguing that the absence of long-run centers of gravitation, and of a tendency for the rate of profit to be equalized across all industries, deprive Kalecki's analysis of the secure objective underpinnings vital for any satisfactory model of a capitalist economy. Others sympathetic to Sraffa, such as Philip Arestis and Marc Lavoie, maintain that a Kalecki–Sraffa synthesis is not only possible but also an urgent theoretical necessity (see SRAFFIAN AND POST-KEYNESIAN LINKAGES).

For the most part, institutionalists have shown no interest in Kaleckian economics for reasons similar to those motivating the hostility of the fundamentalist Keynesians. Kalecki focuses on structure at the expense of agency; he is a formalist, never using words when they can be replaced by an equation; a macroeconomist, who takes little interest in individual or group behavior. And yet there is much in Kalecki of which an institutionalist might approve, above all his insistence on the historical and social specificity of economic analysis and his rejection of the neoclassical claim that "one theory fits all." For Kalecki, capitalism and socialism require very different economic models, as do advanced and backward capitalisms, periods of underemployment and moments of full employment, oligopolist manufacturing and competitive peasant agriculture. He never treated the state as a *deus ex machina*, nor did he ever idealize the Stalinist bureaucracy. In amongst all the algebra is a profoundly political conception of economics, which should have considerable appeal to institutionalists.

See also:

cyclical crisis models; ; Kalecki's macro theory of profits; Kaleckian theory of growth; post-Keynesian political economy: major contemporary themes

Selected references

Feiwel, G.R. (1975) *The Intellectual Capital of Michal Kalecki*, Knoxville, TN: University of Tennessee Press.
Kalecki, Michal (1990–7) *The Collected Works of Michal Kalecki*, 7 vols, Oxford: Clarendon Press.
King, J.E. (ed.) (1996) *An Alternative Macroeconomic Theory: The Kaleckian Model and Post-Keynesian Economics*, Boston: Kluwer.
Sawyer, M.C. (1985) *The Economics of Michal Kalecki*, London: Macmillan.
Steedman, I. (1992) "Questions for Kaleckians," *Review of Political Economy* 4(2): 125–51; see also the discussion in the same issue and in vol. 5, no. 1 (1993) of this journal.

JOHN E. KING

Kalecki's macro theory of profits

In considering KALECKI's theory of profits it is important to bear in mind a number of things. First, the theory deals with the level of profits, not the share of profits in national income. Second, it pertains to the total level of profits in the economy as a whole and is not, in the first instance at least, a theory of the level of profits accruing to an individual firm or industry. Third, the theory does not deal with the "origin" of profits; rather it deals with the "realization" of the surplus in the form of profits. Finally, it is important to note that, although we shall talk about profit income, we really ought to regard the word "profits" as a shorthand for "all non-wage income."

The theory owes a great deal to Marx, especially his analysis of simple and extended reproduction. The clearest and most mature paper on this topic by Kalecki himself is to be found in Kalecki (1971: ch. 7).

Two-sector economy

Attention initially will be confined to the two-sector economy. We assume that the two sectors are fully vertically integrated with respect to raw materials, and that capital goods do not depreciate. For the moment, we will also assume that all profits are saved and that all wages are spent in the current period on wage-goods. To the extent that the workers employed in the wage-goods sector themselves purchase wage-goods, the firms in that sector will be receiving back as revenue no more than they have already paid out as a cost of production. Clearly, in order for firms in the wage-goods sector to receive monies as revenue in excess of their costs of production, there must be spending on their products in excess of the spending undertaken by their own workers, and the size of their profits will reflect the magnitude of that additional expenditure. Given the classical saving assumptions, it is the spending (on wage-goods) of wages earned in the industries outside the wage-goods sector which is the (proximate) source of the profits of the firms in the wage-goods sector. It is this insight which forms the basis for the macro-economic theory of profits.

We have seen that the amount of profits which will accrue to firms within the wage-goods sector will depend upon the amount of spending out of wages (albeit wages paid outside that sector). To the extent that the profits of some firms are no more than the costs of production to some other firms, there can be no profits in the aggregate on this account.

It is investment expenditure, whether "financed" by borrowing or retained earnings, which generates revenue for firms in the economy in excess of their current costs of production. It is the value of this investment expenditure which determines the size of profits in the economy as a whole. We can demonstrate this as follows. Suppose that firms or individual capitalists in the economy borrow or use their retained earnings to finance investment expenditures. The value of their purchases will be divided, within the capital-goods sector itself, between profits and wages. That part which does not constitute the profits of the firms producing capital-goods will (under our assumption of full integration) constitute the wages paid to the workers employed in the capital-goods sector. As we have seen, it is the wages of these workers which, when spent on the products of the wage-goods sector, generate revenue in the wage-goods sector in excess of its costs of production. In other words, it is the wages component of investment expenditure which becomes the profits of the firms in the wage-goods sector. The monies which are outlaid on investment generate an equivalent amount of profits in the economy as a whole, because one part of it increases profits directly in the capital goods sector itself, and the remaining part of it will indirectly increase profits in the industries producing wage-goods.

Model of profits

For those who are happier with symbols, we may set out the model as follows. The value of spending on the output of new capital goods over any period (called the level of investment expenditure and denoted by the symbol "I") will be distributed within the capital-goods sector. We use the symbol W_{cg} to denote the total wages bill paid by firms in the capital-goods sector, and the symbol P_{cg} to denote the profits received by firms in the capital-goods sector. Thus we have total investment emanating from the capital goods sector as:

$$I = W_{cg} + P_{cg} \qquad (1)$$

We have seen that it is the wages of workers in the capital goods sector which, in being spent, generate profits in the wage-goods sector (P_{wg}) of an equivalent amount, that is:

$$P_{wg} = W_{cg} \qquad (2)$$

Inserting P_{wg} for W_{cg} in equation (1) we see that, directly (through P_{cg}) and indirectly (through W_{cg} becoming P_{wg}) investment expenditure of a certain amount will generate profits to firms in the economy of an equivalent amount (P). Hence from (1) and (2):

$$I = P_{wg} + P_{cg} = P \qquad (3)$$

A neat way of summarizing this result is

provided by a saying, attributed to Kalecki, that "workers spend what they get, and capitalists get what they [the capitalists] spend." Implicit in the model is the notion that, within any period, it is the level of investment which is the independent, the active or "causal" element, and the aggregate level of profits which is the "dependent" or "passive" variable. "It is clear that capitalists may decide to consume and to invest more in a given period than in the preceding one, but they cannot decide to earn more" (Kalecki 1971: 78ff).

If we relax our assumption that workers spend all their income and allow for savings by workers out of their wages (S_w), profits will be reduced on that account. Continuing to assume that all profits are saved, we will have:

$$P = I - S_w \quad (4)$$

It is also possible to allow for consumption out of profits (C_p). In this event (4) must be rewritten as:

$$P = I - S_w + C_p \quad (5)$$

As Kalecki (1971: 81ff) shows, it is easy to generalize the model to allow for activities of the government and trade. If this is done we find that aggregate profits are determined as:

$$P = I - S_w + C_p + (G - T) + (X - M) \quad (6)$$

which shows a clear link within each period between the size of the budget deficit and the size of the export surplus, on the one hand, and the aggregate level of profits (before tax) on the other. The appearance of the export surplus in this relationship has an interesting implication for theories of imperialism. For a set of trading partners or, in the last instance, the world as a whole, the sum of exports and imports are equal, and so there can be no additional profits to the trading bloc on this account. Commercial policy acts simply to redistribute profits which arise from each nation's domestic spending propensities, between capitalists of different nationalities.

Kalecki hypothesized that capitalist's consumption was made up of a stable part and a part proportionate to real profits after tax in earlier periods. Given this, and neglecting trade plus government and workers' savings, current aggregate profits will depend upon (a) the size of the autonomous component of capitalists' consumption, (b) current investment, (c) the propensity to consume out of profits, and (d) lagged aggregate profits. Lagged aggregate profits in turn will depend (primarily) on lagged investment. Ultimately, then, current profits will depend upon current and past levels of investment, the autonomous element in capitalists' consumption, and current and past investment outlays. The lagged relationship between these variables was to underpin Kalecki's theories of trend and cycle.

Other uses of the theory

Kalecki's macro theory of profits has been invoked in many aspects of political economy. This includes an examination of financial instability in capitalist economies (Minsky 1979), advances in the theory of taxation (see Kalecki 1937; Asimakopulos and Burbridge 1974), and in attempts to explain the movement of profits (or gross operating surplus) over time in various economies (for a good example see Cowling 1982).

See also:

circuit of social capital; colonialism and imperialism: classic texts; effective demand and capacity utilization; falling rate of profit tendency; Kaleckian theory of growth; monetary circuit; monopoly, degree of; political business cycles; turnover time of capital

Selected references

Asimakopulos, A. and Burbridge, J. (1974) "The Short-Period Incidence of Taxation," *Economic Journal* 74: 267–88.

Cowling, K. (1982) *Monopoly Capitalism*, London: Macmillan.

Kalecki, M. (1937) "A Theory of Commodity, Income and Capital Taxation," *Economic Journal* 47: 444–50; repr. in Kalecki (1971).

—— (1971) *Selected Essays on the Dynamics of*

the Capitalist Economy 1933–1970, Cambridge: Cambridge University Press.
Minsky, H. (1979) "The Financial Instability Hypothesis: A Restatement," *Thames Papers in Political Economy*, Autumn; repr. in H. Minsky, *Inflation, Recession and Economic Policy*, Brighton: Wheatsheaf, 1982, 90–116.

ROBERT DIXON

Kalecki's principle of increasing risk

Introduction

There is a simple intuition behind Kalecki's principle of increasing risk. That is, due to reasons related to the firm's financial structure, investment may cease at a point where there still remain projects that would yield a rate of return higher than the current interest rate. KALECKI believed that, in conditions of developed CAPITALISM, money is predominantly credit money created by the banking system. The principle resulted from his view of the financial markets as essentially being imperfectly competitive. The cost of finance rises with the amount borrowed, and the ease of borrowing is related to the profit and wealth of the borrower.

Even though Kalecki is not usually seen as a monetary economist, he paid more attention to financial issues than is usually recognized (see Sawyer 1985; Arestis 1996). Kalecki's ideas on money and finance were not systematically developed, but Josef Steindl (1989) cogently reminded us that Kalecki did not deny the importance of these factors in any way. However, he saw them as being secondary to, and in a sense derived from, the dynamics of the real sphere of production. A close follower of Kalecki himself, Steindl believed that this was so partly for historical reasons. At Kalecki's time, the long-term interest rate did not change very much, and he could plausibly argue that its influence on investment was not very important.

Kalecki examined the principle in two main places, first in 1937 (Kalecki 1937a, 1937b) and then in 1954 (Kalecki 1954, reprinted in Kalecki 1971; papers which he considered to be his most important). The first concerned the level of entrepreneurial investment, and the second concerned the nature of entrepreneurial capital in relation to the size of the firm.

Reasons for increasing risk

In Kalecki (1937a), two reasons are provided for the increase of marginal risk with the amount invested. The first is that the greater the investment of an entrepreneur, the more his or her wealth position is endangered if the business venture turns out to be unsuccessful. The second reason is the danger of illiquidity. The sudden sale of so specific a good as a capital asset is usually connected with losses. Hence, the amount invested must be seen as an illiquid asset, in the case of a sudden need for capital. Having to borrow in that situation, an entrepreneur would be charged a rate of interest that is higher than the market rate. The amount invested by an entrepreneur is thereby given by the condition that the marginal efficiency of investment is equal to the sum of marginal risk and the rate of interest.

Indeed, Kalecki had already used the principle elsewhere to raise a pertinent objection to Keynes's theory of investment. Kalecki (1937b) read Keynes as arguing that a certain amount should be subtracted from the marginal efficiency of assets to cover risk before comparing it with the current interest rate. For Kalecki, KEYNES, despite his emphasis on the uncertain nature of the future, had not taken into account that the rate of risk of every investment is greater the larger is such investment. Kalecki (1937a) then uses his principle to provide an interesting explanation for the distribution of firm size in an industry. The smaller the amount of his or her own capital that an entrepreneur invests, the greater the risk he or she incurs. Enterprises started in a given industry at a given moment are not of equal size because the personal capital of entrepreneurs is not equal. As access to external finance depends on previously owned capital, business democracy is thus a fallacy.

In Kalecki (1954), in turn, the emphasis is mainly on the size distribution of firms in an industry. Kalecki saw the size of a firm as being constrained by the amount of its entrepreneurial capital, both through its influence on the capacity to borrow capital and through its effect on the degree of risk. In his view, the amount of capital owned by the firm is a factor of decisive importance in limiting the size of a firm. On the other hand, many firms will not use fully the potentialities of the capital market because of the increasing risk involved in expansion. A firm considering expansion must face the fact that, given the amount of the entrepreneurial capital (for instance, a sole trader), the risk increases with the amount invested. For Kalecki, these limitations to investment are applicable in the case of joint stock companies as well.

Indeed, the situation does not change much when a company issues bonds or debentures, the reason being that the greater the issue, the more dividends are impaired in case of an unsuccessful business venture. The situation is similar in the case of an issue of preference shares, a fixed return on which is paid from profit before any return accrues to ordinary shares. Even with respect to the latter, there are limits to a public issue associated with the problem of the maintenance of control by top shareholders. A major limit is the risk that the investment so financed may not increase profits as much as the issue increased the share and reserve capital. Another limit is the extent of the market for shares of a given company.

As the limitation of the size of the firm by the availability of entrepreneurial capital goes to the very heart of the capitalist system, Kalecki would insist anew on the mythical nature of a state of business democracy. The idea that anyone endowed with entrepreneurial ability has equal access to capital is simply fallacious, for the most important prerequisite for becoming an entrepreneur is the previous ownership of capital.

Links with contemporary work

Given the prominent role played by monetary and financial issues in several political economy approaches, Kalecki's principle has been subject to recurrent attention. For instance, Dymski (1996) argues that Kalecki's structural model of investment, which includes the increasing risk notion, can be improved when linked with post-Keynesian monetary theories. Specifically, such a link can provide a better appreciation of financial constraints and credit rationing.

Regarding the kind of credit money endogeneity underlying Kalecki's principle, however, little convergence has been observed. Arestis (1996), for instance, argues that the principle implies that the supply of credit money is endogenous but upward sloping. The reason is that, as more funds are supplied for investment, a higher interest rate will be charged on these loans because their liabilities increase relative to assets and there is thus a higher risk.

Lavoie (1996), in turn, claims that the horizontalist view of credit money endogeneity is compatible with the principle. In this case, the supply of credit is infinitely elastic at interest rates that are determined outside the process of income generation, more precisely by some conventional behavior on the part of the monetary authorities. For Lavoie, the aggregate debt to equity ratio – as a measure of the degree of illiquidity of banks' customers – will not necessarily rise with increased borrowing to finance an output expansion. Indeed, it may eventually fall as a result of increased investment leading to increased profits. There is a close affinity between this principle and the FINANCIAL INSTABILITY HYPOTHESIS.

See also:

endogenous money and credit; interest rates: risk structure; Kalecki's macro theory of profits; Kaleckian theory of growth paradoxes; post-Keynesian political economy: major contemporary themes

Selected references

Arestis, Philip (1996) "Kalecki's Role in Post Keynesian Economics: An Overview," in J.E. King (ed.) *An Alternative Macroeconomic Theory: The Kaleckian Model and Post-Keynesian Economics*, Boston: Kluwer Academic Publishers.

Dymski, Gary (1996) "Kalecki's Monetary Economics," in J.E. King (ed.) *An Alternative Macroeconomic Theory: The Kaleckian Model and Post-Keynesian Economics*, Boston: Kluwer Academic Publishers.

Kalecki, Michal (1937a) "Principle of Increasing Risk," *Economica* 4(November).

—— (1937b) "A Theory of the Business Cycle," *Review of Economic Studies* 4(February).

—— (1954) *Theory of Economic Dynamics*, London: Allen & Unwin; repr. in Kalecki (1971).

—— (1971) *Selected Essays on the Dynamics of the Capitalist Economy*, Cambridge: Cambridge University Press.

Lavoie, Marc (1996) "Horizontalism, Structuralism, Liquidity Preference and the Principle of Increasing Risk," *Scottish Journal of Political Economy* 43(3).

Sawyer, Malcolm (1985) *The Economics of Michal Kalecki*, New York: M.E. Sharpe.

Steindl, Josef (1989) "Reflections on Kalecki's Dynamics," in Mario Sebastiani (ed.) *Kalecki's Relevance Today*, New York: St. Martin's Press.

GILBERTO TADEU LIMA

Kaleckian theory of growth

The Kaleckian theory of growth refers to a body of literature where a long-run equilibrium approach is used for analyzing growth and income distribution on the basis of some key Kaleckian elements. KALECKI himself made little use of equilibrium analysis. His analysis was generally within a framework of BUSINESS CYCLE THEORIES (pure cycles or cyclical growth). For him, "the long-run trend is but a slowly changing component of a chain of short-period situations; it has no independent entity." However, in some places (see Kalecki 1991: 322–37, 411–34) he did discuss a long-run equilibrium (steady-state) growth model. It is rather Steindl (1952: ch. XIII) who made a substantial use of a long-run equilibrium approach along Kaleckian lines. The main momentum came with Robert Rowthorn and Amitava K. Dutt in the early 1980s. Dutt (1990) and Lavoie (1995) provide useful surveys of various Kaleckian models and some doctrinal confrontations with other growth theories.

Oligopoly markets

Kalecki views the oligopolistic market structure as a dominant feature of the modern industrial economy (see MARKET STRUCTURES). Thus, the price of a product in an industry is determined by firms imposing a mark-up on average prime costs (i.e. wages and raw materials costs), which Kalecki considers are more or less constant up to the full capacity level. The mark-up rate reflects the degree of monopoly of the industry and determines the profit margin (and the profit share in the aggregate economy). The level of profits is determined mainly by the level of investment expenditure entrepreneurs implement (see KALECKI'S MACRO THEORY OF PROFITS). It follows that it is pricing and investment behaviors which determine the level of output and employment. The mark-up rate is considered to be relatively insensitive to the state of aggregate demand; fluctuations in economic activity come mainly from fluctuations in investment expenditure.

Only if there exists slowly growing semi-autonomous expenditure, stimulated by "development factors" such as technological innovations and the discovery of new sources of raw materials will the economy grow along a positive long-run trend. This trend is not necessarily a steady-state growth path, but exhibits approximately the same average rate of change as that of the "development factors" (see Kalecki 1991: 435–50). Whether in a steady state or not, however, the long-run trend is normally characterized by less than full employment/utilization of labor and productive equipment.

Key elements or variables

The recent Kaleckian theory of growth differs from Kalecki's own views of growth in that it focuses directly on long-run configurations at the expense of short-run cyclical changes. However, the appellation comes from the fact that some of the distinctively Kaleckian elements constitute its building blocks. The first is the view that firms are price makers, not price takers. While most of the Kaleckian models use mark-up pricing, various procedures of PRICING are compatible with the Kaleckian theory (see Lavoie 1995). The second includes an autonomous investment function. That is, the desired (planned) rate of accumulation is a positive function of the degree of utilization and the (current) rate of profit. The third is the idea that capacity utilization plays a significant role, not only in the short run but also in the long run.

Thus, the key independent variables are the mark-up rate and the parameters of the investment function. Changes in these variables lead to changes in the long-run degree of capacity utilization and correspondingly in the rate of profit. Two important results arise. The first is that the long-run degree of capacity utilization generally diverges from the normal (planned) level, this latter being taken as exogenously given. The implications of this are twofold: (1) the long-run degree of utilization is determined endogenously, and (2) undesired excess capacity can exist even in the long run. The initial emphasis has been on both implications but, as a result of debates (see below), more emphasis is being placed on the first implication. The second result is a higher real wage rate, resulting from a lower mark-up rate, which brings about higher rates of profit and of growth. These two results are in direct contrast to other growth theories, such as neoclassical, neo-Marxian or KALDOR–PASINETTI MODELS OF GROWTH AND DISTRIBUTION (see Dutt 1990). With most of these, long-run equilibrium is characterized by full capacity utilization, and therefore the rate of profit moves inversely with the real wage rate in the long run.

The Keynesian premise

The "Keynesian premise" refers to the proposition that it is savings which adjust to investment, not the other way around. In a short-run equilibrium, savings and investment are equalized through changes in income arising from variations in the degree of utilization of a given productive capacity. The Kaleckian theory generalizes this short-run mechanism to the long run. In the long run, no less than in the short, savings are brought into line with autonomous investment through changes in income. The difference is that, in the long run, changes in income come from variations in the degree of utilization of changing productive capacity. This mechanism sharply distinguishes the Kaleckian theory from some another theories also based on the "Keynesian premise." In the Kaldor–Pasinetti models, the adjustment of savings is realized through changes in the distribution of income rather than in its level. Here a faster rate of growth can come only with a reduction in the real wage rate (and a corresponding rise in the rate of profit). In contrast, the Kaleckian theory provides a vision of a "cooperative" economy, where a higher real wage rate leads to correspondingly higher rates of profit and of growth. This is a vision originating in underconsumptionist theorizing.

Debates

These results triggered some debates (see Dutt 1990; Lavoie 1995). Kaleckians argue that the current degree of utilization influences investment, reflecting the state of effective demand. Then, critics argue, the current rate of profit (decomposable into the degree of utilization and the gross profit margin) should not be included as an additional independent influence on investment. The Kaleckian specification duplicates the influence of effective demand, and also overlooks the adverse cost effect of higher wages on investment (see PROFIT

SQUEEZE ANALYSIS OF CRISES). If the cost effect of wages is allowed for, several regimes are possible on which the distributive relationship depends; the Kaleckian result is only one of the possibilities. However, for the Kaleckians (following Kalecki's view of financing investment), what is important is the ability of firms to invest and this ability is measured by the current, not the future, profitability.

A second debate is on whether the divergence of the realized utilization from normal level can be maintained over the long run. Faced with undesired excess capacity, firms would be willing to revise their current investment/pricing behavior (and they would be able to do so in the long run). The rate of profit in the Kaleckian distributive relationship would refer to its average level over several business cycles, not to its normal level. This has proved a serious charge and a recent Kaleckian formulation allows for the normal level of utilization to respond to the gap from the actual level so that the two levels coincide in equilibrium (the hysteresis effect). This reduces the emphasis on the permanent existence of undesired excess capacity, but strengthens the emphasis on the endogenous determination of the long-run degree of utilization.

Further developments

Various generalizations and applications have been made (for references, see Dutt 1990; Lavoie 1995). The introduction of overhead labor yields more interesting results. Multi-sector models can be used for an analysis of foreign trade. A consideration can be taken of the financial sector and the rate of interest. The conflicting claims theory of inflation can be incorporated. Technical change, exogenous or endogenous, can be analyzed. Obviously, still more generalizations and applications are ahead.

See also:

economic growth; effective demand and capacity utilization; North–South trade models

Selected references

Dutt, Amitava K. (1990) *Growth, Distribution and Uneven Development*, Cambridge: Cambridge University Press.
Kalecki, Michal (1991) *Collected Works of Michal Kalecki*, vol. 2, *Capitalism: Economic Dynamics*, Oxford: Clarendon Press.
Lavoie, Marc (1995) "The Kaleckian Model of Growth and Distribution and its Neo-Ricardian and Neo-Marxian Critiques," *Cambridge Journal of Economics* 19(6): 789–818.
Steindl, Josef (1952) *Maturity and Stagnation in American Capitalism*, Oxford: Basil Blackwell.

MAN-SEOP PARK

Keynes, John Maynard

Keynes (1883–1946) was born in Cambridge. His father, John Neville Keynes, was the registrar at Cambridge University and a distinguished economist and philosopher. His mother served for a time as mayor of Cambridge.

Background

"Maynard," as he was called, was educated at the most prestigious schools in England: Eton and King's College, Cambridge. At Cambridge he studied the classics, philosophy with G.E. Moore, mathematics with Alfred North Whitehead and economics with Alfred Marshall. Keynes also became part of the Society, an exclusive club of intellectuals which later became the Bloomsbury group.

After graduation, Keynes sat for the British Civil Service examination, scoring second highest which meant that he had the second choice of open civil service positions. Although he craved a job at the Treasury, he settled for a post in the India Office where he helped to organize and coordinate British interests involving India. Quickly becoming bored, Keynes returned to Cambridge two years later to teach economics. However, while at the India Office in 1906 he commenced a study on probability which was largely completed by 1911 but only published in 1921 as *A Treatise on Probability* (Keynes 1971–89: vol. VIII).

Public acclaim first came to Keynes following publication of *The Economic Consequences of the Peace* (Keynes 1971–89: vol. 2) in 1919. During the First World War, Keynes served in the British Treasury and was primarily responsible for obtaining external finance to support the British war effort. As the war drew to a close, Keynes was appointed a member of the British delegation at Paris involved in negotiating German war reparations. *Economic Consequences of the Peace* provided an angry critique of the peace treaty. Keynes calculated that Germany could not possibly make good on the British and French demands for reparations; the economic consequence would be the impoverishment of Germany, and rising German hostility toward France and England. The political consequence, which Keynes equally feared, would be the rise of an angry and militant Germany.

The *Tract* and the *Treatise*

Now a figure of national prominence, Keynes turned his attention to questions of economic theory and policy. His *Tract on Monetary Reform* (Keynes 1971–89: vol. 4), published in 1923, warned of the dangers from inflation and looked to central bank control of the money supply as a means of stabilizing the price level. This work also contained Keynes's famous and misunderstood dictum, "in the long run we are all dead." Many have taken this phrase to mean that Keynes was willing to sacrifice long-term economic performance for short-term economic benefits, but this is not what Keynes was driving at. He meant to criticize others who believed that the problem of inflation would eventually remedy itself, without any active government involvement. His point was that rather than waiting for elusive future gains, we should employ policies now to remedy our economic problems.

As unemployment increased in England, Keynes turned his attention to the business cycle. His *Treatise on Money* (Keynes 1971–89: vols 5–6), published in 1930, examined the relationships between money, prices and unemployment. Keynes singled out the saving–investment relationship as the main focus of economic fluctuations. When people attempted to save more than businesses wanted to invest, businesses would soon find themselves with excess capacity to produce goods and too few buyers. On the other hand, when investment exceeded savings, there would be too much spending. This would bid up the price of labor as well as other necessary components of production, and also bid up the price of all consumer goods. Moreover, Keynes stressed that savings decisions and investment decisions were made by different groups of individuals, so the two would not likely be the same. Keynes then argued that the central bank had to keep these two variables equal, and prevent either prolonged inflation or prolonged economic depressions. If savings exceeded investment, the central bank should lower interest rates, thus reducing savings and stimulating borrowing. On the other hand, if investment exceeded savings, the central bank should raise interest rates, thus increasing savings and reducing borrowing.

The *General Theory*

The *Treatise*, though, did not explain how it was possible for an economy to remain mired in a state of high unemployment. This task was left for *The General Theory of Employment, Interest and Money* (Keynes 1971–89: vol. 7), published in 1936. The *General Theory* has been responsible for the development of macroeconomics, and provides the first modern theory of the determinants of output and employment. Although the book says very little about economic policy, it laid the theoretical foundation for government policy makers to employ the economic tools necessary to end the GREAT DEPRESSION of the 1930s.

Keynes begins by attacking Say's Law, the belief that "supply creates its own demand." According to this dictum, unemployment was impossible because, whatever the existing supply of workers, there will be a demand for these workers. Keynes turned Say's Law on its head, arguing that demand determined the supply of output and level of employment. When demand was high, businesses would hire more workers and unemployment would cease to be a problem; but when demand was low, firms would not be able to sell their goods and would cut back on production and hiring.

For obvious reasons, Keynes turned next to a study of aggregate effective demand and the causes of changes in demand. Analyzing the two most important components of demand, Keynes developed the modern theories of consumer spending and business investment.

Keynes identified two broad determinants of consumer spending: subjective factors and objective factors. Among the subjective or psychological factors affecting consumption were UNCERTAINTY regarding the future, desires to bequeath a fortune, and a desire to enjoy independence and power. The objective factors affecting consumption were economic influences such as interest rates, taxes, the distribution of income and wealth, expected future income and, most important of all, current income.

In contrast to the many factors affecting consumption, according to Keynes, business investment depends on just two factors: expected returns on investment and the rate of interest. The former constitutes the benefits from investing in new plants and equipment; the latter constitutes the cost of obtaining funds to purchase the plants and equipment. If the expected rate of return on investment exceeded the interest rate, business firms would expand and build new plants of equipment. However, if interest rates exceeded the expected return, investment would not take place.

Interest rates were determined, according to Keynes, in money markets where banks supplied money, and the demand for money came from portfolio decisions made by people and businesses. They could hold onto money, or hold their wealth in the form of stocks, bonds and other assets. By necessity, the supply of money existing in the economy must be held by someone, and people cannot possibly hold more money than actually exists or gets created.

When people are pessimistic they want to hold money rather than assets, and they attempt to sell assets. The increased demand for money keeps interest rates up, thus holding down investment. Pessimistic sentiments about the returns to investment also keep down the amount of business spending. Likewise, poor expectations about the economy would keep consumption spending down. As a result of this insufficient demand for goods, unemployment would remain a serious economic problem.

Surprisingly, after his presentation of the determinants of aggregate demand, Keynes had little to say about policy. He came out in favor of both money creation and circulation (monetary policy) and government spending and tax cuts (fiscal policy). In a much quoted passage Keynes writes about the need for more houses, hospitals, schools and roads.

In a much maligned passage, Keynes calls for "a somewhat comprehensive socialization of investment" (Keynes 1971–89: vol. 7, 378). While many have taken Keynes to be advocating government control of all business investment decisions, what Keynes really advanced was government spending policies to stabilize the aggregate level of investment in the national economy (Pressman 1987).

The Second World War and after

In the 1940s Keynes returned to advising the British government, and to policy issues surrounding the war effort. He helped negotiate war loans for Britain from the US during the Second World War, and he developed a proposal to help Britain finance the war effort. Rather than raising taxes (which would reduce British incomes), and rather than doing nothing to finance war spending (which would generate inflation due to shortages of goods and high demand), Keynes proposed a plan of compulsory savings or deferred pay. All British citizens with incomes greater than some minimal level would have money taken out of their paychecks and put into special savings accounts to help finance the war. The money in these accounts would then be lent to the government and used to finance the war effort. After the war these forced savings could be withdrawn by British citizens and used for consumption needs.

When the Second World War ended, Keynes worked on the new international monetary arrangements being developed by the victorious governments. Keynes believed that one major cause of the worldwide economic depression in the 1930s was that every country was trying to export unemployment to its trading partners. By running a trade surplus, each country would produce more and create more domestic employment. However, its trading partners would lose because they would import goods instead of producing them.

One way in which countries attempted to generate trade surpluses was through devaluating their currencies. By making foreign monies and goods more expensive, national governments knew that their citizens would buy fewer foreign goods. Similarly, by making domestic money and goods cheaper, devaluation would increase exports.

To prevent competitive currency devaluations, Keynes proposed a system of relatively fixed exchange rates. A modified system was agreed to by the Allied victors at Bretton Woods, New Hampshire in 1944, and became known as the BRETTON WOODS SYSTEM. Bretton Woods required that each country peg its currency to an ounce of gold and keep it there. Because every currency was tied to gold, exchange rates among all currencies were fixed.

A second way to stem the deflationary impact of each country attempting to run trade surpluses was to set up an international mechanism to help clear trade imbalances. Keynes wanted to establish a system that would lend money to countries running trade deficits, and penalize countries running trade surpluses. Both a clearing mechanism (the International Monetary Fund) and a lending facility (the World Bank) were established at Bretton Woods. However, the USA, expecting that it would run huge trade surpluses, would not agree to penalize countries with persistent surpluses. Keynes pushed hard for this policy proposal, but the Americans would not budge (Block 1977).

Ironically, the USA began to run large trade deficits in the 1970s, which continued and grew through to the late 1990s. The mechanisms that Keynes advanced in the 1940s could have helped to deal with this problem, but because the US refused to impose financial penalties on countries running a trade surplus, there is little the US can do in the 1990s to deal with its trade problems, short of reducing demand for all goods and thereby reducing demand for foreign made goods.

Conclusion

Without doubt, no twentieth-century economist has had a greater impact than Keynes. At the theoretical level, he developed macroeconomic analysis. Regarding policy, the many tools employed by central banks and central governments to help control the business cycle, and the international mechanisms that are set up to deal with trade imbalances have their origin in the works of Keynes. Finally, the argument that governments had to use policy tools to improve economic performance is probably his most important legacy.

See also:

fiscal policy; Keynes and the classics debate; Keynesian political economy; Keynesian revolution; monetary policy and central banking functions; post-Keynesian political economy: major contemporary themes

Selected references

Block, Fred L. (1977) *Origins of the International Economic Order*, Berkeley: University of California Press.

Dillard, Dudley (1948) *The Economics of J.M. Keynes*, New York: Prentice Hall.

Hansen, Alvin (1953) *A Guide to Keynes*, New York: McGraw-Hill.

Keynes, J.M. (1971–89) *The Collected Writings*

of John Maynard Keynes, ed. D. Moggridge, 30 vols, London: Macmillan.

Moggridge, Donald (1992) *Maynard Keynes: An Economist's Biography*, London and New York: Routledge.

Pressman, Steven (1987) "The Policy Relevance of *The General Theory*," *Journal of Economic Studies* 14: 13–23.

Skidelsky, Robert (1983–92) *John Maynard Keynes*, 2 vols, New York: Viking Press.

STEVEN PRESSMAN

Keynes and the classics debate

Say's Law and classical economics

John Maynard KEYNES presented his *General Theory of Employment, Interest and Money* in 1936 as a challenge to the classical adherents of Say's Law of markets, claiming classical economics as a special case of his more general theory. Keynes's interpretation of Say's Law was: equality of the aggregate demand price of output as a whole to its aggregate supply price for all levels of output; which is equivalent to the notion that there is a tendency toward full employment.

While noting that Marx coined the term "classical" to describe Ricardo, James Mill and their predecessors back to Petty and Boisguillebert, Keynes extended it to later explicit or implicit adherents of Say's (or James Mill's) Law, "including (for example) J.S. Mill, Marshall, Edgeworth and Prof. Pigou." In a 1937 exchange with Ohlin, Keynes apologized if he had led any reader to suppose that he considered Hawtrey and Robertson classical economists: "I regard Mr Hawtrey as my grandparent and Mr Roberston as my parent in the paths of errancy... Professor Irving Fisher... was the great-grandparent who first influenced me strongly towards regarding money as a 'real' factor" (Keynes 1973: vol. XIII, 202–203n) (see MONETARY THEORY OF PRODUCTION).

Keynes took Pigou's *Theory of Unemployment*, published in 1933, as the outstanding, perhaps the only, explicit exposition of the classical theory, particularly of the two main classical postulates. The first postulate was that the real wage equals the marginal product of labor (the economy is on its labor demand curve); the second was that the utility of the wage equals the marginal disutility of labor (the economy is on its labor supply curve). As Keynes predicted in his preface, those "strongly wedded to what I shall call 'the classical theory'" fluctuated "between a belief that I am quite wrong and a belief that I am saying nothing new" (Keynes 1973: xxi) (he suggested that there was a third alternative). Controversy continues about the fairness of Keynes's representation of the disparate group of economists whom he lumped together as "classical," about what distinguishes Keynesian from classical theory, and which is the more general theory.

Keynes's critique of classical economics

J.R. Hicks's (1937) widely-reprinted "Mr Keynes and the 'Classics': A Suggested Interpretation" ignored both Say's Law and the classical postulates of the labor market, and made only passing mention of UNCERTAINTY. Instead Hicks focused on a three-equation model of aggregate demand. Here the classical theory was a special case, where liquidity preference does not depend on the interest rate (a vertical LL, later LM curve); and Keynes's theory is the special case, where saving depends only on income, not on the interest rate. Hicks argued that Keynes's "General Theory of Employment is the Economics of Depression," relevant to the horizontal segment of the LL (or LM) curve at low levels of income (the liquidity trap), but retracted this last claim in 1945. Modigliani (1944) also considered Keynesian unemployment equilibrium to be a special case, adding either a liquidity trap or an arbitrary assumption of rigid money wages to classical theory.

Keynes offered a sharply different view of what distinguished him from the classics in his reply in the *Quarterly Journal of Economics* (in

February 1937) to four reviews of the *General Theory*. Keynes summed up:

> the main points of my departure [are] as follows: (1) The orthodox theory assumes that we have a knowledge of the future of a kind quite different from that which we actually possess.... The hypothesis of a calculable future leads to a wrong interpretation of the principles of behaviour which the need for action compels us to adopt, and to an underestimation of the concealed factors of utter doubt, precariousness, hope, and fear.... (2) ... I doubt if many modern economists really accept Say's Law that supply creates it own demand. But they have not been aware that they were tacitly assuming it.
>
> (Keynes 1973: vol. XIV, 109–23)

Post-Keynesians, notably Joan Robinson, stressed this article as showing that history and an unknowable future, as opposed to equilibrium, set Keynes apart from the classics.

Writing to Hicks at the end of March 1937, Keynes (1973: vol. XIV, 79–81), while complimentary, criticized the former on two counts: for making investment a function of current income rather than expected future income, and for representing classical economics by the eclectic views of economists who had drifted far from the strict classical view that an increase in the quantity of money cannot affect output. This last criticism, that Marshall's generation had drifted far from strict classicism, had been leveled at Keynes in Pigou's review of *The General Theory* in *Economica*.

Policy versus theory?

The widely-reprinted articles of Hicks and Modigliani persuaded many that Keynesian economics was a special case of a more general classical economics, but a special case relevant to the real world, at least that of the 1930s. A.C. Pigou repeatedly restated the implication of his *Theory of Unemployment* that, in theory, money-wage cuts could eliminate unemployment, even though in practice he continued to share Keynes's preference for aggregate demand expansion through public works as a remedy (as even Say had recommended). In an article in the *Economic Journal* in 1937, Pigou held that lower money wages directly stimulate employment and income, not through lowering the interest rate. But Nicholas Kaldor showed that, in the IS–LM framework, lower money wages and prices increase income by shifting the LM curve, lowering the interest rate.

In the *Economic Journal* in 1943 and *Economica* in 1947, Pigou argued that, as a matter of theory to which he attached no practical relevance, reducing money wages and prices would increase demand to full-employment levels, even in a liquidity trap. This worked through the wealth effect on consumption of the increased real value of money balances and government bonds (a point also raised in the third edition of Gottfried Haberler's *Prosperity and Depression*, which appeared in 1941). Patinkin's influential *Money, Interest and Prices* expressed the consensus of mainstream macroeconomists that the *real balance effect* settled the "Keynes and the Classics debate," with the Keynesian case being just the addition of money wage rigidity to a more general classical theory.

However, KALECKI pointed out as early as 1944 that this real balance effect does not apply to inside money (bank deposits backed by loans). Keynes argued in correspondence with Kalecki that the real balance effect does not apply to government debt if debt service payments are tax-financed. Restricting the real balance effect to outside money (the monetary base) left the real balance effect of lower prices as a very weak equilibrating force, likely to be swamped by dynamic factors considered in Chapter 19 of the *General Theory*: the effect of falling money wages and prices on expectations and on liquidity preference.

Coordination failure and Walras's Law

Robert Clower and Axel Leijonhufvud reopened the debate in the 1960s. They took seriously Keynes's rejection of Say's Law, and its sophisticated version, Walras's Law, and interpreted the economics of Keynes as the economics of coordination failure. Clower and Leijonhufvud critiqued Walras's Law, the notion that the value of excess demand sums identically to zero across all markets, including money. They believed that this law holds only for notional demands, not effective demands. An excess supply of labor in one market need not imply excess effective demand in another market. This is because the wages an unemployed worker doesn't receive aren't part of the worker's budget constraint for goods.

Demand-constrained firms fail to hire workers, expenditure of whose wages would increase demand for output. When markets fail to clear, because too high an interest rate discourages investment, effective demand signals may fail to both coordinate decisions and move the economy to full employment. As Clower said:

> "The sum of all excess market demands, valued at prevailing market prices, is at most zero,"... "Contrary to the findings of traditional theory, excess demand may fail to appear anywhere in the economy under conditions of less than full employment."
>
> (Clower 1969: 292; original emphasis)

Keynes thus differed from classical theory in rejecting Say's Law (in the form of Walras's Law for effective demands) and had sound grounds for doing so.

See also:

effective demand and capacity utilization; Kalecki's macro theory of profits; Keynesian political economy; Keynesian revolution; post-Keynesian political economy: major contemporary themes; unemployment and underemployment

Selected references

Clower, R.W. (1969) "The Keynesian Counter-Revolution: A Theoretical Appraisal," in R.W. Clower (ed.) *Money Theory: Selected Readings*, Harmondsworth: Penguin.
—— (1984) *Money and Markets: Essays*, ed. D.A. Walker, Cambridge: Cambridge University Press.
Hicks, J.R. (1937) "Mr Keynes and the 'Classics': A Suggested Interpretation," *Econometrica* 5(2): 147–59.
Keynes, J.M. (1973–9) *Collected Writings*, vols XIII, XIV, XIX, ed. D.E. Moggridge, London: Macmillan and New York: Cambridge University Press, for the Royal Economic Society.
Leijonhufvud, A.S.B. (1968) *On Keynesian Economics and the Economics of Keynes*, New York: Oxford University Press.
Modigliani, F. (1944) "Liquidity Preference and the Theory of Interest and Money," *Econometrica* 12(1): 45–88; repr. in H. Hazlitt (ed.) *The Critics of Keynesian Economics*, New Rochelle, NY: Arlington House, 1977.
Patinkin, D. (1956) *Money, Interest and Prices*, New York: Harper & Row.
Young, W. (1987) *Interpreting Mr. Keynes: The IS-LM Enigma*, Cambridge: Polity Press, and Boulder, CO: Westview.

ROBERT W. DIMAND

Keynesian political economy

The widely differing theoretical approaches labeled "Keynesian" share John Maynard KEYNES's belief that market forces cannot always be relied upon to keep a capitalist monetary economy at potential output and full employment in the face of fluctuations in effective demand without interventionist demand management by government. This view distinguishes distinctively Keynesian approaches from the more general, pervasive influence of Keynes's ideas indicated by Milton Friedman's often half-quoted statement that "We are all Keynesians now, and no-one is any longer a Keynesian." Keynesian approaches draw selectively on Keynes's *General Theory of Employment, Interest and Money* for inspiration, with great variations as to aspects of the book and directness of contact with the original text.

Broad approaches

Alan Coddington (1983) usefully identified three broad approaches: reductionist, fundamentalist and hydraulic Keynesianism. Reductionist Keynesians seek to reduce Keynesian macroeconomics to the logic of individual optimizing choice. Fundamentalist Keynesians see Keynes's ideas as a fundamental challenge to any reductionist program, stressing such aspects of his message as fundamental UNCERTAINTY. Hydraulic Keynesians constructed aggregate flow models for the forecasting and guidance of aggregate demand management techniques.

Hydraulic Keynesianism

The dominant tendency in the 1950s and 1960s was what Paul Samuelson's introductory textbook (like that by Raymond Barre) presented as the "neoclassical synthesis" of neoclassical microeconomics and hydraulic Keynesianism, a synthesis that Joan Robinson labeled "Bastard Keynesianism." With a simple multiplier model (the 45-degree cross income–expenditure diagram) as an introductory pedagogical device, this approach built upon the Harrod–Hicks–Meade IS/LM model of aggregate demand determination, extended to open economies as the Mundell–Fleming IS/LM/BP model, and to cycles through lagged multiplier–accelerator interaction. Nominal rigidities, unexplained except perhaps by money illusion, accounted for the real effects of aggregate demand shifts, with the consequences of the rigidities described as in Chapter 2 of the *General Theory*.

This approach was embodied in large empirical models, extending to Lawrence Klein's Project Link. The models combined disaggregated national simultaneous equation structural macroeconometric models into a world model. The models are subject to the severe skepticism Keynes expressed about the stability of structural relationships in Tinbergen's 1939 model. Franco Modigliani's life cycle hypothesis of consumption, James Tobin's mean-variance portfolio model of demand for money by risk-averse wealthholders, and the Allais–Baumol–Tobin inventory approach to transactions demand for money explained some aspects of behavior in terms of individual optimization, but this was not done for the approach as a whole. Forecasting and policy failures and reductionist theoretical challenges undermined the dominance of this "Old Keynesianism." However, from this group has emerged an important group of what may be called "Chapter 19 Keynesians" (such as Tobin and Solow) who follow Chapter 19 of the *General Theory* in denying that nominal flexibility ensures convergence to full employment.

Reductionist Keynesianism

The leading American form of reductionist Keynesianism is New Keynesian economics (see Mankiw and Romer 1991), which confronts new classical macroeconomics on its own ground of optimizing individuals. New Keynesians seek rigorous models of nominal and real rigidities based on optimizing individual behavior and rational expectations. But they add imperfect or monopolistic competition and imperfect information leading to multiple, welfare-ranked equilibria, and thereby dropping Keynes's attempt to prove his case even on the classical ground of perfect competition. Mankiw has shown that imperfectly competitive firms may obtain only small benefits from adjusting prices to demand fluctuations, so that even small menu costs (price-adjustment costs) can make prices sticky, with nominal demand fluctuations being reflected in output, not just in prices. Within the New Keynesian approach, John Taylor's explanation of nominal wage stickiness as being due to staggered contracts and workers' concern with relative wages is an independent reinvention of what Keynes wrote in Chapter 2 of the *General Theory*.

The New Keynesian EFFICIENCY WAGES hypothesis that labor productivity depends on the real wage explains why firms may find it unprofitable to cut money wage rates even when faced by persistent involuntary unemployment. The Shapiro–Stiglitz concept of equilibrium unemployment as a device for worker discipline is strikingly reminiscent of Kalecki's view of political aspects of full employment. New Keynesians share the new classical rhetoric of rigorous, consistent microeconomic foundations yet, like the new classicals, run into problems with the formidable conditions for consistent aggregation (see Geweke 1985). New Keynesian theorizing primarily responds to the agenda set by new classical macroeconomics by invoking adjustment costs and imperfect competition, displaying little interest in earlier or alternative Keynesian approaches. A much smaller group of New Keynesian papers (see Section IV of Mankiw and Romer 1991) challenge new classical macroeconomics at a more fundamental level by analyzing coordination failures due to spillovers across markets and complementarities between strategies of agents, but with little reference to relevant work in the other reductionist Keynesian tradition.

The other reductionist Keynesian approach was initiated by Robert Clower, Axel Leijonhufvud's *On Keynesian Economics and the Economics of Keynes*, published in 1968, parts of Don Patinkin's *Money, Interest and Prices* in 1956, and Robert Barro and Herschel Grossman's *Money, Employment and Inflation* in 1976. It rejects Walras's Law (the value of excess demand adds to zero over all markets) as inapplicable to effective demands when agents are quantity-constrained in some markets. If labor is in excess supply, the wages that unemployed workers fail to receive are not part of their budget constraints for demanding goods, and so there is no effective signal to firms that their goods would be demanded if they hired more workers. This amounts to taking seriously Keynes's rejection of Say's Law. Although this group is non-Walrasian in the sense of rejecting Walras's Law for effective demands, economists in this approach emphasize constrained optimization and the interdependence of markets.

This non-Walrasian macroeconomics (also called temporary equilibrium or Keynesian disequilibrium theory) and related approaches flourish in France (Bénassy, Grandmont, Hénin, Laroque, Malinvaud, Younès) and Japan (Iwai, Negishi, Nikaido, Uzawa). However, Robert Gordon notes that:

> An interesting aspect of recent U.S. new-Keynesian research is the near-total lack of interest in the general equilibrium properties of non-market-clearing models... even the most perceptive new-Keynesian commentators tend to forget the central message of these models... that spillovers between markets imply that the failure of one market to clear imposes constraints on agents in other markets.
>
> (Gordon 1990)

Clower and Leijonhufvud have distanced themselves from some of the work they inspired, criticizing both these reductionist approaches for concentrating more on the sources and consequences of nominal rigidities than on effective demand failures (the coordination problem).

Post-Keynesian political economists

This group views the KEYNESIAN REVOLUTION as leading to a fundamental challenge to the choice-theoretic foundations of reductionist Keynesian and new classical economics. Three sharply-differing strands of post-Keynesian fundamentalism all figured in the influential work of Joan Robinson. First, an American strand, centered on the *Journal of Post Keynesian Economics* (founded by Paul Davidson and the late Sidney Weintraub), build directly on some of Keynes's own writings, especially Chapters 12 and 17 of the *General Theory* (on long-term expectation and the essential properties of money), the aggregate demand and supply functions of Chapter 3, his 1937 *Quarterly Journal of Economics* reply to critics and the 1939 critique of Tinbergen. This strand stress the irreducibility of fundamental uncertainty to insurable risk or of a monetary (entrepreneurial) economy to a classical barter economy. This contrasts with New Keynesian disinterest in Keynes's original writings. Minsky's FINANCIAL INSTABILITY HYPOTHESIS is linked with this fundamentalist Keynesian approach.

Second, in the work of G.L.S. Shackle, a fundamentalist Keynesian focus on uncertainty and expectation in an entrepreneurial, monetary economy come close to AUSTRIAN SCHOOL OF POLITICAL ECONOMY concerns with time, limited knowledge and learning through entrepreneurial innovation. Third, Kaleckian short-period macroeconomics is more influential among European, Australian and Indian post-Keynesians, with an emphasis on how income distribution affects spending decisions that recalls Keynes's *Treatise on Money*. The Kaleckian denial that the long period has any meaning except as a sequence of short periods contrasts strongly with the efforts initiated by Pierangelo Garegnani to combine the Keynesian principle of effective demand with a Sraffian long-period analysis of prices of production (Eatwell and Milgate 1983, primarily articles from the *Cambridge Journal of Economics*) (see SRAFFIAN AND POST-KEYNESIAN LINKAGES). Post-Keynesians of all varieties are skeptical of Keynes's belief that, if full employment is maintained by sufficient effective demand, the market will allocate the fully-employed resources properly.

Conclusion

Hydraulic, reductionist and fundamentalist Keynesianism are all rooted in aspects of Keynes: the policy adviser and *ad hoc* model builder, the Marshallian economist and the revolutionary thinker, respectively. They share the belief that markets, especially the labor market, do not always clear without government intervention – in effect, that the Great Depression of the 1930s did occur. They share the belief that responding to this phenomenon requires a theoretical understanding of its causes and consequences, and that this is to be sought in demand deficiency and coordination failure in monetary economies that differ from a barter economy subject to Say's Law. The varieties of Keynesian political economy diverge sharply over whether such an understanding is to be sought within the neoclassical paradigm of optimizing choice under risk by rational individuals, or whether fundamental uncertainty, aggregation problems and irreversibility rule out such neoclassical microeconomic foundations. While much New Keynesian economics has been absorbed into eclectic mainstream macroeconomics, Keynes-inspired research on coordination failure shows a promise of furthering an understanding of monetary economies.

See also:

post-Keynesian political economy: major contemporary themes

Selected references

Bénassy, J.-P. (1993) "Non-Clearing Markets: Microeconomic Concepts and Macroeconomic Applications," *Journal of Economic Literature* 31(2): 732–61.

Coddington, A. (1983) *Keynesian Economics: The Search for First Principles*, London: George Allen & Unwin.

Eatwell, J. and Milgate, M. (eds) (1983) *Keynes's Economics and the Theory of Value and Distribution*, Oxford: Oxford University Press.

Geweke, J. (1985) "Macroeconomic Modeling and the Theory of the Representative Agent," *American Economic Review* 75(2): 206–10.

Gordon, R.J. (1990) "What Is New-Keynesian Economics?," *Journal of Economic Literature* 28(3): 1115–71.

Hahn, F. and Solow, R.M. (1995) *A Critical Essay on Modern Macroeconomic Theory*, Cambridge, MA: MIT Press.

Hall, P. (ed.) (1989) *The Political Power of Economic Ideas: Keynesianism Across Nations*, Princeton, NJ: Princeton University Press.

Mankiw, N.G. et al. (1993) "Symposium on Keynesian Economics Today," *Journal of Economic Perspectives* 7(1): 3–82.

Mankiw, N.G. and Romer, D. (eds) (1991) *New Keynesian Economics*, 2 vols, Cambridge, MA: MIT Press.

Nishimura, K.G. (1992) *Imperfect Competition, Differential Information and Microfoundations of Macroeconomics*, Oxford: Oxford University Press.

ROBERT W. DIMAND

Keynesian revolution

John Maynard KEYNES's *General Theory of Employment, Interest and Money*, first published in 1936 and the debates surrounding it (see KEYNES AND THE CLASSICS DEBATE) transformed how economists theorize about the determination of output and employment in a monetary economy. It set the agenda for modern macroeconomics, even though the mainstream of the discipline has evaded the more unsettling issues raised by the *General Theory*. Keynes's theory of how involuntary unemployment occurs, and of interventionist demand management as the remedy, found a receptive audience, prepared for his message by worldwide mass unemployment in the early 1930s and by ferment in monetary and business cycle theory (*vis-à-vis* Hawtrey, Robertson, the Stockholm School and Keynes's own earlier *Treatise on Money*).

Theoretical novelty

Keynes's novelty was not in his policy recommendations, as countercyclical public works had been preferred to wage cutting as a remedy for unemployment even by Pigou, whose theoretical exercises suggested otherwise. Some, such as Tugwell, advocated financing public works as a remedy for unemployment by cutting other public spending and raising taxes, but failing to grasp the problem of effective demand. Herbert Hoover as Commerce Secretary in the 1920s was identified with plans for public works in depressions, but as US President during the Depression instead pursued a conflicting commitment to a balanced budget. Keynes's revolution was in the MONETARY THEORY OF PRODUCTION underlying his policy views.

His theory challenged both the Marxist view that capitalism cannot be stabilized at full employment; and the Austrian theory (propounded by Hayek and Robbins at the London School of Economics) that depressions are an inevitable reaction to overinvestment, necessary to weed out inefficient firms, and will only be exacerbated by intervention. In contrast to the Austrian view of a self-stabilizing private sector, subject to disruption by policy shocks, Keynes saw a role for demand management to counterbalance the instability of private investment, driven by volatile expectations of future profitability.

Major components of Keynes's theory

Keynes's theory, first presented in his autumn 1933 Cambridge lectures on "The Monetary Theory of Production," had four components: liquidity preference, the marginal efficiency of capital, the propensity to consume and a labor market analysis. The (nominal) rate of interest is determined in the money market, equating the quantity of money to LIQUIDITY PREFERENCE (which depends on expectations). The flow of investment equates the marginal efficiency of capital (expected rate of return over cost on new investment) to the interest rate, and is volatile, as long-period expectations fluctuate in a world of fundamental UNCERTAINTY.

The propensity to consume and the multiplier derived from it were critical to Keynes's analysis, having been developed by Richard Kahn with James Meade in 1931, and independently by R.G. Hawtrey, L.F. Giblin, J.M. Clark and Jens Warming. A level of income is generated at which leakages into saving (and taxes and imports) just equal injections of investment (and government spending and exports). From this analysis of the determinants of effective demand emerges the aggregate demand function, the proceeds which entrepreneurs expect at each level of employment. Keynes's analysis of the labor market yields the aggregate supply function, the expected proceeds that would be just sufficient to induce entrepreneurs to offer the corresponding level of employment, given the wage rate. Keynes thus had a theory of aggregate output and employment, in place of the fundamental equations for the price level of his *Treatise on Money* and in contrast to the Swedish emphasis on prices, as well as to the focus on the cycle in most of KALECKI's essays.

Keynes analyzed the labor market to explain how changes in effective demand affect output and employment, not just prices. In Chapter 2 of *The General Theory*, he accepted the first classical postulate that the real wage equals the marginal product of labor (that the economy is on the labor demand schedule), but rejected the second which equated the utility of the wage and the marginal disutility of labor (placing the economy on the labor supply schedule), allowing for involuntary unemployment (excess supply of labor). Workers resist money wage cuts, not because of money illusion, but because staggered contracts mean that workers accepting a money wage cut have their wages reduced relative to income recipients with unexpired contracts, and because money wage reductions cause prices to fall. Money wage bargains do not lead to market-clearing real wages. A reduction in real wages brought about through higher prices (increased demand) could increase employment without meeting the same resistance, since a simultaneous and equal change in the real value of all nominal incomes would not disrupt relative wages.

Chapter 19 of *The General Theory* argued further that even if prices and money wages were flexible, money wage cuts could not be relied upon to eliminate unemployment because of the effect of deflation on expectations and liquidity preference. Keynes also rejected Say's Law of markets, which he interpreted as holding that an excess supply of labor implied an excess demand for goods, and hence an incentive to hire labor to produce more goods. A decision to refrain from consuming now was simply a reduction in total demand, according to Keynes, and did not effectively signal a demand for other goods at another time.

Influence of Keynes's theory

Keynes's *General Theory* fascinated the younger generation of economists, and for twenty-five years after the Second World War Keynesianism (minus the disturbing concept of fundamental uncertainty) shaped macroeconomic teaching, modeling and policy making in industrialized capitalist countries, with Samuelson's best-selling textbook propounding an uneasy "neoclassical synthesis" of Keynesian macroeconomics and neoclassical microeconomics. Each building block of Keynes's theory generated controversy. The countercyclical real wages implied by Chapter 2 proved empirically elusive, while proponents of simultaneous equations models held that the interest rate was determined as much in the bond market (loanable funds) as in the money market (liquidity preference). New consumption theories weakened the link between consumption and current income, except with imperfect credit markets. Mainstream economists resisted consideration of fundamental or uninsurable uncertainty, as distinct from risk.

The Keynesian revolution shaped subsequent macroeconomic theorizing, whether by force of attraction or of repulsion. It overwhelmed, at least temporarily, alternative approaches to the macroeconomic coordination problem, notably by Kalecki, who related effective demand to class distribution of income, and by Hayek. Keynes provided a theory of how a monetary economy could fail to be self-adjusting, and a sketch of how government could stabilize entrepreneurial capitalism. Amid the mass unemployment of the 1930s, he offered hope of understanding what had gone wrong and how to remedy it. The Keynesian revolution established an agenda for theoretical research that is not yet exhausted.

See also:

Keynesian political economy; post-Keynesian political economy: history; post-Keynesian political economy: major contemporary themes; wage determination

Selected references

Amadeo, E.J. (1989) *Keynes's Principle of Effective Demand*, Aldershot: Edward Elgar.

Asimakopulos, A. (1991) *Keynes's General Theory and Accumulation*, Cambridge: Cambridge University Press.

Clarke, P. (1988) *The Keynesian Revolution in the Making 1924–1936*, Oxford: Clarendon Press.

Dimand, R.W. (1988) *The Origins of the Keynesian Revolution*, Upleadon: Edward Elgar, and Stanford, CA: Stanford University Press.

Hall, Peter A. (ed.) (1989) *The Political Power of Economic Ideas: Keynesianism across Nations*, Princeton, NJ: Princeton University Press.

Kahn, R.F. (1984) *The Making of Keynes' General Theory*, Raffaele Mattioli Lectures, Cambridge: Cambridge University Press.

Klein, L.R. (1947) *The Keynesian Revolution*, New York: Macmillan.

Meltzer, A.H. (1988) *Keynes's Monetary Theory: A Different Interpretation*, Cambridge: Cambridge University Press.

Patinkin, D. (1982) *Anticipations of the General Theory? And Other Essays on Keynes*, Chicago: University of Chicago Press.

ROBERT W. DIMAND

knowledge, information, technology and change

The relationship between knowledge, TECHNOLOGY and ECONOMIC GROWTH has perplexed economists for generations. For neoclassical economic theory, the causes of economic growth in general, and PRODUCTIVITY growth in particular, are still a mystery. Economic growth has been seen as resulting from the input of the "factors" land, labor and capital, with little mention of learning, organization or technological knowledge. Alfred Marshall was thus exceptional when he emphasized in his *Principles of Economics*: "Capital consists in a great part of knowledge and organization.... Knowledge is our most powerful engine of production.... Organization aids knowledge; it has many forms... it seems best sometimes to reckon organization apart as a distinct agent of production" (Marshall 1920: 115).

Standard neoclassical theory

However, the incorporation of knowledge, information, learning and organization into neoclassical theory has proved extremely difficult, in part because of the mechanistic nature of that theory. Learning is generally an irreversible and ongoing process, whereas in classical mechanics, motion is often reversible and equilibrating. Despite much empirical effort, the neoclassical "production function" model still faces a problem in explaining considerable inter-plant and international differences in productivity. Even more striking is the widespread evidence for single industries, showing big sectoral productivity gaps between different countries.

A typical neoclassical response is to suggest that such differences in productivity must be due to either differences in the inputs or mysterious shifts in the production function itself. Attributions of such variations to differences of input have proved problematic. For instance, Clifford Pratten (1976) found that differences in the amounts of machinery appeared to be responsible for no more than one-fifth of the average difference in productivity found in comparable plants in Britain, the USA, West Germany and France. We are led to the conclusion that varied amounts of capital equipment per employee are not the main factor explaining internationally diverse levels of productivity. Extended work on the "growth accounting" approach, for instance by Edward Denison (1979), suggests that "factor inputs," including capital stock, the educational level of the workforce and the amount of expenditure on research and development, explain no more than a small fraction of the US productivity slowdown in the 1970s.

Clearly, neoclassical economists have empirical as well as theoretical difficulties in this area. Although great strides have been made in improving the quality of the data, the measures of such factors as the "quantity" and "quality" of growth are patchy and speculative to say the least. The principal response of many neoclassical economists will be to put further effort into gathering and refining the data and making additional econometric estimations. While such efforts have some value, the underlying theoretical problems with the neoclassical approach should not be ignored.

Endogenous growth

In response to some of the problems in standard neoclassical growth theory, the idea of "endogenous growth" has emerged, due to the work of Paul Romer (1986) and others. In part this replicates some earlier ideas found in the work of Nicholas Kaldor, particularly the emphasis on "learning by doing" and INCREASING RETURNS TO SCALE. Also central to Romer's models are knowledge spillover effects. Instead of the common convergence of growth rates, cumulative divergences of national output and productivity are predicted, seemingly in accord with the available data. However, an amended version of the neoclassical aggregate production function is still at the conceptual foundation of endogenous growth models. Knowledge is still treated as if it were a substance or input.

In fact, the conceptual foundations of both the standard and endogenous growth versions of neoclassical growth theory are still extremely shaky. Although some aggregation is inevitable with such empirical work, the capital theory debates of the 1960s and 1970s show that the concept and measurability of "capital" is highly problematic. Furthermore, even if capital were meaningful and measurable, the arbitrary assumption of a "well behaved" production function remains a great fabrication, supported by the most slender and dubious of evidence (see Harcourt 1972).

Tacit knowledge, learning and organization

Likewise, although the greater attention to knowledge and learning by doing in endogenous growth theory is welcome, the treatment of "knowledge" as if it were a measurable substance is as challengeable as the equivalent aggregation of "capital." Learning is not simply the progressive acquisition of codifiable knowledge, akin to the acquisition or discovery of "blueprint" information. There is also tacit knowledge, as Michael Polanyi (1967) and many others have described. Furthermore, learning is a process of problem formulation and problem solving, rather than the acquisition and accumulation of given "bits" of information from "out there." This process involves conjecture and error, in which mistakes become opportunities to learn rather than mere random perturbations. In general, and acutely within organizations, learning involves the alteration of cognitive frames and mental models of the world (Argyris and Schon 1978).

In addressing production, the problems with neoclassical economics emanate from the deepest conceptual level. In particular, production is treated as a mechanical rather than an "organic" process, and the social and organizational aspects of production are ignored (see SOCIAL AND ORGANIZATIONAL CAPITAL). For instance, and in general, neoclassical theory regards output as mechanically dependent on the number of hours of work that is agreed between employer and employee. However, due to UNCERTAINTY and imperfect knowledge, the amount and efficiency of work has to be imperfectly specified in the contract. It depends not only on the given technology but also upon both the motivation and skill of the workforce and the organization and supervision of management. These, in turn, depend on complex institutional structures and routines and on cultural norms that are inherited from the past (see INSTITUTIONS AND HABITS; CULTURE).

Purposeful behavior and collective knowledge

Instead of further attempts to fit evidence into the "meat grinder" model, where production results from the automatic or mechanical transformation of given inputs, the process of production can be conceived in a different manner. Production can be regarded as a social process involving people with aspirations of their own, in structured social interaction with each other. Instead of the neoclassical symmetry of "factors of production," labor should be seen as an active agency with capital goods as passive instruments. This would follow a number of heterodox writers, including both Karl MARX in *Das Kapital* (vol. 1, ch. 7) and John Maynard KEYNES in the *General Theory*, who have proposed the view that human agents are capable of purposeful behavior but capital goods are not. The owners of labor power and the owners of capital goods are both active and purposeful decision-making agents in the sphere of exchange. But during the process of production, capital goods themselves are passive instruments, subject to the purposeful activity of the workers and managers.

As Thorstein VEBLEN has elaborated, labor is made up of congealed habits or skills, which may take some time to acquire and which depend upon their institutional integument. He drew a number of implications from his conception of habit and routine. For instance, he saw production not primarily as a matter of "inputs" into some mechanical function, but as an outcome of an institutional ensemble of habits and routines: "the accumulated, habitual knowledge of the ways and means involved...the outcome of long experience and experimentation" (Veblen 1919: 185–6). Furthermore, they do not relate to single individuals because the "great body of commonplace knowledge made use of in an industry is the product and heritage of the group" (Veblen 1919: 186). "These immaterial industrial expedients are necessarily a product of the community, the immaterial residue of the community's experience, past and present; which has no existence apart from the community's life, and can be transmitted only in the keeping of the community at large" (Veblen 1919: 348) (see COLLECTIVE SOCIAL WEALTH).

The group-based nature of the immaterial assets of production means that they are not part of the labor contract between employer and employee. They reside in the interstices of the social organization of the firm and its associated community. Economic growth is favored when this social organization facilitates individual learning: "The possibility of growth lies in the feasibility of accumulating knowledge gained by individual experience and initiative, and therefore it lies in the feasibility of one individual's learning from the experience of another" (Veblen 1919: 328).

Early American institutionalists such as John R. Commons and Veblen pointed out that neoclassical capital theory overestimates the tangible assets to the detriment of the intangible. The individualistic and reductionist tendencies in neoclassical theory remove from view the intangible assets of the group. Veblen and Commons thus abandon the capital–labor "factors of production" approach, to propose a conception of production based on the organic interaction of the human workforce with capital goods.

The productivity of an economy is crucially related to the transmission and interpretation of information, and to the growth of different kinds of collective knowledge. For instance, improvements in work organization are often designed to facilitate both the communication of information and the enhancement of collective skills within the plant. Significant increases in productivity can result from better deployment of tasks, a reduction of waste and improved organizational or other skills. Notably, and contrary to both TAYLORISM and Marxian EXPLOITATION theory, these developments are not necessarily associated with an increase in the intensity of work.

Furthermore, the behavior of the firm is not, within the given constraints, entirely determined by, or entirely subject to, the decisions of its managers. Because much of the "expertise" of the firm is embedded in the firm's routines and the habitual skills of its workforce, it is neither completely codifiable and communicable, nor completely manageable from the apex of the organization. Because behavior within the firm and other economic institutions is largely routinized, economic development can appear, for significant periods of time, to be subject to inertia. An adequate theory of the development of productive capabilities must take into account both the social culture and institutions within which habits and routines are reproduced, and the conditions that lead to their disruption or mutation.

Evolutionary transformation and irreversibility

Despite the long-recognized inadequacies of neoclassical theory, an alternative approach to the theory of economic growth and technological change – giving due recognition to knowledge and learning – is still in its infancy. However, substantial progress has been made on the basis of evolutionary models (Dosi *et al.* 1988; Verspagen 1993). Evolutionary economics provides a place for the concept of learning. Unlike neoclassical theory, possible choices are not known and given at the outset. The agent has to discover or create the available options. Technology does not exist as "blueprints," waiting merely to be uncovered. Learning means that economic processes are generally transformative and irreversible. Information problems, and processes of creation and discovery, are central. The switch of metaphor from the mechanical to the evolutionary may thus provide an opportunity to deal with the conundrum of economic growth.

See also:

evolutionary economics: history; evolutionary economics: major contemporary themes

Selected references

Argyris, C. and Schon, D. (1978) *Organizational Learning: A Theory of Action Perspective*, Reading, MA: Addison-Wesley.

Denison, Edward F. (1979) *Accounting for Slower Economic Growth*, Washington DC: The Brookings Institution.

Dosi, Giovanni, Freeman, Christopher, Nelson, Richard, Silverberg, Gerald and Soete, Luc (eds) (1988) *Technical Change and Economic Theory*, London: Pinter.

Harcourt, Geoffrey C. (1972) *Some Cambridge Controversies in the Theory of Capital*, Cambridge: Cambridge University Press.

Marshall, Alfred (1920) *Principles of Economics*, 8th edn, London: Macmillan, 1962.

Polanyi, Michael (1967) *The Tacit Dimension*, London: Routledge & Kegan Paul.

Pratten, Clifford F. (1976) *Labour Productivity Differences in International Companies*, Cambridge: Cambridge University Press.

Romer, Paul M. (1986) "Increasing Returns and Long-Run Growth," *Journal of Political Economy* 94(5): 1002–37.

Veblen, Thorstein B. (1919) *The Place of Science in Modern Civilisation and Other Essays*, New Brunswick, NJ: Transaction, 1990.

Verspagen, Bart (1993) *Uneven Growth Between Interdependent Economies: An Evolutionary View on Technology Gaps, Trade and Growth*, Aldershot: Avebury.

GEOFFREY M. HODGSON